P9-AQG-166

ECKHART PUBLIC LIB.
8401 9100 020 288 2

RULES

1. Books may be kept two weeks and may be renewed once for the same period, except 7-day books and magazines.

2. A fine of two cents a day will be charged on each book which is not returned according to the above rule. No book will be issued to any person incurring such a fine until it has been paid.

3. All injuries to books beyond reasonable wear and all losses shall be made good to the satisfaction of the Librarian.

4. Each borrower is held responsible for all books drawn on his card and for all fines accruing on the same.

Twentieth Century History of Fort Wayne

By John Ankenbruck

United States Bicentennial Edition

Published by Twentieth Century Historical Fort Wayne, Inc.

Fort Wayne, Indiana

1975

Library of Congress Card Number: 75-14666. Printed in the United States.

The Bicentennial Edition of the History of Fort Wayne. A Publication of Twentieth Century Historical Fort Wayne, Inc.

Patrons:

Helen Ankenbruck
James Barrett, Jr.
Phyllis Bulson
Celia Fay
Foellinger Foundation
Frank Freimann Trust
Mrs. William B. F. Hall
Thomas Jehl
Lynn Koehlinger
Kuhne Foundation
Alfred Maloley
Mr. and Mrs. William C. Rastetter, Jr.
Mr. and Mrs. Fred J. Reynolds
Willard Shambaugh
John Spillson

Contents

1. Adventure Into The Unknown 1
2. The Americans Arrive 43
3. A Town Is Born 109
4. Railroads And Black Debris 142
5. City Booms In 1920s 213
6. The Schools 261
7. The Depression Times 285
8. Decade Of 1935-1945 325
9. World Of Sports 370
10. After The War Was Over 407
11. Stable Times 438
12. The Parks 471
13. The Greening Of The City 499
14. Festivals And Easy Money 540

Elected County Officials 583

Notes And Bibliography 588

Acknowledgments 595

Index 597

LAC HURON
LAC MICHIGAN
LAC ONTARIO
LAC ERIE
I. Manitoualin
Michillimakinac
Ancien Païs des Hurons
PAYS DES MIAMIS
Ici etoient les ERIES qui ont été detruits par les Iroquois
l'oyo ou la Belle Riviere
Riviere Ouabache ou de S. Jerome
PAYS DES CHOUANONS
Riviere des Anciens Chouanon
R. Hogohegée selon les Anglois
Cheraquis
Montagnes des Apalaches
PENSIL VANIE
Philadelphie
VIRGINIE
CAROLINE
C. Fear
C. Carteret
La Longue Baye
Charles Town
Edenton
Cap Lookout

Part 1

Adventure Into the Unknown

The written history of Fort Wayne begins at the baptism of a two-day-old boy in the chapel of Chateau St. Louis, which once stood on the very spot in Quebec where the Chateau Frontenac was later built.

"The 21st of the month of January, 1668, has been baptised by me, Henry de Bernieres, cure of this parish, Jean Baptiste Bissot, son of Francois Bissot and Marie Couillard, his wife, born the 19th of the same month and year." That entry on the cold January day high above the St. Lawrence River was made in the records of the Parish of Notre Dame de Quebec by de Bernieres, who in addition to being cure was vicar-general of Quebec, which in those days took in much of a continent, including a place which the baby he was baptising would develop into a wilderness community and eventually be called Fort Wayne.

The baby in the chapel was the great-grandson of Louis and Marie Rollet Hebert, the first French settlers in the New World, and along with Champlain, the founders of Quebec. When the French fleet and most of the settlers temporarily abandoned New France in 1629, the only ones to stay behind were Marie Hebert and her children. (Louis had died following a fall.) Her offspring and those they married included Jean Nicolet, Louis Joliet, the Caveliers (LaSalle), Jean Baptiste Bissot and Francois Marie Morgan Bissot (the Vincennes). They would explore a continent and set up trading posts and forts in previously uncharted lands. Their activities along the rivers and lakes in the wilderness covered an area larger than the whole of Europe.

Even while the French fleet was sailing out of the St. Lawrence, Jean Nicolet was far to the west, exploring the length of Lake Michigan in 1629 and the rivers to the south, possibly including the Maumee. He was followed in a later generation by Nicolas Perrot, Jesuit, who visited the Miami Indians. On Oct. 7, 1675, Jean Baptist Bissot, by that time a little boy of seven, attended the marriage of his older sister, Claire-Francoise, to Louis Joliet who had returned after discovering the Mississippi River. The same Cure, Henry de Bernieres, performed the ceremony as the little boy sat, undoubtedly, in the family pew of the Vincennes. The carved wooden pew was of particular significance because a later legal battle over its ownership is the reason so much is known about the family. It was granted to the Bissot family in 1656. In 1672 King Louis XIV enlarged the estate of Bissot by establishing the seigneury of Vincennes in the New World. Included were large land holdings on the south side of the St. Lawrence opposite the Isle of Orleans.

This tight unit of families within a few years moved over the icy plains, waterways and forests of hemlock and walnut. Beaver was a main object. Paris soon became the fashion center of the Old World partly because of the impact of furs from this far-flung network in America. The Indians were the trappers and soldiers.

LaSalle and Frontenac

It was in 1670s that two of these French aristocrats set out to gain a monopoly on the fur trade in the vast interior. They were Louis de Baude de Frontenac, governor-general of New France, and Rene Robert Cavelier, Sieur de la Salle.

In the process of squeezing out other trading operations, Frontenac and La Salle and others established chains of posts extending from the Arctic wastes to the Gulf of Mexico. Their main bases of operations were however, on Lake Huron and Lake Michigan. Frontenac pulled the political strings while La Salle did the work

In the area south of the Great Lakes, the French had problems. The far-flung Iroquois, with the encouragement of the English, made the territory a deadly one for the French and others, including non-Iroquois Indians.

For this reason, La Salle, Joliet and the others originally took the cold route to the west and south—going through the Straits of Mackinac to Lake Michigan or across Lake Superior in setting up trade down the Mississippi. The shorter route through Lake Erie, up the Maumee, across the portage at three rivers, and down the Wabash to the Ohio and Mississippi, would eventually become a main French water path, but it was to be the last adopted.

To firm up his position on Lake Michigan, La Salle built a fort in 1679 called Fort St. Joseph des Miamis on a river near that lake's southeastern shore. The idea was to control the river traffic down the St. Joseph or the Lake, across the portage to the Kankakee River and eventually to the Mississippi. In traveling in that area, La Salle became acquainted with the Miami and Illinois Indians who at the time occupied land where Chicago, South Bend, Peoria and Niles are now located.

The Better Passage

La Salle was informed by the Indians or already knew that another route, the one up from Lake Erie along the Maumee and across a portage to the upwaters of the Wabash, was easier and quicker for travel both to the northeast to Quebec and southwest down the Mississippi. But there was a serious problem in making use of it. As advice to the French crown at that time said: "Iroquois warfare prevents the obtaining of beaver from the great trade carried on with them in time of peace through the passage by the lakes on the way to the Ottawas, Illinois and Miamis." Mentioned was the slaughter at the portages of both Indians and traders at the hands of the Iroquois.

In his conversations with the Miamis, the blood enemies of the Iroquois, La Salle suggested their moving eastward to the area of the three rivers. He promised a trading mission would be established, which the Indians wanted in those days.

In the following decade, some Miamis did in fact migrate from the Lake Michigan area to the headwaters of the Maumee. A series of bloody conflicts with the Iroquois continued anew. But the Miamis stayed. A partnership between the French and the Miamis, unique in history, was formed. Through marriage and blood lines, the close association was to exist for many generations. A trading post was in operation at the head of the Maumee by 1686.

Captain Vincennes

Jean Baptiste Bissot was not yet 20 years old when he came up the St. Lawrence and crossed over to the French posts on the south shores of Lake Michigan. These were Fort St. Joseph on the southeast side of the Lake and at the Miami Village of Chicagou on the southwest side. He gained friendly relations and trading terms with the Indians at both places and then set up similar relations with the Miamis who were moving to the head of the Maumee. He traveled frequently between the several posts, but at those early years used Fort St. Joseph as his principal base. Records indicate Captain Vincennes (Bissot) rebuilt Post Miami at three rivers in 1697.

When he was 28 years of age, Bissot, who by that time had assumed the title of Sieur de Vincennes, returned to Quebec for an important event. The vestry records show Jean Baptiste Bissot in 1696 married Marguerite, the daughter of Antoine Forestier, the surgeon-general of New France, and Madeleine Cavelier.

To this couple four years later, on June 17, 1700, at Montreal, was born a son. The little boy was named Francois Marie Bissot, and nicknamed Morgan or Marganne in honor of his godfather. When he grew up he would follow in his father's footsteps to the headwaters of the Maumee, and later would establish a post down the Wabash called Vincennes.

In the meantime, Jean Baptiste Bissot returned to Fort St. Joseph to further cement French relations with the Indians. In June, 1701, Antoine de la Mothe Cadillac set out from Montreal with 100 Frenchmen and 100 Indians. Weeks later, he arrived at the straits between Lake Huron and Lake Erie. He picked out a site on July 24, 1701, for the building of Fort Ponchartrain du Detroit. People curried favor in those days as they have in other times. Count Ponchartrain was Minister of Colonies in the Court of Louis XIV.

With the power of France at Detroit, the French posts to the south of the lakes took on increased importance and activity, and moved toward greater conflict with both the British and their allies, the Iroquois. In 1715, Captain Jean Bissot de Vincennes was instructed to move from Fort St. Joseph, north of South Bend near Niles, Mich., to the post at the head of the Maumee. This was just three years after Vincennes had taken an army of Miami Indians, together with forces under the Detroit commander, Captain Dubuisson, to defeat a series of attacks on Detroit by the combined forces of British-encouraged Iroquois and Fox Indians.

Trade apparently flourished along the Maumee and Wabash routes joined by the portage at three rivers. This is demonstrated in the oldest known existing invoice connected with the early days of Indiana and Fort Wayne. With the list of merchandise was the following excerpt, translated from the French:

"Before the undersigned witnesses was present Francois Roye, who acknowledges that the amount established in the statement which precedes was placed on the contract with his brother, Pierre Roye, in the Miami country, amounting to 5,000 livres, Montreal rate, is good and merchantable furs.

"Done at the Miamis, this 12th of May, 1719, in duplicate and said Francois Roye declared his inability to sign made his mark —X.,' Vincennes and another witness, De Sanguir, signed for Roye.

But Vincennes, the French commander in the Miami country since 1696, was coming to the end of a career. Later that same year, there is a letter dated Oct. 28, 1719. It was in the official correspondence of the Marquis De Vaudreuil, governor-general of Quebec, to the Council of the French Marine. "I have learned from the last letter from the Miamis that Sieur de Vincennes had died in their village. These Indians have resolved to not move to the River St. Joseph and to remain where they are. As this resolution is very dangerous on account of the ease they will have in communicating with the English, who are incessantly distributing belts in secret among all the nations by means of Iroquois runners, I have designated Sieur Dubuisson to remain in that place to counteract the effect. The belts have already caused eight or ten Miami canoes to go to trade at Albany."

Vincennes was 51 years old when he died at Kekionga. He was buried near the three rivers at a site now lost with time. One of the most influencial of the early French leaders in the Old Northwest, he was the first prominent European citizen of the community which has become Fort Wayne.

The First Fort

With the growing threats following the death of Jean Baptiste Bissot, the French decided they needed a fort at three rivers to protect their fur trade and military hold. Charles Regnault Dubuisson, who had come to the post from Detroit, was in 1721 instructed to build a stockade. By May, 1722, the log Fort Miamis was up and garrisoned. The commander in the Miami country just prior to building the fort was Eustache Lambert, Sieur Dumont, whose sister was married to Bissot's brother.

A genealogy of the Bissot family was prepared by J. D. Campbell, Montreal historian in 1918 and sent to B. J. Griswold of Fort Wayne. A similar family history was traced by Pierre-George Roy in 1919 at Quebec. It shows the singular involvement of one family in the discovery of much of North America, and in reflection, the importance of the Miami post at three rivers in the French scheme of that era. A portion of the genealogy furnished by Campbell follows:

"Francois Bissot, Sieur de la Riviere, married at Quebec in 1648, Marie, daughter of Guilanne Couillard and Guillemette Hebert, married in 1621. Couillard de l'Epinay was the first Canadian ennobled. Guillemette Hebert was the daughter of Louis Hebert, apothecary, first settler of New France (Canada), who built the first house in Upper Town of Quebec. Next to Champlain, he contributed more than any other to the founding of Quebec. Jean Nicolet, the explorer, had married another of Couillard's daughters.

"Francois Bissot left 12 children. Among these were:

"Louise, married, 1668, Seraphim Marganne de la Valtrie, and officer of the Carignon-Salieres Regiment. It is his son who was godfather to Francois Vincennes, son of Jean Bissot.

"Claire Francoise, married, Oct. 7, 1675, at Quebec to Louis Joliet, discoverer of the Mississippi.

"Francois Joseph Bissot de la Riviere, married, 1698, Marie, daughter of Eustche Lambert, Dumont, Sieur de Clermont, and sister of Captain Dumont, commandant at the Miamis, 1720-21.

"Jean Baptiste Bissot, Sieur de Vincennes, born 1668, married Sept. 9, 1696 to Marguerite, daughter of Antoine Forestier, surgeon, and Madelaine Cavelier. The wedding was at Montreal. Of this marriage were born seven children. Among them was:

"Francois Marie de Vincennes, founder of Fort Vincennes, born at Montreal 17th of June, 1700, burned by the Chickasaws, 1736. In March, 1733, he was married to the daughter of Philippe Longpre of Kaskaskia. He left two daughters, Catherine and Marie Therese. Sometimes signed Marganne de Vincennes, because his godfather was his cousin, Francois Marganne, Sieur de Batilly. It is an old Canadian custom, still in vogue, for a godson to use his godfather's family name as a surname."

The Younger Vincennes

In 1728 Nicholas Joseph de Noyelle was named commandant of Fort St. Philippe, as the fort at the Miami villages was called for a time. He was succeeded by Ensign Charles de Arnaud on June 3, 1732. During this period, the principal French commander at the various posts in the Miami and Illinois country was the younger Vincennes. Among the posts was Fort Ouiatenon, built by Dubuisson in 1722 soon after he completed Fort Miamis. Ouiatenon was on the Wabash near the present city of Lafayette.

During their jousting for advantage both in Europe and America, the French and

British were engaged in a lively contest for trading profits and land control in the North American interior. The no-man's land centered around Lake Erie, with the English and their Iroquois allies to the south and east and the French and the Algonquin tribes to the north and west.

When the French founded Fort Niagara in 1726 on the east end of Lake Erie, their control was enhanced, which in turn stimulated trade and traffic through the Maumee and Wabash corrider which connected the lakes and the St. Lawrence with the interior and the Mississippi.

Young Vincennes was directed in 1731 to proceed further down the Wabash and establish another link in the French power system. This new post was to be oriented toward New Orleans on the Gulf of Mexico. New Orleans is rightfully associated with the early French in America, but it actually was not as old a French community in the U. S. as the place which has become Fort Wayne.

By 1733, Vincennes had completed the erection of Au Poste, later called Fort Vincennes. The young French commander, who's name was to live long in Indiana history, had a short and tragic career. Three years after he founded Vincennes, he found himself on the loosing side of a battle against the Chickasaw Indians. His end was reported by Drouet de Richardville, a French trader whose name would in later years be assumed by leaders of the Miami Indian nation.

"He reports that in this engagement, three of his brothers were killed; that he himself received two gunshot wounds, one in the left arm and one at the base of the stomach, and an arrow wound in his wrist; that he was taken arms in hand by three Chickasaws and brought to a village with 22 French, of whom 20 were burned at the stake, among others: Father Senat, Jesuit; Messrs. d'Artaguette, de Vincennes, de Coulanges, de St. Ange fils, Du Tisne, and Tonty the younger. These gentlemen were burned with Father Senat on the day of the fight, from 3 o'clock in the afternoon to midnight. The other officers who were burned were officers and militiamen." This battle occurred in March, 1736, according to Richardville's report to the Louisiana authorities. In all 40 Frenchmen were lost.

Burning of French Fort

Fort Miamis at the future site of Fort Wayne was having a period of prosperity. Trade through the corridor boomed and some of the later Indians remembered this period as the golden age of French and Indian affairs in the wilderness. The fort itself, however, was not especially well garrisoned. Several visitors to the vicinity in those days remarked on the low condition of both the stockade and the half dozen or more men who were supposedly on duty at the post. It was during this peaceful relationship with the Indians that a war in Europe, called King George's War, broke out in 1744. As the hostilities moved to the New World, the trouble centered in the Great Lakes area.

The war in the hinterlands is remembered as the King Nicolas War, so named because of the leadership of a Huron Chief who took the name of King Nicolas. Under the influence of the British, he made great plans for the wiping out of all the French forts in the northwest wilderness. He was fairly successful in enlisting the aid of many of the tribes for what was to be a surprise stroke. Threatened were some dozen forts from Lake Superior down to the river country below the Great Lakes. As it turned out, the great uprising misfired in just about every instance. In some places, the allied Indians didn't do what they were supposed to do. In others, the French garrisons were informed long in advance of the "surprise" raids and had little trouble beating them off. In all the grand schemes of Nicolas, there was one success. The Indians took Fort Miamis at the headwaters of the Maumee. At that time it was one of the weaker links in the entire chain of French forts in interior America.

The attack took place on Pentecost Sunday, 1747. The Indians rushed the fort and captured the eight-man garrison. The old fort on the banks of the St. Mary's River, just southwest of where the Van Buren St. Bridge was later built, was put to the torch.

Two of the soldiers escaped and the others were believed released later. There is little doubt that the Miami Indians joined in the strike, otherwise it isn't likely that the attack would have occurred. However, at the time of the burning of the first French fort, the Miami chiefs Coldfoot and Hedgehog were at Detroit and the fort commander, Ensign Douville, was on a visit to Montreal.

The destruction of Fort Miamis brought Charles Dubuisson, long-time commandant of Detroit, back to Miamitown. He had originally built the stockade at the St. Mary's portage site in 1721 and upon his return in 1747 partially reconstructed it. He also strengthened the garrison and assigned 30 men to it. Fort Ouiatenon on the Wabash, near where Lafayette was to be later located, was also reinforced.

The Adventurers

The French were moving to the offensive following the failure of the British-inspired Nicolas uprising. Captain Pierre Joseph Bienville de Celeron with 200 French soldiers and a force of Indians crossed Lake Erie and went to the Alleghany River and then down the Ohio. The great squeeze was being put on the British presence and their colonies in North America. Celeron claimed a wide area for France, including another Post Miami which was on the Miami River near the Ohio which had been built by the British. On his return trip, Celeron went overland to Fort Miamis at the headwaters of the Maumee. The year was 1749 and he reported finding the stockade in a condition of decay. With Captain de Celeron on the trip was Father Jean de Bonnecamps who said "The fort of the Miamis was in very bad condition when we reached it. Most of the palisades were decayed and fallen into ruin. There are eight houses, or to speak more correctly, eight miserable huts which only the desire of making money could render endurable." De Bonnecamps, a Jesuit mathematician, explorer and missionary, was professor of mathematics and astronomy at Jesuit College, Quebec. In his eye witness view of life at three rivers in 1749, he said "The French there number 22, and all of them, including the commandant, had the fever. Monsieur Raimond (Capt. Charles D. Raimond who became commandant of Fort Miamis in 1749) did not approve the situation of the fort and maintained it should be relocated on the bank of the St. Joseph, a scant league from the present site."

De Bonnecamps reported that Capt. Raimond wanted him to survey the site for the new fort to be built along the St. Joseph River. But Celeron and De Bonnecamps were anxious to depart. "All that I could do for him was to trace for him the plan of his new fort." Thus we have on his own report to the French government in Paris that De Bonnecamps designed the second Fort built at the future site of Fort Wayne. Also, presumably working from the position of stars, he gave the old fort's latitude as 41 degrees, 29 minutes.

Captain Charles Raimond, who earlier had been in command at Fort Niagara, didn't like the swampy area where the Fort at Miamitown was located along the St. Mary's. He moved quickly to construct the second French Fort Miami on the east bank of the St. Joseph River, about a quarter mile north of the junction with the Maumee. The fortification was erected in 1750.

Louis Coulon

Later that same year, 1750, there arrived at Fort Miami the most illustrous commander since Vincennes a generation earlier. This was Louis Coulon de Villiers, later to be dubbed "The Grand Villiers." He was one of six sons of the long-time commander of Fort St. Joseph near Lake Michigan. He remained at the future site of Fort Wayne for three years, then moved on to launch the French and Indian War, which in turn, became something close to a world war involving much of Europe and parts of Asia. De Villiers came up the Maumee in July, 1750, and strengthened the garrison to 50 men. During his stay, two events tended to increase Miamitown as a key center for both trade and Indian power, and to strengthen the ties between the Miami Indians and the French. The first was the destruction of Pickawillany (sometimes called Post Miami) just north of the Ohio River. In 1752, a French and Indian force came all the way from the Straits of Mackinac, led by the half-breed frontier fighter Charles Langlade, to completely level Pickawillany. This caused many of the Miami Indians who had located there to move to Kiskakon, or Kekionga, at three rivers. The other event was the onset of the smallpox plague of 1753. This dread disease swept across the entire Great Lakes country, reducing the population of the Indian villages and French forces alike. And also some of their English enemies and Indian allies as well. Many of the old Indian villages were abandoned. Some of the survivors tended to concentrate at Miamitown and the vicinity.

Late in 1753, Captain Coulon de Villiers left Fort Miami and made his way to Quebec to prepare for the campaign which was to develop into the French and Indian War. So effective was Coulon in the early phases of the war that he was knighted by the Marquis de Montcalm, the French commander in New France.

French and Indian War

Coulon was the victorious commander in the opening battle of the war. This happened in 1754 when leading an army of French regulars and Indians, including Ottawas, Miamis and Hurons, he moved to head off Colonial forces threatening newly-built Fort Duquesne (later Pittsburgh). In command of the English-Colonial company was the freshly-named colonel at 22 years of age, George Washington.

Le Grand Villiers' younger brother, Coulon de Jumonville, had been killed a few months before at the hands of Washington in a wilderness skirmish in western Pennsylvania.

Captain Coulon went from Fort Duquesne with a force of 650 French and Indians to attack Washington's company of 400 men. They first took to the river in canoes and then traveled overland to a half-built fort, only to learn that Washington had started a retreat two days earlier.

Villiers pressed on with the chase in a driving rainstorm. On July 4, 1754, he caught up with Washington's forces at a place called Great Meadows, where a meager, hastily-constructed stockade called Fort Necessity stood.

A third of Washington's effectives were killed or wounded in a murderous crossfire by Coulon's riflemen, all during what Washington in his report said was "the most tremendous rain that could be conceived." Some of the wounded actually may have drowned in the water-filled trenches around the fort. On the second day Washington capitulated, and after signing away the right of the English to occupy the Ohio Valley for a year and a day, he was allowed to take his defeated troops back east.

Increasingly in the era of Coulon, the Miamis sided with the French in frontier warfare. One day in 1755, more than 250 Miami warriors departed from Kekionga on a trip to Fort Duquesne. These Indians joined in the ambush of the English and Colonial Army of General Edward Braddock. This army of 2,000 was outfitted in England with the express purpose of crushing the French. Washington was second in command. Caught in the wilderness approaching Fort Duquesne, Braddock's army was thrown into disorder and nearly crushed. It was the greatest defeat of a regular army by the Indians in the history of the continent, with the sole exception of a victory by the Miami Warchief Little Turtle in a later generation.

A few years before the English took over the fort on the east bank of the St. Joseph River at Miamitown, the French commander had warned: "Nobody wants to stay here and have his throat cut." As it turned out, few of the French garrison had their throats cut and they departed in one piece. It was a different matter for the British, however, who occupied the fort in 1760. The various forts in the Northwest and Canada were the fruits of victory by the British in the final battles of the French and Indian War.

PAYS
DES
APACHES
ET DES
PADOUCAS
LA LOU
PAYS DES OSAGES
NOVA
MEXICO
LES CADODAQUIOS
LES KANOATINOS
les Padoucas
10 Villages
les Panimaha
les Cansez
les Missouris
les Grimaiches
les Cannesy
les Chacakante
Quiohouhahan
Kanouhanan
Ionhouannes
les Choumans
Cadodaquios
Natchitoches
SIOUX DE L'OUEST
SIOUX DE L'EST
Tintons
les Maha
Caligoa
les Akansas
SINVS
Explicatio Signorum
Habitationes Indorum
Nationes deturbatæ
NOVA Parral
BISCAYA
NOVUM REGNUM LEGIONIS
Rio del Norte
Rio de Flores
Riviere S. Joseph
Pointe aux Serpens
Cap du Nord
Indi errantes et Antropophagi

Novissima Tabula
LVDOVICIANÆ
Jam olim quidem
sub CANADÆ et FLORIDÆ nomine
sub auspiciis Serenissi Ducis Aurelianensis maxime inclarescentis
COLONIÆ GALLICAE
delineata
à Guil. Insulano
LACUS HURON
LACUS sive MICHIGANE
L. MICHIGAN
CANADA sive NOVÆ FRANCIÆ
LACUS ONTARIO
Lac Champlain
IROQUOIS
LAC ERIE ou DU CHAT
Nation du Chat
NOVA YORK
PENSILVANIA
Philadelphia
NEU JERSEY
MARILAND
VIRGINIA
Northampton
Grande Baye de Chesapeack
MARE VIRGINIENSE
CAROLINA
Charles Town
S. Augustin
Ohio ou la Belle Riviere
Algonquins
Les Miamis
Les Tongoria
Portage
Cap de Lookout
Cap Fear
Apalachacolas
Les Caouitas
CANUS

Joliet's rough drawing shows 1673-74 version of Mississippi and Great Lakes.

Section of Italian globe in 1688 is surprisingly accurate, but with man-eating monsters, man-burning Indians and the Mississippi flowing into the Gulf near the Rio Grande.

The beaver, in this old colonial drawing, was the main object of trappers.

On the previous 2 pages is a map printed in Nurnberg, Germany, in 1734 from French, Spanish and English sources which showed the portages and most of the rivers 70 years before the Lewis and Clark expedition.

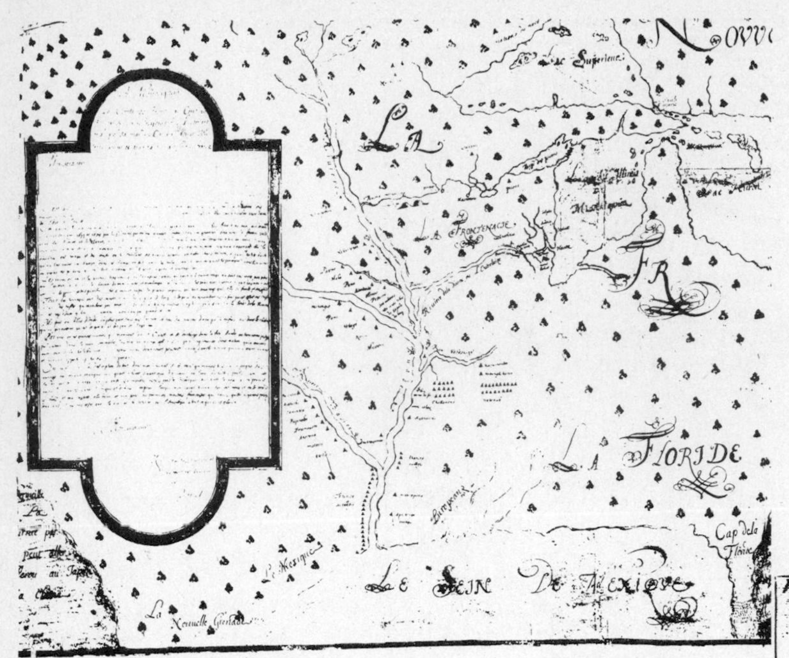

A Beaver 25 inches long from the head to the tail

5. A section from Vincenzo Coronelli's globe of 1688.

British at Fort Miami

English soldiers under Major Robert Rogers came up the Maumee from Detroit and arrived at Miamitown during a December sleet storm. They assumed control of the old French stockade. Ensign Robert Holmes was left in charge. The situation for the fort at Miamitown had always been an uneasy one. It was too close to the smoke and temper of Kekionga, the great Miami village a short distance to the south; and Shawnee and Delaware tribes were increasingly locating in the immediate vicinity.

But things looked calm on the surface. The French, except for a few traders, were completely out of the Great Lakes area. They only had outposts on the Mississippi. The British felt they had a firm hand along the Maumee, Wabash and Ohio Rivers in that year of 1760. But more than a chill breeze was flowing out of the north woods. An Ottawa Indian chief named Pontiac was sending a red-stained tomahawk and a bloody war belt to villages from Lake Superior to the lower Mississippi. The implication was clear to the Indians, but only gradually made an impression on the British. Pontiac had decided it was time for the red man to get rid of the white man.

The Bloody Belt

Robert Holmes at Fort Miami was one of the first of the British officers to get material information on the conspiracy. A friendly Indian told him one day in March, 1763, that the bloody belt of war was at that moment being circulated at Kekionga. He reported the following to Major Henry Gladwyn, the Detroit commander:

> "The bloody belt, being in this village, I have made all the search I could about it, and have found it to be true. I assembled all the chiefs of this nation, and after a long and troublesome spell with them, I obtained the belt, as you will receive enclosed. This affair is very timely stopped, and I hope the news of a peace will put a stop to any further troubles with these Indians who are the principal ones setting mischief afoot. I send you the belt with this packet, which I hope you will forward to the general."

Within weeks, the Indians under Pontiac swept across the entire west. Fort Sandusky, Fort Michilimackinac, Fort St. Joseph, Fort Ouiatenon and Fort Miami fell to the raiders. Some thievery, murder and betrayal of love got into the bloody act at the three rivers. On the night of May 25, three English soldiers who were outside Fort Miami were killed by Indians. Holmes immediately closed the gates to the stockade and the garrison went on the alert. The following day, Jacques Godfroy and several other French traders talked a group of Miami Indians into grabbing two English traders who were taking a cargo of furs down the Maumee. The Frenchmen took the furs and later sold them at Detroit; while the Indians held onto the prisoners. One of the prisoners, Robert Lawrence held at Kekionga, told what happened next. It seems that the garrison at Fort Miami had an Achilles heel —Ensign Holmes' love affair with a pretty Indian girl. According to the story, a Miami chief talked the girl into enticing Holmes out of the stockade.

> "On the 27th day of May, a young Indian girl who lived with the commandant came to tell him that a squaw lay dangerously ill in a wigwam near the fort, and urged him to come to her relief. Having confidence in the girl, Holmes forgot his caution and followed her out of the fort. Pitched on the edge of a meadow, hidden from view by an intervening spur of woodland, stood a great number of wigwams. When Holmes came in sight of them, the treacherous conductress pointed out that one in which the sick woman lay. He walked on . . . two guns flashed from behind the hut and stretched him lifeless on the grass."

One of the English captives, Robert Lawrence, said he was shown Holmes' scalp later that same day.

Fifty-two years later, Laura Suttenfield, who was a resident of old Fort Wayne, met an aged Indian squaw. The Indian woman admitted she was the one who had coaxed the young English ensign out of the fort. She also told Mrs. Suttenfield she was unknowingly with child at the time, and in due course, gave birth to a blond-haired boy, the son of Ensign Holmes.

The English Surrender

When the shots which killed Ensign Robert Holmes, commander of Fort Miami, were heard by the British soldiers in the stockade, a sergeant made the mistake of going out to see what happened. He arrived just in time at the nearby huts of Kekionga to be grabbed by the Indians who were in the process of scalping the dead Holmes. The eight men who remained in the fort along the St. Joseph River took guns in hand and manned the ramparts, awaiting the worst. The Indians were soon at the gates of the fort. These included highly animated Miami Indians headed by the one-eyed Chief Le Gris and Jacques Godfroy, a French trader who was capitalizing on the situation. Godfroy and the Indians demanded the surrender of the garrison. The British soldiers were told the fort would be burned and they would be unpleasantly killed if they didn't give in. Since it was obviously in the power of the Indians to do both, the soldiers after thinking it over for awhile opened the gates and walked out. For some, their chances might have been better with the fort.

Two of the prisoners were dragged off to canoes, and after being taken across the portage, went down the Wabash with an Indian war party and Godfroy. This group eventually arrived at Fort Ouiatenon near the present site of Lafayette. The two prisoners were used there as bodily evidence to convince the commander Lt. Edward Jenkins, that Fort Miami had truly been taken. After appeals of safe conduct, the men of the garrison surrendered to the Indians. The British soldiers credited their lives to a French trader named Francois Maisonville, a longtime resident of Miamitown (now Fort Wayne) who paid the Indians to spare their lives. Maisonville, unfortunately, was later taken prisoner by George Rogers Clark at Vincennes during the Revolutionary War and committed suicide in an American cell.

As hostilities faded, the Ottawa Chief Pontiac came to set up his village here, but the Miamis convinced the famous war chief that it would be better some distance down the Maumee, near present-day Defiance, Ohio. Pontiac was killed four years later by a Peoria Indian near the Mississippi River. As the months passed, several French traders moved their houses inside the palisades. A few Indians also took up residence inside Fort Miami. This was the situation when the next British military presence arrived.

Cost of Scalps

Captain Robert Morris was the emissary of Col. John Bradstreet, British officer sent west to pacify the Indians. After talking with Pontiac further down the Maumee, Captain Morris and his guide, Jacques Godfroy (the same man who had helped set up the murder of Ensign Holmes) proceeded by canoe to Miamitown. Soon after his canoe was pulled onto the muddy river banks at the junction of the three rivers, Morris was grabbed by Miami warriors. First they dragged him to Fort Miami, and after awhile came back for him.

"Two Indian warriors with tomahawks in their hands seized me, one by each arm," Morris later reported. "They dragged me into the water (St. Joseph River) . . led me till we came near the village and there they stopped and stripped me. They then bound my arms with my sash. The whole village was in an uproar."

As Morris stood there, the Indians began arguing among themselves whether to burn him to death or not. One chief, The Swan, was for freeing him. Another, Vesculair, would have none of that nonsense. "Vesculair got up and tied me by the neck to a post. I had not the smallest hope of life when

Pacan, king of the Miami nation . . . mounted a horse and crossed the river, rode up to me. When I heard him call out to those about me and felt his hand behind my neck, I thought he was going to strangle me out of pity, but he untied me, saying: 'I give this man his life'." Pacan was an uncle of Little Turtle, the great Miami chief who put together the most potent Indian armies in America the following generation.

No sooner had Captain Morris gained his freedom, when a group of Kickapoos also made an attempt on his life. The British officer, however, escaped this time, and with Godfroy's help, made it back to Detroit. The idea to garrison the fort was apparently forgotten.

When the English decided to pacify the Indians after the uprising of Chief Pontiac, they didn't rely on half-way measures. They sent west two small armies—one to the northern area of Lake Erie, Lake Huron and Lake Michigan; the other to the south of the hostile Indian country along the Ohio River and Wabash River. Both of these expeditions moved during 1764.

On July 7 of that same year the colonial governor of Pennsylvania issued from the City of Brotherly Love a proclamation. In it, bounties were offered for scalps or capture of hostile Indians in the Old Northwest. It was not unlike the bounties which were later offered in various Indiana counties for hides of foxes and other real or imagined unpopular animals. A difference was, however, that the 1764 bounties were for human beings. A partial pay list follows:

For every male above 10 years, captured, $150.

For every male above 10 years, scalped, being killed, $134.

For every female or male under 10 years, captured $130.

For every female above 10 years, scalped, being killed, $50.

It is difficult to determine just how many of these bounties were collected, or how they distinguished between scalps from Indians above 10 years and those younger. Presumably, it was also difficult to distinguish between scalps of "hostile" Indians and those of "friendly" Indians. It is certain, however, that it was much easier and safer to get the scalps of the friendly tribes, and the records of the time mention raids by bounty hunters on the pacified tribes in the area of Western Pennsylvania. The bounty hunters never made it to Kekionga, where the deserted British Fort Miami was located. In this vicinity, it was the Indians who did all the scalp taking.

Croghan at Miamitown

The following year, 1765, the British decided to try a peace-loving approach with the "hostiles." A man named Colonel George Croghan left Fort Pitt in May and went down the Ohio River, up the Wabash to the future site of Fort Wayne. He wrote about it:

"Within a mile of the Miami village of Kekionga, I was met by the chiefs of that nation who received us very kindly. The most part of these Indians knew me and conducted me to their village where they immediately hoisted an English flag that I had formerly given them at Fort Pitt. The next day they held a council, after which they gave me up the English prisoners that they had.

"The Miami village is situated on both sides of a river called the St. Joseph. This river where it falls into the Maumee River about a quarter of a mile from this place is one hundred yards wide, on the east side of which stands a stockade fort somewhat ruinous.

> "The Indian village consists of about forty or fifty cabins, besides nine or ten French houses, a runaway colony from Detroit during the late Indian war. They were concerned in it, and being afraid of punishment, they came to this spot where ever since they have spirited up the Indians against the English. All the French residing here are a lazy, indolent people, fond of breeding mischief and spiriting up the Indians against the English, and should by no means be suffered to remain here. The country is pleasant, the soil rich and well watered."

Croghan then left Miamitown for Detroit,

going down the Maumee in a canoe. In his prejudice against the French, he had possibly fallen into error. The French traders were at Miamitown long before the Pontiac uprising, and despite that Croghan told his superiors they "should by no means be suffered to remain here," the Frenchmen stayed.

The British continued their political control over the wilderness, but did nothing to restore the decaying fort at Miamitown. The growing importance of the Maumee-Wabash route in trade and Indian power, however, can be noted in the advice to the Crown by Sir William Johnson, in charge of Indian affairs in America, in 1771. He suggested the Home Government furnish the funds to rebuild and garrison the fort at Miamitown.

> "St. Joseph (near Lake Michigan) and Miamis (at the three rivers) have neither of them been re-established. The former is of less consequence for trade than the latter, which is a place of some importance. At the Miamis there may always be a sufficiency of provisions from its vicinity by the river of that name (Maumee is a corruption of the French word for Miami) in the proper season, to protect which the fort can, at a small expense, be rendered tenable against any coupe de mains."

Despite this suggestion, and the increasing trade which was switching from the more westerly lake routes to the Maumee-Wabash waterway and portage, the British fort was never rebuilt.

Indian Power Grows

While the oaken planks in the palisades were coming apart at the seams, Miamitown itself was knitting as a center of Indian activity. Land treaties and warfare further to the east was tending to drive the Indians northwest of the Ohio River, and thus set the stage for a long-term alliance between the Miami and Shawnee Indians. This would eventually make Miamitown the hub of the most potent Indian army in American history, which in turn would be the cause for the building of three more forts there. Perhaps there is need for a perspective regarding events leading to the Revolutionary War. If on the east coast, the issues were taxation, representation and control of trade; the issues on the west fringes of the colonies were more earthly—land speculation and ownership, and the basic privilege of staying alive. In a very real sense, the revolution was a civil war as well as a battle for independence. The English and their descendants were on both sides. In the middle were the Indians.

The English probably made a big mistake in the Treaty of Fort Stanwix in 1768. They turned control of the Indian affairs over to the colonial governors, whose main interest seemed to be in getting settlers into and the Indians out of the western areas of Pennsylvania and Virginia. Also in the treaty, the Iroquois Indians agreed to give up any claims on land east of the Ohio River —again meaning the western parts of Pennsylvania and Virginia. They overlooked one thing. It was the Shawnees who were the main Indians in those areas. As the settlers moved in, the Indians struck back. The scale of massacres increased. Finally, open warfare broke out in 1774, called Lord Dunmore's War, after the colonial governor of Virginia.

Miami Indians from the three rivers went down the Wabash and up the Ohio. Others went across the flatlands and swamps to the southeast where they joined the Shawnees for a series of wilderness conflicts with the colonials. It was a mean little war which the colonial forces won. It had two effects. It set the Ohio River as a semi-permanent boundary between Indian and Colonial lands. It drove the Shawnees and some Delawares further west. Many set up villages along the Maumee. It also put the Indians on the side of the English in the Revolution which broke out in 1775. Even with the war, the English did not rebuild Fort Miami. They did, however, make regular expeditions along the Lake Erie, Maumee and Wabash route, using the portage here. The largest of these was headed by the military commander of Detroit, Col. Henry Hamilton.

Hamilton's Army

Early in the war, Hamilton had talks with the Indians with the aim of attacks on Americans. He set up a pay scale for the scalps of settlers, which earned him the reputation of "hair buyer" along the frontiers. Thus, there was the situation which had the governor of Pennsylvania paying bounties for Indian scalps, and the English commanders further to the west paying for the white scalps. Which was just another way of declaring war of extermination. It turned out that the Miamis were among the best exterminators. Since no settler would have been stupid enough to settle northeast of the Ohio River, the Indians had to go to Pennsylvania and Virginia to get scalps. Kentucky and Tennessee were part of Virginia in those days. It was gory business. Hamilton had little sympathy for the families of the settlers and said their "arrogance, disloyalty and imprudence have justly drawn upon themselves this deplorable sort of war."

In prosecuting the bloody wilderness war, Hamilton soon received at Detroit three volunteers. These were Alexander McKee, Matthew Elliott and Simon Girty. All three were deserters from the American stronghold at Fort Pitt. They had decided the pickings were more interesting on the other side. Both Girty and McKee slipped in and out of Miamitown frequently in setting up raiding parties in the extermination business. Already at Miamitown was Charles Beaubien, a French trader who was interpreter for Hamilton, dealing in both fur of game animals and hair of the colonial variety.

There was great commotion down along the Maumee one dry fall day of 1778 as a whole fleet of flat boats came into Miamitown. Shouts from Indian children mixed with the dust and leaves which were wind-whipped across the three rivers clearing. The great British military expedition from Detroit was stopping to set up a secondary supply depot. Colonel Henry Hamilton, commander of British Fifteenth Regiment and commandant of Fort Detroit, was pushing his campaign to rid the Northwest Territory of all American settlers. His destination was Vincennes, which had been taken a few months before by an impertinent rabble of 400 colonials under George Rogers Clark. In the convoy were 15 large boats and many pirogues and canoes. There were about 180 troops, including regulars and Canadian militia, and numerous Indian volunteers. The inhabitants of the Miami villages watched as crews dragged supplies ashore, including a brass six-pounder cannon and an estimated $50,000 worth of provisions for storage. The colorful red uniforms and flashy swords and weaponry sparkled in the October sun. Many braves in the vicinity eagerly sought to join in the expedition which was to proceed across the portage and down the Wabash. The imperious English officer left his report:

> "On the 24th we arrived at the Miamis Town after the usual fatigue attending such navigation, the water of the Maumee being remarkably low. Here we met several tribes of Indians previously summoned to meet there and held several conferences, made presents, and dispatched messengers to the Shawnees, as well as the nations on our route, inviting them to join us or at least watch the motions of the rebels on the frontiers, for which purpose I sent them ammunition."

Hamilton Meets Le Gris

Hamilton told of meeting Le Gris, the Kekionga chief, and others. "Young men of that nation saluted as usual with several discharges of small arms. Our savages (Chippewa and Ottawa) returned the compliment, after which there was a kind of mock battle with blank powder." The Englishman said Le Gris gave him presents of corn, dried pumpkin and kidney beans, "saying that such coarsefare might serve for my cattle if I could not eat it myself." The colonel reported that the Indians complained "I did not wet the grindstone with rum." Presumably Hamilton didn't want a bunch of drunken savages on his hands. The colonel also gave an insight into early medical practice: "Their priests, who are usually their doctors, are provided with an apparatus very different from our quacks. This is usually carried in the budget and consists of heads, bones and skins of certain animals, preserved birds of a feather, snake skins, wolves teeth, panther claws, eagle talons." He described how the doctor juggled these items, and by pretending to draw out a bear's claw from the diseased part, "seldom fails to . . . perfect the cure." He said some Miamis joined him for his trip southwest.

"Having passed the portage of nine miles, we arrived at one of the sources of the Wabash called the Riviere Petite. The waters were so uncommonly low that we should not have been able to have passed but that at the distance of four miles from the landing place the beavers had made a dam which kept up the water.

"These we cut through to give a passage to our boats, and having taken in our lading at the landing, passed all the boats. The beaver are never molested at this place by the traders or Indians, and soon repair their dam, which is most serviceable work upon this difficult communication.

"With great labor, we next passed a swamp called Les Volets, beyond which the A Boete joins the one we made our way through. The shallowness of the water obliged us to make a dam across both rivers to back the waters into the swamp, and when we judged the water to be sufficiently raised, cut our dyke and passed with all our craft."

Clark Strikes Back

Despite all the arduous labor of his trek through the bush country, Colonel Hamilton and his expedition was destined to end in eventual disaster. The British took Vincennes back with ease. They demanded and received the surrender of the garrison. The Stars and Stripes was run down and the Union Jack was run up. But as they settled in for a quiet winter, and the Indians went back to their villages, there was activity to the west.

Clark brought a hungry force of 170 frontier types from Kaskaskia on the Mississippi across the icy wastes in the dead of winter. On Feb. 7, 1779, he hit Vincennes in surprise attack. On the following day, the British garrison capitulated and Hamilton, the infamous "scalp buyer," was taken prisoner. The English colonel was taken to Williamsburg, Va., and thrown in a dungeon. He lived to be freed in a prisoner exchange at the end of the Revolution. As far as is known, he never again visited the Wabash country or the future site of Fort Wayne. It would have seemed like an excellent opportunity for Clark and his rabble crew to make a move to grab Miamitown and possibly occupy the old French-built fort, which was in somewhat dilapidated condition along the St. Joseph River. They could have moved from there for an attack on Detroit—seeing that Hamilton had taken much of that garrison with him to the Wabash debacle. Clark, however, thought twice about a strike against the Maumee villages and Detroit, and then decided to return to Virginia. He never came to Miamitown. That venture was left to someone else. Where the old frontiersman declined to tred, another with a smaller army and less experience rushed in.

La Balme Massacre

It was the following year, 1780, that August Mottin de la Balme sought his fortune in the North American wilderness. A French cavalry officer commissioned in Paris, La Balme had come to the United States with the Marquis de Lafayette early in the war. After several months along the east coast, he was still a soldier without fortune. He learned in Virginia of Clark's "missed opportunity" and headed west. Both Miamitown and Detroit were prizes. The war was stimulating trade, and also cutting off the usual commerce from American Atlantic ports. The price of furs was skyrocketing in Europe. La Balme might already have had a potential deal going with some French Canadian trading houses along the St. Lawrence. He gathered some adherents at Kaskaskia on the Mississippi headed up the Wabash with about 100 men. Miamitown in the meantime was thriving. In addition to some long-time traders in residence, several new onces had moved in to build storehouses and take advantage of increasing fur profits. The Indian population was growing apace too, and several new villages were going up in the vicinity. Life at three rivers was good.

The tranquility was disturbed on Nov. 3, when Colonel La Balme led his raiders across the portage tracks and sacked Miamitown. Either the Indians were taken by surprise, or they expected the visitors were just passing through. The reaction was swift. Particularly incensed were some of the traders who suffered heavy financial loss in the destruction and thefts. These included Charles Beaubien and Peter LaFontaine, both of whom later married Miami women. Beaubien and LaFontaine insisted that their Indian neighbors revenge the attack and insult, something the Indians were inclined to do anyway.

Under Little Turtle, the Miami War Chief, the Indians caught La Balme's men at a middle-of-the-night encampment along Aboite Creek. It was a massacre. About half the small army was killed on the spot. Few of the others survived more than a couple days. There was only one known survivor, a Monsieur Rhys, La Balme's aide-in-camp. Little Turtle had sent him along with information on the raid to the new British commander at Detroit, Colonel Arent de Peyster, a New York Tory who hated the American cause even more than Henry Hamilton, his English predecessor.

Washington's Dream

That the Great Lakes and Wabash areas were part of the new nation at all was mainly due to the military expedition during the Revolution of George Rogers Clark and the deep interest of George Washington for the inclusion of the territories northwest of the Ohio. On February 8, 1785, Washington wrote to Richard Henry Lee suggesting better mapping of the lakes and river areas and possible control of navigation. "I cannot forbear observing that the Miami Village points to an important post for the Union. The advantages would be unbounded, for I am sure nature has such a display of her bounties in those regions that the more the country is explored the more it will rise in estimation consequently the greater will be the revenue to the Union." The future first president suggested government "mark the way" for expansion westward by the building of a military road. Basic to the effort was a garrison at the three rivers to temper the British influence which was still heavy in the Northwest Territory. Washington's strong arm westward is consistent with the man's early career as a participant in the pre-Revolutionary Indian wars and his diplomatic policies at the conclusion of the Revolution. One cannot help but wonder, however, at his saying: "The expense attending such an undertaking could not be great." Particularly, when one considers the fate of a childhood friend a couple years earlier.

William Crawford grew up in Berkley County, Virginia, in the neighborhood of the Washingtons. Little Billy and George were playmates, and presumably took turns tossing coins across rivers and cutting down cherry trees. Like George, Billy grew up to be a soldier. At the conclusion of the Revolution, Crawford, a colonel, was working out of Fort Pitt. The war was over but the hostilities with the Indians still continued. Colonel Crawford was one of several at the time who saw it his duty to punish the recalcitrant natives. On several occasions he showed he was more eager than most to get out there in the country and cut up the Indian people in the villages. With between 300 and 400 men, he moved west from Pennsylvania in the summer of 1782. It was to be his last jaunt. Colonel Crawford led his men along the south shore of Lake Erie, the aim being to burn out Indian concentrations in that area and along the Maumee River. With the force were Crawford's son and a Dr. Knight, who was notorious for his part in these bloody affairs. Crawford's party never accomplished its mission. Near the present city of Sandusky, Ohio, they were caught and routed by a large group of Indian warriors, mostly Shawnee. With the Indians was Simon Girty, who knew Crawford from the old days when he worked on the American side at Fort Pitt, but now was on the Indian side in about the same mean role Dr. Knight played for the American raiders. Both Colonel Crawford and his young son were captured, but Dr. Knight and most others got away. Soon after, the commander at Fort Pitt sent a letter to George Washingon, July 11, 1782:

"Dr. Knight, a surgeon I sent with Colonel Crawford, returned and he brings a melancholy fate of poor Crawford.

"Crawford and nine others were taken back to Sandusky. The unfortunate colonel, in particular, was burnt and tortured in every manner they could invent. The doctor adds that a certain Simon Girty, who was formerly in our service and deserted with McKee, was present at the torturing. The colonel begged of Girty to shoot him, but he paid no regard."

This sort of thing occurred year after year. Finally, Washington set the ground work for a western campaign aimed at Miamitown, and when elected President, set it in motion. He refers to it in his second annual address to the Joint Houses of Congress. After appointing General Arthur St. Clair governor of the Northwest Territory, the President named General Josiah Harmar to head the expeditionary force of regulars and militia.

Harmar's Drive

To be consistent with announced policy, it would have made as much sense for General Harmar to invade Kentucky and punish the pioneer militia raiders south of the Ohio as to strike against the Indian parties north of the Ohio River. Both were equally guilty of breaking the U.S. edicts against such back-country genocide. As events will show, no such objective enforcement of law and order was ever effected, or even seriously considered. Territorial Governor Arthur St. Clair, frustrated at controlling either the Indians or the pioneers, set up a series of talks with Indian leaders. The trouble was, the main Indian chiefs usually refused to join in the talks. And those that did were often discredited in the eyes of the other Indians. The most stubborn of the Indian chiefs were those of the Miami nation concentrated at Miamitown. Le Gris and Little Turtle consistently refused to meet with the Americans at any of the treaty sites—usually at one fort or another along the Ohio River. To add to St. Clair's and Harmar's discomforture, Miamitown was becoming notorious among Americans as the site where raiding parties originated and prisoners were brought to suffer the tortures of the damned.

To establish at least some communication with the Miamis, St. Clair sent in the spring of 1790 French-speaking representatives, Pierre and Antoine Gamelin, to the lower Wabash to talk with the Indians. The Wabash Indians refused to commit themselves regarding St. Clair's "peace" proposals and told the American representatives they would have to go to Kekionga at three rivers to get any decision from the Indians. The Weas and the Kickapoos told Gamelin: "You know that we can terminate nothing without the consent of our brethern the Miamis. I invite you to proceed to their village and speak to them." It was clear from the advice Gamelin said he received from "one of the head chiefs" that the Miami Confederacy of Indian tribes was becoming effective over a wide area of the wilderness.

Antoine Gamelin, at absolute risk to his life, went up the Wabash, across the portage and to Miamitown at the head of the Maumee. By coincidence, he arrived just a few days after Henry Hay, agent for the British, left Miamitown for Detroit after a similar fact-finding mission for the other side. Hay had spent the entire winter here among the French and Canadian traders and Indians. He had talked with Le Gris and Little Turtle about the American military moves along the Ohio and described the results of Indian raiding parties. He also reported the increasing concentrations of warriors of many tribes, Shawnee, Delaware, Potawatomi Ottawa, as well as Miami, in the three rivers area. Gamelin arrived April 23, 1790, at Miamitown. During the first few days he talked with chiefs of the Shawnees (Blue Jacket) and of the Delawares and Potawatomis.

Le Gris Questions Gamelin

"The next day (April 27) I went to the great chief of the Miamis, called Le Gris. His chief warrior (Little Turtle) was present," Gamelin wrote. To protect themselves, the Miamis had formed a farflung confederation of Indian tribes. When the emissary of the U.S., Antoine Gamelin, came to Kekionga with peace proposals, old Chief Le Gris kept him in the dark. "We cannot give you a positive answer. We must send your speeches to all our neighbors and to the lake nations." Le Gris also told Gamelin that he would have to consult with the commandant at Detroit and that he, Le Gris, wanted all the proposals in writing.

"He promised me that in 30 nights he would send an answer," Gamelin reported. But as far as is known, no answer was ever sent.

One of the methods of keeping the confederacy together, besides getting consent of the various tribes on any course of action, was the use of fear on those who didn't go along. Gamelin said: "Chief Le Gris, chief of the Miamis, asked me in a private discourse what chiefs had made a treaty with the Americans at Muskingum (Fort Harmar)." The life span of any chiefs discovered making land concessions to the Americans was sometimes short. Just three days after Gamelin left Miamitown, an American caught along the Ohio was brought in and burned at the stake. Raids into Kentucky continued.

With Gamelin's report and the new hostilities, Governor Arthur St. Clair ordered General Harmar to get moving on the expedition. On July 15, requests for militia enlistments were circulated in Virginia, Pennsylvania and Kentucky. Harmar already had about 400 regular soldiers. To this was added more than 1,000 militiamen for his main force and 300 more attached to Major John Hamtramck at Vincennes. The American general planned to hit Miamitown from two sides; one army moving directly up from Fort Washington and the other going by way of the Wabash River and striking at Kekionga across the portage from the west. There was great talk of chastising the "inhuman and savage hordes." While the Americans were gathering at the Licking River, across the Ohio from Cincinnati, the Indians were picking up British rifles near the mouth of the Maumee at Lake Erie. The Americans intended to move quickly and in secret, but nobody was fooled.

Harmar's March to Kekionga

On Sept. 26, 1790, the militia moved out of Fort Washington, and on Sept. 30, the regulars joined the march north from the Ohio. Capt. John Armstrong of the regulars and others left records of the campaign. The army under General Harmar marched for 16 days straight. On the afternoon of Oct. 15, Colonel Hardin and an attachment of mounted Kentucky riflemen, "stole in upon the Miami villages, only to find it deserted by men, women and children." Frustrated by finding the Indian villages and traders' building already vacated and burned by the Indians themselves, the militia "soon began to move about in search of plunder." Two days later the main army under General Harmar crossed the Maumee and encamped at Miamitown. Including the militia, the army numbered 1,453 men. The other force, coming up from Vincennes under Major Hamtramck, never made it. That group, totalling about 350 regulars and pioneer auxiliaries, ran short of rations. Some of the men balked at going further, and Hamtramck was forced to return back down the Wabash. At Miamitown, conditions annoyed the general. Both militiamen and officers were chasing about after any stray Indian sighted. Others were scouring the area for items worth grabbing. This resulted in the first official notice by the American government at the site where Fort Wayne now stands. Over the name of General Harmar appeared:

"Camp of the Miami Village, Oct. 18,

1790.

"The general is much mortified at the unsoldier-like behavior of many of the men in the army, who make it a practice to straggle from camp in search of plunder. He, in the most positive terms forbids this practice in the future, and the guards will be answerable to prevent it No party is to go beyond the line of sentinels without a commissioned officer, who, if of the militia, will apply to Colonel Hardin for his orders. The regular troops will apply to the general. All the plunder that may be hereafter collected, will be equally distributed among the army. The kettles, and every other article already taken, are to be collected by the commanding officers of battalions, and to be delivered tomorrow morning to Mr. Belli, the quartermaster, that a fair distributing may take place. The rolls are to be called at troop and retreat beating, and every man absent is to be reported. The general expects that these orders will be pointedly attended to: they are to be read to the troops this evening. The army is to march tomorrow morning early for their new encampment at Chillicothe, about two miles from hence."

Little Turtle Strikes

Most of the troops were apparently under the illusion the Indians weren't going to fight. Getting little action from the Indians at Miamitown, General Harmar, after two days, moved his army to Chillicothe—a Shawnee town located about where Anthony Blvd. crosses the Maumee River today. He hadn't built a fort or even punished the Indians. The troops were restless. While the main army was occupied with the shifting of the encampment a couple miles down river, other soldiers were sent along a trial leading to the northwest. It was suspected, correctly, that villages and trading huts were in that direction along the Eel River. It was on Oct. 19, 1790, that Colonel John Hardin led a force of 300 regulars and militia in search of plunder, following the Indian trail. They went about 10 miles, some getting separated or lost in swamp areas along the way. It was a messy trip. The Americans never did get to the Indian villages. Instead, they ran into a war party headed by Little Turtle, the Miami war chief. The Indians were hidden in a forested area about where U.S. 33 now crosses Eel River. The Indians had deliberately left several fires smoking to draw the troops to the right spot. When raked by rifle shot from the concealed warriors, the surprised militia broke ranks and ran—leaving the small body of regulars behind. It turned out to be a mean skirmish in the thickets and muck of the swampy area. Only six regulars survived. Killed were 22 regulars and nine militia.

This unpleasantness triggered the second official U.S. proclamation within the present city limits of Fort Wayne. Signed by General Harmar, it said:

"Camp at Chillicothe, one of the Shawnee towns on the Omee River, Oct. 20, 1790.

"The party under the command of Captain Strong is ordered to burn and destroy every house and wigwam in this village, together with all the corn, etc. which he can collect. A party of one hundred men, properly officered, under the command of Colonel Hardin, is to burn and destroy effectually, this afternoon, the Pickaway town with all the corn, etc. which he can find in it and its vicinity.

"The cause of the detachment being worsted yesterday has entirely owing to the shameful, cowardly conduct of the militia, who ran away and threw down their arms without firing scarcely a single gun. In returning to Fort Washington, if any officer or men presume to quit the ranks, or not march in the form that they are ordered, the general will most assuredly order the artillery to fire on them. He hopes the check they received yesterday will make them in future obedient to orders."

The next day, the army of more than 1,400 regulars and militia began its march back towards the safety of Cincinnati on the Ohio River. The whole expensive expedition had been bootless to the revenge-minded Kentucky and Pennsylvania militiamen and embarrassing to the general. Harmar couldn't see any safe way to supply a fort so remote in the wilderness. Several dozen men had lost their lives in the campaign.

Aside from some plunder and burning, the Indians were still unpunished. Worse, Indians had, as even the general admitted in his orders, the better of it in the Eel River skirmish. The army moved south for some seven miles before setting up camp for the night where the town of Hoagland is located today. During the evening hours, a scout named David Williams told Harmar and Hardin that the Indians were already returning to Kekionga in considerable number. To salve their frustration, the officers of the U. S. force decided on one final surprise strike against the Miamis. General Harmar ordered 400 men under Colonels Hardin and John Fontaine and Major John Wyllys to make a fast nighttime march back to the three rivers.

Washington's Address

In his second annual address to the joint houses of Congress, Dec. 8, 1790, the First President speaks of the expedition he ordered by General Josiah Harmar into the land of the hostile Indians, "punishing their crimes." Had he known who was getting punishing, some of the following would hardly be in the records:

"It has been heretofore known to Congress that frequent incursions have been made on our frontier settlements by certain banditti or Indians from the northwest side of the Ohio. These with some of the tribes dwelling on and near the Wabash, have of late been particularly active in their depredations, and being emboldened by the impunity of their crimes and aided by such parts of neighboring tribes as could be seduced to join in their hostilities or afford them a retreat for the prisoners and plunder, they have, instead of listening to the humane invitations and overtures made on the part of the United States, renewed their violences with fresh alacrity and greater efforts."

When Washington referred to "A retreat for prisoners and plunder," he meant then-remote Miamitown at the confluence of the three rivers—the destination of the Harmar campaign.

"The lives of a number of valuable citizens have thus been sacrificed, and some of them under circumstances peculiarly shocking, whilst others have been carried into a deplorable captivity.

"These aggravated provocations rendered it essential to the safety of the Western settlements that the aggressors should be made sensible that the Government of the Union is not less capable of punishing their crimes than it is disposed to respect their rights and reward their attachments. As this object could not be effected by defensive measures, it became necessary to put in force the act which empowers the President to call out the militia for the protection of the frontiers, and I have accordingly authorized an expedition in which the regular troops in that quarter are combined with such drafts of militia as were deemed sufficient." Representatives of the western regions were screaming for Federal protection from the Indians of the Miami Confederation, who had killed 1,500 pioneers in the Ohio River area during the preceding few years. But even at that, Washington was careful to mention the Congressional act authorizing his use of military power to invade the Indian lands.

"The event of the measure is yet unknown to me," was the President's rather stilted way of saying he still had no report on the outcome of the battle at Kekionga. "The Secretary of War is directed to lay before you a statement of the information on which it is founded, as well as an estimate of the expense with which it will be attended."

Harmar Meets Disaster

In the meanwhile, back at Miamitown—in fact several weeks before—the American army was in its second try at sneaking up on the Indians. There was no more surprise this time than a few days earlier when the forces of Harmar first hit Miamitown. Mounted riflemen crossed the St. Mary's at about where motorists today go over the Spy Run Ave. Bridge. They aimed to catch the Indians in the rear but were themselves caught by the warriors about a half mile up the St. Joseph. Regulars on foot began moving across the Maumee from the south bank (at a place which has since been called Harmar's Ford, though Harmar wasn't there on the fateful morning). Little Turtle and concealed braves nearly wiped out the soldiers as they attempted to cross the river. Major John Wyllys was killed, as were all but a few of the 60 infantrymen at the spot. Major John Fontaine of the Kentucky militia and a large number of the mounted force also lost their lives. The some 300 survivors, (183 had been killed) fled towards Harmar's camp a half dozen miles to the south. They were met on the way by reenforcements sent by Harmar, but these too turned around and joined the retreat. Later that day, Oct. 22, 1790, General Harmar decided the army would pull out the following morning for the march back to Fort Washington on the Ohio River. There were about 1,200 left to make the trip. There is no record of Indian losses. They had won the victory. They had repulsed the enemy. Instead of a fort being built at Miamitown, it was the Indian villages which were rebuilt.

Federal Outcry

By the time news of Harmar's defeat was reaching the capital cities of the Thirteen States, the Indians were already taking up the offensive. Winter-time raids on Marietta and Cincinnati along the Ohio River and the burning of settlements south of the river brought new cries for Federal protection. The Washington Administration and Congress saw little choice other than to mount another campaign. This time, there was to be no question as to the object of the warfare launched into the Indian country—a permanent stronghold at the seat of Indian power at Miamitown. Money was appropriated not only for the conscription and equipping of a new larger army, but also for the building and supply of the fort-to-be.

As it turned out, getting an army together wasn't so easy. Few reasonable men were willing to risk their necks in the wilderness areas of the hostiles for the measly $2 or $3 a month the army was willing to pay in those days. As a result, the officers of the expeditionary were forced to comb the eastern seaports for the dregs of society and went into the prisons and jail houses with offers of freedom for volunteers. Gradually, the recruits were assembled at Pittsburgh, still the main jumping-off point for both soldiers and pioneers going west. After a few weeks of training, the men were sent in convoys down the Ohio to Fort Washington. They went in convoys, as did all Ohio River traffic, because warriors of the Miami Confederation were making the route a deadly obstacle course. Despite their backgrounds, many of these men would play an important part in the pacification of the enemy—the various Indian tribes of the Old Northwest Territory. From New England and other nonfrontier areas, they were unlikely pioneers. Yet when the chips were down, in the coming battles, they usually held their ground in the face of waves of Indian braves far better than the Kentucky and Pennsylvania militias who were at home in the wild environment. The typical militiamen was an independent soul who, having lived near danger for many years, would move quickly to save his hide for another day; even if that meant throwing down his rifle and running for safety in the face of the enemy. The regulars, perhaps from the jails or wharves of the time, turned out to be the more dependable soldiers. They also paid the heavier price. Casualties among the regulars on both Harmar's and the later campaign of General Arthur St. Clair, ran several times higher than the militia considering the number employed. General St. Clair himself was a rather unlikely frontier leader. Born an aristocraft in Scotland, he became a general in the American Revolution. That he happened to be named governor of the Northwest Territories is in itself a political accident. St. Clair was president of the old Continental Congress which was becoming defunct as the new Constitution of the United States was being ratified by the Thirteen States. In one of its last acts the old Continental Congress in 1787 formed the Northwest Territories—an area which now includes the states of Ohio, Indiana, Michigan,

Illinois and Wisconsin. Since the new institution of the Republic and U. S. Congress would replace the old Continental organization, St. Clair would soon have been out of a job. As St. Clair later would say, he "reluctantly" accepted the position of territorial governor.

After Harmar's failure, St. Clair decided he, himself, would both plan and lead the new campaign to bring the savages to heel. So sure of his success was he, that he even provided for the bringing of large amounts of gold coins for use after his expected victories and the establishing of his fort at the three rivers and portage headwaters. President Washington, however, apparently had some mental reservations about St. Clair. There are in the records several messages aimed at impressing St. Clair with the possible pitfalls of campaigns against the Indians. Pacification of the Indians in the southern part of the United States was going so well in 1791, it just didn't seem reasonable that there should be so much difficulty in the north.

Bolstering St. Clair

The Washington Administration therefore decided to bolster the campaign of General Arthur St. Clair in two ways. First, it was proposed that the permanent line between Indian and pioneer land he moved back from the Ohio River to the Maumee-Wabash Rivers. This was bound to be a popular course, since the numerous new migrants to the Ohio River and Kentucky lands wanted nothing more ardently than the removal of Indians and threats of continuing raids. Also, it looked good on paper. Policy makers could point to a map and draw a line from Lake Erie, across the Maumee and Wabash as far as the Ohio, and over to the Mississippi. They envisioned removing all the tribes to the area northwest of that line. It was believed that difficulties with the "recalcitrant savages" could be overcome by the building of forts, particularly at the portage which joined the Maumee and Wabash Rivers. This would leave vast safe tracts for the veterans of the Revolutionary War and others who had been promised new land holdings by Congress. The second program was designed to split off some of the Indian tribes from the confederacy of the hostiles centered at Miamitown. This was to be by both negotiation with some of the Indians and by separate military attacks against the tribes along the Wabash. Washington's War Department figured if they separated some eastern tribes by treaty and the Wabash Indians by preliminary attacks, St. Clair would be able to march right up the center to Miamitown, disperse the Indians there and build a permanent stronghold as a buffer between Indian and pioneer lands.

Washington Tells Congress

As President Washington mentioned in his third annual address to the Joint Senate and House of Representatives, Oct. 25, 1791: everything seemed to be going according to plan.

"Among the most important of these," Washington said of his executive programs, "is the defense and security of the Western frontiers. To accomplish it on the most humane principles was a primary wish." He described the concluding of treaties and "other proper means used to attach the wavering" Indian tribes; and the adopting of other measures against "those of a hostile description" who apparently were not sufficiently wavering. "Those measures having proved unsuccessful, it became necessary to convince the refactory of the power of the United States to punish their depredations.

"Offensive operations have therefore been directed, to be conducted however as consistently as possible with the dictates of humanity. Some of these have been crowned with full success and others are yet pending.

"The expeditions which have been completed were carried on under the authority and at the expense of the United States by the militia of Kentucky, whose enterprise, intrepidity and good conduct are entitled to peculiar commendation. Overtures of peace are still continued to the deluded tribes, and considerable numbers of individuals belonging to them have lately renounced all further opposition."

The Slashing Raids

The opening expeditions, mentioned by Washington, were quite successful but hardly humane. They were slashing raids in the summer of 1791 against the Indian villages along the Wabash. General Charles Scott led 800 mounted riflemen north from the Ohio River, across the hills of Southern Indiana, in a lightning attack on Ouiatenon along the Wabash, near the present city of Lafayette. The villages of the Weas and Kickapoos were burned to the ground. Further up the Wabash, at the outflow of the Eel River, the Miami village was also destroyed. Scott met little resistance. Thirty-two Indians were slain and 41 prisoners, mostly women and children, were taken. Two months later, on August 1, Colonel James Wilkinson led 500 mounted men in a quick raid on the same villages, and also the village of Kenpacomaque, The Soldier's Miami village six miles above the mouth of the Eel River. Among some 30 prisoners taken along the Wabash was the family of Chief Little Face of the Weas. As did Scott before him, Wilkinson took his men quickly back to the safety of Fort Washington with only minor losses.

After the successful cowing of the Wabash tribes, the time was believed ripe for St. Clair to make his major strike at Miamitown with an army of some 2,000 regulars and militia. But the Indians under the Miami Warchief Little Turtle were not "deluded" as Washington suggested to the members of Congress.

The St. Clair Disaster

Through the months of September and October, 1791, the army of General Arthur St. Clair was making its ponderous way through the wilderness. With 2,000 armed men, calvary and cannon, the general had no doubts that his trip from Cincinnati to Miamitown would be a successful one. To protect the supply route, Fort Hamilton and Fort Jefferson were built in what is now southwestern Ohio. By Nov. 3, the army of St. Clair was well north of both of those stockades. St. Clair set up a camp along a stream—he thought it was the St. Mary's River, but it actually was a tributary of the Wabash. The location was where Fort Recovery, Ohio, is located today. General St. Clair picked this spot as his jumping-off point for the final assault on Miamitown, which was to take place the next day. The Americans were under the illusion that Kekionga and the other Indian villages and trading houses at three rivers were only 15 miles away. Actually, the distance was more than 50 miles. But just how far away was Miamitown was academic at this point. The army of St. Clair had come to the end of the line. During the night, warriors under the Miami Warchief Little Turtle slipped into the immediate vicinity. Large numbers of Indians took up concealed positions to both the west and northeast of the American troops. Among the tribes were the Miami, the Delaware, the Shawnee, the Ottawa, the Wyandot, the Potawatomi and the Kickapoo.

At sunrise on Nov. 4, 1791, the Indians struck. What followed was the most complete defeat of any sizable unit in the history of American arms.

There are numerous reports of the battle —some military and some personal. A young man named Benjamin Van Cleve, who was in St. Clair's quartermaster corps, left an eyewitness account of what it's like to be caught in this sort of situation.

"On the fourth at daybreak, I began to prepare for returning and had got about half my luggage on my horse when the firing commenced. We were encamped just within the lines on the right.

"The attack was made on the Kentucky militia," which was on the other side of the river from the main army position. "Almost instantaneously, the small remnant of them that escaped broke through the line near us and this line gave way. Followed by a tremendous fire from the enemy, they passed me." Van Cleve suddenly found himself between the Indians and the army. He left his pack horse, which had been shot anyway, and made a dash for the position of the regular troops. "My inexperience prompted me to calculate on our forces being far superior to any that the savages could assemble, and that we should soon have the pleasure of driving them." The pleasure of feeling superior was typical of the whole army, but this attitude began to wane. "Not more than five minutes had elapsed when a soldier near me had his arm swinging with a wound." Van Cleve joined some others in a charge, but after firing his ammunition "I looked for the party near me and saw them retreating and half way back to the lines." He followed at a run.

"There were about 30 of our men and officers lying scalped around the pieces of artillery. It appeared that the Indians had not been in a hurry, for their hair was all skinned off.

"Daniel Bonham, whom I regarded as a brother received a shot through the hips. My uncle received a ball near his wrist. The ground was literally covered with dead and dying men.

"Happening to see my uncle, he told me a retreat was ordered. I saw men start on a run a little to the left of where I was. I immediately ran and fell in with them." The retreat turned into a bloody rout. "When we had proceeded about two miles, most of those mounted had passed me. A boy had been thrown from a horse and begged my assistance. I ran, pulled him along about two miles further, until I had become nearly exhausted.

"I took the cramp violently in my thighs, and could scarcely walk, until I got within a hundred yards of the rear, where the Indians were tomahawking the old and wounded men.

"I threw the shoes off my feet and the coolness of the ground seemed to revive me. I began to trot and got before half a dozen persons, I thought it would occupy some time for the enemy to massacre them before my turn would come. By the time I got to Stillwater, some 11 miles, I gained the center of the flying troops," Van Cleve said.

It was every man for himself. Six hundred thirty-two never made it on Nov. 4. Nearly 1,000 died in the campaign. Among those dead and left on the field of battle was General Richard Butler, a hard-as-nails frontier soldier and Revolutionary War veteran who appears in the records for forcing harsh terms on Indians in early treaties.

Left buried under the battlefield was $38,000 in gold coin, originally intended to supply the fort which St. Clair planned to build at Miamitown. It was hidden by Col. William Darke who covered the general retreat. Though searched for many times in later years, the treasure was never found.

Before he left the field of victory, the Miami Warchief Little Turtle told the warriors to jam clay and mud into the mouths of the slain soldiers left to rot at the site. It was meant as a gesture of defiance to all land-hungry Americans who came seeking that which belonged to the Indians.

The U.S. Army Command

"The President of the United States by the advice and consent of the Senate has appointed you Major General and of course commanding officer of the troops in the service of the United States."

Mad Anthony Wayne received the notice April 12, 1792, in a letter from Secretary of War Henry Knox. It may have been the most important single act leading to the defeat of the Indians of the Old Northwest and eventual construction of a permanent fortification at the headwaters of the Maumee. Wayne was not Washington's first choice for the job. Though the President had a high regard for Wayne's Revolutionary War record and his military astuteness; he thought differently about Wayne's more personal qualities. It seems that Washington considered Wayne's ego insufferable and was annoyed with some of his habits—which included frequent night-long drinking parties and some marital infidelities. But Washington's several favored candidates for the job were from Virginia. This made them politically unacceptable because there was already criticism due to the large number of high public officials from that state. Wayne's being from Pennsylvania was, in this instance an asset. It should be noted that Wayne was not only being named to head the campaign against the Indians, but was also commander of the entire army of the United States, such as it was. In the notice of appointment, Knox also told Wayne, "I enclose you the Act of Congress relative to the military establishment." That act was the result of fear which swept eastward from the frontier lands to the capital cities.

So great was the impact of the St. Clair disaster on the young American Republic that the very policies of the Federal Government concerning the old Northwest were thrown into confusion. There was some thought to leave the Indian lands to the Indians, and make the Ohio River the boundry between the wilderness and the territories marked out for the settlers. Several negotiators were sent to both the English governors in Canada and to Indian councils to discuss such possibilities. Washington and some others, however, saw far-reaching consequences of such a course. In the first place, the young nation could hardly afford to succumb to a defeat at the hands of the northwest tribes. It would have been too great a sign of weakness. Further, if the Americans could not control the territories, they risked losing to the British the very lands gained in the Treaty of 1783 following the Revolution. The whole westward expansion of the United States was at stake. Washington pressured through Congress an Act creating and providing for a new army —larger and better provisioned than those previously sent west.

Anthony Wayne took up his command post at Pittsburgh and began the long detailed business of putting together and training an army. "I shall enclose you a schedule of the troops by the next post who have been ordered to march and of those who will be ordered immediately to march to Pittsburgh," Knox wrote Wayne on June 15 of that year. In the meantime, Wayne built Fort Fayette near old Fort Pitt.

Three Plagues

Almost immediately, Wayne was saddled with three plagues: desertions, Indian raids and smallpox. Some of the desertions occurred before the troops even arrived at Wayne's post. "I am however sorry to inform you of the alarming desertions that prevailed in Ashton's detachment and Stake's dragoons, not less than 50 of the former and seven of the latter deserted on their march between Carlisle and Pittsburgh." Wayne also told Knox he would get the names and whereabouts of the deserters so they could be run down. The general was one to leave nothing to chance. At the same time he reported the "eruptive fever" of smallpox and the separation of the infected. Smallpox was also sweeping the Indian lands that year, decimating the villages. "Predatory parties of Indians began to make their appearance in the course of last week. They killed seven people in Ohio County and carried off a number of horses," Wayne said. He also reported the murder of some Indians by a force under Capt. Samuel Brady of the Pennsylvania militia. Wayne was directed to put a stop to the border conflicts during this period of negotiation with the Indians. In the meantime, the general continued to develop and train his army for the major expedition and conflict which he was sure was coming.

At all levels of government, advisors and critics came out of the woodwork. Some were saying he was moving too slow or too fast against the Indians. Others knew better than the commander about which route the army should take for its drive against the Miami villages.

"I cannot agree in opinion with General Rufus Putnam that we ought to carry on part of our operation by the way of Lake Erie," Wayne wrote the War Department in August of 1792. He explained that taking to Lake Erie would invite open British opposition and that "they would prevent us from navigating on that water." He also listed a number of reasons for his being against a fall campaign. There was the question of insufficient numbers of trained men and "because we ought not to risk another defeat with raw troops." He said he was aiming for a spring campaign.

"I consider the Indian a formidable enemy only when he has a choice of time and ground: in the fall of the year he's strong and ferocious and full of spirits—corn is in plenty and venison and other game everywhere to be met with. In the spring he is half starved, weak and dispirited." Wayne mentioned the previous fall attempts and suggested a "strike at him when least expected." He also indicated his growing disgust with all the uninvited advice he was getting. "Permit me to choose the season for operation. Give me time to manoeuvre and discipline the army so as to inspire them with confidence in their own prowess."

Mad Anthony's Plan

The general then outlined his entire campaign, which he would follow, successfully as it turned out, over the next two years. He also reported that his scouting parties had already discovered that several new towns of hostile Indians were being built along the rivers of the wilderness. Clearly, the Indians too were preparing for the American invasion.

Wayne continued: "Whilst the legion was advancing and employed in erecting small intermediate forts at convenient distances between Fort Jefferson (about 60 miles north of Fort Washington at Cincinnati) and the point intended for establishing a strong and permanent post (Fort Wayne), I would make it an invariable rule to halt early each day and to secure my camp before evening with small temporary breast works and abbatis such as to cover the troops —so to enable them to repel every kind of attack of the savages.

"I pledge my reputation as an officer to establish myself at the Miami villages. Our Indian guides, scouts, spies and cavalry, who shall always patrol and hover widely round me, will not suffer the savages to advance undiscovered. Nor will I wait their attack. On the contrary, they shall feel the effects of a nocturnal charge—and I know from experience that they are a contemptable enemy in the night."

Wayne then pointed out his line of march to the Maumee. Congress had provided for an army of more than 4,000 men—a large force in that era. Actually, when Mad Anthony Wayne marched on the towns of the Miami Indian Confederation in 1794, he would have 3,500 men under arms. In the meantime the U.S. continued to send peace emissaries to the Indians. Several of the envoys were killed. Wayne had little thought that negotiations would be successsful. "On Wednesday we had a sham engagement. The rifle corps, highly painted, acted well the part of savages." The simulated battles by Wayne's troops included the crossing of the Allegheny Mountains in surprise actions which were almost too real for comfort, and exacted some minor injuries. "I had no idea that the mind could be so diffusively inflamed by imagination only," Wayne said.

After moving his army from Pittsburgh down the Ohio River to Cincinnati, Anthony Wayne began his drive into the Indian country in earnest. But for each inch of the way there was a price to pay. Working south from the Maumee, the raiding parties of the Miami Confederacy watched for every chance. To protect his army during the advance north, General Wayne proceeded with the construction and strengthening of a series of forts and strongpoints. Moving the army proved less troublesome than the provisioning of the garrisons once they were established.

"The great difficulty at present is that of providing a sufficient escort to secure our convoys of provision and other supplies from insult and disaster, and at the same time to retain a sufficient force in camp to sustain and repel the attacks of the enemy, who appear to be desperate and determined," Wayne wrote on October 23, 1793.

Death Along the Road

The American general had no illusions about things getting better as he moved deeper into the wilderness toward the great swamp to the south of the Miami villages. Just saving the forts from fire and destruction was a major daily concern. The protecting of the large supply trains was becoming a war in itself. In some instances these convoy battles were of considerable size. In a sense, the ability of Wayne to keep open some regular supply lines was his key victory in the entire campaign but at a bloody cost. A typical conflict along the route of the convoys occurred on October 17 of that year. Lt. John Lowry and Ensign Samuel Boyd with a command consisting of about 90 noncommissioned officers and privates, Wayne reported, were proceeding north with 20 wagon loads of food and stores. They were attacked. The Indians hit the wagon train and two army units about seven miles north of Fort St. Clair on the road to Fort Greenville, which Wayne was setting up as winter quarters.

"Those two gallant young gentlemen, who promised at a future day to be ornaments to their profession, together with 13 noncommissioned officers and privates bravely fell, after an obstinate resistance, against superior numbers, being abandoned by the greater part of the escort, upon the first discharge.

"The savages killed or carried off about 70 horses, leaving the wagons and stores standing in the road." In the same report to the War Department, Wayne said he was sending detachments to reinforce four other companies under Col. John Hamtramck, who was bringing another train up from Fort Washington at Cincinnati.

Anthony Wayne had spies working far into the lands of the Old Northeast. He was told at about this time that the "Indians at Au Glaise have sent their women and children into some secret recess, or recesses, from their towns, and that the whole of the warriors are collected or collecting in force." The information Mad Anthony Wayne was receiving was correct. Not only were the usual enemy tribes concentrating in the area of Miamitown, such as the Miami, the Shawnee and the Delaware; but the Indians of the upper Great Lakes, such as the Huron, the Chippewa and the Ottawa, were flowing south in the path of the army. Moving in from the Lake Michigan and Wabash areas were the Potawatomis, the Weas and the Kickapoos. One thing favoring Wayne at this time, however, was the increasing caution of the British. Formerly, they had supported the Indians rather openly. Negotiations in London at the time required the dropping of some of this support and gun supply to the Indians. The main concern of the Home Office in England was that the United States not become involved in the war on the side of the French, and against the British. There was one other circumstance which was working in Wayne's favor. As the general noted at the time, the large influx of Indians created a food and supply problem in the overcrowded villages.

"The savages, however, can't continue long embodied for want of provision. On the contrary, we have by great exertions secured in this camp 70,000 rations. I expect 120,000 in addition by the return of the present convoy, unless they meet with disaster."

Some of the convoys of the Federal Army made it. General Wayne settled down in heavily guarded Fort Greeneville for the winter. In the snow-swept months that followed, hunger stalked the roving bands of Indians in the northwest wilderness.

Fort Recovery

The key battle in Anthony Wayne's drive toward the Maumee and Indian power did not occur at Miamitown or even at Fallen Timbers. Sometimes nearly overlooked by everyone except the Indians and the British was the botched siege of Fort Recovery. The massed Indian army besieged the newly-built American fort for two days in the summer of 1794, and were repulsed by the American garrison. The course of history was changed for two reasons. If the Indians had taken the fort and massacred the more than 300 men defending it, the entire United States campaign would have been blunted and, quite likely, General Wayne would have been relieved of his command. This would have affected the entire American policy and expansion to the West. Also, since Little Turtle, the Miami war chief, gave up his leadership of the confederated Indian tribes soon after this repulse, it had a decided effect on the subsequent actions of the warriors. Not only was the confidence of the Indians shaken, but the clever tactics of earlier days were abandoned—which led to their defeat along the Maumee River near the present city of Toledo.

The Battle of Fort Recovery began to shape up in the bitter cold months of December and January with the building of the stockade along the upper streams of the Wabash River in west-central Ohio, some 50 miles southeast of the three rivers. It was the exact site of the bloody defeat of the army of General Arthur St. Clair in November, 1791. Wayne, at his headquarters at Fort Greeneville, reported to the War Department the use of the cold winter months for erection of the strong point. "Permit me now, sir, to inform you that on the 23rd of December Major Henry Burdeck marched from this place with eight companies of foot soldiers and a detachment of artillery with orders to possess the field of action of the 4th of November, 1791, and there to fortify that which proves to be on the main branch of the Wabash, and not on the St. Mary's as heretofore understood." Wayne said the object was to set up a post for future operations and to afford additional security to the western frontiers as he moved on the Miami villages. He said at the time he expected the Indians to eventually attack the fort and "probably dispute the occupancy of a favorite ground." He therefore decided to strengthen the fort with a small reenforcement of mounted infantry. "Fort Recovery is now furnished with a sufficient garrison well provided with ammunition, artillery and provision, commanded by Capt. Alexander Gibson who will not betray the trust responsed in him."

The Indians Strike

The Indians waited six months before striking. But when they did, it was with more than 2,000 warriors of the Miami, Shawnee, Delaware, Ottawa, Potawatomi, Wyandot, Chippewa and Kickapoo tribes. Wayne reported the action in his usual precise way. "At 7 o'clock in the morning of the 30th of June, one of our escorts consisting of 90 riflemen and 50 dragoons commanded by Major McMahan was attacked by a very numerous body of Indians under the walls of Fort Recovery, followed by a general assault upon that garrison in every direction.

"The enemy was soon repulsed with great slaughter, but immediately rallied and reiterated the attack, keeping up a very heavy and constant fire at a more respectable distance all the remainder of the day; which was answered with spirit and effort by the garrison and that part of Major McMahan's command that had regained the post.

"The savages were employed during the night, which was dark and foggy, in carrying off their dead by torch light, which occasionally drew a fire from the garrison. They nevertheless succeeded so well that there were but eight dead bodies left upon the field—those close under the influence of the fire from the fort." The general said the "enemy renewed the attack on the morning of July 1st but were ultimately compelled to retreat about one o'clock of that day with the loss and disgrace from the very field where they had upon a former occasion been proudly victorious."

Twenty-one Americans were killed in the defense. The Indian losses were unknown, but believed to be high. Wayne said he had Chickasaw and Choctaw scouts in the area at the time who told him "there were a considerable number of British and militia of Detroit mixed with the savages in the assault." He also said it was probably a stroke of luck that the heavy escort for the supply train was at the scene. It ruined the surprise the Indians needed for storming the fort walls and added to the strength of the defenders. With this victory, Wayne began immediate preparations for his main drive to the Maumee.

Mad Anthony Wayne, who had been peculiarly cautious for two years in setting his campaign against the Indians of the Old Northwest, returned to character in the summer of 1794. Within two months he made a series of rapid marches, defeated the Miami Confederacy, and built four forts—the last being Fort Wayne.

It all started on July 28.

Ever the precise militarist, Wayne in a report on July 27 from Fort Greenville informed the War Department of his course of action. "The mounted volunteers actually mustered between the 10th and 16th of this month, 500 of whom are already arrived with Generals Scott and Todd. About 1,000 more are one day's march in the rear under the command of Brig. Gen. Barbee." The 1,500 Kentucky volunteers had been called into service to augment the 2,000 regulars Wayne had at the ready at Greenville. Thus, there were 3,500 men for the final onslaught.

"The Legion will advance at 6 o'clock tomorrow morning."

Fort Defiance

Wayne moved quickly north, going some 25 miles on the first day. The army stopped momentarily at the St. Mary's River near Old Girty Town to build Fort Adams—close by the present location of St. Mary's Lake and St. Mary's, Ohio. The general encountered no resistance from the Indians, and the lack of contact with the enemy disturbed him. He sent scouts and spies ranging far in all directions. Having secured his rear, Wayne stepped off again. First he sent portions of his army in short jaunts in the direction of Miamitown to the northwest and the Maumee Rapids to the northeast. Both of these actions were feints to fool the Indian defenders of the northern wilderness. General Wayne then marched swiftly directly north to the junction of the Auglaise and Maumee Rivers. He arrived at that place August 8 and founded Fort Defiance. This was to be his strongest bastion in the north and gave him control of the Maumee River. He later reported:

"We had built a strong stockade fort at the confluence of the Miamis and AuGlaise, which I have since improved into a regular work, surrounded by a good parapet, sufficient to resist a 24 pounder, with a fraize projecting from the berm over the ditch which is 14 feet wide and eight feet deep.

"In addition to this, I have directed Major Hunt, the commandant to surround the whole to the water edge on each river with a thick abbatis that were ready cut, so the Fort Defiance will support that name should the British and their Indian allies eventually attack."

The conditions for the Battle of Fallen Timbers were taking shape. Warriors of the many tribes were congregated further down the Maumee near the Rapids, a short distance from the present city of Toledo. Nearby was Fort Miami, the British post built earlier that year. Heading the English garrison of about 450 men was Major William Campbell. Wayne sent a peace proposal to the Indians on August 13 by way of a scout named Christopher Miller, holding hostages to secure his safety. Hoping to stall Wayne, the Indians said they would give an answer in 10 days. Wayne, however, was already on the move. Marching along the north shore of the Maumee toward Lake Erie, the American army went as far as the Rapids. They stopped for a day to build Fort Deposit—a small stockade to protect the troops' supplies. All the while, Wayne continued to have scouts and spies infiltrating the forests and watching the waterways. These men included both backwoodsmen and Choctaw and Chickasaw Indians. Many came to bitter ends. Two of the Choctaw spies were caught and strung up to wither away between two oak trees by Indian Creek, later called Spy Run Creek at Fort Wayne. William May, a white spy, was captured and tortured to death. Among the spies and scouts who survived were Simon Kenton, a one-time Virginian turned frontiersman, and William Wells, kidnapped from a Kentucky farm as a boy and the son-in-law of the Miami War Chief Little Turtle.

Warfare on Maumee

As Mad Anthony Wayne continued his relentless push, the Indian situation showed signs of decay. Some of the tribesmen, those from the distant north, had returned to their home villages after the repulse at Fort Recovery. The British were reluctant allies because any action by them would be contrary to the Jay Treaty which was being concluded between the U.S. and England. Most important, the Indian leaders had fallen into disagreement. Little Turtle, who had advised stalling Fabian tactics and the avoiding of direct battle with Wayne's army, was forced out as head of the Confederated warriors. The 1,700 braves waiting Wayne's advance along the Maumee had a new war chief—Blue Jacket of the Shawnees.

It was an August 20, 1794, that Anthony Wayne's army charged at the Indians along the north bank of the Maumee River at a place which has been called Fallen Timbers. The warriors, headed by the Shawnee chief, Blue Jacket, had been waiting for three days for the movement of the Americans. They had taken up positions behind a series of large trees which had been felled by a tornado shortly before. The British Fort Miami was a couple miles further down the river, near present day Toledo. Blue Jacket had some 1,700 braves and a number of Canadians in the area. But because of the long wait, hunger was a problem and several hundred of the Indians were absent on hunting expeditions at the key moment. It was rainy and hot. Wayne described the events.

"At 8 o'clock on the morning of the 20th the army again advanced in columns—the legion on the right, its right flank covered by the Miamis (Maumee), one brigade of mounted volunteers on the left, under Brig. Gen. Todd and the other in the rear under Brig. Gen. Barbee.

"A select battalion of mounted volunteers moved in front of the legion commanded by Major Price." Wayne at that moment was feeling out the Indians. He wanted to be sure of their positions and whether they intended to fight before he commited his main force. General Wayne was directing an army of 3,500 regulars and militia. He got a quick answer. "After advancing about five miles, Major Price's corps received so severe a fire from the enemy, who were secreted in the woods and high grass, as to compel them to retreat." Wayne immediately formed some 2,000 regulars in two lines for a broad advance. In the meantime, he sent the entire 1,500 mounted riflemen into the wilderness to his left in a wide movement to hit the Indians from the inland flank. As the troops advanced, the general ordered the Federal cavalry "to turn the left flank of the enemy next to the river, which afforded a favorable field for that corps to act in." The main army moved up the center in broad ranks with bayonets attached to their rifles. "All those orders were obeyed with spirit and promptitude, but such was the impetuosity of the charge by the first line of infantry that the Indians and Canadian militia and volunteers were drove from all their coverts."

Wayne Tells of Victory

The attack was so successful, some of the troops didn't even have time to get into the battle. Wayne reported the enemy was driven more than two miles in the course of an hour.

"The savages with their allies abandoned themselves to flight and dispersed with terror and dismay, leaving our victorious army in full and quiet possession of the field." The American army went as far as the British fort, where a 450-man garrison was under the command of Maj. William Campbell. Wayne went up to the fort and called for its surrender, saying that it was illegally built in territory of the United States. Campbell refused. Both sides held their fire. Wayne rode slowly on his horse around Fort Miami, carefully inspecting the stronghold as the armed British on the inside looked on. The American general drew off a short distance and directed the destruction of everything in sight, save the fort. The British remained inside the stockade, as they had earlier in the day during the Battle of Fallen Timbers. In the battle of August 20, the Americans lost 33 killed and about 100 wounded. Indian losses were believed to have been about twice that number. It was a complete reversal of the situation three years before when the Indians led by Little Turtle had inflicted a crushing defeat on the American army led by General Arthur St. Clair. American losses in that earlier battle were 20 times greater that at Fallen Timbers.

Disenchantment between the British and

the Indians quickly set in along the Maumee. The defeat itself had not been that costly, but the Indians were disgusted with the failure of both British help and supply. The British, who feared at the time that Wayne would march on Detroit and then Canada, acted superior to the immediate situation. Col. Richard England, British commandant at Detroit, said to John Graves Simcoe, Governor of Upper Canada, "The Indians on this occasion have forfeited every pretension to a warlike or gallant character."

The Scorched Earth

The army of Anthony Wayne took three days to devastate the lower Maumee area before starting the upriver drive to Miamitown. Everything which stood above the ground, in some places even the trees, was leveled in the sweep of the 3,500-man expeditionary force. The main targets were the Indian villages, the posts of the French Canadians and English sympathizers, the corn fields and anything which would support life and resistance to the U.S. presence. The Indians themselves had scattered—most to the north and the west. The victory over the Miami Confederation, coming after a decade of disasters in the Old Northwest, was the most striking event of the young Republic in the 1790's. George Washington was finally vindicated in his determination to keep the west open for American expansion.

The U.S. Senate, through an address to Washington by Vice President John Adams, expressed the public attitude.

"The success of the troops under the command of General Wayne can not fail to produce essential advantages. The pleasure with which we acknowledge the merits of that gallant general and army is enhanced by the hope that their victories will lay the foundation of a just and durable peace with the Indian tribes.

"At a period so momentous in the affairs of nations, the temperate, just, and firm policy that you have pursued in respect to foreign powers has been eminently calculated to promote the great and essential interest of our country, and has created the fairest title to the public gratitude and thanks."

Congress Lauds Victory

The Congress was doubly happy with the success and possible end of the expedition because of the heavy drain on the human and financial resources of the newly-formed Union. This attitude comes through in an address from the House of Representatives to the President.

"We rejoice at the intelligence of the advance and success of the army under the command of General Wayne, whether we regard as a proof of the perseverance, prowess and superiority of our troops, or as a happy presage to our military operations against the hostile Indians, and as a probable prelude to the establishment of a lasting peace upon the terms of candor, equity and good neighborhood.

"We received it with the greater pleasure as it increases the probability of sooner restoring a part of the public resources to the desirable object of reducing the public debit."

The general euphoria led to a rather unusual commitment for a House of Representatives to a President: "We shall on this, as on all occasions, be disposed to adopt any measures which may advance the safety and prosperity of our country."

Back on the frontier, the quest for peace had a stronger flavor—heavy with fire and smoke. It was Wayne's opinion that the wilderness areas could only be pacified by a strong hand. To maintain such a hand, he was determined to further split the Indian power and to secure the army's presence with fort building.

Reporting to the War Department from Fort Defiance, Wayne said, "The Army returned to this place on August 27 by easy marches laying waste the villages and corn fields for about 50 miles on each side of the Maumee. There remains yet a number of villages and a great quantity of corn to be consumed or destroyed upon the Au Glaize and the Maumee above this place which will be effected in the course of a few days. In the interim we shall improve Fort Defiance."

The American general saw continuing the scorched earth policy in the entire valley of the Maumee while preparing for another possible "desperate effort against the army" by Indian reinforcements. Wayne said he was actually hoping for such a battle with any new enemy forces. "This is a business rather to be wished for than dreaded whilst the army remain in force. Their numbers will only tend to confuse the savages and the victory will be the more complete and decisive, which may eventually ensure a permanent and happy peace."

The Indians, however, were more likely at the moment to start fighting among themselves, and any chance of their uniting with the British again was remote. The temper in the northern forests was acid, and a meeting with the British Governor John Graves Simcoe along the Detroit River only added to the acrimony.

Mad Anthony Wayne kept on the move. "As soon as the escort returns with the necessary supplies from Greenville and Fort Recovery, the army will proceed to the Miami villages in order to accomplish the object of the campaign," he said. That object, mentioned by Washington years earlier, was the building of Fort Wayne at the heart of the Indian power.

Anthony Wayne's legions took up the march from Fort Defiance to Miamitown at the three rivers on September 14, 1794. The campaign to break the power of the Indians continued relentlessly, despite sickness, near starvation rations and bitterness among the 3,500-man army. Only fear of lashings and executions, together with fear of the enemy kept the forces under control in the remote wilderness area. The final indignity for many of the men was the lack of whisky. "Provision is nearly exhausted. The whisky has been out for some time, which makes the hours pass heavily," wrote a Lieutenant Boyer. "Hard duty and scant allowance will cause an army to be low spirited, particularly the want of a little wet."

There were other reasons for Wayne's iron hand. His second in command, General James Wilkinson, was conspiring with supply contractors in Kentucky to sabotage Wayne's entire campaign. Wilkinson was later implicated in a suspected treasonable plot with Aaron Burr. Other officers resented Wayne's remorseless discipline, which was meted out to them as surely as to the enlisted men. Of the 319 officers who served under Anthony Wayne during the several years of the preparing and conducting of the campaign against the Miamis and allies, 100 of them came to unhappy ends. Eight were killed by the Indians; four were killed in duels; 13 were dismissed or cashiered after court marshalls; 16 died of the illness and starved conditions in the wilderness; two committed suicide and 52 resigned.

The army moved along the north bank of the Maumee, burning the villages as it went. It was hot and sticky going, particularly since Wayne demanded that a wide road be cut through the forestry—largely thick growths of oak and walnut with massive trunks. Only 11 miles was covered the first day. After two days the legion was as far as the present location of Antwerp, Ohio. The Indians, who had earlier been striking down stragglers and foragers, gave Wayne's troops little trouble at the time, however. Wayne in his report said his men were "cutting and opening a wagon road the whole distance being 48 miles, the general course about west-southwest, without seeing an enemy or meeting with any interruption from them.

"How to account for their inaction or long silence I am at a loss—unless they are awaiting the arrival of Governor Simcoe (British governor of Upper Canada) with the further reenforcement and heavy artillery mentioned in the enclosed information given by a British deserter, corroborated by three others, direct from Fort Miamis."

British Attitude

It was later learned that the Indians of the Miami Confederation were meeting with John Graves Simcoe and other British commanders at the very time Anthony Wayne was moving on Miamitown. Some 1,600 warriors were near Lake Erie, ready to renew the combat. The British, however, didn't furnish artillery to strike at the American forts or the other things the Indians needed. Instead, they were more concerned that Wayne's army would invade Canada.

"If Wayne be permitted to establish himself at Detroit, It may occasion the loss of both Canadas," Simcoe wrote to Lord Dorchester, who had been the prime supporter of the confederacy put together by Chief Little Turtle. Dorchester asked Simcoe if he, Simcoe, "by calling all the force in your power to assemble, you would be in condition to resist Wayne's attack?"

"I think no force in this country could resist Wayne's direct attack," Simcoe answered. "I believe there are few instances of an invading army being suffered to penetrate so far as General Wayne had done without some check." But Mad Anthony Wayne never invaded Canada (at least on this occasion, though he had campaigned in Canada during the Revolution and would assume command peacefully in 1796 of the fortress of Detroit, at the time considered a Canadian stronghold). The American general was busy making things more difficult for the Indians. The British, he said will have "seven to eight thousand additional mouths, including men and women and children, thrown upon them, belonging to the different hostile tribes, whose towns, villages and provisions are totally destroyed and laid waste."

George Ganiere bronze of Little Turtle, the Miami warchief who led the Indian nations in the crucial battles in the Old Northwest.

French explorers, crossing the rivers and lakes from Quebec, are shown in this old print on a fast stream in the wilderness, top. The Indians of the woods and lakes area, as shown in a village, left above, were the soldiers and fur trappers of the Great Lakes area. Robert Cavalier de la Salle, right above, seeking to control the fur trade, urged the Miami Indians to move from the Lake Michigan area to the Maumee. The word Miami literally meant My Friend in French. Costumes of French soldiers during the exploration period are shown at right.

Jean Baptist Bissot de Vincennes, French agent in the Miami Indian country, was the first prominent Frenchman to locate at Three Rivers. He also was in charge of French posts St. Joseph, Mich., and near Lafayette (Ouiatenon). He died at the present site of Fort Wayne in 1719. The burning of Fort Miami along the St. Mary's River in 1747 is also shown in Bill Hammon drawings to the left. Below, an old print shows Indians carrying birch bark canoes over the portage and around the beaver dams between the Maumee and Wabash River. At the bottom of the page are some of totems of Indian tribes, from left, the Iroquois, the Huron and the Illinois. The Huron and Illinois were friends of the Miamis and the Iroquois were the enemy.

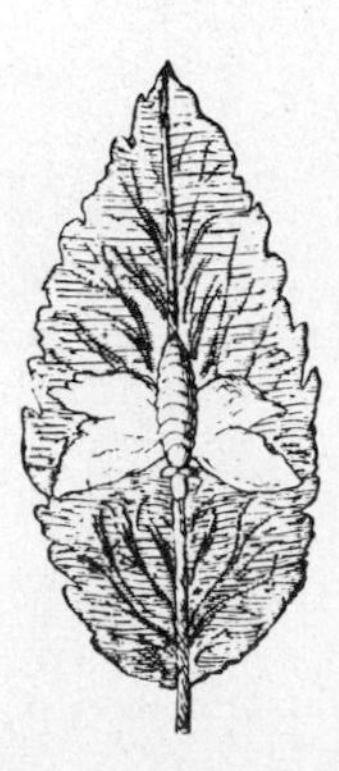

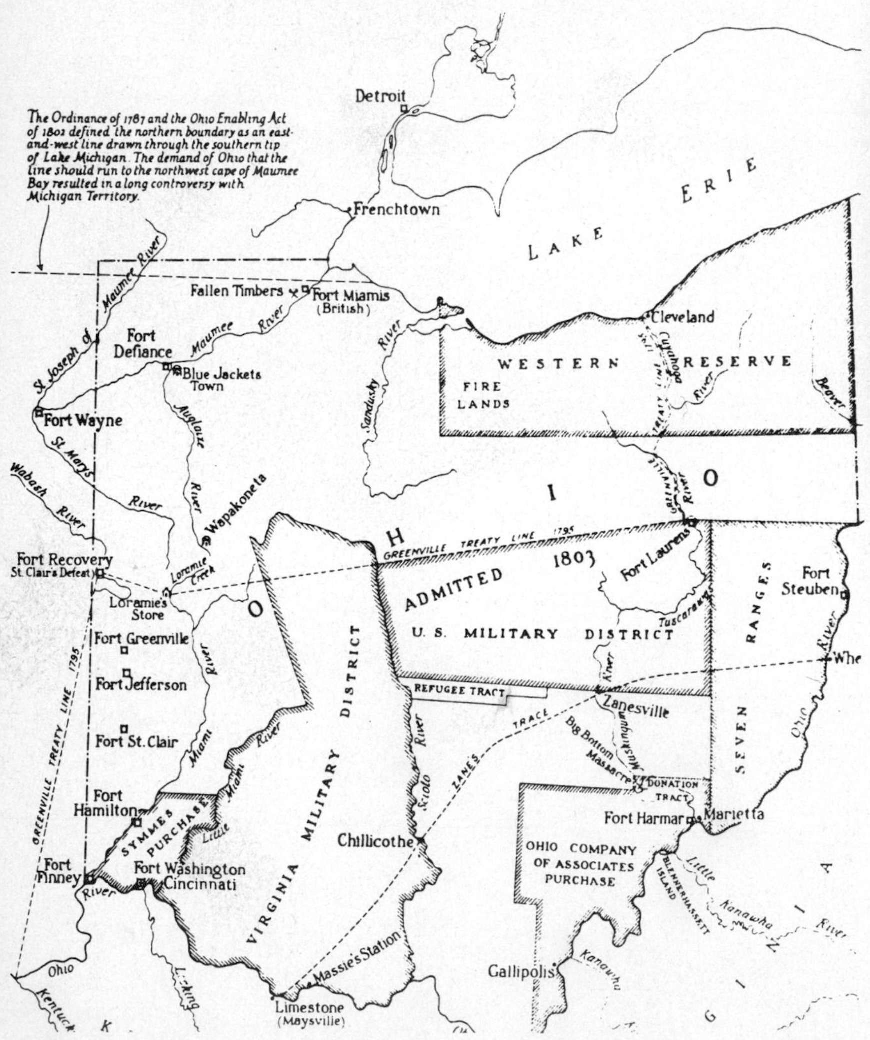

George Washington, soon after becoming the First President in 1789, launched the series of campaigns against the Indians of the Old Northwest. The Miami Warchief, Little Turtle, left above, led the united Indian nations against the U.S. invading forces, defeating the Americans at present Fort Wayne in 1790 and in Western Ohio in 1791. The near-annihilation of St. Clair's army in 1791 was the most decisive defeat of a U.S. military expedition in history.

The Miami Indians waited along the banks of the Maumee River in 1790 as infrantrymen in the army of General Josiah Harmar waded across toward their deaths. General Harmar, below, after the bad experience at the three rivers withdrew to Fort Washington on the Ohio River.

The next army aimed at Miamitown was commanded by Gen. Arthur St. Clair in 1791. St. Clair, shown above, camped on an upper Wabash stream in Western Ohio where his 1,500 soldiers were caught by Little Turtle and his warriors of the Miami, Shawnee, Delaware, Huron, Ottawa, Potawatomi and Kickapoo tribes. The massacre is depicted at left by a Bill Hammon sketch.

General Anthony Wayne (above) was named commanding officer of the Armies of the United States, and after a lengthy campaign, defeated the Indians at Fallen Timbers along the Maumee, a few miles up from Lake Erie. Concepts of the battle are shown to the right and below. The Wayne portrait is by Charles Willson Peale.

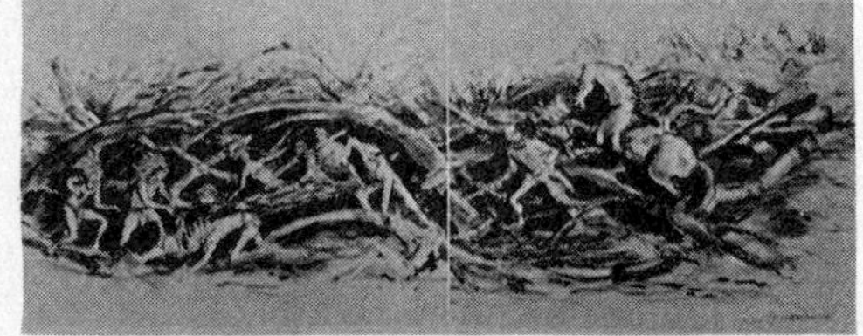

MONGO TRAIL EXTENDED AS FAR AS MACKINAC

GREAT NORTHWEST TRAIL

ST. JOSEPH RIVER

KEKIONGA

NOW DELAWARE AVE.

SITE OF SECOND FRENCH FORT

MAUMEE RIVER

TOLEDO-DETROIT TRAIL

BOAT LANDING

SLOUGH

FORD

RAPIDS

ST. MARY'S RIVER

WABASH TRAIL

Built 1721 SITE OF FIRST FRENCH FORT

MARSH

SECOND AMERICAN FORT, BUILT BY COL. HUNT 1800, BESIEGED BY INDIANS 1812, REBUILT BY MAJOR JOHN WHISTLER 1815.

INDIAN COUNCIL HOUSE—BURNED DURING 1812 INDIAN SIEGE.

THIS WAS LOCATION OF FIRST AMERICAN FORT BUILT BY WAYNE IN 1794.

1813—MAJOR JENKINSON'S MEN MASSACRED.

A FRENCH TRADING POST ABOUT 1680. BISSOT BUILT MILITARY POST 1697.

Fallen Timbers

Maumee River

FORT DEFIANCE

St. Joseph River

Harmar's Defeat

St. Marys River

Auglaize River

FORT ADAMS

St. Clair's Defeat

FORT RECOVERY

FORT GREENEVILLE

FORT JEFFERSON

Ohio

FORT ST. CLAIR

Miami River

FORT HAMILTON

FORT WASHINGTON

Ohio River

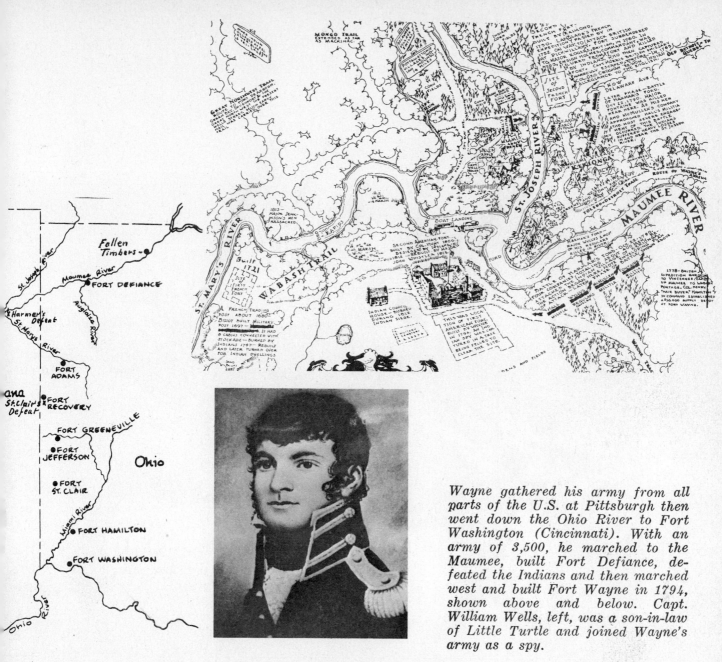

Wayne gathered his army from all parts of the U.S. at Pittsburgh then went down the Ohio River to Fort Washington (Cincinnati). With an army of 3,500, he marched to the Maumee, built Fort Defiance, defeated the Indians and then marched west and built Fort Wayne in 1794, shown above and below. Capt. William Wells, left, was a son-in-law of Little Turtle and joined Wayne's army as a spy.

Wayne Journal

The equistrian statue of Mad Anthony Wayne at Fort Wayne, Indiana, by George Ganiere.

Part 2
The Americans Arrive

At sundown on Sept. 17, 1794, Anthony Wayne and his army of 3,500 men arrived at the source of the Maumee River—the future site of Fort Wayne. They came along the north bank, dragging wagons along the newly-cut road through the wilderness. Scouting parties ranged the entire area, moving back and forth between the marching troops and obscure points in the forest. There was the sound of horses and the curses of men as increasing numbers made their laborious way into the clearing. Otherwise, there was a deathly quiet about the place—for a hundred years known as Miamitown. Numerous Indian dwellings stood just north of the Maumee, on either side of the St. Joseph River. They were all empty. Rough timber houses and storage buildings, belonging to both French traders and Indians, were here and there near the river banks. These too were empty and abandoned.

The sky was overcast and a damp chill wind blew from the west. Mad Anthony Wayne rode his horse slowly through the Kekionga village and its hundreds of Indian houses as far as the remains of old French Fort Miami which still stood on the east side of the St. Joseph. This was the village of Le Gris, the old Miami chief, and was usually considered the largest concentration of hostile Indians in the Northwest Territory. Wayne had learned several years earlier about Le Gris from Antoine Gamelin and other American emissaries. The chiefs of the Wabash and Lake Erie villages would tell American negotiators that they would have to go to see Le Gris if they wanted any answers as to the intentions of the Miami Confederacy. The difficulty was, few wanted to venture that far, and of those who did, even fewer returned. Le Gris, at the moment of Wayne's examination of Kekionga, was some 40 miles to the north in the lake country where he had taken his entire village population. He remained, as he had for half a century, the implacable enemy of intruders into the land of the Miamis. Wayne then crossed to the west side of the St. Joseph where another village stood empty and quiet. This was the village of Pacan, the uncle of the Miami War Chief Little Turtle. It was

here that most of the traders' houses were located—some fairly large and well-fitted, considering the remoteness, and others just one-room huts of rough logs with bark and hide roofs. Wayne decided against either of the village locations for his encampment and fort. He ordered the legion to build temporary protection on the high ground just southwest of the confluence of the rivers. The position commanded a good view of the Maumee River.

One of Wayne's officers, Capt. John Cooke of Pennsylvania, said the army marched 13 or 14 miles on that day before reaching the Miami villages. "We halted more than two hours near the ground where a part of Harmer's army was defeated and directly opposite the point by the St. Joseph and St. Mary's Rivers, until the ground was reconnoitered. It was late when the army crossed and encamped; our tents were not all pitched before dark." The soldiers of Wayne's army continued to flow in from the east. The first night and morning of the American presence at the site of Fort Wayne was described by a Private Bryant. "The road, or trace, was in very bad condition, and we did not reach our point of destination until late in the evening. Being very tired, and having no duty to perform, I turned in as soon as possible, and slept soundly until the familiar tap of reveille called us up, just as the bright sun, the first time for weeks, was breaking over the horizon.

"After rubbing my eyes and regaining my faculties sufficiently to realize my whereabouts, I think I never saw a more beautiful spot and glorious sunrise.

"I was standing on that high point of land overlooking the valley on the opposite shore of the Maumee, where the St. Mary's, the sheen of whose waters were seen at intervals through the autumn-tinted trees, and the limpid St. Joseph quietly wending its way from the north, united themselves in one common stream that calmly flowed beneath." The private's tranquility didn't last long. The general soon ordered breast works to be thrown up around the compound to ward off any possible attacks by the Indians. These were made of earth and required forced digging on the part of most of the men. Others, largely Kentucky horsemen, began the systematic destruction of the villages. Fire swept across the some 500 acres of cleared area. Every building was leveled. Every crop was cut down. The decimation spread in a wider circle. The Delaware village several miles up the St. Mary's was burnt out, as were the Ottawa village some distance up the St. Joseph and any remaining Shawnee dwellings down the Maumee. Wayne kept watch for Indian raiders, but the only people to arrive on that first morning were four deserters from the British Fort Miami on the lower Maumee.

The good feeling that Anthony Wayne had in so easily taking control of the Miamitown area didn't last long. Far in the wilderness, there was the ever-present feeling of danger. This was magnified by the shortage of food and supplies which continued to plague the American army. Getting wagon trains through from the Ohio River sources was always difficult, sometimes impossible. Not only were there the raids by parties of warriors, but the suppliers themselves were conspiring to short Wayne on the materials. The American general was perhaps even more worried by the lack of action of the U.S. Congress in voting added funds to maintain the army in the field. Enlistment periods of many of the troops were running out. Wayne feared that he would be forced to abandon the key locations along the Maumee because of the lack of men. Even the weather was working against him. Just about the time Mad Anthony picked out the site for a fort after arrival at the three rivers, it began to rain, and, rain, and rain. Wayne sent a message to the War Department complaining of the "powerful obstacles" to his completing his mission—the need for supplies and expirations of terms of service. "In the course of six weeks from this day, the First and Second Sublegions will not form more than two companies each, and between this and the middle of May, the whole Legion will be merely annihilated so that all we now possess in the Western Country must inevitably be abandoned unless some effectual and immediate measures are adopted by Congress to raise troops to garrison them." Wayne had originally hoped to build a major fortification at Miamitown. But again, several circumstances were work-

ing against his plans.

Wayne's Fort

"I shall begin a fort at this place as soon as the equinoctial storm is over which at the moment is very severe, attended with a deluge of rain—a circumstance that renders the situation of the soldiery very distressing, being upon short allowance, thinly clad and exposed to the inclemency of the weather," Wayne said.

"I shall at all events be under the necessity of contracting the fortification considerably from the dimensions contemplated in your instructions to me of the 25th of May, 1792, both for the want of time as well as for want of force to garrison it."

To the 3,500 men in the army, the days and nights were hard. "Heavy rains and violent windstorms lasted throughout the night," reported Capt. John Cooke on Sept. 19. The deluge continued the next day and Cooke said the following night was "stormy with frequent hard claps of thunder." Wayne in his journal said, "It rained violently and the wind blew from the Northwest harder than I knew heretofore."

But there were some semblances of normal life during those first few days of the Americans at the confluence of the three rivers. Several of the men built a fish dam across part of the Maumee—presumably to supplement the meager food supplies. The fourth day after arrival was Sunday, Sept. 21, 1794. "We attended divine service," wrote Cooke. "The sermon was delivered by Rev. David Jones, chaplain. Mr. Jones chose for his text, Romans 8:31: 'But what shall we then say to these things? If God is for us, who can be against us?' This was the first time the army had been called together for the purpose of attending divine service since I joined it."

While the Americans were trying to survive in the mud and hunger at Miamitown, most of the Indian warriors still remained on the lower Maumee, near the present city of Toledo. According to information Wayne gained from several British deserters, the Indians were "somewhat divided in opinion; some are for peace and others are for war." This division among the various Indian tribes was to become a permanent condition. They would never again unite as they had done in the Miami Conferedacy under Chief Little Turtle. Because of this, Wayne was able to make complete control of the Old Northwest for the United States. That in turn eventually led to the expansion westward to the Pacific Coast. As the Indian groups began to break up, some returned to their villages, others migrated to Canada. Some, particularly the Miamis and Shawnees, went after the supply trains of Wayne's army, and any stragglers they could find.

Erection of the first American fort at the three rivers was begun Sept. 24, 1794—seven days after the arrival of General Anthony Wayne. Many in the army of 3,500 men had been toiling for several days in the mud, cutting timbers of oak and walnut for the walls of the stockade. "This day the work commenced on the garrison, which I am apprehensive will take some time to complete," reported Wayne at the time. The men were working in squads. Some were digging trenches, others were hauling the heavy tree trunks for implacement. The sounds of axes and straining voices were heard across the wilderness clearing. Some of the pressure was taken off the encampment with the arrival of a supply train carrying 553 kegs of flour, each weighing 100 pounds. Despite the remoteness and dangers of travel in the Indian country, others apparently arrived with the supply convoy. These were the first peddlers and commission merchants who took long risks for the high profits obtainable for desperately needed items at the wilderness posts. They found a ready market. Wayne said "A keg of whisky containing 10 gallons was purchased this day for $80; a sheep for $10; three dollars was offered for one pint of salt, but could not be obtained for less than six." It was good time and place to be in the salt business.

The Iron Hand

Wayne continued to hold his troops under

an iron rein, but that didn't prevent carping on the part of many. Lt. William Clark reported, "The ground cleared for the garrison just below the confluence of the St. Joseph and St. Mary's. The situation is tolerably elevated and has a ready command of the two rivers. I think it much to be lamanted that the commander-in-chief is determined to make this fort a regular fortification, as a common picketed one would be equally as difficult against the savages." This is the same Clark who a few years later would be part of the Lewis and Clark expedition to the Pacific. He was the younger brother of George Rogers Clark, the Virginian who specialized in brutal sweeps across the Ohio at Indian villages. Wayne had put an end to most of that sort of plundering. But the work of the fort continued, despite some desertions, fights and occasional sightings of Indians in the nearby forest. "Every officer, non-commissioned officer and soldier belonging to the square was hauling trees on the hind wheels of wagons," one man wrote. At about the time work was first started on the fort, according to a likely story later told by Private Bryant, the following occurred:

"A squad near where I was at work were engaged in felling a very large and very tall oak standing near the outer edge of the opening. The tree was nearly cut through and tottering in midair when a voice was heard overhead which somewhat startled the men at first; but looking up, they beheld a red varmint perched in the topmost branches.

"This fellow, no doubt, after finding he was caught had made up his mind that it was death anyway, and concluded to take his chances and go with the tree. But as it began to tremble and shake, he got shaky himself and, like Captain Scott's coon, had to come down, and that in a hurry.

"The boys as they watched him scramble down ached to get a shot at him, but they dared not.

"He was a large, fine-looking Indian. In the belt around his waist was a knife and tomahawk. He appeared perfectly undaunted; in fact, assumed an air of defiance, and when marched off to headquarters, seemed well pleased that he had escaped being killed by the falling tree or the bullets of the soldiers.

"He was evidently a spy and had climbed to the top of the tree to see what was going on in camp, little dreaming that his adventure would result as it did. When the tree fell, a buckskin pouch was found filled with parched corn and jerked venison.

"He was held prisoner for some weeks, and one morning it was announced that he was non est. How he escaped was a mystery that was never solved."

From the beginning, a sort of cat and mouse game continued. One of Wayne's spies, Christopher Miller, sighted a band of 16 Indians near the fort construction site on Sept. 26. Wayne sent a patrol of mounted Kentucky riflemen after them. The chase continued to sundown, but all the Indians disappeared unharmed. There was danger back at Fort Defiance too. "The enemy are troublesome about the garrison, and that they have killed some of our men under the walls of the fort," Wayne wrote. Actually, acccording to Capt. John Cooke, eleven men had deserted from Fort Defiance and eight more were missing, either killed by the Indians or deserted. The shadows of fear, death and recklessness growing out of despair stalked American soldiers during the building of the fort at Miamitown. Col. John Hamtramck said to a friend at the time, "The old man really is mad," referring to the commander, Anthony Wayne. Wayne was sitting on a powder keg of problems, but he was in control. He was not mad. Deep in the wilderness with an army too remote for help of any sort, sometimes at starvation levels, surrounded by hostile warriors, and with some of his own officers trying to do him in, the general became harsh and moody.

The Executioner

Anthony Wayne had before him the unfortunate experience of General Arthur St. Clair. That other commander had, three years earlier, suffered a disaster in a similar campaign. Nearly half of St. Clair's army was destroyed by the Indians, partly due to weak discipline. At the key moment, some of

St. Clair's troops were busy chasing down a large group of deserters threatening the very supply lines of the army. Wayne headed off this sort of trouble. His means were not pleasant. To keep some of the officers wary, he named Capt. Edward Butler as an aide. This Butler was the younger brother of General Richard Butler who was killed at St. Clair's defeat. Like his brother, Captain Butler was arrogant, mean and overbearing to both enemy and friend alike, if he had any of the latter. He was hated, but feared, by the other officers.

To give him a firmer hand over the whole army and militia forces, Wayne sought out another man for some specialized work. This was Robert McClellan, then still in his earlier years. This McClellan was to turn up again and again in histories and stories of the entire West. McClellan was one of that hard breed of man nurtured in the realities of the wilderness. With the instincts of an animal he could follow any trail in the forests and swamps. And, as with similar frontiersmen he had a single-minded sense of purpose and independence from the usual attitudes and opinions of society. Wayne named McClellan as one of his scouts, but the real job was something else—discouraging potential deserters. In short, McClellan was the enforcer, the executioner, or hired killer. As it turned out, Wayne didn't have nearly as many deserters as St. Clair, despite the larger numbers in the legion and the longer campaign. But there were enough to keep McClellan busy. He would move about, perhaps being in the area of the new fort one week and at Fort Defiance the next, or one of the other forts which linked the army with the Ohio River. As might be imagined, scant mention of McClellan's operations is made in the official records. One of Wayne's officers, however, Capt. John Cooke, suggests in his journal that he was aghast that anyone would be so stupid as to desert under the circumstances.

"A man deserted from Captain Thompson's company, now commanded by Captain Bines. This desertion seems somewhat extraordinary after McClellan's report to the commander. He had, in accordance with orders, killed one of the deserters he was sent after and had seen two more who were killed and scalped." Presumably the new deserter, likely half starved and desperate to get back to civilization, soon became the hunted in the wilderness. If the Indians didn't get him, McClellan would. The areas of the Old Northwest were vast and uncharted. Here and there, though, there was some activity. Supply trains coming up from Fort Washington at Cincinnati continued to make their way to the three rivers. These were slow-moving units, with one in the fall of 1794 containing 150 bullocks. Heavy guards of several hundred soldiers convoyed the supply train. Otherwise, they would simply amount to supplies for the marauding Indians who dogged every move across their lands. Occasionally someone would make a mistake. Captain Cooke reported one day, much like the others, that "four or five waiters, who had been sent for stores for officers, and who had preceded the escort, were killed about five miles from Greenville. Nelly Bundy was taken at the same time." We will probably never know who Nelly Bundy was.

Work on the fort overlooking the source of the Maumee River continued in October 1794, but a sense of uneasiness pervaded the atmosphere. Something close to insanity seemed to infect most everyone from Anthony Wayne on down to buck privates and wagon loaders. Most first American visitors to the three rivers had a compelling desire to be away from the place. This despite months and years of effort and the terrible cost of getting there. Wayne's attitude was not helped by another near-miss. During one of the violent storms which harassed the army, the top of a large tree cracked and fell a few feet from the general's tent one night. Wayne was still suffering from internal injuries received in the campaign along the Auglaise the previous summer. On the earlier occasion, a tree felled while cutting a road for the legion struck down Wayne. Fights among the men became so common, harsh corrective measures are recorded almost daily. The general put out the order: "Any noncommissioned officer or soldier or follower of the army who shall be detected in firing in the vicinity and hearing of the camp, unless at an enemy, shall immediately receive 50 lashes for a breach of order. Should any commissioned officer be so lost to discipline as to violate the same, he shall be immediately arrested and tried for giving false alarm." People were getting edgy. Wayne kept his word regarding those who attacked either fellow soldiers or the fort's supplies. Privates John Fay Miller, Elivine Crowell and John Hassell received 100 lashes each for cow theft. James Murrow was given 50 lashes for misconduct. Private Michael Burns received 100 lashes for insulting Sergeant Réed. Private David Johnson took 75 lashes across the back for helping to steal cattle. Corporal James Reading was court martialed and sentenced by Wayne to be "hanged by the neck until dead" for cattle theft. He was held prisoner for a period and later taken to Fort Greenville for the execution in front of the troops. At about the same time, a soldier named John Keating was executed by a firing squad as was a deserter from Fort Defiance.

Mutilated Bodies

Wayne pressed harder for rapid completion of the fort. Every man in the regular army was pressed into construction work "not actually on guard or other duty." The Kentucky militiamen were given the job of getting the supplies through. But the difficulties still multiplied. It became common knowledge among the men that Le Gris, the old Miami chief, had moved back into the vicinity. Le Gris and his hungry warriors watched every move in and out of the fort, looking for any chance or weakness.

Wayne was not worried about Le Gris attacking the fort. The general knew from his spies that Little Turtle and most of the other chiefs and warriors were still in the Lake Erie area. But fear gradually took hold of the militiamen whose duty it was to convoy supply trains through the wilderness. On every trip, several of their number would likely disappear. The mutilated bodies of others found along the trails were in each militiaman's nightmares. Lieutenant Boyer reported "the volunteers appeared to be uneasy and have refused to do duty. They are ordered by the commander-in-chief to march tomorrow for Greenville to assist the packhorses, which I am told they are determined not to do." On the next morning the volunteers refused to move out. They were threatened with punishment and loss of all their pay. They finally were coerced into one more convoy trip. Wayne came to the conclusion at this time that it would be better to send the entire 1,500-man militia back home. He could not afford an insurrection at this remote post. Though he needed guards for supply trains, the additional forces were a supply problem in themselves, and a danger to the mission. He wrote to Secretary of War Henry Knox on October 17. "The mounted volunteers of Kentucky marched from this place on the morning of the 14th for Fort Washington, where they are to be mustered and discharged. The conduct of both officers and men of this corps in general has been better than any militia I have heretofore seen in the field for so great a length of time. But it would not do to retain them any longer, although our present situation as well as the term for which they were enrolled would have justified their being continued in service until November 14." Wayne did not like volunteer armies. "The enclosed estimate," he said, "will demonstrate the mistaken policy and bad economy of substituting mounted volunteers in the place of regular troops. Unless effectual measures are immediately adopted by both Houses of Congress for raising troops to garrison the western posts, we have fought, bled and conquered in vain." Wayne, from his headquarters at Miamitown, warned that without added soldiers and extended service of his legion the vast wilderness would "again become a range for the hostile Indians of the West" and "a fierce and savage enemy" would sweep down on pioneers as far as the Ohio River and beyond.

Jacques Lasselle

One man's concern for his brother was to lead to a break in the impasse between General Anthony Wayne and the Miami Indian chiefs. On October 13, 1794, a French-speaking trader named Jacques Lasselle appeared at Wayne's encampment by the three rivers, where construction of the fort was still underway. This Lasselle had with him three Americans who had been held by the Indians. Curious soldiers at the scene quickly recognized two of the prisoners—fellow troopers taken many months earlier during a battle along the convoy routes. As many as 200 soldiers and similar numbers of Indian raiders often fought in these attacks on the American supplies. The other prisoner was a 13-year old girl who had been kidnapped three years earlier by Indians near the Ohio River. It turned out that her sister's husband was among the Kentucky militiamen with Wayne's army. As far as the records show, this is the first time prisoners of the Indians were returned to the Americans during Wayne's campaign. Usually, the Indians either killed the captured soldiers or sold them to the British. Just how Jacques Lasselle talked the Indians into giving up the three prisoners is not known. His brother, Antoine Lasselle, had been a prisoner of the Americans ever since the Battle of Fallen Timbers. The Lasselle brothers, long-time traders at Miamitown, had fought on the side of the Indians—the losing side in that instance. One old account has it that Antoine Lasselle was grabbed from a hiding place under a fallen tree by advancing U.S. regulars who were pursuing the fleeing Indians. It was expected that he would be sentenced to death by an ensuing court-martial. Antoine, however, supposedly noticed a Masonic emblem on Col. John Hamtramck, the judge at the trial. He flashed a Masonic signal to the judge, and was spared the ultimate penalty. Whether the tale is true or not, the Lasselles were good at surviving. Some of their descendants reside to the present day in the Fort Wayne area. Jacques Lasselle risked his life in coming into the American headquarters to trade for his brother. He was taken to General Wayne who quickly saw the potential usefulness of the Lasselles in relations with the tribal chiefs. As events would show, the Lasselles switched to the cause of the United States and became the key persuaders among the Indians for meeting with Wayne at the Greenville Treaty site. Wayne was so convinced of the value of the Lasselles that he reported the development to the Secretary of War, but left blank their names, in fear their identities might fall into the wrong hands.

"I have the honor of transmitting to you a copy of the deposition of a certain (blank), a Canadian prisoner taken in the action of the 20th of August. His brother arrived at this place on the 13th with a flag and three American prisoners, which he redeemed from the Indians with a view of liberating (blank)."

"Enclosed is his narrative given upon oath by which you will see that Governor Simcoe, Col. McKee and the famous Capt. Brant are at this moment tampering with the hostile chiefs and will undoubtedly prevent them for concluding a treaty of peace with the United States if possible.

"I shall, however, endeavor to counteract them through the means of (blank) who have considerable influence with the principal chiefs," Wayne wrote from Miamitown.

Though the British, headed by John Graves Simcoe, governor of Upper Canada, together with Alexander McKee, Simon Girty and other Revolutionary War American turncoats, continued to urge the Indians to battle the U.S. army, events were going in favor of Wayne's side. The American general received a letter about this time from Alexander Hamilton, reporting the conclusion of the Jay Treaty. This meant the English Crown had agreed to stop its support of the Indians and would turn its Northwest forts over to the U.S. In the meantime, the soldiers at the headwaters of the Maumee launched a river boat for a trip to Fort Defiance. According to one report, the boat was 40 feet long and 12 feet wide and was loaded with salt and other supplies.

"She had not proceeded one mile before she ran on a rock and capsized, losing the greater part of her load." said Lt. Clark.

Fort Wayne a Reality

On Oct. 21, Wayne had ordered a halt to work on the nearly-completed stockade and surrounding buildings. He placed Col. John Hamtramck in charge of the companies which were to garrison the fort, making him in effect, commander. On the following morning, there was more than the usual stir about the place. "Colonel Hamtramck marched the troops to the garrison at 7 a.m.," reported Captain John Cooke. "After a discharge of 15 guns, he named the fort by a garrison order, 'Fort Wayne.' He then marched his command into it." Others present reported that the "15 guns" were rounds of cannon fire which echoed across the three rivers. Though Hamtramck is usually credited with naming the fort, he actually was simply reading orders handed to him by Anthony Wayne. The name of the stockade was previously determined during correspondence between Wayne and the War Department. After the reading of the speech and the running up of the Stars and Stripes, there was a volley of three cheers from the assembled troops. General Wayne had stood at a reviewing place near the flag pole during most of the parade and ceremony. By 8 a.m. the deed was done. It was four years to the day since that earlier morning when the Miami Indians under Little Turtle and Le Gris cut down the troops of General Josiah Harmar as they attempted to cross the Maumee. The place of that past disaster to the U.S. Army was in clear view of the new fort on the slight hill just southwest of the confluence of the three rivers.

Following the dedication of Fort Wayne, the general almost immediately began to prepare for his own departure and the extending of the military hold on the Northwest Territory. He was particularly interested in the control of the waterways—the chief route for both war and supplies in the wilderness. "Captain Kibby with a company of spies was directed to proceed up the St. Mary's River to Fort Adams (in Ohio where St. Mary's Lake is located) to ascertain the situation of the river with respect to navigation. He took with him the canoe and three days provisions," wrote Cooke. Apparently Kibby didn't think much of the St. Mary's. "Captain Kibby sent back an express informing the general of the impossibility of navigating the St. Mary's River." Cooke reported on Oct. 25. "He begged permission to return but was peremptorily ordered to continue to Fort Adams." Wayne wasn't having any nonsense about his rivers or whether a person could travel on them.

The main army of Anthony Wayne began its departure from Fort Wayne on October 27, 1794. "At 11 a.m. the army proceeded on the line of march on General Harmar's trace. After four and one-half miles we came to a large swamp," reported Cooke. After proceeding a little further, to a distance of eight and a half miles from the fort, the soldiers camped for the night. The hard march started the following day, Oct. 28, when the army moved 16 miles. The troops continued to the St. Mary's, an area where the woods were reported to be very thick, and went along that stream toward Girty Town, northeast of Fort Recovery. Finally, on Nov. 2, they approached their destination. "In two hours we marched six miles to Greenville; after the discharge of several guns and after three cheers, the men were assigned to their respective huts, which we found very much out of repair," Cooke relates.

Mad Anthony Wayne had completed his war campaign in the Indian country. It was the most significant in American history from the point of view of westward expansion. "Permit me now to inform you that the skeleton of the Legion arrived at this place on the 2nd in high health and spirits after an arduous and very fatiguing but glorious tour of 97 days during which period we marched and countermarched upwards of 300 miles through the heart of an enemy's country, cutting a wagon road the whole way, besides making and establishing those two respectable fortifications," the general wrote to Secretary of War Knox in the November of 1794.

Wayne decided another fort—some eight miles southwest of Fort Wayne—should be built. As long as he had the upper hand, the general saw advantages in tightening his grip over the old travel routes. This meant gaining a complete mastery of the river travel. Only by this means did Wayne think the American military could be sure of its control of the Indian tribes. During the building of the fort at the three rivers,

Wayne spent much of his time moving about the area. He considered the land, Indian trails, the location of the various destroyed villages and the several links between the rivers and streams. Where he did not go himself, he sent others to discover and chart the landscape.

Frontier Plan

It was on Nov. 12, 1794, that Wayne wrote to Secretary of War Henry Knox and urged a complete new plan for the Northwest Territory. He suggested abandoning some of the forts and the Trace which had been used to connect Fort Washington at Cincinnati with the Maumee area. He preferred a route up through present Ohio to connect with the Grand Glaize River and Lake Erie, and then west to Fort Wayne. The key to his entire plan was to be a fortification at the west end of the Maumee-Wabash portage, binding the old French trading roads to the expanding U.S.

"It will afford a much better chain for the general protection of the frontiers—which with a blockhouse at the landing place on the Wabash, eight miles southwest of the post at the Miami villages, which would give us the possession of all the portages between the heads of the navigable waters of the Gulfs of Mexico and the St. Lawrence, and serve as a barrier between the different tribes of Indians settled along the margins of the rivers emptying into each," Wayne said. The general was referring to Little River, the tributary to the Wabash along the western border of Allen County. He had found that it was at this place that the Indian and French travelers had usually started the trek over the land between the Wabash and Mississippi Rivers to the south and the Maumee, Lake Erie and St. Lawrence to the northeast. The east end of the portage was about where Swinney Park is today, though other locations along the St. Mary's River were also used.

It is almost strange to consider today the great part some of these rather small streams played in the early life of the area—before the canals, railroads and highways. Little River and the Aboite Creek, which was also used as a connection with the Wabash, are now ignored backwaters, sometimes not even shown on general maps of the state and area.

The building of this second fortified point in the immediate area was sufficiently important at the time for provision to be made in subsequent treaties forced on the Indians. Wayne set out the land along Little River for U.S. military occupation, and a year later, a four-square-mile plot was surveyed at the location west of the hilly and swampy portage trail. But this was to be the fort which was never built. Through the subsequent years, a condition of peace was maintained with the Indians, except for a couple bloody occasions which will be recounted later. It was probably decided there was no pressing need for the additional blockhouse. Besides, keeping a sufficient number of men to garrison the existing fort was always a problem. Another strong point would have added to the burden.

In the meantime, Colonel Hamtramck, the first commandant at Fort Wayne, was having his own problems. He told Wayne on Dec. 5: "It is with a great degree of mortification that I am obliged to inform your excellency of the great propensity many of the soldiers have to larceny. I have flogged them till I am tired. The economic allowance of one hundred lashes allowed by government does not appear a sufficient inducement for a rascal to act the part of an honest man. I have a number in confinement and in irons for having stolen four quarters of beef on the night of the 3rd. I could wish them to be tried by a general court-martial, in order to make an example of some of them. I shall keep them confined until the pleasure of your excellency is known."

Dividing The Indians

The business of making the most of the disunity among the Indian tribes is told by Wayne in a report on Dec. 23, 1794. "The Wyandots and other Indians in the vicinity of the rapids of Sandusky are completely within our power and their hunting grounds all within striking distance—hence their present solicitude for a suspension of hostilities." The Wyandots, otherwise known as Hurons, were one of the tribes which participated in the Battle of Fallen Timbers and the earlier duels between the Indians and the invading American armies.

"It is however probable that Tarhe (A Wyandot chief usually called The Crane) may now be seriously inclined for peace, being the only surviving principal chief out of four killed in the action of the 20th of August. He himself was shot through the right elbow which has deprived him of the use of that arm." Wayne further said at the time that the Indians along the south shore of Lake Erie who were interested in peace were afraid of the "hostile Indians in the vicinity of Detroit" because of their contracts with the American commander.

"Tarhe says that the present flag is sent without the privacy or consent of those tribes, and expresses some doubts of its safe return should any of the hostile Indians meet it on its way home and discover the object of the mission." What Wayne was really saying was that if The Crane and his fellow travelers should be caught by the Miami or Shawnee raiding parties, it would be a bit of bad luck for both The Crane and Wayne's drive to divide the Indians. Wayne decided to see that The Crane survived long enough to be useful in the coming treaty talks. "I shall endeavor to benefit by this real or affected dread and propose to take them under the immediate protection of the United States, and to build a fortification at the foot of the Rapids of Sandusky as soon as the season and circumstances will permit." As it turned out, The Crane did survive to become one of the Indian signers of the Treaty of Greenville the following summer. In this same report, Anthony Wayne reveals for the first time the possible plan to drive all the Indians out of the American territories. "I have however succeeded in dividing and distracting the councils of the hostile Indians and hope through that means eventually to bring about a general peace; or compel the refractory to pass the Mississippi and to the northwest side of the Lakes." The general, though, doubted that the Indians would move north of the Great Lakes into Canada in any great numbers "because of the inclemency of the Winter season, the sterility of the soil and the scarcity of game." He expected, however, assuming the U.S. could cut the British influence, that the "hostile tribes would either have accepted our invitation to treaty—or have passed to the Spanish side of the Mississippi in the course of this Fall and Winter. Possibly they may yet do the one or the other, as I am informed that their present dependent situation is far from pleasant, nor have we much cause to envy the British the pleasure and expense of supporting and clothing this numerous horde of savages thrown upon them by their own insidious conduct and fortuitous events of war."

Wayne at this time assumed the British were furnishing arms and ammunition in great number to the Indians. Actually, this was not the case. Little Turtle and many of the Indian warriors from the Miamitown and other locations between Lake Erie, Lake Michigan and the Maumee and Wabash areas were in the Detroit vicinity seeking guns from the English military suppliers. For the most part, they received but limited help. This contributed greatly to the decline of the Indian attitude and ability to oppose Wayne. As the winter settled over the Old Northwest, other things were working for Wayne, including Jacques and Antoine Lasselle, the one-time Miamitown traders. "Yesterday a number of chiefs of the Chippewas, Ottawas, Sacs and Potawatomis arrived here with the two Lasselles," reported Col. John Hamtramck from Fort Wayne on Dec. 29. "It appears that the Shawnees, Delawares and Miamis remain still under the influence of McKee; but Lasselle thinks they will be compelled to come into the measures of the other Indians. After the chiefs have rested a day or two, I will send them to headquarters (at Greenville)."

The Great Treaty

To Little Turtle, the Miami war chief, it

was all clear enough. The people with the guns would gain mastery over the people without. In late 1794 in the Northwest Territory, the Indians were the have-nots. It was expected by various Indian chiefs and some of the U.S. officials that the site for treaty talks would be held at Fort Wayne. This was, after all, the destination of the military campaign in the Old Northwest and was considered the seat of power in the wilderness. Wayne, however, was against meeting with any major groups of Indians in the vicinity of Miamitown. Everything in the records indicated he had an aversion for the place which today bears his name. He stayed at the three rivers only long enough to see to the construction of the fort and the appointing of men for garrison duty. He then took himself and the main part of his army to Fort Greenville, about 90 miles to the southeast. He never returned. The general gives his reasoning in a letter to Secretary of War Henry Knox on Jan. 24, 1795.

"There appeared a kind of wish or desire among some of the deputies to hold the treaty at the Miami villages, where the hatchet was first raised, and there they wished to bury it. But this business as easily got over by observing to them that the bloody hatchet would disturb the spirits of the unburied dead, that this ground (at Greenville) was unstained with human gore—that if the hatchet was buried here it never could again be found, because no bloody traces would mark the grave in which it rested."

After explaining what he told the Indians, Wayne proceeded to give his real thinking: "There are many strong reasons to give this place a preference to the Miami villages! The uncertainty of a sufficient number of troops to give protection to the convoys, or to inspire the savages with respect for our force, so as to deter them from making any attempts upon our supplies or posts, should these overtures for peace be only artifice, as suggested by Tarhe.

"This place could be defended by a small body of troops from the citadel against all the Indians in the wilderness. We shall at the same time have strong posts in their rear, well supplied with artillery and ammunition, so as to sustain a long siege—which would not be the case was the treaty to be held at the Miami villages. It might be artfully procrastinated by the savages until our supplies would begin to fail us, the cattle would be always in their power, and should they prove perfidious, we would be placed in a very unpleasant situation." To clinch his argument with the War Department, Wayne said, "It would cost the United States double the sum of money to hold the treaty in that place, than it will at Greenville.,'

Anthony Wayne, however, overlooked nothing to butter up the Indian chiefs. He sent back east for articles to hand out, such as clothing, wampum, paint. He also said if it became an absolute necessity he would go anyplace to secure the treaty. "I am determined to face every difficulty and danger and meet them on their ground, rather than not treat. For I am sick and tired of this kind of war as any man in America, the meekest Quaker not excepted." It had been 12 years since the Americans had first tried to bring the Indian nations of the Miami Confederation under control. Thousands of lives on the frontier had been lost. Two major armies had been defeated. Now for the first time the United States had the upper hand.

Bitter Winter

Fort Wayne, a stockade of the wilderness in the bitter winter of 1794-95, stood at the summit. It was the summit for two reasons. The first was geographical. The other had to do with Indian power on the North American Continent. Even to this day, the community at the confluence of the three rivers is sometimes referred to as the Summit City. This term isn't idle promotion by the civic oriented, nor is it some sort of comparison with other urban centers in the State of Indiana. The term refers to the location as it relates to the flow of inland rivers and lakes which connect the Atlantic Ocean and the Gulf of Mexico. The portage, that eight or 10 miles of flat lands which stood between the Maumee River and the upper tributaries of the Wabash River, was the summit. It was the high point, away from which flowed the waters which were the highways of the wilderness. To the northeast went the Maumee, then Lake Erie and Lake Ontario, the St. Lawrence River to Quebec and beyond to the Atlantic and the ports of the Old World. To the southwest flowed the Wabash into the Ohio River and the Mississippi and finally New Orleans and the Gulf with foreign ports beyond. For the Indians this same site was the place where they had reached the summit of their powers. It was more than a concentration of villages of the Miami, Shawnee and Delaware tribes, though there were seven of these within a few miles of the three rivers. It was the place where the chiefs of many Indian nations of the mid-continent were drawn to plot the preservation of a whole way of life. They came from an area extending from the Ohio River to the Hudson Bay, from Niagara Falls to the Mississippi.

In the early days, the United States was seen as the colonies which occupied a part of the Atlantic Coast area. In the vast interior, no regular political boundaries were recognized. There was a thousand miles of wilderness. But there was continuous activity along its rivers and lakes. The French, and later British, held a rather tenuous sway, but it was Indian country. Many of the Indian peoples, whose very tribal names are beginning to fade, occasionally turn up in old tracts, city names or adventure tales. They include, in addition to the Miami, Shawnee and Delaware, the Wyandot or Huron, the Chippewa, Ottawa, the Illinois, the Peoria, the Mingo, the Kickapoo, the Wea, the Piankashaw, the Potawatomi, the Kaskaskia, the Fox and Sac. Many of these tribes had early banded together, with French encouragement, to do battle with the Six Nations of the Iroquois. This was actually the reason for the founding of Miamitown in the 1690's. The Miamis and allied Indians had moved in from the west and north to take control of the portage and outflowing waters so that the great route from the St. Lawrence to the Mississippi could be used. The area flourished for 100 years prior to the coming of the American armies. Then again, essentially the same tribes that had fought the Iroquois generations before joined in a new confederacy centered at Miamitown to do battle with the white intruders. But after some slashing victories, the Indians were defeated by the Legion of Anthony Wayne. The old trading centers and villages were destroyed. The fort was built at the summit. The trade and travel over the old river route almost immediately began to wither away. Though few of the Indians moved back into the vicinity of the fort, it never again became a center of Indian power. Nor did other concentrations of Indian power of a potency to take on the main army of the United States ever develop any place else on the North American continent.

"I am apprehensive that the Indians have serious intentions of making peace with the United States," wrote Col. Richard England, the British commander at Detroit in January, 1795. The papers of John Graves Simcoe, governor of Upper Canada, reveal that the British were well aware that several of the tribal chiefs were meeting with Wayne at Greeneville. Some of the other Indian nations, such as the Miami and the Shawnee, were holding out in the hopes of forming a new Indian army. These hopes of renewing the attack on the Americans faded, however, when Chiefs Little Turtle, Le Gris and Blue Jacket learned the British would not furnish the arms for a new war. Also, many of the Indian peoples were starving.

"Le Gris, the village chief of the Miami Nation, and one of the commanding trumps in McKee's game, has at last come in," Hamtramck reported from Fort Wayne to Anthony Wayne in March, 1795. "He stood out for a long time. He was four days with me, during which I had an opportunity of examining him with great attention. He is a sensible old fellow, and no ways ignorant of the cause of the war, for which he blames the Americans, saying that they were too extravagant in their demands in their first treaties."

Washington's Advice

In May, 1795, President George Washington sat down with his new Secretary of War, Timothy Pickering, to set plans for the great treaty which was to secure Fort Wayne and the Old Northwest for the United States. They carefully went over a number of things. There were the many records of past agreements with various Indian tribes. They weighed Anthony Wayne's suggestions for the coming council with the Indian nations at Fort Greenville. They discussed secret communications to be made to Lord Dorchester., Governor-General of Canada. Washington was particularly concerned that the huge assembly of Indians might turn into a disaster to the American army at the wilderness outposts. Deep in Washington's memory was the bloody defeat of Gen. James Braddock many years before and the still recent slaughter of the army of General Arthur St. Clair, which cost an even greater number of lives. Pickering relayed the Presidents remarks to Wayne. "From the nature of the case and your representations, a very large concourse of Indians might be expected at the treaty and thence the necessity of being on your guard, notwithstanding the fair and friendly appearance of the late hostile Indians." The Secretary went on to impress Wayne. "This caution, I am sure, you will receive and remember with that respect and attention which on every account is due to the source from which it sprang.

"The uncommonly great assemblage of the Indians which are to be expected and the diminished strength of the legion seemed to have suggested to the President the necessity of extreme caution against any treacherous designs of the Indians during the treaty. To the officers commanding detached posts you will of course give very pointed instructions on this head.

"The treachery of Pontiac, a great chief of one of the Western tribes, towards the English, after they took possession of Detroit about the year 1763, will not be forgotten. Under the guise of friendship he well nigh possessed himself of the fort. And if your information is accurate, that the British agents are at this late hour setting every engine at work to prevent the proposed treaty, you may expect they will not be scrupulous in suggesting the promoting of any treacherous attempt to defeat it."

Anthony Wayne for several months had been trying to impress President Washington and Congress of the need for more men under arms at the western forts. And as an increasing number of Indians began to flow toward the Greenville treaty site, the danger of a possible uprising became more acute. Wayne apparently got his message across. Washington decided to strengthen Wayne's army. "You will receive shortly," Pickering wrote to Wayne on May 23, "a reinforcement of about 330 men from Pittsburgh. Colonel Butler has orders to forward them without delay. Some I hope will be descending the Ohio before my letters reach Pittsburgh. Most of them are recruits from the militia army—fine young fellows, Colonel Butler writes me; and from the temporary service in which they have been engaged since last autumn, I presume they must be tolerably well disciplined. At any rate, they must be greatly superior to common recruits.

"Other recruits are now on the march from New England; which added to some other parties in this state (Pennsylvania), Maryland and Virginia, will make up a corps of at least 200 more.

"Your letter to Lord Dorchester is gone by post for Canada: a regular mail is established from Albany through Vermont to Montreal." Wayne wanted the English governor of Canada to recognize American possession and halt agents in the Indian country from stirring up the warriors. Pickering also told the general, "I furnished the Secretary of State with a copy of Father Edmund Burke's letter to the Wyandots, and he sent it to the British minister, who promised to send it to Lord Dorchester." Some weeks earlier, one of Wayne's spies had obtained the letter Father Burke, a Canadian priest, had distributed to the Indians, saying the United States would suppress the Catholic religion if it got control. From the days of the French, many of the traders and Indians were Catholic oriented. Wayne moved to assure the Indians the Americans would respect the various religions, and asked Dorchester to restrain the activities of Burke and others in the Indian country.

Growing Distrust

As long as there was war, the various Indian nations usually were able to maintain some aim and agreed purpose. With the coming of peace, distrust grew. During the early months of 1795, increasing numbers of the Indian chiefs decided to come to terms with the United States. Others, fearing to be left out of possible concessions and gifts, also went along. Among the Americans, there was unity of purpose as far as the military and government was concerned, but there were growing difficulties with the many adventurers who were interested in land grabs, raids across the Ohio on Indian villages for either plunder or plain bloody revenge. The peace was being further shaken by raiding parties, mostly Shawnee and Miami, who were hitting the American supply lines between Cincinnati and Greeneville, and between Greenville and Fort Wayne. The raids on the supply trains up from the Ohio River and Kentucky were troublesome to Wayne for two reasons. The lesser threat was the loss or delay of needed materials and communications. More important, any hostility was being used by political opponents of the government to try to subvert the treaty negotiations. In the early days of the Republic, there were always groups trying to carve out separate little kingdoms for themselves in the western fringes. In June of that year, two deserters from the British garrison of Fort Miami on the lower Maumee River reported to Wayne that some of the tribal chiefs were meeting with Governor Simcoe and other British officers at "big Rock near the mouth of the Detroit River." Wayne presumed at the time that the English were encouraging the Indians to thwart the treaty negotiations and possibly renew hostile actions. Actually, the Indians received little encouragement of any kind from the British, who also were disagreeing among themselves on what policy to follow in the Northwest Territory.

On June 17, General Wayne wrote to the War Department: "A considerable number of chiefs belonging to the Chippewas, Ottawas, Potawatomis, Delawares, and Pinkashaws are already arrived" at Greeneville to start the great council to settle control of the vast area from the Ohio River, across the Great Lakes and west.

"The Wyandots, Shawnees, Miamis and Hurons are said to be on their way from Big Rock—under the conduct of Blue Jacket. Some of the Michigan and Wabash Indians have reached Fort Wayne on their way in. But I can not as yet form any just estimate of the numbers that may eventually assemble." In the meantime, Wayne "thought it expedient" to constrict his lines and "throw up some additional works to cover the flanks, front and rear" of the places where the Indians were assembling at Greenville. The general, with more than a thousand Indians of the various tribes coming together, was somewhat concerned with security. Within a few days Anthony Wayne was informed by Colonel John Hamtramck of Fort Wayne that Chiefs Little Turtle and Le Gris were on their way to Greenville. The Miami chiefs, together with a large party of warriors, had passed through the three rivers vicinity on their way. The Turtle and his party of 95 Indians arrived at Greenville on June 23. Included in the group were Kekionga and Eel River Miamis, Weas, Piankashaws, Kickapoos and Kaskaskias—all hereditary allies in the Indian wars for a century past. President Washington relayed some final instruction to Wayne regarding his dealing the Indian tribes. He urged the securing of the Ohio area and the posts along the Maumee and Wabash, but not to push too hard as "peace with the four tribes is really the great object of the treaty." Difficulties were to be avoided.

"Although more might be secured to us—for instance some posts at the bottom of Lake Michigan and on the Illinois; yet I should doubt the expediency of touching them at present. When the peace shall once be established, and we also take possession of the posts now held by the British, we can obtain everything we shall want with a tenth of the trouble and difficulty which you would now have to encounter," Secretary of War Pickering advised Wayne.

Greenville Treaty

Fort Wayne was made legal to all concerned on Aug. 3, 1795. This was the date the chiefs of the Indian tribes and the representatives of the United States signed the Treaty of Greenville, sometimes called "The Peace of Mad Anthony." Prior to that time, the young American republic had claimed the Old Northwest by virtue of the Treaty of 1783 with Great Britain at the conclusion of the Revolutionary War. When the fort was built at three rivers and named after Anthony Wayne in the fall of 1794, it stood on contested ground. It was only by the force of arms that the American presence existed. This was all changed with the treaty made with the Indian nations the following summer. In one stroke, the United States took three-quarters of present day Ohio, excepting the northwest portion, and also took a sliver of southeast Indiana. Though the areas now taking in most of Indiana, Michigan, Illinois, Wisconsin and Minnesota remained largely in Indian hands, even strategic points in the Great Lakes area and along some rivers were marked off for U.S. occupation. One such tract was the site of Fort Wayne and the portage terminus to the Wabash River. Other tracts taken include the present sites of Toledo and Defiance, Ohio; Detroit, Chicago, Peoria and Mackinac.

In view of the protracted wars of the previous years, it is almost surprising how readily most of the Indian chiefs gave in to Wayne's demands at the Fort Greeneville treaty talks. Wayne clearly had the gun power and the stronger bargaining hand, so most of the Indian leaders appeared ready to concede most anything and get the whole thing over with. Only Chief Little Turtle of the Miamis disputed Wayne and the American claims. First he tried to talk the other Indian tribes into forming a united front to refuse the huge land demands of the Americans. This failed, partly because some of the Indian chiefs seemed to dislike the Turtle more than the American invaders, and were almost happy to see the Miamis get a comeuppance. Clearly, the old Indian Confederation forged by the Miamis under Little Turtle and Le Gris was dead. Wayne was now calling the shots, and all but a few of the Indians were disposed to go along. But the Turtle pressed on with his arguments—so much so that Wayne complained to the War Department about the Miami chief's "highly-developed sense of litigation." First, the Turtle told Wayne the Americans were pushing too far west with the boundary extending from Fort Recovery to the Ohio River. Wayne countered that such a line was the only way to make clear the boundary between American and Indian lands, though his real reason was to secure the supply lines and forts extending north from the Ohio. Next, Little Turtle said the Miamis had always held sway over an area taking in Chicago, Detroit and covering all land south to the Ohio River. The Miami chief said "those lands were always ours" and said the U.S. had no right to military and other tracts in the Indian lands. Wayne, however, pointed to the locations of French and British forts which had existed along the lakes and rivers, saying in effect, the Indians had given over "as much ground around their forts as their cannon can command." It was an obvious case of power, and Wayne gave little. He did, however, make some minor concessions on the land issue to Little Turtle, presumably to hurry along the talks to a successful conclusion. Still the Turtle pressed on, this time by appealing to avarice. Speaking of control of the profitable portage which connected the Maumee River to the Wabash, the Turtle said: "Let us both own this place and enjoy the common advantages it affords." Wayne then gained the favor of the other tribal chiefs by saying such a concession would require them to pay tribute money to the Miamis for use of the riverways. The other chiefs quickly sided with the American general and against the Miami chief on the issue.

Indian nations participating in the treaty were the Miamis, the Delawares, the Shawnees, the Potawatomis, Wyandots, Chippewas, Ottawas, Weas, Piankashaws, Kickapoos and Kaskaskias. They ceded to the U.S. about 25,000 square miles of land plus 16 other tracts where forts or key communications were involved. The Indians were given $25,000 and were promised an annual allowance.

Power Over Great Lakes

With the power of the Indians somewhat decimated by the Greenville Treaty, the United States moved to take control of the several British forts which remained in the Old Northwest. The outermost military garrisons of the Americans were at Fort Wayne and Fort Defiance. British guns still looked out from Fort Miami on the lower Maumee near present Toledo, Fort Detroit, Fort Michilimackinac at the straits between Lakes Michigan and Huron, and Fort Niagara at the eastern end of Lake Erie. But the days of the English on U.S. territory were nearing the end—mostly because they knew they could not hold them without the support of the Indian armies. In this respect, the Revolutionary War was only now coming to a conclusion in the wilderness areas—some 14 years after the last battles on the East Coast. It was a bitter time for the Indians, that cold winter of 1795-96. Defeated, some traveled back to the upper reaches of the Great Lakes and others attempted to set up new villages in places as yet remote from the intruding soldiers and pioneers from the States to the east. The Miamis, the Shawnees and the Delawares were particularly affected by the destruction of crops and hunting grounds in the areas of the Maumee and Auglaize. Some of the very old and very young were in particularly desperate condition. Colonel John Hamtramck at Fort Wayne wrote on Dec. 13, 1795, about "Ninety old women and children with some very old men who live near us and have no other mode of subsisting but by the garrison. I have repeatedly tried to get clear of them, but without success." Apparently Hamtramck and the other conquerors hadn't foreseen this welfare aspect of taking over the new lands. But like it or not the destitute Indians were still there a month later in January, 1796. "About ninety old women and children have victualled by the garrison. I have yesterday given them five day's provision, and told them it was the last they should have until spring. I was obliged to do so because, from calculation, I have no more flour than will last me until spring. But sir, if other supplies could be got by land, I consider it politic to feed these poor creatures, who will suffer very much for want of subsistence," Hamtramck reported to Wayne. Anthony Wayne had returned to Pennsylvania for the winter. He was received at the cities as the new hero of the Republic. He was praised by President Washington and both Houses of Congress. He was also struck with a stunning disappointment. Mad Anthony had been hoping to be named Secretary of War. Instead, James McHenry was appointed to succeed the retiring Henry Pickering. In his Seventh Annual Address to the Senate and House, Dec. 8, 1795, Washington did, however, show he was taking Wayne's advice about trying to stop the vicious raids by lawless bands which were sweeping into the Indian lands to plunder and kill.

"The provisions heretofore made with a view to the protection of the Indians from the violences of the lawless part of our frontier inhabitants are insufficient. It is demonstrated that these violences can be perpetrated with impunity, and it can need no argument to prove that unless the murdering of the Indians can be restrained by bringing the murderers to condign punishment, all the exertions of the government to prevent destructive retaliations by the Indians will prove fruitless.

"The frequent destruction of innocent women and children, who are the chief victims of retaliation, must continue to shock humanity," Washington said. He urged Congress to provide the means for equal justice in the newly-won lands. "To enforce upon the Indians the observance of justice, it is indispensable that there shall be competent means of rendering justice to them."

But no real actions were ever taken to protect the Indians. The treaty itself was laid before Congress the following day, Dec. 9, and was quickly ratified. The pattern was set for the long-term expansion of the United States to the West, which was eventually to take all the lands of the Indians.

Americans Take Detroit

On May 17, 1796, Colonel John Hamtramck marched from Fort Wayne at the head of an armed force and proceeded down the Maumee. After brief stays at Fort Defiance and Fort Deposit, Hamtramck moved toward Fort Miami, the British military post at the rapids of the Maumee and slighly upriver from Lake Erie. The English were preparing to evacuate Fort Miami, as required by the force of events and the terms of an agreement between the U.S. and the Crown. Hamtramck took possession of Fort Miami on July 11, then proceeded quickly toward Detroit. The Americans took possession of that stronghold on July 13. Earlier, the British commandant had evacuated the Detroit post. After the years of conflict the actual transfer of the military outposts was rather calm and free of acrimony. General Anthony Wayne, who by this time was traveling back west after winter and spring in Pennsylvania, reported the peaceable possession of the two forts to the War Department. "The polite and friendly manner in which the evacuation has taken place is truly worthy of British officers and does honor to them and the nation to which they belong." Wayne enclosed letters from the British, including one from Colonel Richard England, the Detroit commandant who had figured in the Indian battles against the American expeditions. Within a month, Wayne had taken possession of all the British forts on the American side of the line of demarcation between the U.S. and Canada. He sent Major Henry Burdeck with a detachment to occupy Fort Michilimackinac at the straits between Lakes Michigan and Huron; Colonel Hamtramck was put in charge of the fort at Detroit. Also taken were the former British forts of Niagara and Oswego.

Wayne seems to have developed a good relationship with most of the Indians and frontiersmen. After the meetings at Detroit he sent along to the American capitol a list of names of several Indian chiefs who were to embark for a trip to Philadelphia. He made particular mention of two of the chiefs —Blue Jacket of the Shawnees and Little Turtle of the Miamis. It becomes clearer with this letter that the one exception in Wayne's pleasant relationship with the Indian chiefs was Little Turtle.

"Among them is the famous Shawnee Chief Blue Jacket, who it is said had the chief command of the Indian Army on the 4th of November, 1791, against General St. Clair.

"The Little Turtle, a Miami chief who also claims that honor, and who is his rival for fame and power, and is said to be daily gaining ground with the Wabash Indians: he possesses the spirit of litigation to a high degree. Possibly he may have been tampered with by some of the speculating land jobbers —the enclosed original may serve as an instance."

Wayne's pride would never let him admit that in his victory over the Indians at Fallen Timbers, he had not opposed the great war chief of the Miami Confederation, Little Turtle, who had been the leader in the bloody Indian defeat of the Americans under St. Clair in 1791.

Wayne's Young Spy

William Wells was consecutively a Kentucky farm boy, captive and son-in-law of an Indian chief, spy, patroit, landowner and finally victim of an Indian massacre. Wells Streets in Fort Wayne and downtown Chicago are named after him, as is Wells County, Indiana. Whether he was loved or hated depended on the side of the Indian war from which he was viewed. Certainly one friendly view of Wells comes from Mad Anthony Wayne. In one of his last letters before he died in late 1796, General Wayne goes to special pains to praise Wells. In a letter to Secretary of War James McHenry, Oct. 3 from Detroit, Wayne mentions Captain William Wells as one of three interpreters who would accompany various Indian chiefs on a trip to the American Capitol at Philadelphia. The three frontiersmen were Wells, for the Miami and Wabash Indians; Christopher Miller for the Shawnees, and Whitmore Knaggs for the Chippewas, Ottawas and Potawatomis.

"To Mr. Wells," Wayne said, "we are much obliged for bringing about the late treaty. The general was referring to the Treaty of Greenville which brought American control to the entire area from the Great Lakes to the Ohio River.

"Mr. Wells has rendered very essential services to the United States from early in 1793 until this hour by carrying messages, taking prisoners and gaining intelligence. It was he who first brought me an account of the failure of the proposed treaty under the conduct of General Lincoln, Mr. Randolph and Colonel Pickering." Benjamin Lincoln, Beverly Randolph and Henry Pickering had been the special emissaries of President George Washington to a council at Detroit with the British governors and the Indian chiefs. Chief Little Turtle of the Miamis torpedoed the peace mission, which led to a continuation of the war and the defeat of an Indian army at Fallen Timbers along the Maumee River.

Wayne further described Wells' part in the wilderness battles. "In the campaign of 1794, I appointed him captain to the small corps of confidential spies. A few days before the action of the 20th of August, he captured two Indians from whom we obtained interesting information. But, in attempting the same evening to take another small camp of Delawares near Roche de Bout, he received a severe wound from a rifle ball, so near as to shatter the bone of his right arm to pieces, after killing two of the Indians. General Wayne said Wells' wounded arm "continued to exfoliate for upwards of 18 months, by which his arm is so much disabled, as in my opinion, will entitle him to a pension. This in the end may be found as economical, as it will be just and political; for unless the public reward those kind of people, with some degree of liberality, they cannot expect to be served with fidelity in the future." Wayne's account indicated Wells was the most useful of all the spies and scouts who infiltrated the Indian tribes and played such an important part in the American victories and eventual hold on the Old Northwest.

Two months later, Wayne was dead. Apparently, however, his request to the War Department concerning Wells was not ignored. As time went by, Wells was named Indian agent at Fort Wayne and had charge over relations with the various tribes in the entire territory. A section of Fort Wayne, called Wells Reserve, more accurately Wells Pre-emptive, was granted to the former spy and scout at the very location to where he was brought many years before by Chief Little Turtle and where he grew to manhood, marrying Sweet Breeze, the chief's daughter. The land involved in the Wells grant is the part of Fort Wayne which extends north and west of the St. Mary's and St. Joseph Rivers, and includes Spy Run Creek and most of the land from the rivers to Wells St. and State Boulevard. By pre-emptive, the government meant Wells had exclusive right to purchase the property for $1.25 an acre. He occupied the land the few remaining years of his life, but as far as records show, never exercised his rights to purchase the tract which today contains the Filtration Plant, Lawton Park, the city light power facilities and other landmarks.

Wilderness Intrigue

It was in the remote post of Fort Wayne and other frontier holds in the western wilderness that the first great conspiracy to split the United States was being plotted. In fact even while the stockade at the three rivers was being built by Anthony Wayne's legions, one of the main figures in the conspiracy was at the scene. Others involved ranged from the U.S. Senate to the Spanish stronghold of St. Louis on the Mississippi. Wayne's second in command was General James Wilkinson. During the few weeks Wilkinson was here with Wayne and during the entire campaign which led to the defeat of the Indians, Wilkinson was secretly in the pay of the Spanish governor at St. Louis.

Wayne had known for many months that Wilkinson and others were trying to get rid of him. It is likely there were attempts to have Wayne "accidentally" disposed of. The records show that fabricated charges were brought against Wayne in an effort to have him court–martialed and removed. In a private note to Wayne, Secretary of War McHenry wrote on July 9, 1796, that "General Wilkinson has entered upon a specification of all his charges against you both new and old, and will press for a decision inquiry or court-martial." McHenry told Wayne that President Washington was aware of events. Wayne later thanked McHenry for his friendly attitude and said "my presence with the army is very inconvenient to the nefarious machinations of the enemies of the government, and may eventually prevent them from dissolving the Union."

Earlier, Wayne was informed "The President has received information that certain emissaries are employed and paid to gain a knowledge of our military posts in the Western country, and to encourage and stimulate the people in that quarter to secede from the union, and form a political and separate connection with a foreign power." Among the emissaries were two former French generals. It was later discovered that their paths to various American outposts were being promoted by Senator Aaron Burr (later Vice President) ; Senator John Brown of Kentucky; Albert Gallatin, onetime Secretary of the Treasury; and others. In addition to the French military adventurers, the travelers in the wilderness included Judge Benjamin Sebastion, who was in the pay of the Spanish, and Constantin Volney, a French philosopher who became acquainted with Little Turtle, among others. All the conspirators saw General Wilkinson as their military operator in the frontier country.

Actually, the uncovering and blunting of this plot was one of the main reasons for Wayne's coming back West in 1796. Various papers still in existence refer to other "secret" papers and notes. Often codes were used when referring to public figures suspected of the treason. Yet, little hard evidence was gathered at the time, at least by Wayne, who died December 15 of that same year at Presque Isle. He had been on his way across Lake Erie, while sailing back to Pennsylvania.

General Wilkinson

After Wayne's death, the conspirator, General James Wilkinson, succeeded him as U.S. General of the West. The appointment was unfortunate, but in the long run the conspiracy failed because of the distrust of the various parties to it. As early as 1787, Wilkinson was working with the Spanish to detach the Kentucky settlements from the U.S. and make much of the West semi-independent under the influence of the Louisiana government. By the time Wilkinson was under Wayne's campaign authority and at Fort Wayne, the plans for the splitting off of the West were taking a broader and more national shape. Possibly the reason no move was made for an open break was the Presidential ambitions of Aaron Burr, the New York Senator. In the national elections of the year, 1800, Burr tied Thomas Jefferson in electorial votes for the Presidency of the United States. As many will remember, Jefferson was chosen President after numerous votes in the House of Representatives which names Presidents when there is no clear majority. Alexander Hamilton exerted strong influence in the House in order to defeat Burr, even though Jefferson had been a political opponent of Hamilton's for many years. Later, the angry Burr challenged Hamilton to a duel and killed Hamilton at Weehawken, New Jersey. Burr then moved west and tried to put together the smouldering conspiracy. He made an agreement with General Wilkinson, by then at St. Louis and governor of part of the Louisiana Purchase. They aimed to make a kingdom of the approximate area of present Texas and Oklahoma.

Into this near vacuum came Capt. Thomas Pasteur, named to succeed Hamtramck as commandant of Fort Wayne, or so it is usually believed. There is a cloud over this period because some of the American military records were destroyed when the British burned the White House and other government buildings at Washington in 1814. Fort Wayne Historian Bert Griswold notes this phase of uncertainty. Also, the usually reliable French and British sources of early information on the Miamitown area were swept away with the American occupation. Pasteur, who assumed command in the fall of 1796, came from a rather different background than Hamtramck, the first post commander. Hamtramck, short, stocky and tough, was a Canadian of French extraction who had joined the American cause in the vicious backwoods wars during the Revolution. He had been commander of the lonely American post of Vincennes at the time of General Josiah Harmar's ill-fated campaign against Miamitown in 1790. He headed regular brigades in General Arthur St. Clair's disastrous drive toward the Miami villages in 1791, and was with Anthony Wayne in the successful campaign into the Indian country three years later. Later, when Wayne was putting together his army for the expedition into the Western Indian country, he named Pasteur captain of an infantry company. Pasteur served through the entire two-year campaign, and was among the troops which came upon the three rivers and built Fort Wayne in the fall of 1794. He was placed in charge of Fort Knox, a few miles above Vincennes on the Wabash in 1795; but was ordered back to Fort Wayne the following year after Hamtramck moved on to Detroit. Pasteur was promoted to major in 1803, but that was later when he was serving a second term as Fort Wayne commandant.

During the dreary winter of 1796-97, famine and disease stalked the wandering Indians and garrison soldiers alike. In one of his last letters, Wayne asked for medicines and provisions for the garrisons, "with upwards of 400 officers and men sick." There was murmuring in the chill darkness of the fort because of lack of pay and even that was sometimes useless since the traders and Indians still preferred money from European countries, where their main markets were.

Just five years after it was built, Fort Wayne was called "useless" and a "frittering" by the general who succeeded Mad Anthony Wayne as commander in the West. General James Wilkinson, second in command to Wayne when the fort was being built at the headwaters of the Maumee, urged in 1799 the abandoning of practically the entire chain of strongholds built by Wayne in the campaign against the Indians in 1793-94-95. The motives of Wilkinson are suspect, as revealed during a court-martial brought against him in 1811 regarding a vast conspiracy to separate off the American West. But in 1799, Wilkinson was riding high. He was virtual ruler over an area stretching from the Allegheny Mountains to the Mississippi and from New Orleans to Canada. His idea to rub out Wayne's forts was made clear in a letter to Alexander Hamilton on Sept. 4, 1799.

"We at present hold several useless military stations on the northwestern frontier, merely to awe, to conciliate and to watch the Indians, or to aid the transport of public stores in their progress to posts more remote.

"Such are Oswego, Presque Isle, Fort Fayette, Fort Washington, Fort Wayne and Fort Knox. These should be broken up and the troops incorporated, for by such fritterings, we destroy the usefulness of both officers and soldiers and expose ourselves to be beaten in detail."

Wilkinson's Adventures

Wilkinson well knew at the time that George Washington, who had long pushed for western expansion of the U.S., was a dying man at Mount Vernon. The current President was John Adams, who was less interested in western development, and who was also a political ally of Alexander Hamilton. It is possible that Wilkinson had sound military reasons for giving up Fort Wayne and the other forts, but wherever this general is concerned, there are doubts. He suggested "strong works should be erected near the head of the straits which lead from Lake Huron and from Lake Erie" and there should be a "strong regular work at Michilimackinac" at the straits between Lake Michigan and Lake Huron. As Wilkinson proposed, this would have been effective in keeping British noses out of the American side of the Great Lakes. What he didn't say was that the whole frontier territory between the upper lakes and the Ohio River would have been without any sort of regular garrisons and would have been returned to a wild area without American control or communication.

The adventurous general then turned his attention to the Mississippi River area. "We should determine either to defend the country or to abandon it," he told Hamilton. "The imbecility of the Spanish government on the Mississippi," Wilkinson said, would make a main chance possible. "A single individual of heady enterprise, presenting himself with directed credentials, and hoisting a national standard at New Orleans, might depose the Spanish administration in one hour." Wilkinson obviously saw himself as that "single individual of heady enterprise." The game which Wilkinson played for many years almost tests one's credulity, both in regard to his thinking he might actually be able to carve out an interior empire for himself, and that he could scheme for so many years without the national government doing anything about it.

In the guarded conversations and secret messages there was usually the mention of "the baron" or "Hector." This referred to Baron de Carondelet, Governor-General of Louisiana, who was the original mover in the inland scheme. That this was serious business was revealed in the 1811 court-martial. According to testimony in the trial, Wilkinson as early as 1789 was in the pay of the baron. And in the very year, 1794, that Wilkinson was at Fort Wayne for the building of the stockade, he was getting $6,000 as a secret stipend from Carondelet. Hector, Baron of Carondelet, had some initial successes but was finally undone by the turbulent events of European politics. He built up strong fortifications at New Orleans and up-river, taking hold of the then-wild area stretching from the Mississippi River to the Rocky Mountains. Pushing his hand, he sought support for separating off the part of the U.S. which now includes the states of Mississippi, Tennessee, Kentucky and much of the area between the Ohio River and the Great Lakes.

Wilkinson's Court-martial

With the defeat of the Miami confederation by Wayne, Carondelet invited the Indians to join his army, which some of them did. He also had at his command many adventurers and refugees from the French Revolution. Though the Spanish governor, the baron was of French ancestry. In paying General Wilkinson, the baron was buying trouble. In the letter to Alexander Hamilton and in other ways, Wilkinson showed he planned to turn on Carondelet and set up the inland empire for himself. Events, however, moved too fast. Napoleon took over Spain and sold Louisiana to the United States. After the Louisiana Purchase, Wilkinson got himself named governor of the Louisiana Territory.

Astonishingly, he then plotted with Aaron Burr to carve out a new empire in the Mexican territory—now the U.S. Southwest. Tipped off that the plot had been leaked, Wilkinson set up Burr as the fall guy. He had him arrested and declared martial law in the West. It was Burr's trial on treason charges which eventually led to Wilkinson's downfall. Defense attorneys for Burr dug into Wilkinson's past operations. They found evidence which linked him first to the undercutting of Wayne, the conspiracy with and later against Carondelet and finally the plotting with Burr. After Burr's trial, Wilkinson was brought before a court-martial. The charges in part: "That the same James Wilkinson while in the military service and holding the commission of brigadier general in the Army of the United States did corruptly receive diverse sums of money from officers and agents of a foreign power-that is to say from Spanish officers and agents concerned with the administration of the late provincial government of Louisiana . . . in design adverse and hostile to the interests and union of these States."

It was charged that Wilkinson received money at Frankfort, Ky., in 1798; some $4,000 was deposited for him at New Orleans in 1793; he was given $6,000 in 1794; he received $6,333 in 1795; in January, 1796, while Wilkinson was acting general overseeing Fort Wayne and other Northwest posts, he received $9,640 "being sent by the Baron de Carondelet, governor-general of Louisiana, delivered by Thomas Powers to Louisville, Ky." A letter dated January 20, 1796, signed by Baron de Carondelet, and addressed to a Mississippi post commander, said: "Hold at my disposal, to deliver it at the moment and order as may be presented to you by the American General Don James Wilkinson." But Wilkinson was acquited of the charge of treason. The judge advocate said "If the whole scheme of dismemberment" was disclosed to Wilkinson "it does not appear to the court that said Wilkinson to any measure did aid such separation. If he apparently listened to propositions of this nature, it was to advance his pecuniary interest and not injure that of this country." President James Madison approved the acquital Feb. 14, 1812.

Hunt's Fort

Fort Wayne's "minute man" came up the Maumee River in May, 1798, to assume command of the garrison. Colonel Thomas Hunt was the third post comander at Fort Wayne and the man who would direct the building of the second American fort at the three rivers location.

Hunt was a "minute man" in the real sense of the word. A native of Massachusetts, he was one of the men who responded to Paul Revere and the warning that "The British are Coming." Hunt joined the other colonials who fired on the Redcoats at both Lexington and Concord, the battles in April 1775, which marked the beginning of the American Revolution. Later in the Revolutionary War, he participated in the battle of Bunker Hill and the storming of Stony Point. The latter American victory was commanded by a young general named Anthony Wayne, who was thereafter called "mad" for what some considered his rash, but successful, tactics in taking the British stronghold.

When Hunt came to take charge of Fort Wayne, it was not his first trip to the site. He had joined Wayne when the army for the Indian campaign was being formed and was a major during the victory at Fallen Timbers and the building of the original fort at the three rivers in 1794. Prior to taking over at Fort Wayne, Colonel Hunt had been in charge of Fort Defiance, some 50 miles down the Maumee. With him on the move were his wife and two children, Henry and Ruth, who had recently come west from Boston by way of Detroit. Another member of the Hunt family was soon added. On April 11, 1799, there was born John Elliot Hunt, Fort Wayne's first native citizen. At least, he was the first and only child to be born in Wayne's fort. Many others, of course, were born in the some 100 years of earlier French and Indian development of Miamitown.

The following year, 1800, Colonel Hunt began the construction of a new stockade, just to the north of the first Fort Wayne. The original fortification was about where East Berry St. is today, and between Clay and Lafayette Streets. Hunt's fort was built about where East Main St. now ends, the site which was cleared for the new No. 1 Fire Station, and partly occupied by the Norfolk & Western Elevation. It is believed the second Fort Wayne was the approximate size of the first. This would make it about 300 feet square—like a football field only wider. It was apparently well constructed because it was the fort built by Hunt which was later to withstand the only real attacks on Fort Wayne and a desperate siege during the war of 1812.

Colonel Hunt, after his two years at Fort Wayne, moved on to command garrisons at Mackinac and Detroit. All three of his children remained in the Maumee-Great Lakes area, and participated in the development of the former wilderness area. The little boy born in Fort Wayne became an Ohio State Senator and a promoter of the early railroads near Toledo.

Ruth Hunt Marries

The daughter, Ruth, established another first in Fort Wayne, which occurred in 1805 while Colonel Hunt was enroute from Detroit to take command of a fort at Bellefontaine on the Mississippi near St. Louis. She married the garrison surgeon who had arrived at Fort Wayne the previous year. Curiously, William Wells, the son-in-law of Miami War Chief Little Turtle and captain of spies for Anthony Wayne's army, officiated at the ceremony. Wells was Indian agent during some of the Old Fort period. The certificate, in Well's handwriting, said: "Fort Wayne, 4th June, 1805. I do hereby certify that I joined Dr. Abraham Edwards and Ruthie Hunt in the Holy Bonds of Matrimony on the 3rd instant, according to law. Given under by hand and seal the day and year above written. William Wells, Esq." Dr. Edwards and his wife Ruth, the Americans married in Fort Wayne, remained at the fort until 1810. During that time, the couple had three children—all boys born in the fort their grandfather had built some years earlier.

Life in old Fort Wayne could be mean and dirty—despite the general beauty of the untouched countryside, the clear rivers and the many varieties of fur and game animals in the nearby forests. The orderly book of Captain Thomas Pasteur, who returned to Fort Wayne to take command of the garrison in 1802, gives an almost day-by-day account of the harsh realities of stockade life. Pasteur succeeded Colonel Thomas Hunt, the builder of the second fort. With the entry for July 2, we find that Private Factor Bingham "was found guilty of repeated drunkenness and riotous conduct in the barrack room" and that Private George Griscom "was found guilty of absenting himself from duty on the evening of July 1" and that Private John Harrate "was found guilty of being drunk at evening roll call. In consequence, the commanding officer directs that Factor Bingham receive fifty lashes on his bare back, that George Griscom be confined to the fort 15 days when off duty and that John Harrate receive 25 lashes." On this single occasion, because of the recent arrival of the new commander of the fort and the fact that the Fourth of July was to be soon celebrated, the offenders were pardoned.

The Fourth was marked with "five rounds from a piece of ordnance at the break of day . . . at 12 o'clock 16 rounds will be fired from the same piece and at the setting of the sun, one round." Also, "the guard will in the future mount with their hair powdered."

Colonel Hunt had on occasion been accused of too much leniency in the operation of the garrison. Pasteur apparently was bent on correcting any such laxness. On July 6, Private Griscom was again on report—absenting himself from parade. "In consequence of which the commanding officer orders that the prisoner receive 25 lashes on his bare back this evening at roll call." These beatings were administered with a cat-of-nine-tails in front of the entire company. A few days later, a Private Robert Carrey took 50 strokes for "being drunk when in the sick report." Private Bingham was a glutton for punishment. In November, 1802 he took 75 lashes for drunkenness. In the following years he was beaten several more times. Still around in April 1807, he and another private, William Perkins, were given 15 lashes "for going to French Town on the 22nd after the regular time without leave."

French Town

French Town was apparently the place where wayward soldiers went for some diversion. It was located across the river from the fort at the site of present Lakeside. This mixture of Indian huts and trader's shacks was built up on ground burned out in 1794 by Wayne's legions. So foul was the influence on the garrison that soldiers could only go there during the two hours between 11 a.m. and 1 p.m. "and they are not to be there at any other time without particular leave from the commanding officer present."

But for those inclined to the outdoor life, the three rivers was a paradise. If there ever was a question of the amount of wildlife which once was to be found in this area, the records of John Johnson, agent at Fort Wayne, should put it to rest. In the spring months of 1808, he listed on a bill the furs and pelts shipped to Detroit and then east. The deer skins numbered 1,140; the raccoon skins, 26,839; beaver was listed at 26 pounds, there were 773 skins of cats and foxes; 83 otter skins, 251 muskrat skins, 94 bear skins and three wolf skins. On other bills were listed greater numbers of wolves, bucks and does, three buffalo and elk, mink and lynx. Sixty pounds of beeswax was also on one list. These hides and furs were taken in long boats down the Maumee, across Lake Erie and to Detroit. From there they were shipped to Philadelphia. The hunters were the Indians, as had been the case with the French and British traders of earlier years. For exchange, hundreds of items were shipped west. There was scarlet cloth, indigo, salt peter, tobacco, whiskey, spices, German steel, gun powder, knives, hoes, chintz silk scarfs from China, broaches, trinkets, pins, screws and Bibles.

Abundant as was the game in the forest and by the streams of the early American era, it was probably far less than when the French explorers and traders first opened the three rivers as a trading place in the late 1600's. In that earlier time, Frontenac and LaSalle had set up such an efficient trading network, that they literally undid themselves. They shipped so much beaver skin, a prime product in those days, that they glutted the European market, breaking the price structure and bankrupting the two-continent trading system.

The Indiana Story

The story of Indiana starts in the north—along the rivers flowing to the Great Lakes.

The first posts, the first commerce, the early trading, the old French and Indian towns were along the Maumee River in the northeast and the St. Joseph and Calumet Rivers in the Northwest. The next moves were down the Wabash, where Ouiatenon was established near present Lafayette, and a generation later, Vincennes further down river. But most of downstate remained a vast wilderness, scarcely even occupied by the Indians, much less any sort of civilized development. All this began to change with the coming of the Americans and the forcing of the various treaties upon the various Indian tribes. Growth of the Indiana area changed from north to south—establishing a flavor in southern Indiana which exists to the present day. The entire Northwest Territory underwent a quick series of reorganization starting in 1796. First, there was the founding of Wayne County—a vast area extending north from Fort Wayne and taking in what is now Northern Indiana, most of Michigan and parts of Wisconsin.

William Henry Harrison, the young officer who had served with Anthony Wayne, was chosen representative to Congress from the Northwest Territory in 1799. He won the post over Arthur St. Clair, governor of the Northwest Territory and general of the terrible American defeat at the hands of Indians under Little Turtle in 1791. Harrison beat out St. Clair by one elector's vote, 11 to 10, to take the post. St. Clair was to be a loser again in a few years later when the Ohio Territory optioned for Statehood over the objections of St. Clair. In 1800, the Indiana Territory was created. To be more specific, the Ohio Territory was created and everything else was called the Indiana Territory. This latter area included present day Indiana, most of Michigan, all of Illinois and Wisconsin and a part of present Minnesota. Harrison managed to get himself named governor of this vast area north of the Ohio River and taking in much of the Great Lakes vicinity. He chose Vincennes as the territorial capital.

It is with the Harrison era that the new wave of pioneers began to flow across the Ohio River to lands of Southern Indiana. And for a couple decades, the population growth in those vicinities far exceeded that of the older north. The north was still considered Indian country, and there still existed some of the old French flavor. Harrison, a son of one of the signers of the Declaration of Independence, crossed the mountains from Virginia to the Ohio River at the head of a motley crew of 80 men when only 18 years old. He participated in practically every frontier war with the Indians for the next 20 years. In one of his first actions in Congress, he pushed through a bill changing the government's land policy—putting options in small tracts on easy terms within the reach of poor settlers. This, combined with the millions of acres he made available through the treaties with the Indians, stimulated the great surge westward which was to continue for generations. Harrison made numerous trips to Fort Wayne. The first was during the building of the fort in the fall of 1794. He was aide to General Wayne at that time. After being named territorial governor, he negotiated the two so-called Treaties of Fort Wayne with the Miami, Delaware, Potawatomi and other Indians. These treaties further divided the Indians, and were later repudiated by the Shawnees. This was one of the factors leading to the uprising of Tecumseh and the Prophet at the outset of the War of 1812. At that later time, Harrison, by then a general, would lead an army to relieve the siege of Fort Wayne. In his later years, Harrison would come upon hard times. In spite of nearly 50 years on the American frontier as young soldier, representative, governor and general, U.S. Senator and foreign minister, by his old age he was practically destitute. In one of the more ironic turns of American politics, Harrison appeared to be ending his days as an obscure county clerk in Ohio. Then at the age of 68, he was nominated by the Whig Party for the Presidency. Heading torchlight parades and hard cider gambols across the land, he swept to an overwhelming victory over President Martin Van Buren, and became the oldest man ever elected to the Presidency.

The Ugly Truth

In the winter of 1801-2, Miami Chief Little Turtle and Capt. William Wells took a trip back east. They talked with Thomas Jefferson and others at the U.S. Capitol. The Turtle spoke of cementing relations with the American government and finding the means for the Indians to become a normal and useful part of the national society. Wells was interested in becoming Indian agent in the Indiana Territory. The upshot of the trip was that Wells was named agent. He was to operate out of Fort Wayne. The main job of the agent was to pass out Federal grants to the Indians, as provided by the Treaty of Greenville and subsequent agreements. There has ever since been conflicting opinions as to whether Wells was a good pick for the job. There also has been some doubt concerning the value of the grants to the various Indian tribes. The Indian money drew a special brand of traveler to Fort Wayne—the whisky trader. Just as regularly as the Federal grants were passed out to the tribal chiefs, the traders would be on hand. It is these foul types who first founded the town of Fort Wayne, if the description can be properly applied. The earlier Indian and French settlements were on the north side of the rivers—at Lakeside and the Spy Run areas. The American traders began to put together their log shacks just to the southwest of the three rivers, not far from the fort. The first official note of this development mentions "filth and putrefaction." It was on Sept. 13, 1802, that Captain Pasteur found it necessary to issue an ordinance involving the sutlers and inhabitants residing in the vicinity of Fort Wayne:

"Cleanness being one of the greatest promotives of health, the commanding officer is determined to have strictest attention paid to it. He is sorry to observe that those who occupy the public ground near the fort suffer to be diffused every nauseous filth in streets and about their dwellings. He is therefore compelled to order that from and after the seventeenth of the present month, the said sutlers and inhabitants shall keep their lots and streets in front of their houses clean and void of all filth and puterfaction. Secondly, that should any of the said sutlers and inhabitants refuse or neglect to obey this ordinance, they all be deprived of the privileges they at present enjoy."

Fort commanders continued to change rather regularly. In the spring of 1803 arrived Colonel Henry Burdeck. He came directly from West Point where he had been participating in the establishment of the U.S. Military Academy. Burdeck was a veteran of the Revolution and had been with Anthony Wayne on the campaign against the Miami Confederacy. He was the officer who directed the building of Fort Recovery, which withstood possibly the heaviest Indian attack in American history. Burdeck, however, only stayed at Fort Wayne for a few months. Later in 1803, Colonel John Hamtramck, commander at Detroit at the time, died. Burdeck was ordered to assume command of the Detroit post.

Zebulon Pike

Major Zebulon Pike arrived at Fort Wayne in June, 1803. He was descended from an old Pennsylvania family which had received one of the original land grants from William Penn. Like the other commanders at Fort Wayne, he had served in the Revolutionary War, and was one of the survivors of St. Clair's defeat. He was aging a bit by time he came to the three rivers, and had a wife, three sons and a daughter. One of Major Pike's sons, Zebulon Montgomery Pike, was already in the army. The son in his teenage years had worked to supply the American posts in the Indian country, including Fort Wayne. It was during this period that he came under the influence of General James Wilkinson, who was weaving a number of schemes to gain control over wide areas of the inland wilderness. Young Pike, son of the Fort Wayne commandant, went with Wilkinson to the Mississippi and Louisiana Territory. He became Wilkinson's advance man in expeditions to the southwest and Colorado areas. In his western travels, he discovered the peak which today bears his name.

The great struggle for land became more bitter and conniving with each month in the Indian lands and the old territories of the Northwest. To considerable extent, Fort Wayne became a focal point of the conflicting claims, rumors and crimes committed both in the name of poor settlers holding onto their stakes and in the interests of land jobbers and speculators from afar. Millions of acres were the attraction. For the pioneers crossing the Ohio River for farm holdings in that area, the situation was mostly a legal battle. But for those in the distant wilderness of what is now Indiana and Michigan, everyman's life as well as his land was in jeopardy.

The first to feel the uncertainty were the early traders who lived in the Indian country under French or British. When the United States took over the Old Northwest, some migrated to Canada. Others, however, stayed and took their chances under the new government. Finally, on Sept. 3, 1800, these traders, most of French origin, appealed to the U.S. government for both protection from the Indians and the recognition of their claims at distant points along the rivers and Great Lakes. They banded together as the "residents of Wayne County" which extended north from Fort Wayne to the Straits of Mackinac. These families included many who lived or traded at the three rivers, as some of their descendants do to this day. They included Antoine Beaubien; James, Louis and Jacques Peltier; Jacques and Francois Lasselle; Francois and Jacques Lafontaine.

Communication was very poor in the back country. This furnished a staging ground for one of the best means for keeping both the Indians and the government in a constant state of uncertainty, and even inter-tribal warfare. This weapon was the rumor. And in the whole of the Northwest, the prime target for rumors was Chief Little Turtle and his family connections. On July 2, 1802, Secretry of War Henry Dearborn warned Territorial Governor William Henry Harrison of rumors constantly circulating, some designed to stir the Indians, other to stir the settler.

"The origin and progress of the reports which have produced uneasiness among the Indians should be traced, and the real views of those Indians with hostile intentions towards citizens of the United States should be ascertained.

"The report which appears to have been circulated respecting sales of land made by Little Turtle is without the least foundation . . . nor any proposition made on the part of the government or by Little Turtle or any other person for purchasing land in that quarter."

Dearborn at the same time said trading houses at Detroit and Fort Wayne "will be established next autumn."

It was still the government's position at that date that except for certain military tracts, the entire area of northwest Ohio, most of Indiana, Michigan, Illinois and Wisconsin was "Indian Country" and any land claims based on deals with the Indians were unrecognized. This, however, seemed to satisfy few. Typically, the land hungry would go to some Potawatomi or Ottawa chief and tell him Little Turtle was getting rich by trading off lands to various people, and then seek from the backwoods chief land concessions in exchange for whisky, weapons or articles. Though the titles obtained in these deals were illegal, it did not keep the scramble for land from increasing. The bitterness of the Indians became more obvious with each passing day. Chippewa and Ottawa were eying the Potowatomi and Kickapoo Indians. All mistrusted the government and those "favored" tribal leaders such as the Miami operating near Fort Wayne. The government attitude towards the Indians can be seen in a remark by Dearborn: In event of "Indian dupes of their wicked and mischievous acts, and war should be the consequence, the Indians must not expect favor from the United States."

Jefferson Expansion

When President Thomas Jefferson assumed office in 1801, he began expansion of the United States on a scale unequaled before or since. On the surface, it seemed as if various grand land sales to the U.S. were negotiated with ease. Actually, Jefferson saw clearly that the Republic was the only real resident power of the North American continent; and having this confident position, the President skillfully made it attractive for others to go along with his wishes. Fort Wayne, and various Indian chiefs and American officials in the immediate area, became an important part of some deals.

The procedure can be seen in one of the early purchases. Jefferson authorized Secretary of War Henry Dearborn to buy land on the Lower Wabash which contained some salt springs—then considered an important need for future settlers in the frontier area. Dearborn, in turn, told William Henry Harrison, the Territorial Governor, "to embrace every favorable opportunity for sounding the Indians on the subject of ceding the springs with four miles square."

Because of the "hostile views of the Potawatomis and Kickapoos, it is deemed necessary that suitable characters be employed." The Potawatomis and Kickapoos had been resisting land sales in their areas and were "committing hostilities on Citizens of the U.S." As was to be the case on many occasions, the "suitable characters" which Jefferson insisted on being employed were none other than the Miami Chief Little Turtle and his son-in-law, Capt. William Wells, late chief spy for Anthony Wayne. "It is presumed that Little Turtle and Mr. Wells may be employed on such a mission to advantage," Dearborn relayed to Harrison.

In the summer of 1802, the Turtle and Wells went down the Wabash and helped forge an agreement between the Indians in that area and the government, giving the U.S. control of the salt springs. On Jan. 3, 1803, President Jefferson, in a message to the joint Houses of Congress, mentions the land deal, as well as the establishment of a trading house at Fort Wayne.

"To this I have to add that when the Indians ceded to us the salt springs on the Wabash they expressed a hope that we would so employ them as to enable them to procure there the necessary supplies of salt. These springs might at the same time be rendered eminently serviceable to our Western inhabitants by using them as a means of counteracting the monopolies of supplies of salt and reducing the price in that country to a just level." Jefferson also asked Congress for appropriations to cover expenses of developing the springs and this and other "purchases of lands recently made from them."

Unfortunately, not all of the Indians were happy with the gradual loss of country. Dearborn informed Harrison, "It appears that the Potawatomis have not only manifested an unfriendly disposition toward the U.S. generally, but have actually commenced hostilities upon defenseless citizens." The Secretary of War returned in kind the unfriendly disposition. He told Harrison to "demand immediate satisfaction . . . and either deliver the murderers to you or punish with death." Whether the Indians ever turned over the murderers to the U.S. authorities is doubtful. President Jefferson in the meantime moved to ease the way for further land acquisitions. "The minds of the Potawatomis and Kickapoos should be soothed and conciliated with liberalities."

Along the hard frontiers of the Indiana Territory, fear of murder was a day-to-day thing. Both sides were victimized. As an example, in 1802 a reward was offered for the capture of John Williams and a man named Crutchelon who were involved in the killing of Indians.

Adding to the problems was the consumption of whisky which was becoming an uncontrolled thing in the wilderness areas. There are stories on record of whole Indian villages going on drunken rampages—even women and children as well as the men. In this respect, the sales of land were doubly injurious. A vicious circle was created when Indians were paid by the government for various tracts. The money received was often traded for whisky brought in by operators who set up quarters near the payoff points, such as Fort Wayne. This break in the old ways of life made it easier to obtain new land concessions from the tribes. Little Turtle appealed to President Jefferson during a talk in Washington on Jan. 4, 1802, for a prohibition on liquor sales to the Indians. Such a law was passed. Unfortunately, it was ineffectual. The law only applied to the Indian lands. This meant the traders could still take liquor into the back country on the basis that it was going to American settlements and military posts. It was just a simple matter of slipping off into the woods and doing business with Indians after the monthly payoffs at the post.

Fort Dearborn Created

Chicago, the major metropolis of Mid-America, was first founded as an outpost of Fort Wayne and Detroit. It was from Fort Wayne that the original party set out to prepare for the building of Fort Dearborn. At the same time, a winding trail through the wilderness was marked for the use of soldiers and supply trains traveling to and from the Lake Michigan post. The site itself and the very name of the place grew out of the old Miami village of Chikago, as it was then called. Because of this old village and a French fort which was once located there, the Chicago tract was wrested from the Indians at the Treaty of Greenville, over the objections of Little Turtle and Le Gris.

One of the reasons for building a fort on the southwest shore of Lake Michigan was due to the Potawatomi Indians. The Potawatomis had moved into the area and were displaying some hostility to the Americans. The government figured they needed some strength there. On May 26, 1803, Secretary of War Henry Dearborn gave instructions to William Wells at Fort Wayne.

"As we are about to establish a military post at Chikago on the land ceded to the United States, it will be necessary for the purpose of keeping up a communication between that post and Fort Wayne, to have a direct path or bridle road from one post to the other as the nature of the country will admit.

"You will therefore please to take the earliest opportunity of looking out, and designating such a track or path, and you will report your proceeding there to this office, with your opinion of the distance, and whether the natives will have any objection to our improving such a communication for express and driving of cattle."

Actually, there was more to the instructions than simply marking out the road. The War Department was anticipating the possibility of resistance from the Indians concerning the erection of a strong point. Also being weighed was the possible use of various water routes in the supporting of the garrison. Dearborn also told Wells: "You will likewise ascertain how far the river St. Joseph (from South Bend) is navigible for boats, and what will be the probable distance of land carriage between Fort Wayne and Chikago where the post is to be established, and whether there are any other white inhabitants . . . on the St. Joseph or near Chikago. I should wish to have the Little Turtle go with you if he has no objections."

Wells and Little Turtle set out immediately with a party. They followed an old Indian trail from Fort Wayne along what is present Wells St. and traveled a route similar to the present U.S. 33. This wilderness trail took them to the river at South Bend which flows into Lake Michigan at St. Joseph, Michigan. They also charted north of South Bend what was to become known as the Dragoon Trail, so-named because of the soldiers who for years traveled through the vicinity on the route between Fort Wayne and Fort Dearborn.

While Wells and Little Turtle were looking over the site and parleying with the Indians, two other American groups were already moving toward Chikago. These were set in motion by the Secretary of War in a letter to the Detroit commandant.

"The complaints or uneasiness of the Indians relative to the post at Chikago will, I hope, be removed by Mr. Wells, who was ordered there for the purpose early last spring. But, unfortunately, the letter did not reach him until two months after he should have received it, but he set out immediately after receiving the letter, and will undoubtedly be able to convince the Indians not only of our right to make the establishment, but of it being useful to them."

Major John Whistler, who earlier had been on duty at Fort Wayne and would later return to Fort Wayne as garrison commander, was named the first commandant of Fort Dearborn. He and his wife and children set out from Detroit in a schooner, which was also carrying building material for construction of the stockade. They sailed up Lake Huron, through the Straits of Mackinac and down Lake Michigan. At the same time, troops departed from Detroit and marched overland to the Chikago site. The road from Fort Wayne to Fort Dearborn was thereafter called the Dearborn Trail. Wells and Little Turtle prepared the Indians for the building of the fort, and there was no real difficulty at that time. Yet Wells, who helped found the stockade at Chicago, was to be killed by the Indians on the very same spot nine years later during an attempt to rescue Fort Dearborn.

Twenty Hard Years

There ws a strange lack of permanence about Fort Wayne during its first 20 years.

The Indians were grumbling, but generally were still going about their old ways of hunting, fishing and trading off furs. There were cracks, however, in the old power of the chiefs and a certain whisky-prone idleness could be seen among some Indians.

The soldiers had a garrison life of a sort at the fort, but there was a constant series of transfers. A number of the commanders stayed here for less than a year.

In the first decade of the 1800's it is interesting to note that there was not one American family settled in the entire area between Fort Wayne and Fort Dearborn at the present site of Chicago. Settlers were moving rapidly into areas close to the Ohio River, but they were fearful of settling on the more northern lands. They were afraid of the Indians. As this fear increasingly became a block to the growing expectations of the Americans moving west, a policy of sweeping aside the Indians took on a hard shape. The main instrument in this sweep was William Henry Harrison, the Territorial Governor of Indiana. Harrison would always retain the image of an Indian fighter, a respectable term in those days. He was a fairly skilled negotiator with the various tribal chiefs, but his tendency was to press too forceably. There was always the barely concealed threat of violence as he wrested vast land tracts from the Indians. As old correspondence shows, President Thomas Jefferson was constantly telling Harrison to temper his actions with soothing gestures and talks with irritated chiefs.

"It is the opinion of the President of the United States that you ought with little delay as possible to cause a meeting of the Delaware chiefs and some of the principal chiefs of the Miamis and Potawatomis for the purpose of such an explanation of the doings so much complained of, as will satisfy the chiefs generally that the transaction was not only open and fair, but such as they have no right to object to," Harrison was told by the Secretary of War on May 24, 1805. It is obvious that some of the Indians were becoming increasingly hostile to land sales by other chiefs down along the Wabash. Jefferson further advised the governor.

"Should you judge it advantageous to distribute two or three hundred dollars among the Miamis and Potawatomis and others, by way of quieting their minds in relation to the sale of the lands by the Delawares and Piankashaws, you will do it in such manner as you may consider useful."

Before receiving such advice, Harrison sent a letter to President Jefferson accusing Miami Chief Little Turtle and William Wells, the Indian agent at Fort Wayne, of stirring up the tribes to oppose further land concessions. "The Turtle is certainly doing us all the mischief he can, and although he has little or no influence with his own tribe, he has continued to get the chiefs of the Potawatomis altogether under his control (and is) encouraged and supported by the traders and by the agent of the U.S. at Fort Wayne."

After receiving the President's instructions, however, Harrison proceeded to Fort Wayne to sooth and bribe the Indians. He reported to Jefferson on August 29, 1805: "They almost universally consider the era of French establishment in this country as their golden age." From this and other reports, it seems that the civilization of the American Indians peaked in the Great Lakes area during the French period. The French traded with the Indians but made few settlements and didn't demand land from the various tribes. With westward moving Americans, however, it was a different matter.

"Compensation for the tract which has been ceded amounts to about one cent per acre. This was much higher than I could have wished, but it was impossible to make it less," Harrison told Jefferson.' "I pursued your directions relative to the Turtle. You will soon receive from him a letter expressing his great satisfaction at the result of the late conference," Harrison said.

Millions of acres of land were changing hands during this period. As can be seen in the above exchange, Harrison took a vast tract from the Delaware and Wabash Indians, then went to Fort Wayne to pay off the powerful Miami and Potawatomi chiefs so they wouldn't complain too much. It was a matter of playing off one tribe against the other. It is noteworthy that no mention is made of the Shawnees, who were also strong in the area. Under Tecumseh and The Prophet, they were refusing to deal; and instead were gradually beginning to collect what would become a new Indian army.

Old Ways Destroyed

The Northwest Territory was coming apart. Ohio was formed in 1800 and the Michigan Territory was separated off the Indiana Territory in 1805. Of the two, the formation of Michigan under separate government was a more serious blow to the longtime Indian and trading habits of the three rivers area. For more than a century, the old route from the St. Lawrence to the Great Lakes, Detroit, the Maumee and Wabash had been active with Indian canoes and traders' craft. Named governor of Michigan Territory was William Hull, a rather unimaginitive man who usually ignored the French element in his considerations. Since the French-speaking inhabitants were still in the majority, he was asking for trouble.

At Fort Wayne, a series of missionary types came from Pennsylvania and Maryland to teach the Indians the ways of animal husbandry, crafts and land cultivation. Though these people are given lengthy consideration by some historians, they left nothing of permanence. The Indians mostly showed disinterest. The visitors spent part of their time bickering with William Wells, the Indian agent, over who had the right to do what. Typically, after a few years, they went back east.

Another failure was the work of the factor, who was commissioned by the government to operate a "factory" for the benefit of the Indians. This was actually more of an official trading house where the Indians were encouraged to bring their furs and receive various products shipped in from the East in trade. Though some trade was regularly carried on in this manner, the smarter Indians preferred to trade with the British who were still operating out of the upper Great Lakes and from Montreal. The Indians believed they received better prices from the British and often preferred British products to the American ones. The American factor system continued for a number of years, but was eventually abandoned.

The Indians continued to lose more of their lands. In 1807, Governor Hull negotiated with the Ottawa, Chippewa, Wyandot and Potawatomi Indians for the entire southeast portion of the Michigan Lower Peninsula. The Indians were given $10,000 in money and goods and were promised $2,400 annually. Though a dozen years before, the Miami Indians had claimed all the area from Detroit south, they were not even invited to participate in the Brownstown Treaty which ceded the area.

In the summer of 1809, there was a great assembly at the three rivers for what has become known as The Treaty of Fort Wayne. Actually, it was the second treaty at Fort Wayne between the United States and several Indian nations—the other was in 1803. As in the earlier treaty, the main object was to separate the Indians from their lands. Even though the meeting was at Fort Wayne, the lands in question at that particular event were along the Wabash River and in the vicinity of the Ohio River. The taking of the lands in Northern Indiana would come later. Remarking on the Treaty of Fort Wayne, William Henry Harrison wrote to the Secretary of War on Aug. 29, 1809, "I have determined to proceed immediately to Fort Wayne through the tract in question, and to assemble the Miamis, Potawatomis and Delawares at that place."

Nearly 30 million acres changed hands in this and other agreements of the period. The chiefs were paid off and the annual money handouts were promised. It was the beginning of welfare in the United States. The more indolent of the Indians became dependent on regular government stipends. Many of the Indians, however, through resourcefulness, luck or intermarriage, joined in the mainstream of American culture—to an extent that a considerable portion of Americans today have at least a trace of Indian heritage in their veins.

The Prophet Appears

The Indians were people with the usual variations in character, temper and ambitions. During the early days of Fort Wayne, the losing cause of the Indians brought out some of the more individual characteristics.

The Shawnee chief, known as The Prophet, was neither Moses nor Elmer Gantry. But he was both a spellbinder and a leader who promised to lead his people out of captivity. The Prophet was said to be the twin brother of Tecumseh (some records claim they were two parts of a triple birth). Unlike Tecumseh, the one-eyed Prophet was of unstable habits. Like a reformed drunkard, which he was, he railed against the whisky traffic. He was also inclined toward witchcraft. For many years, he was largely ignored as any sort of serious threat on the frontier. Though he would on occasion gain followers, they would usually leave him after a short period. Finally, in the early 1800's, he left his usual haunts in the Ohio country and set up a village along the Wabash and Tippecanoe Rivers, near present-day Lafayette. The Prophet and Tecumseh immediately began to recruit warriors from far and near. The word was also spreading through the territory that any Indian chief who made land concessions to the United States was marked for death. Miami Chief Little Turtle reported at the time that The Prophet was promising the various tribes that he would drive out all the Americans and those Indians which sided with the United States.

Indiana Territorial Governor William Henry Harrison reported in his memoirs that he sent agents to The Prophet to find out his intentions and to settle any difficulties. This is the answer he received in 1808 from The Prophet:

"Let us lay aside this character and attend to the care of our children that they may live in comfort and peace." He then claimed all the area between Fort Wayne and Vincennes. "I have listened to what you have said to us. You promised to assist us. If you give us a few articles, such as needles, flints, hoes, powder, we will take animals that afford us meat with powder and ball."

Powder and flints were not the sort of assistance that Harrison had in mind, particularly since The Prophet had gathered together a considerable force at The Prophetstown at that time. The fortune of The Prophet were an up-and-down thing. Just one year later, William Wells, Indian agent at Fort Wayne, told Harrison that Chippewas, Ottawas and Potawatomis "were hurrying away from The Prophet" and the Shawnee chief only had about 100 warriors left along the Wabash.

William Henry Harrison

Yet, the following spring, Harrison received information from a trader, probably Lafontaine who operated out of Fort Wayne, that The Prophet "was again inciting the Indians to hostilities." He was also beginning to assemble what would eventually be a new Indian army. The trader reported, "The Prophet had 1,000 souls under his control, perhaps 350 to 400 men, principally Kickapoos and Winnebagoes, but some Potawatomis and Shawnees and a few Chippewas and Ottawas." The joining of the Kickapoos, the once strong allies of the Miamis in the earlier Indian wars, was particularly disturbing to Harrison. The Kickapoos, though never numerous, were considered the most skilled and tenacious warriors on the frontier. They were so determined on the warpath that they eventually fought their way to extinction. To further boost his following, The Prophet began a series of dramatic gestures and incantations, including the burning of at least two women who were said to be witches. He decreed that those chiefs who had participated in the land treaties were cursed, and the first to die would be Chief Leatherlips of the Wyandots. The Prophet's stock jumped when the Wyandot chief was found dead a few days later with a crushed skull.

In the meantime, Tecumseh was calling for the war dances, and began a series of trips in the upper lakes and to the Mississippi, beating the drums for war. By early 1811, hundreds of braves were moving to Prophetstown on the lower Tippecanoe. Fear, because of the terrible death tolls in the old days, gripped a thousand miles of frontier. Also, British guns were suddenly turning up in many places in Indian hands.

The "shooting star," as Tecumseh's name was supposed to mean, was gone on the big day down on the Tippecanoe.

Over a month earlier, despite conversation about peaceful settlement, William Henry Harrison had decided the time was right for a strike against the Indians. On October 5, 1811, the Indiana Territorial Governor assembled troops numbering about 1,000 near the Wabash River, some 60 miles north of Vincennes. Further upstream was Prophetstown, a rambling assembly of Indian dwellings providing for warriors from various tribes—the Winnebagoes, Kickapoos, Potawatomis, Shawnees and a few Ottawa and Chippewa. They were in a high state of emotion due to the incantations of their spiritual leader, The Prophet, a one-eyed Indian chief who claimed he "rose up from the place of the dead." Tecumseh, The Prophet's twin brother, had been gone for many weeks on a recruiting expedition—attempting to increase the Indian army and presumably gain more material support from the British in Canada. He apparently believed he had lulled Harrison to inactivity by giving assurances of "peace and happiness." Further, he told his brother to refrain from any hostile action until he returned with added Indian forces. But on the crucial day, Tecumseh was still far from the scene, reportedly down south of the Ohio River someplace.

Battle of Tippecanoe

Harrison had moved up the Wabash, going by a rather indirect route on the northwest side of the river. By Nov. 5, the American army encamped nine or ten miles from Prophetstown, believing they were still undetected by the Indians. The next day, Harrison's troops moved toward the Tippecanoe, stopping less than a mile from Prophetstown. Advance scouts were met at this time by

Indian parties. At this time, Harrison and The Prophet exchanged pleasantries, both sending messages to the other about their peaceful intentions. In their own camps, however, it was a different story. Harrison told his forces to be prepared for an attack, though there is some indication that he really didn't expect one. The Prophet, disregarding the advice of Tecumseh seized the moment. In the cold drizzle of the night, The Prophet called on the spirits of darkness to blind the enemy. He told his warriors that the bullets of the Americans would not hurt them and a great sweep of the white man from the Indian Lands would follow.

It was still raining at about 4 a.m. on Nov. 7 when Harrison's sentries discovered The Prophet's warriors creeping within a few yards of the army encampment. With an exchange of shots in the dark the Indians made a headlong attack on the soldiers' emplacement. The battle, however, did not live up to the promises of The Prophet. By daylight, the warriors had been repulsed, and they soon scattered into the woods. Compared with the earlier campaigns against the Miami Confederacy, the Battle of Tippecanoe was relatively small in sweep or magnitude. The Americans suffered 38 dead and about 150 wounded. Indian losses were believed slightly higher. Involved in the fighting were less than 1,000 soldiers and between 600 and 700 Indians. Harrison, however, reported that he had won a decisive victory and had broken the power of the Indians. He also reported he found new English guns in the possession of some of the fallen Indians.

The combination of the victory over the Indians and evidence of British help was a political windfall to Henry Clay and the other War Hawks who were in the ascendency in Congress. They began stirring wide public support for a war with England and the conquering of Canada. They claimed the only way to resolve the Indian problem was the driving out of the English from Canada, and annexing that portion of North America to the United States.

Following Tippecanoe, Harrison's soldiers completely burned out Prophetstown. The various Indians returned to their tribal homes. All except Tecumseh. Upon returning to the scene, Tecumseh resolved anew his "War upon the living. War upon the dead." He then traveled with a few others upstream, crossing over at the old portage to Fort Wayne. With an audacity which always surprised his opponents, he went to the fort and asked the newly-arrived agent, Benjamin F. Stickney, for guns and powder. It was refused. Tecumseh is believed to have remained in the three rivers vicinity until the following spring. At that time, he openly declared he was on his way to get British guns in Canada and would return with a new Indian army to restore the Indians to their rightful places on the land.

Little Turtle, Peace Die

In the hot, dusty summer of 1812 a series of events quickly changed Fort Wayne and the entire Great Lakes area. The declaration of war by the Americans against the British and the almost simultaneous deaths of Miami Chief Little Turtle and Capt. William Wells meant the end of the rather brotherly approach between the Indians and the American presence at the three rivers.

On June 18, 1812, Congress declared war. Of all the American conflicts, it is probably the least understood. The typical history books will mention freedom of the seas and the impressment of American seamen as prime causes of the War of 1812. A check of the voting records in Congress, however, indicate the realities were quite different. In the House of Representatives, the vote was 79 to 49. In the Senate, the vote was 19 to 13. It is strange that the nation would go to war when opinion was so divided, or when the country was so poorly prepared for it. It is even stranger that anyone could conclude that ocean trade was the cause of war when the Congressmen of the maritime states of New England, New York and New Jersey voted against the war declaration. Voting in favor of hostilities were the War Hawks and the other Senators and Representatives of the western and southern states. Lust for land, fear of the Indians and the belief that Canada was ripe for picking were all part of the thinking of the expansionist-minded westerners. Besides, everyone knew that England was busy in a war with Napoleon and couldn't afford any big campaigns in the North American wilderness.

As war clouds floated across the Indian country, the most successful war chief of the entire frontier era, Little Turtle of the Miami, died of natural causes near the stockade at Fort Wayne. The Turtle, who had been living his last years in a house built for him by the government at his village along Eel River, came to the fort to see the garrison surgeon. It was clear that he was dying, reportedly of the gout—a rather strange disease for an Indian. The Miami chief was 60 years old at the time, and because of his many years of treaty-making and cooperation with the Americans, was no longer popular in the eyes of most of the Indians. He was taken across the St. Mary's River to the home of William Wells, his one-time adopted son, and there died in the open air, as he had requested. It was July 14, 1812.

Little Turtle was buried in an orchard a short distance west of the St. Joseph River, about a half mile north of the fort. The spot is now a yard along Lawton Place. Soldiers from the fort gave military rites to the one-time enemy commander who had later become acquainted with both Presidents George Washington and Thomas Jefferson. A sword and other relics from American leaders were buried with the body. A gold watch, the gift of General Frederick Haldimand, British governor general of Canada during the Turtle's early war days, was retrieved before burial. The Turtle's grandson, Chief Coesse, delivered the funeral oration.

War swept quickly across the frontier, but it did not go as the Americans had hoped. Rather, it was the Indians who went on the offensive, attacking forts and settlements from the upper lakes to the rivers north of the Ohio. As the situation with the U.S. military deteriorated, it was decided that the commander at Chicago should abandon Fort Dearborn to the Indians and move everyone at that place to Fort Wayne. To help in the evacuation and retreat from Fort Dearborn, Capt. William Wells, who by this time had been reduced to sub-agent at the Fort Wayne post, was chosen. Presumably, he volunteered for the job. Captain Nathan Heald, who had earlier been stationed at Fort Wayne, was commandant at Fort Dearborn and was married to Rebekah Wells, niece of William Wells.

Fort Dearborn Massacre

Wells, together with Sgt. W. J. Jordan and some 30 Miami Indians, headed out along the old Dearborn Trail, which is called Wells St. today in Fort Wayne, going west to the south shore of Lake Michigan. When Wells and his party arrived, the fort was already being evacuated. What was to follow would ever be known as the Fort Dearborn Massacre. Bands of Potawatomi and Winnebago Indians, numbering more than 1,000 attacked the soldiers and the several families as they were leaving the fort. The one-sided battle took place in the sand dunes where downtown Chicago is now located. It was August 15, 1812. Few of either of the 70 soldiers or the 27 women and children survived.

Wells was a particular target of the hostile Indians. The Miami Indians with Wells fled. Wells, himself, was cut down by Indian rifle fire. Jordan, who later escaped back to Fort Wayne on a stolen horse, related the end of Captain Wells. "They marched up to where Wells lay . . . and said 'see what I will do with your captain.' Then he cut off his head and stuck it on a pole, while another took out his heart."

Misfortune and death dogged the steps of the Americans in the Great Lakes area as the Indians and the British moved to an early offensive in the War of 1812. Within weeks, Fort Wayne was rendered the most remote post still held by U.S. forces.

Capt. Nathan Heald and his wife Rebekah survived the Fort Dearborn Massacre. Heald, who was commandant at the Chicago stockade at the time, had earlier been commandant at Fort Wayne during the years 1807-10. It was at Fort Wayne that he had met his wife Rebekah, the niece of William Wells. After the slaughter of Wells and many others in the sand dunes outside Fort

Dearborn, the Indians under Chief Blackbird, the Potawatomi, took a number of the survivors in canoes out on Lake Michigan. Captain Heald later described the event:

"On the 16th, this the day after the action, Mrs. Heald and myself were taken to the St. Joseph River (on east shore of Lake Michigan). The journey was performed in three days by coasting the lake, and we remained with them, both being badly wounded and unable to help ourselves, until the 29th of the same month" when they were released. At that date Heald, his wife Rebekah, a Sergeant named Griffith, three Frenchmen and an Indian squaw set out in a birch bark canoe for a 200-mile trip up Lake Michigan to Mackinac Island. The trip took about a month. And when the Americans arrived at Mackinac, they found that the British and Indians had already taken control of that post.

"The 14th of September, we arrived safe at Michilimackinac. I was there paroled by Captain Roberts, the British commandant and permitted to proceed to Detroit with Mrs. Heald and the sergeant," the captain reported. This added another 200 miles to their trip around the lakes. Long before completing the slow, arduous canoe voyage down Lake Huron, the Healds learned of the fall of another American stronghold—Detroit.

At the outbreak of the war, Governor William Hull of the Michigan Territory was named U.S. General of the West. After some preliminary movements, he set out on July 12, 1812, with an army of about 1,800 men. His aim was to take Fort Malden, a British stockade on the east side of the Detroit River. Fort Malden had cannon which controlled much of the river traffic coming up from Lake Erie. After that, the idea was to further invade Canada. Because of the artillery, however, General Hull decided to wait until his own batteries were brought up for the siege. This took about three weeks, and by that time Hull had learned that British reenforcements were on the way from Niagara and he decided to abandon the attack. He took his army back across the river to the Detroit fort.

Tecumseh Rallies Indians

The British force under General Isaac Brock was re-inforced by large numbers of Indians headed by Tecumseh. They quickly moved across the river to the American side and took up positions. Once in control of the area, General Brock asked Hull to surrender. The American general, however, refused at first and an exchange of cannon fire began. The British used both shore batteries and two gun boats. The next day, August 16, General Hull decided to surrender. A factor in the decision was the hope of avoiding a massacre of both the fort residents and the inhabitants of the immediate areas by the Indians. More than 1,000 troops were taken to Montreal as prisoners, including Hull who was later court-martialled by the U.S. for cowardice.

After the fall of Detroit, the Indians under Tecumseh were expected to make quick attacks on Fort Wayne and Fort Harrison (Terre Haute), among the few outposts still in American hands in the Old Northwest. Large numbers of Potawatomi warriors moved into the Fort Wayne area, joining Miami, Shawnee and Delawares who were already giving an unfriendly appearance to the garrison. It was believed the Indians were awaiting Tecumseh and larger numbers of warriors before going on the attack.

At about this time, a series of conflicting orders about the American army command did little to strengthen the American army. William Henry Harrison, the Indiana Territorial Governor, asked at one point for a clarification from the War Department of his own position. General James Winchester was confirmed as commander of the West, succeeding the captured General Hull. On August 30, 1812, the War Department sent a message to Winchester telling him to get his army in the field against the British and Indians and warning him of the moves of the enemy: "The immediate object appears to be the protection of the frontier, for which purpose you will make such disposition of your force as circumstances may render necessary. Fort Wayne, if possible, should be relieved."

Siege of Fort Wayne

The siege of Fort Wayne in the late summer of 1812 did not develop in a big rush of warriors upon the walls of the stockade. Rather, it was a gradual attempt to isolate and strangle the fort. There was some talk of the British bringing in cannon to knock down the timbers of the strongpoint. But this never transpired. As far as is known, only Indians were at the scene.

The post commander, Captain James Rhea, was becoming wary of increasing numbers of Indians in the vicinity as early as July 15. He issued a garrison order: "In the future, as soon as a dancing party of Indians comes within 50 yards of the garrison, the guard will parade and stand with their arms until the party leaves. Every soldier will be in readiness to take hold of his arms in case anything should happen, instantly. It is time for all soldiers to be on the lookout."

In the meantime, the army which would eventually rescue Fort Wayne was already gathering at Cincinnati. The western area of the United States was no longer the remote, unpopulated place that it had been 20 years earlier during the great Indian wars. Both Ohio and Kentucky were now states which, for the time and place, had large migrant populations. These pioneer people seemed almost eager to join a crusade to drive out both British and Indian. Thousands of volunteers from Kentucky and Ohio streamed to Cincinnati and other points to join ranks. William Henry Harrison was activated as general to lead the thrust, though he was annoyed that he was overlooked in the selection of the overall commander in the West. The Indiana Territorial governor went from Vincennes to Cincinnati to take charge.

At about the time of Harrison's arrival, the Americans were just beginning to learn of the series of victories by the British and Indians, as those faster moving forces nearly swept the U.S. presence from the entire Great Lakes area.

"The information received a day or two ago from Detroit is of the most unpleasant nature," Harrison told the War Department in a message from Cincinnati on August 6, 1812. "The loss of Mackinac will probably be followed by the capture of Fort Dearborn. And the suspension of hostilities by Hull's Army, I fear, will give strength to the British party amongst the Indians." Harrison still didn't know how bad things really were. A few days later he said: "In the present posture of affairs it appears to me the one of two plans which I have the honor to submit might be adopted with advantage. The first is to establish a chain of posts upon the Illinois River from the Mississippi to Chicago, and the other, to march immediately a considerable body to Fort Wayne." Harrison at this time enclosed to Washington a letter he had received earlier from William Wells just before Wells left on his fateful journey to Chicago. Wells had told of the coming danger to Fort Wayne. "On June 17, Tecumseh arrived at this place and said he was on his way to Malden (British fort on east bank of Detroit River) to receive from the British 12 horse-loads of ammunition. On July 12, his brother, The Prophet arrived at this place with nearly 100 Winnebagoos and Kickapoos," The arrival of Kickapoos and other Indians from the Wabash area was bad news. They were soon joined by ever larger numbers of Potawatomis moving into the environs of Fort Wayne. And with the death of Little Turtle, old Le Gris took over again as chief of the Miamis, changing their attitude from "friendlies" to "hostiles."

The Siege of Fort Wayne began on August 21 when the Indians began to cut off communications and supplies to the garrison. Through the warning of a trader named Antoine Bondie, an attempt by the Indians to take the fort by subterfuge was frustrated. A week went by as the soldiers in Fort Wayne, numbering slightly less than 100, kept watch as Indians numbering between 500 and 1,000 were on the outside waiting their chance. On August 28, Stephen Johnston, a brother of the factor at the post, and two other men attempted to leave the fort. The Indians shot and killed Johnston, but the other two managed to get back inside the stockade alive. Captain Rhea was furious at the attempt of the three men to leave the post. "The commanding officer is much surprised at any officer sending soldiers out of the garrison to attack Indians at this time without orders. He therefore directs no soldiers be sent out of the garrison." The following day, the Indians of the various tribes destroyed the first community of Fort Wayne—everything but the fort which was protected by gun and gate with its garrison and a number of families which had taken refuge there. The warriors set fire to the factor's house, several buildings of traders and families connected with the fort, and the log house and other structures of the recently-killed William Wells, which were located just north of the St. Mary's River.

As the fewer than 100 men looked out from the log stockade walls of Fort Wayne, very few figured they would ever survive. They knew by this time that Fort Dearborn, Fort Mackinac and Detroit had fallen to the English and Indians. The very buildings around the fort were now ashes—swept in a rage of fire by the Indians who were having the run of the area.

The commander at Fort Wayne, Captain James Rhea, would later be brought before a court-martial on charges of drunkenness during this critical time. But if the garrison orderly book is any indication, the old veteran of the Revolution and many a campaign in the Indian country never completely lost his grip. On Sept. 3, 1812, two weeks after the beginning of the siege, he posted the following garrison order to his men:

"It is earnestly hoped by the commanding officer that for this night everyman will be at his post. Relief is at hand. For on this night, our fame, our honor and everything that is near and dear depends. Be therefore cautious and brave."

Harrison's Army Marches

In spite of Rhea's encouraging sentiments, help wasn't coming all that fast. Harrison only the week before, had still been at Cincinnati trying to put together his force for the expedition into the Indiana and Michigan Territories. "My command consists of three regiment of Kentucky troops . . . and a troop of 12 month volunteers, making an aggregate of 2,100 at this place. Three regiments of infantry, five troops of dragoons and 550 mounted riflemen are also on their way to join me." Harrison was still in the dark concerning some of the fast moving events on the frontier, but he had heard of the fall of Detroit and Fort Dearborn. "I had some hope that the account of the fall of Detroit was not true. By a gentleman who has this moment arrived from Piqua, the taking of Chicago and the massacre of the garrison is also put beyond doubt. Poor Wells has also perished, in endeavoring to save Capt. Heald with his company." As news of continuing disaster flowed into the American headquarters, Harrison told the War Department he was striving "to hasten the march . . . for the purpose of relieving Fort Wayne which was said to be in danger of immediate attack."

"I shall march tomorrow morning with the troops I have here, taking the route of Dayton and Piqua. The relief of Fort Wayne will be my first object, and my after operations will be governed by circumstances. The troops which I have with me, and those which are coming on from Kentucky are, perhaps, the best material that the world has produced. But no equal number of men was ever collected who knew so little of military discipline."

This was another way for General Harrison to say that the soldiers under his command were raw recruits. And since he was moving out in the emergency even before all the troops were gathered, there was nothing he could do about training them. Harrison was also at the moment not the top commander of the American army, a circumstance he was hoping to correct. He would later be named the Northwest Commander, but not until a few more disasters befell the U.S. forces.

"Another letter was received from General Worthington last evening, covering one from Captain Rhea of Fort Wayne stating that a large body of Indians were near the fort and he expected to be attacked that night," Harrison reported the next day. "I shall lose no moment in marching, and I think it more than probably that we shall have to encounter all the Indians who assisted at the taking of Detroit, to whom Chicago surrendered and very large numbers of others who will be induced to join."

Harrison's army grew as he moved north, and numbered about 3,500 as he entered the hostile country. Some of the volunteer Ohio groups ran ahead and used up much of the general's provisions, which didn't help much. By Sept. 11, 1812, Harrison's army was 17 miles from Fort Wayne. "I shall reach it tomorrow, but I have no reason to believe it will not be without a severe contest. No information has been received from the fort since August 3. A small detachment," Harrison said, "which I sent to endeavor to penetrate the fort just returned without accomplishing their object, although they defeated a small party of Indians." Another small force included a friendly Shawnee named Logan. He managed to get to the fort and tell the garrison that help was near. "Logan had gone on in disguise, and passing through the camp of the besieging party, had ascertained their number to be about 1,500. Logan also went to the fort and encouraged the soldiers to hold on, as relief was at hand," wrote John D. White, one of Harrison's soldiers.

Few soldiers in the large expeditionary force slept at the encampment some 17 miles southeast of Fort Wayne. Indian parties, anxious to see the size and condition of Harrison's army, slipped through the forest to spots close to the soldiers, drawing occasional fire from sentries. The situation was described by Robert McAfee: "As soon as the army had encamped this evening, the general with his aides and officer of the day, Colonel Allen, was careful to ride round to examine the ground and inspect the whole encampment, which without delay was strongly fortified with a breast work of logs and the underbrush was cleared away for 30 paces on the outside. The mounted men encamped within the lines. During the night there were a number of alarms, caused by the Indians attempting to approach and examine the camp."

Fort Wayne Rescued

In the meantime, the main body of Indians were making one last attempt to take the fort. Soldiers in the fort described both a hail of bullets from the British guns in the hands of the surrounding warriors and flaming arrows which started fires along the palisades and sheds within the stockade. They had also taken possession of a log military building just outside the fort gates. During this long siege, however, loses of the garrison were light. There were only three reported fatalities, though a large number sustained wounds. An estimated 25 Indians were either killed or wounded. All through the siege period, the Indians had been waiting for the British to arrive with cannon. Had this happened, the battering down of Fort Wayne would have been quickly done and the Indians would have swept into the stockade and dispatched the garrison and others who had taken refuge there. This had not happened. And on the final day, September 12, the Indians were out-numbered three-to-one. "Very early in the morning the whole were in motion," McAfee said of the approaching army, "every man being prepared for action, and expecting to meet the Indians at a well-known swamp about five miles on this side of the fort." This swamp was the northwest fringe of the Great Swamp which in those days extended for nearly 100 miles in Ohio and Indiana between Miamitown and the area to the south.

A dry early fall season helped the rapid movements of Harrison's horsemen and the foot soldiers which followed. They covered the 17 miles to the confluence of the Maumee and were in the fort vicinity "about two hours before sunset." In the entire march, the army encountered only one Indian. And though he became an immediate target, and caused the nervous army to go into battle formation, he slipped away in the swampy thickets of the area.

The chiefs did not wait to do battle with Harrison's army. Following some final activity around the fort, the Indians began to move out of the area. Only a few small parties continued to roam the land between the fort and approaching army on Sept. 12.

And even those had melted into the oak and walnut forests by the time of Harrison's arrival at the stockade. There was general jubilation at the Fort. The garrison and the few families from the stockade flowed out in celebration and relief. The arriving soldiers looked around at the general desolation of the burnt-out area at the three rivers.

Only the fort commander, Captain Rhea, came in for a bad time. He was arrested for intoxication and other supposed misconduct. Harrison, because of Rhea's long service, permitted him to resign rather than face a courtmartial.

Harrison Strikes Out

General Harrison had two goals in mind. First, he wanted to completely annihilate the power of the Indians—even to the point of destroying their means of survival in the territory. Next, he was hoping to launch an invasion of Canada—to conquer that portion of Canada north of the Great Lakes and possibly annex it to the United States. As events were to show, he nearly succeeded.

The army of some 3,500 men milled around the fort, they found nothing in the immediate vicinity but the charred remains of buildings burnt out by the Indians. At distant points, however, there were numerous Indian villages. These drew the interest of Harrison's forces. Two regiments moved out over the old portage and down to the Wabash River as far as the forks where there was a concentration of Miami villages, arriving on September 15, 1812. "They encamped in the town, destroyed all its huts and cabins, and cut up the corn and other vegetables in the field," Robert B. McAfee reported. "The next day the spies discovered several other villages lower down, which were all in like manner destroyed." General Harrison accompanied these raids. Villages near the present towns of Huntington, Wabash, Peru and Logansport were wiped out. Most had been deserted by the Indians upon the approach of the army.

In the meantime another force struck a northwest course to the Elkhart River 60 miles distant where a major concentration of Potawatomi Indians under Chief Five Medals was located. Goshen is now at this site. "On the 16th, having crossed the Elkhart River, above the village about three miles, the line of battle was formed on a plain, thinly timbered," McAfee reported. "Major Johnson's (Richard Menter Johnson, later Vice-President of the United States) mounted battalion was placed in front on the left flank, and Major Dunlap's mounted men on the right front; with orders to advance to the right and left of the town and surround it. The infantry were formed in line of battle, then broke off by heads of companies and followed the others in rapid motion."

However, when the big rush was made on Five Medal's Town, it was found deserted. The Indians had pulled out sometime earlier. Only the body of a dead woman, believed to have been a sorceress because of the odd collection of hawk claws and strange bones about her, was left behind. The soldiers did find quantities of corn, beans, potatoes and other provisions, plus ammunition boxes with labels from London and Malden on them, which the Americans considered proof of British support of the Indian warfare. A newspaper printed in Cincinnati, describing Harrison's army, was also found at the Indian village. After setting fire to everything in sight, the party started the return trip to Fort Wayne.

Harrison, however, wasn't finished. On the 18th, he sent a regiment of dragoons and a company of mounted Kentucky riflemen to the town of Little Turtle, 20 miles west of Fort Wayne where several small lakes are joined by the Eel River. Everything at the site was leveled except a masonry house built for Chief Little Turtle by the U.S. Government some years earlier.

One of the strangest oversights in the typical history course is the major invasion of Canada by American forces under William Henry Harrison during the War of 1812. Much romance and space is devoted to the Lake Erie engagement of Lt. Oliver Hazard Perry, and the Battle of New Orleans directed by Andrew Jackson. Actually, Perry commanded several small sloops which he used with unusual audacity and courage. The only importance of the lake action was, however, in that it helped pave the way for Harrison's campaign to retake Detroit and invade Canada. As for Jackson's victory at New Orleans, the battle came after the peace settlement and its outcome was of little significance in the course of events.

In Canada, the American invasion of that land is not overlooked in the classrooms.

Madison Orders Offensive

Fort Wayne was one of the early jumping-off points for the operations against Canada. Eventually, Harrison's invasion army would become one of the largest to be deployed on the North American Continent until the Civil War.

President James Madison issued his orders to Harrison through the War Department on Sept. 17, 1812. "The President is pleased to assign to you the command of the Northwestern Army which in addition to the regular troops and rangers in that quarter will consist of volunteers and militia of Kentucky, Ohio, 3,000 men from Virginia and Pennsylvania, making your whole force 10,000 men. You will retake Detroit, and with a view to the conquest of Upper Canada, you will penetrate that country as far as the force under your command will in your judgment justify."

By Upper Canada, President Madison meant all of the populated portion of Canada west of Quebec. In the early stages of the war it was the obvious intention of the American government to conquer much of Canada and attach those vast regions to the United States. The expansionist mood of the U.S. in those days was further encouraged by the fact that Great Britain was heavily engaged in Europe in the war with Napoleon, yet despite this, the British in the Great Lakes area were able to take successful rear guard actions and remain a serious threat, in great part due to the fact that the Indians almost universally sided with the English.

By this time, the United States was a much more populous and united nation than at the time of the Revolution. There was a relentless quality to the growth of Harrison's army. Troops came west across Ohio along the south shore of Lake Erie; others moved across the Ohio River and came north; frontier companies marched up the Wabash Valley and down the Maumee from Fort Wayne. Success, however, was to be elusive during the first year of the war.

Harrison was eager to move. On Sept. 27, he relayed his plans: "The mounted force under an officer I shall select for that purpose will take the route from Fort Wayne up the St. Joseph River and across to the waters of the Raisin . . . skip Detroit but sweep the western side of the strait and lake of the Indians who are scattered from Brownstown to the Rapids, rioting upon the plunder of the farms which have been abandoned." The hit-and-run guerrilla tactics were designed to keep the British off balance while Harrison marched up from Ohio for a direct assault on Detroit. Before the mounted raiding parties could move out of Fort Wayne, however, the Americans received news that the British and Indians, some 2,000 strong were already on the offensive—coming up the Maumee and expecting to take Fort Wayne. The actual force consisted of about 200 British regulars under Major Muir from Fort Malden and some 1,000 Indians. General Winchester, who still hadn't heard that he had been superseded by Harrison, as the top American commander, marched his army out of Fort Wayne and down the Maumee Valley to intercept the British and Indians. A short time later, Harrison led other regiments north from St. Mary's Ohio, but the going was slow due to heavy fall rainstorms. The British, who had brought artillery by water as far as the site of Old Fort Defiance, were still advancing down the south side of the river when they heard of the larger American army coming to meet them. Intelligence that further U.S. troops were moving up from the south decided Major Muir on a course of retreat. He moved back about 12 miles above the Auglaize and waited developments. In the meantime, American advance groups and Indian raiding parties were meeting in a series of bloody skirmishes in the forests and along the rivers as the main armies attempted to get into better positions.

Despite the enthusiam of the War Hawks, the slaughter of the Indians and the conquering of Canada weren't to be accomplished overnight. Even General William Henry Harrison, who saw himself in the role of Caesar about to invade Gaul, was annoyed by the lack of realism on the part of some Congressmen. In the fall of 1812, he reported back that he could take Detroit anytime he wanted to, but since the main object was the invasion of Canada, preparations would take a little longer. In his private correspondence, however, Harrison admitted that "My preparations for the principal object of the campaign are progressing, not however with the rapidity correspondent to my wishes." To add to the delays and annoyances, some of the Indians were being troublesome in areas which were supposed to be pacified. Two of these localities were Fort Wayne and Peoria.

"At St. Mary's I found 500 mounted riflemen who had come on to go on the expedition toward Detroit," Harrison said on Oct. 13. "These were dispatched under a Colonel (Allen) Tremble to Fort Wayne." The Indians who reportedly had been collecting around Fort Wayne were gone when the detachment arrived. The rest of the mission was a failure, mostly because of fear and near-mutiny on the part of many of the militia at the prospect of going into the hostile Indian territory. Part of the troop did proceed to the Potawatomi town, now White Pigeon, Mich., and destroyed two villages there. There was no surprise, however, and the Indians had departed earlier.

Burned and Scalped

In the bitter cold January of 1813, American troops moved out of Fort Wayne with supplies to support the winter campaign against the British and Indians north of Lake Erie. General James Winchester, in charge of Harrison's left wing, had by this time rebuilt a stockade near old Fort Defiance, which was renamed Fort Winchester. The raiding force moved down the Maumee as far as the present city of Toledo, then struck across frozen Lake Erie toward Frenchtown, now Monroe, a suburb of Detroit. Frenchtown itself, wasn't much of a target, but the American commanders had been told by Indian spies that the British and Indians planned to occupy the site where the Raisin River flows into Lake Erie. Colonel William Lewis headed the first U.S. detachment of 550 men and was followed by another 110 men headed by Colonel John Allen. The fast-moving U.S. troops and the enemy arrived at the scene at about the same time, and in the skirmish which followed, the Americans successfully drove off the British and Indian party. General Winchester, with another 250 men arrived two days later on January 20.

But the early success was only prelude to disaster. As the American army of some 900 men were consolidating their control of Frenchtown, large numbers of British and Indians slipped into the vicinity, gradually surrounding the American force. On January 22, the attack began. It is reported that the British were even able to bring in several cannons to pour shot upon the U.S. force. Indians with muskets had moved with 300 yards as they opened fire. The Americans, floundering in the heavy snow, attempted to break out to the south. Most were cut down and tomahawked by the numerous Indians who were moving in for the massacre. Among those killed in the early fighting was Colonel John Allen, after whom Allen County, Indiana, is named. Several small parties of the U.S. group succeeded in breaking through the surrounding lines. But due to the heavy snow, the Indians quickly tracked them down, overtaking the exhausted troops in the chill wilderness.

Both General Winchester and Colonel Lewis were captured. After some deliberations between Winchester and the British Commander, Colonel Henry Procter, the American commander decided to surrender to save the remainder of his men from massacre at the hands of the Indians. Most of the prisoners were taken across the ice to Fort Malden on the Canadian side of the Detroit River. Winchester was eventually imprisoned at Quebec. Many of the soldiers were marched across Lake Erie in the intense cold towards Fort Niagara on the lake's far eastern shore. Few made it. The wounded, numbering more than 200 had been left behind at Frenchtown in the care of two medical aides. On the morning after the British departure, the Indians roared into the town, murdered and scalped everyone there, then burned Frenchtown to the ground.

British Riding High

Harrison constructed Fort Meigs on the south bank of the Maumee—across the river from the site of Fallen Timbers where Anthony Wayne had defeated the Indians 18 years earlier. This was to replace Fort Wayne as the jumping-off place for the drives north. It was easier to supply and was closer to the immediate object—the recovery of Detroit.

The British were at their high point in the war on the North American continent. Their Indians allies were more firm than ever. Two American drives into Canada in the East, from New England and New York, had been repulsed. The British were strengthening their hand in the entire Great Lakes area, adding forces at both Chicago and Detroit. In April, 1813, Colonel Procter marched toward Fort Meigs at the head of an army of 2,500 British soldiers and Indian warriors. The aim was to break the back of the American war effort. In the meantime, however, Fort Meigs had been reinforced with Ohio and Eastern troops and Fort Wayne with a draft of Kentucky militia. By the first of May, Procter had succeeded in bringing his army up the Maumee and opened fire on Fort Meigs with cannon batteries. Indians headed by Tecumseh and The Prophet crossed to the south side of the Maumee and cut communications to the American fort from the rear. The attack on the fort continued for five days, all the while Harrison and the other Americans inside the stockade were waiting for rescue.

The men from Fort Wayne and others from Winchester's decimated troops were holed up at Fort Meigs with General William Henry Harrison when they heard that General Green Clay was on the way with reinforcements. Clay's forces consisted of about 1,200 mounted Kentucky militia and were coming from the direction of Defiance. The British under Colonel Procter and the Indians under Tecumseh numbered 2,500. Harrison got word to Clay, instructing him to send 800 men along the north side of the river to silence the British batteries which had been lobbing shells across the river into the stockade. The balance of Clay's men were to join Harrison's men in a rush on several British cannons which had been set up on the south side of the river, just east of the fort. Things went well at first. The north bank detachment under Colonel John Dudley struck with speed and a rush of rifle fire. The British and Indians retreated from the gun positions. The Americans spiked the cannons, temporarily putting them out of commission.

If the Kentucky militia had stopped there and returned across the river to the fort, as instructed, all would have been well. As it happened, about 50 to 60 Indians just out of rifle range appeared to be retreating in halting fashion. It was an inviting target. The 800 Americans went in pursuit. The slow moving Indians were a deliberate ruse set up by Tecumseh. They continued to fall back, deeper into the woods, only firing back an occasional shot. The American militia, hot on the scent, continued after them for two miles. When the militia men found themselves nearly surrounded by 1,500 warriors armed with muskets, their mistake became obvious. Six hundred and eighty of the Americans were either killed or captured. Only a little more than 100 managed to break out and escape across the Maumee to the stockade. The prisoners were taken to old Fort Miami, the one-time British stronghold which by this time was in derelict condition, but sufficient for the holding of captives. A bloody spectacle began, reportedly right under the eyes of the British commander. The Indians, mostly Potawatomi, began to take pot shots from positions along the stockade ramparts at the some 250 prisoners in the compound. The game became more vicious with the tomahawking and scalping of a few more. Between 50 and 60 men died in this fashion before the slaughter was halted—by Tecumseh rather than the British, according to several survivors. The remaining 200 prisoners were taken down river a few miles to a British brig anchored where the port of Toledo is today. All were jammed into the ship's hold. Most survived and were later released. Because of the failure to take Fort Meigs and the fear that communications to the rear across Lake Erie might be cut, Colonel Procter evacuated the area on May 9 and the British returned to Detroit and Fort Malden. The Indians were greatly disappointed. They had expected that Fort Meigs would fall and that the expedition of British and Indians would move upriver to take Fort Winchester (Defiance) and Fort Wayne. Further, they had been promised the entire Michigan Territory by the British. These dreams were fading.

In July, however, the British and Indians returned to the Maumee Valley in even larger numbers—some estimates put the strength at about 5,000. Harrison suspected that the real aim of the offensive was to take Fort Stephenson on the Sandusky River near Lake Erie with the movements up the Maumee a distraction to draw American forces to the wrong place. In any event, Tecumseh led a party of some 800 warriors in a quick slash at Fort Winchester at Defiance and then reappeared at Fort Meigs with some 2,800 braves. At one point, he staged a sham battle in an effort to get the fort gates open. He had a number of Indians dress in frontier clothing and appear to be in a retreating gun battle with Indians, all moving in the direction of the stockade. The Fort Meigs commander, General Clay, was not fooled. Cannon fire from the fort dispersed the Indians. By the end of the month, the British and Indians had moved against Fort Stephenson. The small fort, commanded by Major George Croghan, held out. The British officer, Colonel Procter, pulled out after several days with the expectation that Harrison was moving up with a larger army.

Invasion of Canada

William Henry Harrison accumulated an army of 7,000 men during the summer months of 1813 for his invasion of Canada. Only one thing stood in the way. The American general was on the south side of Lake Erie and the British still had control of the lake.

On Sept. 12, 1813, Harrison received a note: "The United States Brig Niagara, off the Western Sister, Sept. 10, 1813, 4 p.m.

"Dear General, we have met the enemy and they are ours—two ships, two brigs, one schooner and a sloop. Yours with great respect and esteem, Oliver Hazard Perry."

Colonel Richard Johnson, who formerly had been commandant at Fort Wayne, was directed by Harrison to start the general advance. Johnson was to take a regiment of mounted Kentucky volunteers around the western shore of Lake Erie as far as the Raisin River below Detroit, which was soon to be evacuated by the British garrison. Harrison's main army advanced in stages directly across the lake in ships provided by Commodore Perry. Perry had not only defeated the British fleet on the lake, he had accepted the surrender of the added ships.

Starting from Sandusky, the American forces moved according to a detailed "order of debarkation, of march and of battle" as given by Harrison. The first stop was Put-in-Bay and other islands of Lake Erie. On Sept. 27, the army went from the Middle Sister Island to the Canadian Shore. All went well, and expected resistance along the lake's north shore did not materialize. In his first report from Canadian soil, Harrison said from Amherstburg on Sept. 27:

"I have the honor to inform you I have landed the army under my command about three miles below this point at 3 o'clock this evening without opposition and took possession of the town in an hour after.

"General Procter retreated to Sandwich with his regular troops and Indians, having previously burned the fort, navy yards, barracks and public store houses. I will pursue the enemy tomorrow."

A certain relentless quality characterized the following events. Harrison clearly had the upper hand, a fact some of the Indians seemed to recognize since many of them decided against continuing in the field. Not so, however, with Tecumseh and 1,500 warriors who accompanied the some 900 British regulars in the retreat across Ontario.

After moving up to Sandwich on Sept. 28, Harrison sent a brigade across the straits to take possession of Detroit on Sept. 29. The American general also declared martial law in Canada and plotted the pursuit of Procter's army by an overland route. Harrison took an attack force of some 3,500 men for the march up the Thames River, starting on Oct. 2.

"General Procter had posted himself at Dalson's on the right bank of the Thames" some 56 miles from Detroit, Harrison later said. "The baggage of our army was brought from Detroit in boats, protected by three gunboats which Commodore Perry had furnished for the purpose as well as cover the passage of the army over the Thames itself."

As the Americans moved up river, the British and Indians decided to take their stand on dry ground between the river on one side and a swamp on the other. When the battle opened, however, the British under Procter fell back. Tecumseh, at the head of the Indians, elected to hold the ground. In the fighting which began almost immediately, Tecumseh was killed—some say by a pistol shot by Colonel Johnson. The Indian chief was buried on the spot. His brother, The Prophet, survived but never again figured significantly in Indian matters and settled in Canada on a British pension.

The Battle of the Thames, despite the numbers involved, was not especially costly to the American side. Harrison reported 12 killed and 17 wounded. Of the British, he reported 12 killed and 22 wounded. "The Indians suffered most—33 of them having been found upon the ground besides those killed in retreat." Harrison then returned to Detroit and prepared for a further venture in Canada. Late in October, he embarked with 1,500 men for Niagara on the east side of Lake Erie for a push at the British in upstate New York and Ontario. There was little action, however, and the General visited the capital cities in the eastern U.S. and then returned to Cincinnati. The following spring, Harrison resigned his commission in the Army after a disagreement over his authority.

The commandant of Fort Wayne after Richard Mentor Johnson, who was wounded at the Battle of the Thames, was Major Joseph Jenkinson. Jenkinson almost failed to arrive in one piece. It was during the height of Harrison's campaign that Jenkinson's party set out for the stockade at the three rivers. Approaching from the southeast, they put their baggage in several long boats on the St. Mary's River about where Decatur is located today. Going down river to about a half mile from the fort, Jenkinson and several soldiers went ashore to the stockade, leaving others behind to do the unloading. Within minutes, Indians who had been hiding near the bank cut down those in the boats and made off with much of the provisions.

Whistler's Fort

"Whistler's Mother" was not born in Fort Wayne; but his father was. The painter's family were people of accomplishment long before James A. M. Whistler made his mark in the art world, and much of their early story is linked to Fort Wayne.

The artist's grandfather, John Whistler, was the builder of the last military stronghold at Fort Wayne. This stockade, usually called "Whistler's Fort" was started in 1815 and completed the following year. Major John Whistler was commandant here at that time, having assumed the post in 1814. Like many of the army officers of the era, Major Whistler was a veteran of the Revolutionary War—only with one essential difference. He fought on the British side. A native of Ulster, Northern Ireland, he first came over with the army of Burgoyne which invaded the U.S. from Canada and was defeated by forces under Benedict Arnold. Later, Whistler returned to the U.S. and joined the American army. He was an adjutant under General Arthur St. Clair when that expeditionary force met disaster at the hands of Indians under Little Turtle in 1791. Whistler was severely wounded in that battle. Actually, Whistler had a hand in building all three forts at the three rivers, plus Fort

Dearborn at the present site of Chicago. As a lieutenant, he came with Wayne to construct the first fort in 1794. Whistler, later when a captain, was a special officer at Fort Wayne for the building of the second stockade. That was in 1800 during the commandancy of Colonel Thomas Hunt. It was in that same year that John Whistler and his wife, Ann, had a baby boy whom they named George Washington Whistler. This boy, the father of the artist, later graduated from West Point and became one of the major railroad building engineers of the age in the U.S., and eventually headed railroad construction in Czarist Russia, dying in St. Peterburg in 1849. His son, the painter, also attended West Point before going to Paris and a life in the art world of the 19th Century.

Major Whistler also had another son, older than George Washington Whistler, who served here in 1809 and is mentioned in the fort's daily military log book. This son served as commander at Fort Dearborn for a period.

Major Whistler's final assignment at Fort Wayne followed service at Detroit, Fort Dearborn and several Ohio posts. He and his wife, two daughters and son came up the St. Mary's River in 1814 to take up residence in the stockade. During the following year, construction was started on a new military post of rather imposing appearance. The plans for the fort are still in existence. It measured close to two football fields side by side, being about 100 yards square, and part of the timber structure was more than 40 feet high. The approximate location was in the vicinity of the intersection of Main and Clay Streets.

Laura's Story

When Major John Whistler came to Fort Wayne to take charge of the garrison, he was accompanied by William Suttenfield and his wife, Laura. Laura Suttenfield was then 19 years old. A native of Boston, she had come west with her father and met her future husband at Detroit. She was 16 years old when the couple ran off and were married. Suttenfield, usually called "the colonel" was actually a noncommissioned officer who was in charge of the supply trains operating from Piqua, Ohio, to Fort Wayne. But the arrival of the Suttenfields and a few others marked the beginning of the distant American community at the three rivers. The most numerous residents of the vicinity for many years to come, however, would be the Indians and the several French trading families, some of whom also became permanent residents.

Laura, who was to live to the age of 91, has left us with accounts of those early days. Describing her first Fourth of July here in 1814, she said:

"The fort at that time contained 60 men of the regular army, all patriotic and anxious to celebrate one day in the year. They made three green bowers, 100 feet from the pickets of the fort—where Main St. now is—one bower for the dinner table, one for the cooks and one for the music.

"Major Whistler had two German cooks and they prepared the dinner. There were but eleven persons at the table . . . our dinner consisted of one fine turkey, a side of venison, boiled ham, vegetables in abundance, cranberries and green currents. As for dessert, we had none. Eggs were not known here for three years from that time.

"There were three bottles of wine sent here from Cincinnati; but one was made use of. Then there were a few toasts, and after three guns and music, they went into the fort and the ladies changed their dresses.

"Then Major Whistler called for the music, which consisted of one bass drum, two small ones, one fife, violin and flute. There was a long gallery in the fort; the musicians took their seats there. But three of the gentlemen could dance. There were but three ladies present.

"A French four passed off very well for an hour. Then the gates of the fort were closed at sundown, which gave a gloomy appearance. No children, no younger person for amusement, all retired to their rooms. All was quiet and still. The sentinel on his lonely round would give us the hour of the night. In the morning we were aroused by the beating of the reveille."

The Suttenfields lived within the fort walls for a few months, then moved to a house they had built just to the west—the location was at the northeast corner of Columbia and Barr Streets. It was there that their first child, a daugher named Jane, was born in 1816. For neighbors they had Louis Bourie, a fur trader, and his wife Frances who started a bakery just to the west along Columbia St.; and Major B. F. Stickney, the Indian agent who occupied a council house rebuilt in 1816. (The original council house had been destroyed by the Indians in 1812).

Laura Suttenfield, who was to live several decades as a widow, witnessed generations of change in Fort Wayne. So much a part of the town's early days, she lived to become almost a stranger in her own community. Before her death in 1886, still living in the old downtown area, she commented about the vast number of newcomers who had come over the years to constitute the city, "I know no one and but few know me."

A New State

By 1815, Indiana had a population of 63,000—a big increase over the 24,500 population in 1810. This number of Hoosiers was to move up to 147,000 by 1820. Most of these people came up from Kentucky and various southern states and settled in the southern counties of Indiana—setting a character which still exists in some of these counties. Fort Wayne was still a relatively wild post of Indian trading and few pioneers. The whole of Northern Indiana was practically empty of American settlers. They would come later from the east and from across the sea by way of the Great Lakes and rivers, the canal and finally the railroads. But as surely as southern Indiana became populated, there was interest in statehood. An act of Congress was passed on April 19, 1816, authorizing the people of Indiana Territory to form a constitution and state government. The admission resolution was approved by the Senate on Dec. 6, 1816, and signed by the president on Dec. 11, 1816.

There was just one serious tiff. The original Indiana plat called for the northern boundary to be a line from the southern tip of Lake Michigan. Congress moved the state line 10 miles further north. This brought crabbing from the Michigan Territory. But the territorial status and much smaller population of Michigan failed to impress Congress.

Much has been said about the huge riches gathered by Jean Baptiste Richardville, the half-French nephew of Chief Little Turtle. Seldom mentioned, however, were the circumstances which enabled him to accumulate so much wealth while others, both white and Indian, continued in obvious destitution. Richardville, whose Indian name was Pechewa, was indeed wealthy. In an era when pioneer families in the vicinity had difficulty in getting together a few dollars for down payments on government land, Richardville had growing piles of gold coins. Money was a very scarce item in the backwoods, yet Richardville had shipped in a safe or iron strong box in which to store an estimated $200,000 in gold coins. In today's reckoning, this would be like having several million dollars in cash on hand. Further, his land holdings increased as quickly as the land rights of the other Indians were diminishing. Richardville and his family received huge tracts along the St. Mary's and St. Joseph Rivers, and down near the Mississinewa and Wabash. Most any one of these grants exceeded township size. This all in an era when some Indians were living on handouts or the hazards of depleted wildlife and a soldier's pay was a couple dollars a month.

Richardville's timing was good. When he returned to the Fort Wayne area from Detroit after the War of 1812, he presumably was already re-establishing his outlets with the usual Canadian operators who dominated the fur exports. Though there was an American factor, or government operated trading house at Fort Wayne, most of the business by-passed this to take advantage of the better prices of the British-Canadian concerns. An Act of Congress on April 29, 1816, appears to have benefited Richardville, as well as John Jacob Astor, who headed the American Fur Company. The act forbade the trading with the Indians by anyone other than American citizens. This enabled Astor to cut the Canadian competition out of the U.S.

fur trading industry. Next, Astor was able to get legislation favorable to himself which worked to the disadvantage of the American competition. At least one Senator was known to be in Astor's pay. Michigan Governor Lewis Cass time and again made exceptions to the usual trading laws in benefiting Astor. While Astor was granted licenses to operate over wide territories, other traders received little. He even succeeded in getting Congress to abolish the government trading houses, eliminating that weak competition.

One of the common practices at that time, used by Astor as well as the other traders, was the employment of liquor to attract Indians and their furs to the trading posts. Despite laws against the practice, the use of liquor in dealing with the Indians continued to increase during the fur trading era. That Astor's "cartel" dealt heavily in such business, there can be no doubt. Each year, thousands of gallons of liquor were delivered to Mackinac, Astor's headquarters. It was reported that when the fur buying season was at its height, as many as three thousand Indians would be camped along the beaches of Mackinac Island. These were times of rough trading, drunkenness, brawling and murder.

In the area of the Maumee, Richardville managed to prosper during this period, as he had previously done during the British and earlier American periods. His mother, Tacumwa, had managed to gain control of the transportation over the ten-mile portage which connected the Wabash with the Maumee. Richardville continued and enhanced this part of the trading business. There is little question that he had a working arrangment with Astor regarding the movement of furs from the Wabash and Illinois areas. The same Governor Cass of the Michigan Territory, who so consistently served the interests of Astor, was given authority over the Indian affairs at Fort Wayne and other areas where the Miami and Potawatomi Indians were predominent. Cass was the Federal commissioner for Miami treaties of 1814, 1818, 1826 and 1834. It was during these treaties, some occurring while Richardville was officially recognized as the Miami chief, that the vast land holdings of the Miami and related tribes were lost. After the terms of one of the treaties were made known to the Indians, Richardville had to flee for his life to Detroit until tempers cooled.

Whisky and Myths

There is a modern tendency to consider the Indian "whisky disease" as some sort of frontier myth—perhaps nurtured by those who saw advantages in thinking poorly of the Indians anyway. Yet, very consistent and frequent are the accounts in those frontier days of the degeneration of large numbers of Indians involved with liquor drinking. There is the story of the Shawnee Chief Blue Jacket buying kegs of Kentucky spirits, launching a complete village debauch involving the men, women and children for days on end. A Potawatomi chief reportedly told a Federal agent at one point "You take the land, give us the whiskey." Foreign travelers detailed their observation of "the aborigines" lying about the streets of early settlements in drunken stupors. On the other side of the argument, it can be shown that there are people in all walks of life today who are victims of alcohol, with some just as surely to be found on the sidewalks of various urban districts. And it is documented that there were Indians in the old days who were drinkers, yet continued to be among the most astute of tribal leaders. The Miami Chief Le Gris, as an example, put away large amounts of rum at frequent intervals, as reported in the diary of British agent Henry Hay during his stay at Miamitown. Yet at the very same period, Le Gris was the chief given deference by all other tribal chieftains over a wide area, and marked out the course of the Miami Confederation in its early successes against the Americans.

The story of Indian whisky habits, however, fills the records of the pioneer period in the Northwest. A letter, marked "Fort Wayne, August 27, 1817," gives the local view of Major B.F. Stickney, agent at the council house which existed for Indian affairs at that time. Stickney said he recognized "the exalted views of philanthropy of the Kentucky Baptist Society for propagating the gospel among the heathen" but clearly doubted that the great expectations of such missionaries would meet with any soul-satisfying success.

"I have been between five and six years in the habit of daily and hourly intercourse with the Indians northwest of the Ohio, and the great question of the practicability of civilizing them ever before me. That I might have the opportunity of casting in my mite to the bettering of the condition of these uncultivated human beings, and the pleasure of observing the change that might be produced on them, were the principal inducements to my surrendering the comforts of civilized society." But Stickney soon learned the lesson of every other missionary and social worker that ever entered the practical applications of their profession—that people don't always perform as expected. "Upon my entering on my duties, I soon found that my speculative opinions were not reducible to practice. What I had viewed at a distance as flying clouds proved upon my nearer approach to be impassable mountains.

"First, the great and I fear insurmountable obstacle is the insatiable thirst for intoxicating liquors that appears to be born with all the yellow-skinned inhabitants of America; and the thirst for gain of the citizens of the United States appears to be capable of eluding all the vigilance of the government to stop the distribution of liquor among them.

"When the Indians cannot obtain the means of intoxication within their own limits, they will travel any distance to obtain it. There is no fatigue, risk or expense that it too great. In some causes it seems to be valued higher than life itself." Unless the liquor traffic could be halted, Stickney considered any other work among the Indians "fruitless."

He also gives some of the views of Indians at that time, and perhaps intentionally, some of the prejudices of the settlers. He said the Indians had a "firm conviction that the life of the civilized man is that of slavery, and that savage life is manhood, ease and independence." Also, most Indians had an aversion against the habits, dress and customs of the newcomers and held in contempt those Indians who adopted them. "The unfavorable light in which they view the character of the citizens of the United States, believing that their minds are so occupied in trade and speculation that they never act from any other motives . . . they view all white people as enemies and are extremely suspicious of everything coming from them." Stickney said he had about 1,400 Miamis "under my charge" and more than 2,000 Potawatomis within the agency. During the fall and winter, they scattered in the woods, hunting, but assembled in the spring in villages—eleven such places extending from Fort Wayne to Lake Michigan.

Euchred Out of Land

There is little question that the Indians were being euchred out of their patrimony some 150 years ago in these parts. But then, so were a lot of other people. Hundreds of Kentucky pioneers, including Daniel Boone, lost their property to sharpsters who came along with more accurate legal descriptions of the land. The descendants of Daniel Boone and the others are not now making claim for payment on land lost by their great-great-great-great grandfathers. It is the misfortune of the Indians that they were given annuities, reservations and promises. For most, the annuities were stopped; but many continued to live on the reservations and the promises—hoping to get something which wasn't worth the waiting. From a legal point of view, the Indians have a basis for their claims. In 1818, chiefs from Fort Wayne, Eel River and villages along the Wabash trudged to St. Mary's, Ohio (old Girty Town renamed) to meet with the American commissioners; Governor Lewis Cass of the Michigan Territory, Governor Jonathan Jennings of Indiana and Judge Benjamin Parks, also of Indiana. In addition to the Miami and Wea Indians, Wyandots, Shawnees, Ottawas, Delawares, Potawatomis and Senecas participated in the conference. It was the beginning of the end for tribal occupation of ancestoral lands in Indiana, and parts of Ohio, Michigan and Illinois. The entire central portion of Indiana, including most of the land southeast of the Wabash River was given over for pioneer settlement. In that area, only reservations near Logansport, along the Mississinewa and a few other reserves were retained. As for the Delawares, they agreed to migrate out of the territory and to the west within a few years. The Delawares, who player a heavy role in the early crisis days at the three rivers and had numerous villages both here and along the Wabash, thus continued a migration which had originally started on the east coast. They had been forced out of the east, settled in the Miami country during the days of Little Turtle's Confederacy to battle the invading Americans, and now with the Treaty of 1818 were moving on again.

In general, Indian lands were considered to be community property rather than individual holdings. The tribe as a whole owned the land and it could not be sold or taken without presidential approval. The commissioners were representatives of the president in these details. Unfortunately, there were a number of inconsistencies. Certain special favors were made to selected chiefs—usually those of mixed blood through marriage with traders and others. Miami Chief Richardville, as an example, received seven sections of land with individual title. As for the rests of the Indians, who in this one treaty gave up more than 7 million acres of land, they were promised a perpetual annuity of $15,000, plus the services of a blacksmith shop, gunsmith, salt rations and two water mills. It is the perpetual nature of this $15,000 annuity which is the basis of some claims of the Miami descendants to the present day. As in so many other agreements made in that era, the government only honored its commitment for a period of convenience.

A separate treaty had been concluded with the Ottawas and Wyandots at the Maumee River rapids. In that pact, the land between the Maumee and the St. Mary's River was taken. Various money handouts were also promised plus some basic services. The Potawatomis, the most numerous of the Indian tribes at this time, were less effected by the first treaties because their lands towards Lake Michigan were still somewhat distant from the eyes of the land-hungry settlers coming from the south and east.

Raucous Gatherings

Fort Wayne became the scene of some of the wildest gatherings on record following the Indian treaties of 1818. This happened because Fort Wayne was chosen the place for the annual payment of Federal annuities to the Indians—money the government had agreed to give the various tribes for the millions of acres of land being taken. The community at the three rivers at this time normally consisted of several dozen families—the majority of French-Indian half-blood extraction and several others who had come from the east because of military or supply jobs.

But the entire vicinity underwent a startling change as payment day approached. Thousands of Indians—Miamis, Potawatomis, Weas, Kickapoos, Ottawas, Wyandots, Shawnees and Delawares—would begin to stream in from wilderness areas extending from the Wabash to Lake Michigan and the St. Mary's to Lake Erie. There would be Indian squaws and children dragging hides and handmade items, hunters moving singly or in small bands. At the same time, traders and wagon drivers in the several hundreds would roll into the area from the East and South. They would be loaded with kegs of whisky, trinkets, guns, knives, powder, tools—anything which could be used for trading except money. That important item was the reason for everyone being there in the first place, and it would be handed out by the Federal officer.

It was a raucous, disastrous and dangerous combination. Accounts tell of drunken brawls for days on end, rampant naked partying, howling and dancing around fires both at the three rivers clearing and in the nearby forest, rapes, murders, knifings, shootings. On and on it would go until the money was gone.

Fort Wayne was the major payment center in the whole Northwest. And the annuities were paid to the Indians in silver dollars and half-dollars rather than the paper money which was then of somewhat questionable value. Traders described as "low vulgar clowns" infested the place at this time of separating the Indians from their coin.

Isaac McCoy, a missionary who was at the scene, described a drunken Miami woman who threw herself into a fire, burning to death; and many murders near Fort Wayne.

Thomas Scattergood Teas, a Philadelphian, said the "laws of the United States for preventing the introduction of liquors among the Indians are ineffectual.

"A person might remain in the woods within five or six miles of Fort Wayne for a year without being discovered by any white settler. It has been the custom of the traders to bring whiskey in kegs and hide it in the woods about a half-mile from the fort, a short time previous to the paying of the annuity, and when the Indians came to the fort . . . there is whisky to be had," Teas said.

"As soon as they receive their money, they go off in drives to the places appointed, where they frequently buy it at two dollars a pint, till their money is gone, and then pawn their blankets, guns, bracelets and other trinkets till they are sometimes reduced to a state of nudity. In this manner the traders evade the laws with impunity.

"They assemble in groups of 10 to 12, men and women promiscuously, squat on the ground and pass the canteen rapidly around, and sing, whoop and hallo—all laughing and talking at once, with the most terrible contortions. They remind me of Milton's demons. It is not uncommon to see them entirely naked, except a strip of clothing about a foot broad about the middle."

Soldiers Leave Fort

Fort Wayne, which had been the location of the first military outpost in what is now Indiana, was also the last. The soldiers of the fort marched out of the stockade at three rivers on April 19, 1819. It was almost a century after the founding of old Fort Miami by the French during the winter of 1721-22. The reason for the evacuation of the fort was basically a matter of economy and declining need. Though Fort Wayne was still fairly remote from the population centers to the east, and the Indians were still numerous in the area, the strategic purpose of building the fort in the first place no longer existed. The threat of the British and Indians had been permanently eased by the War of 1812 and the gradual settlement of portions of the Old Northwest, particularly in Ohio.

The last commandant at Fort Wayne was Major Josiah N. Vose, a New Englander who was familiar with the three rivers area because of service in the Great Lakes campaigns during the War of 1812. Vose was assigned to succeed Major John Whistler, who had built the final fort, and left for St. Charles, Mo., in 1816. Until Vose arrived on May 31, 1817, the garrison was in the charge of Lt. Daniel Curtis, an infantryman who had been at Fort Wayne for many years, including the period of siege in 1812. By various accounts, Vose brought a sense of religion to the fortification at three rivers which had been fairly lacking since the days of Anthony Wayne. It is regularly documented that a rather loose notion of morality had long been the experience of the Fort Wayne garrison —augmented and encouraged for many years by French Town, which existed on the other side of the Maumee River from the stockade. The base diversions of French Town had contributed to the downfall of many a soldier stationed at the lonely outpost, particularly until the place was burned out by the Indian attacks of 1812. Some of the fort commanders, especially Whistler and Hunt, were at times criticised for being overly broadminded about such matters. Not Vose. As soon as he arrived, he informed his men of his interest in Christian living. According to John Johnston, who was here for a period as Indian agent, Vose started the practice "to assemble his men on the Sabbath Day and read the Scriptures to them and talk with them in a conversational way about religion." Johnston had no doubt that such guidance was in great need at Fort Wayne, and "can only be appreciated by persons familiar with the allurements and temptations of military life." Vose also directed the construction of a council house near the fort for the dealings with the Indians, Benjamin F. Stickney being the Indian agent at that time. Fort Wayne was still a wilderness trading center of a few dozen souls when the day of evacuation came. Therefore there was not a great fanfare or celebration as the military colors came down for the last time. The inhabitants, in fact, were apprehensive about the loss of security which the garrison had long provided. Vose did have on hand, however, two fifes and two drums to mark the occasion. On the final day of service at the fort, the garrison consisted of the commandant, a post surgeon, two captains, a lieutenant, five sergeants and 74 artillerymen and infantrymen, and some others for a total of 96 men. The soldiers moved themselves and the fort provisions to pirogues at three rivers and proceeded down the Maumee. They took with them the dismantled six-pound and twelve-pound cannons which had commanded the waterway. The garrison traveled by water to Detroit.

Land and Pioneers

No sooner had the soldiers departed, when a number of the pioneer families and traders moved into the abandoned stockade. Stickney, the agent, also relocated his council operation into the fort. The other council house was variously used for residences and for the first school set up by Americans a few years later. In one sense, the fort remained a fort even though the army had depated. Families which had moved into the confines of the stockade and had taken up residence in the old soldier quarters continued to maintain a supply of guns and ammunition of their own. They found they slept better that way.

The descendants of Little Turtle and his sister, Tacumwa, became land-rich with Federal grants as the balance of the Miami Indians were either eliminated or shipped west. The removals of the Indians from the Fort Wayne area and Indiana did not happen overnight. Most of the deed was done in three treaties—in 1818, 1826 and 1840. The method of operation was to reward the families of the chiefs—generally intermarried with either early French traders or American soldiers, then shift the balance of the Indians to temporary reservations.

Perhaps the most mysterious character of all was Tacumwa, the one-time beauty of the wilderness whose name, and the names of her children still appear today on abstracts for much of the land in Allen County and downstate along the Wabash. Tacumwa appears in the old records under a number of names. In addition to her Indian name, which meant The Parakeet, she was known as Madame Joseph Drouet de Richardville. A British agent visiting Miamitown before the American campaigns to three rivers referred to her as Marie Louisa, a baptismal name. Later she is known as the wife of Charles Beaubien, a trader implicated in the murders of a number of travelers to Miamitown. Tacumwa and her son, Jean Baptiste Richardville, managed to maintain control of the old Maumee-Wabash portage and much of the area fur trade. When the Federal government got around to the treaties, it was Tacumwa's children and grandchildren through both the Richardville and Beaubien strains who were on the receiving end of vast land grants—some extending for miles along the Wabash and the St. Mary's, and sections along the St. Joseph and Maumee Rivers.

The direct descendants of Little Turtle receiving the government largess were the children of William Wells, the spy for Wayne's army, and his wife, Sweet Breeze, the Turtle's daughter. One of Well's children, Rebecca, married Captain James Hackley, a U.S. Army officer who committed suicide in the early 1820's. Another daughter, Ann, married Dr. William Turner, who was the Indian agent at Fort Wayne.

For the interest of people in the Fort Wayne area today who might be descendants, or have their homes on these land grants, the lists from the treaty records follow:

Jean Baptiste Richardville and family received four square miles along the St. Mary's, now the southwest of Fort Wayne; a square mile at the mouth of the Eel River at the Wabash; a square mile divided by the St. Joseph River on the city's northside; and other sections (square mile) down along the

Wabash in the area of present-day Lafayette.

Ann Turner and Rebecca Hackley received sections along the St. Joseph River. Rebecca's children, Ann and Jack Hackley, received a square mile between the Maumee and St. Joseph's River. Ann Turner and Rebecca Hackley, together with William Wayne Wells, Mary Wells and Jane Turner Wells, received several running miles along thee Wabash River and White River.

Francis Lafontaine, whose wife was Richardville's daughter, Catherine, got two square miles along the St. Mary's and a square mile along the Wabash. Francis Godfroy, also married to a daughter of Richardville, did even better. He received six square miles along the Salamonie River and a section along the Wabash. So did his brother, Louis Godfroy. Josette Beaubien was awarded a square mile along the St. Mary's.

Others given Federal land grants at the treaties, most receiving a square mile or more, include: John Bourie, one of the town founders; Miami Chief Charley; La Gros, a Miami Chief who got four square miles west of Fort Wayne; Charles, Pierre and Therese Gouin; The Crescent, a Miami chief; Peter Langlois and his children, three square miles along the St. Mary's'; Antoine Bondie, two square miles along the Wabash; the children of Antoine Rivarre, two square miles along the St. Mary's; and the son of trader George Hunt, a section on the St. Mary's. The family of Perry Kercheval, one-time clerk to the Indian agent, received land along the Maumee. Eliza Kercheval was named in the grant. She was the daughter of Benjamin Berry Kercheval. The origin of the name of Berry St. in downtown Fort Wayne might have drawn the curiosity of some residents. It turns out that it was not named after a famous admiral or the like. Berry Street got to be what it is because that was the middle name of Benjamin Berry Kercheval, Indian sub-agent.

Isaac McCoy

When Fort Wayne's first school opened, there was a diversity of race, creed and color—all in one room of the old Council House which was about where Main and Lafayette Sts. intersect today. The first class session was held on May 29, 1820, and the teacher was Isaac McCoy, a Baptist missionary. In that first group of children of the frontier villages at the three rivers were 25 pupils. Ten were English-speaking children of American government and pioneer families; six were French-speaking children of the old traders; eight were Indian children who possibly spoke French as well as the Indian dialects; and one was a negro, a child who likely spoke English. A record of the names of the children is no longer available. It was, however, the first schooling in the backwoods area since a generation earlier in the era of the French Catholic missionaries before the English and American periods of control of the Great Lakes. In his second year of operation, in 1821, McCoy received Federal financing and expanded his class to 42 pupils. As far as is known, there was no other school within 100 miles.

McCoy, his wife and their seven children came to Fort Wayne on horseback up the Wabash River route. They had with them a Mr. Lykins, a teacher, and an Indian boy. The group drove a herd of 15 head of cattle and 43 hogs the entire distance from Terre Haute. Their other belongings were carried by flatboat upriver and across the portage. It is said that Chief Richardville saw the safe convoy of the travelers and their wares. The McCoys took up residence in the old fort which had been evacuated by the troops the previous year. The Rev. Mr. McCoy started a small Baptist congregation and regular Sunday church services.

"I preached them in my own house (inside the fort) every Sabbath," McCoy related. He described the locale of that time. "At Fort Wayne was a little village of traders and of persons on the employ of the government, as interpreters, smiths and others, some of whom were French, of Canadian and Indian descent. The nearest settlements of white people were in the State of Ohio, and nearly 100 miles distant." While he was here, one of McCoy's daughters, nine years old, was dragged off and nearly killed by an Indian, before she was rescued by another Indian. The McCoys only stayed at the three rivers for two years, moving to Lake Michigan, at St. Joseph, Mich., to found a school there in 1822.

When the McCoys came to Fort Wayne in 1820, the Indian population of the Northwest —north of the Ohio River and east of the Mississippi River—was officially reported at 47,783. Though official, it is likely that such a figure was inaccurate and on the low side, and related to counts furnished by Indian agents at the various posts. Most of the Indians were concentrated along the shores of the Great Lakes and along the rivers such as the Wabash and the Maumee. Few lived any longer in Ohio or southeast Indiana. The regular Indiana population of that year was 147,000 and the U.S. population was about 9 million.

John Hays, who succeeded Dr. Turner as Indian agent August 14, 1820, reported success with some Indian families in farming. Hays, reportedly the first Jewish resident of Fort Wayne, was succeeded by General John Tipton in 1823.

End of the Indians

The situation for the Indians became worse with each succeeding year. As has been mentioned, their land was taken in a series of treaties, beginning at Greenville in 1795 and continuing through 1840. The Miamis stayed a little longer, some permanently. Most of the Shawnees and Delawares moved west during the 1820's, and the Ottawas had even earlier departed for the northlands. Some of the others, such as the Kickapoos and Illinois Indians became almost extinct, with but a handful going beyond the Mississippi. The Treaty of 1840 provided for the removal to the west of all the Miami Indians except the families of Richardville, Godfroy and their rather numerous relatives and descendants.

It turned out to be dirty business. Many of the Indians refused to move on. This resulted in the government hiring of "removal officers" or gunmen who hunted down the Indians along the rivers and forests of Indiana. Some Indians were killed. Some were dragged to points along the rivers and deposited in flatboats. Others were resigned to the exodus. That was in 1846. The largest group, about 500, were taken in the open boats up the Wabash from Peru, across the portage to Fort Wayne where the canal was being completed. A number of people have given accounts of their watching as the huddled groups of Indians were taken by. The flatboats went as far as Cincinnati. From there, the Indians were loaded on a river boat for a trip down the Ohio, up the Mississippi and then west on the Missouri. At Kansas, the Indian families were dumped ashore during a winter snow storm. Some survived until the following spring.

In one of the final dealings with the Miamis, in 1881, there was listed 318, mostly living in Indiana, but some 40 in Kansas and western Indian Territories. At that time, the old tribal authority was dropped, and the Miamis became regular citizens of the U.S. with full rights and responsibilities.

End of the Fort

Of the three American forts at the three rivers, the last was garrisoned for the shortest time by soldiers, but had the longest twilight existence as a Fort Wayne landmark. It was built in 1815 and occupied by troops until 1819. In overall size, it was believed to have been about the same dimensions of the earlier stockades, but was generally considered to be of better design and construction, and also included more impressive buildings within the complex.

The first American fort, built upon Anthony Wayne's arrival here in 1794, was used for six years. Originally, it was the plan of the U.S. War Department during the Washington Administration to construct a major fortification at Miamitown which would have been the dominant military stronghold in the Old Northwest. These plans were scaled down by Wayne, however, because of the limitations of time and immediate dangers of Indian attacks while the hurried construction was taking place. It was also decided that supply problems were too great to maintain a large garrison in so remote a part of the wilderness. The location of this fort was just north of Berry Street between Clay and Lafayette Streets.

The second stockade, built in 1800 by Col. Thomas Hunt, was a block to the north—the same location as the third fort. It was this second fort which was occupied the longest, 15 years, and withstood the severest tests at the hands of the Indians, including the siege of 1812. Peculiarly, the supposedly less imposing earlier fort had the larger number of soldiers on hand. When Wayne departed Fort Wayne for Greeneville, he provided for 300 to 500 men to man the outpost. Later, during the siege of 1812, there were about 100 men on the ramparts. Slightly less than that marched out of the garrison when the fort was evacuated by the army in 1819.

After the departure of the soldiers, the fort became something of the civic center of the frontier community. It was used by the Indian agents and early officials of one sort or another. After a while, it also served as something of a supply center in that the timbers of the stockade walls were conveniently cut and at hand for building some of the early houses nearby. For a considerable period the old stockade was the site for dealing with the Indians. On May 8, 1822, the uses of the fort were broadened. At that time Congress established a land office at Fort Wayne. Joseph Holman was appointed to the office of register and Capt. Samuel C. Vance was named receiver.

The sale of the lands of what is now downtown Fort Wayne began in 1823. This was called the Old Plat to Fort Wayne and included areas a short distance from the fort but not the tract on which the fort itself stood. The price was set at $1.25 an acre. The military lands at the three rivers were sold, also at $1.25 an acre, in 1830. It was at this time that the government decided to get rid of all the land at the site. This disposal included the blockhouses and palisades and what had been called the military reserve. There were 40 acres in all, 20 of which were platted to the west and became the early community along Columbia Street. This area became known as the County Addition and the balance of the government land, platted in 1835, became known as Taber's Addition. Parts of the old fort complex lasted through the years of the early development of the town and city. Lasting longest was the heavy-timbered multiple-story officers quarters. This was still standing in 1852. In that year, in the interest of development at the site, the last of the fort buildings was demolished. The man who did the deed was John Fairfield.

"The Signing of The Treaty of Greeneville" is a painting in the Ohio State Capital. The Miami Chief Little Turtle is standing left, opposite General Anthony Wayne. More than 1,000 Indians gathered for the treaty in 1795.

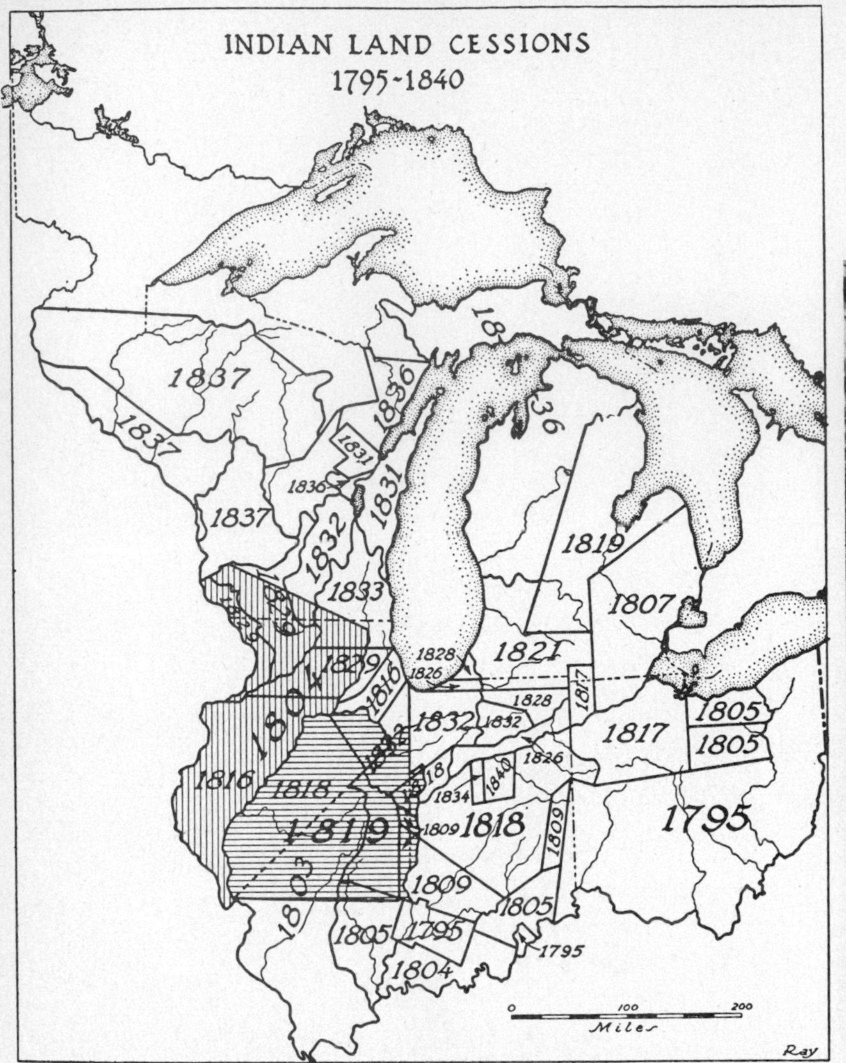

The Indian Land Cessions beginning at Greeneville in 1795 and the Treaties of Fort Wayne in 1803 and 1809 resulted in the loss of the entire Old Northwest over a 40-year period. At left is an old print showing a typical trading post during the period. Above is a bust of Anthony Wayne above the Berry St. entrance of the Allen County, Indiana, Courthouse.

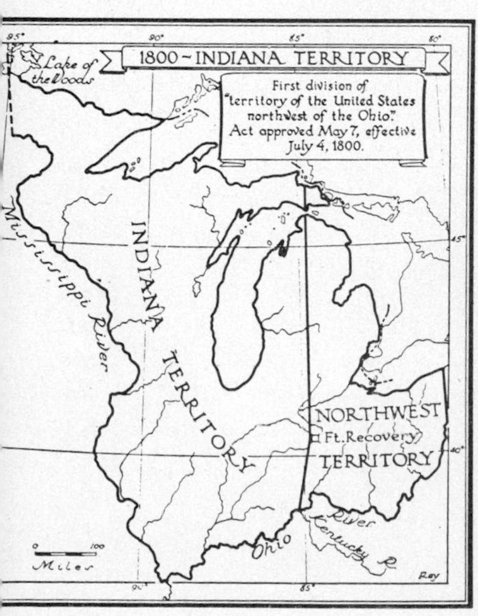

On the days of the annual payoffs to the Indians, called "Treaty Days," hundreds of traders would arrive to sell whisky, trinkets, blankets and other articles to the Indians. Since the Indian Agent was at Fort Wayne for many years, Indians from the entire Northwest Territory would gather for the annual annuity. The maps at left show the Indiana Territory. After the statehood of Ohio, all of present Indiana, Michigan, Illinois, Wisconsin and part of Minnesota was called Indiana.

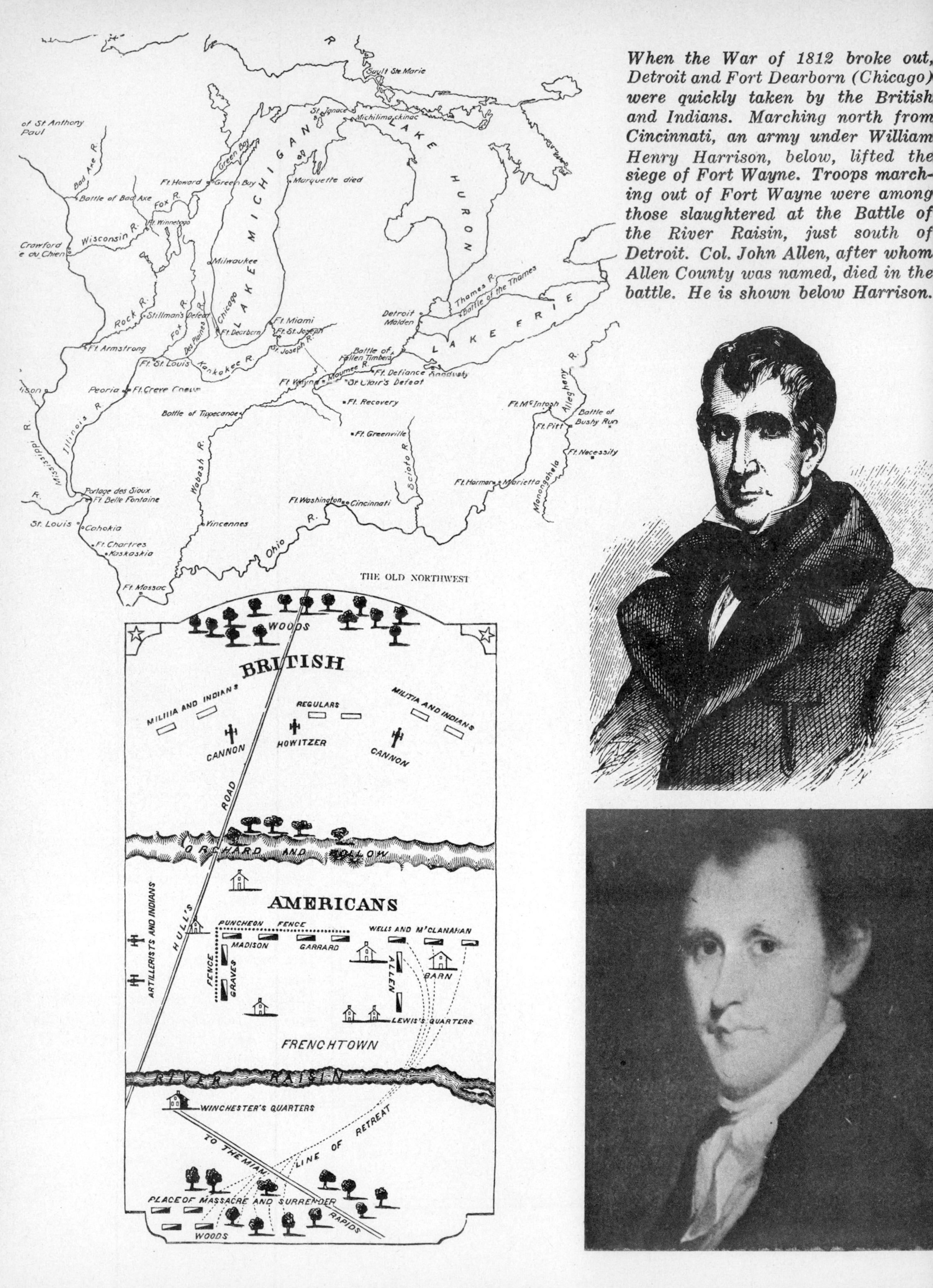

When the War of 1812 broke out, Detroit and Fort Dearborn (Chicago) were quickly taken by the British and Indians. Marching north from Cincinnati, an army under William Henry Harrison, below, lifted the siege of Fort Wayne. Troops marching out of Fort Wayne were among those slaughtered at the Battle of the River Raisin, just south of Detroit. Col. John Allen, after whom Allen County was named, died in the battle. He is shown below Harrison.

The great Shawnee Chief Tecumseh was the relentless enemy of U.S. When war broke, he went from Fort Wayne to Canada to gather forces and returned to defeat American armies at the Raisin and along the Maumee. In 1813, General Harrison took his army across Lake Erie and pursued the British and Indians in Ontario, resulting in the Battle of the Thames where Tecumseh made his last stand. Tecumseh died on the battlefield. He is depicted in a George Ganiere bronze.

1-Court House
2-Offices of Recorder and Sheriff
3-Office of Clerk
4-Offices of Treasurer and Auditor

1816–INDIANA ADMITTED
Indiana enabling act approved April 19, 1816.
Indiana admitted December 11, 1816.
Unshaded portion of Upper Peninsula left out of limits of any state or territory and with no government, 1816–1818.
ILLINOIS TERRITORY
MICHIGAN TERRITORY
INDIANA
OHIO
Mississippi River
Ohio River
0 100 Miles
Ray

The Courthouse Square in Fort Wayne was at the same place as the present Allen County Courthouse. The early layout and buildings are shown in drawings by Bert Griswold. Indiana became a State in 1816.

Chief Richardville

Angeline Chapeteau

Lewis Cass

Jean Baptiste Richardville, son of Little Turtle's clever sister Tacumwa, became Miami chief and a rich man from land and portage fees. His house, still standing south of Fort Wayne, was built in 1827. Angeline Chapeteau was the daughter of a French trader and became a figure in the early town. General Lewis Cass, governor of the Michigan Territory, headed U.S. negotiators in the Indian Treaties at Fort Wayne.

·THE·ORIGINAL·PLAT·OF·FORT·WAYNE·
·1823·

Sam Hanna helped found the town, start the canal and railroads and early commerce in Fort Wayne. Travel, as shown in the old print below, was usually on foot or horseback, but a few took the coach.

Allen Hamilton, right, was an early sheriff, postmaster and banker. Below is Asa Fairfield, an old sea captain who was a developer of parts of the city and operated the first canal boat. The first regular church building was the First Presbyterian built in 1837.

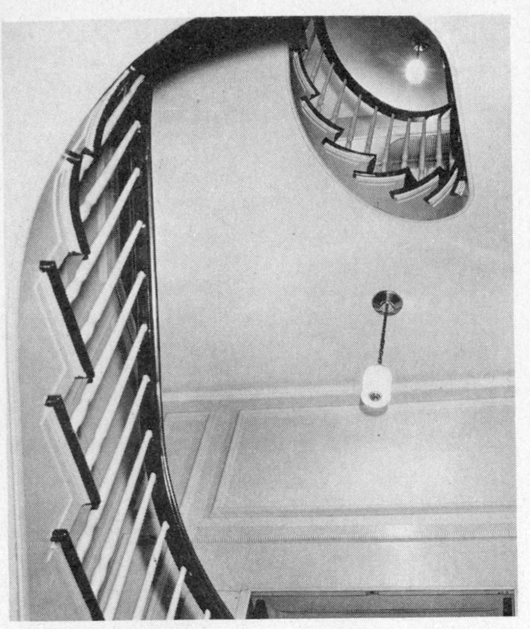

The terrible-tempered William Ewing and his family set up a tra ing apparatus extending from I troit to the lower Wabash. His ma nificient house, built in 1838 Berry and Ewing St., still look new 120 years later when this ph was taken. The stairway was artistic delight and the mansion h nine marble and brick fireplaces

Col. Thomas W. Swinney and his wife, Lucy Taber Swinney, made a charming couple in early Fort Wayne society. Their home on the west edge of town later became the Allen County Historical Museum and much of their land Swinney Park.

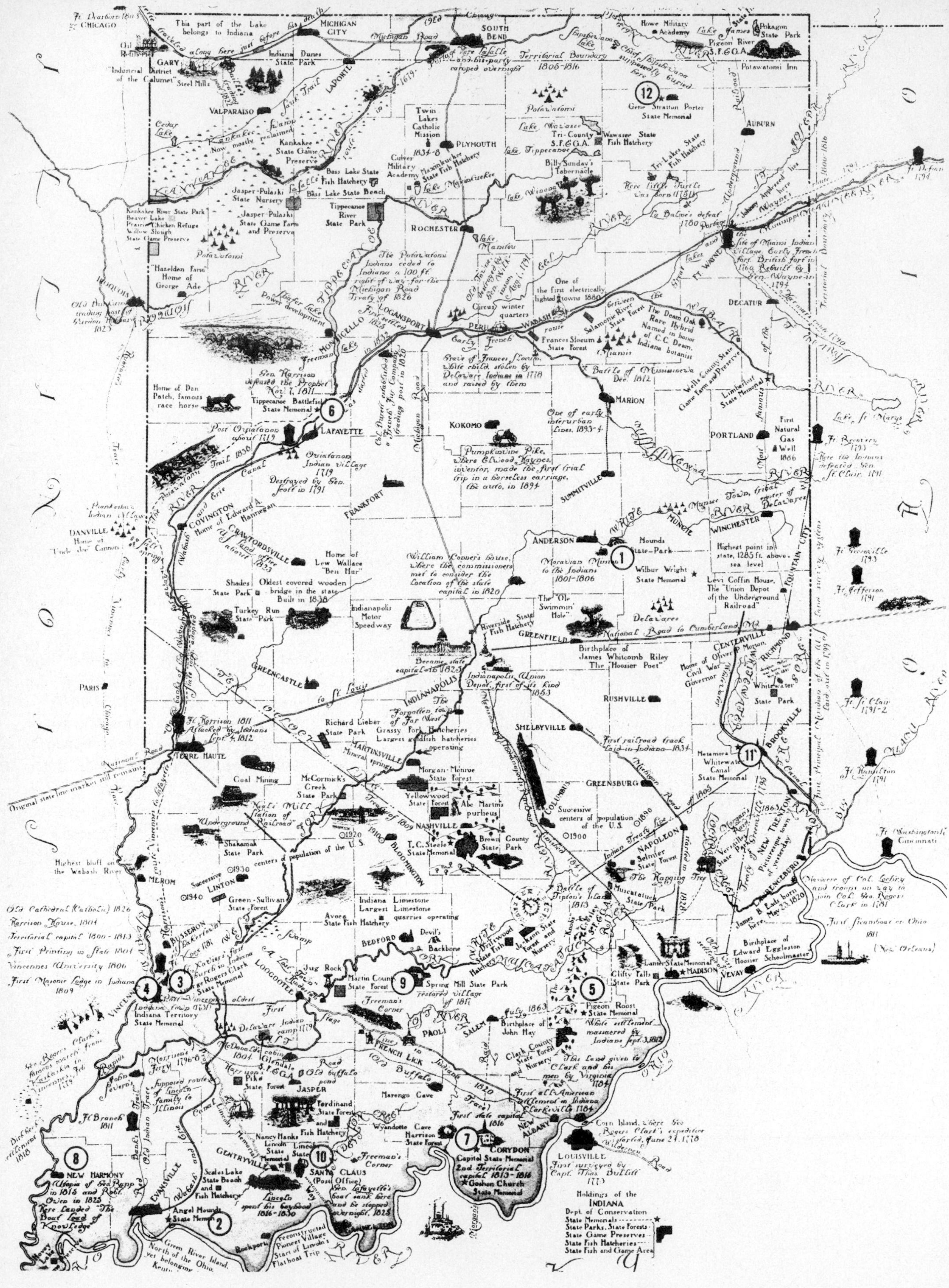

Ft. Dearborn 1803
CHICAGO
This part of the Lake belongs to Indiana
MICHIGAN CITY
Michigan Road
SOUTH BEND
Howe Military Academy
Lake James
Pokagon State Park
Pigeon River S.F.G.G.A.
Oil Refineries
GARY
"Industrial District of the Calumet"
Steel Mills
Indiana Dunes State Park
LAPORTE
Territorial Boundary 1805-1816
Potawatomi Inn
VALPARAISO
Potawatomi
Gene Stratton Porter State Memorial
Cedar Lake
Kankakee State Game Preserve
Twin Lakes Catholic Mission
PLYMOUTH
Lake Wawasee
Tri-County S.F.G.G.A.
Wawasee State Fish Hatchery
AUBURN
Lake Tippecanoe
Tri-Lakes State Fish Hatchery
Culver Military Academy
Bass Lake State Fish Hatchery
Bass Lake State Beach
Jasper-Pulaski State Nursery
Billy Sunday's Tabernacle
Lake Maxinkuckee
Lake Winona
Kankakee River State Park
Beaver Lake Prairie Chicken Refuge
Willow Slough State Game Preserve
Jasper-Pulaski State Game Farm and Preserve
Tippecanoe River State Park
ROCHESTER
Lake Manitou
La Balme's defeat 1780
FT. WAYNE
Site of Miami Indian Village. Early French fort. British fort in 1760. Rebuilt by Gen. Wayne in 1794
Hazelden Farm Home of George Ade
The Potawatomi Indians ceded to Indiana a 100 ft. right-of-way for the Michigan Road Treaty of 1826
Circus winter quarters
One of first electrically lighted towns 1880
DECATUR
Shafer Lake Power development
MONTICELLO
LOGANSPORT
PERU
WABASH
Salamonie River State Forest
The Deam Oak Rare Hybrid Named in honor of C.C. Deam, Indiana botanist
Frances Slocum State Forest
Grave of Frances Slocum, white child, stolen by Delaware Indians in 1778 and raised by them
Battle of Mississinewa Dec. 1812
Wells County State Game Farm and Preserve
Limberlost State Memorial
Gen. Harrison defeated the Prophet Nov. 7, 1811
Tippecanoe Battlefield State Memorial
Home of Dan Patch, famous race horse
LAFAYETTE
MARION
One of early interurban lines. 1893-4
KOKOMO
PORTLAND
First Natural Gas Well 1886
Post Ouiatanon about 1719
Ouiatanon Indian Village 1719
Destroyed by Gen. Scott in 1791
Pumpkinvine Pike, where Elwood Haynes, inventor, made the first trial trip in a horseless carriage, the auto, in 1894
SUMMITVILLE
COVINGTON Home of Edward A. Hannegan
FRANKFORT
CRAWFORDSVILLE
DANVILLE
MUNCIE
WINCHESTER
Highest point in state, 1285 ft. above sea level
ANDERSON
Mounds State Park
Moravian Mission to the Indians 1801-1806
William Conner's house, where the commissioners met to consider the location of the state capital in 1820
Home of Lew Wallace "Ben Hur"
Shades State Park
Oldest covered wooden bridge in the state Built in 1838
Wilbur Wright State Memorial
Levi Coffin House, The "Union Depot of the Underground Railroad"
Turkey Run State Park
Indianapolis Motor Speedway
Riverside State Fish Hatchery
The "Ole Swimmin' Hole"
Delawares
National Road to Cumberland, Md.
GREENFIELD
CENTERVILLE
RICHMOND
Birthplace of James Whitcomb Riley The "Hoosier Poet"
Home of Oliver P. Morton, Civil War Governor
Became state capital in 1825
GREENCASTLE
to St. Louis
INDIANAPOLIS
Indianapolis Union Depot, first of its kind 1853
RUSHVILLE
Whitewater State Park
PARIS
Ft. Harrison 1811 Attacked by Indians Sept. 4, 1812
Richard Lieber State Park
Grassy Fork Hatcheries Largest goldfish hatcheries operating
SHELBYVILLE
First railroad track laid in Indiana 1834
BROOKVILLE
TERRE HAUTE
MARTINSVILLE Mineral springs
Original state line marker still remains
Coal Mining
McCormick's Creek State Park
Morgan-Monroe State Forest
Metamora Whitewater Canal State Memorial
GREENSBURG
Yellowwood State Forest
Abe Martin's purlieus
COLUMBUS
Successive centers of population of the U.S.
"Underground Railroad"
NASHVILLE
T. C. Steele State Memorial
BLOOMINGTON
Brown County State Park
NAPOLEON
Selmier State Forest
The Hanging Tree
NEW TRENTON
Picturesque town of yesterday
Shakamak State Park
centers of population of the U.S.
Highest bluff on the Wabash River
MEROM
LINTON
Green-Sullivan State Forest
Indiana Limestone
Largest Limestone quarries operating
Avoca State Fish Hatchery
Muscatatuck State Park
LAWRENCEBURG
James B. Eads born here, May 23, 1820
Massacre of Col. Lochry and troops on way to join Col. Geo. Rogers Clark in 1781
First steamboat on Ohio 1811
(New Orleans)
Old Cathedral (Catholic) 1826
Harrison House, 1804
Territorial capital 1800-1813
First Printing in State 1804
Vincennes University 1806
First Masonic Lodge in Indiana 1809
BEDFORD
Devil's Backbone
Jug Rock
Martin County State Forest
Spring Mill State Park
Restored village of 1817
Lanier State Memorial
MADISON
VEVAY
Birthplace of Edward Eggleston Hoosier Schoolmaster
Clifty Falls State Park
VINCENNES
Indiana Territory State Memorial
LOOGOOTEE
Freeman's Corner
PAOLI
SALEM
Pigeon Roost State Memorial
Birthplace of John Hay
White settlement massacred by Indians Sept. 3, 1812
Clark County State Forest and Nursery
This land given to Clark and his men by Virginia 1784
FRENCH LICK
Old buffalo pond
JASPER
Pike State Forest
Ferdinand State Forest and Fish Hatchery
Marengo Cave
Wyandotte Cave
Harrison State Forest
First state capital 1816
CORYDON
Capital State Memorial
2nd Territorial capital 1813-1816
Goshen Church State Memorial
NEW ALBANY
Corn Island, where Geo. Rogers Clark's expedition started, June 24, 1778
LOUISVILLE
Ft. Branch 1811
NEW HARMONY
(Utopia of Geo. Rapp in 1815 and Robt. Owen in 1825
Here Landed "The Boat Load of Knowledge"
Nancy Hanks Lincoln State Memorial
Lincoln State Park
GENTRYVILLE
SANTA CLAUS (Post Office)
Scales Lake State Beach and Fish Hatchery
Lincoln spent his boyhood 1816-1830
EVANSVILLE
Angel Mounds State Memorial
Rockport
Reconstructed Pioneer Village Start of Lincoln's Flatboat Trip
Green River Island, North of the Ohio, yet belonging to Kentucky
Holdings of the INDIANA Dept. of Conservation
State Memorials
State Parks, State Forests
State Game Preserves
State Fish Hatcheries
State Fish and Game Area
Ft. Defiance 1794
Ft. Recovery 1793
Here the Indians defeated Gen. St. Clair 1791
Ft. Greenville 1793
Ft. Jefferson 1791
Ft. St. Clair 1791-2
Ft. Hamilton 1791
Ft. Washington Cincinnati
Lake St. Marys

Part 3
A Town Is Born

There is quite a difference between the maintaining of a military post and the building of a town and city. There are any number of places in the United States and in other countries which were at one time of prime strategic importance or the sites of famous contests, yet are today but dim marks along a road or field. In most respects, the type of person to be found in an army garrison, or the hangers-on, are the least likely to found permanent settlements, family and intellectual life and industry.

The same was true with Fort Wayne. There were a number of families connected with the old fort, including some who intermarried with either Miami Indians and/or wilderness traders. Some received land in the treaties and became farmers. A few stayed on in the three rivers community. Generally, though, the frontiersmen, soldiers and foot-loose trader types moved on. They and their sons and daughters became soldiers, homesteaders, explorers and sometimes killers in the West. They climbed Pike's Peak, hired out as guns in the Pacific Northwest, opened river travel and farming in Missouri and claimed water rights in New Mexico. Once the Federal money and the Indian handouts had slacked off, few remained; and of these, only a handful figured significantly in the building of the town. This was left to newcomers who arrived within a few years of the closing down of the garrison in 1819. A surprising number appeared to have some legal orientation. There was an almost universal characteristic for energetic innovation and instinct for commerce.

Two men, more than most others, seem to have brought unusually large shares of the skills of civilization and direction to town growth at Fort Wayne. They were Samuel Hanna and Col. Alexander Ewing. They were more than traders, surveyors or commission agents, as were some of the early arrivals, in addition to the farmers of the virgin lands.

Hanna came in 1819. He was a pioneer, merchant, judge, legislator, canal builder, railroad builder, banker. He was 22 years old when he came to Fort Wayne from St. Mary's, Ohio, a place which was still known by some at that time by the hated name of

Girty Town. His first commercial action was the forming of a trading post in partnership with his brother-in-law, James Barnett.

The family of Alexander Ewing came in 1822 from Troy, Ohio. The members included his wife Charlotte, sister of Capt. William Griffith who was a victim of the Fort Dearborn massacre; four sons, Charles W., who became president-judge of the Circuit Court; William G., the first man to be admitted to the bar in Allen County; George W., who became a leading businessman in early Indiana, Illinois and Michigan; and Alexander H., a prosperous Cincinnati merchant. Also, there were three daughters, Charlotte, married to William Hood; Lavina, married to George B. Walker; and Louisa, married to Charles E. Sturgis. Col. Ewing had been a militiaman and joined General William Henry Harrison in the relief expedition to lift the siege of Fort Wayne in 1812. In his short five years in Fort Wayne after 1822, he founded a tavern and began the real estate holdings of the family in the early era.

Others establishing early trading operations and enterprises at the site were Francis Comparet, who came in 1820; James Peltier, a French Canadian out of Detroit whose family had been on the scene in earlier years before the development of the American community; Louis Bourie, a fur trader from Detroit who did business with the Indians during the days of the fort, operating over the St. Mary's-Wabash portage. Comparet and Alexis Coquillard, who also came from Detroit, were agents of John Jacob Astor's far-ranging American Fur Company. Astor, through the conniving of Governor Lewis Cass of Michigan, gained a virtual stranglehold on fur trading, first in the Great Lakes area and later extending to the Pacific Coast. Coquillard, after a period in Fort Wayne, established a post on the St. Joseph River at South Bend, which was an outpost of the important agency at Fort Wayne.

Paul Taber came in 1819 accompanied by his sons Cyrus and Samuel, and his daughter Lucy. Captain Taber was a sea captain in the war of 1812. When the sale of government lands at $1.25 an acre about Fort Wayne was held on October 22, 1823, Paul Taber was on hand to purchase 240 acres west of the town plat. He gave three tracts of 80 acres each to his three children. Cyrus and Samuel deeded their holding to their sister Lucy. This 240 acres, including the Swinney Homestead built in 1844, eventually became present Swinney Park, the city's first park. Lucy in the meantime had married Col. Thomas W. Swinney who came to Fort Wayne from Piketon, Ohio, in 1823.

John T. Barr, a merchant of Baltimore, and John McCorkle of Piqua, Ohio, had purchased the original fort plat for $2,838.43. The old plat contained a little less than 600 acres, thus the price averaged nearly $5 per acre. Immediately after the sale, Robert Young surveyed and laid out the town.

The most desirable business lots on Columbia St. were 60 by 150 feet, and sold for $100 each. Alexander Ewing, Samuel Hanna and Allen Hamilton bought most of them. Hamilton came to Fort Wayne that same year. He was named the first sheriff here by the governor in 1824 and later formed the first local bank.

In those early days of the founding of the town, the community was just a few yards away from wilderness in point of both time and space. The community itself was far smaller than it had been some 30 years earlier during the heyday of Miamitown. In that earlier French, British and Indian period, before the coming of the Americans, the three rivers community was a central point in the political control of the Northwest. Not only were there the two towns of the Canadian traders on either side of the St. Joseph, just north of the Maumee, but there were thousands of Indians in seven villages in the immediate vicinity. By the early 1820's, hardly a trace of the older community remained. Some Indians were still in the area, but they had largely cleared out of the proximate vicinity during the time of the garrisons. When large numbers of Indians did come to town in the post-fort era, it was usually at the time of the Federal money distributions to the tribes, as provided in the Treaty of Greenville in 1795 or the two Treaties of Fort Wayne in the first decade of the 19th Century.

'Treaty Days'

It might be noted that when those "treaty days" arrived, most of the citizens of the small community were careful to look to their personal security for a spell, while wild times ruled the area.

That Fort Wayne might ever become much of a town was apparently lost on some of the visitors who came by this way in those days.

The Rev. J. B. Finney, a chronicler staying over at the three rivers in 1819, had this to say:

"This was an awful scene for a sober man to look upon. Here were encamped between two and three hundred Indians, one-third, if not one-half drunk; men and women, raving maniacs, singing, dancing, fighting, stabbing and tomahawking one another. There were rumsellers watering their whiskey until it was not strong grog, and selling it for four dollars a gallon, their hired men gathering up all the skins and furs and their silver trinkets . . . and three or four were killed or wounded."

The following year, 1820, Captain James Riley wrote from Fort Wayne to friends back east: "There were at least one thousand whites here from Ohio, Michigan, New York and Indiana trading with the Indians. They brought an abundance of whisky with them, which they dealt out to the Indians freely in order to keep them continually drunk and unfit for business; their purpose being to get the best of them in trade. Horse racing, gambling, drinking, debauchery, extravagance and waste were the order of the day and night."

A topographical engineer named Major Stephen H. Long came to Fort Wayne in 1823 and was similarly unfavorably impressed with the general situation:

"At Fort Wayne we made a stay of three days," he wrote, "and to a person visiting the Indian country for the first time, this place offers many characteristic and singular features. The village is small. It has grown under the shelter of the fort and contains a mixed and apparently worthless population.

"The inhabitants are chiefly of French Canadian origin, all more or less imbued with the Indian blood. The confusion of tongues owing to the diversity of Indian tribes which generally collect near the fort make the traveler imagine himself in a real babel.

"The business of a town of this kind differs so materially from that carried on in our cities that it is almost impossible to fancy ourselves within the same territorial limits; but the disgust which we entertain at the degraded condition in which the white man . . . appears is perhaps the strangest sensation which we experience.

"The village is exclusively supported by the fur trade, which has, however, gradually declined owing to the diminuation of the Indian population. The traders seldom leave town but have a number of Canadians, called engages, in their service who accompany the Indians in their summer hunts, supply them with goods in small quantities, and watch them that they shall not sell their goods to traders other than their employers.

"The furs brought in consist principally of deer and raccoon skins. Bear, otter and beaver have become very rare. The skins when brought in are loosely rolled or tied, but they are afterward made into packs which are three feet long and eighteen inches wide after being subjected to a heavy pressure in a wedge process. Skins are worth: deer, buck, $1.25; deer, doe, $1.09; raccoon, 50 cents; bear, $3 to $5. The values are nominal as the furs are paid for in goods which are passed off on the Indians for more than double the prime cost and transportation. The furs are usually sent down the Maumee to Lake Erie and thence to Detroit, where they are for the most part purchased by the American Fur Company." The American Fur Company was, as mentioned earlier, the politically-favored cartel of John Jacob Astor.

Establishing Law

Through the early 1820's, the legal organization of the community was taking place. In 1822 Samuel Hanna was appointed the first postmaster at Fort Wayne. A regular mail, once a week, was established between the town and Maumee and Piqua, Ohio. Before that time, the local citizenry had depended on the military express, suppliers and travelers and chance.

Even though the court system was finally reaching into the wilderness outposts, some cases were still being resolved by expediency. An example was a murder in 1824. A Miami stabbed and killed an Ottawa at the southwest corner of Clinton and Columbia Streets. The enraged Ottawas formed a war party of several hundred and came thundering in demanding blood or reparation from the Miamis. Chief Richardville called a council of the Miamis and agreed to pay $5,000 out of the Miami annuity. Sam Hanna and James Barnett advanced goods to the Ottawas in that amount, and took an order for the annuity, thus averting impending bloodshed and at the same time turning an honest penny.

The constitution of the State of Indiana, formed in 1816, had provided for the Circuit Courts. Each was to have one president and two associate judges. The Circuit president was chosen by the State General Assembly and the associate judges by electors in the respective counties. By a State Act, Allen County was formed on December 17, 1823. It was named after Col. John Allen who was killed in the American disaster during the War of 1812 at the River Raisin, July 22, 1813. Allen County was organized with its present boundaries, but the Allen Circuit Court also took in territory which later became Wells, Adams and Huntington Counties and all the area north of Fort Wayne to the Michigan line.

The court became activated April 1, 1824, and convened at the house of Alexander Ewing on the fourth Monday of May. This was a log tavern on the southwest corner of Barr and Columbia Streets.

The first County Commissioners were elected on May 22, 1824, as were the associate judges, recorder and clerk. Samuel Hanna and Benjamin Cushman were elected judges. William Rockhill, James Wyman and Francis Comparet were named commissioners, and Anthony L. Davis, clerk. Allen Hamilton was the first sheriff.

At the first session of the court, held in the Ewing Tavern, the business took on an almost family aspect. Charles Ewing was appointed by the court as prosecuting attorney. William G. Ewing was admitted as attorney of the court. The first action of the court was to grant Alexander Ewing a license to keep a tavern in the town of Fort Wayne.

The first grand jury venire was drawn by Sheriff Hamilton. The jurors included John Tipton, Paul Taber, William Suttenfield, Alexander Ewing, James Hackley, Charles Weeks, John Davis, William Probst, Horace Taylor, James Wyman, James Cannon and Peter Felix. Felix was excused by the court and Cyrus Taber and William N. Hood were named to the panel. Tipton was chosen foreman.

At the court's initial session, Francis Aveline, alias St. Jule, became the first foreigner to be naturalized in Allen County as a citizen of the United States. As for the grand jury, the indictments returned differed little from those of similar bodies in the many subsequent years. They included two for adultery, one for playing cards and gambling, one for assault and battery and several for illegal sales of liquor.

The commission to locate the permanent county seat of government met on May 24, 1824. Among the propositions was one from John McCorkle and John T. Barr, who had just laid out the town plat. They offered to pay $500 cash and donate the county the square of land bound by Main, Court, Berry and Calhoun Streets. The offer was accepted which set out the location for the County Courthouse ever since.

The June 6, 1825, court session met with Judge Hanna presiding to hear a case on "a woman taken in adultry." She was sentenced to 15 days in jail, but her paramour was acquitted. At the November, 1825, session, John Tipton pleaded guilty to assault and battery and was fined $3.

The first indictment for murder was against an Indian named Saganaugh. He had stabbed and killed another Indian named Natwatine. Saganaugh was held for a time in the county jail, but the case was continued for several terms and finally dropped by the court.

In addition to the Ewing tavern and house, the court often held session in the tavern of William Suttenfield at Barr and Columbia. This is rather peculiar since Suttenfield appears fairly regularly on old docket sheets on one charge or another—assault, trespass, and intent to steal. In the same 1825 term, Calvin Fletcher was sworn in as prosecuting attorney. In later years he would move to Indianapolis and found the banking firm which still bears his name.

Governor Wallace

In the term of May 12, 1828, which was held at the house of Benjamin Archer, a man who would be eventually elected governor of Indiana was sworn in as prosecuting attorney. He was David Wallace. He was soon elected to the state legislature, then, two terms as lieutenant governor. In 1837 he was elected governor and issued the first Thanksgiving Proclamation in the State of Indiana. He returned to Fort Wayne after his term, but his business ventures were unfortunate, costing him an accumulation of a lifetime and left him poor.

David Wallace was the father of Lew Wallace, a general in the Civil War who was the author of "Ben Hur" and other novels. Lew Wallace, an important figure in Indiana public life, later was named governor of the Arizona Territory during the period of the Range Wars.

Charles H. Test was the first president judge of the Circuit to be elected by the voters of Allen County. The voters numbered 252 in that year of 1830. In his first case as judge, Test presided in the trial of Naw-way-ling-quah, a Miami chief. He was indicted for the murder of Wishmah, a woman slave belonging to the chief. She reportedly was half Indian and half Negro, and had defied him in a drunken rage at Barr and Columbia.

Among those on the jury were two of Indian blood—Jean Baptiste Godfrey and Henry Ossem. The chief was convicted and was sentenced to two years in prison, according to court records.

An interesting, but likely fanciful version of the trial, appears in some unofficial reports. This has it that the chief was sentenced to be executed. He was supposedly told while being held in jail that he might be hanged. To test the situation, he asked for a rope and hung his dog, watching his death struggles. It was not to his liking and he begged to be shot if he had to die. His tribe offered a substitute to take his place—a worthless member of the tribe who they said was a rascal "of no account but would do for hanging." Or so the version goes.

In 1833 the Legislature created several counties in addition to Allen including Cass, Carroll, Lagrange, Elkhart, St. Joseph, LaPorte, Huntington, Wabash and Miami, nearly one-half the area of the State. Whitley County was created in 1834. Noble and Adams Counties were added in 1836. Steuben, DeKalb and Wells were organized in 1837.

The first judge of the Allen Probate Court was William Ewing, appointed in 1830. In 1834 Hugh McCulloch became probate judge. He resigned the following year to become cashier and manager of the Fort Wayne Branch of the State Bank of Indiana. McCulloch came from Indianapolis to Fort Wayne. He soon became president of the State Bank and president of the banking house of Allen Hamilton & Co. In subsequent years he was appointed to the Cabinets of Presidents Lincoln, Johnson and Arthur as Secretary of the Treasury.

The Courthouse

It took a number of years to get a courthouse built in Allen County. But once started, there was a quick series of building up and tearing down of courthouses until the erection of the present one at the turn of the century.

The first steps were taken in 1831. At the May 7 session of the Circuit Court, it was decided to build, and the plans were agreed upon. On August 9 of the same year, the county agent was ordered to let a contract, "to cut the brush and stumps off the public square."

The new courthouse was not completed and occupied until 1847 and was a two-story brick with a steeple. Samuel Edsall was the contractor. This courthouse was deemed inadequate and on June 11, 1858, a levy was ordered of 15 cents on all property for a fund to build a new courthouse. The newspapers of the day said the building "should last for a century at least." The contract was let in 1860. The structure was built under the direction of Virgil Kimball, Ochmig Bird and Louis Wolke and cost a total of $78,000.

In the meantime, the population of Allen County increased 30-fold from a count of 996 in 1830. The prime mover in this rapid growth was the coming of the canals and all the traffic which those canals meant to a wide area of the United States.

The Great Canal

The Wabash-Erie Canal, which was to become the longest stretch of canal in the United States, was begun at Fort Wayne.

When work on the canal started in 1832, Indiana had probably a little more than 350,000 inhabitants, most in the southern part of the state who had migrated down the Ohio River or across from Kentucky. By 1840, the state had 684,000 people and in 1850, more than 988,000. The growth of Illinois was even more phenomenal—157,000 in 1830, some 476,000 in 1840 and 851,000 by 1850.

An early settler in upper Indiana said in later years: "All the immigrants from the East came in by the canal. The boats would take grain to Toledo and bring back immigrants and their goods by the hundred."

With the coming of the canals, the growth of Indiana shifted from the south to the north. The formation of county governments along the Wabash-Canal route was directly related to the rapid increases in population of those areas. In the first three years following the opening of the first section from Fort Wayne to Huntington, five new counties were created. Many people in southern Indiana moved to the north part of the state, attracted by the boom the canal was promising.

The great canal industry began with an act of Congress in 1828 which provided for the sale of public land for such waterways. The proceeds of the sale of these lands, it was hoped, would finance the building of the canals.

The Indiana Legislature wrestled with the question during 1829 and 1830, since the connecting of Lake Erie with the Wabash River and waterways west was one of the national aims of the entire scheme. Land sales were first held at Lafayette and Logansport in 1830, but the results were disappointing. Forty-two thousand acres were sold and brought in only $75,000, an average of $1.78 an acre.

Fort Wayne, however, had already been on the move in initiating a canal with the Treaty of 1826 with the Miami Indians. The agreement provided for the lands of the artificial waterways and at the direction of President John Quincy Adams a survey was ordered.

Colonel James Shriver was detached from the War Department for managing the survey and he chose Fort Wayne as the starting point. That was in 1828. During 1827 and 1828, the survey work was completed from Fort Wayne west as far as the junction of the Tippecanoe River with the Wabash and east along the Maumee as far as Lake Erie. On March 2, 1827, the Federal government granted the land for the road bed of the canal.

By action of the Indiana Legislature, Samuel Hanna, David Burr and Robert John were appointed canal commissioners. The following year, 1829, the Ohio Legislature agreed to the project from the Indiana-Ohio Line, on the east edge of Allen County, to as far as Lake Erie.

Summit City

That Fort Wayne became the focal point in the extensive plans for the creation of a canal system in the middle part of the nation was a matter of geography. The town only had a few hundred people. But it was the summit of the Atlantic Ocean-Gulf of Mexico depression. It was the high point in the natural flow of waterways. Fort Wayne is 198 feet above Lake Erie. Beyond Lake Erie are Lake Ontario and the St. Lawrence and finally the Atlantic. Across a few miles of the old portage to the Aboite and Little Wabash begins the river network flowing down to the Ohio, then the Mississippi, and finally the Gulf. This is the origin of the term, Summit City. Not because Fort Wayne is the highest land in Indiana or the Midwest, but because it is at the high point linking the greatest water-flow depression in North America.

February 22, 1832, Washington's Birthday, was chosen as the day of the great ground-breaking for the canal system. The ceremony took place at Fort Wayne. Hanna and the others took turns spading the traditional shovel of dirt. It was about the only act which made the building of the canals similar to the usual public works. The construction of the canals in the semi-wilderness area remains to this day one of the overlooked wonders of the world. The whole thing was star-crossed from the beginning. It was far more ambitious than there were resources. Disease, larceny, bankruptcy, killings, ethnic battles and plagues of swamp-nurtured insects and cholera and malaria were the real partners of the enterprise. It has been estimated that one man died for every six feet of canal built through Indiana.

But none of this was forseen on that Feb. 22 day of 1832 as most of the people of the small village gathered for the ceremonies. W. G. Ewing painted the future of canal transportation and the area in glowing terms. Henry Rudisill was chairman and David Colerick served as clerk.

The engineering was entrusted to Jesse L. Williams who had learned the profession under an Erie engineer and had worked on canals in Ohio. Workers were offered $10 a month to come to Fort Wayne and hire on as canal laborers. The wages were advanced a bit when too few men showed to fill the crews and replace those who were dying on the job.

In 1834, more than a thousand men were working on the Wabash-Erie canal, mostly on the section just west of Fort Wayne. The canal laborers, a rough and ready lot, outnumbered the regular population several times and altered the entire complexion of life on the near-frontier area. The largest percentage of workers were Irishmen of either Cork or Ulster origins. It proved to be a steamy combination. At one time during that year, they were like two armies edging towards battle, and one incident caused the calling out of the state militia to restore some semblance of peace.

But the work was pushed on mile-by-mile through the oak and walnut forests and along the hillsides and swamps. Money also was being eaten up faster than anyone had anticipated. The total wealth of Indiana at that time was estimated at $80 million. As the costs increased and land sales proved inadequate, public pressure induced the legislature of Indiana to pledge its entire credit. Some $13 million was produced by state-guaranteed notes, and these were to eventually bankrupt the state government.

The first section to be completed in the Wabash-Erie system was the part between Fort Wayne and Huntington. The event was marked with a celebration on July 4, 1835, at both towns. As many people as would fit jammed onto a canalboat for the initial trip from Fort Wayne to Huntington. The crowd included 33 young girls in costume. They moved across the countryside at the usual canalboat speed of three miles an hour.

Bonfires and Parades

The news of the first operations of the canal system in mid-America spread like wildfire. Speculators began a land boom on plots far removed from anyone's visual experience. The State Government proceeded with its out-sized loan plans. Canals projected to Michigan City and other points were talked.

The public was looking forward to a new millennium. Every town with any connection or some potential canal benefit built bonfires and held parades and banquets. Politicians spent hours and days in making orations. Eastern newspapers sang praises of the enterprise of the young frontier states, and made scornful comparisons with the slack backwardness of government and business in places like Massachusetts. Word reaching Europe led to travel plans to the New World to see the latest advances of mankind, which presumably compared with the building of the China Wall and the Pyramids of the Pharoahs.

As the land speculation mania grew through 1836, fortunes were made by the shrewd or lucky gamblers at Evansville and other towns.

But suspicions and distrust began to set in during 1837. Rumors of enormous expenditures began to be circulated. The report came forth that during the first year of the project, nearly $4 million had been spent. The Panic of 1837 put on the cruncher. Land sales dried up, banks began to fail. Money grew scarce. Jesse Williams' report in December of that year said it would cost $23 million more to complete the canal. The following year, Governor Wallace noted that the entire state tax revenues would not pay even half the interest due on the outstanding notes. To compound the matter, even though the Indiana work crept on as far as Logansport, the Ohio portion was not being built—defeating to large extent the entire application of a full canal system.

Work was stopped on the Central Canal system, which caused men to leave the job with sixteen miles of canal built to the south of Indianapolis and eight miles to the north. The problem was bankruptcy, partly due to dishonest dealings. The largest blocks of the canal bonds had been handled by Milton Stapp, a fund commissioner, and Dr. O. Coe, secretary of the commission. Coe had an office in New York and fraudulantly enriched himself by discounting the bonds to Morris Canal and Banking Co., a company which he partly owned. The Morris firm failed. Of the $15 million which the state was supposed to receive, only $8,593,000 was received in cash. The balance was in worthless notes. More than $2 million was reportedly embezzled.

But despite all this, the canal work was pushed on down the Wabash. Script money was used, often called Red Dog because of the color of some of the paper. The script at one point depreciated to 40 cents on the dollar in the canal area and all but worthless elsewhere.

In the meantime, Ohio had made progress in canal building, completing the eastern end of the route to Toledo in 1843. There was great rejoicing when the first boats came in from Lake Erie, for now it seemed that there would at last be profitable operations. Lines of boats brought thousands of new settlers. Business increased rapidly. Docks, elevators, warehouses, hotels and mercantile establishments sprang up at Fort Wayne and other towns. Lafayette became such a busy port that the public square was choked with wagons and teams, some camping for days waiting to make delivery on the boats. By 1844, the fastest packet service in the country was in operation between Toledo, Fort Wayne and Lafayette. The great migrations led to the advance of population centers in Indiana, but even more so in Illinois, particularly after completion of the canal to Terre Haute in 1849. The southern end of the canal finally reached Evansville, 452 miles from Toledo, making it the longest canal in America.

The building of the canal was much more than the cutting of a channel. At Fort Wayne it was actually necessary to build an aquaduct across the St. Mary's River in order to maintain a continuous water level to both the east and west. The aquaduct, near the present West Main St. Bridge, looked like a covered bridge. It was 200 feet long and made of oak timbers supported by stone masonry. It was held together with hand-forged iron bolts. The water level was four and a half feet and the width of the flume was slightly more than 17 feet.

Among the numerous dams needed to provide water grades and reservoirs of impounded water to operate the canal were those at Antwerp, Ohio, and Robison Park, six miles north of Fort Wayne. The dam on the St. Joseph River was 17 feet high and 75 feet wide at the base and 25 feet wide on top. It was made of tree trunks from the forests and filling of stone and gravel. The stone was brought to the site by streams of ox-drawn sledges. A small feeder canal from this reservoir north of Fort Wayne was used to bring the water to the regular Wabash-Erie Canal.

The main canal was usually about six feet deep and between 40 and 50 feet wide.

The boats either came from New York and other Eastern states or were built locally. One Fort Wayne yard reported building five canalboats in a single year, with others being ready for launching.

The grand dedication of the Wabash-Erie Canal was set for July 4, 1843. Fort Wayne was chosen for the ceremonies because it was the place where the construction was begun 11 years earlier.

An editorial in the Fort Wayne Sentinel at that time commented: "We are informed that a very lively interest is felt in this matter by the citizens all along the whole line, and all who can make it conveniently will attend. Several volunteer companies and bands of music will attend, and altogether we presume the celebration will be the largest and most imposing ever witnessed in this state."

Among those sending messages extolling the great event were President Martin Van Buren, Vice President Richard Menter Johnson, Daniel Webster, Henry Clay and General Winfield Scott. Crowds swarmed into town on the weekend prior to the Fourth (a Tuesday) by wagon, canalboat, horseback and on foot. A reporter from a New York newspaper recorded that 100 houses were in the process of being built, mostly wooden but some brick. Laura Detzer, a local historian, believed that more than half the entire county population was in town for the occasion. On Saturday, canalboats from both east and west were lined up along the bank for half a mile. Many were gaily decorated or painted in keeping with the spirit. Taverns and private homes were doing a swinging business.

The main speaker for the observance arrived on a large packet boat on Tuesday morning with the shooting off of an appropriate gun salute. It was Senator Lewis Cass, former governor of Michigan who was running for President, on the Democratic ticket.

When the boat docked at the foot of Clinton St., Senator Cass, a huge, ponderous and vain man, advanced to the gangplank. Looking out over the vast throngs in the dock area, he stepped toward the dock but missed his footing and went plunging into the stagnant and muddy canal.

Cass was sufficiently recovered by 11 o'clock that morning to take his proper place as orator. In the procession were Samuel Edsall, parade marshall; the Toledo Guards which were a flashy unit of the day; veterans of the Revolution and War of 1812; Hugh McCulloch, the reader; and Rev. G. M. Boyd, the chaplain; U. S. Senators A. S. White and Ed Hannegan; political boss Jesse D. Bright; the Defiance Band; the Marion Band; the German Band; a contingent of Miami warriors; the Kekionga Band and many ladies decked out for a fancy occasion.

The canals reached the greatest days of their short years of comparative prosperity with the completion of the link down through Ohio to Cincinnati. The Packet boats operated on schedule. The fare from Fort Wayne to Toledo, a distance of 106 miles, was $3.35; to Cincinnati, a distance of 221 miles, $6.75; to Lafayette, a distance of 104 miles, $3.75. There were first class sleeping berths which were arranged in two rows along the sides of the main compartment. Off of this was a smaller space for the women and children. Men, married or not, were not allowed to enter the woman's space during the sleepy-time hours.

Walnut and Mosquitoes

The canal systems of inland waterways during the 1840's from the Eastern states through Ohio and Indiana were so extensive they were considered a part of the great national military highway. In 1846, a company of Fort Wayne soldiers departed on an eastbound boat on the Wabash-Erie Canal, which turned southward at Defiance Junction on the Miami Canal and floated down to Cincinnati. They were on their way to service in the Mexican-American War. The detachment went from Cincinnati on barge down the Ohio River to the Mississippi and on to New Orleans.

The main canal cargo, however, was bulky materials, grain and other freight. Coal from Terre Haute, lime and building stone from Huntington; pork, flour, wheat and wood products were especially important.

As for the passenger, it was first come, first served as far as the berths were concerned. Late arrivals had to sleep on the floor. When the floor was filled, there still remained the dinner tables which were also converted into beds when occasion required. Sometimes 75 or 80 or even 100 men were closely packed into a room designed for the accommodation of 42. Few found home conditions. The removing of coat and cravat and hat was the usual thing before climbing into the bunk. If unusually fastidious, the gentleman would also divest himself of his trousers and shoes, but passengers going to such extremes were commonly held to be fops or swells.

With the first indications of dawn, the passengers emerged from below deck and sought the open air. The men's washroom was so small as to be inadequate. Both members of the crew and some travelers would drop a bucket over the side of the boat and draw up water for the ablutions. The particular ones would also form a line to secure use of the massive comb and brush which were always chained to the wall of the washroom.

Despite the slowness and apparent monotony of canal travel, it had its pleasant aspects for those traveling for the first time through areas where the scenery was attractive and beautiful. There was the fact that canal travel was very safe.

The crew of a canal boat consisted of the captain, two steersmen, two drivers and the cook. The steersmen worked alternately during the 24 hours. The drivers worked in like manner with the steersmen. The cook worked all the time. The driver, who pushed along the mules or horses which were the locomotive power of canal boats, was the most humble member of the crew. His ambition was to be promoted to helmsman.

An Englishman named J. Robert Beste and his daughter Lucy traveled through Fort Wayne by canal on the Packet Indiana on their way from Terre Haute to Lake Erie. He left a description of the experience in a report published in London.

"After tea, we all began a most murderous attack on the mosquitoes that swarmed on the windows and inside our berths in expectation of feasting upon us. But those on whom we made war were soon replaced by others, and the more we killed, the more they seemed to come to be killed. At last we gave up the task as hopeless and resigned ourselves as well as we could to passing a sleepless night."

His daughter Lucy remarked: "The berths were in tiers three rows high. I was put in the top one. I lay awake but still for a long time. At last I heard everyone turning and sighing with the heat, so I gave way to my own feeling and did so too." Because of the shortness of the berths, the girl had to curl up "and be quite still while the mosquitoes devoured and the heat melted me."

Beste reported: "We passed through scores and scores of miles of woodland that had never heard the ax—passed thousands of acres where trees were rotting in the steaming pool collected about them. I never saw more magnificent timber than shaded the valleys. Great sticks of black oak shot up straight up from the bottoms without a knot or branch until their heads spread out some scores of feet above, like the tufted summits of the Italian pine. At times, partial clearings or little prairies offered vistas in the land beyond, and still the same noble timber everywhere arose."

Johnny Appleseed

All through this period, in fact starting long before the arrival of canal travelers, a man of rather odd appearance and strange but kindly habits had become a regular figure on the dusty streets of Fort Wayne. He is remembered as Johnny Appleseed.

An eyewitness view of Johnny was left by George W. Brackenridge, who came to Fort Wayne with his father in 1830. The elder Brackenridge, Captain Joseph Brackenridge, had been appointed by President Andrew Jackson as registrar of the land office at Fort Wayne.

"An eccentric man by name of John Chapman came to Fort Wayne in the early 1830's during the land sales. He was simply clad, in truth clad like a beggar. His refined features, seen through the grey stubble that covered his face, for he cut his hair and beard with scissors, yet he was not a Nazarene, told of his intelligence. He was serious; his speech clean, free from slang or profanity. He traveled on foot, went about seeking the small fractions of land that occurred in the surveys of public lands. These he purchased and later cleared patches, fenced them with brush, and planted appleseeds; which when grown to sufficient size were bought by the settlers. These fractions became valuable and were bought by owners of adjoining lands. This was not his sole business. He was a convert of the great spiritualist Emanual Swedenborg and a self-appointed missionary. He broke the volumes of a Swedenborg library and separated them into convenient sizes and loaned them to such as would take and read them. When he could find hearers, he would read them. Inspired by their spirit, his voice would rise to the heroic. He believed in communication with spirits, a first, second and third heaven and marriages in heaven. Like his great leader, his diet was bread and milk. He would not sleep in a bed, but on the floor or on the ground. He must have had money, but never exhibited any or looked as though he had any. For undershirts, he wore coffee sacks. He died near here at a farm house," Brackenridge reported.

Actually, Johnny Appleseed had been coming to the Fort Wayne area for some years earlier than 1830, likely by the early 1820's, but there is no record of his first visit. His wanderings in the local wilderness made him a friendly and familiar figure with the Indians and early pioneers.

He was probably born in Springfield, Mass., September 26, 1774. The first appearance of Chapman in the Territory of Ohio was in 1801. Arriving with a horseload of appleseeds, he planted future orchards along Licking Creek in Licking County. He probably continued in this vicinity for the next five years, although it cannot be definitely established as a fact. Western Pennsylvania was the source of supply for his stock of appleseeds. Chapman generally located his nurseries along streams. He planted the seeds and surrounded the sites with brush fences. With an eye to both utility and beauty, the plantings were always made in suitable well-drained soil, the settings were picturesque and well protected by nature. His earliest known nursery was planted about nine miles below Steubenville, Ohio.

No evidence exists that any youth ever jeered at him or that any adult ever took advantage of this lonely and completely defenseless man. He loved children, especially little girls, whom he delighted with precious gifts of ribbon and calico.

Johnny Appleseed's activities in northern Ohio continued during the War of 1812. At that time, most of the Indian tribes in the area were the allies of Great Britain. They terrorized the settlers, burned their homes and tortured luckless prisoners falling into their hands. Johnny, however, roamed freely and without hindrance throughout this large area. He was never harmed by the Indians. On the contrary, he was highly regarded as a great medicine man by the Indians.

He frequently warned American settlers of danger, enabling them to seek refuge in nearby forts and blockhouses. He helped settlers after the surrender of General Hull at Detroit at the outbreak of the war. On one occasion Johnny Appleseed volunteered to go barefoot, bareheaded and unarmed through miles of hostile wilderness to seek assistance for settlers at Mansfield, Ohio.

He was a peaceful man and he never carried a weapon either to kill game or protect himself against man or beast. Abuse of any animal was repugnant to him. He had a special love for horses. If he saw or heard of the ill-treatment of a horse, he offered to buy the animals or find a kinder owner elsewhere. Old, lame or broken-down horses on the frontier were usually abandoned. In the fall, Johnny rounded up such horses and provided food and shelter for them during the winter.

On one occasion while he was planting appleseeds, a rattlesnake struck him. He said later: "Poor fellow, he only just touched me, when I in the heat of my ungodly passion, put the heel of my scythe in him, went away. Sometime afterward, I went back and there lay the poor fellow dead."

Once while camping, he watched as mosquitoes flew into the blazing campfire and were consumed. He immediately dumped water on the flames. He said: "God forbid that I should build a fire for my comfort which should be the means of destroying any of His creatures."

On another occasion he noted that his campfire near a hollow log was disturbing a bear and her cubs, lodged inside. He removed the fire and slept in the snow. While working with a road-building crew one day, the men discovered and destroyed a hornet's nest. One of the hornets got inside Johnny's coffeesack cloak and stung him. The kindly man, though in pain, carefully removed and liberated the wasp. This surprised the fellow workmen, who had expected him to kill the insect. But, he replied, "It would not be right to kill the poor thing for it did not hurt me."

Johnny's Last Days

Chapman became somewhat enfeebled in his old age, but continued his roaming and outdoor ways, mostly in the areas of the St. Joseph and Maumee rivers north and east of Fort Wayne. One day, just before the end of winter, 1845, he learned that cattle had invaded his nursery in St. Joseph Township, 20 miles away. He set out on foot. The exertion proved too great. He was overcome by fatigue and exposure and sought lodging at the home of William Worth. Johnny sat at the cabin door and had a bowl of bread and milk. At nightfall, he entered the house and accepted a quilt and pillow on the floor, but refused the bed offered him. He asked the family to join him in worship and the reading of the Sermon on the Mount. He emphasized the Beatitude: "Blessed are the poor in Spirit for theirs is the Kingdom of Heaven."

In the morning he had a high fever and died that same day.

The obituary for John Chapman was printed March 22, 1845, in the Fort Wayne Sentinel. It said he died March 18, 1845, "at an advance age."

"The deceased was well known through this region by his eccentricity and the strange garb he usually wore," the obituary said. "He followed the occupation of a nursery man and has been a regular visitor here upwards of 20 years. He was a native of Pennsylvania, we understand, but his home, if home he had for some years past was in the neighborhood of Cleveland, Ohio, where he has relatives living. He is supposed to have considerable property yet he denied himself almost the common necessities of life, not so much perhaps for avarice as from his peculiar notions on religious subjects. He was a follower of Swedenborg and devoutly believed that the more he endured in this world the less he would have to suffer and the greater would be his happiness hereafter. He submitted to every privation with cheerfulness and content, believing in so doing he was securing snug quarters hereafter.

"In the most inclemate weather, he might be seen barefooted and almost naked except for when he chanced to pickup articles of old clothing. Notwithstanding the privations and exposure he endured, he lived to an extreme old age, not less than 80 years at the time of his death—though no person would have judged from his appearance that he was 60.

"He always carried with him some work on the doctrines of Swedenborg. He was perfectly familiar with his writings and would readily converse and argue on his tenents, using much shrewdness and penetration.

"His death was quite sudden. He was seen on our streets a day or two previously," the John Chapman obituary concluded.

The body of Johnny was taken from the Worth home in St. Joseph Township, Allen County, Indiana, on the old feeder canal. He was buried at the family burying ground of David Archer on a natural mound near the St. Joseph River, a few miles up river from the town of Fort Wayne. Samuel C. Fletter who attended his dying hours dressed his body, laid it out and made his coffin. These details of death and burial are confirmed by papers filed in Probate Court.

The estate papers of John Chapman still on file in the Allen County Courthouse reveal that at his death he owned two nurseries, one with 15,000 trees in Milan Township, Allen County, and one with 2,000 trees in Jay County, Indiana, as well as several small tracts of land in Allen County. The years following the financial panic of 1837 exacted a toll from Johnny's business. Trees were cheap and brought only two or three cents each. He found it difficult to pay his taxes and some of his real estate was sold for taxes after his death. Thereafter, litigation consumed much of the substance of his estate. It was an ironical ending to the story of Fort Wayne's resident saint, and a figure who has become part of the national folk lore.

1841 1841

WABASH AND ERIE

Transportation Company.

THE subscribers will commence running at the opening of navigation on the Wabash and Erie Caual, a DAILY LINE of boats for passengers and freight from Lafayette, Indiana, to a point in Ohio, 6 miles beyond the Indiana State line; making 146 miles.

The boats will meet *Neil, Moore & Co's.* Line of Stages at the termination of the canal in Ohio, which they will continue to run in their usual good style to the Lake.

Also an excellent line of Boats on the Maumee river will be regularly running from the same place to the Lake for the purpose of carring goods and passengers.

Steamboats and stages are running in all directions from Lafayette and stages running north and south from Logansport, which will afford every facility to travelers that can be required and far exceeding any previous arrangements.

Fare will be reduced so as to meet the expectations of a generous public.

SAM'L. MAHON
L. G. THOMPSON,
F. COMPARET.

N.B.—Stages will be put on between Lafayette and Fort Wayne in connection with the present line to the Lake, as soon as navigation closes in the fall; so that in future there will be no interruption to travelers through this region at any season of the year.

april 14, 1841 1tf

Stage coaches and canal boats were combined to furnish transport said this ad of April 14, 1841, in a Lafayette newspaper of the Wabash and Erie Transportation Company. Construction of the canal was begun at Fort Wayne in 1832.

Johnny Appleseed (Chapman) was to be seen regularly on the streets of Fort Wayne and over much of the Ohio and Indiana area. He visited farmers and Indians alike, planting appletrees and quoting the Bible, as shown in the Bill Hammon stetch above. He was a comical character and universally liked. In the 1871 Harper's Magazine drawing, right above, he is depicted in a dispute with a more conventional preacher. In his last days he depended on friendly pioneers for shelter, reading to them from his Bible, also shown in an old Harper's print.

Johnny Appleseed died in 1845 and was buried in the old Archer Graveyard near the St. Joseph River just north of Fort Wayne. The plot is shown here as it appeared before later improvements. In the photo below, taken May 20, 1949, Gov. Henry Schricker and others dedicate the grave of Johnny Appleseed.

JOHN W. M'ARTHUR,
CITY ENGINEER, COUNTY SURVEYOR,
COMMISSIONER
—OF—
DEEDS AND MORTGAGES.
OFFICE, in Court House.
FORT WAYNE, ALLEN CO., IND.

Engineering, Drafting, and all Instruments of Writing Promptly attended to.

The building of the canal and the trade it stimulated was the main industry of early Fort Wayne. Jesse Williams was the engineer who planned the Wabash-Erie Canal, the longest man-made waterway in the history of the world, extending from Lake Erie to Evansville on the Ohio. Construction of the canal was started at Fort Wayne in 1832 and stimulated a great land speculation.

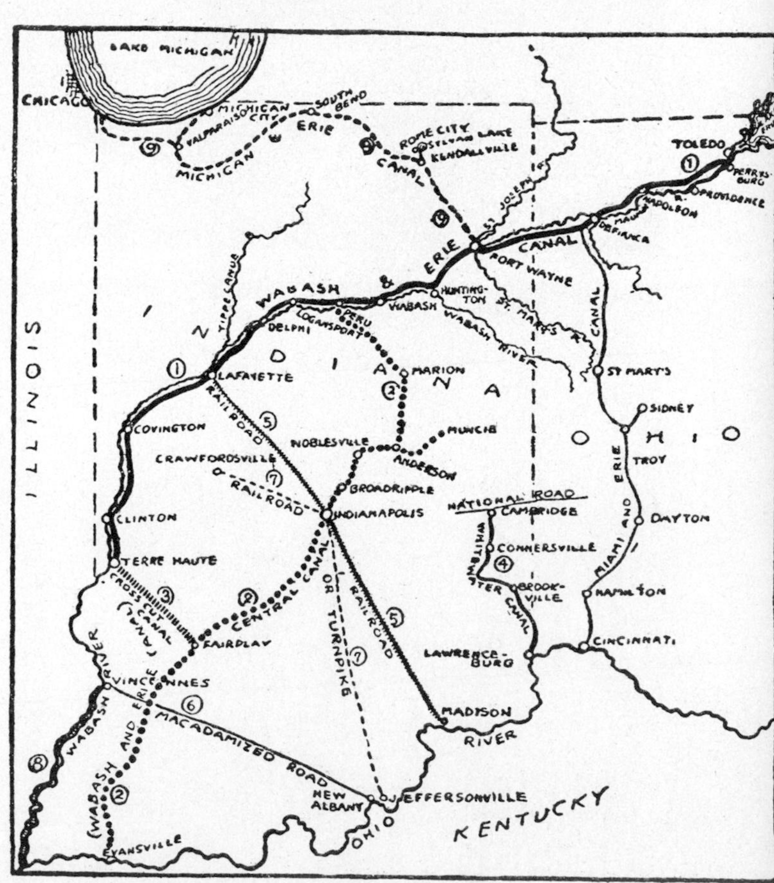

From "History of Fort Wayne" by B. J. Griswold

Indiana's Great Scheme of Internal Improvements

The canal boat of Capt. William H. Ward, standing at the stern, is shown in this old photograph at Fort Wayne. New Industries flourished and populations spread westward along the canal route. Tastes for fancy things came with the trade from the East. Raw materials went back in the opposite direction. Early industries in hides, grains, woolens and furniture, and soon banks, developed along the canal and nearby streets.

J. A. SHOAFF'S

ART GALLERY,

Nort-west corner Calhoun and Main streets, Times Building,

FORT WAYNE, IND.

PARTICULAR ATTENTION PAID TO CARTES DE VISITE

JOHN M. MILLER,

Manufacturer and Dealer in

FINE FURNITURE

Chairs, Husk and Hair Mattresses, Looking-Glass Plates, &c.

Nos. 50 & 52 E. Main Street,

FORT WAYNE, INDIANA.

FIRST NATIONAL BANK,

—OF—

FORT WAYNE, IND.

CALHOUN STREET, OPPOSITE AVELINE HOUSE.

CAPITAL, - - - - - $150,000.

J. D. NUTTMAN, President. W. B. FISHER, Cashier.

DIRECTORS:

J. D. Nuttman,	John Brown,	C. F. G. Meyer,
Samuel Hanna,	Fred. Nirdlinger,	John Orff,
J. M. Miller,	A. S. Evans,	A. D. Brandriff.

The canals began to decline with the coming of the railroads, but they continued in operation through much of the 19th century. The old picture above shows the canal aquaduct coming apart in 1882 under winter snows as the new railroad bridge stands trim and straight just beyond at the Main St. crossing of the St. Mary's River. Youngsters who once swam in the waters of the aquaduct later formed Old Aquaduct Club.

D. O'CONNELL,

PROPRIETOR O'CONNELL'S BILLIARD

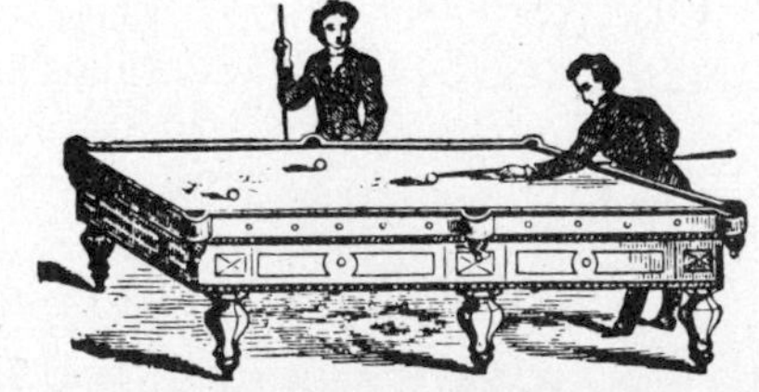

ROOM & RESTAURANT.

East side Calhoun St., bet. Mayer & Aveline Houses,

FORT WAYNE, IND.

A classic example of an early church is the Martini Lutheran Church on the Moeller Road, built in 1853. The Allen County Jail was built in 1850 and expanded in 1870 and was still in use more than 100 years later. In front of the Jail, shown below, were staged the hangings of criminals which drew onlookers from near and far.

The first train to come into Fort Wayne was pulled by "John Bull," an engine shown above. That was in 1854 over the tracks of the Pittsburgh, Fort Wayne & Chicago Railway. The Rockhill House, shown in an 1859 ad, figured to capitalize on rail traveler trade. Within 10 years it became the home of the St. Joseph Hospital.

ROCKHILL HOUSE,

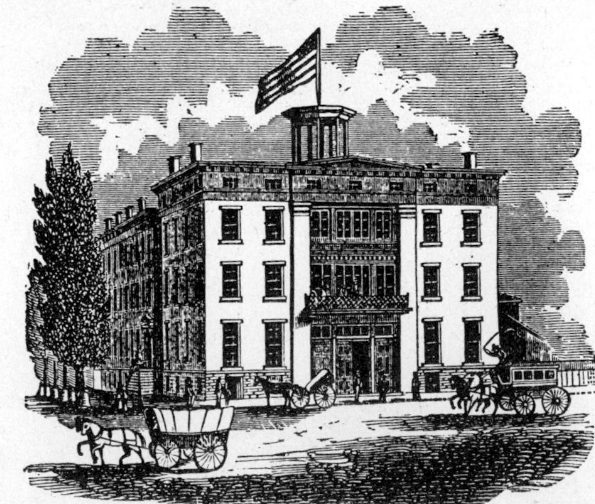

PHILO RUMSEY, Prop.,

Corner of Main and Broadway,

FORT WAYNE, IND.

PITTSBURGH, FT. WAYNE & CHICAGO

RAILWAY.

THE SHORTEST ROUTE FROM CHICAGO TO

NEW YORK, PHILADELPHIA, BALTIMORE, WASHINGTON, HARRISBURGH, & PITTSBURGH.

ALSO THE DIRECT ROUTE TO

BOSTON, ALBANY, BUFFALO, DUNKIRK, CLEVELAND, COLUMBUS, CINCINNATI, WHEELING, DAYTON, and all Cities and Towns between Chicago and the points above named.

FOUR DAILY PASSENGER TRAINS EACH WAY,
(Sundays excepted,) one Express Train leaving every night for the East.

SILVER PALACE CARS LEAVE CHICAGO DAILY FOR NEW YORK,
Without Change of Cars.

There is no Change of Cars between Chicago and Pittsburgh, and but one change between Chicago and Philadelphia, Baltimore, or New York, via Allentown.

☞ **CENTRAL TRANSPORTATION CO.'S SLEEPING CARS** are run on all Night Trains, and Baggage Checked through to all Eastern Cities, and handled free.

☞ To secure the shortest route, greatest comfort, and saving of time, ask for tickets "**VIA THE FT. WAYNE ROAD.**" For sale at all the principal Ticket Offices, and at the Company's Office at Depot.

OFFICERS:

G. W. Cass, President, Pittsburgh; J. N. McCullough, General Superintendent, Pittsburgh; J. P. Farley, Comptroller, Pittsburgh; J. D. Layng, Superintendent of Eastern Division, Pittsburgh; F. M. Hutchinson, Secretary, Pittsburgh; C. E. Gorham, Superintendent of Western Division, Fort Wayne; F. R. Meyers, General Ticket Agent, Pittsburgh; W. P. Shinn, General Freight Agent, Pittsburgh; J. P. Henderson, Treasurer, Pittsburgh; C. H. Miller, Stock Agent, Chicago; W. C. Cleland, General Western Passenger Agent, Chicago; J. P. Brady, Freight Agent, Chicago; J. C. Davis, Agent, Fort Wayne.

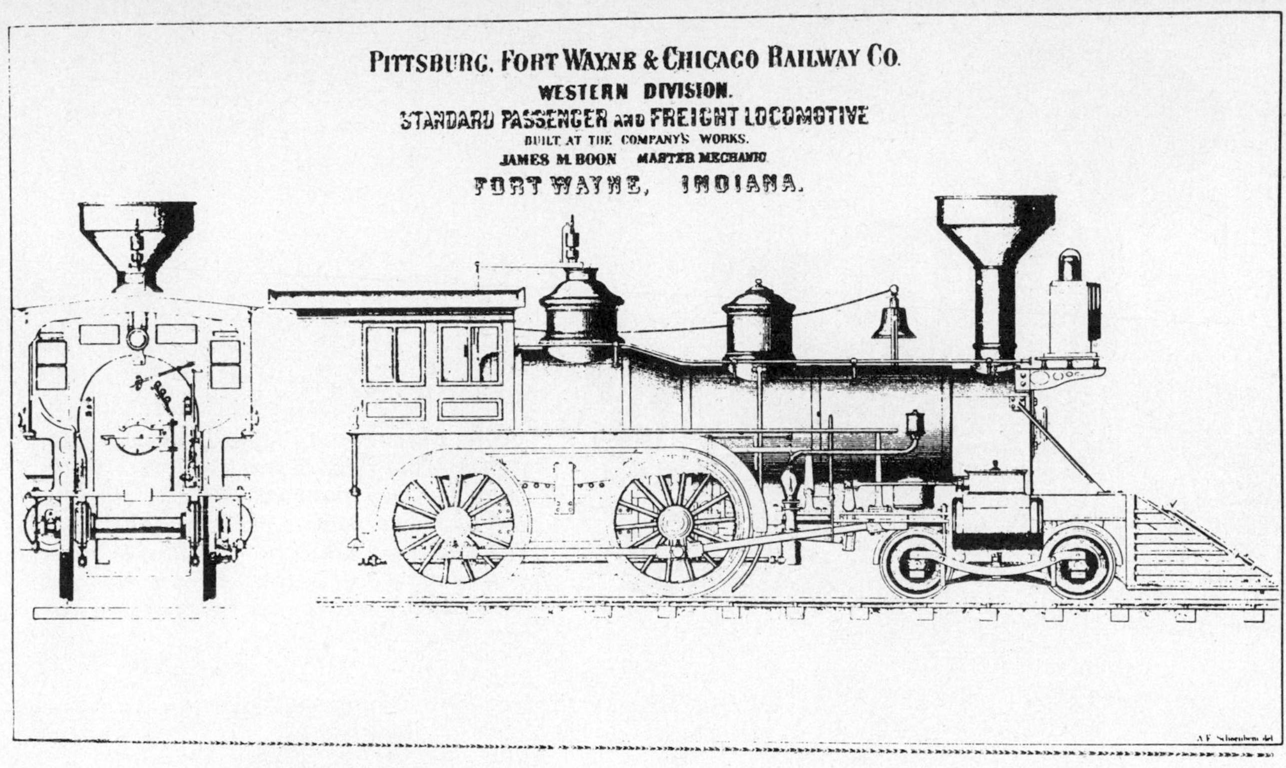

PITTSBURG, FORT WAYNE & CHICAGO RAILWAY CO.
WESTERN DIVISION.
STANDARD PASSENGER AND FREIGHT LOCOMOTIVE
BUILT AT THE COMPANY'S WORKS.
JAMES M. BOON MASTER MECHANIC
FORT WAYNE, INDIANA.

The railway shops soon became the city's largest industry. Engines of master design were manufactured and traveled across the land. Fancy rail cars became the pride of the community and the Bass Foundries became the largest manufacturer of rail wheels in the nation, stimulating new wealth and a rich class in town, which slept on hair mattresses.

HUSK AND MATTRESS FACTORY

JULIUS KEGELMANN,

Manufacturer of and Wholesale Dealer in all kinds of

HAIR and HUSK MATTRESSES

Factory, Corner E. Wayne and Walton Ave.,

FORT WAYNE, IND.

RANKERT & LUTZ,

Bloomingdale Brewery

Manufacturers of

SUPERIOR LAGER BEER,

FORT WAYNE, IND.

ANDREW FOSTER,

Merchant Tailor

21 Calhoun Street,

FORT WAYNE, - INDIANA.

J. M. FOELLINGER,

DEALER IN

FAMILY GROCERIES,

PROVISIONS,

Fresh and Canned Fruits,

OYSTERS,

CIGARS,

TOBACCO, &c.

No. 5 PHŒNIX BLOCK,

Calhoun Street,

FT. WAYNE, IND.

Abe Lincoln of Illinois came into town from Illinois on a Wabash train and stopped over at the old station, below. He took a Pittsburgh, Fort Wayne and Chicago midnight train going east to a Republican convention which led to his nomination for President in 1860.

FORT WAYNE MACHINE WORKS.

Bass & Hanna,

MANUFACTURERS OF

STEAM

ENGINES

From 3 to 100 Horse Power.

BOILERS,

Flued or Tubular, all Sizes.

Saw and Grist Mill Machinery of Every Description,

—AND—

MILL FURNISHING GOODS GENERALLY.

SOLE MANUFACTURERS OF

TICKLER'S PATENT CANE BRUSH SMUT MACHINES.

CAR WHEELS, CHILLED TIRES,

LOCOMOTIVE CYLINDERS,

AND ALL KINDS OF

RAILROAD & CAR CASTINGS BUILDING COLUMNS, GRATES, RAILINGS

&c., &c.,

MADE TO ORDER.

Engines, Boilers and General Machinery

Promptly Repaired.

☞ Competent Millwrights always on hand to furnish drafts and specifications, and superintend putting up our mills.

GEO. BIEMER,

Manufacturer of all kinds of

WAGONS,

Spring Wagons,

EXPRESS WAGONS,

Open Buggies, &c.

REPAIRING

Of all kinds.

Horse Shoeing,

—AND—

GENERAL JOBBING

Attended to.

COR. MAIN AND CLAY STREETS,

FORT WAYNE, IND.

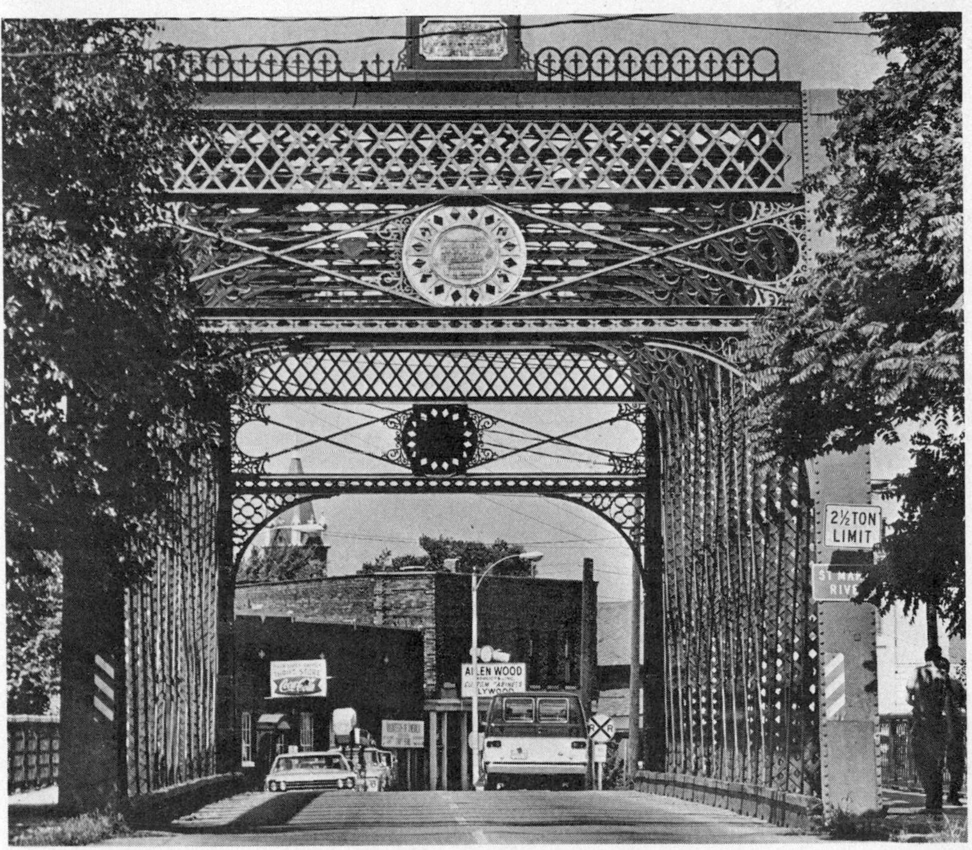

Hugh McCulloch, at left, was named by President Lincoln as Secretary of the Treasury. The mayor of Fort Wayne during the Civil War years was Franklin P. Randall, who is shown in the front yard of his fancy home on Berry St., above. The Wells St. Bridge was built in 1859 and was the first iron bridge over the city's rivers. It was also the last and was still standing in 1975.

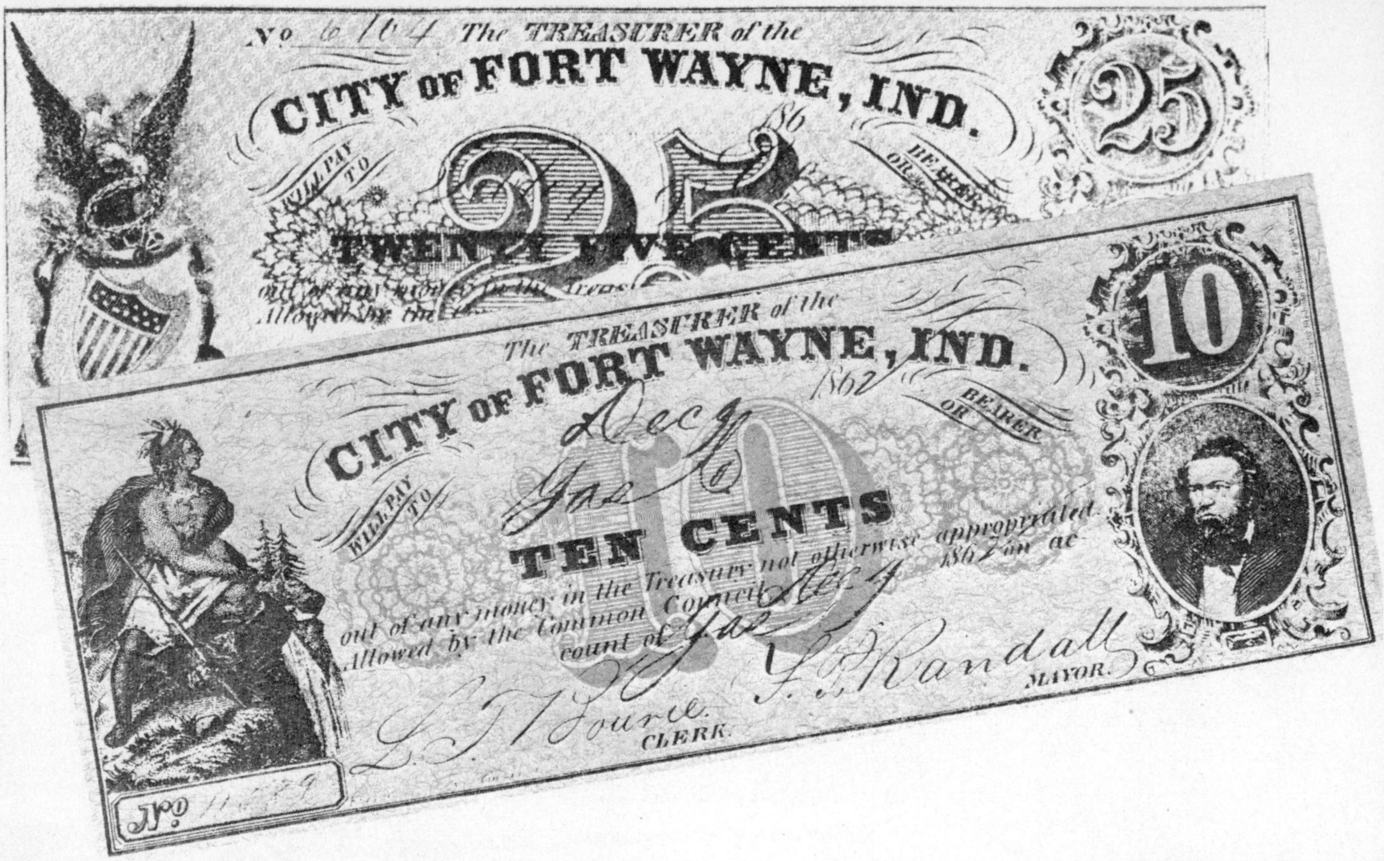

No 6164 The TREASURER of the
CITY OF FORT WAYNE, IND.
WILL PAY TO
OR BEARER
TWENTY FIVE CENTS
25
The TREASURER of the
CITY OF FORT WAYNE, IND.
1862
WILL PAY TO
OR BEARER
TEN CENTS
out of any money in the Treasury not otherwise appropriated
Allowed by the Common Council 1862 on ac
count of
MAYOR.
CLERK.
10
No

LAWTON

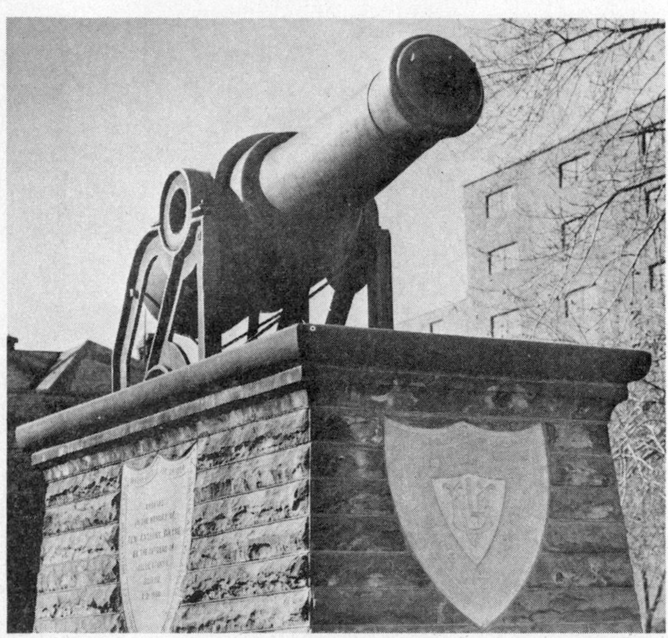

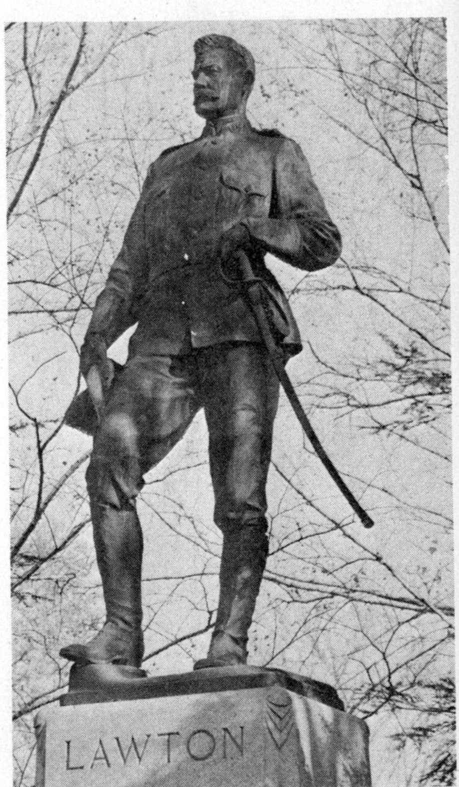

Fort Wayne had its own paper money during the Civil War—due to the metal shortage. Each bill had the picture of Mayor Randall. One of the town's war heros was Henry Lawton who later became a general in the Spanish-American War.

L. FORTRIEDE,
DEALER IN
BOOTS & SHOES,
Repairs Neatly Executed.
32 West Main St., FORT WAYNE, IND.

Mabel Robertson

Railroads expanded in every direction, going north and south as well as east and west such as the earlier lines. Also expanded was the great Bass Works with plants strung along the tracks which later became part of the Pennsylvania System.

THE BASS FOUNDRY AND MACHINE COMPANY'S PLANT, LARGEST CAR WHEEL MANUFACTURER IN THE WORLD

During the 19th Century, the railroad yards and depots were at grade level. This picture shows how the situation looked before there were elevations. At right is the Achduth Veshelom Synagogue which once stood at the southwest corner of Wayne and Harrison Streets.

Starting during the Civil War, the Centlivre Brewing plant grew up between the St. Joseph's River and the old Feeder Canal. The plant operated for a century at the Spy Run Ave. location. An old photo, taken in 1894, shows the beer makers and their new brick building. Identified in the front row, from left, are Heinie Kintz, Pete Mettler, Eddie Franke, Charles Centlivre, Louis Centlivre, Peter Nussbaum, Louis Eckerly and Judy Kieffer.

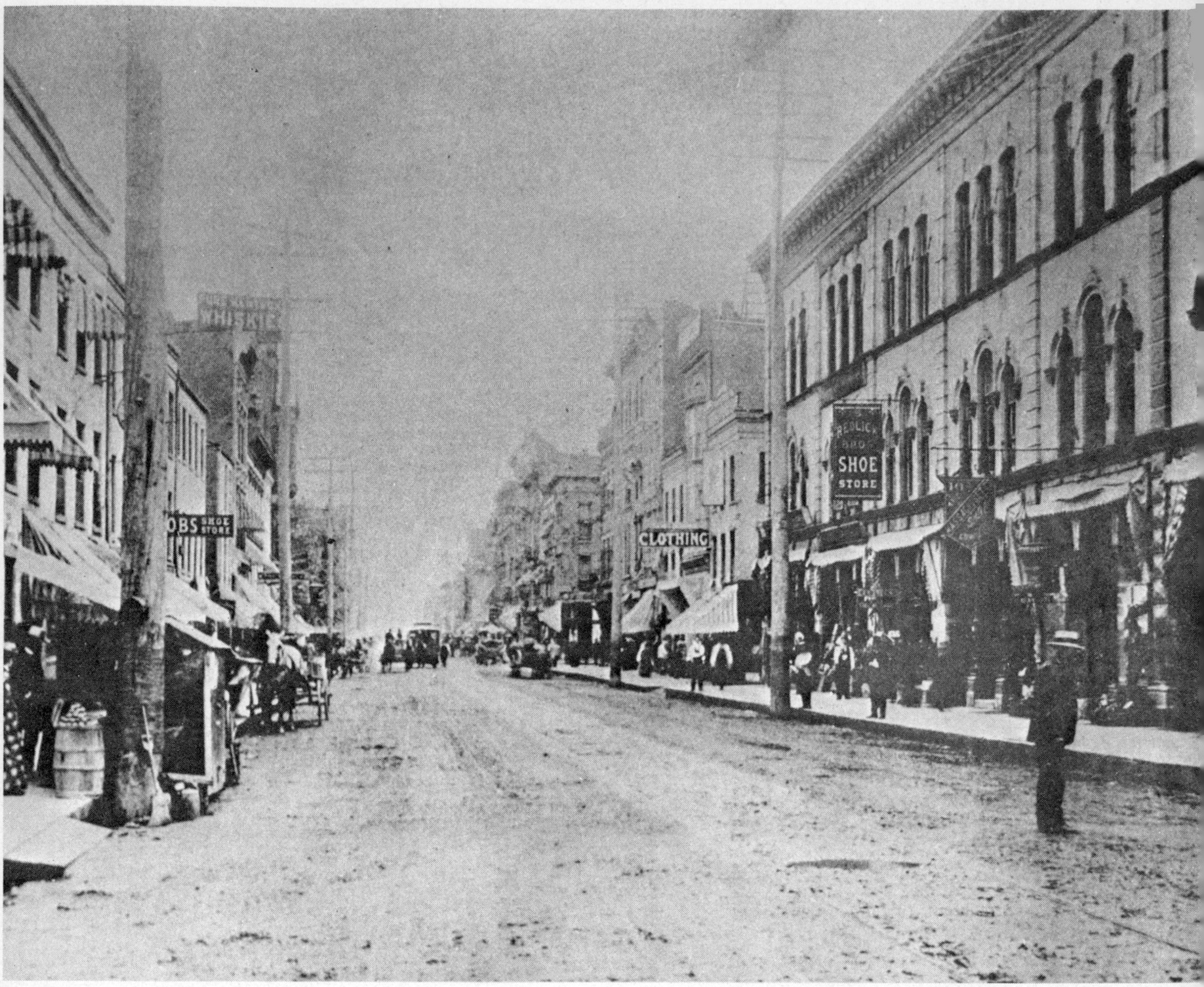

Calhoun St., looking south from Columbia St., was a sea of activity. In the distance is a horse-drawn street car. The street was a mass of mud on rainy days. On the opposite page, the engraving shows the Peter's Lumber Yard along the St. Mary's River with the downtown skyline in the background.

LOUIS PELTIER,

UNDERTAKER

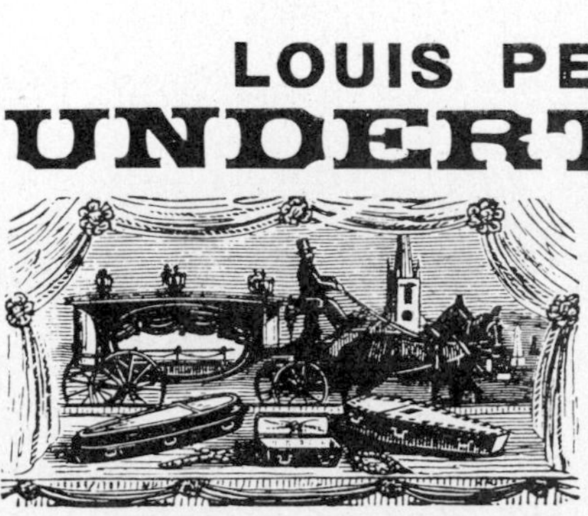

Manufacturer and Dealer in

Coffins, Caskets, Shrouds. Etc.

Hearses and Hacks at all hours, Night and Day, at

No. 17 West Wayne Street,

FORT WAYNE, INDIANA.

CHAS. PAPE, Pres't. WM. FLEMING, Vice-Pres't. WILSON McQUISTON, Sec'y.

THE PETERS BOX & LUMBER CO.

VENEER AND BAND SAWED

BLACK WALNUT, POPLAR AND ASH

LUMBER

Designers and Manufacturers of FURNITURE.

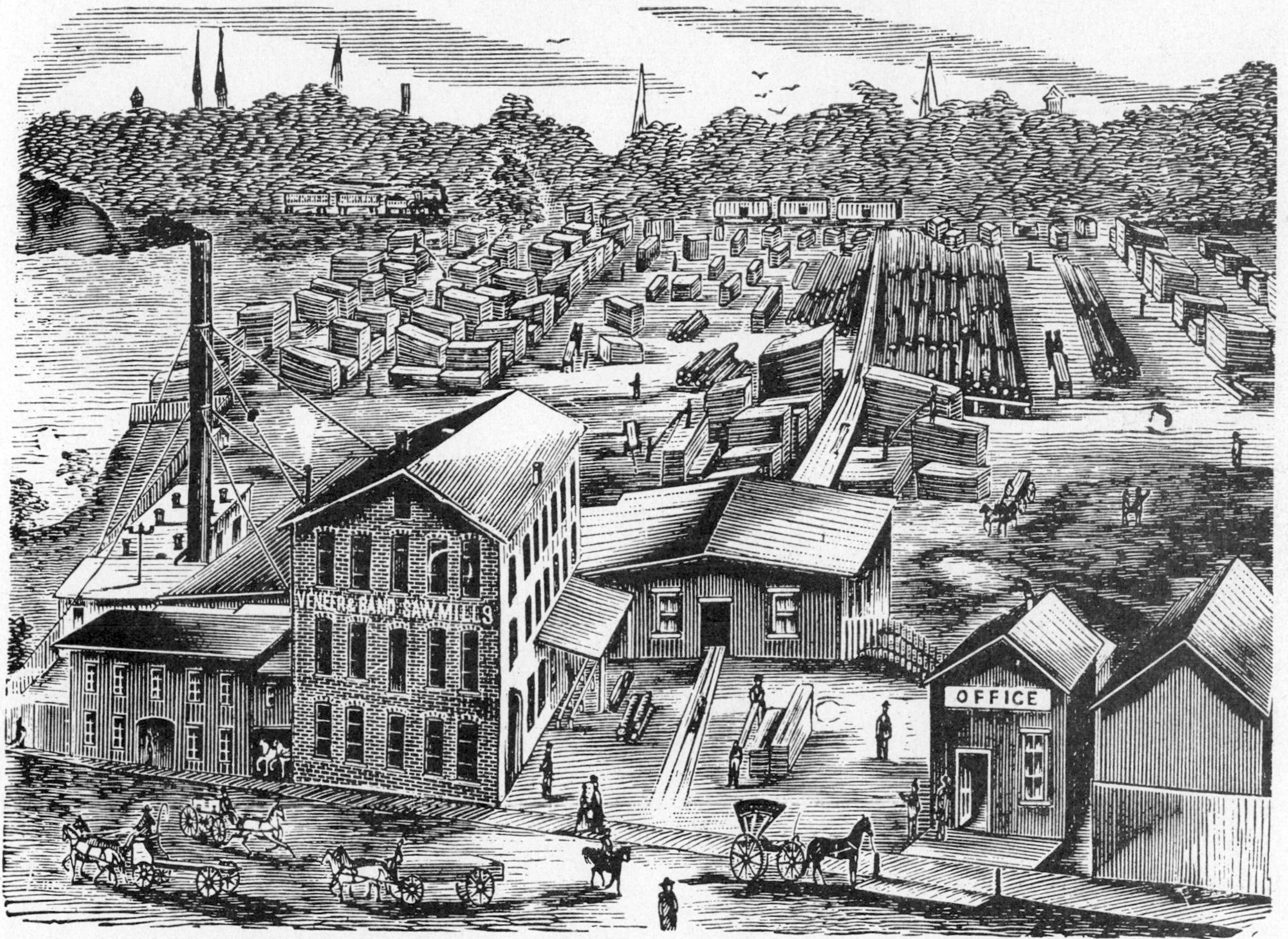

Office, Factory and Mills, 79 to 101 High St.

Furniture and Upholstery

WHOLESALE AND RETAIL.

19 & 21 WEST MAIN STREET,

FORT WAYNE, INDIANA.

The early ostentatious homes were alone East Berry St., above, and a few years later, along West Wayne St., shown at right west of Broadway.

John Bass built his mansion, with lake, buffalo and elk pasture, just northwest of town, later the St. Francis College campus. Hugh McCulloch's house was on Superior St. (then called Water St.)

Allen County Court House.

The Allen County Courthouse, built in 1860 and lasting for 33 years, had treed grounds with famous well, at right.

This scene of activity along the Wabash-Erie Canal at Fort Wayne is from a mural by Robert Grafton which was at one time on the walls of the old First National Bank. Horse teams pulled the canal boats at three miles an hour.

Part 4

Railroads and Black Derbies

In the hard frontier days, overnight travelers would find sleeping places in the old fort or the lofts of open-handed log cabin owners, or possibly at the two or three early taverns. But with the growth of travel in the canal era, more was required. So, along with the burgeoning of the mercantile houses, the hotel industry assumed a more important place in the community.

Practically all this activity and development was on the south side of the canal, for the very sound reason that on the north bank of the canal was the trail for the mules which dragged the canal boats. Near the concentration of docks on the south side of the canal were the commission houses, hotels, saloons and business shops. These were built up along Columbia Street, mostly from Harrison Street to Clinton Street and some extending over to Barr Street. A few others were to the west and south.

According to the notes of Winifred J. Randall, The Lillie Tavern, run by Samuel Lillie, was on Columbia Street just east of Calhoun. The Spencer House, started by John Spencer and operated by Amos Compton was nearby. The Dalman Hotel, later called the Kime Hotel, was built by John Trentman in 1836 at Wayne and Clay Streets. There were several more, but all these pre-canal hotels were really little more than taverns.

It was in the year of 1843, the year of the completion of the Wabash and Erie Canal, that Michael Hedekin built the Hedekin House. It was a stone's throw from the canal on Barr Street just south of Columbia on ground that had formerly been part of the Old Fort site. It was to have the longest life of any hotel in the history of the community. In its last days it was known as the Home Hotel and was finally torn down in the 1960's as part of the general downtown redevelopment project. The Hedekin House, which was little changed over the entire period, was in continual service for 120 years.

The Palo Alto, built in 1839 by Frank Rohle, opened as a tavern in 1840 and was operated for many years by George Maier. It had a fairly long life as a Fort Wayne landmark at the southeast corner of Calhoun and Wayne Sts. until it burned on April 26, 1885.

The Rockhill House, built by William

Rockhill at Main and Broadway in the forlorn hope the railroad would locate its depot in the vicinity, was Fort Wayne's finest early hotel. It stood unfinished for a number of years and wasn't opened until 1854. The 65-room edifice was a discouraging hotel enterprise, but finally in 1868 became the nucleus of the St. Joseph Hospital. As a hotel it had its finer moments. Stephen A. Douglas, the "Little Giant" who opposed Abraham Lincoln for the Presidency, was entertained at the Rockhill House during the campaign. A great parade which took two hours to pass a review stand was the largest social event in the town up to that time. Senator Douglas rode in the carriage of Frederick Nirdlinger, operator of a merchant house on Calhoun Street near Columbia. The Nirdlinger residence, on Main just west of Harrison Street, was the scene of meetings of early Jewish congregations and an important stop on the Underground Railroad. The underground railroad, which spirited Negro slave runaways from the South in the years prior to the Civil War, had its main route from the Ohio River, up through Richmond and on to Fort Wayne, and from Fort Wayne north to Michigan. The most-used crossing point into Canada was from Grosse Isle just south of Detroit and across the Detroit River to Amherstburg, Ontario.

In the years following the opening of the canal, the Fort Wayne area in and about Columbia St. became a sea of horsemen, wagon teamsters, farmers driving herds of hogs, old French backwoods traders with their packs of hides and hosts of travelers, men of the ministry, and sharps and cutthroats, not necessarily in that order. The scene was one of mud-rutted streets and wooden plank walkways. Columbia St. itself took its name, not from Christopher Columbus or national derivative thereof, but from Dana Columbia, who founded a hotel there. It was made of hewn logs and had 20 rooms for boat travelers.

Large commission houses were established by Royal W. Taylor, Joseph J. and David F. Comparet, Samuel and William Edsall, Peter P. Bailey, Jesse L. Williams, and William George and George W. Ewing. A. M. Orbison was warehouseman for Ustial's merchant organization.

The Plank Roads

Hillsdale, Michigan, in those days offered an alternate route for goods and produce going to Lake Erie. To combat this competition, the merchant princes of Fort Wayne contrived to build a plank road to the northern environs. The destination was to be a place called Lima in Steuben County—thus we still hear today of the Lima Road going north from Fort Wayne rather than towards Lima, Ohio, which might appear the more logical direction for such a route in the light of later developments.

Hanna, Hamilton and Ewing each paid about $4,000 in land for the plank road route. Orbison, who had subscribed the only cash, furnished the engineers with money. In 18 months the road was completed to Kendallville and in another year it was extended to Union Mills and Ontario. As soon as Fort Wayne saw the value of this road, other roads were promoted. One road to Bluffton in Wells County was soon constructed. Another to St. Mary's, Ohio, through Decatur was completed in a short time. Another to Columbia City was built.

The population grew from 300 in 1830 to 2,080 in 1840.

The assessed value of property within the limits of Fort Wayne in 1842 was $424,000. Eight years later, the population was 4,285 and the assessed value of property was $892,000.

City Founded

In the meantime, the town became an incorporated city. Franklin P. Randall was asked to prepare a city charter which was approved by the State Legislature on Washington's Birthday, 1840. The charter provided for the election of a president or mayor and a board of six aldermen or City Council which would select other city officeholders and employees. The first mayor of Fort Wayne was George W. Wood, elected March 1, 1840. The board of aldermen was composed of Thomas Hamilton, William Rockhill, William S. Edsall, William L. Moon,

Samuel Edsall and Madison Sweetser. The council named Randall as clerk; George F. Wright as treasurer; Samuel S. Morss as high constable and collector of taxes; John B. Cocanour as lumber measurer; Lucien Ferry as attorney; Robert E. Fleming as assessor and Joseph H. McMaken as street commissioner.

Mayor Wood was reelected in 1841 but retired later that year and was succeeded by Joseph Morgan, chosen in a special election.

Samuel Hanna and James Barnett erected in 1827 the first gristmill near Fort Wayne. This was an important pioneer enterprise as the nearest mills were in Ohio. The mill was located on the banks of the St. Mary's River directly south of the Broadway bridge. The mill was sold several times and in 1888 it was destroyed by fire.

Other enterprises established in this period were the tannery in 1828 by Absalom Halcomb and Isaac Marquis, at the west end of Columbia Street where the Randall Hotel later stood; the cooper shop of Madore Truckey; and the blacksmith shop of Holloway Cushman, on the south side of Berry Street, east of Calhoun Street. All of these establishments furnished employment to a number of residents.

An important manufacturing enterprise which had its beginning in 1830 was the overshot gristmill of Henry Rudisill and Henry Johns, on the St. Joseph River below the site of the State Street bridge, which was then referred to as "one mile north of the town." For many years this establishment, known in later times as the Rudisill mill, served a large territory. The ruins stood until about the year 1910.

In 1834, Jacob Fry, of Pennsylvania, on reaching Fort Wayne, established a tannery and conducted the business in partnership with Henry, David and Robert Work. In this same year a marble works was also established on a site near the canal route at the corner of Fulton and Main Streets. A year later the Summit City Woolen Mills was opened by G. W. Ewing and Louis Wolke and the first sawmill was established by Benjamin Archer. The first planing mill was built in 1836 by John Cochrane.

In the village of Fort Wayne in 1838, all lines of enterprise took on new life, and mills, factories and workshops of many descriptions were established. One of the most important industries in these days were the yards of the canal boat builders, which gave employment to many. The first wagon shop and the first plow factory and steam sawmill were founded in 1838 by the Baker brothers. The following year, Jacob C. Bowser and James Story established the Bowser and Story Foundry and Machine Shop at the southeast corner of Main and Clinton Streets.

William Robinson built a sash factory on Duck Street, operated by water power from the canal in 1841. New industries established during the year 1842 included the sawmills of William Rockhill and Samuel Edsall, on the north side of the canal; and the flouring mill, later known as the City Mills of C. Tresselt and Sons, on the canal at Clinton Street, by Allen Hamilton and Jesse L. Williams.

Early Churchmen

The City of Churches, as Fort Wayne was to be termed at later times, was not especially a Godly place in the eyes of some early visitors. The records indicate the revulsion at the goings on in "Frenchtown" in the days of the garrison and the rather uncivilized behavior in the decade immediately following. But churches did quickly become important in the early 19th Century. And these followed earlier work going back to the French missionary priests such as Father Jean de Bonnecamps in 1749 of the old fur post period; the sermons of Anthony Wayne's soldier-chaplain David Jones; the Quaker workers invited by Chief Little Turtle and the Baptist missionary Isaac McCoy, who started a frontier school for Indian and settlers' children.

Many of the early members of the churches were rather casual about denominational considerations. Mrs. Ann Turner and Mrs. Rebecca Hackley, granddaughters of Little Turtle and daughters of Captain William Wells, are examples. They were baptized in the Maumee River by the Baptist Missionary Isaac McCoy; educated in a Catholic seminary at Bardstown, Kentucky; and then joined as charter members of the First Presbyterian Church when it was formed in 1831.

Among the early missionaries was Rev. John Ross, a Presbyterian from Ohio who arrived in December, 1822. The Presbyterian General Assembly had sent Ross on a three-month mission as an itinerant evangelist. His getting here was a story in itself. Rev. Ross and a trader named Matthew Griggs traveled in a light two-horse wagon. The first night out they were surrounded by howling wolves. Later, intense cold and a raging snow storm forced them to leave their wagon and lead the horses through a blizzard. They stumbled half-frozen into Fort Wayne and awakened Samuel Hanna in the middle of the night for shelter and food.

Father Ross, as the Catholics conveniently dubbed the Presbyterian minister, conducted services and preached in the old fort. He visited at Fort Wayne five times in the succeeding four years, but apparently despaired of developing wide devotion. "There was no place that appeared to me as unpromising as Fort Wayne. There was no Sabbath kept but on the part of a few."

In 1824, the Rev. James Holman, a Methodist minister, came with his family and built a farm home near the St. Mary's River. The people gathered at his home for services. Some years later, in 1830, the Rev. Alexander Wiley established the first Methodist mission in Fort Wayne.

The push toward the founding of a regular Presbyterian congregation started with the arrival in 1825 of James Hanna, father of Sam Hanna, who came from Dayton where he was a church elder. He organized a Sunday School in his son's storehouse, and the class formed the nucleus of a church later established. Allen Hamilton, the postmaster, asked the Home Missionary Society of the Presbyterian Church in Baltimore, to furnish a regular minister. The society sent the Rev. Charles E. Furman in November, 1829. He stayed for six months, didn't form a church, but recommended that move. The Rev. James Chute came to Fort Wayne in June, 1831, from Columbus, Ohio, and on July 1 formed the first permanent church in Fort Wayne. Forty-four persons signed the fellowship list, enabling Chute to remain as minister.

The Presbyterians held services near the corner of Columbia and Harrison Streets in a board shelter, and then moved to a brick schoolhouse on the site where the county jail was later built. Next, services were in the Masonic Hall on the north side of Columbia between Calhoun and Harrison Streets, and in the first courthouse. With the death of Mr. Chute, the Rev. Daniel Jones ministered to the congregation until 1837.

The first Presbyterian Church was built in 1837 at 334 East Berry Street. The pastor, the Rev. Alexander T. Rankin, served from 1837 to 1843 in the 40-foot frame building. The Rev. Jesse Hoover, a Lutheran minister from Woodstock, Canada, came in 1837 as the first teacher in the new Presbyterian school.

Rev. Hoover organized the first Lutheran Church in Fort Wayne. Adam Wefel and Henry Trier were elders and Henry Rudisill and Conrad Nill were deacons. In 1839, the Lutheran congregation began construction of a church on the site of St. Paul's Lutheran Church. Among the teachers in the Lutheran school were Miss Mann, later Mrs. Hugh McCulloch; and Miss Hubbell, later Mrs. Royal Taylor.

For a number of years the Presbyterian, Methodist and Baptist churchgoers worshiped together. The Allen Circuit Court also moved into the church for awhile. The reason was later related by Bert Griswold from various early accounts:

"Since the Courthouse had become unsafe due to faulty construction, the authorities secured the privilege of holding court in the Presbyterian Church until suitable buildings could be built on the square. One day, when court was in session and a large crowd was present, a rumor gained currency that the steeple of the church was not securely supported and would come crashing down on all below. At this session there came a crash and a roar, and the people rushed to the doors and windows to escape the ruins. One man clasped the Bible in his arms and crawled under a bench. Discovering the steeple was still in place, the crowd came back to find the long stove pipe, which stretched from front to back, had fallen."

A falling out of sorts occurred in 1844 when the Presbyterian pulpit became vacant. It introduced into Fort Wayne history a nationally-renowned figure of the pre-Civil War days, the famed abolishionist Henry Ward Beecher.

Beecher, then in his young years, was persuaded by one faction into coming to Fort Wayne to win the allegiance of the First Church members. But the church officers, anticipating the strategy, persuaded Dr. William C. Anderson, an English professor at Hanover College, to move more quickly and fill the pulpit. He arrived April 14, 1844, and took charge. The following Saturday, Beecher arrived from Indianapolis on horseback.

Learning of the situation, Beecher announced to Mrs. Jesse Williams: "I have come to divide your church." He began a series of sermons in the Courthouse, but failing to gain control of the main church group, split off part of the congregation and formed the Second Presbyterian Church of Fort Wayne. It later became known as the Westminister Church. Beecher's sister was Harriet Beecher Stowe, author of "Uncle Tom's Cabin."

Later that same year, First Church decided to build a larger building at a new site. Samuel Bigger, who had just completed a term as governor of Indiana, headed the committee. A lot at the southwest corner of Clinton and Berry Streets was purchased, but traded the following year for a site at the southeast corner of the same intersection. A colonial structure 80 feet long was erected at the direction of a building committee headed by Sam Hanna. The pastor, Rev. H. S. Dickson, laid the cornerstone in October, 185, and the church was finally dedicated in November, 1852.

This church was later enlarged and refined with a $3,500 organ, about half the cost of the original building. It lasted until Dec. 16, 1882, when destroyed by fire. A reporter for the Fort Wayne Sentinel gave vent to some imaginative description:

"The flames entrapped the sacred structure in a weird mantle of flame, shooting athwart the black sky and illuminating the streets roundabout, which were crowded with spectators. Even the famed pyrotechnic displays at the Crystal Palace in London could not approach this carnival of the fire fiend in Fort Wayne. The vast crowd breathlessly awaited the falling of the lofty belfry, which became a red skeleton of framework. The bell tower leaned in the direction of Berry Street and finally fell with a booming crash."

The Cathedral

The establishment of the first Catholic Church in Fort Wayne grew out of the efforts of Rev. Stephen Theodore Badin. This is the same Father Badin who established an orphan's home for Indian children in 1833 at the present site of the University of Notre Dame at South Bend. Father Badin first came to Fort Wayne in 1830 and celebrated Mass and preached at the home of Francis Comparet. In 1831 he assisted in choosing and purchasing a site for a church. Preliminary arrangements in the buying of most of the present Cathedral Square were made on July 18, 1831. The property was deeded by Samuel and Eliza Hanna. In 1837, the first resident pastor, Rev. Louis Mueller built the first church at Cathedral Square. The log building measured 65 by 35 feet.

Father Julian Benoit, a native of France, became pastor at St. Augustine's Church in Fort Wayne in 1840. He also served mission stations at Lagro, Huntington, Columbia City, Warsaw, Goshen, Avilla, New Haven, Besancon, Hesse Cassel and Decatur. By 1846 he had erected a grade school, and Sisters of Providence from Vigo County came as teachers. Later he opened a boy's school at Jefferson and Clinton Sts., and the Brothers of Holy Cross came to assume charge. He also secured a graveyard just west of town, a site later occupied by Essex Wire Company. Some earlier graves were in Cathedral Square. When the Indians were finally ordered out by the Federal government in 1848, Father Benoit went with them on the canal trip to Cincinnati and by riverboat to St. Louis. He reached the Kansas reservation area by stagecoach where he remained for a couple of weeks before returning to Fort Wayne.

St. Mary's Church was organized when a number of German speaking families decided to split off from St. Augustine's. On Nov. 29, 1848, the partially-completed church was occupied, with the Rev. Edward M. Faller named pastor. The following year a school was started near the church at Jefferson and Lafayette Streets.

On September 22, 1857, Fort Wayne became the seat of the Catholic bishop. The diocese included the large share of Indiana north of the Vincennes Diocese, which previous to that date included the entire state. John Henry Luers was appointed first Bishop of Fort Wayne.

The building of the Fort Wayne Cathedral was begun in 1859 at the direction of Father Benoit who was also the architect. It was the same structure which exists today, though the brick exterior was faced with stone in the late 1940's. Thomas Lau was the contractor for the Gothic structure measuring 180 feet by 80 feet. Bishop Luers and Father Benoit dedicated the church in December, 1860. The cost of the project was $54,000. Father Benoit served as pastor for 44 years. He died on January 26, 1885.

The Lutherans

When the Rev. Jesse Hoover organized the first Lutheran church, it was called the First Evangelical Lutheran Church in Indiana. There were 65 names recorded as communicants. With Hoover's death in May, 1838, Henry Rudisill continued to watch over the church's affairs until the arrival some months later of a new pastor. He was Rev. Frederick Conrad Dietrich Wyneken, who had been delegated by the Pennsylvania Synod to look to the needs of German Protestants in all of Indiana. The following year the first church, 40 by 24 feet, was erected on the corner of Barr and Madison Streets.

Pastor Wyneken expressed some of the same negative views on moral conditions in Fort Wayne as mentioned by other early churchmen. "Horror and dismay fills me even now, while writing these lines, when I remember the shamelessness wherewith vice, not hidden in the darkness of night, but in the broadest daylight, struts about in the streets and how I found the grossest indecency and the most disgusting dens of vice conducted by Germans."

At Rev. Wyneken's recommendation, Dr. William Sihler came to Fort Wayne in 1845. It was at his house in Fort Wayne that the Missouri Synod of the Lutheran Church was initiated. Sixteen pastors traveled to Fort Wayne for a meeting in July, 1846. This led to an organizational meeting in Chicago in April, 1847.

In the meantime, part of the congregation wishing services in English held an organizational meeting in March, 1846. This led to the formation of the Trinity English Lutheran Church. At that same time, the original church adopted the name of St. Paul's Evangelical Lutheran Church.

Pastor Sihler was joined in 1875 by Pastor Henry Sauer, who later succeeded as head of the congregation. It was during Pastor Sauer's service that St. Paul's Church was built. The cruciform gothic church was built at a cost of $70,000 and dedicated in September, 1889. The church was destroyed by fire Dec. 2, 1903, and rebuilt by April, 1905.

The Achduth Veshalom Congregation of B'nai Israel was formed in 1848, Rabbi Joseph Solomon was chosen pastor. In the early years the Congregation met at the Nirdlinger house on West Main Street.

The first Episcopal Church was formed on May 26, 1839, by 17 charter members who met in the courthouse. The First Trinity Episcopal Church in 1847 was at the northeast corner of Berry and Harrison Streets. The present church at Berry and Fulton Streets was built in 1865.

The existence of the Methodist Church in Fort Wayne actually began in 1837 when Dr. Alfred S. John arrived on Jan. 10 with a wagon load of saddles and bridles to sell to the Indians. He held services and school in his home or a small brick building which was on Calhoun Street.

It was in 1840 that the first Methodist Church was built. It was at the corner of Harrison and Berry Streets where the Anthony Hotel was later built. It was called the

Berry Street Chapel until 1851, and there after, the Berry Street Methodist Episcopal Church. In 1900 the property at Wayne and Lafayette Streets was purchased and First Methodist Church was dedicated in May, 1903.

St. John's Reformed Church was organized in 1844. A building was up the following year at the corner of Washington Blvd. and Webster Street, a location which served thereafter. The permanent church building was completed in 1871. A two-story school building was erected in 1874 and the parish hall and expansion of the educational unit was in 1904. In 1884, the St. John's Reform congregation was instrumental in the founding of the Fort Wayne Children's Home. It was headed by the Rev. and Mrs. John Rettig.

In the years 1846 and 1847 two church-related colleges were founded in Fort Wayne. They were the community's first institutions of higher learning. One would have a rather short place in Fort Wayne history. The other would become a permanent fixture in the community.

Early Colleges

At a session of the Northern Indiana Methodist Episcopal Conference in 1846, plans were laid for the establishing of Fort Wayne Female College. Samuel Bigger, a former governor of Indiana who had been elected in 1840, presided at the meeting. Bigger, incidently died and was buried at Fort Wayne later in that year of 1846. His grave is still at McCulloch Park (G.E.) since his remains were not removed. Other bodies in that one-time cemetery were disinterred and taken to Lindenwood Cemetery, founded in 1860.

William Rockhill donated the land for Methodist College. The site was at the end of West Wayne Street which in those days butted into College Street as the avenue in front of Fort Wayne College became known. The cornerstone was laid on June 19, 1847, and Dr. Alexander C. Huestis was named first president. For several years, the institution only admitted young ladies, but in 1852 a separate school called the Fort Wayne Collegiate Institute was founded for young men. Soon the two schools were united as Fort Wayne College, but most people continued to call it Methodist College. By 1854 the institution enrolled 256 students. Some years later the college came upon hard financial times and moved to Upland, Indiana, where it became known as Taylor University.

Concordia College in Fort Wayne was developed almost simultaneously. The institution grew out of a trip in 1841 by Pastor Wyneken to Germany. Wyneken interested Dr. William Loehe to move a theological seminary for future Lutheran pastors to America and to locate at Fort Wayne. The transplant from Germany was made in 1847 with the move of 11 students to a four-room house near the parsonage.

In 1848, 15 acres of ground and a brick house on Maumee Ave. near Anthony Blvd. were purchased for the development of the new college. It was to remain the home of Concordia College for more than a century. Dr. William Sihler and Pastor August Craemer worked to enlarge the campus and in 1857 a second synodal school was formed—a normal school for the instructing of young men to be teachers in the Lutheran elementary schools. In 1861, the Concordia Seminary part of the operation was transferred to St. Louis and Concordia College of Perry County, Missouri, was brought to Fort Wayne. In 1865 the normal school was moved to Addison, Ill., and then permanently established at River Forest, Illinois.

Concordia Cemetery was founded during this period across Anthony Blvd. from the campus in 1850. The original graveyard consisted of four and a half acres, but additions were made several times to the acreage in subsequent years.

The Printed Word

Fort Wayne's first newspaper, The Sentinel, began publishing in 1833. The founders were Thomas Tigar and S. V. B. Noel, both of whom moved to the Summit City from

Indianapolis. Tigar, the pioneer editor, was a native of Yorkshire, England. He and Noel were both printers. Noel only stayed for a year, but Tigar stayed with the paper until 1865, except for a four-year span when George W. Wood directed the newspaper affairs. Originally a weekly, the newspaper became the Daily Sentinel in January, 1861. The Sentinel during Tigar's editorship was strongly Democratic, and possibly as a result, Fort Wayne was the main stronghold of Democratic politics in Indiana for many decades.

The Fort Wayne Times, a Whig paper, was established in 1841 by George Wood, then a former mayor. This paper passed into the hands of John W. Dawson in 1854. Dawson was an aggressive newsman who mixed super patriotism and religious zealotry with conservatism on slavery and vitriol regarding other newspaper editors. Tigar, of The Sentinel, showed his dislike for Dawson with the printed observation: "A more corrupt, unprincipled and contemptible object never disgraced the editorial fraternity, and no paper has ever sunk so low and rapidly in public estimation as The Times has since he assumed its direction."

Dawson, the Populist, had the motto "Americans shall rule America." For reasons unexplained, President Lincoln appointed Dawson governor of the Utah Territory in 1861. However, he had a falling out with the Mormons on a moral issue and insult-avenging stagecoach hands are reported as "whipping his excellency at a way station." Governor Dawson fled the territory and returned to Fort Wayne. From then on he expressed dislike for Lincoln and backed Gen. George McClellan, the loser, in the 1864 election. Dawson implied in articles that Lincoln hated the South and was really a traitor to the Constitution of the United States.

Another early newspaper was a German-language weekly named Der Deutsche Beobachter von Indiana, started in 1843. Later German-language newspapers included Der Fort Wayne Democrat and the Freie-Presse Staats-Zeitung, the latter and longest-lasting being published by Herman Mackwitz until 1927.

The "Free" Schools

Public schools were somewhat slower in being started in Fort Wayne than the church-related institutions. Initially, state legislation was needed to provide the financial framework, and for a number of decades they were known as the "free schools." It might also be interesting to Constitutionalists to learn that the very early frontier schools operated by missionaries were partially financed by the federal government, but the public or free schools received no such federal funds and were entirely supported by local tax money.

In 1853, the Fort Wayne City Council chose Hugh McCulloch, Charles Case and William Stewart as a board of trustees to undertake the starting of public schools in the city. The community by that year had some 4,000 residents including 1,233 children of school age, but largely unschooled.

The first step was the renting of the old McJunkin building on the east side of Lafayette Street between Main and Berry Streets. Isaac Mahurin was named principal and M. L. Mahurin was engaged as assistant. The other first public teachers were Mr. and Mrs. A. M. Hulburd who taught in their home at the southwest corner of Wayne and Ewing Streets.

The following year a tax of two mills per $100 assessed valuation was imposed as a school tax. The trustees of that year, James Humphrey, Henry Sharp and Charles French were bent on the construction of regular school buildings. Two were started in 1855 and completed for occupation in 1857. The first public school to open in Fort Wayne was the Clay School at the northeast corner of Washington Blvd. and Clay Street. The date was Feb. 9, 1857. The school was to eventually burn in 1894 and a rebuilt school was destroyed by a great fire in 1930. The second public school, the Jefferson School, opened in September, 1857, at the southwest corner of Jefferson and Griffith Streets. Griffith Street was later renamed Fairfield Avenue. The Rev. George A. Irvin was appointed first Fort Wayne school superintendent. He was described as "a liberal user of the switch as well as of chewing tobacco."

The first public Fort Wayne High School was built in 1867 on Wayne between Calhoun and Clinton Streets, midblock on the north side. It later became known as Old High School in deference to the new Fort Wayne High, which eventually was known as Central High School. Old Fort Wayne High Building served as the school administration office in its later years until razed in 1922 after a fire destroyed most of the building. A few years later one of the city's great movie palaces, the Paramount Theatre, was erected at the site.

First and Finest

In the meantime, several other social changes had occurred in the city and resulted in the establishing of a number of Fort Wayne firsts. The first on-the-beat-type policemen came into existence in 1834 with the founding of "the night watch." The town trustees in June of that year passed an ordinance that "there shall be a watch established to consist of at least four judicious men to be continued as long as may be considered necessary to guard the town from the ravages of fire and to prevent disorderly conduct within the corporation, one half to be posted at 10 p.m. and to stand until 1 a.m. and to be relieved by the marshall or some other persons authorized by the trustees, and the other half, or the remaining two, to stand from thence to 4 o'clock a.m. and be discharged accordingly." These volunteers were closer to vigilantees than regular policemen. Conditions had evidently become so bad with the presence of bawdy houses, saloons and fights and thievery that the nightwatch was given power to stop all persons found on the streets after 10 p.m., and in the absence of a reasonable excuse, to place them in the lockup. It wasn't until December, 1853, that regular paid policemen (they got $1.50 per night) were brought into service. The first Fort Wayne officers were John Hardendorff, Patrick McGee and John D. McGrady.

Before a regular fire deparment was established, there was the hooks and ladders brigade and "each owner of a house within the corporation to procure a fire bucket" was the advice. That was in 1833; and the following year on June 2, 1834, there was formed an engine company, a hose company and a hook and ladder company. Two 24 foot ladders, two 16-foot ladders and one 30-foot ladder were to be made by John Brown, the blacksmith.

In 1839, the town leased from William G. Ewing the northeast corner of Clinton and Main Streets a site for the erection of the first fire station. The "famous Anthony Waynes" fire brigade was formed in 1841 and it consisted of most of the active men in the community. Its proud possession was a Jeffries Gallery Engine with side brakes motivated by horse or human power. It dragged a cart filled with 500 feet of leather hose.

Still, fires were so frequent and destructive that the city council in 1849 passed an ordinance making it unlawful to build wooden structures downtown—between Main, Barr, Harrison Streets and the Wabash and Erie Canal. This edict was a great boon to Benjamin Archer, manufacturer of brick just north of town, the product of whose yard went into the construction of the first brick buildings in Fort Wayne.

Archer's bricks, however, had not been used in the old log jail and debtors' prison on the Courthouse Square. It was destroyed by fire on Saturday night, Feb. 3, 1849. So a "New Jail," as it was called, was built in July, 1849, at the northeast corner of Harrison and Berry Streets. John Grimes furnished the materials and did the work for a price of $270.

But New Jail was less than secure. It was almost immediately broken into by "a gang of desperadoes" as the Sentinel described them, "who rescued the notorious horse thieves, Laertes B. Dean and George Pierce."

Allen County, with a special levy, moved to construct a jail and sheriff's residence on Calhoun Street. It was completed in 1852 and included with a larger building in 1873 on the same site. With later additions and improvements, this jail was still in service 122 years later. The County Jail and the flats in front of the brick structure became the scene of some of the brutal episodes in the history of Fort Wayne. The several hangings in the subsequent years were major public affairs which drew spectators from miles around. Hanging days vied with county fairs, also initiated in the 1850's, as public gatherings. One of the better remembered was the Madden and Keefer hanging of 1855.

The Double Hanging

It was on a sunny April morning; and the high scaffold was standing bare and forbodding at the center of the flat square. The Fort Wayne Sentinel reported: "At an early hour large crowds of persons began to flock in from the country, and before the time appointed for the execution, the jail was surrounded by a multitude of anxious spectators eager to get a glimpse of the awful tragedy. The Mad Anthony Guards under the command of Colonel George Humphrey and a large police force were stationed around the place to keep back the crowd."

The two men awaiting execution were Benjamin Madden and George Keefer. They were convicted of murdering John Dunbar, an old man brutally slain in a lumber yard, and were sentenced to be hanged by Judge E. A. McMahon. Another accomplice, Samuel Romaine, was saved from the gallows by Governor Wright who commuted his sentence to life imprisonment.

The reporter at the scene of the gallows left a first-hand account:

"The two men were brought from the jail and the two ropes which were attached to the crossbeams above were placed around their necks. As the word was given, the main rope was cut and the platform dropped, leaving Keefer suspended in mid-air, his life rapidly ebbing away. Horrible to relate, however, the rope by which Madden was suspended snapped in two and dropped him to the ground with a deep red gash at his throat. The miserable wretch walked around among the horror-stricken and almost paralyzed witnesses, saying: 'Don't murder me, boys!' No one moved until Joel Forbush took Madden and led him again to the scaffold and fastened the rope a second time around his neck. Then a new difficulty presented itself. The platform could not be raised to position because the body of Keefer was still hanging and life was not extinct. The rope having been placed around Madden's neck, he was suspended a second time, but his feet rested upon the ground. Forbush then climbed to the top of the crossbeam and, holding the rope up from the ground with his strong arms, literally hanged Madden himself."

The lake country north of Fort Wayne became such a notorious area of lawlessness and hideouts of criminal gangs that emergency legislation by the Indiana General Assembly was passed to combat it. Cattle rustling, horse stealing, robbery, rape and murder became common over a wide area of Indiana, southern Michigan and western Ohio. A law passed by the Indiana Legislature in 1856 gave power to civilian bands to organize themselves as vigilantes to seek out and capture the criminals. The main law group was called the "Fort Wayne Regulators" and at one time more than 1,000 armed men were in the field, even though the legislation called for not less than 10 nor more than 100 men.

The most notorious leader of the lawless bands was captured in 1857. He was Gregory McDougal. His execution by hanging took place near Diamond Lake in Noble County on January 26, 1858. Another gang in that era reportedly had a stable for stolen horses in a large wooded area just southeast of Huntertown. Numerous extra-official law organizations came into being for a short period. They included the Kekionga Guards, the Perry Rangers, the Lafayette Rangers, the New Haven Vigilants, the Adams Township Rangers, the St. Joe Detectives and the Springfield Detectives. They included a fair percentage of the active men in the various communities and aimed to ward off any possible incursions by marauding bands.

Plague and Progress

The dreaded disease of cholera was sweeping around the world in the 1840's and reached Fort Wayne in 1849. Despite measures by the City Council to rid the town of nuisances and the gathering of the populace in public prayers, cholera racked up its toll. In each of the years of the plague, 1849, 1852 and 1854, there were about 200 deaths reported here. This occurred even though tremendous doses of calomel and cayenne pepper were given by the physicians to the afflicted.

Some left the city and the plague in search of gold with the onset of the Rush of 1849. Frederick Becker made a large number of wagons of the prairie schooner type for Forty-niners who departed from Fort Wayne. Some of the old Fort Wayne families which left Fort Wayne for wealth-seeking in California at that time were those of John Aveline, Charles Colerick, J. A. Bartlett, Sabina Wallace, Louis T. Bourie and James Sheldon.

The first telegraph line, built parallel to the Wabash-Erie Canal, was started in 1848 and in regular operation the following year. The Ohio, Indiana and Illinois Telegraph Co. first completed the line between Toledo and Fort Wayne. The first operator was Chester Griswold who came to Fort Wayne from Dayton, Ohio. The original telegraph office was in the Times newspaper building at the northwest corner of Clinton and Columbia Streets. After about a year, the system became a part of the Western Union Telegraph Company.

These were the great days of the canal when people and produce from 50 miles around flowed into Fort Wayne and to the tight little area of activity surrounding the landings and the wharfs of Columbia Street. The landings were small lakes which served as turn-arounds for the barges of the Wabash-Erie Canal. One landing was located at the northeast corner of Harrison and Columbia Streets. Another was a few blocks east between Barr and Lafayette Streets. It was at these landings and the canal docks in between that the fruits of the wilderness were shipped back to the civilized world to the east and even beyond the ocean.

In those days, civilization for all practical purposes was in two directions—back through the Great Lakes to the Seaboard provinces or downriver to the Ohio, Mississippi and New Orleans. The old folk song about "Fifteen Miles on the Erie Canal" is still sung by school children and preserves the image of the sweat and mule power which lugged the old barges across the landscapes of Ohio, Indiana and Illinois, as well as New York. Some of the flavor of those days was preserved for more than a century by the commission houses and taverns along Columbia Street, a few later restored in The Landing Project of the 1960's.

Fort Wayne was a village of only 300 persons when the building of the canal was started in 1832. By 1841 major extensions had been completed for canal travel in many directions, with the largest link from Lake Erie to Evansville, through Fort Wayne, being the longest man-made waterway in the history of the world. By the start of the Civil War, Fort Wayne was a thriving center of more than 10,000 people.

The first upsurge of growth was due to the canal workers themselves. Irish and German work crews responded to ads in distant places, descending upon the area and some staying permanently. It brought about an era when commission merchants flourished as canal trade and produce consignments reached boom proportions through the 1840's and 1850's, along with the taverns, hotels and bawdy houses. The place was infested with insects and vermin—some of the human variety.

Most of the old downtown churches stem from those years and both churches and mansions of the day were furnished with materials and artifacts brought by canal barge from the East and some originally from European ports.

The First Railroad

A barge brought the product which eventually meant the end of the canals. A crowd that gathered one day in 1852 didn't realize it then, but the steam engine brought in by canal barge was a heavyweight kiss of death. In fact, the Norfolk & Western Railway (the part which formerly was the Nickel Plate Road) runs where the canal used to be.

The iron horse, by means not remembered, was hoisted off the barge and onto railroad tracks which went south on Lafayette St. to the main east-west tracks which had been built. That short run was the beginning of the end of the canal era. The engineer operating the engine on the first run was R. W. Wohlfort. The engine was used for track construction and for several years of passenger service.

The arrival of the engine was the culmination of five years of planning and construction to link Fort Wayne by rail to points east and west. In 1847, Jesse Williams, the chief engineer for the Wabash-Erie Canal, had encouraged the construction of a rail line which would reach to Pittsburgh on the east and Chicago on the west. The Ohio and Indiana Railroad Company was formed on July 4, 1850. The Board of Commissioners of Allen County held a special meeting April 16, 1851, to approve "a subscription of $100,000 . . . for the benefit of said county of Allen to the capital stock of the Ohio & Indiana Railroad Company." The subscription was "to be payable in the bonds of this board" which bore a 7 per cent interest rate. Levies of 20 cents per $100 in assessed valuation in 1851 and of 22 cents in 1852 were imposed. Thus the official records of Allen County show the public through a tax levy helped pay for the original construction of the railroad. The Commissioners named Sam Hanna agent for Allen County to handle the bonds and Robert S. Fleming special agent to vote the county-owned rail stock. Years later, in 1853, Pliny Hoagland was appointed agent in place of Fleming. He was succeeded by Franklin P. Randall in 1855.

For the actual construction work, a contract was let Jan. 28, 1852, to Sam Hanna for the stretch of road between Fort Wayne and Crestline, Ohio, a distance of 131 miles. In September, 1852, a new company, the Fort Wayne and Chicago Railroad was formed at a meeting at Warsaw. Hanna was named president. The two lines were later joined with others to form the Pittsburgh, Fort Wayne and Chicago Railroad, which eventually became the western part of the Pennsylvania Railroad, and finally was merged with the New York Central and became the Penn Central.

The flavor of the era can be seen in a description left by Robert D. Dumm, who rode into Fort Wayne on Nov. 15, 1854, on the first excursion train to come into the city from the east. "It was in the dusk of evening when we arrived, and our first impressions on stepping from the cars were by no means of the most favorable kind. It was before the days of nicholson pavements and our march from the point of disembarkation up Columbia St. was one of continued tramp in mud and water. True, in honor of the occasion, our pathway was lighted by illuminated windows of the stores and shops. Upon our arrival at Colerick's Hall . . . our eyes fell upon large tables filled with the most sumptuous of viands."

Some months later the Pittsburgh, Fort Wayne and Chicago Railroad built the town's first passenger station, a brick structure between Calhoun and Clinton Streets. The station site had been donated by Allen Hamilton. Sam Hanna donated five acres of ground for railroad shops, which some years later became a major industry in the city.

The first moves toward the construction of the Grand Rapids and Indiana Railroad were also taken in Fort Wayne at a meeting on April 26, 1854. The line itself didn't become a reality for several years.

Actually, the oldest rail line to operate through Fort Wayne was the Wabash. However, construction didn't start in Fort Wayne but in Meredosia, Illinois. It was originally known as the Northern Cross Railroad and was started on Nov. 8, 1838. It was one of the first railroads in the world to begin steam operations. A series of mergers involving the Great Western Railroad and the Toledo & Wabash Railroad and the St. Louis, Kansas City and Northern resulted in the Wabash.

James K. McCracken, who became agent for rail lines operating in Fort Wayne in 1863, said since there was only one station, that of the Pittsburgh, Fort Wayne and Chicago, both roads used the same depot. "Often the Wabash trains would seem to arrive on time, but they were in reality 24 hours late," he later recalled.

The Gas Light Era

The gas light era came to Fort Wayne in the mid 1850's. Following a meeting in Colerick's Hall, the place where early minstrel shows and traveling theater groups entertained, the City Council moved to franchise a gas company—The Fort Wayne Gas Light Company. Colerick's Hall, incidently, was on the north side of Columbia between Clinton and Barr Streets.

The gas light firm was capitalized at $65,000, and later at $225,000, beginning March 6, 1855. A plant was established along the canal at the Barr St. junction. First only interior lighting was provided; but in 1857, Fort Wayne's streets were illuminated with gas.

In the autumn of 1859, the first iron bridge in Fort Wayne was built. It was over the St. Mary's River at the foot of Wells St. and cost $3,200. It was designed by Mosley and Company, Cincinnati, Ohio. "In 1860, the bridge fell with a drove of cattle on it," reported T. B. Helm in his 1879 History of Allen County. Some of the cattle were drowned in the stream and a considerable portion of the iron of the ruined bridge remained buried in the mud under the structure. The bridge which was rebuilt later in 1860 is the same structure which continued in use at the site into the 1970's. The County Jail and the Wells St. Bridge established themselves as two of the community's more durable landmarks.

The year 1860 also marked the beginning of another long-term Fort Wayne institution —the Lindenwood Cemetery. In July of the previous year, the city fathers deemed old McCulloch Cemetery along Broadway to be inadequate as a final resting place for increasing numbers in the community. A civic group purchased 152 acres of wild and marshy land two miles west of the courthouse. Isaac Nelson, president of the cemetery organization, and Charles Bond, secretary-treasurer, hired John Doswell as superintendent and landscape gardener. Doswell served in that capacity for 40 years and is largely responsible for the handsome development of the grounds. The dedication of Lindenwood occurred on May 30, 1860. Peculiarly, May 30 was not Memorial Day in those days but came into existence a few years later to commemorate the Civil War dead.

The planking of Calhoun St., "a necessary step to recover it from the dominion of mud that heretofore ruled supreme," according to the Sentinel, was interrupted by the Civil War. The wood planking job was ordered by the City Council in 1857 and the target area was Calhoun from Berry St. to Lewis Street. The planking of Main St. and Harrison St. was begun in 1858. The cost was $1.80 per linear foot for the 40-foot-wide rights-of-way.

Great Axle Works

Other development just prior to the Civil War included the founding of a major industrial operation in the city associated with the growth of the railroads. In 1857, the foundry and machine shops of Jones, Bass & Company were sold to the Pittsburgh, Fort Wayne and Chicago Railroad. This was the beginning of the Pennsy Shops which later became the city's largest industry employing some 1,000 men and existing well into the 20th Century. Among the products was the "Silver Palace" sleeping car costing $20,000 each and renowned throughout the land. William H. Jones and Sion S. Bass were the partners in the original concern. In 1858 John Bass and Edward Force leased a plant from Jones and Bass which was sold the following year to the Fort Wayne Machine Works, headed by Samuel Hanna, Jones, Hugh Bennigen and Neil McLachlan. Jones and McLachlan later moved on to form the huge steel combine. In 1862, John Bass purchased McLachlan's Fort Wayne interests and developed the Bass Foundry and Machine works. In time, he had extensive operations both in Fort Wayne and St. Louis and eventually became the largest supplier of railroad wheels and axles in the world.

The residence of John Bass, which became the campus of St. Francis College in the early 1940's, was a 19th Century showplace. In addition to the mansion, there were lakes, gardens, a wildlife exhibit including elk, buffalo, deer, water fowl and other attractive items in the grand style.

Franklin P. Randall was elected mayor in 1859, and remained in that position during most of the Civil War. Pre-Civil War mayors, after George W. Wood and Joseph Morgan, included Henry Lotz, starting Jan. 1, 1843; John M. Wallace, starting July 1, 1844; M. W. Huxford, starting May 26, 1846; William Stewart, starting Jan. 1, 1849; P. G. Jones, starting Jan. 1, 1852; Charles Whitmore, starting Jan. 1, 1853; William Stewart again on Jan. 1, 1855; and Samuel Morss, starting on Jan. 1, 1857.

Torch Parades

In the years leading up to the Civil War, Fort Wayne experienced some of its bitterest divisions in the community. These included diverse political movements, some populist and conservative; the temperance movement; the merging of splinter parties. The local sentiment proved to be at odds with the national trend.

The remains of the old Whig Party, the Know-nothings, dissident Northern Democrats, the Abolitionists and the Prohibitionists all merged into a new national political party on the American scene. This was the Republican Party which was to dominate events in the United States almost continuously from 1860 to the days of World War I.

New trends made inroads in many ways, with one of the first indications of the power of new politics being state anti-saloon legislation in 1854 which ruled Indiana dry. Torchlight parades against prohibition in Fort Wayne were reported on the night of April 1, 1854. The wets marched to the homes of Jesse Williams and John Hough, Jr., prominent prohibitionists, then marched up Barr St. and buried a keg of whisky in a huge grave. Fort Wayne actually had turned in a majority vote against prohibition and the law was enforced with considerable indifference. "There was scarcely a place in Fort Wayne where a glass of liquor could be obtained," the Sentinel waggishly commented.

The new coalition was called a "buzzards' nest" by Tigar's Democratic-lining newspaper. Dawson of the Times charged Tigar with supporting the foreign element because of his "passion for Dutch girls, lager beer, sauerkraut and sausages" and implied he had an illegitimate child by a certain Kate Vantassel.

Things quickened with nearly a sweep of the newly-formed Peoples Party, as the Republicans were called, of Indiana's Congressional Districts in October, 1854. Democrats lost all but two of the 11 seats. Allen County, swung by a large majority in Fort Wayne, however, went Democratic. Dawson attributed this to 400 illegal votes and a deal made by Sheriff McMullen with Deputy William Fleming, a Catholic, who engineered "his sale to the Papists."

The Kansas-Nebraska issue was irreversibly breaking up the Democrats as the nation moved toward Civil War.

Abe Lincoln in Town

An item in the Daily News of Fort Wayne on February 23, 1860, touches on a significant event in political history and marks the only substantiated visit of Abraham Lincoln to Fort Wayne.

"Hon. Abe Lincoln and wife came from the West this morning at 1 o'clock on the T.W. & W.R.R., and changed cars at this city, west to east. 'Old Abe' looked as if his pattern had been a mighty ugly one."

According to Lincoln historian R. Gerald McMurtry, Lincoln was enroute to New York City to deliver his Cooper Union Address which was scheduled for the evening of Feb. 27, 1860. It was a major step in events which led to his election to the Presidency and the subsequent secession of the South.

Lincoln's train had left the Old Wabash Station at Springfield, Ill., at 10:15 a.m. on Wednesday, Feb. 22. Traveling on a Toledo, Wabash & Western train, he arrived in Fort Wayne an hour late, although he had ample time to catch the Pittsburgh, Fort Wayne and Chicago train at 1:12 a.m. Thursday. The Wabash route then as now was through Decatur, Ill., and Lafayette, Logansport,

Peru, Wabash and Huntington and to Fort Wayne for the eastbound transfer. The wait was undoubtedly in the depot built in 1858 on Baker St. just north of the tracks between Calhoun and Clinton Streets.

But the Presidential candidate of that year of 1860 who was to sweep the majority of votes at Fort Wayne came into town October 2. Stephen A. Douglas, the Little Giant and perennial Lincoln opponent made a speech from the balcony of the Rockhill House on Broadway and then led a giant parade down Main Street for the main event of the day on the banks of the St. Mary's River at the Wells St. Bridge. Along the way, according to George W. Stover who was there, a "great commotion and a float broke into the parade. It was a huge haywagon and on it was a tall, lanky young man dressed to represent Abe Lincoln, and he was splitting rails." The Democrats got the Lincoln wagon out of the way by pouring salt on grass along the roadside, which attracted the oxen hauling the Republican hay float. "The oxen pulled out of line of the parade to lick the salt, and no amount of urging could get them to move on," Stover reported.

Down at the river celebration a huge sawlog, intended to represent Lincoln, was flung into the St. Mary's as a defiant gesture of derision against the Republican candidate. Later in the day at sunset, it was "Everybody to the Court House" where the Democrats hanged a straw figure of Lincoln in effigy.

On Nov. 6, 1860, the people of Allen County and Fort Wayne went to the polls. In the voting, 3,224 ballots went for Douglas; 2,552 for Lincoln; 42 for Breckinridge and 32 for Bell. Four years later, Fort Wayne and Allen County still wouldn't go for Lincoln, then President seeking re-election. The Nov. 7, 1864, vote was 4932 for General George B. McClellan, the Democrat, and 2244 for Lincoln, the Union-Republican standard bearer.

War Cannons

Unrest and expectation of war filled the air in Fort Wayne and other American cities until the actual firing on Fort Sumter on April 12, 1861. At that time, the community generally solidified behind the war effort. Three days after the onset of hostilities, Mayor Randall called a meeting of civic leaders at Hedekin Hall. There was a declaration of unity by those of varying political persuasions.

There were some exceptions, however. An organization called the Order of the Sons of Liberty continued to oppose the war, almost to the point of supporting the South, and at one time even advocated the States of Indiana, Illinois, Michigan and Wisconsin form a Northwest Confederacy and secede from the Union. As late as June 13, 1864, the organization assembled at Fort Wayne to reaffirm the doctrine of states' rights and opposition "to this unholy and unconstitutional war."

Mostly, there was the playing of bands, the booming of cannons and the waving of flags. Military units were formed. Camp Allen on the west bank of the St. Mary's River just south of Main Street was founded as a recruiting place for the region. During the period of the Civil War, Allen County, Indiana, sent 4,103 men to the fields of battle. Of this total, 489 lost their lives.

Col. Sion S. Bass, one of the regimental leaders from Allen County was fatally wounded at the Battle of Shiloh on April 7, 1862. The Daily News reported the return of the body 11 days later and "when the funeral cortege moved, guns were fired, bells tolled, and drums beat. The procession came down Calhoun St. to Wayne St."

Serving with Bass in the Union forces at Shiloh was Lew Wallace, son of the former governor of Indiana David Wallace, a onetime resident of Fort Wayne. Lew Wallace, then a Major General under Gen. U. S. Grant, later became governor of the Arizona Territory during the range wars in the era of Billy the Kid, but is best remembered as the author of "Ben Hur" and other stories.

Lt. Robert S. Robertson, later Colonel Robertson, survived some of the major engagements of the war. On July 8, 1862, according to his diary, at the Virginia Theater "President Lincoln arrived toward evening and reviewed the army by moonlight." He was ordered to Gettysburg toward the conclusion of that decisive battle and later participated in the action at Corgin's Creek. He was wounded on May 12, 1864, during the Battle of the Spotsylvania Courthouse and was shot from his horse on May 31, some 10 miles north of Richmond. Robertson later became a prominent lawyer in Fort Wayne and on Nov. 2, 1886, was elected lieutenant governor on the Republican ticket. This led to one of the more famous donnybrooks of Indiana politics when the Democratic majority in the State Senate refused to recognize Robertson as presiding officer. Robertson also served as a Justice of the State Supreme Court and in 1889 was appointed by President Benjamin Harrison to the election board for the Utah Territory. He was author of books on the Civil War and Indiana and area history and politics.

Colonel Robertson and David N. Foster drafted legislation which led to the law in 1881 establishing the first public library in Fort Wayne. He was on the board of trustees of Indiana University. His daughter, Louise, married William H. Shambaugh, who became a prominent local attorney. Robertson was a collector of rare books, many of which became valuable early gifts to the Fort Wayne Public Library.

James White Career

James Bain White arrived in Fort Wayne by packetboat on the Wabash-Erie Canal in 1854. He was to become a soldier, merchant and banker. A great-grandson, Astronaut Ed White, would carve out a permanent place in world history as the first man to walk in space. After stints at various jobs, including those with Wade C. Shoaff, a merchant tailor; John Brown, who operated the first steam-powered grist mill in Fort Wayne, and the Nirdlinger and Oppenheimer Clothing Store, James White opened a shop of his own at the corner of Main and Calhoun Streets. But with the coming of the Civil War, he joined the regiment of Sion Bass and was named a captain. He fought in the Battle of Shiloh and the Siege of Corinth. He was twice captured by Confederates near Chattanooga and was wounded by a Minie ball in the bloody Shiloh affair. He marched with Union forces to Atlanta.

Back in Fort Wayne in 1866, he opened the White Fruit House and Oyster Depot at No. 12, Berry St., opposite the Avalon House. By 1871, he had moved to 20 West Berry St. and was credited with being the first Fort Wayne merchant to mark goods with a plain price tag—an idea attributed to his wife Maria. A fire on the night of January 6, 1872, caused by a kerosene lamp dropped by an employee, destroyed White's store. He rebuilt nearby, and expanded into a department store operation at Wayne and Calhoun Sts. partly based on the methods of Peter Kiser, operator of a three-story merchandising concern. Nineteenth Century marketing writers credited Kiser and White with being pioneers in the departmentalizing of retail operations. White employed as many as 100 people and did an annual business of half a million dollars—a huge amount for that era. John Wanamaker of Philadelphia and subsequently Macy's of New York, Marshall Field and Carson Pirie Scott of Chicago adopted White's methods of department retailing. In 1872, Captain White and his son John founded the White Wheel Works, a carriage and wagon wheel firm that employed 130 men. In the 1870's, White purchased the Fort Wayne Gazette and 1880 became the owner of the Colerick Opera House. He was a speculator on the Chicago Board of Trade, and in one year, 1881, the records showed his transactions totalled $1,700,000. In 1886, James White was elected to Congress, the first Republican in the usually Democratic District. In 1892, White and his son John who was named president, opened the White National Bank, chartered on April 14 of that year and located at the northwest corner of Wayne and Clinton Streets. This bank in 1905 was merged with the First National Bank, a financial institution which had been founded in 1863 by Samuel Hanna and Joseph D. Nuttman.

Henry Lawton

Henry W. Lawton was a student at Fort Wayne Methodist College when the Civil War broke out. As a volunteer, he joined a regiment formed at Goshen, Indiana, and later returned to join the 13th Indiana Volunteers under Colonel Bass as a drill sergeant. This regiment participated in the bloody battles of Shiloh and Corinth. At Corinth, Lawton was commissioned a captain. Lawton was with the 13th in the battle of Chickamauga Creek and the Tennessee campaign; and was under Generals William Tecumseh Sherman and Philip Sheridan in the battles before Atlanta. So badly decimated was the 13th Indiana Regiment that it was reduced to a battalion.

Henry Lawton became the first Fort Wayne resident to receive the Congressional Medal of Honor. This was bestowed for leading skirmishers in the capture of rifle pits during murderous fire at Atlanta. On March 13, 1865, Lawton was named a colonel—before he was 22 years of age.

As a professional soldier, Lawton participated in the Indian campaigns in the West, including those against the Sioux in 1876, the Utes in 1879, and the Chiricahua Apaches in 1886 and 1887. It was Lawton who led the 1,300-mile pursuit through Arizona and Mexico which resulted in the taking of Geronimo.

Lawton's description of the actual taking of Geronimo was printed later, in the Dec. 19, 1899, issue of the Sentinel. Lawton had walked alone into the camp of the Apache and sat down on a log next to Geronimo. Excerpts follow:

"I turned my attention to the fleas that came skipping along off Geronimo and the buck on my other side to me. By and by, Geronimo asked me what I was there for. I told him to take their surrender. He grunted the others caught his meaning. Then we all thought a long time. They wanted to know what my terms were. I said I had no terms to offer, just surrender; that was all. Geronimo had started the pipe going, and the filthy thing came to me.

"It took hours to arrange it, but finally Geronimo asked to whom were they to surrender. I told him to General Miles. They thought a duce of a long time, and they parleyed a lot. But at last Geronimo said he would go with me to General Miles on the condition that they could have sight of him before deciding." Lawton took Geronimo and a number of his band to San Carlos, where, after having a look, the Apaches gave up.

In his later career, Lawton served in Cuba during the Spanish-American War and was one of the commissioners who received the Spanish surrender at Santiago. He went in 1899 to the Philippine Islands where insurgents, disappointed with the Spanish-American Treaty, attacked Manila. Operating under the overall command of Gen. Arthur MacArthur, General Lawton headed a 4,000-man army on Luzon. Toward the end of a succesful campaign in the mountainous and jungle region, Lawton was fatally hit in the lungs by a Filipino bullet on Dec. 19, 1899. On Feb. 5, 1900, the funeral train arrived in Fort Wayne. Cannons boomed, dirges were played and the cortege went down Calhoun Street. President McKinley and others gave tribute before burial in Arlington National Cemetery. In Fort Wayne, a committee of citizens changed the name of North Side Park to Lawton Park.

Mother George

One of the more fascinating participants in the Civil War from Fort Wayne was not a soldier. It was a middle-aged woman who is remembered as Mother George. She is mentioned in a dozen or more historical works, including A. A. Hoehling's "The Last Train from Atlanta." She was born Elizabeth Hamilton Vermont and was the widow of W. L. George. Her daughter Eliza was probably the wife of Sion Bass, killed at Shiloh, according to research by Hilary Sadler.

Mrs. George, a Fort Wayne landlady, was 54 years old when she joined Union forces as a nurse in 1863 in the Mississippi River campaign in front of Vicksburg. Her letters are superior to most war correspondence reports as she moved with Union forces in the major wilderness engagements. At Chattanooga she reported "An ambulance train brought in 1,200 wounded men. There were 75 with amputated legs and arms, some wounded in the head, in the feet, in every form and manner. They were of the 20th Corps, Hooker's Division.

"Every foot of country here shows it is the theater of war. I am sitting in sight of Lookout Mountain and wondering how our people ever scaled its summit, and for ages to come it will be a wonder."

Mother George may have been the only nurse to move right with the army in some of the fields of battle as General Sherman fought across the bloody miles to Kennesaw Mountain and finally Atlanta. "Our soldiers are becoming exhausted physically, but their spirit is stronger and more defiant than ever. I am perfectly astonished to hear them talk, even while they are writhing with the pain of crushed and amputated limbs," she wrote in 1864.

There were numerous stories from other sources telling of her bravery and tenderness. Yet, Mother George was to survive hospital bombings and perils of the fields, only to be struck down in the last stages of war in circumstances tragic in another way. In the spring of 1865, Mother George was in North Carolina when 11,000 Union prisoners were brought from the terrible stockade at Salisbury. "Two thousand of them had not a whole garment upon their bodies; 200 had lost their feet by frost," she reported at the time. She worked with these suffering and dying soldiers until May when typhoid fever swept through the hospital camp, taking her along with many others. Mother George died May 9, 1865.

In a letter to her daughters in Fort Wayne during 1864, Mother George had sent a legacy: "Strive above all petty considerations to make your home happy, to make it what it should be, a holy, happy place. I want you should kneel down together every night and pray for your absent mother and your suffering country."

The Home Front

Great changes occurred in Fort Wayne during the war years. A new county courthouse was built on the public square; the city's own paper money was issued; a baking powder firm which a century later would be one of the largest in the nation expanded operations; and young Thomas A. Edison took up residence on Columbia Street. Also during the years 1860 to 1862, the community's greatest 19th Century hotel, the Aveline House at Berry and Calhoun Streets was built by Francis S. Aveline. Forty-eight years later it would be the site of the city's most spectacular and tragic fire.

The cornerstone for the fourth courthouse was laid by the county commissioners on May 1, 1861, and the tall brick structure was completed by July 23, 1862. Built at the cost of $78,000, it was surrounded by grass and shade trees. Near the courthouse a new public project occupied the community —an artesian well which was a gathering-place for decades after. When Helm wrote his history in 1879, he spoke of it. "This is one of the notable features of Fort Wayne, attracting the attention of all, inviting the multitude to partake freely of its waters, which are bountiful in their character and possess medicinal virtues of high repute among the many who partake of them."

The sinking of the well was the cause of considerable concern among the city fathers in those days, since the digging and boring went on for several years. Waters were not struck until they were down 3,000 feet. Old prints show a pavilion over the flowing well toward one corner of the Public Square.

A few blocks to the east at the site of the Old Fort, the city purchased the first piece of public park ground in 1863. The triangular plot of one-fifth acre of land near Main and Clay Streets was called Old Fort Park.

Fort Wayne once had its own money as a result of an action by the City Council. On Jan. 1, 1863, the city authorized the issue of city script in the denominations: 50 cents, 25 cents, 10 cents and 5 cents. The need was "occasioned by the drawing out of silver during the rebellion," Historian T. B. Helm reported. The paper money, called 'shinplaster' by contemporaries, bore the portraits of Mayor Franklin P. Randall and City Clerk Louis Bourie.

In that same year, the federal government created a new office: that of controller of the currency. Named to the post was Judge Hugh McCulloch, a Fort Wayne banker. Two years later, in 1865, President Lincoln appointed McCulloch Secretary of the Treasury. He served in that position under three presidents: Lincoln, Andrew Johnson and Chester A. Arthur.

Edison and Baking Powder

The presence of one of Fort Wayne's more famous residents wasn't even noted by reports of the era. A young telegraph operator by the name of Thomas Alva Edison came to Fort Wayne from his former home at Port Huron, Mich., and took a room in a three-story brick building at the northwest corner of Columbia and Calhoun Streets. He reportedly also lived at rooms a block east at Clinton and Columbia. That was in 1864, and after about six months, Edison moved to Indianapolis and then Louisville, Kentucky. The 17-year-old Edison was telegraph operator for the railroad that summer in Fort Wayne.

It was in that same building at Calhoun and Columbia that a baking powder formula was developed which later became a nationally recognized household name. The Hoagland brothers, Joseph and Cornelius, and Thomas M. Biddle developed Royal Baking Powder prior to 1865. Biddle and Cornelius Hoagland continued to operate the drug firm in Fort Wayne while Joe Hoagland moved on to New York to push the sale and manufacture of the product. Several decades later it was the largest in the field.

While the Hoaglands and Biddle were working on their powder formula, crews in 1865 were working on the streets outside for three blocks along Columbia and Calhoun. Wooden block paving called Nicholson was put down to replace the old rattling planks and cover the mud holes which previously were the street environment. These wooden blocks were the city's first paving. Later, they were replaced with red bricks, and finally concrete and asphalt. Some years after the street paving, the old plank sidewalks were replaced at selected places by stone slabs, some of which were still in use a century later.

Making a City

The two decades following the Civil War became known as the lawless years in Fort Wayne, and also the period when major new industries, which were to shape the community until the post World War I era, were largely started.

As to lawlessness, it was an era of murder, body snatching, gang warfare, vigilantes, strikes and mob control. Tickets were sold for hangings. The Chicago Times observed in 1875 that "Fort Wayne by the record is the most lawless town in Indiana." Even Robber Baron Jay Gould was in town long enough to stir trouble with mass firing of workers at the Wabash shops. Gould at that time, just prior to his indictment for alleged gold swindles, had gained control of the Wabash during a series of railroad bankruptcy proceedings.

A mass move against the outlaws occurred in 1867 when an estimated 500 workers from the railroad shops marched on the Ryan Saloon. Edward Ryan, head of a notorious gang of gamblers, pickpocketers and strong-arm robbers, operated from the saloon, also called Carey's, located on Railroad Street between Calhoun and Clinton Streets. As officials looked on, the mob put the torch to Ryan's place, but, according to historical accounts, only Ryan and some of his men were arrested. Ryan skipped bail and disappeared. According to a contemporary, Ryan was a big man, tall and weighing about 240 pounds. He was reportedly tried 11 times for murder but never convicted.

For two weeks in 1877, the city was on edge during the great railroad strike which halted operations of both the shops and train movements. Gangs moved onto the tracks, spiked switches and removed coupling pins from equipment. At 2 a.m. the night of July 22, Mayor Charles Zollinger appeared at the scene and ordered a crowd of some 2,000 to disperse. He threatened "the strong arm of the Law." The crowd laughed at him. Incoming trains were stalled, and these crews were added to the general situation. Workers closed down the H. G. Olds Wheel and Spoke Factory. The strikers pulled engines into roundhouses, took over company and railroad property and set up armed guards on the compounds. Troops were sent from Chicago to Fort Wayne, but they arrived a day after the settlement of the strike, originally caused by wage disputes.

Medical College

On March 10, 1876, the Fort Wayne College of Medicine was founded by Drs. B. S. Woodworth, I. M. Rosenthal, W. H. Myers, C. B. Stemen and H. A. Clark. The college was located at the southwest corner of Broadway and Washington Boulevard. The medical school, despite a splitting off of a rival college which set up classes at the southeast corner of Baker and Calhoun Streets, for a few years, was a great asset to medical practice in the community. The school became rather widely regarded and graduates were highly-respected practitioners in Fort Wayne and numerous other towns.

Almost from the start, however, the presence of the Medical College and the need of the students for cadavers created an uneasy attitude in the general community. The dead were not resting in peace.

An Allen County Grand Jury looked into the matter. Following the investigation, the jury issued a statement criticizing the college "used for the purpose of depositing, concealing and disecting human bodies, a portion of which are stolen from cemeteries or graveyards in this vicinity, in violation of the law, common decency and the proprieties of life." The official report also noted the alleged practice "produced and is producing great excitement, anxiety and indignation, especially among those who have families or have recently lost friends."

Lindenwood Cemetery, a graveyard at Roanoke and others were the targets for the body snatchers. According to information given to the jury, 30 graves had been robbed over a short period. In 1877, ghouls removed a body from Lindenwood which led to the offer of a $1,000 reward for information leading to the capture of the culprits. The body in question was said to have been that of a girl in the prominent Ewing family. In 1879, the body of a Waterloo man was stolen and later was discovered in a trunk on the baggage platform of the Lake Shore Railroad on Wells Street. It was returned to Waterloo but was stolen a second time. Cemeteries in Decatur; Prairie Grove; Delphos, O., and Van Wert, O., were raided. Consternation over the snatching of bodies led to the posting of guards, spring guns and watch towers at the graveyards.

The Fort Wayne College of Medicine continued into the 20th Century. Sister M. Columba, PHJC, who was a young nun working surgery at St. Joseph Hospital soon after the turn of the century, left a record of impressions. She praised the work of Dr. Albert E. Bulson, who was head of the State Medical Assn., and Dr. Miles Porter, on the staff of the college. Among the young interns she remembered Drs. John McArdle and Philip S. Titus. "Dr. Maurice Rosenthal was head of the medical staff at St. Joseph and did a lot for the Hospital. The medical students came every Tuesday and Friday to watch operations." She recalled that occasionally bodies would disappear from the morgue. "Corpses were very hard to get then, but they were necessary for the training of the student doctors." On Oct. 3, 1905, The Fort Wayne College of Medicine was merged with the Indiana College of Medicine to form the School of Medicine at Purdue University.

St. Joseph Hospital was started in 1868 with the purchase of the Rockhill House on Broadway. The Rev. Julian Benoit and Henry Monning headed the association. The Poor Handmaids of Jesus Christ, a German order of nuns, established a mother house there in 1869 to operate the hospital. They later began the city's first nursing school.

The family of Jesse Williams donated funds to build Hope Hospital at Washington and Barr Streets in 1893. The first Methodist unit started at Main and Webster Streets in 1868. Hope moved to the southeast corner of Lewis and Harrison Streets in 1917 and was usually called Methodist Hospital. The Evangelical Lutheran Hospital Assn. founded Lutheran Hospital on South Fairfield Street, in 1904.

There is an old legend concerning Hope Methodist Hospital following its days at the Washington and Barr Street location. It had to do with people reportedly seeing ghosts or white figures through the dark windows. Also, blue lights glowing from the abandoned building on some nights was a peristent but unsubstantiated rumor.

One of the great early fires in Fort Wayne was that at the Comparet Mill, next to the Comparet Basin, which was about two blocks east of the Ormiston Canal Basin which in the mid-20th Century became known as The Landing. The mill was said to have been the finest in the state: six stories high with a corn sheller that turned out 2,500 bushels a day. It burned down on a cold winter night, but firemen saved nearby warehouses. Chief engineer of the Fire Department that night was Frank Vogel and foreman of firemen was Hugh Hogan, father of Harry and Frank Hogan of later prominence in law, banking and national politics. Owner of the mill, D. F. Comparet, was the son of Francis Comparet, the Indian trader of the old fort days.

Park Deals

The State Fair Grounds were once located in Fort Wayne, an enterprise which boosted the park system. In 1864, the city acquired 55 acres on what was then the northern fringes of town for what was hoped would be a permanent site for Indiana State Fairs. But the event was only held there once, in 1865, after which fairs were located at Indianapolis. A pontoon bridge was built across the St. Mary's to link the grounds with the town. Nothing much was done with the land until 1872 when part of it was donated to the Jackson & Saginaw Railroad (later the New York Central and Penn Central). The record of the Common Council of the city of Fort Wayne on the 23rd day of March, 1869, says: "Resolved that there be and is hereby granted to the Fort Wayne, Jackson and Saginaw Rail Road Company twenty acres of land to be surveyed and laid off from the west side of the City Park, to be determined by a line running parallel with the west line of said park from the Saint Marys River to the Feeder of the Wabash and Erie Canal; said grant being made upon the condition that said Rail Road Company shall run its line through and locate its depots for local purposes and all the shops it may find necessary to erect in Fort Wayne." The actual conveying of the property by F. P. Randall, Mayor, to the railroad was on March 26, 1872. Some more of the property was sold off as residential lots, but occasional flood conditions discouraged much of this sale. Finally, the place was called North Side Park and subsequently renamed Lawton Park. Additional land was purchased to extend the park to Spy Run Avenue.

Col. Thomas W. Swinney had provided in his will for a trust for a public park. This said his home and spacious grounds near the St. Mary's River would, upon the death of all his children, become city park property. In 1869, the city purchased 13 lots to the south of the Swinney homestead and added it to the park. During subsequent years starting in 1874, the Allen County Fair Association rented a portion of the Swinney land, including a half-mile race track which once existed there.

Other early parks were Hayden Park, purchased in 1876, and Reservoir Park which was part of the city water system. The lake at the "Res" was formed by the excavation for the hill around the water storage tank. The park contains some 13 acres and the land cost the city $24,000.

The reservoir was a more visible part of a city water system which was authorized in 1879. The waterworks trustees were Henry Monning, Charles McCulloch and C. Boseker. The plan was the subject of a referendum and the vote was 2,593 in favor and 591 against. Work was begun on the system in 1880 and cost $236,865, exclusive of the reservoir. For some reason, the City Council was induced to put the pumping station along Spy Run Creek, which proved inadequate with the first drought the following summer. Water then was tapped from the canal feeder, but it was contaminated. Finally, deep rock wells were drilled which served for many years.

By that time, Fort Wayne had some telephones. In the summer of 1879, Sidney C. Lumbard erected poles and strung wire. He soon had about 100 customers. The Lumbard Exchange was located in the Foellinger Building on the west side of Calhoun St., north of Main Street. Western Union also started a telephone system that year in the Nill Building on the west side of Calhoun north of Wayne Street. Both these early operations folded, but two years later the Fort Wayne Telephone Company began operations which became permanent. In 1886 the Home Telephone and Telegraph Co. was incorporated to expand phone service in the community. It commenced business with 800 customers. Chief promoters were Charles S. Bash, William J. Vesey, Charles McCulloch, Samuel M. Foster, George W. Beers and Christian Hettler. The company grew over the decades until some 70 years later it became a part of the General Telephone System.

Horse-drawn street cars came into use in 1872. The company was called the Citizens Street Railway Company. John Bass was president and Gilbert Bursley was secretary and superintendent. The Fort Wayne Electric Railway Company took over the various horse lines in 1892 and converted to an electrically-operated trolley system.

Murderers and Presidents

On a cool autumn day, October 9, 1883, a throng of thousands converged on the Jail House Flats for one of the great attractions of the era—a hanging. But most of them had to stand in the distance, outside the enclosure, because Sheriff William D. Schiefer issued only 250 tickets. Some of the favored few with tickets sold them at scalpers' prices to the curious. No less than 10 physicians, including Drs. J. M. Dinnen and Miles F. Porter, had choice seats as witnesses.

Sam McDonald, murderer, who was thwarted in an attempt to cut the throat of turnkey Paul Schroeder so he could escape with his brother James, was the main attraction. McDonald had been sentenced by Judge S. M. Hench to hang for the killing of Louis Laurent of Arcola.

McDonald coolly walked up the scaffold and looked over the crowd. He took a last drag from a cigar, blew out a billow of smoke and then handed the butt to the Sheriff. "Gentlemen, I have nothing to say," he said. Then the drop fell. The cigar butt lasted much longer. As late as 1965 it was in the possession of Harry Bender, Allen County councilman and farmer.

The presidential campaign of 1884 drew two future presidents to Fort Wayne, but the candidate of that year who arrived in the city not only was prevented from speaking but was eventually defeated by Grover Cleveland in the election. James G. Blaine, the Republican candidate who was generally believed to be the front-runner, came in with a distinguished entourage. With Blaine were Benjamin Harrison and William McKinley, both of whom would later be elected to the White House. But noisy disorders broke out in the streets of Fort Wayne as Blaine attempted to speak from a balcony of the Aveline House. That night, torchlight paraders of both parties turned into mobs as they came into contact near the corner of Hanna Street and Washington Boulevard. There were fights and profanity, but no one was killed.

Pump Companies

During these years, a farmboy named Sylvanus Freelove Bowser was growing up in Allen County. With three months of schooling and experience selling ice and wrapping paper he was on hard times because of nervous spells which plagued him. At home and idle one cold morning, he became annoyed with the task of lifting a bucket of water by rope from a 70-foot-deep well. Later that same day in early 1885, Bowser conceived the idea for a pump which was to revolutionize the oil and gasoline pump industry and make himself a leading industrialist.

Bowser, with his brother Alexander and Alexander's sons, started his first factory in a cow barn in 1885. The first items were oil tanks and pumps for use in measuring out kerosene in grocery stores. They were immediately successful. By 1888 the S. F. Bowser Co. was formed and a factory was built along East Creighton Ave. near where the old barn stood. In 1894, a fire leveled the Bowser works, but a larger, better factory was built at the same location. Another fire partly destroyed the plant in 1897, and the following year "trusted employees" misused company funds which nearly jeopardized the firm. Bowser, because of this, incorporated in 1899. With the coming of automobiles, sales grew rapidly and operations became world wide. The firm was a pioneer in gasoline handling in garages and later filling stations. By World War I, the company sales were $6,500,00 and double that in the early 1920's. Bowser started his own bank on Creighton Ave., in part to help employees finance homes. It folded in 1931 with many other banks in the Depression. Paternalistic and at odds with union organizations, and overloaded with Bowser family members on the payroll and board of directors, the firm tottered. Bowser lost control in the early 1930's, but the plant remained in operation for another three decades.

Executive headquarters of the Bowser Company were moved to Chicago in 1951. During the final years of operations in Fort Wayne, the firm was headed by Philip W. Smith, Paul Ganz, Fred S. Ehrman, E. M. Kuhl, Richard Piech, Clarence Snow and M. R. Peek. Directors included R. Hosken Damon; James M. Barrett, Jr.; John A. Berghoff; Ehrman; Ganz; Robert V. Gordon; E. Cyril Marsh and Smith.

Fort Wayne's place in the pump world was enlarged in 1891 with the founding of Wayne Pump Company. Actually, when two mechanics, J. J. Becker and W. H. Davis started operations, it was called Wayne Oil Tank Company. Like Bowser, the first products were for the storage and handling of kerosene. The firm won a gold medal at the World's Columbian Exposition held in Chicago in 1893 for the best self-measuring oil pump then on the market. With the coming of the automobile, the firm enjoyed national and international renown in gasoline pumps. The plant was moved from its original location on Lafayette Street to larger quarters on Tecumseh Avenue. Wayne produced the first gasoline pump with a visible dial and in 1933 revolutionized the industry by producing a pump which automatically computed the dollar amount together with the gallons pumped. In 1951, Wayne Pump was merged with the Symington-Gould Corporation.

Pianos and Beer

The most sung-over company in the history of the community was surely the Packard Piano Company, organized in 1871. Originally called the Fort Wayne Organ Company, the firm was put together with $24,000 by Henry F. Talbot, Isaac T. Packard, Lindley M. Ninde, Robert F. Keith, Stephen B. Bond, John H. Bass and Charles D. Bond. Packard was an organ builder in Chicago whose place of business was burned out during the great Chicago fire. Legend has it that he boarded a train and told the conductor to let him off when his money was used up. He apparently ran out at Fort Wayne.

The plant was built at the corner of Fairfield and Organ Avenue. Organ Avenue later was renamed Kinsmoor Avenue. Packard Ave., when laid out later, took its name from the industry. The Company was immediately successful and during the peak years of the 1920's employed more than 300 people in a large brick plant. It had started the manufacture of pianos in 1893 and changed the name of the firm in 1899. Operations were halted on Feb. 6, 1930, with the onset of the Depression. Paul E. Gallmeier and Wilbert Marshall purchased the assets of the firm other than the real estate and continued to market the pianos until 1952, after which a retailer, Ralph Jennings continued to market the product. The old plant was razed in the early 1930's and the land was made a part of the Fort Wayne Park system a few years later.

But the longest-lived of all the Fort Wayne companies, and also not without its songs, was in operation long before the city became known for its pumps and pianos. This was the Centlivre Brewery which began operations in 1862 as the French Brewery. The plant was built along the St. Joseph River north of town and old prints show barges by the river bank for the unloading of grains. Formed by Charles Louis Centlivre, the output was small in the beginning but by the end of the 1870's the brewery was an important local industry. In another 20 years, Centlivre was known as one of the major breweries in the Midwest. Even a fire in 1893 which destroyed much of the plant failed to halt the progress of the company. A larger brick plant replaced the old one. The firm progressed under second-generation Centlivres and their cousins, the Reusses. The Centlivres had horse stables and a race track, river boats and even their own trolley line which connected the north end operation with downtown Fort Wayne along the Spy Run route. The brewmaster from the 1870's to 1910 was Peter Nussbaum who came to Fort Wayne from Chicago after the Great Fire. Turn-of-the Century operators of the brewery were Charles F. and Louis A. Centlivre and Charles Reuss.

The onset of Prohibition, in 1919, put a crimp in the brewery; though a near-beer product called "That's It" was sold for a couple years. Operations were resumed in 1933 with Repeal. Bottles with labels of Nickle Plate and Old Crown became familiar. The last two presidents of Centlivre Brewing Corp. were Charles and John Reuss. John Reuss negotiated a merger of Centlivre Brewing Corp. with a conglomerate of national firms in the mid-1960's, subsequently known as Chris-Craft Corp. At that point, the brewery was renamed Old Crown Brewing Corp. and was employee owned and operated for another decade.

Fort Wayne's circus grounds for many decades was Centlivre Park, just west of the brewery site. Several generations of circus lovers went there to see Ringling Brothers and Cole Brothers and others put on the circuses under the big top. From 1921 to 1954, 53 circuses pitched their tents there. For many years the circuses would come to town on the Pennsylvania Railroad and unload for a circus parade north on Calhoun St. and out Spy Run to the park. It was one of the community's better free shows from the 19th Century until the late 1930's and the onset of World War II. The old circus grounds were in the mid-1960's converted by Herman Centlivre and other members of the family for use as an apartment community. The large complex was named Centlivre Apartments.

Another brewery, the Berghoff Brewing Corp., was started in Fort Wayne in 1887. Eventually, it became even larger than the Centlivre Brewery. The firm was founded by Gustav, Henry, Hubert and Herman Berghoff. Herman Berghoff later established a famous restaurant at Chicago where it was to remain a landmark on Wabash Avenue. The brewery at Fort Wayne was located on Grant Ave., just off Washington Boulevard. The plant prospered until Prohibition, during which time the buildings were used for other purposes. The Berghoff family eventually sold much of their holdings in the Berghoff Brewing Corp., but operated another firm, named the Hoff-Brau Brewery, for more than a decade after Repeal of the Volstead Act in 1933.

Berghoff Brewing Corp. properties were sold to Falstaff Brewing Corp. in April, 1954. In the years immediately following the purchase, Falstaff, a firm headquartered in St. Louis, Mo., spent $2,000,000 in a modernization program at the Fort Wayne plant.

The House of Bursley was founded in 1881 by James M. McKay and Gilbert Bursley. The firm grew and established a large food distribution center at Clinton and Superior Streets. Its trademark "Elf" became nationally known. The firm in a merger became Food Marketing Corporation and located at Interstate Industrial Park.

One of the reasons for much of the early heavy industry in Fort Wayne was the fact that Michigan in the Civil War era was the nation's leading iron producer. Fort Wayne, just south of Michigan and more convenient for the transporting of coal, was a natural location for foundries. Thus Bass and other industrialists became the largest suppliers of railroad wheels and axles, and the railroad shops built engines and cars. That industry spawned other companies, one of which was Kunkle Valve Company.

Kunkle Valve was founded in 1875 by Erastus B. Kunkle. He held a number of patents on safety valves designed for steam engines. The first valves were in use on the main railways in the United States and Canada, plus a number of foreign countries. Later the product line was expanded into valves for boilers, air and gas compressors and pipe lines. The original location was on South Barr St. not far from Old City Hall. In 1921, the company was purchased by Oscar A. Fox, a member of a pioneer family which owned considerable real estate in the downtown area. The firm continued in the valve business in the post World War II era and supplied safety valves for the Submarine Nautilus and other atomic-age naval craft. In the decades from the 1950's through the 1970's, the successive heads of the firm were Louis A. Fox, E. C. Pequignot and H. M. Dykhuizen who would lead the firm in a major expansion in 1974.

Louis Rastetter & Sons Company began operations in 1881 with the manufacture of bentwood buggy and wagon bows and wood felloes for wheel rims. Gradually, the firm moved into complete buggies and carriages, and even made tennis rackets and grandfather clocks. In 1893, Rastetter went into the manufacture of bicycles, again with wooden rims. Even the handlebars were bent wood. Later in 1908, the firm entered the furniture field but continued in the vehicle field, making automobile steering wheels and bows for folding tops on vintage sedans. In the 1920's, the bridge craze drew Rastetter into folding card tables and chairs. By 1950, the company, located at 1302 Wall St., was a large institutional supplier of folding metal and lightweight magnesium and wooden chairs. Grandsons of the founder, William C. Rastetter, Jr., Louis C. Rastetter and Charles A. Rastetter, headed operations during the latter period.

Horton Washers

The world's first contained washing machine was manufactured in Fort Wayne in 1871 by the Horton Manufacturing Company. By 1924, the Horton plant supplied half the world's washing machines. Heading the Horton firm in the 1920's were Henry C. Paul, president; Frank H. Cutshall, vice-president and general manager; and A. F. Ruhl, secretary-treasurer. Paul, when a young man, and John C. Peters had originally organized the Horton Company in 1871. Peters, incidently, was the grandfather of movie actress Carole Lombard, born Jane Peters, who was to become a household name in the 1930's and 40's.

J. C. Eckart opened a cigar factory in the year 1870 and Winslow Pierce and A. J. Emrick engaged in the manufacture of furniture in a factory on Pearl Street. W. Yergens, W. Ranke and Fred Brandt established a factory for making spokes, staves and headings, also in 1870.

In the year 1883 Max Nirdlinger established a factory on West Main Street for the manufacture of baseball bats. His first order was from A. G. Spaulding for 50,000 bats.

Herman and Joseph Freiberger, leather merchants, founded the I. Freiburger & Co. at 119 East Columbia Street. The Freiburgers later became officers in city banking institutions.

Nickel Plate Road

By 1880, the Wabash-Erie Canal was fading to a derelict condition. Gone were the days of the packetboats and travelers who looked through the wild scenery for the possible sight of an Indian. The railroads had taken all the human traffic and practically all the freight as well. One of the few last uses was the floating of firewood from New Haven to downtown Fort Wayne; or youngsters taking dares to wade across the murky stagnant waters.

Finally, the railroads completed the job. In 1880, the portion of the canal through and near Fort Wayne was sold to the New York, Chicago and St. Louis Railroad, known as the Nickel Plate System. The price for the right-of-way was $137,000. The railroad was built in 1881 and 1882 with the roadbed and tracks being directly over the old canal bed.

Originally, the construction of the important east-west trunk line was for the purpose of providing a parallel line to compete with William Vanderbilt's Lake Shore and Michigan Southern Line, later a part of the New York Central System, and to compel the Vanderbilt interests to purchase the Fort Wayne road. Vanderbilt termed the link a "string of dirt leading from nowhere to no place." But the plan succeeded in bringing the desired rail service to Fort Wayne. The Nickel Plate stretched from Buffalo, N. Y., to St. Louis, Mo., and grew to a system of more than 4000 miles of track. It was also one of the more efficient rail systems in mid-America, but one of the continuous points of controversy in Fort Wayne politics because the tracks cut the community in two.

The Vanderbilt interests did purchase the control of the system in October, 1882. William H. Vanderbilt remarked at the time: "The price we paid for it, it ought to be nickel-plated." This is sometimes given as the basis for the nickname of the New York, Chicago and St. Louis Railroad, the Nickel Plate Road. Yet there is an earlier record of the use of the name. An article in the Cleveland Herald of June 18, 1882, raised the issue as to who first applied the name Nickel Plate. According to the report, during the time that the line for the road was being surveyed, the town of Norwalk, Ohio, held strong hopes of securing the road. The town offered inducements and was encouraged in the belief that it would secure the road. But when the system was built, it missed Norwalk and went through Bellevue, Ohio, instead. The people of Norwalk were chagrined. The local newspaper reported the local attitude which decided "the railroad was not that important anyway. It was not the real stuff, merely nickel-plated." The name mentioned in the sour grapes report in the March 10, 1881, issue of the Norwalk Chronicle stuck and was soon adopted as the public label for the Nickel Plate Road.

A long-time problem was resolved after several decades with the Nickel Plate Elevation, as the project was called. At a cost of $9 million—far exceeding the original costs of the land and track construction—the rail right-of-way was raised through the city and a number of underpasses were built. Bonds were issued in 1953, with the city and county each carrying 40 per cent of the cost and the railroad bearing 20 per cent. Mayor Harry Baals turned the first shovel of dirt on Dec. 15, 1953, and the job was completed in 1955.

Even before the end of the canal, and during the construction of the Nickel Plate, one of the community's longest-lived retail businesses was expanding a scant block away. This was Frank's Department Store, founded by Marx Frank in 1869. Frank's operated in Fort Wayne for more than 90 years. During that time, the firm paralleled the growth of the city and spawned other large department store operations either through later members of the family or former employees. Theodore Frank, son of the founder succeeded to the presidency. In the following generation, Eugene Frank and Jack Frank, brothers, succeeded to the head of the firm, with Morton Frank managing the company in the final years in the 1960's. The more familiar location of the Frank Store in its heyday was just northwest of the corner of Calhoun and Berry Streets. The last location was 1017 South Calhoun Street.

Just to the north of Frank's along Calhoun St. across from the Courthouse was Rurode's, a furniture store started by E. C. Rurode.

The Great Mills

In the mid-19th Century, a number of clothing mills became a part of city commerce. The Old Woolen Mill, as it was later called, was on the north bank of the canal, east of where the Nickel Plate Railroad Depot was later built. "The large woolen factory of French, Hanna & Co. is four stories in height, 105 feet in length and 55 feet in width, giving employment to 40 workers," reported William's Fort Wayne Directory for 1864-5, printed by N. P. Stockbridge, 104 Columbia Street. The woolen mill prospered because farmers brought in wool to be made into blankets, flannel, yarn and cloth for pants and other garments. The head weaver was William Kirkham who came to Fort

Wayne from England. Wooden frames for the mill were made by a man named John Paul Dreiser, according to the Winifred J. Randall notes. Among the loom-builder's children were Theodore Dreiser, born in 1871, and remembered as the author of "An American Tragedy" and "Sister Carrie" and other novels; and Paul Dresser, born in 1858, who changed the spelling of his name and created popular songs including "On the Banks of the Wabash" and "My Gal Sal" and others ever-after associated with Indiana and small-town Midwest. The elder Dreiser and his wife Sarah moved to Fort Wayne from Dayton, Ohio, and lived in the city for a number of years before relocating at Terre Haute where the Dreiser children were born. Theodore Dreiser in his memoirs reported his father was foreman of the Fort Wayne Woolen Mill, rather than a loom-builder.

Cloth manufacturing was expanded with the founding of the Wayne Knitting Mills and the Foster Shirt Waist Factory. The firm of Foster Brothers was established in 1868 at Fort Wayne with branches in Terre Haute and Lafayette. A dry goods and furniture store was purchased in 1879 from other members of the family by David N. and Samuel M. Foster. In 1885, David incorporated the furniture company and the following year Sam Foster sold his interest and devoted full-time to his shirtwaist factory which soon became a major industry in the city.

The Wayne Knitting Mills Co. was founded in 1891 by Theodore F. Thieme who previously operated a drug store at the corner of Wayne and Calhoun Streets. The first officers of the knitting firm were Henry C. Paul, Charles S. Bash, William H. Dreier and Thieme. Using both workers and machinery imported from Germany, the mill started operations in rented quarters at the northeast corner of Main and Clinton Streets. The following year the expanding company moved into a new two-story building along the Nickel Plate Railroad near West Main Street.

In 1904 Wayne Knit received national acclaim, walking off with the highest honors in hosiery awards at the St. Louis World's Fair. In 1908 the capital stock reached the $1 million mark. The following year the Thieme Brothers Company was organized for operating a silk hosiery mill in a newly-erected three-story building across from the old plant. Theodore Thieme, the mill manager, succeeded Samuel Foster as president in 1910. The firm was further expanded in 1911 with the acquisition of the Old Fort Knitting Mills.

This all led to a contest of wills between two Fort Wayne men, Sam Foster and Theodore F. Thieme, perhaps without parallel in Fort Wayne finance. It occurred in 1923 and involved the sale of majority holdings of Wayne Knit. The episode was recorded by Charles H. Buesching, banking associate of Foster, in the Clyde Cover papers. Buueschings remarks follow:

"Probably one of the greatest Foster battles during his entire lifetime was the battle that he had with Theodore F. Thieme. He (Thieme) founded the Wayne Knitting Mills back in 1880, but Theodore was always a rather cheerful gentleman and while he was president and had the general managership he preferred to take his investments in preferred stock of the company and Mr. Foster and D. Paul Mossman and others took common stock and it developed that in about 1922 rather spontaneously Theodore Thieme said he was going to sell out to the Munsingwear Corporation of Minneapolis and Mr. Foster did not disagree with that but he asked Mr. Thieme about the price of common and Mr. Thieme said that there would be a good price for the common stockholders and he named the per share that Thieme would pay the common stockholders.

"Thieme invited Foster on a trip west to California and then brought him back by way of Minneapolis where he met the Munsingwear people. F. M. Stone was then the president. And so they proceeded to come home and prepare for getting the stock in and making the sale. I worked 12 days on gathering in the stock and very quickly at the end of the 12th day I was asked to discontinue soliciting stock and on a rather sudden short announcement Mr. Thieme called the deal off.

"Well, in the meantime, Mead, Marley and Mitchell, the auditors for Munsingwear, had been sent in to the Wayne Knitting Mills and took off a complete audit. The first complete outside audit ever taken of the Wayne

Knitting Mill was taken at that time for that reason. Well, Munsingwear had all the rough figures taken off of the local books and took them back to Minneapolis and started compiling. Mr. Thieme never gave Mr. Foster any particular reason why he called the deal off and he took his family and left the city for Florida. Well, while Mr. Thieme was down in Florida, Munsingwear was very disappointed that for no reason at all that he had just called the deal off. In the meantime they compiled this audit and Mr. Stone called on Mr. Foster in person and showed him the audit which reached back 20 years and which revealed to Mr. Foster for the first time to his knowledge of the substantial bonuses that had been taken out of there by the Thieme brothers. Then, as I recall it, also the final deal, had he sold to Munsingwear, Thieme personally would have gotten a very substantial amount of money in person that ordinarily would have gone to stockholders.

"It was by reason of those astounding figures that Mr. Foster immediately declared war on Theodore Thieme. Munsingwear said they were still willing to buy it at the price they offered Mr. Thieme and Mr. Foster said, 'Well we'll sell it to you. I will personally sell it with or without the consent of Mr. Thieme.' Because selling it direct through Foster would have meant six or eight hundred thousand more money for the stockholders; and so, I was put to work again soliciting my same stockholders, working for Mr. Foster, of course, this time and Mr. Foster and the Niezers and the Mossmans and the Wilsons joined and in forty-eight hours they had over 80% of the stock and that deal then was consummated, the sale was made to Munsingwear. There followed some tremendous lawsuits, Thieme suing Foster and one of the suits wound up in Federal Court with a charge of Thieme against Mr. Foster and Mr. Foster against Mr. Thieme.

"That was the battle of the ages, that happened in 1923."

In the following decades, chief executives of Wayne Knit included Fred Stowell, George E. Rutledge, John J. Kronenberg, Thomas Robson and John Archer.

Fort Wayne Electric

General Electric Co. in Fort Wayne had its beginnings in 1881. That was the year when James A. Jenney, inventor of an electric arc lamp and a small dynamo, and his son Charles came to the city seeking a place to manufacture the products. The Fort Wayne Jenney Electric Light Company was organized by Ronald T. McDonald. Officers of the firm included H. G. Olds, president; Perry A. Randall, vice-president; Oscar A. Simons, secretary; and McDonald, treasurer and general manager.

Jenney Electric took quarters in an old boiler shop building of John H. Bass at the southwest corner of Calhoun and Superior Streets. In the first few years, the company also occupied buildings on Superior Street at the foot of Wells Street and on East Columbia Street. The firm enjoyed some renown in the Midwest in the furnishing of cities with street lighting. An example dated 1883 concerns a contract offered to the town of Kankakee, Ill., by the Jenney Electric Co. of Terre Haute. It said in part: "We agree to erect lamp posts . . . said light to be furnished from twilight till midnight on all nights when the moon does not give sufficient light." Jenney lighted the World's Fair grounds in 1884-85 at New Orleans.

The purchase of the old Gause Agricultural works and land along Broadway and the Pittsburgh, Fort Wayne and Chicago Railroad resulted in the permanent nucleus of the expanding firm from 1885 on. This was several years after the advantage of arc lighting had been demonstrated in exhibits for the public in Fort Wayne. It might be called the beginning of the end of the gaslight era. The first incandescent lamps were installed in the Home Billiard Parlor in 1881. That same year, a temporary lighting plant was installed in Library Hall, at the corner of Lewis and Calhoun Streets. It consisted of four lights driven by a traction engine.

In 1888 the Thomson-Houston Electric Co. purchased a controlling interest in the Jenney Electric Company and the firm was subsequently renamed the Fort Wayne Electric Company. In 1888 the entire works were destroyed by fire. The rebuilt plant was in operation in July, 1889. The following year the company purchased a part interest in the Wood arc light system from Thomson-Houston. Accompanied by 100 employees from Brooklyn, N. Y., the young man for whom the system was named, James J. Wood, arrived in Fort Wayne Dec. 3, 1890. The words "Wood System" as well as "Fort Wayne Electric Co." could be seen on old brick factory walls as long as 80 years later at the Broadway works.

Already in Fort Wayne in 1890, having arrived the previous year, was a young man who eventually headed the development of much of the General Electric operation in Fort Wayne. He was Edward A. Barnes, born in India in 1865 and educated in England. He began his electrical career as an associate of the Thomas Edison interests in London in 1884 and joined the Fort Wayne Electric Co. in 1889. He worked his way up from chief inspector to general superintendent, finally retiring in 1931 after 42 years with the company.

In 1892, General Electric Co. came into being with the merging of the Edison firm, Thomson-Houston and other interests. The financial panic of 1893 brought hard times to the Fort Wayne Electric Co. and it went into receivership in 1894. The Fort Wayne Electric Corp. was formed to purchase the assets. The officers were R. T. McDonald, president; Charles S. Knight, vice-president; Charles C. Miller, secretary-treasurer; James Wood, general superintendent; and Fred Hunting, engineering head. This firm folded in 1899 and another company, called the Fort Wayne Electric Works, acquired control. Heading the operation were Henry C. Paul, President; S. D. Green, vice-president; M. F. Westover, secretary; Fred Hunting, treasurer; and James Wood, factory manager. To bring about the reorganization, General Electric Co. had purchased the assets from the receiver. Finally in 1911, the Fort Wayne Works were merged with the parent company and in 1916, the old identity disappeared. It was in the year of 1911 that the Pennsylvania Railroad elevation took place near the Broadway plant of G.E., and at Fairfield Avenue, Harrison, Lafayette, and Hanna Streets, opening the way for the great expansion of Fort Wayne's south side.

It was at the Fort Wayne plant in 1912 that G.E. developed and began production of refrigeration equipment. In 1927 with the building of monitor-top refrigerators, the plant at Winter St. was obtained and the refrigerator production was moved to that location. In the meantime, major new buildings for the production of motors, generators and transformers were built at the Broadway location in 1915 and 1917. A great expansion of plant space occurred in 1941 with the building of the supercharger plant on Taylor Street. Following World War II, G.E. purchased the facility from the government and converted it to a major center for small motor production and wire mill. By the 1950's, the G.E. operations in Fort Wayne had a payroll of more than 9,000. H. A. MacKinnon, G.E. vice-president and chief operating officer in Fort Wayne during the late 1950's and 1960's, commented that Fort Wayne's plant was tied to the evergrowing needs of everything from missiles, computers and milking machines to the endless products of factory and home use.

City Episodes

Franklin P. Randall was not one to be trifled with. When his red brick and stone mansion on East Berry St. burned in 1873, he rebuilt it exactly as before. The original house had been erected five years earlier in 1868—one of the few years of that era when he was not occupied as mayor. The Randall mansion remained a landmark near the city's downtown until 1950.

Judge James L. Worden, a justice of the Indiana Supreme Court returned to Fort Wayne to be elected mayor and began his term on January 1, 1865. He served for less than a year before resigning. Benjamin Saunders served out his two-year term. Henry C. Sharpe, a hat maker, became the first Republican mayor of Fort Wayne in 1867. Franklin Randall in 1869 was returned to office and was re-elected mayor two years later. This completed his five terms as city chief executive.

During this same period, Dr. James H. Smart, starting in 1865, was superintendent of the public schools. He moved on to Indianapolis as state superintendent of public instruction from 1870 to 1880 and then became president of Purdue University.

The Randall mansion was becoming a center for Fort Wayne social events and for meetings of state Democratic politicians. Among the notables entertained at the Randall house were Indiana Governors William Hendricks, Oliver P. Morton and Isaac Pusey Gray. Hendricks was running mate with Presidential candidate Samuel Tilden. Chicago Mayor Carter Harrison and other Illinois Democrats were house guests. The Randall place was ostentatious inside and out. At the iron gatepost was a cannon used by Commodore Oliver Hazard Perry in the Battle of Lake Erie in the War of 1812.

This was the setting for the memorable visit of Governor Blue Jeans Williams, who was addicted to the common manner as many South-of-40 politicians were in Hoosier history. Hundreds of people had gathered to meet the dignitary, Winifred Randall, a relative of the mayor, related. While the band was playing "Hail to the Chief," Governor Williams emerged from the house and proceeded toward a carriage. He stopped momentarily near the gate and blew his nose, without handkerchief, on either side of the sidewalk, "then finished the performance with the expert use of his coat sleeve."

In the 1870's and 1880's, New Year's Day was typically an open-house affair at many of the Fort Wayne homesteads. This was especially true at the Randall place where Mrs. Randall was assisted by Mrs. Sam Morss, Mrs. J. B. White, Mrs. T. J. Hanna, Miss Margaret Colerick, Miss Jessie Hanna, Mrs. Robert Lowry, Mrs. Allan Zollars, Miss Clara Goodwin and Miss Esther McKinnie. Other stops were the homes of Charles Bond on Fairfield Ave., John Bass just northwest of town and those of R. J. Fisher and O. P. Morgan. Regulars at these events were old Fort Wayne family members such as Samuel R. Alden, James M. Barrett, Perry A. Randall, Pliny Hoagland, Fred Beach, J. K. Edgerton and A. P. Edgerton.

Shows of Wealth

In the 1870's, 1880's and 1890's, Fort Wayne was a thriving and bustling community where almost everyone owned his own home. The population grew from 17,718 in 1870 to more than 45,000 in 1900. In 1871, the suburban districts of Bloomingdale and Bowserville were annexed to the city. Bloomingdale was north of the St. Mary's River and west of Wells Street. Bowserville was north of the St. Mary's and east of Wells Street, though in later years the area of East Creighton Ave. near the Bowser Pump Works was sometimes referred to as Bowserville. Frederick W. Kuhne founded his abstract firm in this booming climate.

It was a time of gas light (electric lights came into use in the 1880's but gas remained more prevalent during most of the period) and gaudy shows of wealth by those who had it. The rich tended to be Republican but the Democratic Party was dominant in Fort Wayne, due in part to the heavy concentration of German and Irish in the population who tended to be Democrats.

Social events were usually formal and fancy. Couples in bustles or great coats moved about in buggies and surreys or rigs from the livery stables. In winter, sleighing parties were popular. Adults and children would load into cutters, sleighs, sledges and bobsleds as horses pranced across the snowy landscape.

Perhaps the 19th Century's most famous music hall personality was in Fort Wayne in the winter of 1883. Lillie Langtry joined in the local winter magic as described in a Jan. 20, 1883, issue of the Sentinel.

"Thursday evening about 25 society people enjoyed a sleigh ride around the city until half past ten o'clock, when the whole party repaired to the Nickel Plate Restaurant." Following dinner there were "alluring waltzes" and merry times until the wee hours in the morning, at which time revelers again took to the sleighs under the cold skies. "Among those present were C. B. Woodworth and wife; Theodore Thieme and wife; Robertson J. Fisher and wife; Mrs. Tyler and Mrs. Martha Merriwether; the Misses Lou and Flora Orff, May Robertson, Daisy Myerson,

Josie and Grace Edgerton, Mary Randall; Ed and Mont Orff; Henry Hanna; Ed Edgerton; Colonel Mumby; Samuel R. Alden; Mr. Root; and last but not least, Mrs. Lillie Langtry whose blond beauty and aquiline features were set off by a poke bonnet and a blue-and-gold fascinator borrowed for the occasion."

On the same day, children and the young people were having a taffy pull at the residence of Mr. and Mrs. Max Nirdlinger where "the young men worked gallantly until the golden mass was a luscious creamy white." It was the era of roller skating at the Princess Rink on the corner of Main and Fulton Streets, dancing parties at Ewing's Hall at Main and Harrison Streets and balls at Randall Hall at Harrison and Columbia Streets. Bicycle parties became popular in the 1890's; and on June 22, 1894, the Gazette reported a party on one of the new electric streetcars.

"After the ride over the lines in the city, the club was charmingly entertained by Mrs. M. S. Mahurin. The participants were Messrs. and Mesdames A. Warriner, A. L. Randall, Frank Randall, Elwin Hulse, M. S. Mahurin, P. A. Randal, D.K. and W. Creighton, H. Fischer, O. N. Heaton, Thomas Duncan, Byron Thompson, J. W. Trainer and D. L. Harding; Dr. and Mrs. B. Van Sweringen; and the Misses Luela Boles, Louise Robertson and Abbie Keegan."

For many years the masked balls of the Fort Wayne Saengerbund, a German singing society, were a social institution. These events, starting in 1876, included a Mardi Gras parade with carnival band, "A motley crew of maskers on foot and horseback" who sounded with tin horns and others who poured into the Academy of Music. As late as 1892 the masked ball was still a great attraction and was held at the Princess Rink by that date.

The Women's Club, later the Fort Wayne Woman's Club (1925), was formed in 1892. On Sept. 21, 1894, articles of incorporation were filed. At that date the officers were Mrs. Sara Foster, president; Mrs. Elizabeth Dawson, vice-president; Mrs. Minnie Lauferty, secretary; Mrs. Isabella Evans, treasurer; and directors, Mrs. May Warriner, Mrs. Essie Myers, Miss Merica Hoagland, Mrs. Ella Wilding, Mrs. L. C. Woodworth, Miss Agness Hamilton, Miss Clara Zollars, Mrs. Ellen McGrath, Mrs. Sara Foster, Mrs. Georgiana Bond. Also formed in 1892 was the Fortnightly Club. The first meeting was at the home of Judge Lindley M. Ninde, a place called Wildwood. The discussion group was formed at the suggestion of Mrs. Charles Redway Dryer.

People vied in the giving of elaborate receptions. The man with the most was John Bass who on Dec. 11, 1890, had 500 guests at his home, Brookside, later the St. Francis College Campus. Ladies paraded silk and diamonds across tile floor and past palms and orchids. The men took a bit of fresh air on the frozen lake where the sport of curling had recently been imported from Scotland. David McKay, manager of the Bass farms, was the resident expert on the art of moving the polished stones on the ice and the skillful handling of the brooms.

Weddings were quite large affairs. The Eliza Hanna-Fred Hayden nuptial in 1873 included the sending of 800 admission cards. Reineke's Orchestra played Mendelssohn's "Midsummer Night's Dream" for the marriage of Hattie Rosenthal and Louis Frankel in 1892. When Lillie Morse married Ronald T. McDonald, a whole special train of the Jackson and Saginaw Railroad was chartered for guests for the trip to the Angola wedding site and back.

Tragic Events

The period was not without its tragedies. In 1881 the Clinton St. Bridge over the St. Mary's River collapsed. Killed was Henry C. Hanna, son of Judge Sam Hanna.

In 1887 a boiler explosion crumbled St. Mary's Catholic Church. Two persons died, Anton Evans, the sexton, and Alberta Willard, a 13-year-old girl. She happened to be walking past the front of the church on the way to school when the blast blew off the heavy church doors which crushed her. The church was rebuilt later the same year.

A city ordinance passed in 1885 proved to be a minor tragedy to Fred Woenker, the poundmaster. The new law prevented cows from running at large in the streets. When Woenker attempted to enforce it, he was attacked by angry cow owners, particularly women. He retaliated by filing a number of affidavits against the assailants.

The great street car strike was launched on Memorial Day, 1893. While the regular conductors and motormen were holed up in the Knights of Labor headquarters, scabs operating the cars were being pelted with decayed eggs and other missiles. At the old transfer corner, Main and Calhoun Streets, one of the cars was turned over. Mayor Zollinger issued a proclamation. A mass meeting of some 3,000 persons was held on the Courthouse yard. J. M. Barrett, attorney for the Traction Company, called for enlarged police staffs to protect company property. Sheriff E. F. Clausmeier enlisted a large force of deputies to join city police. The strike was settled on June 15 when the company granted a pay increase from the previous 13½ cents an hour to 15 cents.

In May, 1895, Ringling Brothers Circus was in town, parading down Calhoun Street. A frightened or enraged horse crashed into the street-side crowd, killing Mrs. Eliza LeMay instantly and fatally injuring several other persons. As a result damages of $1,433 were paid to the families of the victims, with Ringling adding $600 more. In the heat of tragedy, the City Council passed an ordinance carefully restricting the conduct of elephants, horses and camels on the streets of Fort Wayne.

In 1895 one of the city's greatest celebrations occurred. A parade five miles long was the central attraction. Memorial arches were erected. One hundred guns were fired by the Zollinger battery. Gas fueled flames from arches proclaimed the festivities at night. A great campfire was in the street in front of the Princess Rink as thousands cavorted about. Governor Claude Matthews and his staff were on hand to join in the festivities. The occasion was the 101st anniversary of the building of the fort by Anthony Wayne. The October 22, 1894, date, the 100th anniversary, had passed by before anyone had noticed.

Mayor Zollinger

Charles A. Zollinger, the Allen County blacksmith, figures big in the life of two communities. He was first president of the board of trustees for the new town of New Haven, incorporated on June 7, 1866, and was seven times elected mayor of Fort Wayne. In addition, he was elected to a two-year term as sheriff of Allen County. That was in October, 1870, when he was still a Republican. Three years later he switched to the Democratic Party and ran a successful campaign for mayor of Fort Wayne, the first of six successive terms.

In 1885, instead of running again for mayor, Zollinger accepted an appointment by President Grover Cleveland as veteran's pension agent for the State of Indiana.

Charles F. Muhler was mayor for a pair of two-year terms, 1886 through 1888. Daniel L. Harding was elected to the 1889-91 term, then was defeated by Colonel Zollinger who returned to local politics for an unprecedented seventh term.

Zollinger was raised to the rank of colonel during his career as a soldier during the Civil War. An immigrant from Germany, the onetime blacksmith apprentice volunteered as a private; participated in the bloody battle of Shiloh; was raised to regimental commander, led troops in the battle of Atlanta and was with Sherman on the March to the Sea. After the war he worked as a blacksmith in New Haven, but soon moved to a job with the Wabash Railroad in Fort Wayne, then into his political career.

Some of the city firsts during the Zollinger years were the city water system, the fire alarm boxes on city streets and the extension of a real sewer system. He also began the community's first regular paid fire department. He named Henry Hilbrecht, Jr., as fire chief, a man who became a permanent fixture in that job. Through it all, Zollinger was a fiscal conservative. He reduced the tax rate which stood at $1 per $100 assessed valuation at the end of his tenure. Zollinger died in harness toward the end of his final term. The date was Dec. 27, 1893.

Henry P. Scherer, a Democrat, served out Zollinger's term until Chauncey B. Oakley became mayor May 1, 1894. Oakley ran as an independent on a "reform" platform and rigidly enforced the laws. He was replaced at the polls after two years by Scherer who served until May 1, 1901.

Old City Hall

It was during Mayor Zollinger's last year in office that the Victorian sandstone City Hall was completed at the corner of Berry and Barr Streets. Its thick walls and fortress-like architecture was to weather four generations of climatc and gibes.

Built on land donated in 1840 by Sam Hanna to the city, the City Hall cost $69,806 to build, including $1,889 for inside furnishings. There was $731.10 left over in the building fund. The architects for the much-maligned design were J. F. Wing and W. S. Mahurin. At the time, however, there was elegant praise for the imposing edifice. And in truth, by the end of its public career in 1971, the structure and its sooty weathered appearance had gained wide affection in the community. On dedication day, April 20, 1893, speeches were made by Herman Michael, chairman of the building committee; ex-Senator J. D. Sarighausen; ex-Senator Charles McCulloch; ex-Mayor C. F. Muhler who had originally pushed the City Hall project; City Attorney William H. Shambaugh; Colonel Oakley; Colonel David N. Foster; and Circuit Court Judge Edward O'Rourke.

South Wayne

Fort Wayne was considerably enlarged on August 14, 1894, when the City Council declared the annexation of South Wayne. This was a territory which extended south of Creighton Ave. between Hoagland Ave. and the St. Mary's River.

The wooded area had long been a favorite ground for the Miami Indians who remained in the precincts during the early town days. The reservations of Richardville, LaFontaine and Beaubien were all along the St. Mary's just south of the South Wayne community. A stream through the area, known as Shawnee Run, disappeared with drainage work. A stone bridge over Shawnee Run had existed along Fairfield Ave., just south of Pontiac Street. The bridge work was still visible under the street, according to Peter Certia who went down the sewer in 1952 to have a look at it. The stream had meandered through what later became Beechwood Circle and environs east and west.

Asa Fairfield, a sea captain from Maine and a privateer in the War of 1812, came to Fort Wayne in 1833. He purchased land in the South Wayne vicinity in 1834 from Benjamin Kerchival and Ann Turner, a granddaughter of Chief Little Turtle and daughter of the fort surgeon. Fairfield prospered as farmer and canal boat operator. It was his boat, the "Indiana," which made the first trip on the Wabash-Erie Canal. The date was July 4, 1834, and the trip was to Huntington and back to Fort Wayne.

In the decade that followed, Asa's sons Cyrus and John watched hundreds of Indians race across the landscape on horseback to the saloon of Old Chief Godfrey. Thousands of wild pigeons weighed down the tree limbs of the forested area. Wild hogs roamed and wolves preyed on them. The area between Creighton Ave. and Rudisill Blvd. was originally called Richardville before being named South Wayne. The first Allen County infirmary was built in the district at Savilla and Broadway. A plank road went along the Indianapolis Road, which was later renamed Broadway.

Some of the streets speak names of early homesteaders Byron Thompson, B. B. Miner and R. S. Taylor. Fairfield sold part of his land in the 1860's to C. D. Bond, George Fox and L. M. Ninde. Cyrus Fairfield ran a soap factory on Broadway. Thompson owned a stirrup factory nearby. Early residents included Judge Fay, Homer Hartman, Edward Colerick, Samuel Stophlet, W. J. Vesey, Dr. Isaac Knapp, G. E. Bursley, O. N. Heaton, and John Ferguson. Early landmarks, also remembered by streets, were Beaver's Mill and Esmond's Mill. The Bond brothers, Charles and Stephen B., both had large homes to the west of Fairfield. James Barrett's place was on the other side of Fairfield.

In order to avoid paying Fort Wayne taxes, the residents of South Wayne incorporated in 1889. Within a few years, however, the costs of Jenney Electric street lights, roads and a water works convinced some of the South Wayners that separate towns don't have all the advantages. A community fight developed. Attorney J. M. Barrett, Sr., won the battle for Fort Wayne by guiding an annexation bill through the State Legislature, providing for a city to annex adjacent territory without majority consent of the annexed. This is the same Barrett who developed the Barrett Bond system for citizen participation in public improvements. The final meeting of the South Wayne Council was on Sept. 1, 1894, at which J. M. Henry, president, permanently adjourned the official community.

At about the same time South Wayne was becoming a part of Fort Wayne, some other residential areas were being developed in the city. Typical of the fine residential areas of the era of the 1890's was that built in what was formerly Williams Park, bound by Creighton Ave., Webster St., Woodland Ave. and Hoagland Avenue. Louis F. Curdes, long-time real estate broker and builder, plotted and sold the Williams Park area. Ten years later in 1905, Curdes opened the Forest Park addition on the northeast side. The fine residential development stimulated and influenced building on the city's northeast side for generations thereafter. The long oval of Forest Park Blvd. was built over the exercise track owned by the Centlivre family and used by the fine show and race horses which the Centlivres maintained for many years.

End of the Swamp

The landscape just southwest of Fort Wayne was changed, starting in 1887. This was the Great Marsh or Portage Marsh over which Indians and fur traders and explorers had floated their canoes on their travels between the Maumee and Wabash rivers. The Portage Marsh was the western portion of the Great Black Swamp which played such a strategic role in the calculations of soldiers and warriors during the great Indian wars of the 18th Century. Portage Marsh spread over parts of Allen, Huntington and Whitley counties. The Great Black Swamp extended as far as the Auglaise River tributaries in Ohio. Through this marsh flowed a sluggish stream known as the Little Wabash or Little River, which emptied into the Wabash near Huntington. At the point where Little River emerged from the swamp, its bed was as wide as the Wabash or the St. Joseph in Fort Wayne. According to the Fort Wayne Gazette, issue of April 9, 1887, "a barren waste of swampland stretches for miles along the (Wabash Railroad) tracks on either side farther than the eye can reach. Clumps of scraggy timber relieve the dreary monotony of the view. Through this great marsh many shallow broad streams run . . . ducks wheel in great squawking flocks, seeking safety from the hunters who pick their uncertain way through the mud and weeds of the treacherous bog." It was a place of desolate beauty, clouds of mosquitoes and plagues of malaria. It all came to an end with the reclaiming of some 35,000 acres of land in what was reportedly the greatest drainage project in the United States up to that time.

On May 20, 1885, the Allen Superior Court approved a plan to drain the swamp and levy the costs against the landowners. The petition had been filed by William Branstrator, George Lawrence, Benjamin Rothschild, Solomon Bash, August C. Trentman, John Sprankel, Henry C. Paul, Charles Aldrich and John C. Peters, all land owners. Six months later a plan was submitted for completing the work and assessing the costs and benefits. The report was filed by the Little River Draining Co. which consisted of Stephen Bond, president of the Old National Bank of Fort Wayne; Boltz and Derheimer, contractors; Henry C. Paul and Solomon Bash. The report had been drawn up by a ditch commission which included O. B. Wiley, county surveyor; W. W. Shoaff and Edward Ely. The great drainage contract became a reality with the awarding of the contract to Boltz and Derheimer for the sum of $137,017 in 1886. The contractors already owned one large steam dredge with which they were clearing Eel River. Joseph Derheimer purchased two more huge steam dredges, costing $10,000 each, according to the contemporary accounts, for the swamp job. In addition to cutting through miles of mud, Bultz and Derheimer removed 93,000 cubic yards of solid rock, all under water, in opening the swamp lands between Fort Wayne and Huntington. Ditches channeled water to both the St. Mary's and Wabash Rivers. This is the same Joseph Derheimer who years earlier had installed the brick sewer system on Calhoun St. which served for a century with portions remaining after the 1971 sewer renewal programs. In July 1889, just three years after the contract was awarded, the limestone barrier near Huntington was blasted and the drainage project was completed. Portage Marsh became history.

Robison Park

Perhaps the greatest impact on the community's recreational habits developed in 1896. The phenomenon was known as Robison Park. It was a time and place of band pavilions, river boats, roller coasters, dancing under the moonlight and theatre-going.

The key to Robison Park was the street car. These vehicles of the Nineties and after would be loaded with young ladies in bustles and gay blades in derby hats. The trip was out Spy Run and then along a route which later became Parnell Ave. to the park some seven miles northeast of town along the St. Joseph River. Located there was a heavily wooded area and a river impounded by a dam originally built to provide feeder waters for the Wabash-Erie Canal.

The park was operated by the street car company, at first known as the Fort Wayne Electric Railway Company when electric cars first ran in town in 1892, but called the Fort Wayne Consolidated Railway Co. after 1895. This firm purchased 265 acres for the park, called Swift Park for a few months, but then renamed in honor of M. Stanley Robison, moving force and first manager of the park.

Robison Park opened on June 13, 1896. The first great attraction was the famous balloonist trio, called aeronauts at the time, consisting of the Leroy Sisters, Victoria and Sadie; and S. L. Hubbard. In an accident high over the crowd, Victoria Leroy and Hubbard, in separate balloons, collided. Hubbard hung on in a descent with one hand and Victoria ended up in a treetop. Both survived that episode, but Victoria was killed a few weeks later at the St. Louis Fair when she plunged 2,500 feet before a horrified crowd of 10,000.

On the first Fourth of July at Robison Park, in 1896, the largest crowd ever up to that date in Northern Indiana, 35,000 people, assembled for the festivities. Though there was a dry rule in the park, liquor dealers including one calling himself Colonel Allen had barges in the river for thirsty customers with the means to travel on water.

A regular steamboat operated on the river for excursion parties until 1905. Named the "Clementina," it was run by Henry, Joe and John Hartman. At that time, the dam broke down, lowering the water level of the river, making large boat operations impossible. Dancing was in the main pavilion where music was provided by a huge orchestron which could be heard across the parklands. It was built by K. A. Engman and played by John Hoke and Ben Ankenbruck. Other times, bands and groups performed. Theatrical performances were staged under a tent which could seat 950 people. The area was lighted for night play. There were steel towers with cable cars attached which swung screaming patrons around in thrilling rides. The roller coaster went up and down along the banks near the river. There were groves, shooting galleries, confection stands, photograph studios, bowling alleys, a merry-go-round and a pony track. A big thrill was the "shoot the chute." This entailed getting into a small flat-bottomed scow with possibly a dozen others on a platform 60 feet high. The scow was then rifled down a 150 foot chute to an exciting landing on the river.

Louis Heilbroner, who planned the activities at Robison Park, was one of the first to introduce motion pictures in the area. These crude early silents, considered a marvel at the time, were developed by Thomas Edison and were operated with his Projectiscope.

The first showing in August, 1897, at Robison Park may have followed earlier showings that same year at the Temple Theater on South Clinton and Wayne Street.

On August 18, 1902, people in Fort Wayne picked up their morning newspaper and read that Carrie Nation had arrived in town on the Lake Erie and Western Railroad. It was a great day for the Anti-Saloon League and large crowds converged on Robison Park for the main rally. Later at the scene, the noted crusader was asked:

"Carrie, have you brought your hatchet?"

"No," she replied, "I have brought an ax this time." She said she was appealing to President McKinley to close down the saloons across the lands. In less than 20 years the movement Carrie Nation set in motion would realize its goal.

The Fort Wayne Traction Company came into being in 1899 following a receivership action and continued to operate the park. For the next 20 years, Robison Park remained a highly frequented recreational area. It all came to an end on April 28, 1920, when Indiana Service Corporation took control of the street car firm. "The figures show 197,232 passengers were carried to the park in 1919; this number of passengers is less than the number carried in four average week days in the City of Fort Wayne at the present time," Robert M. Feustel, receiver for the Traction Company, reported in 1920.

Some of the buildings and concessions at Robison Park were dismantled and moved to Trier's Park on the west side of the St. Mary's River during the 1920's, 1930's and early 1940's. Even the roller coaster at Trier's Park originally came from Robison Park. Trier's Amusement Park was dismantled later as part of the City Park Department and was renamed West Swinney Park.

As for the old Robison Park area, it gradually returned to nature and wildlife. Boy Scouts and others camped there for several decades afterwards, building fires and setting up pup tents near grottos and springs left over from a more glittering era. Still later, motorcyclists roared along the paths and down the hills.

Courthouse Built

The dedication of the Allen County Courthouse was on September 23, 1902. The cost of the building and furnishings was $817--553.59. It is interesting to note that just the remodeling of the interior and some window replacement and sand-blasting on the exterior in 1972 ran half again more than the entire original cost.

But though dedicated in 1902, the Courthouse was seven years in the making, starting with the acceptance of the plans in 1895. It was the fourth Allen County Courthouse, and before construction could begin, there was the razing of the old third Courthouse, built in 1861, and the raising of the tax money for the grand new project.

Actually, there was considerable controversy over whether a new Courthouse should be built at all. Perry Randall suggested the old one was "too good to be thrown away." At this, James M. Barrett, Sr., retorted it was "too poor to be left." Just a few of the drawbacks were the lack of fire safety, poor ventilation and the fact that there was no system of sewerage. In 1894 the Gazette had referred to the "frightful odor" emanating from the Courthouse "which would shame a glue factory or a slaughter house." There was a report of foul gas coming from the basement area and doubts expressed that the water closets there had been "plumbed, cleaned or flushed in the past 30 years."

The first lot of bonds for financing the fourth Courthouse were sold to Paul Brothers and John W. White, both local firms; and White purchased the entire second issue, in both instances representing outside financial concerns. Two local bidders; Christian Boseker and John Suelzer, bid on the entire construction contract, but the general contractor for the job was James Stewart and Company, St. Louis. Brentwood S. Tolan was the architect; A. Hattersley & Sons, plumbing and wiring contractor; William Moellering & Sons, the power house; Louis Schwartzkopf, the tunnel; H. H. Andrews, wood furnishing; C. C. Schlatter, the hardware; Diebold Lock and Safe Co., the vault; W. H. Andrews, interior decorations; Wolf & Dessauer, interior furnishings; and John

H. Welch, the copper box for the corner stone. Inspectors were L. B. Larimore, J. H. Brannan, H. W. Jenson and George Jacoby.

The main materials for the building are Blue Bedford Stone and Vermont Granite, plus white marble. The length of the building is 270 feet, the width being 134 feet, height to clear story cornice being 76 feet, height from the sidewalk to the top of the statue is 225 feet. The statue itself is 13 feet, eight inches. The diameter of the four clock dials is 13 feet.

The cornerstone was laid on Nov. 17, 1897. It was a great day and Indiana Governor James A. Mount was on hand to lead the ceremonies. The city was represented by Louis Peltier, the oldest resident who was born in the old fort in 1813. Col. J. H. Dougall headed the parade. The Rev. Samuel Wagenhals gave the invocation and Charles McCulloch, president of the Hamilton National Bank, gave introductory remarks. Judge John Morris laid the stone—that is, tapped it with a trowel, the stone weighing eight tons. Orations were given by Col. R. S. Robertson, William Breen, as well as Governor Mount and Judge Morris.

During the construction period, William H. Goshorn was building superintendent. Though partially occupied in 1900, the completion and dedication weren't until 1902. Following the invocation by M. Rev. Herman J. Alerding, Bishop of Fort Wayne, addresses were given by James M. Barrett, Sr.; Charles McCulloch; William Bourke Cochran who was a famous orator of the day from New York; Col. R. S. Robertson, the historian. The Rev. David W. Moffett, pastor of the First Presbyterian Church, pronounced benediction.

Italian marble and verde Antique Scagliola were liberally used in the stairs and columns inside the building. The Greco-Roman architecture and interior panels and vaults attracted a number of widely regarded artists of the era. William Barth executed the two reclining sculptured pieces above the first floor tablet. The murals above the ballistrade of Italian marble and on either side of the arched windows of the rotunda were painted by Charles Holloway of Clinton, Iowa. Holloway also painted the "Treaty of Greenville" in Court Room No. 3. Barth, of Fort Wayne did most of the bronze sculptured panels in Superior Court. The fancy "Music" bronze, however was executed by Richard Zeitner of Cincinnati and the "Art" panel by William Ehrman. The paintings of "The Battle of Fallen Timbers" and the portrait of Anthony Wayne in Court Room 3 were done by Florian Piexotto of New York. The three-foot murals above the cornice of the Circuit Court were painted by Carl Gutherz of Washington, D. C. He did much of the mural work in the Congressional Library.

The 20th Century

The end of the 19th Century and the beginning of the 20th Century was truly the end of one era and the beginning of the next. In much of the world, the first decade of the 20th seemed much like the preceding century, but the beginnings of great upheavals were already at work. This was evident in the United States as it was in Fort Wayne.

The official 1900 census gave the city a population of 45,115, which was nearly 10,000 more than the total 10 years earlier. The first few automobiles, looking everybit like carriages only much noisier, were drawing attention along the several brick streets and dusty or muddy roads. Interurbans, short-run intercity electric trains, were just around the corner as high-volume modes of transportation.

The year before, in 1899, the Spanish American War which had been fought mainly in 1898, came to an end with the Treaty of Paris. The U.S. stepped up its place as an international power and assumed control over Cuba and the Philippines. In 1900, the national encampment of the Union Veteran Legion was held in Fort Wayne. The ceremonies included the mounting of a cannon captured from the Spanish during the war. This was placed on a stone pedestal at Old Fort Park.

The 1900 presidential campaign included an appearance in Fort Wayne by Democratic candidate William Jennings Bryan. His opponent, William McKinley, had visited the city in earlier campaigns. The election was a rematch of both candidates and issues of 1896. It was the Cross of Gold and the political bossism typified by Mark Hanna all over again. Actualy the most interesting thing about the campaign was big-business-serving Hanna's failure to kill off the political career of Theodore Roosevelt, who was chosen as Vice Presidential candidate.

The election nationally was a win for the Republicans and the McKinley-Roosevelt ticket. But Fort Wayne voters went the other way. Bryan the Democrat got 10,764 votes to McKinley's 8,250. It was in the following year, on September 6, 1901, in the first year of his second term, that McKinley was assassinated. McKinley was visiting the Pan American Exposition at Buffalo, N. Y., when he was shot by anarchist Leon Czolgosz. The tragic event was a shock to people in Fort Wayne as elsewhere. On Sept. 13, Theodore Roosevelt was sworn in as President. He reversed the government's attitude toward economics business regulation. It was truly the end of an era in U.S. politics which had existed since the end of the Civil War. In the 1904 general election, Fort Wayne delivered one of its few Presidential majorities up to that date for a Republican. Roosevelt was favored over Alton Parker by 10,261 votes to 9,250. It was a local win which neither Abraham Lincoln nor Hoosier candidate and President Benjamin Harrison had been able to bring off.

In the first year of the 20th Century the revolutionary theories of Marx and other socialists were more in evidence in the United States than in Czarist Russia. This condition was not lost on Fort Wayne, as the 1901 city election results show. In that year Henry C. Berghoff, the Democrat, was elected mayor with 5,176 votes. He defeated Charles E. Reese, Jr., the Republican, who received 3,317 votes, and Martin H. Wefel, the Socialist candidate with 716 votes.

Hosey Runs

Four years later Berghoff backed City Councilman William H. Hosey for mayor. It was the beginning of a long career for Hosey as chief executive in Fort Wayne and far greater involvement of government in city affairs. Hosey ran on a platform advocating public ownership of municipal utilities. He denounced any attempt to transfer the water utility to private control and promised to fight the gas utility to gain lower rates. He promised to build a city-owned electric light plant and to elevate the Pennsylvania and Wabash Railroad tracks. In his many years in office, he realized an astonishing number of his goals.

After the Roosevelt margin in Fort Wayne the previous year, the atmosphere didn't appear favorable for Democratic candidates. But Hosey had wide backing. Supporters included Guy Colerick, Julian Franke, Dr. Harry Bruggeman, Tom McLaughlin, James Hayes, Charles McCulloch, William Bayer, Martin Ankenbruck, Robert E. Kelly, Judge Walpole Colerick; plus several Republicans including David N. Foster.

Hosey's opponent was Edward White, banker and son of Civil War hero James White and grandfather of Astronaut Edward White, III. It was reportedly one of the more hostile mayorality races in the city's history. Hosey partisans were offset by Sheriff Jesse Grice, who would succeed Hosey as mayor, and Judge Owen Heaton. Both men were hard Republican campaigners in White's behalf. Hosey, however, won by a fairly comfortable margin, 6,257 votes to White's 4,881. Two Republicans managed to gain office in the election—Judge J. Frank Mungovan and Clerk Benjamin Skelton. The other offices went to the Democrats.

Like all mayors of the turn-of-the-century era, Mayor Hosey spent a good share of time contending with the evils attributed to the more than 100 saloons in the central city area, the floating gambling operations and the inevitable redlight districts. There were some complaints of possible police corruption by Journal-Gazette editor Andrew Moynihan in the final year of Hosey's first term, but the greatest police scandal up to that time was to break during the term of Hosey's successor Jesse Grice.

City Light

City Light had its beginning when the Hosey Administration submitted the question to the voters in 1906. The referendum was overwhelmingly in favor. Construction was begun in 1907 and the plant was in operation in July, 1908. At first, City Light furnished power for only street lighting and municipal needs. A bitter controversy with the Fort Wayne and Wabash Valley Traction Company developed when City Light moved into commercial and residential competition, but the municipal utility prevailed.

Hosey was a great and stubborn believer in rock-well water for the city, despite the receding water table and advice that rivers would furnish a more ample supply. An unfriendly political cartoon in 1907 showed the mayor tossing cats into the Reservoir. This was triggered by the finding of a dead cat when the south side reservoir was being repaired that year. It was during Hosey's first term that the Barr Street farmers market near City Hall was built.

Efforts to elevate the Pennsylvania and Wabash Railroad tracks were stimulated when a Fort Wayne Representative to the State Legislature, William Fruechtenicht, sponsored a bill over the opposition of the railroads. It provided that the city pay 25 per cent of the elevation costs and the railroads pay the rest. The first underpasses were at Calhoun St. and Fairfield Avenue. Actual construction began during Mayor Grice's term, which started in 1910. A singular disaster, the San Francisco earthquake and fire in 1906, drew the interest and charity of Fort Wayne. Mayor Hosey forwarded funds collected in the city for relief of the disaster victims.

The election of 1909 pitted Jesse Grice, the butcher and live stock dealer and former Republican Sheriff, against August Schmidt, controller under Hosey who had the political burden of being a college graduate. Grice won with 7,440 votes—842 more than Schmidt. The Fort Wayne News on Nov. 4, two days after the election, printed a cartoon showing the voters giving Grice a diploma inscribed "Election."

Bricks and Trees

Grice began one of the biggest street-building and sidewalk improvement programs in the history of the community. More than 35 miles of brick paving were laid and some 53 miles of sidewalks. A half century later, many city streets still had the brick underpinning and most of the sidewalks were still in use. Grice also started wide-scale ornamental lamp posts along the streets and in 1912 hired Carl Getz, a Purdue University forestry graduate, to begin the tree and conservation programs along the streets and in the parks. The ornamental lamp posts extended in the downtown area and as far south on Calhoun Street as Creighton Avenue.

Generations later, Clara Philley recalled that she and her sister Virginia watched the Turn-of-the-Century traffic at Wayne and Calhoun Streets. "Wayne St. was paved with cedar blocks and the sidewalk was about three feet above the street. The Barnett Livery Carriage House and Stables was just east of the White Fruit House and Department Store," which was on the southwest of the corner where Stillmans was later located.

"Our great-grandfather, Hiram Philley, brought his family from Vermont in 1832. He bought land from the government, and while his family lived in the Old Fort, he built his home and Inn on the corner of what is now Old Decatur Road and Paulding Road, then known as Piqua Road and Wagner's Lane (sometimes Lovers' Lane). Johnny Appleseed stopped at the Inn."

Serving in the Henry Berghoff administration, starting Jan. 1, 1901, were August Schmidt, clerk and George Louttit and later Robert Dreibelbiss, city judge. Joseph Fox was named controller and William Shambaugh, city attorney. On the board of works were Peter Eggeman, William Doehrman and Henry Zollinger. The board of safety included Louis Kasten, Charles Buck and George H. Wilson. Homer Gorsline was police chief and Henry Hilbrecht was fire chief. Serving with the Hosey administration starting in 1906, were August Schmidt, controller; Edward Lennon, Henry Schwartz and Jesse Brosius, board of works; George Herrman, James J. Hayes and Calvin Rieman, board of safety; Martin Ankenbruck, police chief; and Henry Hilbrecht, fire chief. Serving in the Jesse Grice administration, starting in 1910 were J. Frank Mungovan, city judge; William Jefferies, clerk; W. Sherman Cutshall, controller; and Harry G. Hogan, city attorney. Named to the board of works were Frank Benoy, Henry Hilgemann and E. J. Lennon. Named to the board of safety were Joseph Hutzell, Marion Johnson and William Henderson. Benjamin Elliott was police chief and Henry Hilbrecht, fire chief. Serving in the second Hosey administration starting in 1914, were H. Waveland Kerr, city judge; Gustav Boerger, clerk; William C. Baade, controller; and Guy Colerick, city attorney. The board of works included Frank Singrey, Robert Kelly and Henry Hilgemann; and the board of safety, George Hermann, J. J. Hayes and Calvin Rieman.

Public Library

Despite the best efforts of the intellectual portion of the community, the City Council didn't rush to the support of a Public Library. But by 1904 Fort Wayne finally had a first class library building and depository. Originally efforts for a library came in 1878 by D. N. Foster and R. S. Robertson who drafted state legislation. The bill was defeated that year but passed the General Assembly in 1881. Yet efforts on the local level failed to impress the City Council which refused to levy taxes or appropriate funds. A reading room was established in 1887 by Mrs. Emerine Hamilton and her daughters, Mrs. Mary Williams, Mrs. Ellen Wagenhals and Miss Margaret Hamilton. This was on the south side of Wayne between Calhoun and Harrison Streets. Early librarians were Mrs. S. C. Hoffman, Miss Laura Goshorn, Miss Nannie McLachlin and Miss Tracy Guild.

Finally, after pressure from the Women's Club League, the Council in 1893 agreed to impose a library tax and make a room available in City Hall. Two years later, the library was removed to the residence of Sol D. Bayless at the southwest corner of Wayne and Clinton Streets and in 1898 to the old Brackenridge house at the southwest corner of Wayne and Webster Streets. It was in that year that Miss Margaret M. Colerick became librarian and exercised a guiding hand to library progress for 36 years thereafter.

The building, dedicated on June 7, 1904, and the much-used Public Library until the 1960's, was built following a $90,000 gift by Andrew Carnegie. The total cost was $110,700. Samuel Foster who gave $4,118 was a principal local benefactor. The Young Women's Christian Association provided many of the books in the library's early days.

The years around the turn of the century were productive of more than public buildings. Some major advances in churches, commerce, factories and hotels were changing the face of the community.

The Precious Blood Catholic Church was founded in 1895 with the Rev. Francis Nigsch the first pastor. The West Creighton Avenue Church of Christ was organized with 114 members in 1896. The first pastor was J. V. Updike. The First Church of Christ, Scientist, founded in 1897, listed original members as Mrs. M. L. Brown, Mr. and Mrs. I. N. Woods, Miss Ora Shaver and Miss Emma Rosenthal.

Concordia Evangelical Lutheran Church was formed in 1899 with the Rev. A. H. Lange the first pastor. Msgr. Joseph Delaney, pastor of St. Patrick's Catholic Church for 46 years from its founding in 1890, established a girls' high school at the corner of DeWald and Webster Streets in 1901. Called St. Catherine's Academy, it flourished along with St. Augustine's Academy, located at Calhoun and Jefferson Sts., until the building of Central Catholic High School in 1938 on Lewis Street.

Sam Wolf and Myron E. Dessauer founded the Wolf & Dessauer Department Store in 1896. It would later become the city's most prominent retail establishment at the corner of Washington and Calhoun Streets. The International Business College and the Fort Wayne Business College were consolidated under T. L. Staples in 1899. In that same year the Fort Wayne Drug Company was founded. The grocery wholesale house of

A. H. Perfect and Company was established in 1896.

The Mary Penrose Wayne Chapter of the Daughters of the American Revolution was organized in 1901 with Mrs. Frances Haberly Robertson as regent. The DAR granted the charter the following year. The Fort Wayne Academy of Medicine was established in 1900. In that same year, 1900, Bishop Herman Alerding succeeded Joseph Rademacher. Bishop Rademacher had succeeded Joseph Dwenger as bishop of the Fort Wayne diocese in 1893.

The Van Arnam Manufacturing Co., for a half century a maker of plumbing supplies with a plant on Taylor St., was begun in 1901. The Heit-Miller-Lau Company, for many years headed by Anthony Heit, was formed in 1902. The confectionary maker eventually grew into the Wayne Candies, Inc., a firm by mid-20th Century known nationwide for its candy bars.

The Anthony Hotel, which in a later generation would be known as the Van Orman Hotel, was started in 1905 and completed in 1908. The operator of the hotel in its early years was H. J. Keenan. The hotel became the city's finest and the meeting place and convention center for just about every national political figure and organization of the era. The Hitching Post off the hotel lobby was a favorite gathering spot for Fort Wayne young people and night life until after the World War II years. The nine-story, 263-room hotel cost $500,000.

Across Berry St. from the Anthony Hotel, at the southeast corner of Berry and Harrison Streets, was built the Baltes Hotel, also completed in 1908. It was managed by William Knapp and Charles Moreland. Attached to the south of the building was the Berghoff Gardens, for decades one of the city's finest restaurants.

The Scottish Rite Cathedral at the southeast corner of Clinton St. and Washington Blvd. was erected in 1908 and 1909. The stone building cost $225,000.

Aveline Fire

In the early morning hours of May 3, 1908, the most tragic fire in the history of Fort Wayne claimed the lives of 12 persons in the Aveline House. For 45 years the city's finest hostelry, the Aveline House was built during the Civil War years by Francis S. Aveline and completed in 1863. The original four-story building was later enlarged to six stories. The graceful structure was located at the southeast corner of Berry and Calhoun Streets. The cause of the fire in 1908 was unknown, but the flames swept quickly through the building and billows of smoke choked much of the downtown area. Guests jumped from windows, some to their deaths, others to safety. Many made it to adjoining roof tops. The building was gutted by the fire and remaining parts of the structure were razed.

Railroads were king in the early decades of the 20th Century, and the fastest run of a regular steam train in the history of the world occurred on the Fort Wayne Division of the Pennsylvania Railroad on June 12, 1905. The Pennsy's famed Engine 7002, pulling the crack Chicago-New York Broadway Limited Train, was clocked at 127.1 miles per hour for a measured mile in Ohio just east of Fort Wayne.

The engineer at the controls on the fabled, but true, train run was Jerry W. McCarthy of Fort Wayne. His fireman was Harry R. Tourgee.

The 1913 Flood

Disaster struck Fort Wayne in the fourth year of Mayor Grice's term. This was the great flood of 1913.

The spring thaws were joined by 4.75 inches of rain between 7:25 a.m. March 23 and 9:45 p.m. March 25. The Maumee River crest began to move up rapidly. It went from 6.7 feet on March 23 to 19.6 feet on the morning of the 24th. And still it rose. By March 26 the government gage at the Columbia Street Bridge measured 26.1 feet—an alltime high.

Breaks began to appear in the St. Joseph Blvd. dike. Soon, wide areas were being swept by the flowing tide. Water engulfed more than 2,000 homes. An estimated 15,000 persons were made homeless. Rescue operations were organized. A man helping a family near the West Main Street Bridge was drowned. A greater tragedy occurred during the evacuation of the Allen County Children's Home near the St. Mary's River. A boat capsized and four little girls were drowned. In all, there were six deaths attributed to the flood.

A city relief organization went into motion dispensing aid from a central location. This was headed by Mayor Grice, City Attorney Harry Hogan, City Controller William S. Cutshall and Harry Kauffman, secretary. The City Council appropriated funds and other financial aid came from the Traction Company, the Berghoff Brewery, the Indiana Lighting Company and Home Telephone. A total of 11,187 persons out of a total city population in 1913 of 71,472 received assistance. Other problems included the cutoff of city water and the dangers of disease.

The Mayor declared martial law to control food and prevent looting of abandoned houses. Guards in patrol boats were ordered to shoot looters who failed to obey halt commands.

Bill Hosey, who had returned to employment at the Pennsy Shops during the Grice Administration, reentered the political wars in 1913. He won the election but was a minority vote-getter in a four-way race. He was almost upset by a grocer, Charles H. Buck, who ran on an Independent ticket. Hosey, the Democrat, had 5,584 votes. Buck received 4,240 votes. William H. Boerger, candidate of the growing Socialist faction, got 1,288 votes; and William La Tourrette, the Republican, received 1,015 votes. The Republican Party was split by the Bull Moose schism which began in the 1912 national election. Arthur Parry, lawyer, was chairman locally of the Bull Moose Party, backing Teddy Roosevelt.

Another thing going against the Republicans was the police scandal. Nosing around City Hall at Christmas time, Journal-Gazette Editor Andy Moynihan discovered the Police Chief's desk stacked with gifts. According to Carl J. Suedhoff, long an advertising man who at that time was a news reporter, the gifts apparently came from gamblers and operators of houses on the North Calhoun St. redlight strip. A grand jury investigation which followed led to the indictment of the chief and others. So flagrant was prostitution that electric signs with lewd invitations drew attention to the houses.

Aviator Art Smith

In the meantime, history was being made in aviation. Art Smith, then 21 years old, began construction of an aeroplane in 1910. By the following year he had it in the air for a flight to New Haven and back on October 11. He soon became a widely-known aviator, flying for the Panama-Pacific Exposition in 1915 at San Francisco and in Japan during 1916 and 1917.

In 1913, Gene Stratton Porter moved to Fort Wayne for a short period. The Wabash County native was the author of the novels, "Freckles" and "Girl of the Limberlost," both of which sold more than a million copies. Writer of other popular works, she moved on to Rome City and Geneva, Indiana, and eventually died in an auto crash in 1923 at Los Angeles. Her husband, druggist Charles Darwin Porter, was the brother of Dr. Miles Porter of Fort Wayne. Her sisters, Mrs. Florence S. Compton and Mrs. Ada Wilson, also lived in Fort Wayne.

Theaters began to proliferate in the downtown area. The Majestic had been built in 1904; The Empress, later called the Strand, was erected in 1912. The Palace Theater was opened in 1914. The Majestic was in the 200 block of East Berry Street. The Strand was at the southwest corner of Wayne and Clinton Streets. The Palace was in the 100 block of East Washington Boulevard. Just about every famous stage personality in the world would appear at one or the other of the theaters in the subsequent several decades.

After two decades of agitation, people in Fort Wayne tired of waiting for Congress to act on a national monument in the city in memory of Anthony Wayne. The Allen County Commissioners passed a one-fourth of one cent levy and this money was used in

1916 for the equestrian statue, first located in Hayden Park near Maumee Ave., but moved to Freimann Park downtown in 1973. The bronze statue was executed by George E. Ganiere of Chicago. The statue cost $15,000 and the tablets an additional $900.

The downtown YMCA Building was constructed in 1916 and 1917. The cost for the ambitious project was $341,000, but the facility served for more than a half century thereafter. A center of social events, sports and games, instruction, rooms for travelers and students, and dinners, the "Y" became one of the community's more durable assets. Leading the campaign for building the YMCA were S. B. Bechtel, Arthur F. Hall and Arthur H. Perfect. The largest contribution came from William E. Mossman who gave $50,000. The site at the corner of Washington and Barr Streets was purchased for $42,500. Original officers of the association included Mossman, E. E. Greist, R. H. Mauk and Theodore Wentz.

The 1916 presidential campaign came to Fort Wayne with the Democratic President Woodrow Wilson making a speech from a train to a crowd gathered at the Pennsylvania Elevation. Among those at the Convention earlier in the year was Edward G. Hoffman of Fort Wayne, national Democratic central committee member and secretary. Another delegate to the convention from Fort Wayne was William Breen, an attorney and president of the Peoples Trust & Savings Company. Breen was named president of the Indiana State Bar Assn. in 1903. He was a large benefactor of the University of Notre Dame.

Wilson's opponent, Republican candidate Charles Evans Hughes, stopped in Fort Wayne in 1916 and gave a campaign address at the Palace Theatre. Wilson won the election but lost Allen County in a vote of 10,082 for Hughes and 9,134 for the re-elected President. Thomas Marshall, Wilson's Vice President, had at one time lived in Fort Wayne and attended Central High School. He is best remembered for his slogan: "What this country needs is a good 5 cent cigar."

From June 5 to June 10, 1916, Fort Wayne was in the midst of an historic pageant celebrating the 100th anniversary of Indiana's admission to the Union. An amphitheatre was constructed at the Reservoir to accommodate 14,100 persons. Eleven hundred citizens presented the pageant. Parades through the city and arches downtown marked the event. There was an industrial exposition with two miles of exhibits. Former President of the U.S. William Howard Taft and Indiana Governor Samuel M. Ralston addressed the vast pageant throng and led the floral parade. There were circus acts and carnival days.

The pageant was directed by Donald Robertson and written by Wallace Rice and Kenneth Sawyer Goodman. Indiana Centennial officers were Edward C. Miller, Maurice C. Niezer, R. B. Garmire and Samuel Wolf. The cabinet for the event included William M. Griffin, S. E. Mulholland, Van B. Perrine, Byron Somers, Frank E. Bohn, M. H. Luecke, George M. Haffner, Harry G. Hogan, Charles Niebergall, E. W. Puckett and E. H. Merritt. Committee heads included Frank E. Stouder, Harry Muller, Miss Madge Magee, William Shambaugh, Sol Blair, Samuel Foster, William Scheiman, B. Paul Mossman, James Shields, J. B. Crankshaw, Louis Curdes, E. G. Hoffman, Mrs. Fred McCulloch and Ross Franklin. Directing the music for the pageant was John L. Verweire. The Ballet of Fort Wayne was directed by Miss Muriel Larimore, with Miss Helene Clifford, accompanist.

It was later that summer that a great wave of infantile paralysis swept the country. In Fort Wayne in 1916, orders were issued forbidding the congregation of children under 16 years of age. Bans were placed on schools, churches and theatres. Even newsboys were forbidden to sell newspapers on the streets. The opening of the schools was delayed until October 1 when it was thought that the main threat of the dread malady had passed. Several cases of the disease developed in Fort Wayne that summer. In subsequent decades there would be recurring epidemics of infantile paralysis, with especially crippling attacks in the late 1930's and early 1950's. The development of the Salk and Saban vaccines some years later relieved fear of the disease in Fort Wayne as elsewhere. A mass distribution of the vaccines in 1965 was believed the most complete event, from the point of view of percentage of people participating, of any in the history of the community.

The Great War

In April, 1917, the United States entered the Great War. Since 1914, when Germany and the Central Powers invaded Belgium and France on the Western Front and reversed a Russian invasion on the Eastern Front, much of the world had been drawn into the conflict. The war had become the over-riding interest most everywhere, as reflected in Fort Wayne newspapers of the era. By the spring of 1917, the British were still dying in the mud of Flanders. Nearly one million French and German soldiers were lost the previous year in the shattered area around Verdun. The Yanks, including several thousand from Fort Wayne and the vicinity, would be fighting and dying, particularly in 1918 in battles from the Marne to Argonne Forest.

From the first day of the war declaration, April 6, 1917, to the following June, a total of 4000 men were sent from Fort Wayne to army camps. The first recruits were all enlistees. The draft boards were set up later. A private's pay in those days was $30 a month. The selective conscription registration began on June 5 with the registration of 7,785 men between the ages of 21 and 31 inclusive. The actual draft began July 20.

On May 12, 1917, a medical group called Hospital Unit M, was formed by the Red Cross at Fort Wayne for duty in France. The unit included 21 nurses under the direction of Miss Elizabeth E. Springer. Physicians in the unit included Drs. Allen Hamilton; Henry Bruggeman; Kent Wheelock; John Gilpin; B. W. Rhamy; Dean Metcalf; Charles G. Beall; Charles R. Dancer; Garrett Van Sweringen; Miles Porter, Jr.; B. M. Edlavitch; Herbert Senseny and Harvey Martin.

President Wilson on April 6, 1917, delivered a proclamation which drew wide resentment and controversy, especially in Fort Wayne. It defined as "enemy aliens" all German residents over 14 years of age who had not been naturalized. They were required to register and hold cards and travel was restricted. While not so imposing as the World War II programs of President Franklin D. Roosevelt and Governor Earl Warren against the Japanese in California, the edicts of World War I fed a certain amount of excitement in Fort Wayne and other places with large German populations. Fearing wartime fanaticism, parochial schools which had been conducting some classes in the German language discontinued the practice. People using the German tongue on the streets, which had been quite common, drew wary glances. Actually, the laws of Indiana had even given the ballot to immigrants who had declared their intention to become American citizens and had initiated naturalization procedures. Hundreds of substantial citizens fell into the "Enemy alien" category.

It was a period when thousands of families had "war gardens" on small patches in vacant lots to help with the general food effort. Also women took the places of men in the stores and shops.

News began to flow in from the front. Paul Frank Baer, 24-year-old aviator from Fort Wayne, became America's first ace in World War I. He served with the French Air Service and later with the United States 103rd Aero Squadron. In a period of 45 days he downed 16 German planes, with official credit for nine of them. France gave him the Legion of Honor and the Croix de Guerre. He was the first aviator to receive the U. S. Distinguished Service Cross. In the following decade, Fort Wayne's Municipal Airport was named after Baer.

The news of the Armistice on Nov. 11, 1918, was met with universal celebration and headlines of "Huns Quit" and "Kaiser Flees to Holland" and the like. The celebrations were in contrast with many months of sad reports concerning the men who died in action. Some of the death reports were not received for weeks after the end of hostilities. One hundred and thirty-one men and women from Allen County died in the war. Of the county toll, 94 were from Fort Wayne and the balance from the county towns and rural areas. Of the dead, 117 served in the army and 10 in the Navy. Two were Marines and two women were with Red Cross units. More died of disease than enemy action, 74 compared with 49.

In the city election during the war year of 1917, the Republicans recovered City Hall. The Republicans had nominated W. Sherman Cutshall for mayor to run against Maurice C. Niezer, the Democratic candidate. Cutshall won in the November election and succeeded William Hosey as mayor on January 1, 1918. Cutshall had earlier served as city controller in the administration of Jesse Grice, starting in 1910. For many years Cutshall was a partner in the Chalfant-Cutshall Undertaking Co., located at 801 West Berry Street. J. Frank Mungovan was elected city judge and William T. Jefferies, clerk. J. O. Brown, A. T. Anderson and Cary L. Baird were named to the board of works. B. F. Sarver, J. B. Mills and W. G. Berdelman were named to the board of safety. Creighton H. Williams was appointed city attorney.

Interurban Travel

Interurban railways, electric mass transit vehicles which were to reach their greatest volume in the early and mid-20's and then fade away, suffered a minor crisis in the year following the end of World War I. Patronage had fallen off during the war period and the Fort Wayne and Northern Indiana Traction Company was sold at foreclosure on Dec. 29, 1919. The company was reorganized under the name of the Indiana Service Company.

The story of the interurbans began in 1900. In the subsequent three decades one of the more remarkable transportation construction programs reshaped much of the landscape. "During the heyday of this great electric railway system, more than 18,000 miles of track were in operation in our country," reported historian Roy Bates. "The greatest concentration of these railways was here in the midwest: Indiana, Ohio, Michigan and Illinois. Indiana was in the lead with 2,000 miles of trackage or about one-ninth of the total in operation." It was reported that "an accelerated expansion program began unparalleled in the history of transportation. By 1915 it reached excitable proportions." Fort Wayne was one of the hubs of this growth and investments. Fortunes were made and lost. Hardly a line escaped reorganization.

At first, the cars were of wooden construction, but steel trains made their appearance by 1910. The more prosperous lines had parlor cars, buffets and lounges, in addition to the coaches.

Like some of the railroads in an earlier period, much of the interurban system was built on the old canal right-of-ways. On November 10, 1900, the Huntington Herald Press reported: "A warranty deed in the recorder's office transferred all canal lands yet unsold in Huntington County. The deed conveys to Mr. Aaron W. Dukes the canal in three counties, Allen, Wabash and Huntington, for $15,000. "It is proposed by The Oil Belt Traction Co. to build a line from Huntington to Fort Wayne following the canal towpath." A month later an injunction was filed in Allen County against Charles McCulloch, Henry C. Paul and Charles S. Bash to restrain them from disposing of the towpath of the Wabash and Erie Canal. On December 14, 1900, the city of Fort Wayne granted a franchise to the Fort Wayne and Southwestern Traction Company for an entrance and route on city streets.

Regular service was inaugurated December 12, 1901, when the first electrically driven interurban car made the run from Fort Wayne to Huntington. The downtown terminal in Fort Wayne was at Harrison and Pearl Streets. The southwest route went out of the city by way of Fairfield and Taylor Streets. Service in that direction was completed to Logansport on November 1, 1904. By that time the company was called the Wabash-Logansport Traction Company. Service was pushed to Lafayette in 1907, with the first through run on June 29.

The company had been getting its power to run the trains from a small plant on East Baker Street near Calhoun Street. Directors of the Wabash Valley firm and the Fort Wayne Electric Light and Power Company negotiated a joint venture on Feb. 9, 1905, with a $1 million bond issue to construct a new power plant. The location was on the west side of Spy Run Ave., just north of Elizabeth Street. It became a long time home for the Traction Company and eventually that of Indiana & Michigan Electric Company.

The construction contracts were awarded to John Suelzer. The plant was producing power by May 1, 1907. Though built basically to provide power for the interurban system, the plant almost immediately put the firm in the business of selling light and power to people of the Fort Wayne community.

Utility Merger

In 1911, the most comprehensive merger in the history of Indiana utility companies occurred at Fort Wayne. The surviving company was the Fort Wayne and Northern Indiana Traction Company. Merged with it were the Fort Wayne and Wabash Valley Traction Company, the Fort Wayne Bluffton and Marion Traction Company, the Lafayette and Logansport Traction Company, the Fort Wayne Electric Light and Power Company, the Carrol Electric Light Company and the Fort Wayne Power Company. In addition to the interurban lines, the firm operated street cars in Fort Wayne, Wabash, Peru, Logansport and Lafayete. They also had the Robison Park Line. Electric power for consumers was furnished to several small communities in addition to Fort Wayne. Officials for the firm included James M. Barrett, president; Henry C. Paul, treasurer; Samuel Greenland, general manager; J. J. Brennan, superintendent; H. E. Vordermark, auditor; and Luther Snodgrass, agent.

This entire package was assumed by the Indiana Service Company following the foreclosure of 1919. By this time, Indianapolis had become the interurban capital of the world. More than 400 runs daily were moving in and out of the city over 14 lines. The huge terminal which later was used for buses, was built in 1904 as the interurban terminal. One of the main routes was the one connecting the state capital with Fort Wayne. Originally the trains went by way of Lafayette and up the Wabash Valley route. In later years, however, the heavier traffic was via Marion and Bluffton. Service was also built to Garrett, and from there to Kendallville and Waterloo. This line operated past the Irene Byron Sanitarium along State Road 3. Towns serviced included Huntertown, Auburn, Wallen, Altona, Avilla, and Lisbon. Passenger service continued until 1937, though freight service continued for some years more.

Of the five interurban lines operating out of Fort Wayne, the shortest lived was the line to Decatur, which existed for 20 years from 1907 to 1927. It started out as the Fort Wayne and Springfield Railway Company and after 1915 was known as the Fort Wayne and Decatur Traction Company. Heading the company were James H. Haberly, H. J. Bowerfield, L. F. Eberbach, Samuel Greenfield, all of Fort Wayne, and Homer Ruhl and A. J. Baker of Decatur. The Indiana Service Company acquired the line in 1920.

Speed and Death

A more substantial line was the one which started service on September 22, 1905, between Fort Wayne and Lima, Ohio. It began business as the Fort Wayne, Van Wert and Lima Traction Company. The lease was assigned to the Lima and Toledo Traction Company in 1906 and then to the Ohio Electric Railway Company in 1907, which continued operations until 1920. This 64-mile line served New Haven, Monroeville, Delphos, Dixon, Convoy, Van Wert, Middlepoint and Elida. The trains went from Fort Wayne's downtown out Lewis St., Maumee Ave. and New Haven Avenue. The Indiana Service Company took over operation in 1920. Service was finally abandoned on June 30, 1932.

The fastest and most deluxe service was on the Fort Wayne and Indianapolis run. Parlor-buffet cars traveling through Bluffton and Muncie were named the "Indiana" and "Purdue." These trains over the 125 mile route were operated as the Hoosierland Limited. Similar service between Fort Wayne and Indianapolis, but going through

Peru was called the Wabash Valley Flyer. Running time by way of Bluffton was three hours and 45 minutes. The Peru route took four hours and five minutes, with the natural result that the faster route got the heavier trade.

The worst disaster in the history of interurban travel occurred over the Indianapolis-Fort Wayne run via Bluffton a few minutes after the noon hour on September 21, 1910. So great was the head-on impact that people up to three miles away thought there was an explosion. The northbound car, of the old wooden variety, collided with a new steel car coming from Fort Wayne at a point 18 miles south of the city. The empty south-bound car telescoped the northbound car, killing 41 persons.

Patronage in the middle 1920's reached its last great surge before the ever-increased use of automobiles led to the decline of interurbans in the following decade. Into service in 1924 went new and better cars, named "Little Turtle" and "Anthony Wayne." These had swivel chairs, carpeted floors and table lamps. The competitive line through Muncie swung out Broadway and across a bridge at Oakdale, and out past Indian Village.

The Indiana Service Company alone carried 25,327,000 passengers in 1924 and upped this slightly to 25,667,000 in 1926. The downward trend began in 1927. Though the original terminal was on Pearl St. at the old Randall Hotel, a larger terminal had been established in 1912 in the block bound by Main, Pearl, Webster and Ewing Streets. It served until 1941. All through the 1930's, patronage and revenues declined. There were reorganizations on top of reorganizations, usually resulting in abandoned service. Despite improved Pullman-manufactured cars with observation lounges traveling at 60 miles an hour in the early 1930's, the companies floundered.

The last freight run out of Fort Wayne was on January 13, 1941, over the route to Muncie. At the control was Charles Van Dine, Bluffton, who 31 years earlier was the motorman on the southbound steel car which slammed into the northbound passenger train, resulting in 41 deaths and the worst U.S. interurban tragedy ever.

The last passenger run out of Fort Wayne left the terminal on Main Street at 11 p.m., January 18, 1941. And the very last operation of any kind of interurban train in Fort Wayne was one coming out of Indianapolis the same day. Roy Bates of Fort Wayne rode both trains, the southbound to Bluffton and then catching the northbound car for the final run back to the city.

"On arrival at South Broadway everyone took a turn at blowing the whistle. This continued until our arrival at the terminal on West Main St.," he reported. "We pulled into the terminal at 1:20 a.m. (Jan. 19, 1941). We gave No. 63 a parting salutation. Her lights were switched off. Then the station lights were extinguished."

The corner of Washington Blvd. and the Barr St. Market looked like this in the 19th Century. The city's first telephone lines were just going up. In the background is old City Hall which was torn down to make way for the 1893 City Hall.

Trinity Episcopal Church was built in 1865 at the corner of Berry and Fulton Streets. The city already had fireplugs by the time this picture was taken in 1889. Below is an ad dated 1868 for a German language newspaper.

Indiana Staats Zeitung,

A Tri-Weekly and Weekly German Paper.

The only German Paper in Northern Indiana.

J. SARNIGHAUSEN, - Proprietor and Publisher.

TERMS:

Tri-Weekly, $4 00 Per Annum, In Advance.
Weekly, $2 50 " "

ENGLISH AND GERMAN

JOB PRINTING,

Promptly and Neatly executed at the Lowest Rates.

OFFICE:

N. E. cor. of Columbia & Clinton Sts.,

FORT WAYNE, IND.

THE HORTON M'F'G CO.,

PIONEER BUILDERS OF

Western Washers

AND

Hand Corn Planters

UNEQUALED IN

Quality and Workmanship.

FORT WAYNE, IND.

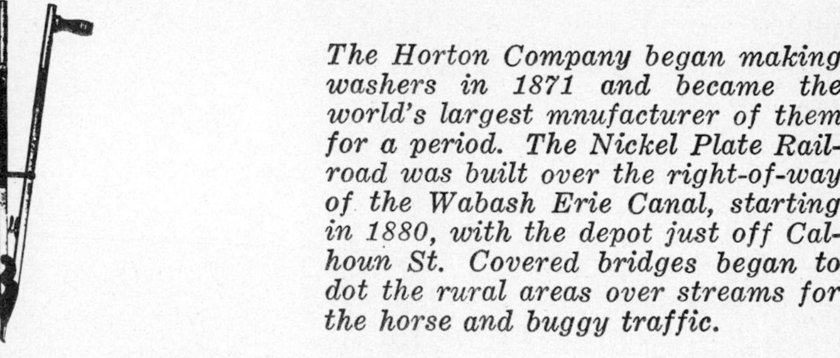

The Horton Company began making washers in 1871 and became the world's largest mnufacturer of them for a period. The Nickel Plate Railroad was built over the right-of-way of the Wabash Erie Canal, starting in 1880, with the depot just off Calhoun St. Covered bridges began to dot the rural areas over streams for the horse and buggy traffic.

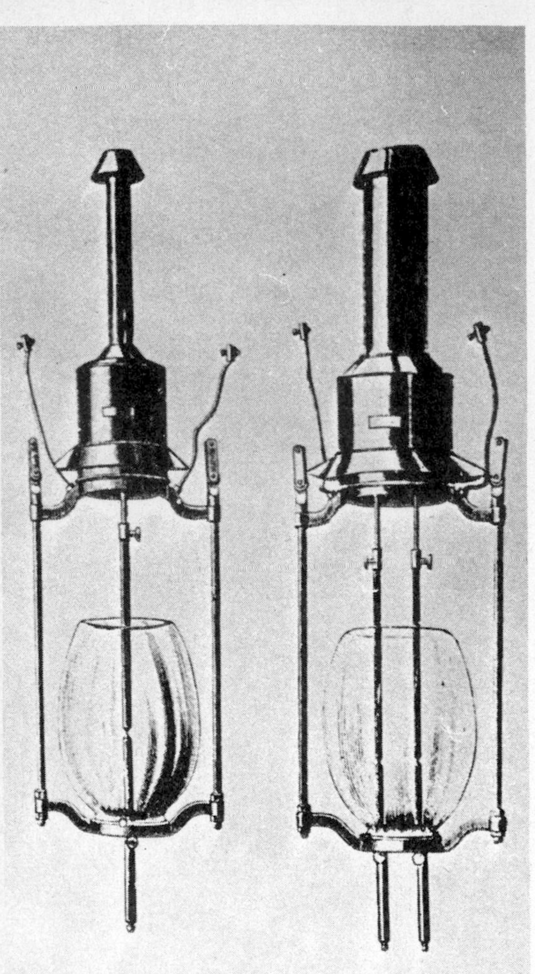

General Electric Company began in Fort Wayne as the Jenney Electric Co. The first building, right above, in 1881 was in the 100 block of West Superior St. The second location was on East Columbia where operations of the electric light maker operated from 1883 to 1886.

Perry Randall, left, was one of the founders of Fort Wayne Electric, as Jenney became known. The firm moved to its Broadway site in 1886 in the buildings of the former Gaus Mowing Machine Co. Buildings shown below along the railroad burned in 1888 and new red brick structures were erected.

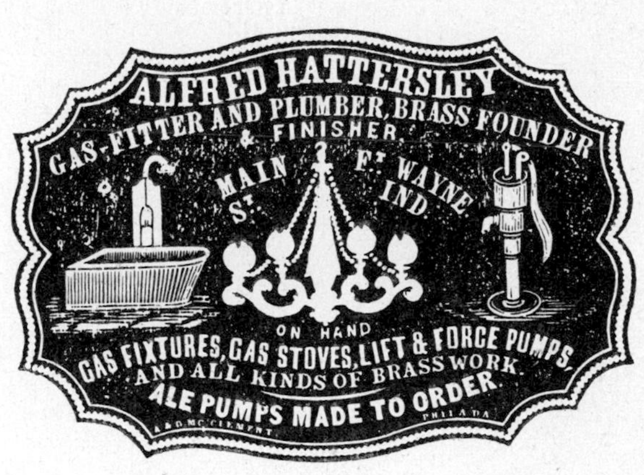

Old downtown to the southeast of the Courthouse as it look in 1888. In the left foreground is the Fire House at Berry and Court, and at Clinton, the old Post Office. In the center horizon are the spires of St. Mary's Catholic, First Presbyterian, and St. Paul's Lutheran churches. At right is an early electric trolley car, advertising a "Free Open Air Concert at Centlivre Park."

S. B. BOND, Pres. C. E. BOND, Treas. G. E. BURSLEY, Sec'y and Gen. Manager.
R. F. KEITH, Superintendent.

FT. WAYNE ORGAN COMPANY,

MANUFACTURERS OF THE

PACKARD

ORCHESTRAL ORGAN

THE PACKARD HAS NO EQUAL.
IT IS POWERFUL, DURABLE and ELEGANT.

IT IS THE CHEAPEST AND BEST.
SEND FOR PRICES.

Office and Factory, - FORT WAYNE, IND.

Fort Wayne Organ Company, with an 1880 ad for this ornate item which was "the cheapest and best," was later named the Packard Piano Company. The plant was located at Fairfield and Packard avenues which later became the site of a city park.

A Nickel Plate steam engine and passenger train starts braking as it passes through New Haven at the turn of the century. The Indiana School and Home for Feeble Minded Youth was built at Fort Wayne on East State Blvd. in 1888.

Charles A. Zollinger established a record by being elected mayor seven times. He was in his last term when City Hall was dedicated in 1893. It was an era of heavy horse traffic along Columbia and Calhoun and numerous saloons. The old 1880 print at the bottom of the page shows the beginnings of the water system.

The old Central Fire Station was going up in 1894 at Main and Lafayette streets. The picture at right shows the same building just before wrecking in 1971. By 1894, Horton had switched to electricity on its famed washers.

Horton
MFG CO
The Horton No. 32 Dolly Type Washer.
The old reliable Horton Dolly Washer with visible accessible mechanism. Horton metal wringer. Cypress tub made complete in Horton modern wood shop. Can be operated by hand in event of power failure.
Shipping weight lbs

The street car tracks to Robison Park,, six miles north of the city, ran along the St. Joseph River. There was a constant coming and going on the Fort Wayne Consolidated Railway cars shown above. The park, known as Swift Park for the first year in 1896 when this picture was taken, was renamed Robison in honor of its founder. At left is a fashionable crowd near the main Robison Park pavilion in 1907.

A white team of fire horses race down Harrison St. on May 21, 1911 to the Mayflower Mills fire. The Air Dome and Majestic Theatre on East Berry St. were in the culture picture in the horse and buggy era.

Sylvanus F. Bowser wanted an easier way to draw up liquids than pulling buckets by hand and founded a minor empire with pumps. His first big manufacturing plant on East Creighton Ave. is shown below with the S. F. Bowser house at left and A. A. Bowser house at right and the delivery crew at the intersection. The plant in the middle picture burned on Christmas Day, 1897, as shown below.

The centennial of the founding of Fort Wayne in 1794 was a little late, but a gala event in 1895 At right, a street car near Columbia St. passes through an arch. On the other end of the pageant route, adjustments in the decorations are being made at Lewis and Calhoun streets.

TO DRINK

A cheap Beer, brewed outside of this city, when Fort Wayne supplies some of the largest cities in the land.

WHY

Pay double prices for imported Beer when a domestic Beer, brewed out of nothing but the choicest Barley and Hops, can be bought at prices not higher than injurious and adulterated goods.

The Herman Berghoff Brewing Co.

PRODUCES IN ITS

Dortmunder, Doppel and Salvator,

Fully as wholesome and pure an article as any imported beer.

THEY DEFIANTLY CHALLENGE THE WORLD

To prove that their claims and affidavits are not true. They invite Chem and Experts to Analyze their Dortmunder and Salvator Beer and to lay claims to th

TELEPHONE 105.

REWARD OF $5,000.

The Berghoff Beer challenge of 1894 was likely met by the rather sober-looking crew of the streetcar company pictured in front of the Main St. and Lindenwood Cemetery trolley. The 100 block of West Columbia St. was anchored by the Randall Hotel on Harrison St.

FROM COURT HOUSE, FT. WAYNE, IND, 2-36

Calhoun St. south from the Courthouse on a snowy day, at top. The Fort Wayne Rifles were getting ready for the Spanish American War in 1898.

The Allen County Courthouse was being torn down when this photo was taken in December, 1896. Below, the construction of the new Courthouse was well underway at Main and Calhoun streets in 1899.

The Allen County Courthouse well completed in 1900 but still lacking the dome, at right. Below is the design in stone for justice on the Courthouse facade.

Miss Liberty reigns on high over the Courthouse and city. Below, policemen in bobbie hats direct traffic as a crowd gathers for a pageant in 1903, in front of the Berry St. entrance to the Courthouse.

The Transfer Corner at Main and Calhoun was a busy place with Interurban Trains, street cars and horse-drawn drays in the first decade of the 20th Century. The Citizens Trust Bank, center of picture on the corner, has a clock which says 5 'til 10 a.m. To the right is the Traction Co. station of the Interurbans at Pearl and Harrison streets. The regular depot was later a block to the west.

The greatest hotel disaster in the history of the city occurred in the early dark hours of May 3, 1908. The Aveline House at the southeast corner of Berry and Calhoun had been a fine hotel since its opening in 1863. Fire of unknown origin raged through the structure. Most patrons escaped or where rescued but 11 lost their lives in the blaze. Large crowds gathered to view the scene after sunrise, as recorded in the picture below.

City Market on Barr St. was erected in 1910 at a cost of $20,000, shown here when new. The stone and concrete pavilion extended from City Hall, built in 1893 in the background, to Washington Blvd. The arch and entrances shown were at Wayne St. Below, cross-country contestants in the Chicago American Vehicle Run pose during a stop at the Courthouse.

Art Smith, early loop artist of the air of world repute, poses with his wife Aimee, above, and in precarious stick position at right. Smith, who built his airplane in 1911, thrilled crowds in the U.S. and abroad both before and after World War I. He was killed in a crash in 1926. At bottom is the great Penn Flyer wreck of Aug. 13, 1911, near Swinney Park at Fort Wayne.

LOOP-THE-LOOP AVIATOR ART SMITH "THE WIZARD OF THE AIR"

The 1913 flood was caused by spring thaws and nearly five inches of rain in two days. The picture above shows efforts on March 25 along St. Joe Blvd. to stem the flow. Much of the city was under water, 15,000 people were homeless, six people died. Jesse Grice, left, was mayor at the time. Below is the crowded street scene as the parade of 1916 Centennial of Indiana Statehood passes down Calhoun.

Part 5
City Booms in 1920s

In 1920 Fort Wayne's population stood at 86,549 persons and the Allen County population as a whole was 114,303. It was an exciting time when the community was on the threshold of growth which considerably exceeded the national average and when the city would take on a character which would last until the post World War II era.

It was the jazz age. A former stevedore named Louis Armstrong was playing Dixieland tunes. Paul Whiteman, who appeared in Fort Wayne a number of times, headed a big name band. Babe Ruth was starting on home run records and building baseball gates. The local breweries, Berghoff and Centlivre were in eclipse because of Prohibition, but bathtub gin was flowing here as elsewhere.

If there was one man who represented the spirit of the early 1920's, it was F. Scott Fitzgerald. The author of "The Great Gatsby," "This Side of Paradise" and other literary works, Fitzgerald and his wife, Zelda, chronicled the Lost Generation from the Old South, the Midwest, New York and Paris. The person more than any other mentioned in connection with the Fitzgeralds during those early years was George Jean Nathan, a native of Fort Wayne. Nathan, a descendant of the old Nirdlinger family, pioneer merchants whose home was the first place of Jewish worship in Fort Wayne, became the best known theatre critic of his generation.

Nathan was born in Fort Wayne in 1882. Writing for several metropolitan dailies and literary magazines, he became THE authority of Broadway drama during the 1920's and 1930's. A man of immense ego, he is remembered as one of the principal characters in the play, "All About Eve." He died in 1958. The George Jean Nathan Award for dramatic criticism remained the richest of them all in U.S. literary arts at $4,500. It was funded in honor of his memory.

It was in 1920 that Warren Gamaliel Harding, who had a number of associations with Fort Wayne, was elected President. Harry Hogan, a Fort Wayne attorney and banker, was one of the political figures at the Republican Convention at Chicago. The term "smoke-filled room" has ever since been associated with the naming of Harding as top nominee. A childhood friend of the Harding family at Marion, Ohio, was in the early 1960's a member of the Fort Wayne Board of Works. He was Berkeley Ward. Despite all the scandals involving Harding, Ward remembered him as a kindly man. "He enjoyed playing poker, having a cigar and a drink, but that didn't make him immoral," Ward said.

"It was a long time ago—40 years, but I still remember one of my visits to the White House," Ward said of a meeting shortly before Harding's death in 1923. "I think he knew his political adversaries were out to get him. Harding said to me that day: 'Berkeley, I have only two friends in this world that I know I can depend on—my wife Florence upstairs and my dog Laddie there on the floor.' "

Hotel Business

In Fort Wayne the year of 1923, a large new hotel was going up at the southwest corner of Harrison Street and Washington Boulevard. It was the Keenan Hotel, operated by James F. Keenan for nearly 50 years. His daughter, Helen Keenan Centlivre, assumed the mangement in 1972. A $2 million modernization program was completed in late 1973. Despite that, the Keenan was closed on May 31, 1974, and razed later in the year.

The 13-story, 214-room hotel was the scene of numerous political and social gatherings for half a century. President John F. Kennedy stayed there in 1959, as did his brother Attorney General and Senator Robert Kennedy in 1960. Senator Edward Kennedy was there for a political meeting in 1972. Earlier, the President's mother, Mrs. Rose Kennedy "liked it so well she stayed for the weekend," according to longtime hotel employee Rosella Boyce.

President Truman stayed here in 1958 and was up early in the morning, slipped outside and walked to Swinney Park before anyone knew where he was," she recalled. "He really had everyone worried for awhile about what had happened to him." Truman, famous for his daily early morning strolls, was 74 at the time.

Other downtown hotels in the 1920's included the Anthony at the northeast corner of Berry and Harrison Streets also operated by James Keenan and managed by Robert McMaken; the Baltes, managed by J. J. Kindler, located at the southeast corner of Berry and Harrison Streets; the Hotel Indiana, at the southeast corner of Jefferson and Harrison; and the Hotel Rich, 1226 South Calhoun Street, operated by Thomas J. O'Dowd. The Randall Hotel, on Harrison Street at the foot of Columbia, was still operated by Winifred J. Randall at that time. The Wayne Hotel, at the site of the original Dana Columbia House, would later be renamed the Jones Hotel by owner Jap Jones, and then in the 1960's the Rosemarie by the owner, John Arnold. The Weber Hotel, operated by Frank J. Morsches, was at 1601 South Calhoun Street and later the site of the Bal-Rou Night Club.

Pavlova at the Palace

Anna Pavlova, or Pavlowa as she was actually listed at the time, appeared in Fort Wayne at the Palace Theater on Dec. 14, 1921. She was regarded then as in subsequent generations as the prima ballerina of the epoch. Her dancing partner that evening was Laurent Navikoff.

Miss Pavlova was one of a host of world-renowned artists who performed on the stages of Fort Wayne beginning in the 19th Century. In the early days, artists traveled and were sponsored by individuals with theaters or any number of musical groups or churches. On Jan. 25, 1890, the presentation of concerts became a more organized effort with the forming of the Morning Musical Society. The moving spirits behind the society were Misses Jane Ninde, Minnie Anderson and Josephine Large. This organization and its successors eventually became the Fort Wayne Community Concert Association formed in 1931, and incorporated in 1957. The first president was J. Ross McCulloch. Other early officers included Walter A. Hansen, Mrs. W. Page Yarnelle, Mrs. W. H. Peltier, Miss Lavon Sperry, Charles Meigs and Mrs. John H. Moring.

Mrs. (Isabelle) Peltier became president of the Community Concert Association in 1937 and continued in that capacity until 1955. At that date she was succeded by Mrs. Hertha Stein Duemling. Ten years later, Mrs. Duemling led the organization of a second concert series in Fort Wayne, the Stellar Concerts. Most of the concerts of both groups were staged at the Scottish Rite Auditorium on West Berry Street between Fairfield Avenue and Ewing Street.

The names of the appearing artists are like a reading of Who's Who in the world of music. Some of the principals were Alma Gluck, Galli Curci, Mary Garden, Geraldine Farrar, Benjiamini Gigli, Antonia Scotti, John McCormick, Marion Talley, Nelson Eddy, Rose Bampton, Lawrence Tibbett, Lily Pons, Richard Crooks, Paul Robeson, Jussi Bjoerling, Jennie Tourel, Marian Anderson, John Brownlee, Lotte Lehman, Lauritz Melchoir, Ezio Pinza, Lucia Albanese, Artric Varney, Charles Kullman, Leonard Warren, Ferruccio Tagliavini, George London, Eileen Farrell, Cesare Siepi, Rise Stevens and Roberta Peters.

The Ballet Russe de Monte Carlo appeared twice in Fort Wayne. John Philip Sousa and his Band gave a concert in Fort Wayne on Sept. 25, 1913. The New York Symphony Orchestra conducted by Walter Damrosch, the Philadelphia Orchestra under Eugene Ormandy, the Boston Symphony under Charles Munch and the Boston Pop Orchestra conducted by Arthur Fiedler all played in Fort Wayne concert halls. The Royal Philharmonic Orchestra of London under Sir Thomas Beecham, the Danish National Orchestra led by Erik Tuxen, the Amsterdam Concertgebouw Orchestra under Rafel Kubelik, and the Florence Festival Symphony Orchestra under Carlo Zecci and Franco Mannino, all entertained local audiences. There were many others, including nearly all the famous orchestras and conductors of the past century of both Europe and America.

Of the great instrumentalists who appeared in Fort Wayne, there has been Fritz Kreisler, Sergei Rachmaninoff, Rudolf Serkin, Adolph Busch, Jose Iturbi, Gregor Piatigorsky, William Primrose, Robert Casadesus, Artur Rubinstein, Ossy Renardy, Yehudi Menuhin, Misha Elman, Jascha Heifetz, Efrem Zimbalist and Van Cliburn.

Temple Theatre Fire

Fort Wayne lost one of its great early music halls on Saturday morning, February 10, 1923, when the Masonic Temple Theatre went up in flames. It was at the northeast corner of Wayne and Clinton Streets.

The Temple Theatre, started in 1879 but not completed until 1884, had opened on Nov. 6 of the latter year with the presentation of Rossini's opera, "Semiramide," by the Emma Abbott Company. "The Temple was Fort Wayne's foremost theatre in the golden age of the American dramatic stage," Frank E. Stouder, manager until 1915 reported at the time of the fire. Stouder managed the Palace Theater from 1915 on. "There was scarcely an actor of note from the tragic Edwin Booth to the comics Weber and Fields who did not know the Temple and did not act there at the height of his career," Stouder said.

Some of the names colorfully advertised by the Temple Theatre billboards and who enlivened the Fort Wayne audiences, capacity approximately 1,000, included: Thomas Keene, Mrs. John Drew, Lillian Russell, Fay Templeton, John T. Kelley, Peter Dailey, John Drew, Richard Mansfield, Ethel Barrymore, the Polish pianist Paderewski who later became president of his country, Otis Skinner, Maude Adams and orator Henry Ward Beecher. It was the site of vaudeville and in 1897 likely the first showing of moving pictures in the city.

The fire, which started in the stage area, was due to a discarded cigarette, according to John Stahlhut, assistant fire chief. There were a number of peculiarities about the Temple fire. The charred remains of a pony, left in the building the evening previously, was found in the debris. On the fourth floor of the theatre building was located the quarters of the Fort Wayne National Guard Unit. Stored there was more than 50,000 rounds of ammunition. When the fire reached the fourth floor, the entire scene took on the aspect of a battlefield. Bullets and shells were crackling and whizzing about the square. An onlooker across the street from the burning theatre was struck in the eye. No firemen were injured by the bullets, but it took more than four hours to subdue the flames.

The beginnings of a concert orchestra in Fort Wayne can be found in the church groups of the Lutherans and others in the community. But the real impetus toward more professional concert performances started with George and Gaston Bailhe who came to the city from France in the first decade of the 20th Century. Their European School of Music was in the 100 block of West Washington Blvd. and later near the corner of Wayne and Webster Streets. During the decade, 1910 to 1920, George Bailhe directed the Bailhe Trio and larger groups in fine music performances. Among pianists featured in the programs of the era were Helen Nussbaum, an instructor at the European School of Music; and Edith Foster, a graduate of the Berlin Conservatory who taught music in the city for many years. During the following decade, in 1933, Gaston Bailhe formed the Fort Wayne Civic Symphony Orchestra. Partially due to these symphonic organizations in the early decades of the Century, the community had a nucleus of talent to make a going thing of a regular philharmonic orchestra in following years.

The Museums

The Fort Wayne Art School received a permanent home in 1921. Theodore Thieme, head of the Wayne Knitting Mills and patron of art as well as a collector, presented his former residence at 1026 West Berry to the Art School. From that building, the school expanded along Rockhill Street with an auditorium and later into houses to the east of the Thieme building. The history of the Art School goes back to 1888 when the first classes were formed by Mrs. Robert C. Bell, wife of an attorney; and J. Otis Adams, a Hoosier artist. Numerous transitional stages of development were experienced by the school, but once settled, there was consistent progress. The aims of the school have been to "provide a qualified faculty to guide the student through planned studio and workshop experiences in order to increase technical ability and aesthetic sensibility," according to the school policy.

The story of the Art Museum is tied to that of the Art School. John Ross, former curator, and Francis Baptist, former director, said much of the emphasis has been on the educational function of the museum, including that of elementary school children and the community as a whole. In 1949, B. Paul Mossman gave a spacious stone and masonry building at 1202 West Wayne St. to house the collection. There are frequent traveling exhibts and shows of art students and faculty.

The Allen County-Fort Wayne Historical Society was founded in 1921 at a meeting held at the Lincoln National Bank on February 2. Samuel Foster presided and Floyd Neff served as secretary. Others participating in the organization were Bert Griswold, Ross Lockridge, Mrs. A. J. Detzer, Miss Flora Wilber, Rabbi A. L. Weinstein and Maurice Niezer. In the following week, a dinner meeting in the auditorium of Wolf & Dessauer served to launch the society in formal fashion. An historical revue was presented by Indiana University Extension students, entitled "The Building of the Wabash and Erie Canal." Addresses were given by visiting notables including John W. Oliver, director of the Indiana Historical Commission; Dr. Harlow Lindley, of Earlham College and secretary of the Indiana Commission; Dr. Frank B. Wynn, commission vice-president; and the Rev. Matthew J. Walsh, president of the University of Notre Dame; and commission members.

The permanent organization of the Historical Society was accomplished on March 23, 1921, at a meeting at Old Fort Wayne High School. William H. W. Peltier was elected president. Other officers named were Bert Griswold, vice-president; Ross Lockridge, treasurer; Mrs. James B. Crankshaw, secretary; and Mrs. Eliza Hanna Hayden, Sam Foster and Jacob M. Stouder, directors. The charter members numbering 208 signed the constitution. The first annual meeting was the following Dec. 6, at which time Griswold succeeded Peltier to the presidency. Lockridge was named vice-president and W. Page Yarnelle, treasurer. The main interest at the meeting centered on the historical collection of the Mary Penrose Wayne Chapter of the Daughters of the American Revolution which at that time was housed on the third floor of the Allen County Courthouse. The problem revolved around the fact that the collection was outgrowing the space in the room at the Courthouse, and the expanding need for court space indicated a new site was needed for the DAR's collection. The DAR invited the Historical Society to take over the function of housing the collection.

In the following year, Ross Lockridge became society president and the organization committed itself to taking over the historical collection. A number of sites were considered for a museum, including the old Swinney homestead on the west edge of the city in Swinney Park. This was the location chosen, but it was several years before the quarters were made ready and occupied. In the meantime, Mrs. Samuel R. Taylor was appointed first curator. She was also elected president of the society in 1923 and was succeeded by David N. Foster in 1924. Other officers at that time included Mrs. Olaf N. Guldlin, Charles J. Steiss, W. Page Yarnelle, Mrs. Eliza Hayden, Mrs. A. J. Detzer, Miss Kathrine Hamilton, Bert Griswold and Jacob M. Stouder. In 1924, the society negotiated and accepted the offer of the Swinney building and concluded an agreement with the DAR giving control of the museum collection to the society, with the DAR getting the privilege of holding meetings at the Swinney site. The old homestead was remodeled under the direction of J. M. E. Riedel, architect. The collection was removed from the Courthouse in 1926 to the Swinney House and the dedication of the place was held on Jan. 17, 1927. The annual meeting on the same day resulted in the election of Frank Bursley Taylor as president. Directors of the museum after Mrs. Sam Taylor include Charles P. Cherry, Mrs. Frances Rawles, Dr. James Kellar, Richard Haupt, David Drury and Gary G. Ernest.

The Building Boom

Trinity English Lutheran Church on West Wayne Street between Ewing Street and Fairfield Avenue, was completed in 1926. The sweeping lines of the late-Gothic stone building dominated the entire neighborhood. The congregation was founded by Henry Rudisill in 1846. Two pastors are especially associated with Trinity, a congregation of 4,000 members and one of the largest in the United Lutheran Church in the United States. They are the Rev. Samuel Wagenhals and Dr. Paul H. Krauss. Wagenhals served as pastor from 1869 to 1920, and was one of the founders of the Chicago Lutheran Theological Seminary. Dr. Krauss, who succeeded Wagenhals upon the latter's death in 1920, served as pastor and pastor emeritus for more than 50 years. Chairman of the building committee which erected Trinity English Lutheran Church in 1926 was John B. Franke, who is remembered for donating to the city the large tract of land known as Franke Park.

A short distance north, at the corner of Fairfield and Berry Street, the Plymouth Congregational Church headed by Dr. Arthur F. Folsom dedicated its church in 1924. The English Gothic edifice in Indiana limestone housed a congregation which reached to about 2,000 members by the 1950's. Blymouth was originally founded in 1870 and the Rev. John Fairbank was the first pastor.

The Catholic Community Center, a building at the southwest corner of Jefferson and Barr Streets, had a short but active career in the history of the city. The building was put up in 1927 for $750,000 after a building fund drive started in March, 1926. Included in the five-story center were two gymnasiums, a music hall, swimming pool, bowling alleys, meeting rooms and accommodations for overnight. The driving force behind the center was Bishop John F. Noll, who became bishop of Fort Wayne on June 30, 1925. Bishop Noll had founded "Our Sunday Visitor," a national Catholic weekly, in 1912. The newspaper in later years reached a circulation of more than 1 million. In 1925, he started "The Priest," a widely distributed magazine among Catholic clergy. He was raised to the rank of Archbishop on Sept. 2, 1953, the only archbishop in the history of Fort Wayne. Other major works of Bishop Noll included the building of the modern St. Vincent's Villa on Wells Street in 1932 and the founding of Central Catholic High School at Lewis and Clinton Streets in 1938. The Catholic Community Center was the scene of numerous sporting events, education and social functions, and theater attractions during the 1920's, 1930's and 1940's. It subsequently served as the Purdue University Center in Fort Wayne, and finally in the mid-1960's until 1968 as the temporary Fort Wayne Public Library. It was then razed.

The Shrine Temple and Auditorium, later renamed the Scottish Rite Auditorium, was built in 1926 at a cost of approximately $1 million. The large auditorium which seated more than 2,000, was more than twice the size of the earlier Shrine Temple Theatre which burned down in 1923. The Shrine, as it was usually called, quickly became the music hall for most major concert events and frequent stage productions. In addition, the lower level of the building was a popular dance hall called the Valencia Gardens during the 1930's and 1940's, and a frequent site for banquets from the 1920's through the 1970's.

The Duemling Clinic, the city's first large medical clinic, was founded in 1922 at 2902 Fairfield Ave. by Dr. Herman A. Duemling, chief surgeon at Lutheran Hospital. The later clinic building, erected in 1973 across Home Ave. from the original structure, was built by a medical group headed by Dr. Eugene Senseny.

Another substantial Fort Wayne landmark was the Masonic Temple, an eight-story Greek edifice of stone built in the 200 block of East Washington Boulevard. The M.W. Grand Lodge, F&AM, laid the cornerstone on October 19, 1923. The Wayne Pharmacal Building, located at the southeast corner of Berry and Ewing Sts., was built in 1924. The seven-story office structure was later called the Medical Center Building. The News-Sentinel Building, at the northwest corner of Washington Blvd. and Barr St., was built in 1925. The two-story, red brick and stone newspaper plant, erected at the direction of Oscar Foellinger, publisher, remained the home of the News-Sentinel until 1958.

First Highways Built

Until the 1920's, there were few paved roads which were suitable for automobile and truck travel. Prior to that time, even routes marked as highways were actually gravel roads which often turned into mud-rutted obstacle courses in bad weather. Travelers in Oldsmobiles, Model T Fords, Marmons and Auburns would take along several sets of tires and tubes, plus extra cans of gasoline as they motored along between the farms and over the hills.

The Indiana Highway Department was created in 1919. Prior to that time, for some 40 years, the matter of roads and highways had been the business of the counties operating under the Three-Mile Gravel Road Law. Extensive use was made of native stone and gravel in Allen County and other counties in the state. When the Indiana Highway System came into being, the State took over a substantial portion of the road mileage. At the beginning, Federal matching funds were made available and a considerable amount of surplus war material was put to use. A three-cent tax was put on gasoline for automotive vehicles, license plates were sold, and funds were split with the 92 county road agencies in the state. By 1926, Indiana had invested $55 million in highways and had laid down 1,500 miles of pavement. In addition there were constructed more than 500 bridges and 3,000 miles of gravel road surface. The State Highway system in 1926 consisted of 4,311 miles out of a total of 73,000 miles of all types of roadways in Indiana. At that date 85 per cent of the state's population was directly served by state roads, including Fort Wayne and Allen County. A

1926 State Highway System map shows U.S. 30 being paved both east and west out of Fort Wayne. U.S. 33 heading northwest and State Road 1 south were also paved. U.S. 27 both north and south were still gravel, as was U.S. 24 which only went southwest.

Airplanes Come to Town

Fort Wayne's first Municipal Airport came into being in 1925 at what was later named Smith Field. The community's history in the colorful early era of flying, however, predates a regular civic airport by more than a decade.

Arthur R. Smith, born in 1890, is popularly regarded as Fort Wayne's first "bird boy" and being the originator of skywriting. He built his own craft in 1911, made out of wooden frames covered with linen. It had a wing span of about 28 feet and was some 21 feet long. It is said his parents mortgaged their home to buy an Elbridge model 399 engine for $1,280.

The reputation of Art Smith was sufficient that 60 years later in the 1970's a national fan club named in his honor was building an authentic replica in a shop across town at Baer Field. Members of the Art Smith Airplane Club building the plane included Billy Parker of Sun City, Ariz.; Bob McComb, an aerobatic pilot for many years; Ralph Bleke; John Fred McComb; George Alford; William Sheets, Harold Kiel and Paul Hobrock all of Fort Wayne. Theodore Hagerman of the Fort Wayne Air Service provided the working space for the rebuilding project.

Smith, himself, had a rather short career, as did many of the early flyers who had carefree attitudes about danger. In addition to skywriting with his primitive craft, Smith engaged in daredevil exploits which thrilled crowds of Sunday spectators in the early 1920's across the land, in Europe and Japan. He was also one of the first pilots employed by the U.S. Post Office for delivering airmail. It was on one of these airmail flights that he was killed in a crash on the night of February 12, 1926, not far from Fort Wayne just across the state line in Ohio.

Actually, the city's first airport, later known as Smith Field, was not originally dedicated in honor of Smith at all, but another flyer whose name is closely linked with Fort Wayne and who became world-renowned as a World War I ace. His name was Paul Baer.

It all happened when efforts to provide the city of Fort Wayne with a municipal airport produced definite results in June, 1925. At that time the Park Commissioners (there was no Board of Aviation Commissioners) bought 156 acres of land north of the city at a cost of $38,000. Fifty-six acres of land were added several years later. The land extended from the Ludwig Road to the Cook Road, west of the New York Central Railroad tracks. The field was formally dedicated to the honor of Paul Baer, who was America's first ace in the Great War, and for much of the war, the U.S.'s leading ace. He was a member of the Lafayette Escadrille, which went to France prior to the declaration by the U.S. to enter the hostilities. He was credited with shooting down 16 German aircraft in a 45-day period.

It was a great day for aviation when the opening of the airport was celebrated. Baer, however, was not there. On hand were pilots from across the land and abroad. The most famous was the French ace, Charles Nungesser, who is listed as one of the half-dozen top air heroes in World War I. Nungesser had 45 victories over the comrades of Baron von Richthofen and Oswald Boelcke of the Kaiser's Flying Circus.

The Municipal Airport, called Paul Baer Airport at the time, was in the 1930's renamed Smith-Baer Airport. The later opening of a larger airport across town to the southwest during World War II by the Army Air Corps led to Baer Field there and Smith Field at the old site. The city didn't get around to forming a Board of Aviation Commissioners until 1929. Prior to that time the Park Board handled the facility as a playground for stunt flyers, balloonists and experiments ranging from people transporters to glider and kite specialists. Driving out to the airport in vintage Hudsons and Hupmobiles to see who was trying some new air trick was regular family recreational fare in those days. Among the early Aviation Commissioners were J. Ross McCulloch, Paul C. Guild, Peter Certia, Arthur Hall, George DeWald and Robert H. Klaehn. The first manager of the airport was Robert Bartell. He was succeeded in 1933 by Capt. Clarence F. Cornish. Other early workers at the municipal airport included Earl J. Miller, Walter Paulmann, Robert Miller, Basil Harter, Harry Winn and Ralph Bleke.

The use of radio was made part of the operation with the opening of a radio station at the field on October 5, 1935. It was reliably reported that 917 transmissions, providing all sorts of information day and night, were made in the first year. Originally, the field was improved with forty miles of field tile for drainage. In 1936 electric lights were installed at the airport to brighten the runways and obstructions. Runways were built and extended in 1936 by WPA workers. The electric lights installed in 1936 replaced the old coal oil lanterns which had been used along the runways prior to that time. Consolidated Aircraft Repair operated the first government-approved service unit at the field.

The Municipal Airport was authorized to issue flying permits on July 1, 1936, ending the informal years of barnstorming regular airport terminals. The issuing of permits was introduced in the name of safety and gave local, state and federal authorities power to suspend permits to use facilities and enforce regulations. The first fatal accident at Fort Wayne's municipal airport took the life of Lt. George Hill, a mail plane pilot, on April 21, 1933. His craft was approaching the field for a landing when it went into a spin at several hundred feet and crashed to the earth.

Mail service at the Municipal Field was inaugurated by the Thompson Aeronautical Corporation on Dec. 6, 1930. The pilot was the same George Hill who was killed at the field 3 years later. In May, 1931, the first regular passenger service was started by the Transcontinental and Western Air, Inc. (TWA) with Fort Wayne being a stop on the daily run between Chicago and Columbus, Ohio. TWA passenger service and all mail service was discontinued in February, 1934, when Postmaster General James Farley of the Franklin D. Roosevelt Administration cancelled air mail contracts as a Depression economy move.

In the first decade of its operation, more than $540,000 was expended by the city on the airport. The biggest portion was for capital improvements, which totaled $390,000. The city sold a $300,000 bond issue; appropriated $172,000 in tax levies and had other improvements through a number of Depression era agencies. These latter included the Federal Emergency Relief Administration, the Allen County Scrip Organization and the Works Progress Administration, which contributed assets with no direct charge upon Fort Wayne taxpayers. Receipts from the sale of gas and oil and space rentals at the airport during the first decade, 1925 to 1936, totaled $64,761. Most of the buildings and runways built in the first 10 years were the same that were being used at Smith Field in the 1970's. As for Paul Baer, Fort Wayne's ace of aces, he died Dec. 9, 1930, when his plane crashed near Shanghai, China.

Lindbergh Buzzes Crowd

August 11, 1927, was the day Charles A. Lindbergh in the Spirit of St. Louis buzzed the Courthouse in downtown Fort Wayne as most everyone in the city gaped upward in the clear morning sun. Fresh from his famous trans-Atlantic solo flight, Lindy was scheduled to stop at Fort Wayne during a flight from Indianapolis to Detroit. As he flew low over the downtown of Fort Wayne, Lindbergh was seen tossing a message packet from his airplane. People on the streets downtown reported even seeing a red ribbon fluttering from the message. Yet when crowds went searching for the message, it couldn't be found.

The News-Sentinel on the day said: "While hundreds of persons sunburned the roofs of their mouths vainly looking for Colonel Charles A. Lindbergh and the Spirit of St. Louis to land at Sweebrock Airport, three miles north of the city on the Lima Road, thousands of others stood on roofs, craned their necks out of windows and gazed upward from the streets at Lindy as he circled about the city and dropped a message near the Courthouse here today.

"At 11:23 o'clock, daylight savings time, a silver dot appeared in the southwestern skies heralding the coming of the famed trans-Atlantic flier. The thousands of sky-gazers in the city were well-rewarded for their glances upward, for Colonel Lindbergh came down within 500 or 600 feet of the ground after he came over Fort Wayne. He was flying high and swift at first, but slowed down and in his extensive and sweeping circles came down as close as he dared to his audience in the city.

"A great many persons saw the Lindbergh message drop from the Spirit of St. Louis and appear to land in the vicinity of the Courthouse. Some observers were positive that it landed on the roof of the Lincoln National Bank Building, but a search failed to bring the missive to light." Later, it was learned a small boy had picked it up; and he was persuaded to make the parchment a part of the city's historical collection.

After buzzing the Courthouse, Lindbergh flew in the direction of Sweebrock Airport north of town. George Sweet of the Sweebrock Aviation Co. had earlier reported receiving a message from a Lindbergh aide that the flier would arrive at the field at about 11:30 a.m. Thousands of people and hundreds of cars were parked at the airport and along roads leading to it. A half-dozen other airplanes were flying about and doing aerial exhibitions in anticipation of the great event.

But Lindbergh never landed at Sweebrock. Presumably wary of the rather wild-flying welcome delegation, Lindbergh swung east when about a mile from the private field and went on to Detroit.

There were a number of privately-operated airports in the vicinity of Fort Wayne during the 1920's and 1930's. Among the owners, in addition to Sweet, was Guy Means who operated the field along State Road 3 a few years later and through the early 1930's. G. S. Means headed automobile agencies for many years in Fort Wayne starting in 1924.

Lincoln National Life

One of the unique companies in the history of the American life insurance industry and certainly in the life of Fort Wayne was coming into its own in 1923—the year it moved into its new headquarters building on Harrison Street. This was the Lincoln National Life Insurance Company.

In the beginning the firm had little about it from which its future success could be predicted. The Fort Wayne newspapers carried stories about an organization incorporated on June 3, 1905, and which operated from a one-room office on Berry Street. The organizers were Samuel M. Foster, president; Arthur F. Hall, secretary; William B. Paul, second vice-president; and Howell C. Rockhill, treasurer. Mentioned in the first reports was that the new company would take over $125,000 of life insurance previously written by the Fraternal Assurance Society of America. In the fall of that year, 1905, Hall received a short note from Robert Todd Lincoln:

"Replying to your note of July 28th, I find no objection whatever to the use of a portrait of my father upon the letterhead of such a life insurance company named after him as you describe; and I take pleasure in enclosing you, for that purpose, what I regard as a very good photograph of him."

The driving spirit behind early and continued success of Lincoln Life was Hall. He came to Fort Wayne from Indianapolis and was the effective chief executive for nearly four decades. A later president, Walter O. Menge, was to describe Hall as "ambitious, dynamic, intelligent and resourceful." By the end of the first decade, the Lincoln came under the influence of another vital idea, the idea of acquiring business through purchase. "This idea, while accepting the fact that the normal process of a life insurance company's growth is through its agents' solicitations, took cognizance of the further fact that a life insurance company may also grow by acquiring the harvest of business gathered in by agencies of other life insurance companies," in the words of Menge.

An unusual circumstance along these lines contributed to the growth which made

Lincoln Life a major American corporation. This circumstance was mentioned in later years by George Bryce, a long-time executive and director of Lincoln.

"Mr. McAndless (A. J. McAndless who became president in 1939) said in various talks that our start in reinsurance business came around 1917 or 1918 when German reinsurance companies which had been active in this country prior to World War I were no longer able to take the business. Somebody had to assume it and Mr. McAndless and Mr. Franklin Mead decided to get into the business," Bryce said.

"Would you say that while we probably are not the originators of the idea of reinsurance, we were one of the main exploiters or developers of that idea," asked Clyde Cover, an attorney with Lincoln.

"I would say so, very definitely," Bryce answered.

"So our success in the reinsurance field was probably attributable to the fact that we got in early and we have had a product which was broad in its appeal to the smaller companies and even to the larger companies?"

"That's true," Bryce concluded.

Forty years later, Lincoln was accepting reinsurance from more than 500 companies throughout the western hemisphere and was a recognized leader in the field.

Franklin Mead was Lincoln's great discoverer and proponent of sound and timely ideas, according to Menge. He developed the idea of substandard life insurance and the idea of indemnity reinsurance. "Without these innovations, the Lincoln might very well have developed with the plodding conservatism which has characterized so many of the 793 American life companies," Menge said. Mead was secretary and actuary, starting in 1911 and was executive vice-president when he died in 1933. Lincoln figures during the earlier growth decades, in addition to Foster, Hall, Mead and McAndless, include Walter T. Shepard, who developed the first agency organization; Alfred L. Dern, Shepherd's successor; and Jerome J. Klingenberger, first lay underwriter in the life insurance industry who was with Lincoln for 41 years.

There was only one sad incident connected with Lincoln Life's new building in 1923. This was the death at the construction site of the son of Fred J. Rump, building contractor. When his son was killed, Rump left the job scene, never to return.

The home office building was expanded in 1929 and 1931 with rear sections to bring the total square feet to 240,000. An even bigger addition was opened in 1960, extending the building to the entire block through to Calhoun Street.

Lincoln Museum

In 1928, the company established its Lincoln Library and Museum, the largest collection of literature and information ever assembled about one man, Biblical characters excepted. The founding Curator, Dr. Louis Warren, was succeeded in 1956 by Dr. R. Gerald McMurtry. In 1932 the heroic Lincoln statue, "Abraham Lincoln—The Hoosier Youth" created by the sculptor Paul Manship, was erected and dedicated in the building entry plaza.

In 1939, Lincoln Life reached the milestone of $1 billion of insurance in force. In that same year, Arthur Hall who had been president since 1923, assumed the position of chairman of the board, a post he held until his death in 1942. Alva J. McAndless, Hall's successor to the presidency in 1939, served as chief executive until his death in 1954.

Walter O. Menge, who at one time had headed the actuarial department of the University of Michigan, served as president of Lincoln Life from 1954 to 1964, and as chairman of the board from 1964 to 1968. Menge once said the place of Lincoln Life in the insurance industry might be condensed in the phrase: "The world is still evolving and unfolding. The importance of this idea which accepts change as natural and inevitable, cannot be over emphasized because life insurance, being largely a response to economic needs, is essentially a handmaid of social advancement."

Lincoln in 1951 purchased the Reliance Life Insurance Company of Pittsburgh, the largest such transaction in insurance history, and in 1957 purchased controlling interest in the Dominion Life Assurance Company in Canada. In 1963, the controlling interest in American States Insurance Company, Indianapolis, a fire-casualty organization, was purchased.

In the fall of 1963, Lincoln formed an European multiple-line reinsurance affiliate known as the Compagnie de Reassurance Nord-Atlantique to handle life, fire and casualty insurance. This move occasioned the visit to Fort Wayne of Jacques Reuff, finance minister of President Charles de Gaulle of France. Reuff was chairman of Lincoln's international affiliate.

Henry F. Rood succeeded Menge as president in 1964 and as chairman in 1968. During the 1960's, Lincoln Life moved toward the $20 billion insurance-in-force figure and was adding to that total at the rate of more than $1 billion a year. Considerable numbers of fortunes were made by Lincoln investors. Menge and Rood became popularly known as the "gold dust twins."

Henry Fairbank Rood, a native of Port Chester, N. Y., joined Lincoln in 1931. In 1948 when a merger formed the Society of Actuaries in the United States, Rood was named the first secretary-treasurer. He conducted the negotiations in the purchase of Reliance Life Insurance Co. with Lincoln in 1951 and was a key figure in expansions involving Dominion Life of Canada, CORENA in Paris and Dominion-Lincoln in London, England, plus the acquisitions of American States and the Lincoln Philippines Life Company.

Lincoln National Corp.

In 1968, the corporate structure of Lincoln National changed when Lincoln National Corporation came into being. The corporation was a holding company for Lincoln's insurance interests, plus LNC Development Corporation, organized to manage, own, develop and invest in real estate. In 1969, LNC acquired Chicago Title and Trust, the largest trust and title operation in the Midwest. Also that year Lincoln formed LNC Equity Sales Corporation, a national distributor of mutual funds; the LNC Investment Management Corporation for fund management; and Medical Information Service, which offers paramedical examinations to insurance and other companies.

Thomas A. Watson became president of Lincoln National Life Insurance Co. in 1968 and succeeded Henry Rood as chief executive officer of Lincoln National Corporation in 1971. Gordon C. Reeves was Lincoln National Corporation president from 1968 to 1971. Gathings Stewart was named Lincoln National Life president in 1973.

Thomas Watson, who was named board chairman of Lincoln Life in 1973, was born at Winona Lake. By interesting coincidence, Watson in his school-boy years was one of the vast crowd standing on Harrison St. that day in 1932 when the Manship statue of the young Lincoln was dedicated in front of the headquarters of the firm Watson later headed. He joined Lincoln in 1945 after U.S. Air Corps service in Europe during World War II. His service as a pilot resulted in his being awarded the Silver Star, the Presidential Citation with clusters, the Air Medal with clusters and the Purple Heart. Watson's career with Lincoln has been broad in both marketing and management within the insurance field and an unusual number of community interests in the areas of human relations, community services and the arts. He has been president or director of the Urban League, the Fine Arts Foundation, Junior Achievement and equal opportunity projects. He was instrumental in the creation of the Lincoln Life Improved Housing Corporation, designed to provide housing ownership for low-income families.

Lincoln National executives who have had extensive roles in shaping the company's progress include Edward Auer, Ronald Stagg, Cecil Cross, Fergus McDiarmid, Lee Wilks, Frank Travers, Henry Persons, Allen Steere, John Phelps and John P. White.

Lincoln in 1974 employed nearly 3,000 persons in its home office operations. In June of that year, Lincoln National announced a further expansion of its home office in Fort Wayne. The plans called for a 200,000 square-foot annex building on the east side of Calhoun St., facing the main company development. Construction was planned for 1975. The $10 million building, seven stories high, was designed with two second-story pedestrian crossovers above Calhoun St. to connect with earlier Lincoln buildings. Thomas A. Watson, LNC president, said the structure would be a public building in that it would house the Lincoln Library and Museum and meeting-dining rooms for civic groups.

International Harvester

In 1922, construction was started on a plant for the International Harvester Company, a manufacturer which would eventually become the largest employer in the Fort Wayne area.

The location of International at Fort Wayne was brought about by perhaps the most united community effort of the city in the 20th Century. It led to the creation of the Greater Fort Wayne Development Corporation which was largely responsible for not only International manufacturing plants but much of what later became called the East End Industries. The effort really began in November, 1919, when the International Harvester Company notified the Fort Wayne Chamber of Commerce that it was seeking a location for a motor truck plant. It was expected the plant would cost as much as $5 million and employ 4,000 to 5,000 men. Production output was scaled at 30,000 trucks annually.

The Fort Wayne people learned that 26 other cities were also competing for the large manufacturing development. The Chamber quickly named a committee consisting of Edward Miller, then postmaster; Robert Feustel, a utility executive; and E. Wesley Puckett, businessman, to carry on negotiations with the Harvester Company. The Fort Wayne group was successful in getting a commitment from I-H officials provided the community could meet certain difficult requirements. The Chamber group agreed to the conditions and signed a contract in May, 1920.

The firm stipulated that a number of services had to be brought to the location east of the Bueter Road and south of Pontiac Street Extended. These services included gas, water, streetcar operations, electricity, telephone, sewers and paved street approaches. The International Harvester would build its own plant. A belt line railroad was to be constructed to connect the plant with the Pennsylvania, Wabash, Nickel Plate and New York Central Railroads. Also, the Chamber was to organize a corporation of ample financial strength capitalized at $750,000 to be responsible for the carrying out of all the obligations under the contract.

According to Albert H. Schaaf, who later reported the events, the housing situation in Fort Wayne in 1920 was "about as acute" as it ever was in the community, and this circumstance much concerned the Harvester officials. They feared the possibility of substantial increases in lot prices and difficulties of employees in securing homes. The Chamber corporation was therefore required to purchase lands in the vicinity of the proposed plant equivalent to at least 400 building sites and to construct up to 1,000 dwelling houses for International workers. "The task of organizing such a company was made all the more difficult because the International would permit no publicity, on the theory no doubt, that the Chamber had assumed a Herculean task, and in the event of failure, the whole matter could be dropped without militating against the selection of some other city," Schaff said.

Hall's Committee

"In this emergency, the Chamber asked that superlative organizer, salesman and civic leader, Arthur F. Hall, to take over." He appointed to his committee Abe Ackerman, representing bankers; Feustel, representing public utilities; Charles B. Fitch, then president of the Chamber of Commerce; Walter Goll, representing manufacturers; Robert Koerber, representing the merchants; Miller, for civic interests; Puckett, representing wholesalers and jobbers; and Albert Schaaf, representing real estate brokers.

The group decided it needed $1 million to launch its program. Thinking big, they approached Louis Fox and W. K. Noble both of whom agreed to head the subscription list with $25,000 each. Four others soon agreed to $25,000 subscriptions. They were Sam Foster, Henry Paul, Gustave Berghoff and Fisher Brothers. John Stillman and Wolf & Dessauer each subscribed $15,000. Eleven individuals or companies subscribed $10,000 including Abe Ackerman, S. F. Bowser, Fred Eckart Packing Company, M. J. Gilmartin, William M. Griffin, A. Hattersly & Sons, Heit-Miller-Lau Candy Co., Hoffman Brothers, William E. Mossman, A. H. Perfect Company and Rurode Dry Goods Company. In all, there were 295 subscribers and a total amount of $945,700. This launched the Greater Fort Wayne Development Corporation. In addition to the original committee members, three other corporation directors were named to the board. They were Frank Cutshall, of Old National Bank; Edward Scheumann, of the First and Hamilton National Bank; and Theodore Wentz, of Lincoln National Bank. Hall was elected president; Ackermann, treasurer; and Schaff, general manager.

The program meant an immediate extension of the community. The County Commissioners extended Pontiac St. more than a half mile east to the Bueter Road and widened Bueter Road from Pontiac to New Haven Avenue. Both streets were made 100 feet wide and paved with concrete, with the assessment for the improvement made countywide. Storm and sanitary sewers were brought to the plant site without expense to the International Harvester Company under a procedure based on Indiana drainage laws and supervised by the Allen Superior Court. The cost was distributed over a considerable amount of real estate to the east of the city limits and south of the Maumee River. The Indiana Service Corporation extended street car lines and power lines to the plant. Northern Indiana Public Service extended gas mains and the Home Telephone Company the telephone service facilities for the new district. An important achievement was getting the four railroads to agree on the beltline railroad, including its financing, construction and operation.

The Development Corporation purchased 298 lots at Pontiac Place, Anthony Blvd. Addition, Eastwood and Shady Brook Park. Forty acres were purchased north of Pontiac and west of Bueter Road, which was later platted and developed as Harvester Park Addition.

"Speed Trucks"

But just as the house building project was about to begin, a business recession set in and International Harvester asked for an extension of time for construction of the first building of the industrial plant. "This was a veritable bomb shell and rumors that our project was doomed to failure became widespread," Schaaf said. "It was only after Cyrus McCormick, Jr., came to Fort Wayne and in a memorable address to a large group of our citizens gave assurance that his company had not abandoned its plans for the Fort Wayne plant, that confidence was restored."

The building of the factory was underway in 1922 and much of the manufacturing operation was started up in 1923. The first year production of "speed trucks" at the company's most modern facility totalled 433. A plant at Akron, where Harvester had earlier produced the trucks, was closed in 1925.

The original manufacturing unit consisted of 200,000 square feet. Later expansion extended the plant to more than 200 acres and in excess of 40 acres of space under roof. Production in 1924, the first full year of production, numbered 6,831 trucks. The firm was producing more than 40,000 trucks annually at the Fort Wayne plant by the midfifties. Separate engineering quarters were erected in 1950 in keeping with advances in testing and research. The Engineering and Laboratories building was located on a 25 acre tract near the Meyer Road. A new $8 million motor truck building and laboratories was formally dedicated and put into operation on September 24, 1952. That facility contained about 250,000 square feet of floor space. In the 1960's, International expanded further with the development of twin assembly lines and development and production of the Scout, a utility automobile which swept the company and Fort Wayne into a new phase of progress.

As for further 1920's development on the East End, the Harvester contributed $20,000 towards a new park in the vicinity. The 10-acre wooded site was named McCormick Park in honor of the founder of International Harvester.

Expanding Industry

The Greater Fort Wayne Development Corporation still had industrial lands, some 90 acres east of the Bueter Road and 60 acres south of Pontiac Street Extended. It was put to good use.

In the spring of 1923, the Fort Wayne group was approached by William C. Spaulding who wanted to locate a factory which would make special truck bodies in the vicinity of International Harvester. Spaulding bought the land and the Development Corporation financed the building. This founded the Truck Engineering Company. Truck Engineering expanded a few years later when it took over the facilities of the Utensils Company, which had been built nearby in 1924. Truck Engineering became a highly successful operation. Clarence A. Croteau, vice-president and general manager of the firm, eventually became company president. After some 30 years, he was succeeded by his son, Jack Croteau, who headed the firm during later periods of innovation and expansion in the trucking industry, particularly by International Harvester.

General Hosiery purchased four acres in 1926 and built a substantial factory. The firm, organized by Henry Herbst, progressed for more than a decade and was sold to Gotham Mills.

A short-lived member of the Fort Wayne industrial community which moved to the East End development in 1927 led to the founding of Rea Magnet Wire Company. The Woodard Engineering Co. came from Zanesville, Ohio, as a designer and maker of machine tools and rolling mill equipment. After a year of operations, the company failed. The property was later leased and subsequently sold to Rea Magnet Wire, headed by Victor F. Rea who had been president of Dudlo Manufacturing Company. The Rea firm steadily enlarged its floor space and capacity. Victor Rea's sons, Samuel and David, eventually became chairman and executive officers of the firm.

Rea Magnet Wire was merged with the Aluminum Corporation of America in 1960, but continued plant operations in Fort Wayne. Rea was part of a magnet wire industry in Fort Wayne which by the 1950's was producing more than half the entire output in the United States. Other large producers by that time included Essex Wire, the Inca and the Indiana Rod and Wire Divisions of Phelps Dodge Corporation and the Wire Mill of the Taylor Street Plant of General Electric Company.

The city's preeminence in the field began with the Dudlo Manufacturing Co., which also was responsible for making Fort Wayne the diamond die center of the world. Dudlo was started by George Jacobs. By 1928 he purchased 15 acres of industrial property for a newly-formed company from the Chamber Development Corporation on the south side of U.S. 30, just east of the Union Railroad. This was the beginning of the Inca Manufacturing Company, as the corporation was named. This firm was purchased in 1930 by the Phelps Dodge Copper Products Corporation.

Phelps Dodge expanded Inca and also its Indiana Rod and Wire Division, a major producer in the Midwest of copper rods, wire and cables. The mills stand on either side of New Haven Avenue. Inca was the world's largest magnet wire plant. The Indiana Rod and Wire Division started operations in Fort Wayne in 1946 in a plant which was completed that year. Much of the Fort Wayne development of Phelps Dodge was directed by S. Allan Jacobs, a corporate vice-president starting in 1941. Jacobs was named president of the Inca Division in 1958 and later chairman of Phelps Dodge Industries. A. F. Van Ranst was named president of Phelps Dodge Magnet Wire Company.

Dudlo was originally started in 1910 at Cleveland and was brought to Fort Wayne in 1911 by George Jacobs, president and general manager of the firm for many years. By the mid-1920's, it had become the largest firm in the country in drawing wire and enameling. At its high point the operation employed more than 3,000 workers. Jacobs sold the firm to General Cables in 1928. The Dudlo Works on Wall St., just east of the St. Mary's River on Fort Wayne's west end near Taylor St., became the home of Essex Wire Corporation.

Farnsworth and ITT

In the fall of 1928 Homer Capehart, a future senator of the United States, lunched at the Chamber of Commerce and talked with representatives of Fort Wayne's Greater Development Corporation. Out of this meeting came the establishment of the Capehart Company on Pontiac Street. Extended, the later development of Capehart Farnsworth Co. and the eventual location of International Telephone and Telegraph Laboratories in Fort Wayne.

Capehart produced some of the finest phonographs of the late 1920's. They were the prestige instrument of the era, with high polished wood wall cabinets and turntables which lifted up the records and turned them over and stacked them as the records were played—an advanced innovation at the time. The machines were also expensive and the company foundered with the onset of the Depression.

In 1938, Philo T. Farnsworth, a genius of the electronic industry, brought his Farnsworth Television and Radio Corp. to Fort Wayne and purchased the Capehart property. The Farnsworth story goes back to 1927 when Philo Farnsworth applied for his first patent covering a completed electronic system of transmitting and receiving television images. While still in his teen years, Farnsworth had evolved the idea for the first electronic television system. He is widely regarded as the father of television.

Farnsworth developed and produced various industrial and commercial products, and during World War II, contributed in the military electronics fields of communications, radar, infrared and early missile guidance systems. The Farnsworth firm was purchased by ITT in 1949 and renamed the Capehart-Farnsworth Corp. It entered the commercial television business and marketed the Capehart receiver for a number of years. Capehart-Farnsworth Corp. was sold in 1956 to the Ben Gross Corporation. ITT, however, continued operations in the Pontiac St. plant and in 1958 expanded with new facilities on the site of old Camp Scott, a World War II installation along Wayne Trace. With the expansion, ITT had more than 250,000 square feet of floor space. This led to the establishing of ITT Federal Laboratories and Kellogg Division in Fort Wayne. Farnsworth Electronics and other ITT operations made operational testing equipment and other apparatus for American missile systems such as Bomarc Interceptor, and other military and space vehicles.

Magnavox

In 1928, the Development Corporation succeeded in attracting the Steinite Company to Fort Wayne. A fancy building was built on the Bueter Road and both the Chamber's development unit and local banks were deeply committed. The firm, which wanted to move from Atchison, Kansas, to Fort Wayne, insisted on donation of the land and a 100 per cent construction loan on the plant consisting of 210,000 square feet. In a weak moment the Development officer capituated to the Steinite terms. "It illustrated that a community can go too far in its quest for growth and industrial payroll," Al Schaaf later commented. In less than two years the poorly managed Steinite company washed out and the Fort Wayne group was stuck with the property and debts.

This situation lead up to the location in Fort Wayne of one of the city's and nation's greatest growth industries, Magnavox Company, in 1929.

Magnavox was founded in 1911 at Napa, Calif., by two engineers in the field of sound, Edwin S. Pridham and Peter Jenson. They were financed by Richard O'Connor, father of the firm's chief executive, Richard A. O'Connor, when the company moved to Fort Wayne. In 1916, the first complete electric phonograph ever produced was introduced by Magnavox. One of its greatest World War I inventions was the anti-noise aircraft transmitters. In 1924 the firm invented a cone speaker with baffleboards, an advance in the loudspeaker industry, and also the moving coil speaker.

The original Fort Wayne plant produced loudspeakers and electrolytic capacitors. The growth of Magnavox was dramatic. From an original staff of about 300, it was to grow to more than 2,000 by the mid-1950's and to more than 4,000 in Fort Wayne alone by the 1970's, in a period when it also had numerous plants in operation in other cities. In the 1930's the plant began the manufacture of quality phonographs and introduced marketing practices which were as innovative as its products. These included direct factory-to-retail systems, which eliminated some of the distributor operations prevalent in the industry. Factory service was also a feature of the company. In World War II, Magnavox was the first electronics firm to receive the Navy E pennant award. Plants were opened in Greenville and Jefferson City, Tennessee; Paducah, Kentucky; Los Angeles, California, and Urbana, Illinois. O'Connor moved up to chairman of the board and Frank M. Freimann became president. Freimann, himself a pioneer in the field of sound, had merged his own operation which had been at Chicago with Magnavox, and had become a company vice-president after the firm located in Fort Wayne.

Pistons and Steel

The advantageous location of Fort Wayne to the auto industry brought Theodore Zollner to the city in 1931. Zollner at that time ran a manufacturing plant at Duluth, Minn., which made pistons for automobiles and trucks. But his transportation costs were high and he wanted something closer to Detroit and other centers of the auto business. Al Schaaf of the Greater Development Corp. drove him out to the East End and showed him a site along Bueter Road, just north of the International Harvester plant. A few days later Theodore Zollner returned with his son, Fred, and they signed an agreement.

Zollner Corp., which had originally been founded in 1912 at Duluth, expanded several times after construction of its 1931 building in Fort Wayne. It became a leader in its field and employed advanced thinking in employee relations. Under Fred Zollner, who succeeded his father as company president, the firm sponsored sports and youth programs, including what was called the Knot Hole Gang in which thousands of youngsters participated. The Zollner Softball and Fastball teams became dominant in national circuits. The Zollner Piston professional basketball teams led the pro circuits out of the dark ages and became world champions in doing so. Some of the Zollner executives included Mrs. Janet Fisher, Blayne Osborne, Otto Adams and Paul Schirmeyer.

Fort Wayne was becoming a sea of industrial activity in the 1920's. The Van Arnam Manufacturing Company was expanding at 2311 Taylor Street. The maker of toilet seats and clothes hampers, it had been founded in 1901 at Coldwater, Mich., and moved to Fort Wayne two years later. John Knott and George Van Arnam headed the company until 1923 when Howard Van Arnam became president. Later executives included Fred K. Horne and Dean B. Needham.

Pollak Brothers began the manufacture of dresses in 1922. Charles MacDougal had originated the company in 1910. Robert Pollak, who came from Cleveland, became a partner in the following year. The firm operated above the Holsum Bakery on Calhoun Street until the bakery building was destroyed by fire in 1920. Pollak Brothers then moved to the southeast corner of Main and Maiden Lane in a building which once had been the Old Turnverein, the German Athletic Club. The Turners moved to the old Hugh McCulloch house on Superior Street, a building which was the last home of the Fort Wayne Medical College. Pollaks expanded at the Main Street site and later opened operations at Bay City, Michigan, and Garrett, Indiana. Robert and Nelson Pollak headed the firm for many years. Later presidents of the firm included David E. Woolner, Joseph Barbieri Sr., and Joseph Barbieri, Jr., until the firm was merged and the Fort Wayne operation closed down in the 1960's.

In April, 1928, Joslyn Manufacturing & Supply Co., purchased the Fort Wayne Rolling Mill Corp. plant, just north of Taylor Street. The origin of the mill dated back to the purchase of land in 1902 from the Rockhill family and the building of a puddle mill. David Lowe of the Rolling Mill firm was credited with making the first bar of steel in Fort Wayne. Joslyn at first limited production to the rerolling of steel. In 1935, it installed its first electric furnace. Seven years later a second electric furnace was installed.

It was during World War II that Joslyn converted its entire facility to the production of stainless steel bars; and in 1943 cold finishing process was added. A wire mill was added in 1946. By 1957 the firm, with Leslie Fry as general manager, employed more than 600 workers.

American Steel Dredge Co., an early manufacturer of steam shovels and river dredges, underwent a number of changes in the late 1920's. The firm had entered business in 1906 at Logansport and moved to Fort Wayne in 1909, building its first of a number of plant operations on West Taylor Street. At first, dipper dredges were built exclusively, but the firm also started making steam shovels in 1912. That was the year the forerunner of the Wayne Crane was introduced.

American Steel Dredge Co. ceased the manufacture of dipper dredges in the late 1920's and was reorganized in 1932 and incorporated. Several years later the plant was enlarged and the production of self-propelled cranes began. The Wayne Crane was designed in 1942 by John G. Rauch, one of the organizers of the company. During World War II, American Steel fabricated steel bases of diesel engines on Navy barges and other war-use fabrications. In the following years, production of cranes and dredges was pursued. American Hoist & Derrick Co. became the surviving corporation in 1955 after a consolidation of American Steel and Dredge with the parent firm. Walter W. Walb, president of American Steel, was named General Manager of the Fort Wayne Division of American Hoist and a vice-president of the parent firm, headquartered in St. Paul, Minnesota. Walter Walb was later named chairman of the American Hoist Executive Committee. Gerald Heller was operating head of a related firm, American Steel Supply Corporation.

In June, 1956, the Crosby-Laughlin Division of American Hoist was located in Fort Wayne in a plant just to the west of the older operation on Taylor Street.

General Dredging Co. was incorporated in 1929 and engaged in the dredging of creeks and ditches in Indiana, Ohio and Illinois. In 1932 the operation was expanded to the building of roads, grading and drainage systems. In 1946 the company started the division known as the Masolite Division for the making of concrete products such as blocks, pre-cast concrete floors and roof systems. Under Ralph W. Walb, president of General Dredging, both the concrete products and the plant to make them underwent a number of expansions beginning in 1957.

Fort Wayne Structural Steel Co., 4022 Northrop Ave., had its beginning in the old Fort Wayne Foundry and Machine Co., which once was a part of the great Bass Foundry family of companies. In 1938 the assets of the old firm were purchased and moved from its location at Superior and Harrison Streets to the Northrop site. The Structural Steel group was headed by John L. Hayner, president; Hubert Hayner, vice-president; and Arnold F. Benz, secretary-treasurer. The firm cut and assembled steel for the building industry and fabricated parts for the trucking industry.

A number of contract shops, makers of tools and dies, have grown up in the wake of larger manufacturers of machines, wire products and other products. The first of these operations was begun in 1913 by Nestor and Gus Fries and L. J. Johnson at Fairfield Ave. and Poplar Street. Many started in the 1920's, including Frank Huth in 1921, Charles Hollman and Jake Goeglein in 1924, Harry Roehm in 1924, and quite a number more during World War II and after. Some of the firms operating in the post-war era, and members of the Fort Wayne Tool & Die Manufacturers Assn., formed in 1957, include Adroit, Fort Wayne Tool & Die, General Tool & Die, Genco Tool, Keller Tool & Die, Merkler Machining, Precision Tool, Quality Tool, Simplex Tool, J. C. Thompson Tool, Toolcraft and United Toolcraft.

Workers Flow In

Fort Wayne's unusual diversification was conducive to business stability during the 1920's, and more particularly in the Depression years of the 1930's. This was largely true because the community was not directly dependent upon one particular industry and therefore was less subject to wide fluctuations and seasonal trends such as experienced at Detroit, South Bend and Gary. The city was, of course, affected by national trends and there was considerable hardship in the Depression, if not such a high percentage of jobless as many other places. The Depression for farmers came earlier than the stock market crash in October, 1929, which signaled the beginning of the great downward slide of the economy. By the mid-20's, farmers in Allen County and other rural areas of the nation were experiencing acute distress. The rural poverty became a long-term thing, driving farm children to the cities and factory-related jobs. It wasn't until the need of food was stimulated by World War II demand that farm recovery set in; but even in the following years the trend toward consolidation and mechanization of farming led to a decline in farm population, but with superior returns on labor and higher income levels. One of the more noticable characteristics of the employee ranks of International Harvester and other East End industries developed in the 1920's is the high percentage of workers coming from rural and smalltown vicinities of Indiana and neighboring Ohio.

Many companies moved to Fort Wayne in the face of an already-tight labor market. The tightness was more apparent than real because of the availability of workers from surrounding areas. There was no other sizable city within an 80 mile radius of Fort Wayne, yet there was considerable population in smaller towns and cities, and rural communities. Both in the 1920's and in the post WWII years (there was little growth of any sort during the 1930's) a number of large firms moved in and set up, almost immediately, fairly large staffs and payrolls. Later ones include Studebaker Corp., U.S. Rubber, Cleveland Graphite Bronze, Magna Power Tool, W. S. Shamban, Peterson Brothers and Stratoflex.

Tokheim Pumps

Tokheim Corp. began operations in Fort Wayne in a small one-story structure in 1918, but expanded quickly during the 1920's. The origin of the firm goes back to 1898 when a Norwegian emigrant named John Tokheim founded an operation at Cedar Rapids, Iowa, for the making of hand pumps. This operation was purchased in 1918 by a group headed by Ralph F. Diserens, then general manager of the Wayne Pump Co., and moved to Fort Wayne. At the same time, the buildings and grounds of the Wayne Spoke and Bending Co. south of the Wabash Railroad on Wabash Ave. were acquired as a place of business. Tokheim Oil Tank & Pump Co. was the name of the firm incorporated in June, 1918.

Diserens was chief executive until his death in 1925. He was succeeded by M. B. Muzen, one of the organizers of Tokheim. Subsequent Tokheim chief executives included C. O. Griffin, Charles M. Niezer, Chester C. Oberly, E. S. Higginbotham, Louis F. Niezer, David Cunningham and Joseph Guidrey. The production of gasoline pumps continued to be a main interest, but in the period following World War II, during which ordance materials were produced, the firm became considerably diversified. A General Products Division and other operations were started. Plants and subsidiaries were established at Shelbyville and Leiden, The Netherlands.

V. M. Nussbaum Electric Co. was founded in 1912 by Victor Nussbaum, one of the backers of Tokheim in 1918 and a long-time Tokheim director. The company, with a plant at 220 East Douglas, installed electric equipment of General Electric and other companies. Herman Nussbaum, brother of Victor, succeeded to the presidency of the firm in 1954.

Armco, a subsidiary of National Mill Supply, Inc., was started before 1920 by S. A. Lehman, father of Harold Lehman who also became president of National Mill Supply, Inc. Armco was designed to handle transformer business.

Wayne Hardware Co., another supply house founded early, operated for more than half a century at Harrison and Pearl Streets. Top officers have included Frank H. Cutshall, John B. Spatz, Robert R. Enoch and Dean Cutshall.

Meats and Sausage

In 1925, Peter Eckrich and Sons was incorporated. The firm had its origin with a small grocery in 1908 at Smith and Wallace Streets. Peter Eckrich, the proprietor, started producing his own sausage at home with a hand grinder. His five sons joined him in the formation of a company to push the meat products. The firm established a headquarters at 2502 Broadway. Corporate officers included Peter Eckrich, president; Clement P. Eckrich, vice-president; John A. Eckrich, secretary-treasurer, and Henry C. Eckrich.

In 1932, the Fort Wayne plant at Osage and Richardson Streets was completed. An earlier plant was in operation at Kalamazoo, Mich., and a second Kalamazoo operation was completed in 1939. By that time officers of the company included Clement Eckrich, president; Paul Foohey, vice-president; and John Eckrich, secretary-treasurer. Herman Eckrich was general sales manager. The firm experienced rapid expansion in Midwest markets. In 1958, a research and development division was completed at Fort Wayne and 10 years later modern office quarters were established along Coliseum Boulevard. The company employment rolls passed the 1,000 mark in the 1950's. Executives during the later expansions included Joseph, Richard and Donald Eckrich, Edward Baker, Duane Daggett, Eugene Eckrich, Harold Stone, Robert Lill, Dr. Roy Tjepkema, Patrick Ciez and Harvey Baker.

Guy A. Laurents Packing Co. was started in 1890 by Alex Laurents and Clarence Hartshorn. The plant at Dwenger Ave. was expanded in the following decades by Guy Laurent and by 1950 was operating in a 60 miles radius of Fort Wayne. Harold Meyers was general manager for many years.

Parrot Packing Co. was organized in 1923 by Frank Parrot, Sr. The original staff consisted of 15 employees which was expanded more than 10-fold in the following decades. The company's plant near the Maumee River has been expanded and modernized a number of times. Executives during the growth years were Joseph Parrot, William Parrot, Leland Parrot and Charles Parrot.

Wayne Paper Box Corp., which had been founded as Fort Wayne Paper Box Co. in 1898, expanded in the 1920's at the corner of Calhoun Street and Superior Street. Officers of the firm included Andrew Burry, E. P. Ruf and R. L. Burry. Fisher Bros. Paper Co., a large wholesale firm, was operating at 120 West Columbia St. in the 1920's and for several decades thereafter. President of the company was Max B. Fisher. Roger I. Fisher, then vice-president, later became president and chairman of the board.

Fort Wayne Corrugated Paper Co. had become a national concern by 1930. The company was started in 1908 in a corner space of the Olds Wagon Works which once existed on Murray Street. The firm began to grow under the direction of Henry C. Paul, John J. Brossard, C. A. Kramer and F. P. Koester. Paper mills at Eaton and Hartford City were merged with the firm, with a larger plant constructed at Hartford City. Other operations were opened at Vincennes, Ind., and Connellsville, Pa., in 1930. An early American manufacturer of the kraft paper products, Fort Wayne Corrugated expanded rapidly after World War II and built a new plant at Rochester, N. Y., in 1952.

Harold Treen, who had joined the firm in 1923, became president in 1943. A large facility was constructed in Chicago, Ill., and the old Hartford City plant was rebuilt and re-equipped. The home office built a headquarters at 1230 South Clinton St., a modernistic building and the first of stainless steel in Fort Wayne. It was later occupied by departments of the Public School Administration. Treen in the meantime served for three years as president of the National Fibre Box

Association. He was a director of the Indiana-Purdue Foundation, and was a benefactor when the I.U.-Purdue Campus was founded. Fort Wayne Corrugated was acquired by Continental Can Co., Inc., in 1955.

McMillen's Feed Empire

The histories of many firms start with a single person who has imagination and the willpower to make an idea work. Dale W. McMillen, a Van Wert, Ohio, farm boy born in 1880, began by mixing and selling dairy, hog, horse and poultry feed on a small scale. In 1916 he came to Fort Wayne and purchased the Transfer Grain Elevator on the west side of the city. By the time he died in 1971 at the age of 91, he had put in motion a host of companies, including giant Central Soya, plus exerting far-reaching influence on the city's park system, recreation and sports activities and numerous civic enterprises. The Wayne Feed Company, which always displayed portraits of Anthony Wayne on its packages, was the first large enterprise. By the mid-1920's, Wayne was shipping 4,000 rail carloads annually. McMillen next headed Allied Mills, Inc., and McMillen Feed Mills, Inc. Some of the executives in these early companies included J. W. Bash, H. D. Egly, J. H. Ball, G. A. Chapman, Roy Hall, Harry E. Offutt, Clyde H. Hendrix, Edward T. Schele and Stewart W. McMillen. Dale McMillen, Jr., was executive vice-president of McMillen Feed. Harold W. McMillen was vice-president and general manager of Central Sugar Co., Inc., yet another enterprise and located at Decatur. A major plant of McMillen Feeds was established at Decatur. The firm's headquarters were in the First National Bank Building, later Fort Wayne National Bank.

In the late 1930's, McMillen became more interested in the potential of the soya bean. In 1937, an extraction plant was relocated from Germany to Decatur and put in operation. Product demand led to the construction of storage, soybean processing and feed facilities at Gibson City, Illinois. Distribution facilities were increased with developments at Madison, Wisconsin, Harrisburg, Pennsylvania, and Marion, Indiana, all in the early 1940's.

Central Soya

Central Soya, Inc., which had been established in 1934, expanded rapidly in the postwar period. Early officers, in addition to Dale McMillen, Sr., who was chairman, include Roy Hall, president; Dale McMillen, Jr., executive vice-president; Offutt, Robert P. O'Brien and David Bunnell, vice-presidents. By the company's 20th anniversary in 1954, it employed more than 2,000 persons. Dale W. McMillen, Jr., was named president and later board chairman. Harold W. McMillen was named president. In 1955 a plant at Chattanooga, Tenn., was opened to boost the firm's interest in the poultry market, an effort which was expanded rapidly in the 1960's. A Chemurgy Division, the main function of which was to research and develop soya bean products for human consumption, grew at a Chicago branch during the 1960's. Central Soya was one of the main tenants to occupy the new Fort Wayne Bank Building in 1970.

In the meantime, Dale McMillen, Sr., was chairman of the campaign in 1925 which led to the establishing of the YMCA camp at Blackman Lake. He was president of the old Farmer's Bank. In the 1950's he launched the Wildcat League, a baseball system where all boys who wanted to play could. It started a national trend.

Central Soya's soya food protein plant at Chicago was opened on Oct. 27, 1959. Harold McMillen, board chairman at the time, related the production to the growing world food problem and future need. He said edible protein resulting from the company's research and development "provides the building blocks of good nutrition and health." Earlier, Central Soya had opened plants in Gibson City, Ill.; Memphis, Tenn.; Marion, Ohio; and Harrisburg, Pa., in addition to the major installation of McMillen Feed at Decatur. Top executives of Central Soya during the middle growth years included Roy Hall, president of Central Soya and McMillen Feeds until 1942; Robert H. Fletcher, president from 1944 to 1948; Fred W. Thomas who became president in 1948; George C. Thomas, vice-president; Bert A. Townsend; E. V. McCann and Norman F. Kruse.

Chamber of Commerce

A number of organizations and associations evolved in Fort Wayne to promote industry and help commerce and the consuming public. In the early days of such associations, the goals were often related to specific functions in the community, but with time, some tended to exert broad influence on human and civic affairs, in addition to business interests.

The building for the Chamber of Commerce was begun in 1926. The site at the northwest corner of Wayne and Ewing Streets had been occupied since 1913 by the First Church of Christ Scientists in the old Charles McCulloch homestead. The Christian Scientist Church was relocated at Fairfield and Pierce Avenues with the erection of an impressive Greek-style structure.

Land for the Chamber building cost $50,000 and the construction costs came to $290,000. The Fort Wayne Woman's Club entered into an agreement with the Chamber and helped raise funds for the project. Moving spirits behind the building program included Louis Fox, Robert Feustal, Arthur Hall, A. H. Schaaf, Thomas J. Kelly and Ben F. Geyer. The architect was Guy Mahurin.

The Fort Wayne Chamber of Commerce had its origins in the old Wayne Club, started in 1893 by F. J. Fisher, and the Fort Wayne Commercial Club, headed by Robert Millard which began meeting in 1899. These clubs were merged in 1910, with Samuel Foster the first president; by 1917, the chamber was an organized unit. The new building completed in 1927 caused some financial difficulties which weren't resolved until 1943. A $125,000 remodeling program in 1964 renewed the interior. The programs of the chamber, which had more than 2,400 members by 1970, was once described by Earl S. (Mike) Ward, executive vice-president for two decades starting in 1945: "Everything the Chamber of Commerce does is aimed at creating new work opportunities." This includes industrial promotion, labor relations, civic and human interests, and in more recent years, task forces in the areas of education, government, roads and race relations. Some of the executives of the chamber have included Paul Trey, Mel Riley, Lucille Zink, Ivan A. Martin, Richard Bickel, John Hall, Lyman Samuels, D. J. Petrucelli and Mary Johnson.

The Credit Bureau of Fort Wayne, Inc., grew out of the Credit Rating Association of the Retail Merchants Bureau started in 1919. Organizers included M. E. Dessauer, Charles Moellering, C. V. Bales and H. E. Bodine. William J. Brutton was long-time secretary, and was succeeded by Bill Brutton, Jr.

The Better Business Bureau was founded in 1920 by local businessmen to "enhance the standing and importance of the city of Fort Wayne, Indiana, as a business and shopping center; to promote integrity and create confidence in advertising, in selling and all phases of business." The incorporators of the non-profit organization were N. Sherman Cutshall; Robert Koerber, Sr.; C. M. Mills; J. W. Greenland; Theodore Frank; Charles W. Walker; Hartwell Gosney; Ernest F. Brinkman; Bert J. Griswold; Henry Achenbach; Oliver Hartman and Charles Bales. The managers included, successively, Charles Walker, Fred Willson, Robert M. Snyder, Thomas A. Hayes, Jack D. Baer, H. C. Dart and C. Lane Breidenstein.

The Taxpayers Research Association, a watchdog of government spending in the interests of the taxpayers and business, was organized in 1934. Angus McCoy, the moving force behind the unit, served as executive secretary from the beginning until 1947, then as president for more than a decade thereafter.

The Toidey Co., the child of Gertrude A. Muller who earlier worked for the Van Arnam Co., was begun in 1924. She was convinced there was a need for a good, folding nursery seat and did something about it. Babies the country over became familiar with Miss Muller's seats. She served as head of the firm until her death in 1954. Plants were located on Taylor St. and at 5908 South Fairfield Avenue. The later building had earlier been the location of the Fort Wayne Riding Academy. During the 1930's and 1940's, men, women and youngsters regularly rode through Foster Park on bridle paths which led from the barn later converted into the Toidey factory. In the 1920's and early 1930's, the Academy Stables were across the St. Mary's River from Foster Park and a stone breakwater in the river enabled horsemen to cross the park. The Sears Pavilion was later built near the old brick stables building.

One of the great Fort Wayne fortunes was made in a relatively short time in the patent medicine field. The Pinex Co. grew out of an old cough syrup formula developed in or brought to the country drug store of B. R. Noll. In 1905, the druggist's son, William H. Noll, formed the company to market the product. National distribution was completed in 1910 and international sales were launched in 1913. A plant existed at 123 West Columbia St. in Fort Wayne and another plant in Toronto, Ontario. The high point in sales was reached by 1920, then began to fall off. In 1916 Bill Noll erected a palatial home of marble and stone in classic Italian architecture at 2500 South Fairfield Ave. which included gold fixtures, ballroom, formal gardens, swimming pool and fountains, largely surrounded by a wall topped with cut stone. It reportedly cost more than $1 million or about the same as the County Courthouse. Noll and his children were well known for effusive parties given at the location. Several Great Danes usually stood guard over the property. The mansion was razed in 1974.

In the early days of the town, the newspapers provided the main shops for printing services too. A firm named D. W. Jones & Son, Steam Book and Job Printers, published Wallace Brice's History of Fort Wayne in 1868. Some of the shops in existence for many years include the Keefer Printing Co., 714 West Washington Blvd., established in 1914 by James H. Keefer. J. Ver Keefer, a son, and James M. Keefer, a grandson, later headed the firm. Old Fort Wayne Printing Co. was founded in 1907 by John Wilding and Herman Heckel. It was reorganized in 1940 by E. C. Dickmeyer and operated until 1948. The Fort Wayne Allied Printing Trades Council, representing labor organizations, was founded in 1903 by John Sessler and Jack Burris.

Big Distributors

By the turn of the century and for several decades thereafter, the distribution houses were king in U.S. commerce. Their place in the scheme of things was reflected in the writings of Sinclair Lewis and others. Quite common was the practice for the great distribution and warehouse operations to start manufacturing operations and factories simply as subsidiaries to supply their own needs. Some of these distributors, such as Mossman Yarnelle in Fort Wayne, had salesmen out covering dozens of states, making regular calls at customer stores as far west as Nebraska. Their high point was reached in the 1910's and 1920's. Like other business operations they suffered in the Depression, but because of changing methods in merchandising in subsequent decades, the large distribution and commission houses never regained their earlier prominence.

Edward F. Yarnelle and Frank Alderman started a heavy hardware house named Alderman & Yarnelle. In 1885 William E. Mossman purchased Alderman's interest and the firm was renamed Mossman-Yarnelle Company. In 1908 the expanding company built its large brick headquarters on Pearl St., just west of Harrison St. and near what was then the depot for the Interurbans. Mossman became president of the Dudlo Manufacturing Co., producers of insulated wire. Edward Yarnelle, who served as president of Mossman-Yarnelle until 1919, was also president of the American Iron, Steel and Heavy Hardware Association. He also was president of Fort Wayne Rolling Mills Co., a supplier for Mossman-Yarnelle. That facility was later purchased by Joslyn Steel Company. B. Paul Mossman, son of William E. Mossman, served as president of Mossman-Yarnelle in the following decade with W. Page Yarnelle, vice-president; Harry E. C. Miller, secretary, and E. H. Roemke, treasurer. Miller's sons eventually assumed management of the company.

Schlatter Hardware Company started business in 1882 at the southeast corner of Clinton and Columbia Streets and remained at the same location until the era of Redevelopment downtown in the 1960's. Christian C. Schlatter founded a small outlet dealing in horsecollars, kerosene lamps, blacksmith tools and wash tubs. The firm grew and grew at the location until it became a hardware supply house of major proportions. It was said at the time of Schlatter's removal to its new Merchandise Place in the northern suburbs near Interstate 69 and State Road 3 in 1967 that it was the single most severe blow to downtown's reputation as a place to get most anything. Successors to Christian Schlatter as head of the firm include John Trier, Harry Schlatter, Birt Hollopeter, C. C. Van Skoik, Ed Williamson and John Williamson. Schlatter's opened several small retail stores in shopping centers with the establishment of the wholesale operation at the north Merchandise Place.

The Perfection Biscuit Company was founded in 1901 by J. B. Franke. The maker of cookies, bread, crackers and cakes was originally located on Barr Street. The large structure which the firm occupied for the next seven decades on Pearl St. was built in 1904. Succeeding top executives of the firm included J. B. Spatz, W. A. Bohn, O. R. Kiefer and H. Leslie Popp.

An earlier bakery which had wide operations in the city and the area during the early decades of the 20th Century was the Haffner Star Bakery Company. It was founded in 1869 by Christian Haffner and later headed by his sons, George, Clarence and Frederick Haffner.

The Edward W. Dodez Dental Supply firm was located at 1425 West Main St. in the 1920's. The firm was later managed by Edward C. Dodez, son of the founder. Edward C. Dodez, along with Robert Nichens, Henry Wahl and Edward Kane founded the Fort Wayne Ski Club, called the Kekionga Ski Club at the time, in 1936. Henry Wahl, in later years a fencing instructor for the Park Board, Indiana Tech and the Indiana-Purdue Regional University, was the city's only certified fencing master.

The Gas Company

A major change in Fort Wayne utility affairs occurred in 1926 when the Fort Wayne Gas Company joined in a merger which resulted in Northern Indiana Public Service Company. The president of Fort Wayne Gas at the time was Henry C. Paul who surely established the broadest sort of business career in the history of the community. He was president and founder of Horton Manufacturing Company in 1871, an organizer and president of Fort Wayne Drug Company in 1899, an organizer and first president of Wayne Knitting Mills in 1891, a president of Fort Wayne Paper Box Co., chairman of Old National Bank, and president of Fort Wayne Electric Works of General Electric from 1899 to the 1905 merger with the parent firm. He was a principal in early traction and interurban companies which operated out of Fort Wayne and which formed part of the basis for electric utilities which became Indiana & Michigan Electric Co., a part of the American Electric Power System.

Paul was a member of the group which formed the Salamonie Mining & Gas Co. in the 19th Century. Others were R. C. Bell, W. W. Worthington, Charles McCulloch, Alfred Hattersley, H. C. Graffe, John Ferguson, B. S. O'Connor and C. S. Bash. This pioneer enterprise in gas explorations and development along the Salamonie River grew to an extensive natural gas operation in the 1890's. By that decade it had more than 207 miles of pipe line, a distribution field of over 200 square miles and was drawing from 115 gas wells. The firm supplied gas for both lighting and heating to a community of 45,000 people—Fort Wayne. This was the firm which developed into the Fort Wayne Gas Company and was merged with Northern Indiana Public Service. Subsequent to the 1926 merger, Thomas J. Kelly was named superintendent for NIPSCO and headed the operations in the Fort Wayne area for the next three decades.

In 1937, the first natural gas line from the Texas Panhandle stretched to Fort Wayne. This line was made through to parts of Ohio and Michigan. With the conversion to natural gas, NIPSCO embarked on a series of improvement and development programs.

The plant on Hale Ave. was modernized and in the years following World War II, more than $6,500,000 was poured into expansion of facilities in the Fort Wayne area. In the subsequent years, gas was stored in rock formations at suitable locations west of Fort Wayne to provide for more even availability of gas supplies. The Fort Wayne Division serves Bluffton, Decatur, Columbia City, South Whitley, and Allen County generally. Division managers after Kelly included Robert L. Kaade, Harley Jenson and P. E. Seybert.

Perennial Politicians

William J. Hosey ran again for mayor of Fort Wayne in 1921. The Republican candidate was Dr. George W. Gillie, who would carve out his own long political career as Allen County Sheriff and Congressman from northeastern Indiana.

In the light of later experience, Hosey had the poorer argument on the main campaign issue in 1921. Fort Wayne had an inadequate water supply. Hosey was still favoring deep rock well water as a source. Gillie was pushing for filtration of river water as a permanent means to assure water for a growing community. Gillie was right but he lost the election. In November, 1921, Hosey was elected to his third term as mayor in a fairly close contest. Hosey had 14,678 votes to 13,182 votes for Gillie. The Democratic mayor appointed Guy Colerick as city attorney for the third time; Julian F. Franke, controller; and John B. Kocks, Otto Bengs and Jesse Brosius to the Board of Works.

In 1922, Mayor Hosey renewed his program for railroad track elevation. The Pennsylvania and Wabash tracks at Lafayette Streets, Hanna Street and Thompson Avenue tral tracks were elevated in 1924 at Sherman were elevated in 1924. The New York Cen- Street. In the winter of 1924-25, Hosey led the fight in the State Legislature to defeat the Penrod Bill, a railroad promoted item which would have halted future rail elevations. Determined to furnish the city citizens with well water, Hosey had several rock wells drilled during the term. City officials included J. Frank Mungovan, judge; Otto W. Koenig, clerk; and Albert Keller, Calvin Rieman and Henry Lapp, board of safety.

In February, 1924, the Board of Public Works let contracts for the construction of Hosey Dam across the Maumee River, just west of the Walton Street Bridge (later Anthony Boulevard). The job was completed in 1925.

The dam was one of Hosey's pet projects in the wake of flooding of the Lakeside area and the problem of low water in Spy Run Creek where the City Light plant had been mistakenly built. The inadequate water supply during dry seasons was a constant problem to City Light because of the need of water to cool the coils of the generator. When the Maumee River Dam was constructed, the mayor decided to include in the project a high-power turbine. However because of technical and economic problems, the plant was never used.

In 1925, Hosey tried again for re-election to the mayor's office. To oppose the Democratic mayor, the Republicans nominated William C. Geake, a lawyer. Hosey stressed his record of economy and the development of the city utilities. Democratic leaders predicted a victory by a 3,000-vote margin. But the Republicans were riding a wave of optimism and national strength at the polls. The old Democratic majority in Fort Wayne was weakening in the face of a Republican Party organization which would remain close to dominant for the next four decades.

William C. Geake was elected mayor of Fort Wayne in November, 1925, by a plurality of 3,150 votes. Geake had 16,822 votes to Hosey's 13,672. Geake named Angus McCoy controller; Louis F. Crosby, city attorney; and William Beck, Tom Snook and W. S. O'Rourke to the board of public works. W. H. Schannen was city judge and L. R. Ellenwood, clerk. Arnold Spiegel, Jacob Bill and August Borgman were named to the board of safety.

The Geake Years

The four-year Geake Administration

which started in January, 1926, experienced possibly the greatest contrasts in city life in the history of Fort Wayne. At first it moved along with growth and activity unparalleled, given the size of the city. It ended with the onset of economic uncertainty, depression and a period of lawlessness which shook the community.

Only one thing was normal. The expectation that the Nickel Plate Railroad was finally to be elevated. On October 26, 1927, newspapers reported a "Definite agreement on the opening of Fairfield Ave., Harrison, Calhoun, Clinton, Lafayette and Clay Streets under the proposed elevation of the Nickel Plate Railroad tracks." Mayor William Geake, members of the board of works, and others met with rail officials. "Members of the board of works expressed themselves as well pleased with the results of the conference wherein it was decided to place the tracks higher than they had asked, permitting a lower per cent grade of the streets under the elevation." Later history shows the actual elevation was some 30 years away.

In the same fall of 1927, more than six million dollars in major building construction was reported underway or recently completed. "It will result in a decided change in Fort Wayne's skyline and will also provide added civic and commercial advantages," The News-Sentinel reported. Three of the buildings involved expenditures of $1 million or more, a large sum in 1927 value of exchange. The biggest project was the Fairfield Manor Apartment House at Fairfield and Creighton Avenues. The Manor was the first high-rise, high-quality apartment building in Fort Wayne and remained the prestige apartment place in Fort Wayne for the next 40 years. It is interesting to note the Manor reportedly cost more to build than the combination of the Fox Theatre and Hotel in the 100 block of West Jefferson St., completed a little earlier. The Fox became the Emboyd and the Hotel Indiana; they also cost in excess of $1 million. The other $1 million dollar project being completed in 1927 was North Side High School near the St. Joseph River at State Boulevard. The Western Gas Construction Co. was spending $750,000 on a new modern plant. It was in 1927 that the Allen County Children's Home north of the city along Lima Road was built at a cost of $175,000. The "New County Infirmary" also along the Lima Road was being completed at a cost of $300,000. Lutheran Hospital was building its Annex at a cost of $300,000; and, some blocks north in the 2400 block of Fairfield, the First Church of Christ Scientists was going up at an estimated cost of $250,000. Other churches being built in 1927 included the Grace Reformed Church at $140,000; the Grace Lutheran Church at $75,000; and the Calvary United Brethren Church at $100,000. The St. Joseph Hospital Nurses Home was built for $150,000. The Erwin and Justin Study Schools both were built in 1927, each costing $140,000, as was the Chamber of Commerce at $275,000.

It was even a big year for the Barr Street Market. "Total receipts from stand rentals at the Barr Street Public Market for the year 1927 were $7,074.75, according to an announcement made today by the Board of Safety. This is the largest business ever reported for the market," according to a newspaper article Jan. 5, 1928.

The market was operated day and night in that era. "Rentals for 120 day stands on the yearly basis was $2,385 and for 121 night stands was $1,815. The day stands rent at $20 a year and $15 per year. Daily and nightly rentals at 25 cents each totalled $2,874.75. The rentals are collected by Henry Geye, marketmaster. Large quantities of produce are displayed and sold at the market by producers of Allen and adjoining counties during the year." The downtown market, which operated from City Hall south to Washington Blvd. six days a week, was an open-sided concrete and stone pavilion with concrete stalls backing to the curb side where farmers' trucks were parked. Being open, it did not operate in severe winter weather. It drew thousands of customers daily. The South Side Market on Warsaw St., being enclosed, operated year-round but on a far more limited weekly schedule.

Fires Sweep Downtown

One of the great fires in downtown Fort Wayne occurred on the night of December

30, 1927, when the old Grand Leader building was gutted. It was on Friday at 9:30 p.m. that the first alarm was sounded. Another alarm went out at 9:33 p.m. and a general alarm at 9:45 p.m. The flames started on the third floor near the elevator shaft and spread from there. All available civic services were brought to bear on the fire but it raged on. "Except for weather conditions last evening, the fire would undoubtedly have done many times more damage. There was comparatively no wind and a downpour of rain at the height of the fire kept sparks which being carried over onto other downtown structures from setting afire," it was reported. Crowds were drawn to the scene but were held back by police. The loss was set at $300,000 by Nathan Goldman, president. The building was owned by J. K. Stillman, New York. The cause of the fire was not determined, according to Fire Chief John Stahlhut. The following year a new Grand Leader Department Store was built at the same site at the southeast corner of Wayne and Calhoun Streets.

Fort Wayne had a series of winter-time downtown fires starting with the Masonic Temple Theatre Fire on Feb. 10, 1923. On January 1, 1924, flames swept through Tepper's Department Store, 110-112 East Berry Street. Tepper's was just east of the site of the great 1908 fire of the Aveline House. The loss in the Tepper fire was estimated at $298,000. On March 7, 1924, a fire at the Patterson-Fletcher Store at Wayne and Harrison Streets caused $73,000 worth of damage. Later that same year, on December 21, 1924, at the height of the Christmas shopping season there was one of the more stubborn fires of the era. This was at the Boston Store, located at 604 South Calhoun Street. The loss was put at $268,000. Just two weeks later, on January 11, 1925, flames swept up from Frank's Department Store and black clouds of smoke flooded the downtown area. The damage to Frank's, at Berry and Calhoun Streets, was estimated at $153,000.

The close proximity of the store fires in a relatively short time indicates that a mad arsonist might have been at work in Fort Wayne. Cause of most of the fires was undetermined. The blazes practically changed the face of the business district. All of them drew crowds running into the thousands. Another situation, on the night of February 4, 1926, was quite a coincidence. A fire alarm drew crews to the Carp & Company Building at 132 West Main St. where flames were already well underway. Within an hour on the same night, a major fire was discovered at the Pickard Furniture Store, 116 East Columbia St., just a block and a half away.

Girls in Trouble

Quite a few girls were getting into trouble during the late 1920's. This was considered something new in social trends and attributed to the general decline in morality. A report presented to Circuit Court Judge Sol A. Wood on Janury 16, 1928, reflected the situation. "Girls are more apt to develop a criminal tendency while they are between the ages of 14 and 17 years," according to a report by Miss Minnie Blue, the girls probation officer. She reported 46 cases. The most common offense among the girls "was immorality, with incorrigibility second." Fourteen of the girls were committed to institutions.

"The most dangerous age for Allen County's boys is 12 to 15 years," it was indicated by Fred Klein, chief probation officer. Charges most numerous against the boys were larceny, loitering and running away. In a 12-month period, 259 boys cases were handled. Seventeen boys were sent to the Indiana Boys School, two to the White's Institute and two to the Gibault Home.

One of the more colorful measures adopted during the Geake Administration was an ordinance: "Persons engaged in practicing phrenology, crystal-gazing, reading of the stars and similar professions were required to obtain a license, paying a fee of $25 a day."

When Mayor Geake took office one of his first actions was to initiate a City Plan Commission in the City of Fort Wayne. Named to the first Planning and Zoning Commission in 1926 were W. Charles Dickmeyer, Fred B. Shoaff, Frank M. Randall, Lee Ninde, Herman Gerdom, Mrs. O. N. Guldin, Henry Herbst, Frank Schramm, William Beck and

Robert B. Hanna. The first acts of the Plan Commission were to adopt a schedule on street widths to prevent more narrow streets in the city; and to require that all new plats provide for the dedication of the river banks to city usage. After an eleven-month study a zoning ordinance and city plan for Fort Wayne land use was adopted on Sept. 1, 1928.

Several advances in fire protection were put into effect. The Fire Prevention Bureau was created in 1926. Shortly after, the installation of fire alarm boxes at city school buildings was begun. Another advance started was the clearing of the streets of overhead obstructions in the downtown area. Many of the utility poles were removed and wires of police and fire alarm systems were put underground in conduit. In 1927, the installation of synchronized traffic lights was begun.

Typhoid and Bad Water

The city was getting increasingly frantic over the short water supply. In the summer of 1925, sections of Fort Wayne were without water for sanitary and household uses. The existence of several industries in the community were also at stake. During 1926, citizens were warned to boil all water used for drinking purposes, an emergency measure which was becoming commonplace, but annoying and dangerous. Typhoid fever was increasingly a threat to public health. Chlorination of well water was started at three plants. To cope with the situation, the Geake administration, starting on January 4, 1926, frantically began to sink new wells. Two wells were sunk in Franke Park and another large well was completed in Lawton Park. Shelters were erected for the wells in Foster Park. Plans were made for a new reservoir to increase the city's water storage. But problems mounted. Four wells at Lawton Park were abandoned when tests showed continual pollution and examination demonstrated faulty casings were responsible. But the construction of a full-fledged filtration plant to use river water was still several years away.

The city election year of 1929 saw the return of the old Democratic warhorse, William J. Hosey, to the political wars. Geake dropped out after his term and the Republicans nominated Jacob Bill as candidate for mayor. In the Democratic primary there was a great falling out of old political allies. Guy Colerick backed John H. Johnson instead of Hosey. David Foster also opposed Hosey because of bitter past disagreements on park policy. The Journal-Gazette, usually Democratic, even refused to support Hosey after he gained the nomination saying the city "has had enough of Hosey." But the News-Sentinel, which didn't like Bill, the Republican, backed Hosey. Despite the clouded political picture both locally and nationally, Hosey won by the largest margin in his career: 19,089 to 15,825 votes for his opponent.

Dams and Filtration

Hosey's last Administration was a mass of problems. The onset of the Depression meant widespread unemployment and PWA crews. Working in the Hosey Administration were Julian Franke, controller; William Fruechtenicht, city attorney; and John Trier, David Erwin and Charles Ramsey, board of works. Conditions were so bad that the city stopped charges by City Light for electricity to light city streets. Economic hardship necessitated a reduction in the city tax rate.

But it was in Hosey's final administration that his crowning achievement occurred. This was the Filtration Plant at Three Rivers and the Pumping Station. There was little choice to act. The water table was falling. Wells were going dry. Hosey's long love for rock well water had to be reversed.

In October, 1930, the firm of Hoad, Decker, Shoecraft and Drury of Ann Arbor, Michigan, was commissioned to design and supervise construction of the new reservoir, dam and filtration plant. Charles R. Wermuth and Sons built the dam and pumping station on the St. Joseph River. John Dehner and Company installed the water mains. Max Irmscher and Sons erected the filtration plant and its pumping station. The filtered water reservoir was constructed by Buesching, Hagerman and Company. The completed plant was capable of processing 20 million gallons of water daily. The project was financed by a bond issue of $2,500,000, which was to be paid out in user charges. The plant at the confluence of the three rivers, with stone architecture and park-like setting, became an attractive city landmark. Superintendent of the Filtration Plant operation from the beginning, including the construction phase, was Leo R. Mathews who came to Fort Wayne from Ann Arbor. Mathews managed the plant for nearly four decades. Shortly after his retirement, he and his son Robert lost their lives when their car crashed into the rear of a truck on a Michigan highway.

Others in the last Hosey Administration, which went into office Jan. 1, 1930, included Bert A. Fagan, city judge; Leonard Pranger, clerk; J. A. Curtin, F. D. Morgan and W. A. Waller, board of safety.

The 1920s meant boom times which opened with the building of monuments to the soldiers of World War I, such as the one at Memorial Park.

On June 30, 1920, Calhoun St. looking north toward Lewis St. was like the picture at left. The immediate block was later the site of the Lincoln Life expansions. Auto servicing was getting big, such as the Fox-Shryock agency which handled White and Studebaker motor cars.

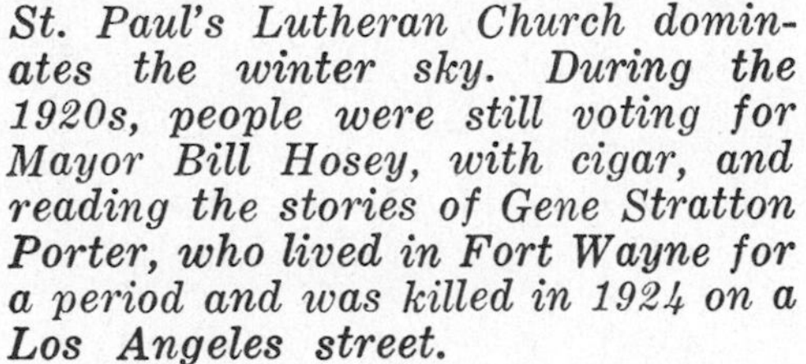

St. Paul's Lutheran Church dominates the winter sky. During the 1920s, people were still voting for Mayor Bill Hosey, with cigar, and reading the stories of Gene Stratton Porter, who lived in Fort Wayne for a period and was killed in 1924 on a Los Angeles street.

Children began to gather at Public Library wagons which visited some of the neighborhoods of the city.

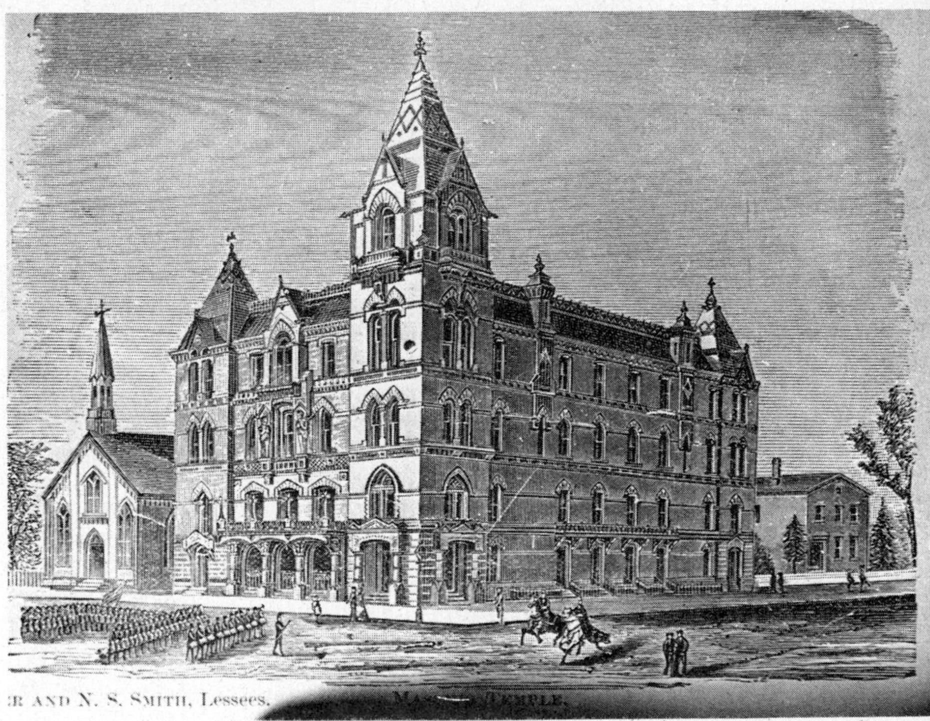

One of the spectacular fires in the city occurred early Saturday morning, Feb. 10, 1923, when the Masonic Temple Theatre went up in flames, as shown on the opposite page. Explosions of ammunition stored by a Reserve Unit on the upper story kept firemen and crowds at bay. The drawing just above shows how the building looked when it was built in 1879.

The reading room of the Public Library on Wayne St. was a busy place in 1924 with girls in Easter hats and boys in short pants, as shown below. At left is the former Henry Olds mansion on West Berry St. which had become the Mizpah Temple. The New Shrine Auditorium was built in 1925. The Plymouth Congregational Church, at Fairfield and Berry, was dedicted in 1925.

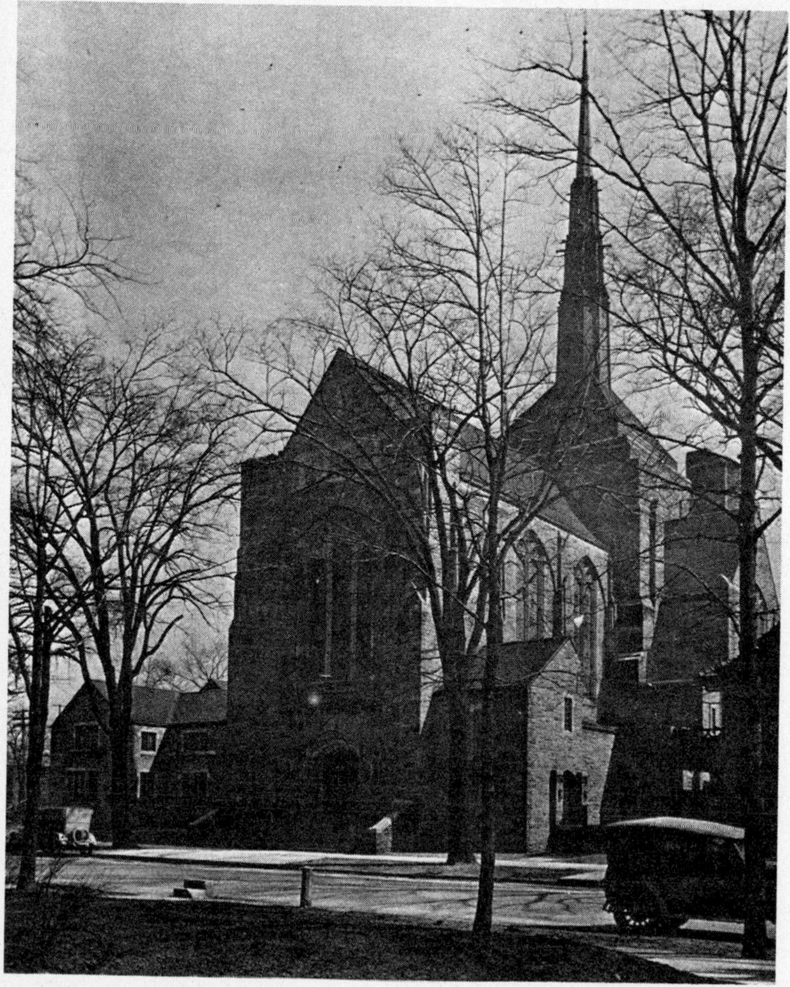

When the building committee and others gathered on June 29, 1924, for the cornerstone laying of the Trinity English Lutheran Church, it was a Who's Who of Old Fort Wayne. The church at Wayne and Ewing streets is shown completed at left. In the group photo: Standing: L to R—C. R. Wermuth, contractor, J. B. Franke, Al C. Wermuth, Rev. Paul H. Krauss, Mrs. Wm. Hahn, W. A. Bohn, Miss Bertha Krudop, Arnold Curdes, Miss Abbie Pfeiffer, J. W. Reynolds, Geo. E. Becker, Gottlieb Heine, Adolph Foellinger, Nestor Fries, Marshall Comincavish. Seated: L to R—E. C. Rurode, Miss Eliza Rudisill, Mrs. Carrie Heller, Mrs. Louise Bostick, Mrs. Sarah Wagner, Mrs. George Thompson, Mrs. E. F. Sites, Mrs. Eliza Ogle, Mrs. J. R. Meriwether.

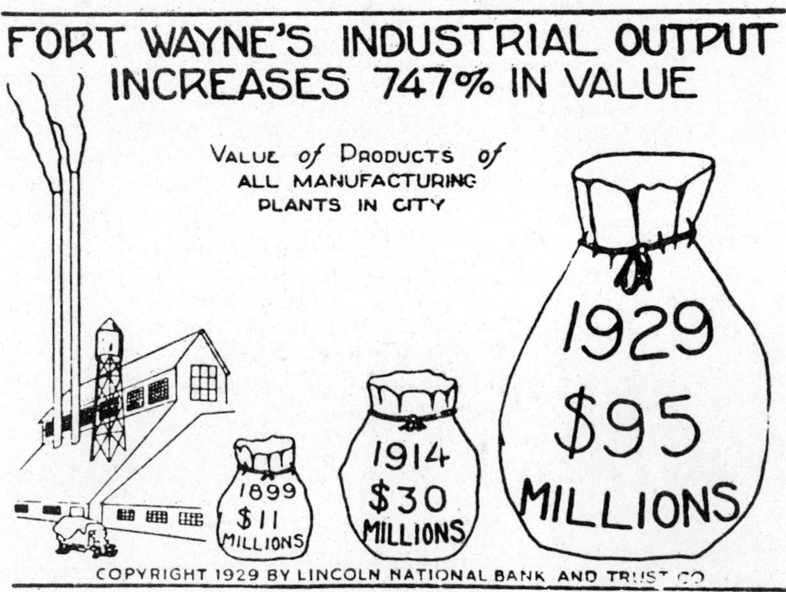

The aerial picture of the International Harvester plant after it was built in the early 1920s was taken before some of the other plant development on the East End. The tremendous growth of the industrial community since the beginning of the Century was reflected in contemporary reports.

Philo Farnsworth, the discoverer of television image projection in a vacuum tube, played a large role in the the Fort Wayne electronics industry, including Capehart-Farnsworth and International Telephone and Telegraph (ITT). Magnavox moved from California to Fort Wyne and located in a plant on the Bueter Road, becoming a national producer of speakers, phonographs and television. Bowser was still making pumps, such as this one being tested on Berry St. near the old Elks Temple.

Radio brings it -
MAGNAVOX tells it
R-3
No wireless receiving set
is complete without the
AC-3-C
MAGNAVOX Radio

B·P·O·E
HAVOLINE OIL

Paul Baer, at right, was the first American ace in World War I. The Fort Wayne native was remembered with the naming of Paul Baer Airport in 1925 (Later renamed Smith Field) and Baer Field of the Army Air Corps built on the other side of town during World War II. But who was "Nungesser in Person" as being eyed on this parade vehicle in the 1100 block of South Calhoun St. in 1925. He was none other than the French Ace of Aces Charles Nungesser (45 kills) who was in the city for the great parade and dedication of Paul Baer City Airport.

At left is the transmitter of Radio Station WOWO which began broadcasts in 1925 at 213 West Main St. Below is the first studio of WOWO on the second floor of the Main Auto Supply Co. The radio station which became WGL began operations a year earlier with studios on the mezzanine of the Keenan Hotel on Harrison St.

Ku Klux Klansmen give a spooky air in 1924 as they circulate at the Interurban depot on West Main St. on a grey winter afternoon. At left is the crew of Parrot Packing Co. which started business in 1923. Below is the view of the northeast corner of Barr and Berry Streets in 1924—later the site of the Telephone Company.

The marble and stone mansion of patent medicine king Bill Noll on South Fairfield, built in 1916, was the scene of high life in the 1920s. When this photo was taken in 1960, it was all but abandonned and finally razed in 1974.

At left is Lindenwood Cemetery as it looked in the late 1920s.

The Lincoln National Life Insurance Building is shown above in 1925, not long after the completion of the building on the east side of Harrison St. The later photo at right includes the Paul Manship statue of the thoughtful young Abe Lincoln and subsequent expansions of the original building.

Flames swept the Grand Leader Department Store on the night of Dec. 30, 1927, at the southeast corner of Wayne and Calhoun Streets. A new store was built and later called Stillman's. Below, firefighters work against flames and smoke at the Frank Dry Goods Company on Calhoun St., across from the Courthouse. It was a cold Jan. 11, 1925.

Even some of the major highways were still gravel in 1926, as the State map shows. Ladies assisted gentlemen at fashionable filling stations as things became more bold in the later '20s. In the meantime, the Chamber of Commerce began its building in 1926 at Wayne and Ewing. Across Ewing, the Wayne Pharmacal Building, later renamed the Medical Center, was already completed.

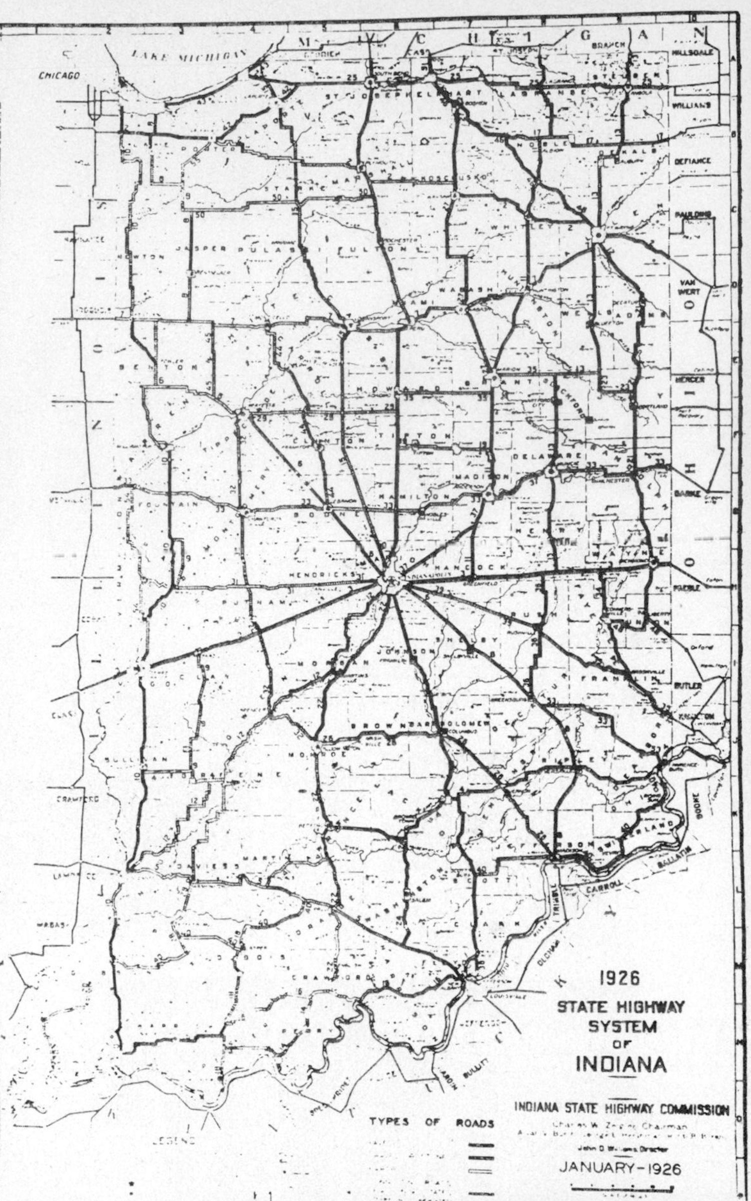

The Public Library Building faced Wayne St. at the corner of Webster in this 1928 picture. The ladies of the library staff posed on the lawn. Standing second from the left is Margaret Colerick, long-time head librarian. Below, is the Journal-Gazette Building as it looked on Jan. 20, 1927.

The great Reo 10,000-mile non-stop run across the country is going west on Washington Blvd. on this rainy day in 1927. The fueling was done on the move by the slick truck and crew. During the same period, the Oakdale Bridge was under construction, with the older Interurban bridge of iron just below over the St. Mary's River.

The Fairfield Manor, the city's first large luxury apartment house, was built in 1928 (shown here in a later photo). The dedication of the Art Smith monument at Memorial Park drew a crowd on August 13, 1928. It honored the flight pioneer.

Fort Wayne High School, the city's first public secondary school was located on the north side of the 100 block of East Wayne St. After Central High was built, the building served as the School Office. In the late 1920s, the site became the location of the Paramount Theatre and still later, Murphy's Store. Horses were the thing in this 19th Century picture.

Part 6
The Schools

A great broadening in the Fort Wayne public schools occurred in the 1920's with the construction of two exceptionally fine high schools: South Side in 1922 on South Calhoun Street and North Side in 1927 at East State Boulevard. But the school story began long before.

After the two early temporary schools were started, the McJunkin School on Lafayette St. near Berry St. and the home of Mr. and Mrs. A. M. Hulburd at Wayne and Ewing Streets, both in 1853, the Public School Trustees turned to more permanent institutions. In 1857 the Clay and Jefferson Schools were opened. The sites, at Clay and Washington Blvd. and at Jefferson and Fairfield, cost $1,300 and $1,170 respectively. School costs were in line with the land scale. The Jefferson School, as an example, cost $5,000. In those days, the public schools were called "the free schools" to distinguish them from the older church-related and private institutions.

By 1866, the public school superintendent reported an enrollment of 1,245 and seating space adequate for but 634. The report said children "stood and sat by turns" and half-days sessions were instituted to alleviate the crowding.

The finding of adequately-trained teachers willing to work for the low pay was always a problem. A training school for Fort Wayne teachers was opened in 1867 and continued until 1886. Another normal school operation to assure staffing the schools was begun in 1897 and discontinued in 1922.

The first public school kindergarten was started in 1899 at the Hoagland School, Hoagland and Butler Avenues. Until 1921, the Board of Trustees for the Fort Wayne Schools met at Old Fort Wayne High School on the north side of Wayne St. between Calhoun and Clinton Streets. After the building was partly destroyed by fire that year, the administration was moved to the Hamilton House at the northeast corner of Clinton and Douglas Streets. In 1928 a regular brick Administration Building was built across the street, at the northwest corner of Clinton and Douglas.

A few school firsts: The plans for the Clay School had overlooked a privy; therefore an added $8.50 was allowed for the first vital facility at the city's first regular public school building. The first telephone was ordered in July, 1896. The business department was inaugurated in 1919. In the meantime, the schools passed from wood-fired stoves, to coal, to oil and gas for heating of classrooms. Lighting went from window light to gas light, to incandescent light to fluorescent.

It was in March, 1913, that the State Legislature passed a bill requiring children between the ages of 7 and 16 to attend school. Prior to that time a considerable proportion of the pupils left school with little more than elementary training. The attendance law led to another school institution—the truant officer. Two were on the payroll by 1921.

The evolution of school attendance laws and rapid growth of interest in education led to child labor laws and more complete record keeping. In 1932 the school census was made a part of the permanent records of the School Attendance Department. The file includes a complete history of every child enrolled in any school, public or parochial.

Gradually, the development of subject matter beyond those of reading, writing and arithmetic became increasingly important in the public school program. Miss Alice Hall was named supervisor of drawing in 1898. An art teacher was made a part of the Central High School staff in 1906. Among the influential art teachers of the Central and South Side art staffs in subsequent decades was Miss Leona Ley. As for elementary school education, Miss Mabel K. Holland was long remembered. Visual education was made a separate department in 1936. Freda Lancaster was the first director. In 1946, Catherine M. Broderick was named director of visual education, geography and history. In 1904, the Fort Wayne Public Schools opened Fort Wayne High and Manual Training School, later named Central High School when South Side was opened in 1922. Woodworking was made available for eighth grade boys in several schools in 1908. In 1911, mechanical drawing was added. Vocational courses were started in 1913. A number of music teachers and directors are remembered. These include John Howard, S. I. Seiffels and Professor William Miles in the early years and Varner Chance and Robert Shambaugh in the mid-20th century. Guidance Counseling was begun in 1929 and among the first several social science teachers in the field was Pauline Van Gorder of South Side. Special education classes were started in 1922, largely because of the interest of Miss Flora Weber. The Fort Wayne School of the Air became an integral part of the class work in 1937 over Radio Station WGL and was continued for more than two decades. Under the leadership of Mrs. H. H. Rogers of South Wayne School, the Parent-Teachers Assn. was begun in 1917.

School Activities

Inter-school athletic competition first came into the picture in the early 1920's in the grade schools. As early as 1891, there were some forms of football rivalries. The first high school newspaper was the Spotlight in 1919 at Central. The South Side Times and the Northerner of North Side were printed soon after the opening of those schools. All three received national recognition, with the South Side Times being considered the outstanding school paper in the nation for several years running during the years of Rowena Harvey, journalism teacher and publication director at South and North from 1922 to 1959. She was the first president of the National High School Teachers of Journalism Assn. and vice-president of the Columbia Scholastic Press Advisory Association. When she died in 1971 she bequeathed $59,000 to the Fort Wayne Education Assn. to be used by students of South Side needing financial aid.

Putting on shows and other entertainments came as early as children and the schools. Drama at the high school level benefited from 1919 to 1951 from the talents of Margery Suter, drama coach, a native of Switzerland with a professional background in theatre. In subsequent years Central High became the city's most active school in drama production under the guidance of Helen Lee. Central Catholic High School became active in drama in 1939 under the Rev. Herman Schnurr. Later CC drama coaches were Helen Riordan, Reid Erekson and Bob Storey.

Robert Wyatt, one-time social science teacher at Central High School, became executive-director of the Indiana State Teachers Assn. in 1938. He was an effective lobbyist at the State Legislature. In 1962 he was named president of the National Education Association. At the time of his retirement as executive of the ISTA in 1971 he was publicly criticized for converting $37,000 in association funds to his retirement benefit. Wyatt had been president of the State Teachers Retirement fund for 25 years.

An unusual experiment in education was launched in 1961 with the Midwest Program on Airborne Television Instruction. Forty-six teachers of the Fort Wayne area used the television school programs offered on two channels transmitted from an airplane which circled over Montpelier, Indiana. Six public schools in Fort Wayne and hundreds of other schools in the Midwest joined the initial programs. Headquarters for the educational development was at Purdue University, with Ohio State and the University of Michigan also preparing the TV instructional sessions.

Public School Openings

Superintendents of the public schools schools since 1856 include George A. Irwin, appointed 1856; E. S. Green, 1863; James H. Smart, 1865; John S. Irwin, 1875; Justin N. Study, 1896; R. M. Himelick, 1917; L. C. Ward, 1920; Merle J. Abbett, 1932; Aaron T. Lindley, 1952; and Lester Grile, 1962. Dr. John Young was acting superintendent for part of 1973.

Schools and their dates of building, after the 1857 opening of the Clay and Jefferson Schools, include Hoagland, 1866; Fort Wayne High School on Wayne St., 1868; Washington School, 1868 and rebuilt in 1910; Harmar, 1868 and rebuilt in 1915; Hanna, 1869 and rebuilt in 1906; Bloomingdale, 1871 and rebuilt in 1964; Miner, 1876; Nebraska, 1876 and rebuilt in 1964; Holton, 1876; McCulloch, 1889; Hamilton, 1891; Franklin, 1891 and a new building in 1923; Lakeside, 1896; South Wayne, 1896 and a new school in 1962; Central High School, 1903 with addition in 1938; Rudisill, 1906; Adams, 1909 with new building in 1925; James Smart, 1910; Riverside, Rolling Mill and Allen County Home Schools were added by annexation in 1919; South Side High School, 1922; Forest Park, 1922; Grasmere Heights, 1925, with new school renamed Frances Slocum in 1936; Harrison Hill, 1925; Oxford, 1925 with new school in 1932 renamed L. C. Ward; North Side High School, 1927; Justin Study, 1927; John S. Irwin, 1928; Elmhurst High School, 1929; St. Joe Center School, 1936; Hillcrest, 1928; Abbett, 1949; Indian Village, 1953; Price, 1953; Southern Heights, 1955; Maplewood, 1956; Northcrest, 1956; Brentwood, 1957; South Calhoun, 1958; Geyer, 1959; Lakeside Junior High, 1959; Northwood Junior High, 1959; Portage Junior High, 1960; Kekionga Junior High, 1960; Fairfield Junior High, 1962; Lane Junior High, 1964; Jefferson Junior High, 1967; Snider High School, 1966; Northrop High School, 1971; Wayne High School, 1971; Blackhawk Junior High, 1972. Also, Franke, 1960; Shambaugh, 1963; Weisser Park, 1964; Holland, 1964; Glenwood Park, 1965; Croninger, 1966; Memorial Park, 1966; Harris, 1968; Haley, 1969; Lindley, 1970; Bunche, 1971; and Young, 1971.

The Fort Wayne Vocational High Center was opened in a remodeled Central High School in 1971 with the transfer of Central High students and staff to other high schools at the time of the 1971 opening of Northrop and Wayne High Schools.

Enrollments in the Fort Wayne public schools reached 5,351 in 1901 and 11,235 in 1925. By 1953 the total was 18,225. The enrollments increased rapidly thereafter due to both annexations and school-age population growth. The highest figure recorded in the Fort Wayne Community Schools was 43,764 in the 1971-72 school year. Some fall-off due to declining enrollments in the beginning elementary grades was noted the following years. Enrollment in the 1973-74 school year was 42,012.

The highest school tax rate on property was $6.15 in 1970. This figure had tapered down to $5.32 in 1973, and was in a trend of further reduction due to increased state tax funding. Expenditures for all purposes by the Community System was $48,020,000 in 1971, the highest up to that date and exceeding the figure of the two following years. Per pupil cost of grades 1 through 12 in 1972-73 was $893.48.

The rated student capacity of the six city public high schools follow: Northrop, 2,600; Wayne, 2,100; North Side, Snider and South Side, 1,900; and Elmhurst with 1,500.

Considered by many as the outstanding educator of the Community Schools for several decades was R. Nelson Snider, principal of South Side High School starting in 1926. Milton Northrop was principal of North Side from 1927 to 1953.

By 1974 the Fort Wayne Community Schools, building-wise, consisted of 43 elementary schools, 12 junior high schools, 6 senior high schools, one vocational school, one special education center, 3 administration buildings, one food service center, one maintenance center and 2 bus garages.

The salaries of teachers and administrators in the public schools are a reflection of changes in times and public financial support of education. The first school superintendent, George Irwin, was granted an annual salary of $900 by the school board in 1856. The annual salaries of the teachers ranged from $550 to $100. Some were presumably part time instructors. By 1926, the salary schedule was set on regular scales: $1,000 per year for starting teachers without experience. $1,400 for inexperienced teachers with B.S. or B.A. degrees, and a maximum of $2,300 with $100 for each year of experience until the maximum figure was reached. In 1975, beginning teachers were making $8,434 a year and the top scale for experienced teacher's with master's degrees was $15,856. The superintendent's salary was $32,000.

School trustees from the beginning in 1853 include: Hugh McCulloch, Charles Case, William Stewart, James Humphrey, Henry Sharp, Charles French, William S. Smith, Franklin Randall, Pliney Hoagland, John M. Miller, Charles Sturgis, William Rockhill, William H. Link, Thomas Tigar, William Edsall, Samuel Edsall, Oliver Morgan, Robert E. Fleming, James Robinson, John C. Davis, Orin Hurd, A. Martin, Christian Orff, Ochmig Birds, Emanuel Bostick, Virgil Kimball, John Irwin, Edward Slocum, Alfred Edgerton, Max Nirdlinger, John Moritz, E. Ely Hoffman, Samuel M. Foster, William P. Cooper, Andrew Boswell, George Felts, Allen Hamilton, W. W. Rockhill, Eugene B. Smith, Charles Bash, Dr. W. O. Cross, Ernest Cook, James H. Fry, Anselm Fuelber, Jesse Macbeth, W. H. Shambaugh, Alfred Randall, Byron H. Somers, Eli Perry, Paul Mossman, Henry J. Bowerfind, James Ford, Mrs. Carl Yaple, Mrs. Harry Fletcher, Mrs. R. Earl Peters, Mrs. L. G. Ellingham, William C. Geake, Dr. L. Park Drayer, William H. Reed, Herman Freiburger, William C. Rastetter, Gottlieb H. Heine, William H. Scheiman, Mrs. Susannah Fonner, Mrs. William Hockett, Ben F. Geyer, W. D. Whipple, David E. Smith, Clyde Reed, Dr. V. H. Hilgemann, Mrs. David Vesey, William T. McKay, Willard Shambaugh, Mrs. Grace Goeriz, August Weigand, W. Page Yarnelle, William C. Gerding, Joseph Kramer, Mrs. Sadie Fulk Roehrs, W. E. Bodeker, Mrs. Marian Rastetter, Gordon Reeves, Walter Dreyer, Walter Hanauer, Charles E. Slater, Mario Funari, Eugene Yargens, Max G. Scott, William E. Miller, Mrs. Fritzy Ober, Mrs. Florence Buirley, Leslie S. Fry, Phillip J. Sanborn, Clarence R. McNabb, Mrs. Charlotte Cooper, Rex Potterf, David Peters, Donald Murphy, Harmon Frye, Lawrence Wyatt, Thomas J. Peterson, Martin Torborg, Mrs. Karl C. Eberly, Jr., Thomas S. Teetor, Dr. W. Lloyd Bridges, Mrs. Helen P. Brown, Dr. Bernard K. Stuart, Dr. Helen C. Lee, and Leonard Goldstein.

A considerable amount of conversion of schools to different grade levels and different scholastic application occurred, particularly in 1970, 1971 and 1972. The use of buses was expanded. Partly to achieve greater racial balance in the high schools and junior high schools, and to make wider use of modern school facilities and equipment, the practice of transporting by bus large numbers of students from the central districts of the city to more outlying locations commenced. The closing of Central High School as a regular high school in 1971 and the simultaneous opening of Northrop and Wayne High Schools was an essential part of the shift.

In the same school years, there was an unusual number of moves by teachers from one school to another. By the 1973-74 school year, the total number of certified personnel in the Community System was 2040. This included 1821 teachers, 147 school administrators, 7 R.V.C. administrators and 65 non-school administrators. The total number of classified personnel, including physical therapists, clerks, school aides, counselor aides, secretaries, food service workers, matrons, custodians, nurses and bus drivers was 1,479.

In the early 1960's there was an evolution in school districting which resulted in four administrative and school taxing districts in Allen County. The consolidations were inducted by State legislation encouraged by the university education departments and the State Office of Public Instruction. The matter was met with considerable controversy, differences as to what should be the surviving school districts, and some opposition to the bureaucratic meddling inherent in the imposition of guidelines for school reorganization. The surviving school administrations in Allen County included the Fort Wayne Community Schools, the East Allen County Schools, the Northwest Allen County Schools and the Southwest Allen County Schools.

A 10-year appraisal of educational characteristics of Allen County was made, based on the 1960 and 1970 census reports. The median education level of the population of Allen County rose from 11.7 years in 1960 to 12.3 years in 1970. In both instances, the figures were higher than the State of Indiana median and the U.S. median for the population as a whole.

Prior to the general school reorganization of the 1960's in Indiana, the county public schools were operated by the township trustees and small towns. There was a county superintendent of public instruction. For many years in Allen County, this post was held by D. O. McComb. The last county school superintendent was Russell Steiner. Following the reorganization, there were three school superintendents in the county in addition to the one for Fort Wayne Community Schools. The East Allen County Schools, which included New Haven, Woodburn, Leo-Grabill, Monroeville and Hoagland, was first headed by Paul Harding. The first superintendent of the Northwest Allen County Schools was Robert Mantock. The first superintendent of the Southwest Allen County Schools was Perry Glancy.

Catholic Schools

The earliest schools were often church-related, mostly financed by mission societies, pioneer families, and on occasion, federal grants. Isaac McCoy, who operated the Baptist missionary school at the Old Fort in 1820 and 1821, received Federal funds in 1821 so he could expand his school to 42 pupils. As we have seen, the pupils were children of government personnel, French traders, Indians and at least one Negro. Other early schools were conducted by Presbyterian, Methodist, Episcopal, Catholic and Lutheran units. In addition there was a scattering of private schools or classes, usually held in log cabins or store buildings. Large parochial school systems were subsequently developed by the Catholic and Lutheran congregations.

The history of the Catholic Schools in Fort Wayne began with the founding of St. Augustine's Academy in 1846. The location was at what later would be called Cathedral Square. At that date, however, Fort Wayne was not the seat of the Bishop, so there was no Cathedral and the parish was called St. Augustine's. The first principal was Sister Mary Magdelen of the Sisters of Providence. There were 60 pupils that first year with 15 of them being boarders. The Brothers School for Boys was founded in 1858 just to the south of St. Augustine's Academy along Calhoun Street. The Brothers School, with further development of parish elementary schools, was converted into a boys high school in 1884 and called Central Catholic. St. Augustine's Academy at that time was made a girls high school. St. Catherine's Academy at Dewald and Webster Sts. adjacent to St. Patrick's Church was a girls high school starting in 1893. St. Mary's Commercial School was opened in 1896 and operated until 1938. Library Hall, where Central Catholic was located, and St. Augustine's Academy and St. Catherine's Academy were closed in 1938 with the opening of a new Central Catholic High School at Clinton and Lewis Streets.

There have been numerous Catholic Schools in the community, in most cases nominally administered by the parish pastor. Some of the early schools are still in operation. In other instances, new parishes and parish schools have supplanted the old. St. Mary's School on South Lafayette opened in 1865. Through most of its history, the Sisters of Notre Dame conducted the school. The Poor Handmaids of Jesus Christ, an order of nuns which began operating St. Joseph Hospital the same year, opened St. Paul's School in 1869 at Fairfield Ave. and Washington Boulevard. St. Peter's School was organized in 1873; St. Patrick's in 1891; Precious Blood in 1898; St. Andrew's in 1911; the Cathedral School in 1915 (the academies handled elementary pupils too prior to that date).

One of the interesting developments was St. Vincent's Villa, an orphanage started in 1887. There were 35 students the first year. This figure expanded to a high of several hundred during the Depression years of the 1930's, then rapidly declined. In the 1930's and 1940's a series of fine school and residence buildings were built at St. Vincent's at the direction of Bishop John Noll. In more recent years, the buildings were used for a multiple of purposes; education, social and administrative functions, day-school classes and a consolidation of parish schools.

St. Joseph's School was opened in 1918; St. Hyacinth's in 1928; St. Jude's in 1929; St. John the Baptist in 1930; Sacred Heart in 1949; Queen of Angels in 1951; St. Charles in 1956; St. Therese in 1956 and St. Henry's in 1957.

Much of the impetus behind the founding of the various parish Catholic schools stemmed from 1879 when Bishop Joseph Dwenger created a Diocesan School Board. Members of the first board included the Revs. Julian Benoit, W. Corby, Edward Koenig, Michael O'Reilly, Henry Meissner, John Oechtering and Joseph Rademacher. In 1882, the Board created six districts in the diocese. Father Oechtering, who later was named president of the school board, wrote the Catechism of Church History which was used in the upper Catholic grades for many years. He also wrote treatises on capital, labor, socialism and several dramas.

When Central Catholic High in 1938 combined both boys and girls in the same school and classes, it was considered an innovation in Catholic education and CC was one of the first parochial coeducational secondary schools in the nation. With the over-crowding in the 1950's, Bishop Leo A. Pursley encouraged the building of additional Catholic high schools. The first, Bishop Luers High School on the Paulding Road on the south fringe of the city, was opened in 1958 and directed by the Order of Franciscans. Bishop Dwenger High School, opened five years later on the north side at Washington Center Road and North Clinton St., was staffed by secular and lay staff under the direction of the Rev. Edward Krason. The white brick structure provided for 1,100 students. The financial burden and declining enrollment of CC located in the downtown area led to the closing of Central Catholic classes after the 1971 school year. Undergraduate students were enrolled in Luers, Dwenger and several of the public high schools, when classes resumed the following fall. There was a big drop in the number of students attending Catholic schools starting in 1966. At that time the number of pupils in a class room was limited to 35. In addition, rising education costs and the decline in the number of teachers of religious orders required the reduction of enrollments. In 1965, the Fort Wayne Catholic Schools were teaching 8,777 pupils compared with 4,455 in 1973, according to a report by Father James Seculoff, school superintendent for the Fort Wayne-South Bend Diocese. There was a slight upturn in 1974 with the addition of about 200 students. Father Seculoff had succeeded Msgr. William Lester as head of diocesan schools.

The Lutheran Schools

After the initial Lutheran School headed

by the Rev. Jesse Hoover began instruction of pioneer children in 1837, there has been steady growth. The first regular Lutheran school at St. Paul's on Barr St. was started in 1839. Emmanuel Lutheran School on West Jefferson St. opened in 1867. Within a few years of that date, Zion Lutheran School at Hanna St. and Creighton Ave. and St. John's Lutheran School on West Washington Blvd. were also in operation.

Between the years 1890 and 1900, Trinity Lutheran School at Huffman and St. Mary's Avenues was opened and Concordia Lutheran School on Alliger St. near Anthony Blvd. came into existence. Shortly after the turn of the century, Grace Lutheran School on Lillie St. and Emmaus Lutheran School on Broadway at Creighton Ave. were established.

Bethlehem Lutheran School on South Anthony Blvd. was opened in 1926 and Mount Calvary in Waynedale was in operation in 1919. Both Holy Cross School on Crescent Ave. and Peace Lutheran on South Fairfield were established in 1946; St. Michael's just to the west of the city was started in 1956; Gethsemane Lutheran School in Crestwood Addition was opened in 1961.

While it has been the usual policy for Lutheran Churches of the Missouri Synod to operate elementary schools, it wasn't until 1925 that there was a regular secondary school building. Classes were held for a small number of students at the Luther Institute at St. Paul's Church starting in 1916. The high school building was put up in 1925 at 1024 Barr St. and used until 1935. From 1935 to 1947, Concordia Lutheran High was located in a building renovated for the purpose at Concordia College Campus on Maumee Ave. and was controlled by the college administration. A change to independent administration was decided upon in 1947 and a new school and laboratory building was completed in 1952 at Maumee and Anthony Boulevard. When the Concordia College campus on Maumee was sold in 1957 to Indiana Technical College, the High School Assn. was forced into a decision. In 1958 an option was taken on Zollner Stadium and 23 acres surrounding it along North Anthony Boulevard. Ground for a new Concordia High was broken in March, 1963, and classes started the following fall.

Offices which serve the entire Indiana District of Lutheran Schools, Missouri Synod, were located in Fort Wayne at Barr and Lewis Sts., with Arthur Amt, district superintendent.

Student enrollment at Concordia High increased from 629 in 1963 to 940 in 1973. Fred Zollner, who had built the stadium on North Anthony in the 1950's for his Fastball Team, donated the facility to Concordia. Carlton Kruse and Edward Koeneman headed a fund drive in 1973 for the expansion of the high school, with completion scheduled for 1975. During the growth of Concordia at the North Anthony site, principal of the high school was Guenther Herzog. The rapid rise in the costs of education had an adverse effect on Lutheran school enrollments in the 1960's. Lutheran School Superintendent Richard Sauer reported the Fort Wayne units lost about 1,000 pupils between 1964 and 1974, reducing total enrollment from 4,800 to 3,800. In the mid-1970's, however, the enrollment had stabilized. No tuition was charged for Lutheran elementary schools, but a $425 fee was charged for high school.

Indiana Tech

Indiana Technical College was organized in 1930 to provide an accelerated engineering program adjusted to the rapid development of the engineering sciences. John Kalbfleisch was the first president and William J. Hess was vice-president and treasurer. There were approximately 100 students in Tech's first class. Degrees were given in electrical, civil, structural and radio engineering after completion of 24 months of study. From the beginning, Tech operated on a year-round program of four terms of 12 weeks each. In 1934, chemical and aeronautical engineering were added. Archie T. Keene became president in 1936 and held the position for the next three decades. For most of its early history, Indiana Tech was located downtown in a building on East Washington Blvd. between Clinton and Barr Sts. where the City Parking Garage was later located, following

the razing of the college building. Tech's greatest growth occurred after World War II with the return of many service men seeking education. In 1948 Tech was reorganized into an endowed institution, a non-profit college. The board of directors established at that time included Arthur Fruechtenicht, Dr. John Caton, William Caswell, Carl Pierson, Donald H. Borger, Paul Hess and Dr. Keene. In the following 10 years, Tech grew to an institution with 56 full-time professors and 83 part-time members of the teaching staff. Liberal arts were added to the program and the course of study was extended to 27 months. Student enrollment was more than 2,000 in the various departments of the school. Tech moved to a new campus in July, 1957. This was the former campus of Concordia College. Concordia had developed a new campus just north of the city along the St. Joseph River. Tech's location between Maumee Ave. and East Washington Blvd. consisted of 20 acres and 23 buildings, some more than 100 years old. Considerable renovation was undertaken and several new buildings appeared including the Dana Science and Engineering Building and the McMillen Building.

Subsequently, the name of the college was changed to Indiana Institute of Technology. Culturally, Tech expanded its interests into many fields. Concerts and musical programs, with community patronage became regular occurrences. Speakers ranged from poet Ogden Nash to rocket inventor Wernher Von Braun. With expanded facilities, Tech moved into a program of intramural and intercollegiate sports.

St. Francis College

Saint Francis College, conducted by the Sisters of St. Francis, moved to Fort Wayne in the spring of 1944. The campus was established at the old John Bass estate on the Bass Road, between the Leesburg Road and Lindenwood Avenue. The college had its origins in a normal college founded in 1890 at Lafayette, Indiana. In the early years at Fort Wayne the small liberal arts college was directed by the academic dean. Revisions were subsequently made in the by-laws and organization of the college and in January, 1952, Sister Mary Evodine was elected by the Saint Francis College Corporation as the first resident president. The student body grew from just 44 students the first term of operation in the city to some 200 the following decade and to a total enrollment of 1,700 by 1974. On April 5, 1957, the college received full accreditation by the North Central Association of Colleges and Secondary Schools. In the meantime, St. Francis became a co-educational institution offering degrees in various areas. The Graduate School of the college was formed in 1960 under the direction of Sister Mary Fridian. Masters degrees in arts and sciences were offered in education, business administration and psychology. Preliminary accreditation was granted in 1961 and full accreditation in 1971.

Concordia College

Concordia Senior College began classes on its modern campus in September, 1957. It was one of 16 institutions of higher learning in the United States owned and operated by the Lutheran Church, Missouri Synod. The college received graduates of synodal junior colleges and transfers from other synodical colleges seeking careers in the pastoral ministry and related church vocations. Graduates of Concordia Senior College receive bachelor of arts degrees. Concordia College grew out of a frontier school founded in 1839 at Dresden, Missouri, by immigrant scholars from Leipzig, Germany. In September, 1861, the students and faculty were moved to Fort Wayne. Dr. William Sihler of St. Paul's Church in Fort Wayne had urged the move and arranged the transfer by special coaches of the Wabash Railroad from St. Louis to where the school had been earlier transferred. In Fort Wayne, Concordia College fell heir to the Maumee Ave. campus which earlier had been occupied by another institution, the Practical Seminary, which had been operated by the Rev. Frederick Wyne-

ken and August Craemer. With additions, the Maumee Campus soon totalled about 25 acres. Among the buildings erected after the move by the college to Fort Wayne were Hansen Hall, Schick Hall, Sihler Hall and Crull Hall. The gym was built in 1927. Ten college presidents served Concordia Junior College prior to the forming of Concordia Senior College and the move to the new campus in 1957. These included G. Alexander Saxer, C. J. Otto Hanse, J. F. Zucker, Rudolph A. Bischoff, Martin Schmidt, Martin L. Luecke, William C. Burhop, Ottomar Krueger and Herbert G. Bredemeier. It was in 1953 that the Lutheran Church, Missouri Synod, decided to sell the old campus and to discontinue the junior college and inaugurate a new program on an expanded campus. There was a considerable period of discussion and some dispute as to the form of the new college and the design of the campus. The result of the inquiries and decisions led to the creation of one of the most unusual college campuses and greatest architectural achievements in the United States. The architect, Eero Saarinen, brought together building lines and materials in a pastoral setting and landscaping which drew the curious and artistic from the world over almost from the moment of construction. The founding of the new campus was under the direction of Dr. Martin J. Neeb and Dr. Bredemeier, the president during the transition period. A large farm and small adjacent acreage were selected as the site north of the Washington Center Road and along the west bank of the St. Joseph River. When originally purchased, the farm was outside the city limits, but was soon annexed by Fort Wayne. The original 186 acres was purchased for $100,000. The total budget of the original complex of buildings on the campus was $7,149,000. Subsequent expansion of the college was completed at an additional cost of $1,250,000. The basic materials in the construction were reinforced concrete, brick, steel, copper, aluminum, glass and clay tile. Saarinen even designed the bricks to be used to conform with his ideas of design and permanence of the structures. Internationally known, Saarinen designed the St. Louis Arch, and the General Motors Technical Center at Warren, Mich.; the auditorium and chapel at the Massachusetts Institute of Technology; the United States Embassy buildings at Oslo, Norway, and London, England; Dulles Airport, Washington, D. C.; Yale University buildings and the Law School at the University of Chicago. Of them all, the Concordia Campus was regarded by many as the most satisfying accomplishment in architectural design in the mid-century.

The Bible College

The Fort Wayne Bible College came into existence on July 12, 1904, when the land on the southern fringe of Fort Wayne along Rudisill Blvd. was purchased. Founded by the Missionary Church Association, the Fort Wayne institution was an outgrowth of a small earlier ministerial college at Bluffton, Ohio, named the Bethany Bible Institute. Founders of the Fort Wayne Bible College were Rev. J. E. Ramseyer, D. Y. Schultz, William Egle, B. P. Lugibihl, Henry Roth and David Roth. Ramseyer was the first president. The first building was dedicated in February, 1905, and was later named Schultz Hall. Some 60 students attended classes the first year at Fort Wayne Bible Training School as the college was then called. In 1929 a women's residence hall, Bethany Hall, was built. In 1931, the name Fort Wayne Bible Institute was adopted. In 1938 the school was incorporated as a theological institute with the offering of academic and college courses. At the same time the School of Music was established as a separate division. Founders Memorial, the third building, was erected in 1941 and became the principal educational unit. Rev. Ransmeyer died in 1944 and Dr. S. A. Witmer, the academic dean, succeeded as college president. The name, Fort Wayne Bible College was adopted in 1950. Academic development led to the accreditation by the Indiana State Department of Public Instruction in 1955. The School of Education was established and teacher training courses were offered. The college's third President, Rev. Jared F. Gerig, assumed office on Jan. 1, 1957. At that time the college had an enrollment of more than 300 students, representing some 25 different religious denominations. Degrees offered by the Bible College include bachelor of arts, bachelor of science, bachelor of religious education, bachelor of sacred music, and bachelor of music education.

International College

International Business College was founded in 1889 by Dr. Tom L. Staples, an immigrant from Canada. At the outset, the school had 20 pupils and one instructor—Dr. Staples. Classes were held in the building at the northwest corner of Washington Blvd. and Calhoun Street. In 1908 the college was moved to the Standard Building on East Berry St. and in 1914 to 120 West Jefferson St., a three-story building which became the school's home for the next half century. Following World War II, the word "Business" was dropped and the title became International College. International was chartered by the State of Indiana to grant bachelor of science degrees in commerce in accounting, executive secretarial, business administration and finance. Subsequently the programs were altered and the name of the school was changed to International Junior College. Dr. Staples was succeeded in 1923 by J. A. Kalbfleisch who served until 1930 when he helped organize Indiana Tech. J. Lyle Tucker became president at that time and served until 1950, at which time he was succeeded by O. A. Dellinger, a long-time teacher who had held stock in the privately-held institution since 1919.

Crosier House

One of Fort Wayne's newest educational institutions, the Crosier House of Studies, has some of the longest links to the past. The Crosier Order itself was founded in Europe in 1210 at the time of the Third Crusade. The property just north of Fort Wayne occupied by the Crosier House of Studies was earlier a pioneer Catholic school called the Sacred Heart Academy. Originally called The Academie by the French settlers who established the place in 1840, it became a boarding school in 1866 under the direction of the Rev. Edward Sorin, CSC, who also founded the University of Notre Dame at South Bend. Sacred Heart received normal school accreditation in 1912 and was a place of education for many girls in the Fort Wayne area. It was made into a boarding school for boys in 1929 but was closed in 1934. The Sacred Heart location, plus an adjacent 160 acre farm, was acquired by the Crosier Order in 1938 from the Sisters of the Holy Cross who had operated the Academy. The old 1866 building was remodeled and on Sept. 12, 1939, the school was opened with an enrollment of 22 students under the direction of Fathers Thomas A. Brandon and Joseph Smerke. Father Brandon, a native of Chicago and the first American member of the Crosier Order, was named first Prior of the House and Minor Seminary in 1942. The philosophy school of the Crosiers was transferred in 1948 from Hastings, Nebraska, to Sacred Heart Seminary. In 1955 the order's theology school was also located at the Fort Wayne institution, at 2620 East Wallen Road near the Old Auburn Road. In the meantime, at the request of Bishop John Noll, the Crosiers had in 1948 assumed operation of Our Lady of the Lake Seminary on the shores of Lake Wawasee, 40 miles northwest of Fort Wayne. The building was erected in 1928 as the Spink-Wawasee Hotel. It was from the Fort Wayne House that four missionaries under Father Francis Pitka set out in 1958 to establish a mission post at Agats, on the wild southern coast of New Guinea. With the expansion of the order and educational activities, a building program was started at the Wallen Road property. The first portion of building was completed in 1957 and further enlargements in 1963. The new quarters were rededicated as the Crosier House of Studies. The American Province of the order was established in 1957, with the first provincial being Father Benno C. Mischke, with headquarters at Fort Wayne. Among those serving prominently as priors, rectors and other capacities in the development of the House of Studies were Fathers Daniel Richard, Leo Sovada, Aloysius Mehr, Martin Schoenberg, Joseph H. Hennen, and Joseph Fichtner. Father Hennen, prior-rector of the House of Studies, said in 1972 that the Catholic seminary attempts to combine academic achievement with personal and communal development and ministerial involvement.

Indiana-Purdue Campus

The Fort Wayne Campus of Indiana and Purdue Universities began classes in September, 1964, but both universities had separate operations in Fort Wayne for many years prior to that time. The Fort Wayne Extension Center of Indiana University was established in 1917. It was the second center of I.U. in the state, founded two years after one in Indianapolis in 1915. The administrative office was in the Allen County Courthouse and classes were held at Central High School. The classes at that time were all held in the evening. In 1925 the office was moved to 114 West Wayne St. and in 1930 to the Dime Trust Bank Building at Clinton and Wayne Streets. In 1939, I.U. purchased a building which formerly housed the Lutheran Institute at 1120 South Barr St. and the building remained the home of the university center until 1964. Originally, I.U. Extension was intended primarily for adults who were employed and could not leave jobs to go to regular college campuses. However, as early as 1927, the curriculum was expanded for fuller student degree work. Frank W. Shockley was the first director but after a few months was succeeded by Floyd R. Neff who held the position until 1951. At that time Ralph E. Broyles became the center's director and continued to conduct Indiana University affairs at Fort Wayne. Dr. Broyles retired as chancellor in 1974. The expansion of the faculty and student enrollment can be seen in comparisons. At the beginning there were nine instructors who taught 12 classes to 142 students. By 1939 there were 65 resident faculty members and 56 associate faculty members who taught 287 sections. The greatest growth occurred in the years following World War II and by 1964 there were 1,335 I.U. students.

Purdue first began operations in Fort Wayne in 1941 as a wartime technical training institute. Conwell J. Poling headed the technical program when he came here in 1942 as assistant professor of general studies. Originally, there were just 30 students who attended classes at Central High School and a couple rooms in the downtown area. In 1946 Purdue opened an extension in the Transfer Building at Main and Calhoun Streets. This was the beginning of regular credit courses permitting students to start education locally and then go on to West Lafayette to complete degree work. In 1947 under the guidance of Al Kettler, a Purdue alumnus and later Trustee, and other interested persons, a large building at the southwest corner of Jefferson and Barr Streets was purchased. The brick structure had formerly been the Catholic Community Center. The purchase was made with funds from local business, industry and individuals and the Purdue Research Foundation. Classes were begun at the site in September, 1947, and the school was renamed Purdue University Center. Dr. Richard Bateman was named director of the new center and subsequently Dr. Leslie A. Willig was named assistant director. Bateman was succeeded in 1960 by Dr. Robert L. Ewigleben who continued to direct the center after its move to the regional campus in 1964. He was succeeded by Dr. Richard D. Smith in 1965 who stayed until 1969 when Dr. Lawrence Nelson became dean and director. In 1970 Dr. Roger J. Manges was promoted to dean and director. In 1964, at the time of its switch to the regional campus, Purdue had 1,462 students.

The joint Indiana-Purdue campus venture had its beginnings in 1957 following a proposal by A. W. Kettler and Walter E. Helmke, Purdue and I.U. trustees for considerable periods. The boards of both universities visited the proposed campus that year and indicated a favorable attitude toward the project. The site originally occupied was a 262 acre tract which formerly had been the Fort Wayne State Hospital farmland. When opened in 1964, all classes and activities were in one building, Kettler Hall. The campus was bound by US-30 Bypass and Indiana State Road 37, next to the St. Joseph's River. In the following eight years, two additional buildings were erected; a $5 million library with 115,000 square feet and a 4.5 million classroom-office-laboratory building with 108,000 square feet and named Neff Hall. In the fall of 1973, a $4 million Student Union, 86,000 square feet, was opened. By that time, the Fort Wayne Campus had more than 5,000 students. Complete baccalaureate degree programs were started in 1966 and two-year associate degree programs had been offered starting in 1964. In the fall semester of 1967-68, a joint agreement between Indiana and Purdue went into effect to pave the way for further development of academic programs. The original purchase of land was 120 acres in December, 1958; which was expanded to 262 acres and then to 412 acres. Ground was broken for the first building in October, 1962. The first class was graduated in a joint ceremony in June, 1968. Long range plans call for construction of an 18-building complex with a capability of serving 15,000 students according to 1974 projections. Participating in dedication ceremonies in 1973, in addition to Purdue President Arthur Hanson and I.U. President John Ryan, were architects Herman Strauss of Fort Wayne and Walter E. Scholer, Jr., of West Lafayette; I.U. Trustee Jeanne S. Miller, Purdue Trustee Walter W. Walb and Dr. Sylvia E. Bowman, I.U. chancellor for regional campuses who began her college teaching career at the old Fort Wayne I.U. extension. On Nov. 8, 1973, Indiana and Purdue Universities approved unification of administrative staffs at the Fort Wayne campus with a single chancellor effective July 1, 1974. Named first chancellor was Dr. Donald Schwartz, who had been acting president of State University College, Buffalo, N. Y.

The I.U.-Purdue Foundation approved in 1975 the acquisition of 20 acres of land by the Indiana Vocational Technical College (Ivy Tech) just to the south of the Regional Campus. Mearle Donica, Ivy Tech dean, said the signing of the deed by Carolyn Gutman, foundation president, was a stepping stone to the building of a $1,400,000 unit to consolidate Ivy Tech's operations. Founded in 1969, Indiana Vocational College had been located in buildings on Maumee Ave., Wells St. and High St. Enrollment grew from 100 students the first year to 790 in 1975. The new building at Coliseum Blvd. and North Anthony Blvd. was expected to be occupied in 1976.

At the top of the page is a drawing of the New Clay School as it was being built in 1894. This school at Washington Blvd. and Clay St. replaced the first regular public school building in Fort Wayne. The first Clay School had burned. So did this one in a spectacular fire in 1930. The middle picture shows the first grade class of South Wayne School about 1928. At bottom is Methodist College built in 1884 at the foot of West Wayne St.

Central High School at Lewis and Barr streets is shown soon after it was built in 1904. Central, originally known as Fort Wayne High, replaced the old Fort Wayne High on Wayne St., shown in the drawing. Below, the pupils of the Wayne Township School line up for the annual picture in front of the rural school, about 1930.

South Side High School, below, was built in 1922 as a one-story school and expanded to two stories after World War II. This picture was taken when street cars were still operating along South Calhoun St. North Side High School, at left, was built in 1927 at East State Blvd. facing the St. Joseph River.

Library Hall, built in 1881 at Calhoun and Lewis, later became Central Catholic High School until 1938. The Cathedral, just behind, had a brick exterior when this picture was taken in the 1890s. St. Catherine's Academy, right, was on DeWald St. and was a secondary school for girls until 1938. Below, buses line up in 1950 on Lewis St. with Central High at left and Central Catholic, built in 1938, in the background beyond Clinton St.

The campus of Indiana Institute of Technology, between Maumee Ave. and Washington Blvd. has some of the old and new. The building at the right of the picture is part of the old Concordia College, begun in 1861. The new building in the background is part of the modern development begun after Tech moved to the campus in 1957. Below is Indiana Technical College building downtown in the 200 block of East Washington Blvd., about 1939. At left bottom is the building at Jefferson and Barr which was originally the Catholic Community Center, then the Purdue University Center following World War II and finally the temporary public library until 1968, after which it was razed.

*The Fort Wayne Bible College, pic
tured above along Rudisill Blvd. o
its 60th anniversary in 1965, was a
expanding part of the city's highe
education. At left is the Crosie
House of Studies on the Wallen Roa
north of the city, built in 1957. Th
Crosier Order took over the old 19t
Century Sacred Heart Academy i
1938. Below, Lynn Koehlinger pre
sents educationist Fred Croninge
with a portrait painted by Grac
Leslie Dickerson as Rex Potter,
long-time head librarian, watche
from the center position.*

The Concordia Senior College campus, one of the outstanding deposits of architecture on the American scene, was completed in 1957. Designed by Eero Saarinen, the placid beauty of the scene is caught on a summer day by Larry Neeb at the campus near the St. Joseph River on the city's north fringe.

Students at St. Francis College, above, dip paddles in a canoe race on the campus lake. The college, moved to the old Bass estate in 1942, expanded with growing enrollment and buildings, such as the hall at upper right. At right is a class activity at North Side High in 1974. At right bottom is Bishop Luers High School, built in 1958 on East Paulding Road.

Concordia High School, right, was built in 1963. Across North Anthony Blvd. is Zollner Stadium which became a part of the school. Below, right, is Bishop Dwenger High School, built in 1962 at North Clinton St. and Washington Center Road Below, left, high school art teachers look over some of the students' creations.

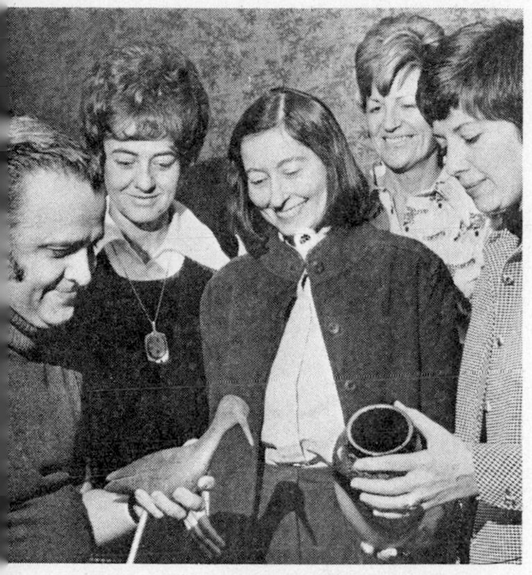

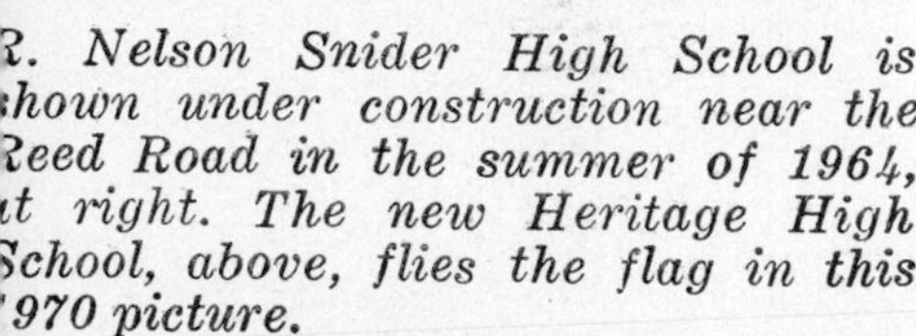

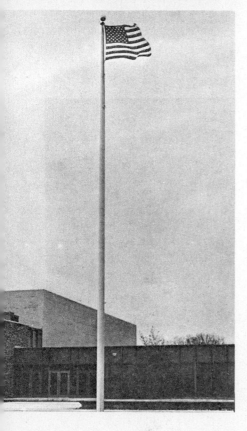

R. Nelson Snider High School is shown under construction near the Reed Road in the summer of 1964, at right. The new Heritage High School, above, flies the flag in this 1970 picture.

At the top of the page is Wayne High School under construction in 1971 near the Winchester Road. At right, students flow out of Northrop High School on a cold winter's day during the 1974-75 term. Northrop was built at the same time as Wayne. In the picture below, college and high school students join in one of the frequent walks for the frequent good causes.

The Indiana-Purdue Universities Campus at Fort Wayne was built along the St. Joseph River north of Coliseum Blvd. The consolidation of earlier extension operations with a new university and campus occurred in 1964. Expansion was to 412 acres with continual building and faculty growth. More than 5,000 students were enrolled by 1973. Projections call for 18 buildings and an enrollment of 15,000 students.

BREAKING GROUND FOR
LINCOLN TOWER BUILDING
AUGUST 16, 1929.

Just two months before the onset of the Great Depression, these gentlemen broke ground for the 22-story Lincoln Bank Tower, for many years thereafter Indiana's tallest building. The date was August 16, 1929. The man with the shovel is Sam Foster, bank chairman. From left are: George Waldschmidt, Willard Shambaugh, Jesse Eschbach, Henry Lepper, E. C. Miller, August Witte, Fred Bueshing, Theodore Buesching, Charles Buesching (bank president), David Foster, William Hagerman, Maurice Rosenthal, Frank Smock, John Disser, Walter Cook, Arthur Perfect, S. E. Mulholland, Samuel Emmett, Alvin Strauss.

Part 7
The Depression Times

Nineteen twenty-nine opened with blue skies. It was nearly universally believed that the greatest era of progress in the history of mankind was at hand. Herbert Hoover, one of the more respected and popular personalities, was the newly-elected President. His promise of "two cars in every garage and a chicken in every pot" seemed reasonable and inevitable. Indiana Governor Ed Jackson gave his final message and, four days later on January 15, Governor Harry G. Leslie was inaugurated. No problem appeared beyond solution. Early in his administration Governor Leslie paroled Howard Buck, Vincennes, former football star at the University of Chicago, so experimental surgery could be performed on his brain to remove his criminal tendencies. The future of the great circuses seemed assured when John Ringling acquired control of five circuses with headquarters at Peru.

But everything wasn't circuses. The farmers were going bankrupt, and their children were growing restless. There were too many chickens and other things, which could hardly be given away. Banks were being robbed to a disturbing degree—a portent of things to come. The president of the National Bank at Sullivan was murdered on the spot. Bank bandit Thomas Burke was shot down at Angola. Two armed bandits secured $5,700 in a daylight robbery of Citizens Bank at Carmel. Gunmen robbed $18,000 from a South Bend Bank. Bandits took $1,200 at the Wolcottville State Bank. The State went on a manhunt for Gene Alger, Indianapolis killer, for the Paris Crossing State Bank holdup. Kirby Davis, Muncie badman, was arrested for robbery of the First National Bank, Angola. LaFontaine State Bank was robbed by a gunman and his moll. The First National Bank, Peru, was robbed of $93,000 by a gang of six or eight men who shot down a watchman and an onlooker. The Citizens Bank of Southport was robbed of $2,300 by two men.

A gang of three men and two women robbed two Kroger stores in Fort Wayne on January 7, 1928. At one of the stores, located at the corner of Calhoun St. and Woodland Ave., they murdered Clem Foley, 50-year-old meatcutter. One of the men, Wayne Williams, was given the death penalty by a jury and sentenced to the electric chair by Judge Sol A. Wood. The others were given prison sentences. Prosecuting the case was Edwin R. Thomas. Defense lawyer was Robert Buhler. In the meantime, the St. Valentine's Day Massacre at Chicago was a red-letter day in the gangster wars.

Black Tuesday, October 29, 1929, on the New York Stock Exchange drew less attention in Fort Wayne newspapers than another October happening—in Big Ten football. Purdue took everything, going untied and undefeated; rolling over Indiana University 32 to 0 in the final game of the season on Nov. 23.

Before the Bust

Manufacturing plants of Fort Wayne turned out goods worth $95 million in 1929, according to estimates based on records of the U.S. Commerce Department. The city's industrial output showed an increase of 747 per cent in value in three decades. According to production records in all mills and factories, the 1914 total was $30 million and the 1899 total was $11 million. Some of the gain was due to inflation of the value of money, but there was also very real progress in both quantity and diversity of industry. The advances in wages paid at Fort Wayne manufacturing plants can be seen in Federal statistics. In 1899 the total paid to workers in city plants was some $3 million. By 1914, the figure had doubled to $6 million. In 1929 the total wages paid by manufacturing units was $21 million, more than triple that of 15 years earlier and seven times the figure just before the turn of the century. "The increase in the wage bill shows why the average Fort Wayne family is able to buy and enjoy many comforts and luxuries that a few years ago were virtually unknown," a local bank reported at the time.

Fort Wayne in 1929 provided employment for 48,000 wage earners and salaried workers in its factories, mills, stores and other commercial organizations. According to the records of the U.S. Census Bureau, the number of men and women occupied in 1900 was 18,000. This figure had advanced to 28,000 by 1910 and to 40,000 by 1920. This high rate of employment, coupled with high educational attainments, led to bank deposits far exceeding the national average. Approximately $668 in deposits was credited on the average in the banks and trust companies for each resident of the city. A comparison was made with average bank deposits for the populations of other cities in 1929. At South Bend the figure was $458; at Evansville, $573; at Indianapolis, $464; at Terre Haute, $440; at Gary, $207; at Toledo, $624; at Dayton, $328.

The Fort Wayne population grew rather quickly during the early decades of the 20th Century. In 1900 the official Census count was 45,115. This advanced to 63,933 by 1910 and to 86,549 by 1920. The special count of 1928 set the figure at 105,300, but local officials claimed it was undercounted and that the 1930 figure would be 117,000. When the 1930 figures on the Census were in, it showed the local promoters were not too far off. The official count was 114,946, or nearly a 30,000 increase in the decade of the 1920's. It is interesting to note that the next 10 years—those of the Great Depression—sharply stunted Fort Wayne's upward population trend. The 1940 Census Bureau count would be 118,410, a bare 3,500 more than the figure 10 years earlier. It was the smallest gain in the history of the city, starting from the mid-1800's.

In 1929, the United States was still a place where the majority of city dwellers were renters. As an example, the proportion of families which owned their homes in Detroit was 38 per cent; in Indianapolis, 35 per cent; in Evansville, 41 per cent; in Chicago the home ownership figure was 27 per cent; in New York, the Nation's largest city, only 13 per cent of the families lived in homes they owned. Fort Wayne was one of the few medium-sized or larger cities with more than a 50 per cent home-ownership figure—a 66 per cent home ownership. It might be thought that back in the 1920's nearly everyone belonged to churches. That was not quite the case. Little more than 50 per cent of the population, approximately 64,000, were enrolled as members of the city's churches. Of the members of the various congregations, 34,560 were women and 29,440 were men.

From the end of the 19th Century, 1899, to 30 years later just before the onset of the Depression in 1929, the average worker's paycheck moved up considerably. In 1899 wage earners in Fort Wayne manufacturing plants averaged $403 for the year. Fifteen years later this annual pay average had gone to only $564. But in the next 15 years, from 1914 to 1929, there was a rather dramatic change in the figure—to an average of $1,339, according to records of the U.S. Commerce Department. The change in pay scales reflected improved methods and worker efficiency. This can be seen in the dollar value output per man and productivity which moved forward 248 per cent. Goods worth $1,728 on the average were turned out by the city's industrial plants in 1899 for each worker on the payrolls. In 1914, output per worker increased to $2,706, government records showed. In 1929 the average was $6,018 worth of goods per man. Women during the same 30-year period joined the work force in increasing numbers. By 1929, there were approximately 11,000 women on the job in Fort Wayne. Women were working as salaried employees, managers and heads of departments, as well as store owners. Manufacturing establishments used the services of 5,060 women, or 46 per cent of all women employed. Clerical occupations furnished employment for 1,870 women or 17 per cent. Some 12 per cent or 1,320 were in professional work, including doctors, lawyers, nurses and school teachers. The stores employed 1,210 women, or 11 per cent, and 1,540 women were working at various other occupations.

Airplanes and Cars

The 1920's, more than any other decade, was the period when sporting airplanes and the family automobile were king. Hundreds of companies were competing with one another in the production of cars of infinite variety. They ranged from high fashion coaches and roadsters to the ubiquitous Model T. The fancy ones would be valued "classics" in later generations. By the end of the 1920's, in 1929, the National Automobile Association reported 122 automobiles were in operation in Fort Wayne for each 100 families. This was one of the highest ownership figures in the U.S. Another reflection on the prosperity of Fort Wayne and the progress in the schools was the investment in school properties, which averaged $401 per pupil in 1929, according to the U.S. Bureau of Education. This was well in excess of Indianapolis at $353 per student; Chicago at $311 per student, or New York at $368 per student. Birth rates were remarkably steady during the 1920's. In 1920 the rate was 20.3 births per 1,000 in the population. In 1928 the birth rate was 20.0. There was an upward bulge in the middle of the decade when the birth rate reached 25.2 in 1924 before tapering off, and then plunging to below 15 in the depth of the Depression during the 1930's. Following World War II and in the 1950's the birth rate again reached and slightly surpassed the 1924 figure, moving to approximately 26 per 1,000 in population. By 1973, the birth rate had again dropped to about 14. Through most of the period from 1900 to 1973, there was a gradual drop in the death rate, as the life expectancy moved upward in years, chiefly due to better nutrition and health services.

The social upheavals and the hardships associated with the onset of the Great Depression will be detailed in due course. It would be a period when more than 30 per cent of the Nation's work force would be unemployed. Mass migrations from the Dust Bowl of the Midwest, the institution of the hobo and the panhandler as commonplace characteristics of city life, and peculiarly, new magnificence in motion pictures were all part of the scene. One set of figures in Fort Wayne lend insight to the family pocketbook and the work opportunities which were so vastly altered by economic circumstances. In 1929, there were 7,538 automobiles sold in Fort Wayne and Allen County. The following year, 1930, the figure had dropped to 4,353. As the economic bind grew tighter the auto sales figure for 1931 was 2,828. In 1932 it hit bottom with only 1,484 cars sold in Fort Wayne and Allen County by all agencies. It was a little better in 1933 and 1934 when only 2,018 and 2,715 cars were sold, respectively. Finally, in 1935, there was limited recovery and 4,707 automobiles were purchased in Fort Wayne. In 1934 and 1935, many regular makes of cars were listed at $299 and $350, new.

The Stable Downtown

There was a remarkable stability in department store and other retail and service companies downtown for many years. Through the 1920's, the 1930's and the 1940's, the majority of firms continued in business in the dominant central district. There were a few changes, but nothing like the mass exodus which was to begin in the 1950's. As an example, Rurode Dry Goods Company was at 708 South Calhoun St. in the 1920's. The president of Rurode's, Earl Groth, opened a new operation called Earl Groth & Co. just two blocks to the south which operated for the next three decades. In the meantime Neisner's Five and Ten Cents Store moved into the old location. During the '30's, Five and Dimes came into their own. There were three practically side by side in the 700 block of Calhoun St., Woolworth's, Kresge's and Neisner's. Also, there was Murphy's on Wayne near Calhoun and Grant's at the southwest corner of Washington and Calhoun. Only Murphy's, much expanded, was still operating downtown and prospering in 1974. Grant's, Kresge's and others moved to shopping centers.

During the three decades, 1920 to 1950, the numerous business establishments downtown were home-owned to a considerable degree. Even the Depression and World War II did little to alter the pattern. It was only in the subsequent two decades that a large proportion of the retail and service operations became links in chain operations and larger corporate enterprises. Some of the stores, however, continued into the 1970's in the hands of families which were downtown merchants in the 1920's. A survey of city enterprises in the late 1920's and early 1930's shows the extensiveness of the downtown activity and some of the principal owners or managers at that time.

Along Calhoun Street

Main and Calhoun was called the Transfer Corner because all the street cars crossed at that point and the conductors gave transfer slips to riders. It was a noisy place. Trolleys clanged and screeched. The larger interurban trains also shuttled noisily back and forth as they began or ended runs to outlying communities.

Riegel's Cigar Store at the northeast corner did a thriving lunch counter business and handled tickets for shows and sporting events. It was operated by Aloysius Riegel, George Kuntz and Frank A. Bougher. At the southwest corner was Meyer Bros. Drug Store. The Meyer Co., which had eight stores at that time, was headed by Gottlieb Heine, Fred C. Heine, Arthur Beuke and Arthur Heine.

To the south of the Transfer Corner along Calhoun St. were Rurode's Dry Goods, S. S. Kresge Co., F. W. Woolworth, Frank Dry Goods Co., Cousins Jewelers and Whelan Drug Co., all on the west side facing the Courthouse. At the southwest corner of Berry and Calhoun was the Old National Bank of Fort Wayne and at the southeast corner, the Citizens Trust Company. Going east along Berry, the stores included Vigran's Ladies Shop, operated by Isador Vigran; the M&N Shoe Store, headed by Dan Myers and Roy Netter; The Lehman Book Store, operated by Anna Taylor, Laura Detzer and Bertha Griebel, and later by Allan McMahan; the Fort Wayne Abstract Co., operated by C. K. Larwill; Home Loan and Savings, headed by Paul Richter, Fred Glusenkamp, Carl Weber, Steve Weber and William J. Hess; the Peoples Drug Store, operated by W. C. Kaiser; and the Wayne Mortgage Loan Co., headed by E. M. Wilson and E. H. Hackman.

At the southeast corner of Clinton and

Berry Sts. was the Post Office and Federal Building. The stone Federal Building on South Harrison St. opposite the Lincoln Life Home Office was built in 1931. To the east on Berry was the Majestic Theater, which was in succession a stage theater, a movie house and the home of the Civic Theatre. Other business establishments in the block included the Fort Wayne Morris Plan (later the Anthony Wayne Bank); the Schneider-Kaiser Washing Machine Co.; William C. Wolf Furnaces; the Dix-Kelly Electric Shop, headed by F. J. Dix, L. W. Kelly and R. E. Kelly; and across on the northwest corner, the Ankenbruck Undertakers. City Hall was on the southeast corner and the Home Telephone and Telegraph Co. on the northeast corner. Home Telephone, which was later merged with General Telephone Co. of Indiana, was headed by Frank Bohn, A. E. Becker, E. C. Bloomeyer, Otto Marahrens and Max B. Fisher. Bell Telephone Co. was just to the east along Berry St., as was Guy Means Buick Agency. On the south side next to City Hall was City Light and Power Works, with Louis A. Centlivre, secretary, Daniel J. Danehy, superintendent, and Merle Gouty, chief engineer.

To the west of Calhoun St. along Berry were The Club and James H. Hart Billiards; Charles W. Anderson Millinery; Sears Roebuck & Co.; John Rabus and Robert Meyer Tailor Shops; the First and Tri-State National Bank Building; the Western Auto Supply Co.; the Clemens Restaurant Co., operated by Herbert Clemens; and the Baltes Hotel at the southeast corner; the Anthony Hotel at the northeast corner; and Meyer Drugs and Dudley S. McClure Real Estate Co. at the northwest corner. Down the street were the B. J. Duesler Music House; the Greyhound Bus Terminal; Art Mosaic & Tile Co. operated by R. B. Kinnane; Getz and Cahill Undertakers; the Elks Temple, and across the street at the Webster St. corner, the Medical Arts Building.

Stores along Calhoun St. between Berry and Wayne Streets included Miller-Wohl Ladies Co. operated by George Arenberg; Vesey Flower Store, headed by W. J., M. S. and David S. Vesey and Ernest Ferguson; the Walk-Over Boot Shop; the Beacon Shoe Store; Berland's Shoe Store; the Nisley Co. Shoes; Fox Jewelry Co.; Hale Hat Co.; Robert Koerber Jeweler; Leon C. Beck Jewelry; H. H. Rogers Optical Co.; Martha Washington Candies; Carl W. Rose Jeweler; A&I Leather Shop, operated by Morris King; Bruder-Calhoun Jewelry Co. and the A. Schulte Cigar Store. Grand Leader Department Store at the southeast corner of Wayne and Calhoun was owned by Stillman's Dry Goods Co. and managed by Clem Melancon. Meyer Bros. Drugs was at the southwest corner.

Patterson-Fletcher

Firms along Wayne, east of Calhoun St. included G. C. Murphy Co.; Northern Indiana Public Service Co.; the Utility Building (Anna Pocock had the cigar counter in the lobby); the Wayne Floral Co. operated by Harry Birkhold; The A&P Grocery; the Summit City Cafeteria, operated by George Collias; the Indiana Service Co.; the Fort Wayne Book Shop, operated by Horace Moses, L. J. Harwood and Mrs. Harriett Moses; Cusma T. David Rugs; Anderson F. Summers Stitching; Strauss Bros. Co. headed by Abe Ackerman and Maurice Brubaker; the Lincoln National Bank & Trust Co.; the Strand Theatre; and at the southwest corner, the 20th Century Lunch, operated by Phil Clauss.

Between Clinton St. and Barr St. along Wayne were the Hilgeman and Schaaf Building; Oliver Conner Barber Shop; the Kindler Hotel; Anna Schueman and Henry Wahl music teachers; James Fuller & Sons violin makers; Pape Bros. Wallpaper Co.; Kroger Grocery; Tom Wing Laundry. In the center of the 100 block on the north side was built in 1931 the Paramount Theatre, one of Fort Wayne's great movie palaces.

West of Calhoun St. along Wayne were Meigs Eye Specialists, operated by Charles Meigs and R. J. Blume; Dominic Manochio Confections; Bazley Meats; Hollywood Cafe operated by Peter Stevens and William Maounis; Howard's, headed by Charles W. Howard; Jay Miller Radio Service; Shine Shoe Co., operated by Nathan Shine, Robert Shiff and Myrtle Shine; the Snowberger Ladies Wear; J. C. Peltier & Son Undertaker, headed by William H. W. Peltier; The Vogue, operated by Oscar Ankenbruck; Bobay Shoe Store, operated by Ambrose Bobay; Rose and Walsh Jewelers, operated by Erwin Rose and Frank Walsh; Miss Julia Emanuel Chemist and Drug Shop; the Roy J. Stirk Bowling Alley; Mrs. Cathrine Brackett Restaurant; the Fort Wayne Drug Co., headed by Henry C. Paul, Henry Bowerfind and Erwin H. Manth; and the Patterson-Fletcher Co. Patterson-Fletcher, which developed into a major department store, was founded in 1906 by Harry P. Fletcher and Mrs. Reuben Patterson, whose husband originally had a store across Calhoun St. from the Courthouse. The move to Wayne and Harrison St. was made in 1917. Subsequently, A. F. Kinnaird became secretary-treasurer; C. Dwight Shirey, advertising manager for many years, became president; Samuel W. Fletcher, department manager, later became chairman of the store and a major industrial and commercial developer in Fort Wayne, Indianapolis and in Michigan. On the southwest corner of Wayne and Harrison was the Central Grocery and on the northwest corner the Packard Music House.

On Calhoun St. between Wayne and Washington Blvd. was located the Winterrowd-Howard Clothing Store, headed by Earl Winterrowd and Henry Howard; The Peoples Trust Building; the Mathias App Shoe Store; D. B. Fishman & Co. Ladies Wear, later headed by Marvin and Stan Fishman; Richman Bros. Co.; The Hutner Co. Men's Wear; the Paris and Hutner's Bon Marche Co., headed by Benjamin J. Hutner, Sidney M. Hutner and Davis S. Hutner; Weisell Baber, Jeweler; Golden's Men's Wear Shop, headed by Charles Golden and later by Ed Golden; and Diamond Bros. Ladies Wear.

Wolf & Dessauer

On the northeast corner of Washington and Calhoun was Wolf & Dessauer for decades one of the highly-reputed department stores in the Nation. Sam Wolf originally started the store with Myron Dessauer in 1896 on Berry Street. The firm was moved into a four-story building on the south side of Berry St. in 1904 until 1919, after which the Berry St. site was utilized for the construction of the 12-story First National Bank Building in 1920. In 1919 Wolf & Dessauer contracted with Oscar Fox for the erection of the seven-story department store building at Calhoun and Washington. The firm was incorporated and the controlling interests sold in 1920. Heading the new Wolf & Dessauer operation for the next several decades were Samuel L. Smith, G. Irving Latz and J. P. Doody. Subsequently, G. Irving Latz, 2nd, Nelson Neiman and William Smith Latz directed Wolf & Dessauer affairs. W&D cut new ground in gracious merchandising services in Fort Wayne. It became a center for Christmas shopping and decoration which attracted people in such numbers that even movement in the store was often difficult. The operation expanded over the years until the entire block from Calhoun to Clinton along Washington was part of the store.

Other businesses on Washington, east from Calhoun Street included: Mrs. Miller's Cafeteria, operated by Luella Miller (Mrs. Miller also operated Mrs. Miller's Tea Room at the southwest corner of Harrison and Jefferson Sts.); Lulu Archer Confections; Chester B. Bryson Barber Shop; the Fawley-Abbott-Bryan Co. Furniture, headed by George Fawley, John Abbott and Edward Bryan; The Palace Theatre; Milton M. Mendelsohn Shoes; and Fred Robbins Barber Shop. On the east side of Clinton St. were the Scottish Rite Cathedral; First Presbyterian Church; Rhoads-Morgan Paint Co., headed by W. M. Leonard, D. F. Michaelis and Oscar Rhoads; Fitch, Fishering, Lumbard and Loos Insurance, operated by C. B. Fitch, George W. Fishering, C. M. Carter and G. L. Loos; The Young Men's Christian Assn. and the News-Sentinel Building. A few of the other businesses on East Washington Blvd. included Grieger, Inc., autos; the Auburn Auto Co. Sales; Arthur G. Koehlinger, locksmith, and Winston F. Koehlinger, bicycle shop; the Chester G. Schiefer Auto Sales; and at the intersection with Clay, Poinsatte Auto Co., headed by Henry J., Albert and William J. Poinsatte.

Busy South Calhoun

On Washington Blvd., west from Calhoun was Grant's; Blackstone Shop, operated by Mary Henline; Cleary & Bailey Printers, headed by Martin J. (Bruff) Cleary, Jr.; Western Union; Montgomery Ward Department Store; Clyde A. Myers Barber Shop; Central Office Equipment Co., headed by Kenneth Brown, Fred Stone, and Fred Wyneken; and the Plaza Cafe, operated by George Condos, Samuel Kamagis and George Christ; and the Keenan Hotel on the southwest corner.

On Calhoun St. between Washington and Jefferson were George T. King, jeweler; the Colonial Theatre, managed by G. Frank Kinkade; the Sweet Lady Pop Corn Shop, operated by Phil Clauss; the Columbia Candy Kitchen, operated by Charles Lambrakis; Sherman Clothes; Israel-Butler Men's Store, operated by Richard B. Butler; the Riley Theatre, operated by Peter Mallers; Maurice R. Miller Windows; Kay Jewelry Co.; Hadley Furniture Co.; the King Trunk and Leather Works, headed by Morris King; Homer R. Gettle Optician; Schloss Tailors; Schroeders Clothing, operated by Edward G. Schroeder; Saul's Clothing; Hillman China Co., Inc., headed by Lee H. Hillman, R. W. Cassidy and B. R. Hillman; Peter G. Kuttner Men's Furnishings; Thom McAnn Shoes; Herman A. William Herbs; W. L. Douglas Shoe Store; Olsen and Ebann Jewelers and the Indiana Frock Shop operated by J. J. Van Vecten.

Along Jefferson west of Calhoun were the Harry Boxberger Phonograph Shop; John L. Guillot Barber Shop; Mrs. Rhoda Depotty Millinery Shop; the Withey Studio of Drama; Ralph Iammarino Confections; Herman P. Pawlisch Shoe Repair; the Jefferson Theater; the Jacobs-Van Sweringen Music House, Inc., headed by Howard Van Sweringen, George Jacobs, George W. Jacobs, Jr.; International College, headed by J. Lyle Tucker, J. N. Fulton and Orvis Dellinger; the Emboyd Theater and Indiana Hotel; and the Sigl Drug Store, operated by Joseph Sigl.

The Fox Theatre and Hotel Building, a $1 million project, was completed in 1927. The Theater on the south side of Jefferson St. was soon renamed the Emboyd, and decades later, the Embassy. The Indiana Hotel operated for four decades. In the 1930's, the Emboyd Theater and the Paramount Theater built in 1931 on East Wayne St., the largest and most ornate movie houses ever built in the city, were operated by Clyde Quimby, one-time vice-president of the Dime Bank & Trust Company. Quimby's wife, the former Helen Kinkade, was a piano player for the old silent movies in the Jefferson Theatre. Quimby at one time had all the major theaters in Fort Wayne. These included the Emboyd, the Paramount, the Jefferson and the Palace. After Quimby's death, Helen Quimby operated the chain and years later built the Clyde Theater in Quimby Village near Bluffton Road, which was managed by Harvey Cocks.

On Calhoun St. across from the Cathedral was the D&N Pharmacy operated by Henry Diebold and C. A. Niebergall, who had four drug stores in the city; Fort Wayne Blue Print and Supply Co., headed by Fred W. Werkman; the Rowlands Furniture Co.; the Pickard House Furnishings Co. operated by Peter, Harry and A. W. Pickard; the Nicholas Andress Shoe Shine Parlor; Will A. Young's Music Store; and at the southeast corner of Calhoun and Lewis, the Belmont Products Co. which sold restaurant supplies until Repeal and was operated by C. H. Schweiters and A. J. Zuber. To the south was Elmer Smith's Tailor and Cleaners; Lanternier Florists operated by Edmund and Clem Lanternier; Mrs. S. Maxie Bradley Millinery; the Vim Sporting Goods, managed by F. Leslie Logan; the Harry M. Boxberger Book Store; the Grand Malt Shop operated by Ben R. Hillman; the Lenkendorfer Coffee Ranch operated by Willard Lenkendorfer. The coffee and peanut shop was originally started by Harry Takimori, a native of Japan who was in business in Fort Wayne until he died in his 90's in 1970. Takimori had numerous clusters of Japanese cherry trees planted in city park areas. Takimori established something of a record when he started a new peanut market in the 100 block of West Washington Blvd. in 1965 when he was 90 years old.

Birth of Radio

The story of early radio in Fort Wayne is the story of two stations, WGL and WOWO, which dominated the local airwaves for a number of decades. General commercial broadcasting began on Jan. 24, 1924, with the call letters WHBJ—which later became WGL. Chester W. Keen, a Fort Wayne businessman, purchased the original equipment in New York and brought it to Fort Wayne. Keen joined forces with Lauer Auto Co. to get the station on the air. Keen broadcast his programs from the mezzanine of the Keenan Hotel. Later Keen bought out Lauer and moved his studio to 1729 South Lafayette St., and changed the call letters to WCWK. On Sept. 1, 1928, Frederick C. Zeig acquired the station from Keen and set up studios on the second floor of the Main Auto Supply Co., 215 West Main St. and changed the call letters to WGL. In the meantime, Zieg, president of Main Auto, worked with Gunnar Elliott in the forming of WOWO—the station with the oldest continuous call letters in the city. The license for WOWO was granted in early 1925 and started on 250 watts. Within a few years WOWO was the most powerful station in Indiana and operating on 10,000 watts, later 50,000 watts. Another early radio station with a rather short existence was WDBV established in three Fort Wayne theatres operated by Clyde Quimby. Frank Freimann, who in later years would join Magnavox and became its president, contracted in 1924 with the Quimby Theatres for the broadcast installation. In the early days, the radios people had in their homes were called receivers. They often had large exposed tubes and speakers, plus aerials strung in the attic.

The infancy of radio included a few hours a day of broadcasts from, typically, a back upstairs room of a sports store on Main Street. The onset of network programs was a gradual thing. Much of the early programming was local in origin and strong on imagination. Soon, the fare became more diversified from both local sources and from the networks. Willis Martin, a Fort Wayne advertising man, recalled that the first remote control broadcast in Fort Wayne was the coverage of the funeral procession of Paul Frank Baer. Baer, America's first World War I ace, was killed in a plane crash in China on Dec. 9, 1930. The body was brought back on ship and the funeral in January, 1931, was the largest military funeral in the history of the city. To give on-the-spot descriptions to the radio listeners, WOWO set up on the portico of the Elks Lodge on West Berry St., overlooking the procession route. The portico was wired to the station's studio back at 215 West Main Street. The announcer was Sam Jackson, who later became a U.S. Senator. In that same season, the first remote control entertainment program was broadcast from the Lincoln Tower at the dedication of the 22-story Lincoln National Bank Building. Al Becker was the announcer for the festivities. The first local network operation was a WOWO broadcast of the Indiana State High School Basketball finals from Butler Fieldhouse, Indianapolis. Gunnar Elliott did the announcing from the scene. He earlier had experimented with sports broadcasts at basketball games in Fort Wayne.

The Hoosier Hop

By the early 1930's, network programs were making a considerable impact on people of all ages. The soap operas came in for the daytime listeners. After school hours, there was Jack Armstrong—the All American Boy, Little Orphan Annie and in early evening, The Shadow. Little children were delighted with the stories of the Singing Lady. Night radio was in its heyday. Eddie Cantor, Charlie McCarthy, Fibber McGee and Molly, Jack Benny and others were masters of the medium. The music of the great orchestras vied with radio theater. Sports announcers Clem McCarthy and Bill Stern brought the exploits of Jimmy Braddock, Max Baer and Joe Louis in boxing; and Notre Dame, Michigan and Purdue on the gridiron. In 1935, a local program originating at WOWO mushroomed into a national hookup with a Hooper Rating of 12—a respectable rating by the service which operated in those days. This was The Hoosier Hop—which gave Fort Wayne a reputation similar to that of Nashville, Tenn., in a later generation. Big attractions on the show included the Blackhawk Valley Boys, Nancy Lee and the Hilltoppers, Judy & Jen and other show stoppers. Harry Smythe was the director. One of the principals of early Hoosier Hops was Shirley Bowersox Wayne, the non-stop fiddler who joined the Olsen and Johnson "Hellzapoppin" show which started in the old Palace Theater. The show, headed by Ole Olsen and Chic Johnson, ran a record number of more than a thousand performances at New York's Winter Garden.

On August 1, 1936, Westinghouse Radio Stations purchased both WGL and WOWO from Zieg and moved the studios from the Main Auto to a new, enlarged facility at the northeast corner of Harrison St. and Washington Boulevard. WGL, which had been linked with the CBS network, was affiliated with NBC. The following year, WOWO was affiliated with NBC and WGL was switched back to CBS. Later, WOWO was associated with ABC. The Farnsworth Radio and Television Co. purchased WGL on May 25, 1945, and moved the studios to 200 West Jefferson Street. On June 17, 1949, the News-Sentinel purchased WGL. At that time the station was affiliated with NBC; but the following year WGL was switched to the ABC network. Pierre Boucheron and Merrill C. Johnson were general managers of the station, successively. Leonard E. Davis, vice-president and general manager of WGL in 1970, announced affiliation with CBS. On Dec. 8, 1971, Helene Foellinger, president of the News-Sentinel Broadcasting Co., Inc.; Davis and others broke ground for new WGL studios, administrative offices and transmitter at 2000 Lower Huntington Road. Carl W. Vandagrift and Edward Wallis were successive general managers of WOWO. Earlier managers of the Westinghouse station were Robert Duffield and Franklin Tooke. Vandagrift, who had originally joined WOWO in 1935, was reappointed general manager of WOWO in 1961 after stints at New York and Cleveland. What was once the tallest structure in the state, WOWO's transmission tower, was brought down in 1954. The 454-foot tower was constructed in 1935 at the intersection of U.S. Highways 30 and 33, just west of Fort Wayne. WOWO built its new transmitter near U.S. 24 in the Roanoke vicinity.

Later Radio

Radio Station WFTW, an independent outlet owned and operated by Fort Wayne Broadcasting Co., went on the air at 1 p.m. Sunday, August 8, 1947. The station used 1,000 watts. The first voice heard was Edward G. Thoms, president and general manager. Other principals of the company included Earl Groth, Sr., C. L. Schust and H. Leslie Popp. In August, 1949, the Fort Wayne Broadcasting Co. purchased WKJG and Northeastern Indiana Broadcasting Co., controlled by William A. Kunkel III and Gilmore Haynie. Hilliard Gates was manager of WKJG. In November, 1949, the Fort Wayne Broadcasting firm discontinued WFTW and continued broadcasting over WKJG. WKJG had been started on Nov. 15, 1947, with studios in the Lincoln Tower. WFTW had studios in the Purdue Center on East Jefferson Street. Operations of the broadcasting company were continued at 3802 South Calhoun Street. Thoms assumed the managership of WKJG and Hilliard Gates, a longtime sports announcer for WOWO, became head of programming and sports on WKJG. WANE, the city's fifth radio station, started broadcasting on March 27, 1948, with studios on the 13th floor of the Fort Wayne National Bank Building. WANE, which affiliated with the CBS network, was owned by Radio Fort Wayne, Inc. Officers included Merlin H. Smith, Charles A. Sprague and Glenn R. Thayer. A 175-foot tower was built on top of the bank building on the south side of Berry Street. In the great wind storm of July 20, 1954, the tower came crashing down the front of the building. In 1966, WANE was sold by the Corinthian Broadcasting Co. to the Shepard Broadcasting Corp. based in Grand Rapids, Michigan. At that time the call letters of the station became WLYV. Herbert J. Weber, general manager of WLYV, was named president of the Shephard Broadcasting Corp. in 1972. Radio Station WPTH, owned by Sarkes-Tarzian, Inc., was located at 3333 Butler Road with Dave Miller, manager. Radio WMEE and WMEF, which formerly had been WKJG Radio, was owned by Northeastern Indiana Radio, Inc., 2915 Maples Road. Burt Sherwood was general manager. WFWR, managed by Edwin Moore, had studios at 424 Reed Road. Creative and diversified radio programming gradually declined during the 1950's and 1960's. Radio, with a few exceptions, became a medium for transmission of popular music on record and tape, occasional news and quiz spots. By 1970, stations were being humorously compared with "one-room bookstores which only sold comic books." But some stations were clearly trying to present more than the lowest denominator in the music field and there were indications of a positive evolution in radio.

The Pre-Panic Banks

In the late 1920's prior to the bank panic in the early 1930's, there were 12 banks serving the financial needs of the people of Fort Wayne. Only two of them would survive the panic and events surrounding the bank holiday without reorganization or bankruptcy proceedings, or simply quitting business. The banks operating in the decade before the Depression, together with the principal officers, included: The Bowser Loan and Trust Co., 1341 East Creighton Ave., O. W. Scheumann, president; William L. Greibel, H. J. Grosvenor, and Jacob Bill, vice-presidents; and H. H. Hesemeyer, secretary. The Broadway State Bank, corner of Broadway and Taylor St., E. A. Barnes, president; M. M. Beaver, vice-president; and George W. Clark, cashier. Citizens Trust Company, Calhoun and Berry Streets, O. N. Heaton, president; W. E. Doud and E. F. Yarnelle, vice-presidents; William B. Gutelius, secretary; and Jesse E. Eschbach, trust officer. The Dime Savings and Trust Co., Court and Berry Streets, Harry Hogan, president; Charles A. Spanley, Oscar A. Fox and W. Clyde Quimby, vice-presidents, and James E. Ruhl, secretary. The East Side State Bank, 1201 Maumee Ave., B. F. Geyer, president; G. A. Berghoff, and H. W. Meinzen, vice-presidents, and Ora M. Blaker, cashier. First and Tri-State National Bank and Trust Company, 119-129 West Berry St., Charles A. Wilding, chairman; C. M. Niezer, president; E. G. Hoffman, H. A. Keplinger, J. R. McCulloch, E. F. Scheumann, E. J. Disser, E. L. Hobrock, H. C. Fair, F. J. Mills, F. C. Heine, G. M. Leslie, E. F. Yarnelle, Max B. Fisher and William C. Rastetter, vice-presidents, and Peter M. Certia, vice-president and trust officer. The Fort Wayne Morris Plan Co., 217 East Berry St., Theodore F. Thieme, chairman; Harry A. Perfect, president; Clinton R. Willson and Maurice Niezer, vice-presidents; Mrs. Grace D. Binder, secretary and manager; and William E. Morton, treasurer. Lincoln National Bank & Trust Company, 719 Court St. and The Lincoln Tower as of 1930, Samuel M. Foster, chairman; Charles H. Buesching, president; George Waldschmidt, Henry W. Lepper, John F. Utt, John J. Disser and Edwin Dickmeyer, vice-presidents; and Oscar H. Bushing, cashier. The North Side State Bank, 1615 Wells St., Walter E. Cook, president; P. C. Dooley, vice-president; and Merle Phillips, cashier. Old National Bank, corner of Calhoun and Berry Streets, Henry C. Paul, chairman; Frank H. Cutshall, president; F. William Hitzeman, vice-president; Stephen Morris, cashier; and C. W. Dannenfelser, trust officer. The Peoples Trust & Savings Company, 913 South Calhoun St., Patrick J. McDonald, president; August E. Becker, vice-president; Donnelly P. McDonald, secretary-treasurer. The South Side State Bank, 2600 South Calhoun St., William C. Rastetter, president; Herman Freiburger, Frank J. Gilmartin and J. B. McKim, vice-presidents; and Fred D. Hoham, Jr., cashier.

In subsequent years, the Dime Savings and Trust would become the Indiana Bank and Trust Co.; the Fort Wayne Morris Plan would become the Anthony Wayne Bank; and the First & Tri-State National Bank would become the Fort Wayne National Bank. Some of the others passed out of existence.

The origins of the Fort Wayne National Bank go back to the community's early financial institutions of the 19th Century. Charles H. Worden brought about a consolidation in 1905 of the First National Bank and the White National Bank. In 1917 the Hamilton National Bank was consolidated with the same institution and Worden was named president of the combined banking firm. In 1919, Worden proposed buying the site of the Barnes Building in the 100 block of West Berry St. which had been formerly occupied by Wolf & Dessauer. The First National Bank Building was erected at the location in 1920. Subsequently, the Tri-State Loan & Trust was consolidated with First National. The Dime Savings and Trust Co., a state bank, was founded by Harry Hogan in 1922, and in 1930 was relocated at the northwest corner of Clinton and Wayne Sts. in a building which previously had housed the White National Bank.

The only two firms to survive the bank panic of the early 1930's without reorganization were the Lincoln National Bank and the Peoples Trust & Savings Company. The Peoples Trust, the city's oldest bank following the Depression was founded in 1903 by William L. Moellering and Patrick J. McDonald. The Lincoln National Bank was founded in 1905 by Samuel Foster, Theodore Wentz, Charles Pfeiffer and Henry C. Berghoff, but was named the German-American National Bank for a short period.

The Lincoln Tower

The story of the erection of Indiana's tallest building just as the Great Depression was setting in has both its financial and human qualities. Charles H. Buesching, president of Lincoln National Bank during the crucial period, described years later the circumstances surrounding the erection of the Lincoln Tower. In 1927, Lincoln had acquired the Lincoln Trust Co. from the Straus Brothers Company, which made Lincoln a $14 million bank.

"That justified at the time thinking in terms of the new building with the result we developed the Lincoln Tower and broke ground for it 30 days after the market crash in 1929," Buesching related. The bank moved in and dedicated the building in November, 1930. How Lincoln Bank came to build such an imposing structure at that time was described by Buesching. He was asked by Clyde Cover if the Tower was his (Buesching's) idea.

"The Tower idea was completely my idea and the design of the building was my idea. In those days we had local architects, Weatherhogg and Mahurin, and my building committee was Arthur F. Hall, Oscar Foellinger, Frank Bond, A. G. Burry and W. F. Griffin, and they all favored the local architects but I simply couldn't enthuse over the designs that they were submitting.

"The designs were clumsy and I realized they would cost just as much money as a more ideal design and just before we were to choose one of the local designs a little runty salesman stepped up to me just fifteen minutes before we went into a meeting with my building committee. He represented Walker and Weeks, a famous architectural firm in Cleveland that had won the world competition design of the World War Memorial in Indianapolis and I told this gentleman, I said, 'Why didn't you show up here 30 days ago?'

"I told him my problem that I was having a meeting and it looked like we would have to choose a local design. Well he said give me a week and I'll give you a design but what kind of a design are you thinking about. I said I wanted a miniature Tribune Tower, the Chicago Tribune. He said I'll have it here within a week.

"So I stepped into that meeting and told the gentlemen that I was not enthused at all about local designs and if there was anything wrong about spending all that money that I would have to eat it, therefore, I was entitled to my own design. So I adjourned that meeting for a week and within a week they chose the Walker and Weeks design.

Floundering Banks

"Mr. Foster was then 80 years old, but little did he know at that time that by the time he moved into that building and he wouldn't be in it four years when the bank would have lost all of its competition, practically all of its competition, and I'll never forget the night that the Old National was merged into the First Tri-State in June of 1931. The bank examiners were in town and they had contacted me, said they might need me before the night was up.

"They were calling a special meeting of the Board of the First Tri-State. Charlie Niezer was President and I told them where they could reach me, so near midnight that night the examiner reached me and asked me to bring a few of my board members with me.

"They needed help in raising the capital required by the controller. So I called Samuel M. Foster, Arthur F. Hall and W. M. Griffin and the four of us arrived there just at midnight in the board room of what is now the Fort Wayne National Bank Board Room.

"There we were advised that the First Tri-State was insolvent and the demand was that two and a half million of new money had to be raised and the capital surplus of the First Tri was being wiped out and up until midnight that night the Board, the outgoing Board of the First Tri-State, had subscribed $1,400,000 of the two and one-half million with $1,100,000 to go and it had to be raised before the next morning at 9 o'clock. And so the examiners said your bank can afford to help out here and buy some of this stuff and maybe some of the other banks will follow and the balance we will have to raise around this Board and who have already subscribed substantially.

"So the examiners sent Mr. Niezer in to us and Mr. Niezer made quite an impassioned plea to the four of us. After he left I suggested that we buy $100,000 worth of stock and Foster, usually being quite conservative, he rather pooh-poohed my stingy offer of only a $100,000 worth of stock. He said they need more money than that, whereupon I told him that I'm responsible for the Lincoln Bank and its investments and things are tough and we can't afford to risk more than $100,000 and if there is any more than that it will have to be taken by you three directors or Lincoln Life, anything above $100,000. I'll never approve more than $100,000.

"Whereupon Foster said 'I will take $20,000' and Mr. Griffin said he would take $10,000 and Arthur Hall said Lincoln Life will take the other $70,000. I said, 'All right, then I am authorized now to announce to the controller here and the examiners that we will take $200,000.'

"They said, 'Yes.' So we called in the chief examiner and told him that I would personally make an announcement before the Board, the outgoing Board of the First-Tri, but I wanted to hear from Frank Cutshall, who was the President of the Old National, and Henry Paul, the Chairman, and they were to take charge the next morning as the new Chairman of the Board and the new President. So he took me in to the Board Room and announced that Mr. Buesching was announcing a subscription but he wanted it confirmed from Frank Cutshall and Henry C. Paul that they would be in charge of management the next morning and that two and one-half million dollars of cash would be subscribed before 9 o'clock the next morning. That announcement was then made to me in the Board Room whereupon I announced the $200,000 subscription of which Lincoln Life finished up with $80,000 instead of $70,000. They took Mr. Griffin's share."

"I see. And that saved the day?" asked Clover of Buesching.

"That was $200,000 from the two Lincolns and Foster and then the Peoples Trust bought, I think $60,000 of stock and the Dime bought $10 or $20 thousand. Those three banks then produced about another $300,000. The balance they got out of the directors and we loaned a hundred thousand in a trusteeship headed by Fred Shoaff. We loaned a hundred and the Indianapolis and Chicago banks loaned the other five hundred and so the result was that money was borrowed, six hundred thousand by a pledge of stock. Well, the bank held them from June '31 until the moratorium was declared on March 3, 1933, and then went into liquidation. So our write off, our charge off on our bank's accommodation to that bank was $200,000."

"Is that so?" Cover said.

"Yes, we wrote that off as a permanent loss. Lincoln Life wrote their $80,000 off as a permanent loss and Samuel M. Foster, of course, wrote his $20,000 off," Buesching said.

"I remember that sequence of failures. The effort to save the—"

"Well, for the time being it saved the situation and they went into receivership in '33 and out of the receivership came what is today known as the Fort Wayne National Bank."

The Power Struggle

"A strange thing in Fort Wayne in all those years the names of Foster and Hall predominated. I'm thinking now of say, beginning 1918 and going on through to 1930. There was that other group, with the exception of Fred Shoaff, who were tied in with the early aristocrats of the city. They usually started with a bank connection. The oldest banks in the city were the Old National, the First National and the Hamilton. Those were the three aristocratic banks, pioneered by the Hamiltons, the McCullochs, the Wordens, the Voors, the Basses. Well the founders of those banks were all a bit clanish. Four national banks and three state banks, while the little German-American Bank organized by Foster was just kind of a dog. It was a dog for many years and the minute the bank opened it started a fight among banks. The leading banks immediately raised the interest rate on savings from 2% to 4% the day the bank opened. Twenty-five years later they were all broke, every one of them except the Peoples Trust. It took 25 years for those chickens to come home to roost with the result that Lincoln Life was organized largely out of Lincoln Bank, big money, Bill Griffin and that type of man," Buesching related.

"Friends of Foster?" Cover asked.

"Friends of Foster. The other banks, they always pooh-poohed Lincoln Life even to the point of recognizing the stock as collateral, and that persisted until the panic. All through Hall's life.

"So while there was no legal relations between the two institutions there was a genuine friendship, kinship?"

"Yes, by reason of the sponsors—well there was Edward Dodez and Joe Hutzell, Griffin, largely out of the Lincoln Bank."

"And the Mossmans?"

"The Mossmans were the only one, I forgot them. The Mossmans were out of the other group," Buesching said. "But very largely—the other banking groups—those that founded them, those that became prosperous, they were sort of away from Lincoln Life and to this day they don't own any of it."

"The panic and all the things that that brought with it—when 1933 came along we had lost all of our commercial bank competition in the city. You see at the time the Lincoln Bank was organized in 1905 we already had four national banks in the city. First National Bank, The Old National Bank, Hamilton National Bank and the White National. We had the Tri-State Loan and Trust which in 1930 was the largest state bank in Indiana outside of the capitol city at Indianapolis. We had the Peoples Trust Company and the Citizens Trust. So there were seven banks in operation at the time the German-American was organized in 1905. When 1933 came along there was only the Lincoln National and the Peoples Trust Company and, of course, by reason of that and the recovery years when we moved into the '40's, why we zoomed naturally and even today in Fort Wayne we have but five banks," Buesching said.

Weathering the Storm

"How did you weather the storm that the others went down under? You must have had a very sound banking position."

"Well, those days during the panic years, beginning about 1930, it was a blessing not to be too large," Buesching continued. "We were a small bank and the bank had always been a good earning bank right from its inception and it has always carried in relation to its deposit liabilities, a comfortable investment of capital and those things in the panic years were of great importance. It was capital that saved the bank. Capital and liquidity, of course, ability to convert to cash."

"The failure of the other banks cast a

shadow over the Lincoln too, didn't it?" Cover asked.

"It created very considerable problems in the way of runs, quiet runs and over a period of three years, three or four years."

"Then when the panic eliminated your competitors you were almost on a straight away weren't you? And you had the beautiful Lincoln Tower as glowing tribute to your strength."

"Well it did not particularly contribute to our strength at all. The facts are—brick and mortar—if you have too much of your capital tied up in brick and mortar it's a weakness. However, we remained solvent and weathered the panic in spite of the building. You understand, of course, you saw our statement of March 4, 1933, the day that Franklin Delano Roosevelt declared the banking holiday, you will find there in order for our bank to maintain its legal reserve that when he closed all the banks of the nation on March 4, 1933, we closed with our full legal reserve intact as the percentage of total deposits. However to do that we resorted to borrowing from various sources. We pledged our Government Bonds, we pledged eligible paper, we pledged mortgages with the Reconstruction Finance Corporation and we borrowed on mortgages from the Lincoln Life on the Lincoln Tower. Lincoln Life loaned us $650,000 on the first mortgage in about 1931. On March 4, 1933, that mortgage was paid down to $450,000. We still owed Lincoln Life $450,000 on March 4, 1933. However when we reopened on March 14, 1933, the deposits zoomed on the up side from then on. It was a very quick recovery and within two years all of our debts were liquidated and deposits have been rising ever since. We were down to $5,000,000 in deposits in March 4, of '33 from a high of $14,000,000 and, of course, we have seen deposits since as high as $132,000,000," Buesching said in 1956.

"Don't you think that notwithstanding the peril that you invited in building more brick and mortar than you actually needed for your banking purposes that that tower has been a symbol of strength and a real asset to you in public relations?"

"I would have to admit that from the standpoint of influence on the public the Tower has added an effect of stability and has generated confidence and, of course, we built that, finished the building in 1930 at a cost of $1,800,000," Buesching concluded.

The financial crisis of the early 1930's was an event of far-reaching consequences which touched most every family and business in Fort Wayne. More than the banks themselves were in jeopardy. Industrial and commercial firms, dependent on banks for their accounts and loans, were in frequent instances driven to insolvency. Individuals with savings deposits found themselves without funds with the failure of some of the banks.

One other financial institution weathered the panic years. This was the Fort Wayne Clearing House Association. The association makes daily clearings between member banks, handling negotiable paper and compiling statistical data of bank credits and debits. It was formed by Henry C. Paul, Samuel Foster, J. H. Bass, Charles McCulloch and J. W. White, all national bank presidents, on Feb. 8, 1905. The original executive-secretary of the unit was Paul F. Kuhne. In subsequent decades A. W. Suelzer was executive secretary.

The First Federal Savings and Loan Assn., 719 Court St., was founded in 1934 upon being chartered by the Federal Government. James H. Haberly was the first president. He was succeeded in 1955 by H. Paul Haberly.

Ice Men Came

In 1930, Fort Wayne was very much the neighborhood town. People had yellow and black cards in their front windows with the figures 25, 50, 75 and 100 on each side. That way the ice man when he came up the street every third day could read from the curbside how large of a block to bring in. If the card was placed in the window so 50 was on top, then 50 pounds of ice was pulled off the ice wagon, flipped on the iceman's leather-protected shoulder with tongs and walked into the kitchen and put in the box. When the iceman came into the house, he always

yelled: "Iceman." In 1930 and for some years thereafter ice wagons were still hauled by horses who seemed to know the route and the right places to stop. There were numerous ice companies, which for some reason, were often also coal companies. A large percentage of homes of that era had coal fired furnaces.

There was little fast traffic on the streets, but there was a lot of noisy slow traffic. The most common motor vehicle was the Tin Lizzie, or Ford Model T. It was inevitably black which Henry Ford said was the color anyone wanted.

But there was other traffic, each with its distinctive sound. Bon-Ton, Leland and other bakeries had their regular and faithful customers in every neighborhood. In each block the driver would stop and pull out trays of his fresh and delightful wares for the housewives and their children who would come out of the surrounding houses. Nearly every morning had its excuses for small get-togethers. Butter and egg men, always with distinctive rural accents, white pants and black purses, would also have their regular rounds. Some of the butcher markets had motorcycle delivery.

A large portion of the streets in 1930 were red brick. The hooves of horses and the iron wheels of wagons made their special music on such surfaces. In the distance, in most parts of town in the fairly confined limits of 1930, could be heard the cadence and shudder of railroad steam engines. More than 100 trains daily operated in and through the city. In addition there was the commotion of the switching in the several railroad yards and around the roundhouses. The main roundhouses were near Gay St. for the Pennsylvania Railroad and just off Fairfield for the Wabash. There were yards east and west of these points and also west of North Clinton St. for the New York Central and just east of town for the Nickel Plate. The steaming passenger trains would sound their high-pitched whistles as would the fast freights as they chugged along their way. All the trains had bells which were clanging almost constantly.

Little boys wore knickers and girls had long black stockings. Few had enough for bicycles. But all could walk and run in relative safety most everyplace they wanted to go in the city. There were parks but not supervised playgrounds. Children in the parks just did what they wanted to do. When the ponds of Lakeside and the Reservoir and other parks froze over, the kids tested the ice. If it supported them they went ice skating. There were no red flags or lights and there were far more days of skating. Also there was an occasional wet leg, and in a few instances, a drowning.

The Neighbor Stores

Every drug store and grocery had its penny candy counters. And each neighborhood had its corner grocery and drug stores. There were no super markets. Everyone in the stores would likely know the other, and speak unless someone had a specific reason for not speaking. Children spent a lot of time in the corner stores, or in going to and from them.

Just how much shopping habits and patterns have changed with the years can be seen by referring to the 1930 City Directory. In that year, there were 268 grocery stores in Fort Wayne—practically all of the family-run neighborhood variety with a few larger operations downtown such as the Central Grocery at Wayne and Harrison Sts. run by Lawrence, Marce and Clarence Freiburger. Of all those 268 grocery stores operating in the 1920's and 1930's, only two are still going at the old stand in 1974. One was Heiny's at 435 West Creighton Avenue. In 1930, it was operated by Lawrence Heiny. In 1974, Lawrence's sons Nicholas and Joe were in charge. Two meat markets were still going in 1974 at the approximate locations as 1930. These were the Bazley Market, 120 West Wayne St., just down the street from the 108 West Wayne location of 1930, and the Kelpin Market, 419 East Lewis St., listed in 1930 at 421 East Lewis. The other grocery store, in addition to Heiny's to be still in business at the same location was Redding's Self Service at 1102 Rivermet Ave. which was operated in 1930 by Elzie D. Redding.

A little farther for most but still within

walking distance of neighborhoods, were the barber shops. They usually were the one or two-seat variety. A hair cut in the early Thirties was 25 cents in the union shops and 15 cents in the others. The magazines were just as out-dated in those years as in later times. Comic magazines hadn't yet made their appearance, but big-little books were the in thing with the young set.

Shoe shops were a little less prevalent than the barber shops—one every six or eight blocks in any direction. Most were manned by a single cobbler, and only the fancy downtown shoe parlors had boot blacks. These were concentrated along Calhoun and Main Streets.

For some reason, every child knew where the houses of prostitution were—always called "whore houses" or "cat houses." On dull afternoons, children found a trek to such locations and pointing out of the ill-reputed houses an always-diverting event. The conversation at such times was always hushed, except for a parting yell by a dare-devil type. Whore houses were big or numerous at three places in those days. Several were upstairs in the red brick buildings along the west side of South Calhoun, from the railroad elevation to Douglas Street. And they really did have red lights, only at the alley entrances. An ancient hotel on north side Columbia St. just up from the Spy Run Bridge was earlier notorious. But the largest concentration of low life in Summit City was along Huff Street. A whole row of houses, with a figure inevitably sitting by a large front window of each, was there. The real name of the street was Hayden, but it was always called Huff St. in the key block and there was hardly a person in town who didn't recognize the implication.

In Shantytown

In 1930, and more during the few years following, vagabonds were commonplace. They were usually called "Tramps" but sometimes by the more romantic name of "hobos." They were men down on their luck who searched along the streets and alleys. Women tramps were rare. There was probably not a street in Fort Wayne in the early 1930's on which tramps wouldn't be trudging along a couple times a week—at least during the warm weather. They would stop at houses for a meal or some other handout. Some would mark "good" houses with pieces of chalk for future reference. It was quite common for people to go out and inspect the siding of the house after such visits and look for the mark and, if there, rub it off. The closer to the railroads, the greater the hobo traffic since the freight rods and empty box cars were the transportation modes of the genre. Fort Wayne was known as one of the Hobo Capitals for a period. Others included Mattoon, Ill., and Harrisburg, Pennsylvania.

It was at this time that Fort Wayne became the location of a Hooverville, or Shantytown as it was actually called. As the Great Depression deepened, the community of the desperate grew. The Shantytown was situated between Calhoun and Clinton Sts., a stone's throw from the County Jail, and in the "flats" area south of the St. Mary's River. This was in the days before Welfare Departments and the only official agencies were the Township Trustees with their soup kitchens. Mostly, those in extreme poverty and on the edge of starvation depended on scrounging and charity of individuals or a few organizations.

At first, only a few families moved into the area. But in 1931 and 1932 hundreds moved in, ever-increasing despite some public complaint about the squatters. They lived in small wheel houses or tar-paper shacks. Inevitably, if a crime was committed in the city, the first place a search was made was in Shantytown. Knowledgeable people of the period, however, reported most residents of the Shantytown were good decent people in dire circumstances. Smoke from their fires would occasionally drift as far as the downtown district, a half dozen blocks to the south. The health conditions were not pleasant. The drifting away from Fort Wayne's Hooverville began almost as soon and quietly as the deposit of humanity had begun. But it was gradual. Old photos by a government agency show a few of the hovels were still scattered about as late as 1937. Soon thereafter they disappeared completely.

People were much more aware of the city environment in 1930 for the very reason that the community was of a much more compact size. According to the 1930 census, Fort Wayne had a population of 115,121—really not so much smaller a number than the 177,000 recorded in the census of 1970. Yet the 1930 population lived within city limits of 17.45 square miles—little more than one-tenth the city area some 40 years later. The map of the city in 1930 shows a fairly square town, four miles long and four miles wide, with hardly any place more than two miles from downtown. Just about the most distant place a person could get from the central business district was Foster Park on the southwest edge of the city. There was little in the way of residential districts and practically no business outside the city limits, other than at the towns of New Haven, Monroeville, Woodburn, Leo, Hoagland, Grabill or Huntertown.

The Gangsters

In the late 1920's and early 1930's a wave of crime and violence struck Fort Wayne unlike anything in the community's previous history. Bank robberies, shootings and killings, and raids involving the illicit liquor business highlighted the era of lawlessness and banditry.

Beginning in 1930, there were a number of spectacular crimes in Fort Wayne or involving Fort Wayne people which continued until gangland shootouts with police and federal agents in 1934.

On August 20, 1930, a Chicago gang led by George (Machine Gun) Kelly, 35, robbed the Broadway State Bank at the northwest corner of Broadway and Taylor Street. Others identified in the robbery included William Naecker, George Smith and Abe Schultz. During the holdup George W. Clark, cashier of the bank, was pistol whipped about the head; and bank customer Theodore Ruby, Blue Lake, was wounded by shotgun pellets. The bandits escaped with $5,912 in an automobile. All four were later captured and returned by Chicago authorities to Fort Wayne for trial. Kelly, Naecker and Smith were tried first, and convicted by a jury. Judge Sol A. Wood of Allen Circuit Court gave each of them 15-year sentences at the Michigan City Prison. Asked if he had anything to say before the passing of the sentence, Kelly replied: "All I can say is that I am innocent. We are victims of a frame-up of the State of Indiana and the Chicago Police Department." Seven guards in the charge of Sheriff George W. Gillie rode shotgun as the trio left Fort Wayne on the way to prison.

One of the more savage crimes involved a former Fort Wayne securities broker who gunned down a Chicago policeman in the early hours of April 13, 1931. F. Guy Sprague, charged with the murder of the police officer, had earlier been indicted at Fort Wayne in 1923 for embezzlement of $1 million from investors. A number of prominent Fort Wayne families and business people were among the heavy losers, according to a grand jury report. Sprague had represented a New York Stock Exchange member for some 10 years in Fort Wayne. In the 1931 killing, Sprague fired two revolver slugs into the midsection of Patrolman Patrick J. Gallagher when the Chicago policeman and two fellow officers interrupted a wild party of Sprague's in a Chicago Hotel. With Sprague at the time was John W. Eidner, also from Fort Wayne.

The Speakeasies

There were a number of indications that bootleggers were operating rather openly in Fort Wayne in the spring of 1931. News reports, grand jury investigations and peculiar shifts in police personnel all pointed to irregularities. On May 28, 1931, County Prosecutor Walter E. Helmke complained to Board of Safety Chairman J. A. Curtin about the removal of Officer Walter Hollman from the dry squad and other frequent shifts which made it difficult to convict bootleggers in Allen County.

"I am aware of the fact that there are hundreds of people who are not in sympathy with the enforcement of the prohibition laws of this state. However, I also know there are just as many, if not more people who believe in the enforcement of all laws as long as they remain upon the statute books. I further feel that no official of this City or this State has a right to permit his personal feelings to control in matters involving the enforcement of the laws." It was a case of a Republican County official complaining to a Democratic City official, but there was little question that the law was hardly being enforced. By 1931, Prohibition had had it. "I feel, therefore, that a grave mistake has been made by the removal of Officer Walter Hollman from the dry squad, assuming, at least, that your Board is in favor of the enforcement of our prohibition law and other vice laws," Helmke told Curtin in a public letter after describing the difficulties encountered by the shifting of dry squad officers after a few weeks.

Apparently they turned to Federal officers for enforcement. Late the night of July 10 and early July 11, 1931, Federal prohibition agents raided numerous speakeasies and roadhouses in Allen County, arresting 24 proprietors, bartenders and musicians. Thirty G-men, divided in small groups and heavily armed, made the raids. Large quantities of whisky, gin, alcohol and beer were seized at all the places raided; and fixtures and equipment were dismantled and seized. Imported spirits, Canadian beer and moonshine had been concealed in "plants" between walls and floors of several buildings. One of the Federal agents, unnamed but called "the Ace" was credited with working under cover in the community, lining up the offenders and methods of operations. Some of the establishments raided included the Orchard Ridge Inn on the Lower Huntington Road; Jimmy Cress's Place at 124½ East Wayne St.; a roadhouse called the Riverside Club on River Road; Woodies Place on East Washington Blvd.; a speakeasy at 306 South Harrison St.; a roadhouse called Bob and Ted's on the Aboite Center Road, and others. The accused were bound over to the U.S. District Court. Most of them claimed they were only musicians or entertainers at the various places and had no knowledge of any illegal operations.

The following night, July 11, 1931, there was "a followup of the county-wide Federal onslaught on liquor places." Agents hit the soft-drink parlor of Sam Hess at 2202 Fairfield Ave. and news headlines the following day told the story of "Big Beer Plant Seized in Raid." Officers seized and destroyed a complete beer manufacturing plant and a large assortment of liquors, 16-gallon kegs of moonshine, two bars, 200-gallon tanks of beer. Quite a number of customers, including a deputy sheriff who at first gave a phony name, were in the place when it was raided. In addition, "Such a large crowd gathered when the raid was staged that it was necessary for police to direct the traffic in front of the place," it was reported.

The gangsters struck back the following night, Sunday, July 12, at the Emboyd Theater. The action was both on the screen and at the box office. While a new gangster film starring Edward G. Robinson called "Little Caesar" was being shown on the silver screen, a real life gunman walked up to theater manager B. L. Clark and pulled a .32 calibre automatic. The bandit forced six people into the Emboyd office and stand with faces to the wall while he scooped some $2,000 in cash from the safe. The outlaw then went out the front door, jumped into a waiting car driven by an accomplice and escaped east on Jefferson Street.

Federal Agents Slain

On July 22, 1931, the Federal agents again pushed their war against the illegal liquor traffic and ran into disaster. In a gunfight near the Stellhorn Bridge two government men were gunned down and killed within minutes. The U.S. special agents killed were John I. Wilson, 40, of Indianapolis, and Walter N. Gilbert, 33, of Cincinnati. The shootout occurred at 8 p.m. along the Lower Huntington Road. Charged with the killings was George Adams, a 35-year-old ex-convict and Leavenworth alumnus. The News-Sentinel of July 23, 1931, described the situation in a manner which would have caused civil libertarians of later generations to throw up their hands. "George Adams, notorious Fort Wayne bootlegger who shot and killed two Federal prohibition agents near Fort Wayne Wednesday evening, held to his constitutional rights and refused to make a statement or answer questions when taken to the police station after his capture early this morning. Adams refused to say anything and was finally locked up and held on a murder charge without bond. His capture came on a tip from U.S. Deputy Marshal Herman Atkins which sent a police squad hurrying to the home of Frank Kenjerski, 1906 East Rudisill Boulevard. They failed to find Adams there but he drove up in a touring car . . . and surrendered without a fight despite the fact that his gun was clutched butt-up between his knees." Officers had trained shotguns on Adams.

The court case was a celebrated one, with a peculiar ending. At the outset, U.S. District Attorney Oliver M. Loomis arrived in Fort Wayne to assist Prosecuting Attorney Walter E. Helmke. Loomis declared: "The government will offer every possible assistance in all of its investigating department and I will offer the assistance of my own office to the prosecutor's office to put this man (Adams) in the electric chair." Newspapers headlined that the cop killer "Must Die Say Loomis, Helmke." The killing drew thousands to the site along the St. Mary's River. "Thousands of cars jammed the nearby highways shortly after the killing of two Federal agents on the Lower Huntington Road Wednesday night. Sirens on ambulances and many police cars as they sped to the scene of the crime acted as magnets to the curious and those in quest of excitement," it was reported. "The news bulletin over WOWO was repeated several times, the name and description of the slayer, together with a description of the car being given. Hundreds of adventuresome motorists, assuming roles of amateur policemen, drove about the vicinity."

When Adams appeared in Allen Circuit Court for the trial he was described as "a typical gangster, suave in the courtroom with diamonds on his fingers and neatly dressed in gangster style." The trial got underway Nov. 3 with Helmke and Dan C. Flanagan handling the government case and David E. Smith and R. C. Parrish the defense attorneys. At the outset, newspapers were speculating on whether Judge Clarence R. McNabb would hand down the death penalty after the jury reached the verdict. The trial dragged on until Nov. 17. Rather incredibly for one accused of killing two Federal agents and having a history of illegal activities, George Adams was only found guilty of voluntary manslaughter, carrying a penalty of 2 to 21 years imprisonment. Three years later he was out of prison and back in the city.

Mayor Harry L. Kelly of Montpelier, Indiana, and T. C. Peterson, the Montpelier city attorney, were arrested on July 28, 1931, in Fort Wayne on a Federal warrant charging conspiracy to violate the National Prohibition Act. Federal agents had raided a race track and concession ground which existed at Montpelier and was operated by the political figures and others. According to charges, liquor and beer was being handled on the premises.

Stink Bombs and Arson

Several other rather unusual cases were handled in Fort Wayne by Federal officials in 1931. On May 15, Henry Stoeff, a wrestler and wrestling promoter in the city was ordered deported to Bulgaria. Accused and convicted of violation of the National Immigration Act, Stoeff was ordered to be at Detroit by May 23 when a whole trainload of aliens were to be taken to New York for embarkation. Also, a Fort Wayne family of four was ordered to appear at Detroit for the same train and for deportation to Germany. They were Mr. and Mrs. Alfred Rommel and their two children, all of 2008 Hillsdale Avenue.

There were also arson and several bombings toward the end of 1931. On September 15, the Shady Grove Dance Hall on Olla Drive near Bass Road was burned down. Two weeks later Deputy Sheriff Charles Coulardot arrested Albert Dollarhite, proprietor of a dance hall on Wayne Trace, for the crime of arson. According to witnesses, Dollarhite had earlier threatened the owner of Shady Grove, Mrs. Olla Lathrop, and had attempted to hire at least two persons to set the fire. Early on the morning of Nov. 7, there was a blast in the lobby of the Creighton Theater, East Creighton Ave. at John Street. Investigating police found a bomb had been constructed with a lead pipe and had been tossed into the theatre. It was the second attempt to bomb the Creighton Theatre. Several months earlier, much of the State Theater on East State Blvd. had been destroyed. Also threatened was the Capitol Theatre in the 100 block of West Main Street. There was considerable difficulty at the time over attempts to unionize theatre employees. A number of movie houses, including the Indiana Theater on Broadway, were emptied by stink bombs or gas bombs during the era.

On June 29, 1934, at about 4:30 a.m., the town marshal of Ligonier was gunned down and killed by four Fort Wayne men. The Fort Wayne men, all captured later the same day, were Virgil Hoffman, 22; Howard Campfield, 32; Walter O'Betzney, 26, and Walter Elliott, 20. They had gone to Ligonier to hijack slot machines. Hoffman was the trigger man. He later told reporters: "We had not gone very far when these two fellows, I guess it was the marshal and the other copper, stepped up and began to question us. There was this big .45 looking at me. Hell, I didn't want to get shot in the face so I knocked it up and as it went off, the slug creased the top of my head. I drew my gun and fired two or three shots. He dropped, but fired one more shot." Hoffman of 720 Anderson Ave., Fort Wayne, was sentenced to life in prison by Judge Robert McNagny of the Noble-Whitley Circuit Court for the murder of Edward Keasey, 58, the Ligonier official.

Dillinger & Company

It was during the greatest heat wave in the history of Fort Wayne with a 106-degree Sunday temperature that news of the slaying of John Dillinger startled people on July 22, 1934. Newsboys could be heard hawking "Extra, Extra," long after midnight along many Fort Wayne streets. No less than three members of Dillinger's gang were from Fort Wayne, and the greatest manhunt in the history of the Nation was rumored to have started with "an information" from one of the three who was bargaining a murder sentence. Though Dillinger never robbed a bank in Fort Wayne, he was in Fort Wayne frequently during his wild years and was sighted in bars along Fairfield Ave. and West Main Street. He and members of his gang raided police stations in three towns nearby. The raids on police stations were called "an innovation in modern banditry" by an INS story out of Indianapolis. "The gang's spectacular exploits against policemen included the following police station holdups: Auburn, Ind., October 16, 1933; Peru, Ind., October 20, 1933; and Warsaw, Ind., April 13, 1934. These raids netted the desperadoes the following armament: 3 machine guns, 19 bullet-proof vests, 3 sawed-off shotguns, 2 riot guns, 13 automatic pistols and revolvers, 7 high powered rifles, sets of handcuffs, and police badges." One of the vests taken at Peru was believed worn by Dillinger in the robbery of the First National Bank at East Chicago. "Dillinger rushed out of the bank with his loot after the East Chicago holdup to find Detective William Patrick O'Malley and other policemen barring the way. The officers fired at Dillinger, but the bullets, according to eye-witnesses, rattled off Dillinger's bullet-proof vest like hail falling off a tin roof. The public enemy then opened up with his machine gun and dropped O'Malley," the INS reported. Other sources said O'Malley was nearly cut in two.

The three bank robbers from Fort Wayne associated with Dillinger were Clifford Mohler, Sam Goldstein and Homer Van Meter. "It was through the arrest of Clifford Mohler and Sam Goldstein, companions of Dillinger, that State Police learned of his operations. Then began the first manhunt," the Associated Press reported. This was in late summer of 1933 just a couple months after Dillinger's release from the State Prison. Clifford Mohler, 36, had been convicted in 1926 in Allen Circuit Court of murdering

Fort Wayne police officer Martin Gephart. He was given a "leave of absence" from his life sentence at the penitentiary in June, 1933, the same month Dillinger was paroled. He was captured August 19 after bank robberies and put in solitary confinement where he reportedly told East Chicago Police Sgt. Martin Zarkovich information which eventually led to the killing of Dillinger. Like Sam Goldstein, Mohler spent much of his life in prison.

Homer Van Meter

After Dillinger was shot by Federal agents outside the Biograph Theatre in Chicago on July 22, 1934, Melvin Purvis, the youthful head of the Chicago Bureau of the FBI (then called the U.S. Department of Investigation), refused to identify the two women who were at the movie with Dillinger. Federal officers said the reason was for their safety because three of Dillinger's chief lieutenants were still at large. The FBI put George (Baby Face) Nelson, Homer Van Meter and John Hamilton at the top of the Most Wanted list. All three were to die in gun battles with police. Van Meter was not believed to have been with the gang which broke into the Lima, Ohio, County Jail on October 12, 1933, killing Sheriff Jess Sarber and freeing Dillinger. But Van Meter was Dillinger's most constant companion and gunman during the wild final months in 1934. Van Meter's name was first linked to Dillinger in news stories on April 13. "Armed with machine guns, two men, positively identified as John Dillinger and his new partner, Homer Van Meter, formerly of Fort Wayne, swooped down on the Warsaw Police Station shortly before 1 a.m. today, and stole three bullet-proof vests and two revolvers after clubbing Night Officer Jud Pittinger, aged 47, and forcing him to open the station." At one point Pittinger grabbed the barrel of Dillinger's gun. "Don't try to take it," Dillinger said. "He (Van Meter) will kill you." Van Meter reportedly wanted to "drill him" but in a fit of anger "struck the officer savagely on the head three or four times with the officer's own gun."

Van Meter, who started his career as a train robber at the age of 19, was at the Michigan City Prison with Dillinger, and like Dillinger, Mohler and several others, was paroled in the great clemency movement of Gov. Paul V. McNutt in the spring of 1933. He was with Dillinger and the others at the shootout with Federal agents at the Spider Lake, Wisc., resort hotel in May, 1934. Two agents died and four were wounded, but all the gangsters escaped. Van Meter came to the end of the line just one month after Dillinger. On the night of August 23 at St. Paul, Minn., he was cut down by the bullets of police who were waiting in an ambush. The body was returned to Fort Wayne by railroad. Secret services were held at the Klaehn Funeral Home on the second floor. An empty casket was taken to the Lindenwood Cemetery, both as a dodge to excessive public curiosity and any possible attempts by fellow gangsters to take the body. Three days later the small family cortege made its way to Lindenwood for the actual burial. The day previously, a Monday evening, two men and a woman in a car with Illinois license plates approached a workman at Lindenwood and asked to see Van Meter's body. The workman told them it was in the vault and locked. "But we wish to see it," one man said. They got out of the car and tried to force the vault door. Unable to gain entrance, they drove off.

Later generations might find it difficult to visualize the impact and boldness of gang crime in the early 1930's. An International News Service story of March 3, 1934, gives a perspective: "So desperate became the crime situation in Indiana that Gov. Paul V. McNutt on October 26 (1933) ordered 640 Indiana National Guardsmen in 70 squads of nine men each to be mobilized as deputy sheriffs in an unprecedented war on the marauding convict gang." Launched was a "road blockade scheme in which flying squadrons of State Policemen and National Guardsmen secretly erected blockades on different roads and stopped all traffic for inspection."

The Federal Building

Bids for the construction of Fort Wayne's new Federal Building, across Harrison St. from the Lincoln Life Building, were taken by the U.S. Treasury Department on August 14, 1931. Construction work began a few weeks later. The plans for the building were prepared by architects Benjamin Morris of New York and Guy Mahurin of Fort Wayne. The new building, for the Post Office and Federal Court, replaced the Old Post Office at the corner of Berry and Clinton Streets. The new building was termed the "most up-to-date facility for receiving and distributing the mail in this part of the country." The three-story limestone structure was in a neo-classical style. The post office occupied the first floor and basement. The second and third floors were given to the U.S. District Court for Northern Indiana, the U.S. District Attorney's Office, the U.S. Commissioner, the Internal Revenue Service, the Federal Bureau of Investigation, the U.S. Army, Navy and Marine Corps recruiting offices. To make room for the Federal Building, which occupied the entire block between Harrison and Webster Sts., a number of structures, mostly aging residences, were razed.

The various Federal offices occupied the building on Harrison St. in 1932. The Post Office had been earlier located at three locations: 608 Clinton St., Court St., and from 1889 to 1932 at Berry and Clinton. Mail delivery was started in 1873. Prior to that time, people went to the post office to get their mail. When mail delivery was started in 1873, five carriers were hired and they delivered 410 letters, 418 newspapers and 11 postal cards on the first day. Also on the staff at that time were five clerks, a postmaster and assistant postmaster. A century later, in 1974, the Post Office was housed in seven buildings, including five substations. In addition there were 11 contract stations located in drug stores and other merchant operations. There were more than 600 employees on the payroll with salaries totalling $3,420,000 per year, handling mail for a 360 square mile area with a population of more than 200,000. Postmaster Eugene Gabriel reported in 1974 that the Fort Wayne Post Office was one of a group of 100 offices that furnish 60 per cent of the entire postal revenue of the country and account for only 30 per cent of the expense of the service. Postmasters at Fort Wayne over the years began with Benjamin Kercheval and Sam Hanna who were successively appointed by President James Monroe in 1820. Prior to Gabriel, the postmaster was Albert N. Smith who held the post from 1951 to 1965.

The separate District U.S. Court for Northern Indiana was created in 1928. The U.S. District Attorneys serving the court since that time through 1974 include, successively: Oliver Loomis; James R. Fleming; Alex M. Campbell; Gilmore Haynie; Joseph Lesh; Phil M. McNagny, Jr.; Kenneth Raub; Alfred Moellering; William Lee, and John Wilks. Secretaries in the U.S. Attorney's office include Jane Keefer and Margaret Long.

The U.S. Court in Indiana, of course, is far older but for more than a century it consisted of only one judicial district. The first appointed Federal judge in Indiana was Benjamin Parke. He was appointed March 6, 1817, by President James Monroe. The first judge named in the 20th Century was Albert Barnes Anderson who was appointed by President Theodore Roosevelt in 1902. Anderson served until 1925 at which time he was succeeded by Robert C. Baltzell. In 1928, when the State was divided into two districts, Baltzell became the first judge for the Southern District. The first judge appointed to the Northern Indiana Federal District was Thomas W. Slick, named on April 21, 1928.

Judge Luther Swygert was appointed in 1943 to succeed Slick. Swygert was appointed by President Franklin D. Roosevelt. Lynn Parkinson was added as a second judge for the Northern District of Indiana by appointment of President Dwight D. Eisenhower. Judge Robert Grant was appointed to succeed Parkinson in 1957. In 1962, Jesse E. Eschbach was appointed by President John F. Kennedy to succeed Judge Swygert. Swygert became Judge of the U.S. Court of Appeals at Chicago. In 1962, President Kennedy also appointed George Beamer to serve on the bench of the Northern District. Beamer's appointment gave the Northern

District three judges. One served in Fort Wayne; one in Hammond and one in South Bend. The District consisted of four divisions, with the fourth Lafayette Division cases being handled by Judge Eschbach. In 1973 Allan Sharpe was appointed by President Nixon to succeed Robert Grant who took senior status in December of that year. Frances T. Grandys was clerk of the District Court in 1974. Serving as deputy clerks for the Fort Wayne office since the 1950's were Jane Wood and Phillip L. Swihart.

Early Relief

To deal with worsening economic conditions and massive unemployment, The Administration of President Herbert Hoover began a number of programs which relied heavily on local organization and subscription. On Nov. 11, 1931, reports in Fort Wayne said: "More than 250 men will be placed at work Tuesday morning and by the end of the month approximately 1,000 will have been given employment through the $417,155 Federated Relief Agency Fund which has been pledged for the relief of the needy unemployed in Fort Wayne this winter." J. B. Wiles, director of the unemployment work, rather overshot on his estimate of the situation. "The splendid oversubscription of the relief agencies fund quota practically marks the end of the depression as far as Fort Wayne is concerned." Workers were "to be paid 35 cents an hour and to work in four eight-hour shifts, three times a month. The limitation on the amount of the time the men can be employed is to provide help to a greater number." Site for work included Bloomingdale Park, Foster Park, Vesey Park, Franke, West Swinney, Lawton and Hamilton Parks, the old Orphans Home on the Bluffton Road, and along the river banks. E. A. Barnes, president of the Federated Relief Agencies, was cited by President Hoover's Administration which said "Fort Wayne was an outstanding city in the American Nation today for caring for its own problem." Arthur F. Hall was general chairman of the fund drive. Other leading relief agency supporters were G. Irving Latz, Robert Koerber, Louis Schwan, Otto Marahrens, the Rev. Louis Rocca, Carl J. Suedhoff, Glen Fuller, Rev. Thomas Conroy and Rabbi Samuel Markowitz. It was the greatest effort in Fort Wayne up to that time to deal with dire human destitution and widespread unemployment; and the first major program to combat the Great Depression locally. But times would get worse and the broader Federal programs of the Roosevelt Administration were still more than a year away.

"Legalized beer made its debut in Fort Wayne at 12:01 this morning," reported Harold K. Milks in the Journal Gazette on April 7, 1933. A front page picture showed the "First Wave of Amber Flood" coming from the Berghoff Brewery. "According to Bernard A. Poelhuis, a brewmaster and superintendent of the Berghoff plant, 15,000 cases of beer will be ready by 7 a.m. today. Almost that much was sent out after midnight by truck," the report said. The picture showed Police Officers Custer Dunifon and Alfred Figel guarding an early shipment. Berghoff was the first brewery to get its product back onto shelves, tables, bars and restaurants. Centlivre was rolling out brew soon thereafter.

There were other diversions for people in Depression-prone 1933. Travelers to Chicago for the "Century of Progress" exhibition came back with stories of bold new things including a fan-dance show which made the name of Sally Rand a household word. Those going the other direction could take in the Ziegfield Follies in New York. Over the radio on June 14, 1934, came the blow-by-blow description by Clem McCarthy telling of the 11th-round knockout of Primo Carnera by Max Baer. The winner of the Nobel Prize for chemistry in 1934 was Harold Clayton Urey, who was born in 1893 at Walkerton, some 25 miles north of Fort Wayne, and who was a frequent visitor to the city. Urey was the discoverer of heavy hydrogen, called Deuterium.

Movie Queens

Hope Harriman was Fort Wayne's first gift to the movie world. Hope was the daughter of Sebastian and Mary Alspaugh, 2131 Cortland Avenue. She began film work in the silents in 1915. She appeared in hundreds of early movies, many of them shorts, and often had a surprised expression looking out from clusters of curls. On the stage she led the chorus in the Ziegfield Follies in 1917. Home for a visit in Fort Wayne in 1930, Hope described her first "talkie" which was being completed in Hollywood. It was entitled "The Wonderful Return" and included the song "After the Ball." Hope said, "Talkies are seven times harder to make than the silent film."

The best remembered film actress from Fort Wayne during the era of the silver screen was Carole Lombard. She began her career as a bathing beauty, but by the mid-1930's was a major film star. She combined happy physical assets with an easy manner and a natural sense of humor. She was born Carol Jane Peters in 1908 at Fort Wayne, Indiana. Her grandfather was John C. Peters who built the Wayne Hotel on Columbia St. in 1887. It was the city's first 100-room hotel and was later known as the Jones and Rosemarie Hotel. Presidents Benjamin Harrison and Rutherford B. Hayes stayed there and William Jennings Bryan spoke from the balcony on Oct. 21, 1896. During her childhood, Carol Jane Peters lived at a house at the southwest corner of Rockhill St. just off West Main Street. At the height of her career in the 1930's, Carole Lombard married Clark Gable, the leading male film star of the period. She was killed in an airplane crash in 1942 while on a War Bond promotion tour.

A number of Fort Wayne people remember Jane Peters (Carole Lombard) in her childhood years. Louis Niezer, born in 1907 just up Rockhill St. from Jane's house was a playmate in those days. Niezer, who later became president of Tokheim Corp. and the Fort Wayne Park Board, had a vivid memory of the great Hoffman Brothers Lumberyard fire of 1917 on nearby West Main Street. The fire, which swept the lumberyard, began about 7 p.m. and drew the interest of youngsters all around, including Niezer, undoubtedly the nine-year-old Jane and many others. Carole Lombard starred with Charles Laughton in "They Knew What They Wanted," directed by Garson Kanin. "Opposite Laughton in the film, and in every way, was the enchanting Carole Lombard, a forthright, down-to-earth and engaging lady," said movie critic George Oppenheimer. She co-starred with Frederic March in Ben Hecht's "Nothing Sacred," directed by William Wellman, and other fine films.

During the 1930's when Carole Lombard was starring in Hollywood, several future entertainers were preparing themselves in Fort Wayne. Herb Shriner was a student at South Side High School. Herb was born in 1918 at Toledo, but grew up in Fort Wayne. Ever the joker, he once said, "I was born in Ohio but moved to Indiana soon's I heard about it." By the late 1940's, Shriner was already a popular figure in entertainment, movies and radio. In the 1950's he had a regular network television show. He always acted the droll hayseed and had a unique manner about him. He was considered by many as one of the most original humorists in show business. Panning the folks back in Indiana was a way of life with Herb. "In my home town," he used to say, "they had a beauty contest and nobody won. They was a pretty lively bunch too. Saturday night 'twasn't nothin' for us to go down and watch a few haircuts." It was probably the best tongue-in-cheek description ever of what high school kids did during the 1930's in Fort Wayne. Working at the Rialto Theatre at Calhoun and Pontiac Streets in the late 1930's was Marilyn Maxwell. Marilyn was born in Iowa in 1922 but moved to Fort Wayne as a girl with her family. She went from ushering movie patrons at the Rialto to respectable parts in movies within a few years. She was a successful actress in the 1940's and a familiar figure in Bob Hope shows, tours and movies in the 1950's. Bill Blass was born in Fort Wayne in 1922. By the 1960's Blass was one of the top designers in the fashion world. Dick York was born in Fort Wayne in 1928, and was a familiar figure in movies and television shows. Pat McVey, a native of Fort Wayne, had a long career in movies and television. A lawyer by training, he practiced a few years in Fort Wayne during the 1930's before trying acting. He was "Steve Wilson of the Illustrated Press" and the detective opposite Victor Jory in "The Detectives" and in many other feature and series roles.

Olsen and Johnson, the comedy team of Hellzapoppin shows in the 1930's, 1940's and 1950's, hailed from Fort Wayne. Ole Olsen and Chic Johnson put together their show in Fort Wayne's Palace Theatre in 1936. They moved on to Broadway and by 1941 the variety and comedy show had run to 1,040 performances. Earl Wilson, national columnist of show people and cafe society, was from Ohio, but a frequent visitor to Fort Wayne where his sister Martha lived and also Wilson's mother in later years.

Edith Hamilton

Edith Hamilton was the descendant of Allen Hamilton, Fort Wayne's first sheriff and an Indian negotiator. Edith, however, may belong with a select few associated with Fort Wayne such as Vincennes, Anthony Wayne, Edward H. White II who carved permanent space for themselves in the world's chronicles. "In the matter of Greek scholarship, our debt to Edith Hamilton is similarly our wealth," the editor's of Time-Life Books once said. "Miss Hamilton was a very great lady of humanistic letters who died in June, 1963, at the age of 96. Her father started teaching her Latin at the age of nine, but she began teaching herself Greek at seven. As a girl, she customarily combed her hair and dressed with a Greek book propped upon her bureau. She grew up in Fort Wayne, Indiana, but the country of her soul awarded her its recognition when she was made an honorary citizen of Athens just four days short of her 90th birthday in 1957." Edith was the first woman student ever admitted to the University of Munich. She went on to become the headmistress of Bryn Mawr School of Baltimore in 1896. But it was not until after her retirement 26 years later that her real vocation began. In 1930, "The Greek Way" appeared. It was immediately seen by scholars and general readers as an authentic and imaginative book on Greek civilization and culture. It was to remain as her most important work and its place in literature grew in the decades since. Other works include "The Roman Way" and "Echoes of Greece."

Holman Hamilton, also a native of Fort Wayne and relative of Edith, is the author of "Zachary Taylor: Soldier in the White House" and "Zachary Taylor: Soldier of the Republic." In his early years, Holman Hamilton worked in Fort Wayne as a newspaperman and then moved on to the academic field and subsequently was named professor of history at the University of Kentucky. Claude G. Bowers, one-time editor of the Journal-Gazette, was the author of a number of books as well as being U.S. Ambassador to Spain and Chile. Among his works were "The Tragic Era—The Revolution After Lincoln," published in 1929; "Beveridge and the Progressive Era," published in 1932; and "Spanish Adventures of Washington Irving," published in 1940. On May 18, 1931, Lee Foster Hartman of Fort Wayne, a son of Lemuel Hartman, was named editor of Harpers Magazine. Hartman was author of "The White Sapphire" and "Frazee," both novels, and a number of short stories. Hiram K. Motherwell, who began his writing career in Fort Wayne, was editor of Theater Guild Magazine. A successful writer during the 1930's, he authored "The Imperial Dollar," "The Theater of Today," and "The Peace We Fought For." Dorthea J. Snow, who was on the News-Sentinel staff during the 1960's, earlier and subsequently authored a number of popular books of particular interest to children. Author Karl Detzer and his wife, part of an old Fort Wayne newspaper and literary family, were long associated with Reader's Digest. Herbert J. Merrill, a poet from Fort Wayne, was published in the Saturday Evening Post, Harpers, the Atlantic and other periodicals; Katherine Neuhaus Haffner was author of fictional works and articles for children; Beth Day, author of modern novels, came from Fort Wayne. Ross F. Lockridge wrote "The Labyrinth of New Harmony" and a biography of Theodore F. Thieme, Fort Wayne industrialist. Ford Frick, who worked on the Journal-Gazette in the 1920's, was named National League Baseball Commissioner in 1951. Bill Gill, a native of Fort Wayne, was working with the Hearst Newspapers in New York in 1913 when he picked up the sinking of the Titanic on a wireless and broke to the world one of the most startling news stories of the epoch. William Rockhill Nelson, a native of Fort Wayne and on the staff of The Sentinel, moved to Kansas City and established in 1880 the Kansas City Star. Louis A. Warren authored a three-volume work on Lincoln, published in 1926. Warren helped found the Lincoln Historical Research Foundation of Lincoln Life in 1928 and was its director.

Auburn and Cord

In the mid-1930's an automobile appeared on the streets of Fort Wayne and other cities which drew wide interest and startled the automotive industry. This was the Cord L810, manufactured at nearby Auburn which for a period in the '20's and '30's was the world's capital in car innovation. The Auburn Company produced Auburns, Cords and Duesenbergs—some of which cost a king's ransom in the Depression and all of which would be worth a king's ransom if still intact a half century later. The company was originally started in 1866 by Charles Eckhart, a buggy maker from Studebaker Works at South Bend who married the daughter of John Ashleman, the man who laid out the town site of Auburn. The switch to autos was in 1901 when the first hand-tooled car was rolled onto the streets of Auburn. Soon, in addition to the Auburn Automobile Company, there was the Zimmerman Co. and the W. H. McIntyre Co. in Auburn. McIntyre made the Cyclecar, a belt-driven front-engine rear-drive car which was unique and tore up early roads. "Harry McIntyre made a record run today in an auto buggy, reaching Wells St. in Fort Wayne in 55 minutes," it was reported in 1909. That was over muddy trails and half-built roads. By 1914 the McIntyre Company employed 400 people in three plants and was shipping to all parts of the U.S. and foreign countries. The Zimmerman Co. produced the DeSoto which later became part of the Chrysler line. Both McIntyre and Zimmerman operations faded by the early 1920's, but the Auburn Company operated by the Eckharts had grown into a million dollar firm which was sold in 1918 to the Rigley banking interests in Chicago. This brought E. L. Cord to the scene. Cord, boy financial wonder and super-salesman of the 1920's, took over Auburn in 1924. By 1929, Auburns and the early classic version of the Cord were the in-cars of the sporting types. Only Duesenbergs, such as owned by Greta Garbo and Gary Cooper, and a few others exceeded them in prestige; and Cord soon acquired Duesenberg Corporation. The early Cord model, the L27 (first built in 1927), introduced front-wheel drive. In 1929, Cord founded the Cord Corporation, designed as a holding company for his expanding interests. Within a few years he controlled the Auburn Automobile Company, Aviation Manufacturing Corp., Auto Aircraft Acceptance Corp., the Duesenberg Corp., Checker Cab Manufacturing Company, Lycoming Engine Co., New York Shipbuilding Corp., and Stinson Aircraft Company. Financial writers in Time Magazine predicted Cord might soon become the greatest industrialist in America. The Great Depression struck, but Cord continued to push his enterprises. He was selling Duesenbergs for $20,000 in years when Fords were going for $400 and Buicks for $600. In the face of worsening conditions, Cord brought out the most original car in automotive history, and one of the more expensive—the Cord L810. It was first manufactured in Auburn in 1935 and at Connersville in 1937. It had streamlined body, front-wheel drive, automatic shift, touch control, V-type 8-cylinder engine, retractable head lamps and over-drive and superchargers for cruising up to 150 miles an hour. The Lycoming engine had aluminum pistons. At one time, as many as 7,000 people a day came just to visit the Auburn plant. But all of Cord's over-extensions and manipulations couldn't defy economic realities indefinitely. All came crashing down in the mid-1930's and the Auburn plant was sold on Dec. 7, 1937. Cord reportedly fled to a guarded estate in California, but later developed broadcasting and real estate holdings. Errett Lobban Cord died January 2, 1974, at Reno, Nev., at the age of 79: and a half century after taking over the Auburn Company.

A Dollar Was A Dollar

If less colorful, Fort Wayne firms were making more permanent progress in the automotive industry in the 1930's. Harvester was holding its own in the truck and farm equipment field. Zollner was making pistons. Essex Wire was making wire assemblies, particularly for the Ford Motor Company. One other vehicle was being made in 1936 and was to become a familiar part of parades in the city and across the land thereafter. It was Black Jack, designed to look like a locomotive engine and built on a 24-foot International chassis. It was the plaything of Voiture 37 of the 40&8, the fun-loving society of World War I veterans of the American Legion. Black Jack was built by Vern Gingher, Al Remy, Jim Smith, John Boehrer, Edwin Krauskopf and Bob Gaskill, with the encouragement of Harry Dwire, all members of 40&8.

There were good times in the old days, everyone's old days, and that applies to the Depression years as any other. All was not soup kitchens. If a child of the 1930's didn't have a television set, he did have quite a few vacant lots in the neighborhood. He saw more of the sky and possibly inhaled more fresh air. The trees blossomed just as surely in the spring of 1934. Children went to school five days a week. And if movies and pictures of the era came in black, white and gray, the real world was in color. A dollar was dear. The old phrase: "Buddy, can you spare a dime" wasn't idle chatter in 1934. It was good for at least two cups of coffee. On a chilly spring Thursday in 1934, the panhandlers along Main St. could duck into Reigel's Cigar Store and get a thick bowl of split pea soup for 10 cents. A noon menu for Thursday fare in 1934 at Reigel's,, then at the northeast corner of Main and Calhoun Streets, shows something of Depression meal economics. The "No. 2 Special Luncheon" offered smoked sausage, Dutch potato salad, sliced tomatoes, bread and butter, coffee, ice tea or milk, all for 25 cents. If the customer wanted to throw caution aside and eat big, there was the No. 1 Noon Luncheon. This consisted of crisp bacon with asparagus tips on toast, Boston cream pie, bread and butter, coffee, tea or milk, all for 30 cents. There was no mention of a hamburger or cheeseburger on the menu—just hamburger joints handled them. Numerous sandwiches were listed on the menu. Boiled ham sandwiches were 10 cents. Beef tenderloin was 15 cents. Corned beef was 15 cents. Wisconsin Swiss cheese was 10 cents.

Later in that same year, a newspaper poll indicated people were already tiring of some of the government Depression measures. Particularly the NRA (National Recovery Act) was losing favor. Out of 86 industrialists, dealers, merchants, shopkeepers and tradesmen interviewed, 63 said they wanted either revision or abolition of the codes. The main complaints were government interference, with the NRA attempting to set work hours, wages and other matters in a spread-the-work effort. Later, the NRA was declared unconstitutional anyway by the Supreme Court.

Toward the late 1930's, the first tentative moves toward that unique American invention, the supermarket, were in evidence in Fort Wayne. The first open-floor, completely self-service grocery with a row of check-out counters was an A&P store at 417 West Creighton Avenue. It was opened in 1938. The large brick building had earlier been a service garage for the Fitch-Potts Packard Company. It was completely renovated for the new purpose; and the existence of a wide parking area for customers was at that time an innovative feature. A&P occupied the building until 1957, after which it was again remodeled and occupied by Maloley Brothers. The building burned in a spectacular fire in the early morning hours of Jan. 3, 1962, with the loss estimated at $235,000. Maloley's built a new supermarket at the site.

Rex M. Potterf was on Dec. 18, 1934, appointed head librarian of the Fort Wayne and Allen County Library. He succeeded the late Miss Margaret M. Colerick who had held the position for more than three decades, since 1898. Potterf, one-time superintendent of the Warren and Huntington Township Schools had been at Central High School starting in 1924 and was head of the social science department at the time of his library appointment.

Baron Long, who was born in Fort Wayne on Aug. 8, 1883, became the leading race track and hotel operator in Southern California. The son of Mason Long, a reformed Fort Wayne gambler and nationally-known writer of the 19th Century, Baron Long worked on the Journal-Gazette in his young years. In 1908 he went to Los Angeles and formed a partnership with James Jeffries who was heavyweight boxing champion. Long started Sunset Blvd. nightclubs and once fired a dancer named Rudolph Valentino. In 1916, Long built the Tijuana Race Track and later the $10 million race track, hotel and casino complex at Agua Caliente. Long headed the syndicate which protested the 1937 seizure of the Agua Caliente properties by Mexican dictator Lazaro Cardenas. For 25 years he owned the Biltmore Hotel in Los Angeles. Long's 120-foot luxury yacht was used in World War II as General MacArthur's headquarters.

The onset of the Great Depression following the crash in late 1929 changed the lives for many years of people in Fort Wayne and other cities. The picture above was taken on a hot summer day in 1930 along Calhoun St. At left is a bread line such as were frequent sights in the land.

Two children look at one of Presiden Herbert Hoover's Emergency Unem ployment Relief Committee signs i late 1930. The measures, howeve didn't stem the deeping unemploy ment and misery. By 1932 thing were hitting bottom and Shant towns, sometimes called Hooverville were springing up as the destitut sought places to live. The paintin by Louis Bonsib, made in 1932, shou the Hooverville between Calhoun an Clinton Streets, north of Superio Note the tank of the old Gas Work in the background of the Decemb scene.

The construction of the U.S. Post Office and Courthouse on South Harrison St. was started in 1931. It replaced the old Post Office at the southeast corner of Clinton and Berry Streets, at left. The Boy Scouts of Troop 4 salute the flag in a ceremony in the early 1930s.

One of the public works was the Van Buren St. Bridge. The top picture shows the scene just prior to construction and the other scene is the after-effect. The old iron structure was soon removed. Below are children gathered at the Public Library for story hour in 1931.

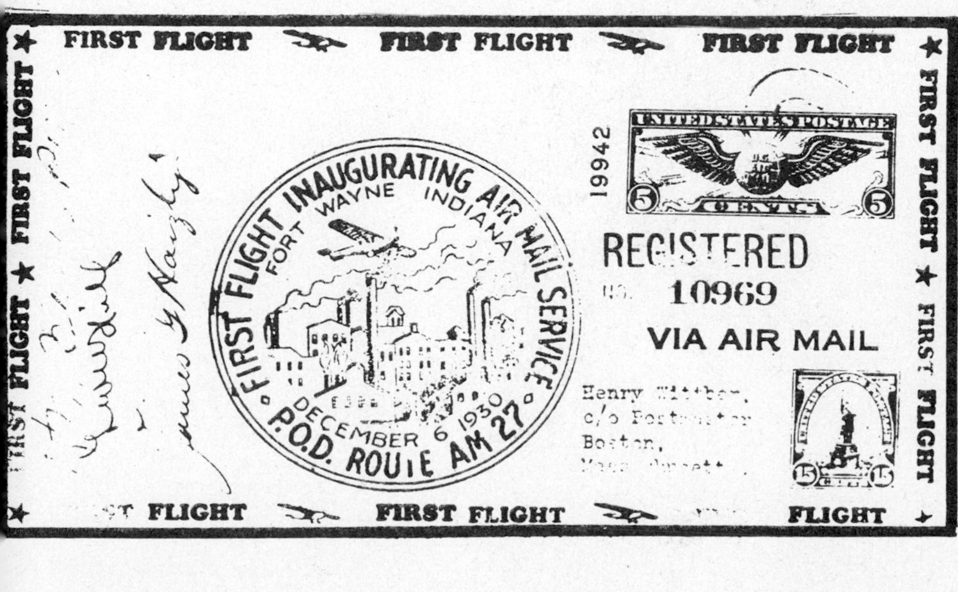

Air Mail Service was started in Fort Wayne and across the country on Dec. 6, 1930. In the cockpit of the airplane above is George Hill, pilot for the first flight out of the city. He is ready to take off from Paul Baer Airport on the Ludwig Road (later renamed Smith Field). At left is the cancelled letter of one piece of mail in the bag on the inaugural flight.

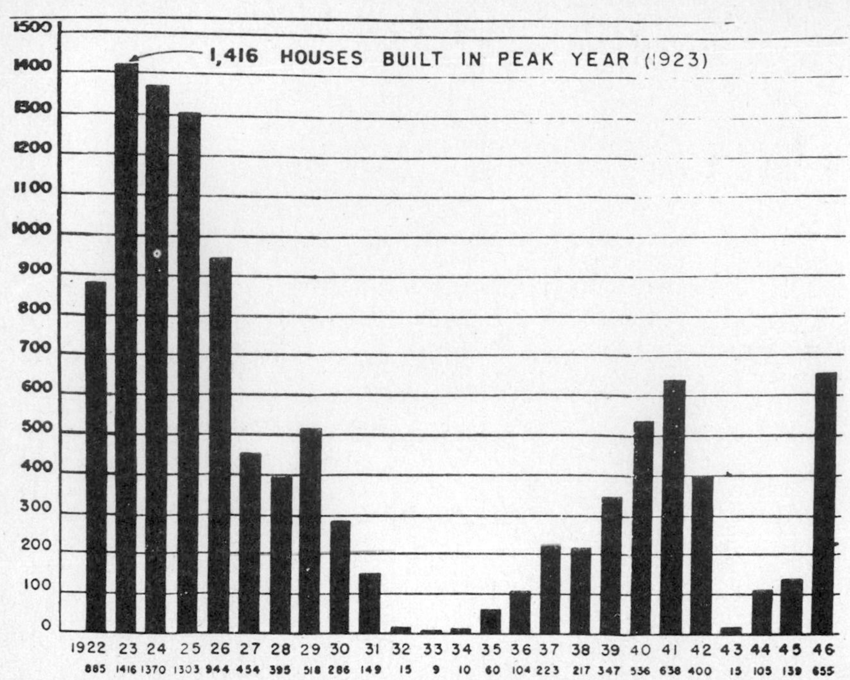

Just how deep the Depression was can be seen in the housing chart of Fort Wayne. From a peak building year of 1,416 new houses in 1923, the rate plunged to just nine during the entire year of 1933, and a very slow recovery the years following. One almost gets the impression that there weren't many fires either from the comfortable picture below at the the No. 8 Engine House on Fairfield Ave., taken about 1932.

Desperado, Van Meter Slug Policeman, Take Revolvers, Steel Vests

Office raided by bandits. — case.

Homer Van Meter.

John Dillinger.

Exterior view of police departm

Homer Van Meter of Fort Wayne was the most constant companion of gangster John Dillinger in the final wild months of the gang in 1934. Cop killer Cliff Mohler and bank robber Sam Goldstein were others from Fort Wayne connected with the Dillinger mob. The News-Sentinel clippings are dated Aug. 13, 1934.

Notorious "Wooden Gun" Bandit And New Partner Escape After Daring Foray; Dragnet Thrown Out.

Night Patrolman Is Injured In Fight

Authorities Fear Epidemic Of Bank Robberies Will Follow Latest Coup Of U. S. Public Enemy No. 1

BY STAFF CORRESPONDENT.

WARSAW, Ind., April 13.—Armed with machine guns, two men, positively identified as John Dillinger and his new partner, Homer Van Meter, formerly of Fort Wayne, swooped down on the Warsaw police station shortly before 1 a.m. today, and stole three bullet-proof vests and two revolvers, after clubbing Night Officer Jud Pittinger, aged 47, and forcing him to open the station.

Officer Pittinger was recovering at his home today from severe cuts on his head, inflicted by blows from his own gun, administered by Van Meter.

All roads in the vicinity of Warsaw were being patroled by State Police officers. Fifteen of them were on duty, deployed over an area of about 15-mile radius, searching vacant lake cottages for a trace of the pair.

State Police Sergt. Walter Menzer, temporarily in charge of the force, said about forty or more state patrolmen would be on duty in the vicinity before nightfall. Lieut. Ray Fisher will be in charge.

Striking with the same calm speed that characterized two similar raids, on the Auburn and Peru police stations, last Fall, Dillinger and Van Meter trapped Officer Pittinger as he walked his beat, near the corner of Center and Buffalo streets, two blocks from the police station.

Both Dillinger and Van Meter covered him with machine guns.

"We want those vests," Dillinger said quietly. As he came closer, Officer Pittinger grabbed the barrel of the machine gun and tried to snatch it from the desperado's grasp. Dillinger held to the gun, but made no effort to regain it, Pittinger said.

"Don't try to take it," Dillinger said. "He (Van Meter) will kill you."

"All right," Pittinger said he replied, "I won't."

Van Meter, snarling an oath, rammed the barrel of his own machine gun into Pittinger's back, and threatened to "drill him." At that

A street car and the first run of an early bus on West Jefferson St. is recalled at right. Below is the replica of Abe Lincoln's cabin which was at Foster Park in the 1930s. At bottom, an unusual photo through a car window catches skaters at Delta Lakes at Lakeside.

The cast and crew of the Old Fort Players, the foreruner of the Civil Theatre, is shown on the stage in March, 1933. The play was "Trewlawney of the Wells." At left is Olsen and Johnson. Ole Olsen and Chic Johnson put together their wild stage review in the mid-30s at Fort Wayne's old Palace Theatre, then moved on to more than 100 performances on Broadway.

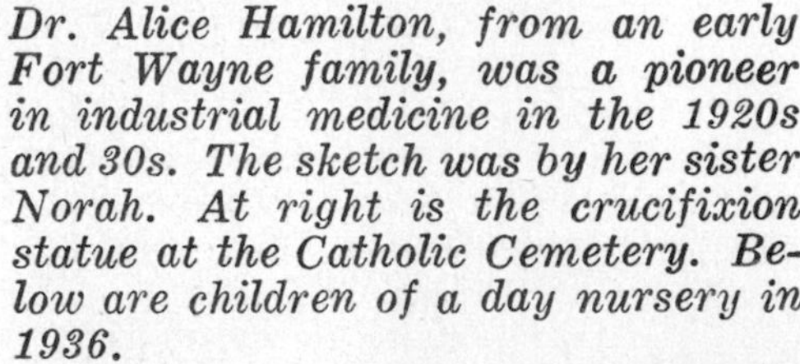

Dr. Alice Hamilton, from an early Fort Wayne family, was a pioneer in industrial medicine in the 1920s and 30s. The sketch was by her sister Norah. At right is the crucifixion statue at the Catholic Cemetery. Below are children of a day nursery in 1936.

Girl Scouts in the 1930s made a lot of fancy things and are busy at work on their patterns and sewing machines, above. At right is the jam of activity at the Barr St. Market in 1935. City Hall is in the background. Below is a 1935 supercharged Auburn 8, which was made 20 miles north of Fort Wayne at the Auburn-Cord Works at Auburn, and was an eye-catcher on city streets.

Swimmers pile into the St. Joseph River in the summer of 1936 at what at the time was called Municipal Beach. In the background is the St Joe River Dam and generator house.

Part 8
Decade of 1935-1945

Bill Hosey, in addition to his four terms, got an extra year in the mayor's chair in 1934. This was due to a move by the Indiana Legislature to skip a year on the elections, which would normally have been held in 1933, as an economy move at a time when civil government was low on funds due to the Depression. Typical of the old City Hall was the odor of cigar smoke and the convenience of handy brass spittoons. There was a feel of permanence about the place and Mayor Hosey added to the coloration of old-time politics. He always had a cigar butt in his mouth which he constantly removed to talk, and then replaced it. Insiders said he actually only smoked about two or three cigars a day, but that he used a box of matches in half a day to keep one lighted. Spittoons were also regular fixtures in the courts, but seemed to disappear after the long tenure of Judge William Schannen.

Mr. Hosey was 80 years old in 1934, but he decided to run for re-election. He cited the record of his accomplishments in his 17 years as city chief executive. The Journal-Gazette was back in his camp and supported him. The election in the fall was razor close, but Hosey lost by 587 votes to his Republican opponent, Harry W. Baals. Baals had been with G.E. for 21 years and had succeeded Edward C. Miller as postmaster in 1922. He would carve out for himself a career in City Hall almost as long as Hosey's had been.

Following the 1934 election, the top Democratic candidates filed for a recount. They were Mayor Hosey, City Clerk nominee Louis J. Voors and City Judge Bert A. Fagan. A month later, Dec. 14, Allen Circuit Judge Clarence McNabb dismissed the proceedings to contest the election of Mayor-elect Harry Baals, Clerk-elect Leonard Ellenwood and Judge-elect William Schannen. On election day, Harry Baals was given 19,575 votes to 18,988 for Bill Hosey. After the recount in 34 contested precincts, Baals added 119 votes to his election-day plurality. The other two Republicans also added votes. In winning the city election in 1934, the Republicans were bucking a national trend which was sweeping with the Democratic Party.

The situation was particularly interesting because since before the days of the Civil War, Fort Wayne was a predominately Democratic community. Several political observers attribute the Republican trend to a high-powered Allen County political organization fashioned by Harry Hogan, at that time a banker and lawyer in the city. Hogan had gained a national reputation as an organizer in both politics and other fields. The Allen County Republican organization he set in motion was to remain nearly dominant until the 1960's. Another peculiarity of the 1934 election was that both city and county offices were voted in the same year. This was due to the Depression-economy move to delay city elections for one year. The Democrats won practically all the county offices and a 5-to-4 majority on the City Council.

Baals assumed office on Jan. 1, 1935. He named Louis Crosby controller, and Walter E. Helmke, city attorney. Robert G. Beams was appointed chairman of the Board of Public Works. William Schannen was city judge and Leonard Ellenwood, clerk. A. T. Anderson and John Johnson were board of works members. Charles Bowen, Ralph Clark and Albert Keller were the board of safety. City councilmen included Frank Wyss, Albert Moran, George Dinnen, Charles Moellering, Arno Spiegel, Harry McMillen, Walter Vetter, Ben Bennet and Gerald Aurentz.

The Shovels of the WPA

Conditions just weren't too good when Harry Baals took over the City Administration. Taxes had been reduced to the minimal services point. Little was going on in the way of building projects or employment expansion. Much of the effort of the mayor was directed toward getting the city a share in the Federally-funded projects which were growing around the nation. In September, 1935, he published a report that the "City Seeks Six Million Federal Aid Funds." Excerpts, which give the flavor of the times, follow:

"If Fort Wayne does not receive its share of Federal relief funds it will not be because the city and citizen's committee has not submitted a sufficient number of worthy projects. The City of Fort Wayne has already submitted projects for Federal relief funds from either the PWA or WPA totaling $6,557,027.41. These include the aid from the PWA on the proposed $5 million sewage disposal plant and interceptor sewer system, and $300,000 from the PWA for improvement to the City Light and Power Works steam generating plant. A total of $1,256,127 is asked from the Works Progress Administration for projects submitted by the Board of Public Safety, the Board of Public Works, Board of Aviation Commissioners and the Board of Park Commissioners. Of this amount $936,265 has been approved and men are now working on the projects. Fort Wayne ranks among the first cities in the United States in its application for work projects under Federal relief funds. The following citizen's committee cooperated in the presentation of the projects: Fred B. Shoaff, chairman; William Kunkle, Oscar G. Foellinger, Clarence O. Van Horn, Harry G. Hogan, Robert E. O.Connor, Stephen B. Fleming, Arthur F. Hall, D. P. McDonald and G. Irving Latz."

Some bald old jokes refer to men "on WPA" leaning on shovels. And true enough, along many a street ditch in Fort Wayne, groups of men could be seen leaning on shovels during those years. They also completed numerous fine public works including buildings, sewers, roads, recreational facilties, art works, and the moving of millions of tons of earth in Fort Wayne and other American cities.

Diphtheria and Typhoid

Another sign of the times was a communication from Dr. Karl C. Eberly, City Health Commissioner: "Another diphtheria death the first week of October (1935), making a total of seven this year, acts as a silent but vivid reminder that our children are not protected. Everyone reading this who has children between the ages of six months and ten years should immediately consult his family physician, if the children are not already immunized. It is a simple and quite painless procedure and, fortunately, causes practically no reaction in children between the ages of six months and five years. On October 4, after only 23 school days, we already had 27 cases of diphtheria."

The Depression days were not without their humor. Otto H. Adams, general office manager of the City Light and Water Utilities, reportedly vouched for the truth of an incident concerning a woman who was a new City Light customer: She asked to buy a jumper cable "because the person that formerly lived in her house had one and it sure saved on the light bill."

In a newspaper private opinion on the evening of Sept. 11, 1935, a writer said: "I cannot think of any more unkind or cutting title to hang on Mayor Baals than calling him 'Economy Baals.' It is like accusing a man of wearing an old-fashioned night shirt or red flannels. I cannot think of any more outrageous practice than for any public official to make even a pretense of practicing economy."

The plague of the early decades of the century, typhoid fever, was at the root of a report in November, 1935: "City Attorney Walter E. Helmke announces successful compromise settlement of 36 typhoid fever damage suits pending against the city for several years." Typhoid was often blamed on contaminated water.

In the decades prior to World War II, city-wide Halloween parades and parties were held in the downtown area. City officials blocked Calhoun St. from auto traffic from Columbia St. to Lewis St. and turned the area over to masked revelers, paraders and dancers. Thousands thronged the streets from early evening to after midnight. The practice was discontinued, however, because the Halloween gathering of such dimensions tended to get out of hand. Injuries and damage became common. In 1935, $5,000 in damage to public and private property was reported. Other years were as bad or worse. Yet, the passing of the great Halloween carnivals downtown were lamented by many.

In April, 1936, the city was recovering from "the severest winter in 40 years." The temperatures were in the neighborhood of 17 below zero for several days running. City officials were complaining that spring flood threats were costing thousands of dollars more than anticipated, and this was added on to "above normal repair costs for reconditioning asphalt pavements and heavy costs to the city's water system in thawing and repairing frozen meters and mains." During the period commencing January 25 and ending March 16, the Water Construction Dept. repaired 32 main line breaks, 71 service leaks and 7 fire hydrants. In addition, 1,234 meters were frozen and 2,650 homes in the city had frozen pipes.

Early in 1936, the City Light power plant was expanded with the help of the PWA. On Jan. 3, the Federal agency gave approval of the plans for the erection of an addition to the plant; including new bus station equipment and the demolition of two steam boilers and the old plant which housed them. Work got underway on Jan. 13 with the removal of two old landmarks—a pair of 111-foot high 60-inch brick smoke stacks. American Steel Dredge Co. and L. I. Griffin Co. handled the removal. Work on the erection of the enlarged power plant building on North Clinton was perfomed by Max Irmscher & Sons. G.E. installed generator equipment. The Federal government furnished 47 per cent of the cost of the PWA project. (Public Works Administration—one of President Roosevelt's alphabetical-sounding Depression measures.) Two City Light Substations were also constructed in the 1936 development.

The Municipal Beach

By the summer of 1936, the City Administration was in a bind. "In February and March of the past winter, when water mains started bursting because of the unusual depth to which the ground had frozen due to the severe weather, the Board of Health immediately emphasized the need of taking restrictive measures to prevent contamination of the water." Both the State Board of

Health and the Federal health agency got into the act. Chemists at the Filtration plant were testing the water every four minutes. One of the measures taken was the elimination of all cross connections of city water mains with lines to private wells or directly with the rivers. Prior to the crisis of 1936, city water lines were still connected with many of the old lines which operated from the well system which served the city prior to 1931.

The Municipal Bathing Beach along the St. Joseph River just below the North Anthony Blvd. dam was opened in July, 1936. As many as 7,000 men, women and children a day reportedly took advantage of the beach during the first summer of operation. The banks were graded and improved with the trucking in of sand. Several life guards were hired to sit in the lifeguard chairs which were provided. Flood lights and diving boards were installed. Mayor Baals announced that further improvements at the site would be made by the 1937 season. It was reported that the initial cost of establishing the beach was only $1,500. There was some local fear, however, that the water might be contaminated. But the Board of Health reported the river was not affected by any sewer contamination during the first summer, and no case of infection or illness traceable to the river was reported during the initial season. Recreation at The Beach was expanded to boxing rings, softball diamonds and the location became the first home of the Zollner Pistons, national champs in the then-popular fastball field. About a decade later, however, swimming at Municipal Beach declined and was abandonned because of uncertain purity of the river water.

A strange find by utility construction crews working under West Columbia St. was reported in September, 1936. Deep underground, the workmen were astonished to break into a room. Well below the usual building levels, and just east of Harrison St., the room measured about 16 by 20 feet, and was 6 feet high. It had 16-inch sandstone walls and arched ceiling. Three doors in the walls had been closed up. The street had been built a number of feet over the ceiling. Some distance away, the men ran into 14-inch timbers which were part of the cribbing of the old canal bank. The only thing found in the strange room was an empty jug and several pieces of broken furniture. They speculated it might have been an old wine celler, a smuggler's place or other illegal operation in the days of the canal. The mystery was never answered.

Mayor Harry Baals turned the switch "which brilliantly illuminates the Paul Baer Municipal Airport with red, amber and green lights." The act at the facility which would later be renamed Smith Field was part of the dedicatory ceremony marking the installation of improved lighting in July, 1936. The installation was a PWA project and cost $10,000.

The Year of Extremes

Also in July, 1936, the City Council met in a special session to pass an ordinance giving authority to the State Highway Commission to construct an underpass at Clinton St. and the Pennsylvania and Wabash Railroads. The city appropriated funds for acquisition of the right-of-way, for the widening, extension and opening of Clinton Street. The actual construction was to be paid by the Federal government. John Dehner, Inc., was awarded a contract by the State Highway Commission for the Clinton St. underpass on a low bid of $276,000. The extension of Clinton St. meant the disappearance of most of Piqua Ave., as the portion of the street was known from Esmond St. south. The year of 1936 goes down in history for the setting of two all-time weather records in Fort Wayne. The hottest temperature, 106.1 degrees, was reported on July 14. The other record had to do with the range in temperature in a single year—a spread of more than 123 degrees. It was 17 degrees below zero on Jan. 23, of 1936.

Some of the worst aspects of the Depression were in evidence in 1936. In October of that year a WPA worker from Fort Wayne won $300 and second prize in a national essay contest. His name was Jack Murray and he was suffering from malnutrition and tuberculosis. "I am a man that doesn't even use tobacco, my wages is all spent for home and today my little children in their shabby clothes are laughed at in school. My good credit of former days is gone and right now I am out of work when a WPA project is finished. It's a loss of at least ten days before we are transferred to another. It's cold facts when I tell you that I have worked many a day on two meager meals that my little children might fare better. This is the new deal, this is the more abundant life. Destruction of pigs, farmers compelled to raise less. Discouragement of business, the very life of any country. Death and the new deal are the same, it makes us all equal." Murray related the situation of a fellow WPA worker who would sneak off to eat lunch alone so others wouldn't see him eating potato peelings. The potatoes themselves were left at home for his wife and youngsters to eat.

Another product of the lengthening Depression was the "Black Legion," a secret, hooded society centered in Detroit, but with branches in Fort Wayne and many other cities. It was an outgrowth of ignorance, poverty, and unemployment. Nearly a score of kidnappings, floggings and conspiracies to murder and incite to riot were charged against members of the Detroit area. In Fort Wayne a 39-year-old man was arrested for carrying a concealed weapon on Nov. 19, 1936, and admitted to having been recruited into the Black Legion. After 11 men were convicted of murder in Detroit in September of that year, the movement faded, though some fear of the night raiders lingered and several movies were made on the subject.

Upsetting Politics

It was a Presidential election year and it was a time of weird politics. On October 10, 1936, a vast rally was held at the Majestic Theatre by the National Union for Social Justice Clubs and Townsend Movement Clubs. The main speaker was William Lemke, North Dakota Congressman and candidate for President on the Union Party ticket. Lemke charged President Roosevelt was trying "to Tammanyize the Nation" and Republican Candidate Alf Landon "never started in this campaign." Lemke said Roosevelt "is not a Communist . . . I would say he is nearer a Fascist than anything else." He said the Democrats were making "every effort to steal the Huey P. Long share-the-wealth support in the state of Louisiana and elsewhere." But when the votes of Nov. 3, 1936, were tabulated, a record high was turned in for a Rooseveltian landslide in Allen County. "President Franklin D. Roosevelt and M. Clifford Townsend, Democrat nominee for Governor, were given the ballot blessings of Allen County citizens by margins that broke all county records. In 1932, Roosevelt defeated Herbert Hoover by 11,371 votes. Tuesday, Roosevelt's margin, according to unofficial vote totals for all precincts of the county, was 14,345," according to a news report. The total official vote cast was 65,556. Democrats swept into every office, with County Prosecutor C. Byron Hayes leading the ticket. FDR drew 39,069 votes; Landon, 24,724; and Lemke a mere 2,502.

It was the season when people were sitting at their radios and hearing reports of a crown crisis and potential abdication of the King of England. "Mrs. Wallis Simpson, fascinating Baltimore-born friend of King Edward of England, won a divorce in a brief hearing at Historic Ipswich Assizes today," reported the Associated Press in the Fort Wayne News-Sentinel on Oct. 27, 1936. "Not since Henry VIII divorced Catherine of Aragon and married the ill-fated Anne Boleyn in 1533, thereby completing the rupture with the Church of Rome, had any severance of marital ties held such far-reaching possibilities," it was reported from London. People in Fort Wayne and around the world later listened to the voice of Edward over crackly radio waves as he gave his abdication speech "for the woman I love."

One thing to be thankful for, according to a Nov. 17, 1936, report in the city, was the price of turkey dinners. "The present wholesale market would justify a retail price for turkeys of 25 cents a pound, fully dressed," a grocer said. He estimated chickens would be about the same and geese at about 22 cents a pound. Other items for the Thanksgiving dinner included potatoes at 18 cents for a half peck, bread at 10 cents a loaf, oysters at 25 cents a pint, a pound of cranberries at 22 cents, a large can of pumpkin for 10 cents; milk at 11 cents a quart and a half pound of butter for 20 cents.

The Christmas Bureau came into existence in 1936, though some of its activities had been carried out since 1926 by the Community Chest. The first place of Bureau operation was the Central Building at 203 West Wayne St. where the Chest officers were located. In those years when there was great need for the bundles of food and toys, packages were furnished at holiday time to many families. Marian Rastetter was group chairman in 1938 through 1943. Margaret Ann Keegan was chairman for the following 10 years. Others active later included Mrs. Richard Blitz, Mrs. Arthur Richard, Mrs. Richard Baird, Mrs. R. Nelson Snider, Chan Ray, Mrs. Edgar O'Hora, Ruth Whearley and thousands of volunteers—housewives, firemen, Marines, students and teachers, workers and business people, professionals and club members.

March of Labor

Labor organizations had their origin in Fort Wayne with 19th century unions such as the Knights of Labor, the cigar makers union, the several railroad unions, the printers union and others. In 1887, 24 labor unions formed the Trades and Labor Council of Fort Wayne, Indiana. In 1897, the group was granted a charter by the American Federation of Labor and in 1902 the group became the Fort Wayne Federation of Labor. Eugene V. Debs, a frequent visitor to Fort Wayne, called the shots in the great American Railroad Union strike of 1894 which affected Fort Wayne and other rail centers in the Nation. The Fort Wayne Industrial Union Council was chartered by the Congress of Industrial Organizations on Nov. 16, 1938. At that time six local CIO unions composed the Council.

It was during the 1930's that the unions had some of their hardest and greatest years. It was during those years that Fort Wayne was the birth site of a major national labor organization—the United Electrical Workers Union (UE). This national organization for workers in the electrical industry was formed in the old Anthony Hotel in 1936 by representatives from various American cities. James B. Carey was named the first president of the UE at the meeting and later the same year the UE became affiliated with the Committee for Industrial Organization, a forerunner of the CIO. When the Congress of Industrial Organization (CIO) was formed in 1938, by John L. Lewis, Carey was named secretary. In later years in a visit to Fort Wayne, Carey said the early history of Local 901 of the union, representing G.E. workers, was one of the glowing pages in the national movement. "Some of the delegates to the 1936 convention probably hitchhiked to get here," he said. That observation on the struggling labor movement during the Depression was underscored by George Gould, long-time international representative of the UE and IUE in the Fort Wayne and Tri-State area. Gould said the first time he saw Fort Wayne was when he came to the city for the 1936 convention and rode into town on a railroad freight car. He became a familiar figure at labor negotiation tables for the next four decades.

The IUE Battle

One of the great struggles within the labor movement developed in 1949 when the majority membership of the Electrical Union attempted to change its Communist-dominated leadership. The actual leadership struggle began in 1946 when a small UE Local (902) headed by James Pascoe charged John Gojack, who headed District 9 comprised of some 30,000 dues-paying members, was secretly affiliated with Communist organizations. Gojack drummed Pascoe out of the UE, but Local 902 went on to become the first Local chartered by the new International Union of Electrical, Radio and Machine Workers (CIO). The IUE had been chartered by the national movement to wrest the labor movement from the grip of Communist-dominated leadership and foster free choice of leadership by the electrical workers. The matter came to a bitter head in 1949 in Fort Wayne when big Local 901, representing G.E. workers, decided to leave the UE and join the IUE. The battle was fought in the union balloting chambers, the streets and the courts. On Nov. 26, 1949, the union membership voted 2,036 to 117 to disaffiliate with the UE and affiliate with the IUE-CIO. Prior to the vote the UE had been expelled from the CIO because of its Communist-dominated leadership. To legally establish itself as bargaining agent and to retain the the assets of the Local, the new IUE affiliate brought action in Allen Superior Court. Bringing the action against Gojack and the old UE leadership, which was attempting to hang on to the assets and bargaining right, where Dallas Smith, president of Local 901, IUE; and Russell L. Johnson; Richard Hurst; Melvin Borcherding; Paulus Adams; Cecil Onion; Virgil Forland; Joseph Kramer and John B. Dennis. In his decision for the new affiliation of Local 901, Special Judge Robert Y. Keegan said "the membership should at all times have complete control of their affairs and not be subject to the dictates of a few people sitting in a distant national office." The UE's grip in Fort Wayne was completely broken in 1957 when workers of the Inca Division of the Phelps Dodge Cooper Products Corp. voted against the UE and joined the IUE. So it was a stange twist in labor history that the same people, such as Carey, Gould and Smith, who first formed the UE in Fort Wayne back in 1936 were largely the same group which broke with it to develop the IUE in the later years.

Over the years, a number of Unions have been prominent in industrial affairs. The American Federation of Hosiery Workers founded a Local as early as 1899 in the local knitting industry. Branch 2 represented workers at the Gotham Hosiery Co. and Branch 121 at the Wayne Knitting Mills. At their height in the years just following World War II the Federation had more than 800 members in Fort Wayne. The largest Local for many years was Local 57 of the United Auto Workers, developed in the 1930's and representing workers at International Harvester Company. Howard Minier of Local 57, UAW, later succeeded Earl Whitehurst and was president of the Central Labor Council for many years. Whitehurst, head of the AFL in Fort Wayne, was the first chairman of the AFL-CIO Council in Fort Wayne, formed in 1956.

The question of racial discrimination in the unions and other areas of business and institutions became more public in the 1950's and 1960's. In 1952 Robert E. Wilkerson, director of the Urban League, reported that of 39 AFL unions affiliated with the Federation only 9 had Negro members. And of those 9, four had no more than four Negro members. The ratio was far better in the CIO affiliated unions and in 1952 the Fort Wayne Industrial Union Council directed an equal rights policy in industry and "non-discriminitory practices by management in our clauses in contracts."

Floods and Bank Nights

At the height of the great floods of January, 1937, along the Ohio River, the city of Fort Wayne drew national attention for the lengths it went to aid flood-stricken people in the Ohio River cities. Seven rail tank cars containing 105,000 gallons of pure drinking water from Fort Wayne's Filtration Plant went to Cincinnati under arrangement by Mayor Baals and Utilities Superintendent Paul Thiele. Water was the most desperate need. Also sent were National Guard units, truckloads of food and clothing, the Nurses Corps and Fire Department equipment. On Jan. 29, 1937, an editorial in the Cincinnati Enquirer said: "Cincinnati bows with respect, admiration, gratitude to Fort Wayne, Indiana. Under the alert leadership of Mayor H. W. Baals, the people of Fort Wayne have sent to Cincinnati six railroad tank cars of water. Today, thousands of gallons of water from one of these cars was made available by the Enquirer to Good Samaritan Hospital. A part of the fire-fighting equipment of Fort Wayne is now in Evansville, Indiana, to help meet the grave crisis there."

In early 1937 the gift of 74 acres of land "in the extreme southeast section of the city" by Mr. and Mrs. Dale W. McMillen was reported by Adolph Jaenicke, park superintendent. The new park land, 40 per cent of which was wooded, was long desired by the Park Board. Because of the lack of funds, however, the board had been unable to act. The gift of land between Oxford St. and Hessen Cassel Road formed the nucleus of McMillen Park, considerably expanded in later years. Also that same year, the Park Board acquired 4 acres at the site of the old Packard Piano factory off South Fairfield and reported the transfer of 16 acres to form an addition to Rockhill Park.

The old Post Office at the corner of Clinton and Berry Streets, was razed in August, 1937. The stone from the historic landmark was trucked out to North Anthony Blvd. where it was used to stem a washout caused by flooding river waters at the North Anthony Dam. The Northern Indiana Public Service Company changed over from manufactured to natural gas late in 1937. The natural gas was piped to Fort Wayne from the gas fields of Texas. At that time, the company reported the switch to natural gas would mean a savings of approximately $185,000 annually to Fort Wayne gas consumers.

A symbol of the 1930's, a time when many people were wishing for miracles, was "Bank Night." Bank Night had nothing to do with banks and little to do with night. It was the evening when various neighborhood theatres would draw a number between features from a large canister. If the lucky holder was in the audience, he would win the big prize—usually about $500. It would be a great day (or Wednesday night) for the winner who would hurry down the aisle to collect. But more often than not, the prize would go unclaimed and another Bank Night audience would go through the same routine the succeeding Wednesday. Late in 1937 there was a move to kill Santa Claus and to enforce anti-lottery laws. Fort Wayne City Councilman Walter Vetter pushed a city ordinance banning Bank Nights. On Nov. 1, 1937, the Fort Wayne Ministerial Association unanimously endorsed the ordinance. On Nov. 2 the City Council held a hearing so the public could express itself on the matter. Rules Chairman Gerald Aurentz asked if there was anyone present wishing to be heard, for or against. There was only silence. The ordinance banning Bank Night was shelved. Two years later, in 1939, there was a test case in Decatur where a grand jury had indicted a theatre owner for operating an illegal lottery. "Decatur's much publicized bank night test case again has been set for trial" it was reported from Adams County Circuit Court. The case drew national attention. Finally, on March 18, 1939, a jury returned a verdict of not guilty, despite the presence of special attorneys of the Indiana Attorney General's Office to prosecute the case. Bank night continued to be popular for several more years in Fort Wayne and elsewhere.

Buddy Filtches a Snipe

On a cold afternoon of January 15, 1938, a newspaper reporter named Charles Baird dressed up like a hobo and headed for the Rescue Mission on Columbia Street. He found the place crowded. He had learned the lingo. Everyone to a tramp is "buddy." The Salvation Army is the "Sally." A cigarette butt is a "snipe." A place to sleep is a "flop." A prospective benefactor is a "score." When Baird reached the mission near the Nickel Plate tracks (that was before the elevation) he was pushed back out the door by a transient type. "We're all filled up. There ain't no more dishes and you have to wait until these guys is finished." The hoboes were eating in shifts in those days. Eventually Baird ate and mixed in the conversation. A dude of a hobo—he had a white silk scarf partially concealing a dirty, tattered shirt—said he had tried bumming meals at restaurants but without luck. Another, who had arrived from Buffalo, N.Y., said "It's terrible, (back East) you can't even walk the streets without being bagged by the coppers. I got run out of three towns on the same day. I'm going to Chicago where they treat you right." Another said: "You ought to try bumming in the South. I just spent 10 days in the Chattanooga Jail. It was lousy. The constable tailed me for five miles." Still another agreed: "The bo's down there are eating their overalls, with shoelace for spaghetti. The best thing I saw down South was a freight train heading North." Several of the "bo's" and the disguised reporter wandered down Columbia St. to Harrison St., then left to Main Street. Baird watched as one of the others shuffled into a place near the corner. "Gimme a pint of the same stuff I had yesterday." The proprietor handed him a bottle. The hobo paid him 37 cents. A little later the 37-cent bottle was passed around. "It ain't bad," one of them said.

The Social Disease War

An unusual local campaign, both for its wide public participation and the nature of the problem, was launched in the spring of 1937. This ws called "The War on Social Diseases." So alarmed was the general public over the issue that more than 2,000 persons attended a mass meeting the following winter in the Shrine Auditorium for a program sponsored by the League Against Veneral Diseases. In the 1930's, prior to the discovery of miracle drugs, venereal diseases could become a stubborn epidemic. According to one report, 1,000 persons in Fort Wayne were infected in a short period by syphilis and gonorrhea. That estimate by the Board of Health launched the campaign of the league which utilized radio, newspapers and a series of public meetings to educate and urge use of a Venereal Clinic which was established.

In May of 1937 the City of Fort Wayne filed suit against the State of Indiana to restrain the State from collecting some $100,000 in taxes levied against the Fort Wayne Municipal Utilities. The Indiana Legislature passed the act in 1933 in an effort to pry tax funds from municipally-owned utilities. Fort Wayne had refused to pay the sum of $23,000 due each year, which with penalties, accumulated to the $100,000 figure. Mayor Baals and the Indiana Municipal League led the fight against the legislation. The suit contested the Constitutionality of the tax law. Baals said it would make as much sense to tax the courthouse or the public library as the public utility. The suit was filed in Allen Circuit Court.

While the city fathers were waiting for the outcome of that battle, the Fort Wayne war against syphilis and gonorrhea was drawing wide attention. The Oct. 28, 1937, edition of the Chicago Tribune devoted considerable space to the matter. "Business and civic leaders of this city are conducting an intensive educational campaign to stamp out syphilis and gonorrhea," the Tribune said in a story filed with a Fort Wayne, Ind., dateline. "With the support of Mayor Harry W. Baals, a League Against Venereal Disease has been organized and today the membership numbers more than 7,000 citizens. Dr. Karl Eberly, secretary and director of the city's public health department, pointed out that in the past, slight attention was paid to the usual laws applicable to venereal diseases, but in the campaign which began last February, citizens have become educated to the symptoms, treatment and control of the diseases through newspapers, radio talks and public mass meetings."

In February, 1938, Circuit Judge Harry H. Hilgemann handed down a decision and a victory for Fort Wayne in its fight against state-imposed taxes on municipal utilities. Judge Hilgemann found the tax law unconstitutional. The ruling was in connection with the suit filed by City Attorney Walter Helmke and Associate Attorney George Leonard to enjoin the state from collecting $108,163 in accumulated taxes on city utilities. Subsequently, legislation was introduced to repeal the tax.

Down the Rain Barrel

An item in the Municipal Review of December, 1937, answers a question which likely was on many people's minds during the existence of the high hill and water tank at Reservior Park. How many gallons? "The old Lafayette St. Reservoir holding 4,800,000 gallons of softened refrigerated water, has been cleaned, inspected and again put into service, according to L. R. Mathews, superintendent of the Three Rivers Filtration Plant. The cleaning was done with a fire stream by a fire crew from Engine House No. 9." William Roebel and Sam Moorhead were in charge of water works crews and Captain Fred Goeglein headed the fire crew. The reservoir held 4,800,000 gallons of filtered water delivered to it from the Three Rivers Filtration Plant through a pipe system. "By continuing to use the Lafayette St. Reservoir . . . water is always available in addition to the 20 million gallons of storage of softened and filtered water in the large underground reservoir at the Filteration Plant," Matthews reported. The great Res tank was cut down and filled in when the top of the hill was leveled in 1959.

The old Reservoir was a holdover from the early days of the Fort Wayne Water Works and was constructed in 1880. In those hard times, homes with baths were charged $10 extra. Hotels got a special low rate if they caught a portion of their water needs in tanks draining from the roof during rain storms. Old billing records show the rate structure before meters came into use. The lack of meters should not be so strange in that even in the 1970's the city of New York still didn't have water meters; and being bankrupt, didn't have the means to install them. In Fort Wayne in the 19th Century, livery stables were charged $2.50 annually for water per horse; soda fountains were levied $5; one family residences were charged $5 with $1 extra for wash basins and $10 extra for bathtubs—an obvious soak the rich policy. Much water was delivered by tank wagon. Two horse water wagons were charged $75 a year and one horse rigs $50 for all the water they could haul. Saloons, of which there were hundreds just in the immediate vicinity of Columbia St., paid $16 a year. The Harmon House, a 41-room hotel, paid an annual fee of $75 provided it used a rain tank. Avalon House, disdaining the rain barrel, was assessed $75 for six months. But all that ended with the installation of meters in the first decade of the 20th Century. And the Res hill finally became little more than a good slope for sled riding by neighborhood children in the winter time.

The most expensive public works project up to that date in the history of Fort Wayne was started September 16, 1938. This was the construction of the $5,322,000 sewage disposal project. For the sake of comparison, the sewer system project cost was nearly double that of the 1931 project to build the Filtration Plant and St. Joe River Dam.

Down in the Sewers

Fort Wayne from its early days had never had an adequate sewerage system nor a sewage disposal plant. The pollution going into the rivers, particularly the Maumee, was no small matter. Time and again efforts to meet the city's sewage disposal needs had been frustrated by politics, indecision and financial considerations. To pay for the system, the city sold bonds totalling $3.5 million. The balance of the cost came from Federal funds. In addition to major public works under the streets to lay sewer lines, the disposal plant on the east edge of the city just north of the Maumee River was constructed. The system, which handled both sanitary flow and surface water meant the elimination for the first time of flooding in some parts of the city during periods of heavy rainfall. Wet basements and cellars were largely eliminated, as was the flooding of some of the intersections and underpasses. The major elements of the project included the Clinton interceptor, the Rudisill interceptor, the St. Mary's interceptor and the Wayne interceptor. A tunnel 40 feet underground was constructed in the Rudisill area for the 10-foot pipe being laid by crews of the Bass Engineering Co. and the Detroit Construction Company. By September of 1939, $3,668,000 in contracts had been let. In addition to the bond financing, the portion funded by the PWA was the largest grant ever issued by the Public Works Administration in Indiana, some $2 million.

The $5 million sewer project was beneficial to Fort Wayne for a reason in addition to the direct public improvement. By 1938 the programs of President Roosevelt directed toward recovery from the Depression were increasingly questionable. Though there was some improvement in economic conditions in 1936 and 1937, there was a severe turndown in 1938. Unemployment became almost as widespread as the early 1930's. It was not until the outbreak of war in Europe in the fall of 1939, and the parallel worldwide demand for material and products, that the Depression ended. The situation is reflected in employment and production statistics in Fort Wayne and throughout the Nation.

It was in November, 1938, that Mayor Baals of Fort Wayne and Harold L. Ickes, Administrator of the PWA and latter Interior Secretary, engaged in a battle of words in the New York Times. In an article in the Nov. 20 issue of the Times, Baals "warned mayors of other cities against a tendency to apply for PWA grants which became financial burdens after their construction." City Attorney Walter E. Helmke, who was with Baals in New Work, told Times reporters that "Mr. Baals' economy program during his first administration had made him the first mayor to be re-elected in the last 30 years in Fort Wayne."

Harold Ickes, one of the Roosevelt braintrusters, was particularly incensed by the headline used in the New York Times story. In the Nov. 25 issue, he said:

"In your issue of Nov. 20 I noted this headline: 'Useless Doodads by PWA Are Scored.' When I read the story it appeared that Mayor Harry W. Baals of Fort Wayne, Ind., had warned the mayors of other cities against a tendency to apply for PWA grants to build useless doodads which become financial burdens after construction. I submit that your heading is misleading and carries an improper reflection upon the Public Works Administration, of which I am head. PWA does not build doodads and even if Mr. Baals really meant PWA, which I doubt, he does not charge that we build doodads. His warning is merely against cities applying for PWA grants in order to build doodads."

All-time Tax Low

By 1938, people in Fort Wayne were paying one of the lowest tax rates in the United States. The city had an astonishing record for reducing its taxes with the onset of the Depression. The downward trend was started by Mayor Hosey and continued by Mayor Baals. In 1933, the total tax rate in Fort Wayne was $2.75 per $100 in assessed valuation. This figure included State, County, Civil City, School, Library and Township levies. The township poor relief accounted for .107 of the figure. The total assessed valuation in the city in 1933 was $148,219,960, and that figure hardly varied until the end of the decade. The tax rate in 1934 was $2.73. In 1935 the city tax rate was down to $2.60 and in 1936 the rate fell to $2.36. The 1937 rate, payable in 1938, was $2.24; and again in 1938, payable in 1939, the same $2.24 tax rate prevailed, the all-time low in the modern era of Fort Wayne. The 1939 rate, payable in 1940, was $2.61—a start on the upward trend which was almost continuous for the next three decades. But even at $2.61, the Fort Wayne rate was by a wide margin the lowest of any Indiana cities in the population class.

It was in 1938 that the city initiated major moves to boost living standards through a Housing Authority. William B.F. Hall, named chairman of the Fort Wayne Housing Authority, said the agency "was first determining whether or not funds could be secured' then a study of the best possible uses for these funds" would be made.

"To date, we have shown sufficient need to obtain from the United States Housing Authority an earmarking of $1,500,000 for a loan (not a grant) for the betterment of housing conditions in Fort Wayne. We have obtained assurance from local investors that we shall have no difficulty in raising our 10 per cent share of the project by the sale of bonds, rather than placing the burden upon our taxpayers." Hall said the WPA would expend $30,000 making a detailed housing census of 1938 conditions. "A similar survey made in 1934 showed conditions slightly worse than the national average and disclosed the surprising fact that only one family out of five in Fort Wayne had individual bathing facilities." Hall said the city's worst housing problems would be uncovered; and the primary purpose would be to improve conditions, "but next to this we feel that the creation of additional employment in our community is of prime importance.

Night Airplane Service

In December, 1938, Fort Wayne entered a new phase in transportation—night airplane service. "For the first time in the history of Fort Wayne, this city now has regularly scheduled night airplane transportation service, affording facilities for passenger, express and air mail," the Aviation Commission reported. "During the past month TWA, due largely to the fact that Fort Wayne has an airport splendidly equipped, meeting the rigid requirements of the Federal Government and its new Civil Aeronautics Authority, included Fort Wayne on its night air route." The Airport had installed electric runway lights and radio for both broadcasting and range in prior months.

On the occasion of the first night flight of air mail, the Mayor of Chicago Edward J. Kelly sent a letter to Fort Wayne, delivered by Capt. Phares McFarren: "Tonight for the first time in air transportation history the great cities of Fort Wayne and Chicago are linked with night air mail, passenger and express service. This air bridge between the two cities, made possible by TWA skyliners, will serve to draw our communities closer together and offer residents of both a convenient, swift and modern travel service that enables residents to spend business days in each city, returning home the same evening," Mayor Kelly said. In historical perspective, the first overland link for Chicago in the days of Fort Dearborn was the Dearborn Trail to Fort Wayne. Similarly, the first rail from Chicago to an outside city was the Pittsburgh, Fort Wayne and Chicago Railroad. The "splendid Municipal Airport" at Fort Wayne mentioned in the 1938 report was the field on the north edge of town which was later named Smith Field, but originally called Paul Baer Airport.

In April, 1939, Fort Wayne's four-year-old fight with the State of Indiana over the taxing of municipal utilities came to a head. Fort Wayne won one battle but lost another. A bill introduced by State Senator Wilbur DeWeese, repealing the tax, was passed by the General Assembly. This freed Fort Wayne from paying the annual tax burden of more than $20,000 which the city had been refusing to pay anyway. But in the matter of back taxes and penalties, it was another situation.

The Indiana Supreme Court reversed an earlier decision of Allen Circuit Court Judge Harry Hilgemann. Hilgemann had ruled the State tax was unconstitutional. The Board of Tax Commissioners had appealed that decision and won the issue in the State Supreme Court. This meant Fort Wayne was ordered to pay the tax and the accumulated penalties through the years which totaled about $150,000. It wasn't until 1941 that the matter was put to rest, at which time the City and the State Tax Board compromised with the city paying $48,000.

The city elections of 1938 pitted Harry Baals, the Republican candidate seeking re-election, against Harry Gottchalk, the Democratic nominee. Gottchalk had been earlier elected county surveyor. But the Republicans swept the city. Baals had 29,163 votes to Gottschalk's 18,338. It was the second term of a nine-man City Council—six districts and three at-large, rather than the 16 councilmen of prior years. The winning city ticket, in addition to Baals, included William H. Schannen, city judge; Leonard Ellenwood, city clerk; and Paul C. Wolf, Arno Spiegel, Harry McMillen, Frank W. King, Harold A. Hart, John Hoelle, Benjamin Bennett, Edward H. Fisher and Charles E. Moellering, all councilmen. Early in his second administration, Mayor Baals named several new officials to city government posts. These included David Lewis, secretary of the Fort Wayne Federation of Labor, to the Board of Public Works; Ernest C. Gallmeier, board member of the Fort Wayne Labor Council and Local 901, UE official, to the Board of

Safety; and Dan C. Flanagan, chairman of the Allen County Republican Central Committee, as associate city attorney. Otto H. Adams was named general superintendent of City Utilities to succeed Paul Thiele, who died in August, 1939. George Eisenhut was police chief and John C. Stahlhut, fire chief.

The Blue Cast Raid

One of the more celebrated raids on a love nest in Allen County occurred on a night late in May, 1939. Twenty-one couples were grabbed by county officers at an old abandoned sanitarium near the Ohio State Line. Reputed to be the largest haunted house in the northeast part of Indiana, the place proved to be full of life. "For years the old Blue Cast Mineral Springs Sanitarium on Road 24, nineteen miles east of Fort Wayne was a celebrated shrine for those seeking to regain the zip and zest of youth" a newspaper reported June 1, 1939. "The magnificant natural beauty spot, nestled on the lofty banks of the Maumee, was never so popular, however, as it has been recently when every night it has been the trysting place for scores of love-bitten couples. Heeding insistent complaints, Sheriff Walter A. Felger and Deputy Sheriffs Walter Adams and Martin Regendanz several nights ago swooped down on the place. Some escaped the carefully-planned raid of the law, but when noses were counted at the county jail, it was determined that 21 couples had been hustled into cars and escorted to the county brig." The 42 young persons ranged in age from 15 to 26 years old. C. Byron Hayes, the county prosecutor, let the 42 captives go with a lecture and their names were never released—which led to all sorts of speculation in the eastern environs of Allen County for many years thereafter. It was widely known in the vicinity that "wholesale love-making" was occurring, according to the sheriff. And all this despite the Blue Cast Springs' reputation as a place for haunting. "Thrill parties have been staged . . . protests of the ghosts against the nocturnal disturbances, practical jokesters frequently smash one of the large windows, the clatter of the shattering glass driving some of the more faint-hearted into veritable hysterics."

Early on the morning of June 24, 1939, Fort Wayne police were startled by a strongman in the 1100 block of Webster St. who crushed with his hands an "iron claw" that officers were using in an attempt to subdue him. Patrolmen Clyde Burton and George Szink had been called to the scene to subdue Al Rogers reportedly in an unruly condition. Rogers reportedly landed a heavy blow on Burton. Szink snapped "the claw" on Rogers' wrist. The claw was a half-inch steel hook police used in those days to deal with difficult customers. Rogers jerked the apparatus away from Szink and broke off the hook. Eventually, officers succeeded in subduing Rogers and cited him for disorderly conduct.

In one of the freak train accidents in the city, two persons were killed and 17 were injured on Oct. 24, 1939. The crash occurred in full view of people in midtown and those working at nearby General Electric plants. A yard engine backed into a passenger train on the Wabash tracks just above Fairfield Avenue. In those days the Wabash roundhouse was just north of the Wabash elevation at Fairfield where the G.E. parking lot was later installed.

There was a time when Fort Wayne's fire chiefs weren't hired and fired with the changes of City Hall politics. The spoils system for fire chiefs came into practice in the late 1940's. The earlier system of tenure can be seen in the retirement of Fire Chief John C. Stahlhut on February 1, 1940. Stahlhut had joined the Fire Department on Feb. 1, 1890, and had served as chief since Jan. 1, 1925. He had served 50 years in the department and 15 continuous years as chief under administrations of both parties. Stahlhut was succeeded by Carter Bowser, a 20-year veteran in the Fire Department. Bowser, who was named State Fire Marshall in 1945 and was in retirement some years later, was killed in the tornado which struck the city in the summer of 1954.

After Franklin D. Roosevelt's landslide victories over Herbert Hoover in 1932 and Alf Landon in 1936, FDR failed to carry a majority in Indiana even though elected to third and fourth Presidential terms nationally. In the election of November, 1940, Wendell L. Willkie of Elwood, Indiana, after one of the more spirited campaigns in history, received 899,466 Hoosier votes compared with 874,063 for FDR. In the 1944 Presidential election in Indiana, Thomas E. Dewey of New York outpolled Roosevelt by a vote of 875,891 to 781,403. Between Roosevelt's 1936 victory and Lyndon B. Johnson's win in 1964, Republican presidential candidates won every Hoosier test.

Fighting Pollution

The city's first real fight against air pollution was begun in the spring of 1941. Until that time smoking chimneys were often seen as a sign of progress, healthy industry and plentiful jobs. It was estimated the smoke was causing $2 million in damage and cleanup costs, in addition to the hazard to health. In the era when coal was still the dominant heating and industrial fuel and the engines of the railroad trains used soft coal in large amounts, Fort Wayne was subject to smog conditions some days of the year unknown in later decades. Mayor Harry Baals named Ermin P. Ruf, vice-president of Wayne Paper Box and Printing Co., as chairman of the Citizens Executive Committee on Smoke Elimination. The program was essentially voluntary with the urging of citizens and companies to find means to clean up exhaust of their own chimneys. R. W. Noland headed a committe of the Fort Wayne Engineers Club with the purpose of dispensing facts in the anti-pollution campaign.

In the late 1930's and early 1940's, recreational opportunities were advanced considerably. Regular buses transported thousands of children free from city locations to the Municipal Beach. The improvement and lighting of the baseball diamonds at the Beach, and the building of bleachers which were regularly packed by thousands for local league ball games, marked a highpoint in Fort Wayne intracity athletics. Six tennis courts at Weisser Park were floodlighted in the summer of 1941 and baseball diamonds at Foster Park were also lighted. In the meantime, the ice skaters shelter at the Reservoir was built under an expanded bandstand and a new rustic-looking shelter was erected at Packard Park.

Public Housing

The first public housing unit of Westfield Village was completed on January 31, 1941. At the outset, 120 family residential units were included in the project on a 15-acre tract north of Taylor St. and between Rockhill Park, Freeman and Morris Streets. The rent for a two-bedroom apartment was $12.50 a month. Three-bedroom units were $1 more and one-bedroom units $1 less. The units were open to low income families only. The units were housed in 48 buildings. The Westfield development, the city's largest venture into public housing, was the second project of the Fort Wayne Public Housing Authority. Originally, in 1939 the Authority had built 50 pre-fabricated houses, erected by WPA Workers, which rented for $2.50 a week. The Housing Authority was created in February, 1938, with William B.F. Hall, chairman. At the time of the Westfield development, Albert Schaaf headed the Authority and John Essig was executive-director. Other members of the Authority included Mrs. Marie Kane, F. Arthur Schack, Hugh Keegan and Walter Goll. Westfield buildings were conventionally built, supervised by A.M. Strauss, architects. Westfield was constructed on a loan of $300,000 made to the local Authority by the U.S. Housing Authority. Cost of the 15-acre tract was $4,000 and construction was let to Max Irmscher & Sons on a bid of $253,000. The per unit construction cost was $1,830. In the early 1940's, many of the units were rented by families of servicemen stationed at Baer Field. Following the war, the units reverted to use by regular low-income families. Westfield Village was razed after more than 30 years of use in 1974. Three smaller housing projects were initiated in 1941. Credit for $200,000 was extended in May, 1941 by the FHA for some 60 units to be built in the

Harvester Park Addition on the city's east side. The aim was to supply homes for expected employees of a new Studebaker Corporation aircraft gear plant which was to be completed in the fall of 1941 in the East End industrial area. The Harvester Park project was a work of Harvester Park Housing Corp. rather than the Public Housing Authority. The Housing Authority, with the apparent success of Westfield Village under its belt, announced plans for two more public developments in the summer of 1941. On June 24, 1941, an ordinance for the apportionment of $375,000 to be allocated to Fort Wayne was introduced in the City Council. Plans set the construction of 62 units between Morris and Catalpa Sts. and 34 units from Catalpa to the Junk Ditch. Design and construction was along the lines of Westfield Village. A portion of the units was earmarked for "white tenants" and the other was termed "the colored project" at the time.

In 1941, James R. Newkirk, a Fort Wayne attorney, was named one of two Indiana delegates to the American Bar Association's policymaking group. Newkirk was president of the Indiana State Bar Association and in 1949 was named to the American Bar Assn. nine-member section on Probate and Trust Law.

America First Crusade

Charles A. Lindbergh was in Fort Wayne to deliver the main address at a massive rally of the America First Committee. An estimated 5,500 persons jammed into the Gospel Temple to hear Lindbergh and another 4,500 or more stood outside on Friday night, October 3, 1941. Lindbergh warned the cheering throng that the Roosevelt Administration was conditioning America for war. He said a governmental gag on free speech would be the next step. The talk was carried on a national radio network. Miss Vera Sessler, secretary of the Anthony Wayne Chapter of the American First Committee, chaired the meeting. Lindbergh was introduced by Mayor Harry Baals and other speakers included the Rev. John A. O'Brien of the University of Notre. O'Brien said Lindbergh was a "Gladiator fighting for truth, for honor, for Justice for America." According to the report, there was an organized effort to incite trouble before the meeting, but no heckling occurred during Lindbergh's speech. "We are in fact governed by one man who has consistently evaded the checks and balances on which representative government balances on which representative government depends—a man drawing more and more dictatorial powers into his own hands." Lindbergh said any effort to invade Europe and crush Hitler "will necessitate turning this country into a military state. We will have to raise an army of 10 million men. It means every family in America will have its wounded and dead." The famous flier warned "that an Administration which can throw us into an undeclared naval war against the will of our people can prevent freedom of speech. Those of us who oppose war do not know what next will be subjected to censorship." Other speakers said they were actually supporting the president "in his solemn declaration to the American people not to send any American boys into a foreign war."

Baer Army Air Base

Late in 1940, rumors that the Army Air Corps was contemplating the location of a major air base at Fort Wayne were circulating around the community. On December 11, 1940, the site of the proposed base was made public. It was to be on a square mile of farm land southwest of the city bound on the north by the Ferguson Road, on the east by the tracks of the old Lake Erie & Western, then known as the Nickel Plate Road and finally the Norfolk & Western Railway, and on the northwest by State Road 3. A short distance east of the tract was State Road 1. Just to the north of the Ferguson Road was another 80-acre tract wanted by the Air Corps for cantonment purposes. According to the original announcement, the cost of the installation would be in excess of $3 million. It was also planned that the City would purchase the land under a $100,000 bond issue and lease it to the Army. Following World War II the Army Air Corps was reorganized and renamed the U.S. Air Force. Construction began in February, 1941. With the deepening of the war in Europe and increasing fears of U.S. involvement, the work was speeded and the size of the project expanded. By summer and fall, the existence of a small city in-the-making could be noted in the area south of Waynedale. On October 26, 1941, it was noted that the size of the air base had been expanded to 907 acres and the expenditure to more than $4 million. "More than 100 buildings of various sizes and intended for a wide variety of uses have been erected. They are designed to house 184 officers and 1,700 enlisted men and provide working space for the personnel in the operation of the air base," it was reported. The base had its own sewage system, water conditioning, filtration plant and fire department. Electricity was obtained from Indiana Service Corporation. There was a complete hospital with professional staff of doctors and nurses. A chapel was built for use by men of various faiths and a modern theatre was equipped. The base had its own post office, establishments, plus telephone and telegraph barber shops, dry cleaning and tailoring installations. The two main runways, each more than 6,000 feet long, formed a giant X on the field. Each was 300 feet wide. The center strips, 100 feet wide and of concrete, were flanked on each side with stablization paving. Twelve underground tanks, each with a capacity of 25,000 gallons, were installed for storing aviation gasoline. A 160 by 200 foot hangar and other service buildings were built on the south side of the field. T. F. Airis, a U.S. engineer, was in charge of the construction, largely carried out by contractors.

The choosing of a name for the new Army Air Base caused a minor flap. The Board of Aviation Commmissioners originally named the air base Anthony Wayne Field. The thinking was that Fort Wayne already had Paul Baer Municipal Airport on the north side of town. But the War Department turned thumbs down and said Anthony Wayne couldn't be used because the policy was to name fields after fliers who had served in the U.S. Air Corps. Finally, on May 13, 1941, the commissioners chose the name Baer Field and submitted it to the War Department. At the same time, the Commissioners changed the name of Paul Baer Municipal Airport to Smith Field. Baer was a World War I ace who had been downed in combat and had spent the rest of the war in a German prison camp. He was killed in an air crash in 1930 in China. Art Smith was an early flight pioneer, stunt man and air mail carrier who died near Montpelier, Ohio, in 1926. According to an Associated Press story, date lined Washington, May 13, 1941, Congressman George Gillie was notified Anthony Wayne's name was out as far as naming the field was concerned. "Because he was born long before flying machines were even seriously thought of, Gen. Anthony Wayne, pioneer warrior and explorer, cannot be honored by having the Army's new Air Corps flying field at Fort Wayne, Indiana, named after him," the AP reported. Gillie said however, he intended to stick with the original request. The Army came back with a list of suggestions which included neither Anthony Wayne nor Paul Baer. By coincidence, the same day Congressman Gillie said he was insisting on Anthony Wayne and the War Department was sending out their own list of possibilities, the Board of Aviation Commissioners at Fort Wayne switched to the Baer Field name. It was soon accepted by all concerned. Dedication of Baer Field was on September 29, 1941. A ribbon was cut by Col. Eugene A. Lohman, the first commanding officer at Baer Field. Three Fort Wayne clergymen participated: Dr. Paul Krauss of Trinity English Lutheran Church; Father S. Joachim Ryder of St. John the Baptist Catholic Church; and Rabbi Irving A. Weingart of B'Nai Jacob Congregation.

The Hottest Fighters

Baer Field became a live airport on December 6, 1941, with the arrival of some of the hottest fighter squadrons in the U.S. "The long-anticipated arrival of pilots and planes of the 31st Pursuit Group at Baer Field took place today when 31 fliers landed their streamlined Airacobras on the runways at the air base. A bright sun and a biting wind, which whipped across the concrete aprons, greeted the pilots here today after they had been delayed in coming to Baer Field since last Monday due to fog and poor visibility," it was reported that day. Within a few more days, between 80 and 100 of the P-39 Airacobras were on the field. "The P-39 used by the 31st Pursuit Group is virtually an arsenal of the air, with weapons suitable for strafing troops, messing up supply depots, halting tanks or nailing bombers," it was reported. The sleek fighter with engines behind the pilot had just been put into service in England. By the stroke of Pearl Harbor, the U.S. was in the war the day following arrival of the squads at Baer Field. Lt. Col. John Hawkins was commanding officer of the 31st Pursuit Group. In addition to the air arrivals, a 54 truck convoy came in at 11:15 a.m. from Fort Bragg, N.C., by way of Columbus, Ohio. A shroud of secrecy was wrapped around Baer Field movements with the new war footing. Tight security was enforced, and by common agreement, the reporting of flights and movements of military personnel was forbidden. It is clear, however, that the numbers located at Baer Field soon ran into the thousands, and many more thousands either visited or were stationed at the base at various times during the war period. The facilities of Baer Field were enlarged. On March 15, 1943, it became an important link in the troop carrier effort. Just how many of the flyers and others at Baer Field later died in the war has never been reported. Many of them became familiar with the city and were remembered by the many friends both at the base and in Fort Wayne. Others returned to Fort Wayne after the war. During the early 1940's, the men and some women, became regular participants in community activities. These included social events, parades, park activities and joint efforts with civil authorities. With the conclusion of the war, the disappearance of this phase of Fort Wayne life occurred almost as fast as it had begun.

At the Airport

A major fire swept a portion of Baer Field on December 4, 1946, almost five years to the day after the activating of the base by the arrival of pursuit squadrons in 1941. The fire started at 3:19 p.m. when an oil heater on the second floor of the 400-foot-long main hangar exploded. The flames, originating on the west end of the huge hangar, were whipped quickly out of control by a south-westerly wind. The hangar, which had cost $212,000 when constructed in 1941, was completely destroyed. Both the Army and the FBI conducted investigations of the cause. There were no deaths in the blaze. When the air field was later turned over to the city of Fort Wayne, some military presence was continued during the following decades. This was the Indiana Air National Guard and its 122nd Tactical Fighter Group. The National Guard developed its facilities along the eastern fringe of the air field. The first civilian terminal building was built on the western side of the field, but the small facility was later replaced with a municipal terminal on the north fringe. The 122nd Tactical Fighter Group went with the changes in aircraft, from the conventional aircraft to the various jets developed in the 1950's, 1960's and 1970's. The air guardsmen were training in F-100 Super Sabre jets in the mid-1970's. Brig. Gen. William R. Sefton was commanding officer of the Baer-Field-based group during much of the post-war period.

Baer Field, which had become a $10 million installation by the end of the war, had successively been occupied by fighter squadrons, medium bomber training units and a staging area for airbourne troop carrier operations. At the peak of personnel, more than 8,000 men and women were based at the field. Following V-E day, the field became a separation center and practically all military presence was ended by early 1947. On Feb. 10, 1948, the War Assets Administration put the field up for sale. Most of the surplus equipment and appointments were sold off in public sales in the following months. The city made application for the airport itself. The acquisition of Baer Field by the City of Fort Wayne was accomplished June 29, 1949, by action of the City Council. In the following days the city took physical control of the 938-acre expanse of Baer Field.

Camp Scott

The War Department on May 8, 1942, announced that a small railroad unit would be located in Fort Wayne. This was the beginning of an installation which would be known as Camp Scott. It was located between Wayne Trace and the Pennsylvania Railroad on the city's east side and had considerable impact on the community during the war years. Among other things, it would later be the site of explosions and mark the only instance of prisonment of foreign prisoners of war at Fort Wayne. "The 130th Railroad Battalion of the United States Army to be mobilized this month will be stationed at Fort Wayne," the original announcement said. The unit consisted of 18 officers and 103 enlisted men. Training was entirely for military railroad operation and maintenance. The date of mobilization was May 15, 1942. Full strength of the railroad operating battalion was set at 800 men, with the nucleus of the operation at Fort Wayne. Lt. Col. John J. Clutz, a Pennsylvania Railroad veteran, was named commander. Camp Thomas A. Scott grew considerably in the following months with the construction of some dozen buildings and the enlargement of the operation. Early on the morning of April 18, 1944, a portion of the city was shaken by two heavy blasts in the Camp Scott area. Telephone lines were jammed with calls to the police and fire departments. It was later reported in the day however, that the explosions were land mines detonated at Camp Scott as part of training exercises. Part of the training at the camp was the preparing of men for overseas work in the detection and demolition of mines. The community learned on Nov. 6, 1944, that Camp Scott had been converted to a new use —the holding of German prisoners of war. Without public notice, the camp had been enclosed with barbed wire and guard towers had been erected. The old railroad battalion had been moved out and the new prisoner-of-war operation was under the command of Lt. Frank Bodenhorn, who formerly had been foreman of carriers at the Fort Wayne Post Office. The German prisoners held at the stockade were used for industrial and farm labor and were paid 80 cents a day in coupons furnished by the government. At the conclusion of the war Camp Scott was closed down and the last seven buildings were sold in 1948. A portion of the area was used starting in 1946 for temporary veteran housing under the Fort Wayne Housing Authority. The operation was closed down in 1949. A portion of the old Camp Scott property was sold to General Industries, a prefabricated home manufacturer.

The Casad Depot, a major World War II operation for the storage of guns and ammunition, was built in 1943 at a cost of more than $5 million. The depot, named after Col. Adam A. Casad, was at a 627-acre site on the Edgerton Road near New Haven. Large quantities of anti-aircraft guns, machine tools, auto parts and ammunition and other ordnance material were stored there. Officials at the Army depot reported at one time that there were twice as many anti-aircraft weapons there as were used in London during the height of the Nazi bombings. The operation was largely manned by soldiers from Camp Scott. In December, 1947, it was deactivated as an ordnance depot but was put back into use in 1948 as an engineering depot. In subsequent years more than 300 persons were employed there until June, 1955, when the depot was closed and the facilities were put to other uses.

"Remember Pearl Harbor"

Sunday, Dec. 7, 1941, the "day of Infamy" on which the Japanese struck Pearl Harbor early in the morning, was an afternoon shock to people in Fort Wayne. From that moment, the consciousness of war was the dominant element in the city and elsewhere in the nation for nearly four years.

In many respects the defense effort had been underway months prior to the entry of the U.S. in the hostilities. The draft was already in existence and quite a number of men were already in training camps or on service duty. Defense Bonds had been marketed for some time, though they were renamed War Bonds. But the war almost immediately became a vigorous pursuit on all levels. The pace of enlistments and the selective service quickened. A new emphasis was placed on war production. Thousands of women went to work in plants, replacing men who were gone and providing the productive power and services for rapid expansion in output. An almost universal fashion for women working in factories became black slacks, white sox with black high-heeled shoes and a scarf on the head half-way back from the forehead.

There was an attitude of total mobilization which extended to the home front. Particularly in the early months of the war, there was an emphasis on civilian defense. City government took the lead in the greatest volunteer movement in the history of the community. Under a general ordinance passed by the City Council, Fort Wayne created a Municipal Defense Council which cooperated with state and national defense councils. Two thousand block wardens were named and instructed; 30,000 homes were listed; manpower was registered and diverse volunteer services were enlisted and charted. Organizations such as the Red Cross were expanded and hundreds of volunteers were recruited for the auxiliary police and fire departments. Mayor Harry Baals, in an address January 23, 1942, outlined the local program. "In the new type of Civilian Defense one of the most vital units is the Defense Warden who furnishes volunteer manpower for our fire and police and other municipal agencies. The wardens will be the organized trained army of civilians who will be ready to meet the remote emergency of invasion, insure the production of war material and stimulate community morale, all within the legal framework." Harry G. Hogan was appointed general warden; D. P. McDonald, Sr. was named chairman of the Executive Committee and Morals and Hygiene Committee; Ernest J. Gallmeyer was chairman of Defense Industries; and James M. Barrett, Jr., was chairman of county volunteers. Particular concern was directed toward the security of the electric and water utilities. Fire Chief Carter Bowser and Police Chief Jule Stumpf headed the fire and police divisions of the Civil Defense. Dr. H. O. Bruggemann was in charge of emergency medical; Robert Beams, emergency public works; and Thomas J. Kelly, emergency utility service. More than 3,000 volunteers and city employees attended classes on first aid, dealing with gas and incendiary bombs and other emergency and disaster measures. An alert system, particularly designed in event of potential air attack, was developed.

The attack by foreign powers never came to Fort Wayne, but on June 20, 1942, much of the volunteer force had the opportunity to practice their emergency skills. Rain, hail and windstorm struck the city in what was described as "one of the worst deluges in Fort Wayne's history, paralyzing power, light, telephone and transportation services." Even the new sewers couldn't handle the water. The rainfall was the largest on record for the month of June. Not only were the underpasses made into small lakes, but even downtown streets such as Berry St. were under a foot or more of water. The street cars weren't running, the lights were out, and the block wardens were out in force.

End of "Jap" Gardens

On May 14, 1942, the Park Commissioners yielded to petitions of several local organizations and individuals and changed the name of the Japanese Gardens in West Swinney Park to the Adolph Jaenicke Gardens. Jaenicke was park superintendant and had been instrumental in the creation of the gardens in 1927. "Protests made to the Park Board asked that the name of the gardens be changed as a rebuke to Japan," it was reported at the time. A sign at the entrance of the gardens had been taken down a few days after the Japanese attack on Pearl Harbor the previous December. "It is now proposed that visitors to the Jaenicke Gardens be educated to consider these oriental features as being Chinese rather than of Jap distinction," it was reported. China was an ally during the war. At the same meeting, the Park Commissioners approved a plan by which soldiers at Baer Field could have free use of the Municipal Golf Course. In 1942, a large Serviceman's Center was established on the north side of Washington Blvd. between Calhoun and Harrison Streets. It was staffed by many individuals and members of local organizations. The center provided entertainment, snacks, dances and other programs for visiting soldiers, sailors and airmen. Hundreds of girls of the Fort Wayne area were hostesses at the center during the war period.

Despite war and rationing, the closest thing to a general strike against taxes in the history of Fort Wayne and Indiana continued into 1942. This was regarding the Indiana Gross Income Tax. Grocers for several years had been refusing to pay the tax and had filed suits against the levy, contending it was unconstitutional. Higher courts had ruled the position of the tax evaders untenable, but the hedging continued. By June, 1942, the Indiana Gross Income Tax Department declared Sheriff Walter A. Felger "has been entirely too lenient" in collecting gross income tax warrants. They cited $61,786 in delinquencies, but actual default in tax paying was believed many times that figure. The State authorities threatened confiscation of business in a drive to clean up delinquencies in Fort Wayne.

War Production

A considerable portion of Fort Wayne business had converted to military production even before the entry of the U.S. in the war in December, 1941. In 1942, practically all the plants were producing war equipment. International Harvester was making trucks and other military vehicles. Tanks and ordnance could be seen passing from or through the city on railroads most every day. General Electric produced a variety of apparatus and motors for aircraft and ground equipment. A huge red brick plant was erected on Taylor St. for the building of superchargers for aircraft. The plant became a permanent part of G.E. operations. Tokheim and Wayne Pump and similar factories built bombs, shells and related items. Small factories did their part. The turning out of wire dies, an essential specialty to the successful war effort, was almost entirely a Fort Wayne thing. Magnavox was active in producing electronic gear. Factories began the three-trick habit with many operating right through the weekends. Amid all the renewed activity, there was rationing of most essentials. Gasoline could be purchased only with government issued stamps. Sugar, meats and some other foods were rationed. Clothes and particularly shoes were rationed. Cigarettes weren't rationed but when "Lucky Strike Green" went to war so did most of the known brands of smokes. People had to be content with "Julips" and other kind of cigarettes and whisky brands seldom heard of before or since.

It was an era of roll-your-own cigarettes and bad booze. High school kids became experts at siphoning gasoline to fuel cars for weekends at Lake James. A wide-open attitude seemed to grip the city. Bars the length of Calhoun St. were crowded and busy, stimulated by soldiers from Baer Field and easier money in local hands. Slot machines made their appearance and were operated openly in spite of laws against gambling. As the war wore on, there was little trouble with the draft. It was the accepted thing for young men to be taken into the armed forces almost immediately after reaching 18 years. Large numbers joined in their 17th year when they could enlist in branches of their own choosing. Juvenile authorities reported some increasing difficulties, however, as roving gangs of teenagers made their appearance. Fort Wayne gained some notoriety in "Stars and Stripes" midway in the war when a "Sex Club on the Banks of the Maumee" made the service newspaper around the world.

A pending crisis was reported on Nov. 2, 1943 in the wake of the strike of the United Mine Workers. The wartime strike led to a major confrontation between UMW head John L. Lewis and President Roosevelt. "Electric utilities of Fort Wayne are today confronted with the greatest coal shortage in history . . . City Light & Power Works being reduced to a 20-day supply and Indiana Service Corporation to a 34-day supply," it was reported. The crisis was soon averted however, with settlement of the strike.

In addition to working in plants, women were for the first time seen in a number of occupations during the war. One instance caused a temporary flap between a cab company and a union. The difficulty centered on Miss Lucille Yost, one of the first women hired by the Safety Cab Company operated by H. B. Schultz. The Truck Drivers Union No. 414 threatened to strike at the hiring of women to replace male drivers. On April 2, 1942, Miss Yost resigned rather than precipitate the strike; but soon thereafter the matter was settled and women driving taxis became commonplace.

The Suspicious Episode

Though the campaign against aliens and foreign-born persons never reached the proportions of World War I, some measures were taken in the early days of World War II. In March, 1942, District Attorney Alexander Campbell launched an intensive check-out campaign against any who might be under suspicion. The office's file was reportedly crammed with FBI reports dealing with foreign-born persons, many of whom were naturalized citizens. Under a new interpretation of the law by Attorney General Francis Biddle, even naturalized citizens could have their citizenship cancelled if it was proven they were participating in activities inimical to the best interests of the country. The "new interpretation" took an almost immediate odd twist in Fort Wayne. The Fort Wayne Industrial Union Council sent a resolution to Attorney General Francis Biddle calling for the Justice Department to investigate the "policies, activities and connections of Willam J. Gross, editorial editor, and others responsible for the editorial policy of the Fort Wayne News-Sentinel." The resolution said Gross had been a member of Verne Marshall's "No Foreign Wars Committee" and noted the department had already taken action against Fr. Charles Coughlin's "Social Justice." Father Coughlin was a very outspoken critic of President Roosevelt. At the same time, Clem Grabner, president of the Industrial Union Council, had solicited help from Senator Robert M. LaFollette, chairman of the Senate Labor and Education Committee, against Gross and Westbrook Pegler, a syndicated columnist in the News-Sentinel. "As a result of the initation of a petition drive on the part of the Fort Wayne Industrial Union Council in pursuit of the removal of Pegler's column from the News-Sentinel, the council incurred the anger of Mr. William J. Gross. Mr. Gross, the editorial editor of the News-Sentinel has been noted for his appeasement, defeatist policies in relation to the national war effort. In an attempt to block the anti-Pegler movement of our organization, Mr. Gross, in a manner not unknown to professional labor baiters, began a vicious red-baiting smear campaign in his editorial columns." The driving edge of the union effort was a committee of three, consisting of Eldon Mee and John Gojack of the United Electrical, Radio and Machine Workers of America, and Howard Minier of the United Auto Workers Local. Gojack was the most active of the group. He later gained control of the UE but his union was largely supplanted by union regulars who formed the International Union of Electrical Workers (IUE) to take back control of the representation from the Communist-dominated leadership.

Ward Answers "Stooges"

Clifford B. Ward, News-Sentinel editor, answered the Council in a column on May 22: "The Commies and their stooges throughout the United States are now out to get Wesbrook Pegler. They are having petitions circulated in many cities to be presented to the newspapers publishing Mr. Pegler's column demanding that these newspapers throw Mr. Pegler's column out the window. This is the typically-indirect sort of attack in which the Commies specialize . . . getting someone besides themselves to boycott his customers. One of the four great principles for which the United States is now fighting is freedom of expression and the Communists in this country don't believe in that freedom, except for themselves."

A little later, on June 1, 1942, in a Good Evening column, Ward commented with broad tongue-in-cheek on the proposed Attorney-General investigation. "Someone, it seems, desires that I, along with others who are responsible for this newspaper's policies, be investigated by Attorney General Francis Biddle. That make me a big-time national villian just like Harry Bridges and Alphonse Capone, better known to his intimates as Scarface. I have said many mean things about Democrats, New Dealers and other miscellaneous persons, and as the investigation may bring out, I have even conspired numerous times with other Republicans to see that only Republicans were elected to office. Unfortunately, these conspiracies on many occasions have failed dismally. So it all boils down to the fact that the only thing that can really be pinned on me is that I am an incorrigible Republican who thinks that Harold Ickes, Madame Perkins and a lot of others at Washington ought to be retired to private life. However, I warn Mr. Biddle that my case isn't as simple as Harry Bridges. Harry can be sent back to Australia, but the best they can do with me is send me back to the south side of the city. Maybe they can force me to become a Democrat by getting me an Admiral's job in the Navy. Despite my admiration for Republicanism, I would sell out to the Democrats for a good Admiral's job. I've always wanted to be piped aboard a battleship."

Also in the news those months were the high rank jobs going to friends of FDR, including an Air Corps generalship to son Elliot Roosevelt. The question of the Attorney General's investigation soon faded. A more substantial case occurred in 1943 which led to the revocation of the citizenship of John Paul Schuchhardt, a Fort Wayne resident who had been naturalized in 1930. During the trial in the U.S. District Court, Schuchhardt was charged with being a member of the German American Bund, believed to have been a Nazi-directed organization. A charter of the bund was introduced during the hearing to show that there was a Branch 28 of the Bund in Fort Wayne as early as 1940. M. Luther Swygert, then assistant U.S. Attorney, prosecuted the case. Special Judge F. Ryan Duffy found for the government and on May 5, 1943, Schuchhardt's citizenship was cancelled. Defense Attorney C. Byron Hayes filed an appeal, but Schuchhardt was returned to alien status.

Floods and Gold Stars

In May, 1943, the greatest flood since the 1913 inundation struck Fort Wayne. The St. Mary's River was three miles wide in some places upstream from the city. Much of the southwest portion of the community was underwater. Some 400 soldiers from Camp Scott joined city crews working all night May 19 to sandbag the Edgewater Ave. dike protecting the Lakeside area. The Maumee River crested at 22.34 feet on that date. The rivers began to recede slowly on May 20. During the crisis, some factories were closed and about 1,500 persons were evacuated from their homes. The roaming waters ranged through districts near Spy Run Creek, West Main St., and the Rolling Mill district. More than 20,000 were homeless in the state.

The real war came home to Fort Wayne in the form of casualties to those in the armed forces and others caught in war zones throughout the world. At first, it was mostly just fear for the safety of men and women volunteering or being drafted for war duty, though some were in immediate danger in the Philippines and other areas of the Pacific. Few Americans, other than Navy personnel, were involved in the European Theatre during the early months of the war. Soon, however, casualty and death figures became a part of the local war reports and the term Gold Star Mother became common—indicating that a member of the family had died in defense of the Nation. The practice was widespread for families to post small, cloth flags on the window with a blue star for each member in the armed forces. A gold star indicated a life lost in the war. As the war wore on, the number of gold stars increased.

Air Ace Bud Mahurin

Fort Wayne had numerous airmen, soldiers who were recognized for unusual or distinguished service during the years 1941 to 1945. Early in the spring of 1942, the U.S. made a daring strike against Tokyo. This is remembered as the Doolittle Raid named after the leader of the group, Brig. Gen. Jimmy Doolittle, a one-time stunt and racing pilot. The Army Air Corps bombers of the Doolittle party took off from a Navy aircraft carrier and bombed Tokyo in a raid which was surprising because the U.S. was still much on the defensive in the Pacific. One of the key men in the Doolittle strike was Lt. Richard E. Miller of Fort Wayne who was a bombardier for the sweep over Japan.

Perhaps the most reknowned military career in the war was marked by Capt. Walker M. Mahurin who became America's Ace-of-Aces in the air war over Germany, was shot down, and made a sensational escape from a Nazi-held territory. Starting in the latter half of 1943, Mahurin established himself as one of the hottest fighter pilots in the European Theatre. By the end of January 1944, Capt. Mahurin had already notched his record with destroying 15 enemy aircraft. He was leading bomber escort wings over Frankfurt, Berlin and other targets. On March 8, 1944, in a raid over Berlin, Mahurin, then 24, shot down three German planes. This brought his total to 20 and set a new mark in the European Theatre making Mahurin the leading American ace. Wire services noted he was only six short of the record set in World War I by Capt. Eddie Rickenbacker. Mahurin always flew a Republic Thunderbolt fighter plane. He went 27 missions at first without hitting anything; then in September 1943, knocked down two Focke-Wulfs over Schweinfurt on the same day. On Oct. 4, 1943, he destroyed three Messerschmitt 110's against great odds and was awarded the Distinguished Service Cross. In a series of articles on Mahurin in the Chicago Herald-American, the ace described a December, 1943 raid over Bremen, Germany. "When I had closed to 100 yards, still firing, I hit the 109's belly tank and the ship blew up. I flew through the debris and flame. I fell in behind another 109. I opened fire and began to take short squints into the sun, hoping I would hit him. Evidently I did because I saw smoke. I fired into the smoke and suddenly the enemy aircraft came into view. Many parts were flying off it." Mahurin was invited to parties at Buckingham Palace where he met the Royal Family and was a leading celebrity of the middle war period. Then it happened. On March 27, 1944, Mahurin was shot down by German aircraft over France. The Ace, with 21 enemy kills to his credit, was last seen bailing out of a flaming fighter and disappearing over the French landscape. Six weeks later Major Mahurin had made his escape from occupied France with the help of the French underground and was back in London. After a visit to Fort Wayne, he was advanced to Lt. Colonel and commanded a squadron in the Pacific, adding two Japanese planes to his his total. Walker (Bud) Mahurin added one more chapter to his Air Corps career during the Korean War. Flying jet fighters, he knocked down three Red MIG's before being shot down over enemy territory in May, 1952. After being reported as missing in action for more than a year, it was unofficially reported he was a prisoner of the North Koreans. He was finally released on August 7, 1953.

The Local Scene

The city election race in 1942 was run at the same time as balloting for county, state and Congressional seats. There were several interesting contests in the May primary. Incumbent Mayor Harry Baals was challenged by Solly K. Frankenstein, an attorney. Alfred H. Randall, an old family name in Fort Wayne politics, and Harry Gottschalk, the Democratic nominee of 1938, sought the city executive post. The voters chose a rerun of the 1938 election pitting Gottschalk against Republican Mayor Baals. It turned out on Nov. 4 election day to be one of the more one-sided Republican sweeps in local politics. The GOP took every city and county office. Congressman George Gillie was elected to a third term by the largest margin ever. He defeated Samuel C. Cleland, the Democrat challenger, by 21,520 votes. In earlier contests, Gillie beat James I. Farley of Auburn in 1938 and Frank Corbett of Fort Wayne in 1940. Harry Baals amassed 21,409 votes to Gottschalk's 13,390 for a margin of 8,019. The mayor led the Republican ticket. Others elected in 1942 to city offices included: Wayne L. Miller, city judge; Leonard Ellenwood, city clerk; and Paul J. Wolf, Arno Spiegel, Harvey McMillen, Frank W. King, Jr., Harold A. Hart, William Knoche, Ben F. Bennett, Edward H. Fisher and Charles E. Moellering, all to the city council. A long career as county coroner began in 1942 with the election of Dr. Edgar N. Mendenhall. Mendenhall, at the time president of the Fort Wayne Medical Society, had earlier been recommended for the post by Dr. A. P. Hattendorf, county coroner who left the job that year for service in the Army Medical Corps. But two of the county commissioners, James T. Johnson and Theodore Goeglein, appointed Dr. Carey B. Parker, a Democrat. Parker served the balance of the year but lost to Mendenhall in the election.

A tragedy struck the downtown area in the spring of 1944 after a fire nearly gutted the Sears Roebuck Store in the 100 block of West Berry Street. The Sears Building was on the south side of the street next to the alley. On April 11, 1944, a brick wall of the Sears building collapsed and crashed across the alley into the Fort Wayne National Bank Building. Masonry rained down on bank personnel and patrons, particularly in the mezzanine area. Five persons were killed and seven seriously injured.

Murders Chill Populace

On a cold and dreary night in February, 1944, the Sheriff of Allen County Walter (Dutch) Adams waited nervously outside a room of St. Joseph's Hospital. A little earlier in the evening, a 37-year-old women had been brought into the hospital. She was near death. The side of her head had been caved in and she was severely beaten generally. Her name was Wilhelmina Haaga. Though in critical condition, the victim was still conscious and the sheriff hoped to question her, if even for a brief moment. He waited while medics worked to save the woman and watched as the family went into the room. At about that time the woman lapsed into a coma and never regained consciousness, though she lived several more days. "To this day, I believe she could have told us something," Adams said years later. Because of the victim's habits and character, he concluded she would not have accepted a ride with someone she didn't know. She was last seen getting into a car on New Haven Avenue. Two hours later she was brutally injured when she crawled to a farm house just east of the city. In little more than a year from that first Feb. 2, 1944, attack, four more women were to be attacked and slain. None of the four was in condition to talk when found. It was the beginning of the most chilling episode in Fort Wayne's criminal history and one which eventually took some strange twists in the courts of the community. In the case of the first murder, the woman had just left work at a war plant in the late afternoon. It was raining at the time.

Several months later a shock went through the city with the discovery of a second murder. A pretty 20-year-old girl was found dead in a field near Taylor Street. She had been strangled and had a broken back. It was May 21, 1944. The girl, Anna Kuseff, had been on her way to work at a war plant at about 11 p.m. It was raining that night. Evidence on the ground showed she had been dragged from the sidewalk some distance in a struggle. The presence of a dog which often accompanied her proved futile. The dog was found dead not far from the body. The murder went unsolved and talk of a mad killer of Jack-the-Ripper proportions swept through Fort Wayne.

It was on a hot, rainy afternoon of August 4, 1944, that a 17-year-old high school girl disappeared. Her name was Phyllis Conine and she was a senior at South Side. There was some conflict in opinion about where she was last seen. It might have been along South Wayne Ave. near Lutheran Hospital while waiting for a bus. Others thought they recognized her at a downtown theatre or in a department store. She was found several days later in an oat field southwest of town. She had been strangled and struck heavily about the head. Officers gave the opinion that a belt had been used in the strangling, as appeared possible in one or both of the earlier attacks. All three killings were termed sex slayings. Fear for women alone on the streets gripped the city. The cases became crime stories of national proportion.

Pearl (Torchy) Lee, 24 was found dead in her walk-up apartment in the 100 block of East Main Street. She had worked at taverns in the neighborhood. When found Feb. 7, 1945, she had been dead for some time—possibly a week or more. Death was variously explained by officials as possibly due to heart disease, or heat prostration, or gas, or maybe cyanide poisoning because the building had been fumigated a number of days previously. There was no verdict of murder in the case of Torchy Lee. There were already three unsolved murders. Officially, Torchy Lee's was never added to that total. Three years later a specialist in pathology became interested in the case. The body was exhumed for a belated post-mortem examination. The specialist, from Harvard University Medical School, said death was caused by intracranial bleeding due to blunt impacts to the head.

The last murder in the series occurred within a block of Torchy Lee's apartment and just a month later. Mrs. Dorothea Howard, 36, was found in a pool of rain water on the morning of March 6, 1945, in an alley. The location was just west of Calhoun St. between Main and Columbia Streets. She had been attacked and brutally beaten about the head but was not dead when found naked at 3 a.m. She was questioned by police and others before she died 11 days later. But she was unable to give much useful information. She reportedly was so drunk at the time of the attack, she couldn't name the assailants or even whether there was one or two men involved.

Bizarre Events in Court

The murders and the peculiarities of the court cases which followed became the largest continuous news story in the history of Fort Wayne. Contemporary reports called the situation one of the most bizarre episodes in the annals of criminal law in the U.S. As the murders mounted and no solutions were forthcoming, something like a psychotic condition gripped much of the community. Several prominent persons with rather eccentric habits were rumored to have committed the brutal crimes. But weeks, months and more than two years went by before any real break came for investigators. And the events which followed were never a completely satisfying resolution.

The city was electrified with the news on June 11, 1947, that a former Churubusco grave digger named Ralph W. Lobaugh had walked into the police station at Kokomo and calmly confessed three murders at Fort Wayne. Lobaugh, 30, said he killed Wilhelmina Haaga, Anna Kuseff and Dorothea Howard. He was brought to Fort Wayne for trial. Lobaugh had been working at a Kokomo factory after leaving the Fort Wayne area. Also indicted in the murder of Dorothea Howard was Charles D. Dodson, who had been a soldier stationed at Baer Field at the time of the crime. Dodson admitted he and a civilian had taken Mrs. Howard, the wife of another soldier, down an alley from a Main St. tavern and there in a cross alley just west of Calhoun St. had disrobed her. Dodson said he attempted to assault her but was scared off by someone approaching in an automobile. He denied beating the woman. Dodson told authorities Ralph Lobaugh was the civilian in the alley that rainy night in March, 1945. Mrs. Howard was found the next morning ravished and fatally beaten. Lobaugh on Oct. 27, 1947, entered a plea of guilty in Allen Circuit Court to the murders of Wilhelmina Haaga, Anna Kuseff and Mrs. Howard. On the same day Judge William Schannen sentenced Lobaugh to death in the electric chair for the three murders. Following the death sentence, Lobaugh denied having committed any of the murders. His case was appealed and the Indiana Supreme Court granted a retrial. Lobaugh, however, failed to act for a retrial and instead appealed to Governor Henry Schricker for a commutation of the death sentence to life imprisonment. Before the weird series of turns in the case were to run their course, Lobaugh would eleven times approach the hour of execution, only to return to his cell after last-minute stays.

While Lobaugh was in the death house at the Indiana State Prison at Michigan City, Fort Wayne police came across information which led to a new suspect in the murder of Dorothea Howard. He was Robert V. Christen, a drug clerk who had worked for many years in the drug store of his father at the corner of Calhoun and Douglas Streets. He was known to have been a man of rather irregular habits. In 1948, Dodson, who had been indicted but never tried with Lobaugh for the Howard killing, was taken to Denver, Colorado, where Christen had relocated. Dodson identified Christen as the man who had been with him in the downtown alley the rainy night in March, 1945, when Mrs. Howard had been slain. He said it was Christen rather than Lobaugh as he earlier had testified. Christen, 38, had also been identified by Gladys Hill, operator of a Main Street house of prostitution, as the man disappearing with Mrs. Howard the night of the murder. Bob Christen was indicted for murder and the trial was held at Columbia City in the Whitley Circuit Court. A jury of 11 farmers and a farmer's wife found him guilty of second-degree murder. Special Judge Lowell Pefley sentenced him to life imprisonment for the slaying of Dorothea Howard. Lobaugh at the time, April, 1949, was still waiting execution for the same murder, among others. Christen's lawyers appealed the case in the Indiana Supreme Court. The conviction was set aside and Christen was freed, but not before another startling turn in the case.

Franklin Click Charged

On the rainy night of August 17, 1949, a 19-year-old mother was dragged from her farm house just southwest of the city and criminally assaulted. Mrs. Simon Sparks said it was about 9:30 p.m. when she was pulled out the back door of the home along the Ditch Road. The assailant had taken his belt and making a noose around her neck had dragged her across the farm yard to a car. With the tightening of the belt about her throat, she had lost consciousness. She later regained consciousness and took the license number of the car as it was going away. Leona Sparks gave the number to the police and it was traced to Franklin Click, 30, who lived along Taylor Street. When Patrolmen Leonard Scrogham and William Bollman arrived they found the car in front of the house, engine warm and tires wet. Inside they found Click, his wife and their five children. The officer said Click rammed his head into the face of Scrogham when they attempted to apply handcuffs. At first Click, a worker at the Sweet Celery Farm which existed at the end of Taylor St., denied the attack. After about 30 hours of relay-interrogation he confessed the kidnapping and attack. He was identified by Mrs. Sparks as the assailant. Later, a 71-year old woman, never publically identified, said Click had earlier abducted and raped her. Then, just two days after the first confession, Click on August 21, 1949, asked his attorney Robert A. Buhler to send his wife, Marie, to his cell in the Allen County Jail. He handed her a written statement:

"My Dear Wife:

"I want you to be the first to know and learn from my own lips that I am a murderer. I am the one and the only one guilty and the only one that murdered Wilhelmina (Billie) Haaga, February 2, 1944; Anna Kuseff, May 22, 1944, and Phyllis Conine, August 4, 1944. No other person was with me or participated in either of these murders. This I know is a terrible confession and I want you to hand this confession to Chief Lester Eisenhut. I understand that by doing so you will be entitled to the reward offered for information leading to the arrest and conviction of the murderer. I am the murderer. You are the first person to whom I have confessed . . you need the money . . May God Help Me . . and you forgive me and be a mother and father to our dear children. I waive any and all my constitutional rights which Mr. Buhler has fully explained to me . . together with any and all rights concerning privileged communication. (signed) Franklin Click."

There was $16,500 in reward money for persons furnishing evidence leading to convictions in the Haaga, Kuzeff and Conine murders. Of this amount, $15,000 had been appropriated by the City Council and $1,500 had been offered by the News-Sentinel. Click would later say he confessed to the crimes in order for his wife to obtain the $16,500 reward. He said officials had convinced him he would get life for the Sparks kidnapping anyway and he could fare no worse by confessing the three slayings. A twist in the situation was that Click's lawyer Robert Buhler had also been the attorney of Ralph Lobaugh whom Buhler was at the time attempting to save from the electric chair. Lobaugh had been given the death penalty for the Kuseff, Haaga and Howard murders. Click was first brought to trial for kidnapping of Leona Sparks. On October 28, 1949, he entered a plea of guilty in Allen Circuit Court on the charge of kidnapping. After questioning, he was sentenced the same day by Judge William H. Schannen to life imprisonment. A plea to have Click declared a criminal psychopath was declined by Judge Schannen. It had been revealed that Click was involved in a truck crash in 1941 and had been hospitalized for head injuries. Both his wife and mother had stated his head injuries bothered him and he was subject to headaches.

Going to the Electric Chair

When Wilheimina Haaga had disappeared in a car on New Haven Ave. after leaving the Inca Manufacturing plant the afternoon of Feb. 2, 1944, Franklin Click was employed at Rea Magnet Wire Co. a couple of blocks away. When Anna Kuzeff was murdered May 22, 1944, in a field west of Fillmore near Taylor St., Click was a neighbor of the Kuseff family. In fact, Click was one of the pallbearers who carried the body of Anna Kuseff to her grave in Prairie Grove Cemetery. Yet, of the three murders to which he had confessed, he was tried for the slaying of Phyllis Conine on Aug. 4, 1944. The obvious reason was that, up to that time, it was the murder to which Lobaugh hadn't confessed. Click was brought back from the Michigan City Prison for the trial which began Nov. 28, 1949. Again, Judge Schannen was on the bench and the Allen Circuit Court was jammed with spectators. Prosecuting the case were Alton L. Bloom and Chester A. Lincoln. The defense lawyers were Robert Buhler, Dan C. Flanagan and Charles Z. Bond. Flanagan, who later would be an Indiana Supreme Court Justice, made both the opening and closing statements to the jury, describing the confession as "phony." Click never took the witness stand. After 11 hours of deliberation, the jury of nine men and three women returned just before dawn, Dec. 1, 1949, and gave a verdict of guilty. The jury recommended the supreme penalty. Judge Schannen immediately sentenced Click to be taken to the State Prison at Michigan City to be electrocuted on March 27, 1950. After Click's death sentence, Ralph Lobaugh at his Michigan City cell said he had also killed Phyllis Conine, the 17-year-old girl for whose death Click had been condemned. Governor Henry Schricker granted Click 12 stays of execution during the balance of the year while attorney's attempted to resolve the riddles in the cases. Franklin

Click, by then 31, walked the short distance from his cell to the electric chair at 12:03 a.m., Dec. 31, 1950. He was electrocuted at 12:05 a.m. and was declared dead at 12:07½ a.m. Thirty minutes before the execution he told Warden Alfred Dowd he hadn't committed the killings. He was described as calm to the end. By that time, Robert Christen had been set free by the Indiana Supreme Court, and had disappeared. Christen had, according to testimony, been the last person seen with Dorothea Howard before she was found murdered in an alley on March 6, 1945. Christen, according to police records, had also been the last person to see Pearl (Torchy) Lee, 24, alive. No indictments were ever returned in the Lee case nor was there a verdict of murder. She had been dead a week or so when found in a room in the 100 block of East Main St. on Feb. 7, 1945, a scant block from where they found Dorothea Howard a month later. Lobaugh's sentence was commuted to life imprisonment where he still remained 30 years after the series of killings. Only one thing seemed reasonably clear regarding the crimes; whoever did them chose rainy nights.

Sam Jackson's Hour

Samuel D. Jackson, then 47, was chairman of the 1944 Democratic National Convention in Chicago. Addressing the national delegates on July 20, 1944, Jackson said America "cannot afford to take a chance" with destiny and urged the election of Franklin D. Roosevelt to an unprecedented fourth term in the White House. "We must not allow the American ballot box to be made Hitler's secret weapon" and said the election of Republican Thomas E. Dewey would mean delay of victory. Jackson was credited with the nomination of Harry Truman as Vice President. During the convention, Jackson banged the gavel and declared a recess at a night session when there was a strong movement to renominate Henry A. Wallace. Later, Truman was nominated instead of the incumbent Vice President and within a year succeeded to the Presidency. Jackson had been Allen County Prosecutor from 1924 to 1928 and Indiana Attorney General in 1940-41. In January, 1944, he was named by Governor Henry Schricker to the U.S. Senate to fill the unexpired term created by the death of Sen. Frederick Van Nuys. At the conclusion of the term Jan. 3, 1945, Jackson returned to law practice in Fort Wayne.

In the final weeks of October, 1944, FDR made a quick campaign tour by train. At Fort Wayne just before noon, he emerged on the platform of the observation car and addressed a huge throng gathered below the Pennsylvania Railroad elevation at Harrison and Baker Streets. Roosevelt looked tired but he flashed his famous grin and held his weathered grey felt hat high overhead. In the November election, FDR defeated Dewey by 25,600,000 to 22,000,000 votes, nationally, but Dewey won Indiana. Five months later Roosevelt died and Truman succeeded to the Presidency on April 12, 1945.

On March 30, 1946, General Henry A. Byroade of Woodburn was named military attache to General George Marshall for a special mission in China. Byroade, who during the war was an OSS officer, went to China in the spring of 1946 and contacted Communist General Lin Piao, commander of more than 100,000 troops in Manchuria. He reportedly obtained an agreement between Generalissimo Chiang Kai Shek and the Red leaders. Later, Byroade served as ambassador to Thailand, Pakistan and other countries.

The Purple Hearts

By 1945, the United States had 12,018,000 men and 270,000 women in the armed forces. Hardly a family in the nation was not personally involved in some activity or through relatives with the war effort. But victory was in sight early that year and people in Fort Wayne were thrilled by headlines on March 22 of Patton's Third Army crossing of the Rhine. Reports of Hitler's death came crackling across the air waves on May 1. Germany's surrender on May 7 was universally acclaimed, but the celebrations were tempered because of the continuing war with Japan. A mixed feeling of wonder, awe and confidence of victory was reflected on city streets with the report on August 6 of a new weapon dropped on Hiroshima, Japan, which obliterated the city; and the second use of the atom bomb on Nagasaki three days later. Victory in Japan Day (V-J Day) was on September 2, 1945. The ending of the war set off dancing in the streets, parades, church bells and services of thanksgiving. There were a couple of days of wild celebrations, plus relief with the end of rationing. In the following weeks, servicemen began to stream home and the Ruptured Duck discharge button became a familiar mark of distinction. Some, however, didn't make it back. The Allen County war dead, including all branches of service, totalled 361. Their names were later listed on a plaque and made a permanent part of the Allen County War Memorial Coliseum.

Most of the city streets were still brick in 1936, such as Clinton St. shown above north of Superior St. on a grey day of early winter. At left are the last of the Civil War veterans as they salute the passing parade on Decoration Day (later called Memorial Day) in 1936. Left to right: W. H. Hannen, Alex Ormiston, Thomas Cragg and John Young.

Johnny Hannon won the first Soap Box Derby which was held in 1935. The event, sponsored by The News-Sentinel and Chevrolet, was held for many years on the Bueter Road hill, shown below as the checkered winners flag comes down and a crowd watches in 1946. At the bottom of the page is Mayor Harry Baals and his family. Baals was mayor during the most of the 1930s.

The Interurbans gradually declined during the 1930s and were replaced by increasing use of buses, as shown on the picture above at the Fort depot in 1938. James Duhamell eyes the competition. The last Interurban out the city was on a run to Muncie in 1941, left, with Eli Applegate, conductor.

Kids wading at the pool of the Municipal Beach near the St. Joseph River was summer fun in 1938. At left are bathing beauties, era 1936, who are being eyed by a few casual gentlemen at the upper right of the picture. Below are radio fans gathered for a program on the green of McCormick Park.

The footbridge across the St. Mary's River was the scene of the Easter outing in 1939. Below is a gathering of many of the physicians of days gone by in Fort Wayne and the area. It is the reunion (the 34th year since the closing of the school) of the Fort Wayne College of Medicine. The event was held at the old Turner Hall on West Superior St., which was the last location of the college. The reunion luncheon was in October, 1939.

Carole Lombard and husband Clark Gable are shown on their farm in 1940. Carole Lombard, a native of Fort Wayne, was Jane Peters before she took her movie name. A top star of the silver screen era, she was killed in a plane crash while on a bond tour during World War II. Below is a crowd at the old Palace Theatre on the south side of the 100 block of East Washington Blvd.

This view from the air of the downtown district in 1940 shows area which changed very little from 1930 to 1960.

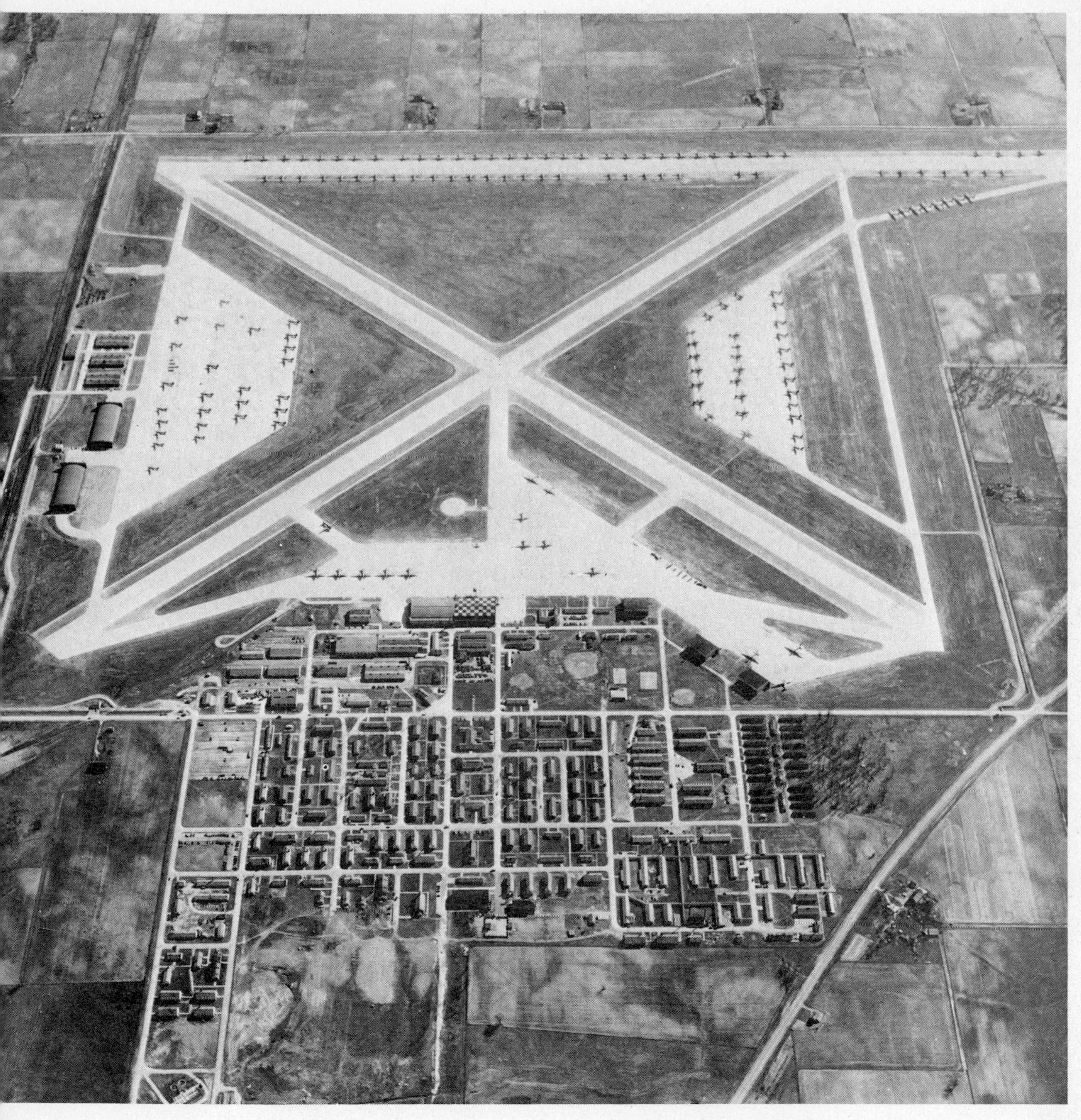

Baer Field, built by the Army Air Forces in 1941, was a major base for fighter squads during World War II. In this 1942 photo of the field and many military buildings, there can be countered 145 armed craft on the ready.

Captain Walker (Bud) Mahurin was America's leading war ace over Nazi Germany during much of World War II. He was shot down, but escaped to fly again. During the war he returned to Fort Wayne for a bond rally. At the luncheon, Mahurin is shown to the left of Mayor Baals while more than $1 million in bonds were sold. At left bottom is a 1942 picture of one of the war gardens which dotted the city. Directly below, crewmen prepare an F-100 Sabre Jet for the Baer Field 122nd Tactical Fighter Group in the post-war era.

The West End Industries coverin
the landscape, above, include Josyl
Steel in the foreground; the G. E
Supercharger plant along Taylor St
built during World War II, center
the Essex Wire Mill, just beyond, an
the G.E. Broadway buildings in th
distance. At left is the way Calhou
St. looked during the war years
north from Washington Blvd.

Factories went on round-the-clock production, including weekends, during the war, such as the winter night scene at the G. E. Broadway plant. To the right is a change of shift in 1945. Below is a 1942 picture of war horses, literally. When gasoline became scarce, the Berghoff Brewery teamed drafthorses to pull beer wagons.

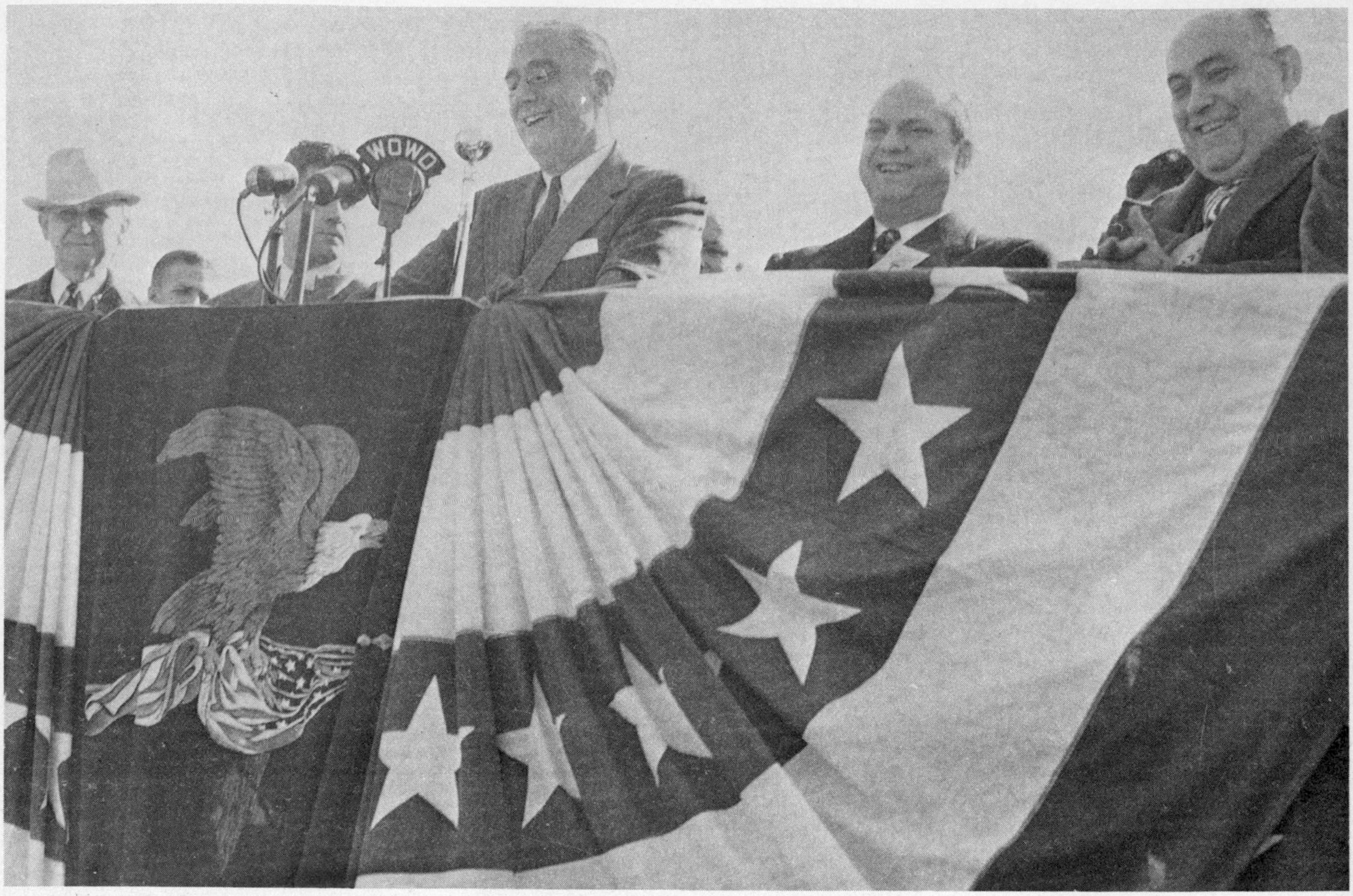

Were you one of the countless heads on Baker St. during the October Presidential campaign of 1944? The crowd on the opposite page is watching Franklin D. Roosevelt making his last rail tour. In the picture above is Indiana Gov. Henry Schricker, FDR, Senator Sam Jackson and National Committeeman Frank McKinney. At right is a houseful of children, more than the 2,900 seats, in the Emboyd Theatre for a 1945 program.

Franklin Click, at right, is shown shortly before he went to the electric chair. Implicated in the series of grisly rape murders which began in early 1944, Click was only one of three unconnected men to be convicted of various of the crimes. Ralph Lobaugh, below, was also sentenced to the chair for three of the five slayings, but his sentence was later communted to life. A third man, Robert Christen, was convicted for one of the killings, but later released. Judge William H. Schannen, right below, sentenced both Lobaugh and Click to be executed.

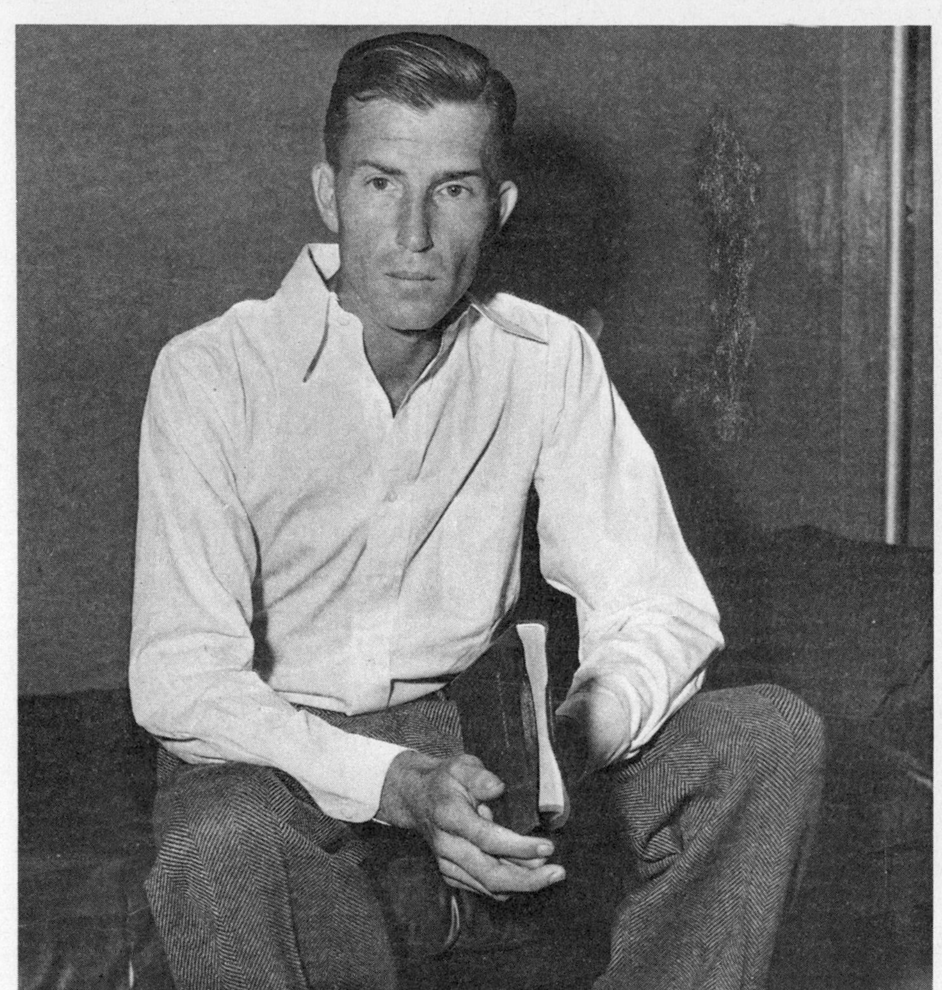

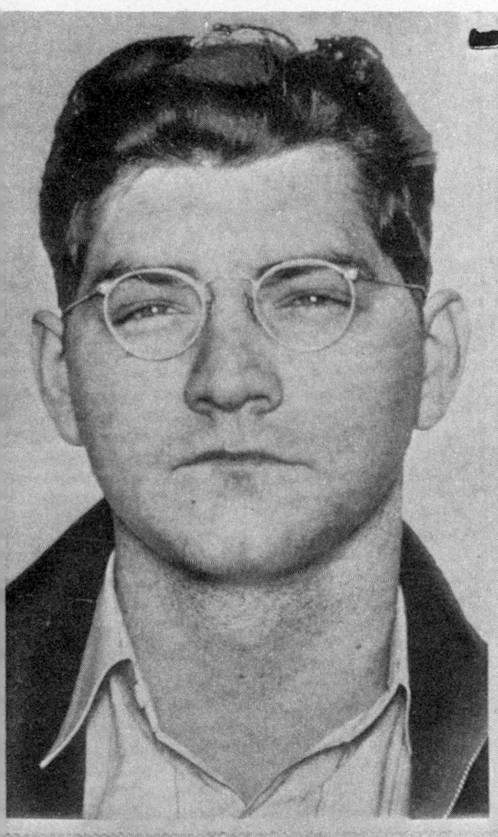

(NY12-AUG.22)--GRANTED STAY--Ralph W.Lobaugh(above),32,former Kokomo, Ind.,factory worker awaiting execution for sex slayings has been granted a 90-day reprieve by Gov. H.F.Schricker. Today at Fort Wayne, Ind., a 30-year-old farm hand signed statements admitting three Fort Wayne sex slayings, two of which had been confessed by Lobaugh.(AP Wirephoto)(See Wire Story)(d21930fis 1949.

Washington Blvd. east of Calhoun as it looked in 1944, the last full year of the war and the beginning of the frightful murders which went unsolved for several years. The building of the News-Sentinel, below, was at Washington and Barr and later became the Foellinger Center for United Community Services. At bottom is Mayor Harry Baals shaking hands of sewer workers deep under the city.

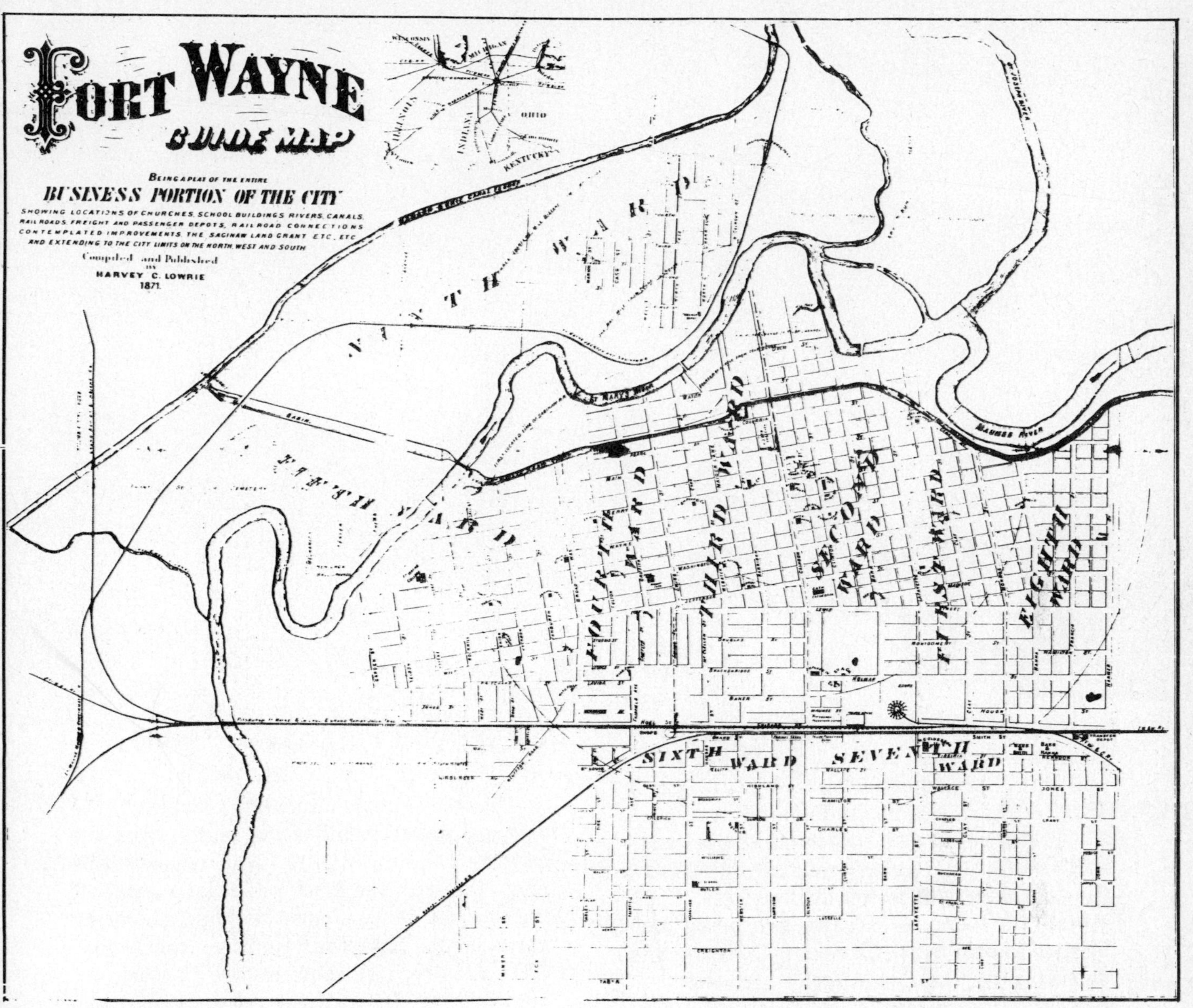

This city map was made in 1871, the same year the first professional baseball league game was played in Fort Wayne. A sharp eye will note the Kekionga Ball Grounds near the St. Mary's River. The game at that location on May 4, 1871, launched the National League. It can also be noted that Superior St. was then Water St., DeWald was Lasselle and West Main St. was known as Cemetery Road.

Part 9
World of Sports

According to the official Encyclopedia of Baseball, the first professional league baseball game in America was played May 4, 1871, at Fort Wayne, Indiana. It was also the first game of the National League, baseball's senior loop. Later that year, in August, the franchise was moved to Brooklyn, N.Y., where the team eventually prospered and became known as the Brooklyn Dodgers, and subsequently the Los Angeles Dodgers.

The 10-team league, called the National Association of Professional Baseball Players, was established on St. Patrick's Day, 1871, in Collier's Cafe on New York's Broadway and 13th Street. "There, in a smoky gaslit hallroom adjoining the saloon, pro baseball suffered its real birth pangs," the encyclopedia reported.

Nine clubs actually started the season: the Philadelphia Athletics, the Boston Red Stockings, the Chicago White Stockings, the Troy Haymakers, the Washington Olympics, the Rockford Forest City, the Fort Wayne Kekiongas, the New York Mutuals and Cleveland Forest City.

First Pro League Game

"It is ironic that the Kekionga club, the only one not to weather the season, won the opening game by 2 to O. Not only was this noteworthy as the first pro league game of record, but it was also the lowest-scoring game in the first four years of the league. Here are the highlights of the "historic inaugural," the Official Encyclopedia of Baseball said:

"The Kekiongas won the toss and sent Forest City (Cleveland) to bat. Bobby Mathews threw the first pitch, a ball. James (Deacon) White was the first batter and he led off the first major league hit, a double. Gene Kimball followed with a fly to second, but when White took too long a lead, Tom Carey pulled an unassisted double play.

"There were several other firsts in that game. In the second inning, Art Allison struck out. However, Jim Lennon (catcher) missed the third strike and Allison reached base safely. Lennon atoned for his error in the home half of the inning by scoring the first run, which also proved to be the winning run. He doubled and came in on Joe McDermott's single. Kekionga had the game clinched by the ninth, but was ready to take its last batting turn anyway when a sudden rainfall caused umpire J. L. Boake to call a halt."

The only other Fort Wayne player to get a hit in the game was first baseman John Kelly. Mathews posted six strikeouts. The official time listed that game for exactly 2 hours before being called in the 9th due to rain.

Chicago quickly displaced Kekionga as league leader by winning its first seven straight games," the official record said. "Unbeaten, the White Stockings invaded New York on June 5 to meet the Mutuals (later Giants) owned by the notorious political potentate, Boss Tweed. Despite a 50-cent admission fee, a record 6,000 crowd jammed the stands, and 3,000 others watched from beyond fences, perched on neighboring roofs or wagons. Pushcart owners charged 10 cents for standing on their vehicles." New York won that game but Chicago later came back, only to lose to the Philadelphia Athletics in the playoff series. In the meantime, the White Stockings had lost their ballpark on the Chicago lakefront in the Great Chicago Fire, October 8, 1871. Fort Wayne's place in the National League was already history. "When the Kekionga franchise wilted in August, the Eckfords (Brooklyn) belatedly decided that professional baseball was here to stay, so they paid their $10 and replaced Kekionga," according to the encyclopedia.

Balls and Grandstands

The first National League game was not played in Old League Park which once stood on the Jailhouse Flats between Calhoun and Clinton Streets. A tract of ground north of Camp Allen, in Nebraska, between the canal and West Main St. was converted into a baseball park for the Kekionga games beginning in 1870 and for several years thereafter. Nebraska was the name given to the section of Fort Wayne west of the Main St. Bridge over the St. Mary's River. The fancy grandstand part of the ballpark was called The Grand Duchess. The Kekiongas were originally organized in 1866 along with a number of other local teams. But the Kekiongas soon cleaned up on the competition in the entire area and were state champs in 1870. One reason for the surge of the Fort Wayne team was that the old Baltimore Orioles were on the road at Fort Wayne when they disbanded. Some of these players became the nucleus of the Fort Wayne Kekiongas which became a part of the National league in the first 1871 season.

Fort Wayne's earliest fame in sports came before the Civil War. William King, a Fort Wayne marksman, became the American champion when he defeated James Shannon and Colonel Blanton Duncan in the 1859 finals at St. Louis. Bill King was then challenged by the European champion, Frere, in pigeon shooting or skeet shooting as later termed. King went to London later that same year and defeated Frere. Queen Victoria awarded King a medal and he was for a considerable period the world's champion.

The city's interest in baseball led to the Summit City Club, founded in 1862 by Charles Brackenridge, William B. Fisher, Thomas B. Shoaff and others. The games were played on land donated for use by Allen Hamilton at the southeast corner of Calhoun and Lewis Streets. By 1867 the local league had a number of teams, including the Kekiongas which in 1871 joined the National League and played in the first organized pro game. The first night baseball game was played at Fort Wayne on June 3, 1883. A pro team from Quincy, Ill., had been challenged by students of the Fort Wayne Methodist Episcopal College. They played before 2,000 fans under the glow of 17 arc lights that furnished the illumination equal to 4,857 gas burners. The lighting stunt was set up by the Jenney Electric Co. to prove the superiority of its products. The arc lights were hung on outfield fences and cast heavy shadows, leading to quite a few errors. Quincy won the game 19 to 11. Later that same year, a World Series game was played in Fort Wayne. "The eyes of a baseball fans of all America were centered upon Fort Wayne in the fall of 1883 when the teams representing Chicago and Providence in the major leagues played the final game of the World Series on a neutral diamond," the historian reported. People from many parts of the country came to the city. Chicago won the game and, of course, the series. There are some disagreements on where both the first night game and the world series game were played. Some sources say they were played at Old League Park, between Calhoun and Clinton Streets, across from the County Jail. But old reports by eye witnesses say the two noted 1883 games were played at Swinney Park; and League Park wasn't built until 1884. Fort Wayne had a team in the Old Northwestern League in 1883 and 1884. Max Nirdlinger, a manufacturer of baseball bats in Fort Wayne, was team president. League Park was rebuilt in 1888 with the organization of the Indiana State League. The city, however, had a Sunday blue law on games so Sunday games were played at Centlivre Park—outside the city limits. Over the years, Fort Wayne had teams in another Northwestern League; the Western League (other teams Columbus, O.; Indianapolis; Milwaukee; Kansas City; Omaha; Toledo); the Interstate League; and finally the Central League which in 1929 became a St. Louis Cardinal farm team. Various owners of the Fort Wayne Chiefs in the Central League, starting in 1903, included Isador Mautner, Claude Varnell, William Klitzke, Carl Vandergrift, Mart C. Wyneken and Chester Schiefer.

Fire Destroys League Park

It was on a hot July 12, 1930, that flames destroyed the Central League Baseball Park in Fort Wayne. Incendiarism was suspected in the fire reported at 1:30 a.m. "The dry wooden grandstands burned like tinder and firemen could do little except keep the blaze confined to the park," it was reported in the News-Sentinel later in the day. Schiefer, who had purchased the ball park the previous year, said persons living nearby said they noticed a strong odor of gasoline about the premises when the fire was discovered. The speed with which the grandstand was consumed and the report that two cars sped away from the scene just before the fire was discovered further indicated arson. Detective Sergeants Peter Junk and Thomas Wunderlich searched for a man who reportedly had fought with ball park attendants the previous afternoon (Friday) over the possession of two baseballs batted into the stands. In those days, a fan who turned in the ball got a free admission tickct. The man wanted to keep the balls. Frame houses across Calhoun St. from the grandstand were in danger from flying sparks and several small roof fires were extinguished and a house on St. Clair St. caught fire. The stiff wind from the east carried sparks as far as the Bloomingdale area where several houses were damaged. The fire, perhaps started by an irate fan because of an argument over fly balls into the stands apparently destroyed the city's last regular professional baseball park. The Fort Chiefs, however, still had league games to play that Saturday and a double header on Sunday, all with the Erie, Pa., ball club. They were played at the Pennsy Diamond which was located on the east side of Anthony Blvd., just north of the Pennsylvania Elevation.

Fort Wayne, after more than 65 years in pro baseball competition, bowed out of organized play after the 1935 season in the Three Eye League. That is, except for the Fort Wayne Daisies, a girl's pro team in the American Girls Baseball League which titillated Fort Wayne fans in the late 1940's and early 1950's. Once the city lost its entry in the regular pro circuits, the players from the community going to the big leagues also grew scarce. In the earlier decades, however, there were numerous top ball players from Fort Wayne, with seven in the majors in 1924 alone. Eugene Hargrave was catcher for the Cincinnati. William Hargrave was catcher for the Washington Senators and Walter Henline was catcher for the Philadelphia Phillies. Eugene Hargrave who played with both the Chicago Cubs and the Reds, started his career in 1913 and ended in 1930 with the New York Yankees. He had a lifetime batting average of .310 in 852 games. William (Pinky) Hargrave caught for the Washington Senators from 1923-25, then played with the old St. Louis Browns, the Detroit Tigers and finished with the Boston Braves in 1933 with a .278 batting average in 650 major league games. Henline joined the New York Giants in 1921; played with the Philadelphia Phillies from 1922 to 1926, the Brooklyn Dodgers from 1927 to 1929 and the Chicago White Sox in 1930. He batted .291 in 740 games. Ralph Miller, who starred for the Fort Wayne Chiefs in baseball and the Fort Wayne Hoosiers in basketball, played three years in the majors, including the 1924 season when the Washington Senators beat the Giants four-to-three in the World Series. Everett Scott was a shortstop for the Boston Red Sox, the New York Yankees, the Washington Senators and the Chicago White Sox. His career spanned 1914 to 1926. He batted .249 in 1,654 games and held the record for consecutive games played until it was broken by Lou Gerhig of the Yankees. William Wambsganss played all the infield spots during a career with the Cleveland Indians between 1914 and 1923 and later was with the Boston Red Sox and the Philadelphia Athletics until 1926. He established an all-time baseball record. He made the only unassisted triple play in a World Series when he was second baseman with the Indians in 1920. He had a .259 batting average in 1,491 league games. Other Fort Wayners in the big leagues included Andrew Woehr, James Hart, Lou Holterman, Max Carey, Earl Bolyard and George Nill.

The Longest Hit

Fort Wayne also stands in some reflected glory because of baseball. Babe Ruth came to town in 1927 and smacked, unofficially, the longest home run in the history of the game. After citing the official long hits by Babe Ruth, Mickey Mantle and others, Sportswriter Carl Wiegman said: "Ruth hit a longer one in Fort Wayne, according to the Bambino's version. He was on a barnstorming tour after the 1927 season and played a game at League Park on North Clinton Street. He belted a ball over the left-centerfield fence and he claimed that the ball landed in a freight car which was passing the park at the time." Wiegman attributed the homer-that-moved-for-miles story to baseball buff Jack Gassert. Yet a person better known the world over than even Babe Ruth once played baseball in Fort Wayne and lived in the city for a season. He was Zane Grey whose name is familiar throughout the world in dozens of languages and on more than 100 million books. Grey came to the city in 1896 and joined the Summit City entry in the Interstate Pro League. Fresh out of the University of Pennsylvania, Grey had not yet started his career as a writer of western novels. He was a 23-year-old outfielder and a native of Zanesville, Ohio, and had been a noted college athlete in several sports. He was no slouch in Fort Wayne during that one season and was the leading hitter in the league, batting .374. In later days, in the 1970's, Fort Wayne was represented in the big leagues by Steve Hargan, a pitcher for the Texas Rangers.

Semi-pro baseball, linked with industrial sponsors, brought glory to Fort Wayne, particularly in the 1940's. Champion teams were managed by John "Red" Braden. The General Electric club won the national semi-pro championships in 1947, 1948 and 1949. Essentially the same team, sponsored by Capehart-Farnsworth, was champion in 1950 and went to Japan to take the world title later in the year. Starting in 1955, Allen Dairy sponsored a Braden-managed club. The following year, 1956, the team won the national crown at Wichita, Kansas, and the world title at Milwaukee. Amateur baseball was played continuously since the Civil War days on various age levels. The Fort Wayne Baseball Federation was started in 1931. Edward "Red" Carrington was the first president. He was also president of the Indiana Amateur Baseball Congress. Little League was started in 1950 and was part of a national organization for youngsters with talent for the game. Another league for youngsters, "so every kid who wants to play can," was organized in Fort Wayne in 1961. This was the Wildcat League founded by

Dale W. McMillen, Sr. By the mid-1960's, more than 6,000 youngsters were playing in the Wildcat League. National attention was attracted with an article in Parade Magazine, and similar leagues were begun in many cities. Organized baseball on the high school competitive schedule was launched in 1971.

Friars and Fighters

A world's championship fight, involving a local boxer, was held at Fort Wayne's Majestic Theatre on Wednesday night, March 17, 1915. According to the St. Patrick's Day billing, the card was headed by Lightweight Champion Freddie Walsh versus Harold (Hal) Stewart of Fort Wayne. Reserved seats cost $3. Walsh won the bout. Stewart, born in 1891 at Payne, Ohio, boxed the top prize fighters of the era, including Steve Ketchell, Three-Fingered Jimmy Murphy and others.

Organized football in Fort Wayne began on Thanksgiving Day, 1890, when the Jenney Electrics beat the Athletics. The Fort Wayne Friars began playing, records show, before 1910 with teams from other cities. Fort Wayne's move into big time football occurred in 1915 with the Friars Club. The team is now in the Pro Football Hall of Fame at Canton, Ohio. The Friars, organized by Steve Callahan, Carl J. Suedhoff, Walter Brase, Howard Wilkins and others, was actually a college all-star team which took on pro teams of the era. The best known players were Knute Rockne and Gus Dorais, who came down from Notre Dame to play for pay. Dorais was the highest paid player on the team, as a quarterback, making $125 a game. Rockne, of course, was the end in the noted passing combination. The Friars played the pro football teams of New York, Detroit, Cleveland, Omaha and Chicago.

The Summit City had a rather unusual champion in 1904—a bird. In that year a homing pigeon owned by Dr. John Schilling of Fort Wayne broke the world's record. The bird went 1,000 miles in five days, two hours and 15 minutes.

Fort Wayne produced a number of fairly successful prize fighters. There was King Wyatt and Frankie Jarr during the 1930's; and Bud Hershey who fought in the 1940's. Wyatt was national Golden Gloves welterweight champ in 1935. But only one local boxer ever won a national or world title two years in a row. He was Bob Burns who turned the trick in the Golden Gloves Tourney. Robert Burns, only 17 years old, won the Fort Wayne elimination and went on to Chicago in 1940 where despite a single loss was chosen as an alternate. In the national finals in New York's Madison Square Gardens, Burns went undefeated and gained the crown. The following year, 1941, Burns went all the way without loss and was crowned national amateur welterweight champion. He won the Barney Ross Sportsmanship Prize also. Fort Wayne was a regular site for Golden Gloves tourneys for 23 years as were 40 other cities in the nation. Thousands of boxers competed annually. The St. Joe Athletic Club sponsored numerous sports activities since its founding in 1899. Sculling on the St. Joseph River was an early specialty. Later, the club sponsored boxing matches and in 1923 developed a football team. The football club, coached by Ralph Shimer, renewed competition after World War II until 1954, playing semi-pro teams from Detroit, Chicago, several cities in Ohio and others. Fort Wayne boxers who won state titles included Moan Baumgartner, Pete LeCrosse and Nick Ellenwood. But the best known event of the St. Joe Club was the annual New Year's Day dip by the Polar Bear Club in the icy St. Joseph's River. The chilly ritual, usually requiring the chopping away of ice, was started in 1926.

Emil Sitko

Emil "Red" Sitko, a native of Fort Wayne, was Notre Dame football's outstanding ball carrier of the modern era. Red Sitko played for Central High School in the early 1940's, starred with the Great Lakes Naval Base team in 1943 and was Notre Dame's leading rusher in 1946, 1947, 1948 and 1949. Notre Dame never lost a game while Sitko was playing for the university. He carried the ball 363 times and gained 2226 yards for an average of 6.1 yards per try. That brought him the nickname of Six-yard Sitko. He scored 26 touchdowns. He played both right halfback and fullback and was named All-American in 1948 and 1949. While at Central High he won nine letters in football, track and baseball and was all-state halfback. Sports writer Jim Costin told the story of Sitko's last college game—in 1949 against Southern Methodist. "It was 20-to-20 late in the contest when the Mustangs kicked off to the Irish and they started a drive deep in their own territory. Notre Dame had a 19-year-old quarterback, Bob Williams, calling the plays. Sitko walked up to him and said, 'Okay, for a kid you're a good quarterback, but you give me the ball every play until I tell you different.' Sitko, 26 at the time, then carried the ball every play until he reached the SMU three, then returned to the huddle and said, 'It's okay now kid, give it to someone else.' He did, N.D. scored and won 27-20." That completed the fourth undefeated season.

During the latter 1940's, Notre Dame and Michigan produced college football's top teams. The All-American quarterback for Michigan's national championship club of 1947 was Bob Chappuis who later moved to Fort Wayne and was an executive at Central Soya. On New Year's Day, 1948, Chappuis led Michigan in the 49-0 slaughter of Southern California in the Rose bowl. In the meantime another football player, a former Central High School standout, was making records at Drake University. He was Johnny Bright, an all-sport star at Central. Bright at Drake in 1949 led the nation in total offense in college football. He later was a top player in the Canadian League.

The Zollner Pistons

Pro basketball grew to manhood in Fort Wayne. In the early days there was the Knights of Columbus team starting in 1919 and the Fort Wayne Hoosiers which was organized in 1925. They were part of the American Professional Basketball League. The Hoosiers played home games at North Side High School Gym and the players included Ralph Miller, Benny Borgman, Shang Chadwick, Hank Kowalczyk and other top players of the day. It wasn't until Fred Zollner organized a team in 1939 and moved into national competition the following year that the city became a moving factor in making basketball a big-time pro sport. Prior to the 1940's, pro basketball had often been something of a traveling exhibition affair. National Basketball League, then the Basketball Association of America, and finally the NBA, were the top leagues thereafter. Fans packed into North Side Gym to see Zollner Piston stars perform, and usually dominate, with a team composed of Bobby McDermott, Paul Curly Armstrong, Buddy Jeanette, John Pelkington, Jerry Bush and Paul Birch. McDermott was the league's leading scorer and competitor, leading the Pistons to victories over Cleveland, Oshkosh and a variety of other squads. The Pistons were world pro champions, and proved it at the end of the 1945 and 1946 season by sweeping a playoff tourney of pro teams in Chicago Stadium. The Pistons continued to hold their own in the major pro league, even after it became a big-city union with the Pistons, a Green Bay entry. Some of the better-remembered players include Larry Foust, Frank Brian, Andy Phillip, Fred Schaus, Jack Kerris, George Yardley, Mel Hutchens, Charlie Shipp, Leo Klier, Ed Sadowski, Charlie Black, Chick Reiser, Bob Kinney and Dick Rosenthall. Jack Molinas became notorious because of a gambling scandal. Perhaps the last memorable hour for the Pistons while they were in Fort Wayne came in 1955 in the National playoffs with the Syracuse Nationals. Actually, none of the playoff games were played in Fort Wayne because the National Bowling Congress was in the city that year and was occupying the Memorial Coliseum arena. Fort Wayne was Western Division leader and Syracuse in the Eastern. The home games were played at Indianapolis and the away games were, of course, played at Syracuse. The series was marred by unruly fans and bad officiating. In the final and seventh game of the playoff at Syracuse,

Fort Wayne had a healthy lead going into the final minutes of play when a rapid series of calls changed the complexion of the game which Syracuse won. The Pistons made the playoff again in 1956, but had less success in the final series against the Philadelphia Warriors, losing four games to one.

Following the 1956-57 season, the team was moved to Detroit. In the 17 years of activity in Fort Wayne, the Zollner Pistons more than held their own. The National Basketball League had been formed in 1937 and almost from the time the Pistons joined in the competition in the 1940's, they were contenders. The biggest single factor was perhaps the purchasing of the services of the old New York Celts star Bobby McDermott in 1940. He encouraged several other top players to come to Fort Wayne and was himself the best long-shot artist in the game. The Pistons at that time introduced a rapid pass style of game which remade the sport. They were league champions in 1943, 1944 and 1945. In 1946, even though Rochester edged Fort Wayne for the league title, the Pistons took the World Title at the Chicago Pro Invitational. The Pistons were in contention during subsequent years, but never again on top.

Sports Capital

Starting in the late 1930's, and particularly in the 1940's and early 1950's, Fort Wayne became a recognized sports capital in the nation. Just why the some dozen-or-so years was a golden era of city sports might be hard to pinpoint. The eminence, however, is obvious from the records on practically all levels. Already mentioned were the national pro basketball champs, embodied in the Zollner Pistons; and the semi-pro baseball titles; and boxers such as Bob Burns. But the same excellence reached through the prep school levels with winners and contenders for state titles an almost-constant habit in three sports.

This was also the era in national popularity of softball, a baseball-like sport which could be played without much equipment, but which faded after about two decades. The Zollner Piston Softball Team, later called Fastball, became so dominent in the pro circuit that they eliminated the competition. The Pistons were organized in 1940 and were disbanded in 1954. During the years in between they had a .869 winning percentage, consistently taking the National Fastball League Championship. Originally, the teams played their games at the Municipal Beach. Zollner Stadium on North Anthony Blvd. was built in 1947. Some of the top Piston fastball players included Leo Luken, Ed Robitaille, Jim Ramage, Hughie and Billie Johnston, Neal Barille, Elmer MacDonald, Bill West and Bernie Kampschmidt.

For seven years, from 1950 through 1956, Fort Wayne was a stop on the Professional Golf Association circuit. The first Fort Wayne PGA Open was in 1950 and was won by Lloyd Mangrum. The first Open was held at Orchard Ridge Country Club and the subsequent pro golf meets were at the Elks Country Club. All were sponsored by the Junior Chamber of Commerce. Other Fort Wayne PGA Open winners include: Jim Ferrier, 1951; Jimmy Clark, 1952; Art Wall, Jr., 1953; Doug Ford, 1954; Dow Finsterwald, 1955; and Art Wall, Jr., 1956. The events were attended by thousands who followed the noted golfers of the era around the links. Attendance was regularly good, but the increasingly-high demands for purses in PGA opens led to the dropping of the tourney after 1956. The Hoosier Celebrities Tournament, an event which combined famous-name golf with famous figures in many lines of activity, was started in 1958. The sporting and social success of the event grew in subsequent years. The top golfers participating included Arnold Palmer, Jack Nicklaus, Gary Player and many others. Honored as Celebrities-of-the-Year with the putting on of the symbolic Red Coat is a list which reads like a history of the times. The Mad Anthonys events at the Fort Wayne Country Club were headed by Tom Hall, Rodger Nelson, Tony O'Connor and others. Some of the honored include Don Miller and the other Four Horsemen of Notre Dame, Bob Griese of Purdue and the

Miami Dolphins, Frank Borman the astronaut who flew around the moon, Network sports commentator Chris Schenkel, Indianapolis Speedway Owner Tony Hulman, Pro Football Coach Webb Ewbank, Notre Dame Coach Ara Parseghian, Michigan's Tom Harmon, UCLA Basketball Coach Johnny Wooden, Song writer Hoagy Carmichael and Entertainer Phil Harris.

For 72 days in 1955, from March 26 to June 5, Fort Wayne was the bowling capital. The event was the 52nd Annual American Bowling Congress. Approximately 31,000 bowlers from throughout the world participated. Attendance was a record for the ABC up to that date. For the tourney at Memorial Coliseum, 38 alleys were constructed in the arena at a cost of $190,000. That took 75,000 feet of maple and 80,000 feet of pine. Detroit won the team championship at the congress. Fred Bujack and Buzz Fazio were top individual scorers. In the local history of bowling, only one team ever won the ABC championship. That was a unit sponsored by Lincoln National Life in 1922. Bowlers on the team were Frank Farnin, Bill Doehrmann, August Greim, Eddie Kraft and Fred Zurcher. The tourney was held at Toledo that year. In 1955, Bobby Carteaux of Fort Wayne turned in the ABC series high of 823 in three frames. Jake Yoder of Fort Wayne scored a perfect game during the ABC singles competition in 1970. Fort Wayne women have made a big impression in bowling. Ermil Lackey was Women's National Bowling champion in 1926 at Milwaukee and Anita Rump won twice—in 1928 at Detroit and in 1930 at Louisville. Garnette Weber and Loranna Franke Kelly set the Women's International Bowling Congress record of 1,230 in doubles in 1937 at Rochester, N.Y.

Memorial Coliseum

Ground was broken for the building of the Allen County War Memorial Coliseum on January 24, 1950. It was dedicated upon completion on Sept. 28, 1952. In the subsequent years the Coliseum was the site of most major sporting events, circuses, ice skating shows and plays, entertainments and musicales; plus great religious gatherings, Presidential political speeches, civic and school events and patriotic observances. The building of the Coliseum grew out of a suggestion by Paul Gronauer, president of the Anthony Wayne Bank, in 1944 made to the Fort Wayne Junior Chamber of Commerce. The Jaycees accepted the challenge and initiated the project for a "living war memorial" for people of the Fort Wayne area. Ramon S. Perry, the Jaycee president, and F. Ellwood Allen, who headed a Park Board Survey on recreation potential, set the framework for a referendum placed on the ballot by the County Commissioners in 1946. The vote was 25,705 in favor and 5,720 against the project. A bill in the 1947 State Legislature, permitting a one per cent ceiling of the assessable property valuation for bonding purposes, was passed to enable the Coliseum project to proceed on the dimensions contemplated. On July 30, 1947, the County Council approved a $100,000 expenditure for a 100-acre building site at the southeast corner of California Road and Parnell Avenue. Later in the year, the County Commissioners entered into a contract with the architectural firm, A. M. Strauss, Inc. to prepare plans. A five-member board of trustees was named in June, 1949, three members by the Commissioners and two by the Circuit Court Judge. The first Coliseum board consisted of C. V. Kimmell, Ramon Perry, Alfred Randall, Otto Adams and James R. Fleming. Don Myers, who had earlier headed the Jaycees' Coliseum promotion effort, was named manager of operations. Bonds in the amount of $3 million were issued to cover construction costs. Bids were taken on Dec. 14, 1949, and the contract was awarded to the Hagerman Construction Co. The First National Bank of Chicago bid on the $3 million bond issue at 1½ per cent interest with a premium of $27,445, an astonishingly low interest figure. The dimensions of the Coliseum were 425 feet in length, 300 feet in width and 87 feet in height from the floor of the arena. There were 7,250 permanent seats and a total capacity of 10,500 patrons.

Fort Wayne Komets

"When the Allen County War Memorial Coliseum opened in September, 1952, the doors also swung open for a new sport in Fort Wayne—ice hockey," said sportswriter Bud Gallmeier a few years later. The sport caught on almost immediately, surpassing the hopes of the initial backers, Ernie Berg and Harold Van Orman, Jr. A total of 186,269 attended Komet Hockey Games during the first season of 1952-3. From the beginning, the Komets were part of the International Hockey League. Other early teams included Louisville, Cincinnati, Troy, Toledo, Cleveland, Indianapolis and Columbus, Ohio. Later, franchises switched around to various other cities, but Fort Wayne consistently maintained high attendance and a healthy record on the ice. By 1974, the Komets were in their 22nd year and were the oldest team in the circuit. When the Komets finished in fifth place the first season, the Cincinnati Mohawks were the leading team. In 1974, the Komets were tops in the league. In all the years in between, the Komets only missed the playoffs four times. The Komets also won the Turner Memorial Cup in 1963 and 1965, once while Ken Ullyot was coaching and the latter date under Eddie Long. The Turner Cup goes to the playoff winner. The Komets were league champions in the 1959-60 season and the 1962-63 season. The hockey team has had many top skaters including Art Stone, Eddie Long, Edgar Blondon, Hartley McCloud, Len Thornson, Robby Irons, Roger Maisonneuve, Glenn Ramsay, Chick Chalmers, Joe Kastelic, Bryan McLay, Bill Mitchell, Greg Jablonski, Guy James, Sid Garant and Brian Walker.

Olympic Gold

The first Fort Wayne athlete to win an Olympic championship was Sharon Wichman in 1968. Sharon, a blonde 16-year-old, won two medals in the swimming events at Mexico City—a gold in the 200-meter breaststroke and a bronze in the 100-meter breaststroke. Daughter of Mr. and Mrs. Francis Wichman and a junior at Snider High School, Sharon Wichman trained with Club Olympia and was a relative unknown at the outset of the Olympic events. On Oct. 19, 1968, she placed third in the 100-meter finals behind Djurdjica Biedov of Yugoslavia and Galina Prozumenshikova of Russia. In the trials for the 200-meter breaststroke, Miss Wichman had the fastest time. In the finals she faced the two swimmers who had finished ahead of her in the 100-meter event. Sharon later related: "Before the finals the girl from Yugoslavia told me to beat the Russian girl. I guess she'd rather see an American win than a Russian. I wasn't confident I could win. I knew I would have a good time, but didn't know how well they'd swim." Sharon was in lane 4; Galina the Russian was in lane 5. "I took the lead in the last 50 meters. I knew I was ahead of Galina, but I didn't know where the Yugoslavic girl was (in lane 1 on Sharon's other side.)" In that swimming final on Oct. 24, 1968, Sharon moved past Bjedov of Yugoslavia at about the 25-meter mark from the finish. Sharon won the gold medal in a time of 2:44.4 for a new Olympic record. She was the first American in Olympic history to take the 200-meter women's breaststroke event.

A decade earlier, another Fort Wayne resident won a world title. He was Capt. Verle Wright who scored highest in the World's Rifle-shooting finals in Moscow, Russia, in 1955.

High School Greats

Fort Wayne high school teams made their charge into the sports limelight in the 1930's and came fairly close to being dominant in Indiana for a number of years. The assault was on the basketball court, track and cross-country, and the gridiron.

Central and South Side High Schools in the early and mid-30's gave indications of state power with individual tracksters and in basketball and football, but it was North

Side which won the first team championship. This was in 1937 when North took the state cross-country title. This started a North Side cross-country dynasty which was to last through 1942. North, coached by Rolla Chambers, went five years without defeat in two-way meets.

Central, in the meantime, was a strong contender in the state basketball tourney. The Central Tigers were beaten in the final game in 1936 and were in the state final four again in 1937. The team's outstanding players, Paul "Curly" Armstrong and Herman Schaeffer, later led Indiana University to its first NCAA championship in 1941. Armstrong also later starred with the Zollner Pistons. Fort Wayne's first Indiana High School Basketball champion was South Side in 1938. Coached by Burl Friddle, the Archers beat Hammond 34-32 in the finals. The players included Dale Hamilton, Jim Glass, John Hines, Bob Bolyard, Jim Roth and Dick Frazell. South beat a tough Muncie Central team to gain the finals. After the final victory in the Butler Fieldhouse, the team returned to Fort Wayne for a riotous city celebration, perhaps only rivaled five years later when a Central victory caused a similar traffic-stopping affair by milling and cavorting thousands in the downtown area. The following year after their State Victory they went undefeated and were ranked Number 1 and odds-on favorites going into the State Tourney. But in one of the great upsets of the era, South was knocked off by an unheralded Ossian High team early in the Regionals.

Central Catholic High School won the State Catholic High School championship three times before parochial schools began competing in the regular State Tourneys in 1943. But the distinguishing thing about the CC record in basketball was its two National Catholic Championships in consecutive years, 1939 and 1940. The National Catholic Tourney was held at Chicago. In the final games of the two years, CC beat Leo High of Chicago and an Indian Prep School from Nebraska. Playing for CC on the two winning teams were Ed Stanczak, George Bitler, Gene Maxwell, Bob Boedeker, Edward Gorman, Bob Heiny, Harold Morthorst, Ed Klotz, Nick Leto, Ed Dehner, Bob Walker and Dick Krouse. The coach was John Levicki.

State Grid Champs

In football, Central came close to the mythical state titles in 1929 and again in 1935, led in the latter year by Steve Sitko who later quarterbacked three Notre Dame teams. Each time, however, Central lost playoffs for the state championship to Horace Mann of Gary and Memorial of Evansville, in respective years. The same thing happened again in 1939 when Central went through its regular season undefeated, only to lose in a playoff. Henry Kulesza, the State high jump titlist, was Central's outstanding back in that year. Central's great basketball and football teams of the 1930's and 1940's were coached by Murray Mendenhall, Sr. It was left to North Side to nail down Fort Wayne's first State football championship. The North Siders came close in 1937 with an undefeated season and were mythical title holders in 1940, also an undefeated season. Actually North Side, coached by Bob Nulf, completely dominated the opposition in 1940 with a backfield consisting of Bob Cowan, Mike Bojinoff and Bob Young. Cowan who also took the 220-yard State track title in 1940 and 1941, scored 159 points on the gridiron in the 1940 football campaign, including 34 points in the final game. He later played for Indiana University and the Cleveland Browns.

In track and field, Rolla Chambers' North Side performers were recognized throughout the state as the team to beat for more than a decade. North tied for the State crown with Horace Mann of Gary in 1939. They took clear titles in 1941, 1942, 1956, 1957 and 1963; and were top contenders most of the years in between. In 1939, Don Kemp won the 880-yard run and North took the half-mile relay. In 1941, Cowan repeated with a win in the 220-yard dash; Ashley Hawk won the mile; Mike Bojinoff took the high hurdles title and North won the mile relay. South Side helped the local cause that year with a win in the half-mile relay and Charles

Feistkorn's 880-yard victory. In 1942 North Side won state again by taking first place in both the mile and half-mile relay events and a win in the mile run by Ash Hawk; plus scoring in a number of other places by the large North team. Hawk was only a sophomore in 1942 and when he won as a freshman the year earlier his time of 4:34 was the fastest ever run in the United States by a high school freshman.

Central's Foursome

Central had big years in 1943 and 1944. A state contender in all major sports both years, the Tigers won the Indiana Basketball Championship in 1943 by beating Lebanon in the final game by a score of 40 to 38. Top Central hoopsters that season were Robert Van Ryn; Murray Mendenhall, Jr.; Charles Stanski, James Blanks, Max Ramsey and Robert Armstrong. In track in 1943, Max Ramsey won state titles in both the 100-yard and 220-yard dashes and Central took the half-mile relay. But despite that effort, Central didn't win the team championship. That came the following year in one of the more unusual episodes in Hoosier sports. Central, which had only come in third place in the Fort Wayne Sectional Track Meet behind North Side and South Side, qualified but a four-man team for the State Finals. In a demonstration of quality rather than quantity, Central's trackmen scored every potential point possible to win the Indiana Track Championship for 1944. Paul Bienz won the 100-yard dash in 10 seconds flat and the 220 in a sensational time of 21.6 seconds. Max Ramsey won the 440-yard run in 50 seconds flat and ran a second place to Bienz' 220 victory. Ramsey and Bienz then teamed with Bill Eshcoff and Bob Mugg for the half-mile relay. Starting the final leg about five yards behind, Ramsey passed and ran away from the competition for a relay victory in 1:31.8, one of the fastest times in many years of State Meets. Others from Fort Wayne winning State titles that year were Ash Hawk of North Side in the mile run and Bill Stults of South Side in the high hurdles. Four years later, a North Side sophomore, Archie Adams, established a U.S. record for a high school student when he won the Indiana Track title in the 200-yard low hurdles in 22 seconds flat. In the meantime, Central had another team in the State Basketball Finals, but missed the title. This was the 1946 team led by Bobby Milton who later played for many years with the Harlem Globetrotters.

C.C. H.S. Football

Central Catholic High developed a state contender on the football field in 1948; and two years later, one of the strongest teams in Indiana annuals. The 1950 CCHS team opened its season at South Bend Washington, then rated in the state's top ten. CC crushed them 27-6 and went on to an undefeated season and the mythical State title. In that season, the Fort Wayne team outscored its opposition 368 to 37. The backfield included Phil Ehrman, Acy Chandler, Tony Martone and Bob Brown. Ehrman later played for Purdue University.

Fort Wayne's individual state track winners date back to 1925 when Al Lomont won the 880-yard run. He was from Central. In 1928 Dick Bell of South Side won the 880 and in 1932 Jack Fleming of South Side won the same event. Bob Clymer of South was the mile run titlist in 1932. Jim Schroff of Central was state high jump winner in 1936 and Allen McMeen of North Side won the 440-yard run in 1937. In the early 1950's, Ron Huffer of New Haven High was state champion in the dashes. During the following decade, Henry King of Central High was the top middle distance runner. In the area of track and field, a number of boys from Fort Wayne schools took individual State titles, including: Sam Sims of Central in the high hurdles in 1949; Everett Tungett of South Side the shotput title in 1950; Dick McComb of North the 200-yard low hurdles in 1951; Warren Anderson of South Side the 180-yard low hurdles and high jump in 1952; Bob Ewing of North Side won the 220-yard dash in 1952 and Bill Griswold of

North won the mile run. Ewing won the 220 again in 1953. Charley Lyons of North Side won the high jump title in both 1954 and 1955. In 1955, North Side's basketball team made it to the State Finals, led by Lyons who later played at Purdue.

North's Track Aces

North Side was back at the top of track wars in 1956. Strong showings by ace hurdler Ron Trowbridge in both hurdles and some team balance put the Redskins within range with a crack mile relay team. But on a rain-soaked track, one Northman fell on the second leg. Then, on the third leg, Ron Bowman moved the Redskins from seventh to second place and Pete Lundell ran to a first place relay victory and the State championship. The following year, North Side had essentially the same team back and scored one of the more conclusive State track wins in the era since the regional eliminations were instituted, scoring 36 team points. Frank Geist won the 880-yard run. Tom Seifert took the shotput title. All of the members of the mile relay team scored well in individual events, then combined for an easy win in the relay. The foursome which came close to national records for the mile event included Frank Geist, Jim Hattery, Ron Bowman and Pete Lundell. In 1963 North Side won the 60th State Track Meet. It was Coach Rolla Chambers' last year, and North marked up 21 points without a first place finish. They did it with a second in the half-mile relay, a third in the mile relay, a second in the mile run by Dave Esterline and a third in the 880 by Steve Konow. But it was enough to win. In 1964, only Don Osdale of New Haven who took first place in the pole vault was a title winner from the local area. But North Side came back in 1965 with an impressive 31 points and it sixth State Track Championship. It was Duane Roe's second year as coach. Jim Hallenbeck took first in the 120-yard high hurdles and fourth in the low hurdles. Howard Doughty won the 180-yard low hurdles and was third in the high hurdles. The half-mile relay team steamed home in a fast 1:29.1 for a big win and 10 points. Running the relay was Paul Paino, Jim Hallenbeck, Steve Balmahn and Howard Doughty. The year of 1965 just missed being a banner year for North Side in basketball when Coach By Hey's quintet went all the way to the final game of the Indiana State Tournament before suffering a loss and ending up second in the state.

South's Second Title

The 1958 South Side basketball team gave Fort Wayne its third state title. Built around seven-foot Mike McCoy, the team was rated by some contemporaries as the greatest team to ever come out of the city. In addition to McCoy, the starting lineup included Tom Bolyard, Carl Stavreti, Rich Miller and Danny Howe. Don Reichert was coach. The toughest game for South on its way to the state title was an afternoon sectional game at Memorial Coliseum against Central, led by John Kelso, also rated in the Indiana Top Ten. South won that game in overtime, 60-56. In the final game of the Indiana Tournament, the Archers defeated Crawfordsville by the score of 63-34, one of the most lopsided state finals on record. Nine years later another South Side team appeared on its way to the Indiana basketball title. The 1967 team, led by Willie Long, was sidetracked in the afternoon game. The following year, South came back with a State Championship in track. The Archers scored 20 points with a win in the 440-yard run by John Lumpp and some good showings by Randy Rhoades, Paul Dekker, Bill Watson and Scott Lougheed.

Wayne and Snider

Wayne High School of Fort Wayne won the Indiana Track Championship in 1973 with a four-man team—duplicating a feat nearly 30 years before by the 1944 Central foursome. John Mitchell won the high hurdles event and took second in a dead heat in the low hurdles. Willie Knox ran to second places in both the 100-yard and 220-yard dashes. Knox and Mitchell then teamed with Wilfred Rouse and Willie Underwood for second in the half-mile relay. With just four men, the team accumulated 42 points. In the same meet, Rick Magley of Fort Wayne Northrop won the mile with a time of 4:18.2. The following year, 1974, Snider High School gained a piece of the State Track Title by tying Gary West, each with 35 points. Rob Goshert of Snider established a state record in the discus with a toss of 169 feet, 10 inches. Snider also got place points from shot-putter Dave Byrne, high jumper Rich Phillips, and runner Wilbert Anderson. Individual winners from other Fort Wayne high schools in the 1974 meet included Gary Hunter of Northrop in the pole vault with a jump of 15 feet 5½ inches; George Doehla of Harding with a shot-put of 58 feet 2 inches; Wilfred Rouse of Wayne in the 180-yard low hurdles in a time of 19.3, and a half-mile relay win by Wayne High. Bishop Luers High School, a regular state contender in football in the 1960's and 1970's, ended the 1973 season with a second-in-the-state ranking.

Northrop Takes State

Before a howling crowd of 17,225 in Assembly Hall in Bloomington, Northrop High of Fort Wayne won the 1974 State Basketball Championship. The Bruins beat Jeffersonville by a score of 59 to 56 in the final game. By winning, Northrop became the third city school to take the title, something no other Indiana community could claim. Earlier winners being South Side, twice, and Central. Coached by Bob Dille, the Bruins went all the way with five men for the clinching victory. The team included Walter Jordan, Tom Madden, Mike Muff, Jim Wimbley and Maurice Drinks. Northrop eliminated Lafayette Jefferson, 71 to 66, in the afternoon game. For the season, Northrop established the finest record in Fort Wayne history with a won-lost record of 28-1.

A move to put Fort Wayne back into the professional basketball picture was made in 1974 by Phil Olofson and Jim Nolan, co-owners. Jack Kerris, former Piston player, was retained as coach of the Hoosiers, the name adopted for the entry in the International Basketball League.

In July, 1974, Bill Kratzert of Fort Wayne was named to the All-American Collegiate Golf Team. Kratzert, a senior at the University of Georgia, had earlier won the Indiana State Amateur Golf Championship.

One annual sporting event, which was also a social and charitable success over the years, was the Fort Wayne Charity Horse Show. As of 1975, the Horse Show was in its 44th year. For most of its existence, the event was held at Covington Manor near the Hamilton Road. The country estate, which offered track and natural hunter courses, was for many years the property of Mr. and Mrs. John Berghoff, and subsequently, the estate of Mr. and Mrs. Donald Perrey. Usually, the Horse Show was a three-day exhibition, opening on Friday evening, with day and evening riding on Saturday, and the concluding hunter tests on Sunday afternoon. The Fort Wayne Horse Show drew fine show horses from much of the Midwest. Hundred of patrons attended the shows each day. By 1958, the proceeds for charity from the Horse Show had exceeded the $100,000 mark, according to Fred Thomas, president of the association at that time. Among the sponsoring organizations were Psi Iota Sorority, the Fort Wayne Junior League, the Jane Addams Society and the Tri Kappa Sorority. Benefiting were the Cancer Society, the League for the Blind, the Child Guidance Center and others.

The World's Professional Basketball Champions moments after the victory in the final playoff game in 1946 at Chicago Stadium. On the Zollner Piston team are, front row: Bud Jeanette, Bob McDermott, Curly Armstrong; second row: Jerry Bush, Reiser, Bob Tough, Charlie Shipp; back row: manager Carl Bennett, John Pelkington, Bob Kinney, Ed Sadowski and owner Fred Zollner.

10950. Fort Wayne Baseball Park, Fort Wayne, Ind.

Fort Wayne Baseball Park was between Calhoun and Clinton, just north of Superior. In the final decades, it was the home of the Fort Wayne entry in the old Central League. The stadium burned on July 12, 1930, in a fire caused by arson by an angry fan. Bobby Mathews, in the Bob Parker cartoon, pitched the first win in the history of professional league baseball. He also is in the record book for pitching the first shutout, a 2-0 victory by Fort Wayne over Cleveland. That initial game was at the Kekionga Ball Park near West Main St. on May 4, 1871. The Fort Wayne franchise in the National League was moved to Brooklyn, N.Y., late in the first season.

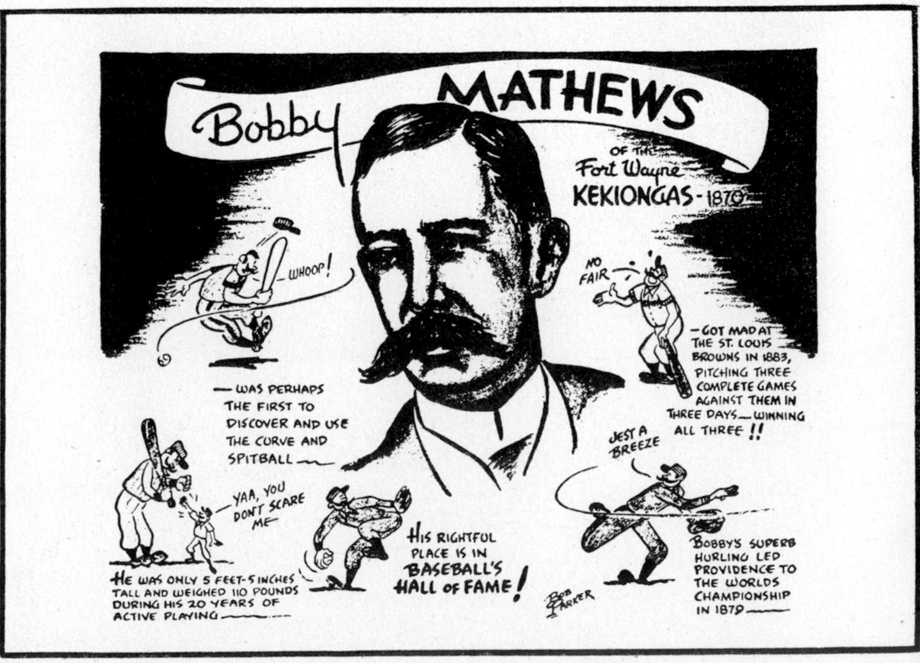

Curve balling Bobby Mathews was the hero of the hour on May 4, 1871.

The photo above shows how baseball teams looked in 1890s. The club is the Fort Wayne entry in the Interstate League and the ball park was at Lakeside, just east of the Delta Lakes. At left is the Rolling Mill Baseball team of the local shop league in 1914. Below is the Fort Wayne Baseball Park under the waters of the 1913 flood.

The 1928 Fort Wayne Chiefs, champions of the Central League, are shown above getting ready for a road trip. At left are the 1946 Zollner Piston Softball League Champions after the tourney win at Cleveland. Front row: John Shaffer, Neal Barille, Sam Lombardo, Hugh Johnston; second row: Jim Ramage, Fred Zollner, Bob Foreman, Bernie Kampschmidt, Curly Armstrong; third row: Chick Goldberg, Harold George, Ed Robitaille, Gene Nickolin; back row: Bob Baker, Leo Luken, Bill West, Diz Kirkendall, Bill Johnston and Carl Bennett. Below is the G.E. Club baseball team of 1948 which won the National Semi-pro championship. Front row, from the left, Olin Smith, Bob Winter, Paul Dyke, John Creavey, Dee Hamilton, John Red Braden, Garland Sewell, Stan Shargey; back row: Charles Wilt, Pete Elko, Len Bobeck, Art Gabrielli, Al Hazle, Hugh Orphan, Bill Brandt, Bill Hardy, John Corriden, Jr., and Charlie Harmon.

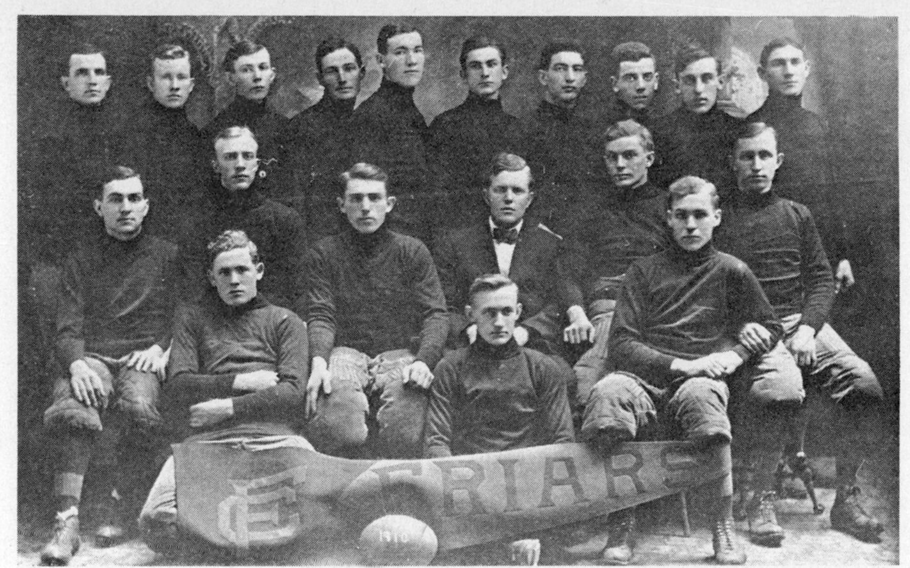

Football teams of the Friars Club represented Fort Wayne in the early part of the Century. In the top picture is the 1910 club and at right is the stellar group of 1911. At bottom is the Fort Wayne Hoosiers team of the American Basketball League in 1928. The team in dark suits is the Chicago Bruins—the competition for the game played at North Side Gym. The Hoosiers, to the right of Mayor William Geake in the center: Ralph Miller, Benny Borgmann, Shimer, Glasco, Rusty Saunders, Chizmadia and Maurice Chadwick.

Fort Wayne Gallery Of Sport

SOME OF OUR FIGHTING BROTHER COMBINATIONS WHO HAVE WON LOCAL GOLDEN GLOVES CHAMPIONSHIPS!

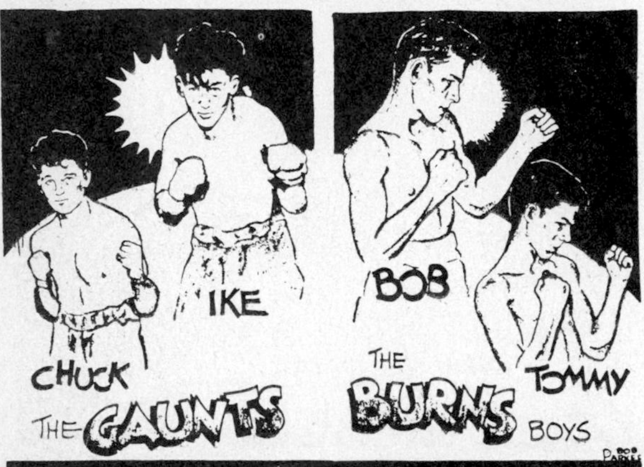

The Golden Gloves Tourney was a big annual event sponsored by the G.E. Club and the Journal-Gazette. Two local fighters were national champions: King Wyatt in 1935 and Bob Burns in 1940 and 1941. At bottom left, in a picture taken in Chicago in 1940, is Hal Stewart and fight mob friends. Stewart, in the center, was a top prize-fight contender from Fort Wayne in the 1912 era. The picture below was taken during the American Bowling Congress held at Memorial Coliseum in 1955. A couple of competitors are warming up at an off moment.

The arena of the Allen County War Memorial Coliseum, shown above with a crowd of more than 9,000 fans, opened in 1952. The building, exterior left, became the site of sporting events, exhibitions and shows of wide interest.

When Bobby McDermott came to Fort Wayne in 1942, the Pistons moved into the big time, winning national pro championships in 1945 and 1946. McDermott was the top basketball player in the U.S. during the period the pro game moved into the mainstream of American sports. Below are Hilliard Gates, announcer; Fred Zollner and Carl Bennett at North Side Gym in the early 1940s where Piston games were played at the time. At the bottom of the page the Pistons of 1955 are packing for the final game of the playoffs at Syracuse, N.Y. Fort Wayne was edged in the seventh game in a bitter contest.

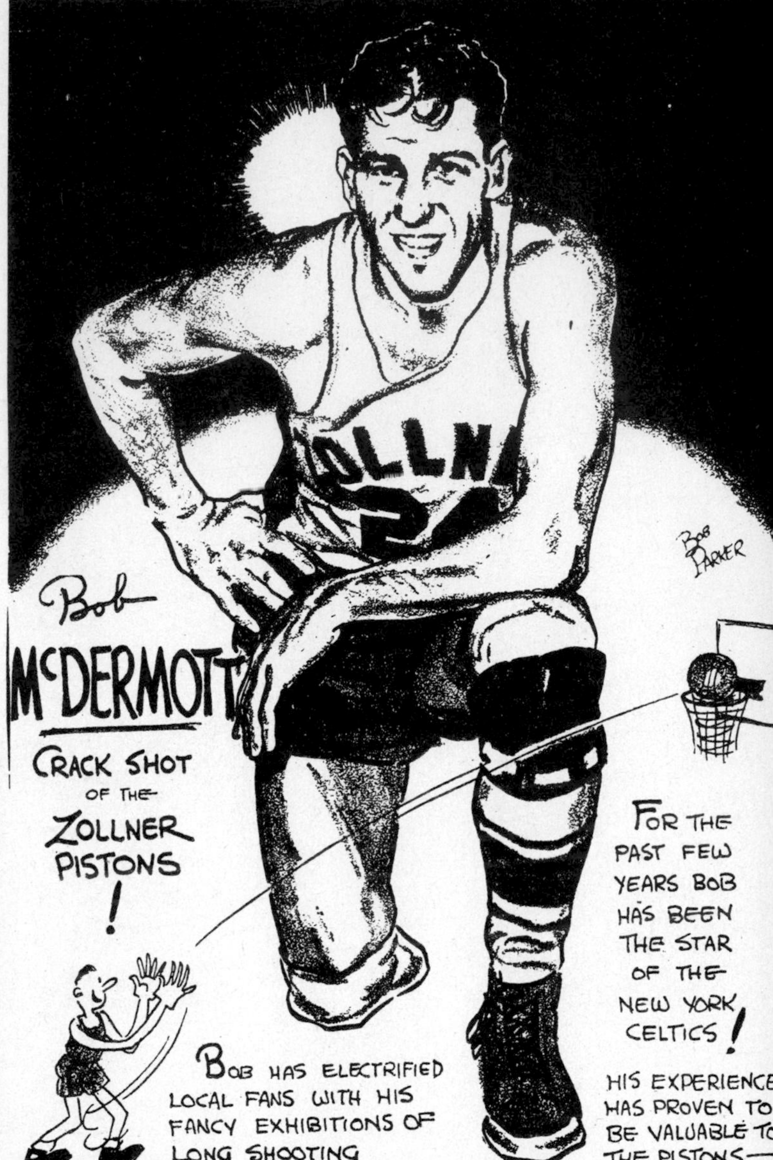

Bob
McDERMOTT
CRACK SHOT OF THE ZOLLNER PISTONS!
FOR THE PAST FEW YEARS BOB HAS BEEN THE STAR OF THE NEW YORK CELTICS!
BOB HAS ELECTRIFIED LOCAL FANS WITH HIS FANCY EXHIBITIONS OF LONG SHOOTING
HIS EXPERIENCE HAS PROVEN TO BE VALUABLE TO THE PISTONS—
BOB PARKER

The final season of the Pistons in Fort Wayne was 1956-57, after which the team was switched to Detroit. The action, upper left, was during that season at the Coliseum. Pro basketball returned to the city with the Fort Wayne Hoosiers in 1974. At left is a Bob Parker drawing in 1941 which depicts the golf pros at Fort Wayne clubs for many years.

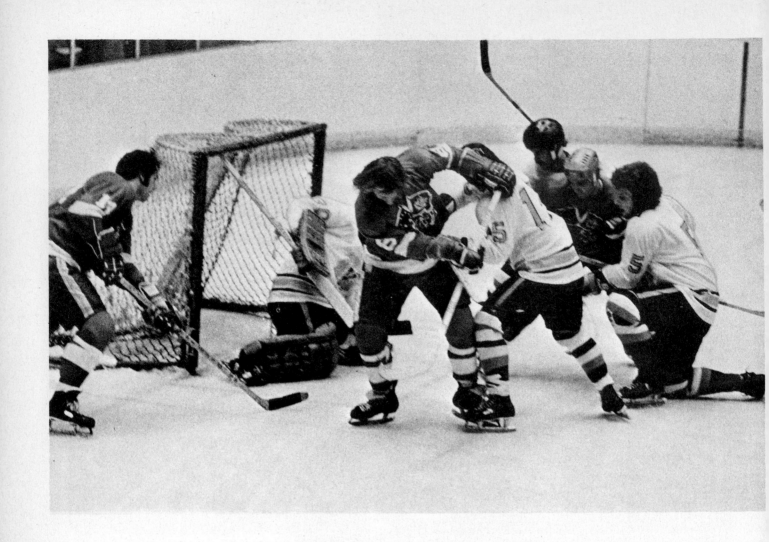

The Fort Wayne Komets began league play at the Coliseum in the 1952-53 season, adding a new dimension to local spectator sports. The team won its first International Hockey League title in 1959-60. Other championship teams skated in 1963, 1965 and 1974.

Sharon Wichman holds the Olympic Gold Medal following her victory in the 1968 event in Mexico City. The only Olympic winner from Fort Wayne, Sharon won the gold for her first place in the 200-meter breast-stroke. The swimmer also won the bronze medal for a third place finish in the 100-meter finals of the 1968 Olympics.

Central High School's basketball team of 1936 went all the way to the final game of the state tourney before faltering. They are lined up at right. Fort Wayne's first state basketball champion was South Side in 1938; pictured below, at Butler Fieldhouse after the victory.

SUNDAY MORNING, NOVEMBER 12, 1939 UNITED PRESS

OTRE DAME MARCH, 7

western; Fordham Beats I

Kulesza Gains; Central Wins Title

The Central Catholic High School basketball team of 1939 is shown after its win at Chicago of the National Catholic Basketball Tournament. C. C. also was National Catholic champ in 1940. At left is Journal-Gazette sports page clipping of 1939 when Central tied for the Indiana State Football chmpionship, but lost in a playoff. The following year, 1940, North Side High dominated Indiana high school football, winning the state title and most games by wide margins. The team is shown below.

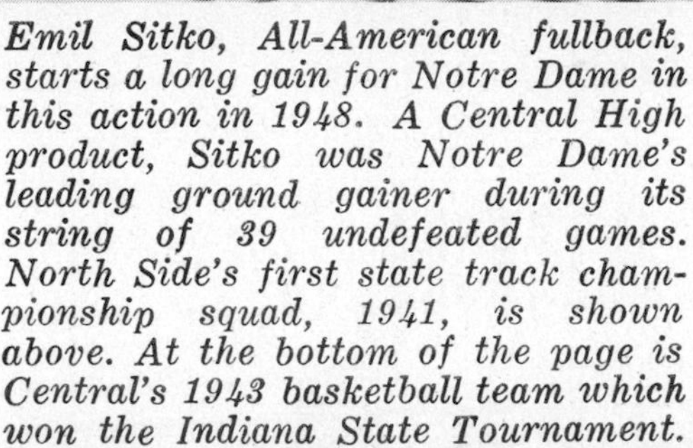

Emil Sitko, All-American fullback, starts a long gain for Notre Dame in this action in 1948. A Central High product, Sitko was Notre Dame's leading ground gainer during its string of 39 undefeated games. North Side's first state track championship squad, 1941, is shown above. At the bottom of the page is Central's 1943 basketball team which won the Indiana State Tournament.

Central's State track championship squad, at left, includes Robert Mugg, Paul Bienz and Max Ramsey in the front row, and Paul Berning, Coach Murry Mendenhall, Sr , and William Eshcoff. This 1944 group won every event it entered in the state finals. Below is part of the crowd on Feb. 24, 1945, outside North Side High School for the Sectional basketball tourney.

The top photo shows Central High School's 1946 basketball team leaving town for the State finals. They finished second in the final game. The center picture is of the 1950 Central Catholic High School football squad which went undefeated and was named Indiana State champs. The 1950 C.C. team and the 1940 North Side team were the city's only State champions in football. At right is the North Side track squad which won the State title in 1957.

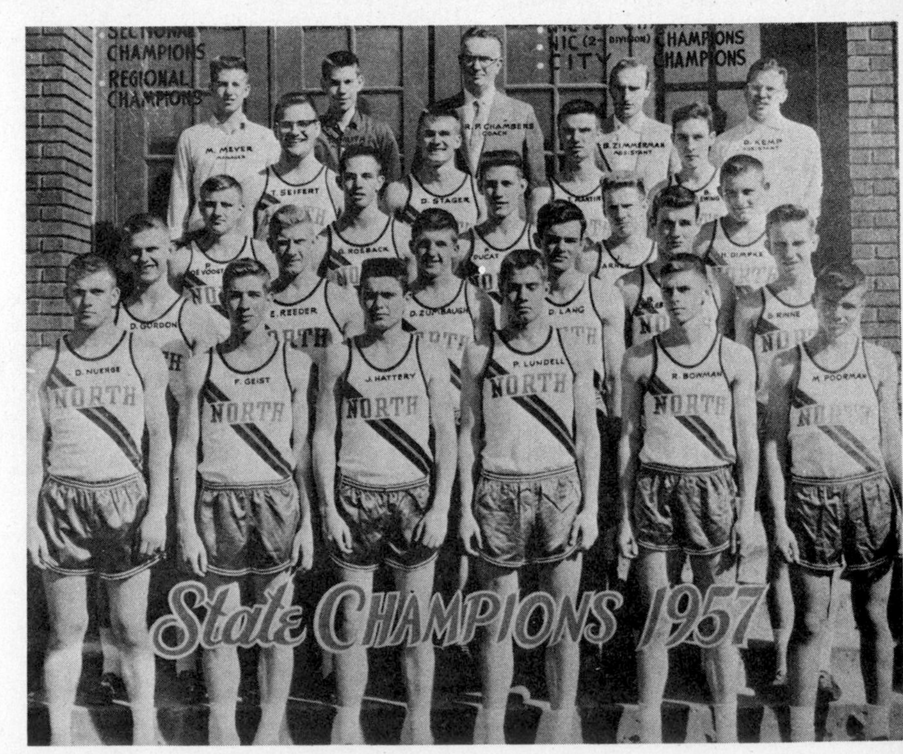

South Side went all the way in 1958. The Archers beat the Number 2 team in the State, Fort Wayne Central, in the Sectional and had little difficulty in winning the rest, as the State Championship smile reflects in the picture above. The Sandeson cartoon shows South on top of the basketball world, with other finalists Springs Valley and Crawfordsville along the victory trail.

Kids learn their basketball early in Hoosierland, such as the clinic, above, being conducted by coach By Hey. At right are two more routine North Side track squads of Rolla Chambers—both State champs. The one is the titlist in 1956 and the other 1963.

Above is the Wayne High School track team which went to State in 1973 and ran away with the championship. North Side and Northrop football squads mix it up in a city series game at Spuller Stadium. Below, high school cross-country runners complete in the Regional eliminations in 1974.

Walter Jordan holds the State trophy as other Northrop High players and fans celebrate victory following the Indiana finals in 1974. The team is lined up below at Bloomington moments after winning the State Basketball Tourney.

There is a big difference between winning and losing. In the photo above the cheering throng of Northrop High records the moment of victory at Bloomington as Northrop takes state in 1974. At left, the faces say North Side High just missed the basketball finals in 1975. Below, the track squad of Snider High School claims No. 1 as they finish in a tie with Gary West in the 1974 State Track finals. The co-titlists marked up 35 points each.

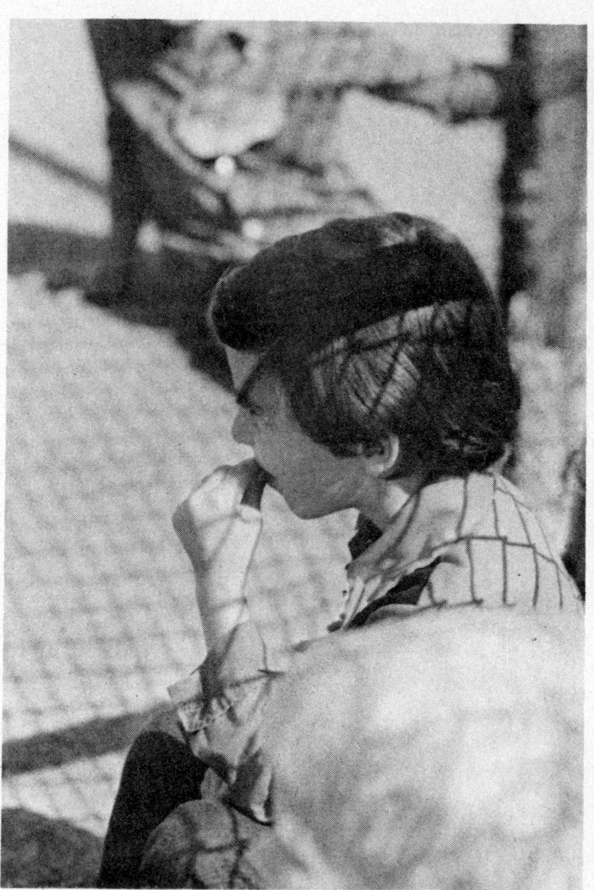

Sports over the years: A base-runner in the Girls Softball League is ruled safe in the 1949 shot at Parkard Park, top. At left is the eternal battle under the backboard. In the mentime, a Little League fan chews his bubblegum.

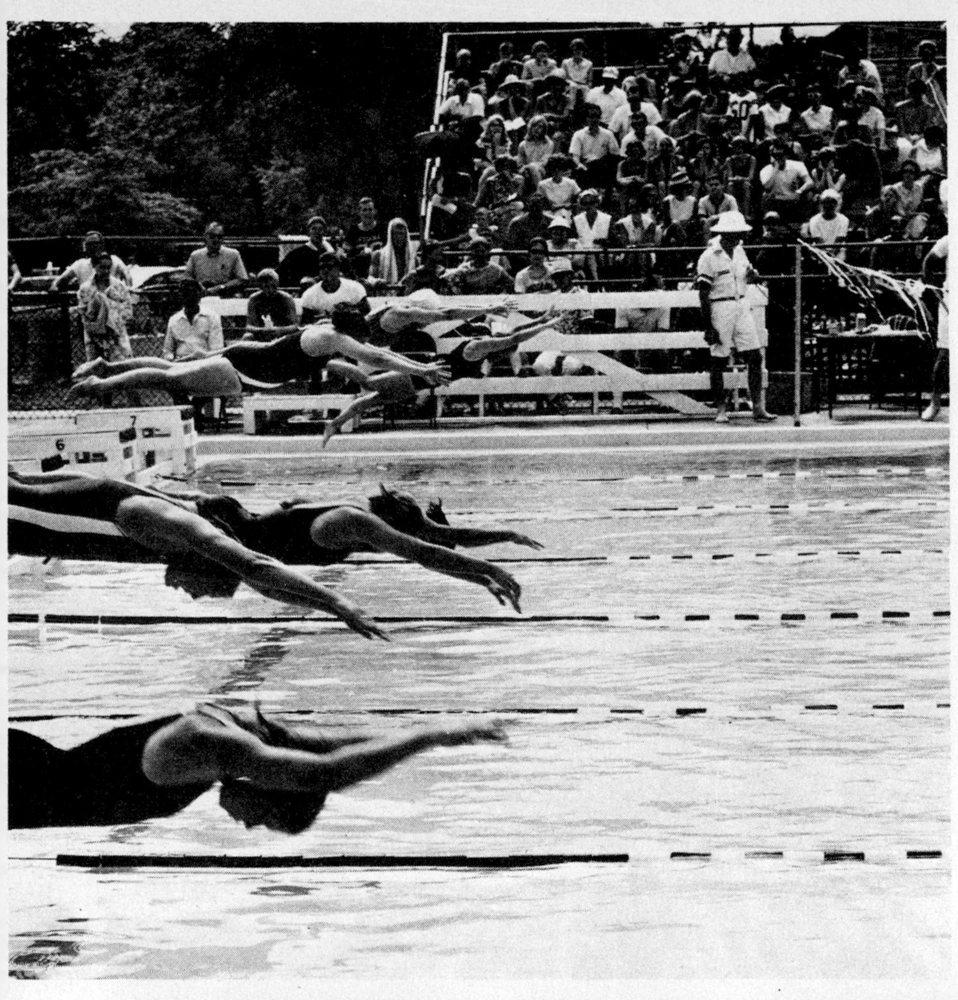

Swimming competition came into its own during the 1960s and the 1967 contest at McMillen Park was typical of the pool meets. The hockey battle at the goal was in 1960 on December ice during park league play.

Bobby sox were for real on the dance floor soon after peace times returned to the local social scene. It was a time when girls were dancing with girls and boys were standing around.

Part 10

After The War Was Over

Interest in the finer things bore immediate fruit with the return of peacetime in the middle 1940's. Until 1945, the Fort Wayne Civic Symphony Orchestra provided opportunity for musicians of the city and area to perform in a series of concerts each year. The Lutheran Choral group was the largest singing group in the community. In May, 1944, a group met in the Chamber of Commerce to initiate the creation of a full-fledge symphony orchestra of high artistic merit. This was the Philharmonic Society of Fort Wayne. Their energies led to the formation of the Fort Wayne Philharmonic Orchestra.

The first move was obtaining the services of Hans Schwieger, a German-born conductor who came to Fort Wayne from New York. With a seasonal budget as high as $100,000 and the initiative of musical director Schwieger in the enlisting of many fine musicians both in the city and elsewhere, Fort Wayne soon had one of the finest city concert orchestras in the nation. The concert series was completely subscribed. "In its first four years, concerts of a calibre never before attained by any local performing group, with some of the world's greatest artists as soloists," were presented, according to a music critic. Another group organized during the Philharmonic's first season was the Philharmonic String Quartet which played at Coffee Concerts, in schools and out-of-town performances. The following year, 1946, the Fort Wayne Philharmonic Chorus was organized. In the spring of 1948, Schwieger accepted a post as musical director of the Kansas City Philharmonic.

He was succeeded by Igor Buketoff who at the time was conducting opera in Paris. In 1949, an innovation was the creation of the Fort Wayne Philharmonic Sinfonietta, a 26-piece orchestra within an orchestra which could travel to smaller music halls in a 75-mile radius of Fort Wayne. Buketoff, who was to remain conductor of the Fort Wayne Philharmonic for more than 20 years, also initiated the Children's Concerts, a popular feature several times each year usually held at the Embassy Theatre rather than the Scottish Rite Auditorium—the regular concert hall. Buketoff developed the World Music Bank, a plan aimed at encouraging international knowledge and performance of contemporary music and sponsored by President Eisenhower's Music Division. The mainstay of support for the Philharmonic was always the regular subscribers and the Philharmonic Women's Committee which was formed early to handle tickets and fund-raising activities.

Fine Arts Foundation

In 1956 The Fort Wayne Fine Arts Foundation was formed to give broader support, not only for the Philharmonic Orchestra but other activities in the arts. The Foundation's office was established in November, 1956, with Richard Gibeau as the first executive-director. The policies and programs of the foundation officers included Samuel A. Rea, chairman; and Allan McMahan, Margaret Ann Keegan, William S. Latz, Edward T. Schele and Mrs. C. Daniel Ingebrand. Members of the foundation included the Philharmonic Orchestra, the Fort Wayne Civic Theatre, The Fort Wayne Art School and Museum, The Fort Wayne Ballet and the Fort Wayne Community Concerts. An early achievement of the Foundation was the "Adventure in the Arts" series over local radio stations. This included programs on stations WOWO, WGL, WKJG and WANE providing classical music, recorded drama and readings, interviews and cultural events. In the spring of 1958, the first Fine Arts Festival was held. The community-wide event presented by the Foundation was a week-long program of concerts, arts, architectural exhibits, drama, dance, music and events at Franke Park. The Festival drew participants and people from a wide area and remained a popular part of the community until merged with the Three Rivers Festival in 1974. Thomas Briccetti became musical director of the Philharmonic in 1970. Among his innovations was the Indiana Chamber Orchestra.

The Civic Theater was one of the earlier arts groups in the city and has a heritage going back to player units of the 19th Century. The Civic Theater is a direct outgrowth of the Old Fort Players, founded in December, 1931. That organization staged its plays in the Fort Wayne Art School, high school auditoriums and even in a room of the Allen County Courthouse. The name, Civic Theater, was adopted in 1940 with the purchase of a permanent home in the old Majestic Theater on Berry St., just east of Clinton Street. It was regarded by some as a sad loss in identity when the commonplace label of Civic Theater was chosen. But the group prospered just the same. A decade later, the Civic moved into the Palace Theater on East Washington Blvd., west of Clinton St.; then into the old Elks Hall, Berry St. and Maiden Lane, and finally the Performing Arts Center in 1973.

Ballet and Opera

The Fort Wayne Ballet, Inc., had its origin in January, 1956, when a small group of ballet fans met at the residence of Margaret Ann Keegan to watch a film of the Sadler Wells Ballet School. Mrs. Walter Lupke, Jr., was made chairman of a steering committee and later the first president. Other early officers included Mrs. L. D. Kurtz, Mrs. Hertha Duemling, Mrs. John Agnew, Mrs. John Spillson, Mrs. Ralph L. Feagles and Walter H. Lupke, Jr. The first director of the ballet was John Neff and the first productions were in the Civic Theater (the old Palace). The first productions were "Les Sylphides," "You Are the Mirror," and "The Skaters."

Beginning in 1950 as the Fort Wayne Light Opera Festival, Inc., an effort which would present summer musicals to thousands over a wide area was brought into existence. The first board was headed by Helene Foellinger, Lee Hillman, Carl J. Suedhoff and Roland R. Schulz. The first shows were "The Merry Widow," "The Red Mill" and "Naughty Marietta" under the direction of William Meader. The first shows used a combination of professional and amateur talent. In 1955 the unit was renamed The Festival Music Theater, Inc., an all-amateur performing group under the direction of Douglas Conway. Performances of the Light Opera and Festival Music Theater were held at the News-Sentinel Outdoor Theatre in Franke Park. It was erected in 1950 and the amphitheater had a seating capacity of 2,500 and a stage 66 feet wide and 45 feet deep. The theater was made possible by a $100,000 gift of the News Publishing Co. through Helene R. Foellinger, president. It was dedicated in memory of Oscar Foellinger, long-time publisher of The News-Sentinel. In the meantime, a number of Fort Wayne composers had works played by orchestras. Marshall Turken, business manager of the Fort Wayne Philharmonic, composed "Jubilation Overture" and heard it played by the Philadelphia Orchestra directed by Jose Iturbi. Mrs. Frank J. Benedict (Helen Quimby) composed "White Dawn" and it was played by the Fort Wayne Philharmonic and the Indianapolis Symphony Orchestra directed by Fabian Sevitsky. Rene Frank, music professor at Fort Wayne Bible College, composed "Passion Symphony" performed by the Indiana University Orchestra and the Indianapolis Philharmonic, and numerous other works composed for orchestras, band and choral groups. One of the more prominent musicians in Fort Wayne was John Escosa, harpist, who played in local concerts and in other cities.

Artists and Soap Boxes

In September, 1947, Dr. Alice Hamilton who had grown up in Fort Wayne became the first woman to receive the Lasker Award of the American Medical Public Health Association. Dr. Hamilton, then 78, was professor emeritus of industrial hygiene at Harvard University and had made exhaustive research into the effects of industrial solvents on liver and bone marrow. Born in New York City in 1869, she was brought to Fort Wayne when a few months old and lived at the Hamilton homestead at Clinton and Montgomery Streets. Among her discoveries were the mine and factory dangers due to lead, phosphorous, Mercury and TNT poisoning.

In 1945 Cliff Milnor began a daily column in the Fort Wayne Journal-Gazette called "Lines and Angles." For the next 27 years it provided a humorous view of the people and foibles in and around Fort Wayne. In the areas of painting, drawing and sculpture, local artists included Homer Davisson, Louis Bonsib, Grace Leslie Dickerson, James McBride, Hector Garcia, Robert Johnson, Leslie Motz, Peggy Brown and Donald Kruse.

The Soap Box Derby was revived on Sunday, July 14, 1946—the first time the event was held since 1941. The race had been cancelled during World War II. Fifty-four boys ran their cars down the Bueter Road course, which had also been the traditional site for the classic since the first race in 1935. Paul Knapp, general chairman, started the 1946 derby, sponsored by The News-Sentinel and Fort Wayne Chevrolet dealers.

Industrial Expansion

During the 1940's a number of industrial expansions occurred in addition to those directly related to production during the war years. Fruehauf Trailer Corp. boosted operations at its plant on East Pontiac St., a block east of Anthony Boulevard. General Electric moved regular motor-building operating into the Super-Charger plant on West Taylor St. and U.S. Rubber took over the plant which had been operated by Studebaker during war years. One of the larger and more permanent industrial citizens to come to Fort Wayne was Dana Corp. The original plant was that of the firm's Salisbury Axle Division. In 1945 it was decided to build a plant in Fort Wayne. Contracts were let in August, 1945, for a manufacturing area of 225,000 square feet with an expected employment roll of 800 men and women. The building was completed and the machinery was moved in 1946 and the firm's axle works at Toledo was transferred to Fort Wayne. Within a dozen years the plant space was doubled and the plant property was expanded to more than 66 acres. The first manager was Virgil R. Stump who served until 1953 when he was succeeded by Norman W. Kimmel. Later Dana division executives included O. L. Giauque, Wade Usher and R. D. Morrison.

Fruehauf had started operations in Fort Wayne on March 19, 1942, in the plant which had been idle for two years previously and had earlier been occupied by the Western Gas Division of Koppers Company. At first, Freuhauf supplied various types of trailers and haulers for the armed forces. With the end of the war, the 150,000-square foot plant was expanded and production of stainless steel trailers was begun at the Fort Wayne Division. Peak employment at the plant reached 1,500 workers.

The Gladieux Oil Sales and Refinery, Inc., on the city's east edge was started in 1948. The firm had earlier been a family business in kerosene deliveries. The 1948 refinery and cracking plant was rebuilt in 1957 with a capacity of 2,000 barrels of crude oil per gallons of refined products. Gladieux operated its own fleet of tank trucks to make scheduled pickups from over 100 crude oil producers in the Indiana, Ohio and Michigan area. The ability to pick up and deliver its own crude was a factor in supply during the international oil crisis which began in late 1973 and continued through 1974. Heading the firm's operation during its development were Ralph E. Gladieux, president; James M. Gladieux, Eugene Fletcher and Russell Sordelet.

Lassus Bros. built its second bulk oil plant in 1947 on Darlene Avenue. The firm grew out of a company founded in 1925 by August J. Lassus, Sr., who began a bulk plant and station at Anthony Blvd. and East Wayne Street. Over the years the firm opened stations to service the public with petroleum products in various parts of the community. Heading the company's operations were A. J. Lassus, Jr., Elmer F. Lassus and William F. Lassus.

The Medical Protective Co., founded in the 1930's as an insurance company for doctors, expanded following World War II. Byron H. Somers was president of the firm located in the Medical Arts Bldg. at Berry and Ewing Streets. The company relocated in a new building at the intersection of Reed Road and St. Joe Center Road in 1950.

The Wolf Bedding Co., manufacturers and upholsters, headed for many years by E. J. Wolf and R. E. Wolf, changed its name to Wolf Corporation. The plant at 710 Schick St. expanded into other fiber products. Richard E. Wolf was named president of the corporation.

Fort Wayne Tool & Die, Inc., headed by Richard G. Nill, manufactured tools at a plant at 1025 Goshen Road. Fort Wayne Pipe & Supply Co. moved into new quarters at 1815 South Anthony Boulevard. The firm was headed by E. J. Trier, president; Wayne L. Thieme, vice-president, and Martin H. Helmke, secretary-treasurer.

The Home Boom

One of the few fine residential areas which continued during the 1930's and into the 1940's was Wildwood Park on the west side, developed by Carl Light. After the doldrums in home building during the Depression and the enforced slack wartime period due to material shortages, a boom began in the late 1940's and continued for the next two decades. Early in the field were John Worthman and Roy McNett in the finer custom home field and Ralph Shirmeyer, Kurt Hanke, George Poag and others in more moderate-priced homes. Shirmeyer developed several large Fort Wayne residential areas with National Homes, a prefabricated design manufactured in Lafayette, Indiana. William B.F. Hall began prefabricated home manufacture in a plant near Wayne Trace which earlier had been occupied by Camp Scott. Hall, president, with Edward Disser and Harold McNight, vice-presidents, expanded the operation which subsequently became known as General Homes and finally General Industries. The firm was merged with Koppers Co. after nearly two decades of operation. As the building industry expanded other builders included Charles

Lebrato, Winfield Moses, Donald Shive, Donald Boharic, Robert Witte, Harold Palmer, William Bostick, Don Feichter, James Klotz, Jack Worthman, Robert Allen and Allen Wise. Richard Curdes developed fine subdivisions in St. Joseph Township.

According to a report of the Fort Wayne Home Builders Association, home building expanded from a 655 figure in 1946, the first year of the post-war boom, to a peak of 1,003 in 1950 before the decline of the Korean War. The building had dropped off to a mere 382 homes by 1955 and then again expanded for a year or two. By the 1960's, a large share of the building was outside the city limits and this trend continued through the 1970's when more than 80 per cent of all building was in the outside area. Secretary of the association for many years, Clem J. Steigmeyer, was succeeded by his son, John Steigmeyer.

The building followed the population trends away from both farm areas and the old urban areas. Even though Allen County's rural population decline between 1950 and 1970 was less than the national average, there was a decline in the county of about 3.5 per cent. Within Allen County there are 20 townships. The fastest-growing townships during the decades leading up to 1970 and after were St. Joseph, Adams, Aboite and Washington—all in the suburban growth area. By 1970 these four townships comprised 34 per cent of the total county population. Wayne Township, which at one time held nearly the entire city area, contained 53 per cent of the county population by 1970. The population within the corporate limit of Fort Wayne grew 9 per cent during the decade 1960-1970. The remaining areas of the county grew 34 per cent. Even at that, much of the city growth occurred through annexation. According to the 1970 U.S. Census, the population of Fort Wayne stood at 177,671 and the Allen County population, a truer measure of the metropolitan population, was 280,455.

Truck Depots

Fort Wayne as a center for trucking and warehousing operations continued to grow in the decades following World War II. These operations were at various locations near highway access and later developed as large operations in the Baer Field area on the south side and Interstate Industrial Park on the north. Further expansion of trucking occurred with the construction of Interstate Highway 69 during the 1960's. Large warehouses were built by W. T. Grant, Kresge, Western Auto and Weatherhead. W. T. Grant first located at 2424 West State Blvd. in 1956 and serviced 270 stores in the Midwest. Kresge located on the Ferguson Road in 1950 in a building covering nearly nine acres and containing 370,000 square feet of floor space. From the site, the firm serviced stores in 26 states. Western Auto was on the Nelson Road and maintained a fleet of trucks servicing stores in five states, starting in 1951. Weatherhead located on Dwenger Ave. in a 75,000 square foot plant in 1951. Norbert Knapke was principal developer in the Baer Field Area.

The first post-war shopping center, a strip of stores along South Anthony Blvd., was planned in October, 1947. Named the Anthony Wayne Village Shopping Center, it was erected by George A. Poag & Associates just north of McKinnic Ave. and was part of a general development of the area, including residential plat and 144 rental housing units. A few years later the Quimby Village Shopping Center was built on the Bluffton Road with principals involved being Helen Quimby Benedict and Harvey Cocks.

Railroad passenger traffic gradually declined with more use of autos, airlines and buses. A Fort Wayne-based intercity transportation firm was ABC Coach Lines, Inc. Officers included J. Earle Wooding, president; Courtland Wilder, vice-president; and Richard Nash, secretary.

Sick Cows

The railroad strike of 1946—the one which drew threats from President Harry Truman to put soldiers in as operators of the nation's trains—had a milky reaction in Fort

Wayne. On May 24, 1946, a news item said "The Fort Wayne Union Stockyards are crowded with bawling cattle today as a result of the railroad strike and by Thursday evening the management was obliged to call a halt to the unloading of livestock from railroad stock cars." The problem was that hundreds of cows were going unmilked. "The yard personnel of the stockyards found it impossible to milk all of the animals, but Humane Officer Wilfred J. Goss and Dr. Charles D. Morrow, veterinarian, volunteered and milked as many of the animals as they could. "The udders of one of the cows were so swollen they would fill a small washtub, and the udders of another big cow were so hot and swollen that I was unable to get milk from them," Goss said. Nine carloads were unloaded from the Nickel Plate and when the Pennsylvania Railroad wanted to unload added carloads, the stockyards called a halt.

During the following year, 1947, Fort Wayne received some reflected glory when twin sisters of a local family won a national title. Marilyn and Joann Voors, 23, were named "most attractive twin" in the land at a convention at Columbus, Ohio.

The Johnny Appleseed Memorial Park became a reality on October 20, 1947, when William T. McKay and Ruth B. McKay donated a tract of land of 12 acres to Allen County. The Commissioners of Allen County accepted the land and the provision that it be improved and maintained as a public park and as a memorial to Johnny Appleseed (John Chapman). The land, just north of the St. Joseph River and east of Parnell Ave., includeld the old Archer Graveyard where Johnny Appleseed had been buried. The Johnny Appleseed Memorial Commission had been created in 1934 by the City Council. The group originally consisted of William Fruechtenicht, Dr. Victor Hilgemann, D. N. Foster and Robert C. Harris. Foster died that year and Charles E. Moellering was appointed. Other early members included William McKay, Arthur A. Herber and John H. Craig. The marker for the grave was placed on May 25, 1935, by the Optimist Club headed by James Menefee, president. The fence was a gift of Stephen Fleming and had been installed around the grave by the Indiana Horticulture Society in 1916. In 1949, the City Council named the area the Johnny Appleseed Memorial Park and Beach. At that time, the grave site was still in a natural state with other old grave stones and markers of the historic Archer plot still in place. In the 1960's, the commission developed the memorial site with modern landscape architecture.

Downtown Fires

At 9 p.m. on Feb. 15, 1947, an unidentified pedestrian walking along West Lewis St. noticed flames and smoke pouring from the rear of buildings just to the north. He sounded the alarm for a fire which destroyed a large business section near the corner of Jefferson and Calhoun Streets. Destroyed was the Weil Building in the blaze which caused damage estimated at about $500,000. The Standard Rug & Linoleum Co., 115 West Jefferson St.; and Rowlands Furniture Company, 1108 South Calhoun St., both suffered losses in excess of $100,000. Meyer Drugs on the corner and Hillman China Co., 117 West Jefferson also had losses. The Warner Beauty College had damages from smoke and water and some 100 girls in training were idled. Fire Chief Fred W. Goeglein said the fire started in the basement and spread up to the fourth floor of the main Weil Building, whose empty brick walls were razed soon thereafter. The fire was the second within a month in the area. The Ryan Building about a block away on West Washington Blvd. was destroyed on Jan. 16, 1947, with a loss of more than $200,000. Police Chief Jule Stumpf pressed all shifts into service in an emergency order during the Weil Building blaze which was out of control for nearly three hours.

Dr. O. T. Kidder was named medical director of Irene Byron Sanitarium in February, 1947. He succeeded Dr. M. H. Draper who had been medical director of the county tuberculosis hospital since 1931. Dr. Kidder remained head of the institution with facilities in six brick structures north of Fort Wayne on the Lima Road until the early

1970's when advances in medical practices rendered obsolete the hospital operation. During its heyday in the 1920's, 1930's 1940's and 1950's the hospital treated thousands of patients needing long-term TB care from a wide area of Northern Indiana.

Parkway Default

A missed opportunity which was to become a legend in Fort Wayne was the Anthony Wayne Parkway, proposed in 1946 and the subject of a referendum on November 5, 1947. Basically, the expressway was a Federal proposal pushed by Governor Ralph Gates which would have resulted in north-south and east-west multi-lane expressways through the center of the city. The east-west route would have been north of the Pennsylvania elevation and the north-south route would have been between Lafayette and Hanna Streets. A large park area and interchange would have been built where the routes crosses. The cost of the project was set at $27 million with the Federal government paying all but $4,085,000 which was to be borne by the city over a 10-year period. It was expected that about 10 years would be involved in constructing the roadway. To make way for right-of-way, 1,536 buildings were to be removed. The Parkway Better Homes Foundation, headed by E. H. Kilbourne, was set up to help in providing new housing. Mayor Harry Baals, the Chamber of Commerce and most civic leaders supported the project. Surprising to some, however, a considerable bloc of resistance to the plan developed. There was an almost open tinge of racism and anti-open housing attitudes expressed by some opponents of the plan for the expressway because it would mean the moving of a considerable portion of Fort Wayne's Negro population. Though the plan was non-partisan, the expressway was associated with the Republican ticket and the opposition was associated with the Democratic ticket. The Republican candidate for mayor in 1947 was Otto H. Adams and the Democratic candidate was Henry Branning. At the top of the ballot was the referendum with which the voters would vote for or against the $27 million Anthony Wayne Parkway. On election day there was the greatest turnout of voters in Fort Wayne up to that time. The expressway plan went down to stunning defeat. It was voted down by a vote of 24,844 to 15,418. Henry Branning and a Democratic city administration were swept into office. In one of its last important acts, the lameduck City Council closed the books on Nov. 10, 1947, on the superhighway project when it adopted a resolution setting aside a previous resolution approving the expressway.

Branning's Team

The 13-year tenure of Mayor Henry W. Baals was brought to an end on Jan. 1, 1948. It was the longest consecutive tenure in the mayor's office in the history of the city. Baals was elected in 1934, 1938 and 1942—the last term being a five-year one to put the city elections back on an off-year schedule. Mayor William Hosey had moved the city election over to an even general election year as a Depression economy measure. Mayor Henry Branning was sworn into office by the newly-elected City Clerk Norbert G. Welch. Welch also administered the oath of office to others elected or appointed to the new city administration. These included John A. Logan, city judge; Arthur Fruechtenicht, city controller; Fred A. Berghoff, chairman, and Richard Hurst and Dayton Abbott, Board of Public Safety; Walter C. Vetter, chairman, and Frank Derck and Chauncey Griffith, Board of Works. Elected to the City Council were Carl Alter, Charles Boyer, F. Wade Boyland, Paul M. Burns, Julian Franke, Elmer E. Fuhrman, Arthur Herber, Edwin Lindenberg and Hilbert Nahrwold. Lester H. Eisenhut was named chief of police and Edward L. Uebelhoer and George Hood, fire chief and prevention chief. Named to the City legal staff were Harry H. Hilgemann, C. Bryan Hayes and Oliver Eggers.

Midwestern United Life Insurance Company was chartered on May 14, 1948, and almost immediately became one of the faster-growing life companies in the United States. The moving spirit and first president of Midwestern was Phil J. Schwanz. Other early officers included Donald B. Grissom, Benjamin W. Hartman, Sam W. Fletcher and Charles A. Lord, Within a decade, Midwestern had nearly $200 million in insurance in force and operations in 40 cities with 550 agents. A few years later Midwestern was further broadened with the merger of Great Northern Life Insurance Co. into Midwestern. Great Northern had been started in Fort Wayne in 1953 by Edward H. Gerber, Frederick R. Tourkow and Robert M. Ryker.

The Fireworks

The largest crowd to gather in Fort Wayne in 1948 was estimated at 125,000 people at the Fourth of July fireworks, sponsored by The News-Sentinel. For a number of decades, the fireworks display consistently drew the biggest annual crowds in the Fort Wayne area. The 1948 event was the first to be held at McMillen Park and it was the second display of the post-war years. Four tons of fireworks were exploded in what several national fireworks manufacturers claimed was the most impressive annual display in the U.S. The large annual fireworks attractions in Fort Wayne had their origin in 1926 when the event was at Irene Byron Sanitarium and sponsored by the Fort Wayne Electric Club and the Fire Department. The News-Sentinel took over the sponsorship at Irene Byron in 1927 when a crowd of 15,000 showed up. The spectacular was then transferred to Foster Park where increasing crowds gathered on the golf course during the 1930's. In 1947 the event was held at Zollner Stadium. After being at McMillen from 1948 to 1971 the fireworks were staged at City Utilities Park near the St. Joseph River and Coliseum parking in 1972 and thereafter. Familiar figures in presenting the fireworks were Oscar Foellinger, News-Sentinel publisher who began regular sponsorship; Helene Foellinger, publisher, who continued them; Tony Vitale, a fireworks artist who came to Fort Wayne for many years to stage the display; and Ralph Heckman, News-Sentinel circulation manager, who was the familiar voice on the microphone during the ceremonies.

Election Trends

Hoosiers gave a bigger vote to Harry S. Truman in 1948 than they did to Franklin D. Roosevelt in 1944, but Thomas E. Dewey was able to edge Truman in Indiana by a vote of 821,000 to 808,000 in 1948, despite Truman's upset victory nationwide. Dwight D. Eisenhower was able to overpower Democrat Adlai E. Stevenson in both 1952 and 1956. The Hoosier vote in 1952 was 1,136,000 to 801,000. The Indiana vote in 1956, providing the greatest margin up to that time in a Presidential election in Indiana, was 1,183,000 for Eisenhower and 784,000 for Stevenson. The Allen County vote in 1956 was more than two-to-one in favor of Eisenhower with a vote of 58,210 to 25,444. Indiana delivered a majority vote to Richard Nixon's losing effort in 1960 with 1,175,000 for Nixon and 952,000 for John F. Kennedy. Allen County was even stronger for Nixon in November, 1960, with a 60,103 for the Republican candidate and 39,235 for Kennedy. Indiana gave Lyndon B. Johnson, the Democrat, a fairly safe margin over Barry M. Goldwater in 1964 with a vote of 1,170,000 to 911,000. The margin in Allen County, however, was very narrow with the Johnson vote at 50,706 and the Goldwater vote of 49,284.

The off-year election of 1950 was one of the more interesting from the Allen County point of view. After Democratic inroads in 1947 and 1948, the Republicans showed considerable strength, sweeping nearly every office. At the top of the ticket was Alexander M. Campbell of Fort Wayne, the Democrat, who opposed Homer E. Capehart, the Republican candidate for U.S. Senate. Capehart defeated Campbell statewide and in Allen County by a vote of 36,878 to 27,304, even though Campbell led the local ticket. Another top vote-getter who went down to defeat in the 1950 election was Edward Kruse who had unseated long-time Republican Congressman George Gillie in 1948. Congressman Kruse, seeking a second term, lost to E. Ross Adair by a vote of 27,277 to 37,083. This was Adair's first Congressional victory and he would be re-elected nine times and serve in Congress for 20 consecutive years.

Campbell and Hiss

Alex Campbell came to national prominence in 1948. Campbell, who had been U.S. Attorney for Northern Indiana since 1941, was named Assistant Attorney General of the United States. He supervised the prosecution of 11 top Communists in New York City. He also participated in the prosecution of Axis Sally and Tokyo Rose, enemy agents in World War II who were convicted of treason. His most famous case involved the prosecution of Alger Hiss, former presidential assistant and secretary of the opening conference of the United Nations. Campbell was in charge of the government espionage case against Hiss. It was Campbell who confronted Hiss with conflicts in testimony given to grand juries. "I think you're lying," Campbell told Hiss. "I don't care what you think," Hiss retorted. Hiss was never tried for espionage but was later convicted of perjury. In addition to being Senate candidate in 1950, Campbell was Democratic National Committeeman from Indiana and chairman of the Allen County Democratic Central Committee. He and his wife Ruby were Palomino horse breeders at nearby Coesse. They rode in the 1968 Tournament of Roses Parade in Pasadena, California, and Campbell died during the trip home.

The Coal Scandals

The Branning Administration may have been the most disastrous in the city's history. There were too many promises, ranging from expansion of the Filtration Plant, City Light and a Garbage Disposal Plant to vast street improvements, annexations, and modernization of the Barr St. Market. The early realizations were hard to discern; and instead the public heard carping that "All of the proceedings entered into by the preceding administration were illegal" regarding thee Nickel Plate elevation. Before the first year of the term was out, Branning sought to double the city budget, proposing to run the civil city tax levy from 91.5 cents per $100 assessed valuation to $1.69. "The Branning Administration, which in the first months of its incumbency inherited city balances totaling more than $2,373,000, today indicated it will almost double the present civil tax levy with its budget for 1949," a news article indicated in the summer of 1948. The city rate was later set at $3.68, including school, county and other departments, which was the highest since 1918. That rate was pared down to $3.45 the following year, but the damage was done. In the meantime, there were reports of shoddy construction jobs by some of the contractors doing city street jobs. From almost the beginning, Mayor Branning became estranged from some of the members of the City Council. Singled out as targets for the mayor's ire were three councilmen who had been openly hostile to some of Branning's policies. There were Edwin Lindenberg, Paul M. Burns and Elmer Fuhrman. None were included on important council committees by Arthur Herber and the Branning-supporting majority.

The gravest issue in the Branning years broke in September, 1950, when Councilman Paul Burns demanded a probe of the coal purchasing practices of the City Administration. The Branning forces moved to shut out Burns by having more friendly councilmen named to the Mayor's investigation of the charges. Burns, however, conducted his own inquiries, making them public. "On June 5, 1950, the City Utilities gave an order to the Martin Coal Co. here for coal at $5.15 per ton," Burns said. "When the coal was delivered the statement to City Light called for a payment of $5.50 per ton. I also have two copies of shipping orders from a West Virginia coal company with car numbers and everything that lists the mine price of this same coal shipped on these cars at $3.50 per ton. I have letters from two coal dealers in Fort Wayne. One of them will furnish coal to the city for $4 a ton and the other for $3.85." Burns said City Light was using more than 80 thousand tons of coal per year. The Martin Coal & Supply Co. had as its president Eugene Martin, former chairman of the Allen County Democratic Central Committee and political ally of Mayor Branning. During August, 1950, checks totaling $46,321 were issued to the Martin firm from city funds. In the following weeks it was revealed a total of $396,000 in city checks had been made out to the Martin firm in the first eight months of 1950. It was learned the coal was shipped directly from mines to City Light, with the city paying the freight, but with a mine cost of $3.50 and the city paying $5.50 per ton. On September 20, 1950, the Indiana State Board of Accounts indicated it would audit the books of the Fort Wayne Municipal Utilities.

The Indictments

On November 10, 1950, the Allen County Grand Jury indicted Mayor Henry E. Branning, Jr., and five others on charges rising out of the coal scandal. The others included Chief of Police Lester H. Eisenhut, City Councilman Charles H. Boyer, Traffic Captain Gregor Klug, City Purchasing Agent Harold F. Battenberg, and A. Eugene Martin, president of the Martin Coal and Supply Co. Fifty indictments were returned by the Grand Jury. Branning and Battenberg were named in 36 indictments which charged conspiracy. Martin was named in 42 true bills, including bribery. Eisenhut and Klug were indicted for perjury. Boyer was charged with accepting bribes. The mayor and the five others surrendered late on the night of Nov. 10 to Sheriff Harold S. Zeis. Eighteen of the indictments involved conspiracy to commit grand larceny involving a total sum of $195,000. It was also alleged that Martin paid Councilman Boyer $7,562 for the purpose of influencing city purchases. Boyer was a salesman for Korte-Baker Company which was involved in other questionable supply transactions with City Utilities. Prosecuting the case for the county was Chester A. Lincoln, who almost immediately ran into difficulty with State authorities who were criticized in the following months for dragging their feet in proceeding with the case. Judge Walter Brubaker of the Kosciusko Circuit Court at Warsaw was named to preside over the indictments on a change of venue from Allen Circuit Judge William H. Schannen. By the end of February, 1952, six months after pre-trial motions, the case still hadn't been tried. David Hogg, one-time Congressman from Northeast Indiana, represented Mayor Branning; Clarence R. McNabb was attorney for Martin. James R. Newkirk represented Boyer; Roland Schulz represented Battenberg; James Jackson represented Eisenhut, and Harold Korn represented Klug. Eventually, the charges against Mayor Branning and others were set aside on the basis that the defendants' constitutional rights had been violated during questioning at Grand Jury sessions.

Despite his court difficulties, Mayor Branning ran for reelection in 1951, but lost by a wide margin in the May primary to Paul (Mike) Burns. After the turndown by his own Democratic party vote, Branning declared he would determinedly continue with his programs. Among the accomplishments of the Branning years were: a lid on gambling which had been wide open in Fort Wayne since the 1930's; the opening of East Berry St. and the establishment of the Police Academy. The Branning Administration boosted salaries of some city officials, as of 1952, to the following totals: City Councilmen, $1,300; City Judge, $6,000; Clerk, $5,400; Board of Works members, $6,000; and Board of Safety members, $1,200. The Mayor's salary remained at $8,800. Also, late in 1950, the beginning of the end of one of Fort Wayne's oldest and commonest institutions loomed into sight. This was the street car token which had been a part of daily commerce since the days of the horse-drawn cars of the 19th Century. On Nov. 22, 1950, the Fort Wayne Transit, Inc., petitioned the Indiana Public Service Commission to eliminate the three-for-a-quarter token fare and establish a regular 10-cent fare with the ordinary dime as the common deposit for a bus ride.

The new G. C. Murphy store at the northeast corner of Wayne and Calhoun Streets was opened on October 25, 1950. Work on the building was started in 1948 with the razing of a long-time downtown landmark, the old IOOF Building which had been there since 1890 and was a heavy, dark brown stone structure. The new Murphy Bldg. had frontage along Calhoun St. of 110 feet and along Wayne of 182 feet, with 112,970 square feet of floor space. H. M. Spreuer, store manager, later reported the operation in Fort Wayne was the largest volume-wise in the Murphy chain. The four-story building, with a front of limestone and red granite trim, was designed by A. M. Strauss architects.

North Bypass

Work on U.S. 30 Bypass, a road around the north and east sides of Fort Wayne, was begun in 1950. The highway would later be renamed Coliseum Boulevard. Basic aspects of the project were the connecting and improving of the old Bueter and California Roads and the development of a cloverleaf interchange on the east end of the city. Bids were opened on August 29 by the Indiana State Highway Commission and construction on an east-west leg was begun in September. Plans provided for the altering of a number of city streets, including the angling of Jefferson St. through Hayden Park to Maumee and the developing of superior one-way routes on Washington Blvd. and Jefferson St. until they joined in a four-lane express road to the east-end cloverleaf. The immediate purposes of the project were to advance traffic movement along Bueter Road from the east end industries and provide a route for through highway traffic around the north of the city. At the direction of Federal engineers, considerable right-of-way was acquired for an angle route in a northwest to southeast slant to join the Bueter and California Roads and provide what was then termed as the Circumurban Highway. The Bypass in subsequent years provided the scene for the greatest commercial and industrial development of the community and eventually became a hopelessly clogged emporium of cross-traffic, signals and sluggish mixture of local shoppers in automobiles and highway truck rigs.

Eating Out

Until the postwar years, eating places consisted mainly of a few fine restaurants and numerous lunch rooms and neighborhood taverns. The principal restaurants were downtown. These included the Berghoff Gardens on Harrison St., south of Berry, operated by Nicholas and Cleo Spillson; Mrs. Miller Tea Room at Jefferson and Harrison which later was known as the English Terrace; the dining rooms of the Anthony Hotel (The Van Orman Hotel operated by Harold Van Orman after 1946) and the Hotel Keenan. The Hobby House at 213 East Jefferson St. was operated by Phil Clauss, who soon opened another Hobby House at Wayne near Barr Street. Clauss developed a chain of restaurants, including a large Ranch House on North Anthony Blvd. and later numerous Kentucky Fried Chicken outlets. He served on the KFC Corp. board of directors from 1951 to 1969. The Dutch Lunch, 616 South Clinton St., was a familiar gathering place for politicians and newsmen for many years. Operated by Henry Heemsoth, Dutch's was in business until redevelopment swept the block away in the late 1960's. The city's first large drive-in restaurant of wide popularity was Gardner's at Jefferson and Webster Streets, operated by Frank Willis and Mrs. Josephine Gardner. Perhaps the greatest popularizer of drive-ins was Don Hall who began a drive-in on the Bluffton Road just west of the Oakdale Bridge in 1949. Hall, who in his early years had worked in Hall's Meat Market at 1938 South Calhoun St., soon expanded his restaurant chain with both drive-ins and specialty restaurants in various parts of the city. Hall's Gas House Restaurant, at Superior and Spy Run Ave., the site by the St. Mary's River where the old gas works once stood, became a widely-known eating place in Fort Wayne and the area. The Azar family also started with a store on Calhoun St., a grocery in the 2600 block, but in subsequent generations developed large restaurant enterprises. The first Azar Big Boy Restaurant was at 2440 West Jefferson St. near Swinney Park and opened in 1954. Other restaurants were opened downtown and in seven other locations. In the mid-1960's Alex and David Azar built a large commissary at 1010 Colseum Blvd. to service the various outlots. Azar's expanded in other northern Indiana communities and in other states. In 1972 Alex Azar opened The Moonraker, a fine eating place at Coliseum Blvd. and Parnell Avenue. By 1974 Azar's had 1,500 employees and $20 million annual sales. Steve Gouloff operated the Paramount at Fairfield and Kinsmoor Avenues, adding to the city's reputation for fine steak houses in the 1950's and 1960's. Younger brothers Ted Gouloff and Tom Gouloff moved on to found their own restaurants. George Mallers founded The Phoenician in the Georgetown Shopping Center and Peter's in Northcrest, both in the early 1970's. The fine restaurant establishments complimented movie theaters Mallers had at the locations, the two Holiday Theaters at Northcrest and the two Georgetown Square Theaters at the other site. Of all the restaurants in Fort Wayne developed in the decades following World War II, the one with the widest reputation for excellent cuisine was Cafe Johnell, operated by John and Jane Spillson at Calhoun St. and Woodland Avenue. The restaurant, listed in national publications as one of the two finest eating places in Indiana, used a mostly French menu with painstaking preparation and comfortable dining atmosphere.

The fast service industry wasn't limited to restaurants and automatic laundries, of which there was a major rash starting in about 1950. There were also the automated auto washes which appeared in most sides of the community. The first large completely automatic fast-wash operation was Mike's Car Wash, founded by Joseph and Edward Dahm in 1948 at Calhoun St. and the Pennsylvania Elevation.

Veteran's Hospital

Work on the $5 million Veteran's Hospital at Lake Ave. and Randallia Drive was largely completed by the end of 1949. Final equipping and dedication of the VA unit was in 1950. Construction on the project was begun in early 1948. A $4,682,000 contract was let for the main construction to the Gust K. Newberg Construction Co. of Chicago. The 200-bed, five story concrete and brick structure was designed by architects A. M. Strauss, Fort Wayne, and Giffels and Vallet, Detroit. W. A. Sheets Sons, Inc., constructed five staff quarters buildings. The VA hospital was built for veterans with service-connected disabilities. Veterans with war-time service but without war-connected disabilities were eligible for hospitalization if unable to pay for regular hospital care and on a space-available basis. The structure included, in addition to rooms and wards, an auditorium, library, game room, vocational and occupational therapy rooms, plus a chapel and service quarters.

Newspaper Changes

A change in local newspaper publication occurred in 1950. This included several corporate changes and the creation of Fort Wayne Newspapers, Inc., for unified production of both evening and morning newspapers. In real terms, it meant the financially-sound News-Sentinel would furnish printing and other services for the Journal-Gazette on a contractural arrangement. The two newspapers remained separate and independent editorially. At the time of the production merger, the News-Sentinel had a daily evening circulation of 81,292 and the Journal-Gazette had a daily morning circulation of 69,895 and Sunday circulation of 85,847. The printing plant used was in the News-Sentinel Building built in 1926 at

Washington Blvd. at Barr St., which later became the Foellinger Center for United Community Services. The Journal-Gazette was located at the southeast corner of Clinton and Main Streets. The origins of the News-Sentinel began with the Sentinel founded in 1833, the city's oldest newspaper, and the News, founded in 1884. The Journal, established in 1868 by Thomas Taylor and Sam Hanna, absorbed the Gazette in 1899, a paper which had its origins in 1863. In a twist with the years, the Sentinel when first published by Thomas Tigar in 1833 and for nearly a half-century thereafter, was a staunch Democratic paper. Hanna and Taylor founded the Journal as a Republican paper. In the 20th Century, the News-Sentinel was consistently Republican and the Journal-Gazette, Democratic. In 1916 the Journal-Gazette was purchased by Lew Ellingham and Edward G. Hoffman. William Kunkel published the Journal-Gazette from 1935-1948. The Sentinel publication was taken over by Edward A.K. Hackett in 1880. The News, formed in 1874 by William Page and Charles Taylor, was sold in 1892 to a company formed by Clarence Bicknell, Ernest Bicknell and Alvin Hert. After Charles Bicknell's death in 1920, Oscar G. Foellinger became president and general manager of the News Publishing Company. Oscar Foellinger remained publisher of the News-Sentinel until 1936 when he died during a Canadian hunting trip. At that time, his daughter, Miss Helene R. Foellinger, became president and publisher. At the time of the 1950 merger of production operations, officers of Fort Wayne Newspapers, Inc., the agency corporation, were Miss Foellinger; Miller Ellingham, then vice-president of the Journal-Gazette; and Henry C. Page, News-Sentinel business manager. Directors included Helene Foellinger; Mrs. Richard S. Teeple, a sister of Miss Foellinger who together with her husband and two others died in a 1951 airplane crash; and Virgil M. Simmons, president of the Journal-Gazette. James R. Fleming was co-publisher with Simmons at the Journal-Gazette.

On July 26, 1956, ground was broken at 600 West Main St. for a new building for the publishing of the Fort Wayne newspapers. Designed by Naess & Murphy, Chicago architects, the building was constructed by A. C. Wermuth, Inc. The building stretched 505 feet from Fulton to Van Buren Streets and was 200 feet wide. The office portion of the structure, of light grey brick, was two stories. The center area housing the 10-unit press was roughly three-stories high. The building contained more than 100,000 square feet of space. The structure was completed in March, 1958. Editorial offices of the News Sentinel were on the second floor and the Journal-Gazette on the first floor. The contract negotiated in 1950 between The News Publishing Co. and the Journal-Gazette Co., establishing Fort Wayne Newspapers, Inc., as the agency corporation was renewed in August, 1974. Under the contract, the agency corporation provided business and production departments for The News-Sentinel and the Journal-Gazette. Helene R. Foellinger, publisher of The News-Sentinel, continued as president of Fort Wayne Newspaper, Inc.; Richard G. Inskeep, publisher of the Journal-Gazette, as vice-president; and Elmer C. Roemke, secretary-treasurer. Clifford B. Ward, editor of The News-Sentinel for 21 years, retired in 1965. He was succeeded by Ernest E. Williams. At the Journal Gazette, Miller Ellingham was succeeded as editor by Richard Inskeep, who in turn was succeeded by Larry Allen. Robert Johnston was business manager for Fort Wayne Newspapers, Inc. He was succeeded by Duane Jacobs who was named general manager. Prior to the 1958 relocation in the newspaper plant at 600 West Main St., the News-Sentinel was located at the northwest corner of Washington Blvd. and Barr St. The Journal-Gazette was located at the southeast corner of Clinton and Main Streets.

New Churches

Renewed interest in church construction was much in evidence in the 1950's. A principal addition to the downtown church scene was the First Presbyterian Church which was being relocated at the northwest corner of Wayne and Webster Streets. Formerly, the church was at Washington and Clinton. Constructed was a brick structure in colonial architecture. Actually there were five units to the building complex. The main church and associated halls were complimented by the McMillen Chapel across a courtyard near the corner. The membership of the church, some 1,100 prior to that time, was more than doubled. Pastor of First Church starting in 1950 was Dr. John W. Meister, who later became prominent in national Presbyterian offices. He left Fort Wayne to become, in 1967, executive secretary of the Council on Theological Education of the United Presbyterian Church. Soon after arriving at Fort Wayne, in January, 1950, however, Dr. Meister became the center of one of the more serious religious controversies in Fort Wayne. On Nov. 11, 1951, Dr. Meister presided at a "Religious Freedom Rally" at which Paul Blanshard, touring for Protestants and Other Americans for Separation of Church and State, was the main speaker. Blanshard attacked what he termed the "encroachment" of the Catholic Church on American political and educational life. At the time, President Truman was considering appointing an ambassador to the Vatican. The new First Presbyterian Church was dedicated in 1956. The sanctuary, chapel, education building, office unit and fellowship hall cost some $2,300,000.

In the meantime, in 1955, St. John the Baptist Catholic Church on South Fairfield was completed at a cost of $800,000; Trinity English Lutheran Church at Wayne, Ewing and Fairfield, completed in 1956 a $600,000 addition for education; Trinity Episcopal Church added an educational wing and parish house in 1956. B'nai Jacob Synagogue was built at Fairfield and Pierce Avenues, with the brick and stone structure combining modern lines with traditional character. Rabbi Seymour Weller served the congregation. In 1958, Dr. Frederic A. Doppelt announced plans for a new temple of the Achduth Vesholem Congregation on a 10-acre tract along Old Mill Road near Foster Park. Dr. Doppelt had come to Fort Wayne in 1940. Since 1916, the Jewish Congregation had been located in a building completed in 1917 at the northwest corner of Wayne St. and Fairfield Avenue. The new Temple on the south side of the city along Old Mill cost in excess of $800,000. In 1956, the Plymouth Congregational Church began construction of a $560,000 addition for education and other improvements at the site on West Berry St.

Baptist Churches

The First Baptist Church built its Fairfield Ave. edifice just south of Creighton Ave. in 1950, and the old Cutshall mansion just to the south of the church was used for church and educational activities. Prior to 1950, the First Baptist congregation had attended a church on West Jefferson St. since 1867. In 1946 the Union Baptist Church was created by a merger of the earlier Mount Olive and Greater Mount Olive Baptist Churches which went back to the 19th Century. The Dr. Clyde Adams headed the Union Church. Pilgrim Baptist Church, located at 1331 Gay St., was headed for many years by the Rev. John Dixie.

St. Paul's Lutheran Church, Missouri Synod, completed its administration and new educational buildings in 1956 at a cost of $500,000. The Redeemer Lutheran Church at Rudisill Blvd. and Harrison St. built an education unit at $200,000 in 1957 and installed a fine new pipe organ in the sanctuary in 1958. St. Jude's Catholic Parish built in 1968 a new modern church-in-the-round at the corner of East State Blvd. and Randallia Drive. Churches of contemporary architecture built in the decade between 1955 and 1965 include St. Michael Lutheran Church on the Getz Road; North Highlands Church of Christ at 1414 Archer Ave.; Peace Lutheran Church at 5000 South Fairfield Ave. and the Unitarian Meeting Hall at the foot of old Mill Road. The Cathedral on Calhoun St. was faced with limestone and the McDougall Chapel was built on the Square near Lewis St. and the Diocesan Office Building on the Square near Jefferson Street. Msgr. Thomas Durkin was Cathedral rector.

The merger of the Wayne St. Methodist Church, located at Wayne and Broadway, with the First Methodist Church was accomplished in 1968. In a sense it was a reuniting because the two congregations had been divided by conference action more than a century earlier in 1849. The uniting led to the erection of a new sanctuary and other buildings on East Wayne St. in 1972. Dedication of the First Wayne Street United Methodist Church was on Feb. 11, 1973. Heading the ceremonies were Ralph T. Alton, Bishop of the Indiana Area; A. Hunter Colpitts, district superintendent, and John D. Wolf, senior pastor. The contemporary building with a ten-story pylon tower holding a carillon of four bronze bells was designed by Harold Wagoner and erected by the Hagerman Construction Corp.

Sol Wood Home

The Sol A. Wood Home for Boys and Girls was completed and put in operation in January, 1953. Built at a cost of $300,000 at the direction of Circuit Court Judge William H. Schannen, the home (officials frowned on the term "detention center") was designed as a more human keep than the County Jail for wayward youth. The building at 2929 Wells St. was designed by architects Fred Pohlmeyer and John Martindale. It had two wings—one for girls and one for boys—and was located near Spy Run Creek on a five-acre plot. "With the approach of spring, officials hope to develop the plot both as a garden spot and a place for outdoor recreation for the children," it was reported at the time. The center was named after Sol A. Wood, a former Circuit Court Judge.

Bowmar Instrument Corp., a firm which grew quickly into a major supplier of electronic and engineering devices and later mini-calculators, was born in 1951 at Fort Wayne. Bowmar was started by Edward A. White who earlier was head of the electromechanical section of Farnsworth Electronics Corp. At first, the company had one employee and its entire business was producing precision potentiometer housings for a single customer. Bowmar moved from its original garage location to a loft at Smith Field. Within two years the staff was up to 30 people and the operation was moved to 2415 Pennsylvania Street. A separate division was located in a small building along the Seddlemeyer Road. Finally, in 1957, the company operations were consolidated in a new plant on the Bluffton Road, north of the Baer Field area. That plant has been expanded a number of times and the firm began operations in various other states. In addition to White, who remained chief executive of Bowmar, and his wife, Joan, a director, other principals of the firm included Robert C. Ahlersmeyer, Edward W. Hartman, Ernest Cornelius, George McCarthy, James Young, Fred Bienz, G. H. Durkee, Dennis Mason, William Meazell and W. R. Santa. Space-age electronic components and development of hand-size calculators in subsequent years made Bowmar a nationally-recognized firm. On Feb. 14, 1975, Bowmar Instrument Corp. filed for court protection under the Federal Bankruptcy Act because of failure to meet interest payments on $35 million in obligations, nearly half due to the New York Life Insurance Co. Edward White, chairman and president, and William Meazell, chief financial officer, resigned. Richard Brown was named acting chief operating officer.

Actors of the Civic Theatre are on stage for "Star Wagon" in 1945.

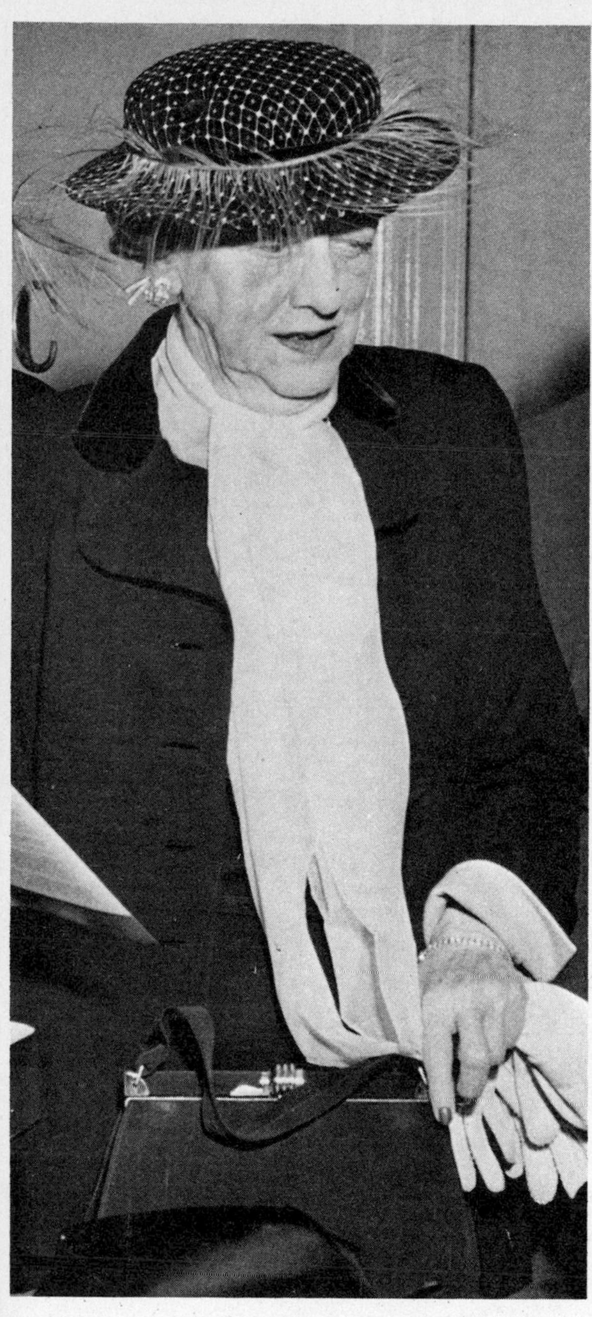

Mrs. Isabelle McClure Peltier headed the association which formed the Fort Wayne Philharmonic Orchestra in 1945. Below is Hans Schwieger, the first conductor of the Fort Wayne Philharmonic which began concert performances in late 1945. On the

Above is Igor Buketoff, on the far right, shown with some of the performing artists of the orchestra. Buketoff succeeded Schwieger as conductor and remained at the post for two decades. Others with Buketoff, from left, are Hugo Gottesmann, Ernest Zala, Mac Marlow and Robert Sametini.

Gen. George C. Marshall, Secretary of State and founder of the Marshall Plan for European recovery, looks out from a rail car to Fort Wayne well-wishers on the night of Jan. 20, 1947. It was an era when old men were getting down to some serious card playing, such as the game below.

The natural scene at left was taken at Franke Park in the spring of 1947. Note the wild geese on the waters of the pond. Below is the Fortnightly Club at a meeting in 1947. Mrs. Hertha Duemling, left, is giving the talk at a regular session of the literary group.

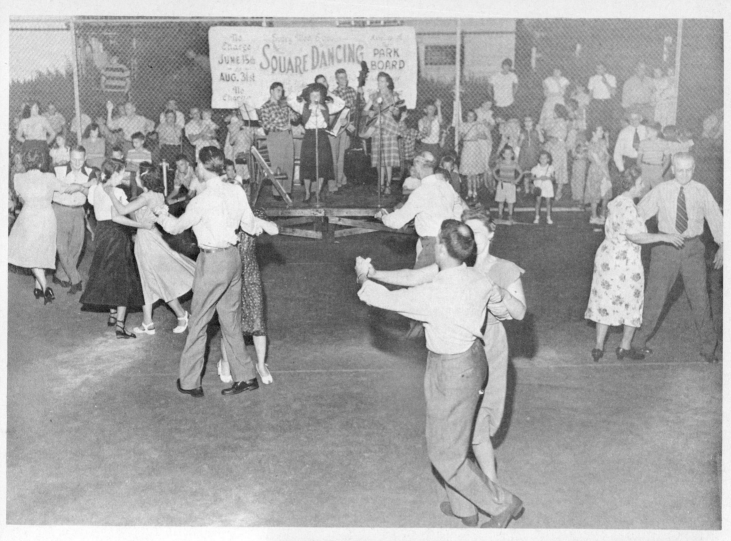

The fiddles were afiddling and the dancers were swinging in squares the night of June 23, 1949, when this picture was taken at the Lafayette Playground. To the right is Henry Branning as he looks over the election returns of Nov. 4, 1947, and discovers he has been elected mayor.

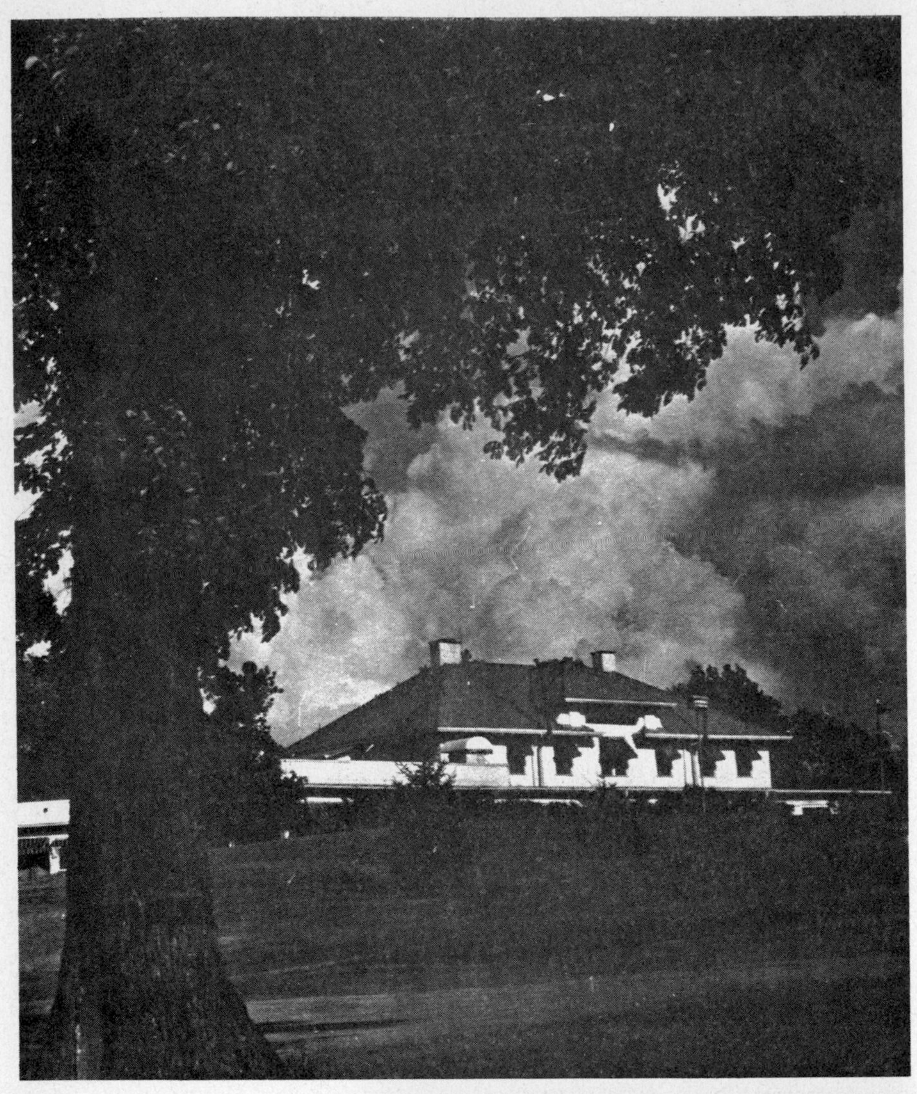

The Fort Wayne Country Club as it looked on a hot summer afternoon in 1948. Below are the people participating on one of the city's lasts. It is the last run of a street car in Fort Wayne, June 27, 1947.

All eyes are on the kites except one as these youngsters compete in a 1949 kite contest. At right is a political cartoon in The News-Sentinel on Sept. 17, 1951, depicting a costly Allen County Farm operation. The county operation was discontinued later.

INDIANA, MONDAY, SEPTEMBER 17, 1951

Nothing Left But an Appetite!

The First Baptist Church on South Fairfield Ave. was built during 1949 and 1950. In the background is the Fairfield Manor. Below is a procession down Calhoun St. on June 29, 1950, celebrating the silver jubilee of Bishop John Noll. The bishop, in the center of the picture, was the only archbishop in the history of the Fort Wayne diocese.

The huge Santa and sleigh on the side of the Wolf & Dessauer Building at Washington Blvd. and Calhoun St. was a familier Christmas sight to shoppers for many years. At right is a Sandeson cartoon warning of a United Fund deadline on Halloween. Called the Community Chest, then the United Fund and later the United Way, the community charity drive was a regular success and financed numerous agencies.

Cloudy And Cold Today With Few Snow Flurries

THE JOURNAL-GAZETTE

Ruark Goes To Jail For Refresher Course In Penology

FOUNDED ... ASSOCIATED PRESS WIREPHOTO — FORT WAYNE, INDIANA, SATURDAY MORNING, NOVEMBER 11, 1950 — ASSOCIATED PRESS UNITED PRESS — PRICE FIVE CENTS

MAYOR, CHIEF INDICTED!

Allies Link Up Across North Korea Waist

SEOUL, Korea (AP)—The U. S. Eighth Army and the [illegible] Corps linked up Friday across the 100-mile waist of North Korea.

Chinese Reds continued withdrawing in Korea under [illegible] Allied air attacks while building up their reserves [illegible]

[illegible]

point for Chinese Communist troops coming into Korea.

U. S. F-80 jets scored at least one direct hit with a 1,000-pound bomb on the rail-highway bridge at Sinuiju. No mention was made of attacks on a new railway bridge across the Yalu at that point.

U. S. Navy planes from the carrier Philippine Sea bombed the bridge spans Thursday and U. S. B-29s attacked them as well as the city itself the day before. Pilots reported the city was 90 per cent destroyed by the B-29 attack with fire and explosive bombs.

While the Chinese were withdrawing from the front, an Intelligence officer at Gen. MacArthur's Tokyo headquarters said Chinese troops were still crossing the Yalu River from Manchuria into Korea in a steady volume.

Allies Probe All Fronts

Allied troops, now in a continuous line across the narrowest part of North Korea, cautiously probed ahead on all fronts.

U. S. Efforts To End Phone Strike Fail

Sabotage Reports Mount As Unions Continue 'Hit-Run' Picketing Plan

NEW YORK, (UP) — Day-long efforts to end the nationwide telephone strike failed last night as reports of sabotage mounted.

Federal mediators met with representatives of the Western Electric Company and the CIO Communications Workers of America throughout the day. A joint meeting of both sides ended in deadlock, but mediators said another would be held "not later than 3 p.m. Sunday."

New York police reported last night that the "receiving units" of 28 pay telephones in Pennsylvania Station and an unknown number of phones in bars, grills and stores had been removed by "unknown persons."

Southwestern Bell said a three-inch cable carrying 150 pairs of wires to Springfield, Mo., Newspapers Inc. was sliced with an ax. Service was restored after eight hours. At Minneapolis, [illegible] Bell said a main telephone cable had been cut.

Flying Police Wedges

In Philadelphia, police squads of 40 men formed flying wedges at two garage-warehouses to permit equipment-laden trucks to pass through picket lines. Two pickets were injured when they allegedly were knocked down.

Some 17,000 key employes of the Western Electric Company, who make, install and maintain telephones, struck in 43 states at 6 a.m. local time across the nation Thursday. Joseph Beirne, president of their union, the CIO Communications Workers of America, said the strike would continue until "substantial" wage increases are granted.

Wages Not Discussed

Maggiolo said wages were not discussed at the New York meeting. The union has been demanding an estimated 39-cents-an-hour pay boost. The company said it had offered an average 11¼ cents an hour increase.

Because the Western Electric strikers do not have enough strength to picket all telephone exchanges, they have adopted a unique picketing scheme—they picket one exchange for several hours, then move on to another.

MAYOR HENRY E. BRANNING, JR.

Martin, Battenberg, Boyer, Klug Named In Conspiracy Case

By PHIL NICAR

(Other Pictures On Page 9)

Mayor Henry E. Branning, Jr., four other city officials including the chief of police and a member of the City Council, and the president of a Fort Wayne Coal Company were indicted yesterday by the Allen County Grand Jury, climaxing seven weeks of investigation into city purchases of coal and other materials.

Others indicted included:

Chief of Police Lester H. Eisenhut.

Charles H. Boyer, city councilman.

Traffic Capt. Gregor Klug.

Harold F. Battenberg, City Utilities purchasing agent.

A. Eugene Martin, president of the Martin Coal and Supply Company.

Fifty-two secret indictments were returned by the Grand Jury against the six individuals.

In addition, the grand jury submitted a voluminous 15-page report detailing its activities and outlining what it described as abuses of the city's purchasing policies.

Branning Named In 36

Branning and Battenberg each were named in 36 of the indictments, which charged conspiracy. Martin was named in 42 true bills. He was charged with bribery in addition to conspiracy.

Chief Eisenhut and Capt. Klug each were indicted for perjury. One indictment against each was returned.

The mayor and others all voluntarily surrendered late last night to Sheriff Harold S. Zeis in his courthouse office. They had arranged bonds to cover their appearance. Martin's bond was set at $11,000, the mayor's, Battenberg's at $9,000 each and Eisenhut and Klug's at $1,000 each.

Councilman Boyer was the last of the six to appear at the sheriff's office. He, too, furnished $7,000 bond early this morning. Boyer was indicted for accepting bribes, seven true bills being returned, while nine indictments were returned against him on the general conspiracy charge arising out of the city's purchasing policies.

Charge False Testimony

The two police officers, the indictments charged, gave false testimony before the grand jury.

Nine of the indictments returned against Branning, Battenberg and Martin charged conspiracy to commit a felony by obtaining signatures of members of the Board of Works to purchase orders by false representations. Involved in these indictments were purchase orders calling for expenditure of sums totalling $17,852.84.

The 18 indictments concerning the purchase of coal technically charge conspiracy to commit grand larceny. The total sum involved is $195,461.11.

Nine other indictments in which Branning, Martin, and Battenberg are named, arising out of the city's purchases from the Korte-Baker Company, Inc., concerned transactions involving purchases totalling $38,647.40.

'Influencing Action'

The bribery indictments against Martin allege that he paid City Councilman Boyer, a salesman for the Korte-Baker Company, $7,542.40 for the purpose of "influencing

Continued on Page 8.

POLICE CHIEF EISENHUT

CHARLES H. BOYER

A. EUGENE MARTIN

CAPT. GREGOR KLUG

Attorney General Rebukes Criticism By Grand Jury

[illegible] Emmett McManamon, Indiana attorney general, said last [illegible] the [illegible] Grand Jury which criticized him for not giving a legal opinion had used an improper and [illegible] approach in seeking the opinion during its investigation.

The Jury's statement was made [illegible] a probe of the Fort Wayne [illegible] purchasing methods.

However, Chief Prosecutor C. A. [illegible] presented a far different [illegible] of the matter.

"[illegible] two weeks I tried to reach [the] attorney general and fix a [time] it was convenient for him to [appear] before the grand jury," [illegible] said.

[illegible]

prosecutor as to the medium provided by the law for such an opinion.

"I would have been unfair to them and the public generally if I had attempted to give them a hasty opinion on such meagre facts as were available to me at that time and without prior information or notice of their request.

"The prosecutor was in error in approaching our office by the method of a subpena, and if such gesture was intended for political reasons it was a gross misuse of the fine American institution of the Grand Jury which grants no immunity to anyone.

"The law compels the attorney general to confer with and advise the various prosecutors as to the duties of their office, and in this instance when they so sorely needed help and advice we were ready and willing if he had acted properly in his approach.

"Our opinions are rendered after an exhaustive search of the law and the facts presented to us, and for it to be official in character the request should be in writing, as the answer is required to be."

The attorney general was subpenaed and appeared before the grand jury.

Straight 10-Cent Bus Fare Asked

The Indiana Public Service Commission will hold a hearing November 22 to consider an application by Fort Wayne Transit, Inc., to establish a regular 10-cent fare and to eliminate the present three-for-a-quarter token fare on Fort Wayne Transit buses.

Donald H. Walker, president of Fort Wayne Transit, also announced that a new wage agreement with Division 682 of the Amalgamated Association of Street, Electric Railway and Motor Coach Employes of America, had been signed.

Walker said that the agreement provides pay increases of 8 cents per hour effective November 1, 1950, and an additional 2-cent increase on May 1, 1951. The contract will expire January 31, 1952.

Continue School Rate

If the new rate schedule is approved, the present three-for-a-quarter tokens will be eliminated and all fares on the transportation company's system in the city will be paid for in cash. The present 5-cent school fare and free transfers will continue.

In announcing the wage contract and fare increase request, President Walker stated: "Increased living costs have produced a trend toward higher wage scales. Our long sessions of collective bargaining negotiations led finally to the signing of an agreement providing increases for our employes comparable with increases in transit wage scales for companies in conditions similar to ours.

"In the entire year 1949 our net

Continued On Page 2.

TIBET APPEALS INVASION TO U.N.

NEW DELHI (UP)—A report circulated by usually reliable sources said today that the government of Tibet had sent an appeal to the United Nations against the Chinese Communist invasion.

The Indian cabinet went into emergency session yesterday and informed sources believed Tibet's appeal for intervention by the U. N. was discussed.

Almost no direct news came from Lhasa. It had been reported that a Communist spearhead had reached heights overlooking the city.

PURCHASING METHODS ATTACKED

Text Of Grand Jury's Report To Judge Schannen

[illegible] William H. Schannen, [illegible] Allen Circuit Court. [illegible]

[illegible] the members of the Allen County Grand Jury respectfully [submit] this report.

[illegible] our duties on the 26th [day of] September, 1950, the day [illegible] as grand jurors, [illegible] after convening in [the] Grand Jury room that the [illegible] consideration and [illegible] concerned sales of [coal] to the City of Fort Wayne. [None] of us had any knowledge [illegible] of this matter [other] than that which had appeared in the press, and we learned [that] the Prosecuting Attorney's [Office] had no further knowledge [illegible]. A witness was subpenaed [that] day and from interrogation [of] this witness our inquiry [branched] out.

Our investigation has disclosed [illegible] that the expose by the press [concerning] sales of coal to the City of Fort Wayne, Ind., originated for political purposes. The Grand Jury was greatly hampered in their efforts in this matter by [reason] of the expose by the press [illegible] the matter being presented to the Prosecuting Attorney's Office or to a Grand Jury. We learned early in our investigation that excessive profits had been made upon the sale of coal to the City of Fort Wayne, Ind. We requested and obtained the services of an auditor to audit [the] books that were obtained by Grand Jury subpena. As this audit progressed we continued to examine witnesses, basing our work from day to day upon information obtained from witnesses from day to day. From the evidence thus learned our attention was directed to other items sold to the City of Fort Wayne, Ind., other than coal.

Policy For Number Of Years

We wish to call the Court's attention to a practice that has been in effect in the City of Fort Wayne concerning purchases by the Board of Works and Board of Safety for a number of years. The statutes of the State of Indiana provide that the Board of Works of the City of Fort Wayne may purchase without ratification or approval by the City Council any and all items, including equipment, supplies, and labor, where the amount of the purchase does not exceed $2,000.00.

The practice for a number of years by the present administration, as well as preceding administrations, has been to break down the items to be purchased in such manner that no purchase order exceeds $2,000.00. In order to accomplish this, purchases have been made as follows: Coal was purchased in five carload lots on each purchase order, the average tonnage and price of coal being such that five cars of coal would be less than $2,000.00. The City Light Plant of the City of Fort Wayne uses an average of five cars of coal per day, the yearly consumption is approximately 90,000 tons. We find that although a verbal contract was made from time to time by the Purchasing Agent of the City of Fort Wayne for coal for more than five cars at a stipulated price, that purchase orders were drawn for five cars even though a number of purchase orders were given to the supplier at the same time. For example, the vendor of coal might receive purchase orders for fifty cars of coal in the same envelope or he delivered to him directly and at the same time, but there would be ten orders of five cars each.

Paid Direct For Service

In the purchase of equipment we learned that equipment amounting to thousands of dollars was purchased from the same concern or company or dealer at the same time with a definite understanding as to the total price for all the equipment, but purchase orders were prepared for individual items so that no purchase order exceeded $2,000.00; that where the equipment was installed by the vendor, the agents and employes of the vendor were placed upon the pay roll of the City of Fort Wayne and paid direct for their services in installing the equipment, when in truth and in fact the entire contract for all of the equipment and the installation of it was in a definite sum and definitely understood by the city officials and by the vendor at the time.

An audit prepared by the Auditor of the City of Fort Wayne, Ind., disclosed that from the 1st of January, 1948, until the 1st of September, 1950, the total purchases by the Board of Works without City Council approval for the three utilities—water, light and sewage—not including any labor costs, amounted to $6,165,859.82; that during that same period of time the purchases by the City of Fort Wayne, Ind., with the approval of the City Council amounted to $2,556,168.25.

Our investigation disclosed that only those items which could not be broken down into less than $2,000.00 were the ones approved by the City Council. For example, a bulldozer costing approximately $8,000.00 was purchased by Council approval for the sole reason

ON OTHER PAGES

Comic Page	18
Crossword Puzzle	12
Deaths	2
Editorials	4
Feature Page	5
Market Page	12
Radio Program	5
Society Page	7
Sports	10-11
Theaters	8
Tri-State Area News	8
Vital Statistics	3
Woman's Page	6

GRAND JURORS END LONG INVESTIGATION—Members of the Allen County Grand Jury yesterday concluded its investigation of city purchasing methods, returning a 15-page report on its findings and 52 indictments against six individuals. Seated, left to right, are Paul W. Lehmon, R. R. 11, Mrs. Kathryn [illegible] Gerbers, Woodburn, and Leonard J. Jenne, 2127 North Clinton Street; standing, C. A. Lincoln, deputy prosecutor, who assisted in the investigation, Charles O. Wisel, R. R. 1, Roanoke, foreman of the grand jury, Howard L. Means, R. R. 1, Grabill, and Russell W. James, 733 Third Street. The picture was taken

Queen Mother Ill; 83

LONDON, (AP)—Queen Mother Mary is confined to her home at Marlborough House with a slight cold, it was announced. The queen mother, who is 83, is the mother of King George VI and the widow of King George V.

WEATHER

INDIANA — Partly cloudy and cold with a few snow flurries extreme north today; tonight partly cloudy and continued cold; tomorrow partly cloudy and a little warmer.

LOWER MICHIGAN — Cloudy with occasional snow flurries today and tonight; tomorrow considerable cloudiness

The dedication of the Allen County War Memorial Coliseum in 1952 was actually a series of events. At right are Bob Hope, Marilyn Maxwell, the movie queen who came from Fort Wayne, and Coliseum manager Don Myers. Officials of veterans organizations and city and county government participated in the formal dedication ceremony, below.

Bathing beauties of the era are shown decorating the dedication of the McMillen Park swimming pool in the picture above. That was a couple years before the dedication of the Coliseum in 1952, the entrance of which is shown on a snowy evening.

The Church of Our Saviour on West Rudisill Blvd. was built in 1951. In the 1950s, there was a movement to rename Main St. to Lincoln Blvd. But Mayor Branning rode the idea out of town, according to a contemporary political cartoon in The News-Sentinel.

SUMMARY OF THE FORT WAYNE MARKET—as published by SALES MANAGEMENT—5-10-54

City	Population 1-1-54 Sales Mgmt.	Families 1-1-54 Sales Mgmt.	Effective Buying Income 1953	E.B.I. per Family 1953	Total Retail Sales 1953	Retail Sales per Family 1953	Food Sales 1953	Gen. Mdse. Sales 1953	Furn., H. H., Radio Appliance Sales 1953	Automotive Sales 1953
Fort Wayne	139,000	44,600	$277,166,000	$6,214	$236,591,000	$5,305	$ 48,898.000	$39,825,000	$14,795,000	$ 50,046.000
County	**FORT WAYNE AND ITS RETAIL TRADING AREA—ABC—13 COUNTIES**									
Adams	23,200	6,800	$ 31,666.000	$4,657	$ 24 087,000	$3,542	$ 5,326,000	$ 1,002 000	$ 1,700.000	$ 4,885,000
Allen	197,100	61,900	371,904,000	6,008	266,640,000	4,308	56,281,000	41,148,000	14,873,000	54,737,000
DeKalb	27,000	8,600	38,409,000	4,466	25,200,000	2,930	6,451,000	1,739,000	1,229,000	4,228.000
Huntington	32,400	10,500	45,982,000	4,379	37,099,000	3,533	8.518,000	5,022,000	1,792,000	5,606,000
LaGrange	15,800	4,500	17,555,000	3,901	11,478,000	2,551	2,731,000	567,000	485,000	2,289,000
Noble	26,400	8,200	35,151,000	4,287	32,901,000	4,012	6,471,000	1,420,000	1,202,000	9,032,000
Steuben	18,400	5,700	24,794,000	4,350	23,531,000	4,128	4,881,000	1,261,000	564,000	5,978,000
Wells	20,400	6,500	28,597,000	4,400	20,102,000	3,093	4,489,000	967,000	1,470,000	4,438,000
Whitley	19,900	6,400	27,260,000	4,259	21,391,000	3,342	4,418,000	955,000	684,000	4,878.000
Defiance (Ohio)	26,700	8,200	40,056,000	4,885	35,256,000	4,300	7,744,000	1,787,000	1,683,000	9,943,000
Paulding (Ohio)	15,200	4,700	18,134,000	3,858	10,323,000	2,196	2,595,000	284,000	687,000	2,485,000
Van Wert (Ohio)	27,500	8,900	42,066,000	4,727	31,052,000	3,489	6,995,000	1,876,000	1,310,000	5,882,000
Williams (Ohio)	26,400	8,600	37,286,000	4,336	32,480,000	3,777	7,379,000	1,584,000	1,406,000	6,102,000
TOTAL	476,400	149,500	$758,860,000	$5,076	$578,740,000	$3,885	$124,279,000	$59,612,000	$29,085,000	$120,483,000

The overhead photo of Cathedral Square was taken after the building of McDougal Chapel, with the round roof, and the Diocesan Office to the north of the church front. The old Gas Works buildings on Superior St. were finally sold in 1955. Some were razed and others became Hall's Gas House restaurant. Ethel Waters, popular singer and actress for 40 years, during one of her several appearances in Fort Wayne.

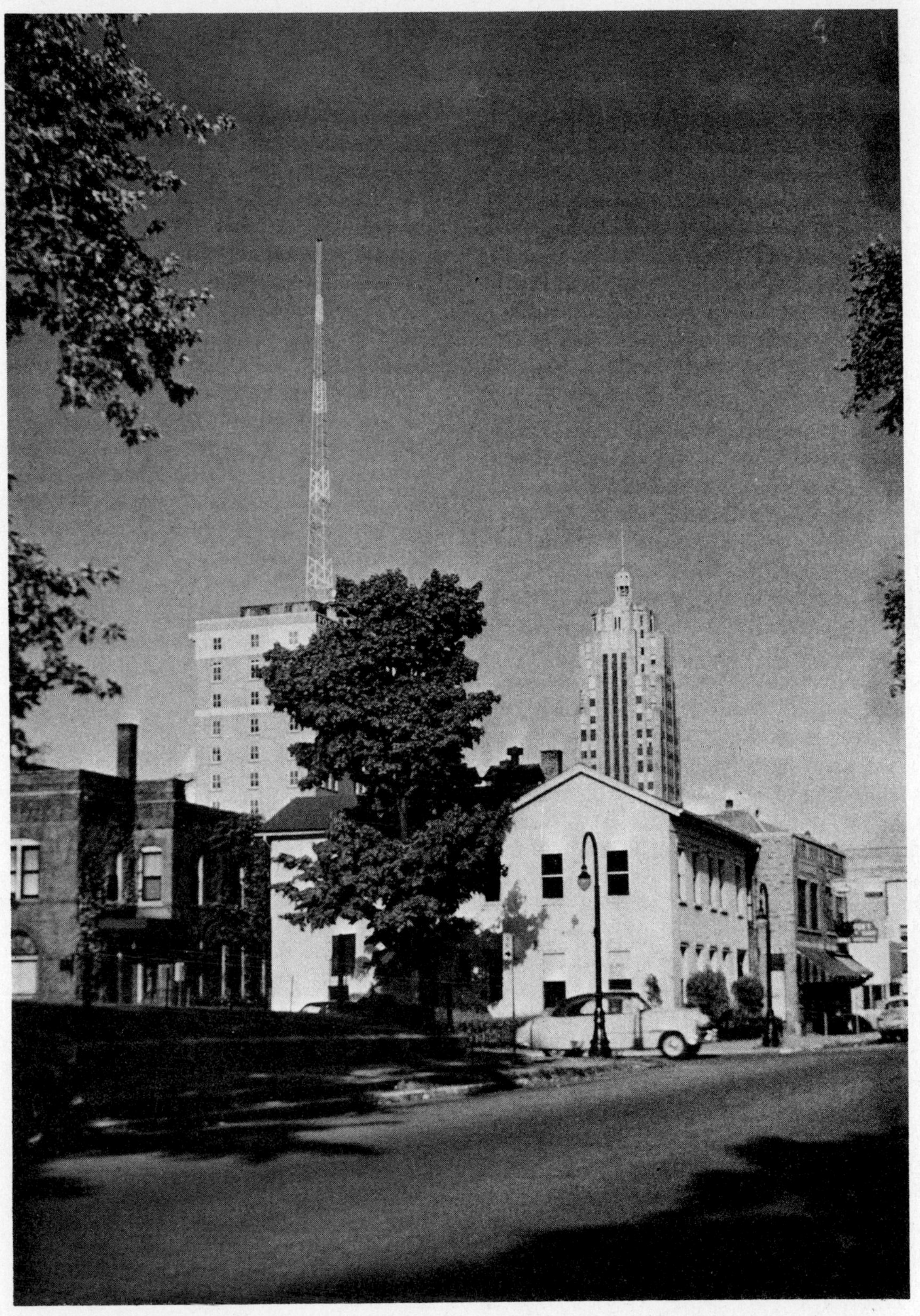

The view from West Wayne St. at Webster St. about 1949.

Part 11
Stable Times

Former Mayor Harry Baals came out of retirement in 1951 to face Paul (Mike) Burns, the Democratic councilman who had unseated Mayor Henry Branning in the spring primary election. Baals kicked off his campaign in a rally at Foster Park and promised to return the city to tax economy and elimination of waste. Republican leaders boosting the Baals campaign included Lloyd Hartzler, county chairman; Robert Meyers, city chairman; Frank King, Jr.; and Paul Gick, heading the rally. Burns waged an uphill battle because much of the regular Democratic apparatus under Branning control was openly opposed to Burns. Burns and his campaigners, headed by City Chairman Jerome O'Dowd, were very active and a sample election poll in late October, 1951, indicated but a slight percentage edge for Baals. The election turned out to be a victory for Harry W. Baals in the closest official vote in the history of the mayor's race. Baals drew 20,804 votes to the Burns total of 20,542. It was the fourth election victory for Mayor Baals. Other winners in the city election were Alton L. Bloom, city judge; Carl E. Miller, city clerk; and councilmen Ben F. Bennett, Jack Dunifon, Fred Feustel, Max Crosley, John Robinson, Charles Derrickson, Paul Gick, Robert Dahman and Edward Degelman. There were several changes in the Baals Administration from his City Hall appointments of earlier terms. Robert E. Meyers was named city controller. Bernard Swanson Sr., chairman, and Robert G. Beams and Orin Darling were named to the board of public works. Frank Butters, Otto Brunner and Walter Krull were named to the board of safety. Alfred Figel was named police chief and Clinton Baals appointed fire chief. Paul W. Philips, William F. MaNagny and Thomas A. Gallmeyer were named to the city legal staff.

The Old Poor Farm

The County Farm, an institution with roots which went back to the poor farm for the indigent elderly of the previous century, went up for sale on April 28, 1952. The sale of the property six miles north of the city near State Road 3 had been urged for more than two years. The County Commissioners were reluctant to let go of the small patronage item and argued that it provided meat and dairy products for inmates and patients at the Allen County Infirmary, the Irene Byron Sanitarium and the County Children's Home. County Councilman Sam Fletcher, however, said the County Farm had operated at a 10-year loss of $400,000 even though it was tax exempt. He said it would be a great savings to simply buy the needed products from farmers and put the property on a tax-paying basis. Six hundred and forty-five acres of land went up for auction with some 50 bidders on hand. In addition, 135 head of cattle, a wide variety of machinery and about 200 hogs were listed. The liquidation of the Allen County Farm brought in $224,081 to the county general fund. About 77 acres of the farm were retained to provide possible future expansion of the several county institutions just west of the Lima Road in the north section of the county.

The community was shocked with the news of a double killing on the night of August 7, 1952, at a Union St. apartment. Ira D. Snouffer a prominent attorney who had been the 1951 Democratic candidate for city judge, and Mrs. Elsie Marie Phillips, 33-year-old drug clerk were found dead. A verdict of murder and suicide was given by Coroner H. Paul Miller. The coronor said Mrs. Phillips had shot Snouffer, 48, in the heart with a 25-calibre pistol, then put a bullet into her own temple. The bodies were not found for two days, before which there had been a citywide search for the missing attorney.

On the Platform

General Dwight D. Eisenhower arrived in Fort Wayne on Sept. 15, 1952, at 9 a.m. for a major address during his quest for the Presidency. The Monday morning talk was on the first leg of a 12-day, 12-state campaign tour. Eisenhower urged 5,000 in a crowd at Pennsylvania Station to cast their votes to end the Korean War "that the Democratic Administration fumbled." The five-star general spoke from a platform which had been erected on the south side of Baker Street. Police Chief Alfred Figel and Fort Wayne's finest blocked off Baker from Calhoun St. to Webster St. and Harrison from Brackenridge to Murray Streets. On the platform with Eisenhower were City Controller Robert Meyers, County Auditor Fred Wissman, Congressman E. Ross Adair, Attorney Dan C. Flanagan and Judge Alton Bloom. The Eisenhower reception compared favorably with an estimated 3,000 persons who heard President Harry Truman at the same location on June 4, 1948, during a 10-minute campaign stop.

Adlai Stevenson, Democratic candidate for President, addressed a crowd of 4,000 on Nov. 1, 1952. He stepped off his 15-car campaign train at Fort Wayne with Gov. Henry Schricker, Senate candidate, at his side. He said "Congress makes the laws" and the farmer is prospering "due to Democratic price supports." With Stevenson on the platform were J. Robert McDonald, County Democratic chairman, Edward Kruse, Superior Court Judge, and his wife Joan. Two days earlier, Senator Robert Taft, campaigning for Dwight Eisenhower, met Republican leaders at Baer Field and addressed a capacity crowd at Quimby Auditorium. Meeting the Taft plane were Mayor Baals; Clifford B. Ward, News-Sentinel editor; Lloyd Hartzler, county chairman; Dorothy Raver, vice-chairman; and Harold Korn and Dan Kelly, co-chairmen of the Taft rally. As mentioned earlier, Eisenhower took Allen County by huge margins in both 1952 and 1956 on his way to Presidential terms.

Death and Life

The worst air crash in the immediate Fort Wayne vicinity occurred on April 28, 1951, just south of Baer Field. Eleven persons lost their lives when a DC-6 transport of United Air Lines went down in a wooded area near the Pleasant Center Road.

Among the dead were two Fort Wayne men, Dr. H. Clive McAlister, 55, and Maurice Oyer, 34. Eight passengers and a crew of three were aboard. The Civil Aeronautic Board later ruled a severe downdraft was responsible for the crash. Weather conditions resulting from a severe thunderstorm with gusts up to 85 miles per hour had caught the craft as it was approaching Baer Field on a Cleveland-Chicago flight.

The first Christ Child Festival in Fort Wayne was in December, 1951. It became a unifying force in the community thereafter during the pre-Christmas season. Held annually at the Coliseum, the festival drew participation of churches, 4-H, civic groups and thousands of men, women and children who attended displays, acted in yuletide plays and gave colorful life to Christmas as celebrated around the world.

Junior Achievement of Fort Wayne and Allen County was born on July 8, 1953. It was a program designed to give high school students experience in running corporations of their own. Over the years thousands of students participated, creating companies which designed, produced and sold products; and in addition served in the corporate jobs typical of industry. Most major firms in the community and educational leaders worked with the JA companies and sponsored the programs. Directors of JA included J. William Kennedy, Charles Robison and Bob Wells. By the 20th anniversary of JA, the program was known as Junior Achievement of Northeastern Indiana. Adult officers included Lynn Koehlinger; Kenneth Maxfield; Donald McConiga; Neil McKay; Robert Kempton; Carl Gunkler, Jr.; Alden Irmscher and Charles McFall.

In October, 1953, Sears Roebuck opened a major new department store at Rudisill Blvd. and Clinton Street. It was the center piece in a shopping district which flourished on the south side of the city extending from Clinton to Calhoun St. along Rudisill. The three-level Sears Store had more than 75,000 square feet of selling space and 48 departments. The store replaced a downtown operation in the 100 block of West Berry St. where Sears had been located for 25 years.

Parkview Hospital

Parkview Hospital was dedicated Sunday, Nov. 8, 1953. It was a new milestone in hospital service in Fort Wayne. The total cost of the new hospital and the Parkview-Methodist School of Nursing was $5 million. The location at Randallia Drive and East State Blvd. provided room for future expansion. Clyde J. Cover, president of the Parkview Board of Directors, headed the program which began with construction in August, 1952. Fund drives in 1942, 1950 and 1952 provided the financial backing for the hospital. The new Parkview was equipped to handle 240 adult patients and 36 infants. At the outset, personnel and patients from the old Methodist Hospital were transferred to Parkview. The history of the hospital parallels the growth of the community. In 1878 Fort Wayne City Hospital was opened with 16 beds in a building located at the northeast corner of Lewis and Hanna Streets which earlier had been the residence of the Tapp family, and later became the home of American Legion Post 82. In 1883 the hospital was moved to the old Oliver Hanna Homestead at the corner of Washington and Barr Streets where the YMCA was located in later years. In 1891 the name was changed to Hope Hospital. In 1917 the hospital was moved to the newly-constructed Ways Sanitarium at 119 West Lewis St. and renamed Methodist Hospital in 1922. Beginning in 1942, when a fund campaign headed by Byron Somers netted $600,000, plans for the new hospital began to take more definite form. The 1950 fund campaign was headed by Harold W. McMillen and Sam Fletcher and was over-subscribed for a total of $1,250,000. With more than $1,800,000 on hand and promise of matching grants from the Federal government, construction plans were begun. A fund campaign in 1952 netted another $2,660,000. Parkview was constructed without wards. All rooms were either private or two-bed. The hospital and school of nursing were built on an 18-acre wooded tract. The general contractor was Hagerman Construction Corp. The Parkview-Methodist School of Nursing building was completed in early 1954 at a cost of

$600,000. The two-story building was complete with classrooms, living quarters, lounges and other facilities to accommodate 120 students. Officers and directors of the hospital at the time of the creation of Parkview included Clyde Cover; C. Dwight Shirey, vice-president; Earl L. Carvin, treasurer, and Louis E. Wade, secretary. Other board members included E. Ross Adair; A. A. Berry; David Cunningham; Joseph W. Dye; C. Thomas Evans; Clyde Flowers; Dr. J. W. Fox; Ben F. Geyer; D. L. Haffner; Verling Harrold; Archie T. Keene; Edgar H. Kilbourne; Robert Koerber, Jr.; Harry Lowery; Fred McLucas; Harold McMillen; C. H. Matson; Dr. A. Wesley Pugh; C. L. Schust; Dr. Brooks B. Shake; Herman Sigrist; Lucius Somers; A. P. Teter; Kenneth Triggs and Walter W. Walb. Donald C. Carner was hospital administrator. He was succeeded by Stanley Nelson and later by Mark Slen who remained administrator for the following two decades. The original building has a center rise of six stories with the main wing of four stories, and a front wing of two stories. In 1957, the hospital was expanded with the addition of three stories on the center and main wings. The improvement, which cost $1,650,000, was completed in 1959 under the direction of Ermin P. Ruf, board president; and Clyde Cover, building committee chairman. Parkview was again expanded in 1966 with a $1.5 million program. Main areas of enlargements were radiology, laboratory and dietary departments and other ground floor extensions. Other improvements and expansions at Parkview, including extensive emergency service facilities and out-patient clinics, were built at various times. In 1973, plans began for a three-year expansion, including an outpatient clinic and short-term care units with 100 to 150 beds just to the east of the hospital proper.

Lunchhour Bandit

The colorful and dastardly career of "The Lunchhour Bandit" came to an end in 1954 in the U.S. District Court for Northern Indiana at Fort Wayne. Subject of national magazines and a wide search by police and the FBI, the identity of the Lunchhour Bandit was discovered after the almost accidental arrest of his driver in the Waynedale area. George M. Miller, the driver, was picked up for drunken driving and the subsequent investigation led to the arrest of Bernard LaClair. Bank robber LaClair had become infamous for walking calmly into banks during the lunchhour, when employees and customers were coming and going and holding them up. Banks robbed were at Berlin, Conn.; Dunkirk, Ohio; Hamlet, Bourbon and Evansville, Ind., and Springfield, Mass. Federal Judge Luther Swygert gave LaClair a 30-year sentence to Fort Leavenworth Prison and fined him $50,000. Miller, the driver, drew 20 years.

Television Era

Fort Wayne, which could lay a claim to being the cradle of the nation's television industry, was in the ironic position of watching TV grow into big business without a station of its own. Capehart-Farnsworth Corp. and Magnavox Co. were both important pioneers and producers in the television industry. Philo F. Farnsworth, who in 1927 applied for the first patent covering a completed electronic system of transmitting and receiving television images, had been a member of the local community since 1938. But it wasn't until 1953 that the first television station went into operation in Fort Wayne. The first telecast was on Nov. 21, 1953, over WKJG-TV. The awarding of the license had followed several years of legal jockeying by the radio stations and other interests. WKJG-TV, operated by Northeastern Indiana Broadcasting Co., built a 750-foot tower, weighing more than 100 tons of steel, on West State Blvd., a general location which was to become TV row in Fort Wayne.

The onset of television programs stimulated an immediate retail boom in TV sets of all kinds. Prior to 1953, video reception was from the distance and required high towers for dependable reception. Many local taverns had became gathering places during the late 1940's and early 1950's by having reception equipment not usually available, except at high cost, in the home. It was an era when prize fights on television were particularly popular. With the onset of local television, the pattern began to change. TV became home entertainment. Movie houses began to suffer. The first Indiana State Finals of the High School Tourney to be carried locally was in the spring of 1954. (Bobby Plump of Milan dumped in the winning basket in the final seconds to nip Muncie Central.) The station operated on Channel 33 and affiliated with the NBC network.

The TV Ripoff

Fort Wayne's second television station actually was conceived in Waterloo, born in Auburn, and didn't get located in the city until two years later. The station was WIN-T and the granting of the license appeared to be a fast ripoff to enrich the original licensees who soon sold the station. The FCC authorized the station at Waterloo in 1953 but telecasting didn't begin until Sept. 26, 1954. The station was owned by a consortium of Cleveland and Detroit interests who formed Tri-State Television, Inc. WIN-T affiliated with the CBS television network and broadcast over Channel 15. A tower with antenna 910 feet above the ground was built five miles south of Auburn. In 1956, Tri-State sold the station to Universal Broadcasting Co., Indianapolis, which owned Radio Station WANE at the time. A number of different figures were given out as the sale price. Within two months, stories cropped up that the station had been resold in a combination involving several stations and at a total price of $10 million. A House subcommittee inquiring into the operations of the FCC was told that station WIN-T was sold in two months at a substantial profit. The station became WANE-TV. The transfer of Channel 15 was one of three under investigation. On August 8, 1956, Universal sold WANE-TV and Radio, WISH Radio and TV at Indianapolis to the Indiana Broadcasting Corp., owned by Jock H. Whitney of New York. Purchase of the properties totaled $10 million, according to the report given to the House committee. In March, 1957, Whitney announced the formation of Corinthian Broadcasting Corp. to operate WANE-TV in Fort Wayne and other stations in the corporate system. R. Morris Pierce remained as manager of WANE-TV and Reid Chapman of WANE-Radio. The following year, 1958, Chapman succeeded to the post of vice-president and general manager of the combined WANE operations. In the meantime, television and radio stations WKJG were sold in January, 1957, by the Northeastern Indiana Broadcasting Co. Clarence Schust, president of the firm, reported the sale to an Elkhart group headed by John F. Dille. Hillard Gates was subsequently named general manager. Calo Mahlock became program manager and Jack Gray, news manager. Richard Florea later was named WKJG-TV news manager. Florea also served as president of the Allen County-Fort Wayne Historical Society.

Later Television

In 1957, two high television towers were added to the landscape of northwest Fort Wayne. WANE began transmitting from an 836-foot high tower on West State Blvd. on Sept. 17, 1957. On Sept. 28, 1957, the city's third television station went into operation—WPTA operating on Channel 21 and affiliated with the ABC network. The station was owned by Sarkes-Tarzian, Inc., Bloomington. Studios and transmission tower were built on the Butler Road. Ronald Ross, who for many years was program manager for WOWO Radio Station, was named general manager of the new TV outlet. Among the television people with Fort Wayne associations were Ray Scherer, NBC White House and London correspondent who earlier worked at the Journal-Gazette; Ann Colone, who began her TV show on WANE in 1958; Robert J Keefe, WANE-TV promotion manager who became executive-secretary of the National Democratic Party organization. The sale of WKJG-TV to a Lansing, Mich., firm for $4 million was announced in August, 1973. Federated Media, Inc., sold the station to Gross Telecasting, Inc. Hilliard Gates, vice-president and general manager of WKJG-TV, continued in the same capacity under the new ownership structure. A fourth television station in Fort Wayne, and the first one on an educational channel, was announced in 1974 with broadcasting starting in January, 1975. Wallace Fosnight, president of Fort Wayne Public Television, Inc., reported the station would operate on Channel 39 with publically-subscribed funds at $80,000 to cover initial costs. The station was designed to bring the community diversified non-commercial television programs to enhance the cultural, educational and entertainment fare for viewers in the Northeast Indiana area.

Nickel Plate Elevation

The elevation of the Nickel Plate Railroad tracks was hailed at the time of its dedication in 1955 as "Fort Wayne's greatest improvement in 40 years." There was considerable truth to the observation because the tracks and freight traffic just north of the downtown had acted as a barrier to the growth of the north side of the city for generations. Prior to the elevation, the population center of Fort Wayne had moved south of Creighton Avenue. Following the elevation, the massive expansion of the north side of the city began and it was in that area that some of the largest new residential and commercial districts were developed. The elevation cost $9 million. The project was originally talked in 1923 when the Board of Works called for elimination of the grade crossings by the Nickel Plate. Proposals were regularly made and engineering surveys became routine.

Finally, in 1947, Mayor Harry Baals signed an agreement with the railroad to elevate the tracks at seven crossings. Bonds were issued in 1953 and the first shovelful of dirt was turned on Dec. 15, 1953. The city and county each bore 40 per cent of the cost and the railroad paid 20 per cent. Temporary rail tracks were laid so freight and passenger traffic could be maintained during construction on the regular right-of-way. The track grade on the two-mile elevation began near Coombs St. and continued west of Fairfield Avenue. With the elevation, most of the remaining traces of the old Wabash-Erie Canal disappeared. The Nickel Plate, later merged with the Norfolk & Western Railway, had been built in 1882 on the old canal route. The dedication of the elevation was attended by city dignitaries in October, 1955.

Last of Trolleys

The spread of the city had a number of effects. One was a change in public transportation within the city and its eventual decline. Many changes had occurred since the first horse-drawn street car worked its way back and forth on Calhoun St. between Main and Creighton. Electric trolley cars went into service on July 9, 1892, and the trolleys continued in service until a final run on June 27, 1947. In the meantime, electric trolley coaches had gradually taken over much of the service starting in the early 1940's.

The era of the trolley coaches was easily the finest years of public transportation in Fort Wayne. Fast, quiet and efficient, the coaches were far superior to the later motor coaches, but had a serious drawback. They were expensive and the overhead wiring needed for their use was even more expensive at a time when the area of the city was spreading outward and the patronage was declining due to increased use of automobiles. Fort Wayne Transit, a firm developed to handle the urban transportation function after the old Traction Co. (by that time named the Indiana Service Co.) was merged with Indiana & Michigan Electric Company in 1948. Donald Walker, president of Fort Wayne Transit, reported in the mid-1950's that the switch to motor buses was inevitable. At that time, 1957, there were 41 motor buses and 59 trolley coaches in service in the city. Within a few years the coaches were eliminated and the overhead wiring was sold off. The less desirable buses continued in operation for a declining market until 1968 when Fort Wayne Transit notified the city that operations were to halt. The city government then purchased the system.

Meyers Becomes Mayor

Mayor Harry W. Baals died on the night of May 9, 1954. Thus ended a career of more than 15 years as the city's chief executive. Baals had always been a low-key individual who was respected for his kindly interest in people and his conscientious ways in government. Succeeding to the Mayor's Office was Robert E. Meyers, city controller. Meyers assumed the title of Acting Mayor for the balance of the term. Meyers was a lawyer and the son of Judge and Mrs. Edward W. Meyers. At the time of the son's assumption of the mayor's post, the elder Meyers was serving his third four-year term on the Bench of Allen Superior Court. One of the immediate jobs of Bob Meyers was the seeing through the Nickel Plate Elevation which had been in the works for a number of years. In the meantime, the elections of county and state officials in 1954 strengthened the Republican hold on the area. E. Ross Adair defeated Fred Greene by a 37,661 to 24,541 vote in the Congressional race. The narrowest race of the major county offices involved the county auditor's post. Robert L. Shambaugh, a Democrat, nearly unseated George C. Bond who had come under fire because of questionable financial practices. Bond, however, survived with a vote of 31,421 to 30,360 for Shambaugh.

Robert Meyers received little opposition in the primary election of 1955. The Democrats nominated Alfred W. Moellering, 27-year-old attorney for their candidate for mayor. Interest in the election campaign appeared to be somewhat slack compared to some of the earlier city campaigns. On election day, Nov. 8, 1953, Meyers was swept into office by the largest margin in the history of city politics. The vote was 24,243 to 13,290. Not only did the Republicans elect their mayoralty candidate, but they picked up two Demoratic seats on the City Council for a clean sweep of the city offices. The total ballot was 37,950, somewhat short of the 41,000 cast four years earlier. Alton L. Bloom was elected city judge; Walter C. Meyers, clerk; and Jack Dunifon, Paul C. Wolf, James P. Davis, Jr., Emmit Bliss, Charles Derrickson, John Robinson, Paul Gick, Robert Dahman and Willard Redmond, all councilmen.

Juvenile Matters

There was an upsurge in interest in air raid protection in the mid and late 1950's. Twenty-five air raid sirens were installed in 1955 at the direction of Col. Chester Lichtenberg, director of Civil Defense in Fort Wayne and Allen County. Mark Jury, manager of the Red Cross chapter; Mrs. Alda Jane Carson, chief warden; and Lt. Kenneth Waldrop of the Police Department; and Leon Swager, industrial representative, prepared plans for disaster relief.

Another problem was returning—a new wave of juvenile trouble, or at least fear of gang trouble. Rumors led to some 50 to 60 calls a day to police officers by people seeking information on gangs supposedly operating in the city. On Oct. 19, 1955, William Schannen, judge of Allen Circuit Court, said, "There is no room for Jacket Clubs here." A tip to police said two gangs, the Sons of Satan and the East Side Gang were planning a battle. But it never materialized though police did find some 60 youths milling about. There was also a girls' group called the Daughters of Desire. Nothing was reported, however, to compare with the juvenile upheavals of 1943. In that wartime year 780 juvenile cases were handled in the courts. An all-time high of 323 underage boys were put in jail cells as police attempted to control the city. The county total listed as delinquent in 1943 was 642. By

1949, the delinquent count was down to 452 and the number of young offenders jailed was down to 102. Also, a change in pattern was noted, with a marked decrease in violence and threats to authority, but an increase in sex offenses. By 1955, the trend was further noted, with increased involvement of girls in the organization and boys affecting "Duckcuts" or "Balboa" haircuts, but not much criminality of a violent nature.

Archbishop Noll Dies

A churchman who had figured prominently in Fort Wayne for many years, Archbishop John F. Noll, died on July 31, 1956. He was succeeded by Bishop Leo A. Pursley, D.D., who was installed in the Cathedral as Sixth Bishop of Fort Wayne by Archbishop Paul Schulte of Indianapolis on Feb. 26, 1957. Bishop Pursley had been named auxiliary bishop of the diocese by Pope Pius XII on July 22, 1950, and had been ordained bishop on Sept. 19, 1950, by Amleto Cardinal Cicognani, apostolic delegate to the United States. In 1957, the Diocese of Gary was created, taking four northwestern Indiana counties from the Fort Wayne Diocese. The Fort Wayne-South Bend Diocese was redesignated in 1960 consisting of 14 counties in Northeastern Indiana with 89 parishes and 160,000 Catholics. Bishop Pursley became publisher of Our Sunday Visitor in 1956.

Essex Wire

Essex Wire Corp. moved its headquarters to Fort Wayne in 1955. The firm was established in 1930 at Detroit and took over the old wire plant at Wall St. and the St. Mary's River for Fort Wayne operations. By the mid-1960's, Essex was operating seven divisions and 39 plants and had warehouses in 17 states. The main business of Essex was the manufacture of wire and electric current-carrying devices for a wide range of products including automotive use, construction, electricity utilities and various manufactured products. Early chief executives included Walter F. Probst and Addison E. Holton, the founder. Probst came to Fort Wayne in 1955 and succeeded Holton as president three years later. Other Essex executives included C. Harold Phillips, vice-president and general manager of the Fort Wayne plant starting in 1950; W. J. Shea, executive vice-president of the corporation; J. W. Stewart, vice-president; T. P. Sharples, vice-president, Frank Gallucci, director of industrial relations. Subsequent expansions included the purchase of the main Studebaker plant at South Bend in 1964 which gave the firm 800,000 square feet of manufacturing area for the C-P Fittings Division of Essex. In December, 1964, Essex Wire Corp. filed a petition with the Securities and Exchange Commission with the aim of listing for trading on the New York Stock Exchange. The corporate structure of the firm at that time included 5 million shares of stock and sales of more than $200 million annually. Paul W. O'Malley was named president; Probst, chairman and chief executive officer; and Ove W. Jorgensen, executive vice-president.

By November, 1973, Essex had increased its sales four-fold. At that time Essex began negotiation of a merger with United Aircraft Corp., headquartered in East Hartford, Conn. Terms of the agreement called for the exchange of five shares of Essex common for one share of new convertible preferred stock of United. Essex International sales for the first nine months of 1973 were $624 million and earnings were $32 million compared with United Aircraft's sales of $1,654 million and earnings of $43 million for the same period. Combined sales of Essex and United for 1973 were $3,134,000,000 which made the firm the 30th largest in the nation. Elected to the United's board of directors were Probst, O'Malley and Jorgensen. O'Malley was elected board chairman of Essex International in December, 1974.

The Lutheran Hospital

The new Lutheran Hospital was dedicated on Sunday, April 15, 1956. Actually a major expansion program, the $3 million building adjacent to the older wing facing Fairfield Ave. was the beginning of a series of Lutheran Hospital improvements in subsequent years, including the Moellering Unit on South Wayne Ave. a decade later. The doors to the 105-bed unit dedicated in 1956 were formally opened by Henry Frey, president of the Hospital. The Rev. Wilfred J. Schnedler, chaplain, officiated. The main speaker was Dr. Leonard Scheele, surgeon general of the United States. The expansion of Lutheran Hospital began with a fund drive launched in 1952. The five-story addition was of red brick, stone and marble construction.

Max Pohlmeyer & Associates were architects and Theodore Hagerman of Hagerman Construction Co., the builders. Walter E. Helmke, who headed the fund drive, was master of ceremonies at the dedication program. Speakers included Mayor Robert Meyers; J. B. Martin, of the Indiana State Board of Health; E. C. Moeller, administrator; Edgar Kruse, assistant administrator; The Revs. Herbert Lindemann and Herbert Luecke, members of the board; W. C. Dickmeyer, president of Wayne Candies, Inc.; Earl S. Ward, executive of the Chamber of Commerce; E. Robert Leach, president of the Fort Wayne Federation of Labor; Cecil Onion, president of the Fort Wayne Industrial Union Council; Rabbi Frederic Doppelt; Dr. N. H. Gladstone; Dr. Paul Krauss; R. Nelson Snider of the School of Nursing Advisory Committee; Dr. L. J. Mortenson, president of the medical staff; Miss Helen Succop, Nursing School head; Mrs. Walter H. Lupke, Sr., head of the hospital Ladies Aid; The Rev. Edwin A. Nerger, pastor of St. Paul's Lutheran Church. Included in the expansion were new clinical labs, headed by Dr. Walter Griest, and a new X-ray department headed by Dr. Juan Rodriguez. Lutheran Hospital first came into existence in 1904 with the purchase of the old Judge Ninde homestead, after about three years of organizational work. The old brick house provided about 25 beds for nursing care. In 1905 the cornerstone for the first construction was laid at the site facing Fairfield Avenue. Residences for nurses were built in 1915 and 1918. The west wing of the hospital was added in 1927. It was a 90-bed structure, and aside from several limited improvements to the hospital, that was the basic building complex until the 1956 expansion, which gave Lutheran Hospital a 400-bed capacity. The Nurses Home on Home Ave. was built in 1948 and dedicated in 1950.

Indiana Bank Born

A major change in ownership of the Dime Trust & Savings Bank occurred on June 1, 1956. The restructure of the bank led to the establishment two years later of the Indiana Bank & Trust Company. At the time of the sale of controlling interests of the Dime Bank in 1956, the financial firm was doing business at the northwest corner of Wayne and Clinton Streets. In addition to Harry G. Hogan, president, the bank directors included Lester Dailey, Louis A. Fox, Ernest Gallmeyer, Walter E. Helmke, Richard Nill, Arthur Rose, James Ruhl, Charles Spanley and August H. Witte. Hogan had been president and board chairman for 32 years. The sale price of the bank was approximately $1 million based on the $80 per share price on 12,500 shares of stock. The principals of the purchasing group were F. E. Schouweiler, Gerald Zent, Haywood Davis, David S. Hutner and Dr. Maurice Rothberg. On January 16, 1957, Richard T. Doermer was elected president of the Dime Bank to succeed Harry Hogan who had retired at the first of the year. Directors named at that time included Doermer, Chester Anderson, James M. Baker, Dailey, Gallmeyer, Hutner, Sol and Maurice Rothberg, Nill, Ruhl, Schouweiler, Spanley and Zent. Gallmeyer, Spanley and Ruhl were vice-presidents, as was Herman Fenker who was also trust officer. Later in 1957, construction of a new bank building was begun at the northeast corner of Clinton St. and Washington Blvd., the first new bank headquarters construction in the city since the onset of the Depression. The new seven story Indiana Bank was built in conjunction with the erection of the City Parking Garage.

The property, owned by the FPC Realty Co., had formerly been the location of the First Presbyterian Church. The FPC Realty Co. constructed both parking garage and bank building and leased the parking premises to the City of Fort Wayne and the bank structure to Indiana Bank. Three stories were added to the bank building in 1966, making the office building 10 stories high. The exterior of the building was improved with granite facing and other features in 1974. By 1974, assets of the Indiana Bank had reached $197 million and deposits, $173 million. Top officers at the end of the 18-year period included Richard T. Doermer, president; William G. Kemp, executive vice-president; Darrell L. Blanton, senior-vice president; Roy E. Grimmer, Jr., vice-president; and Denis L. Koehlinger, vice-president and trust officer.

Two Firsts

Darl Dee Parker, 27, and an accomplice walked into the Rudisill Branch of the Lincoln National Bank on Oct. 18, 1957, and made off with $50,100. The daylight robbery, one of the largest in the city's history, was the beginning of some noteworthy escapades by Parker. He was captured five months after the robbery during a running gun battle with FBI agents. While awaiting trial in the Allen County Jail, Parker obtained a gun which had been smuggled to him, forced a deputy to surrender his uniform, shot the lock off the jail door and jumped into a car driven by Frederic Bolton, a postal clerk. With a gun at Bolton's head, Parker got as far as Hicksville, Ohio, where a roadblock had been set up. In the shoot out with police, Parker was injured. He later was sentenced to 50 years in prison and was sent to Alcatraz, the maximum security prison in San Francisco Bay. In December, 1962, Parker and a cellmate sawed bars and dove into the Bay. Parker was picked up far out on a rock, but his cellmate made it to the mainland, the only convict to ever escape from the infamous Federal keep.

The first annual Parades of Homes in Fort Wayne was in 1956. The event, sponsored by the Home Builders Association of Fort Wayne, became a regular event usually staged in late summer or early fall. The early Parade was in the Woodhurst Addition off South Fairfield. In subsequent years the Parade shifted to locations in various parts of the city and suburban area, with the northeast developing area the more frequent site. The homes, usually about 12 to 18 new structures, drew thousands annually to view trends in home design, construction and furnishings.

Waynedale Annexed

The 1956 election was a sweep of the Republicans in the county and state. Harold Handley was elected governor and all the seats in Allen County remained with the Republicans. E. Ross Adair, Fourth District Congressman, defeated Democrat challenger F. Dean Bechtol by a 55,059 to 28,402 vote in Allen County and a margin of wide proportion Districtwise. A factor in the landslide victory was the election of President Dwight Eisenhower over Adlai Stevenson by more than two-to-one in Allen County. Early in 1957 the move to annex Waynedale, in the talking stage for some years, took a positive turn. On June 25, 1957, the Fort Wayne City Council voted unanimously in favor of the annexation ordinance. The measure meant the taking of 5.27 square miles of the southwest area and the boosting of the city population by nearly 6,000 persons. There was just one dissenting note at the council session. Charles Churchward, who said he was a friend of the late Abner Elzey, founder of the Waynedale community, told the councilmen: "I don't see this council has done anything to be proud of." Churchward said it was "Elzey's dream that the community eventually be incorporated." He charged proponents of the annexation plan were "newcomers to Waynedale who have had practically nothing to do with making a town out of it." The Waynesdale Civic Association, headed by Max Farrell, had opposed the annexation for more than a year during the study stage. Farrell was instrumental in having a poll conducted among Waynesdale residents in early 1957 on the questions of town incorporation or annexation to Fort Wayne. Farrell's group indicated they would be guided by the decision of the majority of voters. Results of the poll announced in February showed 723 in favor of annexation and 633 in favor of incorporation.

Paving the Streets

Paving, street work and the producing and spreading of asphalt in Fort Wayne and the area has been an industry in itself, particularly with the urban spread in the post-war period and the improvement of secondary roads and parking space. Several of the companies, usually family operated but with extensive staff and equipment, worked from various locations. The L. W. Dailey Construction Co. and Dailey Asphalt Products Co., opened a large asphalt plant on the Thomas Road near the Pennsylvania Railroad in 1957. Brooks Construction Co., 1123 Barthold St., was headed by John F. Brooks, L. E. Ginn, Bruce Wilson and L. E. Marsh, and later James E. and Robert Brooks.

John Dehner, Inc. and related construction and paving companies were headed by John Dehner and his sons Edward Dehner and Gerald Dehner. The firm operated from 1206 Clark St. and had plants near the California Road and Ardmore Avenue. Hipskind Asphalt Corp, 6525 Ardmore Ave., was headed by J. Henry Hipskind, president, Dan and David, and Jerome Hipskind. In the highway construction business, one of the larger firms in the state for many years was the J. C. O'Connor & Sons, Inc., 2104 Miner Street. Robert E. O'Connor was president; Ralph Magee, treasurer; and T. L. Asbury, secretary. In a merger in the 1960's, Don Perrey became head of the firm. A major supplier of basic construction material was May Stone & Sand, Inc., with pits and production plant on the Ardmore Avenue. Heading the May firms were Paul Seitz, William May, Art Bolinger, William Backus and Dave Davis. The Paul C. Brudi Stone and Gravel Co., 2110 Lower Huntington Road, was later headed by Lester Doell.

The Old Fort Supply Co. was for many years a familiar supply house on Clay St. just south of the Nickel Plate Elevation. The firm also operated a ready-mix concrete plant on Anthony Blvd., north of the Pennsylvania Railroad. The firm grew into a major firm based in Fort Wayne and Colorado. The offices and show rooms of Old Fort were moved to enlarged quarters at 2001 Anthony Blvd. and the corporate identity of the parent firm was changed to Old Fort Industries, Inc., with headquarters and major installations at 2013 South Anthony. Officers of Old Fort Industries included F. E. Schouweiler, his sons Edwin Schouweiler and W. Dale Schouweiler, Vernon Adams, Edwin Hermening and Roger Perkins. Alen Wyss became president of Old Fort Supply, Inc. Ottenweller Co., Inc., a steel fabrication and welding shop at 115 East Superior St., was descended from a family blacksmith shop operated by Ed Ottenweller. The firm was later headed by Nelson Ottenweller.

Food Marketing

Food Marketing Corp., a food distributor with roots in Fort Wayne's 19th Century business life, became part of a major national grocery supplier in the mid-20th Century. The firm became the largest wholesaler in the tri-state area with the merger of earlier companies, the principal one of which was the G. E. Bursley & Co. The Bursley firm was headed for many years by Neil A. McKay, president; H. B. Safford, vice-president; J. M. McKay, secretary; Frank L. Smock, treasurer, and later, William T. McKay, treasurer. Prior to locating in a large modern plant at Interstate Industrial Park, the firm was headquartered at Clinton and Superior Streets adjacent to the Nickel Plate Railroad. Following the local consolidation, the company was headed by George W. McKay, president;

Paul E. Painter, board chairman; D. M. Lochner, vice-president; John Chenoweth, treasurer; Neil McKay, Jr., secretary; Carl Mesing, controller; Donald F. Murphy, general manager; and A. J. Cumming, sales manager. George McKay subsequently became president of the Minnesota-based parent firm, Super Valu, into which FMC was merged. Murphy was later president of Food Marketing. The merger with Super Valu Stores was consumated in October, 1963. The construction of FMC's warehouse at Interstate Industrial Park, a 225,000-square-foot facility, was completed in 1962 at a cost of $1,250,000. Other large food wholesale firms in Fort Wayne included A. H. Perfect Co., headed by E. E. Jordan; and Dilgard Frozen Foods, Inc., managed by Howard Couch. Dilgard's storage and distribution operation at 830 Hayden St. was the state's largest frozen food distribution center when it opened in 1963.

Barr Street Market

The Barr Street Market, a Fort Wayne landmark since the early days of the city, was razed in 1958. The birth of the market occurred in 1837 when Sam Hanna donated the land for City Hall and the market. A combination City Hall and market building was built in 1855 at a cost of $2,800. The facility was enlarged with the growth of activity over the years. Two stone pavilions which were to be a focal point of farmer-market activity and a familiar strolling area for thousands of housewives and their children were erected in 1910. The cost was $20,000. The market drew farmers for many miles around in Indiana and Ohio during the early decades of the century, through the Depression and World War II, before slowly declining during the 1950's. The pavilion nearest City Hall was torn down in 1957 and the remaining pavilion between Wayne and Washington along Barr St. (it was always called the Barr Street Market, not the Farmer's Market, during its era) was razed the following year. Trees were planted where the main walkway used to be between the rows of stalls. The streets were turned over to parking spaces. Parking meters were installed. In 1973 a partial restoration of the market renewed activity in the area just north of Wayne Street.

The disclosure that a ring of Fort Wayne policemen had committed scores of burglaries over a several-year period rocked the community in 1958. The first arrest was on June 13 and six more soon followed. The crimes included safe cracking, stolen cars and breakins. Most of the defendants received prison sentences.

Three spectacular fires destroyed major buildings in 1958. The 101-year old MacDougal Building at the northwest corner of Berry and Calhoun Streets burned on the last week in December. The Fort Wayne Waste Paper Co., 301 East Columbia went up in a spectacular blaze on May 13. A loss of $1 million occurred June 16 when fire leveled a plant of General Industries, Inc. near Wayne Trace.

For several months in 1958 and 1959, considerable amount of public attention was trained on a suit filed against the City of Fort Wayne making an agreement to lease the City Parking Garage from the FPC Realty Co. (First Presbyterian Church). The suit was brought by Robert E. O'Connor, of the J. C. O'Connor & Sons, Inc., a major road building firm, and Solly Frankenstein, an attorney. Frankenstein questioned members of the Board of Works and other city officials at length regarding the contract and parking garage plans, and possible eventual losses to the taxpayers.

New W & D Store

Wolf & Dessauer opened a new store at Wayne and Clinton Streets on Feb. 2, 1959. The opening of the modern department store building meant the closing of the old store at Calhoun St. and Washington Blvd. where W&D had operated since 1919. Completion of the new building, four broad stories which extended from Clinton to Barr Streets, took 16 months. Wolf & Dessauer's decision to build a new store downtown—

reversing the trend to suburban shopping centers—had triggered the largest realty deal in the downtown section up to that time. The Downtown Realty Co., which built and owned the four-story and basement structure, put together properties of 10 owners. The decision to build had been announced Aug. 30, 1957. Before construction, a number of landmarks dating back to the 1890's were razed. These included the Salem Evangelical Reformed Church, the Kindler Hotel and the Pape Paint Shop. The department building, faced with white brick and tile, was designed by A. Epstein & Sons, Chicago, and constructed by Hagerman Construction Corp. The cost was set at $6.6 million. Heading the firm at the opening were Nelson K. Neiman, board chairman; G. Irving Latz, 2nd, president; William Smith Latz, secretary; Chester M. Leopold and Edward Giese, vice-presidents; and James A. Mason, Leo C. Mascotte, James M. Barrett, Jr., Howard L. Storch and Kenneth Noll. Officers in the Realty company included Edgar H. Kilbourne, chairman; and Earl G. Schwalm and James M. Barrett, III.

The Great Fire

Several of the old buildings on the north side of Washington Blvd. were kept in operation for the company's appliance and television departments, services and officers. It was these buildings which burned in the great W&D fire of Feb. 10, 1962. Breaking out in a store room at 113 East Washington shortly before the noon hour, the fire raged out of control and threatened the entire block. At least eight persons, including two firemen, were hurt and Fire Chief Howard Blanton reported a huge crowd drawn to the site hampered the fire crews. Smoke billowed hundreds of feet in the air and engulfed the entire downtown area. Five buildings, extending to Clinton St., were destroyed or damaged. The fire burned out of control for more than 10 hours. The loss was placed at more than $2 million. The fire was believed to have started in a carpentry shop at the rear of a furniture repair shop. Freezing temperatures at nightfall created an eerie and treacherous scene of hanging ice as firemen continued to pour water into the flaming buildings. An estimated 3,800,000 gallons of water were used at the fire. The old seven-story building at Calhoun and Washington was mostly saved when fire doors automatically closed, though a wooden superstructure on top the building crashed over into a three-story building to the east. All the heavily damaged and destroyed buildings were leveled in the aftermath. A few years later, the main building at the northeast corner of Calhoun and Washington was torn down by the owners, the Fox Realty Company. The name of Wolf & Dessauer disappeared from the Fort Wayne mercantile scene on Dec. 1, 1969, with the purchase of the interests by the L. S. Ayres Department Stores, Inc. W&D by that time had two operations, the 350,000 square-foot downtown store and a new store in the Southtown Mall. The acquisition gave Ayres six stores in the city, including two discount stores then under construction. City Stores, Inc., a national chain had earlier purchased controlling interest in W&D and it was this firm which sold its interest to L. S. Ayres. Hans T. French was manager of Fort Wayne Ayres branches.

The Cracker Barrel

Sitting on an old cracker barrel at Coesse General Store just west of Fort Wayne, Herb Shriner said "Even the crackers are good." The network television humorist who grew up in Fort Wayne chose Coesse for the filming of a show depicting the good life in smalltown America on March 4, 1959. Mrs. Edith Hunsacker, operator of the general store, became an instant actress on the TV special on CBS. About half the town population of 151 either were in the show or watched as cameras whirled and lights flickered. Shriner said he picked Coesse, because it was "as typical as an Indiana town can be, with all the color; and no jail, no saloon, no hard feeling and no homely girls."

In May, 1959, roadblocks were set up along the California Road (U.S. 30-bypass) as a touch of the old west returned to the scene. A renegade herd of cattle had broken out of corral, crossed the road and ran wild in the Franke Park area. The Sheriff's posse headed by Capt. Robert Bender (later sheriff) and five deputies mounted up and played cowboy to run down the 36-odd head of cattle. With Bender were Pat McLain, Nick Vandervort, Oren Simon, Ray Bower and Darwin Biehl. The steers had come from the farm of Elmer Kolmertin, where a few years later Interstate Industrial Park was located.

Adventurous travelers in the summer of 1959 left records of both success and tragedy. On June 20, 1959, Ed Kammeyer and Neil Sowards pulled their canoe out of the Maumee River after completing an upstream trip from Lake Erie. They then began the trek over the Maumee-Wabash Portage of old fur trading days and continued down the Wabash in their "courer-de-bois" canoe. Though not the only persons to ever make the journey, the pair did succeed in going down the Ohio and Mississippi Rivers all the way to the Gulf of Mexico. That same summer, Kurt Isken, a 24-year-old electrical engineering student of Indiana Tech, left Fort Wayne for an expedition to headhunter country in the Amazon jungles. By September he had disappeared from remote parts of Equador and reportedly was filming mock war scenes among Amazon natives. Early the next year the body of Isken was found along the unmarked Chimarra River, a tributary in the upper reaches of the Amazon. The student film-maker had been shot in the back, presumably for his camera equipment and clothes.

The State School

Ground breaking ceremonies for the Parker Place expansion of the Fort Wayne State School were held in August, 1959. The event was the beginning of a $25 million building program covering more than six years. It subsequently meant a mass exodus from the Old State School buildings on East State Blvd. east of Parnell Avenue. The Indiana School for the Feeble-Minded Youth, as the state institution was long known, was originally founded in 1879 at Knightstown and was located in Fort Wayne in 1888. The Gothic-style brick buildings and black iron fence were a familiar part of the north side scene for several generations. By the 1920's, the institution had about 1,600 "inmates" and operated some 1,000 acres of farm land and facilities of academic and craft training. With the creation of the Parker Place campus on a 270-acre tract east of St. Joe Road, modern techniques and care were brought to the patients. Later the institution was renamed the Fort Wayne State Hospital and Training Center. By 1965 about 1,500 patients were at the old State Blvd. institution and 1,000 in the new Parker Place facilty. Heading the State School program during the transition period beginning in 1959 were Bernard Dolnick, superintendent; Jerome Henry, chief social worker who later became superintendent of the State Reformatory at Pendleton; Mrs. Cless Stodtman, head of crafts. Earlier officials at the State School included Alexander Johnson, Luther Hurley and Dr. Iona C. Hamlett.

In the City of Churches, as Fort Wayne was sometimes called, some of the largest gatherings were of a religious nature. In the fall of 1959, Dr. Oswald C. J. Hoffmann addressed a Lutheran Hour Rally of more than 10,000 in the Coliseum. He warned that the greatest problem in life was the attempt "of so many people to be satisfied with material gain." More than 2,000 adults and children from city and area Lutheran churches participated in a massed choir. During the same season a Catholic throng filled the Coliseum to capacity to attend a Mass service and hear church leaders plead for faith and charity in the beginning of the ecumenical movement proposed by Pope John XXIII. Choirs, both adult and school children, represented the parishes of the community at the programs which continued for about a decade. Bishop Leo A. Pursley of Fort Wayne-South Bend, later joined other Catholic bishops of the world at the two sessions of the Vatican Council which led to major revisions in Catholic practices.

Adams. The firm prospered and eventually located at the southwest corner of Wayne and Harrison Streets.

Tomahawk Heads

Two large tomahawk heads, embedded in the sidewalk, were uncovered along Main St. in February, 1959, with the tearing down of brick structures on the north side of the street. Kenneth Peters, foreman of L. I. Griffin & Sons, noticed the relics as the crew was demolishing the Old Union Hall, also known as the Swinney Building, just across from the Courthouse. It remained a mystery who embedded the worn-by-the-years tomahawk heads, each about the size of a human hand. The City engineering Dept. could only report the sidewalks were laid sometime prior to 1894, so the grey stone articles had to be placed in the concrete before that year.

In early 1959, the Brotherhood Mutual Life Insurance Co. moved into new, modern quarters on U.S. 30-Bypass (Coliseum Blvd.). The firm had been founded in 1939 and in less than 20 years had reached the $100 million figure in life insurance in force. The location of the company, later renamed Mutual Security Life, along the Bypass stimulated construction of one of the city's more satisfactory groups of office buildings in the immediate area. The architecture of the Mutual Security building was a refreshing functional design by Orus Eash. The small pond and fountain in the yard became in later years a regular stop for Canadian geese on their seasonal pilgrimages north and south—an unexpected occurrance to the designer, perhaps, but a natural curiosity to many people in the area. Officers of the Mutual Life firm during its growth years included Maurice M. Rupp, Peter Rupp, Lester C. Gerig, Arlo K. Gump, Ezra Steiner and David Hogg.

Franklin National Life Insurance Company began business as American Security Life Insurance Co. in March, 1957. Heading the operation were Louis Palumbo, Vito Palumbo, Emerson Fisher and James D.

Burns Elected Mayor

The 1959 city election campaign drew considerable fireworks, particularly in the Democratic Primary in May. In the mayoralty race were Paul Mike Burns, who had narrowly lost the 1951 race; W. Robert Fleming, who had just missed a 1958 Congressional victory by a recount margin and who had the Democratic machine support; and H. N. (Bert) Clauss, former president of the Fort Wayne Chamber of Commerce. Much of the pre-primary maneuvering involved a "unity" campaign among Democrats which was widely interpreted as pro-Fleming and knock-out-Burns. But when the primary votes were in, Burns was nominated by 7,453 votes to 3,193 for Fleming, his closest competitor. The Republicans nominated Richard Fishering for mayor. Mayor Robert Meyers had declined to run for re-election. In the November general election, Burns was elected mayor in a close battle to bring a Democratic into City Hall. Burns' victory margin over Fishering was 1,127 votes.

Burns named Jerome O'Dowd city attorney and George Gable, city controller. Appointed to the Board of Works were Paul Roembke, chairman and Berkeley Ward and Charles Sidle. John H. Logan was elected City Judge and Eugene Gabriel, clerk. Elected to the City Council were John Nuckols, John Robinson, William Hinga, Herbert Tipton, Robert Dahman, Verlin Buchanan, Carl A. Alter, Patrick W. Donahue and Julian F. Franke, Jr. Appointed to the Board of Safety were H. N. Clauss, chairman, and Arden Ober and Robert Neal, and later, John Lombard, chairman. Associate city attorneys included Robert Hines, Giles Pierre and John E. Hoffman, Jr. Paul Clark was chief of police and William Dileo, inspector. Howard Blanton was named fire chief.

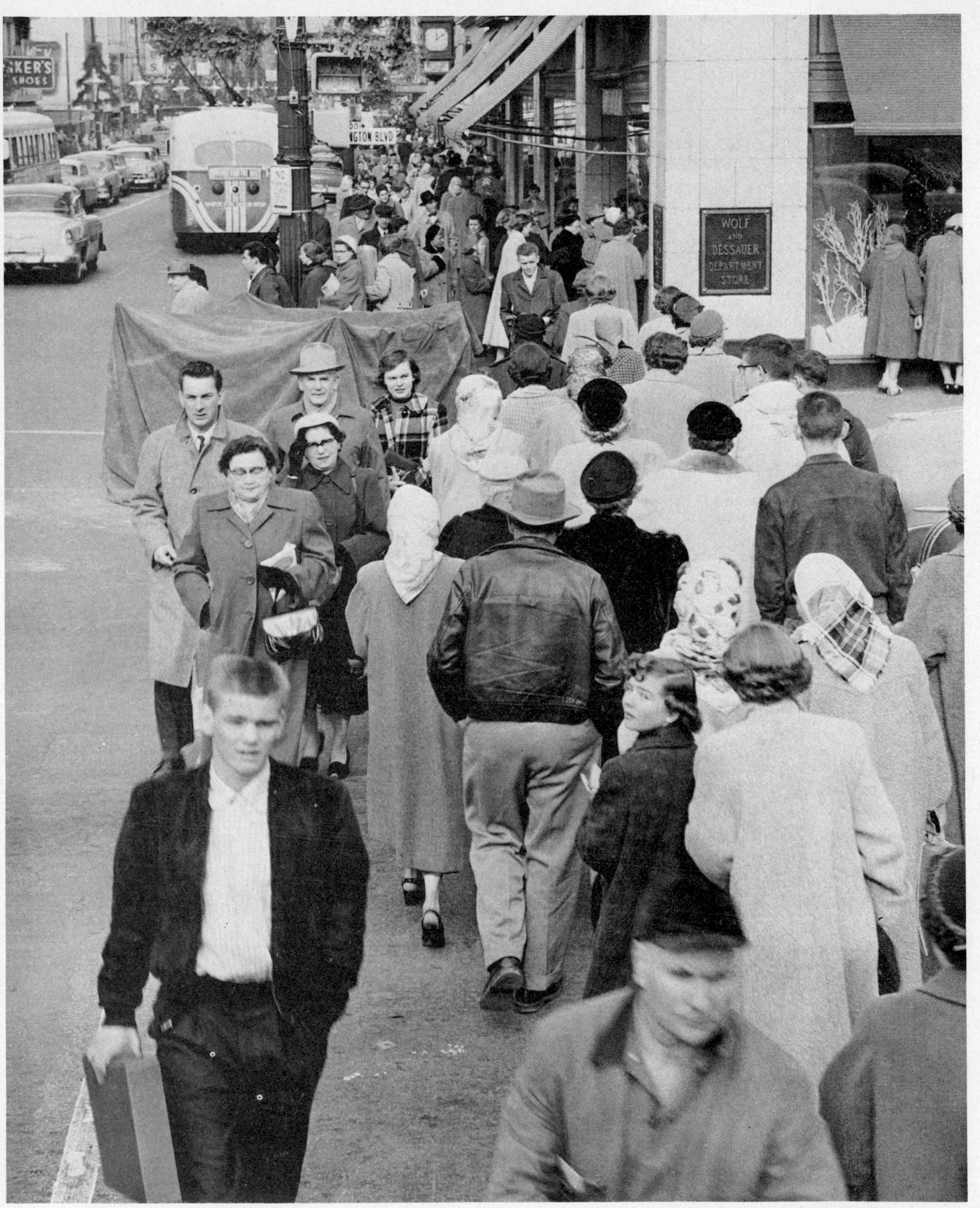

When downtown was busy at Calhoun and Washington in the 1950s.

Gen. Dwight Eisenhower, campaigning for the presidency, addressed a massed Baker St. crowd on Sept. 15, 1952. President Harry Truman and daughter Margaret, at right, stump here for the Stevenson ticket in 1952. Below, Mary Meyers, Dorothy Raver and Marian Adair great Mrs. Eisenhower.

Vote for
STEVENSON
and
SPARKMAN

At left is Eisenhower in 1952 from another angle. Above, Custer Dunifon, in uniform, and others watch bike safety techniques. Below, a crowd of shoppers in 1955 at Wayne and Calhoun St. The electric trolley coaches were the best public transit the city ever had. The Murphy and Grand Leader stores and others were busy.

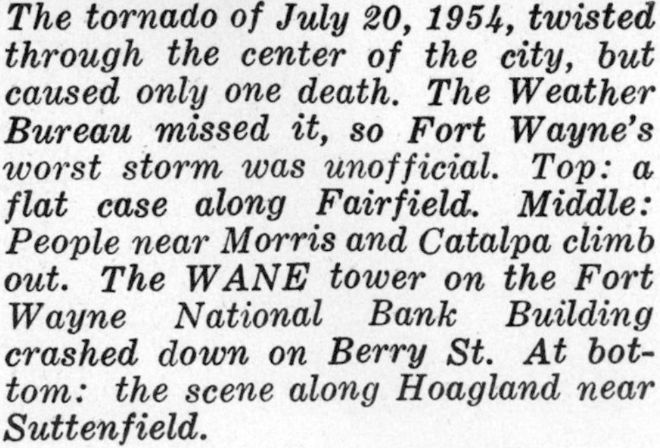

The tornado of July 20, 1954, twisted through the center of the city, but caused only one death. The Weather Bureau missed it, so Fort Wayne's worst storm was unofficial. Top: a flat case along Fairfield. Middle: People near Morris and Catalpa climb out. The WANE tower on the Fort Wayne National Bank Building crashed down on Berry St. At bottom: the scene along Hoagland near Suttenfield.

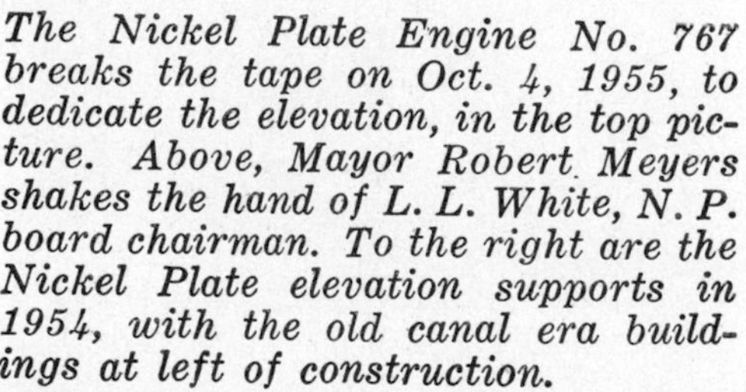

The Nickel Plate Engine No. 767 breaks the tape on Oct. 4, 1955, to dedicate the elevation, in the top picture. Above, Mayor Robert Meyers shakes the hand of L. L. White, N. P. board chairman. To the right are the Nickel Plate elevation supports in 1954, with the old canal era buildings at left of construction.

The First Presbyterian Church spires at Wayne and Webster Streets replaced the 1884 church at Washington and Clinton. Removing the old cornerstone in 1955 were: from left, M. J. Larimore, Page Yarnelle, A. W. Kettler (kneeling), Frank Blosser, Frank Smitley and Leslie Fry.

OUR RIP VAN WINKLE AWAKES!

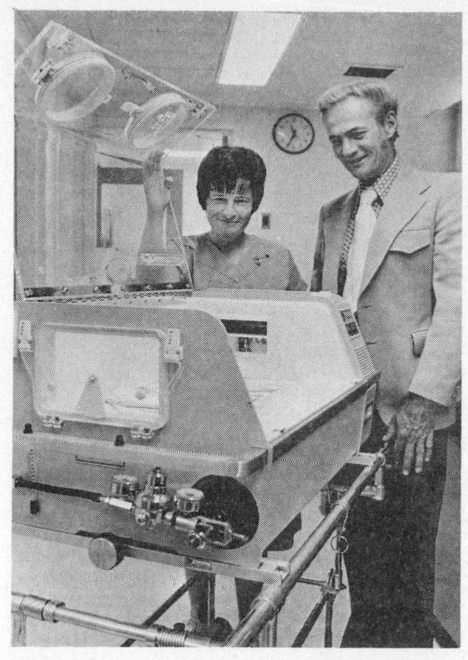

The evolution of Parkview Hospital. At left is Fort Wayne City Hospital in 1878 at Lewis and Hanna Streets. Below it is Methodist Hospital at Lewis near Harrison St. in 1954, before razing. At bottom is a view of Parkview Hospital at State Blvd. and Randallia Drive. Parkview, built in 1953, is shown with additions as of 1975. Just above, Nancy Nicholas, R.N., and Ronald Hardisty, March of Dimes chairman, study an incubtor in the intensive care unit.

The Civic Theatre moved from the old Majestic at Berry St. in 1957. Demolition crews cleared the stage before the 1904 building was razed. The Civic moved to the Palace on East Washington Blvd., a grand dame of stage and movies since 1914. At bottom is Bud Burger in a room under the Embassy Theatre stage with pictures he kept of Palace entertainers and others in his theatre work over the years. Directly below is banjoman Eddie Peabody who was on stage at the Berghoff Gardens in 1958.

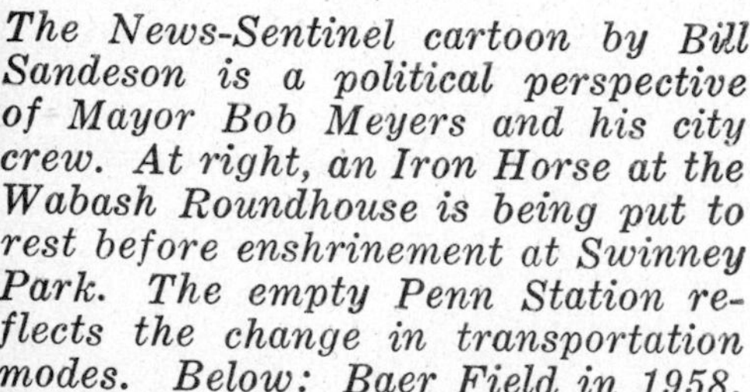

The News-Sentinel cartoon by Bill Sandeson is a political perspective of Mayor Bob Meyers and his city crew. At right, an Iron Horse at the Wabash Roundhouse is being put to rest before enshrinement at Swinney Park. The empty Penn Station reflects the change in transportation modes. Below: Baer Field in 1958.

"Even the crackers are good," said Herb Shriner in March, 1959, at the Coesse General Store during the filming of an NBC-TV show. The entertainer returned to home territory to capture a piece of disappearing America.

The day the old Barr St. Market came down was March 29, 1957. The great water tank, there since 1880, was dozed 1959 at the Reservoir Park near Lafayette and Creighton. The last man to die in the electric chair in Indiana was convicted wife-murderer Richard Kiefer, at right. He is shown after he received the death sentence in 1957 in Circuit Court, with deputy prosecutor Jack Danehy in background.

Until the 1950s, all major shopping activity was downtown. Changes were slow at first, then the exodus. An early center was the Quimby Village on the Bluffton Road, below. Sears built at Rudisill and South Clinton in 1953, the interior at right. Northcrest was already a busy place along Coliseum Blvd. by 1961, shown at bottom.

OFFICE OF CITY TRAFFIC ENGINEER

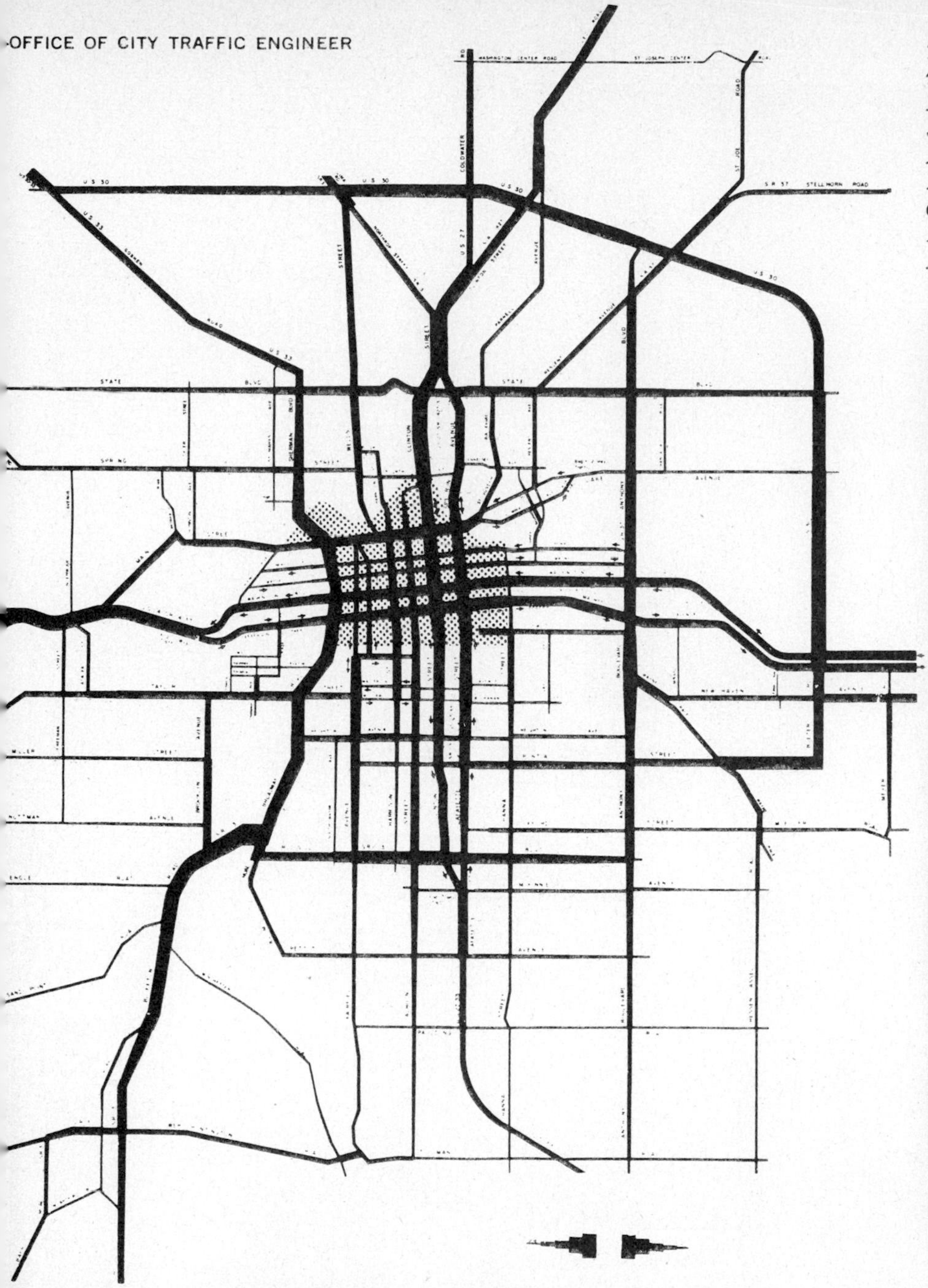

RAFFIC VOLUMES, 1960 ANNUAL AVERAGE WEEK DAY

The changes in traffic patterns are reflected in the city study at left. Below, crews in 1958 work to remove some of the damage of the Dutch Elm Disease which stripped many areas. At bottom is the Moritz Fruit Store, at the time in a building dating from 1860 which was soon removed, at Main and Clinton Streets.

The morning-after smile of Paul Mike Burns on his election as mayor in November, 1959. Above Burns and members of his legal staff, including: City Attorney Jerome O'Dowd, seated, and from left, Robert Hines, Giles Pierre, Warren Wyneken and John E. Hoffman, Jr. Below: The cartoon marks the move of the News-Sentinel to a new building at 600 West Main St. in 1958, and also its 125th anniversary as a newspaper. On the opposite page are two massive audiences at the Coliseum for religious events starting in 1959. At top is the crowd for the Lutheran Hour and at bottom activity of a Catholic celebration.

Jack Kennedy, seeking the presidency, walks onto stage at the Scottish Rite on Oct. 3, 1959, with William Hinga and County Chairman Alex Campbell at the podium. Below: Lyndon Johnson at a campaign talk at Baer Field in 1960.

Richard Nixon basks in the October sun and cheers of the crowd on Berry St. in 1960.

Carl Sandburg, shown with Mrs. S. Allan Jacobs in 1960, talked and sang at a Moring Lecture program, and put in a few plugs for Kennedy. At right, an arrow marks the spot where an electrical transformer was lashed to the GR&I track over a ravine. It was found just before arrival of the Nixon train on Oct. 28, 1960. It would have derailed the train near Butler Road.

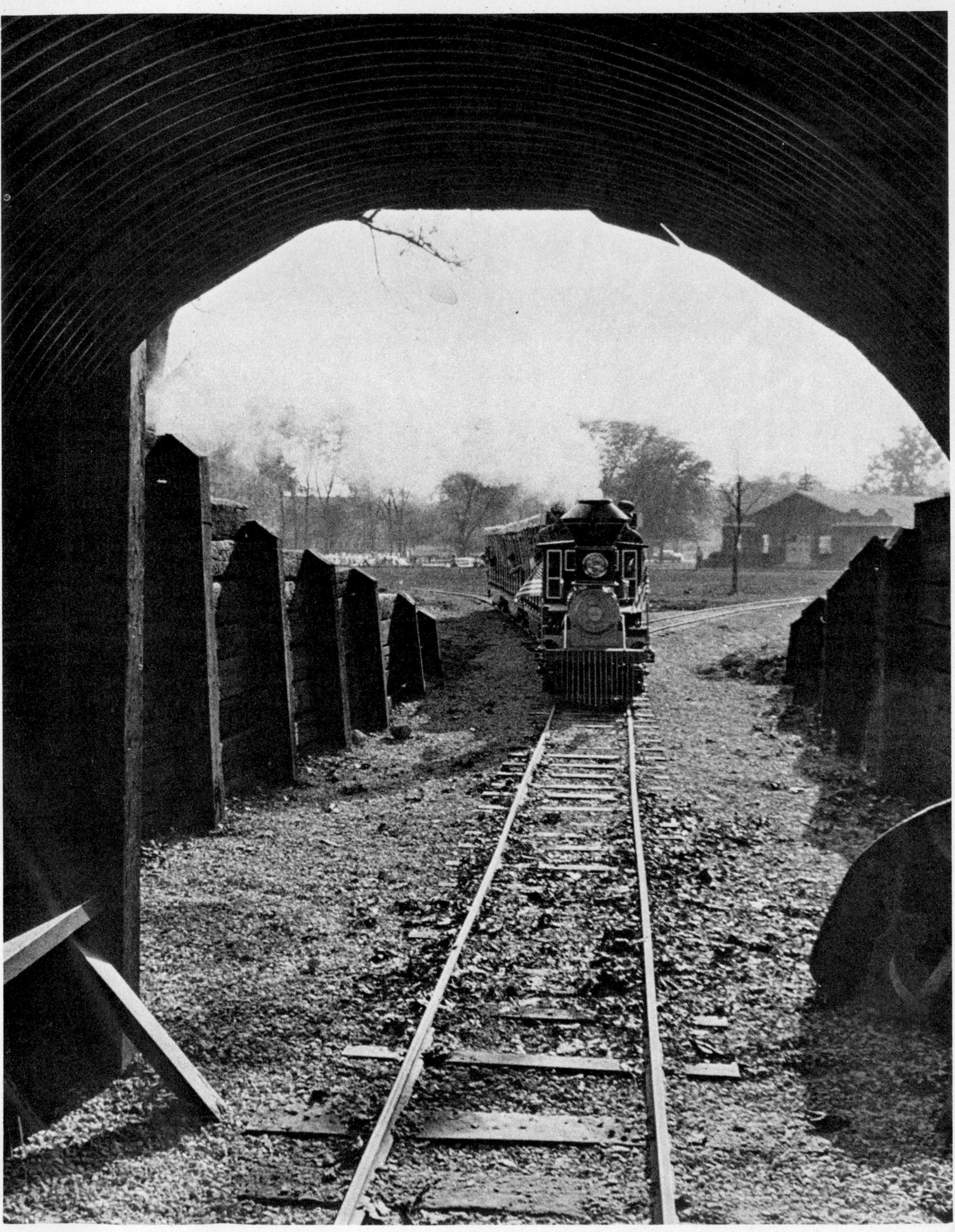

Part 12
The Parks

On the occasion of the 50th anniversary of Fort Wayne's Park system under an organized Park Board, Mayor Robert E. Meyers in 1955 cited the unique position of the city parks as developed since 1905. "In addition to the outstanding service of our Park Boards, many public spirited organizations and individuals have given generous support to this program. For example, in 1905 Fort Wayne had eight parks with a total of 110 acres. Naturally, in those early years there was little organizerd effort in recreation and supervision as we know them today. Today, Fort Wayne has 47 parks totaling an acreage of 1205. A year round program involving the full and part time services of 225 persons has been developed under the direction of Martin Nading, Jr., superintendent of recreation and secretary; Howard L. Von Gunten, superintendent of parks and city forester; Harry S. Grabner, assistant superintendent of recreation; and David Gillie, assistant superintendent of parks. This growth of our city's park system has been possible through the generous gifts of valuable lands as park sites. In the past 50 years, approximately 51 per cent of park land has been donated to the city by such public spirited individuals as Sam and David Foster, John B. Franke, D. W. McMillen, Sr., Fred B. Shoaff, A. W. Kettler, to name but a few. The donations of land is only part of the story. Organizations and private companies have made possible important facilities on our parks such as the News-Sentinel Open Air Theatre in Franke Park, zoo development, pavilions, artifical lakes, historic monuments, equipment and countless other contributions large and small which make possible our well-rounded program."

Mayor Meyers mentioned the vision of Col. David N. Foster who became the first president of the Park Board in 1905. Foster, himself, had gathered a history of the early days of the parks. It follows in somewhat telescoped form since mention of some of the development has already been made in this work.

"The history of the Fort Wayne park system dated back to 1863 when for $800 the city purchased what we know as Old

Fort Park—a half-acre of ground which was a part of the original fort, built in 1794 and named Fort Wayne in honor of its builder, General Anthony Wayne, whose equestrian statute stands in Hayden Park. (Moved to Freimann Park in 1973.) The late Henry M. Williams was a moving spirit in procuring this historical spot, and at his own expense he built the fence about it and erected the fine flag staff. It had to be fenced for in those days the cows, pigs and geese roamed our city streets," Foster said in his 1926 report.

Subsequent park development included the purchase of Lawton Park for use as an Indiana State Fair Grounds in 1866 (It was called North Side Park until the turn of the century); and Swinney Park, partly through the last will of Colonel Thomas W. Swinney and partly through purchase of adjacent lots with the total cost to the city being $26,000 with the first purchase taking place in 1869. Lawton and Swinney remained the largest parks for many years. With added land purchased along Fourth St. in 1918, Lawton had 40 acres. Swinney Park contained 46 acres during much of the early period. Hayden Park was purchased in 1876, with one lot donated by Mr. and Mrs. Fred Hayden. As earlier mentioned, Reservoir Park was acquired for $24,000 in 1880 for the building of the water reservoir to provide pressure in the city water system. The lake was formed by the excavation made to build up the banks of the reservoir.

McCulloch Park was formerly a city cemetery. The land along Broadway near the General Electric Works was given to the city by Hugh McCulloch, Secretary of the Treasury in President Abraham Lincoln's Cabinet. Williams Park on South Calhoun St. and Piqua, was given to the city by Henry M. Williams and his wife. Orff Park, a small plot purchased in 1892 from John Orff for $5,500, is along West Main St. but only a tiny triangle remains because much of it was taken up with the relocation of the West Main St. Bridge. Guildlin Park was purchased in 1897 for the location of a water pumping station and cost $7,000. The Station was subsequently built on the other side of the St. Mary's River and the land was made into a park. It contains about six acres and was named after O. N. Guildlin because he outfitted it with a children's playground at his own expense. The play equipment later was destroyed by flooding winter river ice.

Lakes and Gardens

Lakeside Park was acquired in 1908. The ground was donated by the Fort Wayne Land Improvement Co. and the Forest Park Co., but $7,800 was paid by the city for grounds improvements. Henry J. Doswell, long-time superintendent of Lindenwood Cemetery, drew the plans for the Park which consists of 27 acres. The two Delta Lakes, carved out so earth could be used for the river levies, are 12 feet deep. The sunken gardens were originally created at a cost of $17,500, paid by a special assessment on Lakeside residents. Weisser Park, or 15 wooded acres of it, was purchased in 1909 for $10,500 and a few years later 10 more acres were added. Also in 1909, the Fort Wayne Land & Improvement Co. donated to the city the park strips along the north side of the Maumee River and the east line of the St. Joseph's River as far north as the Tennessee Bridge. This involved more than 18 acres of land and about three miles of river bank. In 1912 the city acquired Camp Allen Park, a three-acre tract on the northwest bank of the St. Mary's River, south of Main Street. It had been the site of a camp for concentrating Union soldiers during the Civil War.

In 1912 Sam and David N. Foster and their families donated Foster Park to Fort Wayne. Extending along the St. Mary's River for some two miles. The original wooded section contained 67 acres. Shortly after, another 40 acres extending the park as far as the Stellhorn Bridge was donated by the Fosters. In the early 1920's the Park Board purchased 111 additional acres of land at a cost of $123,000, making the park an area of 218 acres. In all, the park has four miles of river bank. In the large area was located the Municipal Golf Course and a $16,000 pavilion. In subsequent years, swings and other play equipment, tennis courts, a replica of Abe Lincoln's Birth Cabin, and a cable foot bridge were developed at the park. A break in the natural envirnoment of the park occurred in 1972 when developers and government, with concurrence of the Park Board, brought about the construction of the Baer Field Freeway across a south section of the park; together with a bridge over the river.

Several other early parks included Vesey Park near Spy Run Avenue. John H. Vesey donated five acres in 1912 and the Park Board enlarged the park to 12 acres a few years later at a cost of $6,500. Bloomingdale Park included 10 acres west of Wells St., south of the Lake Erie Railroad and north of the bank of the St. Mary's River, purchased for $10,000. Sieling Park was donated in 1915 by Dietrich Sieling and is the grassy tract at New Haven Ave. and Wayne Trace. Pontiac Park was donated by developers of the vicinity, and is the 100-foot wide strip running for four blocks east of Anthony Boulevard. Hirons Park was donated by Albert R. Hirons and is the small plot at Piqua and Fairfax Avenues. Rockhill Park, which was part of the old Rockhill farm property, was donated by the Fort Wayne Commericial Improvement Company. The 15-acre wooded area was between the Pennsylvania Railroad and Wildwood Park on the west side of the city. Gravel Pit Park was five acres near Memorial Park and cost the city $15,000. Roosevelt Park was an acre and a half acquired in 1918 at the west edge of the West Main St. Bridge. Klug Park was donated to the city by Nicholas Klug in 1918 and was a heavily-wooded area of two and a half acres in the Driving Park Addition.

Old Trier's Park

West Swinney Park has a history which has been rather unique for several reasons. The land, consisting of 50 acres west of the St. Mary's River from the older Swinney Park, was procured in 1918 for $37,000. The late David Foster, then Park Board president, said in 1926 that West Swinney "is the most popular of all our parks because of the amusement concessions put in by George F. Trier, under a rental of a portion of the land." In fact, during the 1920's and 1930's, the park became popularly known as Trier's Park. It was the city's only full-scale amusement park, aside from the privately-operated Robison Park of the previous generation. Many of the concessions at Trier's Park, including the roller-coaster, came from the earlier Robison Park. The cost of building the concessions, which also included a fun house, thrill rides, a house of mirrors and a dance hall, was more than $125,000. The Park Board also installed a swimming pool at the site—the Park Board's second pool after the onc at Lawton Park. Trier's Park became a sea of children on the annual Kid's Day when all rides were two cents. There were also special events such as a greased pole with prizes for the more nimble and quick. Other diversions included pony rides around a small track, miniature airplane rides, and a ferris wheel. Several of the big bands of the era played at the dance hall. The roller coaster was a subject of fear and controversy. It was widely rumored to be "condemned" or unsafe, but it rolled on. It did, however, rattle like it was about to jump the tracks on every trip. This added a certain amount to the zest as the string of coaches flitted human cargo through dives and around loops. The carts set up vibrations which nearly defied a youngster's knuckles to stay latched to the safety bar. Girls' screams were part of the environment. Use of the aging amusement park faded in the years after World War II. The end came on June 22, 1953, when fire destroyed much of what was left of amusement properties. "The last spectacle of the old amusement park, witnessed by just a fraction of the throngs it used to draw, presented a deep puzzle for those in charge of the investigation—Fire Chief Clinton Baals, Asst. Chief Maine Graft and Detective Sgt. Gerald Clark, arson investigator for the police department," according to news accounts. Incendiarism was believed to have caused blazes which destroyed the dance hall, fun house and north trestlework of the roller coaster (called The Cyclone) which had thrilled countless thousands in its noisy rushes along the tracks. The Jaenicke Gardens in West Swinney Park were developed by Adolph M. Jaenicke, park superintendent from 1917 to 1948, who also develped the Lakeside Rose Gardens. Only the Jaenicke Gardens were known as The Japanese Gardens until shortly after Pearl Harbor.

Memorial Park was a 35-acre tract purchased in 1918 for $40,000. It was named in honor of the service men and women of World War I. A feature of the park was the wooded grove in the upper portions of the land upon which was planted a tree for each soldier, sailor, marine and nurse from Allen County who was killed or died while in service during the war. It was intended as a living memorial of an individual nature. A large crowd was on hand for the dedication of the heroic stone and statue memorial when it was completed in 1920. After World War II, a monument was erected in Hamilton Park to commemorate veterans of that war. Three Rivers Park consisted of four acres when purchased for $15,000 in 1920 and was to be later expanded in connection with Hosey Dam near Anthony Boulevard. Hanna's Ford Park, containing about two acres above Centlivre Brewery along the St. Joseph River was donated by Mr. and Mrs. Joseph Hanna.

Franke Park

Franke Park, destined to become the city's largest park, began with a gift of 80 acres in 1921 by John B. Franke, president of the Perfection Biscuit Company. By 1974, the park contained 282 acres. Among the features of Frank park were three pavilions, toboggan and sledding areas, a two-mile hiking trail, The News-Sentinel Outdoor Theatre, the Jack Diehm Museum of Natural History, archery ranges, baseball diamonds, tennis courts and tree nursery.

One of the expansions of Franke Park occurred in 1952 when 54 acres were donated on the west side for the Shoaff Nature Preserve. The Franke Park Children's Zoo evolved in the mid-1960's from an earlier bird sanctuary and native animal exhibit. The Zoological Gardens proved to be an immediately popular attraction and by 1971 more than 280,000 persons annually were attending the zoo. This led to an expansion with the purchase in 1971 of 22 acres east of the present zoo for a drive-through African veldt which was being developed in 1974. Numerous individuals and organizations gave funds exceeding $350,000 and help in the expansion of the colorful zoo. The outdoor theater, constructed in 1948 and 1949, was built with donated funds in memory of the last Oscar Foellinger, publisher of the News-Sentinel. The Diehm Museum of Natural History, a gift of Berlen Diehm, was built in 1963 and later expanded.

The lake at Franke Park, a manmade body of water, came into existence in 1939. The 13-acre body of water, which quickly became one of the most popular features of Fort Wayne's park system, was stocked with fish and the south fringe became a bird sanctuary. Ice skaters, who previously crowded the Reservoir and the Delta Lakes at Lakeside Park, made use of Franke Park from the first winter. Later, toboggan slides and a small ski jump were provided. In 1947, heavy dredging equipment was moved back in to expand Shoaff Lake and improve the banks. Fishing for children was expanded. A feature of the Children's Zoo, which was opened on July 3, 1965, was a miniature train which circled around part of the lake. Among the beautiful growth along the shores are Japanese Cherry trees, gifts of Harry Takimori. The Soap Box Derby Track in the northwest portion of the park was donated and constructed in 1969 by civic organizations and others. Heavily used by racers in the summer, it is probably given greater wear with wintertime sledding.

After the acquisition of the city's two early large parks, Foster and Franke, in addition to the gradual expansion of Swinney, the park system grew rapidly. In 1917, there were only 160 acres of park. By 1926, the system had expanded to 28 park areas and 615 acres with a total valuation of $1,250,000. During those early years, there were numerous people who made possible the advances in beauty, recreation and natural environment. David Foster served as president of the Park Board until 1934 when he was succeeded by Fred B. Shoaff. Adolph Jaenicke was superintendent from 1917 until 1948 and a master of horticulture and landscape architecture. Adolf K. Hofer, a civil engineer, served as parttime engineer for the Park Board from 1915 to 1932. He laid out many areas of the city south of Rudisill Blvd. and north of North Highlands which show far greater planning insights than that of later years after the Plan Commission came into being. Carrie Snively organized and supervised the first play ground in Fort Wayne in 1908. She served the Park System as supervisor of play grounds from 1923 to 1954. Carl J. Getz succeeded Jaenicke as park superintendent in 1948.

A number of smaller parks were acquired during the 1920's and 1930's. These included Indian Village Park, a 10-acre site on the west side of the St. Mary's River, in 1926; McCormick Park, in connection with the International Harvester Co. development, was acquired in 1927; Lafayette Place Addition Park, six-acre tract on the south side, was obtained in 1929; Hamilton Park, with more than 16 acres, was acquired in 1930; and Packard Park, the site of the old piano factory along South Fairfield and consisting of 4½ acres, was purchased in 1937.

McMillen Park

The start of one of the city's major parks, McMillen Park on the southeast side of Fort Wayne, occurred in 1937. The park was made possible by the donation of land by Mr. and Mrs. Dale W. McMillen, Sr. Subsequent donations of land and facilities by the McMillen family and the McMillen Foundation extended the use of the park and it became one of the most heavily utilized recreational areas in the city. The 168-acre park included a 25-meter swimming pool and shelter, eight ball diamonds, two football fields, one soccer field, an 18-hole golf course with nine lighted for night play, an ice-skating rink, tennis courts, playground, horseshoe courts, lighted basketball courts and pavilions and shelters. McMillen Park has been the site of some of the largest community events, including the News-Sentinel Fourth of July Fireworks, organized competition in swimming, and the Twelfth Night Burning of the Greens—12 days after Christmas when thousands would bring holiday trees for a giant fire. The practice was discontinued in 1971 after agitation by various persons claiming the ecology was being threatened. The outdoor artificial ice rink at McMillen was built in 1956 and was designed to provide skating surfaces and other facilities for four months of the year and other uses in other seasons. The original cost of the rink was in excess of $150,000 with two-thirds of the cost provided by the McMillen Foundation.

Shoaff Park, 169 acres north of the city between the St. Joseph's River and St. Joe Road, was acquired in 1955 and 1956. Practically the entire park area, 160 acres, was purchased with a donation by Mr. and Mrs. Fred B. Shoaff. Park Board funds were used to buy the other 9 acres. The pavilion at Shoaff Park was built with funds provided in the will of Mrs. Ella Conklin. Plans for the building were furnished by T. Richard Shoaff as a donation to the city. Subsequent features of Shoaff Park included an 18-hole golf course, club house, a second pavilion, camping area and picnic equipment, a lighted ball diamond, tennis and basketball courts, archery range and fishing pond for children. Shoaff Park has 1.3 miles of river bank and a boat ramp. The natural features of the park are especially attractive to adults, including woods and river landscape.

Broadening of the park system was remarkably consistent for many years. Two swimming pools were installed in 1948. The pool constructed at Memorial Park cost $95,000 and the pool at McMillen Park cost $105,000. Though the Indiana General Assembly gave the Park Board responsibility for playgrounds and recreational activities in 1923, it wasn't until after World War II that the park began the setting up of large staff in the recreational and supervisory area. In many respects, the change reflected a different attitude in parks and recreation. In the earlier days, the parks were available but the recreation was almost completely a matter of individual inclination and creation. In later decades, an emphasis was increasingly placed on instruction, supervision, entertaining and educational programs such as crafts, day camps, supervised games and swimming instruction. Safety was stressed. These changes are reflected in Park Board budgets. Where in early decades, the number of park staff and salaries were quite modest, by 1971 the expenditure for personal services had passed the $2 million mark with a figure of $2,013,455. Staff expenditure took about 80 per cent of the entire tax revenue for the Park Board during the same, and a typical year, which amounted to $2,547,000. An early recreational center was the Jefferson Center acquired by the Park Board from the public school system in 1945. For many years it served as headquarters for the Park Department and as a recreational place for the elderly and the children, as well as teen groups. Among the programs were theatre, dancing, fencing, crafts, games and meetings. From the Jefferson Center recreational programs and playground activities were expanded in many localities in the community, including both park facilities and school properties.

Acres of Space

Park expansions in the 1950's included Psi Ote Park in the Indian Village vicinity, a nine acre tract donated by the sorority in 1953. Lions Park on the north side about a half-mile east of Anthony Blvd. was donated by the Lions Club. It included 14 acres acquired in 1953. Kettler Park, the gift of Mr. and Mrs. Alfred W. Kettler, was donated in two stages, 1947 and 1957. The south end park was furnished with multiple recreational facilities. The three-acre Brewer Park, deeded to the city by Township Trustees, was acquired in 1958. The site of the grave of the Miami Warchief Little Turtle, a lot facing Lawton Place, was donated in 1959 by Mary Catherine Smeltzly. Three large properties were obtained by the Park Board in the 1960's, some of which were programmed for future use. It all began with the purchase of 81 acres of land west of South Anthony Blvd. and along Tillman Road at a cost of $122,100. This land was sold in 1966 to Southtown Mall, Inc., for $230,000 plus 70 acres along Tillman Road earlier known as the Tillman Dump, and renamed Tillman Park. In the same year the trade was altered so the Park Board could acquire 110 acres on North River Road, east of the city. This land was renamed Maumee Park.

In 1967 the Park Commissioners purchased 145 acres adjacent to Interstate Highway 69 at Kroemer and Leesburg Roads. The rolling land with a small stream and some heavy timber cost $83,098. It was known as the Buckner Farm property, and was left in its natural state with any development to be planned later. During the 1960's and 1970's the Park Board received or purchased a number of sites for plazas and vest-pocket parks such as Turpie Playlot, Salon Plaza, Seiling Park, Bass Playground and others. In 1973 and 1974, a formal park was created in the downtown area at a site near the original forts of the Old Northwest campaigns. This was Freimann Park, made possible by a bequest in the will of Frank Freimann, former president of Magnavox Company. The land was provided through a federally-assisted redevelopment program. The Freimann funds, of $750,000, were used for actual park development including floral displays, fountain and pool, and appropriate landscaping. A principal in the Freimann Trust was G. M. Ungaro. He was a long-time associate of Freimann from Chicago and was vice-president and secretary of the Magnavox Company. In 1973, the equestrian statue of Anthony Wayne, created by George Ganiere in 1916, was moved from Hayden Park to Freimann Park at Main and Clinton Streets.

Dutch Elm Disease

One of the plagues of the Park Department for many years was the Dutch Elm

Disease. In fact, it was a city plague of large proportion. Fort Wayne had been a heavily-wooded community prior to the onslaught of the elm disease. Large elms, some many feet in diameter and up to 200 years old, dotted the landscape and gave a number of avenues cathedral-like ceilings. The onset of the disease was gradual. Increasingly, the typical browning and drooping of the foliage was noticed by the mid-1950's. In its 1956 annual report, the board noted that "The Forestry Department was again compelled to spend a large part of its time attempting to control Dutch Elm disease and the results have given us some encouragement." The board said 9,791 trees were sprayed. Including trimming and cutting, the crews served 15,245 trees that year out of an estimated 72,000 trees along city streets. Though the Board was still hoping for "success" in combating the tree disease that year, it was a forlorn hope. The disease was relentless and by the middle of the following decade, it was the removal of dead trees which was the most demanding activity. By 1971, the board reported "The Dutch Elm Disease epidemic is no longer an emergency in Fort Wayne. This year we removed 242 diseased elms." The epidemic ended because only few and scattered elms were left. Many places were still rather bare, but new tree growth of other varieties were establishing themselves. More than 1,000 trees were planted by the Park Board that year and increasing numbers by the mid-1970's. In 1971, Martin Nading retired as park superintendent and was succeeded by Robert C. Arnold. Other staff heads included Dennis Noak, asst. superintendent; Phillip Bennell, asst. for recreation; Helen Ogden, office manager; and H. James Haley, business manager and secretary.

By 1974, the total acreage of parks in Fort Wayne or under Fort Wayne Park Commission authority was 1,668, or approximately nine acres of parkland for every 1,000 residents. According to a master plan of the park system, prepared by Angela Derheimer, park planner, future interest of the Park Board will include hiking and bicycle trails, greater use of rivers after improvements are made in water quality and bank areas, and increased opportunities involving historical attractions such as the restoration of the Old Fort near the three rivers.

Park Commissioners, since the organization of the board in 1905, together with the first and last year of service, follow: David N. Foster, 1905 to 1934; Ferdinand Meier, 1905 to 1912; Joseph Singmaster, 1905-12; Oscar Tresselt, 1905-12: Louis Dorn, 1912-16; E. F. Yarnelle, 1912-29; Louis Fox, 1912-22; Abe Ackerman, 1914-25; William Brewer, 1916-21; John C. Trier, 1921-29; Frederick B. Shoaff, 1922-61; William Lennart, 1923-26; Samuel Wolf, 1930-35; Byron Hattersley, 1930-40; Dr. A. F. Hall, Jr., 1934-36; Joseph P. Doody, 1936-39; A. W. Kettler, Sr., 1936-49; Arthur W. Rose 1939-48; Ervin Zern, 1941-48; Byron Novitsky, 1948-71; Trygve Storm, 1949-64; Sidney Patterson, 1950-53; Helen W. Sweet, 1953-60; Alfred W. Kettler, Jr., 1954-61; Louis F. Niezer, 1961-writing; Harold W. McMillen, 1962-71; Morton C. Frank, 1965-72; Howard S. Watters, 1971-72; William J. Moody, 1972-73; Richard N. Allen, 1972-73; A. L. Berk, 1973; Alberta H. Robinson, 1973; and Paul A. Leamon, 1974.

County Park Department

The Allen County Park and Recreation Board came into existence in 1965 with action by the County Commissioners and County Council. The first board was organized on July 23, 1965. That board included Thomas E. Dustin, president; Jack Danehy, vice-president; Arnold Roemke, secretary, and Richard T. Blitz, Guy Beerbower and Russell Steiner. In 1973, John F. Popp succeeded Dustin on the board. The County Park Board acquired the Fox Island Nature Preserve in 1972 at a cost of $194,000. The tract southwest of the city contained 381 acres of land. The nature preserve area within Fox Island contained sand dunes and marshes dating back to the glacial era. In November 1973, the County Park Board announced plans to set aside 219 acres of the park area for nature study.

James Barrett, III, a member of Acres, a conservationist organization, said the State act was to create long-term continuity in the nature preserve. Park Board President Richard Blitz reported a master plan for the entire park would be enacted by the board after the establishing of the nature preserve, voted on Nov. 10, 1973. On Nov. 11, 1973, the formation of a private foundation to expand park systems in Fort Wayne, New Haven and Allen County was announced. Called the Fort Wayne-Allen County Park Foundation, Inc., the organization was designed to funnel gifts and bequests for expanding and developing park and recreational facilities. Incorporators and initial developers were Richard N. Allen, chairman, and Helene Foellinger, Harold W. McMillen, Byron F. Novitsky and William V. Sowers.

Riding through Foster Park along the bridle path was popular sport when this shot was taken in 1936.

The City Forestry crews were out in full form soon after the turn of the century, doing a spraying job on the trees. Cannons became part of the Lawton Park scene in 1901.

Crowds of youngsters were swimming at the West Swinney Park pool in July, 1938, as a steam engine chugs past the G.E. plant in the background.

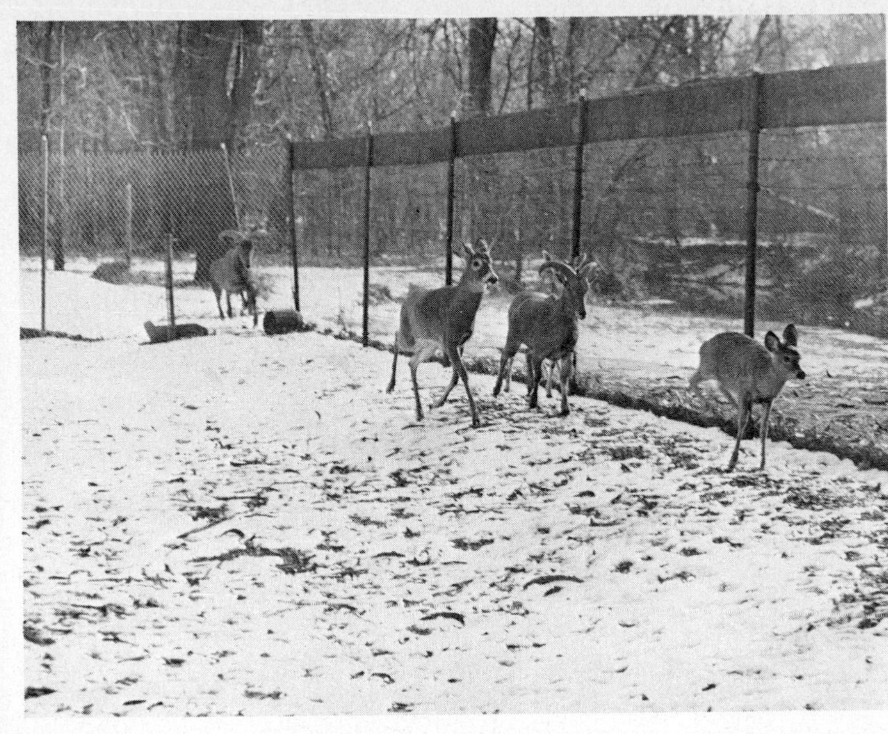

Deer scamper about on the snowy turf of Franke Park on December 13, 1954.

The rose gardens and pool had pristine beauty when this picture was taken in 1938 at Lakeside Park.

Children watched the antics of the small Franke Park wild life exhibit that existed in 1955.

Park contributions where honored in 1957 at the 50th Anniversary of the Park Department. Left to right are A. W. Kettler, Fred B. Shoaff, Helene Foellinger and D. W. McMillen, Sr. Dancers make for a sprightly pace in one of the open air festivals at the parks.

Pool shooters, at left, at a recreation center, and kite flyers at Franke Park, above, get ready. A little girl in the meantime was attracting the swans of the lake in 1960.

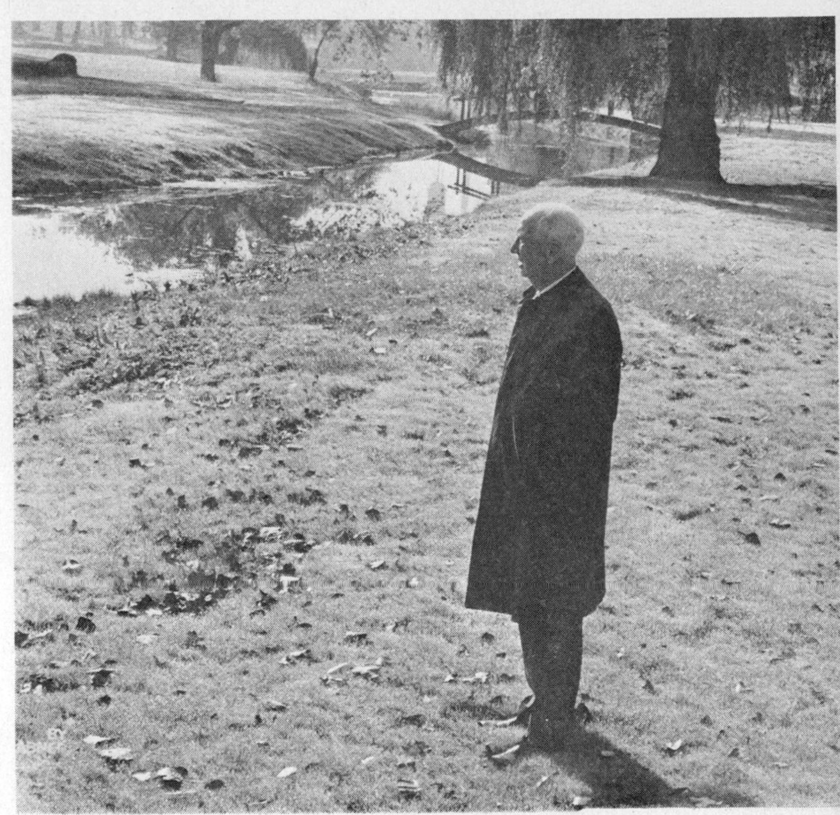

Jaenicke Gardens on a fall day of 1968 with Alex Jaenicke, son of a park designer Adolph Jaenicke, in the foreground.

Afternoon patrons take in a bit of music at the News-Sentinel Outdoor Theatre at Franke Park.

The Fourth of July fireworks drew upwards of 100,000 people annually to city parks and the display sponsored by The News-Sentinel. In the middle pictures, young chess players and swimmers make the most of things. At right are skaters at McMillen rink during the holidays of 1970.

A lot of history can be seen in Fort Wayne parks. Two boys stand on the battlefield of Harmar's defeat by the Indians under Little Turtle in 1790, part of the Maumee parkstrip. Statue at Lawton Park commerates troops assembled for the Civil War. The grave of Governor Sam Bigger was the only one left in the old cemetery which became McCulloch Park after the other bodies were removed to form Lindenwood.

The great water storage tank built in 1880 was part of the city's first real water system, and the hill at Reservoir Park formed up the sides.

'he cold St. Mary's River leaves icy emains in Swinney Park in Febru- ry, 1959.

big elm along West Main St. comes own in 1952, with crews sawing runk.

'he great storm of July 20, 1954, reated a big removal job, such as his one along Fairfield Ave.

John Collis, head of the park board woodworking, left, shown with Earl Miller in this 1949 picture.

Skilled hands render flowers at the Jefferson Center in 1966.

A boy, below, looks to see if the new Freimann Park pond has any fish in 1974.

Winter or summer, the Soap Box Derby Hill at Franke Park gets lot of wear. The winter scene in 1968 and the derby run in 1974.

One group of children, top, get on and another group, below, step off the train at Franke Park in 1964.

This boxer at the Dog Show is getting final instructions from his young master.

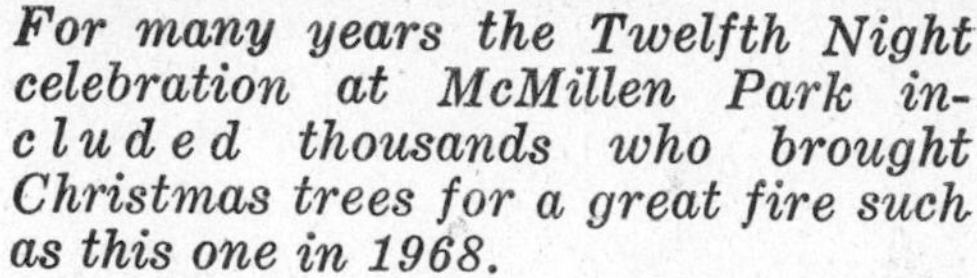

For many years the Twelfth Night celebration at McMillen Park included thousands who brought Christmas trees for a great fire such as this one in 1968.

The pavilion at Shoaff Park in 1958 reflected light and lines. A girl swimmer in a park pool in 1967 displays breast stroke technique.

Bear cubs in a tree draw a crowd in 1965 at the Children's Zoo.

The entrance to the Zoo at Franke Park had a stockade motiff similar to the forts built during the Anthony Wayne era.

On the opposite page, work progress at the Clown Factory in the Sears Pavilion in July, 1974, has the clown watching the little girl.

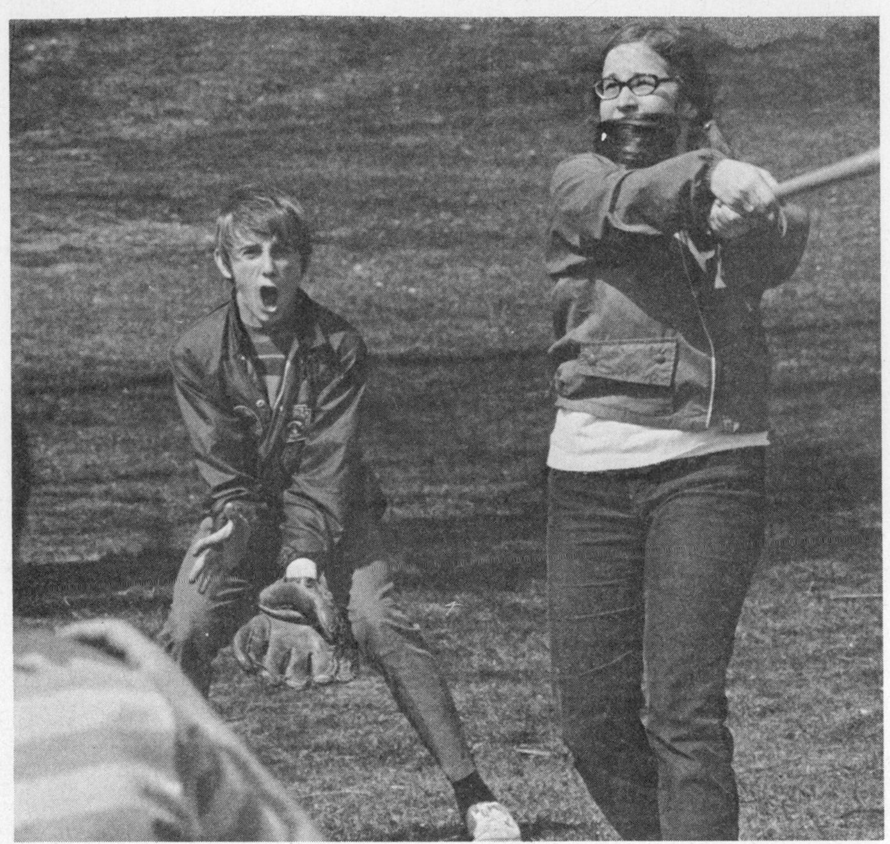

Getting out early at the ball park, strong-armed types lay into the baseball in this game on a March afternoon.

Faces are at work during Three Rivers Festival time.

An old timer forms the stone for a park fireplace in 1955.

On the opposite page, tennis takes over on March 21, 1975.

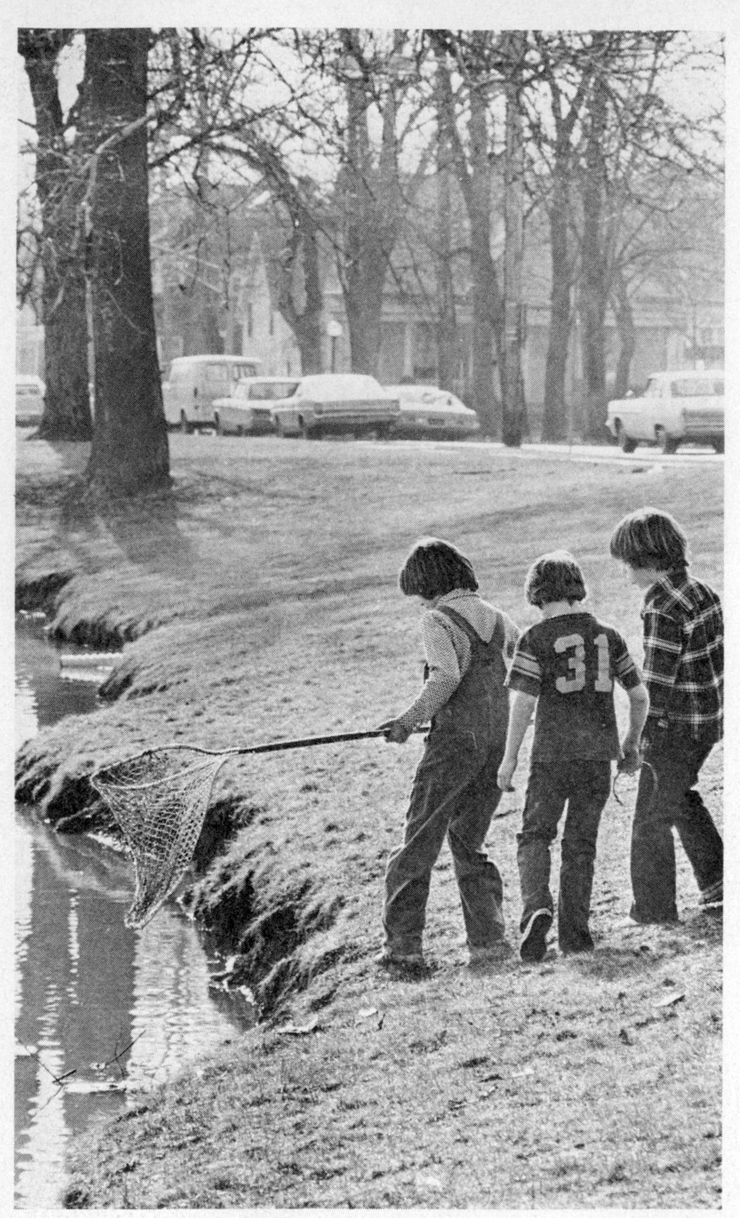

Would-be fisherman are out early in 1975 seeking their fortunes in the Delta Lakes at Lakeside.

Below, a girl sits in placid wonder in 1955 in the midst of the Lakeside rose gardens.

Directly below, is the Diehm Museum of Natural History which was burned by an arsonist in early 1975.

The eternal first playground activity of little children is the swing, as in this evening picture taken about 1950 by Harry Grabner of the Park Department.

Freimann Park, with its fountains and the City-County Building in the background, become part of the downtown landscape in 1973.

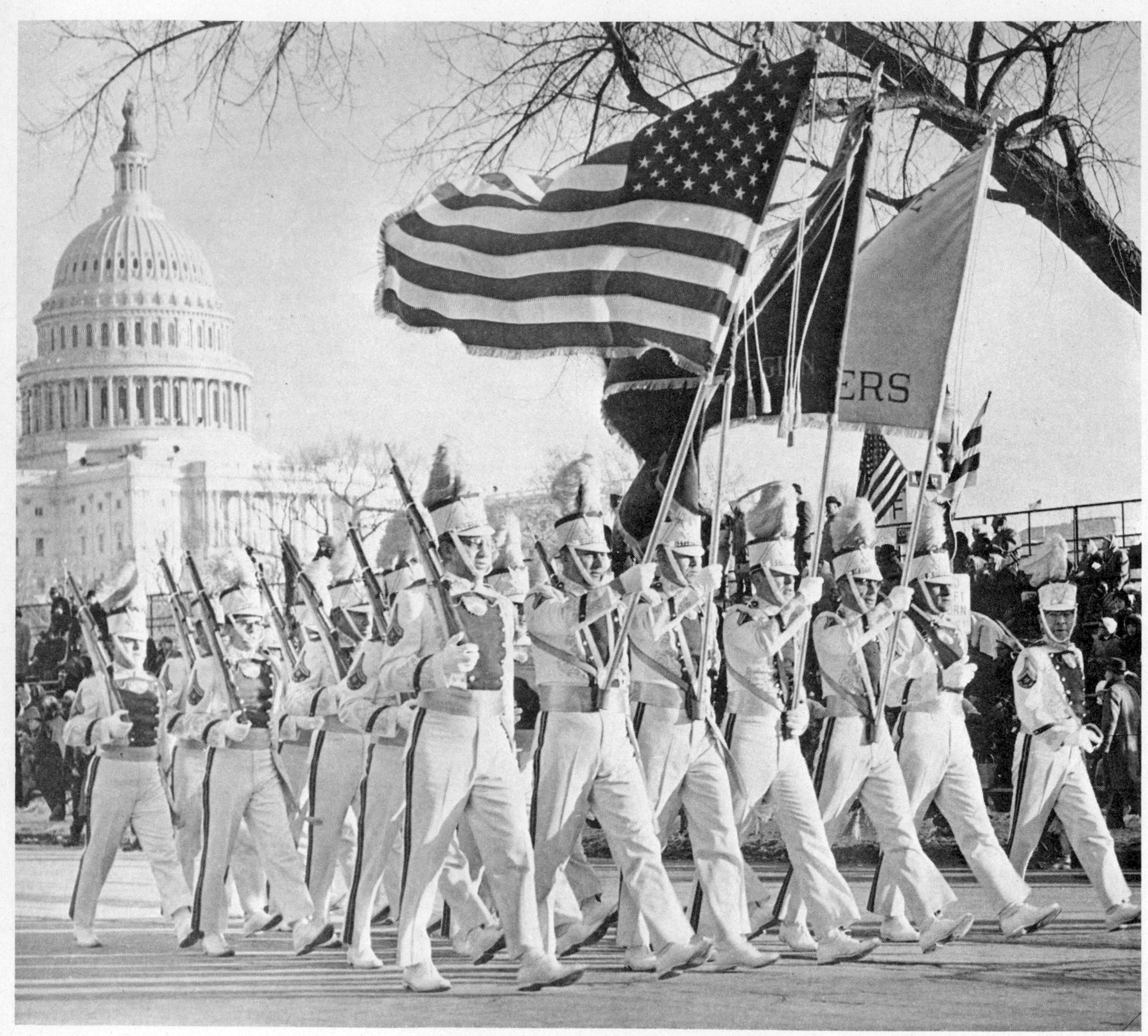

The color guard of American Legion Post 82, led by Sylvester Yaney, march in the cool January sun at Washington, D.C., for the inauguration of President John Kennedy in 1961.

Part 13
The Greening of the City

The flight of retailing activity from downtown to the shopping centers began in the late 1950s and continued at an increasing pace in the 1960s. The reasons included the spread of the residential areas, excessively high property taxes downtown, the need for more parking space for shoppers, the sweep of parking from downtown curbs; and the conveniences of shopping in more modern and nearby facilities at the suburban centers. The County Plan Commission in a master plan submitted in 1959 estimated growth patterns in Allen County with an expected 1975 population of 300,000. It proved to be fairly accurate, in view of later census reports. Richard Gucker was county plan director at the time and was succeeded by Jack Suter in 1965. The City of Fort Wayne had earlier made provision for the expanding use of water in the urban community. Mayor Robert E. Meyer had lowered the gates at the new Cedarville Dam on September 2, 1954. This was the first step in filling the reservoir at Cedarville which soon formed a 500-acre lake. By that time the daily consumption of water had reached 32 million gallons. Cedarville Dam, 135 feet across and 30 feet high was built with three steel gates and was constructed by Wermuth Incorporated. The dam, 10 miles up the St. Joseph River from Fort Wayne, cost $440,000 to build and $200,000 for the right-of-way of flooded land. The trend toward shopping centers was nationwide. After the initial neighborhood centers such as Quimby Village on the Bluffton Road, the Poag Center on South Anthony and the Rudisill Center developed by Joe Goldstine & Son (Robert Goldstine), the plazas became larger in scope. The Southgate Plaza, north of Pettit Ave. and east of Calhoun St., was opened April 18, 1955. It contained 40 store units at the outset on an area of 40 acres. Developed by the American Shopping Centers, Inc., it was the city's first large center and provided parking for 2,500 cars. Major stores included Stillman's, J. C. Penney, F. W. Woolworth, W. T. Grant, The People's Trust Bank, Richman Brothers, Walgreen Drug Stores and Kroger Supermarket. Just across U.S. Highway 27 to the east was built Eavey's Market, the largest grocery of its single-room type built in the nation up to that time. Built by Henry J. Eavey, it contained 80,760 square feet of space. In subsequent years the building was occupied by Scott's, a grocery firm headed by Donald G. Scott and Francis Scott.

More Shopping Centers

On the north end of the city an early center was the North Anthony Shopping Center developed by the Triangle Investment Co. and others. In the area were located a Peoples Trust Branch, Rogers Markets and Marsh Foodliner whose store space was later occupied by Maloley Brothers, supermarkets. The first large retailing center on the north fringe was Northcrest Shopping Center, developed by Sam Fletcher. Constructed in 1958, Northcrest contained 80 acres and cost more than $2 million. Located just north of Coliseum Blvd. and west of North Clinton St., the center included Montgomery Ward, Kroger, Patterson-Fletcher, Howards, F. W. Woolworth, W. T. Grant, Schlatter Hardware and Ream-Steckbeck Paints. Montgomery Ward and other major stores opened in March, 1960. Rental agent Norbert B. Knapke said during initial construction the Northcrest area would have more than 22 stores, a figure which proved to be only the beginning for the center. In 1959, the Skyline Plaza on U.S. Highway 30 west was built by American Shopping Center, the same firm which developed Southgate. It was designed to have 38 retail units and parking for 2,000 cars. It was one of the few shopping centers which didn't expand much with the passing years.

Early in 1960, Rea Magnet Wire Co. was merged with Aluminum Corporation of America. In September, 1960, R. L. Whearley succeeded Sam Rea as president of Alcoa's Rea subsidiary.

Expanding Decade

Industrial expansion moved up a pace in 1960. New industries coming into the area included the B. F. Goodrich Co., Wabash Fibre Box, Metallurgical Processing C., Massoud Marine, Maritime Plastics, Kwik-Lok Corp. and ITT-Kellogg. In mid-year James Crozier was named director of the Fort Wayne Redevelopment Department and together with the board members initiated urban renewal, the largest early projects being the Hanna-Creighton Area and the Downtown-Main St. clearance. In June of 1960, 18 civic leaders were appointed by Mayor Paul Burns to explore a proposed Fort Wayne-Allen County Building. Though the Building Authority never succeeded in erecting the major government office structure as proposed, their work led to the eventual construction of the City-County Building by the two branches of government. The Goodrich tire plant east of the city along U.S. Highway 24 near Woodburn, was a multi-million structure which by 1962 was employing 1,000 workers. Of major significance in 1960 was the production of a new vehicle by International Harvester Co., the Scout, a small utility vehicle which soon became part of the national automotive scene. International took over the old U.S. Rubber plant to increase production space.

The 1960s were years of almost continuous expansion of Fort Wayne industry and population. During the 1960-70 period net migration accounted for approximately 30 per cent of the population increase while only 20 per cent increase in immigrants was experienced on a national level. Of 14,592 persons moving into the county during the decade, more than 80 per cent moved in during the last half of the decade, reflecting the quickening pace of business and industry in the later 1960s. The Allen County population in 1960 was 232,196. By 1970 the population figure had reached 280,455. The city population in 1970 stood at 177,738, indicating a much smaller rise than the county and up from 161,000 in 1960. During the 1960s, practically all the city population gain was due to annexation and in the central area of the city there was a net population loss. The resident labor force advanced steadily during the decade. The 1960 labor force numbered 91,882 in the county as a whole, which was 58 per cent of the population 14 years and over. From 1960 to 1970, the labor force grew 30 per cent, reaching 119,000 persons in 1970. As a percentage of the population, 14 years and older, the labor force grew to 60 per cent. The labor force in the city alone numbered 77,317 in 1970, but was no longer considered an adequate yardstick of urban employment in Fort Wayne-related job market. Females constituted 39 per cent of the labor force in Allen County by 1970. The County Plan Commission forecast an Allen County population of 331,000 by 1980 and 394,000 by 1990. The forecasts, made after the 1970 census, were soon rendered obsolete by declines in the birth rate noted in 1973 and 1974 and the slackening of school enrollments in the early grades.

Interstate Park

The Interstate Industrial Park, north of Coliseum Blvd., was developed in 1961 by Sam Fletcher and Theodore Hagerman. It played a large roll in the expansion of industry during the 1960s. Interstate was planned with all the access and utilities required for quick location of production units, plus the ability to furnish buildings as needed by industries. In just eight years the 425-acre development provided for 51 occupants in 55 buildings with a total of 1,646,000 square feet of space. This total was further expanded on an additional 70 acres purchased. The Magnavox Co. located operations in four plants at Interstate. One of the largest food distributors in the Midwest, Food Marketing Corp., located its facilities on 35 acres of Interstate Park. It built 383,000 square feet in its center where it serviced 253 retail supermarkets and 12,000 institutional customers. In the Baer Field Industrial area, Scott Paper Co. in 1969 completed a new plant as did Carnation Milk Co. The Magnavox Co. completed a $3 million corporate headquarters building on a 60-acre tract at the west edge of the city near State Road 14 and Interstate 69. The building was dedicated March 23, 1970, by Robert Platt, president; Jack W. Schrey, senior vice-president and other company and civic leaders. It contained 287,000 square feet of space and put Magnavox at three locations in Fort Wayne, employing 5,500 persons. General Telephone expanded in 1969 north of the city near U.S. Highway 27 and I-69. The Data Services Corp., a subsidiary of General Telephone and Electronics, completed a $2 million data center, the first of six planned in the Nation.

Midwestern United Life Insurance Co. began construction on its new headquarters building west of the city on June 15, 1961. The firm had formerly been located at the southeast corner of Berry and Webster Streets. The new site was south of U.S. Highway 24-West on a 60-acre tract. Phil J. Schwanz, MULIC president, named Leo Daly of Omaha, Neb., as architect, and Humbrect & Associates of Fort Wayne as associate architects. The multi-million dollar modern structure included relief along its exterior depicting historical events in Fort Wayne; and a lake with water jet was a feature of a wide lawn area to the front of the building. The exterior made use of glass, steel, aluminum and stone. Midwestern at the time had assets of $27 million and $370 million of insurance in force. In little more than another decade, the insurance figure was boosted to more than $1 billion. Midwestern ran into some court difficulties in the wake of the death of an Indianapolis securities dealer, Michael Dobich, whose airplane crashed July 19, 1965. Judge Jesse E. Eschbach of the U.S. District Court for Northern Indiana ruled that Midwestern was liable for some $1.6 million in stock that Dobich had failed to deliver. The case dragged on until October, 1969, when the 7th U.S. Circuit Court of Appeals in Chicago upheld the ruling of lower courts that Midwestern must pay the 354 investors whose stock the bankrupt dealer, Dobich, had failed to deliver.

Harvester Growth

The expansion of International Harvester included a new master parts distribution center on a 320-acre site at the northeast corner of Meyer and Moeller Roads. The building, started in 1960, eventually covered 15 acres, 625,000 square feet, and became the company's largest and the world's largest parts distribution facility. In May, 1960, International purchased another 109 acres on Meyer Road adjoining the Truck Engineering Department Building. In 1963, H. A. Ehrman, manager of the Fort Wayne truck plant, announced a $5 million expansion at the location. More than 240,000 square feet of space were added, 194,000 to the assembly division and 42,000 to the machining division. In 1966, the former International Telephone and Telegraph Corp. building on Oxford St. was acquired, adding 160,000 square feet and 40 acres to the Fort Wayne operation. In 1970, a Vehicle Emissions Laboratory, located on the Meyer Road, was opened to push the firm's environmental protection programs. In the meantime the Scout, the first of which rolled off the assembly line on Nov. 30, 1960, passed the 100,000 mark in July, 1964. By the end of the decade, Fort, Wayne International operations were producing 61,000 trucks and Scouts annually. Employment was more than 8,000 with a weekly payroll of about $1.9 million.

General Electric Co. plant expansions were somewhat limited during the 1960s and subsequent years, but there was almost continuous improvement in Fort Wayne departments in line with technical advances and product improvements. Employment remained fairly constant over much of the period at about 7,000 employees. A new building was constructed at Wall and College Streets for warehousing operations in connection with the Specialty Transformer Department. Ground was broken in December, 1968, for the 40,000 square foot facility, completed in the summer of 1969. Fred H. Holt, GE vice-president and general manager of the Appliance Components Division, was the chief executive locally for the company. Others included Carl H. Rinne, general manager of the Specialty Transformer Department; William I. Hamilton, manager of employee and company relations; Robert W. Trickey, manager of manufacturing for the Transformer Department; D. J. Bowater, manager of the Apparatus Department; Van Williams, general manager of the General Purpose Motor Dept.; W. C. Bates, manager of the Small Motor and Generator Dept.; W. A. Rutledge, general manager of the Specialty Motor Division; D. J. Harbour, manager of the Specialty Transformer Department.

Microfilm Scandal

County Commissioner Sam Cook was indicted on March 2, 1960, by an Allen County Grand Jury in what became known as the microfilm scandal. Cook had been a political figure since 1943. He served two terms as county treasurer and three terms as commissioner. The Grand Jury charged Cook with accepting a bribe and an unlawful interest in a public contract. Earlier the State Board of Accounts had reported the county had overpaid $92,795 for microfilming of old records in the County Clerk's office. The bribery indictments said Cook "did receive and accept the sum of $450 in money from Christian Salomon." Salomon was president of Fort Wayne Microfilm, Inc. In order to save space it had been decided to microfilm records and dispose of the original voluminous documents. Much of the film was so poorly done, however, that it was unreadable. In the process many original county records were lost. Christian V. Salomon and his wife Maxine received suspended 2-to-14 year sentences from Judge Wiliam H. Schannen of the Circuit Court. The sentences were suspended on condition the defendants pay to the county auditor $21,000 in restitution. Their firm had received $140,000 for microfilming in an original contract of $25,000. Subsequently, Circuit Court Judge W. O. Hughes set aside charges against Cook.

Kennedy-Nixon Visits

The year, 1960, was one of the most stimulating Presidential election seasons ever;

and left its mark on Fort Wayne. On Feb. 22, 1960, Robert Kennedy, brother of Presidential hopeful John F. Kennedy, came to town. The event was the Gridiron Banquet of the Fort Wayne Press Club which for many years was a sounding board and entertainment gathering for the great and near-great of the public community. Kennedy said his brother, Senator John Kennedy, considered the Indiana primary a very important one; but wished that some of the opposition felt the same way. He said Senator Stuart Symington, (D-Mo.) "seemed to be avoiding any public test in the primaries and was evidently relying on appointment by the politicans at the national convention." Kennedy also said Sen. Lyndon Johnson (D-Texas) was considered the principal opponent because of convention votes already promised to him. In the May Democratic primary, Kennedy swept to a one-sided victory in Indiana. John Kennedy was nominated by the Democrats and Richard M. Nixon by the Republicans at respective national conventions. Nixon drew the biggest crowd in Fort Wayne that year, and one of the largest ever to gather for a political talk in the city. The entire area of Berry St. on the south side of the Courthouse was flooded with people as Nixon gave a major campaign address in late September, 1960. The appearance of Nixon came at a time when both he and Kennedy were rated an identical 45 per cent preference figure in public polls with 10 per cent undecided, and just one week before the noted television debate by the two candidates. On election day, Kennedy won nationally with an advantage in popular vote of less than one per cent; but Nixon carried the majority vote in Allen County.

One of the oddest occurances in Allen County in 1960 drew little comment at the time. Mrs. Mary Elizabeth Veit, 94, of Fort Wayne, was naturalized as a citizen of the U.S. by U.S. Clerk Kenneth Lackey. The peculiar thing was that Mrs. Veit was born in Allen County in Jefferson Township in 1866 and had lived on a farm near Monroeville or in Fort Wayne all her life. It was discovered, however, that she had lost citizenship under an old law when she was a June bride in 1888 to a German citizen from Bavaria. Even though the marriage occurred in Allen County, a woman marrying an alien lost citizenship under the law repealed in 1922.

National Air Races

For ice-skating fans, 1960 was a year to remember. Freezing weather hit early and the young skating set was out on the icy ponds two weeks before Christmas, playing hockey, pull-away or just standing around with cold toes. It was one of those seasons when too many Christmas trees were on the market. Those shoppers who waited could pick up good living-room size trees for $1 each. The area landscape was liberally decorated with heavy pre-Christmas snowfall. The early onset of winter had followed a busy summer in Fort Wayne. Jimmy Miller won the National Air Race Championship at Baer Field, flying over the course at an average speed of 199.145 miles per hour. Miller received the Thompson Trophy, presented by Roscoe Turner, three-time national air race champ. Col. Turner said the large crowd at Baer Field, numbered at some 6,000, made Fort Wayne one of the more air-minded cities in the U.S. A double fatality when two air racers collided at the July 4 contest, however, curtailed the future of the event. During the carnival, Judy Cole of Cole Bros. Air Show, stood on the wing during loops and other stunts as a biplane was flown by Bill Adams. The Cole family, located in Fort Wayne, were prominent in stunt flying and air shows on an international basis.

Country Music was drawing capacity crowds at the News-Sentinel Outdoor Theatre at Franke Park in the 1950s and 1960s. Started in 1953, the festival drew contestants and fans from a wide area and by 1960 was at the height of its popularity. Beverly Jean Grotrian, 20, from Hoagland, was crowned Miss Country Music that year. Sharon Huffman, 17, of Fort Wayne, was crowned Miss Country Music of 1961. The annual event, sponsored by the Park Board, was directed by Charles "Smoky" Montgomery, local radio personality. Among other Country Music winners were Ardala Huffman in 1958 and Joyce Miller in 1959. Entertainment in another field struck Fort Wayne in 1960 with the making of a movie by the Galbreath Pictures, headed by Richard Galbreath a Fort Wayne musician, photographer and film maker. Production started after the arrival of Lisa Gaye who had earlier starred in "Rock Around the Clock" and other Hollywood films. Miss Gaye played the lead role in the feature film the story of a beauty queen who ended up in prison. The film developed considerable local interest because much of the cast was drawn from the Civic Theatre and the shooting of the film was on Fort Wayne locations. The picture, however, was an artistic and commercial failure.

Carl Sandburg Plays Guitar

On Nov. 14, 1960, Carl Sandburg came to Fort Wayne and quoted poetry, sang songs accompanying himself with a guitar and discussed history, past and current. "Carl Sandburg, wearing his 82 years like a graceful mantle, thrilled a Moring Lecture Series audience here Monday," a contemporary news story reported. An overflow crowd at the Fort Wayne Art School listened as the poet spoke in gravelly, serious tone with a hint of humor. He talked of Abraham Lincoln and television. "Toward the end of the program, he played the guitar and sang a few tunes—mostly of the old West. He has a singing-talking style that is both melodious and effective, quite in the spirit and character of the balladiers of past years. He gives of himself casually. He seems to like people. He seems to like life, with or without people," it was reported. Chairman of the Moring Lecture Series was Mrs. S. Allan Jacobs. Choreographer Agnes de Mille, movie actress Agnes Moorehead and anthropologist Margaret Mead appeared on the series.

The Burns-Robinson Tiff

One of the memorable verbal battles of Fort Wayne political life occurred on Wednesday night, Sept. 14, 1960, in Old City Hall. The combatants were Mayor Paul Mike Burns and long-time City Councilman John Robinson. Members of the City Council, Board of Works and other Fort Wayne and New Haven municipal leaders were in process of approving an agreement by which Fort Wayne would furnish water to New Haven. Much of the session was devoted to the reading of the agreement by City Attorney Jerome O'Dowd. "I don't buy your thinking," Republican Robinson told Democrat Burns. Robinson had been urging that annexation of the East End industries be made part of any water agreement.

"I don't buy yours, but we're going ahead anyway," the mayor replied. "We're not going to contaminate New Haven water with Republican politics."

"They might purify it," Robinson said. "It would be nauseating and might be a violent physic," Burns retorted.

Robinson then said the mayor was "dreaming if you think the water is going to be a palliative so you can annex New Haven." Under the terms of the agreement Fort Wayne was to furnish New Haven water and pay for a feeder line to the New Haven system and New Haven users would pay the regular city water rate plus a 35 per cent surcharge. Robinson, in a final jab at the plan, called for the dismissal of a New Haven suit in Circuit Court to annex the East End industrial area and a halt to a practice where "they bootlegged into a Fort Wayne sewer."

Last Man Walks Last Mile

On June 15, 1961, at 12:15 a.m., the last man to die in the electric chair in Indiana walked the "last mile" at the Michigan City State Prison. He was Richard Kiefer, 40, of Fort Wayne. Kiefer was arrested after a three-state hunt in 1957 for the murder of his wife, Pearl, and his five-year-old daughter. According to Warden Ward Lane, the condemned man walked under his own power and said nothing. The execution actually began at 12:11 a.m. Six charges of 2,300 volts were sent through Kiefer's body before he was pronounced dead by two doctors at 12:15 a.m. Kiefer was tried and convicted of the murder of his wife in the basement of their home on Burgess Street. In fact he was twice tried and sentenced to death for the brutal hammer and knife slaying. He was convicted in 1958, but won a new trial on appeal to the Indiana Supreme Court. In the second trial, a jury of seven men and five women returned a verdict of guilty in Allen Circuit Court on June 19, 1959. Judge William H. Schannen read the death penalty to Kiefer. Keifer was never tried for the little girl's death. Supporting the first-degree murder verdict was evidence that Kiefer, after striking the wife and daughter with a hammer, went upstairs for a hunting knife and returned to the basement to finish the slayings. Prosecutor J. Byron Hayes, Robert Parrish and Jack Danehy handled the government's case. Defense Counsel Barrie Tremper won the retrail on an appeal to the Indiana Court; and following the second conviction after the State Court refused to review the case, won a six-week stay of execution from the U.S. Supreme Court. After the refusal of a petition of review by the High Court, the execution date was reset.

The Bomb Shelters

Early in 1961, people were becoming concerned about the potential threats of a nuclear attack by enemy powers. There was a surge of bomb shelter building and calls for government action. A survey in Fort Wayne in February, 1961, revealed attitudes. "Do you think the Federal, State or City governments, or any other agency, has provided any real plan for you or your family to save yourselves in case of atomic attack?" Only 17 per cent of persons answering said they thought the government had definitely provided useful survival measures. Another 46 per cent said "No" and 37 per cent didn't know. Women were less confident than men with only 9 per cent seeing government in a positive role. During the year, the Bay of Pigs fiasco occurred and even the shortage of Havana cigars was noticed in Fort Wayne. In July, 1961, a Marine officer returned to visit his family from Vietnam where a struggle was just beginning. Capt. James Turner and two other Marine officers were in South Vietnam to help train troops who were dealing with Communists infiltrating from the north. "Since 1958 the guerrilla activities have been stepped up." One of only three Marine Corps military advisors in Vietnam, the Fort Wayne native was prophetic in observing South Vietnam faced long-term threats from the Communist North Vietnamese and Chinese Reds. On October 10, 1961, a citizens group met in downtown Fort Wayne, and called for mass education in nuclear survival. Participating were Elwood Roth, Civil Defense chief; Deputy Sheriff Robert Bender; Fire Chief Howard Blanton; and Robert Schram, Robert Kelley, Bennie Patton and Al Snyder. The marking of fallout shelters and the deposit of a packaged field hospital in the basement of the Post Office followed the program of the unit.

The only known fire to be delivered to Fort Wayne came into town on June 22, 1961. Belching smoke and acrid fumes, a Railway Express boxcar rolled into the elevated Pennsylvania Terminal at 7:30 a.m. with the No. 52 Fort Pitt passenger train of the Pennsy. Thirty sections of 50-foot hose were needed to bring sufficient water to the scene. District Chief Walter Roemke said damage was heavy on the train coming out of Chicago.

Jostling, peering pickets, massed at the main gate of Magnavox Company successfully repulsed two attempts by law enforcement officers to open plant gates on September 1, 1961. Finally on a third try, about 15 policemen and sheriff deputies led by Police Chief Paul Clark and Sheriff Custer Dunifon succeeded in clearing a way for waiting cars of supervisory and salaried employees. Two pickets were hustled across Bueter Road to a paddy wagon. They and four others in the wagon were released a little later by agreement between police and Allied Industrial Workers Union officials George Skelton and Jack Koch. The strike was the first at Magnavox since 1945.

Save City Light

A new citizen's organization was formed in 1961 which was to figure in Fort Wayne politics for more than a decade but eventually fail on its avowed purpose. The group was Citizens for City Light. It hoped to prevent the decline or sale of the city-owned electric utility. The moving spirits behind the formation were Robert E. Bauer, Dalton Ferguson, Wayne Kepler, David Gearhart, David Erwin and Edward Smith. Bauer, original chairman, said, "Fort Wayne is going to be out of the power business in a few years if we don't do something about it." Kepler said City Light money "has been siphoned off for contributions to the general tax fund or anything that comes along."

On another front, uneven property taxes in the city were seen as effecting development and business downtown. Fred Hunter, chairman of a committee of the Fort Wayne Board of Realtors, said the unit was studying land values. "Development of downtown or any other area is going to be determined by economic factors," Hunter said, pointing out that heavier taxes could make it unprofitable to build, rent or locate in the high-cost area. At that time, 1961, land value for tax purposes on Calhoun St. downtown was $5,000 per front foot, or 100 times greater than the $50 per front foot for a shopping center on Rudisill Boulevard. Public officals did too little about the problem, before or after that period, however, with the result that empty store fronts appeared along much of downtown. The city's total assessed valuation in 1960 was $315 million, which included personal property such as automobiles and household goods which were figured at the time, in addition to land and buildings.

In December, 1961, the last of an ancient institution was still on the streets of the city. Aaron Kelso with his wagon and his white horse named "Beer" was doing daily rounds of hauling. Kelso's horse was the last regularly-licensed city workhorse. The second last licensed workhorse, a black one, had died the previous year and had been owned by Kelso's brother. Kelso had been on the route for 33 years but said things were getting pretty tight, particularly in the winter. He said having a horse shod cost $10 in the city. "If it was me, I'd put a horse out to pasture before I'd pay $10 for shoes," Kelso said. Kelso's wife Rose said "You can't buy a sack of corn with cobs on for less than a dollar. I know because I pay the bill." Kelso kept his horse in his garage behind his home on Hayden Street. Riding with him often on his rounds were his sister's little great-grandchildren.

Some Surprises

Considerable surprise was expressed in the community on March 23, 1961, with the resignation of Fort Wayne Community Schools superintendent Aaron T. Lindley. Lindley, whose salary of $25,000 made him the highest paid public official in Indiana at that time, resigned to accept a $8,400 associate professorship at Purdue University. Only Willard Shambaugh, school board chairman, appeared to have prior knowledge of Lindley's plan to resign. The school board voted Lindley a $10,000 grant as terminal compensation. This grant drew criticism from Mayor Paul Burns who said the board was being overly generous with the taxpayers' money. The school board later rescinded the grant. Lester L. Grile succeeded Lindley on August 1, 1961, as superintendent at an annual salary of $16,000. Shambaugh said even if the $10,000 terminal grant had been paid, the difference in salaries would have soon more than compensated for the amount.

Bank robberies were fairly epidemic in the early 1960s. On Feb. 23, 1961, at 10:40 a.m., a lone bearded bandit stepped into the busy little Grabill Bank and seized $9,900 in less than five minutes and vanished despite a widespread blockade. Bank teller Judy Shaw described the robber as "a creep" and carrying a shotgun with sawed-off butt. On April 17, 1961, a "skinny, nervous" gunman in Levi pants robbed the Waynedale Branch of the Peoples Trust Bank. Armed with a pistol, the bandit fled east with $5,200, according to Mrs. Joan Yawn, teller, and R. F. Rodenbeck, branch manager. FBI agents captured Richard C. Ruip in a shootout near Canton, O., and charged him with the crime. On October 25, 1962, a redhaired outlaw with a snub-nosed gun robbed the Gateway Plaza Branch of the Indiana Bank. Mrs. Mary Cerney, lone teller at the bank, said the gunman stuffed $10 and $20 bills totalling $2,130 in a white bag.

One of the major public works in Northern Indiana began at Fort Wayne on May 10, 1962. This was Interstate Highway 69 which eventually became a major link from Indianapolis on the south and central Michigan on the north. Some 50 pieces of heavy road quipment were moved onto the project as more than 2 million cubic feet of concrete were poured in the 4.3 miles of dual highway and three cloverleaf interchanges just west of the city. Following that first portion of I-69, construction was pushed toward completion of the 160-mile route. Original schedules called for I-69 to be open from Indianapolis to the Indiana State Line north of Angola by 1966, but the actual completion was not until 1971.

In the 1962 general elections, E. Ross Adair was re-elected to Congress. His Allen County vote was 45,542 compared with 35,574 for Ronald E. Ross, his Democratic opponent. Republicans swept county offices. In the state, however, 1962 was the year Birch Bayh unseated long-time Republican Senator Homer Capehart by a narrow 9,375 margin out of a record combined vote of 1,801,800. Thomas Gallmeyer, a Fort Wayne attorney, quit the post of State Republican chairman on Nov. 20, 1962. The 122nd Tactical Fighter Wing of the Air National Guard, based at Baer Field, returned from France in early 1962. The Fighter Wing had flown to France on an emergency basis 10 months earlier during the Berlin Wall crisis and was stationed at Chambley Air Base in France.

Banking and Houses

Charles H. Buesching, chairman and chief executive officer of the Lincoln National Bank & Trust Co., was stricken and died Jan. 11, 1962, during a testimonial dinner in his honor. Succeeding Buesching as chairman of Lincoln Bank was Willard Shambaugh, long-time board member. Earl G. Schwalm continued as president. Later presidents of Lincoln Bank included Charles Kelly, Lloyd Beatty, Clyde E. Flowers and Robert A. Morrow. Carl A. Gunkler was senior vice-president and board member. By the end of 1973, Lincoln had total deposits of $372,892,000 and assets of $431,979,000, the largest in the city on both counts. Directors, in addition to Flowers, Morrow and Gunkler, were Shambaugh, chairman; and Alexander Azar, Conrad Balentine, Albert Beckwith, Norbert G. Berghoff, Earl Brenn, Dale Doehrman, Helene Foellinger, Theodore Hagerman, S. Allan Jacobs, Robert M. Kopper, Clifton E. McCormick, Harold W. McMillen, William F. McNagny, Louis H. Meyer, D. G. Jack Norton, H. Leslie Popp, Walter Probst, Henry F. Rood and Fred Zollner.

In January, 1962, the Fort Wayne-Allen County Chapter of the Red Cross awarded a $225,000 contract for construction of a new center at Coliseum Blvd. and Parnell Avenue. The Red Cross had until that time been located at the northwest corner of Berry and Ewing Streets in the old Ewing mansion. It was the finest old home in Fort Wayne—a three-story brick building of classic Georgian design. Built in 1838 by William G. Ewing, the home had nine fireplaces, partitions 18 inches thick and mounts which once held shutters to be drawn during Indian raids. For many years prior to Red Cross occupancy, it had been the family home of Dr. Eugene Bulson. It was razed for a car lot after the Red Cross moved out.

Colonial Mortgage Co., Inc., was a home-financing firm at 927 South Harrison St. operated by officers of General Industries, the prefabricated house manufacturer. Officers of Colonial were moved to new quarters at 333 East Washington Blvd. Heading the firm were William B.F. Hall,

D. G. Jack Norton, James Griffin, E. J. Disser and Cletus Rumschlag.

Zeis Elected Mayor

The 1963 city elections were among the more hotly contested in recent decades. In the May primary Mayor Paul M. Burns defeated Democratic opponents, Clara Luecke and Carlos Campbell, easily enough. The Republicans in the primary had more of a contest. John H. Cooper, formerly of the Board of Works, had informal backing of the regular party organization. Harold S. Zeis, former sheriff and former superintendent of the Indiana State Police, had wide recognition. Robert W. Dahman, former city councilman, waged an energetic campaign; as did a darkhorse, Oral Ballinger. When the votes were in, Zeis won the nomination with an 8,557 vote. This compared with 6,526 for Cooper; 4,759 for Dahman and 152 for Ballinger. County Central Committee Chairman Orvas Beers said the primary battle indicated a strong Republican turnout and predicted victory in the fall election. The Nov. 5 election, however, proved to be a very close contest. Zeis won with a plurality of 1,233, or about 51 per cent of the vote. Zeis drew 27,368 votes to 26,135 for Burns. Joseph Christoff was elected city judge and Walter C. Meyers, clerk. Elected to the City Council were John Nuckols, John Robinson, William T. Hinga, Herbert Tipton, Phil Steigerwald, Verlin H. Buchanan, Jack Dunifon, Celia Ann Fay and Edwin J. Rousseau. Zeis named Ivan McKathnie as city controller; J. Robert Arnold, city attorney, and David Heaton, associate city attorney. On the Board of Public Works were Fred Ehrman, chairman, and Robert Dahman and George Gable. The Board of Safety included: Robert E. O'Reilly, chairman, and Melvin Heckman, John Braden and E. Neil Maginity. Chester Ricketts was named police chief. Martin Luepke was fire chief. Ursula Miller was administrative assistant to the mayor. Donald Figel later succeeded Ricketts as police chief. Edward C. Loraine succeeded Luepke as fire chief in 1967. Paul Goodwin and Fred Ray served as fire prevention chiefs, successively. Police work underwent a considerable number of changes during the 1960s. By 1970, the Police Department made 11,488 emergency runs. This meant police were answerthe needs of distressed people about every 40 minutes, 24 hours a day, seven days a week throughout the year. The Police Academy was established in the former Seyfert Building on South Lafayette Street. New officers were given 12 weeks of training in crime and safety control, human considerations and use of weapons. The Fort Wayne Police Laboratory was established in 1966. The number of the force was increased from 247 in 1964 to 289 in 1971. The number in the Fire Department was increased from 250 to 270 during a similar period.

In August, 1964, the Fire Department celebrated its 125th anniversary with an estimated 50,000 people witnessinng various demonstrations during a week-long schedule. During the great snow emergency of Feb. 25, 26 and 27, 1965, the Fire Department maintained limited but vital services at a time when all usual transportation in the city had broken down. Medical staff were delivered to hospitals and food and medical supplies were delivered on fire equipment. Large scale renewal of equipment and construction of fire stations included: eight new pumpers purchased from International Harvester in 1966; new stations at Interstate Industrial Park in 1966, at 3400 Reed Road in 1967, at 1500 Coliseum Blvd. in 1968. The new No. 1 Engine House at the northwest corner of Main and Lafayette Sts. was built in 1971. Of modern architecture, it was similar to the original designs of Louis Kahn for the building of the Fine Arts Center (Kahn abandonned the original architectural concept and adopted something else for the actual building of the Performing Arts Theatre).

Urban Renewal

The $6 million Three Rivers renewal got underway in the summer of 1965 with approval by the Redevelopment Commission of plans for the twin, 14-story luxury apartments. Prior to that, starting in 1962, the site had been cleared through the Redevelopment process, employing local funding. The total site consisted of about eight acres bound by Lafayette St., the Norfolk & Western Railway elevation and the junction of the St. Mary's and St. Joseph Rivers to form the Maumee. The financial resource for the Three Rivers Apartments was Indiana & Michigan Electric Company. Prior to the program, there were eight structures at the site in varying degrees of utility, largely of the decaying warehouse variety. Prior to acquisition, the property was assessed at $203,000. Following the improvement the value for assessment purposes was set at $1,405,000. The cost of land and demolition was $666,000. It was sold in 1964 to developers for $250,000.

The stage for the construction of the City-County Building was set in July, 1965. The area included some 24 acres running east from Calhoun St. for more than three blocks, one and a half blocks deep from Main St. to the N&W. The area consisted of 101 parcels of real estate, much of it still with the flavor of the old days of the Wabash-Erie Canal. Several of the buildings were occupied by major business interests, but the majority lightly-used 19th Century structures and some all but abandoned. The cost of the Main St. Project was shared by the Federal Government and the City of Fort Wayne, with the federal share being about three-fourths of the total $6.8 million cost. The City County Building was financed completely with local public funds. The structure, between Calhoun and Clinton Sts., just north of the County Courthouse, required three bond issues totaling $9.1 million issued by the Allen County Commissioners and County Council. Architect for the building was Herman Strauss of A.M. Strauss, Associates, and general contractor was Hagerman Construction Company. Ground for the City-County Building was broken on Oct. 10, 1968. Directors of the Redevelopment Commission during most of the planning and construction stages of the major projects were James Crozier and Wayne Schacht, in succession. The City-County Building was dedicated Sept. 25, 1971. Trustees for the Redevelopment Commission at the time of the completion of the Main St. Project were Alden L. Irmsher, Dr. H. L. Pearson, C. V. Sorenson, Cecil Onion and John D. Shoaff. Commissioners included Donald H. Walker, Max Scott, Donald P. Eckrich, William F. Borgmann and Harold Stith.

The Great Dream

Soon after the Main St. Redevelopment was first initiated, it was envisioned that Fort Wayne would have a Fine Arts Center of cultural dimension that drew national attention. A number of architects of international repute visited the city to discuss project designs. Louis I. Kahn, Philadelphia architect who had designed the Yale Art Gallery, Medical Research Buildings at the University of Pennsylvania and other distinguished buildings, was selected for the Fort Wayne work. The entire area from Clinton to Lafayette north of Main was to be used. Kahn soon displayed models for the series of buildings contemplated for the arts complex. The financial support needed for the major undertaking fell short, however. Plans were scaled down. Eventually the great concept was abandonned. The western half of the land area was given over for use as a downtown park. The eastern portion of the site was the location for the single theatre building called the Center for Performing Arts. Kahn was architect for the building, but it was quite different from his original designs for the Fine Arts Center. Freimann Park, between the City-County Building and the Performing Arts Theatre, was financed in large part by a gift bequeathed by Frank Freimann, who was president and board chairman of Magnavox Company. Designed as a formal park, it soon became a place of rest and beauty in the downtown area, and the sight for various popular programs. The focal points were the pool with fountain and the equestrian statute of Anthony Wayne which was moved from old Hayden Park to Freimann Park in

1973.

The Hanna-Creighton Urban Renewal Project was the city's largest in terms of land area. It was aimed at providing new and better residences for citizens. Located southeast of the central business district, the area was bound by Hanna, Creighton, Anthony and the Pennsylvania Elevation. Much of the district was considered blighted though much of it was not. The Project officially began in October, 1964. The area contained 112 acres and 532 buildings and 583 dwellings units. The original plan was to replace some of the housing, renew other units and to keep the better family-owned residences. This approach was abandonned, however, as being financially unfeasible. The whole area was leveled. Several thousand persons were relocated or sought homes in other areas of the community. The impetus behind the project was the availability of Federal money of which several million was used to acquire the land, raze the structures and in relocation efforts. The city's cost in that phase of the project was $264,000. Afterward, construction of streets and utilities to serve the area, originally estimated at $800,000, ran to more than $1 million. The estimated cost of redeveloping a portion of the area was $5.5 million. For redevelopment, 47 acres were set aside for housing, 28 acres for industrial use, 10 acres for a school site and 11 acres for commercial use. About 30 acres were developed by the Inter-Church Housing Corporation with FHA-financed apartment units for limited income families. The Federal Government originally committed $3,395,000 to the project and added funds were switched from the Main St. project.

The Rolling Mill Project, initiated in 1966, was directly related to industrial development. The 40-acre area was north of Taylor St. and between the N&W Railway on the east and the Penn-Central on the north. The project led to a new manufacturing plant of Joslyn Stainless Steel Co. which had an older factory in the immediate vicinity. Prior to redevelopment, the area was a mixture of housing, commercial and industrial property and some blighted area. The total cost of acquisition, fees, demolition and relocation adjustments was $1,096,000. The sale of the land realized $181,000. Assessment for tax purposes before renewal was $245,000. Assessment after renewal was $1,167,700. Joslyn planned a $10 million expansion and began construction in December, 1966. The first building of the steel mill was longer than three football fields. The Joslyn expansion was expected to eventually boost employment by 2,000 workers. Paul A. Lauletta, president of Joslyn, reported the completion of a portion of the expansion in 1974. The nation's largest centerless grinder and the world's most powerful abrasive saw for forging billets were part of the new production machinery at the mill.

Sober Days

The long weekend of Nov. 23-25, 1963, was one of the more sobering of the age in Fort Wayne and communities across the land. News that President John F. Kennedy was assassinated in the early afternoon of Friday, Nov. 22, 1963, while proceeding in a Dallas, Texas, motorcade, halted all normal activity in the city. Churches conducted memorial services and civil leaders issued appropriate statements. Most people followed mournful and shocking events on television. Vice President Lyndon Johnson succeeded to the presidency; and attention was trained on the funeral proceedings at the Capitol and White House. Sunday morning the television audience saw on live video the shooting of assassin Lee Harvey Oswald by Jack Ruby as Dallas police were taking Oswald down a hallway in a Dallas public building. The sun was shining on a cold Monday Nov. 25, in Washington as world leaders followed the caisson to the Arlington burial site of John Kennedy. In Fort Wayne, it was a quiet day and mostly cloudy.

On Feb. 22, 1964, police reported the arrest of Larry Joe Chamberlain of Fort Wayne for the $61,623 robbery of the East State Blvd. Branch of Indiana Bank. It was the largest robbery in the state since the heyday of John Dillinger. In 1964, Seyfert Foods began construction of its new headquarters and plant at Interstate Industrial Park. Also during the year Edward Thoma succeeded Archie Keene as president of Indiana Institute of Technology and Helene Foellinger was re-elected president of Junior Achievement.

On August 21, 1964, at Franke Park, the national pow-wow of the Grand Council of North American Indians convened. Indians from many parts of the nation came to the three-day conclave. It was an extremely dry spell and medicine men prayed for rain. It came 4 days later.

The Berghoff Gardens, for many years a landmark restaurant in Fort Wayne, burned late June 3, 1964. According to Fire Chief Martin Luepke, one fire damaged the stage area and another fire was in ductwork in another part of the building. The restaurant, which connected with the Baltes Hotel at the southeast corner of Harrison and Berry Streets, had been closed for some years and a teen club and other business interests had been using the premises. The hotel and restaurant had been built in 1908. The property was purchased in 1957 by Gene Himelstein from Beatrice Baltes Flynn. The four-story hotel had 60 rooms and was operated by Jake Kindler.

The Candidates

Lar Daly, candidate for President of the United States, arrived in Fort Wayne in April, 1964, in a green 1952 Chevy with rain-spattered campaign posters hanging out of the trunk. Pulling up in front of the Indiana Hotel, the Democratic aspirant emerged in a stovepipe hat and red, white and blue sash to push his campaign in the May 5 Indiana primary. The reception committee consisted of one bellhop and a newspaper reporter. "The issues are clearly drawn. It's Gov. Matthew Welsh sitting in for President Lyndon Johnson on civil rights and Gov. George Wallace of Alabama for state's rights," Daly said of the Indiana primary. Daly, of Chicago, was a perennial also-run as a candidate but recalled he received 41,000 votes in the 1960 Indiana primary against John F. Kennedy.

When George Wallace arrived in the city that same spring, the scene was quite different. A crowd approaching mob proportions surged as sirens screamed and the Wallace motorcade pulled up at the Berry St. entrance of the Van Orman Hotel. It was a period of civil rights strife in the South and Wallace was making his first national campaign tour. Fort Wayne police, headed by Capt. Richard Schmeding, formed a wedge around Wallace to assure his safety to the hotel ballroom where Wallace spoke to a small crowd, his words nearly drowned out by shouts of a larger crowd outside. Wallace said he was launching his candidacy for the Presidency to rescue the people in the states from a growing oppression of central government in Washington. In the general election in 1964, most of the contests were close. Lyndon B. Johnson, running on the Democratic ticket for a return to the White House, narrowly defeated Republican Senator Barry Goldwater in Allen County, though Johnson won by a landslide nationally. Johnson had a county vote of 50,706 to 49,284 for Goldwater. Incumbent Congressman E. Ross Adair turned back Democratic challenger Max Hobbs by a vote of 51,483 to 47,926.

Anthony Wayne Bank

The Anthony Wayne Bank Building was completed in 1964. The 15-story office building, at a cost of more than $2.5 million, was located at the northeast corner of Clinton and Berry Streets. The bank occupied the first two floors and the next four floors of the concrete structure were devoted to parking space. Anthony Wayne experienced remarkable growth following the expansion of banking facilities. Formed in 1944 out of the old Morris Plan firm, Anthony Wayne by the end of 1973 had more than $50 million in deposits and total resources of $83 million. Paul G. Gronauer was president during the building period. The board of directors in 1973, in addition to Gronauer, included Harold A. Lehman, Nan A. Dahm, Phil J. Schwanz, L.H. Weilemann, John A. Rogers,

Oral F. Ice, Dr. Ralph W. Elston, John Williamson, Allan E. Bloom, Nord Krauskopf, Carl Bennett, Adrian Bixby, Fred Marolf, Jr., Carl S. Seibel and Gerald Dehner. Earlier presidents include Theodore Thieme and Harry Perfect in the Morris Plan period, and Clint Willson and A. Everett Bloom, after 1943. Miss Grace Binder was executive vice-president for many years.

American Federal Savings and Loan Assn. completed its first facility at the corner of Clinton St. and Rudisill Boulevard. By 1970, the association was operating at three locations, on the Coldwater Road across from Glenbrook Shooping Center and in New Haven. Assets at that time were over $14 million and savings at $13,934,000. Officers included Thomas A. Gallmeyer, president and board chairman; Paul Yergens, senior vice-president; William Riethmiller, vice-president and secretary, and Alexander Azar, treasurer.

Palm Sunday Tornadoes

From the point of view of weather, 1965 goes down as a year of disaster for Fort Wayne and Indiana. In February of that year, a record fall of snow stopped the city in its tracks and blanketed much of Northern Indiana. The Palm Sunday Tornadoes ripped across Central and Northern Indiana on April 11, 1965, killing 140 persons and causing damage estimated at $125 million. Fort Wayne was cut off from most of its electric supply when 11 different lines of Indiana and Michigan Electric Company were knocked down by the tornado sweeping north and south of the city. Fort Wayne, almost peculiarly, was not hit by any of the several tornadoes which ripped near Elkhart and the lake country to the north and through Berne to the South. Jess Halsey of the Baer Field Weather Station said the Palm Sunday tornadoes were the worst wind disasters in 40 years. On March 18, 1925, some 689 persons in Missouri, Illinois and Indiana were killed. The Palm Sunday tornadoes were spawned when balmy 73-degree weather was overtaken by cold air high over the Great Lakes area, causing a cyclonic action of spinning air at times in excess of 300 miles per hour.

In 1965, Governor Roger Branigan named Mrs. Hertha Duemling of Fort Wayne as the Indiana representative at the first conference of state art leaders in Washington, D.C. Mrs. Duemling was executive director of the Indiana Arts Commission and president of Fort Wayne's Stellar Concert Series.

Poverty Warfare

The Economic Opportunity Council, a federally-financed spearhead of the war on poverty, came into increasing public attention and participation in 1965. The EOC was described as a government unto itself, since it operated parallel to regularly-elected public offices, but was not locally subject to them. The council, its staff and those on receiving ends of the services included a considerable percentage of community interests and residents. The programs included Head Start, Legal Services, Neighborhood Youth Corps, Economic Development, Emergency Food and Medical Services, Youth Development, Foster Grandparents, Neighborhood Services System, Planning and Research, Public Services Careers Program, and the Community Mobilization Program. By 1970, the EOC was operating on an annual budget of $1.8 million in Fort Wayne and Allen County. Named executive director in 1965 was William G. Williams who remained in that position for six years. Chairmen and program directors included Howard Minier, Nadene Petrecelle, Esther Burhop, Dr. Clyde Adams, Bernice Bradley, David Miller, Louise Sanders, Calvin Keys, Larry Payne, Rosey Metrailer, Famious Williams, Joseph Daniel, Willie French, and Leon Simpson. The decline in federal funding of EOC became evident in 1972. Merle Bennett, chairman of the Allen County EOC, was succeeded in 1974 by John Bonsib. Interest continued to focus on reports of discrimination in employment and housing.

Other officials of the organization included Nicholas Roembke, James Henderson, Dorothy Holt, Emil Brown, Rev. Otha Aden, the Rev. Mack Magree, William Turner, Mrs. Joann Dunson, Clem Trevino, Rev. Thomas O'Connor, Mary Brunner, Robert Smith, and Benjamin Eisbart.

White's Space Walk

Edward H. White, III, stepped into a new element—space—on June 3, 1965, as he and fellow astronaut James A. McDivitt orbited the earth in a Gemini 4 capsule. White, a member of an old Fort Wayne family dating back to the Civil War, became the first man to propel himself in space. People the world over watched on TV at the blast off of the space vehicle and heard on radio as White made his famous venture outside the craft and his swim in space. Motion pictures of the space walk were shown upon the return from the 62-orbit, four-day mission. Peculiarly, the Russians later released films of what they claimed was a space walk by a cosmonaut earlier than the American trip. The lighting and movements in the Russian film, however, lacked the open space quality of the White film and doubt was cast on the authenticity of the claim. Ed White was born in San Antonio, Texas, while his father Air Force General Edward White, II, was stationed there. The mother of the astronaut was the former Mary Haller, who in her younger years was a teacher in the Fort Wayne public school system. Ed White attended West Point, as did his father. The astronaut's great-grandfather was Capt. James B. White, who after the Civil War founded a department store and wheel works in Fort Wayne. The astronaut, being an "army brat" because of his father's military career, only spent summer vacations during his childhood in Fort Wayne. However, he registered his car at Fort Wayne, was a registered voter in Allen County until 1957 and considered the city his permanent residence. The astronaut was a colonel when he and McDivitt were propelled into space by a nine-story Titan 2 rocket from Cape Kennedy, Florida. When Ed White floated into space it was human breakthrough into a new element, and marked a permanent place for him in the records of mankind.

Edward White, III, the first man to move in space outside a space ship, and two fellow astronauts, perished in a Jan. 27, 1967, fire on Apollo I during a simulated count down at Cape Kennedy, Florida. Hoosier Astranaut Virgil (Gus) Grissom and Comdr. Roger B. Chaffee, like Grissom a Purdue University graduate, died with White in the flash fire of the space craft. Grissom, a familiar figure in Fort Wayne, was the second astronaut to make a journey into space and the first to make two space trips. White, Grissom and Chaffee were preparing for a later flight to the moon at the time of the tragedy.

Two natural gas explosions rocked the community in 1966. On Feb. 3, a series of two or more blasts shortly after 10 a.m. wiped out two homes and heavily damaged five others. For 16 blocks around the corner of Broadway and Kinsmoor Ave., families were evacuated. Three women went to the hospital with critical burns. They were Dorothy Swain, 47, Mrs. Regina Otis, 38, and Mrs. Clara Shipley, 77, all of the Broadway residential area. Mrs. Swain died a week later. The gas explosions had erupted from faulty mains under the street and spread fire and debris over the snowy landscape. There was fear at the time that five children had been in one of the houses which had blown apart. But later it was discovered they had fortunately gone elsewhere shortly before the explosion. The following summer, on Aug. 23, a gas explosion leveled the brick office building of Phelps Dodge Corp. on New Haven Avenue.

St. Joseph Hospital

St. Joseph Hospital's largest expansion program, the building of the main Broadway wing, was completed with dedication ceremonies on May 1, 1966. The $6 million improvement was initiated by a fund drive which began in 1960. A new nine-story building along Broadway to replace the old 1912 structure at the location and a four-story wing on Van Buren St., plus a convent structure at Van Buren and Main St., were basic constructural elements. Including modernization of the Berry St. wing, the project boosted St. Joseph's capacity to 400 beds and 60 bassinets. Sister M. Odillia, administrator during the planning stage, said a public subscription campaign and federal funds would finance the improvement. Heading the fund drive were Donnelly P. McDonald, Jr., chairman; and Dr. Stephen C. Michaelis, Rt. Rev. Msgr. Thomas L. Durkin, Sister M. Wilma, Ralph Shirmeyer and Richard Rosenthal. Bishop Leo A. Pursley was honorary chairman. Associate chairmen of drive committees were Drs. Justin Arata, Joseph Baltes, R. Morton Bolman, Robert Brosius, Charles J. Cooney, Virgil Levy, John Nill, Maurice Rothberg, Joel W. Salon and Robert Schmoll. Others included Edward J. Griesedieck, Jr.,; Norbert Knapke; C. Edwin Schouweiler; Martin Torborg; Joseph Colligan; Thomas J. O'Reilly; William Latz; Rev. William M. Faber and Rev. John Moskal. Architect for the project was Joseph Hulfeld of A.M. Strauss & Associates. Construction was awarded to Irmsher & Sons, Inc., on May 22, 1962. Leo M. Ford was chairman of the lay advisory Board and Russell Roache, building coordinator. Sister M. Joann, administrator, and John Hurley, associate administrator, Bishop Pursley and D. P. McDonald, Jr. headed dedication ceremonies in 1966. The hospital had its origin in 1869 with the occupation of the Old Rockhill House by the Order of Poor Handmaids of Jesus Christ. The chapel and motherhouse, built in 1881, were razed to make way for construction completed in 1966. Hospital buildings erected in 1892 and 1912 were also razed. The main Berry St. wing, built in 1928 and 1929, remained but the entrance was closed off and the interior modernized, with the top floor of the seven-story building a surgical center. The new entry way, facing Broadway, was at the center of the nine-story wing and serviced by a driveway and canopy.

On June 9, 1966, a proposed 134-page updated Fort Wayne building code was presented to the City Council by the Fort Wayne Engineers Club. A 41-member committee spent eight months in preparing the new code—nearly a third more compact than the old one. S. J. Antalis, chairman of the committee, said the building regulations took into consideration state and federal recommendations. Engineers, architects, public officials, builders and consultants spent 1,500 man hours putting together the first comprehensive overhaul of the building code in 40 years.

The 1967 city elections were pretty much a rerun of the test in 1963. Mayor Harold Zeis, the Republican, won re-election by a narrow margin over former Mayor Paul Mike Burns. Fuad G. Bonahoom was elected city clerk; Larry T. Miller, city judge. On the city Council the second Zeis term were John Nuckols, John Robinson, Thomas G. Adams, Herbert Tipton, Phil Steigerwald, William K. Geake, Jack K. Dunifon, Celia Ann Fay and Edwin Rousseau. Ivan McKathnie was renamed controller and J. Robert Arnold, city attorney. Associate city attorneys included Robert Meyers, David Heaton and Philip Davidson. During the term, Edward V. Elkins succeeded to the board of works, the original members being Fred S. Ehrman, chairman, and Robert Dahman and George Gable, with Kenneth McGraw, secretary.

The Big Malls

The Glenbrook Shopping Center was started in 1965 on the city's north side, near U.S. 27 and the Coliseum Boulevard. The major development in retail commerce was designed as a $7 million project with 70 stores. It was later expanded beyond the original dimensions. In addition to a high-quality operation and structure, the mall became a regular scene for social and cultural interests of the community. Major store operations include L. S. Ayres, Sears Roebuck, Howards, Hutners, Walgreens and many other retail and service operations. The developer was Landau, Heyman & Clay,

Inc., Chicago. The architectural firm was Schenkel & Shulz, Inc., Fort Wayne and the contractor was Construction Control Corp. With a 265,000 square foot addition started in 1974, the total shopping center space was brought to 950,000 square feet. According to Edwin Rousseau, resident manager, the shopping center with the expansion contained 80 retail stores and parking for 5,200 cars. Among the stores in the new addition was J. C. Penney Co. which occupied 175,000 square feet of space.

The Southtown Mall, announced in 1966, was a $7 million shopping center of comparable dimension with Glenbrook. Bulldozers and heavy equipment moved in to start construction on March 16, 1967. The site was near U.S. 27 and Tillman Road the developer was Melvin Simon, Indianapolis. Wolf & Dessauer, Montgomery Ward and J. C. Penney established major department stores. Wolf & Dessauer later became L. S. Ayres. The architect was Daverman and Associates, Detroit. Store operations included Patterson-Fletcher, G. C. Murphy, Maloley Bros., Hutner's and other retail and service firms. Al Zacher, representative of the developers, said employment was to exceed 3,000 persons and parking was provided for 4,200 cars. The entire complex, including a wide mall, was enclosed and air-conditioned. Local educational, and social events of general interests became regular fare in the mall area.

Ground-breaking ceremonies on November 2, 1967, was the beginning of Georgetown Square Shopping Center on the northeast side of the community. The center, originally comprising 60,000 square feet of shopping space, underwent almost continuous expansion beyond the six-acre site in subsequent years. Georgetown, on East State Blvd., was developed by Jehl Bros., Inc. headed by Thomas, Paul C. and Leo Jehl. Located at the center were Lincoln National Bank, Rogers Market, Franklin Variety, two theatres and other stores and service shops. Branches of the Public Library and First Federal Savings and Loan were built. A major addition was completed in 1973, bringing the number of business establishments to 45. Stores included Hutners, Stucky Brothers, Ream-Steckbeck, Reader's World Bookstore, Keltsch Pharmacy and others. In early American design, the shopping center was built by William Cranmer, general contractor. The architect was Humbrecht, Sherbondy and Associates. Expanding shopping centers were established at Maplecrest Road and State Road 37 northeast—the Maplewood Shopping Center; The Canterbury Green Shopping Center, St. Joe and St. Joe Center Roads near the Canterbury Green Apartment Complex; the Washington Square Shopping Center at North Clinton and Washington Center Roads; and the Times Corner Shopping Center, started by Charles Weyrick at U.S. 24 West and Covington Road.

Changing Downtown Activity

By the mid-1960's, fewer people were going downtown for shopping purposes but more were going for other business and government purposes. Years earlier, the central business district of the city was heavily devoted to retail business. Office, government and other commercial uses were relatively small by comparison. According to studies by the Downtown Fort Wayne Association, 70 per cent of the downtown area in 1950 was devoted to retailing. In the same era the office interests occupied about 20 per cent and government about 10 per cent of downtown land. By 1966, the pattern was clearly different. Retailing was using about 50 per cent of the property, financial, professional and offices were occupying about 30 per cent and government and education, about 20 per cent. In the early 1970s, retailing was a minority use, and offices, financial institutions, cultural, educational and government uses comprised approximately 60 per cent. Yet, building by both private and public interests continued in the central area. The new Sheraton Inn was built in 1968 at the corner of Washington Blvd. and Lafayette Street. The modern hotel dramatically changed the east downtown appearance. John Truemper, president of Schinnerer & Truemper, Inc., the builders, described the construction of the

13-story hotel as a pre-cast concrete method which would raise the superstructure in 90 days. The ground breaking of the $3.75 million project of Fort Wayne Investment Co. was in August, 1967. It had 225 rooms and swimming pool. The hotel filed bankruptcy proceedings in 1971 and later was sold for approximately $2,750,000 to a partnership headed by David P. Schenkel.

Public Housing

In August, 1967, the city's design for the 100-unit Beacon Heights apartments received Federal approval from the Chicago Regional Office of the Department of Housing and Urban Development. The program for the elderly was a project of the Fort Wayne Housing Authority. The apartments were on the city's northeast side on Beacon St. near Hobson Drive just south of East State Boulevard. The one-bedroom efficiency apartments for elderly individuals and couples featured a community and craft center. The development on a two-acre plot was near shopping, transportation and medical service. The cost, in excess of $1 million, was mostly in Federal funds. Federal approval for 97 units of the McCormick Place improvement was received in July, 1968. The one and two-story buildings cost a total of $1,250,000 in Federal funds. The site was at Edsall Ave., Schele Ave. and McCormick Avenue. The new apartment complex replaced the old "tin village" which had previously existed at the location since the early 1940s. Included in the McCormick Place development were homes ranging from one to five bedrooms and a community building for children's play and social activities. The first of the Brookmill Court units were ready for occupancy in early 1969. The 25 units were part of a 108-family public housing complex eventually built on the south side of the Covington Road, a quarter of a mile west of Brooklyn Avenue. The total cost of the Federally-assisted project was $1.8 million. Families displaced by urban renewal in other parts of the city were given first priority for occupying the new Brookmill units. The 18 townhouse type buildings were arranged in clusters, usually three or four, and placed around a community building in the 11-acre tract. Rents depended on the tenents' ability to pay. The board of the Commission at the time of the project included Dr. N. L. Salon, chairman; Otto H. Adams, secretary and executive director; and Robert Troutman, Jackson Lehman, Albert Jennings, Dorent Elliott, Robert Meyers and Lloyd Neuman.

Some Hot Days

The Metropolitan Human Relations Commission was created by an ordinance of the City Council and came into existence on July 1, 1970. The aims of the commission were to foster healthy relations among the various cultural, racial, ethnic, social and religious groups in the city; and to advise and assist departments in assuring justice and equal opportunity for citizens of Fort Wayne. The Human Relations Commission was a successor to the Mayor's Commission on Human Rights which had existed for some 10 years. The making of the Commission a regular branch of City government was stimulated by events in the summer of 1966. A series of marches on City Hall and downtown posed the potential for violence as was being experienced in many urban centers. On July 2, 1966, more than 600 chanting demonstrators in a heated mood paraded in 100-degree temperatures to Wayne and Calhoun Streets for a rally and speeches. It was the fourth consecutive demonstration in as many days, but not the last as several more confrontations occurred in following days. The principal organizer of the demonstrations was the Rev. Jesse White. City Councilman John Nuchols, the Rev. Ralph Larson and others spoke at the rallies. In the wake of the events, Mayor Harold Zeis announced the city could seek added employment opportunities for Negroes, recruitment for Police and Fire Departments, better street lighting in the east end, a crackdown on prostitution and Negro representation on the School Board. Another step was the naming of Dr. Huey Pearson to the Redevelopment Commission. A potential crisis occurred on the Labor Day weekend of 1970. The mayor declared a city-wide curfew on two successive nights. Trouble was limited to a few teenage gangs breaking in store fronts along Lewis St. and damage to equipment of a radio station. On the nights of the curfew, Sept. 5 and 6, the city looked like "a virtual ghost town" according to a newspaper comment. An event with potential trouble-making possibilities was on Palm Sunday, 1971, at Foster Park. More than a thousand young people were running about and causing disturbances in the general area of the park. There was a mob-like quality to the gathering which was dispersed by city police with some difficulty. Successive executive secretaries of the Human Relations Commission were Alvin Wesley, Carl Benson, James W. Bryant and Ralph Larson.

In the effort to protect the rivers and streams, the Three Rivers Pollution Control Board was created in 1968, with staff furnished by the Board of Public Health. Dr. Oliver Kaiser was designated water pollution officer to inforce safe standards and was also named air pollution control officer.

Workers at General Electric leave plant gates on Broadway on a hot summer afternoon during era of full employment. The metropolitan population jumped 26 percent between 1950 and 1960.

POPULATION CHARACTERISTICS

1960 CENSUS

	Metro Area	Urbanized Area	Fort Wayne
Number	232,196	179,571	161,776
% Increase from 1950	26.4%	28.0%	21.1%
% Non-White	5.2%	6.7%	7.4%
% Under 18	37.5%	36.2%	35.4%
% 18-64	54.1%	55.0%	55.2%
% 65 and Over	8.4%	8.9%	9.4%
Male 14 and Over % Married	72.5%	72.0%	71.2%
Female 14 and Over % Married	67.0%	65.1%	63.9%
18 years old and over % male	47.5%	46.9%	46.7%
In Group Quarters	2.4%	2.5%	2.8%

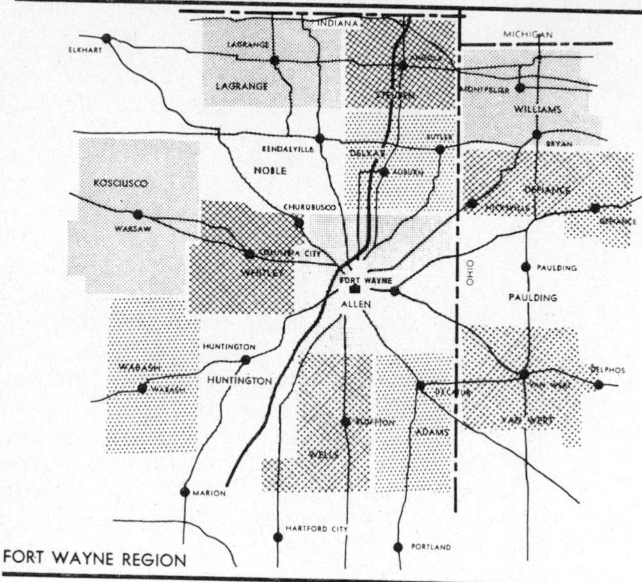

5,000 POPULATION AND OVER

City	Population	Daily Circulation	% Home Coverage	Sunday Circulation	% Home Coverage
Fort Wayne, Ind.	161,776	73,576	100%	41,946	71%
Huntington, Ind.	16,185	3,449	67%	3,018	58%
Defiance, Ohio	14,553	475	11%	795	19%
Wabash, Ind.	12,621	673	17%	949	24%
Van Wert, Ohio	11,323	1,344	37%	1,804	49%
Decatur, Ind.	8,327	2,859	100%	2,672	100%
Hartford City, Ind.	8,053	118	5%	305	12%
Bryan, Ohio	7,361	878	36%	998	41%
Warsaw, Ind.	7,234	1,019	42%	1,344	55%
Portland, Ind.	6,999	898	36%	967	39%
Kendallville, Ind.	6,765	1,780	85%	1,455	69%
Auburn, Ind.	6,350	2,142	100%	1,731	84%
Bluffton, Ind.	6,238	2,065	99%	1,975	95%

2,500 TO 5,000 POPULATION

City	Population	Daily Circulation	% Home Coverage	Sunday Circulation	% Home Coverage
Columbia City, Ind.	4,803	2,557	100%	1,981	100%
Angola, Ind.	4,746	2,316	100%	1,448	100%
North Manchester, Ind.	4,377	1,119	88%	899	71%
Garrett, Ind.	4,364	1,763	100%	1,097	79%
Montpelier, Ohio	4,131	647	46%	497	35%
New Haven, Ind.	3,396	666	70%	352	37%
Hicksville, Ohio	3,116	1,178	100%	910	92%
Paulding, Ohio	2,936	766	84%	710	78%
Berne, Ind.	2,644	1,063	100%	677	80%
Ligonier, Ind.	2,595	750	86%	522	60%

1,500 TO 2,500 POPULATION

City	Population	Daily Circulation	% Home Coverage	Sunday Circulation	% Home Coverage
Butler, Ind.	2,176	1,033	100%	610	90%
LaGrange, Ind.	1,990	1,007	100%	603	94%
Montpelier, Ind.	1,954	258	40%	312	48%
Winona Lake, Ind.	1,928	152	24%	103	16%
Syracuse, Ind.	1,595	431	80%	452	84%

Sources: 1960 U. S. Census—A. B. C. Audit Report 12/31/62

Map and census table shows towns of the area. Below is the major Decatur plant of Central Soya.

The mature set in crazy hats gathered at the Jefferson Center on Sept. 11, 1960. Below is the City Parking Garage and Indiana Bank & Trust Co. as it looked in 1961, soon after the building was completed along Clinton St. To the right across Washington Blvd. is the old 1908 stone building of the Scottish Rite Cathedral which was razed in 1967. The new Scottish Rite Building at Berry St. and Fairfield Ave. was dedicated in November, 1964. At the bottom of the page is the old Centlivre Hotel, later known as the Milner Hotel, a railroaders stopover, just before wrecking in 1963, and Mayor Burns and the last trolley bus riders on June 10, 1960.

Shoppers cross the street at Clinton and Wayne on a busy day in 1961. The block-long Wolf and Dessauer Department Store building opened in 1959. It later became part of Ayres group of department stores. On the opposite page is the great W&D fire just as it was getting a good start on Feb. 10, 1962. The flames raged on into the night, taking three store buildings on the north side of Washington Blvd. between Calhoun and Clinton, and for a period threatened the whole block.

27
33
1
3
30
24
37
14

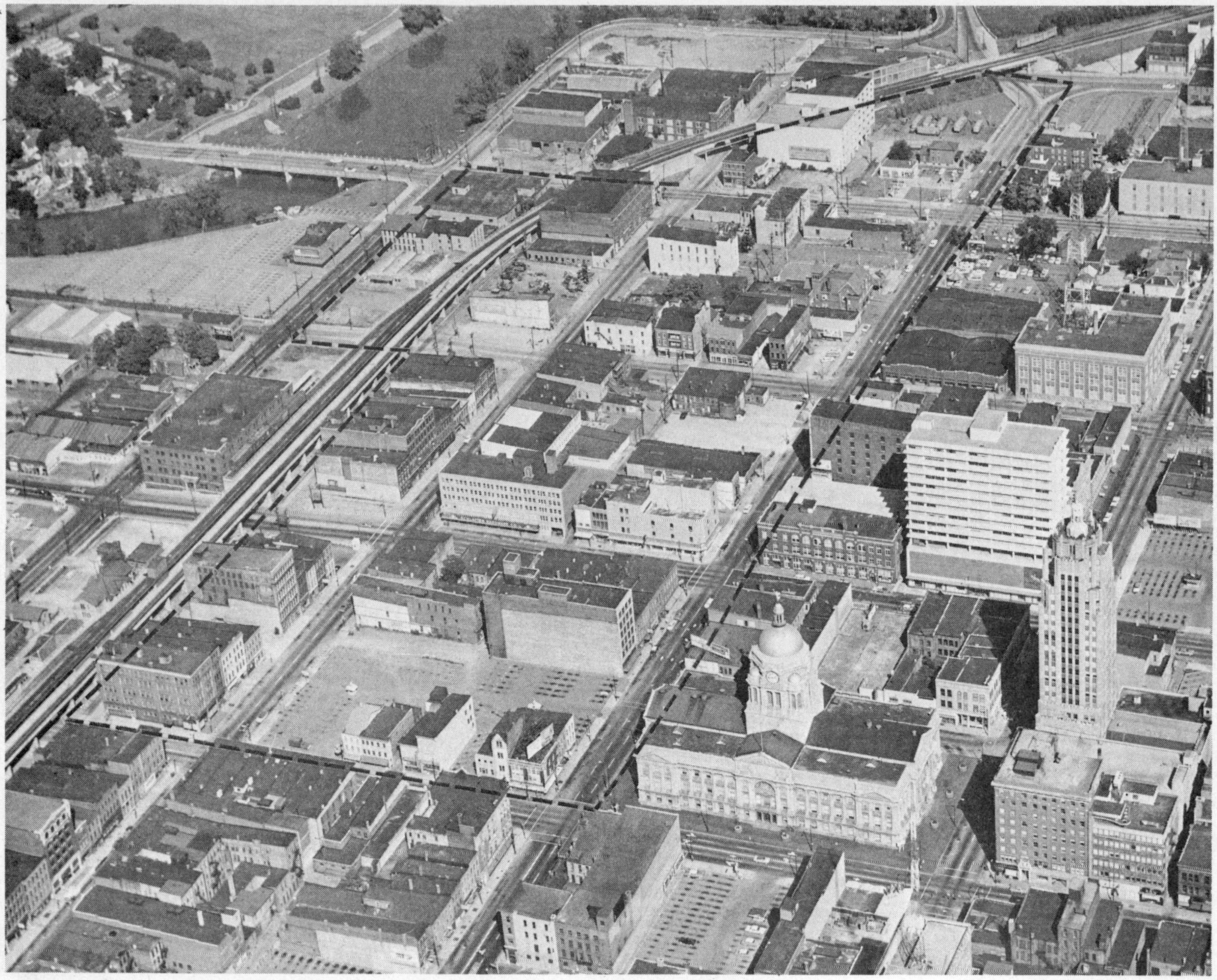

This view from the air shows part of the downtown area as it looked in 1964 with Courthouse, Lincoln Bank Tower and the recently-completed Anthony Wayne Bank Building at right-center. The doted area north-east of Main and Calhoun Streets and the area beyond to the rivers was marked for razing and redevelopment. The first new major buildings were the Three Rivers Apartments, shown at left.

A closer look at what disappeared in the Main St. Redevelopment Project. At top is a rat haven along old Columbia St. The street itself at this location soon disappeared. Middle: Some store fronts along Columbia. The Hedekin House (Home Hotel) and other Canal Era structures were swept away. At bottom is a view from Main and Calhoun where the City-County Building was later built.

Vice Presidential candidate William Miller on the 1964 campaign stop with Congressman E. Ross Adair at right.

Crewcut lads in another kind of race.

The Fort Wayne Newspapers Building on West Main St. buried under the big snow of Feb. 25, 1965. The building, the home of The News-Sentinel and the Journal Gazette, was completed in 1958.

The new nine-story Broadway wing of St. Joseph Hospital was going up in 1964, just before the old hospital building was taken down. Sisters Margery and Arnoldine rescue a relic from the old chapel which has just been removed in the photo above.

Something less than choice homesites in the Rolling Mill area are shown just before redevelopment. Steel for the Joslyn Stainless Steel plant points skyward in 1967 at the site near Taylor St. Below, some characters watch the removal of familiar places.

The Mutual Security Life Insurance Co. along Coliseum Blvd.

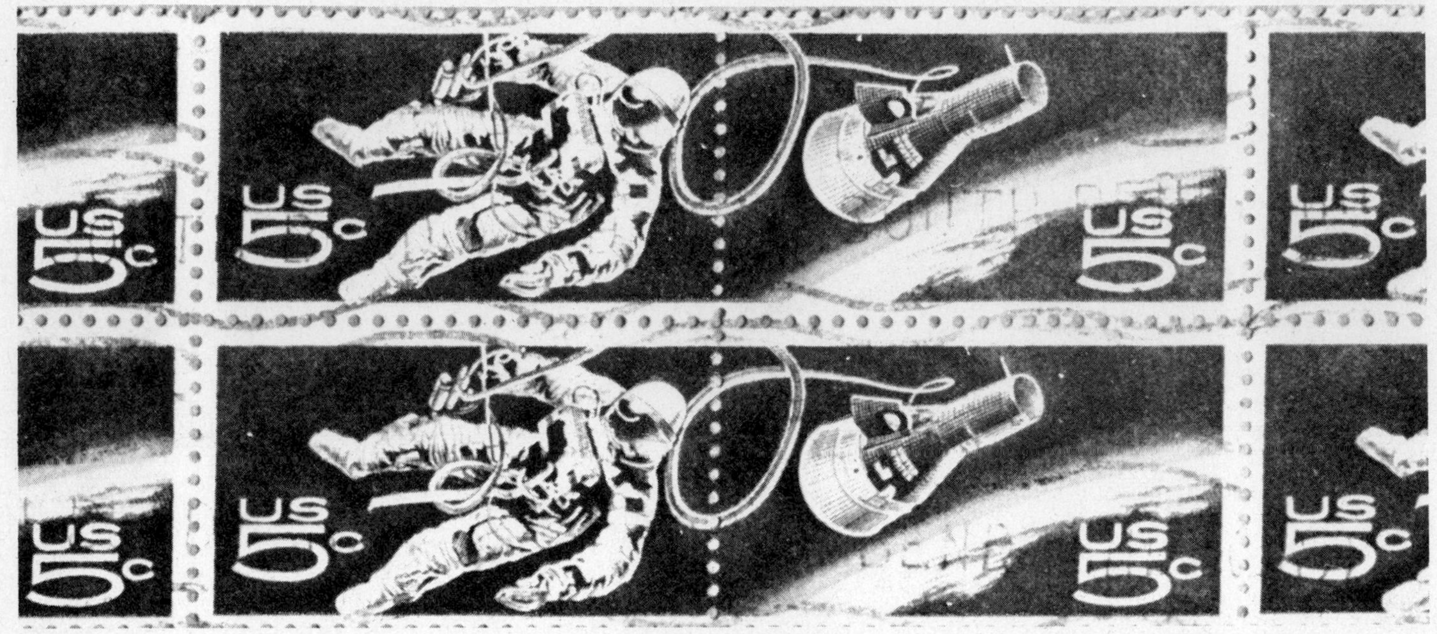

A U.S. Postage Stamp issue marked the space walk of Edward H. White on June 3, 1965. Astronaut White, of an old Fort Wayne family, was the first man to step into space. Two years later he was killed during a rocket misfire preparatory to the moon mission.

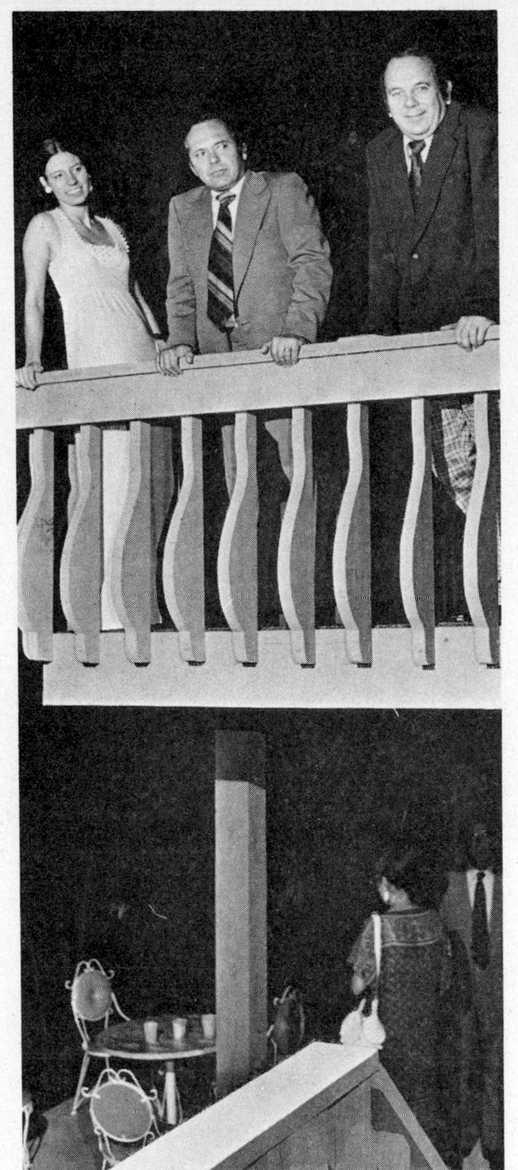

Casual observers of the Parade of Homes look from a balcony. The Parade drew thousands during the 1950s, 1960s and 1970s.

Bicycling on the south side of town.

Skilled Wildcat League action in 1963.

Sledding on the north side after a heavy snow in 1963.

The Lutheran Hospital was expanded almost continually during the 1960s. Note the additional floors on the picture at right compared with the scene at top, both on the Fairfield Ave. side of the hospital. The Moellering Unit was built along South Wayne Ave. to the rear of this structure.

A bit of old city was preserved in the gaslight atmosphere of The Landing at 100 West Columbia St. At left, the Three Rivers Apartment Buildings and the Filtration Plant on either side of rivers.

This 1967 view of Calhoun St. going south from Wayne St. was a landscape quickly changing. On the right, below, is a photo of the suburban headquarters of the Midwestern United Life Insurance Co. along U.S. 24 West. Directly below, Mayor Zeis gives a grimace and heave to the first dirt for the sewerage ponds near Lakeside. With him, from the left, are Marshall Wetsell, Jerry Kannane, Fred Ehrman and Robert Dahman.

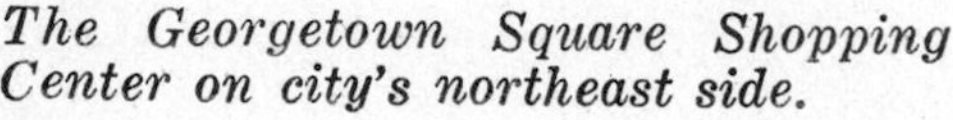

The Georgetown Square Shopping Center on city's northeast side.

Newsmen record the start of the 26-story Fort Wayne National Bank Building in 1967.

Fort Wayne National's hole as it looked on March 10, 1967, with the old bank and the Van Orman Hotel in the background. Bank planners at left include: seated, Russell Daane, and from left, Dale W. McMillen, Jr., John D. Shoaff, Paul Shaffer, Harley Jenson, Mayor Harold Zeis and Joseph Miller.

Government Plans War On Pep Pills, Goofballs—Page 4A

CLOUDY, COLDER TONIGHT
SNOW, CLOUDY FRIDAY

The News-Sentinel

CITY EDITION

FORT WAYNE, INDIANA, 46802 THURSDAY, FEBRUARY 3, 1966

50 PAGES—4 SECTIONS

BLAST RIPS BROADWAY AREA

[IN]FERNO ON BROADWAY—Flames shoot skyward where houses at 3328 and 3404 Broadway formerly stood. Explosions at 10:21 a.m. demolished both houses today. This view is looking west from Kinsmoor Ave. Three women, including two residing in the destroyed houses, were injured. Houses on the north and south side of the those destroyed caught fire as well as the house on the east side of the street at 3401 Broadway. A service station sign near middle right of picture was blown out by the blast.

3 Injured, 5 Homes Destroyed as Police Evacuate 16 Blocks

(OTHER PICTURES ON PAGE 4B)

By JOHN ANKENBRUCK, JERRY GRAFF, AL CAHILL AND ROBERT THOMPSON . . .

A series of two or more natural gas explosions shortly after 10 a.m. today blasted two homes to splinters, completely destroyed three other houses, and sent three women to the hospital with critical or serious burns.

In addition to the five homes destroyed, several others were damaged in varying degrees either by fire, water, or flying debris, and police and firemen evacuated an area of about 16 square blocks between the 2900 and 3600 blocks of Broadway, and Broadway and Beaver Ave.

Seriously or critically burned were:

Mrs. Dorothy Swain, 47, 3330 Broadway.

Mrs. Regina Otis, 38, 3406 Broadway.

Mrs. Clara Shipley, 77, 3404 Broadway.

At 1:30 p.m., the condition of Mrs. Swain was reported critical by hospital attaches, and the conditions of Mrs. Shipley and Mrs. Otis were said to be "serious."

Although the exact sequence of events was difficult to reconstruct, Fire Department records indicated their first call was received at 10:22 a.m., reporting an explosion at a manhole in the street at Broadway and Kinsmoor Ave.

While fire units were en route to the scene, perhaps a minute or two later, the William Shipley residence, 3404 Broadway, and the Arthur Swain residence, 3330 Broadway, were blown apart and fire erupted in nearby houses.

All available police and private ambulances in the city were rushed to the scene, and it was feared for a time that five children had been caught in the exploding homes.

However, Mayor Harold Zeis said that a search by firemen indicated there were no children in the two homes, and it later was reported that the children were safe at neighbors.

Homes destroyed or severely damaged by fire included those at 3401 Broadway, 3328 Broadway, and 324 Broadway. In addition, several other homes in the vicinity were damaged by flames or flying debris.

The Board of Public Safety immediately issued an order for the evacuation of houses in a 16-block area in the vicinity of the explosion, since firemen feared that gas accumulations might occur in them and result in a chain of blasts.

Firemen broke out windows in nearby houses to speed ventilation, and residents of other

(Turn to Page 13A, Column 1)

Mossler Handyman's Testimony Shakes Aunt Candy's Calm

By H. D. QUIGGS

MIAMI (UPI) — Mrs. Candace Mossler grimaced and whispered nervously to her attorney today when a Negro handyman calmly uttered the testimony which the state regards as the key in its attempt to send her and her darkly handsome nephew and alleged lover, Melvin Lane Powers, to the electric chair.

Testifying as the fifth state witness in the 14th day of the trial, Roscoe Brown, a 17-year employe of the Mosslers, told how he scrubbed kitchen surfaces with soap and water the afternoon before the post-midnight stab-murder of multimillionaire Jacques Mossler, 69, Candy's husband.

Under questioning by State Attorney Arthur E. Huttoe, who was admonished once by Judge George E. Schulz for leading the witness, Brown told of two telephone calls in which Mrs. Mossler implored him to "tell the truth" and say that he did not clean the kitchen.

It was on a surface which Brown says he cleaned a few hours before the murder that fingerprint experts, dusting after the murder, found a palm print of Powers. That is circumstantial evidence with which the state hopes to tie the six-foot three-inch figure of 29-year-old Powers into the minds of the all-male jury as the murderer.

Brown, a middle-aged man in a blue suit, began his testimony by pointing an indentifying finger at the impassive Powers at the defense counsel table.

The slaying took place at 1:45 a.m., June 30, 1964, the state contends. In mid-July, Brown said, while Mrs. Mossler was in Rochester, Minn., he got a phone call from her.

"She told me to tell the truth, and that the day I went over

(Turn to Page 13A, Column 3)

House Panel Okays New G.I. Benefits

Permanent Housing, Education Benefits Provided in Bill

WASHINGTON (AP) — A new GI bill offering permanent education and loan benefits for men and women serving in the armed forces was approved today by the House Veterans Committee.

The bill would affect immediately 3.5 million veterans who served since early in 1955, the date benefits for Korean War veterans ended.

The first-year cost for the bill was estimated at $355 million, far more than the administration has proposed. The administration is backing a bill that would limit benefits to veterans who served in dangerous areas.

Chairman Olin E. Teague, D-Tex., said the committee approved the bill unanimously, although Republicans made numerous attempts to increase the benefits.

The bill would provide:

— Up to 36 months of education or training, on the basis of one month for each month spent in the service.

— Allowances of $100 a month for single veterans, $125 for [illegible]

(Turn to Page 13A, [illegible]

U.S. Planes Bomb Red Points in North

[SAIGON] (UPI) — U.S. planes [pierc]ing North Viet Nam anti-aircraft and missile defenses strengthened during the 37-day bombing lull hit military targets 60 miles northwest of Hanoi today. In the ground war [fou]r major offensives had put more than 3,000 Communists out of action.

The biggest success was scored by troops of the U.S. 1st Cavalry Division in "Operation Masher" along the coast 300 miles northeast of Saigon. The operation inflicted an estimated 800 casualties on the enemy of which 707 were confirmed dead. The total estimated dead was

It was the second highest toll ever inflicted on Viet Cong and North Vietnamese regulars. The 1st Cavalry killed 1,500 Communists, including most of two North Viet Nam regiments, in the Ia Drang Valley and on the slopes of Chu Pong Mountain last November. Estimates there were 2,000 dead. That was the heaviest loss ever suffered by the North Vietnamese.

"Operation Masher" was renamed Operation White Wing today, perhaps signalling a new phase of a campaign that also netted 120 Viet Cong captured, 906 suspects detained and an estimated 300 or more wounded.

The two other offensives were Operation Van Buren by the 101st Airborne. To date it has killed 343 Viet Cong and detained 493 suspects in fighting along the coast below the 1st Cavalry section. Operation Mallet carried out by U.S. 1st Infantry troops 25 miles southeast of Saigon has killed an estimated 80 to 90 Viet Cong including two today.

American losses in the four offensives were described as light to moderate.

Two New Missions

U.S. Air Force F105 fighter-bombers streaked through low clouds on two missions over North Viet Nam today in the fourth day of raids since the lull ended Monday.

On one mission the Thunderchiefs sank or set fire to two barges on the Song Ma River 60 miles northwest of Hanoi, the northernmost strike since resumption of the raids.

A spokesman said U.S. Navy planes in Wednesday attacks sank a North Vietnamese patrol boat 40 miles south of the key port city of Haiphong. Most of the other raids were further south where Air Force planes hit a storage area near the port city of Vinh while Navy planes pounded highways and other communications.

Hundreds of American, South Vietnamese and South Korean troops have been participating in the coastal sweep 300 miles northeast of Saigon since last Friday.

The highest previous enemy death toll was 699 in the U.S.

(Turn to Page 13A, Column 2)

Chief Lupke Saw Blast From Truck

By SAM JACOBS

"I came around the corner and all of a sudden I heard a terrific explosion. I looked and saw two houses on the west side of Broadway in flames and a wall of flame stretching all the way across the street."

This was the way Fort Wayne Fire Chief Martin Lupke, an eyewitness to the explosions and fires which injured three persons and destroyed five homes in the area of Broadway and Kinsmoor Ave., described the scene.

Lupke was at Fire Station No. 11 at Rudisill Blvd. and Lafayette St. when the call came in that there had been a gas explosion. He hitched a ride on one of the fire trucks and got there just as the second explosion occurred.

Immediately all of the ladder trucks in the city were called to the scene as well as three pump trucks.

Flames by this time has spread from the original two where the fire has occurred — that of Mrs. William Shipley, 3404 Broadway

(Turn to Page 13A, Column 3)

Aides Crowd Emergency Corridor

By ELIZABETH WILLIAMS

The emergency corridor of Lutheran Hospital was crowded with aides and nurses following the explosion in a residential neighborhood a few blocks away.

Three people had been brought in from the ambulance entrance and immediately were wheeled into emergency rooms to be worked on by teams of doctors and nurses.

Those in the corridor gathered in clusters, talking in hushed whispers and apprehensively glancing at the double glass doors for more disaster patients to be brought in.

A crisp voice came over the loud-speaker system.

"There will be no smoking, please, in the hospital area. Absolutely no smoking anywhere in the hospital."

The guard at the emergency entrance shook his head and said, "Just three, but all of them women, and they looked pretty badly burned. One was worse than the others — her hair, face, legs and arms were bad."

He told how the first two had been brought in by squad car right after the explosion. The

(Turn to Page 13A, Column 3)

Henry Ford Daughter's 'Expecting'

ST. MORITZ, Switzerland (UPI) — Automobile heiress Charlotte Ford Niarchos is expecting a baby this summer, her secretary announced today.

Miss Ford, daughter of Henry Ford II, and Greek shipping magnate Stavros Niarchos have been honeymooning in St. Moritz since their marriage in Mexico Dec. 16.

Neither Niarchos nor his bride were available for comment, but the secretary said Mrs. Niarchos plans to have the baby in New York, where her mother lives.

Hedy Lamarr Fired From Starring Role

HOLLYWOOD (AP) — Hedy Lamarr has been fired from her first starring role since 1951, the film's producer said today.

Bert I. Gordon said he took the action not because of the actress' arrest last week on a shoplifting charge but because "nervous exhaustion" has made her unavailable.

A spokesman for Gordon said the producer was negotiating with Merle Oberon, now in Mexico, to replace Miss Lamarr. Miss Oberon, like Miss Lamarr, was a reigning star of Hollywood's golden era of the 30s.

"With a picture costing in excess of $1 million, it is impossible financially to delay production any longer on Miss Lamarr's scenes," Gordon said.

He added that a car was sent to pick up the 51-year-old screen beauty Wednesday, but the driver was told by a housekeeper that Miss Lamarr had entered [We]stwood Hospital due to nervous exhaustion.

Miss Lamarr was to costar with Don Ameche in "Picture Mommy Dead," playing the mother of a 16-year-old. The script called for her to be burned to death.

She was arrested a week ago in the parking lot of a Los Angeles department store and accused of petty theft of items totaling $86. She was due for arraignment Wednesday but her attorney was granted a one-week continuance of the case.

Funds Sought for Safe Car

WASHINGTON (UPI) — Sen. Abraham A. Ribicoff, D-Conn., predicted today that there would be enough funds in President Johnson's forthcoming safety program for development of a prototype safety car.

Ribicoff made the prediction after New York State legislators showed a Senate subcommittee plans for a safety car which they said could save at least 200,000 lives in the next 10 years.

The New York legislators [illegible]

designed to prevent most injuries and deaths, even in a head-on collision between cars doing 50 miles an hour.

State Sen. Edward J. Speno asked the federal government to quickly provide $3.6 million to help his state design, make and crash test the proposed vehicle.

The plans were eagerly adopted by members of Ribicoff's Senate executive reorganization subcommittee.

Ribicoff said the President [illegible]

within a few days a safety program which would include a substantial fund for research.

He said this fund would include enough money for the prototype and added that the project should get priority.

Sen. Jacob K. Javits, R-N.Y., said he and Sen. Robert F. Kennedy, D-N.Y., will introduce within a few days a bill to provide federal sponsorship of the project.

At the end of the hearing, Kennedy suggested that the [illegible]

in 5 per cent of their profits to help design the safety car.

The New Yorkers doubted that the manufacturers would agree to contribute but Kennedy said "Let's ask."

Speno, Chananau, and state Sen. Simon J. Liebowitz made their presentation to the Senate executive reorganization subcommittee, which is holding hearings on the federal role in traffic safety.

Chananau said "We have proof that a car can be built [illegible]

that will prevent 75 per cent of injuries and fatalities at crash-impacts of 50 miles an hour, 75 per cent in side collisions, 90 per cent in rollover accidents, and 90 per cent when a car runs into the rear of another."

The feasibility study was conducted by the Republic Aviation Division of the Fairchild Hiller Corporation with $100,000 appropriated by the New York Legislature.

Today's Reading Guide

LeMay Raps U.S. Policy

Retired Air Force General Says More Expensive Targets Should Be Hit in North Viet Nam, Page 1C.

WILLIAM C. FOSTER, U.S. DELEGATE TO DISARMAMENT CONFERENCE IN GENEVA, GREETED SOVIET PREMIER ALEXEI N. KOSYGIN'S ATOMIC CURB PROPOSAL: "We welcome the interest shown by Premier Kosygin in the work of the disarmament committee. The message will be studied with care." Story on Page 10D.

William C. Foster

SIR PATRICK DEAN, BRITISH AMBASSADOR TO THE U.S., IN EXPLAINING BRITAIN'S REASON FOR CONDUCTING A SMALL AMOUNT OF TRADE WITH NORTH VIET NAM: "—even if it is with countries with which we disagree very much. Trade is one of the ways of breaking down barriers." Story on Page 12A.

★ WELL WORTH YOUR READING TIME ★

The weight of public opinion throughout the world is the one key factor that could force the United Nations to take over an active role in the Viet Nam peace offensive, Columnist David Lawrence writes on Page 7-A.

National poll discloses big majority of public, including rank-and-file union members, oppose President Johnson's proposed repeal of 14B — the right-to-work law, according to Columnist William F. Buckley, Jr. on Page 7-A.

Lebanon's pact for French jets pushes Arab air forces near the same level as Israel, and girds the UAC for a military showdown with the Tel Aviv government by 1970. Story on Page 10A.

Amusements	2B, 3B	David Lawrence	7A
Area News	4B, 5B	Life Begins at 40	7A
William F. Buckley	7A	Markets	7D, 8D
Comics	6B	Radio-TV Programs	2C, 3C
Crossword Puzzle	7C	Roesner, Elmer	8D
Daily Investor	8D	Society	2D, 3D, 5D
Deaths	6D	Sports	4C, 5C, 6C, 7C
Editorials	6A	Statistical Summary	13A
Good Evening, C. B. Ward	1D	Weather Map	1B
Russell Kirk	6A	Woman's Page	4D

Today's Chuckle

A camping enthusiast pays good money to do all the things he griped about in the Army.

THE WEATHER

NORTHERN INDIANA — Partly cloudy tonight with a low between 10 and 18. Partly cloudy Friday with a chance of some snow flurries. High Friday 25 to 32. Saturday's outlook calls for partly cloudy with little temperature change and some snow flurries near Lake Michigan.

OHIO—Increasing cloudiness tonight with a low of 10 to 18. Considerably cloudy Friday with light snow and turning a little colder.

MICHIGAN—Mostly cloudy with light snow or snow flurries probable tonight and Friday. Low tonight 10 to 15. Turning a little colder Friday.

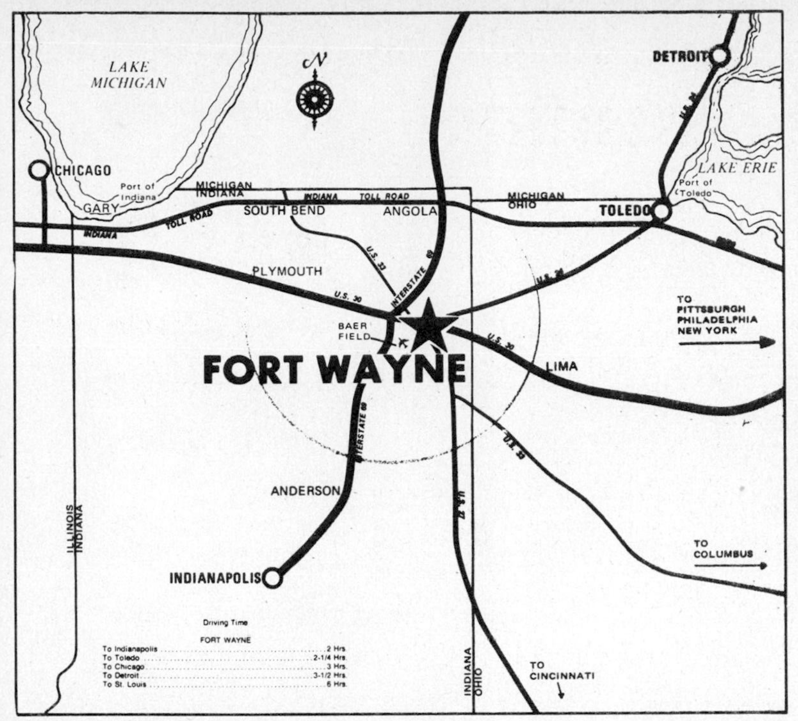

Major Roads of Tri-State Area, and jet transportation comes to Baer Field in 1967.

The Southtown Mall interior, above, and the architect's drawing of Southtown, at left, became part of the local picture in 1967 The Glenbrook Center, on the north side, below, was two years older.

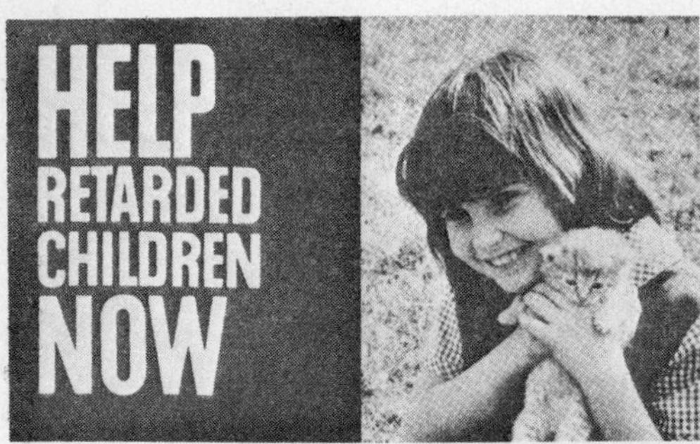

Kim Fisher of the Johnny Appleseed School was National Poster Child of 1967.

Van Cliburn here in 1968.

Bishop Leo A. Pursley and Auxiliary Bishop Joseph Crowley.

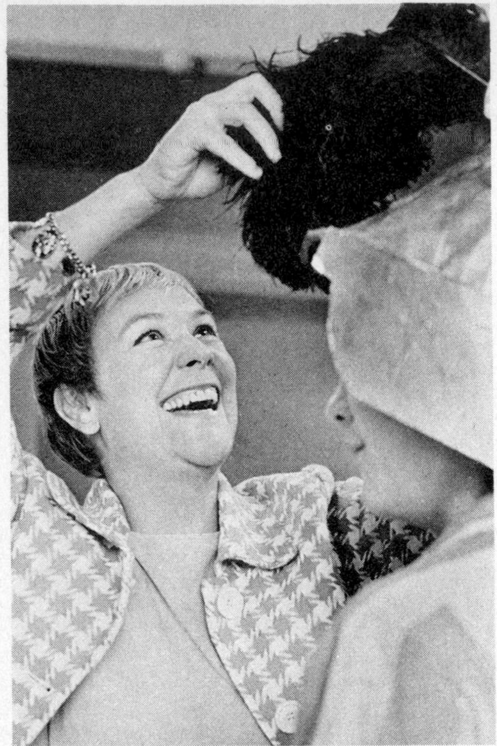

Jean Warfield of Civic Theatre adjusts a costume in 1968.

Sen. Robert Kennedy takes a stroll at Baer Field, May 5, 1968, during the Presidential primary.

Public Transportation Corp. was formed by the city in 1968 and women drivers followed. At left at International Harvester in 1970, a milestone: from the left, G. C. Berg, William Rodgers and Rex Bear of the UAW, Works Manager H. A. Ehrman, and R. L. McCaffrey. Pictured below is a little girl in the spring sun at Lakeside, May 2, 1968.

The new Library Building was going up in September, 1967. At the cornerstone laying on Oct. 29, 1967, were Dr. Paul Krauss, Mayor Zeis and Head Librarian Fred J. Reynolds, left to right. Below, the Library dedication along Webster St. on Aug. 21, 1968.

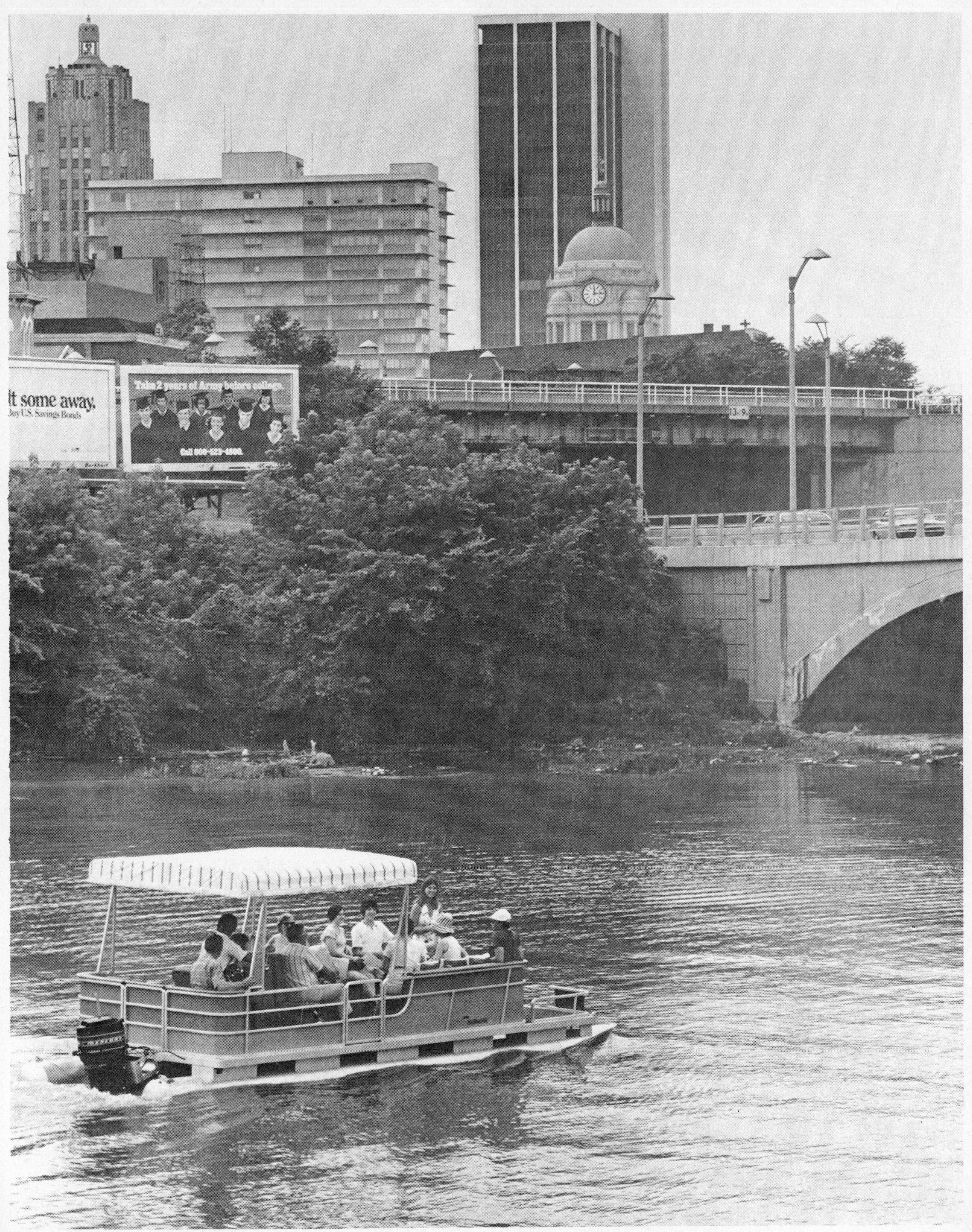
lt some away.
Buy U.S. Savings Bonds
Take 2 years of Army before college.

Part 14
Festivals and Easy Money

While the Redevelopment Commission was taking down the old to make way for the new in the Main St. area, that part of Fort Wayne's old downtown looked like a good place to make war movies. There was enough debris, stark walls and empty space to roll a few tanks and support a troop of snipers. Old Columbia St., the town's center of activity in the days of the Wabash-Erie Canal, was being erased from the scene, except for one block west of Calhoun Street. During the days of wrecking in the winter months of 1967 and 1968, hardly a day went by without some ancient commission house or other structure once associated with canal trade biting the dust. Many of the old buildings had had their day in the sun. One of the buildings leveled was at the northwest corner of Columbia and Lafayette Streets. This was a pile of brick, wood and mortar which had almost as many lives as the rats which occupied the neighborhood. In the final decades of its existence, it was the home of Rescue Mission. Back in the 1890s and early 1900s the activities of the Victorian structure had a rather scarlet hue. Old folks were still around in 1968 who remembered passing the place on their way to school when they were children at the Turn of the Century. In those early days the children would gawk at the prostitute types leaning out the windows or sitting around laughing near the back entrance during off hours. Still earlier, the building was a four-story hotel catering to the canal trade. People, such as Tom Edison, likely walked by it daily in the Civil War days. With the other brick buildings, such as the old blacksmith shops, fruit houses, feed shops, junk yards, lofts which once had been woolen mills and decaying warehouses, it all came down. The rats, which possibly were descendants of those coming in with the canal packet boats of old, were the last to move out. As iron balls of wrecking crews began to crash in old walls, the rats could be seen on dreary winter mornings scurrying across the ancient brick street to seek new homes. After 1968, possibly the rats were the only living link to most of old Columbia St. where a century and a half earlier the world's longest canal had its birth.

The Landing

One block of Columbia St. was saved—the part from Calhoun to Harrison St. which became known as The Landing. That name was chosen because the canal turnaround and docks were once at the northeast corner of Columbia and Harrison. The prospect of complete demolition of old Fort Wayne was viewed with alarm by some in the community; and the effort of salvaging a small portion was stimulated by Mrs. Edward (Joan) White and historian Roy M. Bates. An initial architectural survey was made in the fall of 1963 by the senior class of the Notre Dame School of Architecture. In September, 1964, Mayor Harold Zeis named a commission for preservation and restoration. Mrs. White headed the commission. Others playing a role in restoring the block included Fred Reynolds, Edward Kane, Edward Dodez, Ruth Whearley, Kenneth Keller, James Fleming, John E. Arnold, William Jones, Troy Yeoman, Fred Ehrman, the City Park Department, Northern Indiana Public Service Co. and many people and firms volunteering services and material. Gas lights were installed and trees were planted. The dedication of The Landing with a torchlight parade was on Oct. 23, 1965.

The elections in 1966 were a sweep for Republicans in both Allen County and in the state. E. Ross Adair was returned to Congress with a vote in the county of 49,516 compared with a vote of 27,387 for his Democratic opponent, J. Byron Hayes.

New Library

On August 21, 1968, the new Fort Wayne Public Library was dedicated. The modern two-story building with white vertical concrete formation and dark vertical windows extended from Wayne St. to Washington Blvd. and had its main entrance on Webster Street. It was a focal point on the downtown's west side and a part of the central city rebirth. It was described as "a major environmental element in the fabric of the city" by Carl L. Bradley of Bradley and Bradley architects. Library Board President Charles Slater, Mayor Zeis and Chief Librarian Fred Reynolds presided at the placing of the cornerstone. The total cost of the library was $4,120,000, a figure which included the site, the building costs, the equipment and furnishings. With a total area of 173,000 square feet, the building extended 294 feet along Webster St., 121 feet on Wayne St. and 247 feet on Washington Boulevard. Housing one of the finest community libraries in the nation, the building had reading and study space for approximately 600 persons and meeting rooms for an additional 227. Provided was open shelf space for 222,000 volumes and closed stack and storage space for 1,278,000 volumes. In the storehouse of knowledge were convenient facilities for adult research and study, a west wing for school use of junior and senior high school students; colorful atmosphere for children; a department for books and periodicals of a business and technical nature; and a gallery for fine arts, including material on painting, sculpture, music and a loan program of art works. The library contained an historical genealogy department of unusual depth, developed over the years by Fred Reynolds and members of the staff. It was regarded as one of the three most extensive genealogy collections in the United States. Microfilm equipment and records of publications and materials, and a technical processes department were included to encourage continuing renewal of library wealth and use. Fred Reynolds succeeded Rex Potterf as head librarian in 1960. The new library replaced a library building of Greek revival architecture which stood at the corner of Wayne and Webster since 1904. To make way for the new library, the old structure was razed and the library was housed in the old Purdue Building at Jefferson and Barr Streets from 1965 to 1968. The general contractor for the library was C. A. Lehman & Sons. Basic financing of the building was a $2,900,000 bond issue in 1964. The library board at the time included Charles E. Slater, Allan J. Tremper, Arthur J. Meyer, Helen Knobluch, Phillip Sanborn, Willard Shambaugh and Florence A. Buirley, secretary.

Presidential contenders beat paths across Fort Wayne in 1968. Senator Eugene McCarthy gave a witty talk at the Gridiron Banquet in April. Governor Roger Branigan, a stand-in for President Johnson, visited several times. Senator Robert Kennedy took a last ride on the Wabash Cannonball. He came to Fort Wayne on May 6 just a month before he was assassinted on the night of the June California primary. Hubert Humphrey, the eventual Democratic nominee, campaigned in the city. Both Richard Nixon and his Republican running mate, Spiro Agnew, waved to crowds watching their motorcades. When the votes were counted in November, the Nixon-Agnew ticket won easily in Allen County and took the state and national election. Incumbent Congressman E. Ross Adair won election to his 10th and final term by beating Democrat J. Edward Roush by a 55,001 to 50,002 vote in Allen County and carrying the district. At the April Gridiron Dinner at Cutter's Chalet, the Roastmaster was George Kinne, an advertising man who "does this sort of thing as well as I have seen," according to a Boston columnist who saw Kinne in action.

Jets and Buses

On Feb. 21, 1967, Fort Wayne formally entered the jet age with the inauguration of regular jet service by United Air Lines. Actually jet aircraft had been around the city for many years in the hands of the Air National Guard at Baer Field, but the jet service was new to passenger flights. The service was non-stop between Fort Wayne and New York to the east and one-stop (South Bend) to Chicago. Air travel had advanced rapidly in the eight years from 1963 to 1971, with Baer Field handling some 400,000 passengers annually by 1971 compared with 150,000 in 1963. Lengthening of the runways and the installation of newer radar controls and other electronic equipment provided greater safety at the terminal for air transportation. The main trunk lines operating through Fort Wayne were United Air Lines and Delta Air Lines. A new operation, Hub Air Lines, Inc., joined the Fort Wayne service in 1966. Hub, a division of George Bailey Co., Inc., Fort Wayne, provided a feeder service to a number of midwestern metropolitan centers, including Chicago, Detroit, Cincinnati and Indianapolis.

On March 1, 1968, the Fort Wayne Public Transportation Corporation came into existence. Prior to that date the City Council passed legislation for the creation of a tax-subsidized company to provide public transport in the city and the two-mile fringe area. As a practical matter, the city took over the operation of the city bus system from Fort Wayne Transit, Inc., a private company which had operated street car and bus service for many years. Fort Wayne Transit, due to the changing modes of transportation and financial losses on bus service, had notified the city government it planned to discontinue service. In purchasing the bus operation in the summer of 1968, the PTC borrowed $650,000 from Fort Wayne National Bank to be paid back from revenues and taxes. On Sept. 30, 1969, the bus corporation received $876,850 in Federal funds under the Urban Mass Transportation Act. During the period of expansion and upgrading of service, 40 new buses were purchased. But despite an immediate boost in riders, the old trend of decline in bus patronage reasserted itself. Based on a 35-cent fare, the PTC reported 1,200,000 passengers in the first six months of 1971, down from 1,600,000 during a similiar period a year earlier when the fare had been 25 cents. Thomas Black, general manager of PTC, reported low fares were necessary to maintain patrons. It was agreed the buses were needed for general city services, particularly for the elderly, school students and others without cars. In 1972, a tax levy was boosted and 12 cents per $100 assessed property valuation was set for the next couple years. The PTC board at the time included James Kelley, chairman; Richard Allen, Shockley Lockridge, John S. Littlejohn, Charles Sidle, Robert Benninghoff and Cecil Ellis.

Fifty-one passengers of the Penn-Central Limited were injured in a derailment on Sept. 10, 1968, at 1:38 p.m. near the Pontiac-Wayne Trace Elevation. Four coaches jumped the tracks and crashed. There was a total of 129 passengers abroad the train, which was traveling from New York to Chicago. In an unrelated report, one of the oldest names in country and western music died on Sept. 19, 1968. He was Clyde (Red) Foley who took ill after doing a show on a Fort Wayne stage and returned to his motel where the singer died.

Forts and Tourists

In early 1966, an ambitious program to reconstruct the Fort Wayne stockade, which had existed at three rivers from 1794 to 1819, was outlined by the Allen County-Fort Wayne Historical Society. It was estimated at the time the project would cost about $750,000. The plan called for the building of the Old Fort on the north bank of the St. Mary's River near Spy Run Ave. The land, once called Wells Reserve or Preemptive, after the Captain William Wells who was a spy for General Anthony Wayne and son-in-law of Chief Little Turtle, was directly across the river from the actual location of the original fort. An Indian village and French trading center dating back to the 1600s had also been at the chosen site. The building plans, at a somewhat advanced cost, were to bear fruit with construction nine years later.

The Tourism Council of the Greater Fort Wayne Area met for the first time on Dec. 7, 1967, and organized for tourist promotion in 1968. Fort Wayne was the first city in Indiana to have an organized council. Lynn Koehlinger was named chairman. The name of the Council was subsequently changed to Fort Wayne Convention and Visitors Bureau.

In July, 1969, the Three Rivers Festival was launched. It was a citywide celebration which almost immediately became a regional attraction. The annual week-long celebration combined stunts, historical meaning, street dancing, river events and a parade several miles long. Mrs. Joan C. White headed the organizing group. In 1972 a governing board, Three Rivers Festival, Inc., was formed to make the event permanent. A focal point of the festival was the Landing, but programs were almost continuous in parks, theatres and public places. The great race down the St. Joseph River to the junction of three rivers was a popular and colorful attraction with some 700 craft of strange design and several thousand participants at the watery game. Crowds along the river banks for this event alone numbered 60,000 or more, with some estimates running to 100,000 people.

Controlling Pollution

Work was started in 1969 on a $2.5 million program to reduce the flow of pollutants into the Maumee River. The aim was to find an economical way to control pollution rather than to build separate sanitary and storm drains in all parts of the city. The plan adopted called for the building of lagoons to receive the overflow from combination sewers during times of heavy rainfall and flooding, rather than having the overflow going directly into the river. The first lagoon was completed in 1971 north of the Maumee River near Lake Ave. on the city's northeast side. The 40-acre terminal pond provided tertiary treatment during dry periods to increase the efficiency of the Water Pollution Control Plant. In 1972, a grant of $1,057,000 was received from the Environmental Protection Agency for research and development of a phosphate removal program at the Sewage Treatment Plant. Heading the water-protection projects were Ron Bonar, city engineer; Paul Brunner, superintendent of the Water Pollution Control Plant; Harry Siegel, assistant superintendent; and Richard Koos, chief chemist. A whole series of sewer improvements and enlargements were built in the city in the 1960s and 1970s. The largest single sewer, 102 inches in diameter, was installed as much as 50 feet underground through the central part of the city. Called the Downtown Storm Relief Sewer, it was designed to relieve flooding of underpasses and basements in much of the central and south portions of the city and take flow to the Maumee River. The $3.9 million project was completed in 1972. It was financed with a $2.4 million bond issue and $1.5 million in federal funds.

The largest expansion of water resources in Fort Wayne since the building of the Filtration Plant in 1931 was begun in May, 1966. The two-phase program was scheduled to cost $15 million. On April 25, 1967, the City Council initiated a $3 million bond issue to construct major water lines in the city and to boost pumping facilities at the Filtration Plant. Three 14-million gallon per day pumps, adding a total of 42 million gallons, were installed. Thus a new total capacity of 111 million gallons per day was created. One of the more important developments in the second phase of the water expansion was the $2,102,000 Hurshtown Reservoir. The construction furnished the city with a two billion gallon reservoir. A component of the storage was a 10-million-gallon-per-day pumping station, which lifted water from the St. Joseph River into the pond. The site was a 340-acre tract near the river just above Leo and Grabill. Construction began in 1968 and the filling of the reservoir started in 1970. In the spring of 1971, a leak developed in the reservoir which required its draining and repair. In the decade beginning in 1964, more than 400,000 feet of water mains were built in Fort Wayne. This brought the total footage of service mains in the city utility system to more than 3 million feet, or approximately 573 miles. During the period, H. A. Kerby was chief water engineer; Paul Fulkerson, superintendent of the Filtration Plant; and Glen R. Patrick, chief chemist.

In the Vineyards

Fort Wayne Future, an attempt to involve all Fort Wayne residents in the planning for the growth of the city, was launched on Nov. 21, 1968. Sponsoring organizations included The News-Sentinel, the City of Fort Wayne, the Chamber of Commerce, the League of Women Voters, the Fort Wayne Society of Architects and the WKJG Broadcasting Stations. Dr. Reginald R. Isaacs, senior faculty member of Harvard University's Department of City and Regional Planning, and Walter Blucher, Harvard and MIT planning consultant, participated in the initial conference. Many phases of urban life and potential were discussed. Panelists included Martin Torborg, William H. Watson, Robert Y. Adams, Paul Philips and Howard Watters. At the session, attended by 350 persons representing various walks of city life, it was suggested the city was adrift without strong direction and that more forceful roles needed to be assumed in planning and moving the city toward what it perceived as its goals. Ernest E. Williams, editor of The News-Sentinel was named chairman of the steering committee of Fort Wayne Future. Named as chairmen of the task forces were Paul Philips, government; Charles Redd, human relations; Martin Torborg, education; Herman Steegman, industrial development; Howard Watters, transportation; and Conrad Jankowski, physical planning. The task forces held public hearings on their various reports and sought to involve civic, church, service, and social organizations in planning for future developments in the community. In October, 1969, John E. Hoffman, Jr., an attorney, succeeded Williams as chairman of the steering committee. In subsequent years the Fort Wayne Future task units studied and recommended courses of action in the downtown development, race relations, education, employment opportunities and civic participation.

In terms of man hours, one of the great labor strikes in Fort Wayne ended on Jan. 30, 1970. The contract dispute between the General Electric Company and the International Union of Electrical Workers had begun with the onset of the strike 94 days earlier. More than 7,200 employees of local GE plants were out during the last two months of 1969 and the first month of the new year. The return to work came with the ratification of a new labor pact by Local 901, IUE. But the longest large strike of the decade was still going on at the time. This was the walkout by workers at the Phelps Dodge Magnet Wire Corp. which began on Jan. 16, 1969. It wasn't until June 24, 1970, nearly a year and a half later, that Local 963, IUE, came to terms with the plant management.

Two locally-owned supermarket firms became fairly dominent in Fort Wayne in the decades after World War II. Maloley Bros. and Rogers Markets were so highly successful in grocery service that national chains had difficulty staying in the competition. Rogers Markets, Inc., was started in 1944 by W. W. Rogers with a store on West Jefferson Street. Two years later a self-service operation was built on East Pontiac St. and in 1947 a store at Fairfield and Kinsmoor Avenues. From that time the growth was to key locations in the city and in selected shopping centers. W. W. Rogers became chairman of the firm, Harry Rogers president, and John Rogers, vice-president. By the end of 1971, the firm was operating 10 stores in the area. Maloley Bros. was operating 13 supermarkets and two stamp redemption centers by 1972, with stores in Fort Wayne, New Haven, Kendallville and Bluffton. The Maloley chain headed by Alfred and Michael Maloley, had remarkable growth in the post-war years. Early stores were at 2730 South Calhoun St. and at the corner of Broadway and Huestis Avenue. In 1945, the firm bought the old Kayser Grocery at the southeast corner of Jefferson St. and Broadway and the Beyer Grocery Co. operation which at that time was located at Harrison and Columbia Streets. In subsequent years the Maloley Brothers went from leasing existing buildings to the establishing of large new supermarket operations in developing shopping centers. A consistently successful feature of the Maloley operations was the bakery goods which were produced in the firm's own plant. Another growing grocery chain was Scott's Foodlanes, headed by Don Scott. For many years, Scott operated at the corner of Fairfield and Taylor St., but that operation was eventually closed down while operations were opened at four locations, the largest at Old Dectur Road, on the south side.

Fort Wayne National

Fort Wayne National Bank officially opened the doors of its new 26-story building at Calhoun and Berry Streets on May 11, 1970. Two days earlier, the bank had completed major transfers of cash and other materials from the old location on the south side of Berry Street. Officials at the bank opening included Russell M. Daane, chairman of the bank board of directors; Paul Shaffer, bank president; and Mayor Harold Zeis. Construction of the building, the city's tallest, began in 1967 with excavations and the sinking of steel piers in the earth below. The cost was set at $4.4 million. The structure was 340 feet high. It was originally designed and engineered by Kelley & Marshall, Inc., Tulsa, Okla., and owned by that firm; and Cities Service through a subsidiary, called Trans-American Investment Group. City Services later purchased total ownership and the building was held by Fort Wayne Bank Building, Inc. Fort Wayne National Bank in 1974 purchased the building through a wholly-owned subsidiary, FWNB Realty Co. A feature of the opening ceremonies in 1970 was the pouring of waters from both the Atlantic Ocean and the Gulf of Mexico into the 30-foot waterfall in the main lobby, making the waterful national in character and symbolic of the old role of the Maumee-Wabash portage which linked waterways extending to both the Atlantic and the Gulf. The building, with modern lines, was built of stone, brick, marble, glass, steel and other materials. The major tenant, in addition to the bank, was Central Soya, Inc. There were six levels of parking to accommodate 284 cars and the two top floors of the building were occupied by the Summit Club, a business and professional organization which came into existence with the building. Fort Wayne National Bank purchased for $36,000 the old Van Orman-Anthony Hotel Building in 1973, at that time empty and condemned, as a future site for a parking lot.

Fort Wayne National Bank had been formed in 1933, organized out of First National Bank, which in turn had been formed from several of the early prominent banks in the city. Fred S. Hunting, one-time general manager of the Fort Wayne General Electric plant, was named bank president. He was succeeded by Wendell C. Laycock after serving for 14 years. Russell Daane became president after Laycock and subsequently became chairman. Paul Shaffer succeeded Daane as president and was named chairman. Other top officers in 1973 included William V. Sowers, executive vice-president and senior trust officer; Jackson R. Lehman, senior vice-president; Robert B. Quance, vice-president and cashier; and Thomas E. Quirk, senior vice-president and trust officer. Directors of the bank in 1973 included Edward Auer; James M. Barrett, III; Russell Daane; James D. Edgett; Donald B. Grissom; Joseph Guidrey; Frederic H. Holt; Lynn Koehlinger; G. Irving Latz, 2d; Wendell Laycock; Leo C. Mascotte; Dale W. McMillen, Jr.; Joseph W. Miller; Lyall D. Morrill; Louis F. Niezer; Jack W. Schrey; Paul Shaffer; John D. Shoaff; William V. Sowers; Gathings Stewart; A. F. Van Ranst; Walter W. Walb and Don A. Wolf. At the end of 1973, assets were $309 million and deposits were $289 million, about three times the figures 10 years earlier.

Central Soya Expansion

The construction of the Fort Wayne National Bank meant the relocation of Central Soya's executive offices from the old bank building to the new structure. Central Soya in the decade prior to 1970 had become a widely-held firm with stock traded on the New York Stock Exchange. By 1971, sales totalled $751 million for the year and the firm employed 7,180 persons. On Oct. 1, 1971, Harold W. McMillen, long-time chairman, retired. Dale W. McMillen, Jr., succeeded to the chairmanship and was named chief executive officer of the company. Top executives and directors included Joseph F. Jones, president; Douglas G. Fleming, Robert B. Parrott and Burt A. Townsend, all executive vice-presidents; John L. Andreas, vice-president; Richard C. Rastetter, senior vice-president of the Continental Illinois National Bank of Chicago; and John D. Shoaff, general counsel for Central Soya.

Waterfield Mortgage Company, Inc., headed by Richard H. Waterfield, moved its headquarters into the former Fort Wayne National Bank Building at 123 West Berry Street.

In the 1970 state and county elections, J. Edward Roush of Huntington unseated 10-term Congressman E. Ross Adair. Roush, a Democrat, had previously served in Congress and first ran in the Fourth District in 1968 because of a change in District boundaries. Adair, the Republican, drew 43,022 votes in Allen County compared with 46,979 for Roush. The district margin for Roush was slightly larger. The Republicans held most county offices but the Democrats picked up the Wayne Township posts. A high point in the pre-election campaign was an address by President Richard M. Nixon during an overflow Republican gathering at the Coliseum on Oct. 20, 1970.

A series of racial disturbances occurred in late June, 1970, in the section of the city just southeast of downtown. Mayor Harold Zeis invoked an old curfew law on July 1, following violence of several evenings running in which 16 persons were injured and instances of arson were reported. The curfew cleared the streets from 10 p.m. to 5 a.m. On July 12, a 17-year-old girl died of injuries received when the auto in which she was a passenger was pelted with stones and bricks at Chute St. and Maumee Ave. at 11:15 p.m., July 5. The curfew was again invoked during the Labor Day weekend, giving the city a strange air of quiet and inactivity.

People and Wages

The statistical summary of Fort Wayne and Allen County, as of 1970, was reported by the U.S. Bureau of the Census. There were 177,738 inhabitants of Fort Wayne and 280,455 in the metropolitan area, or approximate county area. The Fort Wayne labor force numbered 76,400 or about 62 per cent of the population, 16 years and older. The county figure was 118,062 in the labor force or about 63 per cent of the population, 16 years and older. The number in manufacturing was 33 per cent of the total 114,325 persons holding jobs in the metropolitan area. Whites comprised 89 per cent of the city population. Negroes were 10.6 per cent and persons of foreign birth amounting to 8.7 per cent with the largest groups coming from the United Kingdom and Germany. Median income of all Fort Wayne families was $10,399 and Negro families, $8,142. Among the population 25 years and older, 56 per cent were high school graduates, including 21 per cent with some college. Owners lived in 67 per cent and renters in 33 per cent of housing units of the city. In the county area, 73 per cent lived in owner homes. The median value of owner-occupied homes in the city was $13,626; and in the county as a whole, $15,530. More than 89 per cent of households in the city in 1970 had a telephone; 97 per cent had a television set; 34 per cent had air conditioning; 16 per cent had a dishwasher and 85 per cent of the households had an automobile.

In the meantime, old landmarks were disappearing. In 1970, the Moellering Gristmill at 6203 Fairfield Ave. disappeared. The firm was started in 1900 by Fred Moellering and Charles Stellhorn. During the last 25 years, the mill was operated by Melvin Gerka and C. Merle Engelman. The mill ground wheat and corn and sold grains.

Construction of the Performing Arts Theatre, which was started on June 1, 1970, entailed a fund drive which lasted for several years. The 767-seat structure, by Louis Kahn, cost about $4 million by the time it was completed on Oct. 5, 1973. Major gifts included $150,000 from the Central Soya Foundation and the McMillen family in 1971, which was in addition to $100,000 given earlier by the same interests. General chairman of the drive was Clyde J. Cover. Others heading the fund raising included James Anglin; John Croker, Jr.; Helene Foellinger; Robert G. Irish; G. Irvin Latz 2d; Mrs. William McNagny; Milford Miller, Jr.; Donnelly P. McDonald, Jr.; Kenneth Kurtz; John D. Shoaff, and Newell Wright. The theater was a project of the Fort Wayne Fine Arts Foundation, organized in 1955. The brick and concrete structure was located on land obtained through the Main St. Redevelopment Project, the site being just east of Freimann Park and the City-County Building. Among officers and board members of the foundation, in addition to those mentioned, were Robert Kaag, Hans French, Mrs. Eugene Senseny, Harold W. McMillen, Samuel Rea, Thomas Watson, Norman Ballinger, Harry Crawford, James Zid, Mrs. Noble Schlatter, Roger Manges, Darrell W. Huntley, George Dodd, Richard Adams, Edward Downing, Mrs. Carter Dunstone, Larry Reeves, Arthur Richard, Mrs. Alberta Robinson, Gay Schmidt, Walter Tharp, Jr. and Richard VerWiebe.

Lebamoff Becomes Mayor

The 1971 City Elections pitted Republican Mayor Harold Zeis, seeking a third term, against Ivan Lebamoff, a lawyer who was Democratic County Central Committee Chairman. Zeis had no real opposition in the primary. It appeared that former mayor Paul Burns might run on the Democratic ticket, but chose to seek a council seat instead. Lebamoff received some competition from Famious Williams, but won the primary handily. In the fall election, the Democratic Party gained City Hall and most of the Council seats. Lebamoff defeated Zeis with a vote of 33,190 to 29,568. Others selected included Charles W. Westerman, clerk; and Paul M. Burns, Vivian Schmidt, Samuel J. Talarico, John Nuckols, Donald Schmidt, William Hinga, Eugene Kraus, Jr., Winfield Moses, Jr. and James S. Stier, all councilmen. Appointed to the Board of Works in the Lebamoff Administration were Dr. Jerry Boswell, chairman and William G. Williams and Ronald Bonar. Edward Kamnikar was named city controller. The Board of Safety included Thomas Casaburo, chairman, and Bob Wire and Corrinne Brooks.

David Keller was named city attorney; Thomas Casaburo, public safety director; E. Owen Donnelly, director of community development and planning; David Kiester, administrative assistant to the mayor. Albert Bragalone and Robert Gebhard were successively named chief of police and Walt Roemke and Tom Heckman, successive fire chiefs.

The 1972 general elections drew wide interest and heavy turnout at the polls. The spring primary resulted in former State Senator Allan Bloom defeating former Indiana Secretary of State William Salin in a close test for the Fourth District Congressional nomination on the Republican ticket. At the State Republican Convention, Otis Bowen of Bremen was chosen as candidate for governor over Phillip E. Gutman of Fort Wayne. Gutman was State Senate President Pro-Tem. On Oct. 3, 1972, Vice President Spiro Agnew arrived at Baer Field and led a motorcade to the City-County Building where he addressed a crowd boosting the Nixon-Agnew ticket. On Oct. 6, 1972, Senator Edward Kennedy gave a press conference at Baer Field and spoke at a Democratic luncheon at the Keenan Hotel. He later addressed an audience at Concordia Senior College in favor of the election of Democrats George McGovern and Kennedy's brother-in-law Sargent Shriver. The November election had some odd twists. Bowen was elected governor and the Nixon-Agnew ticket swept McGovern-Shriver by a two-to-one margin in Allen County on the way to a second term in the White House. J. Edward Roush, however, won a fairly close test with challenger Allan Bloom, 58,528 to 53,810 in Allen County, as the Democrat retained his Congressional seat.

"The Fort Wayne Story"

The Watergate inquiry following the 1972 election campaign led to one of the more curious episodes, which became nationally known as "The Fort Wayne Story." During the Senate hearing, reference was made on August 1, 1973, to a memo by Presidential Assistant H. R. Haldeman on Feb. 10 in which he said "There's also the question of whether we should let out the Fort Wayne story now." According to The Washington Post on August 2, no mention of George McGovern was made publicly at the Senate Watergate hearings, but reporters got some answers from McGovern. The Senator said the Fort Wayne Story was a reference to a birth certificate in the city records of Fort Wayne that lists "George S. McGovern of Mitchell, S.D." (McGovern's hometown) as the father of a child born out of wedlock in the early 1940s. McGovern denied he was the father. The Washington Post confirmed the existence of such a birth certificate, and contacted the child's mother, who also denied that McGovern was the father. "I don't know who listed his name on the birth certificate," the woman said. She was a contemporary of McGovern at Mitchell and had come to a Fort Wayne hospital to have the child. There was an unconfirmed report that evidence of the birth and parentage was at Parkview Hospital in the old Methodist hospital portion of the records, but the Parkview authorities declined to reveal information on the matter. McGovern's father had been a Methodist minister at Mitchell, S.D., in the early 1940s. McGovern told the Post he became aware of his name on the birth certificate in the spring of 1972, before he became a Presidential nominee. He said he had a copy of the birth certificate read to him over the telephone. It was later revealed that a member of Fort Wayne Mayor Lebamoff's staff had made a copy of the certificate available to persons unnamed. McGovern told the Post the woman had been visited in 1961 by FBI agents when the FBI was conducting a backcheck on McGovern before his appointment to a Federal position. At that time, 1961, the woman acknowledged that McGovern was listed on a Fort Wayne birth certificate as father of one of her children.

A strange train of events followed. Fort Wayne newsmen, in attempting to confirm the story, were refused looks at the Board of Health records and were told McGovern's name was not on the records. Since this contradicted reports by all other parties involved, a court order was granted to inspect the accuracy of the public records. Attorneys for the News-Sentinel and City Administration inspected the Fort Wayne Health Department records and found the name for the father had been eradicated with a chemical from the birth certificate in question. After the instance of tampering with records at the department in Fort Wayne, interest turned to the State Board of Health which also held birth records. The State Health Board refused to open the records and the State Attorney General filed motions to block further investigative processes in the courts. Senator McGovern called the inquiry "outrageous and scurrilous" and an attempt to divert attention from Watergate. "This incident is said to have happened more than 30 years ago when I was a teenager growing up in South Dakota. As for the alleged changing of records in Fort Wayne, neither I nor any person acting for me has even seen these records." In subsequent months, articles in Newsweek and other national publications attempted to suggest the existence of McGovern's name on the Fort Wayne records was a "dirty trick" of the 1972 election campaign. However, it was already on record that the existence of McGovern's name on the record was an accepted fact as early as 1961, and well before his nomination.

Things Abuilding

Much of the growth in the 1970s consisted of large apartment and condominium complexes. In 1972 Realamerica Homes, Inc., began construction of the Covington Creek Condominiums near Covington Road just west of Time Corners on the southwest edge of the city. The development was headed by Duane Bobeck, Neil Diver, Bill Martin and Don Johnson. At the 49-acre site, 304 housing units were planned at an estimated cost of $11 million. Already expanding at that time on the opposite fringe of the city was Canterbury Green Apartment Homes, still larger and including a population of some 4,000 by 1974. Canterbury Green, between St. Joe Road and the St. Joseph's River, just north of the Indiana-Purdue Campus, had an 18-hole golf course, swimming pools, tennis and handball courts. It was developed by Palmer-Eckrich Companies. The $22 million town house project on 175 acres was started in September, 1969.

Ground was broken Dec. 5, 1972, on General Telephone Co. of Indiana's new headquarters building at 8001 U.S. 24 West. The two-story steel and concrete structure was located on an 85-acre tract. The $8 million building was designed to house more than 800 employees and included lounge, cafeteria and parking for 830 cars. When completed in 1974, Albert E. Beckwith, president of General Telephone, said the firm planned a total of $63 million in capital improvements in the state. Among the improvements was the expansion and renewal of the firm's Fort Wayne Division offices at 303 East Berry Street. Two additional floors brought the height of the building to five stories; and a mental sheath was installed around the microwave tower on top of the structure. Donald W. Prigmire, vice-president-operations, and Donald McConiga, division manager, reported extensive installation of phone cables and conduit throughout the division.

On March 3, 1972, the Walton Ave. Bridge was closed down. One of the old iron bridges over the Maumee River, the bridge had long since become the Anthony Blvd. Bridge in common acceptance with the only reminder of the older name of the street being a sign high on the bridge structure. At first it was thought the bridge could be repaired, but the general deterioration led to the reconstruction of the bridge. Later in the year, another bridge over the Maumee was opened after widening and improvements. This was on Nov. 21, at Columbia Avenue just east of Main Street.

Hot and Dirty

During the hot summer days of 1972, officials were active. On Aug. 18, 71 persons were arrested during a raid by Federal agents on the Zig-Zag Night Club at Harrison St. just south of the Wabash elevation. The raid was a key part of a drive against illicit drug traffic. On August 29, after two nights of destruction by vandals and roving gangs of teenagers, Mayor Ivan Lebamoff met with some 500 persons at the Hanna Homestead Park urging peace and quiet.

The Baer Field Thruway, long a bone of contention because of opposition to the route which cut across a piece of Foster Park and southend residential areas, and the fact it didn't exactly go to the Municipal Terminal, was completed in 1972. Another sometimes unpopular move in connection with Baer Field was the imposition of a local $1 tax on air travelers. The tax was later removed at Federal regulatory direction.

The City made moves to curb the proliferation of nude dancing, stores which sold obscene books and dirty pictures, and massage parlors which were really fronts for prostitution. In July, 1972, the City Council passed an ordinance aimed at the offenders. The Lebamoff Administration later attempted to close down massage parlors and number of arrests were made. For the most part, however, the objectionable book stores, X-rated movie houses, nude-dance joints and parlors of prostitution continued to operate.

Room Service

The expansion of hotels, motels and highway inns continued in 1972 at an increased pace. The $3 million Marriott Motor Hotel and Win Schuler Restaurant, at Interstate 69 and U.S. 27 North had opened in June, 1970. The six-story, 149-room hotel was later expanded. Late that same year, the Hospitality Inn, a $2 million motor hotel at Interstate 69 and State Road 3, was nearing completion. The 160-room inn was on a seven-acre site at Merchandise Place. The Merchandise Place was developed by Schlatter Hardware Company. Other major installations were those of Graybar Electric Co., Pittsburgh Plate Glass Go., National Mill supply Co., Central Electric Co. and H & W Electric Co. The $2.5 million Ramada Inn at I-69 and State Road 14, west of the city, was built in 1972. The 150-room motel was near the Magnavox headquarters in the immediate vicinity. Motels built in 1973 included Days Inn, a 121-room operation; and Motel 6, a 106-room hotel, both near I-69, Coliseum Blvd. and U.S. 30 West. The 130-unit Imperial House on the Washington Center Road near State Road 3 was completed in 1974.

The physical expansion in and around the city was in large part caused by the continued expansion of industry and employment. The average unemployment rate in 1972 was 3.6 per cent, well below the national average. By September, 1973, the unemployment rate was down to 2.5 per cent. Total employment in the county was 137,800, up nearly 6,000 in just one year. One of the city's oldest businesses quit operations in 1973. It was Pierre's Dry Goods Co., 1214 Broadway, which was founded by Peter Pierre after he came to Fort Wayne in 1851.

The Living and the Dead

In the early 1970s, a number of events involving Fort Wayne people were reported. Richard B. Sturges was listed as president of Food Marketing Corporation. Richard Hire, president of Hire's Auto Parts announced the opening of his fourth outlet, a 40,000-square-foot center on South Anthony Boulevard. Mrs. Nan Elliott Dahm announced the construction of the Gunnar Elliott Ice Arena on Racquet Drive, with the faciliy named for Paul Gunnar Elliott, a long-time Fort Wayne sportsman and beer distributor. Richard Grosh, a native of Fort Wayne and dean of engineering at Purdue University, was named president of the Rensselaer Polytechnic Institute in New York. Frederick R. Tourkow, a Fort Wayne attorney, was elected president of the National Shrine to the Jewish War Dead, Washington, D.C. Zollner Corp., on Coliseum Blvd., added 20,000 square feet to accommodate its air conditioning products.

Falstaff Brewing Corp. doubled its beer production and added ale to its product line after completing a $2 million expansion at its Fort Wayne plant, making the local operation the largest of the firm's seven breweries.

On May 1, 1971, the Wabash Cannonball passed through Fort Wayne on its last run between Detroit and St. Louis. The N&W passenger train was long a fixture on the American rail scene and the subject of legend and song.

The brother-in-law of Fort Wayne's Mayor Ivan Lebamoff was murdered on Nov. 10, 1973. George Spahiev, 47, was fatally shot at the Variety Liquor Store, 3322 North Clinton St., by a bandit during a robbery attempt. Spahiev managed the store. Dallas Wayne Howard, 22, of Waterloo, was convicted the following May in Kosciusko Circuit Court of the crime.

Some of the proposed city developments ran into public resistance in 1973. After Mayor Ivan Lebamoff announced plans for the widening of Rudisill Blvd. on the south side and Anthony Blvd. on the east side neighborhood residents formed committees and opposed the moves. The main objections were the possible loss of trees and the greater numbers of trucks which would be using the routes. In May, plans to expend $1 million in Federal urban renewal funds in the east-central neighborhood and a west-central area, just west of Broadway and south of Jefferson, were announced. Some objections were raised to the east site chosen by the Redevelopment Commission and a somewhat different tract near Harmar St. and Washington Blvd. was chosen. The year of 1973 was a hard one from the point of weather. More than nine inches of snow fell on March 17. Then later in the year, on Dec. 19, a near-record 14 inches of snow smothered the city. In between times, on May 10, four tornadoes were sighted streaking across Fort Wayne, touching down in several places, damaging homes and other buildings and many trees, but without causing any deaths. On July 21, more than 3000 homes were evacuated on the southwest edge of town after rail cars on the Penn-Central derailed. They contained vinyl chloride which exploded, creating flaming clouds high over the area. In September, Mr. and Mrs. Walter Probst contributed $200,000 for the African Veldt addition to the Park Board's Zoo at Franke Park. For the first time since the onset of Prohibition 54 years earlier, alcoholic drinks could be sold on Sunday, as a result of a new State Law which became effective in 1973.

The old Barr St. Market opened in a small way in August, 1973, after an absence of 16 years. Farmers and a few handicraft and other venders occupied stalls between Wayne St. and the old City Hall Building. The market opened at a time when shortages of beef and price controls were the rule at supermarkets. Later in the year, the international oil crisis, brought on by price rigging and embargoes by Arab and other oil producing nations, caused price run-ups and shortages of gasoline at service stations. In November, 1973, the Park Board announced a $325,000 grant from the Foellinger Foundation for the rebuilding of the Outdoor Theatre at Franke Park. It was originally dedicated as the News-Sentinel Outdoor Theatre in 1949. The stage-building portion of the theatre had been destroyed in a fire on Dec. 15, 1972, which was believed caused by arson. Through the early and mid-1970s, arson continued to be a problem as a number of park buildings were destroyed.

Two Hotels Blasted

In Fort Wayne, 1974 will be remembered as the year of the big hotel blasts. The city's two largest hotel buildings were demolished by explosions. The first to go was the Anthony Hotel at the north-east corner of Berry and Harrison Streets. Known as the Van Orman Hotel and managed by Harold Van Orman from the mid-1940s, the 1950s and until 1968, it had been the city's leading meeting place and reception center for most of its 65 years. At 10 a.m. on Sunday, Jan. 13, workmen of Controlled Demolition, Inc., Baltimore, Md., detonated 294 charges strapped inside the eight-story hotel. Nine seconds later here was nothing but a pile of rubble and a cloud of dust as awed spectators looked on in the zero weather. The property had earlier been purchased for back taxes by the Fort Wayne National Bank. Martin, Inc., had the wrecking contract. The 52-year-old Keenan Hotel, at the southwest corner of Washington Blvd. and Harrison St., was demolished at 9:25 a.m. on Sunday, Oct. 20, 1974. The same demolition teams which brought down the old Anthony leveled the Keenan. The 13-story brick and stone Keenan fell in a slow-motion collapse, victim of 330 pounds of high velocity gelatin in 252 electrically-controlled charges. The hotel was owned and operated for many years by James Keenan. The demolition was ordered by his daughter, Mrs. Helen Keenan Centlivre, because of declining revenues and fire regulation problems at the downtown hotel.

On Jan. 21, 1974, a fire caused more than $1 million in damage at the Peter Eckrich and Sons, Inc., plant at Osage Street. The flames started in a tank of cottonseed oil and spread quickly. More than 200 employees were evacuated and three firemen were injured. A more far-reaching tragedy was the tornado of April 3 during which five Fort Wayne residents were killed when their car was thrown into Lake Freeman near Monticello, Indiana. The twisters, none of which hit Fort Wayne, took the lives of some 50 Hoosiers. The people from the city who died included Dr. Donald Richards, 37, language director at the I.U.-Purdue Campus; Margaret Stump, 18; Jackie McKelleb, 17; Sharon Miller, 18; and Elizabeth Scalf, 17.

Old buildings, and what to do with them, were much in the news. The end of the Irene Byron Sanitarium loomed in sight on Jan. 11, when Tom Katsanis, superintendent of the County Hospital and Health Center on the Lima Road, said four of the buildings were closed down. The other building was converted to hospital use after changes in medical practice led to the discontinuation of the old tuberculosis sanitarium. County Council President Max Shambaugh questioned the expending of public money to continue the maintenance of the buildings. John Heiny, County Welfare Director, reported no welfare money was available to renovate the structures for other uses.

On March 10, local artists performed in the old Embassy Movie Theatre in the 100 block of West Jefferson to kick off the Save-the-Embassy drive. Duo-harpists John Escosa and Joe Longstreth, organist Buddy Nolan and film maker Col. John Craig headed the program. Gretchen Wiegel, Bobbie Martin and Robert Goldstine headed the group which aimed to raise $250,000 to purchase the unused property which included the 2,800 theatre and Indiana Hotel building. The Philharmonic Orchestra and other artistic organizations considered using the one-time movie palace. In the meantime, Mayor Ivan Lebamoff was trying to interest private organizations in using and preserving the old, empty City Hall Building, built in 1893 and located at Berry and Barr Streets.

Mind and Body

The United Community Services, a descendant of the Community Chest founded to help the neglected in the 1920s, continued a steady growth in volunteer donations and services for half a century. Most of the financial support came from workers in business and industry who made regular contributions from pay envelopes. The donations grew from a few thousand in the early years to several million annually by the 1970s. Headquarters of the UCS after 1958 was at Washington Blvd. and Barr St. in the building which had earlier been occupied by The News-Sentinel and had been made available by a Foellinger Foundation grant. United Fund drives each year occupied hundreds of civic leaders, businessmen and others. The fund supported numerous charities and social services which helped men, women and children in numerous circumstances and problems involving health, education and family. In 1973, Lisle D. Hodell, a former G.E. executive, was president of United Community Services which administered the funds and represented the community regarding services and agencies. Vice-presidents included A. L. Berk, James

B. Griffith, Thomas J. Blee, Levan Scott, and William I. Hamilton. Lloyd S. Stubbins was secretary and Jack W. Schrey, treasurer. Almaron M. Wilder, Ph.D., was executive administrator.

Construction of a $3 million Fort Wayne Mental Health Center began in late 1974 after more than seven yers of planning. Jerome O'Dowd, a lawyer, headed the planning group for the center which was to serve mental patients and others in Allen, Adams and Wells countries. The center construction began on a 15-acre site, part of 47 acres near East State Blvd. and Parnell Ave. which for nearly a century had been the location of the old Fort Wayne State School. Funds for the center were mainly from Federal and State sources, with $100,000 coming from local sources including the Fort Wayne Foundation, headed by John D. Shoaff, and the United Way, headed by Richard Sturgis. Center officials included Dr. William Lyon, board president and Dr. Robert Greenlee, director of the center. The center was designed to offer educational, occupational and recreational therapy programs, socil retraining, 24-hour emergency service in a 12-bed unit for short-term care.

End of City Light

The sale of City Light to Indiana & Michigan Electric Co. became one of the controversial issues in 1973 and 1974. Due to the changes in technology and the aging of the City Light plant, the public-owned utility had been purchasing increasing amount of power from I&M, a subsidiary of the American Electric Power System. By the end of 1973, City Light was buying more than 80 per cent of its energy needs from I&M. Mayor Ivan Lebamoff described the situation: "It's like selling the family farm for the highest dollar the day before the bank forecloses the mortgage." The mayor decided the issue should be decided at a public referendum at the May, 1974, Primary Election. Under the terms of the proposed agreements, I&M would lease City Light for $55 million over a 35-year period, plus pay cash for materials and transportation equipment of the City Light Utility. At the time, City Light had about 35,000 customers in the city. The balance of electric service in the city and most of it in the area was furnished by I&M. In the weeks prior to the vote, public discussion was widespread, but strong organized opposition failed to materialize. On election day of May 6, the voters cast 17,589 votes in favor of the lease and 10,386 votes against. On Friday, September 13, 1974, Mayor Lebamoff and Robert M. Kopper, I&M vice-president, signed the 35-year lease of the 66-year-old City Light Utility. The City Council had passed a resolution calling for the lease by a 6-1 margin. The favorable votes were cast by John Nuckols, William Hinga, James Stier, Paul Burns, Vivian Schmidt and Samuel Talarico. The lone dissenter was Winfield Moses, Jr. City Light's Lawton Park generating plant was shut down on March 1, 1975, after 66 years of operations at the site next to Spy Run Creek.

Peoples Trust Bank

The building of a major bank and office complex downtown was related to the City Light sale issue. On April 19, the Peoples Trust Bank and Indiana & Michigan Electric Co. announced plans for a $30 million, twin-towered downtown headquarters. Donnelly P. McDonald, Jr., bank president, and Robert Koppers, executive vice-president of the utility, unveiled an architectural model which included two office towers, one 28 stories and the other 20 stories high. Provisions were made in the designs for a 250-unit hotel and commercial activities. The total square footage of the development was set at about one million. Construction was tentatively planned for 1975 in the block bound by Calhoun, Clinton, Wayne Sts. and Washington Boulevard. Features of the complex were to include an outdoor ice skating rink and a tree-lined plaza.

The Peoples Trust, founded in 1903 and the oldest bank in operation in the city, had been seeking to expand and consolidate its downtown operations for some years. Donnelly P. McDonald, Sr., was president of the bank from 1941 to 1963 when he was succeeded by Donnelly P. McDonald, Jr. Except for the first couple of years of its existence, the Peoples Trust was located in a six-story building on the east side of Calhoun St., midway between Wayne and Washington, with an identifying large clock over the front entrance. The top officers included Lawrence Mullen, Neil A. McKay, Leo Ford, George Keller, George H. Kinne, Charles Diamond, Paul Underwood, Hiram Nally, and Richard Burrows. In early 1974, bank deposits totalled $197,500,000 and assets were listed at $221,336,000. The figures were listed for Financial Incorporated, a holding company which had been created to broaden the bank's activities. Directors included Harold L. Bobeck, Paul Clarke, David Cunningham, Thomas J. Eckrich, Robert Goldstine, Richard G. Inskeep, Alden Irmsher, George Kowalczyk, John F. Lassus, Von E. Livingston, Alfred Maloley, Donnelly McDonald, Jr., Henry J. Moellering, Donald F. Murphy, Charles Seyfert, R. Nelson Snider and Frank Travis. Many of the bank's 12 branches were housed in buildings with a pyramid design which drew attention nationally and were featured in world expositions.

Stillman's Department store at the southeast corner of Wayne and Calhoun Streets closed in August, 1974. Also closed were the firm's store at Southgate Shopping Center and a warehouse at 4111 North Clinton Street. Stillman's known as the Grand Leader until the 1950s, was a downtown fixture for more than 60 years. The end came because of bankruptcy proceedings filed in New York against the parent company, Interstate Stores. The store operations in Fort Wayne, however, had been profitable to the end, according to Frank Pavelich, general manager. Robert Stillman, a spokesman for the family owning the property, reported negotiations to sell the propery to Indiana & Michigan Electric Co. and the Peoples Trust Bank which were planning a large bank and office complex in the block.

Judges and Bonds

In the 1974 elections, the results were mixed with both political parties winning some offices. J. Edward Roush retained his Congressional seat over Republican challenger Walter P. Helmke. Charles (Bud) Meeks, Republican, won the sheriff's office and Republicans retained control of the Courthouse. Allen Superior Court Judges Robert M. Hines, Robert L. Meyers and Alfred W. Moellering were confirmed in office under the procedure providing for appointed judges being periodically subject to voter approval. Hines and Meyers were the first appointive judges, under the reorganization of the Allen County Courts by State Legislation, and had been sworn in on Dec. 1, 1971.

The Fort Wayne Development Commission, an agency of City government which financed local business and industrial buildings on tax-exempt, municipal-type bonds, engaged in its first ventures in 1974. The first large facility which drew on the commission's financing process was Kunkle Valve Co. which began construction of a manufacturing and office building on March 15, 1974, at 8100 Bluffton Road. Mayor Lebamoff termed the event a milestone because "it is a major breakthrough for the commission." Clifton McCormick, former president of General Telephone Co. of Indiana, was commission president. Horace Dykhuizen, Kunkle president, said the firm, which had been founded in 1875, had outgrown its plant at 101 South Clinton Street. The new one-story building of steel and masonry covered 80,000 square feet of floor space. Other buildings financed with commission bonds were Patton Electric Co. and the Dahm Auto Wash at the Glenbrook Shopping Center.

Sewage and Ice Skates

The expansion of water pollution control in the Fort Wayne area led to formation of a $34 million project in late 1974. In

December, ordinances providing a $7 million bond issue for the city's share of the financing were introduced in the City Council. The balance of the money was to come from Federal and State agencies. Introduced at the time was a $2.5 million bond issue for expansion of the water filtration plant and St. Joe River dam improvements. Dr. Jerry Boswell, chairman of the board of works, reported public hearings would be held on the bond issues and on water and sewer rate increases. The sewage-treatment project followed agreements with the city of New Haven on the acceptance of New Haven sewage by the Fort Wayne Pollution Control Plant. New Haven Mayor Herbert Brudi and New Haven City Attorney Arthur H. Fruechtenicht negotiated the pact with Fort Wayne officials. The U.S. Corps of Engineers and the Environmental Protection Agency participated in the plans to solve local sewer expansion and protection of Maumee River waters flowing into Lake Erie. In 1972, the Indiana Stream Pollution Control Board had ordered New Haven to abandon its own sewer treatment facilities and to send affluents to Fort Wayne treatment plants.

Reservoir Park, a site of recreation since 1880 on the city's south side, was rebuilt in 1974. William J. Cooper, Wayne Township Trustee, committed $122,000 in federal revenue sharing money to the building of a community center at Clinton St. and Creighton Ave. at the park's northwest corner. The lake, long a favorite place for ice skating and fishing by children, was emptied; then deepened and rebuilt along the shore line.

In June, 1974, Gov. Otis Bowen approved long-range plans for the building of I-69 Bypass around the south and east of Fort Wayne. Portions of the route, long seen as a major relief to truck and other congestion and traffic through the city, had earlier been included in the State Statutory Highway Program. The 11-mile segment from U.S. 30 in the New Haven area, north to the Dupont interchange with regular I-69, was the last to be made part of the planning process. It was expected that completion of the express route would take about 10 years. In September, 1974, N.V. Philips, a huge Dutch electronics concern, gained a controlling interest in Magnavox Company. The move was made through the Philips American subsidiary, North American Philips Corp., based in New York. By October 3, Philips reported having 83 per cent of the Magnavox stock in hand and continued to offer $9 a share for the remainder. Magnavox, long a leading U.S. electronics firm headquartered in Fort Wayne for 40 years, had been under some pressure because of the generally-depressed condition of the electronics industry. The sale was a surprise, however, to most people locally. The firm employed some 4,000 workers in the Fort Wayne area.

The long-planned Fort Wayne Regional Corrections Center was about ready for the construction stage in November, 1974, when it ran into opposition by residents of the East State Blvd. area where the center was to be located. The main objections were to the presence of a jail on the old State School property where a series of buildings were planned. The purpose of the center was to furnish treatment for some 80 persons convicted of crimes, but believed capable of responding to treatment, education and some working conditions. The center would also replace the County Jail, a 100-year-old institution which was a concern of the community. The center was designed to hold 120 pre-trial prisoners. The price tag on the Corrections Center was set at about $5.5 million and construction was to start in 1975.

The U.S. Bicentennial

The Committee of '76, an Advisory Board on the celebration of the National Bicentennial, was appointed by Mayor Lebamoff in early 1974. Ladonna Huntley was named chairman of the committee and launched the planning for diverse events and activities focusing on 1776 and the entire range of local and area participation in connection with the American Revolution. Among the principals and chairmen of the committee programs were Charles Walker, Arthur Hayes, Fred J. Reynolds, and Jack Dunifon, all members of the State Bicentennial Commission; Earl Klingenberger, Leonard Vosmeier, Russell Oettel, Richard Katt, Ben Eisebart, Dee Marquart, Charles Hall, William Nash, Barbara Hutmacher, Evelyn Williams, Ruth Whearley, David Drury, Joseph Levine, Frank Lansing, Phyllis Florea, Andrea McFadden, William Anthis, James Haw, Donna Jean Darby, Patricia Griest, Carolyn Gutman, William Small, Gabriel Delobbe, Darrell Huntley, Sharon Dodd, Karen Anderson, Cathy Choka, Lucy Green, Gary Ernest, Mel Quinn, Harriet Miller, William Watson, David Tanner, William Casteel, Brian Dunnigan, Maureen Grinsfelder, Robert Morrow, Don Petrucelli, Burton Sherwood and John Vaughn. Chris Schenkel, ABC network sports commentator, was named honorary commissioner. Board members also included Thomas Alter, Robert Arnold, Douglas Baugh, Merle Bennett, Beatrice Borders, Mary Ball Brant, Sharon Eberhard, Richard Friedrich, Max Gecowets, Sharlene Kraus, Ruth Lane, William G. Williams, Pat Yoder, Harold Vizino, Steve Shine, Wesley Bayshore and Bill Hausman.

As a Bicentennial Project Hector Garcia was commissioned to create a large statue of Chief Little Turtle in 1975. The bronge figure was to be about nine feet tall. Also in 1975, former State Senator Walter P. Helmke of Fort Wayne was named chairman of the Indiana Revolution Bicentennial Commission.

The largest public works project on record in Fort Wayne was approved Jan. 20, 1975, by the City Council. The $34 million program included expansion of sewage treatment plants and the building of secondary treatment facilities and sewer line extensions, boosting the capacity of 30 million gallons a day to 60 million gallons. The project was funded with $27 million in Federal and State money and $7 million in local bond issues. Sewer bills to people in the city were advanced 24 per cent to help pay for the improvement. Contractors furnishing low bids were the Hagerman-Shambaugh Construction Co. with a bid of $20,768,000 for the plant expansion and John Dehner, Inc., $4,584,779 for the overflow ponds and $5,305,637 for the sludge lagoons.

Arson Abounds

Fire destroyed the last of Fort Wayne's grand old hotels when flames swept through the Rosemarie on The Landing the night of Feb. 3, 1975. The heavy damage to the hotel and the six-story Bash Building across Columbia St. at the corner with Harrison St. dealt a blow to the attempt to preserve The Landing as a piece of 19th Century Fort Wayne. The Rosemarie, long known as the Wayne Hotel and the Jones Hotel, was built in 1887 by John C. Peters, who was the grandfather of movie actress Carole Lombard. Torchlight political parades had passed by the entrance; and Presidents Benjamin Harrison, James Garfield and Rutherford B. Hayes had stayed there. The fire broke out in the upper stories of the four-story hotel. Flames coming out the roof and windows flashed across the downtown landscape. The fire was contained after about two hours, but the building was labeled a total loss—estimated at $250,000. The hotel had 35 residents, but all were cleared out without serious injury. The Bash Building, occupied by Old Fort Draperies and other shops, and earlier the home of P&H Supply Co. and Protective Electric Co., burned on both Monday and Tuesday nights, Feb. 3 and 4. Fire inspectors attributed the fires to arson. Feb. 3 was a night of fires. The Third Presbyterian Church at Harrison and Tabor Streets was found ablaze at about midnight. Volunteer fire units from outlying districts were brought to the church blaze as most city crews were occupied with the two large fires on Columbia Street. Rev. Philip Nygaard, pastor, estimated the Third Presbyterian loss at $175,000. The stone church building was built in 1900.

Arson was also reported as the cause of a fire which destroyed the Diehm Museum of Natural History at Franke Park on Feb. 17, 1975. Flames were reported about 4 a.m., but the fire was too far along to save the structure and the loss was estimated at $1 million. Doors were jimmied and gasoline was used to set the blaze, according to firefighters. The museum was constructed in 1963. It was the sixth fire in park buildings attributed to arson over a four-year period.

Ground was broken on September 26, 1974, for the Harrison Office building at the northwest corner of Harrison and Berry Streets. The eight-story structure, a project of the Harrison Realty Co., was designed to have commercial operations on the first level and offices on the seven upper stories. The concrete building was put together much like a child's blocks with large walls and corner sections lifted and dropped into place by cranes.

Old Fort Recreated

On Nov. 19, 1974, the rebuilding of the Old Fort was begun just a stone's throw from the St. Mary's River. Keith Barker, president of Historic Fort Wayne, Inc. turned the first shovel. To be recreated was a full-scale replica of the fort which was built near the three rivers in the frontier days. The actual fort chosen for the attraction was the third American Fort, and the fifth fort originally built at the old seat of Miami Indian power, and was called Whistler's Fort because it was built in 1815 by Capt. John Whistler who was commander at the time. It was the only sockade for which plans were still in existence; so in the interests of authenticity, the Whistler fort, or last fort of the old garrison, was chosen for reproduction. The actual site, a four acre tract between the river and Spy Run Ave., was across the St. Mary's River from the location of the original fort. The site was close, however, and was the one-time location of an old Miami Indian villiage and French trading posts. The cost was about $1,200,000, including land and building. The rebuilding of the Old Fort followed research by members of the Allen County-Fort Wayne Historical Society and meticulous study of maps, drawings and plans to insure accuracy and authenticity. The restoration was to go beyond the constructing of a fort. Included in plans were colorful pioneer types, soldiers and trappers, shops and houses of pioneer vintage and period facilities for tourists and educational purposes. The project to recreate the Old Fort was talked for several generations. The Historic Fort Wayne group, headed by Barker, Lynn Koehlinger and Charles Walker, worked for a half-dozen years to raise funds and initiate construction plans. The Old Fort was scheduled for opening in 1976. The celebration of the Bicentennial in Fort Wayne was officially launched with a flag-raising ceremony by Mayor Lebamoff and Commission Chairman Ladonna Huntley on Jan. 24, 1975, at the City-County Building.

As the 20th Century passed the three-quarter point in Fort Wayne, the tempo and atmosphere of the city was quite another thing from a generation earlier, and a world apart from the turn-of-the-century city. Downtown was no longer a place people went to in the evenings. The fringes of the city were no longer rural. The pulse of the community was a fragmented article. Humpty-Dumpty had fallen from the wall and all the little parts grew legs and scattered in diverse directions.

Standing at the old Transfer Corner, Main and Calhoun Streets, a person could see nothing being transferred. The term had faded from use as surely as the old over-head trolley lines had disappeared. Only an occasional old building was in sight, with bare brick sides and crumbling lettering of enterprises long forgotten. The wide spaces were now occupied by stone government buildings, tall banks and fresher concrete. Teeming numbers of people were never seen, but a constant flow of individuals or couples went business-like from one building to another. Few vagrants any longer spent their hours around Courthouse Square or along Main Street. It was much cleaner and duller in that part of the city. Business activity continued a few blocks along Calhoun, Clinton, Berry and Wayne Streets, but faded fast beyond the constricted zone. Social life had deserted downtown except for the days of occasional festivals.

The clubs, restaurants, theatres and pageants had moved to a donut-shaped area which surrounded what had been the city prior to World War II. Exhibitions and people crowded shopping center malls. Impatient traffic swung along routes in the clogged donut. A thousand traffic signals were the most conscious environmental factor. Children walked less to play or school, and hardly ever wandered as far as downtown. Suburbia was a disjointed series of enclaves with attractive lawns and protection within; but surrounded by dangerous expressways and stretches of wasteland without sidewalks. The parks had more staff and planned activity, but less natural space.

The vitality of the community could be seen pumping in the growth of major corporations, diverse organizations, colorful arts and a constant flow of dreams sometimes partially realized. A consensus, though, was hard to come by on just what kind of human operaion the city was supposed to be. So many of the changes tended to make Fort Wayne a place rather than a town. Where at one time most roads led to the center of the city, by 1975 the roads were leading outward and not necessarily to any place in particular.

Yet, there was a spirit and harmony in 1975, perhaps more evident than in earlier times. It could be seen in the meeting places of the outlying areas. Downtown, men, women and their children came Sunday mornings and joined in spirit at old St. Paul's Lutheran, the colonial First Presbyterian, the greystone English Lutheran, the modern comfortable United Methodist and other churches. People still gathered to sing the songs of Christmas Eve at the Cathedral.

The Three Rivers Festival began to be an annual event in 1968 and activities involved most of the community. The great raft race drew as many as 100,000 people to the banks of the St. Joseph River. Hundreds of odd craft with varying floating qualities and thousands of participants went into the water. The race began at City Utilities Park and finished at the three rivers.

The Wabash Cannonball, a train of legend which went through Fort Wayne on the route between St. Louis and Detroit, took its last run through town on April 29, 1971, on the N&W line. Below left: The junking of cars continued as usual and people who no longer took trains were riding the buses. Below: a common sight starting in the late 1960s–groups protesting something as the bearded types at the Allen County Courthouse. On the opposite page, a heavy duty International truck manufactured in Fort Wayne chugs past city promotion.

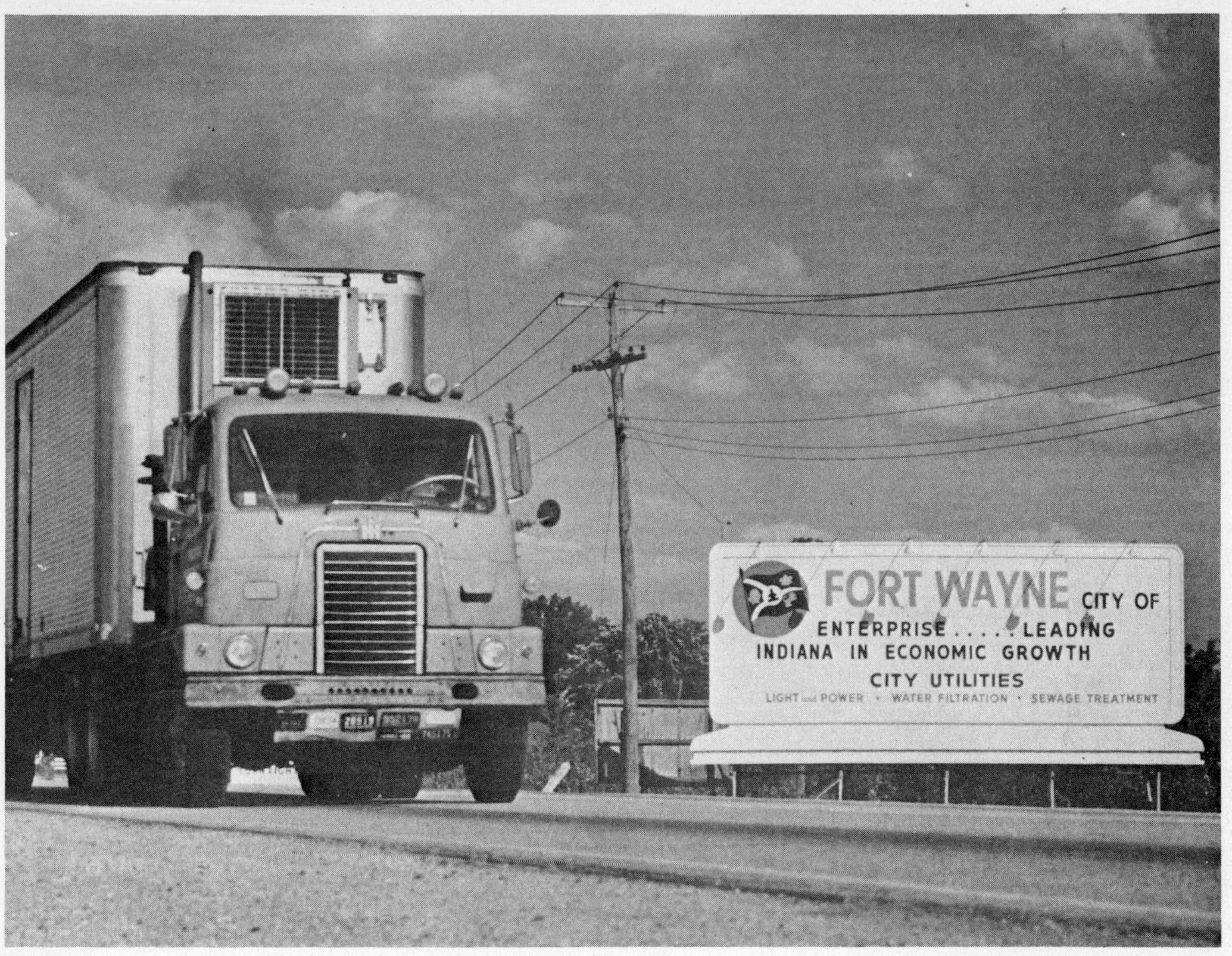

The following table shows the growth of the new Metro Area and the 15-county Retail Trading Zone as related to the 1960 and 1970 U.S. Censuses.

	POPULATION 1970	1960	% CHANGE	OCCUPIED HOUSEHOLDS 1970	1960	% CHANGE
Fort Wayne (City)	178,021	161,776	10.0%	57,627	50,149	14.9%
New Metro Area (1973)						
Allen County*	280,455	232,196	20.8%	85,720	68,743	24.6%
Adams	26,871	24,643	9.0%	7,982	7,010	13.8%
DeKalb	30,837	28,271	9.1%	9,466	8,479	11.6%
Wells	23,821	21,220	12.3%	7,529	6,504	15.7%
Total Metro	361,984	306,330	18.1%	110,697	90,736	21.9%
Area Counties						
Huntington	34,970	33,814	3.4%	11,069	10,391	6.5%
Kosciusko	48,127	40,372	19.2%	15,389	12,463	23.4%
LaGrange	20,890	17,380	20.2%	5,828	4,716	23.5%
Noble	31,382	28,162	11.4%	9,696	8,420	15.1%
Steuben	20,159	17,184	17.3%	6,455	5,301	21.7%
Wabash	35,553	32,605	9.0%	10,856	9,871	9.9%
Whitley	23,395	20,954	11.6%	7,299	6,276	16.3%
Defiance, O.	36,949	31,508	17.3%	10,675	8,931	19.5%
Paulding, O.	19,329	16,792	15.1%	5,676	4,897	15.9%
Van Wert, O.	29,194	28,840	1.2%	9,511	8,839	7.6%
Williams, O.	33,669	29,968	12.3%	10,667	9,233	15.5%
15-County Totals	695,601	603,903	15.2%	213,818	180,074	18.7%

* Central County

The City-County Building, shown at left during early construction in 1968, was dedicated Sept. 18, 1971, below. Other pictures show level workman hands and the lockup in the basement.

A bird's eye view of downtown in the summer of 1971 when the City-County Building was being completed. The 1973 News-Sentinel cartoon shows Mayor Lebamoff trying to decide what to do with old City Hall at Berry and Barr. Historical Society President Max Hobbs later proposed making it a historical and art museum.

Congressional candidate Allan Bloom, Governor Otis Bowen and Vice President Spiro Agnew met at Baer Field Oct. 3, 1972. Below is Main St. character Jimmy Richardson at the piano. The Mame cast completes the picture.

photo by gabriel delobbe

The Theatre Workshop Summer Musicals
Producer – Robert E. Behr
Associate Producer – Larry Wardlaw

Choral Director
KAREN TAYLOR

Musical Director
BARRY ASHTON

Technical Directors
MICHAEL MINICK
TIM SCHLIE

Costumer
MARGARET BLOOM

Stage Manager Margaret Geyer
Lighting Design Patrick Behr

1971 SEASON

MAME

Book by Jerome Lawrence and Robert E. Lee
Music and Lyrics by Jerry Herman
Entire Production Staged and choreographed by
BRUCE CURLESS

Ann Colone Donna Meek Taps Hines
Steve Morgan Jeoff Benward Milt Folds
Mary Bosk David Barngrover John Cronkhite
Kevin Behr Margaret Achleman David Ramm
Peppe Russell Roger Waters Kathy Belschner
Bruce Turner John Bechtelheimer Jerry Duguid
Carol Howell Ruth Ann Johnstone Rosalie Geller
Janine Griffis Susan Mahoney Dan O'Connell
John Silverman Larry Reynolds Bob Behr Tim Cooley
Dorothy Christman Bonnie Hart James J Goheen
Sylvia Bechtelheimer Janine Burke Delane Fielden Diana Moilanen
Jennifer Hanselmann Julie Hanselmann Elaine Duesel Janet Ankenbruck Lisa Haram Margaret Ankenbruck

"General, Are The Supply Wagons Coming?"

The Anthony Wayne statue was moved to the new Freimann Park on June 7, 1973, a location next to the under-financed Performing Arts Theatre. The interior arches of the theatre are shown during the building phase. Architect Louis Kahn, in the bottom picture, was on hand for the dedication Oct. 5, 1973.

At top is the First Wayne St. United Methodist Church going up in 1972, with the Sheraton Hotel to the right. Directly above is the interior of the Methodist Church completed in 1973. At left, Rabbi Seymour Weller of Bnai Jacob and Succoth Festival participants.

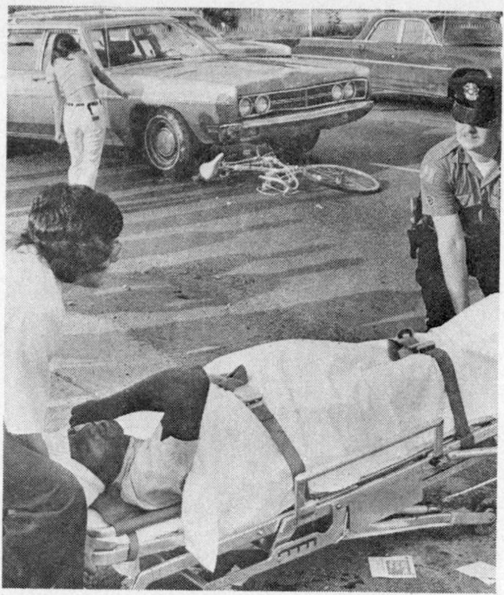

At left: A hot day of 1974 along Harrison St. and police to the rescue of a bike rider hit by a car at Clinton and Murray Streets. The Reform Jewish Temple is shown as it looked in 1974. Below is the scene along Berry St. after the Dec. 20, 1973, snow storm, with Courthouse and Anthony Wayne Bank in the background.

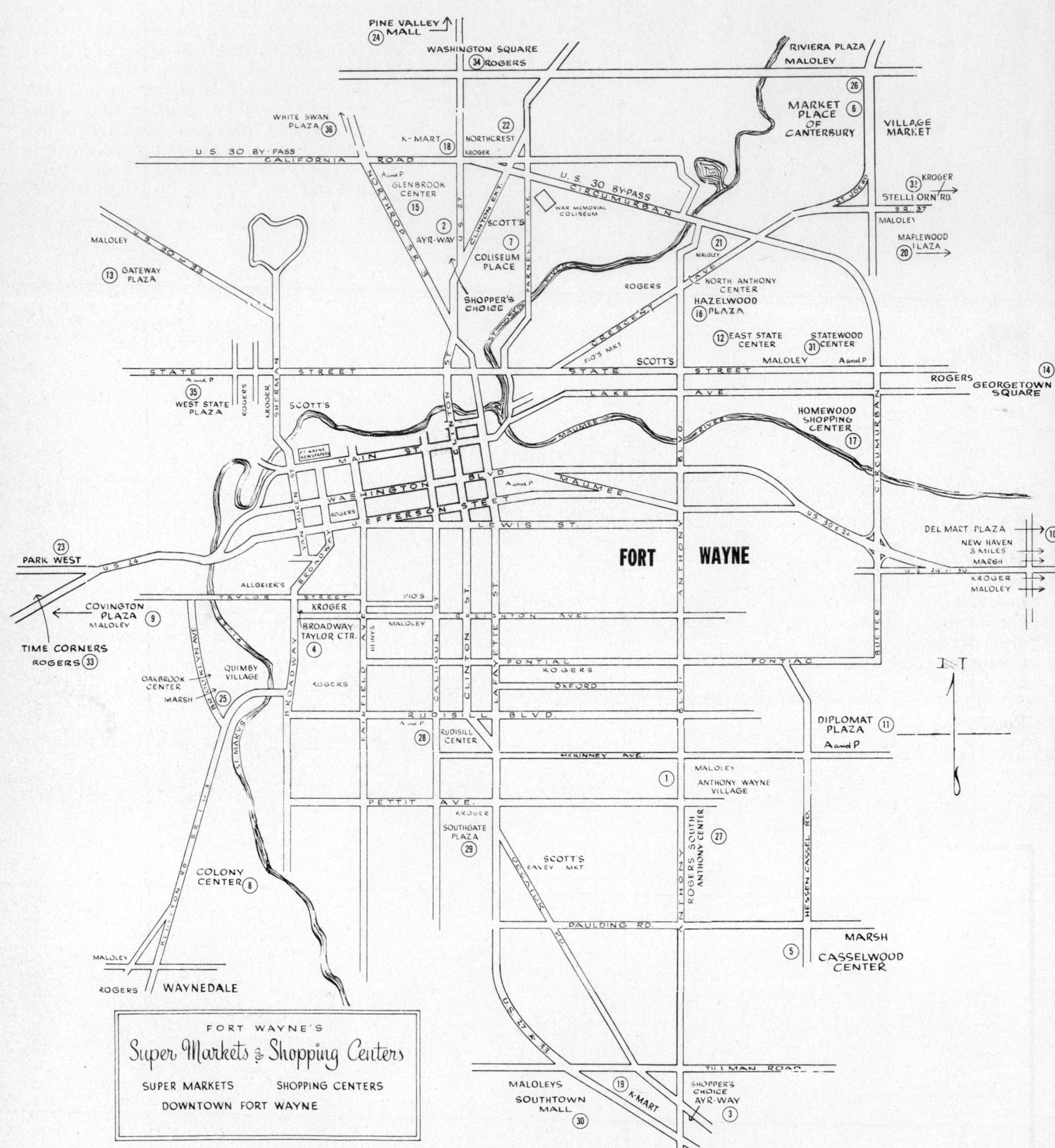

PINE VALLEY MALL
24
WASHINGTON SQUARE
34 ROGERS
RIVIERA PLAZA
MALOLEY
26
MARKET PLACE OF CANTERBURY
6
VILLAGE MARKET
WHITE SWAN PLAZA
36
K-MART
18
NORTHCREST
22
KROGER
U.S. 30 BY-PASS
CALIFORNIA ROAD
A and P
GLENBROOK CENTER
15
NORTHROP S.R. 3
U.S. 27
CLINTON EXT.
PARNELL AVE.
WAR MEMORIAL COLISEUM
U.S. 30 BY-PASS
CIRCUMURBAN
ST. JOE RD.
32 KROGER
STELLHORN RD.
S.R. 37
MALOLEY
MAPLEWOOD PLAZA
20
MALOLEY
U.S. 30 & 33
13 GATEWAY PLAZA
2
AYR-WAY
SCOTT'S
7
COLISEUM PLACE
SHOPPER'S CHOICE
21
MALOLEY
ROGERS
NORTH ANTHONY CENTER
HAZELWOOD PLAZA
16
12 EAST STATE CENTER
STATEWOOD CENTER
31
CRESCENT AVE.
FIO'S MKT
SCOTT'S
MALOLEY
A and P
STATE STREET
ROGERS
14
GEORGETOWN SQUARE
A and P
35
WEST STATE PLAZA
ROGERS
KROGER
SHERMAN
SCOTT'S
LAKE AVE.
HOMEWOOD SHOPPING CENTER
17
MAUMEE RIVER
CIRCUMURBAN
FT. WAYNE NEWSPAPERS
MAIN ST.
CLINTON
BLVD.
WASHINGTON
ROGERS
JEFFERSON STREET
A and P
MAUMEE
US 30 & 24
LEWIS ST.
VAN BUREN
BROADWAY
DEL MART PLAZA
10
NEW HAVEN 3 MILES
MARSH
U.S. 24 & 30
KROGER
MALOLEY
FORT WAYNE
23
PARK WEST
US 24
ALLGEIER'S
TAYLOR STREET
FIO'S
KROGER
COVINGTON PLAZA
MALOLEY
9
TIME CORNERS
ROGERS 33
BROADWAY-TAYLOR CTR.
4
MALOLEY
CREIGHTON AVE.
HEINYS
CALHOUN ST.
CLINTON ST.
LAFAYETTE ST.
ANTHONY BLVD.
BUETER
PONTIAC
ROGERS
OXFORD
OAKBROOK CENTER
MARSH
25
QUIMBY VILLAGE
BROOKLYN AVE.
ROGERS
FAIRFIELD AVE.
RUDISILL BLVD.
A and P
28
RUDISILL CENTER
DIPLOMAT PLAZA
11
A and P
McKINNEY AVE.
MALOLEY
1
ANTHONY WAYNE VILLAGE
ST. MARYS RIVER
PETTIT AVE.
KROGER
SOUTHGATE PLAZA
29
ROGERS SOUTH ANTHONY CENTER
27
SCOTT'S
EAVEY MKT
DECATUR RD.
HESSEN CASSEL RD.
COLONY CENTER
8
BLUFFTON RD. S.R. 1
PAULDING RD.
MARSH
5
CASSELWOOD CENTER
MALOLEY
ROGERS
WAYNEDALE
U.S. 27 & 33
TILLMAN ROAD
MALOLEYS
SOUTHTOWN MALL
30
19
K-MART
SHOPPER'S CHOICE
AYR-WAY
3
N
FORT WAYNE'S
Super Markets & Shopping Centers
SUPER MARKETS
SHOPPING CENTERS
DOWNTOWN FORT WAYNE

Mayor Lebamoff and downtown promoters meet at Wayne and Calhoun in 1974 to plan renewal, above. In the meantime, autos jam the parking area around Glenbrook Center along Coliseum Blvd. and trees come down at expanding Canterbury Green at St. Joe Road and St. Joe Center Road.

WORK FORCE SUMMARY

Fort Wayne Area (Allen County) — (in Thousands)

ANNUAL AVERAGE*

Employment Status	1972	1971	1970	1969	1962
TOTAL WORK FORCE	136.9	133.0	134.3	131.8	103.3
Unemployed	4.9	6.1	5.1	2.7	4.0
% Unemployed	3.6%	4.6%	3.8%	2.0%	3.8%
Employed	131.9	126.7	128.2	127.6	99.2
In Non-farm Industries	123.7	117.7	119.2	118.5	89.0
MANUFACTURING	44.0	42.2	44.2	45.2	37.0
Durable	35.5	33.7	36.0	36.9	30.6
Primary Metals	3.2	3.0	3.3	3.3	———
Non-electrical Machinery	5.0	4.5	5.1	5.1	3.5
Electrical Machinery	13.0	13.0	14.5	14.1	11.5
Transportation Equipment	11.8	10.9	10.7	11.8	9.9
‡ All Other Durables	2.5	2.3	2.4	2.6	8.6
Non-Durable	8.5	8.5	8.2	8.3	6.4
Food Products	3.4	3.6	3.5	3.6	3.5
‡ Printing and Publishing	1.2	1.1	1.2	1.2	———
Rubber & Misc. Plastics Products	2.7	2.6	2.3	2.4	———
‡ All Other Non-Durables	1.2	1.2	1.2	1.1	———
NON-MANUFACTURING	79.7	75.5	75.1	73.3	52.1
Contract Construction	5.8	4.9	5.1	5.8	4.1
Trans., Com. and Util.	8.8	8.4	8.3	8.0	6.9
Wholesale and Retail Trade	28.3	27.4	27.7	26.9	19.3
Fin., Ins. and Real Estate	6.8	6.8	6.6	6.2	4.8
Service and Misc. and Mining	17.3	15.6	15.4	15.1	9.9
Government	12.7	12.4	12.0	11.3	7.1
All Other Non-Agricultural	6.4	7.7	7.8	7.8	8.0
Agricultural	1.8	1.3	1.2	1.3	2.2

* *Indiana Employment Security Division and U.S. Department of Labor.*
‡ *Broken out of "All Other Mfg." 1968.*

Two views of the central area of the city in 1974: at left looking south and below looking northeast. In the meantime, a noon crowd relaxes at Freimann Park.

photo by gabriel delobbe

THEATRE WORKSHOP
DEPARTMENT OF PUBLIC PARKS
9th Season — 1972 — 73 — 41st Production

Musical Director: Robert Zehr
Choreographer: Jordan Hamm
Stage Manager: Barbara Jimenez

"CABARET"
by
JOE MASTEROFF, FRED EBB
JOHN VANDRUTEN, JOHN KANDER

Directed by
Larry Wardlaw & Rebecca Jewel

Nancy Williams
Helen Grimes
Mary Wishmeyer
Becky Munro
Kevin Demetroff

Candy Summers
Jeffrey Pike
Scott Simmons
Jeffery Ray
John Wilson
Robert Behr
Mary Bosk
Janie Davis
Jill Armstrong
Anne Welle-Strand

Larry True
Michael McVey
Michael Greene
Wayne Schaltenbrand
Donna Warren
Wynne Begun
George Koegel
Sharon Maher
Ed Dunlap
Elaine Duesel

Leg art one step ahead of Mack the Knife moves in Cabaret, across top of page. Just above are Christmas shoppers near North Highlands Apartments. The prices at left reflect the gasoline crisis which struck in late 1974, boosting prices from 30 cents to 50 cents a gallon, and higher.

This July crowd takes things easy while waiting for the parade. Later in 1974, the buildings in the block across Calhoun St. were razed to make way for Lincoln National Life expansion. Below, a Wabash, Indiana, float glides down Harrison St. But the parade was too long for baby.

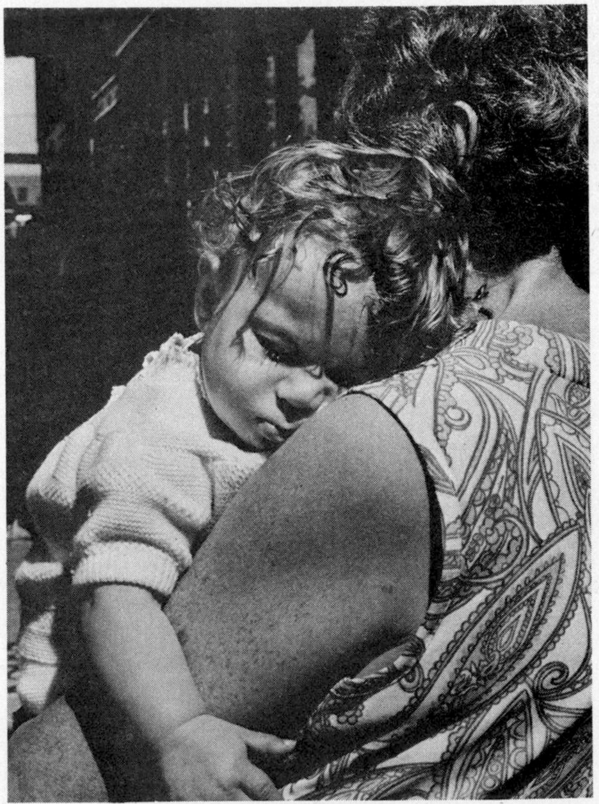

Donnelly P. McDonald, Jr., president of Peoples Trust Bank, and Robert Koppers, I&M vice-president, study model for a highrise downtown banking, office and shopping center in 1974. Below left is the General Telephone of Indiana headquarters built in 1972 west of the city. The girl below with the armed police officer is actually a boy caught in the act of armed robbery at a drug store.

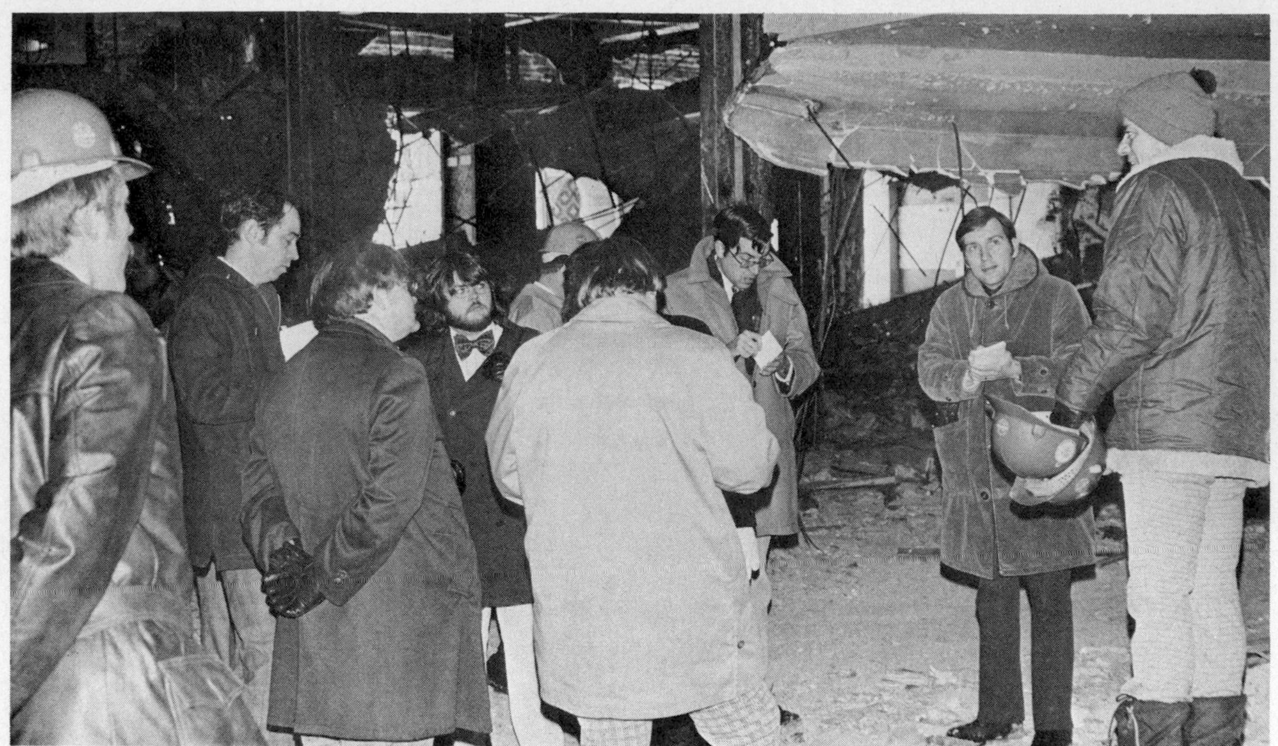

Newsmen, above, gather under the Van Orman Hotel at Berry and Harrison Streets just before the Sunday, Jan. 13, 1974, blast. Later in the year on October 20 the Keenan Hotel at Washington Blvd. and Harrison was also brought down in a controlled demolition explosion, with the result shown below.

On the opposite page, the Van Orman and Keenan come-downs make spectacular displays.

HOT

ADAMS

JUNIOR CHAMBER OF COMMERCE—JACK SOSENHEIMER

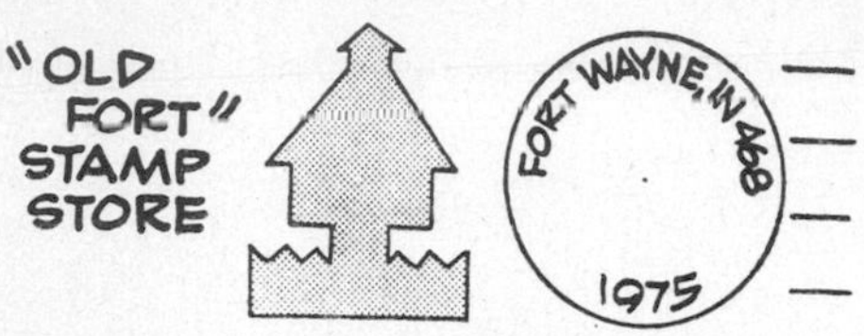

Art work by N-S staff artist Jerry Stewart

'Old Fort Wayne' Slated for Stamp?

Old Fort Wayne may debut as a collector's item— as a once-only special stamp cancellation.

Fort Wayne Postmaster Eugene J. Gabriel says, first, permission must be granted from Chicago Regional Postal authorities to reopen the Old Fort Stamp Store as a "philatelic center" at the Harrison Street Post Office.

The reconstruction of old Fort Wayne was underway in 1975 along the St. Mary's River. The drawing at top shows the fort design. The actual ground breaking was Nov. 19, 1974, with the ceremony pictured below. At left is a news story announcing the Old Fort stamp. In the meantime, Mayor Lebamoff and Ladonna Huntley, city Bicentennial chairman, raise the birthday flag on Jan. 24, 1975. Later in the year Governor Otis Bowen named Walter P. Helmke of Fort Wayne as chairman of the Indiana American Revolution Bicentennial Commission.

The fire of the Rosemarie Hotel, a stop-over place for three 19th Century Presidents, occurred Feb. 3, 1975. Arson was believed the cause of the hotel fire and another at the old Bash Building across Columbia St. Below, one-time basketball player Robert Armstrong, a Republican, is shown in a Sandeson political cartoon challenging Mayor Ivan Lebamoff after the May primary

"Politics Is A Game!"

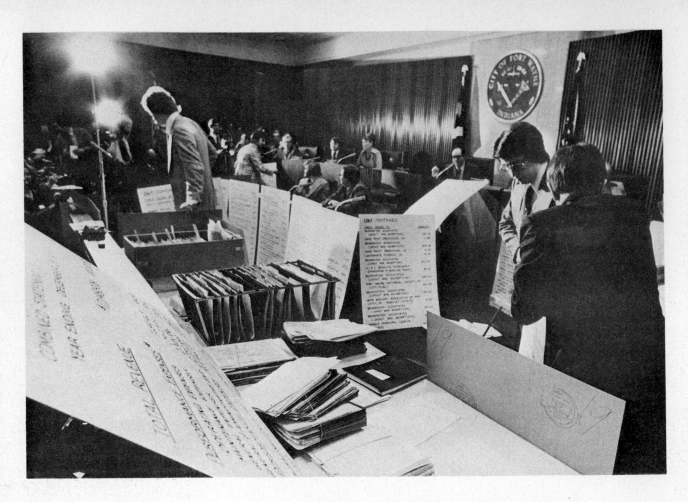

"I Brought Along Our Friend!"

One of the main controversies to develop in 1975 was over the use of City Utility funds by members of the City Administration for entertainment, travel and other purposes. It caused some excitement, confrontations and lots of paper at the City Council, shown above. The News-Sentinel cartoon, at right, depicts Mayor Lebamoff and Dr. Jerry Boswell, Board of Works chairman, on utility business.

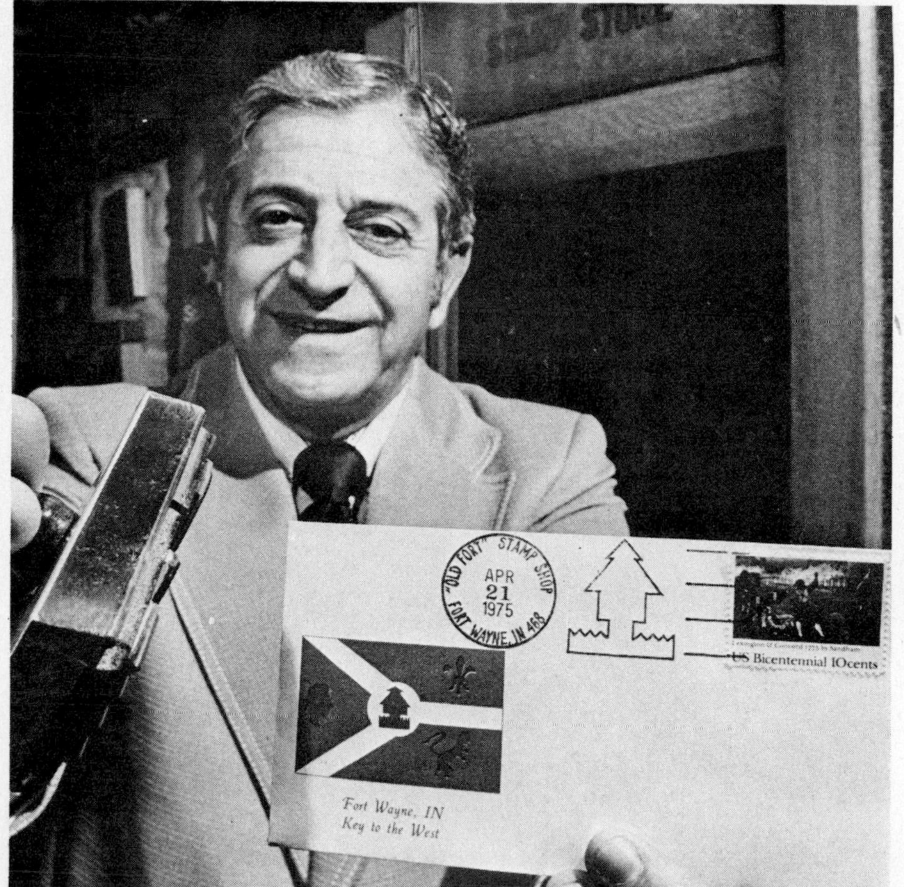

The rededication of the Allen County Courthouse, renewed after 75 years, was on Law Day, May 1, 1975. This interior shot from the third floor under the rotunda shows Walter E. Helmke, event chairman, at the lectern. Seated to his right are Governor Otis Bowen and Senator Birch Bayh. Others participating include state and county justices, county and city officials and quite a few onlookers from various angels. At left in the hands of Postmaster Eugene Gabriel is a letter with the Old Fort cancellation stamp of Fort Wayne, dated April 21, 1975.

Elected County Officials

Indiana State and Allen County officials elected or receiving majority votes in Allen County from 1900 to 1974, according to records of County Clerk Robert D. Hanson.

Election in 1900

Governor—John W. Kern (Winfield T. Durbin elected)
Lt. Governor—John C. Lawler
Secretary of State—Adam Heineerger
Rep., U.S. Congress—James M. Robinson
State Senator—George V. Kell
State Representatives—Charles L. Drummond, George W. Louttit, George B. Lawrence
Prosecutor—Emmett V. Emrick
Judge of Superior Court—John H. Aiken
County Sheriff—George W. Stout
County Assessor—William Eggemann
County Commissioners—August R. Schintker, Martin L. Moudy, Charles E. Orff
County Councilmen—William Franke, George W. Breckenridge, Charles Dalman, William Rorick, William H. Ringwalt
County Treasurer—John H. Rohan

1904

Governor—Jay F. Hanly
Lt. Governor—Hugh T. Miller
Secretary of State—Daniel E. Storms
Rep., U.S. Congress—James M. Robinson, Newton W. Gilbert
State Senator—John W. Tyndall, Hiram M. VanSweringen
State Representatives—Michael Sheridan, Albert R. Parker, Thomas M. Grake
Prosecutor—Daniel B. Ninde
County Sheriff—Jesse Grice
County Treasurer—Jacob Funk
County Commissioners—William Hockmeyer
ounty Recorder—George L. Ashley

1906

U.S. Senate—William Rinke
Rep., U.S. Congress—John W. Moor
Secretary of State—James F. Cox
State Representatives—Albert R. Parker, William Fruechtenicht, William S. Wells
Prosecutor—Albert E. Thomas
Judge of Superior Court—Owen W. Heaton
County Treasurer—William H. Scheiman
County Clerk—Joseph N. Mason
County Auditor—George W. Lindemuth
County Sheriff—Jesse Grice
County Assessor—William Eggemann
County Commissioners—William F. Franke, Joseph Tonkel, John B. Wyss
County Councilmen—Hiram B. Roller, Louis A. Cenlivre, William Smith, Jacob Gable, George W. Coverdale, Valentine L. Shaffer, Martin V. Metcalf

1908

Governor—Thomas R. Marshal
Lt. Governor—Frank J. Hall
Secretary of State—James F. Cox
Rep., U.S. Congress—Cyrus Cline
State Senator—Stephen B. Fleming, William J. Vesey
State Representatives—William S. Wells, Adolf Roggen, Robert B. Shirely
Prosecutor—Albert E. Thomas
County Treasurer—William H. Scheiman
County Recorder—Robert E. Kelly
County Sheriff—Arron M. Reichelderfer
County Commissioners—James D. Butt, John B. Wyss

1910

U.S. Senate—Frank Greenwall
Rep., U.S. Congress—Cyrus Cline
Secretary of State—Louis G. Ellingham
State Representatives—Adolf Roggen, Clifford J. Moran, William H. F. Moellering
Prosecutor—Harry H. Hilgemann
Judge of Superior Court—Carl Yaple
County Treasurer—Jay Herman Bueter
County Clerk—William E. Gerding
County Auditor—Calvin H. Brown
County Sheriff—Arron M. Reichelderfer
County Assessor—William Eggemann
County Commissioners—William F. Franke
County Councilmen—Louis Centlivre, Ira J. Grubb, James J. Hayes, George H. Viberg, William Reddin, Valentine Shaffer, Albert J. Black

1912

Governor—Samuel M. Ralston
Lt. Governor—William P. O'Neil
Secretary of State—Louis G. Ellingham
Rep., U.S. Congress—Cyrus Cline
State Senator—Stephen B. Fleming
State Representatives—Clifford J. Moran, William H. F. Moellering, Charles W. Koenig
Judge of Circuit Court—John W. Eggemann
Prosecutor—Harry H. Hilgeman
County Treasurer—Jay H. Bueter
County Recorder—Alan Hursh
County Sheriff—Amiel C. Gladieux
County Commissioners—Albert J. Black, Samuel D. Butt, William C. Schweir

1914

U.S. Senate—Benjamin F. Sively
Rep., U.S. Congress—Cyrus Cline
Secretary of State—Omer L. Cook
State Senator—Ochmig Bird
State Representatives—Michael Kinder, John B. Wyss, Joseph Tonkel
Judge of Superior Court—Carl Yaple
Prosecutor—Frank A. Emrick
County Treasurer—William J. Reinke
County Clerk—David C. Stout
County Auditor—Will Johnson
County Sheriff—Auriel C. Gladieux
County Assessor—William Eggemann
County Commissioners—Henry A. Wetzel, William C. Schweir
County Councilmen—Byron A. Hattersley, Louis A. Centlivre, George H. Viberg, William J. Reddin, Valentine Shaffer, Noah Amstutz, J. C. Wertz

1916

Governor—James P. Goodrich
Lt. Governor—Edward D. Bush
U.S. Senate—Harry S. New (long term), James E. Watson (short term)
Rep., U.S. Congress—Louis W. Fairfield
Secretary of State—Edward Jackson
State Senator—Glenn Van Auken, William Bowers
State Representatives—Melville M. Clapp, Francis E. Moore, Richard M. Vesey
Prosecutor—Levi A. Todd
County Treasurer—William F. Reinke
County Recorder—Elias H. Bookwalter
County Sheriff—George W. Gillie
County Commissioners—Adolf W. Lepper

1918

Rep., U.S. Congress—Louis W. Fairfield
Secretary of State—William A. Roach
State Senator—William Bowers
State Representatives—Charles A. Phelps, Richard Brandt, Jr., Richard Vesey
Prosecutor—Levi A. Todd
Judge of Superior Court—William N. Ballou
Circuit Court Judge—Sol A. Wood
County Treasurer—Ernest G. Kampe
County Clerk—Kent Sweet
County Auditor—Angus C. McCoy
County Recorder—Frank Cunnison
County Sheriff—George Gillie
County Assessor—Louis W. Oser
County Commissioners—Frank J. Poirson, A. J. Baker, Henry Hilgeman
County Councilmen—Henry A. Miller, Owen E. Garman, Al P. Smith, Alfred J. Pembrook, Charles F. Johnston, John B. Wyss, Orion H. Lake

1920

Governor—Warren T. McCray
Lt. Governor—Emmitt F. Branch
Attorney General—Ulysses S. Lesh
U.S. Senate—James E. Watson
Rep., U.S. Congress—Louis W. Fairfield
Secretary of State—Edward Jackson
State Senator—Lee Hartzell
State Representatives—Nathan C. Ross, Donald C. Rulo, Charles F. Tilden
Prosecutor—Louis F. Crosby
County Treasurer—Ernest Kampe
County Sheriff—Albert A. Abbott
County Commissioners—A. J. Baker, Gustave Hilgeman

1922

U.S. Senate—Samuel M. Ralston
Rep., U.S. Congress—Charles W. Branstrator
Secretary of State—Daniel M. Link
State Senator—Robert B. Shirley
State Representatives—Waldemar E. Eickhoff, Howard M. Hobbs, Arthur Ortlibb
Prosecutor—Samuel D. Jackson
Judge of Superior Court—Charles J. Ryan
County Treasurer—Thomas J. Connelly
County Clerk—Elmer Strum
County Auditor—John H. Johnson
County Recorder—Georgia H. Blume
County Sheriff—Louis C. Bobilya
County Assessor—Clayton Lindemuth
County Commissioners—Thomas Sheehan
County Councilmen—Thomas Dunkel, William Miner, John B. Wyss, Edwin A. Bittler, Henry A. Rockhill, Henry Grotrian, William Bruick

1924

Governor—Carlton E. McCulloch (Elected: Emmett F. Branch 1924-25; Ed Jackson 1925-29)
Lt. Governor—Fred H. Van Orman
Rep., U.S. Congress—David Hogg
Secretary of State—Fredrick E. Schortemeier
State Senator—Edward O'Rourke
State Representatives—H. O. Barr, Glenn P. Gardner, Harry W. Rowe
Circuit Court Judge—Sol A. Wood
Prosecutor—Samuel D. Jackson
County Treasurer—W. S. Roebuck
County Sheriff—Henry Marlin
County Commissioners—Orin H. Lake, A. J. Baker, Eli Slussman

1926

Rep., U.S. Congress—David Hogg
State Senator—Otto W. Koenig
State Representatives—Edward J. Braun, Payne Morgan, George Stolte
Prosecutor—Edwin R. Thomas
Judge of Superior Court—Charles J. Ryan
County Treasurer—Thomas J. Connelly
County Clerk—Louis C. Rippe
County Auditor—John H. Johnson
County Recorder—Adolf C. Bieberich

County Sheriff—Guy Emrick
County Assessor—Clayton A. Lindemuth
County Commissioners—Charles Miller, Jacob H. Able
County Councilmen—Thomas J. Sheehan, Henry A. Wetzel, John B. Wyss, Edmond A. Bittler, Hugh McFadden, Henry C. Grotrian, William Bruick

1928

Governor—Harry G. Leslie
Lt. Governor—Edward D. Bush
U.S. Senate—Arthur R. Robinson
Rep., U.S. Congress—David Hogg
Secretary of State—Otto G. Fifield
State Senator—Lee J. Hartzell
State Representatives—A. Everett Bloom, Lettie M. Ferguson, Louis E. Gerding
County Treasurer—Kent Sweet
County Sheriff—George Gillie
County Commissioners—Orin H. Lake
Prosecutor—Walter E. Helmke
Judge of Superior Court—George H. Leonard

1930

Rep., U.S. Congress—Thomas P. Riddle
Secretary of State—Frank Nayr, Jr.
State Senator—Harry M. Williams
State Representatives—Eugene Martin, Payne Morgan, George Stolte
Prosecutor—Otto W. Koenig
Judge of Superior Court—Charles J. Ryan
Circuit Court Judge—Clarence R. McNabb
County Treasurer—Fred W. Eggeman
County Clerk—Alma H. Reed
County Auditor—F. William Ortlieb
County Recorder—Adolf B. Bieberich
County Sheriff—Fred G. Lunz
County Assessor—Frank P. Sordelet
County Commissioners—Clarence Roy, Charles Miller, Jacob Gable
County Councilmen—William P. Bruick, Thomas J. Sheehan, John B. Wyss, Henry G. Wetzel, Henry A. Rockhill, Henry G. Grotrian, Martin Goeglein

1932

Governor—Paul V. McNutt
Lt. Governor—M. Clifford Townsend
Rep., U.S. Congress—James Farley
Secretary of State—Frank Nayr, Jr.
State Representatives—Edward J. Braun, Pat J. Cain, Alfred H. Randall
Prosecutor—Otto W. Koenig
Judge of Superior Court—Harry W. Muller
County Treasurer—Fred W. Eggeman
County Sheriff—Fred G. Lunz
County Commissioners—William B. Johnson, Paul P. Kinder

1934

Rep., U.S. Congress—James Farley
State Senator—Martin J. Cleary
State Representatives—Edward J. Braun, Allan C. Lamont, Payne Morgan
Prosecutor—Byron Hayes
Judge of Superior Court—Charles J. Ryan
County Treasurer—Clifford H. Borgman
County Clerk—Alma H. Reed
County Auditor—F. William Ortlieb
County Recorder—Pat J. Cain
County Sheriff—George W. Gillie
County Assessor—Frank P. Sordelet
County Commissioners—Clarence B. Roy
County Councilmen—William P. Bruick, Jacob H. Gable, John B. Wyss, Edmond A. Bittler, Henry A. Rockhill, Fred H. Gable, Martin Goeglein

1936

Governor—M. Clifford Townsend
Lt. Governor—Henry Schricker
Rep., U.S. Congress—James I. Farley
Secretary of State—August Mueller
State Senator—Alfred H. Randall
State Representatives—Edward J. Braun, Arthur J. Gladieux, Charles F. Lenz
Prosecutor—C. Byron Hayes
Judge of Superior Court—Harry W. Muller
Circuit Court Judge—Harry H. Hilgeman
County Treasurer—Clifford H. Borgman
County Sheriff—Herman C. Holle
County Commissioners—Clarence E. Roy, William A. Johnson, Paul B. Kinder

1938

State Senator—Wilbur A. DeWeese
State Representatives—W. O. Hughes, Harold E. Korn, Garth H. Vernor
Prosecutor—James O. Ballou
Judge of Superior Court—Edward W. Meyers
County Treasurer—Walter E. Klebe
County Clerk—Dorothy Gardner
County Recorder—Lester E. Garman
County Sheriff—Walter A. Felger
County Assessor—Elmer M. Cook
County Commissioners—Carl O. White, James T. Johnson
County Councilmen—Richard T. Blitz, Ralph K. Snyder, Harry E. Wineland, Josephine Black, Joseph B. Corbat, Glenn H. Lake

1940

Governor—Glenn R. Hillis (Elected: Henry F. Schricker)
Lt. Governor—Charles M. Dawson
U.S. Senate—Raymond E. Willis
Rep., U.S. Congress—George W. Gillie
Secretary of State—James M. Tucker
State Senator—Lucius Somers
State Representatives—W. O. Hughes, Harold E. Korn, Charles A. Phelps
Prosecutor—James O. Ballou

Judge of Superior Court—George H. Leonard
Judge of Appellate Court—Dan C. Flanagan
County Treasurer—Walter E. Klebe
County Sheriff—Walter A. Felger
County Commissioners—Clay F. Spalding

1942

State Senator—Charles A. Phelps
State Representatives—W. O. Hughes, Harold E. Korn, Paul C. Moellering
Prosecutor—A. Everett Bloom
Judge of Superior Court—Edward W. Meyers, D. Burns Douglass
Circuit Court Judge—William H. Schannen
County Treasurer—Walter A. Felger
County Clerk—Dorothy Gardner
County Auditor—John A. Browar
County Recorder—Lester Garman
County Sheriff—Walter C. Adams
County Assessor—Elmer M. Cook
County Commissioners—Clay F. Spalding, Erven Knight, James Liggett
County Councilmen—Richard F. Blitz, Lawrence Heiny, Ralph K. Snyder, Winifred Spalding, Glenn Stouffer, Elsworth Snider, Carl Rekeweg

1944

Governor—Ralph F. Gates
Lt. Governor—Richard T. James
U.S. Senate—Homer E. Capehart (long term), William E. Jenner
Rep., U.S. Congress—George W. Gillie
Secretary of State—Rue J. Alexander
State Representatives—W. O. Hughes, Harold E. Korn, Paul C. Moellering
Prosecutor—A. Everett Bloom
Judge of Superior Court—George Leonard
Judge of Appellate Court—Dan C. Flanagan
County Treasurer—Walter A. Felger
County Sheriff—Walter C. Adams
County Commissioners—Erven Knight, James A. Liggett

1946

U.S. Senate—William E. Jenner
Rep., U.S. Congress—George W. Gillie
Secretary of State—Harry E. McClain
State Senator—Dorothy Gardner
State Representatives—W. O. Hughes, Harold E. Korn, Paul C. Moellering
Prosecutor—Alton L. Bloom
Judge of Superior Court—Edward W. Meyers
County Treasurer—Samuel Cook
County Clerk—Elton L. Marquart
County Auditor—Fred C. Wissman
County Recorder—Carl Rekeweg
County Sheriff—Harold Zeis
County Assessor—Elmer M. Cook
County Commissioners—William E. Roussey
County Councilmen—Winifred Spalding, Glenn Slof-fer, Elsworth Snider, Glenn H. Lake, Richard T. Blitz, Chauncy L. Griffith, Ralph K. Snyder

1948

Governor—Henry F. Schricker
Lt. Governor—Rue J. Alexander
Rep., U.S. Congress—Edward H. Kruse, Jr.
Secretary of State—Alfred Anthony Ferrini
State Senator—Lucius Somers
State Representatives—W. O. Hughes, Harold E. Korn, Paul E. Mollering, Bernard Swanson, Jr.
Prosecutor—Alton L. Bloom
Judge of Superior Court—George H. Leonard
Judge Circuit Court—William H. Schannen
County Treasurer—Samuel Cook
County Sheriff—Harold S. Zeis
County Commissioners—Emmet Harper, Erven Knight, Charles E. Freiburger

1950

Rep., U.S. Congress—E. Ross Adair
State Senator—Dorothy Gardner
State Representatives—Richard B. Fishering, W. O. Hughes, Paul E. Moellering, Bernard Swanson, Jr.
Prosecutor—John Reiber
Judge of Superior Court—Edward W. Meyers
County Treasurer—Willis Hite
County Clerk—Elton L. Marquart
County Auditor—Fred C. Wissman
County Recorder—Carl Rekeweg
County Sheriff—Harold S. Zeis
County Assessor—Elmer Cook
County Commissioners—Erven Knight, Samuel Cook
County Councilmen—Richard T. Blitz, Samuel Fletcher, Donald L. Myers, Winifred Spalding, Thomas H. Kendall, Lester Gerardot, Glenn H. Lake

1952

Governor—George N. Craig
Lt. Governor—Harold W. Handley
U.S. Senate—William E. Jenner
Rep., U.S. Congress—E. Ross Adair
Secretary of State—Crawford F. Parker
State Senator—Lucius Somers
State Representatives—Richard B. Fishering, W. O. Hughes, Paul C. Moellering
Prosecutor—John G. Reiber
Judge of Superior Court—Harold E. Korn
County Treasurer—Willis D. Hite
County Commissioners—P. E. Henebry

1954

Rep., U.S. Congress—E. Ross Adair
State Senator—Dorothy Gardner
State Representatives—Robert H. Berning, Richard B. Fishering, W. O. Hughes
Prosecutor—Glen J. Beams
Judge of Superior Court—Robert E. Leonard

Judge Circuit Court—William H. Schannen
County Clerk—Robert K. Hawkins
County Recorder—Dorothy E. Raver
County Sheriff—Harold S. Zeis
County Assessor—Elmer M. Cook
County Commissioners—P. E. Henebry, Erven Knight, Samuel Cook
County Councilmen—Richard T. Blitz, Samuel W. Fletcher, Carl Suedhoff, Max P. Shambaugh, Thomas H. Kendall, Lester F. Gerardot, Ezra Shanebeck

1956

Governor—Harold W. Handley
Lt. Governor—Crawford F. Parker
U.S. Senate—Homer E. Capehart
Rep., U.S. Congress—E. Ross Adair
Secretary of State—Frank A. Lenning
State Senator—Lucius Somers
State Representatives—Robert H. Berning, Richard B. Fishering, W. O. Hughes, D. P. McDonald, Jr.
Judge of Superior Court—Harold E. Korn, Lloyd S. Hartzler
County Treasurer—Harland E. Pressler
County Commissioners—Erven Knight, Samuel Cook

1958

Rep., U.S. Congress—E. Ross Adair
State Senator—Chester K. Watson
State Representatives—Edward Degelman, Eugene E. Smith, Charles H. Young
Prosecutor—J. Byron Hayes
Judge of Superior Court—William L. Burger
County Clerk—Elmer Smith
County Auditor—Robert Shambaugh
County Recorder—Richard Hartman
County Sheriff—Custer A. Dunifon
County Assessor—C. Ross Lindemuth
County Commissioners—Fred W. Meyers
County Councilmen—J. Alban Becker, Edmund P. Sanborn, Orville R. Sturm, Ruth R. Turner, Clifford J. Reuille, Russell E. Huber, Lester F. Gerardot

1960

Governor—Crawford F. Parker (Elected: Matthew E. Welsh)
Lt. Governor—Richard O. Ristine
Rep., U.S. Congress—E. Ross Adair
Secretary of State—Charles O. Hendricks
State Auditor—Dorothy Gardner
State Senator—Lucius Somers
State Representatives—William A. Berning, Dale J. Myers, Walter H. Summers
Judge of Superior Court—Harold E. Korn, Lloyd S. Hartzler
Judge Circuit Court—W. O. Hughes
County Treasurer—Harland E. Pressler
County Commissioners—Harry B. Amstutz, Glenn H. Lake, John R. Hartman

1962

Rep., U.S. Congress—E. Ross Adair
State Senator—Allan E. Bloom
State Representatives—William A. Berning, Arthur C. Hayes, Samuel A. Rea
Prosecutor—Walter P. Helmke
Judge of Superior Court—Dale J. Myers
County Clerk—Elton L. Marquart
County Auditor—Walter H. Summers
County Recorder—Dorothy E. Raver
County Sheriff—Custer A. Duniforn
County Assessor—Melvin A. Azar
County Commissioners—Glenn H. Lake, John R. Hartman
County Councilmen—John Ankenbruck, Louis W. Bonsib, William S. Latz, Charles H. Weyrick, Harry W. Bender, Max Shambaugh, Edgar Bohn

1964

Governor—Roger D. Branigin
Lt. Governor—John M. Ryan
U.S. Senate—D. Russell Bontrager
Rep., U.S. Congress—E. Ross Adair
Secretary of State—John D. Bottorff
State Auditor—Mark L. France
State Senator—Chester K. Watson
State Representatives—William A. Berning, Elmer MacDonald, John R. Sinks, Arthur C. Hayes, Samuel A. Rea
Judge of Superior Court—Frank J. Celarek, Lloyd S. Hartzler
County Treasurer—Chester L. Graffis
County Commissioners—Fred W. Meyer

1966

Rep., U.S. Congress—E. Ross Adair
State Senator—Allen E. Bloom, Dean Kruse
State Representatives—Arthur C. Hayes, Wm. S. Latz, Thomas V. McComb, Samuel A. Rea, John R. Sinks
Prosecutor—Walter P. Helmke
Judge of Superior Court—Dale J. Myers
Judge Circuit Court—W. O. Hughes
County Clerk—Elton Marquart
Conty Auditor—Walter Summers
Cunty Recorder—Dorothy E. Raver
County Sheriff—Robert A. Bender
County Assessor—Melvin A. Azar
County Commissioners—Glenn H. Lake, Charles H. Weyrick
County Councilmen—John V. Ankenbruck, Louis W. Bonsib, Richard Ellenwood, Fredrick R. Hunter, Mervin Ehle, Max P. Shambaugh, Alvin C. Burkett

1968

Governor—Edgar D. Whitcomb
Lt. Governor—Richard E. Folz
U.S. Senate—William D. Ruckelshaus

Rep., U.S. Congress—E. Ross Adair
Secretary of State—William N. Salin
State Senator—Phillip E. Gutman
State Representatives—Arthur C. Hayes, Wm. S. Latz, Thomas V. McComb, Samuel A. Rea, John R. Sinks
Judge of Superior Court—Frank J. Celarek, Harold E. Korn
County Treasurer—Chester L. Graffis
County Commissioners—Richard M. Ellenwood

1970

Rep., U.S. Congress—J. Edward Roush
State Senator—Walter P. Helmke, Thomas V. McComb
State Representatives—Arthur C. Hayes, William S. Latz, Elmer MacDonald, Samuel A. Rea, John R. Sinks
Prosecutor—Arnold Duemling
Judge of Superior Court—Alfred W. Moellering
County Clerk—Robert D. Hanson
County Auditor—Dorothy E. Raver
County Recorder—Irene Swihart
County Sheriff—Robert A. Bender
County Assessor—Walter H. Summers
County Commissioners—Charles N. Hoemig, Charles Weyrick
County Councilmen—Irwin C. Bandemer, Vance L. Amstutz, Max Shambaugh, Roger J. Bruck, Louis Bonsib, Cook Lougheed, Ronald Kleopfer

1972

Governor—Otis R. Bowen
Lt. Governor—Robert D. Orr
Rep., U.S. Congress—J. Edward Roush
State Senator—Phillip E. Gutman
State Representatives—Wm. S. Latz, Elmer MacDonald, Richard W. Worman, Victor Zimmerman, Jack K. Dunifon, Thomas E. Fruechtenicht, John R. Sinks
Judge of Superior Court—Louis L. Bloom, Frank Celarek, Philip R. Thieme
Judge Circuit Court—Herman Busse
County Treasurer—Dorothy E. Myers
County Commissioners—Richard M. Ellenwood

1974

Rep., U.S. Congress—J. Edward Roush
State Senator—Woodrow Wilson, Graham A. Richard
State Representatives—Richard W. Worman; James J. Sherron; Elmer MacDonald; Victor Timmerman; Thomas E. Fruechtenicht; Richard L. Worden, Sr.; John R. Sinks
Prosecutor—Arnold H. Duemling
County Clerk—Robert D. Hanson
County Sheriff—Charles B. Meeks
County Auditor—Joan Uebelhoer
County Recorder—Irene E. Swihart
County Assessor—Barton C. Blosser
County Commissioners—Vance L. Amstutz, Jack K. Dunifon
County Councilmen—James H. Blanks, Sr.; Richard W. Kees; Edwin J. Rousseau; Edwin Nieter; Carl J. Suedhoff, Jr.; Gloria Goeglein; Richard L. Summers

Notes and Bibliography

The notes and bibliography of this volume are in chapter sequence and the approximate order the reader will encounter in the work proper.

Part 1

Record of the Parish de Notre Dame de Quebec, 1668; Archives Publiques, Ottawa, Canada. Baptism of Jean Baptiste Bissot.

Acts, 1763, Archives Publiques de Quebec, Ottawa, Canada: "On the 24th of January, 1656, the vestry board of the parish de Notre Dame de Quebec conceded to Francois Bissot, Sieur de la Riviere, a pew of six feet in length and three and one-half in depth in said church to possess for himself and his heirs in perpetuity in consideration of 100 livres once paid.
"On the 8th of April, 1729, Francois Bissot . . . brought action against the vestry board of Quebec to compel it to put him in possession of the pew of his father (Jean Baptiste Bissot, son of the original Francois Bissot.)" The suit serves to establish that Francois, or Francis Morganne Vincennes of Fort Miami (Fort Wayne) and Au Poste (Vincennes, Indiana) was the son of Jean Baptiste Bissot de Vincennes, the founder of Miamitown, later Fort Wayne.

Acts, Series M, Archives Publiques de Quebec, Ottawa, Canada. Statement by Frederick Haldimand, governor-general of Canada, 1786, confirmed to Sieur Joseph Roy, siegneur and proprietor of the seignory of Vincennes. The Haldimand statement reports the Roys got the Vincennes fief in 1749; and also traces the granting of the original Vincennes fief to the Bissots on Nov. 3, 1672, by King Louis XIV.

J. D. Campbell, the Vincennes Genealogy. The previously unpublished report by Campbell, Montreal, Canada, was sent to B. J. Griswold, Fort Wayne historian, on Feb. 8, 1918. Copy in Fort Wayne Public Library, Fort Wayne, Indiana.

Pierre-Georges Roy, Le Sieur de Vincennes; a

genealogy. Charrier & Dugal, Quebac, 1919.

J. D. Campbell, French Commandants at Fort Wayne. Notes from the French Council of Marine, Paris, reported by Campbell at Montreal in 1918.

Charles Poinsatte, Fort Wayne 1716 to 1829, a history thesis at the University of Notre Dame (1951).

Francois Roye, letter from Miamitown, May 12, 1719. The letter for the illiterate Roye (later Roy) was actually written by Jean Baptiste Bissot and is the oldest existing document of Fort Wayne. It was given by J. D. Campbell, Montreal, to B. J. Griswold, Fort Wayne, in 1919. In just 30 years after the 1719 date, the Roy family succeeded to the Vincennes title and estates in Quebec.

Moreau St. Mery, Historique de la Louisiane, Vol. 24. Richardville's report on the death of Vincennes and others in 1736.

De Celeron de Bienville, Journal in 1749.

De Bonnecamps, S.J., Journal, Oct. 17, 1750; Archives of the Marine, Paris, France. Jean de Bonnecamps was professor of mathematics at Jesuit College, Quebec, before returning to France in April, 1759.

Coulon de Villiers, Journal, in The Olden Time, ed. Neville B. Craig.

Walter O'Meara, Guns at the Forks, Prentice Hall (1965).

Charles H. Bartlett and Richard Lyon, La Salle in the Valley of the St. Joseph. Fort Wayne Public Library Publication.

Elbert Jay Benton, Wabash Trade Route. Fort Wayne Public Library Publication.

Daniel Boone, Memoirs, Missouri Historical Papers, St. Charles, Mo.

Wallace A. Brice, A History of Fort Wayne, Jones & Sons (1868).

Pierre F. X. Charlevoix, History of New France, Paris, 1744, Francis P. Harper.

Willis F. Dunbar, Michigan, Wm. B. Eerdmans Publishing Co. (1965).

B. J. Griswold, The Pictorial History of Fort Wayne. Robert O. Law Company, Chicago (1917).

Charles Hanna, The Wilderness Trail. The Knickerbocker Press (1911).

Thomas Hutchins, Papers of Sir John Johnson, Vol. 10. Albany (1951).

J. Alton James, The Life of George Rogers Clark. Univ. of Chicago Press (1928).

Louise P. Kellogg, The Old Northwest. Wisconsin Historical Society (1935).

Thomas T. McAvoy, The Catholic Church in Indiana. Columbia University Press (1940).

Francis Parkman, Count Frontenac and New France Under Louis XIV. Little, Brown and Co. (1907).

Howard H. Peckham, Pontiac and the Indian Uprising. Princton University Press (1947).

Milo M. Quaife, Journal of Henry Hay. The Citadel Press (1962).

Henry R. Schoolcraft, History of the Indian Tribes, Lippincott (1851).

Charles E. Slocum, History of the Maumee River Basin. Defiance, Ohio (1905).

General Arthur St. Clair, Papers edited by W. H. Smith. Robert Clark and Co. (1882).

Anthony Wayne, Correspondence on the Northwest Campaign. War Department Archives.

General James Wilkinson, Memoirs of My Own Times. Philadelphia (1816).

War Department, Official Communications, 1783-1794.

George Washington, Messages and Papers of the President.

Calvin M. Young, Little Turtle, the Great Chief of the Miamis. Greenville, Ohio.

U.S. Territorial Papers, Volumes on the Northwest Territory..

Part 2

Portions of Parts 1 and 2 appeared in the author's "Five Forts," News Publishing Co., Fort Wayne, 1973.

The main sources for Part 2 are the American and Canadian military histories as preserved in government archives at Washington, D.C., and Ottawa, Canada. Wherever possible, at-the-scene accounts are used as told in the diaries and journals of Capt. John Cooke, Private Bryant, Lt. William Clark, General James Wilkinson and Anthony Wayne's correspondence with Col. John Hamtramck and others. Similarly, the correspondence of William Henry Harrison with both his subordinates and with the War Department and the accounts of Robert B. McAfee are essential to the 1812 War period.

American State Papers, Anthony Wayne correspondence with Secretaries of War Henry Knox, Timothy Pickering and James McHenry.

American State Papers, William Henry Harrison correspondence with Secretary of War Henry Dearborn.

Canadian Archives, Ottawa, Papers of John Graves Simcoe, governor-general of Upper Canada, 1795.

Canadian Archives, Ottawa, Lasselle Letters.

Bert Anson, The Miami Indians. University of Oklahoma Press (1970).

John D. Barnhart, Valley of Democracy. Indiana University Press (1953).

Wallace A. Brice, History of Fort Wayne. Jones and Sons (1868).

Lewis Cass, Inquiries of the Indians. Detroit (1823).

John B. Dillon, A History of Indiana. Bingham and Doughty (1859).

Capt. Allan Dougal, Death of Captain Wells. Fort Wayne Gazette (1887).

Randolph C. Downes, Council Fires on the Upper Ohio. University of Pittsburgh Press (1940).

Willis F. Dunbar, Michigan. Wm. B. Eerdmans Publishing Co. (1965).

Logan Esarey, Messages and Letters of William Henry Harrison. Indiana Historical Bureau, Indianapolis (1922).

B. J. Griswold, The Pictorial History of Fort Wayne. Robert O. Law Co., Chicago (1917).

B. J. Griswold, Fort Wayne, Gateway of the West, 1802-1813. Indianapolis (1927). This is essentially a collection of journals by the commandants, agents and factors at Fort Wayne.

Benson J. Lossing, The Pictorial Fieldbook of the War of 1812. Harper Brothers (1868).

Robert B. McAfee, History of the Late War. Historical Publications Company (1919).

Isaac McCoy, History of the Baptist Indian Missions. Washington (1840).

Ora Brooks Peake, A History of the United States Indian Factory System, 1795-1822. Sage Books (1954).

Charles C. Royce, Indian Land Concessions. Washington (1899).

Charles E. Slocum, History of the Maumee River Basin. Defiance, Ohio (1905).

Gayle Thornbrough, Indian Agency at Fort Wayne. Indiana Historical Society (1961).

Constantin F. S. Volney, The Aboriginal Tribes of America. J. Conrad and Co., Philadelphia (1804).

James Wilkinson, Memoir of My Own Times. Philadelphia (1816).

George Washington, Messages and Papers of the President.

John Adams, Messages and Papers of the President.

Jefferson, Messages and Papers of the President.

U.S. Territorial Papers, Volumes on the Northwest Territory and Indiana.

Joseph Levine, John Jacob Hays. Indiana Jewish Historical Society, Fort Wayne, Ind. (1973).

Part 3

Outline of Fort Wayne History, 1750-1860. Fort Wayne Daily Sentinel (July 10, 1874).

First Presbyterian Church in Fort Wayne. Staff publication of the Fort Wayne Public Library (1959).

Fort Wayne Sentinel (May 10, 1841).

R. S. Robertson, The Organization of Allen County. Brant & Fuller, Madison, Wis. (1889).

Bessie K. Roberts, Thomas Swinney. Allen County-Fort Wayne Historical Society paper, Fort Wayne (1963).

Jesse L. Williams, The Summit City. Fort Wayne Gazette (1873).

Rex M. Potterf, Wabash and Erie Canal. Fort Wayne Public Library (1970).

Harold W. Thompson; Body, Boots & Britches. J. B. Lippincott Co. (1939).

Fort Wayne on the Old Canal. Staff publication of the Fort Wayne Public Library (1952).

Johnny Appleseed, Orchardist. Staff publication of the Fort Wayne Public Library (1963).

W. D. Haley, Johnny Appleseed. Harper's Magazine (November, 1871).

A. Banning Norton, History of Knox County, Ohio (1862). Notes on Johnny Appleseed.

J. Richard Beste, The Wabash, or Adventure of an English Gentleman's Family in the Interior of Indiana. London (1855). Gives a colorful and personal view of canal travel.

B. J. Griswold, Pictorial History of Fort Wayne. Robert O. Law Co., Chicago (1917).

Part 4

The Winifred J. Randall Collections (she operated the Randall Hotel on Harrison St. at the foot of Columbia St.) detail much of the colorful early beginnings of the canal houses and inns. She also mentioned the beginnings of the woolen mills and the part the father of Theodore Dreiser and Paul Dresser had in the mills, a fact confirmed by Dreiser's memoirs. She said he was a loommaker; Dreiser said his father was manager. The notes include recollections of William Buckles, Charles Freese, Charles Comparet and Julia Baker Stapleford. The collection was published by the Allen County-Fort Wayne Historical Society with reprints by the Public Library in 1960.

The notes on the Swinney and Tabor families were compiled by Bessie Keeran Roberts under the title, "Donor of Fort Wayne's First Park." The paper of the Historical Society was reprinted by the Public Library in 1963.

The booklet, "First Presbyterian Church in Fort Wayne," was compiled in 1959 from older historical works and newspaper sources by the Allen County-Fort Wayne Historical Society and printed by the Public Library.

"The Catholic Church in Fort Wayne," a 1961 publication of the Fort Wayne Public Library, draws on earlier historical works and articles to outline Catholic development from the French period to 1900.

Mildred L. Burger compiled the "Short History of the Lutheran Church-Missouri Synod in Fort Wayne, Indiana," a booklet of the Fort Wayne Public Library (1967).

Richard L. May, Notes on the Formation of the Republican Party in Fort Wayne, Indiana, 1852-1858. The source for conflicts of the Temperance Movement and early newspaper editors Thomas Tigar and John Dawson. Fort Wayne Public Library reprint (1967).

B. J. Griswold, Pictorial History of Fort Wayne, Robert O. Law Co. (1917). Also used in railroad development pertaining to the Wabash, was Norfolk and Western Magazine (Oct. 15, 1973).

R. Gerald McMurtry, Fort Wayne's Contacts with Abraham Lincoln. Fort Wayne Public Library booklet (1966).

"Colonel Sion S. Bass, 1827-1862." Report published by the Fort Wayne Public Library (1958).

"Colonel Robert S. Robertson, 1839-1906." Undated compilation by the Fort Wayne Library staff, based on earlier records including Robertson's own historical works, Valley of the Upper Maumee River; Recollections of the War.

"Captain James B. White." Sketch based on earlier records and undated publication by the Fort Wayne Public Library.

"Major General Henry W. Lawton of Fort Wayne, Indiana." Booklet, Fort Wayne Public Library (1954).

Hilary A. Sadler, "Mother George, Fort Wayne's Angel of Mercy." Originally published in the Fort Wayne Journal-Gazette, revised printing Fort Wayne Public Library (1964).

T. B. Helm, History of Allen County (1879).

David L. Drury, Historical Narratives. Fort Wayne Journal-Gazette (1973). Notes on growth of Pennsylvania Shops and John Bass Foundry.

Merle Rice, The History of the Pennsylvania Railroad's Fort Wayne Shops. Allen County-Fort Wayne Historical Society publication, reprinted Fort Wayne Public Library (1966).

Nickel Plate Road, 1959 Annual Report of the New York, Chicago and St. Louis Railroad; partial reprint, N&W Magazine, March, 1974.

Fred J. Reynolds, Anatomical Materials. Quest Club paper on 19th Century body snatching, excerpts in the News-Sentinel, Fort Wayne (1973).

Sister M. Columba, PHJC, an interview, The News-Sentinel, Fort Wayne (1962). Sister Columba joined St. Joseph's Hospital surgical ward in 1895 while the Fort Wayne Medical School was still nearby.

Richard V. Pierard, Sylvanus F. Bowser. Thesis reprinted by the Fort Wayne Public Library (1964).

The Gilded Age in Fort Wayne, 1870-1900. Compilation of earlier news reports and reminiscences of the social scene, published by the Fort Wayne Public Library (1955).

Christmas and Other Gala Days, reminiscences of the old Franklin P. Randall home in the 1880s. Allen Cunty-Fort Wayne Historical Society publication, reprinted by Fort Wayne Public Library (1964).

"Colonel Charles A. Zollinger, Seven-time Mayor of Fort Wayne." Undated publication of the Fort Wayne Public Library.

Roy M. Bates, Robison Park—1896-1919. Publication of the Allen County-Fort Wayne Historical Society, reprinted by the Fort Wayne Public Library (1964).

Frank D. Walter, South Wayne. Originally published in the Fort Wayne Daily News (1908), ed. Rex Potterf, Fort Wayne Public Library (1966).

Georgiana W. Bond and Ada C. Fenton, Guide to the Allen County Court House. Fort Wayne (1913).

Rex M. Potterf, Allen County's Courthouses. Old Fort News, Fall (1970) by Allen County-Fort Wayne Historical Society.

"Fort Wayne Up to Date." 20th anniversary publication of the Fort Wayne News (1894).

Clara E. Philley, "We Remember." Letter (Oct. 10, 1974).

"Gene Stratton Porter, Best-Seller." Publication of the Fort Wayne Public Library.

William P. Cooper, Colorful Journalism in Fort Wayne, Indiana. Old Fort News (1966) by Allen County-Fort Wayne Historical Society.

"Jesse A. Grice, Sheriff and Mayor." Publication of the Fort Wayne Public Library (1957).

"William J. Hosey, Fort Wayne's Dedicated Mayor." Publication of the Fort Wayne Public Library (1957).

Statistical information of the war dead of Fort Wayne: Fort Wayne News-Sentinel (Sept. 4, 1921); Journal-Gazette (Sept. 10, 1921).

Roy M. Bates, Interurban Railways of Allen County, Indiana. Published by the Allen County-Fort Wayne Historical Society, reprint Fort Wayne Public Library (1958).

Rex M. Potterf, Little River Drainage Project. Publication of Allen County-Fort Wayne Historical Society, reprinted by Fort Wayne Public Library (1968).

Part 5

News-Sentinel Progress Edition, May 27, 1958. The broadest reference work available on Fort Wayne developments in the first half of the 20th Century is the 180-page newspaper edition edited by Ernest E. Williams. It has been used extensively in this work, particularly in the areas of schools, industry, the arts, sports, commerce, churches and some government activities. Authors of the articles, some on the News-Sentinel staff and others associated with community organizations, include: Helene R. Foellinger, Clifford B. Ward, Williams, Henry Flowers, Russ Oleson, Robert Manth, Tom Cooksey, Sue Webber, Herbert Miller, Marjorie Barnhart, Richard P. Smith, Al M. Cahill, Glenn Hopper, Robert L. Thompson, Bill Ringle, Charles Keefer, Jim Costin, Robert D. Adams, Marty Sullivan, Roger Doran, Celeste Roudebush, Richard Gibeau, Mollie Simpson, Monica Marshall Agnew, Don Myers, John Ross, Albert Diserens, Jack Keyser, Sharon Weaver, Marshall Turkin, Bud Gallmeier, Ben Tenny, Carol Heyn, Helen Riordan, Floyd R. Neff, Robert F. Shambaugh, Richard Gerig, Herbert G. Bredemeier, Earl S. Ward, Paul Trey, Mrs. Arthur Thieme, George Wascovich, James P. Conroy, Elmer Voelkel, C. C. Collins, Paul E. Paino, C. G. Shira, George B. Wood, Frederick Fagley, Thomas Zehr, Kay Howard, Frank Lansing, William Mahoney, Richard Gucker, Rex Potterf, William Johannsen, S. Marie Heiney, Sam Cook, Mrs. Karl Mavis, Ken Weaver, George Tetherly, C. Lane Breidenstein, Stan Knapp, Lucille Zink, Tim M. Conner, Paul G. Gronauer, Richard T. Doermer, Mary Jane Somers, Charles Robison, Evangeline Fox, Dorothy Morehouse, Jerry Stewart and William Sandeson.

Fort Wayne News-Sentinel (Feb. 10, 1923). Details on the Masonic Temple Theatre.

Fort Wayne Journal-Gazette (Feb. 11, 1923). American and European performers on the Temple Theatre stage.

Indiana Sesquicentennial of American Independence Bulletin, Indiana (1926); Indiana Historical Bureau, Indianapolis (1926).

Fort Wayne Up to Date. 20th anniversary publication of Fort Wayne News, Fort Wayne, Indiana (June, 1894). Details development of the Salamonie Mining & Gas Co.

Walter O. Menge, The Heritage of Fifty Years, an address presented June 27, 1955, at Lincoln National Life Insurance Company's Golden Jubilee Convention, Chicago. Emancipator Magazine (June, 1955).

Clyde Cover Papers, Interview with George Bryce, September 11, 1958, Fort Wayne, Indiana. Unpublished.

Kenneth B. Keller, Flying Memorial to Art Smith. Fort Wayne Journal Gazette (Oct. 21, 1973).

Fort Wayne Municipal Airport, article on opening and first decade. The News-Sentinel, Fort Wayne, Indiana (Dec. 26, 1936).

Albert H. Schaaf, Quest Club Paper on the Greater Fort Wayne Development Corporation (Oct. 10, 1947). Fort Wayne Public Library.

Fort Wayne News-Sentinel (August 11, 1927). Charles Lindbergh's flight over the Allen County Courthouse in the Spirit of St. Louis.

Fort Wayne News-Sentinel (Dec. 31, 1927). The Grand Leader fire and other fires in the mid-1920s.

Fort Wayne News-Sentinel (Oct. 26, 1937). The Agreement for elevation of the Nickel Plate Railroad.

Report of Activities of the City Government, 1920-1927, Fort Wayne, Indiana.

Part 6

Ernest W. Cook, Fort Wayne School History Traced for 106 Years. The News-Sentinel, Fort Wayne (June 19, 1926).

Our Public School, 1853-1953, publication of the Fort Wayne Public Schools on the 100th anniversary of the system.

Fort Wayne Community Schools, Personnel Statistics. Leaflet of the Fort Wayne Community Schools (Sept. 14, 1973).

Statistical Report 74, Fort Wayne Community Schools.

Sample Classes of Airborne TV. The News-Sentinel, Fort Wayne (July 4, 1961).

Allen County Comprehensive Plan, Volume One, Allen County Plan Commission (July, 1973).

Mildred Burger, Short History of the Lutheran Church-Missouri Synod in Fort Wayne, Indiana. Fort Wayne Public Library (1967).

The Catholic Church in Fort Wayne. Allen Conty-Fort Wayne Historical Society, reprinted by Fort Wayne Public Library (1961).

Jerome W. Rausch, OSC, The Crosier Story—A History of the Crosier Fathers in the United States. Crosier Press, Onamia, Minn. (1960).

The Journal-Gazette, Fort Wayne (May 12, 1973). Indiana-Purdue Hosts Open House.

The News-Sentinel, Fort Wayne (Nov. 8, 1973). IU-Purdue OK Joint Administration.

Becky Richards, The News-Sentinel, Fort Wayne (Feb. 14, 1975). Ivy Tech Land Acquisition.

Part 7

Lincoln National Bank Thirty-year Fort Wayne Progress Report, published 1929 at the groundbreaking of the Lincoln Tower, Fort Wayne. Details city economic and population advances, comparatively with national trends as reported by the U.S. Department of Commerce.

The News-Sentinel, Fort Wayne (Jan. 23, 1964), 40th Year of WGL Radio Marked.

Parade Magazine (Aug. 24, 1947), WOWO Hoosier Hop Famous.

Clyde Cover Papers, interview with Charles Buesching, Sept. 19, 1958, Fort Wayne, Indiana, unpublished. An inside view and unusual insight into the bank panic of the early 1930s in Fort Wayne.

The News-Sentinel, Fort Wayne (Oct. 29, 1930). Conviction of George Kelly and others of the Broadway Bank robbery, Fort Wayne, Indiana.

The International News Service, Chicago, Ill. (April 15, 1931). Fatal shooting of Officer Patrick Gallagher by F. Guy Sprague.

The News-Sentinel, Fort Wayne (May 28, 1931). Public criticism of weak enforcement of Prohibition Law in Fort Wayne.

The News-Sentinel, Fort Wayne (July 23 and Nov. 17, 1931). The gun-battle killing of two Federal agents and trial of George Adams.

The News-Sentinel, Fort Wayne (Nov. 7, 1931). Bombings of local movie theatres.

International News Service, Chicago, Ill. (July 23, 1934). The killing of John Dillinger and "most wanted" status of gangsters Homer Van Meter and George (Baby Face) Nelson.

Associated Press, Indianapolis, Ind. (May 5, 1934). Arrests of Clifford Mohler and Sam Goldstein launches manhunt for Dillinger.

The News-Sentinel, Fort Wayne (July 24, 1934). Killing of Police Officer Martin Gephart by Clifford Mohler and information of Mohler linked to shooting of Dillinger at Chicago.

The News-Sentinel, Fort Wayne (April 13, 1934). Dillinger and Van Meter raid on the Warsaw Police Station.

The News-Sentinel, Fort Wayne (Aug. 29, 1934). Strange funeral of Homer Van Meter.

The News-Sentinel, Fort Wayne (July 22, 1931). Bids for construction of a new Post Office and Federal Court Building to be opened August 14.

The News-Sentinel, Fort Wayne (Nov. 11, 1931). One thousand men to be given jobs by funds of Federated Relief Agencies.

The Journal-Gazette, Fort Wayne (April 7, 1933). Harold K. Milks report of the end of Prohibition in the city.

The News-Sentinel, Fort Wayne (1930). Silent movie queen Hope Harriman visits mother in Fort Wayne.

Earl Wilson, The Journal-Gazette (Sept. 17, 1973). Notes on Herb Shriner.

C. M. Bowra, Introduction to The Greek Way by Edith Hamilton; Time, Inc., New York (1963).

The News-Sentinel, Fort Wayne (March 25 and April 1, 1959). Report of growth of Auburn industry and Cord era.

Gene Rugh, The News-Sentinel, Fort Wayne (May 19, 1973). Black Jack of Voiture 37 of the American Legion 40&8.

United Press, Los Angeles, Calif. (Dec. 30, 1937). Baron Long Heads Syndicate Protesting Mexican Seizure of Gambling Resort.

Part 8

The News-Sentinel, Fort Wayne (Feb. 2, 1950). Judge Rules in IUE and UE case.

Robert Wilkerson, Report of Fort Wayne Labor Movement, Urban League publication (1952).

The News-Sentinel, Fort Wayne (Oct. 14, 1936). WPA worker in prize-winning letter.

Marilyn S. Steele, Christmas Bureau; Old Fort News, Fall (1972). Allen County-Fort Wayne Historical Society publication.

The News-Sentinel, Fort Wayne (Nov. 20, 1936). Activities of Black Legion In This City Aired by Prisoner.

The News-Sentinel, Fort Wayne (Oct. 10, 1936). Lemke Raps New Deal in Address Here.

The News-Sentinel, Fort Wayne (Nov. 4, 1936). Entire Democratic County Ticket is Swept to Victory.

Municipal Booster, a news bulletin of Fort Wayne City Government: editions published on July 20, 1935; September, 1935; October, 1935; November 1935; March, 1936; April, 1936; July, 1936; February, 1937; March, 1937. Fort Wayne, Indiana.

Municipal Review, a publication of the Fort Wayne City Light and Water Utilities, editions published May, 1937; August, 1937; November, 1937; February-March, 1938; May-June, 1938; September, 1938; February, 1939; April, 1939; May-June, 1939; September-October, 1939. Fort Wayne, Indiana.

Municipal Review, a publication of the Fort Wayne City Light and Water Utilities, editions published April, 1941; February, 1942; April, 1942; July 1942. Fort Wayne, Indiana.

The News-Sentinel, Fort Wayne (June 1, 1939). Sheriff rounds up 42 at "Haunted House" love oasis.

The News-Sentinel, Fort Wayne (May 15, 1942). Japanese Garden renamed Jaenicke Gardens.

Emery Applegate, Jr., The News-Sentinel, Fort Wayne (Oct. 4, 1941). 10,000 Hear Lindburgh at America First Rally.

The News-Sentinel, Fort Wayne (Jan. 31, 1941). First of Westfield Village Homes Completed.

The News-Sentinel, Fort Wayne (March 15, 1941). Public Housing projects underway in Fort Wayne.

The News-Sentinel, Fort Wayne (Dec. 11, 1940). Site designated for proposed Army Air Corps Base southwest of Fort Wayne.

The News-Sentinel, Fort Wayne (May 13, 1941). Aviation Board switches from Anthony Wayne Field to Baer Field for new air base name.

Associated Press, Washington (May 13, 1941). War Department informs Congressman George Gillie name of Anthony Wayne for field is out.

Fort Wayne Journal Gazette, Fort Wayne (Oct. 26, 1941). Baer Field Rapidly Nears Completion.

The News-Sentinel, Fort Wayne (Sept. 29, 1941). Clergy, Military dedicate Baer Field Chapel.

The News-Sentinel, Fort Wayne (Dec. 6, 1941). Pilots and Planes of Pursuit Group Arrive at Air Base.

Fort Wayne Journal Gazette, Fort Wayne (Dec. 5, 1946). Main Baer Field Hanger Destroyed in Spectacular Fire.

The News-Sentinel, Fort Wayne (May 8, 1942). Railway Unit of Army to Train Here—beginning of Camp Scott.

The News-Sentinel, Fort Wayne (Nov. 6, 1944). German War Prisoners at Camp Scott—Towers and Barbed Wire Built.

The News-Sentinel, Fort Wayne (Aug. 15, 1949). Camp Scott closed as emergency veteran housing project of Fort Wayne Housing Authority.

The News-Sentinel, Fort Wayne (Feb. 15, 1951). Casad Ordnance Depot.

The News-Sentinel, Fort Wayne (March 30, 1942). District Attorney moves against foreign-born citizens.

The News-Sentinel, Fort Wayne (May 28, 1942). Union Council seeks investigation of News-Sentinel editorial policy makers.

Clifford B. Ward, The News-Sentinel, Fort Wayne (June 1, 1942). Editor answers proposed Attorney General investigation.

The News-Sentinel, Fort Wayne (Feb. 25, 1943). Trial of John Paul Schuchhardt, accused of German-American Bund membership.

The News-Sentinel, Fort Wayne (May 20, 1942). Lt. R. E. Miller with Doolittle Over Tokyo.

Associated Press (Jan. 31, 1944). Capt. Walker M. Mahurin as top U.S. air ace in Europe.

The News-Sentinel, Fort Wayne (March 9, 1944). Capt. Mahurin sets record in air war over Germany.

The News-Sentinel, Fort Wayne (April 10, 1944). Capt. Mahurin Shot Down Over France.

Chicago Herald-American (May 1, 1944). The story of American air ace Walker Mahurin.

The News-Sentinel, Fort Wayne (Nov. 4, 1942). Mayor Baals Re-elected in Republican Sweep of City and County.

Charles Keefer, The News-Sentinel (Aug. 22, 1949). Investigations of the Kuzeff, Haaga and Conine Murders.

Herbert Miller, The News-Sentinel, Fort Wayne (Dec. 29, 1950). Thin Hope for Condemned Slayer.

Robert Thompson, The News-Sentinel, Fort Wayne (Dec. 30, 1950). Franklin Click Goes to the Electric Chair.

(INS), Chicago (July 20, 1944). Chairman Sam Jackson's Speech at the 1944 National Democratic Convention.

(AP), Nanking, China (Sept. 26, 1946). General Henry Byroade completes mission as special envoy to China.

Part 9

Description of the first professional big league baseball game, which historians clearly state was played at Fort Wayne, was taken from The Official Encyclopedia of Baseball, Revised Edition, by Hy Turkin and S. C. Thompson A. S. Barnes and Co., New York (1956).

Carl Wiegman, Fort Wayne Journal Gazette (1974). Column on Fort Wayne baseball players in the major leagues and Babe Ruth's longest home run.

Old Fort News, Spring (1972), Allen County-

Fort Wayne Historical Society publication. Zane Grey's baseball career in Fort Wayne.

The News-Sentinel, Fort Wayne (July 12, 1930). League Park Fire.

Fort Wayne Journal Gazette (March 31, 1974). The 75 years of the St. Joe Athletic Club.

Jim Costin, The News-Sentinel, Fort Wayne (Dec. 17, 1973). Red Sitko Finally Stopped.

Jim Costin, The News-Sentinel, Fort Wayne, 1974 Here and There column 1915 Fort Wayne Friars in Pro Football Hall of Fame.

Bud Gallmeier, The News-Sentinel, Fort Wayne, 1958 Progress Edition. New Coliseum Open Door to Success in Ice Hockey.

Jim Costin, The News-Sentinel, Fort Wayne, 1958 Progress Edition. The story of the Fort Wayne Open of the Professional Golf Assn.

The News-Sentinel, Fort Wayne (Oct. 28, 1968). An interview with Sharon Wichman, Olympic gold medal winner.

The News-Sentinel, Fort Wayne (July 12, 1930). Louis Heilbroner and Frank Biemer report of Fort Wayne teams in professional league baseball.

Kerry Hubartt, The News-Sentinel, Fort Wayne (June 4, 1973). Wayne's four-man track team wins state title.

Jim Costin, The News-Sentinel, Fort Wayne (March 23, 1974). Northrop is No. 1 in the Indiana Basketball Tourney.

Part 10

The News-Sentinel, Fort Wayne (May 5, 1946). Stockyard Crowded with Bawling Cows During Rail Strike.

Old Fort News, Nos. 1-2 (March-June, 1945). Allen County-Fort Wayne Historical publication. Johnny Appleseed Source Book by Robert C. Harris.

The News-Sentinel, Fort Wayne (Feb. 5, 1947). Fort Wayne on Threshhold of New Transportation Era.

The News-Sentinel, Fort Wayne (Nov. 12, 1947). City Council Cancels Expressway Action After Voters Turn Down Parkway in Referendum.

Indiana Almanac and Fact Book, ed. Edward A. Leary, Indianapolis, Indiana (1968).

Raymond J. Berghoff, M.D. Biographical Sketch of Alexander Campbell. Fort Wayne, Ind., undated.

Edwina Essex, The News-Sentinel, Fort Wayne (July 6, 1948). Fourth of July Fireworks Display.

Fort Wayne Journal-Gazette (Jan. 12, 1949). Branning Gives Report.

The News-Sentinel, Fort Wayne (Sept. 22, 1950). Council Airs Coal Profits.

Fort Wayne Journal-Gazette (Nov. 11, 1950). Mayor, Chief Indicted.

The News-Sentinel, Fort Wayne (Aug. 2, 1950). Work on Circumurban Highway to Begin.

The News-Sentinel, Fort Wayne (Oct. 25, 1950). New Murphy Store Opened.

The Wall Street Journal (Feb. 14, 1975). Bowmar Instrument filed under Federal Bankruptcy Act.

Part 11

The News-Sentinel, Fort Wayne (Sept. 15, 1952). Gen. Dwight Eisenhower in Fort Wayne Today.

The News-Sentinel, Fort Wayne (Nov. 7, 1953). Opening of Parkview Hospital.

Robert Thompson, The News-Sentinel, Fort Wayne (Jan. 24, 1953). Opening of Sol Wood Home.

The News-Sentinel, Fort Wayne (Oct. 21, 1955). Essex Wire moves headquarters to Fort Wayne.

The News-Sentinel, Fort Wayne (April 12, 1956). New Lutheran Hospital.

The News-Sentinel, Fort Wayne (June 1, 1956). Controlling interest purchased in Dime Bank.

The News-Sentinel, Fort Wayne (June 26, 1957). City Council Votes Annexation of Waynedale.

Fort Wayne Journal-Gazette (Sept. 17, 1974). The story of Darl Parker who robbed Lincoln Bank Branch in 1957.

The News-Sentinel, Fort Wayne (Feb., 1959). Tomahawks Found in Main St. Sidewalk.

The News-Sentinel, Fort Wayne (March 4, 1959). Herb Shriner at Coesse for TV film.

The News-Sentinel, Fort Wayne (Jan. 24, 1959), New W&D Store to Open. (Feb. 10,1962), W&D Fire Rages. (Dec. 1, 1969), Ayres Purchases W&D.

Bob Kaser, Michigan City, report in The News-Sentinel, Fort Wayne (June 15, 1961). Electrocution of Richard Kiefer.

Indiana 1926, pub. by Indiana Historical Bureau. The beginnings of the Fort Wayne State School traced.

Carmen Dent, The News-Sentinel, Fort Wayne (May 1, 1965). Expansion of State School Progresses.

Part 12

A Pictorial History of Fort Wayne Parks and Recreation, 1905 to 1955, published by the Board of Park Commissioners with the 1956 annual report.

Fort Wayne's Park System from 1863 as told by Col. D. N. Foster, The News-Sentinel, Fort Wayne (June 19, 1926).

The News-Sentinel, Fort Wayne (May 22, 1957). Editorial on Shoaff Park.

The News-Sentinel, Fort Wayne (June 22, 1961). Feature on the old days in Trier's Park.

The News-Sentinel, Fort Wayne (June 23, 1953). Arson Indicated in West Swinney Park Fire.

George Tetherly, Park and Recreation (Dec. 1968). Article on development of park activities at Fort Wayne.

Board of Park Commissioners, Annual Report (1971), Fort Wayne.

Park Master Plan, Board of Park Commissioners, Fort Wayne (1974). Prepared by Angela Derheimer.

Highlights of the Fort Wayne Park Department for the Period of 1946 to 1970, an outline of the Park Board, Fort Wayne (1970).

Park Board Log, a journal containing entries detailing land acquisitions from 1863 to 1974.

Fort Wayne Journal-Gazette (Jan. 12, 1967). County Park Board elected officers.

Fort Wayne Journal-Gazette (Nov. 7, 1973). Fox Island Nature Preserve planned.

The News-Sentinel, Fort Wayne (Nov. 27, 1973). County-wide Park Foundation organized.

Part 13

The News-Sentinel, Fort Wayne (Sept. 15, 1960). Verbal Clash Over New Haven Water.

The News-Sentinel, Fort Wayne (Sept. 1, 1961). Police Quell Picket at Magnavox Strike.

The News-Sentinel, Fort Wayne (Nov. 15, 1961). Citizens for City Light Formed.

The News-Sentinel, Fort Wayne (July 29, 1960). Star Arrives for Local Movie.

The News-Sentinel, Fort Wayne (Nov. 15, 1960). Carl Sandburg Pleases Audience.

The News-Sentinel, Fort Wayne (March 3, 1960). Sam Cook Charged with Bribery.

The News-Sentinel, Fort Wayne (Feb. 22, 1960). Robert Kennedy at Gridiron.

Helene Foellinger, report in Markets of America, New York (1970).

The People of Allen County, report of Allen County Plan Commission (July, 1973).

The News-Sentinel, Fort Wayne (May 22, 1962). Contract Awarded for St. Joseph Hospital.

The News-Sentinel, Fort Wayne (June 4, 1964), the Berghoff Gardens Burns.

The News-Sentinel, Fort Wayne (March 16, 1967). Southtown Mall Groundbreaking.

Part 14

Roy M. Bates and Kenneth Keller, The Columbia St. Story, Fort Wayne Public Library publication (1970).

William Ferguson, The News-Sentinel, Fort Wayne (Nov. 22, 1968). Fort Wayne Future Finds City Adrift.

The News-Sentinel, Fort Wayne (Feb. 3, 1966). Gas Blast Rips Broadway Area.

Clara E. Philley, Note on old Wayne Street letter, Oct. 28, 1974.

Carol Heyn, The News-Sentinel, Fort Wayne (Aug. 28, 1967). Construction of Sheraton Inn.

Jerry Graff, The News-Sentinel, Fort Wayne (April 10, 1974). New Haven, Fort Wayne Sewer Pact.

Bob Woodward and Carl Bernstein, The Washington Post (Aug. 2, 1973). Leak Involving McGovern on Fort Wayne Birth Record.

William A. Ferguson, The News-Sentinel, Fort Wayne (Aug. 2, 1973). Memo Ties Sen. McGovern to Illegitimate Child Here.

Chuck Crumbo, Fort Wayne Journal-Gazette (March 15, 1974). Kunkle Plant Financing by City Unit.

Roger Metzger, The News-Sentinel, Fort Wayne (May 8, 1974). Referendum leads to City Light Lease to I&M.

Gary Graham, The News-Sentinel, Fort Wayne (Sept. 13, 1974). Lease Signed by Mayor and I&M.

Sam Smith, The News-Sentinel, Fort Wayne (June 12, 1974). Details on $55 million lease.

The Wall Street Journal (Sept. 16, 1974). Dutch concern takes over Magnavox.

Dell Ford, Fort Wayne Journal-Gazette (Oct. 21, 1974). Keenan Hotel Demise in Seconds.

The News-Sentinel, Fort Wayne (Nov. 15, 1974). Old Fort Groundbreaking to be Nov. 19, 1974.

Dick Isenhour, The News-Sentinel, Fort Wayne (Feb. 4, 1975). Fire Destroys Rosemarie.

Roger Metzger, The News-Sentinel, Fort Wayne (Feb. 4, 1975). Lost Landmarks.

Acknowledgments

The board is grateful for the numerous individuals and organizations who aided in furnishing information and materials for the completion of this volume. They include people from every walk of life in the city. The staffs of the Public Library, headed by Fred J. Reynolds; Willard Heiss of the Indiana Historical Society; the Allen County Historical Museum, Helen Berg, Doris Perry and others were particularly helpful. Picture credits include: The Fort Wayne Public Library, Allen County Historical Society, Fort Wayne Park Board, Fort Wayne Redevelopment Commission, Fort Wayne Plan Commission, Allen County Plan Commission, Fort Wayne Board of Works, The News-Sentinel, The Journal-Gazette, Fort Wayne Community Schools, the Chamber of Commerce, Robert Parker, Carl Hartup, John Stearns, Argil Shock, John Sorensen, Dailey Fogle, Bob Gwaltney, Jr., H. Brooks Dawson, Jim Berger, Dale Stedman, Wesley Pusey, Robert L. Bastress, Harry Grabner, Mrs. J. O. Dreher, Frank Delisle, Watters Studio, National Aeronautics and Space Administration, Gabriel Delobbe, Neuman Studio, Bob O'Reilly, Allen Lomont, Pius Lankford, Clyde Butler, the U.S. Air Force, Fort Wayne Transit, Inc., Midwestern United Life Insurance Co. for drawings by Bill J. Hammon, Nick Longworth, Don Rust, City Directories from 1859 to 1887, Sheldon Hines and Dean Musser.

Many other events and people played important roles in the progress of Fort Wayne, but are not mentioned because of physical limitations, something the author regrets. Also, there may be errors in facts or names, due either to the writer's error or source material. People almost beyond number aided in providing material and the completion of this book. The author is grateful to each of them.

Index

A & P Grocery 289
A. C. Wermuth, Inc. 419
A. H. Perfect and Co. 182
A. H. Perfect Co. 225
A. H. Perfect Co. 449
A. Hattersley & Sons 177
A. Hattersly & Sons 225
A. Schulte Cigar Store 289
A&I Leather Shop 289
A&P Store 311
Abbett, Merle J. 263
Abbott, Albert A. 584
Abbott, Dayton 413
Abbott, John 290
ABC Coach Lines 411
Abdication Speech 329
Able, Jocob H. 585
Academy of Music 172
Achduth Veshalom Congregation 147
Achduth Vesholem Congregation 420
Achenbach, Henry 233
Ackerman, Abe 225
Ackerman, Abe 289
Ackerman, Abe 477
Adair, E. Ross 439
Adair, E. Ross 441
Adair, E. Ross 507
Adair, E. Ross 511
Adair, E. Ross 541
Adair, E. Ross 542
Adair, E. Ross 586
Adair, E. Ross 587
Adair, E. Ross 588
Adams Township Rangers 151
Adams, Archie 380
Adams, Bill 503
Adams, Dr. Clyde 420
Adams, George 302
Adams, George 303
Adams, J. Otis 216
Adams, James D. 452
Adams, Otto 228
Adams, Otto 377
Adams, Otto H. 327
Adams, Otto H. 337
Adams, Otto H. 413
Adams, Otto H. 516
Adams, Paulus 331
Adams, Richard 547
Adams, Robert Y. 544
Adams, Thomas G. 514
Adams, Vernon 448
Adams, Walter 337
Adams, Walter C. 586
Rev. Otha Aden 513
Admas, Dr. Clyde 512
Adolph Jaenicke Gardens 343
Adultery 112
Agnew, Mrs. John 408
Agnew, Spiro 542
Agnew, Spiro 548
Ahlersmeyer, Robert C. 421
Aiken, John H. 583
Air Base 340
Air Corps Bombers 347
Air Crash 439
Air Guardsmen 341
Air Mail 336
Air Pollution 338
Air War 347
Airborne Television Instruction 263
Aircraft 344
Airmail Flights 219
Airplane Service 336
Airplanes 219
Airplanes 287
Airport 219
Airport 336
Airport 341
Alcatraz 447
Alden, Samuel R. 171
Alden, Samuel R. 172
Alderman & Yarnelle 234
Alderman, Frank 234
Aldrich, Charles 175
Ale 551
Alerding, Bishop Herman 182
Alerding, Rev. Herman J. 178
Alexander, Rue J. 586
Alexander, Rue J. 586
Alford, George 219
Alger, Gene 285
Alconquin Tribes 5
Allen County Children's Home 237
Allen County Fair Association 162
Allen County Formed 112
Allen County Infirmary 439
Allen County Officials 583
Allen Hamilton & Co. 113
Allen, Col. John 112
Allen, Colonel John 83
Allen, F. Ellwood 377
Allen, Larry 419
Allen, Richard 542
Allen, Richard N. 477
Allen, Richard N. 478
Allen, Robert 411
Allied Mills, Inc. 232
Alspaugh, Mary 308
Alspaugh, Sebastian 308
Alter, Carl 413
Alter, Carl A. 452
Alter, Thomas 556
America First Committee 339
American Electric Power System 235
American Federal Savings and Loan 512
American Federation of Hosiery Workers 331
American Fur Company 88
American Fur Company 110
American Hoist & Derrick Co. 229
American Iron, Steel 234
American Legion 311
American Security Life Insurance Co. . . 452

American States Insurance Co. 223
American Steel Dredge Co. 229
American Steel Dredge Co. 229
American Steel Dredge Co. 327
Amstutz, Harry B. 587
Amstutz, Noah 584
Amstutz, Vance L. 588
AMT, Arthur 267
Amusement Park 473
Anderson F. Summers Stitching 289
Anderson, A. T. 186
Anderson, A. T. 326
Anderson, Albert Barnes 306
Anderson, Chester 446
Anderson, Dr. William C. 146
Anderson, Karen 556
Anderson, Minnie 214
Anderson, Warren 380
Anderson, Wilbert 382
Andreas, John L. 546
Andrews, H. H. 177
Andrews, W. H. 177
Anglin, James 547
Ankenbruck Undertakers 289
Ankenbruck, Ben 176
Ankenbruck, John 587
Ankenbruck, Martin 179
Ankenbruck, Martin 181
Ankenbruck, Oscar 290
Annual Pay 287
Antalis, S. J. 514
Anthis, William 556
Anthony Hotel 182
Anthony Hotel 289
Anthony Hotel 551
Anthony Wayne Bank 289
Anthony Wayne Bank 294
Anthony Wayne Bank 511
Anthony Wayne Parkway 413
Anti-Saloon League 177
Apartments 516
Appleseed, Johnny 118, 180, 412
Appleseeds 119
Aquaduct 116
Arata, Dr. Justin 514
Archer Graveyard 412
Archer, Benjamin 113
Archer, Benjamin 144
Archer, Benjamin 150
Archer, David 120
Archer, John 169
Arenberg, George 289
Armstrong, Capt. John 19
Armstrong, Paul 379
Armstrong, Paul Curly 375
Armstrong, Robert 380
Army Air Corps 340
Army Air Corps 340
Arnaud, Ensign Charles De 4
Arnold, J. Robert 508
Arnold, J. Robert 514
Arnold, John 214
Arnold, John E. 541
Arnold, Robert 556
Arnold, Robert C. 477
Arson 303
Arson 473
Arson 556
Art Mosaic & Tile Co. 289
Art Museum 216
Art School And Museum 408
Art Smith Airplane Club 219
Asbury, T. L. 448
Ashleman, John 310
Ashley, George L. 583
Asphalt 448
Assault and Battery 112
Astor, John Jacob 88
Astronaut 513
Athens 309
Atkins, Herman 303
Auburn Auto Co. Sales 290
Auburn Automobile Co. 310
Auburns 218
Auburns 310
Auer, Edward 223
Auer, Edward 546
Aurentz, Gerald 326
Aurentz, Gerald 332
Auto Aircraft Acceptance Corp. 310
Auto Sales 288
Automobile 164
Automobile 287
Automobile 301
Automobile 310
Automotive Industry 310
Avalon House 157
Avalon House 334
Aveline Fire 182
Aveline House 159
Aveline House 182
Aveline, Francis 112
Aveline, Francis S. 159
Aveline, Francis S. 182
Aveline, John 152
Aviation Manufacturing Corp. 310
Azar Big Boy Restaurant 418
Azar, Alex 418
Azar, Alexander 507
Azar, Alexander 512
Azar, David 418
Azar, Melvin A. 587
Azar, Melvin A. 587
B. F. Goodrich Co. 500
B. J. Duesler Music House 289
B,nai Jacob Synagogue 420
Baade, William C. 181
Baals, Clinton 438
Baals, Harry 325, 333, 336
Baals, Harry 348
Baals, Harry 413
Baals, Harry 438
Baals, Harry 443, 444
Baals, Mayor Harry 167
Baber, Weisell 290
Backus, William 448
Badin, Rev. Stephen Theodore 146
Baer Field 219
Baer Field 340
Baer Field 421
Baer Field 503
Baer Field 542
Baer Field 550
Baer, Jack D. 233
Baer, Max 307
Baer, Paul 219
Baer, Paul Frank 185
Baer, Paul Frank 292
Bailey, Peter P. 143
Bailhe, Gaston 216
Bailhe, George 216
Baird, Cary L. 186
Baird, Charles 332
Baird, Mrs. Richard 330
Baker Brothers 144
Baker, A. J. 187
Baker, A.J. 584
Baker, A. J. 584
Baker, A. J. 584
Baker, Edward 231
Baker, Harvey 231
Baker, James M. 446
Bakeries 299
Bakery 235
Bal-Rou Night Club 214
Balentine, Conrad 507
Bales, C. V. 233
Bales, Charles 233
Ball Club 372
Ball Park 372
Ball, J. H. 232
Ballerina 214
Ballet 408
Ballet 408
Ballet Russe De Monte Carlo 215
Ballinger, Norman 547
Ballinger, Oral 508
Balloons 176
Ballou, James O. 585
Ballou, William N. 584
Balmahn, Steve 381
Baltes Hotel 182
Baltes Hotel 289
Baltes Hotel 511
Baltes, Dr. Joseph 514
Baltzell, Robert C. 306
Band Pavilions 176
Bandemer, Irwin C. 588
Bandits 285
Bank Deposits 286
Bank Examiners 296
Bank Night 332
Bank Robberies 301
Bank Robberies 506
Bank Robbers 304
Banking Holiday 298
Bankruptcy 294
Banks 294
Banks 297
Baptist 144
Baptist, Francis 216
Barbee, Brig. Gen. 30
Barber Shops 300
Barbieri Jr., Joseph 228
Barbieri Sr., Joseph 228
Barille, Neal 376
Barker, Keith 557
Barnes, E. A. 294
Barnes, E. A. 307
Barnes, Edward A. 170
Barnett Livery Carriage House 180
Barnett, James 112
Barnett, James 144
Barr Street Market 237
Barr Street Market 449
Barr Street Public Market 237
Barr, H. O. 584
Barr, John T. 110
Barr, John T. 112
Barrett Bond System 175
Barrett Jr., James M. 164
Barrett, J. M. 173
Barrett, J. M. 175
Barrett, James 478
Barrett, James M. 171
Barrett, James M. 177
Barrett, James M. 178
Barrett, James M. 187
Barrett, James M. 343
Barrett, James M. 450
Barrett, James M. 546
Bartell, Robert 220
Barth, William 178
Bartlett, J. A. 152
Baseball 370
Baseball 372
Baseball Bats 166
Baseball Bats 372
Baseball Diamonds 338
Bash Building 556
Bash, C. S. 235
Bash, Charles 264
Bash, Charles S. 163
Bash, Charles S. 168
Bash, Charles S. 186
Bash, J. W. 232
Bash, Solomon 175
Bash, Solomon 175
Basketball 375
Basketball 381
Basketball Championship 380
Basketball Championship 382
Basketball Tourney 379
Basley Meats 289
Bass Foundry 229
Bass, Col. Sion S. 156
Bass, J. H. 298
Bass, John 154
Bass, John 163

Bass, John 171
Bass, John H. 164
Bass, Sion 157
Bass, Sion S. 154
Bastress, Robert L. 596
Bateman, Dr. Richard 271
Bates, Roy 186
Bates, Roy 188
Bates, Roy M. 541
Bates, W. C. 502
Bathing Beach 328
Bathing Beauty 308
Bathtubs 334
Battenberg, Harold F. 416
Battle of Fallen Timbers 30
Battle of the Thames 86
Battle of Tippecanoe 74
Bauer, Robert E. 506
Baugh, Douglas 556
Baumgartner, Moan 374
Bayer, William 179
Bayless, Sol D. 181
Bayshore, Wesley 556
Bazley Market 299
Beach 328
Beach, Fred 171
Beacon Heights 516
Beacon Shoe Store 289
Beall, Dr. Charles G. 185
Beamer, George 306
Beams, Glen J. 586
Beams, Robert 343
Beams, Robert G. 326
Beams, Robert G. 438
Beatty, Lloyd 507
Beaubien, Antoine 68
Beaubien, Charles 17
Beaubien, Charles 93
Beaubien, Josette 94
Beaver, M. M. 294
Beaver,s Mill 174
Bechtel, S. B. 184
Bechtol, F. Dean 447
Beck, William 236
Beck, William 238
Becker, A. E. 289
Becker, August E. 294
Becker, Frederick 152
Becker, J. Alban 587
Becker, J. J. 164
Beckwith, Albert 507
Beckwith, Albert E. 549
Beecher, Henry Ward 146
Beer 302
Beer 551
Beerbower, Guy 477
Beers, George W. 163
Beers, Orvas 508
Beeswax 66
Bell Telephone Co. 289
Bell, Dick 380
Bell, Mrs. Robert C. 216
Bell, R. C. 235
Belmont Products Co. 291
Below Zero 328
Bender, Harry 163
Bender, Harry W. 587
Bender, Robert 505
Bender, Robert A. 587
Bender, Robert A. 588
Benedict, Helen Quimby 411
Benedict, Mrs. Frank J. 409
Bengs, Otto 236
Bennet, Ben 326
Bennett, Ben F. 348
Bennett, Ben F. 438
Bennett, Benjamin 336
Bennett, Carl 512
Bennett, Merle 556
Bennigen, Hugh 154
Benninghoff, Robert 543
Benoit, Father Julian 146
Benoit, Julian 266
Benoit, Rev. Julian 161
Benov, Frank 181
Benson, Carl 517
Benz, Arnold F. 229
Berdelman, W. G. 186
Berg, Ernie 378
Berg, Helen 596
Berger, Jim 596
Berghoff Brewery 183, 307
Berghoff Brewing Corp. 165
Berghoff Gardens 182
Berghoff Gardens 417
Berghoff Gardens 511
Berghoff, Fred A. 413
Berghoff, G. A. 294
Berghoff, Gustav 165
Berghoff, Gustave 225
Berghoff, Henry 165
Berghoff, Henry 180
Berghoff, Henry C. 179
Berghoff, Henry C. 295
Berghoff, Herman 165
Berghoff, Hubert 165
Berghoff, John 382
Berghoff, John A. 164
Berghoff, Norbert G. 507
Berk, A. L. 477
Berk, A. L. 552
Berland,s Shoe Store 289
Bernieres, Henry De 1
Berning, Robert H. 586
Berning, Robert H. 587
Berning, William A. 587
Berry Street Methodist Episcopal Church 148
Berry, A. A. 441
Bethany Bible Institute 269
Bethlehem Lutheran School 267
Better Business Bureau 233
Beuke, Arthur 288
Bicentennial 555
Bickel, Richard 233
Bicknell, Clarence 419
Bicknell, Ernest 419
Bicycle Parties 172
Bicycle Shop 290
Bicycles 166
Biddle, Thomas M. 160
Bieberich, Adolf B. 585
Bieberich, Adolf C. 584
Biehl, Darwin 451
Bienz, Fred 421
Bienz, Paul 380
Big Ten 286
Bigger, Samuel 146
Bigger, Samuel 148
Bill, Jacob 236
Bill, Jacob 239
Bill, Jacob 294
Binder, Miss Grace 512
Binder, Mrs. Grace D. 294
Bingham, Private Factor 65
Biograph Theatre 305
Birch, Paul 375
Bird, Ochmig 114
Birds, Ochmig 264
Birkhold, Harry 289
Birth Certificate 548
Birth Rates 287
Birth Records 549
Bischoff, Rudolph A. 269
Bishop Dwenger High School 266
Bishop Luers High School 266
Bishop of Fort Wayne 445
Bissot Family 4
Bissot, Francois 1
Bissot, Francois 4
Bissot, Francois Marie 3
Bissot, Francois Marie Morgan 1
Bissot, Jean Baptiste 1
Bissot, Jean Baptiste 3
Bissot, Jean Baptiste 4
Bitler, George 379
Bittler, Edmond A. 585
Bittler, Edwin A. 584
Bixby, Adrian 512
Black Jack 311
Black Legion 329
Black, Albert J. 583
Black, Charlie 375
Black, Josephine 585
Black, Thomas 542
Blacksmith Shop 144
Blackstone Shop 291
Blair, Sol 184
Blaker, Ora M. 294
Blanks Sr., James H. 588
Blanks, James 380
Blanton, Darrell L. 447
Blanton, Howard 450
Blanton, Howard 452
Blanton, Howard 505
Blass, Bill 308
Blee, Thomas J. 553
Bleke, Ralph 219
Bleke, Ralph 220
Bliss, Emmit 444
Blitz, Mrs. Richard 330
Blitz, Richard 478
Blitz, Richard F. 586
Blitz, Richard T. 477
Blitz, Richard T. 585
Blitz, Richard T. 586
Blitz, Richard T. 587
Blockhouses 119
Blondon, Edgar 378
Bloom, A. Everett 512
Bloom, A. Everett 586
Bloom, Allan 548
Bloom, Allan E. 512
Bloom, Allan E. 587
Bloom, Alton 439
Bloom, Alton L. 351
Bloom, Alton L. 438
Bloom, Alton L. 444
Bloom, Alton L. 586
Bloom, Everett A. 585
Bloom, Louis L. 588
Bloomeyer, E. C. 289
Blosser, Barton C. 588
Blucher, Walter 544
Blue Bedford Stone 178
Blue Cast Springs 337
Blue Jacket 31
Blue Jacket 54
Blue Jacket 56
Blue Jacket 59
Blue Jacket 89
Blue Law 372
Bluffton 143
Blume, Georgia H. 584
Blume, R. J. 289
Board of Works 596
Bob and Ted,s 302
Bobay Shoe Store 290
Bobay, Ambrose 290
Bobeck, Duane 549
Bobeck, Harold L. 554
Bobilya, Louis C. 584
Bodeker, W. E. 264
Bodenhorn, Frank 342
Bodine, H. E. 233
Body Snatchers 161
Boedeker, Bob 379
Boehrer, John 311
Boerger, Gustav 181
Boerger, William H. 183
Boharic, Donald 411
Bohn, Edgar 587
Bohn, Frank 289
Bohn, Frank E. 184
Bohn, W. A. 235
Bojinoff, Mike 379
Boles, Luela 172
Bolinger, Art 448
Bollman, William 350
Bolman, Dr. R. Morton 514

Bolton, Frederic 447
Boltz and Derheimer 175
Bolyard, Bob 379
Bolyard, Earl 373
Bolyard, Tom 381
Bomb Shelters 505
Bombings 303
Bonahoom, Fuad G. 514
Bonar, Ron 543
Bonar, Ronald 547
Bond, C. D. 174
Bond, Charles 154
Bond, Charles 171
Bond, Charles 174
Bond, Charles D. 164
Bond, Charles Z. 351
Bond, Frank 295
Bond, George C. 444
Bond, Mrs. Georgiana 172
Bond, Stephen 175
Bond, Stephen B. 164
Bond, Stephen B. 174
Bondie, Antoine 78
Bondie, Antoine 94
Bonham, Daniel 25
Bonnecamps, Father Jean De 6
Bonnecamps, Father Jean De 144
Bonsib, John 512
Bonsib, Louis 409
Bonsib, Louis W. 587
Bontrager, D. Russell 587
Bookwalter, Elias H. 584
Boone, Daniel 90
Bootlegger 303
Bootleggers 301
Borcherding, Melvin 331
Borders, Beatrice 556
Borger, Donald H. 268
Borgman, August 236
Borgman, Benny 375
Borgman, Clifford H. 585
Borgmann, William F. 509
Boseker, C. 162
Boseker, Christian 177
Bostick, Emanuel 264
Bostick, William 411
Boston Cream Pie 311
Boston Store 238
Boswell, Andrew 264
Boswell, Dr. Jerry 547
Boswell, Dr. Jerry 555
Bottorff, John D. 587
Boucheron, Pierre 293
Bougher, Frank A. 288
Bounties 13
Bounties 15
Bourie, John 94
Bourie, Louis 88
Bourie, Louis 110
Bourie, Louis 159
Bourie, Louis T. 152
Bowater, D. J. 502
Bowen, Charles 326
Bowen, Otis 548
Bowen, Otis 555
Bowen, Otis R. 588
Bower, Ray 451
Bowerfield, H. J. 187
Bowerfind, Henry 290
Bowerfind, Henry J. 264
Bowers, William 584
Bowers, William 584
Bowling 377
Bowman, Dr. Sylvia E. 272
Bowman, Ron 381
Bowmar Instrument Corp. 421
Bowser and Story Foundry 144
Bowser Loan and Trust 294
Bowser Pump Works 171
Bowser Works 164
Bowser, Alexander 164
Bowser, Carter 337
Bowser, Carter 343
Bowser, Jacob C. 144
Bowser, S. F. 225
Boswer, Sylvanus Freelove 163
Bowserville 171
Boxers 374
Boxing 292
Boyce, Rosella 214
Boyd, Ensign Samuel 28
Boyd, Rev. G. M. 117
Boyer, Charles 413
Boyer, Charles H. 416
Boyland, F. Wade 413
Brackenridge, Charles 371
Brackenridge, George W. 118
Braden, John 373
Braden, John 508
Bradley, Bernice 512
Bradley, Carl L. 541
Bradley, Mrs. S. Maxie 291
Bradstreet, Col. John 12
Brady, Capt. Samuel 26
Bragalone, Albert 548
Branch, Emmett F. 584
Brandon, Thomas A. 270
Brandt Jr., Richard 584
Brandt, Fred 166
Branigan, Roger 512
Branigan, Roger 542
Branigin, Roger 587
Brannan, J. H. 178
Branning, Henry 413
Branning, Henry 438
Branning, Henry E. 416
Branstrator, Charles W. 584
Branstrator, William 175
Brant, Mary Ball 556
Brase, Walter 374
Braun, Edward J. 584
Braun, Edward J. 585
Breckenridge, George W. 583
Bredemeier, Herbert G. 269
Breen, William 178
Breen, William 184
Brenn, Earl 507
Brennan, J. J. 187
Brewer, William 477
Breweries 551
Brewery 165
Brewery 307
Brian, Frank 375
Briccetti, Thomas 408
Bridge 549
Bridges, Dr. W. Lloyd 264
Bright, Jesse D. 117
Bright, Johnny 375
Brinkman, Ernest F. 233
Broadcasting 292
Broadcasting 293
Broadway Limited Train 182
Broadway State Bank 294
Broderick, Catherine 262
Bronze Bells 421
Brooks Construction Co. 448
Brooks, Corrinne 547
Brooks, James E. 448
Brooks, John F. 448
Brooks, Robert 448
Brookside 172
Brosius, Dr. Robert 514
Brosius, Jesse 180
Brossard, John J. 231
Brotherhood Mutual Life Insurance Co. 452
Brothers School For Boys 265
Brothers, Paul 177
Browar, John A. 586
Brown, Bob 380
Brown, Calvin H. 583
Brown, Emil 513
Brown, J. O. 186
Brown, John 150
Brown, John 157
Brown, Kenneth 291
Brown, Mrs. Helen P. 264
Brown, Mrs. M. L. 181
Brown, Peggy 409
Brown, Richard 421
Broyles, Ralph E. 271
Brubaker, Maurice 289
Brubaker, Walter 416
Bruck, Roger J. 588
Bruder-Calhoun Jewelry Co. 289
Brudi, Herbert 555
Bruggeman, Dr. Harry 179
Bruggeman, Dr. Henry 185
Bruggemann, Dr. H. O. 343
Bruick, William 584
Bruick, William 585
Bruins 382
Brunner, Mary 513
Brunner, Otto 438
Brunner, Paul 543
Brutton Jr., Bill 233
Brutton, William J. 233
Bryan, Edward 290
Bryand, JameW. Bryant, James W. 517
Bryce, George 222
Bryn Mawr 309
Buchanan, Verlin 452
Buchanan, Verlin H 508
Buck, Charles 180
Buck, Charles H. 183
Buck, Howard 285
Buesching, Charles H. 168
Buesching, Charles H. 294
Buesching, Charles H. 295
Buesching, Charles H. 507
Bueter, Jay H. 583
Bueter, Jay Herman 583
Buggies 171
Buggies and Carriages 166
Buggy Maker 310
Buhler, Robert 286
Buhler, Robert 351
Buhler, Robert A. 350
Building Code 514
Buirley, Florence A. 542
Buirley, Mrs. Florence 264
Bujack, Fred 377
Buketoff, Igor 407
Bull Moose Party 183
Bulson, Dr. Albert E. 161
Bulson, Dr. Eugene 507
Bundy, Nelly 47
Bunnell, David 232
Burdeck, Colonel Henry 67
Burdeck, Major Henry 29
Burger, William L. 587
Burglaries 449
Burhop, Esther 512
Burhop, William C. 269
Burke, Father Edmund 55
Burke, Thomas 285
Burkett, Alvin C. 587
Burns, Michael 48
Burns, Paul 415
Burns, Paul 438
Burns, Paul 500
Burns, Paul 506
Burns, Paul 547
Burns, Paul 553
Burns, Paul M. 413
Burns, Paul M. 415
Burns, Paul M. 508
Burns, Paul Mike 416, 452
Burns, Paul Mike 504
Burns, Paul Mike 514
Burns, Robert 374
Burr, Aaron 33
Burr, Aaron 61
Burr, David 114
Burris, Jack 234
Burrows, Richard 554
Burry, A. G. 295
Burry, Andrew 231
Burry, R. L. 231
Bursley, G. E. 174

Bursley, Gilbert 163
Bursley, Gilbert 165
Burton, Clyde 337
Bus Station 327
Bus System 542
Buses 411
Bush, Edward D. 584
Bush, Edward D. 585
Bush, Jerry 375
Bushing, Oscar H. 294
Business District 515
Busse, Herman 588
Butler Fieldhouse 379
Butler, Capt. Edward 47
Butler, General Richard 25
Butler, Richard B. 291
Butt, James D. 583
Butt, Samuel D. 583
Butters, Frank 438
Byme, Dave 382
Byroade, Henry A. 352
Cadillac, Antoine De La Mothe 3
Cafe Johnell 418
Cain, Pat J. 585
Callahan, Steve 374
Calvary United Brethren Church 237
Camp Allen 156
Camp Allen Park 472
Camp Scott 227
Camp, Thomas A. Scott 342
Campbell, Alex 415
Campbell, Alex M. 306
Campbell, Alexander 345
Campbell, Carlos 508
Campbell, William 30
Campfield, Howard 304
Canal 114
Canal Bonds 116
Canal Building 116
Canal Lands 186
Canal Trade 540
Canal Travel 118
Canalboats 117
Cannon, James 112
Canoe 451
Canterbury Green 549
Canterbury Green Shopping Center 515
Capehart-Farnsworth Corp. 227
Capehart-Farnsworth Corp. 441
Capehart, Homer 227
Capehart, Homer E. 586
Capehart, Homer E. 587
Capitol Theatre 304
Capone, Alphonse 346
Card Tables 166
Carey, James B. 330
Carey, Max 373
Carey, Tom 370
Carl W. Rose Jeweler 289
Carnation Milk Co. 501
Carnegie, Andrew 181
Carner, Donald C. 441
Carnera, Primo 307
Carrey, Private Robert 65
Carrington, Edward 373
Carrol Electric Light Co. 187
Cars 287
Carson, Mrs. Alda Jane 444
Carteaux, Bobby 377
Carter, C. M. 290
Carvin, Earl L. 441
Casaburo, Thomas 547
Casaburo, Thomas 548
Casad Depot 342
Casad, Adam A. 342
Case, Charles 149
Case, Charles 264
Cass, Lewis 89
Cass, Lewis 110
Cassidy, R. W. 291
Casteel, William 556
Caswell, William 268
Cat Houses 300
Cathedral 558
Cathedral Square 146
Catholic Church 146
Catholic Community Center 217
Catholic Community Center 271
Catholic Religion 55, 451
Catholic Schools 265
Cathrine Brackett Restaurant 290
Caton, Dr. John 268
Cattle Rustling 151
Cavelier, Madelaine 4
Cavelier, Madeleine 3
Cavelier, Rene Robert 2
CBS 293
Cedarville Dam 499
Celarek, Frank 588
Celarek, Frank J. 587
Celarek, Frank J. 588
Celeron, Captain Pierre Joseph Bienville De 6
Cenlivre, Louis A. 583
Census Bureau 286
Centlivre 307
Centlivre Brewery 165
Centlivre Brewing Corp. 165
Centlivre Family 175
Centlivre Park 165
Centlivre, Charles Louis 165
Centlivre, Helen Keenan 214
Centlivre, Helen Keenan 552
Centlivre, Herman 165
Centlivre, Louis 583
Centlivre, Louis A. 289
Centlivre, Louis A. 584
Central Catholic High School 181
Central Catholic High School 218
Central Catholic High School 263
Central Catholic High School 266
Central Catholic High School 379
Central District 288
Central Electric Co. 550
Central Grocery 290
Central Grocery 299
Central High School 262
Central High School 271
Central League 372
Central Office Equipment Co. 291
Central Soya 232
Central Soya 545
Central Soya 546
Central Sugar Co. 232
Century of Progress 307
Cerney, Mrs. Mary 507
Certia, Peter 220
Certia, Peter M. 294
Chadwick, Shang 375
Chaffee, Roger B. 513
Chalfant-Cutshall Undertaking Co. 186
Chalmers, Chick 378
Chamber of Commerce 233
Chamber of Commerce 237, 596
Chamberlain, Larry Joe 510
Championship Fight 374
Chance, Varner 262
Chandler, Acy 380
Chapman, G. A. 232
Chapman, John 118
Chapman, John 120
Chapman, Reid 442
Chappuis, Bob 375
Charity Horse Show 382
Charles McCulloch Homestead 233
Charles R. Wermuth and Sons 239
Charles W. Anderson Millinery 289
Checker Cab Manufacturing Co. 310
Chenoweth, John 449
Cherry Trees 474
Cherry, Charles P. 217
Chester B. Bryson Barber Shop 290
Chester G. Schiefer Auto Sales 290
Chicagou 3
Chickasaw Indians 5, 29, 30
Chief Little Face 24
Children,s Zoo 474
Chinese Reds 505
Chippewas 52
Choctaw 29
Choctaw 30
Choka, Cathy 556
Cholera 151
Chris-Craft Corp. 165
Christ Child Festival 440
Christ, George 291
Christen, Robert V. 350
Christmas 503
Christmas Bureau 330
Christoff, Joseph 508
Chrysler Line 310
Church of Christ 420
Churches 144
Churches 419
Churchward, Charles 447
Chute, Rev. James 145
Cicognani, Amleto Cardinal 445
Ciez, Patrick 231
Cigar Factory 166
CIO 330
Circuit Court 113
Circus 165
Cities Service 545
Citizens Street Railway Company 163
Citizens Trust Company 288
Citizens Trust Company 294
City Election 186
City Hall 174
City Hospital 440
City Light 180
City Light 236
City Light 239
City Light 506
City Light 553
City Light and Power Works 289
City Mills 144
City Parking Garage 446
City Parking Garage 449
City Records 548
City Utilities 415
City-County Building 500
City-County Building 509
Civic Theatre 289
Civic Theatre 408
Civic Theatre 504
Civil Defense 444
Civil Defense 505
Civil Rights 511
Civil War 156
Civilian Defense 343
Clapp, Melville M. 584
Clark, B. L. 302
Clark, Dr. H. A. 161
Clark, George Rogers 12
Clark, George Rogers 17
Clark, George Rogers 45
Clark, George W. 294
Clark, George W. 301
Clark, Lt. William 45
Clark, Paul 452
Clark, Paul 505
Clark, Ralph 326
Clarke, Paul 554
Classical Music 408
Clausmeier, Sheriff E. F. 173
Clauss, H. N. 452
Clauss, H. N. 452
Clauss, Phil 289
Clauss, Phil 291
Clauss, Phil 417
Clay School 149
Clay, General Green 84
Cleary & Bailey Printers 291
Cleary Jr., Martin J. 291
Cleary, Martin J. 585
Cleland, Samuel C. 348
Clemens Restaurant Co. 289
Clemens, Herbert 289
Cleveland Graphite Bronze 230

Click, Franklin 350
Clifford, Miss Helene 184
Cline, Cyrus 583
Cline, Cyrus 583
Cline, Cyrus 583
Cline, Cyrus 584
Clinton St. Bridge 172
Cloth Manufacturing 168
Clothes Hampers 228
Clyde A. Myers Barber Shop 291
Clyde Theater 291
Clymer, Bob 380
Coal Companies 299
Coal Scandals 415
Cocanour, John B. 144
Cochran, William Bourke 178
Cochrane, John 144
Cocks, Harvey 291
Cocks, Harvey 411
Coe, Dr. O. 116
Coesse General Store 450
Coldfoot 6
Cole Brothers 165
Cole, Judy 503
Colerick Opera House 157
Colerick, Charles 152
Colerick, David 115
Colerick, Edward 174
Colerick, Guy 179
Colerick, Guy 181
Colerick, Guy 236
Colerick, Guy 239
Colerick, Judge Walpole 179
Colerick, Miss Margaret 171
Colerick, Miss Margaret M. 181
Colerick, Miss Margaret M. 311
Colerick's Hall 153
Colerick's Hall 154
Collias, George 289
Colligan, Joseph 514
Colone, Ann 442
Colonial Mortgage Co. 507
Colonial Theatre 291
Colpitts, A. Hunter 421
Columba, Sister M. 161
Columbia Candy Kitchen 291
Columbia City 143
Columbia St. 540
Columbia St. 556
Columbia, Dana 143
Columbian Exposition 164
Communist 330
Community Chest 330
Community Concert Association 214
Community Concerts 408
Community Schools 596
Community Services 552
Compagnie de Reassurance Nord-Atlantique 223
Comparet Mill 162
Comparet, D. F. 162
Comparet, David F. 143
Comparet, Francis 110
Comparet, Francis 112
Comparet, Francis 146
Comparet, Francis 162
Comparet, Joseph J. 143
Compton, Amos 142
Compton, Mrs. Florence S. 183
Computers 170
Concordia College 148
Concordia College 267
Concordia Evangelical Lutheran Church 181
Concordia Lutheran High 267
Concordia Lutheran School 267
Concordia Senior College 268
Condominiums 549
Condos, George 291
Congress of Industrial Organizations 330
Congressional Medal of Honor 158
Conine, Phyllis 349
Conine, Phyllis 351
Conklin, Mrs. Ella 475
Connelly, Thomas J. 584
Conroy, Rev. Thomas 307
Conspiracy 416
Contract Dispute 544
Controlled Demolition, Inc. 551
Conway, douglas 409
Cook, Elmer 586
Cook, Elmer M. 585
Cook, Elmer M. 587
Cook, Ernest 264
Cook, Omer L. 584
Cook, Sam 502
Cook, Samu 586
Cook, Samuel 587
Cook, Walter E. 294
Cooke, Capt. John 44
Cooke, Capt. John 45
Cooke, Capt. John 45
Cooke, Capt. John 47
Cooke, Captian John 50
Cooney, Dr. Charles J. 514
Cooper Shop 144
Cooper, John H. 508
Cooper, Mrs. Charlotte 264
Cooper, William J. 555
Cooper, William P. 264
Coquillard, Alexis 110
Corbat, Joseph B. 585
Corbett, Frank 348
Corby, W. 266
Cord Corporation 310
Cord L810 310
Cord, E. L. 310
Cord, Errett Lobban 311
Cords 310
Corinthian Broadcasting Co. 293
Cornelius, Ernest 421
Cornerstone 178
Cornish, Capt. Clarence F. 220
Corps of Engineers 555
Couch, Howard 449
Cough Syrup 234
Coughlin, Fr. Charles 345
Couillard, Guilanne 4
Couillard, Marie 1
Country Music 503
County Clerk's Office 502
County Courthouse 112
County Farm 438
County Farm 439
County Park Department 477
County Plan Commission 499
County Records 502
Courthouse 113
Courthouse 159
Courthouse 177
Courthouse 509
Courthouse Square 150
Cousins Jewelers 288
Cover, Clyde 222
Cover, Clyde 441
Cover, Clyde J. 440
Cover, Clyde J. 547
Coverdale, George W. 583
Cowan, Bob 379
Cows 173
Cows 412
Cox, James F. 583
Crackers 235
Craemer, August 269
Craemer, Pastor, August 148
Craig, Col. John 552
Craig, George N. 586
Craig, John H. 412
Crankshaw, J. B. 184
Crankshaw, Mrs. James B. 217
Cranmer, William 515
Crawford, Harry 547
Crawford, William 17
Credit Bureau of Fort Wayne, Inc. 233
Creighton Theater 304
Creighton, D. K. 172
Creighton, Mrs. D. K. 172
Creighton, Mrs. W. 172
Creighton, W. 172
Crime 303
Crime 305
Criminal History 348
Criminally Assaulted 350
Croghan, Colonel George 13
Croghan, Major George 85
Croisier House of Studies 270
Croker, John 547
Crosby, Louis 326
Crosby, Louis F. 236
Crosby, Louis F. 584
Crosier Order 270
Crosley, Max 438
Cross of Gold 179
Cross, Cecil 223
Cross, Dr. W. O. 264
Croteau, Clarence A. 226
Croteau, Jack 226
Crowell, Elivine 48
Crozier, James 509
Cumming, A. J. 449
Cunningham, David 230
Cunningham, David 441
Cunningham, David 554
Cunnison, Frank 584
Curdes, Louis 184
Curdes, Louis F. 175
Curdes, Richard 411
Curtin, J. A. 240
Curtin, J. A. 301
Curtis, Lt. Daniel 92
Cushman, Benjamin 112
Cushman, Holloway 144
Cusma T. David Rugs 289
Cutshall, Dean 231
Cutshall, Frank 225
Cutshall, Frank 296
Cutshall, Frank H. 166
Cutshall, Frank H. 231
Cutshall, Frank H. 294
Cutshall, N. Sherman 233
Cutshall, W. Sherman 181
Cutshall, W. Sherman 186
Cutshall, William S. 183
Cyclecar 310
D. B. Fishman & Co. Ladies Wear 290
D. C. Zollner Corp. 550
D. W. Jones & Son 234
D & N Pharmacy 291
Daane, Russell 546
Daane, Russell 546
Daane, Russell M. 545
Daggett, Duane 231
Dahm Auto Wash 554
Dahm, Edward 418
Dahm, Joseph 418
Dahm, Mrs. Nan Elliott 550
Dahm, Nan A. 511
Dahman, Robert 438
Dahman, Robert 444
Dahman, Robert 452
Dahman, Robert 508
Dahman, Robert 514
Dahman, Robert W. 508
Dailey Asphalt Products Co. 448
Dailey, Lester 446
Dalman Hotel 142
Dalman, Charles 583
Daly, Lar 511
Daly, Leo 501
Damon, R. Hosken 164
Dana Columbia House 214
Dana Corp. 409
Dance Hall 473
Dancer, Dr. Charles R. 185
Danehy, Daniel J. 289
Danehy, Jack 477
Danehy, Jack 505
Daniel, Joseph 512
Dannenfelser, C. W. 294
Dar 182

Dar . . . 217
Darby, Donna Jean . . . 556
Darling, Orin . . . 438
Dart, H. C. . . . 233
Data Services Corp. . . . 501
Daughters of Desire . . . 444
Davidson, Philip . . . 514
Davis, Anthony L. . . . 112
Davis, Dave . . . 448
Davis, Haywood . . . 446
Davis, James P. . . . 444
Davis, John . . . 112
Davis, John C. . . . 264
Davis, Kirby . . . 285
Davis, Leonard E. . . . 293
Davis, W. H. . . . 164
Davisson, Homer . . . 409
Dawson, Brooks . . . 596
Dawson, Charles M. . . . 585
Dawson, John W. . . . 149
Dawson, Mrs. Elizabeth . . . 172
Day, Beth . . . 309
Daylight Robbery . . . 447
De Wald, George . . . 220
De Weese, Wilbur . . . 336
De Weese, Wilbur A. . . . 585
Dean, Laertes B. . . . 150
Death Sentence . . . 350
Death Sentence . . . 351
Debtors, Prison . . . 150
Decline in Morality . . . 238
Degelman, Edward . . . 438
Degelman, Edward . . . 587
Dehner, Ed . . . 379
Dehner, Edward . . . 448
Dehner, Gerald . . . 448
Dehner, Gerald . . . 512
Dehner, John . . . 448
Dekker, Paul . . . 381
Delaney, Msgr. Joseph . . . 181
Delaware . . . 24
Delawares . . . 14
Delawares . . . 52
Delisle, Frank . . . 596
Dellinger, O. A. . . . 270
Dellinger, Orvis . . . 291
Delobbe, Gabriel . . . 556
Delta Air Lines . . . 542
Delta Lakes . . . 472
Democratic . . . 325
Democrat . . . 179
Democrat . . . 183
Democrat . . . 236
Democrat . . . 414
Democratic . . . 171
Democratic . . . 419
Democratic . . . 452
Democratic . . . 511
Democratic . . . 547
Democrats . . . 346
Dennis, John B. . . . 331
Deposits . . . 298
Depot . . . 156
Depot . . . 234
Depression . . . 230
Depression . . . 234
Depression . . . 237
Depression . . . 285
Depression . . . 294
Depression . . . 307
Depression . . . 311
Depression . . . 446
Der Fort Wayne Democrat . . . 149
Derailment . . . 543
Derby Hats . . . 176
Derck, Frank . . . 413
Derheimer, Angela . . . 477
Derheimer, Joseph . . . 176
Dern, Alfred L. . . . 222
Derrickson, Charles . . . 438
Derrickson, Charles . . . 444
Desoto . . . 310
Dessauer, M. E. . . . 233
Dessauer, Myron . . . 290
Dessauer, Myron . . . 181
Detroit . . . 32
Detzer, Karl . . . 309
Detzer, Laura . . . 288
Detzer, Mrs. A. J. . . . 216
Detzer, Mrs. A. J. . . . 217
Development Commission . . . 554
Diamond Bros. Ladies Wear . . . 290
Diamond, Charles . . . 554
Dickerson, Grace Leslie . . . 409
Dickmeyer, E. C. . . . 234
Dickmeyer, Edwin . . . 294
Dickmeyer, W. C. . . . 446
Dickmeyer, W. Charles . . . 238
Dickson, Rev. H. S. . . . 146
Diebold Lock and Safe Co. . . . 177
Diebold, Henry . . . 291
Diehm Museum of Natural History . . . 556
Dileo, William . . . 452
Dilgard Frozen Foods, Inc. . . . 449
Dille, John F. . . . 442
Dillinger, John . . . 304
Dillinger, John . . . 305
Dillinger, John . . . 510
Dillinger,s Gang . . . 304
Dime Bank & Trust Company . . . 291
Dime Savings and Trust Co. . . . 295
Dime Trust & Savings Bank . . . 446
Dime Trust Bank Building . . . 271
Dine, Charles Van . . . 188
Dinnen, George . . . 326
Dinnen, J. M. . . . 163
Dipper Dredges . . . 229
Diptheria . . . 326
Disaster . . . 512
Diserens, Ralph F. . . . 230
Disser, E. J. . . . 294
Disser, E. J. . . . 508
Disser, Edward . . . 410
Disser, John J. . . . 294
Diver, Neil . . . 549
Dix-Kelly Electric Shop . . . 289
Dix, F. J. . . . 289
Dixie, Rev. John . . . 420
Dobich, Michael . . . 501
Doctors . . . 410
Dodd, George . . . 547
Dodd, Sharon . . . 556
Dodez, Edward . . . 297
Dodez, Edward . . . 541
Dodez, Edward C. . . . 235
Dodson, Charles D. . . . 349
Doehla, George . . . 382
Doehrman, Dale . . . 507
Doehrman, William . . . 180
Doehrmann, Bill . . . 377
Doell, Lester . . . 448
Doermer, Richard T. . . . 446
Doermer, Richard T. . . . 447
Dollarhite, Albert . . . 303
Dolnick, Bernard . . . 451
Dominic Manochio Confections . . . 289
Dominion Life Assurance Co. . . . 223
Dominion Life of Canada . . . 223
Donahue, Patrick W. . . . 452
Donica, Mearle . . . 272
Donnelly, E. Owen . . . 548
Doody, J. P. . . . 290
Doody, Joseph P. . . . 477
Dooley, P. C. . . . 294
Doppelt, Dr. Frederic A. . . . 420
Doppelt, Rabbi Frederic . . . 446
Dorais, Gus . . . 374
Dorchester, Lord . . . 55
Dorn, Louis . . . 477
Doswell, Henry J. . . . 472
Doswell, John . . . 154
Double Killing . . . 439
Doud, W. E. . . . 294
Dougall, Col. J. H. . . . 178
Doughty, Howard . . . 381
Douglas, Stephen A. . . . 156
Douglass, D. Burns . . . 586
Downing, Edward . . . 547
Downtown . . . 288
Downtown . . . 499
Downtown . . . 506
Downtown . . . 515
Downtown . . . 540
Downtown Fort Wayne Assoc. . . . 515
Draft . . . 185
Draft Boards . . . 185
Draper, Dr. M. H. . . . 412
Drayer, Dr. L. Park . . . 264
Dreher, Mrs. J. O. . . . 596
Dreibelbiss, Robert . . . 180
Drier, William H. . . . 168
Dreiser, John Paul . . . 168
Dreiser, Theodore . . . 168
Dresser, Paul . . . 168
Dreyer, Walter . . . 264
Drinks, Maurice . . . 382
Drive-In Restaurant . . . 417
Drug Store . . . 299
Drug Stores . . . 291
Drug Traffic . . . 550
Drummond, Charles L. . . . 583
Drunken Brawls . . . 91
Drunken Rampages . . . 70
Drury, David . . . 217
Drury, David . . . 556
Dryer, Mrs. Charles Redway . . . 172
Dubuisson, Captain . . . 3
Dubuisson, Charles . . . 6
Dubuisson, Charles Regnault . . . 4
Ducks . . . 175
Dudley S. McClure Real Estate Co. . . . 289
Dudley, Colonel John . . . 84
Dudlo Manufacturing Co. . . . 226
Dudlo Manufacturing Co. . . . 234
Duemling Clinic . . . 218
Duemling, Arnold . . . 588
Duemling, Arnold H. . . . 588
Duemling, Dr. Herman A. . . . 218
Duemling, Mrs. Hertha . . . 408
Duemling, Mrs. Hertha . . . 512
Duemling, Mrs. Hertha . . . 215
Duesenberg Corporation . . . 310
Duesenbergs . . . 310
Duffield, Robert . . . 293
Dukes, Aaron W. . . . 186
Dumm, Robert D. . . . 153
Dumont, Captain . . . 4
Dunbar, John . . . 151
Duncan, Mrs. Thomas . . . 172
Duncan, Thomas . . . 172
Dunifon, Custer . . . 307
Dunifon, Custer . . . 505
Dunifon, Custer A. . . . 587
Dunifon, Jack . . . 438
Dunifon, Jack . . . 444
Dunifon, Jack . . . 508
Dunifon, Jack . . . 555
Dunifon, Jack K. . . . 514
Dunifon, Jack K. . . . 588
Duniforn, Custer A. . . . 587
Dunkel, Thomas . . . 584
Dunnigan, Brian . . . 556
Dunson, Mrs. Joann . . . 513
Dunstone, Mrs. Carter . . . 547
Durbin, Winfield T. . . . 583
Durkee, G. H. . . . 421
Durkin, Msgr. Thomas . . . 420
Durkin, Rt. Rev. Msgr. Thomas L. . . . 514
Dustin, Thomas E. . . . 477
Dwenger, Bishop Joseph . . . 266
Dwenger, Joseph . . . 182
Dwire, Harry . . . 311
Dye, Joseph W. . . . 441
Dykhuizen, H. M. . . . 166
Dykhuizen, Horace . . . 554
Earl Groth & Co. . . . 288
Eash, Orus . . . 452
East End . . . 339
East End Industries . . . 224

East Side Gang 444
East Side State Bank 294
Eating Out 417
Eavey, Henry J. 499
Eavey,s Market 499
Eberbach, L. F. 187
Eberhard, Sharon 556
Eberly Jr., Mrs. Karl C. 264
Eberly, Dr. Karl 333
Eckart, J. C. 166
Eckhart, Charles 310
Eckrich, Clement P. 231
Eckrich, Donald 231
Eckrich, Donald P. 509
Eckrich, Eugene 231
Eckrich, Henry C. 231
Eckrich, Herman 231
Eckrich, John 231
Eckrich, John A. 231
Eckrich, Joseph 231
Eckrich, Peter 231
Eckrich, Richard 231
Echrich, Thomas J. 554
Economic Development 512
Economic Opportunity Council 512
Edgerton, A. P. 171
Edgerton, Alfred 264
Edgerton, Ed 172
Edgerton, Grace 172
Edgerton, J. K. 171
Edgerton, Josie 172
Edgett, James D. 546
Edison, Thomas 170
Edison, Thomas 176
Edison, Thomas A. 159
Edison, Thomas Alva 160
Edison, Tom 540
Edlavitch, Dr. B. M. 185
Edsall, Samuel 114
Edsall, Samuel 117
Edsall, Samuel 143
Edsall, Samuel 144
Edsall, Samuel 264
Edsall, William 143
Edsall, William 264
Edsall, William S. 143
Edward of England 329
Edward W. Dodez Dental Supply 235
Edwards, Dr. Abraham 65
Eggeman, Fred W. 585
Eggeman, Peter 180
Eggemann, John W. 583
Eggemann, William 583
Eggemann, William 584
Eggers, Oliver 413
Egle, William 269
Egly, H. D. 232
Ehle, Mervin 587
Ehrman, Fred 508
Ehrman, Fred 541
Ehrman, Fred S. 164
Ehrman, Fred S. 514
Ehrman, H. A. 502
Ehrman, Phil 380
Eickhoff, Waldemar E. 584
Eidner, John W. 301
Eisbart, Benjamin 513
Eisebart, Ben 556
Eisenhower, Dwight D. 439
Eisenhut, George 337
Eisenhut, Lester 351
Eisenhut, Lester H. 413
Eisenhut, Lester H. 416
Elected Officials 583
Election 179
Election 444
Election 502
Election of 1909 180
Election Trends 414
Elections 508
Elections 541
Elections 547
Electric Arc Lamp 169
Electric Chair 286
Electric Chair 303
Electric Chair 350
Electric Chair 351
Electric Chair 504
Electric Club 414
Electric Streetcars 172
Electric Trolley 443
Electrical Union 330
Elkins, Edward V. 514
Elks Country Club 376
Elks Lodge 292
Elks Temple 289
Ellenwood, L. R. 236
Ellenwood, Leonard 325
Ellenwood, Leonard 326
Ellenwood, Leonard 336
Ellenwood, Leonard 348
Ellenwood, Nick 374
Ellenwood, Richard 587
Ellenwood, Richard M. 588
Ellingham, Lew 419
Ellingham, Louis G. 583
Ellingham, Miller 419
Ellingham, Mrs. L. G. 264
Elliott, Benjamin 181
Elliott, Dorent 516
Elliott, Gunnar 292
Elliott, Matthew 15
Elliott, Paul Gunnar 550
Elliott, Walter 304
Ellis, Cecil 543
Elm Disease 476
Elmers Smith's Tailor and Cleaners 291
Elston, Dr. Ralph W. 512
Ely, Edward 175
Elzey, Abner 447
Embassy Theatre 408
Embassy Theatre 552
Emboyd 237
Emboyd 302
Emboyd Theater 291
Emmanuel Lutheran School 267
Emmaus Lutheran School 267
Emrick, A. J. 166
Emrick, Emmett V. 583
Emrick, Frank A. 584
Emrick, Guy 585
End of the Canals 152
Enemy Aliens 185
Engelman, C. Merle 547
Engelman, Gerka 547
England, Col. Richard 32
English Lutheran 558
English Surrender 12
Engman, K. A. 176
Enoch, Robert R. 231
Ensign Douville 6
Episcopal Church 147
Equestrian Statue 184
Erekson, Reid 263
Ernest, Gary 556
Ernest, Gary G. 217
Erwin and Justin Study Schools 237
Erwin, David 239
Erwin, David 506
Eschbach, Jesse E. 294
Eschbach, Jesse E. 306
Eschbach, Jesse E. 501
Escosa, John 409
Escosa, John 552
Eshcoff, Bill 380
Esmond's Mill 174
Essex Wire 226
Essex Wire Company 146
Essex Wire Corp. 445
Essex Wire Corporation 227
Essig, John 338
Esterline, Dave 381
European School of Music 216
Evangelical Lutheran Hospital Assn. 162
Evans, Anton 172
Evans, C. Thomas 441
Evans, Mrs. Isabella 172
Evodine, Sister Mary 268
Ewigleben, Dr. Robert L. 271
Ewing Tavern 112
Ewing, Alexander 110
Ewing, Alexander 112
Ewing, Bob 380
Ewing, Charles 112
Ewing, Col. Alexander 109
Ewing, G. W. 144
Ewing, George W. 143
Ewing, W. G. 115
Ewing, William G. 112
Ewing, William G. 150
Ewing, William G. 507
Ewing,s Hall 172
Execution 505
Explosions 342
Explosions 551
Expressway 413
F. W. Woolworth 288
F. W. Woolworth 499
Faber, Rev. William M. 514
Factories 286
Fagan, Bert A. 240
Fagan, Bert A. 325
Fair, H. C. 294
Fairbank, Rev. John 217
Fairfield Manor Apartment House 237
Fairfield, ASA 174
Fairfield, Cyrus 174
Fairfield, John 96
Fairfield, Louis W. 584
Fairfield, Louis W. 584
Fairfield, Louis W. 584
Fallen Timbers 60
Falstaff Brewing Corp. 165
Falstaff Brewing Corp. 551
Farley, James 585
Farley, James I. 348
Farmer's Bank 232
Farnin, Frank 377
Farnsworth Electronics 421
Farnsworth Radio and Television Co. ... 293
Farnsworth, Philo F. 441
Farnsworth, Philo T. 227
Farrell, Max 447
Father Senat 5
Fawley-Abbott-Bryan Co. 290
Fawley, George 290
Fay, Celia Ann 508
Fay, Celia Ann 514
Fay, Judge 174
Fazio, Buzz 377
FBI 305
FBI Agents 447
Feagles, Mrs. Ralph L. 408
Federal Agents 302
Federal and State Money 556
Federal Annuities 91
Federal Building 306
Federal Funding 512
Federal Funds 516
Federal Judge 306
Federal Money 510
Federal Relief Funds 326
Federation of Labor 330
Feed 232
Feed Shops 540
Feichter, Don 411
Feistkorn, Charles 379
Felger, Walter A. 344
Felger, Walter A. 585
Felger, Walter A. 586
Felix, Peter 112
Felts, George 264
Fencing Master 235
Fenker, Herman 446
Ferguson, Dalton 506
Ferguson, Ernest 289
Ferguson, John 235
Ferguson, Lettie M. 585

Ferrini, Alfred Anthony 586
Ferris Wheel 473
Ferry, Lucien 144
Feustal, Robert 233
Feustel, Fred 438
Feustel, Robert 224
Feustel, Robert M. 177
Fightner, Father Joseph 271
Fifield, Otto G. 585
Fifty Indictments 416
Fiegel, Alfred 307
Figel, Alfred 438
Figel, Alfred 439
Figel, Donald 508
Fighter Squadrons 340
Fights and Profanity 163
Filtration Plant 239
Filtration Plant 239
Filtration Plant 334
Filtration Plant 555
Financial Institution 298
Financial Institutions 515
Fine Arts Center 509
Fine Arts Foundation 408
Fine Arts Foundation 547
Finney, Rev. J. B. 111
Fire 182
Fire 304
Fire 308
Fire 311
Fire 348
Fire 372
Fire 450
Fire 505
Fire 511
Fire 552
Fire 556
Fire Chiefs 337
Fire Department 150
Fire Department 508
Fire Prevention Bureau 239
Fires 237
Fires 412
Fires 449
Fireworks 414
Fireworks 475
First Airport 219
First and Hamilton National Bank 225
First and Tri-State National Bank 294
First Baptist Church 420
First Church of Christ Scientist 181
First Church of Christ Scientists 233
First Church of Christ Scientists 237
First County Commissioners 112
First Electric Furnace 229
First Evangelical Lutheran Church 147
First Federal Savings 515
First Federal Savings and Loan 298
First Gristmill 144
First High-Rise 237
First Incandescent Lamps 169
First Iron Bridge 154
First Mayor 143
First Methodist Church 421
First National Bank 157
First Native Citizen 64
First Night Baseball 371
First Planing Mill 144
First Plow Factory 144
First Postmaster 111
First Presbyterian 558
First Presbyterian Church 145
First Presbyterian Church 290
First Presbyterian Church 419
First Presbyterian Church 447
First Public School 149
First Recruits—1917 185
First Sawmill 144
First School Superintendent 264
First Shopping Center 411
First Telegraph Line 152
First Telephone 262
First Trinity Episcopal Church 147
First Wagon Shop 144
Fischer, H. 172
Fischer, Mrs. H. 172
Fisher Bros. Paper Co. 231
Fisher Brothers 225
Fisher, Edward H. 336
Fisher, Edward H. 348
Fisher, Emerson 452
Fisher, F. J. 233
Fisher, Max B. 231
Fisher, Max B. 289
Fisher, Max B. 294
Fisher, Mrs. Janet 228
Fisher, Robertson J. 171
Fisher, Roger I. 231
Fisher, William B. 371
Fishering, George W. 290
Fishering, Richard 452
Fishering, Richard B. 586
Fishering, Richard B. 587
Fishing 555
Fishman, Marvin 290
Fishman, Stan 290
Fitch—Potts Packard Co. 311
Fitch, C. B. 290
Fitch, Charles B. 224
Fitch, Fishering, Lumbard and Loos Insurance 290
Flanagan, Dan C. 337
Flanagan, Dan C. 351
Flanagan, Dan C. 439
Flanagan, Dan C. 586
Fleming, Douglas G. 546
Fleming, Jack 380
Fleming, James 541
Fleming, James R. 306
Fleming, James R. 377
Fleming, James R. 419
Fleming, Robert E. 144
Fleming, Robert E. 264
Fleming, Robert S. 153
Fleming, Stephen 412
Fleming, Stephen B. 326
Fleming, Stephen B. 583
Fleming, W. Robert 452
Fleming, William 155
Fletcher, Calvin 113
Fletcher, Eugene 410
Fletcher, Harry P. 290
Fletcher, Mrs. Harry 264
Fletcher, Robert H. 232
Fletcher, Sam 440
Flethcer, Sam 500
Fletcher, Sam 501
Fletcher, Sam W. 414
Fletcher, Samuel 586
Fletcher, Samuel W. 290
Fletcher, Samuel W. 587
Flood 1913 182
Flooding 334
Flooding 472
Flooding 543
Flooding 544
Floods 331
Floods 346
Florea, Phyllis 556
Florea, Richard 442
Flowers, Clyde 441
Flowers, Clyde E. 507
Flynn, Beatrice Baltes 511
Focke-Wulfs 347
Foelinger, Helene 408
Foellinger Building 163
Foellinger Center 419
Foellinger Foundation 551
Foellinger Foundation 552
Foellinger, Helene 293
Foellinger, Helene 414
Foellinger, Helene 478
Foellinger, Helene 507
Foellinger, Helene 511, 547
Foellinger, Miss Helene R. 419
Foellinger, Oscar 218
Foellinger, Oscar 295
Foellinger, Oscar 409
Foellinger, Oscar 414
Foellinger, Oscar 474
Foellinger, Oscar G. 326
Foellinger, Oscar G. 419
Fogle, Dailey 596
Folding Nursery Seat 233
Foley, Clem 286
Foley, Red 543
Folsom, Dr. Arthur F. 217
Folz, Richard E. 587
Fonner, Mrs. Susannah 264
Fontaine, John 21
Fontaine, John 22
Food Marketing Corp. 448
Food Marketing Corp. 501
Food Marketing Corp. 550
Foohey, Paul 231
Football 374
Football 380
Forbush, Joel 151
Force, Edward 154
Ford, James 264
Ford, Leo 554
Ford, Leo M. 514
Foreign-Born 345
Forest Park 175
Forest Park 338
Forestier, Antoine 3
Forestier, Antoine 4
Forestier, Marguerite 3
Forland, Virgil 331
Fort 557
Fort Adams 30
Fort Adams 50
Fort Dearborn 71
Fort Dearborn 87
Fort Dearborn 110
Fort Defiance 32
Fort Defiance 45
Fort Defiance 45
Fort Defiance 49
Fort Defiance 58
Fort Defiance 59
Fort Defiance 64
Fort Deposit 59
Fort Detroit 58
Fort Duquesne 7
Fort Duquesne 7
Fort Greenville 28
Fort Greenville 30
Fort Greenville 53
Fort Greenville 55
Fort Hamilton 24
Fort Jefferson 24
Fort Knox 62
Fort Malden 77
Fort Malden 82
Fort Meigs 84
Fort Miami 6
Fort Miami 11
Fort Miami 14
Fort Miami 30
Fort Miami 44
Fort Miami 56
Fort Miami 58
Fort Miami 59
Fort Miamis Ouiatenon 4
Fort Michilimackinac 11
Fort Michilimackinac 58
Fort Michilimackinac 59
Fort Necessity 7
Fort Niagara 5
Fort Niagara 6
Fort Niagara 58
Fort Niagara 84
Fort Ouiatenon 6
Fort Ouiatenon 11
Fort Pitt 15
Fort Ponchartrain Du Detroit 3
Fort Recovery 28
Fort Recovery 33

Fort Recovery 50
Fort Recovery 57
Fort Recovery 67
Fort Sandusky 11
Fort St. Philippe 4
Fort St. Clair 28
Fort St. Joseph 3
Fort St. Joseph 3
Fort St. Joseph 11
Fort St. Joseph Des Miamis 2
Fort Vincennes 5
Fort Washington 19
Fort Washington 47
Fort Washington 51
Fort Wayne 5
Fort Wayne 50
Fort Wayne 58
Fort Wayne 62
Fort Wayne 64
Fort Wayne 67
Fort Wayne 70
Fort Wayne 78
Fort Wayne 82
Fort Wayne 88
Fort Wayne Abstract Co. 288
Fort Wayne Academy of Medicine 182
Fort Wayne Air Service 219
Fort Wayne and Chicago Railroad 153
Fort Wayne and Decatur Traction Co. .. 187
Fort Wayne and Northern Indiana Traction Co. 187
Fort Wayne and Southern Traction Co. .. 186
Fort Wayne and Springfield Railway Co. 187
Fort Wayne and Wabash Valley Traction Co. 187
Fort Wayne Bible College 269
Fort Wayne Bible Institute 269
Fort Wayne Blue Print 291
Fort Wayne Bluffton and Marion Traction Co. 187
Fort Wayne Book Shop 289
Fort Wayne Broadcasting Co. 293
Fort Wayne Business College 181
Fort Wayne Cathedral 147
Fort Wayne Chiefs 373
Fort Wayne College of Medicine 161
Fort Wayne Collegiate Institute 148
Fort Wayne Commercial Club 233
Fort Wayne Consolidated Railway Co. .. 176
Fort Wayne Corrugated Paper Co. 231
Fort Wayne Daisies 372
Fort Wayne Drug Co. 181
Fort Wayne Drug Co. 235
Fort Wayne Drug Co. 290
Fort Wayne Education Assn. 262
Fort Wayne Electric Co. 170
Fort Wayne Electric Company 169
Fort Wayne Electric Light and Power Co. 187
Fort Wayne Electric Railway 163, 176
Fort Wayne Electric Works 170
Fort Wayne Electric Works 235
Fort Wayne Extension Center 271
Fort Wayne Female College 148
Fort Wayne Friars 374
Fort Wayne Gas Co. 235
Fort Wayne High School 150
Fort Wayne Jenney Electric Light Company 169
Fort Wayne Komets 378
Fort Wayne Machine Works 154
Fort Wayne Medical College 228
Fort Wayne Methodist College 158
Fort Wayne Microfilm, Inc. 507
Fort Wayne National Bank 232
Fort Wayne National Bank 294
Fort Wayne Newspapers, Inc. 418
Fort Wayne Organ Company 164
Fort Wayne Paper Box Co. 231
Fort Wayne Paper Box Co. 235
Fort Wayne Park 164
Fort Wayne PGA Open 376
Fort Wayne Power Co. 187
Fort Wayne Public Library 218
Fort Wayne Regulators 151
Fort Wayne Riding Academy 234
Fort Wayne Rolling Mill Corp. 229
Fort Wayne Rolling Mills Co. 234
Fort Wayne Saengerbund 172
Fort Wayne Ski Club 235
Fort Wayne State School 451
Fort Wayne Structural Steel Co. 229
Fort Wayne Telephone Company 163
Fort Wayne Tool & Die 229
Fort Wayne Tool & Die 410
Fort Wayne Tool & Die Manufacturers Assn. 229
Fort Wayne Traction Co. 177
Fort Wayne Transit, Inc. 416, 443
Fort Wayne Transit, Inc. 542, 596
Fort Wayne Woman's Club 172
Fort Wayne Woman's Club 233
Fort Wayne Works 170
Fort Wayne, Van Wert and Lima Traction 187
Fort Winchester 85
Fortnightly Club 172
Forts 95
Forty-Niners 152
Fosnight, Wallace 443
Foster and Hall 297
Foster Grandparents 512
Foster Park 234
Foster Park 301
Foster Park 472
Foster Shirt Waist Factory 168
Foster, D. N. 412
Foster, David 239
Foster, David 471
Foster, David 475
Foster, David N. 157
Foster, David N. 168
Foster, David N. 174
Foster, David N. 179
Foster, David N. 217
Foster, David N. 472
Foster, Edith 216
Foster, Mrs. Sara 172
Foster, Mrs. Sara 172
Foster, Sam 217
Foster, Sam 225
Foster, Sam 472
Foster, Samuel 168
Foster, Samuel 184
Foster, Samuel 216
Foster, Samuel 233
Foster, Samuel 295
Foster, Samuel 298
Foster, Samuel M. 163
Foster, Samuel M. 168
Foster, Samuel M. 221
Foster, Samuel M. 264
Foster, Samuel M. 294
Foster, Samuel M. 296
Foundry and Machine Shops 154
Fourth of July 87
Fourth of July 176
Fourth of July 414
Foust, Larry 375
Fox Indians 54
Fox Jewelry Co. 289
Fox Theatre 237
Fox Theatre 291
Fox, Dr. J. W. 441
Fox, George 174
Fox, Louis 224
Fox, Louis 233
Fox, Louis 477
Fox, Louis A. 166
Fox, Louis A. 446
Fox, Oscar 290
Fox, Oscar A. 166
Fox, Oscar A. 294
France, Mark L. 587
Frank Dry Goods Co. 288
Frank, Eugene 167
Frank, Jack 167
Frank, Marx 167
Frank, Morton 167
Frank, Morton C. 477
Frank, Rene 409
Frank, Theodore 167
Frank, Theodore 233
Frank's Department Store 167
Frank's Department Store 238
Franke Park 217
Franke Park 471
Franke Park 474
Franke Park 511
Franke Park 551
Franke, J. B. 235
Franke, John B. 217
Franke, John B. 471
Franke, John B. 474
Franke, Julian 179
Franke, Julian 239
Franke, Julian 413
Franke, Julian F. 236
Franke, Julian F. 452
Franke, William 583
Franke, William F. 583
Frankel, Louis 172
Frankenstein 348
Frankenstein, Solly 449
Franklin National Life Insurance Co. ... 452
Franklin, Ross 184
Fraternal Assurance Society of America . 221
Frazell, Dick 379
Fred Eckart Packing Company 225
Fred Robbins Barber Shop 290
Freiberger, Herman 166
Freiberger, Joseph 166
Freiburger, Charles E. 586
Freiburger, Clarence 299
Freiburger, Herman 264
Freiburger, Herman 294
Freiburger, Lawrence 299
Freiburger, Marce 299
Freie-Presse Staats-Zeitung 149
Freimann Park 472
Freimann Park 476
Freimann Park 509
Freimann, Frank 292
Freimann, Frank 476
Freimann, Frank 509
Freimann, Frank M. 228
French and Indian War 7
French Brewery 165
French in America 5
French Traders 11
French Traders 265
French, Charles 149
French, Charles 264
French, Hanna & Co. 167
French, Hans 547
French, Willie 512
Frick, Ford 310
Fridian, Sister Mary 268
Friedrich, Richard 556
Friemann Park 184
Fries, Gus 229
Fries, Nestor 229
Frontenac, Louis De Baude De 2
Frozen Food 449
Frozen Pipes 327
Fruechtenicht, Arthur 268
Fruechtenicht, Arthur 413
Fruechtenicht, Arthur H. 555
Fruechtenicht, Thomas E. 588
Fruechtenicht, Thomas E. 588
Fruechtenicht, William 180
Fruechtenicht, William 239
Fruechtenicht, William 412
Fruechtenicht, William S. Wells 583
Fruehauf Trailer Corp. 409
Fruit Houses 540
Fry, Jacob 144
Fry, James H. 264
Fry, Leslie S. 264
Frye, Harmon 264
Fuelber, Anselm 264

Fuhrman, Elmer 415
Fuhrman, Elmer E. 413
Fulkerson, Paul 544
Fuller, Glen 307
Fulton, J. N. 291
Fun House 473
Funari, Mario 264
Funk, Jacob 583
Fur Trade 2
Fur Trader 110
Fur Trading 89
Furman, Rev. Charles E. 145
Furniture 166
Furs 111
G. C. Murphy 417
G. C. Murphy 515
G. C. Murphy Co. 289
G. E. 331
G. E. Bursley & Co. 448
G-Men 302
Gable, Clark 308
Gable, Fred H. 585
Gable, George 452
Gable, George 508
Gable, George 514
Gable, Jacob 583
Gable, Jacob 585
Gable, Jacob H. 585
Gabriel, Eugene 452
Galbreath, Richard 504
Gallagher, Patrick J. 301
Gallmeier, Ernest C. 336
Gallmeier, Paul E. 164
Gallmeyer, Ernest 446
Gallmeyer, Ernest J. 343
Gallmeyer, Thomas 507
Gallmeyer, Thomas A. 438
Gallucci, Frank 445
Gambler 312
Gambling 344
Gamelin, Antoine 18
Gamelin, Antoine 19
Gamelin, Antoine 43
Gamelin, Pierre 18
Gangland Shootouts 301
Gangs of Teenagers 550
Gangster 303
Gansters 301
Gangsters 305
Ganiere, George E. 184
Ganz, Paul 164
Garant, Sid 378
Garcia, Hector 409
Garcia, Hector 556
Gardens 343
Gardens 472
Gardner, Dorothy 585
Gardner, Dorothy 586
Gardner, Dorothy 587
Gardner, Glenn P. 584
Gardner, Mrs. Josephine 417
Garman, Lester 586
Garman, Lester E. 585
Garman, Owen E. 584
Garmire, R. B. 184
Gas Explorations 235
Gas Explosions 513
Gas House Restaurant 418
Gas Light 154
Gas Lights 541
Gaskill, Bob 311
Gasoline 344
Gasoline Pumps 164
Gassert, Jack 373
Gates, Hillard 442
Gates, Hilliard 293
Gates, Ralph F. 586
Gaye, Lisa 504
Geake, William 237
Geake, William C. 236
Geake, William C. 264
Geake, William K. 514
Gearhart, David 506
Gebhard, Robert 548
Gecowest, Max 556
Geist, Frank 381
Gemini 4 513
Genealogy 541
General Cables 227
General Dredging Co. 229
General Electric 235
General Electric 344
General Electric 409
General Electric 546
General Electric Co. 169
General Electric Co. 170
General Electric Co. 170
General Electric Co. 226
General Hosiery 226
General Industries 342
General Industries 449
General Telephone Co. 289, 501
General Telephone Co. 549
General Telephone Co. 554
General Telephone System 163
General Tool & Die 229
George, W. L. 158
George, William 143
Georgetown Square Shopping Center ...515
Gerardot, Lester 586
Gerardot, Lester F. 587
Gerber, Edward H. 414
Gerding, Louis E. 585
Gerding, William C. 264
Gerding, William E. 583
Gerdom, Herman 238
Gerig, Lester C. 452
Gerig, Rev. Jared F. 269
German Aircraft 347
German American Bund 346
German Athletic Club 228
German Cooks 87
German-American Bank 297
German-American National Bank 295
Geronimo 158
Gethsemane Lutheran School 267
Gettle, Homer R. 291
Getz and Cahill Undertakers 289
Getz, Carl 180
Geye, Henry 237
Geyer, B. F. 294
Geyer, Ben F. 233
Geyer, Ben F. 264
Geyer, Ben F. 441
Ghouls 161
Giauque, O. L. 410
Gibault Home 238
Gibeau, Richard 408
Gibson, Capt. Alexander 29
Gick, Paul 438
Gick, Paul 438
Gick, Paul 444
Giese, Edward 450
Gilbert, Newton W. 583
Gilbert, Walter N. 302
Gill, Bill 310
Gillie, David 471
Gillie, Dr. George W. 236
Gillie, George 348
Gillie, George 584
Gillie, George 585
Gillie, George W. 301
Gillie, George W. 584
Gillie, George W. 585
Gillie, George W. 586
Gilmartin, Frank J. 294
Gilmartin, M. J. 225
Gilpin, Dr. John 185
Gingher, Vern 311
Ginn, L. E. 448
Girls Baseball League 372
Girty, Simon 15
Girty, Simon 18
Girty, Simon 49
Gladieux Oil 410
Gladieux, Amiel C. 583
Gladieux, Arthur J. 585
Gladieux, Auriel C. 584
Gladieux, James M. 410
Gladieux, Ralph E. 410
Gladstone, Dr. N. H. 446
Gladwyn, Major Henry 11
Glancy, Perry 265
Glass, Jim 379
Glenbrook Shopping Center 512
Glenbrook Shopping Center 514
Glusenkamp, Fred 288
Godfrey, Jean Baptiste 113
Godfroy, Jacques 11
Godfroy, Jacques 12
Goeglein, Fred 334
Goeglein, Fred W. 412
Goeglein, Gloria 588
Goeglein, Jake 229
Goeglein, Martin 585
Goeglein, Theodore 348
Goeriz, Mrs. Grace 261
Gojack, John 330
Gojack, John 345
Gold Coin 25
Gold Coins 88
Gold Star Mother 347
Gold Swindles 160
Golden , Charles 290
Golden, Ed 290
Golden's Men's Wear Shop 290
Goldman, Nathan 238
Goldstein, Leonard 264
Goldstein, Sam 304
Goldstine, Robert 552
Goldstine, Robert 554
Golf 376
Golf Course 475
Goll, Walter 224
Goll, Walter 338
Good 5 Cent Cigar 184
Goodman, Keneth Sawyer 184
Goodrich, James P. 584
Goodwin, Miss Clara 171
Goodwin, Paul 508
Gordon, Robert V. 164
Gorman, Edward 379
Gorsline, Homer 180
Goshert, Rob 382
Goshorn, Miss Laura 181
Goshorn, William H. 178
Gosney, Hartwell 233
Gotham Hosiery Co. 331
Gotham Mills 226
Gottchalk, Harry 336
Gottschalk, Harry 348
Gouin, Therese 94
Gould, George 330
Gouloff, Steve 418
Gouloff, Ted 418
Gouloff, Tom 418
Gouty, Merle 289
Grabill Bank 506
Grabner, Harry S. 471, 596
Grace Lutheran Church 237
Grace Lutheran School 267
Grace Reformed Church 237
Grafee, H. C. 235
Graffis, Chester L. 587
Graffis, Chester L. 588
Grake, Thomas M. 583
Grand Larceny 416
Grand Leader 554
Grand Leader Building 238
Grand Leader Department Store 289
Grand Lodge, F&AM 218
Grand Malt Shop 291
Grand Rapids and Indiana Railroad ...153
Grandfather Clocks 166
Grandstands Burned 372
Grandys, Frances T. 307
Grant, Judge Robert 306
Gravel Pit Park 473
Gravel Road 218

Gravel Roads 218
Gray, Jack 442
Graybar Electric Co. 550
Great Black Swamp 175
Great Marsh 175
Great Northen Life Insurance 414
Great War 185
Great Western Railroad 153
Green, E. S. 263
Green, Lucy 556
Green, S. D. 170
Greene, Fred 444
Greenfield, Samuel 187
Greenland, J. W. 233
Greenland, Samuel 187
Greenlee, Dr. Robert 553
Greenville 47
Greenville Treaty 57
Greenville Treaty 58
Greenwall, Frank 583
Greibel, William L. 294
Greim, August 377
Grey, Zane 373
Greyhound Bus Terminal 289
Grice, Jesse 179
Grice, Jesse 180
Grice, Jesse 186
Grice, Jesse 583
Gridiron Banquet 503
Griebel, Bertha 288
Grieger, Inc. 290
Griesedieck, Edward J. 514
Griest, Dr. Walter 446
Griest, E. E. 184
Griest, Patricia 556
Griffin, Bill 297
Griffin, C. O. 230
Griffin, James 508
Griffin, W. F. 295
Griffin, W. M. 296
Griffin, William M. 184
Griffin, William M. 225
Griffith, Alexander H. 110
Griffith, Capt. William 110
Griffith, Charles W. 110
Griffith, Chauncey 413
Griffith, Chauncy L. 586
Griffith, George W. 110
Griffith, James B. 552
Griffith, William G. 110
Griggs, Matthew 145
Grile, Lester 263
Grile, Lester L. 506
Grimes, John 150
Grimmer, Roy E. 447
Grinsfelder, Maureen 556
Griscom, Private George 65
Grissom, Donald B. 414
Girssom, Donald B. 546
Grissom, Virgil 513
Griswold, Bert 61
Griswold, Bert 145
Griswold, Bert 216
Griswold, Bert 217
Griswold, Bert J. 233
Griswold, Bill 380
Griswold, Chester 152
Grocery 299
Grocery Supplier 448
Gronauer, Paul 377
Gronauer, Paul G. 511
Grosh, Richard 550
Gross, William J. 345
Grosvenor, H. J. 294
Groth, Earl 288
Groth, Earl 293
Grotrian, Beverly Jean 503
Grotrian, Henry 584
Grotrian, Henry 585
Grubb, Ira J. 583
Gucker, Richard 499
Guidrey, Joseph 230
Guidrey, Joseph 546
Guild, Miss Tracy 181
Guild, Paul C. 220
Guildin Guildlin Park 472
Guildlin, O. N. 472
Guldin, Mrs. O. N. 238
Guldin, Mrs. Olaf N. 217
Gump, Arlo K. 452
Gunkler, Carl 440
Gunkler, Carl A. 507
Gunnar Elliott Ice Arena 550
Gunned Down 304
Gutelius, William B. 294
Gutherz, Carl 178
Gutman, Carolyn 556
Gutman, Phillip E. 588
Guy A. Laurents Packing Co. 231
Guy Means Buick Agency 289
Gwaltney, Bob 596
H & W Electric Co. 550
H. G. Olds Wheel and Spoke Factory 161
H. H. Rogers Optical Co. 289
Haaga, Wilhelmina 348
Haberly, H. Paul 298
Haberly, James H. 298
Hackett, Edward A. K. 419
Hackley, Ann 94
Hackley, Captain James 93
Hackley, Jack 94
Hackley, James 112
Hackley, Mrs. Rebecca 144
Hackley, Rebecca 94
Hackman, E. H. 288
Hadley Furniture Co. 291
Haffner Star Bakery Co. 235
Haffner, Christian 235
Haffner, Clarence 235
Haffner D. L. 441
Haffner, Frederick 235
Haffner, George 235
Haffner, George M. 184
Haffner, Katherine Neuhaus 309
Hagerman Construction Co. 509
Hagerman-Shambaugh Construction Co. 556
Hagerman, Theodore 219
Hagerman, Theodore 501
Hagerman, Theodore 507
Haircuts 308
Haircuts 445
Halcomb, Absalom 144
Haldeman, H. R. 548
Hale Hat Co. 289
Hall, Arthur 220
Hall, Arthur 222
Hall, Arthur 233
Hall, Arthur F. 184
Hall, Arthur F. 221
Hall, Arthur F. 224
Hall, Arthur F. 295
Hall, Arthur F. 296
Hall, Arthur F. 307
Hall, Arthur F. 326
Hall, Charles 556
Hall, Don 417
Hall, Dr. A. F. 477
Hall, Frank J. 583
Hall, John 233
Hall, Miss Alice 262
Hall, Roy 232
Hall, Roy 232
Hall, William B. F. 335
Hall, William B. F. 338
Hall, William B. F. 410
Hall, William B. F. 507
Hallenbeck, Jim 381
Haller, Mary 513
Halloween Parades 327
Halsey, Jess 512
Hamilton National Bank 178
Hamilton National Bank 295
Hamilton, Alexander 49
Hamilton, Alexander 61
Hamilton, Allen 110
Hamilton, Allen 112
Hamilton, Allen 144
Hamilton, Allen 145
Hamilton, Allen 264
Hamilton, Allen 309
Hamilton, Col. Henry 14
Hamilton, Colonel Henry 15
Hamilton, Dale 379
Hamilton, Dr. Alice 409
Hamilton, Dr. Allen 185
Hamilton, Edith 309
Hamilton, Holman 309
Hamilton, John 305
Hamilton, Miss Agness 172
Hamilton, Miss Kathrine 217
Hamilton, Miss Margaret 181
Hamilton, Mrs. Emerine 181
Hamilton, Thomas 143
Hamilton, William I. 502
Hamilton, William I. 553
Hamlett, Dr. Iona C. 451
Hammon, Bill J. 000
Hamtramck, Col. John 45
Hamtramck, Col. John 49
Hamtramck, Col. John 50
Hamtramck, Colonel John 56
Hamtramck, Major John 19
Hanauer, Walter 264
Handley, Harold W. 586
Handley, Harold W. 587
Hanging 163
Hangings 151
Hanke, Kurt 410
Hanly, Jay F. 583
Hanna, Eliza 146
Hanna, Eliza 172
Hanna, Henry 172
Hanna, Henry C. 172
Hanna, James 145
Hanna, Judge Sam 172
Hanna, Miss Jessie 171
Hanna, Mrs. T. J. 171
Hanna, Robert B. 239
Hanna, Sam 146
Hanna, Sam 153
Hanna, Sam 174
Hanna, Sam 306
Hanna, Sam 419
Hanna, Samuel 109
Hanna, Samuel 110
Hanna, Samuel 112
Hanna, Samuel 144
Hanna, Samuel 146
Hanna, Samuel 154
Hanna, Samuel 157
Hannegan, Ed 117
Hanse, C. J. Otto 269
Hansen, Walter A. 215
Hanson, Robert D. 588
Hanson, Robert D. 588
Harbour, D. J. 502
Hardendorff, John 150
Hardin, Colonel John 20
Harding, D. L. 172
Harding, Daniel L. 173
Harding, Mrs. D. L. 172
Hardware Supply House 235
Hargrave, Eugene 372
Hargrave, William 372
Harmar, General Josiah 18
Harmar, General Josiah 21
Harmar, General Josiah 50
Harmon House 334
Harper, Emmet 586
Harpers Magazine 309
Harrate, John 65
Harriman, Hope 308
Harris, Robert C. 412
Harrison, Benjamin 157
Harrison, William Henry 66
Harrison, William Henry 69
Harrison, William Henry 73
Harrold, Verling 441
Harry Boxberger Phonograph Shop 291

Harry M. Boxberger Book Store 291
Hart, Harold A. 336
Hart, Harold A. 348
Hart, James 373
Harter, Basil 220
Hartman, Benjamin W. 414
Hartman, Edward W. 421
Hartman, Henry 176
Hartman, Homer 174
Hartman, Joe 176
Hartman, John 176
Hartman, John R. 587
Hartman, Lee Foster 309
Hartman, Lemuel 309
Hartman, Oliver 233
Hartman, Richard 587
Hartshorn, Clarence 231
Hartup, Carl 596
Hartzell, Lee 584
Hartzell, Lee J. 585
Hartzler, Lloyd 439
Hartzler, Lloyd S. 587
Harvester 311
Harvester Park Housing 339
Harvey, Rowena 262
Harwood, L. J. 289
Hassell, John 48
Hates, Arthur C. 587
Hattendorf, Dr. A. P. 348
Hattersley, Alfred 235
Hattersley, Byron 477
Hattersley, Byron A. 584
Hattery, Jim 381
Haupt, Richard 217
Hausman, Bill 556
Havana Cigars 505
Haw, James 556
Hawk, Ash 380
Hawk, Ash 380
Hawk, Ashley 379
Hawkins, Robert K. 587
Hay, Henry 18
Hayden Park 162
Hayden Park 472
Hayden, Fred 172
Hayden, Fred 472
Hayden, Mrs. Eliza 217
Hayes, Arthur 555
Hayes, Arthur C. 587
Hayes, Arthur C. 588
Hayes, Byron 585
Hayes, C. Bryan 413
Hayes, C. Byron 329
Hayes, C. Byron 337
Hayes, C. Byron 585
Hayes, J. Byron 505
Hayes, J. Byron 541
Hayes, J. Byron 587
Hayes, J. J. 181
Hayes, James 179
Hayes, James J. 181
Hayes, James J. 583
Hayes, Thomas A. 233
Hayner, Hubert 229
Hayner, John L. 229
Haynie, Gilmore 293
Haynie, Gilmore 306
Hays, John 95
Head Start 512
Heald, Captain Nathan 76
Health Department 549
Hearst Newspapers 310
Heaton, David 508
Heaton, David 514
Heaton, Judge Owen 179
Heaton, Mrs. O. N. 172
Heaton, O. N. 172
Heaton, O. N. 174
Heaton, O. N. 294
Heaton, Owen W. 583
Heavy Hardware Association 234
Hebert, Guillemette 4
Hebert, Louis 1
Hebert, Louis 4
Hebert, Marie Rollet 1
Heckel, Herman 234
Heckman, Melvin 508
Heckman, Ralph 414
Heckman, Tom 548
Hedekin Hall 156
Hedekin House 142
Hedekin, Michael 142
Hedgehog 6
Heemsoth, Henry 417
Heilbroner, Louis 176
Heine, Arthur 288
Heine, F. C. 294
Heine, Fred C. 288
Heine, Gottlieb 288
Heine, Gottlieb H. 264
Heineerger, Adam 583
Heiny, Bob 379
Heiny, John 552
Heiny, Lawrence 299
Heiny, Lawrence 586
Heiss, Willard 596
Heit-Miller-Lay Candy Co. 182, 225
Heit, Anthony 182
Heller, Gerald 229
Helmke, Martin H. 410
Helmke, Walter 333
Helmke, Water E. 271
Helmke, Walter E. 301
Helmke, Walter E. 303
Helmke, Walter E. 326
Helmke, Walter E. 446
Helmke, Walter E. 446
Helmke, Walter E. 585
Helmke, Walter P. 554
Helmke, Walter P. 556
Helmke, Walter P. 587
Helmke, Walter P. 588
Hench, Judge S. M. 163
Henderson, James 513
Henderson, William 181
Hendricks, Charles O. 587
Hendrix, Clyde H. 232
Henebry, P. E. 586
Henebry, P. E. 587
Henline, Mary 291
Henline, Walter 372
Hennen, Father Joseph H. 271
Henry, J. M. 175
Henry, Jerome 451
Herber, Arthur 413
Herber, Arthur 415
Herber, Arthur A. 412
Herbs, Herman A. William 291
Herbst, Henry 226
Herbst, Henry 238
Herman P. Pawlisch Shoe Repair 291
Hermann, George 181
Hermening, Edwin 448
Herrman, George 181
Hershcy, Bud 374
Hert, Alvin 419
Herzog, Guenther 267
Hesemeyer, H. H. 294
Hess, Paul 268
Hess, Sam 302
Hess, William J. 288
Hettler, Christian 163
Hides and Furs 66
Higginbotham, E. S. 230
High School Teams 378
High Schools 261
Highway Inns 550
Highways 218
Hilbrecht, Henry 173
Hilbrecht, Henry 180
Hilbrecht, Henry 181
Hilbrecht, Henry 181
Hilgeman, Gustave 584
Hilgeman, Harry H. 583
Hilgeman, Harry H. 585
Hilgeman, Henry 584
Hilgemann, Dr. V. H. 264
Hilgemann, Dr. Victor 412
Hilgemann, Harry 336
Hilgemann, Harry H. 333
Hilgemann, Harry H. 413
Hilgemann, Harry H. 583
Hilgemann, Henry 181
Hill, Gladys 350
Hill, Lt. George 220
Hillis, Glenn R. 585
Hillman China Co. 412
Hillman China Co., Inc. 291
Hillman, B. R. 291
Hillman, Ben R. 291
Hillman, Lee 408
Hillman, Lee H. 291
Himelick, R. M. 263
Himelstein, Gene 511
Hines, John 379
Hines, Robert 452
Hines, Robert M. 554
Hines, Sheldon 596
Hinga, William 452
Hinga, William 547
Hinga, William 553
Hinga, William T. 508
Hipskind Asphalt Corp. 448
Hipskind, Dan 448
Hipskind, David 448
Hipskind, J. Henry 448
Hipskind, Jerome 448
Hire,s Auto Parts 550
Hirons Park 473
Hiss, Alger 415
Historical Society 216, 596
Hitching Post 182
Hite, Willis 586
Hitzeman, F. William 294
Hoagland Brothers 160
Hoagland School 261
Hoagland, Joe 160
Hoagland, Miss Mercia 172
Hoagland, Pliney 264
Hoagland, Pliny 153
Hoagland, Pliny 171
Hobbs, Howard M. 584
Hobbs, Max 511
Hobby House 417
Hobo 332
Hobo Capital 300
Hobrock, E. L. 294
Hobrock, Paul 219
Hockett, Mrs. William 264
Hockey 378
Hockmeyer, William 583
Hodell, Lisle D. 552
Hoelle, John 336
Hoemig, Charles N. 588
Hofer, Adolf K. 475
Hoff-Brau Brewery 165
Hoffman Brothers 225
Hoffman, Dr. Oswald C. J. 451
Hoffman, E. Ely 264
Hoffman, E. G. 184
Hoffman, E. G. 294
Hoffman, Edward G. 184
Hoffman, Edward G. 419
Hoffman, John E. 452
Hoffman, John E. 544
Hoffman, Mrs. S. C. 181
Hoffman, Virgil 304
Hogan, Frank 162
Hogan, Harry 162
Hogan, Harry 183
Hogan, Harry 213
Hogan, Harry 294
Hogan, Harry 295
Hogan, Harry 326
Hogan, Harry 446
Hogan, Harry G. 181
Hogan, Harry G. 184
Hogan, Harry G. 326
Hogan, Harry G. 343

Hogan, Harry G. 446
Hogan, Hugh 162
Hogg, David 416
Hogg, David 452
Hogg, David 584
Hogg, David 585
Hoham, Fred D. 294
Hoke, John 176
Holland, Miss Mabel K. 262
Holle, Herman C. 585
Hollman, Charles 229
Hollman, Walter 301
Hollopeter, Birt 235
Holloway, Charles 178
Hollywood Cafe 289
Holman, Joseph 96
Holman, Rev. James 145
Holmes, Ensign Robert 11
Holmes, Ensign Robert 12
Holsum Bakery 228
Holt, Dorothy 513
Holt, Fred H. 502
Holt, Frederic H. 546
Holterman, Lou 373
Holton, Addison E. 445
Holy Cross School 267
Home Billiard Parlor 169
Home Building 410
Home Building 411
Home for Boys and Girls 421
Home Hotel 142
Home Loan and Savings 288
Home Missionary Society 145
Home Ownership 286
Home Telephone 183
Home Telephone and Telegraph Co. 163
Home Telephone and Telegraph Co. 289
Hood, George 413
Hood, William 110
Hook and Ladder Company 150
Hoover, Rev. Jesse 145
Hoover, Rev. Jesse 147
Hoover, Rev. Jesse 267
Hop Hope Hospital 161
Hope Hospital 440
Hope Methodist Hospital 162
Horne, Fred K. 228
Hornets 120
Horse Show 382
Horse Stealing 151
Horse-Drawn Street Cars 163
Horsecollars 235
Horses 119
Horton Manufacturing Co. 235
Horton Manufacturing Company 166
Hosey, Bill 325
Hosey, William 186
Hosey, William 413
Hosey, William H. 179
Hosey, William J. 236
Hosey, William J. 239
Hospital 440
Hospital Unit M 185
Hospitality Inn 550
Hotel 291
Hotel 511
Hotel 540
Hotel 551
Hotel Business 214
Hotel Indiana 214
Hotel Indiana 237
Hotel Rich 214
Hotels 334
Hotels 550
Hotels 556
Hottest Temperature 328
Hough, John 155
House of Bursley 165
Housing 338
Housing 512
Housing Authority 516
Howard, Charles W. 289
Howard, Dallas Wayne 551
Howard, Dorothea 349
Howard, Dorothea 352
Howard, Henry 290
Howard, John 262
Howard, Mrs. Dorothea 349
Howard's 289
Howe, Danny 381
Hub Air Lines 542
Hubbard, S. L. 176
Huber, Russell E. 587
Huestis, Dr. Alexander C. 148
Huffer, Ron 380
Huffman Brothers Lumberyard 308
Huffman, Ardala 504
Huffman, Sharon 503
Hugh McCulloch House 228
Hughes, W. O. 502
Hughes, W. O. 585
Hughes, W. O. 586
Hughes, W. O. 587
Hulburd, A. M. 261
Hulburd, Mr. and Mrs. A. M. 149
Hulfeld, Joseph 514
Hulse, Elwin 172
Hulse, Mrs. Elwin 172
Human Relations Commission 516
Human Rights 516
Humphrey, Col. George 151
Humphrey, Hubert 542
Humphrey, James 149
Humphrey, James 264
Hunsaker, Mrs. Edith 450
Hunt, Col. Thomas 96
Hunt, Colonel Thomas 64
Hunt, Colonel Thomas 87
Hunt, George 94
Hunt, John Elliot 64
Hunt, Ruth 64
Hunt, Ruthie 65
Hunter, Fred 506
Hunter, Fredrick R. 587
Hunter, Gary 382
Hunting, Fred 170
Hunting, Fred 170
Hunting, Fred S. 546
Huntley, Darrell 556
Huntley, Darrell W. 547
Huntley, Ladonna 555
Huntley, Ladonna 557
Hurd, Orin 264
Hurley, John 514
Hurley, Luther 451
Hurons 52
Hursh, Alan 583
Hurst, Richard 331
Hurst, Richard 413
Hutchens, Mel 375
Huth, Frank 229
Hutmacher, Barbara 556
Hutner Co. Men,s Wear 290
Hutner, Benjamin J. 290
Hutner, David S. 446
Hutner, Davis S. 290
Hutner, Sidney M. 290
Hutzell, Joe 297
Hutzell, Joseph 181
Huxford, M. W. 155
I. Freiburger & Co. 166
I. U. Extension 271
Ice Hockey 378
Ice Man 298
Ice Skates 554
Ice-Skating 503
Ice, Oral F. 512
Immigrants 114
Inca Manufacturing Co. 226
Incandescent Light 262
Indian Exodus 95
Indian Lands 26
Indiana & Michigan Electric Co. 187
Indiana & Michigan Electric Co. 235
Indiana & Michigan Electric Co. 509
Indiana & Michigan Electric Co. 553
Indiana Bank & Trust Co. 446
Indiana Bank and Trust Co. 294
Indiana Boys School 238
Indiana Broadcasting Corp. 442
Indiana College of Medicine 161
Indiana Frock Shop 291
Indiana Hotel 291
Indiana Hotel 552
Indiana Lighting Co. 183
Indiana Rod and Wire 226
Indiana Rod and Wire Divisions of Phelps Dodg 226
Indiana Service Co. 289
Indiana Service Co. 186
Indiana Service Corp. 177
Indiana State Fair Grounds 472
Indiana State Fairs 162
Indiana State Finals 442
Indiana State Prison 350
Indiana Technical College 267
Indiana Theater 304
Indiana-Purdue Campus 271
Indians 90
Indians 93
Indians 110
Indians 111
Indigent Elderly 438
Industrial Expansion 409
Industrial Expansion 500
Industrial Hygiene 409
Industrial Park 448
Industrial Union Council 330
Industry 286
Infantile Paralysis 184
Inflation 286
Ingebrand, Mrs. C. Daniel 408
Inland Waterways 117
Insects and Vermin 152
Inskeep, Richard G. 419
Inskeep, Richard G. 554
Insulated Wire 234
Insurance 410
Inter-Church Housing Corp. 510
International Business College 181
International Business College 270
International College 291
International Harvester 224, 225
International Harvester 344
International Harvester 500, 501
Interstate Highway 69 507
Interstate Industrial Park 411
Interstate Park 501
Interurban 187
Interurban Railways 186
Interurbans 178
Intoxication 90
Invasion of Canada 85
Ioof Building 417
Irene Byron Sanitarium 187
Irene Byron Sanitarium 412
Irene Byron Sanitarium 414
Irene Byron Sanitarium 552
Irish and German Work Crews 152
Irish, Robert G. 547
Irishmen 115
Irmschler, Alden 440
Irmsher, Alden 554
Iron Bridges 549
Irons, Robby 378
Iroquois 2
Iroquois 14
Irvin, Rev. George A. 149
Irwin, George A. 263
Irwin, John 264
Irwin, John S. 263
Isaacs, Dr. Reginald R. 544
Isken, Kurt 451
Israel-Butler Men's Store 291
ISTA 263
ITT 227
ITT-Kellogg 500
IUE 331
J. C. O,Connor & Sons, Inc. 448

J. C. Peltier & Son Undertaker 290
J. C. Penney 499
J. C. Penney Co. 515
J. C. Thompson Tool 229
Jablonski, Greg 378
Jack Diehm Museum 474
Jacket Clubs 444
Jackson & Saginaw Railroad 162, 172
Jackson, Ed 584
Jackson, Edward 584
Jackson, James 416
Jackson, Samuel D. 352
Jackson, Samuel D. 584
Jacobs Jr., George W. 291
Jacobs-Van Sweringen Music House 291
Jacobs, Duane 419
Jacobs, George 291
Jacobs, Mrs. S. Allan 504
Jacobs, S. Allan 226
Jacobs, S. Allan 507
Jacoby, George 178
Jaenicke, Adolph 332
Jaenicke, Adolph 475
Jaenicke, Adolplh M. 474
Jail and Sheriff's Residence 150
James Fuller & Sons 289
James H. Hart Billiards 289
James Stewart & Co. 177
James, Guy 378
James, Richard T. 586
Jankowski, Conrad 544
Japanese Cherry Trees 291
Japanese Gardens 343
Jarr, Frankie 374
Jay Miller Radio Service 289
Jaycees 377
Jeanette, Buddy 375
Jefferies, William 181
Jefferies, William T. 186
Jefferson School 149
Jefferson School 261
Jefferson Theater 291
Jefferson, Thomas 69
Jeffries Gallery Engine 150
Jehl, Leo 515
Jehl, Paul C. 515
Jenkins, Lt. Edward 12
Jenner, William E. 586
Jenner, William E. 586
Jenner, William E. 586
Jenney Electric 175
Jenney Electric Co. 169
Jennney Electric Co. 371
Jenney, James A. 169
Jennings, Albert 516
Jennings, Jonathan 90
Jennings, Ralph 164
Jenson, H. W. 178
Jenson, Harley 236
Jet Age 542
Jimmy Cress's Place 302
Joann, Sister M. 514
Joe Goldstine & Son 499
John Dehner and Co. 239
John Dehner, Inc. 448
John L. Guillot Barber Shop 291
John, Dr. Alfred S. 147
John, Robert 114
Johns, Henry 144
Johnson, Alexander 451
Johnson, Chic 293
Johnson, Colonel Richard 85
Johnson, David 48
Johnson, Don 549
Johnson, James T. 348
Johnson, James T. 585
Johnson, John 92
Johnson, John 326
Johnson, John H. 239
Johnson, John H. 584
Johnson, John H. 584
Johnson, L. J. 229
Johnson, Lyndon 510
Johnson, Lyndon B. 511
Johnson, Marion 181
Johnson, Mary 233
Johnson, Merrill C. 293
Johnson, Richard Menter 81
Johnson, Robert 409
Johnson, Russell L. 331
Johnson, Will 584
Johnson, William A. 585
Johnson, William B. 585
Johnston, Billie 376
Johnston, Charles F. 584
Johnston, Hughie 376
Johnston, Robert 419
Joliet, Louis 1
Joliet, Louis 4
Jones and McLachlan 154
Jones Hotel 214
Jones Hotel 556
Jones, Bass & Company 154
Jones, David 144
Jones, Jap 214
Jones, Joseph F. 546
Jones, Rev. Daniel 145
Jones, Rev. David 45
Jones, William 541
Jones, William H. 154
Jordan, E. E. 449
Jordan, W. J. 76
Jordan, Walter 382
Jorgensen, Ove W. 445
Joslyn Manufacturing & Supply Co. 229
Joslyn Stainless Steel Co. 510
Joslyn Steel Co. 234
Journal-Gazette 239
Journal-Gazette 310
Journal-Gazette 312
Journal-Gazette 418, 596
Julia Emanuel Chemist and Drug Shop . . 290
Junior Achievement 440
Junior High Schools 264
Junk, Peter 372
Jury, Mark 444
Juvenile Matters 444
Kaade, Robert L. 236
Kaag, Robert 547
Kahn, Louis I. 509
Kaiser, Dr. Oliver 517
Kaiser, W. C. 288
Kalbfleisch, J. A. 270
Kamagis, Samuel 291
Kammeyer, Ed 451
Kamnikar, Edward 547
Kampe, Ernest 584
Kampschmidt, Bernie 376
Kane, Edward 235
Kane, Edward 541
Kane, Mrs. Marie 338
Kaskaskia 17
Kaskaskia 54
Kastelic, Joe 378
Kasten, Louis 180
Katsanis, Tom 552
Katt, Richard 556
Kauffman, Harry 183
Kay Jewelry Co. 291
Kayser Grocery 545
Keasey, Edward 304
Keefe, Robert J. 442
Keefer Printing Co. 234
Keefer, George 151
Keefer, J. Ver 234
Keefer, James H. 234
Keefer, James M. 234
Keefer, Jane 306
Keegan, Abbie 172
Keegan, Hugh 338
Keegan, Margaret Ann 330
Keegan, Margaret Ann 408
Keegan, Robert Y. 331
Keen, Chester W. 292
Keenan Hotel 214
Keenan Hotel 291
Keenan Hotel 292
Keenan Hotel 548
Keenan Hotel 552
Keenan, H. J. 182
Keenan, James 214
Keenan, James 552
Keenan, James F. 214
Kene, Archie 511
Keene, Archie T. 267
Keene, Archie T. 441
Kees, Richard W. 588
Keith, Robert F. 164
Kekionga 4
Kekionga 7
Kekionga 11
Kekionga 12
Kekionga 13
Kekionga 15
Kekionga 19
Kekionga 21
Kekionga 24
Kekionga 43
Kekionga 56
Kekionga Club 370
Kekionga Guards 151
Kell, George V. 583
Kellar, Dr. James 217
Keller Tool & Die 229
Keller, Albert 236
Keller, Albert 326
Keller, David 548
Keller, George 554
Keller, Kenneth 541
Kelley, James 542
Kelley, Robert 505
Kelley, Robert E. 179
Kelly, Charles 507
Kelly, Dan 439
Kelly, George 'Machine Gun' , ... 301
Kelly, Harry L. 303
Kelly, John 371
Kelly, L. W. 289
Kelly, Loranna Franke 377
Kelly, R. E. 289
Kelly, Robert 181
Kelly, Robert E. 583
Kelly, Thomas J 233
Kelly, Thomas J. 235
Kelly, Thomas J. 343
Kelpin Market 299
Kelso, Aaron 506
Kelso, John 381
Keltsch Pharmacy 515
Kemp, Don 379
Kemp, William G. 447
Kempton, Robert 440
Kendall, Thomas H. 586
Kendall, Thomas H. 587
Kendallville 143
Kennedy, J. William 440
Kennedy, John 503
Kennedy, John F. 510
Kennedy, Robert 542
Kenton, Simon 30
Kentucky Baptist Society 90
Kentucky Fried Chicken 417
Kepler, Wayne 506
Keplinger, H. A. 294
Kerby, H. A. 544
Kercheval, Benjamin 306
Kercheval, Benjamin Berry 94
Kercheval, Eliza 94
Kercheval, Perry 94
Kerchival, Benjamin 174
Kern, John W. 583
Kerr, H. Waveland 181
Kerris, Jack 375
Kerris, Jack 382
Ketchell, Steve 374
Kettler, A. W. 271
Kettler, A. W. 471
Kettler, A. W. 477
Kettler, Al 271

Kettler, Alfred W. 476
Kettler, Alfred W. 477
Keys, Calvin 512
Kickapoo 24
Kickapoo 54
Kickapoo 69
Kickapoos 13
Kickapoos 28
Kid's Day 473
Kidder, Dr. O. T. 412
Kidnappings 329
Kiefer, O. R. 235
Kiefer, Richard 504
Kiel, Harold 219
Kiester, David 548
Kilbourne, E. H. 413
Kilbourne, Edgar H. 441
Kilbourne, Edgar H. 450
Kimball, Gene 370
Kimball, Virgil 114
Kimball, Virgil 264
Kime Hotel 142
Kimmel, Norman W. 410
Kimmell, C. V. 377
Kinder, Michael 584
Kinder, Paul B. 585
Kindergarten 261
Kindler Hotel 289
Kindler Hotel 450
Kindler, J. J. 214
Kindler, Jake 511
King Nicolas War 5
King Trunk and Leather Works 291
King, Frank 438
King, Frank W. 336
King, Frank W. 348
King, George T. 291
King, Henry 380
King, Morris 289
King, Morris 291
King, William 371
Kinkade, G. Frank 291
Kinkade, Helen 291
Kinnaird, A. F. 290
Kinnane, R. B. 289
Kinne, George 542
Kinne, George H. 554
Kinney, Bob 375
Kirkham, William 167
Kiser, Peter 157
Klaehn Funeral Home 305
Klaehn, Robert H. 220
Klebe, Walter E. 585
Klebe, Walter E. 586
Kleopfer, Ronald 588
Klier, Leo 375
Klingenberger, Earl 556
Klingenberger, Jerome J. 222
Klitzke, William 372
Klotz, Ed 379
Klotz, James 411
Klug Park 473
Klug, Gregor 416
Knaggs, Whitmore 59
Knapke, Norbert B. 500
Knapke, Norman 514
Knapp, Dr. Isaac 174
Knapp, Paul 409
Knapp, William 182
Knickers 299
Knight, Charles S. 170
Knight, Erven 586
Knight, Erven 587
Knights of Labor 173
Knights of Labor 330
Knobluch, Helen 542
Knoche, William 348
Knot Hole Gang 228
Knott, John 228
Know-Nothings 155
Knox, Henry 25
Knox, Willie 382
Koch, Jack 506
Kocks, John B. 236
Koehlinger, Arthur G. 290
Koehlinger, Denis L. 447
Koehlinger, Lynn 440
Koehlinger, Lynn 543
Koehlinger, Lynn 546
Koehlinger, Lynn 557
Koehlinger, Winston F. 290
Koeneman, Edward 267
Koenig, Charles W. 583
Koenig, Edward 266
Koenig, Otto W. 236
Koenig, Otto W. 584
Koenig, Otto W. 585
Koenig, Otto W. 585
Koerber Sr., Robert 233
Koerber, Robert 224
Koerber, Robert 307
Koerber, Robert 441
Koester, F. P. 231
Kolmertin, Elmer 451
Koos, Richard 543
Kopper, Robert M. 507
Kopper, Robert M. 553
Koppers Co. 410
Koppers, Robert 553
Korn, Harold 416
Korn, Harold 439
Korn, Harold E. 585
Korn, Harold E. 586
Korn, Harold E. 587
Korn, Harold E. 588
Kowalczyk, George 554
Kowalczyk, Hank 375
Kraft Paper Products 231
Kraft, Eddie 377
Kramer, C. A. 231
Kramer, Joseph 264
Kramer, Joseph 331
Krason, Rev. Edward 266
Kratzert, Bill 382
Kraus, Eugene 547
Kraus, Sharlene 556
Krauskopf, Edwin 311
Krauskopf, Nord 512
Krauss, Dr. Paul 340
Krauss, Dr. Paul 446
Krauss, Dr. Paul H. 217
Kroger 500
Kroger Grocery 289
Kronenberg, John J. 169
Krouse, Dick 379
Krueger, Ottomar 269
Krull, Walter 438
Kruse Jr., Edward H. 586
Kruse, Carlton 267
Kruse, Dean 587
Kruse, Donald 409
Kruse, Edgar 446
Kruse, Edward 439
Kruse, Norman F. 233
Kuhl, E. M. 164
Kuhne, Frederick W. 171
Kuhne, Paul F. 298
Kulesza, Henry 379
Kunkel, William 419
Kunkel, William A. 293
Kunkle Valve Co. 554
Kunkle Valve Company 165
Kunkle, Erastus B. 166
Kunkle, William 326
Kuntz, George 288
Kurtz, Kenneth 547
Kurtz, Mrs. L. D. 408
Kuseff, Anna 348
Kuseff, Anna 351
Kuttner, Peter G. 291
Kwik-Lok Corp. 500
L. I. Griffin Co. 327
L. S. Ayres 450
L. S. Ayres 514
L. S. Ayres 515
L. W. Dailey Construction Co. 448
L,Epinay, Couillard De 4
La Balme Massacre 16
La Balme, August Mottin De 16
La Clair, Bernard 441
La Riviere, Francois Joseph Bissot De . . 4
La Salle, Sieur De 2
Labor Baiters 345
Labor Force 547
Labor Movement 331
Lackey, Ermil 377
Lackey, Kenneth 503
Lafayette and Logansport Traction Co. . . 187
Lafayette Rangers 151
Lafayette, Marquis De 16
Lafontaine, Francis 94
Lafontaine, Francois 68
Lafontaine, Jacques 68
Lafontaine, Peter 17
Lake Erie Railroad 473
Lake, Glenn H. 585
Lake, Glen H. 586
Lake, Glenn H. 587
Lake, Orin H. 584
Lake, Orin H. 585
Lakeside Park 472
Lakeside Rose Gardens 474
Lambert, Eustache 4
Lambert, Eustche 4
Lambrakis, Charles 291
Lamont, Allan C. 585
Lancaster, Freda 262
Land Sales 114
Land Sales 115
Land Use 239
Landon, Alf 329
Lane, C. 233
Lane, Ruth 556
Lange, Rev. A. H. 181
Langlade, Charles 7
Langlois, Peter 94
Langtry, Lillie 171
Lankford, Pius 596
Lansing, Frank 556
Lanternier Florists 291
Lanternier, Clem 291
Lanternier, Edmund 291
Lapp, Henry 236
Large, Josephine 214
Larimore, L. B. 178
Larimore, Miss Muriel 184
Larson, Ralph 517
Larson, Rev. Ralph 516
Larwill, C. K. 288
Lasselle, Antoine 49
Lasselle, Francois 68
Lasselle, Jacques 49
Lasselle, Jacques 68
Lassus Bros. 410
Lassus, August J. 410
Lassus, Elmer F. 410
Lassus, John F. 554
Lassus, William F. 410
Last Passenger Run 188
Lathrop, Mrs. Olla 304
Latz, G. Irvin 547
Latz, G. Irvin 290
Latz, G. Irving 307
Latz, G. Irving 326
Latz, G. Irving 450
Latz, G. Irving 546
Latz, William 514
Latz, W lliam S. 408
Latz, William S. 587
Latz, William S. 588
Latz, William Smith 290
Latz, William Smith 450
Latz, Wm. S. 587
Latz, Wm. S. 588
Lauer Auto Co. 292
Lauferty, Mrs. Minnie 172
Laurent, Guy 231
Laurent, Louis 163
Laurents, Alex 231

Lawler, John C. 583
Lawrence, George 175
Lawrence, George B. 583
Lawrence, Robert 11
Lawton Park 158
Lawton Park 162
Lawton Park 472
Lawton Park 473
Lawton, Henry W. 158
Laycock, Wendell 546
Laycock, Wendell C. 546
Le Crosse, Pete 374
Le Gris 15
Le Gris 18
Le Gris 19
Le Gris 19
Le Gris 43
Le Gris 48
Le Gris 50
Le Gris 54
Le Gris 56
Le Gris 57
Le Gris 89
Leach, E. Robert 446
Leader Department Store 238
League of Women Voters 544
Leamon, Paul A. 477
Leaninon Leaning on Shovels 326
Leather Merchants 166
Lebamoff, Ivan 547
Lebamoff, Ivan 551
Lebamoff, Ivan 552
LebraktoCharleLebrato, Charles 410
Lee, Dr. Helen C. 264
Lee, Helen 263
Lee, Richard Henry 17
Lee, Torchy 349
Lee, Torchy 352
Lee, William 306
Legal Services 512
Legalized Beer 307
Lehman Book Store 288
Lehman, C. A. 541
Lehman, Harold 231
Lehman, Harold A. 511
Lehman, Jackson 516
Lehman, Jackson R. 546
Lehman, S. A. 231
Lemay, Mrs. Eliza 173
Lemke, William 329
Lenkendorfer Coffee Ranch 291
Lenkendorfer, Willard 291
Lennart, William 477
Lenning, Frank A. 587
Lennon, E. J. 181
Lennon, Edward 180
Lennon, Jim 370
Lenz, Charles F. 585
Leon C. Beck Jewelry 289
Leonard, George 333
Leonard, George 586
Leonard, George 585
Leonard, Robert E. 586
Leonard, W. M. 290
Leopold, Chester M. 450
Lepper, Adolf W. 584
Lepper, Henry W. 294
Leroy, Victoria 176
Lesh, Joseph 306
Lesh, Ulysses S. 584
Leslie, G. M. 294
Leslie, Harry G. 285
Leslie, Harry G. 585
Lester, Msgr. William 266
Leto, Nick 379
Levine, Joseph 556
Levy, Dr. Virgil 514
Lewis, Colonel William 83
Lewis, David 336
Ley, Miss Leona 262
Library 311
Library 541
License Plates 218
Lichtenberg, Chester 444
Life Insurance Industry 221
Liggett, James 586
Light, Carl 410
Lill, Robert 231
Lillie Tavern 142
Lima and Toledo Traction Company 187
Lincoln Historial Research Foundation .. 310
Lincoln Library and Museum 222
Lincoln Life 296
Lincoln Life 298
Lincoln National Bank 216
Lincoln National Bank 225
Lincoln National Bank 295
Lincoln National Bank 447
Lincoln National Bank 507
Lincoln National Bank & Trust Co. 289
Lincoln National Bank & Trust Co. 294
Lincoln National Life Insurance Company 221
Lincoln Tower 293
Lincoln Tower 294
Lincoln Tower 295
Lincoln Trust Co. 295
Lincoln, Abraham 155
Lincoln, Benjamin 60
Lincoln, Chester A. 351
Lincoln, Chester A. 416
Lindbergh, Charles A. 220
Lindemann, Herbert 446
Lindemuth, C. Ross 587
Lindemuth, Clayton 584
Lindemuth, Clayton A. 585
Lindemuth, George W. 583
Lindenberg, Edwin 413
Lindenberg, Edwin 415
Lindenwood Cemetery 148
Lindenwood Cemetery 161
Lindenwood Cemetery 472
Lindley, Aaron T. 263
Lindley, Aaron T. 506
Lindley, Dr. Harlow 216
Link, Daniel M. 584
Link, William H. 264
Linwood Cemetery 154
Liquor Drinking 89
Little Turtle 7
Little Turtle 13
Little Turtle 17
Little Turtle 18
Little Turtle 18
Little Turtle 20
Little Turtle 24
Little Turtle 25, 30
Little Turtle 43
Little Turtle 45
Little Turtle 52
Little Turtle 54
Little Turtle 56
Little Turtle 57
Little Turtle 59
Little Turtle 60
Little Turtle 66
Little Turtle 67
Little Turtle 68
Little Turtle 69
Little Turtle 78
Little Turtle 86
Little Turtle 88
Little Turtle 93
Little Turtle 93
Little Turtle 144
Little Turtle 174
Little Turtle 543
Little Turtle 556
Little Turtle's Confederacy 91
Littlejohn, John S. 542
Livery Stables 171
Livery Stables 334
Livestock 412
Living Standards 335
Livingston, Von E. 554
LNC Development Corporation 223
LNC Equity Sales Corporation 223
LNC Investment Management Corporation 223
Lobaugh, Ralph 351
Lobaugh, Ralph 351
Lobaugh, Ralph W. 349
Lochner, D. M. 449
Lockridge, Ross 216
Lockridge, Ross F. 309
Lockridge, Shockley 542
Loehe, Dr. William 148
Log Jail 150
Logan, F. Leslie 291
Logan, John A. 413
Logan, John H. 452
Lohman, Col. Eugene A. 340
Lombard, Carole 166
Lombard, Carole 308
Lombard, Carole 556
Lombard, John 452
Lomont, Al 380, 596
Long, Baron 312
Long, Eddie 378
Long, Margaret 306
Long, Mason 312
Long, Stephen H. 111
Long, Willie 381
Longpre, Philippe 4
Longstreth, Joe 552
Longworth, Nick 596
Loomis, Oliver 306
Loomis, Oliver M. 303
Loos, G. L. 290
Loraine, Edward C. 508
Lord, Charles A. 414
Lotz, Henry 155
Lougheed, Cook 588
Lougheed, Scott 381
Louis Rastetter & Sons Co. 166
Louis Schwartzkopf 177
Louitt, George W. 583
Louttit, George 180
Lowe, David 229
Lowery, Harry 441
Lowry, Lt. John 28
Lowry, Mrs. Robert 171
Luecke, Clara 508
Luecke, M. H. 184
Luecke, Martin L. 269
Lueke, Herbert 446
Luepke, Martin 508
Luepke, Martin 511
Luers, John Henry 147
Lugibihl, B. P. 269
Luken, Leo 376
Lulu Archer Confections 290
Lumberyard 308
Lumpp, John 381
Lunchhour Bandit 441
Lundell, Pete 381
Lunz, Fred G. 585
Lunz, Fred G. 585
Lupke, Mrs. Walter 408
Lupke, Mrs. Walter H. 446
Lupke, Walter H. 408
Lutheran Choral 407
Lutheran Hospital 162
Lutheran Hospital 237
Lutheran Hospital 445
Lutheran Hour 451
Lutheran Institute 271
Lutheran Schools 266
Luxury Apartments 509
Lycoming Engine 310
Lycoming Engine Co. 310
Lyon, Dr. William 553
Lyons, Charley 381
M&N Shoe Store 288
Mac Donald, Elmer 587
Mac Donald, Elmer 588
Macbeth, Jesse 264
MacDonald, Elmer 376
MacDougal Building 449
MacDougal, Charles 228

Machine Guns 304
Machine Guns 305
Mackinac Island 89
Mackinnon, H. A. 170
Mackwitz, Herman 149
Mad Anthony Guards 151
Mad Killer 349
Madden and Keefer Hanging 151
Madden, Benjamin 151
Madden, Tom 382
Magee, Miss Madge 184
Magee, Ralph 448
Maginity, E. Neil 508
Magley, Rick 382
Magna Power Tool 230
Magnavox 228
Magnavox 292
Magnavox 344
Magnavox Co. 441
Magnavox Co. 501
Magnavox Co. 501
Magnavox Co. 505
Magnavox Co. 509
Magnavox Co. 555
Magree, Rev. Mack 513
Mahlock, Calo 442
Mahurin, Guy 233
Mahurin, Guy 306
Mahurin, Isaac 149
Mahurin, M. L. 149
Mahurin, M. S. 172
Mahurin, Mrs. M. S. 172
Mahurin, W. S. 174
Mahurin, Walker M. 347
Maier, George 142
Mail 111
Mail Delivery 306
Main St. Project 509
Maisonneuve, Roger 378
Maisonville, Francois 12
Majestic Theater 289
Majestic Theater 408
Majestic Theatre 374
Malaria 175
Mallers, George 418
Mallers, Peter 291
Malls 514
Malnutrition 328
Maloley Bros. 545
Maloley Brothers 311
Maloley, Alfred 554
Maloley, Michael 545
Managny, William F. 438
Manges, Dr. Roger J. 271
Manges, Roger 547
Manslaughter 303
Manth, Erwin H. 290
Mantock, Robert 265
Manual Training School 262
Manufacturing 286
Maounis, William 289
Marahrens, Otto 289
Marahrens, Otto 307
Marble Works 144
Marganne, Francois 4
Marine Corps 505
Maritime Plastics 500
Market 237
Market 551
Market Building 449
Markowitz, Rabbi Samuel 307
Marlin, Henry 584
Marolf, Fred 512
Marquart, Dee 556
Marquart, Elton 586, 587
Marquis, Isaac 144
Marriott Motor Hotel 550
Marsh Foodliner 500
Marsh, E. Cyril 164
Marc Marsh, L. E. 448
Marshal, Thomas R. 583
Marshall, Thomas 184
Marshall, Wilbert 164
Martha Washington Candies 289
Martin Coal Co. 415
Martin, A. 264
Martin, A. Eugene 416
Martin, Bill 549
Martin, Bobbie 552
Martin, Dr. Harvey 185
Martin, Eugene 416
Martin, Eugene 585
Martin, Ivan A. 233
Martin, J. B. 446
Martin, Willis 292
Martone, Tony 380
Mary Penrose Wayne Chapter DAR 217
Mary Penrose Wayne Chapter-DAR 182
Mascotte, Leo C. 450
Mascotte, Leo C. 546
Masked Balls 172
Mason, Dennis 421
Mason, James A. 450
Mason, Joseph N. 583
Masonic Emblem 49
Masonic Hall 145
Masonic Temple 218
Masonic Temple Theatre 215
Masonic Temple Theatre Fire 238
Massage Parlors 550
Massoud Marine 500
Mathews, Bobby 370
Mathews, Leo R. 240
Mathias APP Shoe Store 290
Matrimony 65
Matson, C. H. 441
Mauk, R. H. 184
Maurice R. Miller Windows 291
Mautner, Isador 372
Max Irmscher & Sons 239, 327
Max Irmscher & Sons 338
Maxfield, Kenneth 440
Maxwell, Gene 379
Maxwell, Marilyn 308
May Stone & Sand, Inc. 448
May, William 30
May, William 448
Mc Alister, Dr. H. Clive 440
Mc Andless, Alva J. 222
Mc Ardle, Dr. John 161
Mc Bride, James 409
Mc Cann, E. V. 233
Mc Carthy, Clem 307
Mc Carthy, Eugene 542
Mc Carthy, George 421
Mc Carthy, Jerry W. 182
Mc Clellan, Robert 47
Mc Cloud, Hartley 378
Mc Comb, Bob 219
Mc Comb, Dick 380
Mc Comb, John Fred 219
Mc Comb, Thomas V. 587
Mc Comb, Thomas V. 588
Mc Comb, Thomas V. 588
Mc Coniga, Donald 440
Mc Coniga, Donald 549
Mc Cormick Jr., Cyrus 225
Mc Cormick, Clifton 554
Mc Cormick, Clifton E. 507
Mc Coy, Angus 233
Mc Coy, Angus 236
Mc Coy, Isaac 144
Mc Coy, Isaac 265
Mc Coy, Mike 381
Mc Cray, Warren T. 584
Mc Culloch Cemetery 154
Mc Culloch Park 472
Mc Culloch, Charles 162
Mc Culloch, Charles 163
Mc Culloch, Charles 174
Mc Culloch, Charles 178
Mc Culloch, Charles 179
Mc Culloch, Charles 186
Mc Culloch, Charles 235
Mc Culloch, Charles 298
Mc Culloch, Hugh 117
Mc Culloch, Hugh 149
Mc Culloch, Hugh 264
Mc Culloch, Hugh 472
Mc Culloch, J. R. 294
Mc Culloch, J. Ross 215
Mc Culloch, J. Ross 220
Mc Culloch, Judge Hugh 160
Mc Culloch, Mrs. Fred 184
Mc Culloch, Mrs. Hugh 145
Mc Dermott, Bobby 375
Mc Diarmid, Fergus 223
Mc Divitt, James A. 513
Mc Donald, D. P. 326
Mc Donald, D. P. 343, 587
Mc Donald, Donnelly 554
Mc Donald, Donnelly P. 294
McDonald, Donnelly P. 514
Mc Donald, Donnelly P. 547
Mc Donald, Donnelly P. 553
Mc Donald, Patrick J. 294
Mc Donald, Patrick J. 295
Mc Donald R. T. 170
Mc Donald, Robert 439
Mc Donald, Ronald T. 169
Mc Donald, Ronald T. 172
Mc Donald, Sam 163
Mc Fadden, Andrea 556
Mc Fadden, Hugh 585
Mc Fall, Charles 440
Mc Farren, Phares 336
Mc Gee, Patrick 150
Mc Govern, George 548
Mc Grady, John D. 150
Mc Grath, Mrs. Ellen 172
Mc Graw, Kenneth 514
Mc Intyre, Harry 310
Mc Junkin School 261
Mc Mc Kathnie, Ivan 514
Mc Kay, David 172
Mc Kay, George 449
Mc Kay, George W. 448
Mc Kay, J. M. 448
Mc Kay, James M. 165
Mc Kay, Neil 440
Mc Kay, Neil 449
Mc Kay, Neil A. 448
Mc Kay, Neil A. 554
Mc Kay, Ruth B. 412
Mc Kay, William 412
Mc Kay, William T. 264
Mc Kay, William T. 412
Mc Kay, William T. 448
Mc Kelleb, Jackie 552
Mc Kim, J. B. 294
Mc Kinnie, Miss Esther 171
Mc Lachlan, Neil 154
Mc Lachlin, Miss Nannie 181
Mc Lain, Pat 451
Mc Laughlin, Tom 179
Mc Lay, Bryan 378
Mc Lucas, Fred 441
Mc Mahan, Allan 288
Mc Mahan, Allan 408
Mc Maken, Robert 214
Mc Meen, Allen 380
Mc Millen Chapel 420
Mc Millen Feed 232
Mc Millen Feed Mills, Inc. 232
Mc Millen Feeds 232
Mc Millen Park 414
Mc Millen Park 475
Mc Millen Sr., Dale 232
Mc Millen Sr., Dale W. 374
Mc Millen, D. W. 471
Mc Millen, Dale W. 232
Mc Millen, Dale W. 332
Mc Millen, Dale W. 475
Mc Millen, Dale W. 546
Mc Millen, Harold 441
Mc Millen, Harold W. 232
Mc Millen, Harold W. 232
Mc Millen, Harold W. 440
Mc Millen, Harold W. 477

Mc Millen, Harold W. 478
Mc Millen, Harold W. 507
Mc Millen, Harold W. 546
Mc Millen, Harold W. 547
Mc Millen, Harry 326
Mc Millen, Harry 336
Mc Millen, Harvey 348
Mc Millen, Stewart W. 232
Mc Murtry, Dr. R. Gerald 222
Mc Nabb, Clarence 325
Mc Nabb, Clarence R. 264
Mc Nabb, Clarence R. 416
Mc Nagny, Judge Robert 304
Mc Nagny, Mrs. William 547
Mc Nagny, Phil M. 306
Mc Nagny, William F. 507
Mc Nett, Roy 410
Mc Night, Harold 410
Mc Nutt, Paul V. 305
Mc Nutt, Paul V. 585
Mc Vey, Pat 308
McAfee, Robert 80
McClain, Harry E. 586
McCorkle, John 110
McCorkle, John 112
McCoy, Angus C. 584
McCoy, Isaac 92
McCoy, Isaac 94
McCracken, James K. 153
McCulloch, Carlton E. 584
McCulloch, Hugh 113
McDougal, Gregory 151
McKee, Alexander 15
McKee, Alexander 49
McMahon, E. A. 151
McMaken, Joseph H. 144
McNabb, Clarence R. 585
Mead, Franklin 222
Mead, Mr. Franklin 222
Meader, William 408
Meager Meals 329
Means, G. S. 221
Meat Markets 299
Meazell, William 421
Medical Arts Building 289
Medical Center Building 218
Medical Information Service 223
Medical Practice 15
Medical Protective Co. 410
Medical Services 512
Mee, Eldon 345
Meeks, Charles 554
Meeks, Charles B. 588
Mehr, Father Aloysius 270
Meier, Ferdinand 477
Meigs Eye Specialists 289
Meigs, Charles 215
Meigs, Charles 289
Meinzen, H. W. 294
Meissner, Henry 266
Meister, Dr. John W. 420
Melancon, Clem 289
Memorial Coliseum 377
Memorial Park 474
Mendenhall, Dr. Edgar N. 348
Mendenhall, Murray 379
Mendenhall, Murray 380
Menefee, James 412
Menge, Walter O. 221
Menge, Walter O. 222
Mental Health Center 553
Merchandise Place 550
Merkler Machining 229
Merrill, Herbert J. 309
Merritt, E. H. 184
Merriwether, Mrs. Martha 171
Merry-Go-Round 176
Mesing, Carl 449
Messerschmitt 110 347
Metallurgical Processing Co. 500
Metcalf, Dr. Dean 185
Metcalf, Martin V. 583
Methodist Church 147
Methodist College 148
Methodist Hospital 162
Methodist Hospital 440
Methodist Mission 145
Metrailer, Rosey 512
Meyer Bros. Drugs 289
Meyer Co. 288
Meyer Drugs 412
Meyer, Arthur J. 542
Meyer, Fred W. 587
Meyer, Louis H. 507
Meyer, Robert 289
Meyer, Robert E. 499
Meyers, Edward W. 444
Meyers, Edward W. 585
Meyers, Edward W. 586
Meyers, Fred W. 587
Meyers, Robert 438
Meyers, Robert 439
Meyers, Robert 446
Meyers, Robert 452
Meyers, Robert 514
Meyers, Robert 516
Meyers, Robert E. 438
Meyers, Robert E. 444
Meyers, Robert L. 554
Meyers, Walter C. 444
Meyers, Walter C. 508
Miami Canal 117
Miami Confederacy 43
Miami Confederation 21
Miami Confederation 22
Miami Confederation 32
Miami Confederation 53
Miami Confederation 59
Miami Confederation 63
Miami Indians 7
Miamis 2
Miamis 15, 24
Miamis 52
Miamitown 16
Miamitown 43
Miamitown 80
Michaelis, D. F. 290
Michaelis, Dr. Stephen C. 514
Michigan City Prison 301
Michigan Territory 88
Microfilm 541
Microfilm Scandal 502
Midwestern United Life 413, 501, 596
Mike,s Car Wash 418
Miles, William 262
Military Vehicles 344
MilinMachineMilking Machines 170
Milks, Harold K. 307
Millard, Robert 233
Miller-Wohl Ladies Co. 289
Miller, Carl E. 438
Miller, Charles 585
Miller, Charles 585
Miller, Charles C. 170
Miller, Christopher 30
Miller, Christopher 45
Miller, Christopher 59
Miller, David 512
Miller, Earl J. 220
Miller, Edward 224
Miller, Edward C. 184
Miller, Edward C. 325
Miller, George M. 441
Miller, H. Paul 439
Miller, Harriet 556
Miller, Harry E. C. 234
Miller, Henry A. 584
Miller, Hugh T. 583
Miller, Jeanne S. 272
Miller, Jimmy 503
Miller, John Fay 48
Miller, John M. 264
Miller, Joseph W. 546
Miller, Larry T. 514
Miller, Lt. Richard E. 347
Miller, Luella 290
Miller, Milford 547
Miller, Ralph 375
Miller, Rich 381
Miller, Robert 220
Miller, Sharon 552
Miller, Ursula 508
Miller, Wayne L. 348
Miller, William E. 264
Mills, C. M. 233
Mills, F. J. 294
Mills, J. B. 186
Milnor, Cliff 409
Milton M. Mendelsohn Shoes 290
Milton, Bobby 380
Miner, B. B. 174
Miner, William 584
Mineral Springs Sanitarium 337
Mingo 54
Mini-Calculators 421
Minier, Howard 331
Minier, Howard 345
Minier, Howard 512
Mischke, Benno C. 270
Missiles 170
Missionary Church Association 269
Missouri Synod 147
Missouri Synod 269
Mitchell, Bill 378
Mitchell, John 381
Model T 287
Moeller, E. C. 446
Moellering Gristmill 547
Moellering, Alfred 306
Moellering, Alfred W. 444
Moellering, Alfred W. 554
Moellering, Alfred W. 588
Moellering, Charles 233
Moellering, Charles 326
Moellering, Charles E. 336
Moellering, Charles E. 348
Moellering, Henry J. 554
Moellering, Paul C. 586
Moellering, Paul C. 586
Moellering, William H. F. 583
Moellering, William L. 295
Moffett, Rev. David W. 178
Mohler, Clifford 304
Molinas, Jack 375
Monitor-Top Refrigerators 170
Monning, Henry 161
Monning, Henry 162
Montcalm, Marquis De 7
Montgomery Ward 291
Montgomery Ward 500
Montgomery, Ward 515
Montgomery, Charles 504
Moody, William J. 477
Moon, William L. 143
Moonshine 302
Moor, John W. 583
Moore, Edwin 294
Moore, Francis E. 584
Moorhead, Sam 334
Moran, Albert 326
Moran, Clifford J. 583
Moran, Clifford J. 583
Moreland, Charles 182
Morgan, F. D. 240
Morgan, Joseph 144
Morgan, Joseph 155
Morgan, O. P. 171
Morgan, Oliver 264
Morgan, Payne 584
Morgan, Payne 585
Moring, Mrs. John H. 215
Moritz, John 264
Mormons 149
Morning Musical Society 214
Morrill, Lyall D. 546
Morris Canal and Banking Co. 116
Morris Plan 289, 294
Morris Plan 511
Morris, Benjamin 306

Morris, Captain Robert 12
Morris, Judge John 178
Morris, Stephen 294
Morrison, R. D. 410
Morrow, Robert 556
Morrow, Robert A. 507
Morsches, Frank J. 214
Morse, Lillie 172
Morss, Mrs. Sam 171
Morss, Samuel 155
Morss, Samuel S. 144
Mortenson, Dr. L. J. 446
Morthorst, Harold 379
Morton, William E. 294
Moses, Horace 289
Moses, Mrs. Harriett 289
Moses, Winfield 411
Moses, Winfield 547
Moses, Winfield 553
Moskal, Rev. John 514
Mosquitoes 118
Mossman, B. Paul 184
Mossman, B. Paul 216
Mossman, B. Paul 234
Mossman D. Paul 168
Mossman, Paul 264
Mossman, William E. 184
Mossman, William E. 225
Mossman, William E. 234
Motels 550
Mother George 158
Motherhouse 514
Motherwell, Hiram K. 309
Motor Buses 443
Motz, Leslie 409
Moudy, Martin L. 583
Mount Calvary School 267
Movie Houses 291
Movie Palaces 289
Movie Queens 308
Movie Theaters 418
Movies 308, 504
Moynihan, Andrew 179
Moynihan, Andy 183
Mrs. Miller Tea Room 417
Mrs. Miller's Tea Room 290
Mrs. Rhoda Depotty Millinery Shop 291
Mueller, August 585
Mueller, Rev. Louis 146
Muff, Mike 382
Muhler, C. F. 174
Muhler, Charles F. 173
Mulholland, S. E. 184
Mullen, Lawrence 554
Muller, Gertrude A. 233
Muller, Harry 184
Muller, Harry W. 585
Mumby, Colonel 172
Mungovan, J. Frank 181
Mungovan, J. Frank 186
Mungovan, J. Frank 236
Mungovan, Judge J. Frank 179
Municipal Airport 185
Municipal Airport 219
Municipal Beach 327
Municipal Golf Course 472
Municipal Terminal 550
Munsingwear Corporation 168
Murder 304
Murder 505
Murder 551
Murder Charge 303
Murders 348
Murders 349
Murphy, Donald 264
Murphy, Donald F. 449
Murphy, Donald F. 554
Murphy, Jimmy 374
Murray, Jack 328
Museums 216
Musicians 87
Mutual Security Life 452
Muzen, M. B. 230
Myers, Dale J. 587
Myers, Dan 288
Myers, Donald L. 586
Myers, Dorothy E. 588
Myers, Dr. W. H. 161
Myers, Mrs. Essie 172
Myerson, Daisy 171
Mystery 328
N. V. Philips 555
Nading Jr., Martin 471
Nading, Martin 477
Naecker, William 301
Nahrwold, Hilbert 413
Nally, Hiram 554
NASA 596
Nash, Richard 411
Nash, William 556
Nathan, George Jean 213
Nation, Carrie 177
National Air Races 503
National Bank 545
National Banks 297
National Fibre Box Association 231
National Homes 410
National League 371
National Mill Supply Co. 550
National Mill Supply, Inc. 230
National Mill Supply, Inc. 231
Natural Gas 235
Natwatine 112
Nayr Jr., Frank 585
NBC 293
Neal, Robert 452
Neeb, Dr. Martin J. 269
Needham, Dean B. 228
Neff, Floyd 216
Neff, Floyd R. 271
Negro 265
Negro 516
Negro Members 331
Negro Population 413
Negroes 547
Neighborhood Services 512
Neighborhood Youth Corps 512
Neiman, Nelson 290
Neiman, Nelson K. 450
Neisner's Five and Ten 288
Neizer, Maurice C. 186
Nelson, Dr. Lawrence 271
Nelson, George 305
Nelson, Isaac 154
Nelson, Stanley 441
Nelson, William Rockhill 310
Nerger, Rev. Edwin A. 446
Netter, Roy 288
Neuman, Lloyd 516
New Haven 504
New Haven Vigilants 151
New Jail 150
New Library 541
New York Central 153
New York Shipbuilding Corp. 310
New York, Chicago and St. Louis Railroad 166
New, Harry S. 584
Newkirk, James R. 339
Newkirk, James R. 416
News Publishing Co. 419
News-Sentinel 239
News-Sentinel 345
News-Sentinel 351
News-Sentinel 414
News-Sentinel 418
News-Sentinel 471
News-Sentinel 474
News-Sentinel 544
News-Sentinel 549
News-Sentinel 551
News-Sentinel 552, 596
News-Sentinel Broadcasting Co. 293
News-Sentinel Building 218
News-Sentinel Building 290
News-Sentinel Outdoor Theatre 409
Newspaper 418
Nichens, Robert 235
Nicholas Andress Shoe Parlor 291
Nickel Plate Elevation 443
Nickel Plate Railroad 237
Nickel Plate Restaurant 171
Nickel Plate Road 152
Nickel Plate Road 167
Nickel Plate System 166
Nicolet, Jean 1
Nicolet, Jean 4
Niebergal, Charles 184
Niebergall, C. A. 291
Nieter, Edwin 588
Niezer, C. M. 294
Niezer, Charles M. 230
Niezer, Charlie 296
Niezer, Louis 308
Niezer, Louis F. 230
Niezer, Louis F. 477
Niezer, Louis F. 546
Niezer, Maurice 216
Niezer, Maurice 294
Niezer, Maurice C. 184
Nigsch, Rev. Francis 181
Nill, Conrad 145
Nill, Dr. John 514
Nill, George 373
Nill, Richard 446
Nill, Richard G. 410
Ninde Homestead 446
Ninde, Daniel B. 583
Ninde, Jane 214
Ninde, Judge Lindley M. 172
Ninde, L. M. 174
Ninde, Lee 238
Ninde, Lindley M. 164
Nirdlinger and Oppenheimer Clothing Store 157
Nirdlinger Family 213
Nirdlinger, Frederick 143
Nirdlinger, Max 166
Nirdlinger, Max 172
Nirdlinger, Max 264
Nirdlinger, Max 372
Nisley Co. Shoes 289
Nixon, Richard 542
No. 2 Special Luncheon 311
Noble, W. K. 224
Noel, S. V. B. 148
Nolan, Buddy 552
Nolan, Jim 382
Noland, R. W. 338
Noll, Archbishop John F. 445
Noll, B. R. 234
Noll, Bishop John F. 217
Noll, Kenneth 450
Noll, William H. 234
Norfolk & Western Railway 152
North American Indians 511
North Bypass 417
North Side High School 237
North Side Park 162
North Side Park 472
North Side State Bank 294
North Vietnamese 505
Northcrest Shopping Center 500
Northeastern Indiana Broadcasting Co. .. 441
Northern Cross Railroad 153
Northern Indiana Traction Co. 186
Northerner 262
Northwest Confederacy 156
Norton, D. G. Jack 507
Norton, D. G. Jack 508
Notre Dame 375
Novitsky, Byron 477
Novitsky, Byron 478
Noyelle, Nicholas Joseph De 4
NRA 311
Huckols, John 516
Nuckols, John 452
Nuckols, John 508
Nuckols, John 514
Nuckols, John 547

Nuckols, John 553
Nulf, Bob 379
Nussbaum, Helen 216
Nussbaum, Herman 230
Nussbaum, Peter 165
Nussbaum, Victor 230
Nuttman, Joseph D. 157
Nygaard, Rev. Philip 556
O'Conner, Robert E. 326
O'Brien, Rev. John A. 339
O'Brien, Robert P. 232
O'Connor, B. S. 235
O'Connor, Rev. Thomas 513
O'Connor, Robert E. 448
O'Dowd, Jerome 438
O'Dowd, Jerome 452
O'Dowd, Jerome 553
O'Dowd, Thomas J. 214
O'Hora, Mrs. Edgar 330
O'Malley, Paul W. 445
O'Malley, William Patrick 304
O'Neil, William P. 304
O'Neil, William P. 583
O'Reilly, Bob 596
O'Reilly, Michael 266
O'Reilly, Robert E. 508
O'Reilly, Thomas J. 514
O'Rourke, Edward 584
O'Rourke, Judge Edward 174
O'Rourke, W. S. 236
Oakley, Chauncey B. 173
Oakley, Colonel 174
Ober, Arden 452
Ober, Mrs. Fritzy 264
Oberly, Chester C. 230
Ochmig, Bird 584
Odillia, Sister M. 514
Oechtering, Father 266
Oechtering, John 266
Oettel, Russell 556
OffottHarrE. Offutt, Harry E. 232
Ohio and Indiana Railroad Company 153
Ohio Electric Railway Co. 187
Ohio Indiana and Illinois Telegraph Co . . 152
Oil Belt Traction Co. 186
Oil Crisis 551
Old Buildings 540
Old Crown Brewing Corp. 165
Old Fort Industries, Inc. 448
Old Fort Knitting Mills 168
Old Fort Park 159
Old Fort Players 408
Old Fort Recreated 557
Old Fort Supply Co. 448
Old Fort Wayne Printing Co. 234
Old National Bank 225
Old National Bank 235
Old National Bank 288
Old National Bank 294
Old Northwest 13
Old Turnverein 228
Old Union Hall 452
Old Woolen Mill 167
Oldest Business 550
Oldest Newspaper 419
Olds Wagon Works 231
Olds, H. G. 169
Oldsmobiles 218
Oliver Conner Barber Shop 289
Oliver, John W. 216
Olofson, Phil 382
Olsen and Ebann Jewelers 291
Olsen and Johnson 293
Olsen and Johnson 309
Olsen, Ole 293
Olympic Championship 378
Onion, Cecil 378
Onion, Cecil 331
Onion, Cecil 446
Onion, Cecil 509
Opera 408
Optimist Club 412
Orbison, A. M. 143
Orchard Ridge Country 376
Orchards 119
Order of Poor Handmaids 514
Orff Park 472
Orff, Charles E. 583
Orff, Christian 264
Orff, Ed 172
Orff, Miss Flora 171
Orff, Miss Lou 171
Orff, Mont 172
Organ Avenue 164
Organ Builder 164
Ormiston Canal Basin 162
Ornamental Lamp Posts 180
Orr, Robert D. 588
Ortlieb, Arthur 584
Ortlieb, F. William 585
Osborne, Blayne 228
Osdale, Don 381
Oser, Louis W. 584
Ossem, Henry 113
Oswald, Lee Harvey 510
Otis, Mrs. Regina 513
Ottawa 24
Ottawa 69
Ottawas 52
Ottenweller, Ed 448
Ottenweller, Nelson 448
Ouiatenon 24
Outdoor Theatre 551
Overshot Gristmill 144
Oyer, Maurice 440
P & H Supply Co. 556
Pacan 13
Packard Music House 290
Packard Piano 164
Packard Piano Factory 332
Packard, Isaac T. 164
Packet Boats 117
Paddy Wagon 505
Page, Henry C. 419
Page, William 419
Paino, Paul 381
Painter, Paul E. 449
Palace Theater 214, 290, 309
Palace Theater 408
Palm Sunday Tornadoes 512
Palmer, Harold 411
Palo Alto 142
Palumbo, Louis 452
Palumbo, Vito 452
Panhandler 287
Panhandler 311
Panic 294
Panic 297
Panic of 1837 116
Pape Bros. Wallpaper Co. 289
Pape Paint Shop 450
Paper Box and Printing Co. 338
Parades of Homes 447
Parakeet 93
Paramount Theatre 150
Paramount Theatre 289, 291
Paris and Hutner's Bon Marche Co. 290
Park Board 596
Park System 471
Parke, Benjamin 306
Parker, Albert R. 583
Parker, Albert R. 583
Parker, Billy 219
Parker, Crawford F. 586
Parker, Crawford F. 587
Parker, Darl Dee 447
Parker, Dr. Carey B. 348
Parker, Robert 596
Parkinson, Lynn 306
Parks, Benjamin 90
Parkview Hospital 440
Parrish, Robert 505
Parrot Packing Co. 231
Parrot Sr., Frank 231
Parrot, Charles 231
Parrot, Joseph 231
Parrot, Leland 231
Parrot, William 231
Parrott, Robert B. 546
Parry, Arthur 183
Pascoe, James 330
Passenger Flights 542
Passenger Trains 299
Pasteur, Capt. Thomas 61
Patrick, Glen R. 544
Patterson-Fletcher Co. 290
Patterson-Fletcher Store 238
Patterson, Mrs. Rueben 290
Patterson, Sidney 477
Patton Electric Co. 554
Patton, Bennie 505
Paul C. Brudi Stone and Gravel Co. 448
Paul, Henry 225
Paul, Henry 296
Paul, Henry C. 166
Paul, Henry C. 168
Paul, Henry C. 170
Paul, Henry C. 175
Paul, Henry C. 175
Paul, Henry C. 186
Paul, Henry C. 187
Paul, Henry C. 231
Paul, Henry C. 235
Paul, Henry C. 290
Paul, Henry C. 294
Paul, Henry C. 298
Paul, William P. 221
Paulmann, Walter 220
Pavelich, Frank 554
Pavement 218
Pavlova, Anna 214
Payne, Larry 512
Peace Lutheran Church 420
Peace Lutheran School 267
Peanut Market 291
Pearl Harbor 342
Pearson, Dr. H. L. 509
Pearson, Dr. Huey 516
Peek, M. R. 164
Pegler, Westbrook 345
Pelkington, John 375
Peltier, Jacques 68
Peltier, James 68
Peltier, James 110
Peltier, Louis 68
Peltier, Louis 178
Peltier, Mrs. Isabelle 215
Peltier, Mrs. W. H. 215
Peltier, William H. W. 216
Peltier, William H. W. 290
Pembrook, Alfred J. 584
Penn Central 153
Penn-Central Limited 543
Pennsylvania Railroad 182
Pennsylvania Railroad 412
Peoples Drug Store 288
Peoples Party 155
PeapleTrusPeoples Trust 297
Peoples Trust & Savings Co. 295
Peoples Trust & Savings Co. 184
Peoples Trust & Savings Co. 294
Peoples Trust Bank 507
Peoples Trust Bank 553
Peoples Trust Building 290
Peoria 54
Pequignot, E. C. 166
Perfect, Arthur H. 184
Perfect, Harry 512
Perfect, Harry A. 294
Perfection Biscuit Co. 235
Perfection Biscuit Company 474
Performing Arts 509
Performing Arts Center 408
Performing Arts Theatre 547
Periodicals 541
Perjury 416
Perkins, Roger 448
Perkins, William 65
Perrey, Don 448

Perrey, Donald 382
Perrine, Van B. 184
Perrot, Nicolas 1
Perry, Doris 596
Perry Rangers 151
Perry, Eli 264
Perry, Lt. Oliver Hazard 81
Perry, Ramon 377
Perry, Ramon S. 377
Persons, Henry 223
Peter Eckrich and Sons 231
Peter Eckrich and Sons 552
Peters, Carol Jane 308
Peters, David 264
Peters, Jane 166
Peters, John C. 166
Peters, John C. 175
Peters, John C. 308
Peters, John C. 556
Peters, Kenneth 452
Peters, Mrs. R. Earl 264
Peterson Brothers 230
Peterson, T. C. 303
Peterson, Thomas J. 264
Petrecelle, Nadene 512
Petrucelli, D. J. 233
Petrucelli, Don 556
Peyster, Colonel Arent De 17
Pfeiffer, Charles 295
Phelps Dodge Corp. 513
Phelps, Charles A. 584
Phelps, Charles A. 585
Phelps, Charles A. 586
Phelps, John 223
Philharmonic Chorus 407
Philharmonic Orchestra 552
Philharmonic Sinfonietta 407
Philharmonic Society 407
Philips, Paul 544
Philips, Paul W. 438
Philley, Hiram 180
Phillip, Andy 375
Phillips, C. Harold 445
Phillips, Merle 294
Phillips, Mrs. Elsie Marie 439
Phillips, Rich 382
Phonographs 227
Piankashaw 54
Pianos 164
Pichard Furniture Store 238
Pickard House Furnishings Co. 291
Pickard, A. W. 291
Pickard, Harry 291
Pickard, Peter 291
Pickering, Henry 60
Pickering, Timothy 55
Pickets 505
Piech, Richard 164
Pierce, George 150
Pierce, R. Morris 442
Pierce, Winslow 166
Pierre, Charles 94
Pierre, Giles 452
Pierre, Peter 550
Pierre's Dry Goods Co. 550
Pierson, Carl 268
Pike, Major Zebulon 68
Pilgrim Baptist Church 420
Pinex Co. 234
Pipe & Supply Co. 410
Pistons 228
Pitka, Father Francis 270
Pittinger, Jud 305
Pittsburgh Plate Glass Co. 550
Plan Commission 596
Plane Crash 292
Plank Road 143
Plank Walkways 143
Platt, Robert 501
Plaza Cafe 291
Plumbing Supplies 182
Plymouth Congregational Church 217
Plymouth Congregational Church 420
Poag, George 410
Pocock, Anna 289
Poelhuis, Bernard A. 307
Poinsatte Auto Co. 290
Poinsatte, Albert 290
Poinsatte, Henry J. 290
Poinsatte, William J. 290
Poirson, Frank J. 584
Polar Bear Club 374
Police Academy 508
Police Department 508
Policemen 150
Poling, Conwell J. 271
Political Parades 556
Pollak Brothers 228
Pollak, Nelson 228
Pollak, Robert 228
Pollution 334
Pollution 338
Pollution 543
Pollution Control 517
Pollution Control 555
Pontiac 11
Pontiac 12
Pontiac 55
Pontiac Park 473
Poor Farm 438
Poor Handmaids of Jesus Christ 161
Poor Handmaids of Jesus Christ 266
Poor Relief 335
Pope John XXIII 451
Popp, H. Leslie 235
Popp, H. Leslie 293
Popp, H. Leslie 507
Popp, John F. 477
Population 213
Population 286
Population 411
Population 500
Population 547
Portage Marsh 175
Porter Jr., Dr. Miles 185
Porter, Charles Darwin 183
Porter, Dr. Miles 161
Porter, Dr. Miles 183
Porter, Gene Stratton 183
Porter, Miles F. 163
Post Office 306
Postmaster 306
Potawatomi 24, 52
Potawatomi 54
Potawatomi 69
Potawatomis 89
Potawatomis 90
Potterf, Rex 264
Potterf, Rex 541
Potterf, Rex M. 311
Poverty 300
Practical Seminary 268
Pranger, Leonard 240
Precious Blood Catholic Church 181
Precious Blood School 266
Precision Tool 229
Prefabricated Homes 410
Press Club 503
Pressler, Harland E. 587
Price Controls 551
Prigmire, Donald W 549
Printing 234
Prisioners of War 342
Privy 262
Prize Fighters 374
Pro Basketball 375
Probate Court 113
Probst, Walter 507
Probst, Walter F. 445
Probst, William 112
Procter, Colonel Henry 83
Productivity 287
Professional Work 287
Prohibition 155
Prohibition 302
Prohibition 303
Projectiscope 176
Prostitute Types 540
Prostitution 300
Protective Electric Co. 556
PSI OTE Park 476
Public Health 333
Public Housing 338
Public Housing 516
Public Library 181, 596
Public School Openings 263
Public Schools 149
Public Schools 261
Public Square 159
Public Transportation Corp. 542
Public Works 326
Public Works Project 556
Puckett, E. W. 184
Puckett, E. Wesley 224
Pugh, Dr. A. Wesley 441
Pump Industry 163
Purdue Research Foundation 271
Purdue University Center 218
Purple Hearts 352
Pursley, Bishop Leo A. 266
Pursley, Bishop Leo A. 445
Pursley, Bishop Leo A. 451
Purvis, Melvin 305
Pusey, Wesley 596
Putnam, General Rufus 26
PWA 239
PWA 326
PWA 327
PWA 334
Pyramid Design 554
Quaker 53
Quality Tool 229
Quance, Robert B. 546
Quebec 1
Quimby Theatres 292
Quimby Village 499
Quimby, Clyde 291
Quimby, Clyde 292
Quimby, W. Clyde 294
Quinn, Mel 556
Quirk, Thomas E. 546
Rabus, John 289
Raccoon Skins 111
Racial Balance 264
Racial Discrimination 331
Racial Disturbances 546
Racism 413
Radar Controls 542
Rademacher, Joseph 182
Rademacher, Joseph 266
Radio 220
Radio 292
Radio 293
Radio Fort Wayne, Inc. 293
Radio Station WGL 262
Railroad 224
Railroad 299
Railroad Strike 412
Railroad Track Elevation 236
Railroad Tracks 153
Railroads 166
Railway Elevation 509
Railway Express 505
Raimond, Capt. Charles D. 6
Ralph Immarino Confections 291
Ralston, Samuel M. 583
Ralston, Samuel M. 584
Ramada Inn 550
Ramage, Jim 376
Ramsay, Glenn 378
Ramsey, Charles 239
Ramsey, Max 380
Ramseyer, Rev. J. E. 269
Rand, Sally 307
Randal, Mrs. P. A. 172
Randal, P. A. 172
Randall Hotel 144
Randall Hotel 214
Randall Mansion 171

Randall, A. L. 172
Randall, Alfred 264
Randall, Alfred 377
Randall, Alfred H. 348
Randall, Alfred H. 585
Randall, Alfred H. 585
Randall, Frank 172
Randall, Frank M. 238
Randall, Franklin 170
Randall, Franklin 264
Randall, Franklin P. 153
Randall, Franklin P. 155
Randall, Franklin P. 159
Randall, Franklin P. 170
Randall, Mary 172
Randall, Mrs. A. L. 172
Randall, Mrs. Frank 172
Randall, Perry 177
Randall, Perry A. 169
Randall, Perry A. 171
Randall, Winifred 171
Randall, Winifred J. 214
Randolph, Beverly 60
Ranke, W. 166
Rankin, Rev. Alexander T. 145
Rastetter, Charles A. 166
Rastetter, Louis C. 166
Rastetter, Mrs. Marian 264
Rastetter, Richard C. 546
Rastetter, William C. 166
Rastetter, William C. 264
Rastetter, William C. 294
Rationing 344
Raub, Kenneth 306
Raver, Dorothy 439
Raver, Dorothy E. 587
Raver, Dorothy E. 588
Raver, Robert K. 587
Rawles, Mrs. Frances 217
Ray, Chan 330
Ray, Fred 508
Rea Magnet Wire Co. 226
Rea Magnet Wire Co. 500
Rea, David 226
Rea, Sam 500
Rea, Samuel 226
Rea, Samuel 547
Rea, Samuel A. 408
Rea, Samuel A. 587
Rea, Samuel A. 588
Rea, Victor 226
Rea, Victor F. 226
Reader's Digest 309
Reader's World Bookstore 515
Reading, James 48
Ready-Mix Concrete 448
Real Estate 509
Receivership 297
Reconstruction Finance Corporation 298
Red Cross 507
Redd, Charles 544
Reddin, William 583
Reddin, William J. 584
Redding, Elzie D. 299
Redeemer Lutheran Church 420
Redevelopment Commission 509
Redevelopment Commission 540, 596
Redevelopment Project 547
Redlight Strip 183
Redmond, Willard 444
Reed, Alma H. 585
Reed, Clyde 264
Reed, William H. 264
Reese, Charles E. 179
Reeves, Gordon 264
Reeves, Gordon C. 223
Reeves, Larry 547
Refinery 410
Refrigeration Equipment 170
Regendanz, Martin 337
Reiber, John G. 586
Reichelderfer, Arron M. 583
Reichert, Don 381
Reigel's Cigar Store 311
Reinke, William F. 584
Reinke, William J. 584
Reiser, Chick 375
Rekeweg, Carl 586
Reliance Life Insurance Co. 222
Relief Agency 307
Remy, Al 311
Renewal 508
Renters 286
Republican 171
Republican 179
Republican 183
Republican 236
Republican 414
Republican 419
Republican 511
Republican 548
Republican Party 155
Republicans 325
Republicans 452
Rescue Mission 540
Reservoir 162
Reservoir 180
Reservoir 184
Reservoir 334
Reservoir 544
Reservoir Park 162
Reservoir Park 472
Reservoir Park 555
Residential Areas 410
Restaurant 418
Retail Merchants Bureau 233
Retailing 499
Retailing 515
Reuff, Jacques 223
Reuille, Clifford J. 587
Reuss, Charles 165
Revolutionary War 14
Revolutionary War 57
Revolvers 305
Reynolds, Fred 541
Reynolds, Fred J. 555, 596
Rhamy, Dr. B. W. 185
Rhea, James 78
Rhoades, Randy 381
Rhoads-Morgan Paint Co. 290
Rhoads, Oscar 290
Rice, Wallace 184
Richard, Arthur 547
Richard, Father Daniel 270
Richard, Graham A. 588
Richard, Mrs. Arthur 330
Richards, Dr. Donald 552
Richardville, Catherine 94
Richardville, Drouet De 5
Richardville, Jean Baptiste 93
Richardville, Madame Joseph Drouet De 93
Richman Brothers 290, 499
Richter, Paul 288
Ricketts, Chester 508
Riddle, Thomas P. 585
Riedel, J. M. E. 217
Riegel, Aloysius 288
Riegel's Cigar Store 288
Rieman, Calvin 181
Rieman, Calvin 236
Riethmiller, William 512
Rifle-Shooting 378
Riley Theatre 291
Riley, Captain James 111
Riley, Mel 233
Ringling Brothers Circu 165, 173
Ringling, John 285
Ringwalt, William H. 583
Rinke, William 583
Rinke, William 583
Rinne, Carl H. 502
Riordan, Helen 263
Rippe, Louis C. 584
Ristine, Richard O. 587
Rivarre, Antoine 94
River Dredges 229
Riverside Club 302
Roach, William A. 584
Roads 310
Robbery 285
Robbery 447
Robert Koerber Jeweler 289
Robertson, Col. R. S. 178
Robertson, Col. R. S. 178
Robertson, Donald 184
Robertson, Louise 172
Robertson, Lt. Robert S. 156
Robertson, May 171
Robertson, Mrs. Frances Haberly 182
Robinson, Alberta H. 477
Robinson, Arthur R. 585
Robinson, James 264
Robinson, James M. 583
Robinson, John 438
Robinson, John 444
Robinson, John 452
Robinson, John 504
Robinson, John 508
Robinson, John 514
Robinson, Mrs. Alberta 547
Robinson, William 144
Robison Park 176
Robison Park 473
Robison, Charles 440
Robison, M. Stanley 176
Robitaille, Ed 376
Robson, Thomas 169
Rocca, Rev. Louis 307
Rocket 513
Rockhill Family 229
Rockhill House 142
Rockhill House 156
Rockhill House 161
Rockhill Park 332
Rockhill Park 473
Rockhill, Henry A. 584
Rockhill, Henry A. 585
Rockhill, Henry A. 585
Rockhill, Howell C. 221
Rockhill, W. W. 264
Rockhill, William 112
Rockhill, William 142
Rockhill, William 143
Rockhill, William 144
Rockhill, William 148
Rockhill, William 264
Rockne, Knute 374
Rodenbeck, R. F. 507
Rodriguez, Dr. Juan 446
Roe, Duane 381
Roebel, William 334
Roebuck, W. S. 584
Roehm, Harry 229
Roehrs, Mrs. Sadie Fulk 264
Roembke, Nicholas 513
Roembke, Paul 452
Roemke, Arnold 477
Roemke, E. H. 234
Roemke, Elmer C. 419
Roemke, Walt 548
Roemke, Walter 505
Rogers Market 515
Rogers Market 500
Rogers Markets, Inc. 545
Rogers, Al 337
Rogers, Harry 545
Rogers, John 545
Rogers, John A. 511
Rogers, Major Robert 11
Rogers, Mrs. H. H. 262
Rogers, W. W. 545
Roggen, Adolf 583
Rohan, John H. 583
Rohle, Frank 142
Roller Coasters 176
Roller Skating 172
Roller-Coaster 473
Roller, Hiram B. 583

Rolling Mill Project 510
Romaine, Samuel 151
Rommel, Alfred 303
Ronsib, Louis 588
Rood, Henry F. 223
Rood, Henry F. 507
Rood, Henry Fairbank 223
Roosevelt Park 473
Roosevelt, Franklin D. 352
Rorick, William 583
Rose and Walsh Jewelers 290
Rose, Arthur 446
Rose, Arthur W. 477
Rose, Erwin 290
Rosemarie 214
Rosemarie 556
Rosemarie Hotel 308
Rosenthal, Dr. I. M. 161
Rosenthal, Dr. Maurice 161
Rosenthal, Hattie 172
Rosenthal, Miss Emma 181
Rosenthal, Richard 514
Rosenthall, Dick 375
Ross, John 216
Ross, Nathan C. 584
Ross, Rev. John 145
Ross, Ronald 442
Roth, David 269
Roth, Elwood 505
Roth, Henry 269
Roth, Jim 379
Rothberg, Dr. Maurice 446
Rothberg, Dr. Maurice 514
Rothschild, Benjamin 175
Rouche De Bout 60
Roundhouses 299
Rouse, Wilfred 382
Roush, J. Edward 542
Roush, J. Edward 546
Roush, J. Edward 554
Roush, J. Edward 588
Rousseau, Edwin 514
Rousseau, Edwin 515
Rousseau, Edwin J. 508
Rousseau, Edwin J. 588
Roussey, William E. 586
Rowe, Harry W. 584
Rowlands Furniture Co. 291
Rowlands Furniture Co. 412
Roy J. Stirk Bowling Alley 290
Roy, Clarence 585
Royal Baking Powder 160
Royal Philharmonic Orchestra 215
Roye, Francois 3
Roye, Pierre 3
Ruby, Theodore 301
Rudisill Center 499
Rudisill, Henry 115
Rudisill, Henry 144
Rudisill, Henry 145
Rudisill, Henry 147
Rudisill, Henry 217
Ruf, E. P. 231
Ruf, Ermin P. 338
Ruf, Ermin P. 441
Ruhl, A. F. 166
Ruhl, Homer 187
Ruhl, James 446
Ruhl, James E. 294
Ruip, Richard C. 507
Rulo, Donald C. 584
Rump, Anita 377
Rump, Fred J. 222
Rumschlag, Cletus 508
Rupp, Maurice M. 452
Rupp, Peter 452
Rural Poverty 230
Rurode Dry Goods Co. 225
Rurode Dry Goods Co. 288
Rurode, E. C. 167
Rust, Don 596
Rutledge, George E. 169
Rutledge, W. A. 502
Ryan Saloon 160
Ryan, Charles J. 584
Ryan, Charles J. 585
Ryan, Edward 160
Ryan, John M. 587
Ryder, Father S. Joachim 340
Ryker, Robert M. 414
S. F. Bowser Co. 164
S. S. Kresge Co. 288
Saarinen, Eero 269
SAC 54
Sacred Heart Academy 270
SACS 52
Sadowski, Ed 375
Safe Cracking 449
Safety Cab Co. 345
Safford, H. B. 448
Saganaugh 112
Saint Francis College 268
Salamonie Mining & Gas Co. 235
Salaries 416
Salem Evangelical Reformed Church 450
Salin, William 548
Salin, William N. 588
Salomon, Christian V. 502
Salon, Dr. Joel W. 514
Salon, Dr. N. L. 516
Salt 45
Salvation Army 332
Samuels, Lyman 233
Sanborn, Edmund P. 587
Sanborn, Phillip 542
Sanborn, Phillip J. 264
Sandburg, Carl 504
Sanders, Louise 512
Sanitarium 337
Santa, W. R. 421
Sarber, Jess 305
Sarighausen, J. D. 174
Sarkes-Tarzian, Inc. 294
Sarkes-Tarzian, Inc. 442
Sarver, B. F. 186
Sash Factory 144
Sauer, Pastor Henry 147
Saul's Clothing 291
Saunders, Benjamin 170
Sausage 231
Sawed-Off Shotguns 304
Saxer, G. Alexander 269
Scalf, Elizabeth 552
Scalping 84
Scalps 12
Scalps 15
Schaaf, A. H. 233
Schaaf, Al 228
Schaaf, Albert 338
Schaaf, Albert H. 224
Schacht, Wayne 509
Schack, F. Arthur 338
Schaeffer, Herman 379
Schannen, Judge William 325
Schannen, W. H. 236
Schannen, William 325
Schannen, William 326
Schannen, William H. 336
Schannen, William H. 351
Schannen, William H. 416
Schannen, William H. 421
Schannen, William H. 502, 505
Schannen, William H. 586
Schannen, William H. 587
Schaus, Fred 375
Scheiman, William 184
Scheiman, William H. 264
Scheiman, William H. 583
Schele, Edward T. 232
Schele, Edward T. 408
Schenkel, Chris 556
Schenkel, David P. 516
Scherer, Henry P. 173
Scherer, Ray 442
Scheumann, E. F. 294
Scheumann, Edward 225
Scheumann, O. W. 294
Schiefer, Chester 372
Schiefer, William D. 163
Schilling, Dr. John 374
Schinnerer & Truemper, Inc. 515
Schintker, August R. 583
Schirmeyer, Paul 228
Schlatter Hardware Co. 235
Schlatter, C. C. 177
Schlatter, Christian C. 235
Schlatter, Harry 235
Schlatter, Mrs. Noble 547
Schloss Tailors 291
Schmeding, Richard 511
Schmidt, August 180
Schmidt, August 180
Schmidt, Donald 547
Schmidt, Gay 547
Schmidt, Martin 269
Schmidt, Vivian 547
Schmidt, Vivian 553
Schmoll, Dr. Robert 514
Schnedler, Rev. Wilfred J. 446
Schneider-Kaiser Washing Machine Co. .. 289
Schnurr, Herman 263
Schoenberg, Father Martin 271
Scholer Jr., Walter E. 272
School for the Feeble-Minded Youth 451
School of Nursing 440
School Reorganization 265
School Tax 264
School Trustees 264
Schools 261
Schools 263
Schortemeier, Fredrick E. 584
Schouweiler, C. Edwin 514
Schouweiler, Edwin 448
Schouweiler, F. E. 446
Schouweiler, F. E. 448
Schouweiler, W. Dale 448
Schram, Robert 505
Schramm, Frank 238
Schrey, Jack W. 501
Schrey, Jack W. 546
Schrey, Jack W. 553
Schricker, Henry F. 585
Schricker, Henry F. 586
Schroeder, Edward G. 291
Schroeders Clothing 291
Schroff, Jim 380
Schuchhardt, John Paul 346
Schueman, Anna 289
Schultz, Abe 301
Schultz, D. Y. 269
Schultz, H. B. 345
Schultz, Roland 416
Schulz, Roland R. 408
Schust, C. L. 293
Schust, C. L. 441
Schust, Clarence 442
Schwalm, Earl G. 450
Schwalm, Earl G. 507
Schwan, Louis 307
Schwanz, Phil J. 414
Schwanz, Phil J. 501
Schwanz, Phil J. 511
Schwartz, Dr. Donald 272
Schwartz, Henry 180
Schweir, William C. 583
Schweir, William C. 584
Schweiters, C. H. 291
Schwieger, Hans 407
Scorched Earth 32
Scott Paper Co. 501
Scott, Don 545
Scott, Donald G. 500
Scott, Everett 373
Scott, Francis 500
Scott, General Charles 24
Scott, Levan 553
Scott, Max 509
Scott, Max G. 264
Scott's Foodlanes 545

Scottish Rite Auditorium 218
Scottish Rite Cathedral 182
Scottish Rite Cathedral 290
Script Money 116
Scrogham, Leonard 350
Sears Roebuck 289, 348
Sears Roebuck 440
Sears Roebuck 514
Sebastion, Benjamin 61
Second Television Station 442
Seculoff, Father James 266
Securities 501
Seibel, Carl S. 512
Seiffels, S. I. 262
Seitz, Paul 448
Self-Measuring Oil Pump 164
Self-Service Grocery 311
Senseny, Dr. Eugene 218
Senseny, Dr. Herbert 185
Senseny, Mrs. Eugene 547
Sessler, John 234
Sessler, Miss Vera 339
Severest Winter 327
Sewage 554
Sewage Disposal 334
Sewage Treatment 556
Sewage-Treatment 555
Sewer System 176
Sewers 543
Sex Slayings 349
Seybert, P. E. 236
Seyfert, Charles 554
Shady Grove Dance Hall 303
Shaffer, Paul 545
Shaffer, Paul 546
Shaffer, Valentine 583
Shaffer, Valentine 584
Shaffer, Valentine L. 583
Shake, Dr. Brooks B. 441
Shamban, W. S. 230
Shambaugh, Max 552
Shambaugh, Max 587
Shambaugh, Max 588
Shambaugh, Robert 587
Shambaugh, Robert L. 444
Shambaugh, W. H. 264
Shambaugh, Willard 264
Shambaugh, Willard 506
Shambaugh, Willard 507
Shambaugh, Willard 542
Shambaugh, William 180
Shambaugh, William 184
Shambaugh, William H. 157
Shambaugh, William H. 174
Shanebeck, Ezra 587
Shantytown 300
Sharp, Henry 149
Sharp, Henry 264
Sharpe, Allan 307
Sharpe, Henry C. 170
Sharples, T. P. 445
Shaver, Miss Ora 181
Shawnee 14
Shawnee 18
Shawnee 24
Shawnee 31
Shawnee Run 174
Shawnees 14
Shawnees 52
Shea, W. J. 445
Sheehan, Thomas 584
Sheehan, Thomas J. 585
Sheets, William 219
Sheldon, James 152
Shepard Broadcasting Corp. 293
Shepherd, Walter T. 222
Sheraton Inn 515
Sheridan, Michael 583
Sherman Clothes 291
Sherron, James J. 588
Sherwood, Burt 294
Sherwood, Burton 556
Shields, James 184
Shiff, Robert 289
Shimer, Ralph 374
Shine Shoe Co. 289
Shine, Myrtle 290
Shine, Nathan 289
Shine, Steve 556
Shipley, Mrs. Clara 513
Shipp, Charlie 375
Shirely, Robert B. 583
Shirey, C. Dwight 290
Shirey, C. Dwight 441
Shirley, Robert B. 584
Shirmeyer, Ralph 410
Shirmeyer, Ralph 514
Shive, Donald 411
Shoaff Park 475
Shoaff, Fred 297
Shoaff, Fred B. 238
Shoaff, Fred B. 326
Shoaff, Fred B. 471
Shoaff, Fred B. 475
Shoaff, Frederick B. 477
Shoaff, John D. 509
Shoaff, John D. 546
Shoaff, John D. 547
Shoaff, John D. 553
Shoaff, T. Richard 475
Shoaff, Thomas B. 371
Shoaff, W. W. 175
Shoaff, Wade C. 157
Shock, Argil 596
Shockley, Frank W. 271
Shoe Shops 300
Shooting Galleries 176
Shopping Center 515
Shopping Centers 499
Shortages 551
Shrine Temple and Auditorium 218
Shrine Temple Theatre 218
Shriner, Herb 308
Shriner, Herb 450
Shriver, Colonel James 114
Sidewalk Improvement 180
Sidle, Charles 452
Sidle, Charles 543
Siegel, Harry 543
Sieling, Dietrich 473
Sigl Drug Store 291
Sigl, Joseph 291
Sigrist, Herman 441
Sihler, Dr. William 148
Sihler, Dr. William 268
Sihler, Pastor 147
Silk and Diamonds 172
Silver Palace Sleeping Car 154
Simcoe, John Graves 32
Simcoe, John Graves 33
Simcoe, John Graves 49
Simcoe, John Graves 54
Simmons, Virgil M. 419
Simon, Oren 451
Simons, Oscar A. 169
Simplex Tool 229
Simpson, Leon 512
Simpson, Mrs. Wallis 329
Sims Sam 380
Singmaster, Joseph 477
Singrey, Frank 181
Sinks, John R. 587
Sinks, John R. 588
Sitko, Emil 374
Sitko, Steve 379
Sively, Benjamin F. 584
Skelton, Benjamin 179
Skelton, George 506
Skywriting 219
Slater, Charles 541
Slater, Charles E. 264
Slater, Charles E. 542
Slen, Mark 441
Slick, Thomas W. 306
Slocum, Edward 264
Sloffer, Glenn 586
Slot Machines 304
Slot Machines 344
Slussman, Eli 584
Small, William 556
Smart, Dr. James H. 171
Smart, James H. 263
Smeltzly, Mary Catherine 476
Smerke, Joseph 270
Smith Field 219
Smith Field 340
Smith, Al P. 584
Smith, Albert N. 306
Smith, Art 183
Smith, Art 340
Smith, Arthur R. 219
Smith, Dallas 331
Smith, David E. 264
Smith, Dr. Richard D. 271
Smith, Edward 506
Smith, Elmer 587
Smith, Eugene B. 264
Smith, Eugene E. 587
Smith, George 301
Smith, Jim 311
Smith, Merlin H. 293
Smith, Philip W. 164
Smith, Robert 513
Smith, Samuel L. 290
Smith, William 583
Smith, William S. 264
Smock, Frank L. 448
Smog 338
Snider, Elsworth 586
Snider, Mrs. R. Nelson 330
Snider, R. Nelson 264
Snider, R. Nelson 446
Snider, R. Nelson 554
Snodgrass, Luther 187
Snook, Tom 236
Snouffer, Ira D 439
Snow 551
Snow, Clarence 164
Snow, Dorthea J. 309
Snowberger Ladies Wear 290
Snyder, Al 505
Snyder, Ralph K. 585
Snyder, Ralph K. 586
Snyder, Robert M. 233
Soap Box Derby 409
Soap Box Derby 474
Soap Operas 292
Social Diseases 333
Socialist Candidate 179
Socialist Faction 183
Soda Fountains 334
Soft Coal 338
Softball 376
Sol Wood Home 421
Soldiers 344
Solomon, Rabbi Joseph 147
Somers, Byron 184
Somers, Byron H. 264
Somers, Byron H. 410
Somers, Lucius 441
Somers, Lucius 585
Somers, Lucius 586
Somers, Lucius 587
Sons of Liberty 156
Sons of Satan 444
Sordelet, Frank P. 585
Sordelet, Frank P. 585
Sordelet, Russell 410
Sorenson, C. V. 509
Sorenson, John 596
Sorin, Rev. Edward 270
Sousa, John Philip 215
South Side State Bank 294
South Side Times 262
South Vietnam 505
South Wayne 174
Southgate Plaza 499
Southtown Mall 515

Sovada, Father Leo 270
Sowards, Neil 451
Sowers, William V. 478
Sowers, William V. 546
Sowers, William V. 546
Space Walk 513
Spahiev, George 551
Spalding, Clay F. 586
Spalding, Winifred 586
Spanley, Charles 446
Spanley, Charles A. 294
Sparks, Leona 350
Sparks, Mrs. Simon 350
Spatz, J. B. 235
Spatz, John B. 231
Spaulding, A. G. 166
Spaulding, William C. 226
Speakeasies 301
Spencer House 142
Spencer, John 142
Sperry, Miss Lavon 215
Spiegel, Arno 326
Spiegel, Arno 336
Spiegel, Arno 348
Spiegel, Arnold 236
Spillson, Cleo 417
Spillson, Jane 418
Spillson, John 418
Spillson, Mrs. John 408
Spillson, Nicholas 417
Spink-Wawasee Hotel 270
Spoils System 337
Sports Broadcasts 292
Sprague, Charles A. 293
Sprague, F. Guy 301
Sprankel, John 175
Springer, Miss Elizabeth E. 185
Springfield Detectives 151
St. Andrews School 266
St. Augustine's Academy 265
St. Augustine's Church 146
St. Catherine's Academy 181
St. Catherine's Academy 265
St. Clair Disaster 24
St. Clair, Arthur 66
St. Clair, Arthur 86
St. Clair, General Arthur 18
St. Clair, General Arthur 22
St. Clair, General Arthur 29
St. Clair, General Arthur 45
St. Clair, General Arthur 55
St. Clair, General Arthur 62
St. Clair, Governor Arthur 19
St. Francis College 154
St. Francis College 172
St. Joe Club 374
St. Joe Detectives 151
St. John The Baptist Catholic Church 420
St. John's Lutheran School 267
St. John's Reformed Church 148
St. Joseph Hospital 143
St. Joseph Hospital 161
St. Joseph Hospital 266
St. Joseph Hospital 513
St. Joseph Hospital Nurses Home ...237
St. Louis, Kansas City and Northern .153
St. Mary's Catholic Church 172
St. Mary's Church 147
St. Mary's Commercial School 265
St. Michael Lutheran Church 420
St. Michael's Lutheran School 267
St. Patrick's Catholic Church 181
St. Patrick's School 266
St. Paul's Church 267
St. Paul's Church 268
St. Paul's Evangelical Lutheran Church 147
St. Paul's Lutheran 558
St. Paul's Lutheran Church 145
St. Paul's Lutheran Church 420
St. Paul's Lutheran School 267
St. Paul's School 266
St. Peter's School 266
St. Vincent's Villa 218
St. Vincent's Villa 266
Stagg, Ronald 223
Stahlhut, John 215
Stahlhut, John 238
Stahlhut, John C. 337
Stahlhut, John C. 337
Stanczak, Ed 379
Standard Building 270
Standard Rug & Linoleum Co. 412
Stanski, Charles 380
Staples, Dr. Tom L. 270
Staples, T. L. 181
Stapp, Milton 116
State Banks 297
State Fair Grounds 162
State Finals 380
State Hospital and Training Center ...451
State Prison 304
State Tax Board 336
State Theater 304
Statue of Little Turtle 556
Stavreti, Carl 381
Steak Houses 418
Steam Dredges 176
Steam Engine 152
Steam Shovels 229
Stearns, John 596
Stedman, Dale 596
Steegman, Herman 544
Steere, Allen 223
Steigerwald, Phil 508
Steigerwald, Phil 514
Steigmeyer, Clem J. 411
Steiner, Ezra 452
Steiner, Russell 477
Steiss, Charles J. 217
Stemen, Dr. C. B. 161
Stevens, Peter 289
Stevenson, Adlai 439
Stewart, Gathings 223
Stewart, Gathings 546
Stewart, Harold 374
Stewart, J. W. 445
Stewart, William 149
Stewart, William 155
Stewart, William 155
Stewart, William 264
Stickney, Benjamin F. 93
Stickney, Major B. F. 88
Stickney, Major B. F. 89
Stier, James 553
Stier, James S. 547
Stillman, J. K. 238
Stillman, John 225
Stillman, Robert 554
Stillman's Department Store 554
Stillman's Dry Goods Co. 289
Stink Bombs 304
Stinson Aircraft Co. 310
Stith, Harold 509
Stock 501
Stockade 543
Stockyards 412
Stodtman, Mrs. Cless 451
Stoeff, Henry 303
Stolte, George 584
Stolte, George 585
Stone, Art 378
Stone, F. M. 168
Stone, Fred 291
Stone, Harold 231
Stophlet, Samuel 174
Storch, Howard L. 450
Storey, Bob 263
Storm, Trygve 477
Storms, Daniel E. 583
Story, James 144
Stouder, Frank E. 184
Stouder, Frank E. 215
Stouder, Jacob M. 217
Stouder, Jacob M. 217
Stouffer, Glenn 586
Stout, David C. 584
Stout, George W. 583
Stowell, Fred 169
Straits of Mackinac 2
Straits of Mackinac 7
Strand Theatre 289
Stratoflex 230
Straus Brothers Co. 295
Strauss Bros. Co. 289
Strauss, A. M. 418
Strauss, Herman 272
Stream Pollution Control Board 555
Street Cars 443
Street Car Strike 173
Street Work 448
Street-Building 180
Strike 545
Strong-Arm Robbers 160
Strum, Elmer 584
Stuart, Dr. Bernard K. 264
Stubbins, Lloyd S. 553
Stucky Brothers 515
Studebaker Crop. 230
Studebaker Works 310
Study, Justin N. 263
Stults, Bill 380
Stump, Margaret 552
Stump, Virgil R. 410
Stumpf, Jule 343
Stumpf, Jule 412
Sturges, Richard B. 550
Sturgis, Charles 264
Sturgis, Charles E. 110
Sturgis, Richard 553
Sturm, Orville R. 587
Succop, Miss Helen 446
Suedhoff Jr., Carl J. 588
Suedhoff, Carl 587
Suedhoff, Carl J. 183
Suedhoff, Carl J. 307
Suedhoff, Carl J. 374
Suedhoff, Carl J. 408
Suelzer, John 177
Suelzer, John 187
Summers, Richard L. 588
Summers, Walter H. 587
Summers, Walter H. 588
Summit City Cafeteria 289
Summit City Club 371
Summit City Woolen Mills 144
Sunday Mornings 558
Super Valu Stores 449
Supermarket 311
Suter, Margery 262
Suttenfield, Laura 12
Suttenfield, Laura 87
Suttenfield, Laura 88
Suttenfield, William 87
Suttenfield, William 112
Suttenfield, William 113
Swager, Leon 444
Swain, Dorothy 513
Swamps 115
Swanson Jr., Bernard 586
Swanson, Bernard 438
Swedenborg 119
Swedenborg 120
Sweet Lady Pop Corn Shop 291
Sweet, George 221
Sweet, Helen W. 477
Sweet, Kent 584
Sweet, Kent 585
Sweetser, Madison 144
Swift Park 176
Swihart, Irene E. 588
Swihart, Phillip L. 307
Swimming 378
Swinney Building 452
Swinney Homestead 110
Swinney Park 214
Swinney Park 217
Swinney Park 472
Swinney, Col. Thomas W. 110

Swinney, Col. Thomas W. 162
Swinney, Thomas W. 472
Swygert, Luther 306
Symington-Gould Corporation 164
Symphony Orchestra 407
Szink, George 337
Taber, Cyrus 110
Taber, Paul 110
Taber, Paul 112
Taber, Samuel 110
Tacumwa 89
Tacumwa 93
Takimori, Harry 291
Takimori, Harry 474
Talarico, Samuel 553
Talarico, Samuel J. 547
Talbot, Henry F. 164
Talkie 308
Tanner, David 556
Tannery 144
Tarhe 52
Tarhe 53
Tax 336
Tax Rates 335
Taxis 345
Taxpayers Research Association 233
Taylor University 148
Taylor, Anna 288
Taylor, Charles 419
Taylor, Frank Bursley 217
Taylor, Horace 112
Taylor, Mrs. Royal 145
Taylor, Mrs. Sam 217
Taylor, Mrs. Samuel R. 217
Taylor, R. S. 174
Taylor, Royal W. 143
Taylor, Thomas 419
Teachers 264
Teamsters 143
Teas, Thomas Scattergood 92
Tecumseh 73
Tecumseh 85
Teenage Gangs 517
Teeple, Mrs. Richard S. 419
Teetor, Thomas S. 264
Telegraph 160
Telegraph Office 152
Telephone System 163
Television 441
Temple Theater 177
Temple Theatre Fire 215
Ten Cent Store 288
Tennis Courts 338
Tennis Rackets 166
Tepper Fire 238
Tepper's Department Store 238
Test, Charles H. 113
Teter, A. P. 441
Thanksgiving Proclamation 113
Tharp, Walter 547
Thayer, Glenn R. 293
The Club 289
The Dime Savings and Trust Co. 294
The Dutch Lunch 417
The Empress 183
The Fort Wayne Allied Printing Trades Council 234
The Fort Wayne Gas Light Company 154
The Fort Wayne Story 548
The Fort Wayne Times 149
The Landing 162
The Landing 541
The Landing 556
The Lumbard Exchange 163
The Majestic 183
The Moonraker 418
The Palace 183
The Phoenician 418
The Prophet 73
The Sentinel 148
The Sentinel 310
The Strand 183
The Vogue 290
Theater 291
Theater Guild Magazine 309
Theatre 509
Thiele, Paul 331
Thiele, Paul 337
Thieme Brothers Company 168
Thieme, Philip R. 588
Thieme, Theodore 168
Thieme, Theodore 171
Thieme, Theodore 216
Thieme, Theodore 512
Thieme, Theodore F. 168
Thieme, Theodore F. 294
Thieme, Theodore F. 309
Thieme, Wayne L. 410
Third Presbyterian Church 556
Thom McAnn Shoes 291
Thoma, Edward 511
Thomas, Albert E. 583
Thomas, Edwin R. 286
Thomas, Edwin R. 584
Thomas, Fred 382
Thomas, Fred W. 233
Thomas, George C. 233
Thompson Aeronautical Corporation .220
Thompson Trophy 503
Thompson, Byron 172
Thompson, Bryron 174
Thompson, Mrs. Byron 172
Thoms, Edward G. 293
Thomson-Houston Electric Co. 169
Thornson, Len 378
Three Rivers Apartments 509
Three Rivers Festival 543
Three-Mile Gravel Road Law 218
Thrill Rides 473
Thunderbolt Fighter 347
Tigar, Thomas 148
Tigar, Thomas 264
Tigar, Thomas 419
Tilden, Charles F. 584
Tillman Park 476
Times Corner Shopping Center 515
Timmerman, Victor 588
Tipton, Herbert 452
Tipton, Herbert 508
Tipton, Herbert 514
Tipton, John 112
Titus, Dr. Philip S. 161
Tjepkema, Dr. Roy 231
Toboggan Slides 474
Todd, Levi A. 584
Todd, Levi A. 584
Toidey Co. 233
Toilet Seats 228
Tokheim Corp. 230
Tokheim Corp. 308
Tokehim Oil Tank & Pump Co. 230
Tokheim, John 230
Tolan, Brentwood S. 177
Toledo & Wabash Railroad 153
Toledo Guards 117
Tom Wing Laundry 289
Tomahawk Heads 452
Tomahawking 84
Tonkel, Joseph 583
Tonkel, Joseph 584
Tooke, Franklin 293
Toolcraft 229
Torborg, Martin 264
Torborg, Martin 514
Torborg, Martin 544
Torchlight Parade 163
Torchlight Parades 155
Tornado 552
Tornadoes 512
Tornadoes 551
Tourgee, Harry R. 182
Tourkow, Frederick R. 414
Tourkow, Frederick R. 550
Tourrette, William La 183
Townsend Movement 329
Townsend, Bert A. 233
Townsend, Burt A. 546
Townsend, M. Clifford 585
Track and Field 379
Trackmen 380
Traction Company 173
Traction Company 183
Traders 66
Traders 91
Traders 111
Traders 143
Trades and Labor Council 330
Trading Post 110
Tragic Events 172
Trailers 410
Train Accident 337
Trainer, J. W. 172
Trainer, Mrs. J. W. 172
Trains 187
Tramps 300
Transfer Building 271
Transfer Corner 288
Transfer Corner 557
Transfer Grain Elevator 232
Transportation 336
Travers, Frank 223
Travis, Frank 554
Treaty 52
Treaty of Fort Stanwix 14
Treaty of Fort Wayne 73
Treaty of Greenville 57
Treaty of Greenville 110
Treaty of 1840 95
Treen, Harold 231
Tremble, Colonel Allen 83
Tremper, Allan J. 542
Tremper, Barrie 505
Trentman, August C. 175
Trentman, John 142
Tresselt, Oscar 477
Trevino, Clem 513
Trey, Paul 233
Tri-State National Bank Building 289
Tri-State Television, Inc. 442
Triangle Investment Co. 500
Trickey, Robert W. 502
Trier, E. J. 410
Trier, Henry 145
Trier, John 235
Trier, John 239
Trier, John C. 477
Trier,s Amusement Park 177
Trier,s Park 473
Triggs, Kenneth 441
Trinity English Lutheran Church 147
Trinity English Lutheran Church 217
Trinity English Lutheran Church 420
Trinity Episcopal Church 420
Trinity Lutheran School 267
Trolley System 163
Trolleys 443
Troutman, Robert 516
Trowbridge, Ron 381
Truant Officer 262
Truck Engineering Co. 226
Truckey, Madore 144
Trucking 411
Trucks 551
Truemper, John 515
Trysting Place 337
Tuberculosis Hospital 412
Tucker, J. Lyle 270
Tucker, J. Lyle 291
Tucker, James M. 585
Tungett, Everett 380
Turken, Marshall 409
Turner, Ann 94
Turner, Ann 174
Turner, Dr. William 93
Turner, James 505
Turner, Mrs. Ann 144
Turner, Ruth R. 587
Turner, William 513
TWA 220

Twelfth Night....................475
Tyler, Mrs.......................171
Tyndall, John W..................583
Typhoid Fever 239
Typhoid Fever 327
U. S. Rubber 230
U. S. District Attorneys 306
Uebelhoer, Edward L. 413
Uebelhoer, Joan 588
Ullyot, Ken 378
Underground Railroad 143
Underwood, Paul 554
Underwood, Willie 382
Unemployment 307
Union 331
Union Party 329
Union Soldiers 472
Union Veteran Legion 178
Unitarian Meeting Hall 420
United Air Lines 542
United Aircraft Corp. 445
United Auto Workers 331
United Auto Workers 345
United Electrical 345
United Electrical Workers 330
United Lutheran Church 217
United Methodist 558
United Presbyterian Church 420
United Toolcraft 230
Universal Broadcasting Co. 442
Updike, J. V.....................181
Urban League 331
Urban Renewal 508
Urban Renewal 510
Urban Renewal 516
Urey, Harold Clayton 307
Usher, Wade 410
U S Airforce 596
Utensils Co......................226
Utility Companies 187
Utility Poles 239
Utt, John F. 294
V. M. Nussbaum Electric Co. 230
Vagabonds 300
Vagrants 557
Valencia Gardens 218
Valentino, Rudolph 312
Van Arnam Manufacturing Co. 182
Van Arnam Manufacturing Co. 228
Van Arnam, George 228
Van Arnam, Howard 228
Van Auken, Glenn 584
Van Cleve, Benjamin 24
Van Gorder, Pauline 262
Van Horn, Clarence O. 326
Van Meter, Homer 304
Van Meter, Homer 305
Van Orman Hotel 182
Van Orman Hotel 511
Van Orman Hotel 551
Van Orman, Fred H. 584
Van Orman, Harold 378
Van Orman, Harold 551
Van Ranst, A. F. 226
Van Ranst, A. F. 546
Van Ryn, Robert 380
Van Skoik, C. C. 235
Van Sweringen, Dr. and Mrs. B.....172
Van Sweringen, Dr. Garrett 185
Van Sweringen, Hiram M. 583
Van Sweringen, Howard 291
Van Vecten, J. J. 291
Vance, Capt. Samuel C. 96
Vandagrift, Carl W. 293
Vanderbilt Interests 167
Vanderbilt, William H. 167
Vandergrift, Carl 372
Vandervort, Nick 451
Variety Liquor Store 551
Varnell, Claude 372
Vaudreuil, Marquis De 3
Vaughn, John 556
Veit, Mrs. Mary Elizabeth 503
Veneral Diseases 333
Vermont Granite 178
Vermont, Elizabeth Hamilton 158
Vemor, Garth H. 585
Verweire, John L. 184
Verwiebe, Richard 547
Vesey Flower Store 289
Vesey Park 473
Vesey, David S. 289
Vesey, John H. 473
Vesey, M. S. 289
Vesey, Mrs. David 264
Vesey, Richard M. 584
Vesey, W. J. 174
Vesey, W. J. 289
Vesey, William J. 163
Vesey, William J. 583
Veteran Housing 342
Veteran,s Hospital 418
Vetter, Walter 326
Vetter, Walter 332
Vetter, Walter C. 413
Viberg, George H. 583
Viberg, George H. 584
Vigilantees 150
Vigran, Isadoi 288
Vigran,s Ladies Shop 288
Villiers, Coulon De 7
Vim Sporting Goods 291
Vincennes 3
Vincennes 16
Vincennes 19
Vincennes, Francois 4
Vincennes, Francois Marie De 4
Vincennes, Sieur De 3
Vinyl Chloride 551
Vitale, Tony 414
Vizino, Harold 556
Vogel, Frank 162
Voiture 37 311
Volney, Constantin 61
Von Gunten, Howard L. 471
Voors, Joann 412
Voors, Louis J. 325
Voors, Marilyn 412
Vordermark, H. E. 187
Vose, Major Josiah N. 92
Vosmeier, Leonard 556
W. A. Sheets Sons, Inc. 418
W. H. Mc Intyre Co. 310
W. L. Douglas Shoe Store 291
W. T. Grant 499
Wabash and Erie Canal 186
Wabash Cannonball 542
Wabash Cannonball 551
Wabash Fibre Box 500
Wabash Railroad 173
Wabash Valley Traction Co. 180
Wabash-Erie Canal 114
Wabash-Erie Canal 116
Wabash-Erie Canal 152
Wabash-Erie Canal 166
Wabash-Erie Canal 174
Wabash-Erie Canal 443
Wabash-Erie Canal 509
Wabash-Logansport Traction Co. 186
Wade, Louis E. 441
Wage Earners 287
Wagenhals, Mrs. Ellen 181
Wagenhals, Rev. Samuel 178
Wagenhals, Rev. Samuel 217
Wagoner, Harold 421
Wahl, Henry 235
Wahl, Henry 289
Walb, Ralph W. 229
Walb, Walter W. 272
Walb, Walter W. 441
Walb, Walter W. 546
Waldrop, Lt. Kenneth 444
Waldschmidt, George 294
Walgreen Drug Stores 499
Walgreens 514
Walk-Over Boot Shop 289
Walker, Bob 379
Walker, Brian 378
Walker, Charles 233
Walker, Charles 555
Walker, Charles 557
Walker, Charles W. 233
Walker, Donald H. 509
Walker, George B. 110
Wallace, David 113
Wallace, David 156
Wallace, George 511
Wallace, John M. 155
Wallace, Lew 113
Wallace, Lew 156
Wallace, Sabina 152
Waller, W. A. 240
Wallis, Edward 293
Walsh, Frank 290
Walsh, Freddie 374
Walsh, Rev. Matthew J. 216
Wambsganss, William 373
Wanamaker, John 157
Wane 293
Wane 442
Wane-TV 442
War of 1812 88
Ward, Berkeley 214
Ward, Berkeley 452
Ward, Clifford B. 345
Ward, Clifford B. 419
Ward, Clifford B. 439
Ward, Earl S. 233
Ward, Earl S. 446
Ward, L. C. 263
Warehouses 540
Warehousing 411
Warner Beauty College 412
Warren, Dr. Louis 222
Warren, Louis A. 310
Warriner, Mr. A. 172
Warriner, Mrs. A. 172
Warriner, Mrs. May 172
Wash Tubs 235
Washing Machines 166
Washington 23
Washington Square Shopping Center .515
Washington, George 7
Washington, George 17
Washington, George 54
Washington, George 60
Waste Paper Co. 449
Water 334
Water 504
Water Meters 334
Water Pollution 554
Water Pollution Control 543
Water Resources 544
Water Supply 239
Water Wagons 334
Waterfield, Richard H. 546
Watergate 548
Waterworks 162
Watson, Bill 381
Watson, Chester K. 587
Watson, James E. 584
Watson, Thomas 547
Watson, Thomas A. 223
Watson, Thomas A. 224
Watson, William 556
Watson, William H. 544
Watters, Howard 544
Watters, Howard S. 477
Watters Studio 596
Wayne 31
Wayne Candies 182
Wayne Club 233
Wayne Crane 229
Wayne Feed Co. 232
Wayne Floral Co. 289
Wayne Hardware Co. 231
Wayne Hotel 214
Wayne Hotel 308
Wayne Hotel 556

Wayne Knitting Mills 168
Wayne Knitting Mills 216
Wayne Knitting Mills 235
Wayne Knitting Mills 331
Wayne Mortgage Loan Co. 288
Wayne Oil Tank Company 164
Wayne Paper Box Corp. 231
Wayne Pharmacal Building 218
Wayne Pump Co. 230
Wayne Pump CoCompany 164
Wayne Spoke and Bending Co. 230
Wayne St. Methodist Church 420
Wayne, Anthony 25
Wayne, Anthony 28
Wayne, Anthony 32
Wayne, Anthony 43
Wayne, Anthony 53
Wayne, Anthony 58
Wayne, Anthony 59
Wayne, Anthony 309
Waynedale Annexed 447
WCWK 292
WDBV 292
WEA 54
Weaver 167
Weber Hotel 214
Weber, Carl 288
Weber, Garnette 377
Weber, Miss Flora 262
Weber, Steve 288
Weddings 172
Weeks, Charles 112
Wefel, Adam 145
Wefel, Martin H. 179
Weigand, August 264
Weil Building 412
Weilemann, L. H. 511
Weingart, Rabbi Irving A. 340
Weinstein, Rabbi A. L. 216
Weisser Park 472
Welch, John H. 178
Welch, Norbert G. 413
Weller, Rabbi Seymour 420
Wells St. Bridge 156
Wells, Ann 93
Wells Wells, Bob 440
Wells, Rebecca 93
Wells, William 30
Wells, William 59
Wells, William 65
Wells, William S. 583
Welsh, Matthew 511
Welsh, Matthew E. 587
Wentz, Theodore 184
Wentz, Theodore 225
Wentz, Theodore 295
Werkman, Fred W. 291
Wertz, J. C. 584
Wesley, Alvin 517
West Creighton Avenue Church of Christ 181
West Point 87
West Swinney Park 177
West Swinney Park 473
West, Bill 376
Westerman, Charles W. 547
Western Auto Supply Co. 289
Western Gas Construction Co. 237
Western Union 291
Western Union Telegraph Company ..152
Westfield Village 338
Westinghouse Station 293
Westover, M. F. 170
Wetzel, Henry A. 584
Wetzel, Henry A. 585
Weyrick, Charles 588
Weyrick, Charles H. 587
WFTW 293
WFWR 294
WGL 292
WHBJ 292
Whearley, R. L. 500
Whearley, Ruth 330
Whearley, Ruth 541
Whearley, Ruth 556
Wheel Works 513
Wheelock, Dr. Kent 185
Whelan Drug Co. 288
Whig Party 155
Whipple, W. D. 264
Whiskey 89
Whiskey 91
Whiskey 111
Whisky 70
Whisky 302
Whisky Trader 67
Whistler, Capt. John 557
Whistler, James A. M. 86
Whistler, John 86
Whistler, Major John 92
Whistler's Fort 86
Whitcomb, Edgar D. 587
White Fruit House and Oyster Depot .157
White III, Edward 179
White National Bank 157
White National Bank 295
White Wheel Works 157
White, A. S. 117
White, Carl O. 585
White, Edward 179
White, Edward A. 421
White, Edward H. 309
White, Edward H. 513
White, General Edward 513
White, J. W. 298
White, James 157
White, James 179
White, James 370
White, James B. 513
White, James Bain 157
White, John D. 80
White, John P. 223
White, John W. 177
White, Mrs. Edward 541
White, Mrs. J. B. 171
White, Mrs. Joan C. 543
White, Rev. Jesse 516
White's Institute 238
White's Store 157
Whitmore, Charles 155
Whore Houses 300
Wichman, Francis 378
Wichman, Sharon 378
Wiegel, Gretchen 552
Wilber, Miss Flora 216
Wildcat League 373
Wilder, Almaron M. 553
Wilder, Courtland 411
Wilding, Charles A. 294
Wilding, John 234
Wilding, Mrs. Ella 172
Wildwood Park 410
Wildwood Park 473
Wiley, O. B. 175
Wilkerson, Robert E. 331
Wilkie, Wendell L. 338
Wilkins, Howard 374
Wilkinson, Colonel James 24
Wilkinson, General James 33
Wilkinson, General James 68
Wilkinson, James 60
Wilks, John 306
Wilks, Lee 223
Will A. Young's Music Store 291
Willard, Alberta 172
William C. Wolf Furnaces 289
William Moellering & Sons 177
Williams Park 175
Williams Park 472
Williams, Bob 375
Williams, Creighton H. 186
Williams, David 21
Williams, Ernest E. 419
Williams, Ernest E. 544
Williams, Evelyn 556
Williams, Famious 512
Williams, Famious 547
Williams, Harry M. 585
Williams, Henry M. 472
Williams, Henry M. 472
Williams, Jesse 153
Williams, Jesse 155
Williams, Jesse 161
Williams, Jesse L. 115
Williams, Jesse L. 143
Williams, Jesse L. 144
Williams, John 70
Williams, Mrs. Jesse 146
Williams, Mrs. Mary 181
Williams, Van 502
Williams, Wayne 286
Williams, William G. 512
Williams, William G. 547
Williams, William G. 556
Williamson, Ed 235
Williamson, John 235
Williamson, John 512
Willig, Dr. Leslie A. 271
Willis, Frank 417
Willis, Raymond E. 585
Willson, Clint 512
Willson, Clinton R. 294
Willson, Fred 233
Wilma, Sister M. 514
Wilson, Bruce 448
Wilson, E. M. 288
Wilson, Earl 309
Wilson, George H. 180
Wilson, John I. 302
Wilson, Mrs. Ada 183
Wilson, Woodrow 588
Wimbley, Jim 382
Win-T 442
Winchester, General James 83
Wind Disasters 512
Wine 87
Wineland, Harry E. 585
Wing, J. F. 174
Winn, Harry 220
Winterrowd-Howard Clothing Store ..290
Winterrowd, Earl 290
Wire, Bob 547
Wise, Allen 411
Wissman, Fred 439
Wissman, Fred C. 586
Withey Studio of Drama 291
Witmer, Dr. S. A. 269
Witte, August H. 446
Witte, Robert 411
WKJG 293
WKJG 442
WKJG-TV 441
WMEE 294
WMEF 294
Woehr, Andrew 373
Woenker, Fred 172
Wohlfort, R. W. 153
Wolf & Dessauer 177,.181
Wolf & Dessauer 216
Wolf & Dessauer 225
Wolf & Dessauer 290
Wolf & Dessauer 295
Wolf & Dessauer 449
Wolf & Dessauer 515
Wolf Bedding Co. 410
Wolf, Don A. 546
Wolf, E. J. 410
Wolf, John D. 421
Wolf, Paul C. 336
Wolf, Paul C. 444
Wolf, Paul J. 348
Wolf, R. E. 410
Wolf, Sam 181
Wolf, Sam 290
Wolf, Samuel 184
Wolf, Samuel 477
Wolke, Louis 114
Wolke, Louis 144
Women,s Club 172

Women,s Club League 181
Wood Fired Stoves 262
Wood, George W. 143
Wood, George W. 149
Wood, George W. 155
Wood, James 170
Wood, James 170
Wood, James J. 170
Wood, Jane 307
Wood, Judge Sol A. 286
Wood, Judge Sol A. 301
Wood, Sol A. 584
Wood, Sol A. 584
Woodard Engineering Co. 226
Woodies Place 302
Wooding, J. Earle 411
Woods, Mr. & Mrs. I. N. 181
Woodworth, C. B. 171
Woodworth, Dr. B. S. 161
Woodworth, Mrs. L. C. 172
Woolen Factory 167
Woolen Mills 540
Woolner, David E. 228
Worden Sr., Richard L. 588
Worden, Charles H. 294
Worden, James L. 170
Work, David 144
Work, Henry 144
Work, Robert 144
Worker 287
Workhorse 506
World War I 185
World War I 345
World War II 340
World,s Fair 169
Worman, Richard W. 588
Worthington, W. W. 235
Worthman, Jack 411
Worthman, John 410
WOWO 292
WOWO 442
WPA 326
WPA 335
WPA Workers 220
WPTA 442
WPTH 293
Wrecking Crews 540
Wright, George F. 144
Wright, Newell 547
Wright, Verle 378
Wunderlich, Thomas 372
Wyandot 24
Wyandots 51
Wyatt, King 374
Wyatt, Lawrence 264
Wyatt, Robert 263
Wyllys, Major John 21
Wyllys, Major John 22
Wyman, James 112
Wyman, James 112
Wyneken, Fred 291
Wyneken, Frederick 268
Wyneken, Mart C. 372
Wyneken, Pastor 148
Wyneken, Rev. Frederick Conrad Dietrich 147
Wynn, Frank B. 216
Wyss, Alen 448
Wyss, Frank 326
Wyss, John B. 583
Wyss, John B. 584
Wyss, John B. 585
X-Rated Movie Houses 550
Yaple, Carl 583
Yaple, Carl 584
Yaple, Mrs. Carl 264
Yardley, George 375
Yargens, Eugene 264
Yarnelle, E. F. 294
Yarnelle, E. F. 294
Yarnelle, E. F. 477
Yarnelle, Edward F. 234
Yarnelle, Mossman 234
Yarnelle, Mrs. W. Page 215
Yarnelle, W. Page 217
Yarnelle, W. Page 217
Yarnelle, W. Page 234
Yarnelle, W. Page 264
Yawn, Mrs. Joan 507
Yeoman, Troy 541
Yergens, Paul 512
Yergens, W. 166
YMCA 232
YMCA 440
YMCA Building 184
Yoder, Jake 377
Yoder, Pat 556
York, Dick 308
Yost, Miss Lucille 345
Young Men,s Christian Assn. 290
Young Women,s Christian Association181
Young, Bob 379
Young, Charles H. 587
Young, Dr. John 263
Young, James 421
Youth Development 512
Zacher, Al 515
Zarkovich, Martin 305
Zeig, Frederick C. 292
Zeis, Harold 514
Zeis, Harold 516
Zeis, Harold 541
Zeis, Harold 545
Zeis, Harold 546
Zeis, Harold 547
Zeis, Harold 586
Zeis, Harold S. 508
Zeis, Harold S. 586
Zeis, Harold S. 587
Zeitner, Richard 178
Zent, Gerald 446
Zern, Ervin 477
Zero Weather 552
Zid, James 547
Ziegfield Follies 307
Ziegfield Follies 308
Zig-Zag Night Club 549
Zimmerman Co. 310
Zimmerman, Victor 588
Zink, Lucille 233
Zion Lutheran School 267
Zollars, Miss Clara 172
Zollars, Mrs. Allan 171
Zollinger, Charles A. 173
Zollinger, Henry 180
Zollinger, Mayor Charles 160
Zollner Corp. 228
Zollner Piston Softball Team 376
Zollner Pistons 375
Zollner Stadium 267
Zollner Stadium 376
Zollner Stadium 414
Zollner, Fred 228
Zollner, Fred 375
Zollner, Fred 507
Zollner, Theodore 228
Zoological Gardens 474
Zuber, A. J. 291
Zucker, J. F. 269
Zurcher, Fred 377
20th Century Lunch 289